Church of England Record Society
Volume 18

FROM THE REFORMATION TO THE PERMISSIVE SOCIETY

A MISCELLANY IN CELEBRATION OF THE 400TH ANNIVERSARY OF LAMBETH PALACE LIBRARY

This volume of the Church of England Record Society, published in celebration of the 400th anniversary of the foundation of Lambeth Palace Library, is a tribute to the value of one of the world's great libraries to the scholarly community and its importance for the history of the Church of England in particular. Thirteen historians, who have made considerable use of the Library in their research, have selected texts which together offer an illustration of the remarkable resources preserved by the Library for the period from the Reformation to the late twentieth century. A number of the contributions draw on the papers of the archbishops of Canterbury and bishops of London, which are among the most frequently used collections. Others come from the main manuscript sequence, including both materials originally deposited by Archbishop Sancroft and a manuscript purchased with the help of the Friends of Lambeth Palace Library in 2007. Another makes use of the riches of the papers of the Lambeth Conferences. Each text is accompanied by a substantial introduction, discussing its context and significance, and a full scholarly apparatus. The themes covered in the volume range from the famous dispute between Archbishop Grindal and Queen Elizabeth I, through the administration of the Church by Archbishop Laud and Archbishop Davidson's visit to the Western Front during World War I, to the involvement of the Church in homosexual law reform.

FROM THE REFORMATION TO THE PERMISSIVE SOCIETY

A MISCELLANY IN CELEBRATION OF THE 400TH ANNIVERSARY OF LAMBETH PALACE LIBRARY

EDITED BY

Melanie Barber and Stephen Taylor
with Gabriel Sewell

THE BOYDELL PRESS

CHURCH OF ENGLAND RECORD SOCIETY

First published 2010

A Church of England Record Society publication
Published by The Boydell Press
an imprint of Boydell & Brewer Ltd
PO Box 9, Woodbridge, Suffolk IP12 3DF, UK
and of Boydell & Brewer Inc.
668 Mt Hope Avenue, Rochester, NY 14620, USA
website: www.boydellandbrewer.com

ISBN 978–1–84383–558–5

ISSN 1351–3087

Series information is printed at the back of this volume

A CIP catalogue record for this book is available
from the British Library

The publisher has no responsibility for the continued existence or accuracy
of URLs for external or third-party internet websites referred to in this book,
and does not guarantee that any content on such websites is,
or will remain, accurate or appropriate.

This publication is printed on acid-free paper

Printed in Great Britain by
CPI Antony Rowe, Chippenham and Eastbourne

Contents

Illustrations

All illustrations are reproduced by permission of Lambeth Palace Library, except where otherwise indicated.

Contributors

Melanie Barber joined the staff at Lambeth Palace Library in 1966. She became Deputy Archivist in 1967 and then Deputy Librarian and Archivist in 1971, retiring in August 2002. She was a member of the Council of the Church of England Record Society from its foundation in 1991 until 1994, when she became its Executive Secretary.

Arthur Burns is Professor of Modern British History at King's College London and vice-president of the Church of England Record Society. He is one of the directors of the *Clergy of the Church of England Database 1540–1835* and co-investigator on 'Building on History: the Church in London' knowledge transfer project. He is currently working on a study of Christian socialism in Thaxted in the twentieth century.

James P. Carley is a Distinguished Research Professor at York University in Toronto and an Associate Fellow at the Pontifical Institute of Mediaeval Studies. He has written on *The Libraries of King Henry VIII* (2000) and on *The Books of King Henry VIII and His Wives* (2004). His edition, translation, and study of John Leland's *De uiris illustribus* will appear in 2010.

Patrick Collinson is Regius Professor of Modern History, Emeritus, at the University of Cambridge, and is a Fellow of Trinity College. He previously held chairs at Sydney, the University of Kent at Canterbury, and Sheffield. He has the CBE and is a Fellow of the British Academy. His books include: *The Elizabethan Puritan Movement* (1967 and 1990), *Archbishop Grindal 1519–1583* (1979) and *The Religion of Protestants. The Church in English Society 1559–1625* (1982). His biography of *Elizabeth I* (2007) originated as the longest article in *The Oxford Dictionary of National Biography*. He was the first president of the Church of England Record Society.

Kenneth Fincham is Professor of Early Modern History at the University of Kent. His first book, *Prelate as Pastor* was published in 1990, and since then he has edited *Visitation Articles and Injunctions of the Early Stuart Church 1603–1642* in two volumes for the Church of England Record Society and, most recently, co-authored with Nicholas Tyacke, *Altars Restored: the Changing Face of English Religious Worship 1547–c.1700* (Oxford, 2006). He is one of the directors of *The Clergy of the Church of England Database 1540–1835*.

Robert G. Ingram is Associate Professor of History at Ohio University. He is the author of *Religion, Reform and Modernity in the Eighteenth Century* (2007) and co-editor of *Religious Identities in Britain, 1660–1832* (2005).

Hugh McLeod is Professor of Church History in the University of Birmingham. He edited the twentieth-century volume of the *Cambridge History of Christianity* (2006) and is the author of *The Religious Crisis of the 1960s* (OUP 2007).

Charlotte Methuen is Lecturer in Church History and Liturgy at Ripon College Cuddesdon, and Lecturer in Ecclesiastical History at the University of Oxford. Before moving to Oxford, she taught at the Universities of Bochum and Hamburg, and was Director of Training for the Diocese in Europe. She is currently working on a study of George Bell and the ecumenical movement between the first and second world wars.

Dr **Richard Palmer** was Librarian and Archivist of Lambeth Palace Library from 1991 to 2010. He was formerly Curator of Western Manuscripts at the Wellcome Institute and honorary lecturer in the history of medicine at University College London. His publications have been mainly concerned with medicine in the early modern period, especially in Venice and northern Italy.

Professor emeritus **M. H. Port**, Queen Mary, University of London, has written at length on nineteenth-century public buildings, including churches. His *Six Hundred New Churches. The Church Building Commission 1818–1856* (2nd edn, Spire Books, 2006) explores in detail one of the principal factors in the revival of church-building.

Michael Snape is Senior Lecturer in Modern History at the University of Birmingham. He has published extensively on the subject of war and religion in the modern world and on the Church of England in the eighteenth century. His recent books include *The Royal Army Chaplains' Department, 1796–1953: Clergy Under Fire* (2008), *God and the British Soldier: Religion in the British Army in the First and Second World Wars* (2005) and *The Redcoat and Religion: The Forgotten History of the British Soldier from the Age of Marlborough to the eve of the First World War* (2005). He is Honorary Secretary of the Church of England Record Society.

Gabriel Sewell is Deputy Librarian at Lambeth Palace Library.

Sarah Stockwell is senior lecturer in imperial and Commonwealth history at King's College London. Her publications include: *The Business of Decolonization: British Business Strategies in the Gold Coast* (2000); co-edited with S. R. Ashton, *Imperial Policy and Colonial Practice, 1925–1945,* (British Documents on the End of Empire Series, HMSO, 1996); her edited collection *The British Empire. Themes and Perspectives* (2008); and, co-edited with Robert Holland, *Ambiguities of Empire* (2009). She is currently working on the history of the domestic Anglican Church and empire in the twentieth century.

Stephen Taylor is Professor of Early Modern History at the University of Reading. He is one of the directors of *The Clergy of the Church of England Database 1540–1835* and co-investigator of 'British state prayers, fasts and thanksgivings, 1540s to 1940s'. Among his recent publications is *The Entring Book of Roger Morrice. Vol. IV: 1687–1689* (Woodbridge, 2007), and he is currently working on studies of politics and religion in early Hanoverian England and (with Kenneth Fincham) religious conformity in the 1640s and 1650s. He has been Honorary General Editor of the Church of England Record Society since 1994 and a member of Council since its foundation in 1991.

Dr **Peter Webster** is Editorial Controller of British History Online, at the Institute of Historical Research, University of London. He has published widely on the arts and the Church of England in the twentieth century. His study of Archbishop Michael Ramsey is to be published by Ashgate.

Preface

In 2010 Lambeth Palace Library, one of the world's great libraries, celebrates the 400th anniversary of its foundation. The Church of England Record Society has a considerably shorter history, having been founded less than twenty years ago. From its origins, however, the Society has been closely linked with the Library. The Society was the brainchild of Dr Geoffrey Bill, then Librarian and Archivist, who overcame the scepticism of some eminent historians to establish a new record society in the unpropitious climate of the early 1990s. His successor, Dr Richard Palmer, and the staff at Lambeth have been unfailingly supportive ever since. Each year the Society's annual general meeting has been held in the magnificent, yet congenial, surroundings of the Great Hall. And, of course, manuscripts from the Library's collections have played an important part in the Society's publication schedule. It seemed entirely appropriate to the Society's Council, therefore, that we should publish a miscellany volume as part of the 400th anniversary celebrations. The aim of this volume is to bring together a selection of documents drawn from the collections at Lambeth Palace Library and edited by a group of junior and senior historians who have spent a considerable amount of time working in the Library. As such, the volume is a tribute from the academic community to one of the institutions that, through its collections and staff, does so much to make our professional lives not only possible, but also a pleasure. It is also intended to offer an illustrative sample of the resources held by the Library for the period from the Reformation to the late twentieth century. A number of contributions thus draw on the papers of the archbishops of Canterbury and bishops of London. Others come from the main manuscript sequence, including both materials originally deposited by Archbishop Sancroft and a manuscript purchased with the help of the Friends of Lambeth Palace Library in 2007. Another makes use of the riches of the papers of the Lambeth Conferences.

The idea for this volume came originally from Melanie Barber, known to many of the Library's users as a long-serving Deputy Librarian and Archivist who retired after thirty-six years' service in 2002. For many people Melanie *was* the Library. My own first experience of the Library was in 1981. It was only after I had gained admission and Melanie had identified some key documents among the uncatalogued Secker papers that it emerged that I was still an undergraduate. At that time, undergraduates were only granted access in exceptional circumstances and were entirely forbidden the use of manuscripts. To circumvent these regulations, imposed rigorously by Geoffrey Bill, Melanie stood beside me, turning the pages, as I read Secker's speech against the Quaker Tithe Bill of 1736. Melanie's association with the Church of England Record Society dates from 1991. She was one of the founding Council members and has subsequently served the Society with enormous commitment as its Executive Secretary since 1994. The conception of this volume is largely Melanie's: she identified most of the contributors and worked with many of them to select appropriate documents from among the wealth of manuscripts preserved in the Library. Unfortunately, during the period in which contributions came in and the volume passed through the press, ill health has prevented Melanie from continuing in her editorial *rôle*. Gabriel Sewell, the Deputy Librarian at Lambeth, has kindly taken on much of the burden of chasing contributors and ensuing that the volume was ready to go to press. I am particularly grateful to her for her hard work. For the same reason, it has not proved possible to include the definitive list of Lambeth Librarians, on the construction of which Melanie has expended much effort. It is hoped that it will be possible to publish it elsewhere in due course. I would also like to thank the contributors for their understanding in working to a very tight deadline, to Richard Palmer for his support, to Clare Brown, Assistant Archivist at Lambeth, for her work with the photography, and to Linda Randall for copyediting the whole text.. The Society is grateful to the Isobel Thornley Fund for a grant towards the cost of publishing the Dorothy L. Sayers's correspondence, and to the Anglo-Catholic History Society for a generous subvention. The volume as a whole, however, remains very much Melanie's achievement and, while it is unusual to dedi-cate a book to one of its editors, it seems entirely appropriate to do so in this case.

Stephen Taylor
July 2009

1

THE PROPHESYINGS AND
THE DOWNFALL AND SEQUESTRATION
OF ARCHBISHOP EDMUND GRINDAL 1576–1583

Edited by
Patrick Collinson

1 Copy of the letter of submission by Archbishop Grindal to Queen Elizabeth I, for refusing on grounds of conscience to suppress puritan prophesyings, 21 January 1581 (LPL, MS 3470, fo. 78)

Introduction

The context of events

The Lambeth papers which follow in this collection concern at their epicentre Edmund Grindal (1519–83), native of remotest Cumbria, in the days of Edward VI protégé of Bishop Nicholas Ridley and destined to be his successor, a Germanically inclined Marian exile and disciple of Martin Bucer of Strasbourg, and in the reign of Elizabeth successively bishop of London, archbishop of York and archbishop of Canterbury.[1] When on Christmas Eve 1575 the queen consented to Grindal's translation to Canterbury, a suspiciously long time after the death in May of his predecessor, Matthew Parker, and perhaps with reluctance, there were high hopes in some quarters that this would mean 'change', a word borrowed from a modern transition of power. Parker's occupation of Augustine's chair had been marked not only by what we now call conservatism, but by a progressively pessimistic inertia and an inclination to retreat into the scholarly pursuits where he was most at home. Far from settling the disputes within the church as to the direction in which it was going, the Parker regime, obliged to be somewhat repressive in its insistence on strict prayer book conformity, was a provocation to those who favoured what they called a 'further reformation', an advance on the religious settlement of 1559. Grindal was the man to make a change. William Cecil, Lord Burghley, marked him out for preferment almost before the last breath was out of Parker's body. He was 'the meetest man to succeed'. 'Take my proxy for my poor voice.' One of Burghley's colleagues, almost certainly Sir Walter Mildmay, chancellor of the exchequer, wrote optimistically to Grindal, still in the north: 'It is greatly hoped for by the godly and well-affected of this realm that your lordship will prove a profitable instrument in that calling … I know it will be hard for you to do that good that you and your brethren desire. Yet (things discreetly ordered) somewhat there may be done.'[2] There is the strong implication in the letter that only one august person stood in the way of the hoped for progress.

Yet within little more than a year things went horribly wrong, in part because things had not been 'discreetly ordered'. Grindal had been provoked into writing such a letter to the queen as Elizabeth never expected to receive from any subject, least of all from an archbishop, her creature, a letter of 6,000 words which contemporaries referred to as his 'book to the queen'. In modern parlance, Grindal had

1 There is an extensive collection of letters and other papers relating to Archbishop Grindal in *The remains of Edmund Grindal*, ed. W. Nicholson, Parker Society (Cambridge, 1843). John Strype published his *The life and acts of the most reverend father in God, Edmund Grindal* in 1710. It was republished in Oxford in 1821, the edition cited here. My own *Archbishop Grindal 1519–1583: the struggle for a reformed church* was published in London and Berkeley in 1979. My article on Grindal in *The Oxford dictionary of national biography* (*ODNB*) corrects and elucidates a number of points. See also Patrick Collinson, 'The downfall of Archbishop Grindal and its place in Elizabethan political and ecclesiastical history', in Collinson, *Godly people: essays on English protestantism and puritanism* (London, 1983), pp. 371–97.
2 Collinson, *Archbishop Grindal*, pp. 219–24.

chosen to read the riot act to his sovereign, and the result was that he was deprived of most of the functions of his office, and would have been deprived *tout court*, dismissed, if Elizabeth's councillors and courtiers had not striven by might and main to prevent that scandalous outcome.[3]

The occasion of the affair, the fatal letter and all that followed from it, lay in an innovation in the Elizabethan church known as the 'exercise of prophesying', or 'exercise' for short. 'Occasion' may be a more appropriate word than 'cause', since what we may call the Grindal affair marked a watershed in the affairs of the Elizabethan church, a tectonic shift in the politics of both court and country. The politics behind it implicated the favourite of the hour, the religiously conservative Sir Christopher Hatton, who in the course of the 1580s would lend his weight to the reactive policies of Bishop John Aylmer of London, Archbishop John Whitgift and Hatton's chaplain, Richard Bancroft.[4]

But we need to focus on prophesying. This was a gathering at regular intervals, monthly or fortnightly, of the clergy of, as it might be, the vicinity, within a day's journey on horseback, of a suitable church, typically in a market town. Two or three sermons were preached by the more qualified of the ministers, supervised by a moderator. The term 'prophesying' had biblical authority, but came more immediately from practice in the reformed church at Zurich, a model for the Elizabethan church. The institution was a composite of several elements, and it served more than one purpose. It was a kind of open university for the less learned clergy, encouraging them to become acceptable preachers; and to that end written 'exercises' were set, performed and examined in something like our modern pedagogical sense, a widespread practice which continued long after Grindal's spat with the queen, under the auspices of Grindal's successor, Archbishop John Whitgift.[5] And then prophesyings were an occasion for 'conference' among the clergy, not only on the doctrine preached but on other matters of common interest, often concerning 'discipline', conference and discipline being loaded words in the Elizabethan religious lexicon. And the prophesyings provided a feast of sermons which in the early Elizabethan church were otherwise in short supply. That attracted a lay auditory, which included persons of some local consequence, making them a forceful demonstration of the ascendancy of the reformed religion in an environment still often hostile, or indifferent. And they were good for market town business. But the prophesyings had their enemies, who told tales which from time to time reached the ears of the queen, reports of disorders of the kind associated with what was beginning to be called 'puritanism'.[6]

3 *Ibid.*, pp. 233–65.

4 Brett Usher, *William Cecil and episcopacy, 1559–1577* (Aldershot, 2003), pp. 131–43, and Usher's article on Bishop John Aylmer in *ODNB*. See also Sir Harris Nicolas, *Memoirs of the life and times of Sir Christopher Hatton* (London, 1847).

5 Patrick Collinson, *The Elizabethan puritan movement* (London and Berkeley, 1967), pp. 170–1. A more detailed account of clergy exercises (in this sense) will be found in my unpublished London Ph.D. thesis of 1957, 'The puritan classical movement in the reign of Elizabeth I', pp. 244–73. The practice in various dioceses was regularized, particularly in the orders 'for the better increase of learning in the inferior Ministers and for more diligent preaching and catechisinge', drawn up by convocation in 1586/7, under the leadership of Archbishop John Whitgift, and following as a model practice in the diocese of Lincoln (in the aftermath of the suppression of prophesying).

6 Collinson, *Archbishop Grindal*, pp. 233–6; 'Letters of Thomas Wood, puritan, 1566–1577', ed. Patrick Collinson, in his *Godly people*, pp. 45–107.

The canons and formularies of the church knew nothing about prophesyings. But they had been authorized by the bishops in many dioceses, including Parker's own diocese of Canterbury, the county of Kent.[7] In one of the documents printed below, either Grindal or someone sympathetic to his cause claimed that the exercise had been introduced first in the diocese of London, by Grindal, in, it would seem, 1562, a picture which can be coloured in from the reports of four of the archdeacons of the diocese.[8] Much later, in the early days of the new Jacobean regime, the Canons of 1604 stipulated that no minister or ministers should 'presume to appoint or hold any meetings for sermons, commonly termed by some prophecies or exercises, in market towns or other places', unless they had 'the license and direction of the bishop of the diocese first obtained'.[9] In fact many Jacobean bishops did license such things, now often called 'lectures by combination', preached according to a rota by the clergy of the neighbourhood, and after 1577 normally involving only one sermon, but otherwise resembling in all respects the earlier prophesyings. Meanwhile, in the northern province, immune from the ructions of 1576 and the queen's opposition, a region where, by common consent, popery was a greater problem than puritanism, prophesyings and combination lectures flourished, nothing less than a notable part of the regional culture.[10] But in the context of the Grindal affair, Elizabeth denied that bishops had the power to allow such proceedings. In his notes on the case, Sir Walter Mildmay (whatever may have been his personal sympathies) wrote: 'a thing not sufferable that any shall set up any things in the Church without public authority. Neither hath the bishop such power.'[11]

It is fair and necessary comment that whereas prophesyings and combination lectures enjoyed episcopal licence, it was often pressure from the grass roots, clerical and lay, which secured that licence, the tail wagging the episcopal dog.[12] Nor are the views of those who regarded the prophesyings with suspicion as the source of what we should call radicalism to be lightly dismissed. The presence of the laity

---

7   Cathedral Archives and Library, Canterbury, MS Z.5.1, fos. 164v–171r, contains the orders of prophesying, with the names of the participants, held in the Kentish deaneries of Ospringe and Sittingbourne, Lympne and Sandwich, and Ashford; as well as the orders for Buckinghamshire in the diocese of Lincoln, and for Eye, in the diocese of Norwich. There is another copy of the Buckinghamshire orders in Cambridge University Library, MS Ff.v.14, fos. 85r–87r. For details of the orders of prophesying in many other places, see Collinson, *The Elizabethan puritan movement*, pp. 171–6.

8   Lambeth Palace Library (LPL), MS 2003, fos. 12, 16, 23 (for the archdeaconries of Essex, St Albans and London); digest of a report from the archdeacon of Colchester, British Library (BL), Add. MS 21565, fo. 26. There is no report extant from the archdeaconry of Middlesex.

9   *The anglican canons, 1529–1947*, ed. Gerald Bray, Church of England Record Society 6 (Woodbridge, 1998), pp. 362–5.

10 Patrick Collinson, 'Lectures by combination: structures and characteristics of church life in 17th-century England', in his *Godly people*, pp. 467–98.

11 Northamptonshire Record Office, MS F.(M),P,70.b.

12 Bishop Cooper of Lincoln noted on a draft of the Hertfordshire order: 'These orders of exercise, offered to me by the learned of the clergy of Hertfordshire, I think good and godly' (Collinson, *The Elizabethan puritan movement*, p. 174). For similar evidence of the response, thirty years later, of Bishop John Jegon of Norwich to local initiatives in favour of combination lectures, see Collinson, *Godly people*, pp. 481–2. For evidence of similarly reactive rather than proactive actions by an earlier bishop of Norwich, Edmund Scambler, see 'The combination lecture at Bury St Edmunds', in *Conferences and combination lectures in the Elizabethan church: Dedham and Bury St Edmunds 1582–1590*, ed. Patrick Collinson, John Craig and Brett Usher, Church of England Record Society 10 (Woodbridge, 2003), pp. 151–80.

was particularly contentious.[13] As we shall see, Grindal insisted that they be present at the exercises, while equally insisting that no layman be permitted to speak (which may imply that sometimes they had).

In the churches of foreign 'strangers' in Elizabethan London, prophesying had been the occasion for lively lay participation. As bishop of London in the 1560s, Grindal knew all about this, and feared it. More conservative defenders of the exercises, including the young Francis Bacon, thought that they should be confined to the clergy. Even if they made up a passive, receptive audience, conservative minds suspected, perhaps with some reason, that lay hearers might hear things that they had better not hear, and might want to discuss those things amongst themselves once out of the church and earshot, their Geneva bibles at the ready. Grindal, on the other hand, for whom conscience and the obedience which went with a sound conscience were things needing to be activated and stirred up by the dynamism of the Gospel, believed the prophesyings to be the solution, or an important part of the solution, to the problem of how to turn an inert, ignorant, still by inclination 'popish' and potentially disloyal mass into an informed, godly, reformed and obedient community. Under the surface there was a profound political and ideological difference, the difference between what we have begun to call the ideology of monarchical republicanism and its more repressive, authoritarian and simply monarchical opposite. Grindal was an ecclesiastical monarchical republican.[14]

This all came to a head in the summer of 1576, when Elizabeth was informed of certain disorders involving named preachers, and locations, in Northamptonshire and Warwickshire, and in particular of 'the over busy dealing' of the preachers at Southam in south Warwickshire. Her concern may have been aroused in part by the exotic, and perhaps alarming, word 'prophesying', or 'prophecies'. In his letter, Grindal acknowledged that this was a semantic problem. The terms were 'very odious in our dayes to some because they are not rightly understood'. Elsewhere Grindal, or someone who sounds like him, wrote that some preferred to call them 'exercises', wishing to dissociate themselves from 'prophesying'.[15] However, Elizabeth's hostility had to do with more than mere semantics. Grindal was summoned to court and into the presence of the queen to answer for his stewardship on two

---

[13] Among those who believed that the exercises should be renewed, for the benefit of the clergy only, see Francis Bacon, writing *c.* 1589: 'I know prophesying was subject to great abuse ... But I say the only reason of the abuse was, because there was admitted to it a popular auditory, and it was not contained within a private conference of ministers' ('An advertisement touching the controversies of the Church of England', in *Francis Bacon*, ed. Brian Vickers (Oxford, 1996), p. 13). On the matter of the presence of the laity, see Peter Iver Kaufman, *Thinking of the laity in late Tudor England* (Notre Dame, IL, 2004), pp. 121–37, 'Prophesyings and the people'. Kaufman's conservatively minded critique of the prophesyings provides a necessary counterweight to my own perhaps over-Grindalian apologetics. However, he distorts the balance of forces for and against by referring throughout to Grindal's contention having been with something called 'the government'. Would that it had been that simple!

[14] Collinson, *The Elizabethan puritan movement*, pp. 169–70; Patrick Collinson, 'Calvinism with an anglican face: the stranger churches in early Elizabethan London and their superintendent', and 'The Elizabethan puritans and the foreign reformed churches in London', both in *Godly people*, pp. 213–72; Kaufman, *Thinking of the laity*, pp. 123–5; John F. McDiarmid (ed.), *The monarchical republic of early modern England: essays in response to Patrick Collinson* (Aldershot, 2007), especially Peter Lake, ' "The monarchical republic of Queen Elizabeth I" (and the fall of Archbishop Grindal) revisited', pp. 129–47.

[15] See pp. 39–40 below.

occasions, on 12 June, immediately after those damaging reports from the midlands had been received, and on 18 November.[16] In between, Grindal collected reports on the prophesyings from the bishops and began to prepare a book-length, scholastic defence of the practice. But on the occasion of the second interview Grindal was not permitted to speak and was obliged to listen to a tirade in which Elizabeth revealed her attitude towards preaching itself, which was ambivalent to say the least. Hence some of the most anguished passages in Grindal's letter. Apparently the queen had said that three or four preachers should be sufficient for a whole county. The publicly authorized homilies were safer. 'But surely I cannot marvel enough, how this strange opinion should once enter into your mind, that it should be good for the Church to have few preachers. Alas, Madam!' But for that, Grindal might have sidestepped the issue, as other bishops had done two years earlier, with the quiet encouragement of the privy council.[17] But this was just too much. Denied the opportunity to offer the queen counsel by word of mouth, Grindal was driven to the fatal mistake of doing so on paper. For Peter Lake, the resultant débacle is a reminder that the ideology of 'monarchical republicanism' 'very seldom dared to speak its name'.[18] On this occasion, it did utter. But with what consequences!

In writing his 'book to the queen', Grindal had, literally at his elbow, a pattern in the letters of one of the great fathers of the church, the distinctly prickly St Ambrose of Milan, addressing the Roman emperors, Theodosius and Valentinian. His copy of the works of Ambrose survives, heavily annotated, with particular passages marked for direct quotation. It was a fatal mistake. Ambrose and the emperor were not related in the same way as an Elizabethan bishop to the supreme governor of the Church of England. Ambrose could declare that matters of religion belonged in synods, not in palaces. Ambrose could say that these things should be left to the churchmen who understood them best. Ambrose could even excommunicate an emperor, a unique occurrence. Grindal could not hold his sovereign to the ultimate account, except rhetorically, which he proceeded, gratuitously and unwisely, to do: 'Remember Madame that you are a mortall creature.'[19]

Grindal's 6,000 words boiled down to one simple declaration of obedient disobedience. He would not pass on to the bishops of his province an order from the queen to suppress the prophesyings. She would have to do that herself. (And she

---

16 See pp. 40–1 below.
17 Collinson, *Archbishop Grindal*, pp. 235–6. LPL, MS 2003, fo. 27, is a letter from Bishop Sandys of London to the privy council, dated 13 July 1574, the archbishop (Parker not Grindal) having informed him that 'hir Majestie doeth thincke it convenient that suche exercises should ceasse'. Stanford Lehmberg in his edition of documents from MS 2003 (see p. 12 below) followed a misdating of the letter to 1576, as if Grindal should have advised Sandys of the queen's desire to have the prophesyings suppressed. A letter from William Masters, chancellor of the diocese of Norwich, to the Norfolk gentleman Sir Christopher Heydon casts some circumstantial light on the events of the summer of 1574. Bishop Parkhurst of Norwich had been charged by Archbishop Parker 'in her Majesties name' to put down the prophesyings in his diocese, whereupon Masters took appropriate action. But Heydon's son had proceeded to London, where he obtained letters signed by two privy councillors and Bishop Sandys 'for the restitution' of the exercises (Inner Temple Library, MS Petyt 538.47, fo. 28).
18 Lake, '"The monarchical republic revisited', p. 144.
19 Patrick Collinson, 'If Constantine, then also Theodosius: St. Ambrose and the integrity of the Elizabethan *ecclesia anglicana*', in *Godly people*, pp. 109–33; Collinson, *Archbishop Grindal*, pp. 242–5. Grindal's annotated copy of the 1538, Basle, edition of the *Opera* of St Ambrose is preserved in the Library of Queen's College, Oxford.

did.) 'Beare with me, I besech yow Madame, if I chuse rather to offend your earthly Majestie then to offend the heavenly Majestie of god.' If in consequence she chose to remove him from his office, so be it. In the words of le Maréchal Bosquet: 'C'est magnifique, mais ce n'est par la guerre.' The consequences of Grindal's magnificent letter were disastrous. There is evidence that after the despatch of the letter via the earl of Leicester more than a week passed before it was shown to the queen, a week in which Leicester and Burghley attempted a diplomatic compromise which would have excluded the laity from attendance at the prophesyings, converting them into purely clerical conferences: a deal which Grindal found unacceptable.[20] Then five months went by in which nothing happened, except that the primate continued to perform his primatial responsibilities, consecrating the next generation of bishops, Edwin Sandys as archbishop of York, John Aylmer as bishop of London, John Whitgift, who would succeed him as archbishop, as bishop of Worcester; and setting up his metropolitan visitation. But Grindal was warned to stay away from court, the royal command suppressing the 'innovations' of 'all such prophesyings' was promulgated, and on 27 May 1577, on a formal appearance before the privy council, Grindal was suspended, sequestered and put under what was effectively house arrest at Lambeth. His repeated refusal to recant was deemed 'a second offence of disobedience, greater than the first'. Only on 25 August 1578 was there a partial relaxation of his sentence. Grindal was permitted to use his other residence at Croydon.[21] (Lambeth would have needed cleaning out.) The wheel of historiography has turned full circle since anglican historians expressed disdain for what for one of them called Grindal's 'puritan crankiness'.[22] A more recent historian has called Elizabeth's suspension of Grindal 'the single most irresponsible decision that she ever took' in the supposed defence of her church.[23] It set the stage for a history of conflict never quite resolved, which just might have been averted. There was at the time, and still is in some quarters, another analysis of the situation: the prophesyyings were dangerous, too dangerous to be tolerated in a monarchical and hierarchically regulated commonwealth. Did the seventeenth century need a revolution? The stakes were that high.

The formal deed of sequestration, if there was one, has not survived, and the exact terms and conditions of the archbishop's restraint are far from clear, except that he was 'removed from the exercise of all ecclesiastical jurisdiction'.[24] All the formal acts which would normally have been issued under his hand and seal were now to be executed by his principal officers, exercising what was termed 'the vicarageship of the archepiscopal see of Canterbury'. On the evidence of Grindal's Register and a letter from the privy council in this collection, from the end of 1581 these powers were vested in Dr William Aubrey.[25] And yet there was much that

20 Collinson, *Archbishop Grindal*, pp. 246–7.
21 *Ibid.*, p. 249; and see pp. 40–1 below.
22 W. H. Frere, *A history of the English church in the reigns of Elizabeth and James I* (London, 1904), p. 192.
23 Usher, *William Cecil and Episcopacy*, p. 152.
24 See pp. 40–1 below.
25 LPL, Grindal's Register, II, fo. 406; and pp. 29–30 below. On arriving at Lambeth, Grindal had initiated an investigation into the state of his various courts spiritual. Thomas Yale, the author of a report of fifty-five numbered paragraphs, made an honest assessment: 'I am not so able to advertise your Grace how to remedy the disease of these delays as to make them known unto you' (Collinson, *Archbishop Grindal*, pp. 230–1).

Grindal could still do, in spite of his sequestration, and much that he was required to do on terms which were often quite humiliating. The exchange of letters with Sir Francis Walsingham in this collection is a revealing illustration of that. Grindal was frequently instructed to take administrative action, 'notwithstanding your present sequestration'.[26] He was to investigate popish recusancy, to order special prayers after the earthquake of 1580, to oversee the collection of money for the relief of Geneva,[27] to sort out a variety of storms in ecclesiastical and academic teacups[28] and even to confer with other bishops about the weighty matter of the views of John Dee on the new Gregorian calendar.[29]

So far as the queen was concerned, the formality of Grindal's sequestration was but the overture to his deprivation, an event which her closest advisers feared would have had the gravest repercussions, domestic and international. Grindal's troubles coincided with what was perceived to be a dangerous corner in the prospects for protestant England. It was now increasingly clear that the threat of catholic revanchism, internal and external, was not going away. Events in the Netherlands were coming to a critical head. And, to the dismay of many, it appeared that Elizabeth's preferred route of escape from these dangers was to marry the French duke of Anjou, a catholic, of course. On 9 January 1578, Sir Francis Knollys wrote to Sir Thomas Wilson: 'But if the bishop of Canterbury shall be deprived, then up starts the pride and practice of the papists...And then King Richard the Second's men [viz., corrupt flatterers, evil counsellors] will flock into Court apace and will show themselves in their colours.'[30] Until recently, historians have overlooked a significant coincidence of initiatives in the climacteric year, for Grindal, 1577. The regime now turned its attention to the catholic threat, with the bishops required to stir themselves anew, and to report on the extent of popish recusancy in their dioceses. The motive for what looks like a careful balancing act is not hard to detect. The result was that a priest, Cuthbert Mayne, became the first of the Elizabethan catholic martyrs; and in East Anglia, in the context of the royal progress of the summer of 1578, drastic steps were taken to remove county government from catholics and crypto-catholics and to put it into the hands of reliable protestants.[31]

---

26 Collinson, *Archbishop Grindal*, p. 270.
27 On the relief of Geneva, see Simon Adams and Mark Greengrass (eds.), 'Memoires et procedures de ma negociation en Angleterre (8 October 1582- 8 October 1583), by Jean Malliet, councillor of Geneva', in *Religion, politics and society in sixteenth-century England*, Camden 5th ser. 22 (Cambridge, 2003), pp. 165–96.
28 See papers having to do with a dispute between Canterbury Cathedral and Queens' College, Cambridge, together with a page of notes in Grindal's hand (resembling in form the notes he made in connexion with the prophesyings): 'Reasons for my awarde'; BL, Add. MS 32092, fos. 13–20.
29 Sir Francis Walsingham to Grindal, 18 Mar. 1582, 29 Mar. 1583, Grindal and other bishops to Walsingham, 4 Apr. 1583; BL, Add. MS 32092, fos. 26–9. Walsingham had required Grindal to confer on the matter with such bishops 'as are presently about London'. There seems to have been some expectation that they would regard the new calendar favourably. But Grindal, Aylmer of London, Piers of Salisbury and Young of Rochester responded, from Lambeth: 'We are not to deale with or in anye wise to admitt it before mature and deliberate consultation had not only with a provinciall assemblie of the clergie and convocacion of this Realme but also with other reformed churches which professe the same Religion that we doe.'
30 Collinson, *Archbishop Grindal*, pp. 257–8.
31 Peter Lake, 'A tale of two episcopal surveys: the strange fates of Edmund Grindal and Cuthbert Mayne revisited', *Transactions of the Royal Historical Society*, 6th ser. XVIII (2008), 129–63; Patrick Collinson, 'Pulling the strings: religion and politics in the progress of 1578', in *The progresses,*

Meanwhile a strange Kafkaesque quadrille was played out, with much intrigue and subterfuge, appearances before the council in Star Chamber, which might well have led to deprivation, called off when Grindal was advised to plead diplomatic illness. The archbishop's hopes were regularly raised, buoyed up by what he called 'court promises', but as often dashed.[32]

It all came to a head in January 1581 with the recall of parliament, the first for five years, and with parliament the convocation of Canterbury, over which the archbishop of Canterbury would normally have presided. The privy council (four councillors, Burghley, Leicester, the earl of Sussex and Sir Thomas Wilson) instructed Grindal to depute his presidency of convocation to the bishops of London, Winchester and Lincoln.[33] In practice it was Aylmer of London, Hatton's bishop, who stood in for Grindal. The stone which the builders had rejected now became the head of the corner. The plight of their metropolitan induced a rare sense of solidarity in the clergy. When the prolocutor of the Lower House was presented to the bishops in the Upper House, normally a mere formality, Tobie Matthew, the dean of Christ Church, a polished rhetorician and one of Elizabeth's favourite divines, made an eloquent and even passionate appeal for an initiative which might lead to the archbishop's rehabilitation. This was followed by a supplication to the queen from both houses, composed by Matthew, which vigorously defended Grindal's reputation and pleaded that the queen should raise up an archbishop now broken and feeble, and restore the church to him and him to the church. Twelve of the bishops, almost the entire effective episcopate of the province, memorialized the queen on their own account, affirming that the cloud under which their metropolitan, 'summus in Ecclesia Anglicana sacerdos Dei', laboured was a cause of shame and injury, 'detrimentum'.[34]

While this was going on, Grindal was presented with a form of submission, apparently devised by the man who would succeed him, Whitgift, together with John Piers of Salisbury, a future archbishop of York and a sound Whitgiftian, a copy of which is included in this collection.[35] This was a total and humiliating climb down. The Lambeth copy contains the marginal note 'Copie of my lo: g. of Cant: his submission', and this is in Grindal's hand, as are the initials at the foot 'subscribed E.C.'.[36] Grindal's first biographer, John Strype, who saw another copy of this document without endorsement or date, and who placed it (incorrectly) in 1582, assumed that Grindal had actually submitted in these terms. And perhaps, from the presence of his handwriting on the Lambeth copy, we should think so too. But if so it was not the case, as Strype thought, 'that from henceforth our archbishop had his sequestration taken off, and was restored to the exercise of his ecclesiastical jurisdiction'. That never happened.[37]

    pageants, and entertainments of Queen Elizabeth I, ed. Jayne Elisabeth Archer, Elizabeth Goldring and Sarah Knights (Oxford, 2007), pp. 122–41.

[32] Collinson, *Archbishop Grindal*, pp. 253–67.

[33] LPL, MS 3470, fo. 71; BL, Add. MS 29546, fo. 56r.

[34] Collinson, *Archbishop Grindal*, pp. 273–4; LPL, MS 3470, fo. 76; another copy printed in Edward Cardwell (ed.), *Documentary annals of the reformed Church of England* (2 vols., Oxford, 1844), I, 441–6.

[35] See pp. 37–9 below.

[36] Copies of the submission in BL, Add. MS 32092, fo. 22, and Add. MS 29546, fos. 56v–7r, an eighteenth-century copy which seems to have been taken from LPL, MS 3470.

[37] Strype, *Grindal*, pp. 403–4.

In 1583 the queen sent Grindal a New Year's gift, a standing cup. That may indicate that by then he had made some form of submission. He was by now in very
poor health, his eyesight failing. In the early months of 1583 there were attempts in
which Burghley, for one, was actively involved, to arrange an honourable resignation. But there were all sorts of impediments and other complicating factors and it
was not to be. Grindal died at Croydon on 6 July, still archbishop of Canterbury.[38]
Not until 1928 would an archbishop of Canterbury succeed in resigning his office.

---

[38] Collinson, *Archbishop Grindal*, pp. 276–8.

Documents

Editorial conventions

For the most part, the original orthography, punctuation and capitalization have been retained. I acknowledge gratefully the great help of Elisabeth Leedham-Green with the Latin translations, and with solving some teasing palaeographical puzzles, with which Diarmaid MacCulloch has also been helpful.

All the documents which follow belong to a family of manuscripts in Lambeth Palace Library (LPL) familiarily known as the Fairhurst papers, or Laud–Selden–Fairhurst papers. They were present in the Library at the time of the fall of Archbishop Laud, were removed by John Selden, passed later into the hands of his friend and executor Sir Matthew Hale, were then dispersed (some finding their way into the Petyt Manuscripts in the Inner Temple Library) and the bulk otherwise lost to sight until those which remained in the Gloucestershire home of the Hale family were discovered and acquired in the 1930s by the Lancashire businessman James Fairhurst. We can safely credit Archbishop Richard Bancroft, the founder of LPL, with the initial conservation of these and other Elizabethan ecclesiastical muniments.[1] After the Second World War the papers found their way, by dribs and drabs, into the sale room. For some time part of the collection was in the keeping of St Paul's Cathedral Library (where I consulted it in 1953), and they are referred to in some publications of the time as St Paul's 'Additional Manuscripts'.[2] But St Paul's failed to make good the purchase and its loss was Lambeth's gain. In 1963 the late Geoffrey Bill succeeded in acquiring for his Library the greater part of the collection, and another tranche, including most of the documents published here, was purchased in 1988, with a few strays following in later years.

In 1965, with the encouragement of Dr Bill, Professor Stanford Lehmberg, then of the University of Texas at Austin, later of the University of Minnesota, published in the *Historical Magazine of the Protestant Episcopal Church* papers relating to the prophesyings from what was by then LPL MS 2003, together with one of the orders of prophesying allowed by Bishop Thomas Cooper of Lincoln, from MS 2007.[3] Perhaps because the edition was prepared from microfilm, it left a good deal to be desired. But to date this remains the only version available in print of the responses of the bishops to Grindal's request for information about the prophesyings, and other related documents. (There are eighteenth-century copies of the letters in the British Library (BL), Add. MS 29546, sometimes cited but never published.)

---

[1] Implicit in the LPL catalogue of these muniments. Prominent in the Fairhurst papers are many documents connected with Bancroft's dealings with the appellant priests in the context of the late Elizabethan archpriest controversy. See the listings in Bodleian Library, MS Tanner 88, fos. 20–60; and D. M. Barratt, 'The library of John Selden and its later history', *Bodleian Library Record*, III (1951), 128–42.

[2] P. Renold (ed.), *The Wisbech stirs (1595–1598)*, Catholic Record Society 51 (London, 1958); Patrick Collinson (ed.), *Letters of Thomas Wood, puritan, 1566–1577*, Bulletin of the Institute of Historical Research, Special Supplement no. 5 (1960).

[3] Stanford E. Lehmberg, 'Archbishop Grindal and the prophesyings', *Historical Magazine of the Protestant Episcopal Church*, XXXIV (1965), 87–145.

The bishops' letters

These letters are unique, in that on no other subject did almost all the Elizabethan bishops of the province of Canterbury share their views with the archbishop. They were replying to a letter from Grindal requiring reports on the prophesyings dated 25 June 1576, a fortnight after his appearance at court. (But Thomas Bentham of Coventry and Lichfield refers to 'three severall letters'.[4]) Of the eleven episcopal replies printed by Lehmberg from MS 2003, eight were more or less favourable to the exercises. Bishops William Bradbridge of Exeter and Richard Curteys claimed not only to have approved of them, but to have taken an active part themselves. Bradbridge thought their continuance 'right necessarye'. 'Greate profitte growethe therbye.' Curteys, who reported that the exercises in Sussex had begun only in his own time as bishop, thought them 'not onlye commendable, but necessarye'.[5] Edwin Sandys of London strongly implied his approval by forwarding letters from his archdeacons, providing us with much detailed and circumstantial knowledge of what may have gone on in the exercises.[6] Bentham of Coventry and Lichfield was another who found the exercises 'not onlye profitable … but also verye necessarye'; although Bentham was not very well informed, and had learned for the first time about the notorious exercise at Southam, in Warwickshire, the source of those adverse reports to the court,[7] only the day before he heard that Grindal had 'restrayned' it.[8] Richard Davies of St David's reported that the exercise was unknown in his part of Wales, and given the severe shortage of learned ministers, could not be introduced without 'confusion, disorder and inconvenience'. But he thought that in England it would 'edifye and may be profitably contynewed'. Nicholas Robinson of Bangor was of the same opinion.[9] Thomas Cooper of Lincoln recounted what had happened in 1574, when, like Sandys, he had turned a blind eye to an earlier order of suppression. He suspected that the current complaint had originated with 'one or two of some countenance and easie accesse vnto the prince, that haue smale liking to that, or anie other thing whereby religion maie be further published'. 'And so to suspect, I haue greater cause than I maie convenientlie put in writing.' He claimed to have kept a very careful eye on the exercises, and believed 'it better that theie should be kepte', but for the clergy only.[10] Gilbert Berkeley of Bath and Wells (in a letter endorsed in Grindal's hand) was another who thought prophesying 'very proffitable'. 'The order that my Lord Bisshoppe of Lincolne hathe taken for the settinge forthe of the exercise is very good.'[11] Edmund Ghest of Salisbury (another of Grindal's endorsements) was unhappy about the word 'prophecy', an apostolic gift no longer to be found in the church, but offered a scholarly and conservative defence of some sort of clerical exercise.[12]

Since they are not found in the Lambeth archives, but only in the digest of the letters in BL, Add. MS 21565, fo. 26, I include here the summary of what Grindal

---

4 LPL, MS 2003, fo. 5.
5 *Ibid.*, fos. 8, 4.
6 *Ibid.*, fos. 25, 23, 16–18, 12–13.
7 Collinson, *Archbishop Grindal*, pp. 233–4.
8 LPL, MS 2003, fo. 5.
9 *Ibid.*, fos. 31–2, 1.
10 *Ibid.*, fos. 29–30.
11 *Ibid.*, fo. 2.
12 *Ibid.*, fos. 33–4.

was advised by the bishop of Rochester (John Piers) and by the archdeacon of Colchester, the scarcely crypto-puritan George Withers:

> Episcopus Roffens. he alloweth it amongst the ministers with some moderator, to see what doctrine taught who (the lecture to the people being ended) may geve his sentence yf he think good of that which hath ben taught of the reader, and add of his owne as he thinketh best for the further confirmacion of the doctrine and the edification of the people.

> Archidia. Colcesten. The continaunce cannot but be profitable to the churche for all ministers are constreyned to this exercise; the vnlearned to study and confer-ence whereof many growe to reasonable abilitie. thei of the old stampe openly to renounce popery. ministers priuily slaundering the religion stablished finde les credit with the people. the people come to knowledge and reape comfort by those wholsome exhortations.

Only John Scory of Hereford and Richard Cox of Ely were frankly hostile (although Edmund Scambler of Peterborough, whose diocese was in the firing line might well have been – we do not hear from him). Scory had put down two or three exercises, 'partlie because I feared that might happen in my dioces which I heare to have happened in some others', where Thomas Cartwright's puritan 'platform' had been laid 'vnder coulor of such exercise'. At Shrewsbury, for example (and did Bentham know about this?), one of the moderators of the exercise had made a long discourse comparing the bishops to the scribes and Pharisees, who hated and persecuted Christ because he told them the truthe. 'I neither lyke the name of prophecie, nor yet th'order I heare to be vsed.'[13] Cox was brutal. 'To what end your questions tende I can not tell. This I can tell: the worlde is full of new fangles and fancyes.'[14] Both Scory and Cox were elderly, world weary and veterans of the Edwardian church and the Marian exile.

Among the additional Fairhurst papers acquired by Lambeth in 1988, there is a volume, now MS 3470, containing further evidence of the prophesyings and of Grindal's troubles, and it is from this collection that most of the documents which follow are taken. They include two letters not found in MS 2003 and Lehmberg's edition (although there are copies in BL, Add. MS 29546), and they are published here for the first time: letters from Bishop Richard Cheyney of Gloucester and John Aylmer, from 1561 rector of Cossington, Leicestershire, and in 1576 still arch-deacon of Lincoln. Both are of some interest. Cheyney's favourable account of what he calls 'exercises of learning' seems out of character, since he is known as theo-logically the most conservative, even crypto-catholic, of the Elizabethan bishops. He has been called 'idiosyncratic', 'an unwilling protestant'. Archbishop Parker had wanted to get rid of him, and in 1571 had excommunicated him for refusing to subscribe to the Thirty-Nine Articles.[15] Perhaps Cheyney was doing no more than toe what he took to be the party line in the autumn of 1576. Aylmer's letter, the only letter written directly to Grindal from someone below the rank of bishop, is evidence, if we needed it, of the bulldog-like animosity to puritanism which within

---

[13] *Ibid.*, fo. 10.
[14] *Ibid.*, fo. 7.
[15] Caroline Litzenberger, *The English Reformation and the laity: Gloucestershire, 1540–1580* (Cambridge, 1997), pp. 106–10; Usher, *William Cecil and episcopacy*, pp. 91–3; *ODNB*, art. Cheyney.

months would make him the queen's (and Sir Christopher Hatton's) favoured candidate for the bishopric of London, after many years in the wilderness, the consequence in all probability of his ill-judged reply to John Knox's *First blast of the trumpet against the monstrous regiment of women*, Aylmer's *Harborowe for true and faithful subiects* (1559).[16] Aylmer's letter is also grounds for the justified suspicion that when his bishop told Grindal that the complaints about the exercises had originated 'not many miles off', and involved 'some that seeke to creepe in fauour not onlie by their owne well doenges, but by the discrediting of others well doenges', he had his archdeacon of Lincoln in mind.[17] But Aylmer's letter is otherwise precious evidence of what might be called the methodology of radical puritanism in its east midlands heartland, particularly of the activities of what Aylmer called 'rangers and posting apostles'.[18]

1. Richard Cheyney, bishop of Gloucester, to Archbishop Edmund Grindal, 15 September 1576, autograph: LPL, MS 3470, fo. 20r

My dutie humblie remembred to your grace. for answer touchinge thexercise of learning vsed in my diocese. there haue been quiet meetinges in two places. thone hathe ceassed thease twoo yeares by occasion of the moderators departing owt of the diocese, his name is Mr Wynfeld.[19] Of late I caussed thother to cease, hearing what a doe had been in Northamptonshire and considering the weaknes in learning of the moderator whose name is Mr Becke[20] a preacher no graduate, but verie honest and zealouse, well mynded, but vnhable to wealde such a matter. His exercise was kepte once in a fortnight or thre wekes. The honest and quiet men of the cleargie haue encreasid their learning, by occasion of thexercise. I can like the continuance

---

16 When Grindal had been named for York in 1569, Archbishop Parker had wanted Aylmer to replace him in London. 'I think certainly the Queen's Highness should have a good, fast, earnest servitor at London of him.' But, according to Brett Usher, there was then 'a Stop Aylmer' campaign, organized jointly by Leicester and Cecil. Usher further believes that Aylmer would not have become bishop of London except for the circumstances of Grindal's disgrace; and that Cecil (Lord Burghley) came to regard his elevation 'both as an unmitigated disaster and as an error of political judgment' (Usher, *William Cecil and episcopacy*, pp. 109–10, 141–2; *ODNB*, art. Aylmer).

17 LPL, MS 2003, fo. 29. On Cooper and Aylmer in 1577, Usher, *William Cecil and episcopacy*, pp. 141–2.

18 'Apostle' implies an itinerant preaching minister without a fixed cure. According to the best Calvinist principles, this was an irregularity, but one which radical Elizabethan puritans must have regarded as legitimate, in the conditions in which they found themselves, which included, in Northamptonshire in the mid-1570s, the suspension and deprivation of some leading preachers. The successor to the 'apostles' named in Aylmer's letter, ten years on, was a certain William Fludd, a shadowy figure who allegedly rode about Northamptonshire 'like an apostle or patriarch...always taking upon him to be a chief director' (Collinson, *The Elizabethan puritan movement*, pp. 324–5).

19 William Wyngfeld, MA, was instituted rector of Buckland in the diocese of Gloucester on 21 July 1573 (The National Archives (TNA), E331, Glouc. 2). I owe this reference to John Craig.

20 Jacobus Becke was instituted as perpetual curate of Chirche Staneway (Stanway) in the diocese of Gloucester on 6 Apr. 1564 (TNA, E331, Glouc. 2). I owe this reference to John Craig. Becke will have been put into Stanway by the lord of the manor, Richard Tracy (by 1501–69), son of the evangelical pioneer William Tracy of Toddington and a true chip off the old block, author in the 1540s of a number of protestant pamphlets (*The history of parliament. The House of Commons 1509–1558*, ed. S. T. Bindoff (3 vols., London, 1982), III, 471–3). For evidence of nonconformity at Stanway, and that Tracy had himself preached in the parish (and taken part in prophesying?), see Litzenberger, *The English Reformation and the laity*, pp. 114–15.

so they medle not with matiers in controversie and have a moderator that excelleth
in learninge, and admitt no laye man to speake in theire exercise. In their so doinge
I promised them my helpe and furtheraunce because it maketh them more redie
in the scriptures and more apte to instruct and teache god[s] people comitted to
their charge. Lastlie I would wishe that every minister that resortethe to thexercise
prouide a paper booke, wherin he maye note what scriptures or other good learning
is brought for the matter, or commune place propounded: and those commune places
to be sett downe by your g[race] and the learned fathers with thaduise of other the
best learned in euerie diocese and so to be deliuered to the learned moderatours in
places where exercise is had.[21] God blesse your grace with all his good gyftes and
graces. From Gloucester the xvth of September 1576. Your G[race] to commaunde
in C[hristo].

Ric. Glouc.

Endorsed on fo. 21v, in Grindal's hand: 'Epis[copus] Glocestrensis de Exercitiis
Ministrorum'.

Another copy in BL, Add. MS 29546, fo. 56r.

2. John Aylmer to Archbishop Edmund Grindal, 25 September 1576, holograph:
LPL, MS 3470, fo. 22

my duty humbly remembered vnto your grace. Yt maye please yow to understand
that since my coming in to lecester Shire I have observed the Course of this courset
I praye god I maye not saye this cursid world and I assure your grace I have fownd
great boldnes in the meaner sorte which will er[e] yt be longe bringe great confusion in the Church if yt be not speedyly preventyd. There is of late a ranke of
rangers and posting apostles that go from shire to Shire from exercise to exercise
namely patchet[22] standon[23] etc. accompanyed cowntenaunced and backed with Sir

---

21 Cheyney recommends what was to become standard practice, after the suppression of the prophesyings. For similar arrangements in the archdeaconries of London and St Albans before 1576, see the
letters to Bishop Sandys from John Mullins, archdeacon of London, and David Kemp, archdeacon of
St Albans, LPL, MS 2003, fos. 23, 16–18.
22 'patchet' must be Eusebius Paget, rector of two Northamptonshire livings, Old from 1569 and and
Lamport from 1572, until his deprivation for nonconformity in 1574. Besides his leading *rôle* in the
prophesyings, especially at Southam, Paget ministered in the household of his uncle and patron, John
Isham, and was the true author of one of the most popular and enduring of catechisms, attributed
to 'Robert Openshawe'. In 1581 the patronage of the earl of Bedford and the influence with Sir
Richard Grenville of Francis Hastings, brother of the earl of Huntingdon, secured Paget the rectory
of Kilkhampton in Cornwall, where his collaboration with the radical Scottish preacher David Black
landed him in further trouble (Francis J. Bremer and Tom Webster (eds.), *Puritans and puritanism in
Europe and America: a comprehensive encyclopedia* (Santa Barbara, 2006), art. Paget). Sir Walter
Mildmay's papers contain the (undated) record of Paget's examination before the High Commission
(Northamptonshire Record Office, MS F. (M.) P. 56).
23 Nicholas Standon had been deprived of a London living in the first drive against nonconformity of
1566, and was an early member of the London conference organized by John Field. By 1573 he was
in Northamptonshire, enjoying the patronage of George Carleton (see n. 25) at Overston, where the
book of common prayer had been abandoned in favour of communal psalm-singing and preaching,
a matter of concern to Bishop Edmund Scambler of Peterborough (W. J. Sheils, *The puritans in the
diocese of Peterborough 1558–1610*, Northamptonshire Record Society 30 (1979), pp. 28–9, 127).

R. Knitley[24] Mr Carlell[25] and others out of Warw[ickshire] northampton and other Shires to Ashby where Gilby is busshopp[26] to Lecester where Johnson is superin-tendent[27] to another place where the monke Anderson reigneth[28] to Covent[ry] etc. and there are BB. [bishops, 'rayled at' – BL, Add. MS 21565] dressyd metropoli-tanes wondred at for ther visitacions for ther officers ther pompe ther not visiting and what not as within this fourtenight patchett and Standen bestowed them at Lec[ester] and one of no small birthe and cowntenaunce when I urged him to shewe me some instants ['instances' – BL, Add. MS 21565] of sp[iritu]all faultes of ['in' – BL, Add. MS 21565] sp[iritu]all men in the Clergye ['in the Clergye' omitted, 'persons' – in BL, Add. MS 21565] he said that the Archb[ishop] of Cant[erbury] diffred not from a pope, and that Idolatrously he kept in his gallery an old busshpp with a Crosse what I replyed and who he is I will tell your grace another time. I have my selfe some parishioners that refusing my communion because wee kneele resorte to a walking communion[29] at Lecester ministred by an ignorant man. your graces inquisition was by my L[ord] of Lincolne commytted to one Sparke[30] and Willoke[31] who them selfes never minister the communion because they will were no surplesses. and use standing communions with other disorders/ therefore yowr grace had neede take heede howe yow credytt the certificates/ I heare that my L[ord]

---

24 Sir Richard Knightley, a prominent friend and patron of radical puritanism, from under whose roof 'Martin Marprelate' would later publish some of his libels (*ODNB*, art. Knightley).

25 'Carlell' must be George Carleton, another puritan militant (and MP) with connexions to the Marprelate affair (*ODNB*, art. Carleton).

26 Anthony Gilby, 'Father Gilby', given his age and seniority, was a leading figure in what might be called the first wave of Elizabethan puritanism. He lived under the secure protection of the earl of Huntingdon at Ashby de la Zouche. See extensive references in Collinson, *The Elizabethan puritan movement*.

27 'Johnson' presents problems. There were three Robert Johnsons prominent in different ways in the Elizabethan church and puritan movement, one of them Robert Johnson, rector of North Luffenham, Rutland, from 1574, later archdeacon of Leicester, a man of considerable wealth, benefactor of Emmanuel College, Cambridge, and founder of the schools of Oakham and Upppingham. But Aylmer must be referring to Jefferie Johnson, at this time a preacher in Leicester funded by the earl of Huntingdon. In his letter to Grindal of 27 July 1576, Bishop Cooper of Lincoln wrote that 'Leicestre towne' was 'the worst place and that which alwaies I haue most suspected'. 'One Johnson that is a moderatour there' was 'somewhat a rash man and so moche as he dare inclined to nouelties' (LPL, MS 2003, fo. 30).

28 Who was 'the monke Anderson'? Possibly David Anderson, a prominent Scottish preacher active in the London parish of St Botolph's Aldgate from 1583. I owe this suggestion to John Craig.

29 To receive the communion walking past the table resembles some continental Lutheran practice but may have been less common in Elizabethan England than receiving seated, either around the table (rather than kneeling), perhaps especially in small rural churches, or in the pews or other seats in the church, with the elements taken down (the practice with baptists today). There is evidence of standing, or walking, communions from Moreton Corbet in Shropshire, Watford and Whiston in Northamptonshire, and even from the Temple Church in London in Walter Travers's time. According to 'the order of Northampton', the work of the Genevan veteran Percival Wiburn, the people 'for the dispatche of manye, doe aryse from their pewes and so passe to the Communyon table, where they receave the sacrament, and from there in lyke order to their place' (Collinson, 'The puritan classical movement in the reign of Elizabeth I', pp. 745–6). The order of Northampton is in TNA, SP 12/78/38.

30 Thomas Sparke was a prominent puritan who represented the cause both in a disputation with Arch-bishop Whitgift and other bishops at Lambeth in 1584 and at the Hampton Court Conference in 1604. After Hampton Court he in effect changed sides, publishing in 1607 his *Brotherly perswasion to unitie and uniformitie* (*ODNB*, art. Sparke).

31 'one Willoke' was no nonentity. A Scot, John Whillock co-authored with John Knox the *First book of discipline* of the reformed Scottish kirk, and in 1567 served as moderator of its General Assembly. He was rector of Loughborough, Leicestershire, from 1562 to 1585 (*ODNB*, art. Willock).

of Lincoln hath inhibited thes ['the' – BL, Add. MS 21565] exercises which I must ['needs' – BL, Add. MS 21565] saye dyd moche proffytt the yonger sorte of mynistres if they could have ben bridled from glauncing and girding at ther superiors which is hard to be done for envy is a cancre in the nature of man. They are in some hope to have the said exercises restored but your grace and my L[ord] of Lincoln had neede well considere of yt/

This bearer being a man of my bringing vp and now an honest and diligent preacher is to be a sewter to your grace for a plurality for ii little benefyces being lesse than a mile out from another ['one from the other' – BL, Add. MS 21565] of very small valewe, wherin I besech your grace stand his good L[ord] and the rayther in respecte of this my humble sewte. Thalmighty send your grace good and longe helth to the glory of god and the profytt of his Churche. Cosington in Lec[stershire] 25 of septembre 1576.

Your graces humbly to command in [Christo]

John Elmer

Endorsed on fo. 23v, in Grindal's hand: 'Mr Aelmer off the propheti in Leycestershyre/ off Pagett Standon etc.'

Another copy, BL, Add. MS 29546, fo. 56v.

Grindal's letter to the queen

Grindal begged the queen to read with patience 'this that I now sende written with myne owne rude scribbling hand', quoting St Ambrose in an epistle to the emperor Theodosius (no. 51 of his collected letters): 'Scribo manu meo quod sola legas' – 'That you alone may read it.' Yet no holograph of the letter survives, only a number of fair copies.[32] What seems to have happened was this. From a letter which Grindal addressed to Burghley on 16 December 1576 it appears that his letter to the queen was written on 8 December.[33] Yet most copies are dated 20 December. That would seem to be the day when the letter was finally shown to the queen. In the interval between these two dates copies had been made, primarily, it would seem, for the benefit of members of the privy council. The copy in the Lansdowne MSS in the BL (Lansdowne 23, no. 12, fos. 24–9v) is endorsed in Burghley's hand '20 December 1576 Epistola Edmundi Cantuar Arch. ad D. Reginam.' An almost identical copy in the Northamptonshire Record Office, Fitzwilliam of Milton papers (MS F.(M).P.54) was Sir Walter Mildmay's.[34] Lehmberg printed the copy in LPL, MS 2014, fos. 17–22. Given the occasion, it would be nice to use the same version in this edition. But the LPL copy is post-Elizabethan, and at many points corrupt. The following extracts follow MS Lansdowne 23, a text which was printed, with fair accuracy, in

---

[32] The tag from Ambrose occurs in no. 51 of his Epistles, a celebrated rebuke to the emperor Theodosius, following the atrocity of a massacre at Thessalonica, and calling upon him to do penance (*The letters of S. Ambrose bishop of Milan*, Library of Fathers of the Holy Catholic Church (Oxford, 1881), p. 328).

[33] Grindal, *Remains*, p. 391.

[34] Endorsed in Mildmay's hand: 'from D. Grindall Archb. of Canterbury'.

The remains of Edmund Grindal, *ed. W. Nicholson, Parker Society (Cambridge, 1843), pp. 376–90.*

3. Archbishop Edmund Grindal to Queen Elizabeth, [8 December 1576]

[fo. 24r] With most humble remembrance of my bounden dewtie to your Majestie: yt maye please the same to be advertised that the speeches which it hath pleased yow to delyver vnto me when I last attended on your Highness concerninge abridgeing the number of preachers, and the vtter suppression of all learned exercises and conferences amonge the ministers of the Churche, allowed by their bisshoppes and ordinaries have exceedingly dismayed and discomforted me: Not so much for that the said speeches sounded very hardly against myne owne person, being but one perticular man and not much to be accompted of, but most of all for that the same might both tende to the publike harme of gods church, (whereof your highnes ought by office to be *Nutricia* [nurse]), and also to the heavie burdening of youre owne conscience before god if they shold be put in strickt execution. It was not your Majesties pleasure then the tyme not servinge thereto, to heare me at any length concerninge the said two matters then propounded. I thought it therefore my dutie by writing to declare some parte of my minde vnto your highnes, beseaching the same with pacience to read over this that I nowe send written with myne owne rude scribbling hand which semeth to be of more length then it is indeed. For I saye with Ambrose, *Scribo manu meo quod sola legas.* [Margin: Ambrosius ad Valentinian. Imperat.]

Madame first of all I must and will duringe my life confesse that there is noe earthly creature to whome I am so much bounden as to your Majestie who notwithstanding myn insufficiencye (which comendeth your grace the more) hath bestowed vppon me soe many and so great benefytes as I cold never hope for much lesse deserve. I doe therefore according to my most bounden dewtie with all thankes gyvinge beare towardes your Majestie a most humble faythfull and thankefull harte, and that knoweth he which knoweth all thinges. Neither doe I ever intende to offend your Majestie in any thinge, vnlesse in the cause of god and of his Church by necessitie of office and burden of Conscience I shall therevnto be enforced. And in those causes which I trust in god shall never be vrged vpon me if I shold vse desemblinge or flattering silence I shold very evill requite youre Majestie's so many and so great benefittes for in so doinge both you might fale into perill towardes god and I my selfe into endlesse damnacion. The prophet Ezechiell termeth vs ministeres of the Church *Speculators* and not *Adulatores* yf we see the sworde cominge by reason of any offence towardes god we must of necessitie give warning or els the bloode of those that perrishe will be required at our handes. I beseeche your Majestie thus to thinke of me that I doe not conceyve any evell opinion of you although I cannot assent to those two articles ther propounded.

...

[fo. 24v] But surely I cannot marvaile enough how this strainge opynion shold once enter into youre minde that it shold be good for the church to have five [LPL, MS 2014, 'fewe'] preachers. Alas Madame, is the scripture more playne in any one thinge, then that the gospell of christ shold be plentyfullie preached and that plentie of laborers shold be sent into the lords harvest, which being great and

large standethe neede not of a fewe but many woorkemen [margin: Math[ew] 9]...
And in this place I beseech your Majestie to note one thing necessarie to be noted
which is this, If the holy goste prescribe expressely that preachers shold be placed
oppidatim [in every town], how can it well be thought that thre or four preachers
maie suffice for a shyer.

Publick and continuall preaching of godes word is the ordinarie meane and
instrument of the salvation of mankinde. S Paule calleth it the ministerie of reconciliation of man vnto god [margin: 2 Cori[nthians] 5]. By preaching of godes word,
the glorie of god is enlarged, fayth is nourished, and charitie increased. By it the
ignorant is instructed, the negligent exhorted and incyted, the stubborne rebuked,
the weake conscience comforted [margin: Psalm 30] and to all those that sinne of
malicious wickednes the wrath of god is threatened. By preaching also due obedience to Christian princes and magistrates is planted in the hartes of subiectes. For
obedience procedeth of conscience conscience is grounded vppon the word of god,
the worde of god worketh his effect by preaching, so as generally where preaching
wanteth obedience failteth [margin: Ro[mans] 13.5/ Ro[mans] 16.19]. No prince
ever had more lively experience hereof then your Majestie hath had in your tyme
and maie have dayly.

Yf your Majestie come to your Citie of London never so ofte, what congratu-
lacion, what ioye, what concourse of people is there to be seene. Yea, what acclamations and prayers to god for your longe lyfe and other manifest significations
of inwarde and vnfayned love, ioyned with most humble and hartie obedience are
there to be heard? Wherof cometh this Madame but of the continuall preaching of
godes word in that Citie, whereby that people hath bin plentifully instructed in theire
duetyies towardes god and your Majestie? On the contrary what bredd the rebellion
in the North? Was it not papistrie and ignoraunce of godes word through want of
often preaching, and in the tyme of that rebellion were not all men of all states that
made profession of the gospell most redie to offer their lyves for your defence. In so
much that one poore parish in Yorkeshyre which by continuall preaching had been
better instructed then the rest (Hallifax, I meane) was redie to bring three or four
thousand hable men into the fielde to serve you against the said rebelles.

[fo. 25v] How can your Majestie have a more lyvely tryall and experience of
the contrarye effects of much preaching and of lyttle or no preachinge, the one
working most faythfull obedience and the other most vnaturall disdobedience and
rebellion.

But it is thought of some that many are admitted to preach and few be able
to do it well. That vnable preachers be removed it is verie requisit if abilitie and
sufficiency maie be rightly weighed and iudged, and therein I trust as much is and
shall be done as can be. For both I for myne own part (lett it be spoken without any
ostentacion) I am verie carefull in allowing such preachers onely as be able and
sufficient to be preachers, both for their knowledge in the scriptures, and alsoe for
testimonie of their good lyfe and conversacion. And besides that, I have given very
greate charge to the rest of my brethren the bishops of this province to do the lyke.
We admitt no man to the office that eyther professeth papistrie or puritanism, generally the graduates of the vniversities are onely admitted to be preachers vnlesse it
be some fewe which have excellent giftes of knowledge in the scriptures ioyned
with good vtterance and godly persuation. I my self procured above fortie learned
preachers and graduates within lesse then vi yeres to be placed within the diocesse
of Yorke, besides those I found there, and there I have lefte them. The frutes of

whose travell in preaching your Majestie is lyke to reape dayliie by most assured duetifull obedience of your subiectes in those partes.[35]

...

[fo. 26r] Now where as it is thowght that the reading of the godly homelies set foorth by publicke authoritie may suffice I continue of the same minde I was when I attended laste vppon your Majestie. The reading of homelies hath his comoditie but is nothing comparable to the office of preaching ... Exhortations reprehensions and perswasiones are vttered with more affection to the moving of the hearers in sermons then in homelies. Besides homelies weare devised by the godly Busshoppes in your Brothers tyme only to supplie necessitie for wante of preachers and are by the statute not to be preferred but to geve place to sermons whensoever they maye be had, and were never thowght in them selves alone to conteine sufficient instruction for the Churche of England ... Yf every flocke might have a preachinge pastor (which is rather to be wisshed then hoped for) then were reading of homelies altogether vnnecessary. But to supplie that want of preaching of godes word which is the foode of the soule growing vppon the necessities before mentioned bothe in your Brothers tyme and in your tyme, certen godly homelies [fo. 26v] have bin devised, that the people should not be altogether destitute of instruction, for it is an ould and a trewe proverbe, better halfe a loafe then no breade.[36]

...

Now for the second point, which is concerning the learned exercise and conference amongst the ministers of the church I have consulted with divers of my Brethren the Busshoppes by letters who think the same as I doe a thinge profittable to the Churche and therefore expedient to be continued and I trust your Majestie will thinke like when your highnes shall have been enformed of the manner and order thereof, what authoritie it hath of the scriptures, what comodity it bringeth with it and what incomodities will followe yf it be cleane taken awaye. The authors of this exercise are the Busshoppes of the dioces where the same is vsed who both by the lawe of god and by the Cannons and Constitutions of the Churche now in force have authoritie to appoint exercise to their inferior ministers for increase of learning and knowledge in the scriptures as to them seemeth most expedient for that pertaineth *ad disciplinam clericalem*.[37] The tymes appointed for the assembly is once a moneth or

---

35 Grindal's York Register and Institution Act Books record, separately, 'ordines speciales', men whom the archbishop had hand-picked to spearhead the reform of the north. There is some unintentional irony in what he reported to the queen. Among these special men was one Christopher Shute, from Grindal's college of Pembroke Hall. Shute would be vicar of Giggleswick for half a century, from 1576 to 1626. The fruit of Shute's travails in preaching was a radical religious tradition in the Craven district of Yorkshire which in the seventeenth century fed into Quakerism.

36 An alternative to the publicly approved Homilies of the Church of England was provided by the sermons of the Zurich reformer Heinrich Bullinger, known in England as his *Decades*. First published in England in 1577, they were promoted in the diocese of Lincoln by Bishop Cooper. Somewhat pointedly, the anonymous tanslator, one 'H.I., student in Divinitie', lambasted those 'Phanaticall fellowes' who would not allow homilies or sermons to be read in churches, 'be they never so sound, pithie and effectuall'. I owe this information to John Craig. Did this implicitly refer to Grindal's views on the matter?

37 Grindal seems to be deliberately conflating exercises, in the sense of purely clerical exercises, of the kind which would be very widely adopted, and enforced, in the time of his successor, Archbishop Whitgift, with the more controversial prophesyings.

once in xii or xv dayes, at the discretion of the ordinary. The tyme of the exercise is two howers the place the church of the town appointed for the assembly the matter intreated of is as followeth. Some text of Scripture before appointed to be spoken of is interpreted in this order. First the occasion of the place is showed, 2 the ende 3 the proper sense of the place 4 the proprietie of the woords and those that be learned in the tongues shewing the diversities of interpretations, 5 where the like phrases are vsed in the scriptures, 6 places in the scriptures seeming to repugn are reconciled, 7 the argumentes of the text are opened 8 it is also declared what vertues and what vices are theare towched and to which of the Commandementes they pertaine 9 how the texte hath bin wrested by the adversaries if occasion so require 10 And last of all what doctrine of fayth or manners the texte doth conteyne. The conclusion is with the prayer for your Majestie and all estates as is appointed by the booke of Common praier and a psalme.

These orders following are allso observed in the said exercise first twoe or three of the gravest and best learned pastors are appointed of the bushopp to moderate in every assembly noe man may speake vnless he be firste allowed by the Bushopp with this proviso that no laye man be suffered to speake at any tyme no controversie of this present tyme and state shall be moved or delt withall yf any attempte the contrary he is put to silence by the moderator. None is suffered to glaunce openly or covertly at persons publique or private: neither yet any one to confute an other. [fo. 27r] If any man vtter a wrong sence of the Scripture he is privately admonished thereof and better instructed by the moderators and other his fellowe Ministers. Yf anye man vse immodest speaches or irreuerent gestures or behavior or otherwise be suspected in lyfe, he is likewise admonished as before. Yf any man willfully doe breake these orders he is presented to the Busshop to be by him corrected.

...

Howsoever reporte hath bin made to your Majestie concerning the rest of these exercises, yet I and others of your Busshoppes whose names are noted in the margent hereof[38] as they have testified vnto me by their letters, have found by experience that those prophittes and commodities following have ensued of them.

[fo. 27v] The ministers of the Churche are more skillful and reddy in the scriptures and apter to teach their flockes. 2. It withdraweth them from Idlenes and wandring gaming, etc. 3 Some afore suspected in doctrine are browght herby to open confession of the treuth. 4 Ignorant ministers are drawen to studie if not for conscience yet for shame and feare of discipline. 5 The opinion of laye men as towching the Idlenes of the Clergie is hereby removed. 6 Nothing by experience beateth downe popery more then that Ministers as some of my brethren certefye growe to such good knowledge by meanes of these exercises that where afore were not three able preachers now ar xxx[tie] meate to preache at Poules Crosse and xl or l besides able to instruct there own cures. So as it is found by experience the best meanes to increase knowledge in the simple and to continue it in the learned. Only backward men in relligion and contemners of learning in the countries abroade doe freatt against it which in truthe dothe the more commend it. The dissolution of it wold breade triumphe to the adversaries and greate sorowe and griefe vnto

---

38   A marginal note specifies the archbishop of Canterbury, and the bishops of London, Winchester, Bath and Wells, Coventry and Lichfield, Gloucester, Lincoln, Chichester, Exeter and St Davids.

the favourers of Religion…And althoughe some fewe have abused this good and necessary exercise ther is no reason that the malice of a fewe shuld preiudice all. Abuses may be reformed and that which is good may remaine. Neither is there eny iust cause of offence to be taken yf divers men make divers senses of one sentence of scripture, so that all the senses be good and agreeable to the analogie and properties of fayth.

…

I truste when your Majestie hath considered and well weied the premisses, you will reste satisfied and iudge that no suche inconveniences can growe of these exercises as yow have bin enformed but rather the cleere contrary. And for my owne parte I am well assured, bothe by reasons and argumentes taken out of the holy scriptures and by experience the certeine seale of suer knowledge, that the said exercises for the interpretation and exposition of the scriptures and for exhortation and comfort drawen out of [fo. 28r] the same are both profittable to encrease knowledge amonges the ministers and tendeth to the edyfieng of the hearers. I am forced with all humilitie and yet plainely to professe that I can not with safe conscience and without the offence of the Majestie of god give my assent to the suppressing of the said exercises. Much lesse can I send out any iniunction for the vtter and vniuersall subvertion of the same. I saie with St Paule I have no power to destroye but only to edefie [margin: 1 Cor[inthians] 10] and with the same Apostle, I can do nothing against the truth but with the truth.

Yf it be your Majesties pleasure for this or any other cause to remove me out of this place I will with all humilitie yeld thereunto And render againe to your Majestie that I received of the same … And what should I winne if I gayned (I will not saie a bishoprycke but) the whole world and lose myne owne soule.

Beare with me I besech yow Madame, if I chuse rather to offend your earthly Majestie then to offend the heavenly Majestie of god. And now being sorie that I have bine so long and tedious to your Majestie, I will drawe to an end most humbly praying the same well to consider these two short petitions following.

The first is that yow wold reserue all these ecclesiasticall matters which touch religion or the doctrine and discipline of the Church vnto the bishops and divines of your realm, according to the example of all godly Christian Emperours and princes of all ages, for in deede they are to be iudged (as an auncient Father wryteth) *in ecclesia seu sinodo non in palatio*.[39] When your Majestie hath questions of the lawes of your realme yow doe not decyde the same in your Court but send them to your iudges to be determined. Lykewise for doubtes in matters of doctryne or disciplyne of the Church the ordinari waie is to referre decesions of the same to the bishops and other head ministers of the Church. Ambrose to Theodosius vseth these wordes, *Si de causis pecuniariis comites tuos consulis quanto magis in cause religionis sacerdotes domini aequum est consulas*.[40] [fo. 28r] The said Ambrose so much commended in all histories for a godlye Bishope, goeth yet further and

---

[39] 'In the Church, or the synod, not in the palace.' For the Ambrosian ideology expressed in this and other passages, see S. L. Greenslade (ed.), *Early Latin theology*, Library of Christian Classics 5 (London, 1956), pp. 178–81.

[40] 'If in financial matters you consult your Courts, how much more fitting is it that in the causes of religion you should consult the Bishops of the Lord?' (Epistle 40, to the emperor Theodosius, in *The letters of S. Ambrose*, p. 267).

wryteth vnto the said Emperor [Constantinus] in this forme, *Si docendus est episcopus a laico quid sequitur?*[41]

... Would to god your Majestie wolde follow this ordinarie course, yow shold
procure to your self much quyetnes of mind better please god, avoyd many offences
and the Church should be more quietly and peacabely governed, much to your
comfort and commoditie of your Realme.

The second petition I have to make to your Majestie is this, that when you deale
in matters of fayth and relligion or matters that touch the Church of Christ which is
his spouse, bought with so deare a price yow wold not vse to pronounce so resolutye
and peremptorilie *quasi ex authoritate* as ye maye do in civill and externe matters,
but allwaies remember that in godes causes the will of god (and not the will of any
earthly creature) is to take place ... In godes matters all princes ought to bowe their
scepters to the sonne of god, and to aske councell at his mowth what they ought
to do ...

Remember, Madame that yow are a mortall creature, looke not onely (as was said
to Theodosius) vppon the purple and princely arraye wherewith you are apparelled
[margin: Theodoret eccles. hist. 5.cap 8] but consider withall what it is that that
is covered therewith. Is it not flesh and blood? is it not dust and ashes? is it not a
corruptible bodie which must returne to his erth againe (god knoweth how sone) ...

Wherefore I besech you, Madame, *in visceribus Christi*, when yow deale in these
religious causes, set the majestie of god before your eyes, [fo. 29r] layeinge all
earthly majestie aside, determyn with yowr self to obeye his voice and with all
humilitie saye vnto him, *non mea sed tua voluntas fie*[42] God hath blessed yow with
great felicitie in youre raigne nowe many yeres beware you doe not impute the same
to your owne [LPL, MS 2014 'witt'] desertes, or policie, but gyve god the glory ...

Ye have donne many thinges well, but except ye percever to the ende ye cannot
be blessed. For yf ye torne from god then god will turne awaye his mercyfull coun-
tenaunce fron you, and what remayneth then to be loked for, but only a terrible
expectacion of godes iudgmentes and an heapeing vp of wrath against the daye of
wrath.[43] But I trust in God youre majestie will alwaies humble youre self vnder his
mightie hand and goe forward in the zealous setting forth of godes true religion
allwaies yelding dewe obedience and reverence to the word of god the onely rule of
fayth and religion. And if ye soe doe, although god hath iust Cause many waies to
be angry with yow and us for our unfaithfullness [LPL, MS 2014 'vnthenkefulnes']

---

[41] 'If a layman may teach a Bishop, what may follow?' (Epistle 21, to the emperor Valentinian, *ibid.*,
p. 138.) Earlier in the same letter: 'When have you ever heard, most gracious Emperor, that laymen
had judged a Bishop in a matter pertaining to the Faith?'

[42] 'Not my will but thine be done' (Mark 14.36).

[43] This apparently threatening language was within a convention of prophetically judgmental rhetoric, and by no means unique to Grindal's letter. See, for example, John Hales's oration to Queen
Elizabeth at the beginning of her reign, printed by John Foxe in the 1576 edition of *Acts and monuments*; and much admonitory material in Thomas Bentley's *The monument of matrones* (1582). See
Patrick Collinson, 'Windows in a woman's soul: questions about the religion of Elizabeth I', in his
Elizabethan essays (London, 1994), pp. 87–118. Lest this should be thought to be a matter of male
chauvinism, it should be noted that James VI and I seems to have been subjected to the same sort
of pulpit rhetoric in a sermon preached by Bishop Tobie Matthew at Newcastle on his way south in
1603, Matthew's text, 1 Chronicles 15, 1–2: 'The Lord is with you, while ye be with him, and if ye
seke him, he wil be founde of you, but if ye forsake him, he wil forsake you' (Peter E. McCullough,
Sermons at court: politics and religion in Elizabethan and Jacobean preaching (Cambridge, 1998),
p. 103).

yet I doubt nothinge but that for his own names sake, and for his own gloryes sake, he will still hold his mercyfull hand over vs, shield and protect vs under the shadowe of his winges, as he hath done hetherto. I beseeche god our heavenly father plentifullie to power his principall spirite vpon yow, and alwaies to direct your hart in his hollie feare. Amen.

Archbishop Grindal in defence of the prophesyings and of his own actions

Grindal had an analysis made of the letters he had received from the bishops.[44] *He wrote a substantial apologetic treatise on the subject of the prophesyings, which is contained in LPL, MS 2014, fos. 72–80 and MS 2007 fos. 126–44. There is a synopsis of the four chapters on fo. 72v of MS 2014, 'Ordo huius tractatus de exercitiis'. The fourth chapter is headed 'Quod prophetia sit ritenenda', 'that prophesying may be retained'. The hand is that of a chaplain, or other amanuensis, with interpolations in Grindal's hand. There is further, related, material in MS 2872. LPL, MS 3470, fos. 32–9v contains summary Latin notes for the treatise in Grindal's hand, dated 16 March 1577, and consisting for the most part of 'Objections' and 'Responses'. Are these the only surviving working materials for a book in the hand of an archbishop of Canterbury from this period? And, in addition to this labour, Grindal composed a set of 'Orders for reformation of abuses about the learned exercises and conferences amongst the ministers of the Church'.*[45] *Amongst other corrective reforms, Grindal closed the door against the participation of the likes of Aylmer's 'posting apostles'; and ruled, 'ante omnia', that no lay person be suffered to speak publicly in those assemblies.*

Material in LPL, MS 3470 fos. 24–9, partly in Grindal's, partly in a scribal hand, 'Instances againste the argument of indifference', addresses the case that since prophesying was 'a thing indifferent', 'adiaphora', it was legitimate for authority to suppress it. The vestiarian controversy of the mid-1560s had seen extensive debate about things indifferent: did ecclesiastical vestments and other 'ornaments' fall within that category, but did their enforcement against the consciences of nonconformists rob them of their indifference? It is remarkable that Grindal's 'Instances' place him full-square on the 'puritan' side of this argument, remarkable in that the puritanism of Thomas Cartwright had no more resolute an opponent.[46] *In these commonplaces, Grindal addresses situations which might arise in an established Church such as the Church of England, in which it would be legitimate for a bishop to disregard an order 'though he be commanded', the position in which Grindal found himself.*

---

[44] BL, Add. MS, 21565, fo. 26.
[45] Grindal, *Remains*, pp. 373–4.
[46] On the vestments controversy and the issue of adiaphora, see John H. Primus, *The vestments controversy: an historical study of the earliest tensions within the Church of England in the reigns of Edward VI and Elizabeth* (Kampen, 1960), and Bernard Verkamp, *The indifferent mean: adiaphorism in the English Reformation to 1554* (Athens, OH, 1977); and, most relevantly, with particular reference to St Paul's distinction between lawfulness and expediency in 1 Corinthians, and its applicability to the concept of 'edification', John S. Coolidge, *The Pauline renaissance in England: puritanism and the Bible* (Oxford, 1970). Grindal told Cecil in 1570 that Thomas Cartwright and his kind must be 'bridled by authority'. As for Cartwright himself, 'he hath a busy head, stuffed full of singularities' (Grindal, *Remains*, pp. 304–5). So much for the puritan archbishop!

4. Instances againste the arg[ument] of indifference: LPL MS 3874, fos. 24–9

> Instances against this argument (They are not to
> be condemned that suppresse prophecies, ergo they
> ought to be iustified in so doing, or ergo, you
> being commaunded ought to suppresse them.)
> and first of thinges not merely indifferent.

1. Divers churches of Germanie professing the Gospell and having roodes[47] in their churches.

2. The crosse and candlestikes in the Q[ueen's] Chappell.[48]

3. St Paul his purifying, or circumcising Timothie, whereas yet he would not circumcise Titus.

4. The Auncient Fathers in dissolving second mariages.

5. Joseph for swearing by the lyfe of Pharao, wheras Polycarpus chose rather to dy, then to sweare by Caesars foirtune.

6. The Auncient fathers that ministred the euchariste vnto infantes.

7. The churches in Germanie that proffesse the Gospell and yet refuse the vse of excommunication.

8. The Christian princes that permitt the Jewes to lyve and exercise their religion within their dominions, whereas Ambrose doth vehemedntly defend the byshop that had burnt the Jewishe Synagog,or at the lest refused to reedifye it at the Emperours commaundement.[49]

> Other instances of thinges by their owne nature
> indifferent, and yet in respect of circumstances
> are not indifferent to be done though they
> be commanunded.[50]

---

[47] 'Roods' were crosses, especially the great crucifixes, flanked by images of Mary and John, which had been all but eliminated from English churches, but survived (as they still do) in Lutheran Germany.

[48] The cross and candlesticks in the Elizabethan Chapel Royal were a long-running bone of contention, the subject of a notorious passage in a sermon preached before the queen by the dean of St Paul's, Alexander Nowell, which Elizabeth scandalously interrupted. To my knowledge, this is the only occasion on record when a bishop (no less than the archbishop of Canterbury) declared these ornaments to be, not indifferent, but simply unlawful.

[49] No. 40 of the Epistles of Ambrose addressed the emperor Theodosius on the subject of the destruction of a Jewish synagogue at Callinicum on the distant Euphrates at the instigation of the local bishop. Theodosius had ordered restitution, which Ambrose ruled to be out of order. It was in the context of this letter that Ambrose asserted that it was the part of a bishop to speak his mind, and of an emperor to listen (Collinson, 'If Constantine, then also Theodosius', *Godly people*, p. 111).

[50] 'in respect of circumstances' touches the heart of the puritan objection to the vestments and other ornaments, the relevant circumstance in that case being the offence to the consciences of 'simple gospellers'.

1. To be maried or not is an indifferent thing, yet to give an iniunction that ministers should not marie, is not indifferent.[51]

2. The often or seldome administration of the sacramentes is indifferent, yet were it not indifferent for a B[ishop] in a churche established to inioyne that they should only once be mynistred in ii yeres though they were commaunded.

3. The number of preachers in one citie is indifferent, yet for a B[ishop] by commaundement to take order that in suche a citie as london is or Antioche was where there were many godly preachers and prophetes, and the multitude of Christians so great, all the rest should be restrayned saving one, were not indifferent.[52]

4. The age of preachers indifferent, yet is it not indifferent for a B[ishop] in considering the great necessitie of the churche and the excellencie of giftes in men of lesse yeares, to ordeyne vpon coimmaundement that none should be admitted to preache before he be 30 yeares ould alledging the example of Christe.

5. To eate is indifferent, yet it is not indifferent to commaund the weake conscience to eate fleashe on friday or to eate thinges offred to Idolls.[53]

6. The place of publick prayer and administration of the sacramentes is in nature indifferent, yet for a B[ishop] in a churche established, where the gospell hath free successe, and where there be convenient churches for the purpose, to ordeyne that thei should be vsed in privat mens houses or in the feldes or desertes, were not indifferent, thoughe he were commaunded.[54]

1. Cor[inthians] . 10 [.23]. In rebus adiaphoris id tantum licet quod expedit, et quod aedificationem conducit. Omnia mihi licet, sed non omnia conducent: omnia mihi licent, sed non omnia aedificant.[55]

[Scribal hand]   Instances against this argument (it is no mater or article of fayth ergo we ought to yeld vpon commaundement.)

1.   All the former instances serve against this argument.
2.   The commaundement that a woman of synguler lerninge should preache.

---

[51] This point is close to the bone. Although Elizabeth had not issued an injunction forbidding clerical marriage, her objection to it had been made clear from time to time, especially in 1561, when Archbishop Parker, himself a married man (but the last married archbishop of Canterbury for well over a century), felt obliged to write to Cecil: 'I was in an horror to hear such words to come from her mild nature and Christianly learned conscience.' 'We have cause all to be utterly discomforted and discouraged' – a curious prolepsis to Grindal's 1576 letter (*Correspondence of Matthew Parker*, ed. J. Bruce and T. T. Perowne, Parker Society (Cambridge, 1853), pp. 156–7).

[52] An obvious reference to the queen's alleged remark that three or four preachers should suffice for a shire.

[53] St Paul to the Corinthians on the thorny question of eating meat offered in sacrifice to idols was at the heart of the vestiarian controversy of the 1560s. See Coolidge, *The Pauline renaissance in England*.

[54] The Latin arguments which follow are mostly in Grindal's own hand.

[55] Geneva Bible: 'All things are lawefull for me, but all things are not expedient; all things are lawfull for me, but all things edifie not.'

[Grindal's hand]

3.   That women goe covered in the Congregation, is no matter
                     of faythe, and yett wer it nott well to geve a Contrarie
                     commaundement.[56]
                                    (abducit a veritate infirmos fieri potest vt
                     Scandalum vel (credant infirmii (quod supprimantur
                                    (prophetiae) illicitas et perniciosas esse,
                                    (cum antea pias et licitas putarint.
                                    2 (Confirmat in errore nempe illicitas
                                    (impias et perniciosas esse prophetias.

                     Vtrumque qunatum fieri potest vitandum.[57]

Either is to be avoided as far as possible.

Scandali Definitio

                     Scandalum spirituale, est obex in via spirituale disponens
                     ad Ruinam spiritualem.
ex summa Silvest[ri]   vel
                     Scandalum est dictum vel factum minus rectum (id
                     est secundum se malum, vel habens speciem mali)
                     praebens alteri occasionem ruinae.[58]

     Panorm[itanus =- Tudeschi] in Clementiniarum de prebendis Lib. 3[59]

                     Scandali occasio nemini offerenda[60]

Mat[hew] 18 [.6]   Qui scandalizaverit vnum de pusillis istis qui in me
                     credunt, expedit ei vt suspendatur mola asinaria in collo
     eius
                     et demergatur in profundum maris.[61]

ibid. v. 7   Vae mundo a scandalis. Necesse est enim vt veniant
                     scandala, verumtamen vae illi homini per quem scandalum
                     venit.[62]

---

[56] The Latin arguments which follow are in Grindal's hand.

[57] Translation: 'Scandal/offence either (1) seduces the irresolute from the truth: it may be that the irresolute may believe the prophesyings, because they are suppressed, to be illicit and pernicious, although
previously they thought them pious and legal, or (2) confirms them in their error, viz. in thinking the
prophesyings to be illicit, impious and pernicious.'

[58] Translation: 'Definition of scandal [from Sylvester's *Summa summarum quae siluestrina dicitur]*
Spiritual scandal is an obstacle in the path of spirituality, leading to spiritual ruin, or Scandal is an
evil statement or action (that is either evil in itself, or having the appearance of evil leading to the
chance of ruin for another. Addit abstinendum esse "Si Scandalum de verisimili exoritur videatur"'.

[59] Translation: 'Panormitanus adds [source as above] that it is to be avoided "If the scandal seems to be
rooted in truth."'

[60] Translation: 'Nobody should be the object of offence.'

[61] Geneva Bible: 'But whosoever shall offend one of these little ones which beleeue in mee, it were
better for him, that a milstone were hanged about his necke, and that he were drowned in the depths
of the sea.'

[62] Geneva Bible: 'Woe be unto the world because of offences: for it must needes bee that offences shall
come, but woe be to that man by whom the offence commeth.'

Mark 9 [.43]   Si scandalizaverit te manus tua, abscindi illam, etc.[63]

Rom[ans] 14 [.13]   Non ergo amplius invicem iudicemus, sed hoc iudicate
                      magis, ne ponatis offendiculum fratri vel scandalum.[64]

1 Cor[inthians] 8 [.9] Videte ne licentia vestra offendiculum fiat infirmis.[65]

ibid., v. 13   Non manducato carnem in aeternum etc. [final sentence of
                      verse].[66]

ibid. v. 12   Vulnerantes conscientiam infirmorum in Christum
                      peccantis (paraphrase).[67]

1 Cor[inthians] 10 [.32] Sine offensione sitis Iudaeis et gentibus et ecclesiae Dei.[68]

2 Cor[inthians]] 6 [.3] Nemini damus vllam offensionem, vt non vituperetur
                         ministerium nostrum.[69]

                      Christus ne scandalum daret tributum solvit.[70]

                      Paulus (Timotheum circumcidit
                              (Titum noluit circumcidere.[71]

1 Cor[inthians] 9 [.5–12] Paulus potestate (circumducendi vxorem) ne quid
                           offendiculum sua non est vsus (stipendium accipiendi)
                           det Evangelio Christi.[72]

The practicalities of the situation

5. The privy council to Archbishop Grindal, [blank] December 1580, autographs:
LPL, 3470, fo. 66

After our harty commendacions to your grace, Whereas D. Awbrey[73] hathe the exercise of the offices of vicar generall to your grace, and of the Court of Audience,
togither with an other ioyned in the same with him, and but during pleasure only,

---

63 Geneva Bible: 'Wherefore, if thine hand cause thee to offende, cut it off etc.'
64 Geneva Bible: 'Let vs not therefore iudge one another any more but vse your iudgement rather in
    this, that no man put an occasion to fall, or a stumbling blocke before his brother.'
65 Geneva Bible: 'But take heede lest by any meanes this power of yours be an occasion of falling to
    them that are weake.'
66 Geneva Bible: 'I will eat no flesh while the world standeth [that I may not offend my brother.'
67 Geneva Bible: 'Now when ye sinne against the brethren, and wound their weake conscience, ye sinne
    against Christ.'
68 Geneva Bible: 'Give none offence, neither to the Jewes, nor to the Grecians, nor to the Church of
    God.'
69 Geneva Bible: 'We giue no occasion or offence in any thing, that our ministery should not bee repre-
    hended.'
70 Translation: 'Christ, lest he give offence, pays tribute.'
71 Translation: 'Paul (a) circumcised Timothy, (b) was not willing to circumcise Titus.'
72 Translation: 'Paul did not use his power (a) to travel with a wife [or, perhaps, simply to marry –
    'ducendi'], or (b) to accept a stipend, lest he should offend against the Gospel of Christ.'
73 William Aubrey (c. 1525–95) retained his office of sole vicar-general under Archbishop Whitgift.

which D. Yale[74] heretofore enioyed wholy him selfe alone and for his lyfe: Forasmuch as this estate of D. Awbreys, being so maymed and vncertain, he accompteth him selfe nowe in worse case and condicion then yf he were only an advocate as he was before, And for that he is so meet and sufficient a man to supply the places, as your grace knoweth and one of whome her majestie hathe allready shewed her good lyking to that purpose, and for that he myndeth (as he saithe) leaving his practise to bende him selfe wholy to that service, yf he may be placed in them as D. Yale was: We hartely pray your grace (notwithstanding any motion made by any of vs vnto you for any other heretofore) that you will graunt D. Awbrey alone a patent of those offices during lyfe, and that you will wryte to the dean and Chapitre of Cantur[bury] for a confirmacion thereof vndre their common seale,[75] Wherein your grace (as we are perswaded) shall do your selfe a good tourn in being furnished of so fitt a man, and give us cause right hartely to thancke you for him, and to be ready allwayes to requyte your favor to him any wayes we can. Thus we committ your grace to the allmightye, From the Court the   of december, 1580.

Your graces loving frendes.

T[homas] Bromley: canc. (lord chancellor)

E. Lyncoln   R. Leycester
Chr: Hatton   Fra: Walsingham

6. The privy council to Archbishop Grindal 16 January 1580[1], autographs: LPL, MS 3470, fo. 76

After our right hartie commendacions to your Lordship we have receaved your letter which yesterdaie yow wrote vnto vs. And forasmuche we perceave that your Lord-ship untill such a time as her Majestie shalbe pleased to restore you vnto th'exercise of your Jurisdiction appertaininge vnto that ? cannot be present in the Convocation house: and neverthelesit is thought convenient that for the more orderlie proceed-inge in that assemblie your Lordship should depute some of your brethren the Bish-oppes to supplye your place: We have thought meete, on her Majesties behalf, to praye yow to directe forth a Commission vnto our verie good Lordes the Bisshoppes of London, and Winton, and Lincoln, for the purpose aforesaid. Which we praye yow to sende vnto them, assone as yow conventientlie maye. And so we bidd your Lordship right hartie Farewell. From Westminster the xvith of January 1580.

Your Lordship's lovinge Frendes

W. Burghley   T. Sussex   R. Leycester Tho[mas] Wylson

---

74 Dr Thomas Yale, as Grindal's chancellor the presiding judge of his Court of Audience, had honestly advised the archbishop: 'In your Grace's Court of Audience, as in all other your courts, so things be out of order that few thinge be as they should be' (Collinson, *Archbishop Grindal*, p. 230).

75 Evidence that, on his sequestration, Grindal had been obliged to surrender his own seal, so that a formal matter of this kind had to be sealed by the dean and chapter of Canterbury.

'Notwithstanding your present sequestration'

'Turning up the heat on the Catholics'[76]

Following an initiative by Bishop John Aylmer (who had been promoted with a mission statement requiring him to deal with catholic and puritan opponents of the ecclesiastical status quo with equal severity),[77] the bishops were required by the privy council (with Walsingham in the driving seat) to enquire into the extent of popish recusancy. These initiatives were taken in the summer of 1577, and they offer a mirror image to the alarm felt at court about the 'puritan' prophesyings in the previous summer of 1576.[78] 'Notwithstanding his sequestration', Grindal was included in these investigations which continued through 1580 and 1582, at a time when the Jesuits Robert Persons and Edmund Campion entered the country, with Campion brought to a sensational trial and executed. The letter to Archbishop Grindal and the other bishops of 1 Apr. 1582 followed on the heels of the 1581 parliament, which had enacted a severe penal code against Catholics, including a measure which imposed sharply increased fines and other penalties for absence from church: £20 a month, rising to £40 for the second month of absence, £100 for the third, with the penalties of praemunire for persistent recusancy.[79]

7. The privy council to Archbishop Grindal, 16 December 1580, autographs: LPL, MS 3470, fo. 67

After our righte hartie comendacions vnto your good Lordship. The Queens Majestie finding the dailie inconvenience growing vnto the Realm by the education of great nombers of yonge gentlemen and other her subiectes in the partes beyonde the seas where for the moste parte they are misled and nowrished in papistrie with soch Instructiones as maketh them to mislike of the governement of this Realme, and so liklie to become undewtifull subiectes, so as retorninge home, manie of them doe not onlie them selves refuse to yeilde obedience vnto her Majesties lawes and proceadinges in matters of religion established by the Parlamant but by their evell example corrupte soche others as are wel disposed: the contagion whereof beginneth to extend yt self so farr within the Relme, as if some speedie remedie be not hadd for the preventinge of the mischeeff that maie in tyme followe thereof, it cannot be but dangerouse vnto her Majestie and her estate. She therefore intendinge to take some presente order therein as well by prohibitinge that none but soche whose parentes are knowen to be well affected in Religion and will vndertake for the good education of their Children shalbe suffered to departe out of the Realme, and that with the speciall lycense of her Majestie as also by revoking of those that are presentlie in the partes of Spaigne, Italie, Fraunce and other places not having her Majesties lycense: Hathe geven comaundement that your Lordship vppon the receipte hereof shall call before yow the persons within your diocesse whose names are contained in the scedule written on thother syde of this letter, notifienge vnto them the inconveniences above mencioned and forthwith to take bondes of them and everie of them in good somes of money to her Majesties use, for the callinge home

---

[76] Lake, 'A tale of two episcopal surveys'.
[77] Nicolas, *Hatton*, p. 56.
[78] Lake, 'A tale of two episcopal surveys'.
[79] J. E. Neale, *Elizabeth I and her parliaments, 1559–1581* (London, 1953), pp. 378–92.

of their sonnes or frindes to be retorned into the Realme within three monethes after the saide bondes taken, at the farthest: Yow shall also geue direction vnto your Archdeacon or to the ministers of everie parishe within your diocesse to inquire particularlie what other personnes within their parishes have at this presente anie of their sonnes, and other kinssfolkes vnder their charge beyonde the seas, in what places and vnder whose charge thei be, how longe they haue ben absent, whether they are departed the Realme without license or not, and with as muche expedicion as possiblie yow maie, to certefie the same vnto vs, with the names of the parentes, their degrees and dwelling places, that therevppon the like order maie be taken with them yf anie soche then shalbe for revokinge of their Childeren and frindes that is taken with soche as are alreadie knowen vnto her Majestie and vs. and yf anie shalbe founde vnwillinge to delyver readie and plaine answere hereunto, then to comaunde them to appere before vs, and thereof to certefie vs: Wherein we praie your Lordship that soche care and dilligence be vsed as the necessetie thereof dothe requier: And so we bidd yow right hartelie farewell: From Whitehall the xvith of december 1580.

Postscript: Allthough we send yow not herewith the scedule mencoined
in this letter, yet we praie yow faile not to geue order that
inquirie be made what personnes within the same have their sonnes or kinssfolkes
beyond the seas and thereof to certefie vs according to the direction of
our said letters.

                                   Your Lordships verie loving freindes
T. Bromley canc.   W. Burghley   E. Lyncoln
                                   R, Leycester Hounsdon
F. Knollys   Jamys Croft
Chr. Hatton   Tho: Wylson
                                 Fra: Walsingham
(Sir Thomas Bromley, lord chancellor, Lord Burghley, the earl of Lincoln, the earl of Leicester, Lord Hunsdon, Sir Francis Knollys, Sir James Croft, Sir Christopher Hatton, Sir Thomas Wilson, Sir Francis Walsingham)

8. The privy council to Archbishop Grindal, 1 April 1582, autographs: LPL, MS 3470, fo. 80

After our hartie commendacions to your Lordship. Wheras the Queens Majestie is geven to understande, that notwithstandinge manie favourable meanes heretofore vsed for the reducinge and retayninge of her highnes subiectes in their due obedience: the same hathe hitherto verie litle preualyed, but that diuers remaine still obstinate in refusinge to come to the Churche, and conforme them selues in matters of religion, accordinge to her Majesties Lawes: Albeit we doubt not but that accordinge to our former letters yow haue made trewe and perfecte certificates of all such persons, within your diocesse, vnto the Justices etc. and that they haue thereuppon caused them to be proceaded with accordinge to lawe: yet to thintent we maye particularly vnderstande, howe thinges haue passed both in your diocesse and else where: we haue for certaine good consideracions thought meete to require yow (as we haue don the like to the rest of the Bishoppes) to cause in everye parishe within your diocesse, a diligent searche and enqurie to be made of all such persons as sithe the ende of the last Session of Parlament haue forborne to come to the Churche, and hauinge ben therof laufullie convicted, doe nevertheles not conform them selues as they ought to doe, and thereupon to cause a certificate to be made in writinge, subscribed with your hande, and the handes of some of the Justices of peace of the Shire, where euerye suche offender hathe his residence, to th'intent that the same maie be according to the meaninge of the Lawe deliuered over into the Courte commonly called the Kinges Benche, in the next Easter Terme. Wherin we praie yow to vse as much expedicion as yow maye, and to addresse the said Certificates vnto vs, first in some convenient time before or at the beginninge of the said Terme, to th'intent that we maye peruse and consider the same as cause shall require. And so on her Majesties behalf willinge and chardginge yow, that herof yow make no default: we bidd yow right hartelie Farewell. From Greenich the first of Aprill 1582.

Your lovinge frendes

T. Bromley: canc.   E. Lyncoln   T. Sussex
                                          Hounsdon

F. Knollys   Jamys Croft

Chr: Hatton   Fra: Walsyngham
[Sir Thomas Bromley, lord chancellor, the earl of Lincoln, the earl of Sussex, Lord Hunsdon, Sir Francis Knollys, Sir James Croft, Sir Christopher Hatton, Sir Francis Walsingham]
(subscribed) 'L. Archb: of Canterbury'

A question of money

In 1580 the process of refining and strictly defining Lutheran orthodoxy in the German principalities which adhered to the Confession of Augsburg came to a head in the acceptance and promulgation of a 'Book of Concord', incorporating an earlier 'Formula of Concord'. The book was published on the fiftieth anniversary of the Augsburg Confession, 25 June 1580. If that was what the diplomatic mission to which Sir Francis Walsingham refers in this correspondence was all about, it would appear to have been too little and too late, since the acceptance of the Book of Concord had already ruled out any union between the two major strands of prot-estantism, Lutheran (evangelical) and reformed. It represented a slamming of the door.[80] However the king of Denmark, recently promoted to the Order of the Garter, did continue to offer Queen Elizabeth his good offices in 'establishing agreement among the reformed churches'. But in truth the seasoned diplomat Daniel Rogers, son of the Marian proto-martyr John Rogers, born at Wittenberg and later a student at Wittenberg under Philip Melanchthon, had other fish to fry. He was being sent as an ambassador to the emperor Rudolf II and the Imperial Diet, meeting in Nurem-berg. Poor Rogers! On his way to Nuremberg he was captured in the duchy of Cleves and held to ransom by an opportunistic warlord, and this led to no less than four years spent in a Dutch prison, under the orders of the prince of Parma and King Philip II.[81]

---

80 *The Oxford encyclopedia of the Reformation*, ed. Hans J. Hillerbrand (New York and Oxford, 1996), art. 'Formula of Concord'; Diarmaid MacCulloch, *Reformation: Europe's house divided 1490–1700* (London, 2003), pp. 352–4.

81 *Calendar of state papers foreign, 1579–80*, nos. 417, 441, 459–60, 472, 476; *Calendar of state papers foreign*, Jan. 1581 – Apr. 1582, nos. 79, 83, 126, 157, 239, 617; *ODNB*, art. Rogers.

It would seem that Walsingham was using the theological slice of Rogers's agenda as an excuse for requiring the church to cover his expenses. In spite of what he called Grindal's 'cold answer' to the demand that he contribute £300 from his own pocket, in October 1580 the senior clergy of the province of Canterbury, bishops, archdeacons and cathedral deans, were collectively taxed to fund Rogers's journey, raising a little over £300, of which Grindal's share was £12.[82]

Walsingham has not been alone in finding Grindal's plea of poverty a little hard to understand, or accept. In my biography of the archbishop, I suggested that as bishop of London he had netted a total revenue of about £12,000, at York upwards of £9,000, as archbishop of Canterbury perhaps £20,000: in twenty-four years as a bishop possibly a total of £40,000. Grindal was unmarried (unlike most Elizabethan bishops) and had little in the way of family to provide for. And yet the greater part of these revenues was used up in Grindal's lifetime, although it is to his credit that he died free of debt. There is no evidence that Grindal was a careless manager of his affairs: to the contrary. But questions remain which can probably never be satisfactorily answered.[83] *Walsingham's confession, in his second letter, to having been torn between silence and his conscience must be a snide reference to Grindal's letter to the queen, and suggests that Mr Secretary was not lacking in a black sense of humour.*

9. Sir Francis Walsingham to Archbishop Grindal from Ostend, 29 August 1580, autograph: LPL, MS 3470, fo. 60

It may please your grace, Whereas her Majesty is given to vnderstand by the King of Denmark that certaine of the Princes of the Empire at the instigation of a few divines of the Augustane confession haue a meaninge very shortly to proceede to the signing of the booke called *Corpus doctrinae* tending to the condemnacion of all other churches that professe the relligion reformed, publishing of the same, vnlesse by her majesties mediacion it may be stayed at the least so long vntill a Synode may be called wherein the deputies from all churches which are lyke to be interessed thereby may be heard. Forasmuch as her highnes is well pleased to send a fitt messenger to the said Princes to stay that intended proceeding, for the care she hath of the good estate of the Gospell and advauncement thereof, and by reason of the great charges she is put vnto by the troubles of Irlande hath thought good to haue the charge of the said messager defrayed by the state of your profession and to that effect hath caused the B[ishop] of London to be written vnto for the colleccion of three hundreth poundes, which accordingly he will performe with all convenient diligence, but shall not be able to effect it in so short tyme as the messager is to be dispatched in, neyther can of him self for want of hability as his L[ordship] pretendeth disburse so much before hande (as the necessity of the busines requireth) vntill he may haue it rembursed, These are therfore to pray your grace to find the meanes eyther by your self or your frendes that the said messager may be furnished with the said somme, that through want thereof the busines so greatly importing the state of the whole church may not be hindered, nor yn losse by exchange be sustayned which otherwyse of necessity must be if order be not taken that he may haue the

82 TNA, SP 12/143/21.
83 Collinson, *Archbishop Grindal*, pp. 295–308.

said somme to make ouer before his departure. The discommodity whereof I do partly feele my self, hauing ben content for the furtheraunce of that service to give him credit for one hundreth poundes before hand for the which I am constrayned to pay interest. And so not doubting but your grace will haue that care that the cause requireth I leaue youe to the grace of God from the Doulet [?] at Ostend this 29 of August 1580

Your G[race] to commande

Fra: Walsingham

Endorsed by Grindal, fo. 61v: 'Mr. Secret. Wals. to laye owte money for Mr. Rogers jowrney into Germanie 29 August 1580 … cum resp. mea 2 Septemb.1580.'

10. Margin: Copie of my l[ord] g[races] letter to Mr Secret[ary] Walsingham

2 Sept[ember] 1580.

Sir your letter of the xxixth of Auguste laste I receaved this seconde of September. / I am sorie that those troublouse divines vnder pretense of the Augustane confession, goe aboute to disturbe the peace of the Churche, and interrupte the cowrse of the gospell, for those inconvenyences muste nedes followe (so farr as man can iudge) if their devises maye take effecte. / her Ma[jes]ties care for the staye thereof is highlie to be commended, and I truste godd shall geve good successe to the same. / For the disbursinge of so muche money aforehande as ye write, I muste of necessitie praye to be excused: No man knoweth better than you that my L[ord] of Yorke hadd of me latelye fower hundreth poundes for dilapidacions,[84] a good parte whereof, I was compelled to borrowe of a Frende for a tyme, and so am lefte at this presente scarselye able to susteyne myne ordynarye charges till my revenue come, at myne Auditte after Michellmas, and I have no suche creditt with the Marchauntes as to take vpp any money of them and I am lothe to Enter into theyr bookes for interest etc. / yf creditt be to be vsed, my L[ord] of London, who shall have the receipte of the money contributed, is the meetest man in myne opynion to take it upp: I shalbe contented with all my harte to beare my parte of the charges that shall growe that waye, as well as of the principall. / Thus praieng you to accepte of this my necessarie ['excuse' erased] answer, I take my leave, and commende you to the grace of god. From Croydon this seconde of september 1580.

11. Sir Francis Walsingham to Archbishop Grindal, 17 September 1580, from the court, autograph: LPL, MS 3470, fo. 63

There are extensive marginal notes in Grindal's hand, merely high-lighting and analysing scholastically the points in Walsingham's letter, perhaps because the hand is scarcely legible. Grindal's marginalia are supplied in italics.

---

[84] *Ibid.*, pp. 302–6.

7 Sept[ember] 1580
inhabilitie of y{ou}r
owne, or by
y{ou}r creditte
required by my L[ords]

loquar an sileam? [shall I
speak or remain silent?]
he shuld offende
conscience by silence

1.the cause
2. my place
3. my affliction
4. the greate lyelyhood
off my habilitie for a
farre greater summe

these four made it
strange to him to
receive so colde an
answer

prooffe of the first
cause, which needeth nott

probatio 2ᵈᵒ viz off my
place
which shulde moeve
me in this daungerous
case

[cer]tim sub Cruce
[admitten]do [dando?] est
³ᵃ causa

4ᵒde habilitate viz
So longe enjoinge lyvinges

After I receyved your G[races] letter by the which you
declared youre in habylte to fvrnishe eyther of your
owne or otherwyse by your credyt the 300L requyred by
my Lords for the performaunce of Mr Da{niel} Rogers
iorney I rested a longe season dowbtefull whether I myght
acquaynt your L[ordship] with the greefe I conceyved
therby or suffre the same to passe vnder sylence/
but in the ende I concluded with my selfe that I
should in a kynde of sorte offende my owne
consyence by concealyng of the same. And therefor my
good L[ord] in somme this yt wants. Fyrst when I
considered the cawse of the gentlemans employment The
place your L[ordship] houldeth in the churche
of god within this realme under her Maj[es]tye: The late
afflycton it hathe pleased god to laye upon you; And the
great lykleyhod of your abyltytye to be in state to have
fornished a farre greater somme yt seemed verye straing
vnto me to receave from your L{ordship} so cowld an
awntswer. For fyrst towching the cawse what can be
greater then to have so dayngerowse a scysme to take
place emongest the professores of the gospell as to see
some of the pryncypall and best qualefyed persons
so transported with passyon as to have pvt on a
determynatyon to proceede to the intemprating of
ther fellow professours, especyally at this tyme
when owre common ennemyes are entred into a
confederacye for the rootyng owt of the professors
thereof with lykelehod to perfourme the same yf the
extre[me] rage of ther furye thorowghe gods goodness in
mercye be not stayed. Nowe consyderinge the place your
L[ordship] howldethe within this realme being the
pryncypall pyller of this chirche under her Ma[jes]tye
and seing not only this chirche lyke to be condempned
·but also the generall cawse of relygyon (according to
mans judgement) to be in dayngere to be
overthrowen, what cause myght move your L[ordship]
to imploye not only your substaunce and credyt but also
your lyfe, yf this may not especyally at this tyme
when yt hath pleased god to laye his crosse vppon
you which doth commonly[season mens myndes
and make them the more apte to imbrace causes
as pretending to the mayntenaunce and fvrtheraunce of
relygyon. Lastly towching your L[ordship's] abylyte yt
were straing or almost incredible yf you that hathe
possessed so longe a season thos lyvinges your
L[ordship] hath enjoyed (and having of late more
cause to spare then other your predecessors) shoulde
not be able to fornishe so smawle a somme to so good
a pvrpose. This my good L[ord] I doe not wryte with a

mynde to offende you (being the man of your cawlyng
whom I have honored above others) but only to
acquaynte you with my greafe and growndes of
the same, which I hope as yt is but well and
Christianlye meant by me so yt wyll be
both well and charitably acceptd by your G[race]
whome I doe recomende vnto the protectyon of the
almyghtye most humbly takyng my leave At the
coorte the xvii of Sep[tember] 1580

> Your G[race's] to command
> Fra: Walsingham

12. Archbishop Grindal to Sir Francis Walsingham, 23 September 1580, holograph:
LPL MS 3470, fo. 65

Sal[utem] in Christo./ I perceave the ['grieffe' erased] offense ye gather of my
Last Letters, groweth especiallye apon an opinion ye have conceived off my greate
wealthe, gathered by occasion off my restraynte etc. / I thinke it is nott goode that
one off vs, in suche cases, shoulde narrowly iudge off another. And therfore I praye
you iudge frendlye and well of me, and off my Late answer and thynke, that I had
goode growndes to write to you as I dyd, allthowghe I doo nott now descende to
particularities for answering your l[etter]. / I have hearde off some others of goode
callynge, which have bene fullye perswadett that my Receiptes are farre greater
and my Expenses farre lesse then they be indede Apon which occasion in Januarie
Laste I willed myne officers to Examyne my state, and trulye to make a brieffe
Extracte off the same: which was done, and hathe bene shewed to some off my
goode frendes, who apon view thereoff have confessed, thatt I was nott in so goode
case for wealthe as they before had conceived. / I have sente unto you by this bringer
['some shorte notes concerning the premisses' erased] the said Extracte which I
praye you (iff your leysure serve therto) to view, and consider, for your further
sattisfaction. Thus forbearynge to troble you with anie longer writynge, and prayeng
you still to contynew my honorable goode frende, as of olde, I take my leave, and
commende you to the grace and protection off the Allmightie. from Croydon, this
23. of Septembere 1580.

No signature to this copy. At the foot: 'To Mr. Secretarie Walsingham.'

Archbishop Grindal's submission

*The Fairhurst MSS contain a document endorsed '21 Jan. 1580 [1581] Copie of
my lor[d's[g[race[of Cant[erbury] his submission'. It is signed in Grindal's hand:
'subscribed E.C.' Another copy of the submission is in BL, Add. MS 32092, fo. 22.
This is endorsed (fo. 23v) 'A forme of submission devised and sente by the Biss-
hops of Sarum and Worcester [John Piers and John Whitgift] 21 Jan. 1580 [1581].'
Significant differences between the two versions are noted in this transcription, MS
Add 32092 in bold type. The background to the démarche initiated by Piers and
Whitgift would appear to be supplied by fo. 73 of LPL MS 3470, which is sadly so
badly damaged that only a few sentences and phrases can still be read. According*

*to the catalogue of the Fairhurst papers this was a letter to Bishops Piers and Whit-
gift. However, the document is not in the form of a letter, and an endorsement in
Grindal's hand appears to read: '------- sent by the B[isho]ps of Sarum and [Wor]
cester as a charge ------------ the Archbishop'. The document rehearses Grindal's
offence in not complying with the queen's commandment in respect of the exercises,
emphasizing the presence of 'vulgar and unlearned people', who had made 'inter-
pretacions of their owne'. It then proceeds to outline what must be done to repair the
situation, anticipating that the queen 'vppon hoape of his better regarde hereafter
to obey her commaundemene' will 'receive him to her former favor, and to license
him to exercise his place in parlamente as his Jurisdiccion in the convocacions nowe
to be hadd of his Clergie, as in all other thinges incidente to his Archiepiscopall
office'. However, whether or not Grindal made his submisision in the terms devised
for him by the two bishops, it is clear that he did not resume his normal presidency
of Convocation, nor in all those other things incident to his office.*

13. LPL, MS 3470, fo. 22

The Archbisshop of Cant[erbury] beinge advertised of the cause of her Majesties
offence, as is sett downe by the L[ords] of the Counsell [**as before is recyted**], and
of her gratiouse inclination towardes him vpon his humble submission [**acknowledging of his faulte**], dothe confesse that he hathe bene and is moste hartelie sorie
that her Majestie hath bene offendid with him [**to have offended her Majestie**], as
a matter more grevouse to him then any worldlie calamytie./ And though he refused
to execute her Majesties commaundemente by reason of scruple of conscience [**and
though his offence beganne rather of some scruple of conscience**] which moved
him to thinke that the said exercises might have bene in some pointes reformed and
so contynued [**tollerated**]: Yet vnderstandinge that her Majestie herein did vse the
advice and allowance of certen Bishoppes his Brethren [**Yet consideringe that he
seeth that her Majestie herin did nothinge but with the advice and allowance of
certen Bishoppes his Brethren**] who by likelihode certefied that they hadd in their
owne dioces [**who by likelihoode hadd in their own diocese**] founde the same more
hurtfull then profitable: And for that he is perswaded [**well assured**] that her Majestie
hadd therein a sincere and godlie meanynge to the quietnes of the [**her**] people: And
that also her commaundemente was not against any positive Lawe or constitucion
of the Realme [**of the Churche**]: He can not but thinke and speake honorablie and
and duetifullie of her Majesties doinges as of a godlie Prince meanynge well to the
Churche and her People in this her Majesties dyreccion and commaundemente./
[BL, **Add. MS 32092 omits** 'he can not but thinke…commanudemente'] And as
he is moste hartelie sorie that he hath incurred her Majesties grevouse offence for
not observinge that her commaundemente [**he is hartelie sorie that herein he did
offende her Majestie in not executing her Majesties commaundement at that
time**], so dothe he moste humblie and lowlie beseche her highnes [BL, Add. **MS
32092 replaces** 'so dothe he moste humblie and lowelie beseche' with 'Beseeching']
not to impute the same to any obstinate intente or meanynge to disobey her Majestie
but onelye that he was then [**then was sumwhat**] moved in conscience to be an
humble sutor to her Majestie to be spared from beinge the speciall instrumente
in suppressinge the said exercises./ [BL, **Add. MS 32092 omits** 'to be an humble
sutor…the said exercises', **and has instead:** 'moved in conscience to have them
ceasse.'] And to the intente her Majestie maye thinke that he meante no disobedy-

ence in any mayntenaunce of them to continewe contrarie to her commaundemente he dothe praie her Majestie to be trulie enformed howe he him self did in his owne Bisshopricke, and other peculier Jurisdicions, suffer no suche exercises to be vsed after the time of her Majesties said commaundemente. [BL, **Add. MS 32092 omits** 'after the time of her Majesties said commaundemente'.]

Archbishop Grindal's own account (?) of the progression of his troubles

The Latin document which follows presents the story in a very favourable light. It is not signed or endorsed, but if not composed by Grindal himself, it must be the work of a sympathizer.

14. LPL, MS 3470, fo. 40

In nonnullis huius regni Diocesibus mos erat, ex Episcoporum, quibus illae parent, authoritate ac voluntate susceptus, ut statis certisque temporibus, Ministri ecclesiarum, numero triginta, aut quadraginta, aut etiam plures ad ea opppida convenirent, quae eis celebriora erant, et ipsis magis propinqua atque opportune. In eo autem conuentu, post Divinum minime precibus imploratum, Ecclesiastica bini aut terni (1 Cor. 14), norman a D Paulo prescriptum observantes, ecclesiaeque Primitivae consuetudinem renovantes, Scripturae locum aliquem ordine ac vicissitudine quadam interpretabant praesente etiam atque audiente populo, qui his diebus ad has loca et confluere maxima frequentia, et Ministros dicentes attente ac modeste audire, et ex illorum sermonibus maximam consolationem, fructumque percipere consuevit, id quod ex Literarum, quas hic vna misimus, Exemplari articulatius constare potest. Genus hoc Scripturam isto modo, et more, quem diximus, interpretendarum, a quibusdam Prophetia, ab aliis ad jugiendam verbo invidiam, Ministrorum Exercitatis dicebatur, qua primo in Dioccesi Londiniense annis abhinc plus minus sedecim ab Archiepiscopo hoc ipso Cantuariensi, qui tum episcopus erat Londiniensis instituta, ab eoque post in Eboracensem Diocessum, dum illam provinciam Archiepiscopus obtineret, introducta fuit, atque hoc modo in multas praeterea Dioecses sparsa latius manavit. His prophetiis Regia Maiestas offensa propter minus veros ad ipsius Celsitudinem perlatos de illarum vitiosa et intoleranda tractatione rumores, Archiepiscopo hinc ipsi Cantuarensi dedit in mandatis, circiter mensem Junium, anno 1576. Vt eas penitus tollendas atque abrogandas curaret. Archieposcopus tempus postulavit deliberandi, et reliquas collegas suos provinciae suae Episcopos per Literas consulendis, quod impetratum est. Epioscopi fere omnes rescipserunt (uno alteroue excepto) eas Prophetias, seu Exercitationes, ecclesiae utillisimas, quaeque perpetuo celebrarentur dignisssimas sibi videri responderunt. Regia Maiest. 18 Novemb. 1576 omnem Archieiscopo longiorem consultationem denegans, ei aperte disertque praecepit, vt Prophetias illas omnes universim sine mora profligaret etc. Archiepiscopus non permissus, vt coram, quid sibi videretur, exponeret, 10 Decemb. 1576 Literas ad Regiam Maiest. paulo luculentiores dedit: in quibus postquam et Regiae Maies. summa in se beneficia recoluisset, et suam in ipsius Maiest. fidem, obseruatiamque declarasset, cum utilitates illas, quae ex prophetiiis ad ecclesiam pervenerant, commemoravit, tum quantopere plerisque Episcopis probarentur, narravit promisitque se operam libentissime daturum, ut quicquid in illis minus recte, et praeter ordinem fieret, congerentur: postremo conclusit, quandoquidem in illae sive prophetiae siue Exercitationes, erant et Scripturarum authoritate constituae [margin: 1 Cor[inthians]. 14], et in ecclesia primitiva celebratae, et ab antiquissimis patribus approbatae atque tractatatae et in plerisque nostrorum temporum Reformationibus, ac purioribuus ecclesiis instaurate deinde cum experientia et re constaret easdem plurimum ad Evangelium propagandum, aedificandamque ecclesiam valuisse: futurumque esset, vt illarum viniversa abrogatiio infinitas calumniae et offensiones excitaret, piroum pectora dolore afficeret, veritatis inimicos laetitia perfunderet: denique cum Archiepiscopus, quod ipse boni [bene?] extruxerat, hoc modo destruere videretur, ad sempiternam ministeriii sui labem, at conscientiae vulnus: se nullo modo integra salvaque conscientia posse committere, vt illarum se vbique abroganarum ministrum praeberet: Quare humillime rogare, vt in ea re sibi venia daretur. Atque hoc ipsum Archiepiscopus Dominis consiliariis semel atque iterum diuersis temporibus declarauit, coram ad id euocatus. Posthaec Regia Maiest. litteris ad omnes regni episcopos singulatim scriptis Prophetias illas intermitti iussit: quod ubique statim factum est, nec quicquid Archiepiscopus vnquam contra tentauit aut egit. Maii 29 1577 Archiepiscopus ex Regiae Maiest. mandato a Domiinis consiliariis relato, omni fuit ecclesiasticae iurisdictionis functione priuatus ac summotus, et domi se suae continere iussus: itaque semper hactenus ab illa die fecit, et sex etiam mensibus, quanquidem offensam in se Regiam Maiest. sensit, sponte sua fecerat. Augusti modo 25 proximo hoc anno 1578 permissum ei fuit, vt alteris suis aedibus Croydonensibus vti posset, quae Lambetha absunt mille passus sex.

Atque hic rei status est.

Translation

In several dioceses of this realm it was the custom by the authority and will of the bishops concerned, that at regular and certain times the ministers of the Church, thirty or forty in number, or even more, would gather together at the more populous towns, and those which were nearest and most convenient for them. In that gathering however, after short prayers for divine blessing, two or three preachers (1 Cor. 14), following the rule laid down by St Paul, and reviving the custom of the primitive Church, they would, in order and in turn, interpret some passage of scripture to the people also there and listening who, on these days, both flock to these places in great numbers and listen to the ministers' words attentively and quietly, and were seen to receive from those sermons the greatest consolation and profit, insofar that, from the example of letters which we have sent along with this only from here it can quite lovingly be agreed. This kind of interpretation of scripture, in this fashion and in a way which we direct, is called by some 'prophesying', by others, wishing to avoid that word, an exercise of the ministers, which exercise was first introduced in the diocesee of London some sixteen years ago, more or less, by this present archbishop of Canterbury, both when he was bishop of London, and then when as archbishop of York he occupied that province, and in this way it spread more widely, scattered into many other dioceses. The Queen's Majesty, offended by these prophesyings on account of less than true rumours relayed to her highness concerning them with a vicious and intolerable report, commanded the present archbishop of Canterbury, about the month of June 1576, that he should take pains that they be utterly removed and abolished. The archbishop asked for time to consider, and by letters to consult the bishops in his province, his brethren, and this was granted. Almost all the bishops wrote (with one or two exceptions) that these prophesyings or exercises were most useful to the Church and reported that they seemed to them most worthy of being retained. The Queen's Majesty, on 18 November 1576, denied the archbishop any longer consultation, and openly and clearly commanded him that all those prophesyings should be overthrown everywhere without delay, etc. The archbishop not being permitted to explain in person how it seemed to him sent to the Queen's Majesty letters a little more explicit, in which, after he had recalled her Majesty's great favours to him, and his own trust in her Majesty, and made declaration of his obedience, he both recited the great benefits to the Church which had arisen from the prophesyings and recounted how much they were esteemed by most of the bishops, and promised that he would most willingly exert himself to see that anything that occurred in them that was less than correct, or against good order, would be dealt with. Finally he concluded that, seeing that these prophesyings or exercises were both sanctioned by scriptural authority [margin: 1 Cor[i thians]. 14] and were performed in the primitive Church and were approved and treated of by the most ancient Fathers, and were instituted in most of the best reformed and pure churches of our time, therefore it was evident both from experience and from fact that they were and would be of the greatest value in the propagation of the Gospel and in the building up of the Church, and that their total aboliton would cause infinite objections and offences, would strike sorrow into the hearts of the godly and overwhelm with joy the enemies of the truth. Finally, as the archbishop had himself well established them, so he would be seen to be destroying them, to the eternal dishonour of his ministry and injury to his conscience. Therefore he could not with a clear and safe conscience present himself as the agent of their abolition in every place. Therefore he humbly begged that she would grant her indulgence in this matter. And this the archbishop once and again stated to the Lords of the Council at various times when summoned before them for that purpose. After this, in letters sent to all the bishops in the realm individually,[85] the Queen's Majesty ordered these prophesyings to be stayed, which was forthwith everywhere done, nor did the archbishop at any time attempt or do anything against it. On 27 May 1577 the archbishop, brought before the Lords of the Council by Her Majesty's coimmand, was deprived of and removed from the exercise of all ecclesiastical jurisdiction, and ordered to remain within his house, and so from that day has remained, and indeed for six months before that, since he was sensible of the Queen's Majesty's offence with him and did so of his own accord. But on 25 August of the next year, 1578, he was allowed to use his other residence, at Croydon, which is six miles from Lambeth.

And this is the state of the matter.

---

85 *recte* all bishops of the province of Canterbury. The northern province was not included in the queen's order.

2

'ACCURATELY AND EXQUISITELY MADE': GEORGE ABBOT'S PREFACE TO THE 1612 CATALOGUE OF LAMBETH PALACE LIBRARY

Edited by
James P. Carley

In as much as both pietie to God & his Church, & also iustice amongst men doth require, that the holy actions of our Predecessors should be recorded wth gratefull memory, & that the vse of such things, as by their laſt wills and Teſtament, they haue left ad pios vsus, should be preserved to succeeding ages, I haue thought it fit, hauing now in my custodie a notable & famous Librarie in the Archbishop of Cantorburies house at Lambeth to set downe to posteritie, who was the Author & beginner of the same, & what the purpose & intendiment was of the Doner and beſtower of thoſe bookes. Let all men therefore present & to come knowe and vnderſtand, that Richard Bancrofte Dr of Diuinity, firſt, Bp of London, & afterward promoted to the Archbishopricke of Cantorburie, being for many yeares a greate gatherer togethor of bookes, did voluntarily & of his owne motion (as in his life time he had oft foretold that he would) by his laſt Will and Teſtament, giue and bequeath vnto his Succeſſors the Archbishops of Cantorburie for euer, a greate & famous Librarie of bookes of Diuinitie, & of many other sortes of learning, but wth request & intreaty, that the Kings Matie within the space of two yeares would gratiously take order, ÿ theſe Bookes might safely be continued to poſterity, that so the good and religious intention of him that was the beſtower, might not be fruſtrated & annihilated. The Kings Matie therefore, that is to say, James by the grace of God, King of Greate Britaine, France & Ireland, Defender of the faith, with his Royall affection embracing this good purpose of the foresaid Archbishop, & according to the greate wiſdome, religion, and learning, which God hath giuen vnto his Highneſſe, conceauing it to be a monument of fame wth in his Kingdome, and of greate vse to himſelfe and his Succeſſors, as well as to the Church of God, that in a place so neare vnto his Royall Palace theſe bookes should be preſerued, did, after mature deliberation commend the care and conſideration hereof vnto Sr Fraunces Bacon knight his Maties Solliciter, that he should thinke vpon some course how the cuſtody of this Library might be iſtablished, and that by the negligence of thoſe that come after, so excellent a worke might not be fruſtrated, to the hurt of the Church, and Common wealth. Sr Fraunces Bacon therefore, as a man learned, and a true louer of learning (for by both thoſe titles the King was pleased to ſtile him) after good conſideration, did hold it fitt, that a Catalogue of the Bookes should be accuratly and exquiſitly made, that it might be knowne in the ages to come, what were thoſe Bookes which the foresaid Archbishop Bancrofte did leave vnto his Succeſſors, and that this Catalogue should be sent vnto the Deane and Chapter of the Cathedrall Church of Cantorbury, that it may

2 Opening page of Archbishop Abbot's preface to the 1612 catalogue of Lambeth Palace Library (LPL, LR/F/1)

Introduction*

In part as a result of bitter religious disputes, the second half of the sixteenth century saw more and more English protestant scholars returning *ad fontes* in the humanist tradition of textual scholarship: printed editions, as became increasingly evident, could be manipulated for polemical purposes and needed to be closely scrutinized for accuracy. The new trend, which mirrored the work of continental catholic apologists, culminated in the efforts of Thomas James (1572/3–1629), librarian to Sir Thomas Bodley and religious controversialist, who established, with the backing of Bodley (and perhaps to a lesser extent of King James I), a team of scholars to collate manuscripts and printed editions of the fathers. This project was launched – with the blessing (and financial support) of Richard Bancroft, to whom James had briefly served as a chaplain – on 1 July 1610, a matter of months before the archbishop's death on 2 November 1610.[1] James's preliminary account, *A treatise of the corruption of scripture, councils and fathers, by the prelats, pastors, and pillars of the church of rome, for maintenance of popery and irreligion*, was published in 1611 (*RSTC* 14462) and is described by Nelles as 'nothing short of a manifesto of state-of-the-art textual criticism'.[2] The *Treatise* provided a number of examples, by James's reckoning, of the way catholic scholars had falsified readings of the early church fathers to serve their own ends.[3] Early in Elizabeth's reign, for example, Francis Milles, clerk of the signet and a fellow of All Souls College, Oxford, heard a sermon given at Abingdon by John Jewel, bishop of Salisbury – a theologian

*   I include as well the section of Richard Bancroft's will concerning the disposal of his books. I am grateful to Melanie Barber for asking me to write this article. Growing out of the Seventeenth History of the Book Lecture I gave at UCLA on 13 May, 2008 it also represents an introduction to my intended critical edition and study of the library catalogues of John Whitgift and Richard Bancroft. I am deeply indebted to Ann Cox-Johnson's pioneering study on 'Lambeth Palace Library 1610–1664', *Transactions of the Cambridge Bibliographical Society*, II (1954–8), 105–26. Other useful bibliographical studies are M. R. James's 'Lambeth Palace Library', *ibid.*, III (1959–63), 1–31; and Geoffrey Bill, 'Lambeth Palace Library', *The Library*, 5th ser., XXI (1966), 192–206. See also Joseph Black, 'Pamphlet wars: the Marprelate Tracts and "Martinism", 1588–1688', Ph.D., University of Toronto, 1996. Gabriel Sewell provided electronic images of the documents for me as well as answering a variety of questions. A number of other individuals have read drafts and have made helpful suggestions and corrections: Joseph Black, Ken Fincham, Paul Nelles, Richard Ovenden, Richard Palmer, Bill Sherman, Jennifer Summit and Colin Tite. I thank them here.
1   See Paul Nelles, 'The uses of orthodoxy and Jacobean erudition: Thomas James and the Bodleian Library', *History of Universities*, XXII (2007), 21–70; also Jennifer Summit, *Memory's library. Medieval books in early modern England* (Chicago and London, 2008), pp. 221–33. James was made a chaplain to Bancroft after Bodley advanced his interests in 1609: see Richard Palmer's very helpful 'In the steps of Sir Thomas Bodley: the libraries of Lambeth Palace and Sion College in the seventeenth century', *Lambeth Palace Library. Annual Review* (2006), 53–67, at 56–7.
2   For the quotation see Nelles, 'The uses of orthodoxy', 43. The treatise was dedicated to George Abbot, Bancroft's successor as archbishop of Canterbury: James considered Abbot's elevation as an act of divine providence. See Palmer, 'In the steps of Sir Thomas Bodley', 57.
3   On patristic texts collated by James see N. R. Ker, 'Salisbury Cathedral manuscripts and Patrick Young's catalogue', repr. from *Wiltshire Archaeological and Natural History Magazine*, LIII (1949–50), 153–83, in his *Books, collectors and libraries. Studies in the medieval heritage*, ed. Andrew G. Watson (London and Ronceverte, 1985), pp. 175–208, at pp. 178–9.

greatly admired by Bancroft – in which Jewel quoted the reading '[praeparatus est] exercitus sacerdotum' (an army of priests) from a passage in the *Registrum epistularum* of Gregory the Great.[4] This was a crucial phrase in terms of Jewel's anti-Roman polemic: it indicated that when the Antichrist came there would be an army of (catholic) priests ready to receive him. Recently issued printed editions of the *Registrum*, however, gave the reading 'exitus sacerdotum' (a departure [or killing] of priests), which could be interpreted to mean that the arrival of the Antichrist led to the departure or end of true (i.e. catholic) priests. The disparity, with its profound polemical implications, troubled Milles. As a result, according to James,

> it so pleased God to put into his mind, to seeke in the *Manuscripts*: and remembring they had one in the *Librarie*, of good antiquitie, in that *Coll.* whereof he then was *fellow*, hee did so; went up into the *Librarie*, found the words there as Bishop Jewel had reported them: which was no small comfort unto him.[5]

Triumphant, in fact, Milles caused a public placard to be displayed, affirming that Jewel's was the true reading and alleging as his authority 'an ancient *Manuscript* in *Alsoules College*'. Ker has argued that this incident may have helped bring back a taste for manuscripts in university circles and thus to have led indirectly to the restocking of the college libraries, such as Archbishop Matthew Parker's at Corpus Christi College, Cambridge, with the salvaged manuscripts from the dissolved monastic libraries.[6] Certainly it was a crucial episode as far as James, in the next generation, was concerned. It showed very clearly why reliable editions based on trustworthy exemplars were required: it was the only way to expose the duplicity of the papists.[7] Because James and his fellow apologists believed that the doctrinal purity of the primitive English church assured that the manuscripts it had produced were more reliable witnesses than those found elsewhere, moreover, it seemed especially urgent that the English tradition be preserved and recorded.[8]

Although many were individually formed, Elizabethan collections were not meant, nevertheless, to be personal collections – they were not private hoards. Why? In another section of *A treatise on the corruption of scripture* James observed that

---

[4] See *A treatise of the corruption of scripture*, part 2, pp. 78–80. In 1609 James borrowed a manuscript of Gregory's letters from Lambeth: see Palmer, 'In the steps of Sir Thomas Bodley', p. 53. On Jewel's sermon of 1559, 'challenging' the catholics to prove their doctrines through recourse to the early fathers see Nelles, 'The uses of orthodoxy', 24–5.

[5] *A treatise of the corruption of scripture*, part 2, p. 79.

[6] Ker discusses the textual tradition and describes the manuscript used by Milles: see his 'The provision of books', in *The History of the University of Oxford*, III: *The collegiate university*, ed. James McConica (Oxford, 1986), pp. 441–77, at pp. 446–7.

[7] Apart from James see, for example, the comments of William Crashaw, *Falsificationum romanarum et catholicarum restitutionum tomi primi liber primus* (London, 1606), sig.¶3v: 'my accusation against the Romish Church is, that they have razed the records, and falsified the monuments of mens writings, altering the bookes of learned men after they are dead, adding and taking out at their pleasures: and namely, taking out such words, sentences, and whole discourses, as make against them, and adding the contrarie, even whatsoever they can imagine to make for them: so that the crime is no lesse then corruption and forgerie in the highest degree' (cited by Nelles, 'The uses of orthodoxy', 34).

[8] The motives of the seventeenth-century polemicists were thus very different from those of the early antiquaries such as John Leland or those of the ex-monks who preserved manuscripts in the belief that their houses would be refounded in the near future: see my 'The dispersal of the monastic libraries and the salvaging of the spoils', in *The Cambridge history of libraries in Britain and Ireland*, I: *To 1640*, ed. Elisabeth Leedham-Green and Teresa Webber (Cambridge, 2006), pp. 265–91.

For, whiles they [books] are in private mens hands, though their care be never so commendable in preserving them in their life times; yet what use can be made of them, or how may their authorities be vouched, which are not alwaies to be seene whiles they are living; and when they die, may easilie miscarie, by falling into the hands of such as regard them not. *Cicero* was an eloquent man in his time; yet his sonne proved but a Dunce: the father may be a worthy lover of Antiquity; it is a chance whether the sonne wil follow the fathers steppes.[9]

This is a real call for new and stable forms of institutional libraries to serve as replacements for the dissolved monastic libraries of the middle ages and must, of course, be read in the context of Sir Thomas Bodley's establishment of the Bodleian Library in 1602 and Bancroft's gift to Lambeth of his collection in 1610.[10]

Much has been written about Parker's donation of manuscripts and printed books to Corpus Christi College, Cambridge – where he had been master until deprived in Mary's reign – in 1575.[11] Parker was succeeded as archbishop in 1576 by Edmund Grindal, who died in 1583, leaving a large portion of his library to Queen's College, Oxford. Like most donors, English and continental, Elizabeth's first archbishops turned to established foundations, which had long histories and thus guaranteed continuity, when they disposed of their collections. A new archiepiscopal library would be too great a risk – it would be at the mercy, as Bancroft would later point out, of the whims of subsequent archbishops – in spite of the multiplying attempts to justify the policies, and very existence, of the Church of England through the use of theological and historical texts.[12]

Grindal's successor in 1583 was John Whitgift. A graduate of Pembroke College, Cambridge, briefly master of Pembroke and then of Trinity as well as vice chancellor of the university, Whitgift was a theologian and a gifted scholar, concerned to maintain a learned ministry. Like his recent predecessors, most notably Thomas Cranmer and Parker, Whitgift was an inveterate collector both of medieval manuscripts and printed books.[13] His library was a major one, made up of some 6,000 books including at least 200 manuscripts. A catalogue, identified as such only in 1956, survives at Trinity College Dublin, but it has never been edited. William O'Sullivan, who first recognized the catalogue for what it was, suggested that it was 'compiled in 1588 or very shortly after' and *c*. 1588 does, in fact, provide a *terminus ante quem non*, since there are a number of books that can be shown to have come from the library of the martyrologist John Foxe who died on 18 April 1587.[14]

---

9   *A treatise of the corruption of scripture*, part 5, p. 13.

10 For Bodley see Nelles, 'The uses of orthodoxy', 22–3; on 41 he describes the Bodleian as a 'quasi-national library'.

11 See most recently Timothy Graham, 'Matthew Parker's manuscripts: an Elizabethan library and its use', in *The Cambridge history of libraries*, ed. Leedham-Green and Webber, I, 322–41. Graham characterizes Parker's initiative as 'a nationally co-ordinated initiative to salvage the written record of England's medieval past' (p. 322).

12 See *inter alia* Benedict Scott Robinson, '"Darke speech": Matthew Parker and the reforming of history', *Sixteenth Century Journal*, XXIX (1998), 1061–83; also Felicity Heal, 'What can King Lucius do for you? The Reformation and the early British church', *English Historical Review*, CXX (2005), 593–614.

13 On Cranmer's collection see David G. Selwyn, *The library of Thomas Cranmer* (Oxford, 1996).

14 On the catalogue, now Dublin, Trinity College, MS E.4.13, see O'Sullivan, 'Archbishop Whitgift's library catalogue', *Times Literary Supplement*, 3 Aug. 1956, p. 468.

The catalogue is arranged alphabetically, by first letter only, but there are some ambiguities: writings by Thomas More, for example, are listed under both 'M' and 'T'. A change that occurred during the course of the sixteenth century in a number of libraries, although it was by no means universal, was the physical separation of manuscripts and printed books.[15] When an alphabetical inventory of Henry VIII's library at Westminster Palace was drawn up in 1542, books and manuscripts were housed together helter-skelter, but in Whitgift's catalogue the manuscripts for the most part appear as distinct units within alphabetical groupings and are signalled as 'script:'.[16] When Whitgift came to divide up his collection in his will, moreover, he distinguished clearly between printed books and manuscripts.

The catalogue was set out as a working document and spaces were left for additions; these occur in several hands. The last to be entered was a book published in 1604, the year of Whitgift's death: it is a copy of Abbot's *The reasons which Dr Hill hath brought for the upholding of papistry ... unmasked*. In toto, then, the catalogue was actively maintained for more than fifteen years.

Like his predecessors Whitgift turned to academic foundations when he considered the disposition of his library and he bequeathed the majority of his manuscripts to Trinity College, Cambridge, where he had been master from 1567 until 1577.[17] Duplicates were to go to Peterhouse, where he had been a fellow from 1555 until 1567, providing 'they have not the same authors before'.[18] According to the benefactors' book at Trinity 149 came to the college, but it does not appear that any got to Peterhouse.[19]

As the catalogue indicates, printed books formed the bulk of Whitgift's collection. Although Whitgift left Bancroft 'all my [hand] written bookes in paper touching matters of learning or anie concerning matters of the Church', nowhere in the will does Whitgift even mention the collection of printed books, let alone offer them to Bancroft. No doubt these went to members of his family with the rest of his estate and they may have in turn sold them to Bancroft.[20]

[15] See David McKitterick, 'Libraries and the organization of knowledge', in *The Cambridge history of libraries*, ed. Leedham-Green and Webber, I, 592–615, at 610: 'The strength of tradition, and the fact that many people saw no need to separate the two, is to be seen in the influential publications of Gesner, who mingled manuscript and print. In most libraries, the two media were not systematically separated for several generations.'

[16] There is a similarity to John Caius's catalogue of Cambridge University Library, published in his *Historia Cantebrigiensis academiae* (1574), where manuscripts and printed books were 'listed separately but under the same subject-heads' (McKitterick, 'Libraries and the organization of knowledge', p. 592). Summit (*Memory's library*, p. 210) notes that the firm separation of manuscripts and printed books in Bancroft's library anticipated later developments.

[17] On the reasons why Whitgift may have transferred books to Trinity (and by extension left his collection to the college) see Philip Gaskell, *Trinity College Library: the first 150 years* (Cambridge, 1980), p. 80: 'In removing Canterbury manuscripts to Cambridge, Whitgift followed the example of Archbishop Parker. No doubt the two archbishops – and Dean Nevile after them – believed that Canterbury's monastic books would be safer in academic libraries in Cambridge than exposed in the cathedral library to the possible bigotry or carelessness of their successors.' It was, as we shall see, this possible bigotry or carelessness that Bancroft set out to circumvent.

[18] See David Pearson, 'The libraries of English bishops, 1600–40', *The Library*, 6th ser., XIV (1992), 221–57, at 256.

[19] Pembroke College received Whitgift's Complutensian Bible and the works of Thomas Aquinas.

[20] In 'The libraries of English bishops' Pearson suggests that 'presumably he purchased them by agreement with the relatives who shared the residue of Whitgift's estate' (256).

In his will Bancroft, who was Whitgift's former household chaplain as well as his executor, bequeathed his own collection, more than 6,000 separate items, of which at least 472 were manuscripts, 'unto my successor and to the archbishops of Canterbury successively for ever'.[21] The bequest was conditional, however, on provisions for its strict preservation: if these were not met, the books would go 'unto his majesties colledge to be erected at Chelsey, yf it be erected within theis six yeares; or otherwise I geve and bequeath them all to the publick library of the University of Cambridge'.

Parker had considered the Cambridge University Library a fit repository for a portion of his collection and had donated 100 volumes, printed and manuscript, to the library.[22] Bancroft also had strong links with Cambridge, where he had received his education – BA (Christ's College, 1567); MA (Jesus College, 1572); and D.Th. (1585) – and the University Library thus provided an obvious fallback position for the disposition of his collection.[23] His naming of Chelsea College as his preferred choice in the event that things did not work out at Lambeth may, however, provide a clearer indication of his long-term ambitions for the library he had assembled.

The chief promoter of Chelsea College was Matthew Sutcliffe (1549/50–1629), a former fellow of Trinity College, Cambridge, dean of Exeter Cathedral and a man with whom Bancroft had been long associated: Bancroft had, for example, made use of Sutcliffe's *Treatise of ecclesiastical discipline* (1591) in his own tracts defending the episcopal structure of the Church of England.[24] King James was patron: he laid the foundation stone on 8 May 1609 and gave financial support as well.[25] Formally incorporated by charter on 8 May 1610 as 'King James's College at Chelsey', the establishment was to consist of a provost and nineteen fellows nominated by the king, of whom seventeen were to be in holy orders. Sutcliffe was the first provost, and the original fellows included historians William Camden and John Hayward, author of *The first part of the life and raigne of King Henrie IIII.*[26]

The chief function of the college, as *A briefe declaration of the reasons that moved King James of blessed memory, and the state, to erect a colledge of divines, and other learned men at Chelsey* (London, 1645) made clear, was to provide a means of responding to the catholic institutions of polemic that were springing up on the continent:[27]

---

21 In 1605 the Bodleian contained 5,600 volumes: see Nelles, 'The uses of orthodoxy', 49.

22 See Graham, 'Matthew Parker's manuscripts', 337. As Graham observes, Parker's benefaction 'was a key element in the restoration of the library planned by Andrew Perne, master of Peterhouse'.

23 In 1629 Cambridge University Library contained 'barely 1,000' volumes: see Palmer, 'In the steps of Sir Thomas Bodley', 54.

24 On Chelsea College see D. E. Kennedy, 'King James I's College of Controversial Divinity at Chelsea', in *Grounds of controversy. Three studies in the late 16th and early 17th century English polemics*, ed. D. E. Kennedy (Melbourne, 1989), pp. 97–126; Jesse M. Lander, *Inventing polemic. Religion, print, and literary culture in early modern England* (Cambridge, 2006), pp. 201–21.

25 See Kennedy, 'King James I's College', p. 103, on the king's benefactions.

26 In *William Camden. A life in context* (Woodbridge, 2007) Wyman H. Herendeen suggests that Chelsea College 'was designed to be a think-tank for Protestant policy and polemic, with John Hayward and William Camden recommended as the resident "historiographers"' (p. 425).

27 On the equivalent continental establishments see Nelles, 'The uses of orthodoxy', 46. Nelles notes that the founding of the Ambrosiana in 1607 must have posed a particular threat: 'the library was armed with a college of *doctores*, and the college constitutions published in 1610 mapped out a plan of studies intended to augment the majesty of the Holy Church through the cultivation of studies oriented around scholastic theology, scripture, polemic, and ecclesiastical history'.

That a select number of Divines and others should be gathered together into one body, and united with one form of Lawes, and there maintained, who being furnished with Bookes, and directed by men of experience and action, might alwaies be ready to maintaine our Christian faith, to answer the Adversaries Calumniations as well against Religion as the State, to defend the Majesty of Kings and Princes, against the usurpation of Popes, the liberty of Christians, against the yoke of Superstition, to supply the defect of teaching where Appropriations have devoured the Ministerie, by teaching and conference to convince the obstinate Papist and Atheist, and by all lawfull meanes to maintaine truth, and discover falshood.[28]

It thus complemented James's enterprise in Oxford and it is possible that Sutcliffe hoped that the two initiatives could work together to combat papistical polemic.[29] For James's scheme the Bodleian Library was crucial – it was from the beginning well 'furnished with Bookes' – and presumably Sutcliffe must have been concerned about where the essential reading for his college would be found. Without books, as *A briefe declaration* makes clear, the institution could not function effectively.

For many years Bancroft had followed a policy of limited toleration towards catholics.[30] As a result of the abortive Gunpowder Plot, however, and after some prominent defections to Rome, he became more outspoken in his opposition to the papists and it is in this context that one must see his support for Chelsea College.[31] In 1653 Arthur Wilson named him as the progenitor (as did Fuller after him) stating that his '*design* was to answer all *Popish Books*, or others, that vented their *malignant spirits* against the *Protestant Religion*'.[32] His library was essential to the protestant cause – Geoffrey Bill observes that 'Books were the weapons of controversy, and a library was the proper place for an arsenal of them'[33] – and it was his natural concern to maintain its integrity after his death and to bestow it where it could most effectively be used. By naming Lambeth Palace rather than Chelsea College itself

---

[28] *A briefe declaration*, pp. 2–3.

[29] See Nelles, 'The uses of orthodoxy', 39. The sorts of research generated by the 'Library and Academy' proposed by Sir Robert Cotton, Sir James Ley and John Dodderidge to Elizabeth at the end of her reign were also meant to be put at the disposal of the state in its dealings with the international community: see Kevin Sharpe, *Sir Robert Cotton, 1586–1631* (Oxford, 1979), pp. 27–8.

[30] Indeed in 1604 there was a bill, which was suppressed, accusing him of treason for having permitted the printing of appellant books. On this topic see Patrick Collinson, 'Bishop Richard Bancroft and the succession', in *The question of succession in late Elizabethan England*, ed. Susan Doran and Paulina Kewes, forthcoming.

[31] In his *The church-history of Britain* (London, 1655) Thomas Fuller cited the college, the foundation of which he attributed to Bancroft, as evidence for Bancroft's committed protestantism and support of the anglican middle way: 'as a two-edged sword, [it] was to cut on both sides to suppresse *Papists* and *Sectaries*'. Writing when the archiepiscopacy and Lambeth Palace functioned no more, Fuller also maintained that Bancroft had left his library to the college: 'was he never observed in his own person to aim at the enriching of his *Kindred*, but had intentions to make *pious uses* his *publick Heire*, bequeathing his *Library*, the confluence of his own collections with his Predecessours, *Whitgift, Grindoll, Parkers*, to *Chelsey-Colledge*; and if that took not effect, to the publick *Library* in *Cambridge*, where at this day they remain' (sig. H h h h 1r).

[32] Arthur Wilson, *The history of Great Britain, being the life and reign of King James the First* (London, 1653), H3r. As Debora Shuger has observed, Bancroft argued in 1610 that 'misliked' books should be confuted in print. This was precisely the function, as King James himself had stated, of Chelsea College: see *Censorship & cultural sensibility. The regulation of language in Tudor-Stuart England* (Philadelphia, 2006), p. 240.

[33] Bill, 'Lambeth Palace Library', 193.

– which would have obvious use for it – as his first choice for its institutionaliza-tion, he was possibly looking at the Oxford model: Bodley's library stood separate from James's collation project but was meant to provide the storehouse that made the project possible.[34]

As his desire to preserve the integrity of his collection stirred Bancroft to suggest alternative homes for his books if a permanent library were not founded at Lambeth, so too did it cause him to put a restriction of the date of completion of Chelsea College. His concerns were, in fact, well-founded and, in spite of its auspicious beginnings, the death of Prince Henry in 1612 seems to have been a blow.[35] Although in 1615 Thomas Cooper would write confidently about its progress, things were not as rosy as he portrayed them.[36] On 5 May 1616 the king wrote to Abbot, stating that although the buildings were well begun more funding was required and he commanded the archbishop to write to his bishops who were in turn to solicit funds from their clergy and 'other of their Diocese'.[37] Within two years after Sutcliffe's death in 1629, moreover, the Court of Chancery decreed that Sutcliffe's gifts were to revert to his natural heirs as a result of the delay of work on the college.[38]

Like Parker before him Bancroft showed himself anxious to maintain the integ-rity of the collection if it ended up at Lambeth and to prevent loss of books.[39] He therefore recommended that 'his most excellent majesty and his most royall successors, when they receave the homage of any Archbishop of Canterbury, first

---

[34] As Bodley wrote to James in 1606: 'your cause is good, your leasure is good, and so is your will, I am sure, and likewise your means, by reason of your library' (quoted in part by Nelles in 'The uses of orthodoxy', 36, from *Letters of Sir Thomas Bodley to Thomas James*, ed. G. W. Wheeler (Oxford, 1926), p. 155).

[35] See Kennedy, 'King James I's College', p. 101.

[36] *The art of giving* (1615; *RSTC* 5692), p. 89: 'And are not the foundations laid of another famous Colledge, by the pious and magnificent authority of our Soveraigne Lord King *James*, the most constant enemy of Antichrist, and defender of the true Christian, ancient, and Apostolike faith, for the maintenance of such worthies of our Church, to employ their studies in refuting the adversary, and justifying the truth of Jesus Christ? Is not a good part of that Colledge alreadie erected? Is it not still furthered and undertaken by the Soveraigne Majesty, who for the glory of GOD will finish that glorious worke.' See also Cooper's commendation of the Bodleian: 'Is not that glorious Library, exceeding the Vatican, or any now extant in the World, furnished with all sorts of bookes, and constant mayntenance for a Keeper therof, and continuall supply for the same, a very true and blessed monument of the bounty of these times, a very lively fruit of the true Religion of Jesus Christ? Shall not the memory of deuout *Bodley* be blessed for euer?' (p. 91). Cooper, it seems, was an advocate of the rhetorical question.

[37] See Kennedy, 'King James I's College', p. 114.

[38] See *ibid.*, p. 115; on the proviso in his will, p. 104.

[39] Existing collections, as he would have noted, seemed particularly vulnerable to new bibliographical schemes. In the petition drawn up by Cotton, Ley and Dodderidge, it had been suggested 'that it may please her Maiesty to bestow out of her gratious library sutche & so many of her bookes concerning history & Antiquity as yt shall please her highnes to graunt for the better furnishing of this library' (quoted in Richard Ovenden, 'The libraries of the antiquaries (c. 1580–1640) and the idea of a national collection', in *The Cambridge history of libraries*, ed. Leedham-Green and Webber, I, 527–61, at 549). Likewise King James himself had promised Bodley around 1604/5 'the choice of any books that I shall like in any of his houses of librarys'. When, much to Bodley's displeasure, he later changed his mind Bodley crossly observed 'And if I may not enjoy that gift of his manuscripts I doubt I shall not undertake that collation of the Fathers' (quoted in my 'Henry VIII's library and the British Museum duplicate book sales. A newly discovered de-accession', in *Libraries within the library. The origins of the British Library's printed collections*, ed. Giles Mandelbrote and Barry Taylor (London, 2009), pp. 11–23, at p. 13).

to procure him to enter bondes to leave all the said bookes to his successor'.[40] His concerns, moreover, seem to have been prescient. Bancroft appointed Samuel Harsnett (1561–1631) as one of his chaplains soon after his elevation to the bishopric of London in 1597 and other preferments followed. Harsnett was consecrated bishop of Chichester by Bancroft in 1609 and Bancroft named him and George Abbot as overseers of his will (Bancroft's nephew and namesake was the sole executor). Some twenty years later Harsnett left his own collection of books to the corporation of Colchester with the proviso that a suitable room be found to provide reading facilities for the local clergy and other divines as well.[41] The collection seems to have remained almost intact in spite of various vicissitudes and it is now housed in the Special Collections Room at the Albert Sloman Library at the University of Essex.

As has long been noted, Harsnett owned a number of books that can be shown through binding or other marks to have previously belonged to Whitgift and Bancroft.[42] Apart from these there are many others that passed through Bancroft's collection, many deriving in turn from Whitgift: books previously owned by John Foxe, Robert Dudley, earl of Leicester, Sir Christopher Hatton, Henry Fitzalan, earl of Arundel, John, Lord Lumley, Thomas Wakefield, first regius professor of Hebrew at Cambridge, and from less well-known individuals as well.[43] There are several books from the royal library, including Hervé Nédellec's commentary on Peter Lombard's Sentences (Venice, 1505).[44] Writing to James Montagu, bishop of Bath and Wells, on 5 December 1610, Patrick Young, the king's librarian, stated that Bancroft had the royal books on loan, and they were therefore not his to give away.[45] It is thus almost certain that the royal books came to Harsnett after Bancroft's death: borrowed themselves, they would not have been gifts during the archbishop's lifetime. Presumably the other Harnsett books, which (as far as I can tell) do not

[40] John Evelyn would observe (inaccurately) in a letter written in 1689 to Samuel Pepys that the library was 'replenished with excellent books, but that it ebbs and flows like the Thames running by it, at every prelate's accession or translation': quoted in 'Library of Lambeth Palace Library', *The Gentleman's Magazine* (Aug. 1834), 151–4, at 153.

[41] 'I give unto the bayliffes and incorporacion of the towne of Colchester all my librarie of bookes, provided that they prepare a decent roome to sett them up in, that the clergie of the towne of Colchester and other divines may have free accesse for the reading and studieing of theme': quoted in Pearson, 'The libraries of English bishops', 242. See also my '"A great gatherer together of books": Archbishop Bancroft's library at Lambeth (1610) and its sources', *Lambeth Palace Library. Annual Review* (2001), 51–64, at 57. Like Harsnett after him Bancroft no doubt intended his library to serve the clergy, above all the local clergy of London: see Bill, 'Lambeth Palace Library', 194.

[42] See, for example, Gordon Goodwin, *A catalogue of the Harsnett Library at Colchester* (London, 1888), who notes Whitgift and Bancroft bindings.

[43] Apart from my 'Archbishop Bancroft's library at Lambeth', see Julian Roberts, 'Extending the frontier: scholar collectors', in *The Cambridge history of libraries*, ed. Leedham-Green and Webber, I, 292–321, at 310–11. On Wakefield's books see my 'Religious controversy and marginalia: Pierfrancesco di Piero Bardi, Thomas Wakefield and their books', *Transactions of the Cambridge Bibliographical Society*, XII (2002), 206–45. Tom Freeman and I are preparing an article on Foxe's collection.

[44] This carries an inventory number, no. 1128, characteristic of Henry VIII's library at Westminster, on which see my *The libraries of King Henry VIII* (London, 2000), pp. lxvi–lxxiii. I discovered this book after I had completed *The libraries of King Henry VIII* and it does not appear in the volume.

[45] The letter is printed in Johannes Kemke, *Patricius Junius (Patrick Young) Bibliothekar der Könige Jacob I. und Carl I. von England* (Leipzig, 1898), pp. 5–6. On the episode see most recently my 'Henry VIII's library and the British Museum duplicate book sales', pp. 13–14. As Young put it in a rather backhanded compliment: 'Tantus enim amor librorum ei fuit, ut loca omnia lustraret, et bibliothecas priuatorum hominum scrutaretur, ac prece aut pretio, quae rariora essent, in suam transferret, ita ut nec Regiae perpercerit.'

appear in the 1612 catalogue, must have gone missing between 1610 and 1612, that is, during the period of the settlement of Bancroft's estate. A calculation of the size and extent of Bancroft's collection must, therefore, go beyond Abbot's catalogue and take into account the Harsnett materials.

In spite of pledging that 'I will keepe these bookes to the best of my power safely as a precious treasure and not willingly suffer any of them to be taken away', Abbot rejected Bancroft's recommendation that bonds be posted, maintaining that it would be impossible to guarantee the preservation of

> all and every booke and volume ... because it may and hath fallen out that some booke may be sent for by the king himselfe or may for a time be taken out for some publicke use of the church, with a purpose to returne it againe (besides all other casualties unto which all things in this mortall life are subject) when, notwithstanding all the care and diligence which the archbishop possibly can use, this booke or books may...not be returned unto the librarie againe; in which or the like case it is not agreeable unto reason, that a bond or obligation of some thousands of pounds should be forfeited, but that the value of this booke or bookes which are lost ... should be made good to the library againe.[46]

Part of the problem, as Abbot discreetly pointed out, was that the king himself took a rather predatory interest in the disposition of the collection. This is not surprising since James was an avowed admirer of libraries. According to Robert Burton:

> when he came to visit our Uniuersity of Oxford [in 1605], & ... came to see that famous Library, renued by *Sir Thomas Bodley*, in imitation of *Alexander*, at his departure brake out into that noble speech, If I were not a King, I would be an University man. *And if it were so that I must be a prisoner, if I might have my wish, I would desire to have no other Prison then that Library, and to bee chained together with my fellow writers.*[47]

Considering himself no mean scholar and proud to be associated with his 'fellow writers', James thus saw Bancroft's library as a complement to the royal library,[48] claiming that it would be 'of great use to himselfe and his Successors, as well as to the Church of God, that in a place so near unto his Royall Palace these bookes should be preserved'. Its strengths in the fields of contemporary theology would compensate for possible gaps in the king's own collection, which consisted in large part of inherited books maintained under the keepership of Patrick Young.[49]

---

[46] See Graham, 'Matthew Parker's manuscripts', 338–40, on details of Parker's elaborate instructions to ensure that his benefaction to Corpus Christi College, Cambridge – some 433 manuscripts and more than 800 printed books – be kept intact.

[47] *The anatomy of melancholy* (London, 1621), pp. 352–3. See Summit, *Memory's library*, p. 219, for an alternative version of the text.

[48] In spite of his precipitate offer to Bodley James later set about increasing the holdings of his collection and in 1622 he commissioned Patrick Young to make inventories of the contents of cathedral libraries and these were used to arrange for the transfer of books to London: see Ovenden, 'The libraries of the antiquaries', p. 528.

[49] Although Bancroft fully supported Thomas James's editorial project, and even though he was chancellor of the University of Oxford, he did not consider the Bodleian as an alternative home for his own collection. One reason may be that he realized that London needed a comparable library and that the king himself would wish to make use of it.

Abbot also stated that James himself was, at least indirectly, responsible for the production of the catalogue under the supervision of Sir Francis Bacon (1561–1626). Bacon was an obvious choice.[50] A former pupil of Whitgift at Trinity, he had advanced rapidly under the new king and was appointed solicitor-general in 1607, and then clerk of the Star Chamber in 1608.[51] He also advocated a reform of institutions of learning as well as the founding of new libraries and colleges. In his *Of the proficience and advancement of learning*, published in 1605 and dedicated to the new king, he stated that 'Libraries are as the Shrynes, where all the Reliques of the ancient Saints, full of true vertue, and that without delusion or imposture, are preserved, and reposed.'[52] He was anxious that books be read and used rather than left untouched and he associated protestantism with this active process:

Martin Luther conducted (no doubt) by an higher providence, but in discourse of reason, finding what a Province he had undertaken against the Bishop of Rome, and the degenerate traditions of the Church, and finding his owne solitude, being no waies ayded by the opinions of his owne time, was enforced to awake all Antiquitie, and to call former times to his succors, to make a partie against the present time: so that the ancient Authors, both in Divinitie, and in Humanitie, which had long time slept in Libraries, began generally to be read and revolved.[53]

In one sense, as David McKitterick has observed, the comparison of books to relics suggests a conservative attitude towards libraries, but the further contrast between waking and sleeping, as well as Bacon's suggestion that reading leads to 'revolution', indicates the significance of the library in his new scientific world.[54]

Bacon was more concerned with the advancement of learning than with its preservation *per se* – he was anything but an antiquary – but he was also well aware of the dangers of 'information overload' (as Jennifer Summit has put it) and thought deeply about how to organize knowledge, including the library, to make it readily accessible. With the proliferation of books, like the proliferation of ideas, scientific cataloguing became essential.[55] The orderly marshalling of pertinent facts, which is what the library allows us to do once it has been properly organized, represents

---

[50] For a useful summary of his career see Markku Peltonen's entry in the *Oxford dictionary of national biography*.

[51] Bacon later attacked Whitgift and disputed bitterly with Bancroft, who suppressed his *Certain considerations touching the better pacification and edification of the Church of England* (1604). Nevertheless, in 1608 he considered Bancroft as a potential supporter for his experimental work: see Lisa Jardine and Alan Stewart, *Hostage to fortune. The troubled life of Francis Bacon* (London, 1998), p. 302.

[52] Bacon, *The advancement of learning*, second dedication, fo. 2v. Bacon goes on to call for 'New Editions of Authors, with more correct impressions, more faithfull translations, more profitable glosses, more diligent annotations, and the like.' This, of course, is precisely what Thomas James was setting out to do.

[53] *The advancement of learning*, bk 1, fo. 17v.

[54] See McKitterick, 'Libraries and the organization of knowledge', in *The Cambridge history of libraries*, ed. Leedham-Green and Webber, I, 592–614, at 607.

[55] On Bacon's method as it relates to libraries see Summit, *Memory's library*, pp. 197–230. In his *Cogitata et uisa de interpretatione naturae, siue de scientia operatiua* (1607) he argued for new forms of organizing the branches of knowledge, recommending the gathering together of a 'great storehouse of facts'; after which 'the material collected should be sorted into orderly Tables, so that the understanding may work upon it and thus accomplish its appropriate task' (quoted, with useful discussion, from Benjamin Farrington, *The philosophy of Francis Bacon. An essay on its development from 1603 to 1609 with new translations of fundamental texts* (Chicago, 1964), in *Memory's library*, p. 211).

'literate experience', and it is only after this has been accomplished that induction can take place.[56] In the very year that the Lambeth catalogue was completed, moreover, Bacon wrote an unfinished paper entitled 'Descriptio globi intellectualis', in which he provided the beginnings of a classification scheme for the sciences: knowledge as a whole, in other words, was to be catalogued.

Bacon's *rôle* at Lambeth was limited to finding a way to honour Bancroft's stipulation that the collection be preserved without, nevertheless, resorting to the extreme measures the archbishop had recommended. There is no indication that Bacon had anything to do with the actual compilation of the present catalogue: not surprisingly it does not in any way reflect his theories of the organization of knowledge.[57] Abbot's catalogue was, in fact, an old-fashioned one. It was probably based, moreover, on the catalogues Bancroft himself had had made during his lifetime.[58] In effect a shelf-list, it corresponds to the order in which Bancroft stored the books.[59] In fact 'my study over the cloisters' was not an ideal location – the light was not good and according to a nineteenth-century account, made after it was converted to a reading room, 'in winter only men like Captain Parry and his crew [of arctic explorers] could make use of such a place'.[60] Nevertheless, it was here that the books resided, apart from one short interlude during the Commonwealth,[61] until 1828 when the printed books were transferred to the renovated Great Hall under Archbishop William Howley's supervision.[62]

Beginning with theology, the catalogue was arranged around the four walls of the room according to a number of traditional categories, each arranged alphabeti-

---

56 See Farrington, *The philosophy of Francis Bacon*, p. 99.

57 See Summit, *Memory's library*, p. 137, on contemporary theories of cataloguing: these 'reflect seventeenth-century preoccupations with the taxonomy and right ordering of knowledge, as well as with the idea that the individual book or text is made meaningful by the classifications and taxonomies through which it is ordered and navigated'. See also McKitterick, 'Libraries and the organization of knowledge', p. 603: 'They [new schemes of classification in the seventeenth century] ignored alphabetical ordering by author (as, for example, in Gesner's bibliographical work of the 1540s) just as the natural world was reduced into classifications based on analysis and, increasingly, on observation.'

58 On Bancroft's catalogues see Young's letter to Montagu (ed. Kemke, *Patricius Junius*, p. 6): 'Reliquos [of the books Bancroft borrowed from the royal library], quorum magnus est numerus, adhuc habet, quos quoniam in suos catalogos retulerat, et de nouo cum suis insignibus compingendos curauerat, ambigo, an pro suis habuerit, an uero se mortuo melius habitos ac quasi rediuiuos ad ueterem dominum redire uoluerit.'

59 As McKitterick observes: 'there are always two fundamental ways (with many further subsidiaries) of arranging books: one on the actual shelves, the other on paper and according to the priorities chosen by the individual for a particular selection, and for the particular purposes of the moment' ('Libraries and the organization of knowledge', p. 593; see also pp. 605–6).

60 Quoted from John Cave-Browne, *Lambeth Palace and its associations* (Edinburgh, 1882), p. 56 n. 3, by Robin Myers in 'Dr Andrew Coltée Ducarel, Lambeth librarian, civilian, and keeper of the public records', *The Library*, 6th ser., XXI (1999), 199–222, at 201–2.

61 The catalogue made before the collection was to be sent to Cambridge was presented to the House of Commons on 29 Apr. 1647. It too was a shelflist and 'The order of classes is the same as Bancroft's catalogue, the authors being arranged alphabetically within their class' ('Lambeth Palace Library', 115–16). The basic organizational principles of the library had not changed, in other words, since Bancroft's death.

62 For a lyrical description of this new location, 'carried into effect with great taste by Edward Blore, esq. the celebrated architect', see the 1834 article on 'Library of Lambeth Palace'. Signalled out was the new heating system: 'The room is heated by pipes under the floor, and the warm air is admitted into the room through fourteen brass gratings, between every division of the library. At either end of the hall is a suitable fire-place' (152). The manuscripts went to 'a fire-proof room, over a newly built internal gateway, abutting on the south side of the hall' (154).

cally.[63] Within the individual groupings (or sub-groupings) books were separated by size.[64] Placed in the theology section ('in parte Occidentali' and overflowing 'in parte Australi') were Bibles, works by the fathers (construed fairly generally as in the case of the *Reuelationes* of St Bridget of Sweden), protestant books, protestant controversy, biblical commentary by catholics, by catholics and protestants, and then by protestants alone, as well as a few Hebrew commentaries, catholic books ('libri pontificii'), catholic books of controversy (including Henry VIII's *Assertio septem sacramentorum aduersus Martinum Lutherum*), sermons and scholastic theology.[65] Also on the south wall were books of canon law, civil law and common law as well as 'libri Humanioris literaturae' (which included Bacon's *The advancement of learning*).[66] History books were found 'in parte Orientali' (and Foxe's *Acts and monuments* was placed in this category as well as Jacobus de Voragine's *Legenda aurea*). Manuscripts were kept separately 'in parte Boreali', along with books of the Roman liturgy, puritan books, 'libri Pontificiorum' (under which was found both *The insitution of a Christian man* and *A necessary doctrine and erudition for any Christian man*) and dictionaries.[67]

The individuals who prepared the catalogue and whose signatures, dated 24 April 1612,[68] appear at the conclusion of the catalogue were Gervase Nidd, William Baker and Walter Dobson.[69] Nidd, who was a graduate of Trinity College, Cambridge, received his doctor of divinity in 1613. An ecclesiastical licenser between 1611 and 1616 , he was a chaplain to Abbot in 1612–13, and it was he whom Abbot instructed to supervise the preparation of the catalogue.[70] William Baker was a secretary to

---

63 Cox-Johnson notes that 'the library was housed in a gallery which was built over the four sides of a cloister. The inner walls were 75 feet long and apparently were lined with book-shelves' ('Lambeth Palace Library', 107). For a summary of books contained in each grouping see Roberts, 'Extending the frontier', p. 311; also Summit, *Memory's library*, p. 210. The alphabetical principles were not always clear, and there were sometime ingenious solutions such as 'of our' [in margin] 'Lady the mirrour' for *The myrroure of our lady* (London, 1530).

64 As McKitterick observes, 'In most libraries, private and institutional, and as one of the arrangements most economical of space, ordering by size is a frequent phenomenon' ('Libraries and the organization of knowledge', pp. 594–5).

65 Concerning the arrangement see Palmer, 'In the steps of Sir Thomas Bodley', p. 59: 'The books were arranged as if in battle order, with sections of Protestant books, Catholic books, Protestant works of controversy, Catholic works of controversy, Protestant commentaries, Catholic commentaries, Protestant liturgies, and Catholic liturgies. There was also a section of Puritan books, including the scurrilous Marprelate tracts whose printers and authors Bancroft had hounded so zealously...Arranged around the cloisters at Lambeth they must have been an impressive sight, well-ordered and bristling with intent.' As Collinson observes, moreover, 'Bancroft was a natural conspirator who warmed to conspiracy, and for whom intelligence gathering was second nature' ('Bishop Richard Bancroft and the succession'). The library reflects this mentalité.

66 For the most part the literature section was devoted to the classics but it did include medieval authors, albeit in printed editions, such as Boethius, Bartholomaeus Anglicus and Geoffrey Chaucer.

67 At the Bodleian the books were organized alphabetically within faculty: theology, law, medicine and the arts. Summit observes that the reversal of law and medicine within the hierarchy was a deliberate decision in order to give precedence to the former: 'the order of the books in the Bodleian – and the catalogue that records it – follows the order of knowledge in the *universitas scientiarum*' (*Memory's library*, pp. 228–9).

68 According to the preface Bancroft had requested King James to make provision for the integrity of the collection 'within the space of two yeares'.

69 For details see Cox-Johnson, 'Lambeth Palace Library', 107 n. 2.

70 On Nidd see *Clergy of the Church of England database*, ID 31361; also Cyndia Susan Clegg, 'Checking the father: anxious paternity and Jacobean press censorship', in *Printing and parenting in*

Abbot, who described him as 'as gentle a man as ever served any master' in his will, and was, as Abbot requested in the will, the scribe of Abbot's own catalogue.[71] Dobson, who was the scribe of this catalogue, was a witness to Bancroft's will, by which he received a legacy of £40. He acted as Abbot's receiver and like Baker appears in his will, Abbot piously hoping that 'hee hath not utterly lost his time under mee'. In 1644 he made a list of books in Laud's private study just before they were taken away to Westminster.[72]

In the preface to the catalogue Abbot made it clear that Bancroft's bequest was the seventeenth-century equivalent of seed money. His successors were expected to contribute to the enterprise, beginning with Abbot himself who observed:

> whereas I have diverse bookes of mine owne, and may (God blessing me) have from time to time many more, which are not left in this library by my venerable predecessor, my meaning, I say is, to adde these unto this studie, and so to encrease that number which my predecessor left, to the greater use and more ample benefite of those that shall succeede me.

And, although he did give books elsewhere, Abbot's own chief benefaction was to Lambeth: 39 manuscripts and 2,627 printed books.[73] He was justly proud of the collection Bancroft had put together, and which he was steadily augmenting, boasting in a letter of 31 August 1614 to William Trumbull, English agent to the Spanish Netherlands, that

> I have perused the Catalogue of the Library left by the late Archduke of Arscott but find not any thinge therein which I much desire. For I may let you know, that I myselfe have a Library at Lambith, not much inferiour unto that of any private man in Europe, for which the See of Canterbury is beholding to my last Predecessour: and I do continually increase it to my no small expense.[74]

early modern England, ed. Douglas A. Brooks (Aldershot, 2005), pp. 291–302, at p. 293; also *eadem*, *Press censorship in Jacobean England* (Cambridge, 2001), pp. 190–1.

71 On Baker, apart from Cox-Johnson, see Cyndia Susan Clegg, *Print censorship in Caroline England* (Cambridge, 2008), p. 154.

72 See Cox-Johnson, 'Lambeth Palace Library', 112.

73 On his will, dated 23 July 1632, see Pearson, 'The libraries of English bishops', 232. Concerning his library Abbot stated 'I have many books in the great study or library at Lambeth marked with these two letters G.C. I give and bequeath those to that Library for the use of the Archbishops of Canterbury in succession' (quoted in Cox-Johnson, 'Lambeth Palace Library', 107). He also requested his successors to keep the collection as safe as he had done. For a tabulated subject breakdown of the collection in 1633 see Cox-Johnson, 'Lambeth Palace Library', 108.

74 Quoted by Cox-Johnson, 'Lambeth Palace Library', 110. On Trumbull (d. 1535) – to whom Abbot was a supporter – see Robert Hill, 'Ambassadors and art collecting in early Stuart Britain.The parallel careers of William Trumbull and Sir Dudley Carleton, 1609 – 1625' (*Journal of the History of Collections*, XV (2003), 211–28). Passonate about books himself Trumbull acquired works of art for English patrons. Several individuals, including Robert Carr, Viscount Rochester, were interested in the collections of the duke of Aarschot (d. 1612) and in August 1614 Trumbull sent Sir Thomas Lake a catalogue of Aarschot's books which Lake may have passed on to Abbot: see Hill, 'Ambassadors and art collecting', 215. Imran Uddin provides a gist of the letter to Trumbull taken from the calendar of Trumbull's papers: it includes the following statement not quoted by Cox-Johnson: 'But if that manuscript of Cardinal Wolsie's treaty at Calais be to be had, buy it for me.' See 'William Trumbull: a Jacobean diplomat at the court of the archdukes in Brussels, 1605/9–1625', Ph.D., Katholieke Universiteit Leuven, 2006, pp. 54–5.

As his dedication of this burgeoning library 'to the service of God and his Church, of the kings and common wealth of this realme' suggests, moreover, he saw the library as both national and public in a way that the royal library, for example, could never be.[75] As in so many other ways, it resembled the Bodleian in this.

Editorial conventions

The following are not diplomatic editions. I have not noted corrections in the original hand and I have expanded '&' to 'and'. I have followed modern usage for the vowel and consonants denoted by i/j and u/v (as I have also done in my quotations from contemporary printed texts in my introduction). Punctuation, capitalization and paragraphing are also mine. Both texts have been printed with modernized spelling in A. C. Ducarel, *The history and antiquities of the archiepiscopal palace of Lambeth* (London, 1785), pp. 47–52.

---

[75] See Palmer, 'In the steps of Sir Thomas Bodley', 54. Palmer also observes that 'Parliament always referred to it as "the publick library belonging to the archiepiscopal see of Canterbury"' (66).

Texts

1. Lambeth Palace Library, CM XII/2: probate copy of Richard Bancroft's will, dated 28 October 1610; proved 12 November 1610

I have excerpted the clause relating to his library.

Item, I geve all my bookes in my study over the cloysters unto my successor and to the archbishops of Canterbury successively for ever, if he my next successor will yeild to such assurances as shal be devised by such learned councell as my supervisor and executor shall make choyce of for the continuance of all the said bookes unto the said archbishops successively according to my true meaning; otherwise I bequeath them all unto his majesties colledge to be erected at Chelsey, yf it be erected within theis six yeares; or otherwise I geve and bequeath them all to the publick library of the University of Cambridge. Touching this my bequest and legacy there may be some defect in the same, which I desire may be so supplied as that all my said bookes may remayne to my successors, for that is my chiefest desire. And yf it might please his most excellent majesty and his most royall successors, when they receave the homage of any Archbhishop of Canterbury, first to procure him to enter bonds to leave all the said bookes to his successor, my desire herein would be greatly strengthned. Item, I geve to my next successor all the mappes and pictures in my gallery at Lambeth, and all my writinges and papers concerninge church causes which are in my paper study and in my great study.[1]

2. Lambeth Palace Library, LR/F/1. fos i–ii: Abbot's preface to the catalogue of Richard Bancroft's library

Written in Dobson's hand, the preface is dated and signed by Abbot (G. Cant). The catalogue exists in two copies as was mandated by Bacon, one to be stored with the dean and chapter of the cathedral church of Canterbury and the other kept at Lambeth. Both, now at Lambeth, retain their original binding, rebacked, with Abbot's arms, but it is not known which is which. I have used LR/F/1 as my copy text and have listed all variants from LR/F/2, even though these consist exclusively of orthographic variants.

In as much as both pietie to God and his Church, and also justice amongst men doth require that the holy actions of our predecessors should be recorded with gratefull memory, and that the use of such things, as by their last wills and testament, they have left *ad pios usus*, shoud[a] be preserved to succeeding ages, I have thought it fit,[b] having now in my custodie[c] a notable and famous librarie[d] in the Archbishop of

---

[a] should – LR/F/2.
[b] fitt – LR/F/2.
[c] custody – LR/ F/2.
[d] library – LR/F/2.

---

[1] On the fate of papers kept in the Archbishops' study after the Civil War see Bill, 'Lambeth Palace Library', 201–3.

Canterburies house at Lambeth,[e] to set[f] downe to posteritie who was the author and beginner of the same, and what the purpose and intendment was of the doner and bestower of those bookes.

Let[g] all men therefore, present and to come, knowe[h] and understand that Richard Bancrofte Dr of Divinity,[i] first Bishop of London, and afterward promoted to the Archbishopricke of Canterburie,[j] being for many yeares a greate gatherer together of bookes, did voluntarily and of his owne motion (as in his lifetime he had oft foretold that he would) by his last will and testament, give and bequeath unto his successors, the Archbishops of Canterburie[k] forever, a greate and famous librarie[l] of bookes of divinitie and of many other sortes[m] of learning, but with request and intreaty, that the King's Majestie within the space of two yeares would gratiously[n] take order that these bookes might safely be continued to posterity, that so the good and religious intention of him that was the bestower might not be frustrated and annihilated.[o] The King's Majestie therefore, that is to say James, by the grace of God, King of Greate Britaine, France, and Ireland, Defender of the Faith, with his royall affection, embracing this good purpose of the foresaid Archbishop, and according to the greate wisedome, religion, and learning which God hath given unto his Highnesse, conceaving it to be a monument of fame within his kingdome, and of greate use to himselfe and his successors, as well as to the Church of God, that in a place so neare unto his royall palace these bookes should be preserved, did, after mature deliberation commend the care and consideration hereof[p] unto Sir Frauncis Bacon, knight, his Majesties solliciter, that he should thinke upon some course, how the custody of this library might be established and that by the negligence of those that come after, so excellent a worke might not be frustrated to the hurt of the Church and Commonwealth.

Sir Frauncis Bacon therefore, as a man learned and a true lover of learning[2] (for by both those titles the king was pleased to stile him), after good consideration did hold it fitt that a catalogue of the bookes should be accurately and exquisitely made that it might be knowne in the ages to come what were those bookes which the foresaid Archbishop Bancrofte did leave unto his successors, and that this catalogue should be sent unto the Deane and Chapter of the Cathedrall Church of Canterbury,[q] that it may / [fo. iv] be there layd up in archivis, and this writing or instrument registred there, that so after the death of every archbishop, it may be knowne what were the bookes which were commended to his trust. And also that a copie or duplicate of this booke or catalogue should remaine in the library itselfe at Lambith, that the succeeding archbishop from time to time might be acquainted with those bookes, which are in his custody, and carefully looke to the conservation of them. But it did not seeme fitt that any greate bond should be entred by the new archbishop comming in for the restitution by his heyres[r] or executors, of all and every booke

e	Lambith – LR/F/2.	l	library – LR/F/2.
f	sett – LR/F/2.	m	sorts – LR/F/2.
g	Lett – LR/F/2.	n	graciously – LR/F/2.
h	know – LR/F/2.	o	annihillated – LR/F/2.
i	Divinitie – LR/F/2.	p	heereof – LR/F/2.
j	Canterbury – LR/F/2.	q	Canterburie – LR/F2.
k	Canterbury – LR/F/2.	r	heires – LR/F2.

2   'true … learning': Abbot is perhaps quoting Plato, *The republic*, 2. 311.

and volume which was and is conteyned[s] in that library, because it may and hath fallen out that some booke may be sent for by the king himselfe[3] or may for a time be taken out for some publicke use of the church, with a purpose to returne it againe (besides all other casualties unto which all things in this mortall life are subject) when, notwithstanding all the care and diligence which the archbishop possibly can use, this booke or bookes may (by some accident, or default of another) not be returned unto the librarie[t] againe; in which or the like case it is not agreeable unto reason, that a bond or obligation of some thousands of pounds should be forfaited, but that the value of this booke or bookes which are lost (and the losse thereof might have ben hindred)[u] should be made good to the library againe. In these termes these bookes comming unto me who, by the mercy of God and gracious favour of my soveraigne King James, do succeede in this archbishopricke[v] of Canterburie,[w] I have held it my duety[x] simply and in the sight of God to make the world acquainted with that which I doe[y] or shall do in this behalfe. And therefore I have first caused a catalogue of all these volumes to be written into two bookes, the one whereof I send unto the Deane and Chapter of the Cathedrall Church of Canterbury, and the other I retaine in the library heere, but both to the uses aforesaid. These catalogues I have caused to be compared accurately with the bookes and volumes themselves and then each of them with other, and in testimony of the faithfulnesse which hath ben used heerein, I have caused their names to be subscribed with their owne hands, whose helpe[z] and diligence I did use in this businesse. In the next place my purpose is, and I doe[aa] here solemnly and holilie[bb] promise and vow it, that during my life or the tyme[cc] that I shall have charge over them, I will keepe these bookes to the best of my power safely as a precious treasure and not willingly suffer any of them to be taken away, to be defaced or mutilated,[dd] or to receave any other detriment, from the which I may preserve them. And thirdly my / [fo. iir] intendment is that whereas I have diverse bookes of mine owne, and may (God blessing me) have from time to time many more, which are not left in this library by my venerable predecessor, my meaning, I say, is to adde these unto this studie and so to encrease[ee] that number which my predecessor left, to the greater use and more ample benefite[ff] of those that shall succeede me. And of these bookes by me given, and to be given, I shall alsoe[gg] leave a catalogue written in the same library,[4] that those who[hh] come after may see that I have not ben a diminisher or dissipator of that which was commended to my trust, but rather an enlarger and increaser of the same. It remaineth now, that I doe[ii] pray and beseech those which shall succeede me in this archishopricke, which

s   conteined – LR/F2.
t   library – LR/F2.
u   hindered – LR/F2.
v   archbishoprick – LR/F2.
w   Canterbury – LR/F2.
x   duetie – LR/F2.
y   do – LR/F2.
z   help – LR/F2.
aa do – LR/F2.

bb holily – LR/F2.
cc time – LR/F2.
dd mutulated – LR/F2.
ee increase – LR/F2.
ff benefitt – LR/F2.
gg also – LR/F2.
hh which – LR/F2.
ii do – LR/F2.

3   In 'Lambeth Palace Library', 195, Bill points out that 'one of the worst offenders was the King, who borrowed books from Lambeth without returning them'. Cox-Johnson suggests that James had informed Bacon that he intended to borrow books ('Lambeth Palace Library', 106).
4   The two copies of the catalogue of books given by Abbot are found with copies of Bancroft's catalogue as LR/F/5 and LR/F/6.

by these presents I doe,[jj] and in the bowells of Christ Jesus[5] do adjure, as they will answere unto me and[kk] my predecessor in that fearefull day of God, that with the like care and diligence they looke to the preservation of this library and, setting aside all subtletie or fraude or pretence which worldly[ll] wisedome may devise to the contrary, they do suffer them, as far[mm] as lyeth in them, to descend from age to age and from succession to succession, to the service of God and his Church, of the kings and commonwealth of this realme and particularly of the archbishops of Canterbury.[6] And God, who knoweth heerein the integritie of my hart,[nn] blesse this purpose and endeavour of my predecessor, and myselfe, and blesse all them unto whome the care of this may any waies[oo] appertaine, to the honor of his name, the good of his Church, and their owne everlasting comfort. Amen. Octobr: 15 1612.

G. Cant.

3. Lambeth Palace Library, LR/F/1, fo. 78v (LR/F/2, fo. 91v)

Conclusion to the catalogue.

Aprilis 24o 1612
Collatione accurata per nos quorum nomina subscribuntur facta, reperimus hunc uerum esse indicem uoluminum et librorum omnium, qui ad perpetuum usus (si Deus uoluerit) archiepiscoporum Cantuariensium relicti sunt in Bibliotheca Lambethana, ex testamento D. Richardi Bancroft piae memoriae Archiepiscopi Cantuariensis, qui obiit in Domino 2o Novembr: Anno 1610

Gervasius Nid
Gulielmus Baker
Gualterus Dobson

[jj] do – LR/F2.
[kk] and to – LR/F2.
[ll] worldly – LR/F2.

[mm] farre – LR/F2.
[nn] harte – LR/F2.
[oo] wayes – LR/F2.

[5] 'bowells...Jesus': Philippians 1:8.
[6] Palmer suggests that 'the dedication to the King and Commonwealth meant that in some sense the Library was to be both national and public' ('In the steps of Sir Thomas Bodley', 54). He also observes that 'Parliament always referred to it as the publick library belonging to the archiepiscopal see of Canterbury' (66).

3

ANNUAL ACCOUNTS OF THE CHURCH OF ENGLAND, 1632–1639

Edited by
Kenneth Fincham

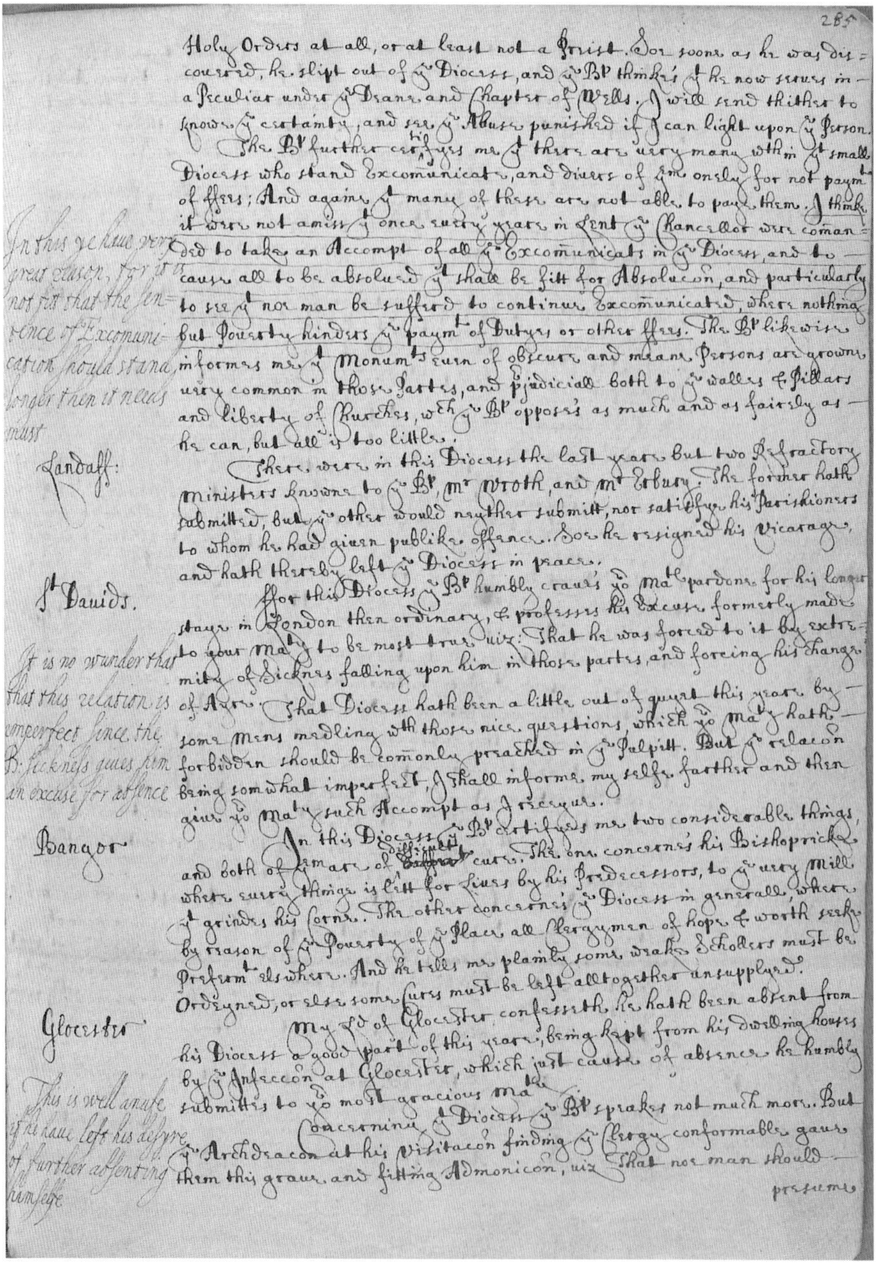

Holy Orders at all, or at least not a Priest. For soone as he was dis=
covered, he slipt out of my Diocess, and my Bp thinkes he now serues in
a Peculiar undre the Deane and Chapter of Wells. I will send thither to
know the certainty, and see the Abuser punished if I can light upon the Person.

The Bp further certifyes me that there are very many within that small
Diocess who stand Excomunicate, and diuers of thē onely for not paym̄t
of ffees; And againe that many of these are not able to pay them. I thinke
it were not amiss that once every yeare in Lent the Chancellor were coman=
ded to take an Accompt of all the Excomunicats in the Diocess, and to
cause all to be absolued that shall be fitt for Absolucōn, and particularly
to see that noe man be suffred to continue Excomunicated, where nothing
but Pouerty hindreth the paym̄t of Dutyes or other ffees. The Bp likewise
informes me that Monum̄ts euen of obscure and meane Persons are growne
very common in those partes, and prjudiciall both to the walles & Pillars
and liberty of Churches, wch the Bp opposeth as much and as fairely as
he can, but all is too little.

Landaff:

There were in this Diocess the last yeare but two Bp refractory
ministers knowne to the Bp, mr Wroth, and mr Erbury. The former hath
submitted, but the other would neither submitt, nor satisfye his Parishioners
to whom he had giuen publike offence. Soe he resigned his Vicarage,
and hath thereby left the Diocess in peace.

St Dauids.

For this Diocess the Bp humbly craues yo Matꝭ pardons for his longer
stay in London then ordinary, & professeth his Excuse, formerly made
to your Matie to be most true viz. That he was forced to it by the extre=
mity of Sicknes falling upon him in those partes and forcing his change
of Ayre. That Diocess hath been a little out of quyet this yeare, by
some Mens medling with those nice questions, which yo Matie hath
forbidden should be comonly preached in the Pulpitt. But the relacōn
being somewhat imperfect, I shall informe my selfe farther and then
giue yo Matie such Accompt as I receyue.

Bangor

In this Diocess the Bp certifies me two considerable things,
and both of them matter of curse. The one concernes his Bishopricke,
where euery thinge is lett for Leirs by his Predecessors, to the very Mill
that grindes his Corne. The other concernes the Diocess in generall, where
by reason of the Pouerty of the Place all Clergymen of hope & worth seeke
Preferm̄t elswhere. And he tells me plainely some weake Schollers must be
Ordeyned, or else some Curs must be left alltogether unsupplyed.

Glocestr

My Ld of Glocestr confesseth, he hath been absent from
his Diocess a good part of this yeare, being kept from his dwelling houses
by the Antecōn at Glocester, which just cause of absence he humbly
submitts to yo most gracious Matie.

Concerning the Diocess the Bp speakes not much more. But
the Archdeacon at his visitacōn finding the Clergy conformable gaue
them this graue and fitting Admonicōn, viz That noe man should
presume

Margin annotations (left):

In this ye haue very
great reason, for it is
not fit that the sen-
tence of Excomuni-
cation should stand
longer then it needs
must

It is no wunder that
that this relation is
imperfect since the
Bp sicknes giues him
an excuse for absence

This is well aduised
if he haue left his desyre
of further absenting
himselfe

Introduction

In December 1629 Charles I issued a series of instructions to the episcopate of England and Wales, the last clause of which required the archbishops of Canterbury and York to submit an annual account on the observance of these orders in their provinces.[1] These 'accounts', 'certificates' or 'returns', as they were variously known,[2] represent a remarkable annual record of diocesan affairs in the 1630s, unparalleled in the sixteenth- and seventeenth-century Church of England. They also contain royal marginalia, which is a central source for understanding the exercise of the royal supremacy by Charles I. The certificates for Canterbury province are well known and much cited, for they were first printed in 1695, and reprinted in William Laud's *Works* in 1853, but those from York province have never been published, and as a result have been largely overlooked.[3] Yet the presentation and, in many ways, the content of the two sets of provincial accounts are strikingly dissimilar, and put together they offer new perspectives on the operation of the Laudian reformation across all twenty-seven dioceses of England and Wales, and provide new insights into Charles I's relationships with successive archbishops. This edition prints, for the first time, all surviving annual reports from both provinces from 1632 to 1639.

Charles I endured humiliation abroad and uncooperative parliaments at home in his first four years as king. The failure of the 1628–9 parliament, and the decision to end the conflict with Spain and France, allowed him to concentrate on domestic affairs, and approve a series of initiatives to tackle what his regime viewed as the underlying problems of ineffective government and unchecked dissent in both church and state. Charles's support for the anti-Calvinist interest had been signalled by some key preferments, including the promotion of William Laud and Richard Neile to the privy council in 1627, and Samuel Harsnett to the archbishopric of York in 1628–9, but any major reform of the church could not be contemplated so long as the king was trying to bargain with a Calvinist-dominated House of Commons for supply. Now, in 1629, with parliament dissolved and wars at an end, significant religious changes could be discussed, formulated and disseminated.

The royal instructions were compiled by Archbishop Harsnett of York and Bishop Laud of London, in consultation with the king, and issued under his name in late December 1629.[4] They were intended to address a wide range of perceived ills in the church: bishops were ordered back to their dioceses, and once there were to protect their temporalities, ordain with care, enforce the royal moratorium on discussing predestination in the pulpit, nurture conformist clergy, encourage the laity to attend

---

1   Printed below, pp. 79–80.
2   See below, pp. 81, 87, 100.
3   H. Wharton (ed.), *The history of the troubles and tryal of … William Laud* (1695), pp. 519–64; J. Bliss and W. Scott (eds.), *The works of … William Laud DD, sometime lord archbishop of Canterbury* (The Library of Anglo-Catholic Theology, 7 vols., Oxford, 1847–60), V, 309–11, 317–70. The only scholar to make extensive use of the York returns is Andrew Foster. See ch. 8 of his 'A biography of Archbishop Richard Neile (1562–1640)', D.Phil. thesis, Oxford, 1978, and his later writings on Neile.
4   The fullest account we have of the origins and enforcement of the royal instructions is J. Davies, *The Caroline captivity of the church* (Oxford, 1992), pp. 27–31, 126–71.

prayers and catechizing as well as sermons, detect unauthorized use of chaplains, and above all 'take greate care' to regulate lecturers. Finally, on the second of January each year, the two archbishops were to report to the king on the observance of the instructions.[5] In January 1635 an expanded version of these instructions was circulated. It incorporated the royal order on leasing policy of June 1634,[6] required the reporting of 'any notable alteration or other Accident' affecting the doctrine or discipline of the church and gave the bishops a deadline – 10 December each year – for submitting their individual certificates to their provincial. The author of these additions was probably Laud, by now archbishop of Canterbury.[7]

Collectively, these instructions articulate some characteristic Laudian concerns, notably the desire to safeguard clerical wealth and curb nonconformist lecturers, but they also disclose some Caroline preoccupations. The requirement that bishops reside in their sees was part of a broader drive by Charles I to dispatch the governing classes back to their seats, there to dispense justice and hospitality; while the submission of annual accounts was matched by the command, in the Book of Orders of January 1631, that JPs return quarterly reports on their activities.[8] The Caroline regime laid out an ambitious agenda for its representatives in the dioceses and shires, and demanded that they account for their exercise of royal authority. Just how valuable the information gathered by the two archbishops actually was, and the uses to which it was put, will be considered below.

Annual accounts were delivered to the king at the start of each year from January 1631 to January 1640, and the scheme was abandoned in late 1640 as the Laudian reformation collapsed and Laud himself was impeached. Thirteen out of a possible twenty reports for 1630 to 1639 are extant. Two are missing for Canterbury province (relating to 1630 and 1631) and a further five for York province (relating to 1630–2, 1634 and 1637). Six of these seven were evidently compiled, and subsequently lost, to judge from comments in surviving accounts and other correspondence. There is a reference to the missing certificates from Canterbury province for 1630 and 1631 in Archbishop Abbot's report for 1632, when he observed that he had mentioned 'these two last yeeres past' the problem of Roman Catholics visiting Holywell, and noted that this year Bishop Owen of St Asaph 'doth not forgett to touche it againe'.[9] There were teething problems, however, in the northern province. In March 1631 Archbishop Harsnett of York informed Bishop Bridgeman of Chester that he was still awaiting the latter's account for 1630 and in the meanwhile had sent the king an incomplete and 'lame reporte of mine owne', which cannot now be traced.[10] The see of York was vacant from Harsnett's death in May 1631 until March 1632, and it is appears that no certificate for the northern province in 1631 was compiled and submitted to the king. Harsnett's successor Neile returned a certificate each year, and we can trace references to his three accounts – for 1632, 1634 and 1637 – which

5   See below, pp. 79–80.
6   See below, p. 80 n. 8.
7   See below, pp. 80–1.
8   K. Sharpe, *The personal rule of Charles I* (Yale, 1992), pp. 414–17, 459–62. From 1633 JPs' reports were required biannually.
9   See below, p. 82. Abbot's report for 1630 is also mentioned in a letter of 27 Mar. 1631 from Harsnett to Bishop Bridgeman of Chester: Staffordshire Record Office (SRO), Weston Park MSS, D1287/9/8 (A/93).
10 *Ibid.* Shortly after his move to York, Neile checked with Bridgeman that he had actually submitted a certificate to Harsnett: SRO, D1287/9/8 (A/93), Neile to Bridgeman, 11 Apr. 1632.

have not survived. Those for 1632 and 1634 are mentioned in Neile's certificates the following year, for 1633 and 1635,[11] while his covering note for the 1637 return, but not the return itself, is preserved in State Papers.[12]

Eight of the ten original accounts for Canterbury province, one by Abbot and seven by Laud, were acquired by Archbishop Sancroft in 1678–81, bound together with other papers of Laud, Sheldon, Sancroft and Chillingworth, and housed as 'Wharton M' in Lambeth Palace Library. The volume narrowly escaped accidental destruction by Archbishop Tenison's executors after his death in 1715, and returned into private hands. It was recovered for the library by Archbishop Herring in 1757, and subsequently was catalogued as 'MS 943', which remains its modern reference number.[13] Three sets of the annual accounts (for 1634, 1636 and 1637) were also recorded in Laud's Register, and there are a number of contemporary copies of some but not all of the Canterbury returns.[14] In contrast, the five original accounts for York province are preserved in the State Papers series in the National Archives, and no other copies are known, while the personal archives of Archbishops Harsnett and Neile have been dispersed and largely lost.[15]

The annual reports of each archbishop were compilations of the certificates returned by their suffragan bishops, who in turn drew on information supplied by their subordinates in the diocesan administration. Archdeacons, traditionally the *oculi episcopi* or eyes of the bishops, were a vital source of intelligence, particularly in larger dioceses such as York, Lincoln or Norwich where much episcopal authority was devolved to the archdeaconries.[16] In 1635 Juxon of London complained that three of his five archdeacons had made no return to him, 'soe he can certifye nothinge but what hath come to his knowledge without theyr helpe'. Matters did not improve much thereafter, even though Juxon was appointed lord treasurer in 1636 and became more dependent than ever on his archdeacons.[17] They could be important, too, in smaller dioceses such as Gloucester. Bishop Goodman was absent from his diocese for much of 1638, so his return to Laud relied heavily on the report of Hugh Robinson, archdeacon of Gloucester.[18] The episcopate also looked to other officials for help. In Exeter diocese rural deans remained active agents of the bishop, and were required by Bishop Hall 'in their severall divisions to observe and certify'

11 See below, pp. 87, 106–7. In correspondence with Bridgeman, Neile acknowledged receipt of his certificate for 1634, which is also now lost: SRO, D1287/9/8 (A/93), Neile to Bridgeman, 7 Jan. 1635.

12 The National Archives (TNA): PRO, SP 16/379/19. In correspondence with Laud, Neile also mentioned his return for 1637: Lambeth Palace Library (LPL), MS 943, p. 562.

13 LPL, MS 943, pp. i–ii, 237–41, 855; LPL, LR F.40, fo. 57r.

14 LPL, MS 943, pp. 105–7, 247–96; Laud's Register I, fos. 215r–216r, 254r–256r. For copies, see: British Library (BL), Harleian MS 787, fos. 21r–23v, 32r–38r (accounts for 1634, 1636 and 1637 among the papers of Laud's secretary William Dell), Add. MS 39288, fos. 8v–9r, 10r–11r (accounts for 1632 and 1633); Pierpont Morgan Library, New York, MA 664, pp. 53–68, 104–36 (accounts for 1634, 1636 and 1637 in a commonplace book from the Cecil-Stamford-Towneley MSS).

15 TNA: PRO SP 16/259/78, 312/84, 345/85.I, 412/45, 441/93. No accounts were transcribed into Neile's archiepiscopal register (Borthwick Institute (BI), REG/32).

16 For one such archidiaconal return, from Henry Wickham, archdeacon of York, to Archbishop Neile in 1635, see BI, BP C+P XXVII.

17 See below, pp. 102, 126, 143. Juxon's predecessor, Laud, had encountered similar difficulties: H. R. Wilton Hall (ed.), *Records of the old archdeaconry of St Albans* (St Albans and Hertfordshire Architectural and Archaeological Society, St Albans, 1908), p. 155.

18 See below, p. 135.

him, each September, about 'the performances or neglectes' of the royal instructions.[19] Laud, in his own diocese of Canterbury, expected 'all my under officers' to
supply him with knowledge of local events, including William Somner, the diocesan
registrar, who reported on 'the life and conversation' of the clergy. In August 1636
Laud chided Somner for failing to submit his return, and required him 'to give me
notice before the end of November next, of all ministers in the diocese that are
unconformable in doctrine or discipline, or disorderly in life'. Somner was also to
remind the vicar-general, the archdeacon of Canterbury 'and other inferior officers'
to do likewise.[20] As late as October 1640 Laud was still pursuing Somner, this time
wanting a list of Roman Catholics and news of the behaviour of Thomas Wilson,
the nonconformist minister of Otham.[21] In their reports for 1633–7, both Laud and
Neile also made extensive use of information gleaned during their metropolitical
visitations of the two provinces.[22]

A majority of the annual accounts were incomplete as some suffragans failed
to submit their certificates on time, especially in the larger province of Canterbury. It is unclear how many reports reached Abbot for his report on 1632, and his
brief summary mentions only five dioceses. Laud's appointment to Canterbury in
September 1633, rather surprisingly, did not put the southern episcopate on their
mettle, and no fewer than nine bishops missed the deadline for Laud's first account,
including his close allies Curle of Winchester and Bancroft of Oxford, and all had
their knuckles rapped on the orders of the king.[23] It may have been this experience
which led to the inclusion, in the revised royal instructions of January 1635, of a
specified date of 10 December each year for episcopal reports to reach the archbishops.[24] Rates of return certainly improved from the low-point of 1633, and Laud's
last two certificates of 1638 and 1639, barring vacancies, were complete. In the
north, Archbishop Harsnett had faced real difficulties extracting certificates from
Bridgeman of Chester,[25] but his successor Neile returned full reports on all but one
occasion.[26] The most persistent defaulters were Wright of Coventry and Lichfield,
who failed to submit on time for four successive years (1634–7), Goodman of
Gloucester and Thornborough of Worcester, both of whom made no return on three
occasions. All three can be found enforcing the royal instructions in their dioceses,
but none was close to Laud or the king, and Goodman and Wright in particular faced
criticism and complaints at court.[27]

Most bishops, however, returned certificates to their archbishop each year, which
were then assembled into a single report and dispatched to the king. There is a sharp

[19] Devon Record Office (RO), Chanter 57, fo. 7r–v; see J. F. Chanter, *The life and times of Martin Blake*
      (London, 1910), pp. 49–50.
[20] Laud, *Works*, VII, 268–9; see also TNA: PRO, SP 16/330/16.
[21] Canterbury Cathedral Archives, Dcb/J/Z/3/14, fo. 41r. For Thomas Wilson (c. 1601–53), see his entry
      in the *Oxford dictionary of national biography (ODNB)*.
[22] SRO, D1287/9/8 (A/92); TNA: PRO, SP 16/274/12, 293/28; Laud, *Works*, VI, 405–6; see below, pp.
      89–92, 95–8, 103, 116–17.
[23] See below, p. 87.
[24] See below, p. 81.
[25] SRO, D1287/18/2 (P399/52), Harsnett to Bridgeman, 30 Mar. 1630, D1287/9/8 (A/93), Harsnett to
      Bridgeman, 27 Mar. 1631, and Neile to Bridgeman, 11 Apr. 1632.
[26] The exception was 1635 and the defaulters were Morton of Durham, and Parr of Sodor and Man: see
      below, pp. 109–10.
[27] Davies, *Caroline captivity*, p. 135; K. Fincham (ed.), *Visitation articles and injunctions of the early
      Stuart church 1603–1642* (2 vols., 1994–8), II, 45, 53, 69, 85, 96–7; see below, pp. 73, 117.

contrast in the editorial practices of the archbishops in the two provinces. For York, Neile usually reproduced the certificates from his suffragans 'in the same forme, and words, as I had them from themselves, geving credit to them', as he explained in January 1634. Five years later, he apologized to the king for such 'large narrations', and having promised that this year he would proceed 'by a more compendious way; yet not omitting any thing of substance that they have certified', then transcribed the diocesan reports virtually *in extenso*! The notable exception was Neile's last account, for 1639, which stated baldly that the royal instructions were fully observed in the northern province.[28]

The position is more complicated for the province of Canterbury. This was primarily a function of size: whereas Neile had charge of five dioceses, Laud was reporting on twenty-two in his province, so compression was essential. We possess just five of the original certificates that suffragan bishops sent to Laud – one from Williams of Lincoln (for 1636), three from Wren at Norwich (1636 and 1637) and then Ely (1639), and one from Montagu of Norwich (1638) – and a comparison of these with the entries in Laud's provincial account allows us to explore his rôle as editor.[29] From this admittedly small sample, it seems that Laud usually provided an accurate summary of these diocesan reports, but occasionally did suppress comments and proposals. Although Laud and Williams were locked into a protracted and bitter dispute on the matter, Laud faithfully relayed his report on problems arising from the introduction of the railed altar, though he omitted Williams's belated assurance that he was busy organizing the collection of arrears of payment for the rebuilding of St Paul's Cathedral.[30] Since this was a minor matter, its omission is not significant.

Wren's three reports presented a challenge of their own. Laud described Wren's certificate of 1636 as 'a very carefull and punctuall Accompt, very large, and in all Particulars very considerable', which is also true for those of 1637 and 1639. Laud's summary of each of Wren's certificates, in turn, was fairly full and notably longer than entries for other dioceses.[31] Although Laud expunged much of the detail, and in 1637 declined to report 'somthinge…not fitt to be related here', he overlooked little of any substance. The major omission was Wren's innovative response in Norwich diocese in 1636 to clause 6 of the instructions, requiring bishops to 'countenance' conformist clergy and through them to monitor the conduct of lecturers and preachers. Wren's answer was to establish a hand-picked group of fifty-nine commissioners 'of the gravest, ablest and most orderly divines' to encourage conformity and 'where contempt and obstinacie appears, forthwith to give me knowledge therof'.[32] It was a sensible scheme, in view of the size of Norwich diocese and Wren's absence at court, and the item was probably excluded for reasons of space.

More revealing is Laud's treatment of Montagu's lengthy account of his first impressions as the in-coming bishop of Norwich in 1638. Much of the certificate,

---

28 See below, pp. 89, 137, 148–9.
29 Laud, *Works*, VI, 476–7; LPL, MS 943, pp. 615–27; TNA: PRO, SP 16/337/19; Bodleian Library, Oxford (Bodl.), Tanner MS 68, fos. 316r–317r.
30 Laud, *Works*, VI, 476–7; see below, p. 115; K. Fincham and N. Tyacke, *Altars restored: the changing face of English religious worship 1547–c.1700* (Oxford, 2007), pp. 152–3, 155, 158–9, 176–81, 196–8, 207–9.
31 See below, pp. 112–14, 127–9, 144–6. Other lengthy certificates, to judge from Laud's summaries, were returned by Skinner of Bristol and Towers of Peterborough, both, like Wren, enthusiasts for the new order. See below, pp. 130–1, 146–7.
32 See below, p. 129 and n. 350; TNA: PRO, SP 16/337/19; Fincham (ed.), *Visitation articles*, II, 161–4.

as Laud correctly reported, complained of the impoverishment of the see in the sixteenth century by long leases and unfavourable exchanges. However, Montagu had various suggestions how the king might restore the wealth of the bishopric, which Laud did not pass on, and there is no evidence that he pursued the ideas elsewhere.[33] Montagu went on to berate the practice of receiving communion at the rails, which had been introduced by his predecessor Wren, who had excommunicated 'many' who had refused to comply. In Montagu's view, the requirement was 'unnecessary, inconvenient, cumbersome or irregular', without warrant of 'Lawe, Articles, Advertisements, Canons, Injunctions', and he looked for direction from Laud and the king. Montagu here put his finger on a serious problem – the absence of any authoritative source for the increasingly controversial matter of reception at the rails – and his trenchant objections opened the prospect of public divisions emerging on the issue among Laud's own supporters among the episcopate. Laud moved quite adroitly, first obtaining Wren's view of Montagu's claims about the disputes in Norwich diocese, and then, in his annual report, summarizing the problem, while concealing Montagu's personal opposition to receiving at the rails. Laud went on to recommend to the king that it continue as 'the most decent and orderly waye', observed in the chapel royal and 'now allmost every where else'. He also assured the king, based on information from Wren, that only a handful were excommunicated or suspended for refusing to obey. Charles duly agreed, and a major plank of the Laudian reformation was upheld in a diocese which Laud had long regarded as a nest of puritans.[34] As we shall see, Laud regularly steered the king towards a particular view, but in this case, owing to the chance survival of Montagu's report, we can appreciate that the decision ran counter to the personal views of the suffragan.

If we compare the contents of the two provincial sets from Canterbury and York, some interesting similarities and differences emerge. Accounts from both provinces regularly included information not directly related to the royal instructions, including opposition to the restoration of St Paul's Cathedral and the enforcement of the Book of Sports,[35] material which from 1635 usually appeared as answers to the new clause 12, a catch-all item requiring each bishop to 'give notice of any notable alteration or other Accident within his diocesse, which may any wayes concerne either the doctrine or the discipline of the Church established'.[36] Both Neile and Laud drew attention to the poverty of the clergy, although the latter returned to the topic time and again. Following his metropolitical visitation of seven dioceses in 1634, Laud found 'one great Complaint, and very fitt to be redressed', namely the stipends of poor vicars, which scarcely covered the costs of food and clothing. The following year he reported the moves by Williams of Lincoln to augment 'fower or fyve Small Vicarages' and expressed the hope, not for the first time, that the king would take up the project. Laud's accounts later in the decade echoed these concerns.[37] Despite the claims of some revisionist historians, the importance of the London Court of High Commission in imposing discipline stands out from the accounts for Canterbury province. Time and again Laud referred to prosecutions of offenders through

[33] See below, p. 135; LPL, MS 943, pp. 620–4.
[34] LPL, MS 943, pp. 625–7; TNA: PRO, SP 16/406/99; see below, p. 136; Fincham and Tyacke, *Altars restored*, pp. 215–17.
[35] See below, pp. 82, 96, 106–7, 114.
[36] See below, p. 81.
[37] See below, pp. 98, 103, and also pp. 89, 127, 133, 135.

the court, including nonconformists such as the magistrates of Boston, and puritan ministers such as Samuel Ward, William Erbury and Cornelius Burges.[38]

A constant refrain in reports from the northern province was the restoration of church fabric and furnishings, launched by Archbishop Neile in his metropolitan visitation of 1632–3 of the dioceses of York, Carlisle and Chester. Neile presented it as fulfilling the call in the royal proclamation of October 1629 to repair churches, even though he had devised its detailed provisions, including uniform pews, chancelwise seating and railed altars.[39] A similar campaign got underway a little later in the decade in the southern province, but only featured once in their annual accounts.[40] Neile, by contrast, went out of his way to record its progress in the north, even quoting from a letter from Bridgeman of Chester in 1636, reporting that he had continued what Neile had begun, and 'have brought most of the Churches in my Dioces to uniformitie, and decencie', with Cheshire alone spending more than £4,000 on repairs and beautification.[41]

Most singular of all, however, was Neile's description for 1633 of the diocese of Sodor and Man, giving basic information on its size, jurisdiction, value and practices but making no mention at all of the royal instructions. It was a clear attempt to educate Charles I on an obscure corner of the northern province, at a time when the see was vacant, and the criticisms it contained of the late bishop, John Phillips, were intended to point up the need for an energetic and reforming successor.[42] Laud found its content useful enough to acquire his own copy.[43]

On completion, the provincial reports were sent to the king via the two secretaries of state, Sir John Coke for Canterbury province, and Sir Francis Windebank for the province of York. Why two secretaries were used, rather than one, is not clear. The certificates from Abbot and Laud were usually dated 2 January, the date of submission specified in the instructions, while those from York were often a little late. As we have seen, Harsnett submitted his account for 1630 in March 1631, while Neile's return for 1637 was sent from Yorkshire on 19 January 1638 and arrived in London in mid-February.[44] The king then read and usually wrote marginal notes on the accounts, which was his customary practice with papers of state,[45] and then on occasion discussed their content with the two archbishops.

---

[38] Sharpe, *Personal rule*, pp. 377–9; see below, pp. 97, 103, 104, 111. High Commission features less prominently in the certificates from York province: see pp. 89, 90, 93, 107.

[39] A. Foster, 'Church policies of the 1630s', in *Conflict in early Stuart England*, ed. R. Cust and A. Hughes (London, 1989), pp. 201–5; Fincham and Tyacke, *Altars restored*, p. 238; and see below, pp. 107, 124.

[40] Fincham and Tyacke, *Altars restored*, pp. 237–49; and see below, p. 136.

[41] J. F. Larkin (ed.), *Stuart royal proclamations, volume II...1625–1646* (Oxford, 1983), pp. 248–50; and below, pp. 90, 107, 120–1, 124.

[42] See below, pp. 93–4 and n. 108. Neile was not alone in censuring Phillips, who in his lifetime had the rare distinction of being checked by both metropolitans, Matthew of York and Abbot of Canterbury: BI, PREC BK 4, pp. 54–5; SRO, D1287/18/2 (P399/27A), Abbot to Phillips, 8 Feb. 1627.

[43] TNA: PRO, SP 16/265/45–6. These copies contained additional information about the lands and wealth of the bishopric.

[44] See above, p. 66; TNA: PRO, SP 16/379/19. The 1637 certificate was late because Neile had received a cursory report from Bridgeman of Chester and wrote, on 4 Jan. 1638, asking for a fuller response and saying he would delay submitting his certificate until he had received Bridgeman's enlarged account: SRO, D1287/9/8 (A/93).

[45] Sharpe, *Personal rule*, pp. 201–7.

We have not fully recognized the novelty of a supreme governor carefully examining reports on diocesan affairs, year by year. There were plenty of precedents for the circulation of royal injunctions and orders, none at all for annual returns being scrutinized and often annotated by the monarch. It was an exercise of the supremacy which underlined Charles I's conscientious care of religion, and demonstrated his personal investment in the Laudian reformation of the church. He regarded the royal orders as 'my Instructions' and looked to his archbishops not just to supply an annual account but also 'from tyme to tyme' keep him abreast of developments in the two provinces.[46] The annual reports were expected to arrive on time, and the king was critical of both archbishops and bishops who were late. In December 1630 he reminded Harsnett of York that his provincial report was due very shortly, and told Neile on his appointment to York in 1632 that he had found some 'slackness' in Harsnett's submission of certificates, a comment which Neile passed on to his suffragans.[47] Laud usually ended his account with a list of bishops who had yet to deliver their reports, and Charles I's reaction in 1634 to this was typical: 'As soone as may bee gett thease Bishoppes certificats.' When Wright of Coventry and Lichfield pleaded in 1638 that his late submission 'was but a slip of forgetfulnes', Charles retorted that Wright had 'slipt in the same way before' and he did not like his commands to be 'so slightly regarded as to be so easily forgotten'.[48] Charles read Abbot's provincial account for 1632 the day after it was delivered, and was delighted with it. As Sir John Coke reported, the king 'much reioyced to receive soe good a testimonie of the state of the Church Goverement under your iurisdiction'.[49] It was a rare expression of warmth from Charles to Abbot, and although it suggests some naïvety on the part of the king, given the short and complacent tone of the report, it was clearly exactly what Charles wanted to hear. Abbot may have had a better understanding of Charles than the king had of his archbishop. Although Charles did not annotate this annual account, he was to do so regularly thereafter, with comments often accompanied with underlining of key passages. There are just two exceptions – the certificate for Canterbury for 1635 which he never saw, owing to the illness of Sir John Coke,[50] and the return for York for 1636. Did this also fail to reach the king?

There are significantly more annotations on the accounts from Canterbury than from York, which may reflect Charles I's closer relationship with Laud than with Neile, especially after the summer of 1636 when the latter left London and the court to reside permanently in the north. But it also reflects different strategies of presentation. Neile was content, for the most part, to transcribe the rather mechanical returns from his suffragans, and in his own reports on York diocese rarely solicited the king's advice. Laud, in contrast, summarized and shaped the entries for each diocese, often using them to raise questions or problems for the king to resolve, and regularly adding his own recommendation for action. Often Laud couched his requests in neutral language, but sometimes he reached for phrases which would

[46] See below, p. 148; SRO, D1287/9/8 (A/93), Harsnett to Bridgeman, 11 May 1630.
[47] SRO, D1287/9/8 (A/93), Harsnett to Bridgeman, 27 Mar. 1631, and Neile to Bridgeman, 11 Apr. 1632.
[48] See below, p. 87; Laud, *Works*, VII, 413.
[49] BL, Add. MS 39288, fo. 9r.
[50] LPL, Laud's Register I, fo. 241r–v.

resonate with Charles, raise his political hackles and ensure his support. Thus in his bid for help against the Stranger churches, Laud described them as 'great Nurseyes of Inconformity' and enjoying 'a Separation…from both Church and State', while his proposal that the cases against Bastwick, Burton and Prynne might need to be transferred from High Commission to Star Chamber made reference to 'Treason' and 'Sedition in the Common wealth'.[51] Almost invariably the king endorsed Laud's suggestions, among much else promising to give the backing of Star Chamber and the judges to the archbishop's moves against puritan pamphleteers and separatists, to protect Bishop Wren from his critics in Norwich diocese, and to prevent the laity from hiring and firing lecturers.[52] Such ready support was, for Laud, an invaluable weapon against the forces of opposition and obstruction to his reforms, and for Charles, the practical expression of the trust he placed in Laud's judgment and understanding of the church.

Only once did the king's views appear to cross those of Laud. In 1636 Bishop Williams of Lincoln reported that a Bedfordshire clergyman had dug up a gravestone and erected it as an altar, which Williams claimed he had quietly removed. Laud's comment was this was a bold move by the minister to do so without consulting Williams, but Charles was sceptical of Williams's tale – 'This may prove a boulde part in the Bishope and the poore Prist in no falte' – since Williams had been found recently to be peddling half-truths by the privy council, and he ordered Laud to 'examine this further'. Whether Laud actually saw this as a check is another matter. Given his entrenched rivalry with Williams, which he was at pains to conceal, and his inclination to back rather than criticize his suffragans to the king, it is perfectly possible that Laud penned his entry in the expectation that he would appear to be even-handed and still have Williams incur Charles's censure. In any case, the king's instincts were not misplaced, since on one (hostile) account Williams had theatrically broken up the gravestone rather than dispose of it discreetly, and Laud himself may have assisted the clergyman, Jasper Fisher, in his promotion to a royal chaplaincy later that year.[53]

The king's independence of mind is evident elsewhere, which makes his customary willingness to second Laud's proposals all the more significant. Charles was quick to censure bishops who – like Williams – had aroused his suspicions. Godfrey Goodman's failed bid in 1633 to become bishop of Hereford and his subsequent request to have a coadjutor at Gloucester had not impressed the king, who taxed him the following year for setting up as well as disbanding lectureships: 'I must bee satisfied that the occasions were verie necesary otherwais he shall answer it.' Charles turned down Goodman's request in 1638 to travel abroad to improve his health, and when Laud reported his absence from Gloucester diocese that same year in order to avoid the plague, Charles observed tartly that 'This is well anufe if he have left his desyre of further absenting himselfe.'[54] Both Bridgeman of Chester and Potter of Carlisle were marked men: they had been criticized for lax government by Archbishop Neile in his account of 1633, and in the same year Bridgeman had been charged with

51 See below, pp. 95, 111–12; R. Cust, *Charles I: a political life* (London, 2005), pp. 135–6.
52 See below, pp. 86, 110, 111–12, 114.
53 See below, p. 115; Fincham and Tyacke, *Altars restored*, pp. 254–5; LPL, MS 1030, fos. 96r–97v.
54 See below, pp. 100, 135; G. Soden, *Godfrey Goodman, bishop of Gloucester 1583–1656* (London, 1953), pp. 210–23, 279–82.

embezzlement by the king and had to buy his way out of trouble.[55] Charles criticized Bridgeman's statement in 1635 that he had 'done his best endevor' to enforce attendance at divine service. 'But whether is it performed or not' was the king's response. Charles reacted sharply to Potter's complaint the same year that churchwardens were failing to present absentees from church: 'This I take to his falce [fault], for he should cale to the Churchwardens to doe ther deutie.' The fact that Potter had the audacity to hint elsewhere in his report that he might be promoted to a better see could not have helped.[56] On occasion, Charles settled problems himself. Having read Neile's complaint about the profanation of a Lancashire chapel by a royal official, the king noted that he had commanded Windebank to sort out the issue.[57] The king did not always choose to respond to requests for support; and on occasion wanted additional information, such as an explanation for the growth of recusancy in Winchester diocese in 1637.[58] Nor would he buy Archbishop Neile's long explanation of the administrative difficulties both Bridgeman of Chester and Potter of Carlisle faced in enforcing conformity in the north-west, and their inclination to win puritans around with mildness rather than coercion, a policy which they believed would be counterproductive and only encourage the sizeable Catholic population. It was a very measured account by a seasoned bishop of the problems of ruling the northern church, but Charles's comment was terse and dismissive: 'The neglect of punishing Puritans breedes Papists.'[59]

The annual accounts, with the king's comments upon them, were presumably returned to the archbishops via the two secretaries, although the only certain evidence we have of the administrative process is the note from Coke to Abbot reporting the king's pleasure on reading his return for 1632, and Neile's thanks to Windebank in January 1638 for relating 'His Majesties well allowing of my last yeares Certificate'.[60] The marginalia itself indicates that royal involvement did not stop here. Charles sometimes asked Laud to be his aide-mémoire. For the Stranger churches, for example, he wrote on the 1634 report: 'Putt mee in mynd of this at some convenient tyme when I am at Councell and I shall redress itt.' Laud, in turn, could state in another certificate that he would brief Charles I more fully elsewhere on the problems associated with the dean and chapter of Rochester.[61] Laud also pursued matters which had not elicited a royal annotation in the accounts. Charles did not comment on the vexed issue of the correct placing of the communion table in parish churches, raised by Williams in his diocesan report of 1633, so shortly afterwards Laud pressed the king for a ruling. Similarly, Charles and Neile seem to have discussed the report on York province for 1633 after its submission.[62]

---

[55] See below, pp. 89, 92; B. W. Quintrell, 'Lancashire ills, the king's will and the troubling of Bishop Bridgeman', *Transactions of the Historic Society of Lancashire and Cheshire*, CXXXII (1983), 67–102.

[56] See below, pp. 108, 109. In 1636 Charles refused Potter permission to leave his diocese during the plague: F. E. Boas (ed.), *The diary of Thomas Crosfield* (London, 1935), p. 93.

[57] See below, p. 91.

[58] See below, pp. 94, 126, 128–9.

[59] See below, pp. 92–3.

[60] BL, Add. MS 39288, fo. 9r; TNA: PRO, SP 16/379/19.

[61] See below, pp. 95, 85.

[62] See below, p. 86; Laud, *Works*, VI, 350; Fincham and Tyacke, *Altars restored*, pp. 197–8; SRO, D1287/9/8 (A/93), Neile to Bridgeman, 21 Mar. 1634.

Just as the annual accounts represent the upward movement of information through the hierarchy of the church from the rural deans to archdeacons, bishops and archbishops to the supreme governor, so we can trace the downward flow of the royal responses to them. On occasion, both Laud and Neile wrote to their suffragans, quoting Charles I's annotations and requiring compliance with his orders. The fullest example we have is Neile's lengthy letter to the hapless Bridgeman of Chester in March 1634. Neile had reported frankly to the king on the shortcomings which his metropolitical visitation of 1633 had unearthed in Chester diocese, and now he wrote to relay Charles's reactions and commands. While 'well pleased' with Bridgeman's care of Wigan church, the king had been 'much moved' by the ruinous state of churches and chapels, and ordered them to be surveyed according to the proclamation of 1629. The secular use of consecrated places was to stop, and the king 'requireth to be the next yeare certified, what is done for reformation thereof'. Neile enclosed with this letter the detailed report of his visitors to the diocese, and urged Bridgeman to add 'your strength and vigilancy' to the reforms that they had started, so that he and Bridgeman could give a good account next year to the king. In July 1634 Neile wrote again, expressing confidence that the work of reform was proceeding, and reminding Bridgeman that 'His Majestie will expect such a certificate hereafter, as I have in your name promised'.[63] There is no doubt that Bridgeman's co-opting into the fold of reforming bishops owed much to the leverage that Neile could exert through the annual accounts.

How does the considerable evidence for royal involvement in this annual audit of the instructions of 1629 inform current historiographical debates over the respective *rôles* of Charles I and Archbishop Laud in ruling the Church of England in the 1630s? The traditional view that Laud controlled the church in the 1630s has been challenged by those who see Charles I the initiator and motor for religious change, and Laud merely his ecclesiastical handyman and his master's voice.[64] This stark binary choice, which replicates contemporary debates over monarchical authority and the power of evil councillors, in turn has been countered by the suggestion that their working relationship is best viewed as a partnership of prince and primate.[65] The view that Charles was dominant and domineering receives some support from his proprietorial view of the instructions, his insistence on full and punctual reports, his detailed annotations and the evidence they contain of his independence of mind – checking various bishops, brushing aside Neile's apologia for Bishops Bridgeman and Potter, questioning Laud's support for Williams, demanding more information.

63 Laud, *Works*, VI, 349–50; see below, p. 86; SRO, D1287/9/8 (A/93), Neile to Bridgeman, 21 Mar. and 17 July 1634; D1287/9/8 (A/92). Not all royal comments reached the suffragans. Charles criticized Potter's complaint about the negligence of churchwardens, and Potter repeated the point the following year, evidence that he knew nothing of the royal rebuke (below, pp. 109, 120).

64 Sharpe, *Personal rule*, ch. 6; Davies, *Caroline captivity*, especially pp. 5–45, 288–318. The two disagree on Charles's impact: while Sharpe sees it as beneficial, Davies characterizes it as effectively malign.

65 K. Fincham and P. Lake, 'The ecclesiastical policies of James I and Charles I', in K. Fincham (ed.), *The early Stuart church, 1603–1642* (Basingstoke, 1993), pp. 44–7; K. Fincham, 'William Laud and the exercise of Caroline ecclesiastical patronage', *Journal of Ecclesiastical History (JEH)*, LI (2000), 69–93; Fincham and Tyacke, *Altars restored*, ch. 5; and see the judicious account in Cust, *Charles I*, pp. 133–42.

But it is as important to acknowledge that only once did Charles I dispute Laud's advice, and on every other occasion was prepared to throw his political weight behind the archbishop's recommendations. As he wrote in response to a request from Laud, 'I ... will express my pleasure (if need be) what way you will.'[66] This high degree of trust, both in accepting Laud's counsel and leaving him to implement it, is quite striking. Moreover, the artful manner in which Laud expressed some requests for political support demonstrates his acute understanding of the king's outlook and vulnerabilities, and makes it hard to regard him as merely a docile royal servant. Indeed, the annual reports suggest that it was Laud rather than the king that usually made the running. Rather than plump for either Charles or Laud as the architect of religious change, it seems more plausible to characterize their relationship as a partnership, certainly unequal – after all, Charles was both king and supreme governor, Laud his nominee as archbishop – but one built on trust and mutual dependence. Charles often relied on Laud's suggestions and the technical knowledge which underpinned them, commanding the archbishop on one occasion 'to show me the way to overthrou' lay control of lectureships, and on another telling Laud that the problems at Rochester Cathedral 'must bee remedied one way or other'; while Laud, with no power-base of his own, needed the considerable political authority that Charles could wield, and in the event he acquired, *inter alia,* the support of Star Chamber against Bastwick, Burton and Prynne, and saw off the threat to ecclesiastical jurisdiction from the Council of the Marches.[67] Moreover, the format of the annual accounts, whereby Laud was able to obtain the king's explicit command for a course of action he wished to take, fitted perfectly with the archbishop's wish to protect himself from critics by appearing to be not the initiator but the executor of royal policy.

So what did these yearly certificates contribute to the government of the church in the 1630s? At his trial in 1644, Laud was upbeat about their benefits, claiming that there was no 'better or safer way to preserve truth and peace in the Church' than through the submission of annual accounts to the supreme governor, who otherwise would remain 'a great stranger to all Church proceedings'.[68] Historians have been more sceptical.[69] While it is perfectly true that the yearly returns gave Charles I a better understanding of diocesan government than his predecessors had enjoyed, the information he received was patchy, filtered and sometimes misleading. Not all bishops made returns; many of those submitted were perfunctory, the episcopal counterpart to the churchwardens' return of *omnia bene*; they could be downright inaccurate, as Neile discovered when his officials visited Carlisle and Chester dioceses in 1633 and found 'things much differing' from the diocesan certificates submitted the previous year;[70] Potter of Carlisle even submitted the same return two years in a row, but for the addition of a final sentence, commenting on church repairs in the diocese;[71] archbishops were usually reluctant to criticize their suffra-

---

[66] See below, p. 96.
[67] See below, pp. 85, 86, 111–12, 117.
[68] Laud, *Works*, IV, 274.
[69] C. Carlton, *Archbishop William Laud* (London, 1987), pp. 105–6; Davies, *Caroline captivity*, pp. 31–2.
[70] See below, p. 89.
[71] See below, pp. 108–9, 119–20.

gans; sometimes there was little continuity between one report and the next;[72] above all, the impression was conveyed that the threat from puritan nonconformity was insignificant.

Abbot's notorious claim in his report for 1632 that there was no 'inconformable Minister' left in the Church of England was echoed over the next few years by suffragans from Llandaff, St Asaph and Gloucester; Williams stated in 1635 that he knew of 'but one unconformable man' in the whole diocese of Lincoln, Juxon wrote that there was only one 'noted Refractory Person' throughout London diocese in 1638, while in 1639 Towers reported that there were no more than 'seven or eight' who 'seeme refractory to the Church' in Peterborough diocese.[73] Clearly some bishops were either poorly informed or determined to convey the impression that they had local nonconformists under control. Laud himself occasionally expressed some mild surprise at these comments, observing on the absence of nonconformists in Gloucester in 1634 that 'if it be true, is a great Clearinge of those Partes, which have of late been soe much suspected', but did little else to correct this distortion.[74] Occasionally, there were hints of greater disorder and resistance in the second half of the 1630s, which in retrospect take on a significance which few may have recognized at the time: Wren's reforms encountering opposition in Norwich diocese, Laud's complaint in 1636 of the 'factious and malitious Pamphlets against the Bishoppes', one of which (by Prynne) was available in Exeter diocese, rumours from 'the Preciser Faction' in the West Country in 1637 that the Scottish liturgy 'hath in it sundry notorious pointes of Popery', and the report for 1639 that people in numerous dioceses had 'of late' begun refusing to receive communion at the altar rails.[75] Overall such straws in the wind did not provide a genuine balance to the reassuring tones of most certificates. We should acknowledge that the annual accounts were not intended to be an accurate census of nonconformity, but that may be how the king saw them, to judge from his final comment on the certificates, of January 1640, just ten months before the start of the puritan backlash on the opening of the Long Parliament: 'I hope it is to be understoode that what is not certified here to be amiss is right, tuching the observation of my Instructions, which granted, this is no ill Certificat'.[76]

In other respects, however, the annual accounts aided and abetted the Laudian reformation. They strengthened the ties between the archbishops and their suffragans, enabling Laud and Neile to be much more active and informed metropolitans than their predecessors; thus Laud used the information about dilapidations at Rochester Cathedral of 1633 in his visitation there the following year, and, based on a complaint from Skinner of Bristol about his predecessor but one, Robert Wright, now of Coventry and Lichfield, got drawn into a dispute in 1638 between them about evidences and leases.[77] As the senior metropolitan, Laud may have read or received a copy of Neile's annual reports and thereby kept abreast of events in the northern province. Certainly, as we have noted, Laud obtained an enlarged version

---

[72] Thus in 1636 Laud promised Charles I that he would report, next year, on his forthcoming visitation of London diocese, but in the event never did: see below, pp. 112, 126.

[73] See below, pp. 82, 86, 99, 100, 103, 132, 147.

[74] See below, p. 100.

[75] See below, pp. 112–14, 111, 116, 130–1, 142.

[76] See below, p. 148.

[77] See below, pp. 85, 130 and n. 362; TNA: PRO, SP 16/260/90.

of Neile's report on the bishopric of Sodor and Man for 1633, and in January 1638 Neile informed him that since his report for 1637 'little differeth from the certificates of the former yeares', he would not trouble him with its contents.[78] Suffragans, in turn, could not lose sight of the royal instructions since, year on year, they had to account for their observance. The king's authority could also be mobilized to protect the jurisdiction of the church from the laity and secular powers, and the prerogative courts and common law judges could be enlisted against nonconformists and separatists; in other circumstances, it could be used by archbishops to chivvy their suffragans into action or dragoon them into line. In short, with a devolved system of ecclesiastical government, the annual reports gave the two archbishops new opportunities of command and control, which both Laud and Neile were quick to exploit.

Editorial conventions

The royal instructions of 1629, expanded in 1635, are printed at the start of this edition, since the annual accounts on their observance make frequent reference to them. Archbishops Laud and Neile presented their accounts from the two provinces rather differently, which has been preserved in the lay-out below, with Charles I's underlining of key passages reproduced in the text and his annotations italicized and placed in the margins, just as they appear in the originals. Each is headed *C.R.*, i.e., *Carolus Rex*, initials which he sometimes used in his marginalia.

The original spelling, capitalization and punctuation have been retained and standard contractions have been expanded.

In preparing this edition, I am grateful for the assistance of Graham Anderson, David Crankshaw, Alison Fincham, Andrew and Julia Foster, John Hawkins, Mark Jenner, Peter Lake, Matthew Reynolds, Stephen Taylor, Nicholas Tyacke and the staff of Durham Cathedral Library, and Staffordshire and Devon record offices. I dedicate it to Melanie Barber, who first suggested that I re-edit Laud's annual accounts.

---

[78] See above, p. 71; LPL, MS 943, p. 562.

Documents

The royal instructions of 1629

Charles Rex.[1]
Instructions for the most reverend Father in god, our right trusty and right intirely beloved counsellor George Lord Archbishopp of Caunterbury[2] concerneing certaine orders to be observed and put in execution by the severall Bishopps in his province.

1. That the Lords the Bishopps be commanded to theire severall sees there to keepe residence excepting those which are in necessary attendance at courte.
2. That none of them reside uppon his land or lease that he hath purchased, nor on his *commendam* if hee hold any, but in one of his Episcopall houses, if hee have any,[3] and that hee waste not the woods when any are left.
3. That they give charge in their trieniall visitations, and at other convenient tymes, both by them selves and the Archdeacons that the declaration for setling all questions in difference[4] be strictly observed by all parties.
4. That there be especiall care taken by them all that theire ordinations, be of solumne, and not of unworthy persons.
5. That they take greate care concerneing the Lecturers in theire severall diocesse, for whome wee give these speciall directions followeing.
   I. That in all Parishes the afternoone sermons be turned into catischisming, by question and answer, where, and whensoever there is not some great cause apparent to breake this auncient and commendable order.
   II. That every Bishop ordaine in his diocesse that every Lecturer doe read divine service according to the litturgie appointed by authority in his surplice and hood before the Lecture.
   III. That where a lecture is set upp in a markett towne it may be read by a company of grave and orthodoxe divines neere adioyneing; and in the same diocesse and that they preach in gownes, and not in cloaks as too many doe use.
   IV. That if a corporation doe mayntaine a single lecturer hee be not suffered to preach till hee professe his willingnes to take upon him a liveing with cure of soules, within that corporation, and that hee doe actually take such benifice or cure, soe soone as it shalbe fairely procured for him.

---

[1] TNA: PRO, SP 16/153/100.I. For another copy, with slight variations, see LPL, MS 943 pp. 103–4, printed in Laud, *Works*, V, 307–9.
[2] George Abbot, archbishop of Canterbury 1611–33.
[3] All bishops had at least one, with the exception of Oxford, for which see below, p. 81.
[4] The royal declaration for the peace of the church, printed in London in 1628–9 and prefixing the articles of religion of 1563, reprinted in Fincham (ed.), *Visitation articles*, II, 33–4.

6.   That the Bishops do countenance and incourage the grave and orthodoxe divines of theire clergie, and that they use meanes by some of theire clergie, or others that they may have knowledge how both Lecturers, and preachers within their diocesse behave them selves in theire sermons, that soe they may take order for any abuse accordingly.

7.   That the Bishopps suffer none under Noble men, and men qualified by the lawe to have any private chapplaine in his house.

8.   That they take speciall care that divine service be diligently frequented as well for praiers and catichismes, as sermons, and take perticular note of all such as Absent them selves, as Recusants, or otherwise.

9.   That every Bishop that by our grace and favor, and good oppinion of his service shall be nominated by us to another Bishopricke, shall from that day of nomination not presume to make, any lease for three lives, or one and twenty yeares, or concurrent lease or any way renewe any estate, or cutt any wood, or tymber, but meerely receive the paid rents due, and quitt the place: for wee thinke it an hatefull thing that any mans leaveing the Bishopricke, should almost undoe the successor. And if any man shall presume to breake this order wee will refuse to give our royall assent, and keepe him at the place hee hath soe abused.

10. Lastly wee comand you to give us an accompt every yeare the second daie of January of the performance of these our command.

Dorchester.[5]

The royal instructions of 1635

Instructions[6] for the most Reverend Father in God, our Right trusty and Right entirely beloved Counsellor William Lord Archbishopp of Caunterbury[7] concerneing certaine Orders to be observed by the severall Bishopps of his Province.

[Clauses 1–9 are identical to those of 1629.]

10. That every Bishop give his Metropolitane a Strict Accompte yearly of their Obedience to Our late Letteres[8] prohibiting them to change any Leases from yeares into lives. And that they faile not to certifie, if they find that the Deane, or Deane and Chapter, or any Archdeacon or Prebendary etc within their severall Diocesses, have att any tyme broken our Commandes in any Particular conteyned in the aforesaid Letteres.

11. That every Bishopp to whome in regard of the smale Revenewes of his Bishopricke Wee either have already or shall hereafter not only give power, but Command to receive and hold as in *Commendum* [*sic*] any Lease expired, or neer expiringe, and belonginge to their See, or any ecclesiasticall Benefice

---

5   Dudley Carleton, Viscount Dorchester (1574–1632), one of the secretaries of state.
6   LPL, Laud's Register I, fo. 217r–v.
7   William Laud, archbishop of Canterbury 1633–45.
8   See Charles I's letter to Laud, dated 22 June 1634, in LPL, Laud's Register I, fos. 202v–203r, printed in D. Wilkins, *Concilia magnae Britanniae et Hiberniae ab...MDXLVI ad...MDCCXVII*, IV (1737), 493.

or Benefices, or other Promotion, with Cure or without, being in his or their owne guift, by Letteres given under our Signett, and sent to those Bishopps respectively, doe likewise give an Accompt yearly to his Metropolitane, that he doth not putt any of the aforenamed Benefices, or other Preferment out of his *Commendum*, to give to any sonne, kinsman, freind or other, upon any pretense whatsoever, thereby to frustrate Our Gracious Intentions to those severall Sees, and the succeeding Bishopes therein.

12. That every Bishopp respectively do likewise in his yearly Accompt to his Metropolitan, give notice of any notable alteration or other Accident within his diocesse, which may any wayes concerne either the doctrine or the discipline of the Church established.

13. That whereas John Bancroft Doctor in Divinity and Bishopp of Oxford hath very worthily att his owne proper Costs and Charges, built a House for Himselfe, and the Bishops of Oxford successively (by Our both leave and Incouragement) upon the Vicaridge of Cuddesden neer Oxford, which Vicaridg is in the Patronage and guift of him and his Successors. And whereas Our further will and pleasure is, that the said House togeather with the Vicaridge aforesaid, shall ever be held in *Commendum* by the Bishopps of Oxford successively. That therefore the said Bishop for the tyme being doe yearly give his particular Accompt of his holding both the House and Benefice aforesaid, to the end that Wee and our Successors may upon all occasions bee putt in minde of keeping that House and Vicarage to the See of Oxford, att all tymes of change, when or howsoever that Bishopricke shall become void.[9]

14. Lastly Wee command every Bishopp respectively to give his Accompt in writing to his Metropolitan, of all these our Instructions, or as many of them as may concerne him, att or before the tenth day of December yearely. And likewise that you out of them make a Breife of your whole Province, and present itt to Us every year by the second day of January followinge, that soe Wee may see how the Church is governed, and Our Commandes obeyed. And hereof in any wise faile you not.

January 19 1634 *Computi Angliae*[10]

Canterbury province, 1632

May it please your most excellent Majesty.[11]

The yeere is at an end, *redit orbis in orbem, Et moritura ruit perituri machina mundi.*[12] But the Account of the Church-affaires for the last yeere must not be forgotten.

To speake generally unto the Articles heeretofore propounded by your Majesty, it is enough to say that the Bishops for ought it appeereth unto mee, have lived at home

---

9   Since this clause related to the bishop of Oxford, other bishops ignored it in their reports to their provincial. See TNA: PRO, SP 16/337/19; Bodl., Tanner MS 68, fos. 316r–317r; and below, pp. 107–9, 137–41.

10 1635 new style.

11 LPL, MS 943, pp. 105–7, in the hand of William Baker, Abbot's secretary; endorsed 'Archbishop of Canterbury accompt Abbott 1632' (p. 108).

12 'The world comes back in full circle and the workings of the doomed earth rush to their destruction.'

and in their Episcopall Houses: saving onely my Lord of St Davids,[13] who by his wives sicknesse,[14] but especially by a Law sute which concerneth him for all that hee hath, as hee informeth, was constrained to keepe heere.[15] But now that vexatious sute being ended, hee promiseth to repaire home, and there to reside, that there shall bee no iust occasion of complaint against him.

Of Arminian pointes[16] there is no dispute: And Ordinations of Ministers for ought that I can learne, are Canonically observed. The rules for Lecturers are strictly kept.

Care is had that divine Service is religiously read and frequented, saving by certaine Separatists about London, who for their persons are contemptible, but fitt to bee punished for their willfull obstinacy, which wee do with moderation; yet yeelding them meanes to conferre with learned men, whiche wee hope will prevayle with some of them.[17] And so it may bee said of the rest of the Articles, that I finde no noted transgression of them.

There is not in the Churche of England left any inconformable Minister which appeereth, and yet the Lord Bishops of London[18] and Lincolne[19] have bene forced to deprive two or three,[20] whom no time can tame not instruction conquer, according to the rule, *Immedicabile vulnus ense recidendum est*.[21]

There was one Burges a physitian[22] who opened his mouth wide against the repairing of Pauls Churche; but hee hath bene so castigated, that as I trust very few other will bee encouraged to walke in his waies, and to blaspheme so holy a worke.[23]

There hath bene these two last yeeres past, mention made of Papists frequenting Hollywell or Saint Winifreds well in Wales.[24] And the Bishop of St Asaph[25] doth not forgett to touche it againe in these wordes, There hath bene there all this Summer

---

13 Theophilus Field, bishop of St David's 1627–35.

14 Alice Field.

15 In *c.* 1630–1 Archbishops Abbot and Harsnett had recommended to Charles I that for similar reasons Field be allowed to remain temporarily in London. TNA: PRO, SP 16/159/50; see also 16/174/96, and below, p. 86.

16 A reference to clause 3 of the 1629 instructions. His telling choice of phrase indicates Abbot's conviction that the threat to the peace of the church came from Arminian opinions, rather than from both Arminian and Calvinist positions. This is also the only mention in the annual accounts of 'Arminian' views.

17 See S. R. Gardiner (ed.), *Reports of cases in the courts of Star Chamber and High Commission* (Camden Society, n.s., 39, 1886), pp. 278–81, 284–6, 292–5, 302, 308–10, 315.

18 William Laud, bishop of London 1628–33.

19 John Williams, bishop of Lincoln 1621–41.

20 In London diocese, principally Thomas Weld, vicar of Terling, and Nathaniel Ward, rector of Stondon Massey, deprived respectively in Jan. and Dec. 1632. See T. Webster, *Godly clergy in early Stuart England* (Cambridge, 1997), pp. 189–90, 195–9; and below, p. 84.

21 'The incurable wound must be cut out'. See Ovid, *Metamorphoses*, X, 189.

22 John Burgess junior, physician, of Sutton Coldfield, Warwickshire, where his father, John Burgess (1563–1635), the celebrated puritan nonconformist, was rector.

23 Burgess had maintained that 'it was no deed of charitie to give to the repaire of that church, that he would rather give tenn shillings to the pulling of it downe than five shillings to repaire it' and that re-building 'was rather an Acte of Magnificence than Religion'. On 29 Nov. 1632 he was fined £500 by High Commission, to be put to the repair of St Paul's, and finally submitted to the sentence on 30 Jan. 1634. Cambridge University Library (CUL), MS Dd. 2.21 (High Commission act book, 1631–4), fos. 85v, 92r, 99r, 118v–119r, 126v, 218v–219r, 263v, 289v; MS Mm 1.36, p. 265.

24 See A. Walsham, 'Reforming the waters: holy wells and healing springs in protestant England', in D. Wood (ed.), *Life and thought in the northern church c. 1100 – c. 1700*, Studies in Church History, Subsidia, 12 (1999), pp. 233–4. See also below, pp. 86, 117.

25 John Owen, bishop of St Asaph 1629–51.

more then ordinary concourse of People, and more bold and open practise of super-stition. Where it is not to bee forgotten, that at that well a greate parte of the powder-treason was hatched.[26] And therefore my humble opinion is, that serious letters should bee directed from your Majesty or privy Counsell, to the Lord Presi-dent of Wales[27] and his fellow-Commissioners, that at Sommer next some course should bee taken for the repressing of this Confluence, being indeed no better then a Pilgrimage.

The Lady Wotton in Kent hath sett up a bolde Epitaph upon her Lords Tombe, and will not bee perswaded to take it downe. Wee have therefore called her into the highe Commission, where by excuse of sickenesse shee hath not yet appeared. But at the next Terme (God willing) wee intend to proceede with her, whiche is but necessary for the avoydeing of scandall in the Country.[28]

These few are the most observeable thinges, whereof I can give your Majesty any reckoning. And if there were any thinge else worthy the reporting I should not conceale it. But there being nothing more, it may bee the greate comfort of your Majesty, that in so large and diffuse a multitude both of men and matters, upon strict examination there is so little exorbitancy to bee found.

Lambeth January 2 1632[29]   Your Majesties humble servant
                                     G: Cant:[30]

Canterbury province, 1633

January 2 1633[31]
May it please your most sacred Majesty.

According to your Royall Commandes, I doe here upon the second of January 1633 *Computi Angliae* present my Accompt, of, both the Diocess and Province of Canterbury, concerning all those Church-affaires which are conteyned within your Majesties most gracious Declaration[32] and Instructions, published out of your most Princely and Religious care to preserve Unity in orthodox Doctryne, and Conformity to Government in this your Church of England.

---

26 A manicule appears in the left-hand margin at this point. See W. H. Sherman, 'Towards a history of the manicule', in R. Myers, M. Harris and G. Mandelbrote (eds.), *Owners, annotators and the signs of reading* (London, 2005), pp. 19–48.

27 John Egerton, first earl of Bridgewater (1579–1649), appointed president of the Council of the Marches and Wales in 1631.

28 Margaret Wotton, widow of Edward First Baron Wotton (1548–1628) had erected the following inscription over her husband's tomb in Boughton Malherbe church: 'Charissimo suo Conjugi Domino Eduardo Wotton Catholico Baroni de Marchei Mestima sua uxor Domina Margareta Wottonae Catholica filia Domini Philippi Wharton Baronis de Wharton hunc Lapidem posuit' and had ignored orders by Archbishop Abbot to obliterate 'Catholico' and 'Catholica'. After being threatened with a fine of £500, she co-operated and High Commission was certified on 9 May 1633 that the two offending words had been removed. CUL, MS Dd. 2.21, fos. 127r, 129r, 157r.

29 1633 new style.

30 George Abbot, archbishop of Canterbury 1611–33.

31 LPL, MS 943, pp. 247–50, in the hand of William Dell, Laud's secretary, and endorsed '1633 January. Lord Archbishop of Canterburies accompt to his Majesty. Arch Bishop Laude at his first entrance with the kings Apostills in his owne hand etc.' (p. 250). The year is 1634 new style.

32 See above, p. 79, n. 4.

Canterbury.   And first for my owne Diocess of Canterbury, I hear of many thinges amiss, but as yet my tyme hath been soe short, that I have had noe certaine knowledge of any thing fitt to certify, save onely that some of my Peculiars in London are extremely out of Order.

London.   For the Bishopricke of London, it is Certifyed that my Lord the now Bishop[33] hath not receyved Complaint against any of his Clergy since his comming to that Sea, which was since Michaelmas last. For all the former part of this first yeare I must give your Majesty Accompt for my self, being then Bishop there.

And first having heretofore after longe patyence and often Conference, proceeded against Nathanyel Warde Parson of Stondon in Essex, to Excommunication and Deprivation, for refusing to subscribe to the Articles established by the Canon of the Church (of which I certifyed the last yeare) I have now left him still under the Censure of Excommunication.[34]

I did likewise convent Mr John Beedle Rector of Barnstone in Essex, for omitting some partes of Divyne Service, and refusing Conformity.[35] But upon his Submission, and promise of reformation I dismissed him with a Canonicall Admonition onely.

Since my Returne out of Scotland[36] Mr John Davenport Vicar of St Stevens in Colmanstreet (whom I used with all moderation, and about two years since, thought I had setled his Judgment, having him then at advantage enough to have put extremity upon him, but forbare it) hath now resigned his Vicarage declared his Judgment against Conformity with the Church of England, and is since gone (as I heare) to Amsterdam.[37]

Bath and Wells.   For Bath and Wells, I fynde that the Lord Bishop[38] hath in his late Visitation taken a great deale of paines to see all your Majesties Instructions observed. And particularly hath put downe diverse Lecturers in Market Townes, which were Beneficed men in other Bishoppes Diocesses. Because he found that when they had preached factious and disorderly Sermons, they retyred into other Countyes, where his Jurisdiction would not reach to punish them.[39]

His Lordship hath likewise sent up a List of Romish Recusants which were presented at his late Visitation, which he saith are for the most part, but of mean Condition, and those not many considering the Greatnes of that County.

Rochester.   In this Diocess the Towne of Mawling, and that whole Deanery were very much out of Order, but the Archdeacon[40] by my Lord the Bishops[41] command hath setled them.

---

[33] William Juxon, bishop of London 1633–60.

[34] See above, p. 82 and n. 20.

[35] See Webster, *Godly clergy*, pp. 199–200; and below, p. 132.

[36] Laud had accompanied Charles I to Scotland in June–July 1633: see Laud, *Works*, III, 217–18.

[37] John Davenport (1597–1670) went to Amsterdam in Dec. 1633; see his entry in *ODNB*.

[38] Wiliam Piers, bishop of Bath and Wells 1632–70.

[39] Laud endorsed this practice of removing lecturers beneficed in other dioceses, and in a letter of May 1634 recommended it to Bishop Thornborough of Worcester and claimed he had himself always observed it: Worcestershire RO, b 716.093 BA 2648/10 (ii), p. 83. See, however, Davies, *Caroline captivity*, pp. 152–3.

[40] Elizeus Burges, archdeacon of Rochester 1625–51/2.

[41] John Bowle, bishop of Rochester 1630–7.

My Lord likewise brought Mr Throgmorton the Vicar of Mawling[42] into the High Commission, where he submitted himself, and receyved a Canonicall Admonition.[43]

I likewise certifye your Majesty that the Bishop complaine's, that the Cathedrall Church suffer's much for want of Glass in the Windowes,[44] and that the Churchyard lye's very undecently, and the Gates downe; And that He hath noe power to remedy these thinges, because the Dean and Chapter refuse to be Visited by him, upon pretence of theyr Statutes are not confirmed under the Broad Seale, with some other circumstances, with which I shall acquaint your Majesty more at large.

C.R. This must bee remedied one way or other concerning which I expect a particular account of you

Peterburgh. Concerning this Diocess, wheras your Majesties Instructions require that Lecturers should turne theyr Afternoone Sermons into Catechizing by waye of Question and Answere, some Parsons and Vicars make a doubt whether they be bound to the like Order, because Lecturers onely be named as they pretend. But your Majesties expression is cleare for Catechizing generally, and my Lord the Bishop[45] will presently settle this Doubt.

There is one Mr Elmes in that Diocess who being not qualifyed by Lawe keep's a Schoolmaster in his House, and use's him as a Chaplaine to preach a Lecture upon Sundayes in the afternoone, in the Church of Warmington.[46] But by this tyme, if the Bishop keep his promise that Abuse is rectifyed.

Coventry and Lichfield. The Bishop[47] complaines that the Peculiars of his Diocess (wherin he hath noe power) are much out of Order, and I easily beleive it, but the Remedy will be hard, because I knowe not in whom the Peculiars are, but shall enforme my self.

His Lordship farther certifye's that he hath suppressed a seditious Lecture at Repon.[48] And diverse monthly Lectures, with a Fast and a Moderator (like that which they called Prophecying in Queen Elizabeth's tyme). As alsoe the Running Lecture soe called, because the Lecturer went from Village to Village, and at the end of the weeke proclaimed where they should have him next, that his Disciples might followe. They say this Lecturer was ordeyned to illuminate the darke Corners of that Diocess.

C.R. If they bee darke Corners in this Dioces it were fitt a trew light should illuminat it and not this that is falce and uncertaine

---

[42] Robert Throckmorton, vicar of West Malling.

[43] Archbishop Abbot had admonished Throckmorton to conform on 15 Nov. 1632: see CUL, MS Dd. 2.21, fo. 105v. Despite this, Throckmorton was again in trouble in July 1634 for nonconformity: Centre for Kentish Archives, DRB/Pa 33, fos. 139v, 145v and *passim*.

[44] At Laud's visitation of Rochester Cathedral in 1634, the dean and chapter stated that they had left the repair of the windows until they had completed a major restoration programme costing over £1,000, 'else they would have bene broken agayne before the reparations had been fynished', and were now about to restore the glass; in response, Laud urged them to do so 'without delaye'. V. J. Torr, 'Rochester Cathedral in 1634', *Archaeologia Cantiana*, LXXVIII (1963), 49, 52.

[45] Augustine Lindsell, bishop of Peterborough 1633–4.

[46] William Elmes (d. 1641). See *Victoria County History Northamptonshire*, III (1930), 114, 121.

[47] Robert Wright, bishop of Coventry and Lichfield 1632–43.

[48] Repton, Derbyshire.

St Davyds.   My Lord of St Davids[49] is now Resident in his Diocess, and hath soe
been ever since the last Springe:[50] And professe's that he will take
great care hereafter to whom he give's holy Orders.

His Lordship certifye's that he hath suspended a Lecturer for his Inconformity;
And that they have but few Romish Recusantes.

St Asaph.   The Bishop of St Asaph[51] returne's that all is exceeding well in his
Diocess, save onely that the number and boldnes of some Romish
Recusants increaseth much in many Places, and is much incouraged by the
superstitious and frequent Concourse of some of that Party to Holywell, otherwise
called St Winifreds well. Whether this Concourse be by waye of Pilgrimage or noe,
I knowe not, but I am sure it hath longe been complained of without Remedy.[52]

Landaff.   My Lord the Bishop[53] certifye's that he hath not one refractory
Nonconformist, or Schismaticall Minister within his Diocess. And
that there are but two Lecturers, and that they both are lycensed Preachers.

Lincolne.   My Lord the Bishop of Lincolne[54] signifye's that the Company of
Mercers in London, trusted with the guift of one Mr Fishburne, sett up
a Lecturer in Huntingdon with the Allowance of £40 *per annum* to preach every Saturday morninge (being Market day) and Sunday in the afternoone, with a proviso in his Graunt from them, that upon any dislike they may have of him, he shall at a month or a fortnights warning give over the Place, without any Relation to Bishop or Archbishop.

C.R. Certainlie I cannot hould fitt that anie Lay Person or Corporation whatsoever should have the Power thease Men would take to themselves; for I will have no Preest have anie necessitie of a Lay dependancie, wherefore I command you to show me the way to overthrou this and to hinder the performance in tyme to all suche intentions[55]

My most humble Suite to your Majesty is, that noe lay man whatsoever, and least of all, Companyes or Corporations may under any pretence of giving to the Church, or otherwise, have power to put in, or put out, any Lecturer, or Other Minister.

His Lordship likewise complaine's of some in Bedfordshire that use to wander
from theyr owne Parish Churches, to followe Preachers affected by themselves, of
which he hath caused his Officers to take speciall care. As for the placing of the
Communion Table in Parish Churches, his Lordship professe's that he takes care of
it according to the Canon. These two last are noe part of your Majesties Instructions,
yet since his Lordship hath been soe carefull to reporte them to me, I take it my duty
to express that his Lordships care to your Majesty.[56]

---

[49] Theophilus Field.

[50] See above, p. 82.

[51] John Owen.

[52] See above, p. 82, and below, p. 117.

[53] William Murray, bishop of Llandaff 1627–40.

[54] John Williams.

[55] Charles I's annotation is incomplete, owing to damage to the manuscript, so the transcription here also draws on *Troubles and tryal of...William Laud*, p. 528.

[56] For an exchange of letters between Laud and Williams on Charles I's response to these points, see Laud, *Works*, VI, 349–51.

Hereford and   These two Diocesses are voyde, and I had no Certificat before the
Bangor.   Death of the Bishoppes.[57]

All the Bishoppes above mentioned (which are all that have yet certifyed) doe agree that all other thinges in your Sacred Majesties Instructions conteyned, are carefully observed, and particularly that of avoyding factious medling with the prohibited Questions.

From any of the rest of the Bishoppes within my Province I have not as yet receyved any Certificat at all. Namely

	Salisbury[58]	Winchester[59]
C.R. As soone as may bee	Norwich[60]	~~Ely[61]~~
gett thease Bishoppes	Worcester[62]	Chichester[63]
certificats	Oxford[64]	Glocester[65]
	Bristol[66]	Exeter[67]

Soe I humbly submitt this my Certificat.

W: Cant:[68]

Ely.   The Lord Bishop of Ely[69] certifyes that he hath had speciall care of his
         Majesties Instructions, and that He doth not know that they are broken in
his Diocess in any poynt.

W: Cant:[70]

York province, 1633

To the Kings Most Excellent Maiestie, The Certificate of your Maiesties most humble, and obedient servant and Chaplaine, Richard, Archbishop of Yorke.[71]

It pleased your Sacred Maiestie gratiously to allow of the Certificate, which I made the last yeare,[72] of the condition of Church affaires in my Dioces of Yorke, what I found to be amisse, and how putt into a way of reformation: for which your favourable acceptance of that my service, I geve your Maiesty most humble, and dutifull thanks. I now crave your Maiesties like favourable acceptance of this Information, how things now stand both in mine owne Dioces, and in the rest of the Diocesses of the Province of Yorke.

---

[57] Francis Godwin, bishop of Hereford, died in Apr. 1633, and David Dolben, bishop of Bangor, died in Nov. 1633.
[58] John Davenant, bishop of Salisbury 1621–41.
[59] Walter Curle, bishop of Winchester 1632–47.
[60] Richard Corbet, bishop of Norwich 1632–5.
[61] A late arrival, added as a postscript.
[62] John Thornborough, bishop of Worcester 1617–41.
[63] Richard Montagu, bishop of Chichester 1628–38.
[64] John Bancroft, bishop of Oxford 1632–41.
[65] Godfrey Goodman, bishop of Gloucester 1625–56.
[66] George Coke, bishop of Bristol 1632–6.
[67] Joseph Hall, bishop of Exeter 1627–41.
[68] William Laud, archbishop of Canterbury 1633–45.
[69] Francis White, bishop of Ely 1631–8.
[70] William Laud.
[71] TNA: PRO, SP 16/259/78, endorsed 'Certificate of the Lord Archbishop of Yorke to his Majesty'.
[72] Missing, assumed lost.

For mine owne Dioces,[73] I humbly assure your Maiestie, that things have hitherto well succeeded in the way of that amendment, which I then intimated taken: for the due observation of your Maiesties Declaration,[74] the performance of your Instructions, and the executing of Divine Service according to the Booke of Common Prayer, and the Canons, and Constitutions of the Church. And for the perfecting, and continuance thereof, I shall (by Gods grace) use all care, and diligence, that becometh me on my part; and will exact of all my inferior officers that vigilance, and industry, that to them belongeth.

For the rest of the Diocesses of the Province, I humbly present to your Maiestie the ensuing Informations.

Durham.

Of Durham Dioces, I have received of my Brother of Durham, this that followeth,

A list of the Lecturers in the Dioces of Durham, *Anno Domini* 1633.

Durham.	Christian Sherwood,[75] Master of Arts, Lecturer in the Cathedrall Church of Durham, and St Nicholas parish there.
Newcastle upon Tine.	Robert Jennison,[76] Doctor in Divinitie, Lecturer of Allhallowes Church there.
	Thomas Stevenson,[77] Master of Arts, Lecturer of St Nicolas Church there.
Tinemouth.	William Alder,[78] Master of Arts, Lecturer there.
St Hulda alias Shields.[79]	Patrick Watt,[80] Master of Arts, Lecturer there.
Barwick.[81]	Richard Hunt,[82] Master of Arts, Lecturer there.

All these Lecturers are conformable to the doctrine, and discipline of the Church of England, so farr as I could be informed.

Tho: Duresme.[83]

---

73 Of York.

74 See above, p. 79 n. 4.

75 Presented by the dean and chapter of Durham to St Oswald's Durham, 1631, chaplain in the royalist army, rector of Bishop Wearmouth 1644–6, ejected, and died 1652. See J. and J. A. Venn, *Alumni Cantabrigienses Part I*, IV (Cambridge, 1927), p. 64; A. G. Matthews, *Walker revised* (Oxford, 1988), p. 143.

76 Robert Jenison (1583–1652); see his entry in *ODNB*.

77 Vicar of Stamfordham, Northumberland, in 1635; resigned his lectureship at Newcastle in 1639 'upon a distaste and discontent' about the town's 'fiery zealots harsh carriage towards him'; later an active royalist. See *Calendar of state papers domestic (CSPD) 1639–40*, pp. 169, 385–6; Matthews, *Walker revised*, p. 291.

78 Vicar of Aughton, Yorkshire, from 16 July 1620, and vicar of Tynemouth from 24 July 1633. See 'William Alder' (CCEd Person ID 112690), *The clergy of the Church of England database 1540–1835* <http:// www. theclergydatabase.org.uk>, accessed 18 June 2009.

79 St Hilda's South Shields.

80 Vicar of Norham 1615–43, and still lecturer at St Hilda's in 1637. See 'Patrick Watt' (CCEd Person ID 112689), *The clergy of the Church of England database 1540–1835* <http://www. theclergydata­base.org.uk>, accessed 18 June 2009; W. H. D. Longstaffe (ed.), *The acts of the High Commisssion Court within the diocese of Durham* (Surtees Society, 34, 1858), p. 173 and n. a. The lectureship is not mentioned in Morton's list for 1638: see below, p. 139.

81 Berwick upon Tweed.

82 Unidentified.

83 Thomas Morton, bishop of Durham 1632–59.

Yet I must confesse to your Maiestie I have reason to suspect some of them, not to be so conformable, as they ought to be, touching your Maiesties Declaration, and Instructions published.[84]

Chester and Carlile.

I the last yeare presented to your Maiestie such Certificates, as I received from my Bretheren, the Bishops of Chester,[85] and Carlile,[86] in the same forme, and words, as I had them from themselves, geving credit to them: But, having this last summer visited those Diocesses,[87] I find things much differing from the said Certificates; as in particulars following;

1. Many men never admitted into Holy Orders, permitted to serve Cures in Chappells of Ease (where (indeed) the stipend is so small, that no man of sufficiencie will accept thereof): But all these through out both Diocesses are interdicted, and the Inhabitants required, either to provide a Minister in Orders to serve there, or els to make their repayre to their parish Church.

2. The publick prayers of the Church so generally neglected, as if all Religion were but in a sermon.

3. The Booke of Common Prayer so neglected, and abused in most places by chopping, changing, altering, omitting, and adding at the Ministers owne pleasure, as if they were not bound to the forme prescribed. In sundry places, the Booke of Common Prayer was so unregarded, that many knew not how to reade the Service according to the Booke. And, as in the publick prayers, so likewise in the administration of the Sacraments, the formes, rites, and ceremonies prescribed, very much neglected; and many were found, that thought themselves well-deserving and conformable men, though they observed not the Booke, and Orders prescribed, so long as they did not oppose them. The most of which have ben made to see, and acknowledge their faults; and many of them, upon promise of reformation, craved pardon for that which was past, and have undertaken to make due certificate of their performance of that amendment, they have promised. Some others are suspended; and some of them are bound over to answere their offenses at the High Commission at Yorke, and some have left the country.

4. It was found, that in the performance of your Maiesties commandement for catechising, the Catechisme of the Booke of Common Prayer hath ben in many places neglected, and divers other new-fangled Catechismes, no way authorized, brought into the Church. But order is geven for the use of the Catechisme of the Booke of Common prayer, and none other.

---

84 Of these six lecturers, Jenison was already well known to Neile from his time as bishop of Durham (1617–28) and was suspended by him for nonconformity in 1639: K. Fincham, *Prelate as pastor* (Oxford, 1990), p. 245; A. Foster, 'Archbishop Richard Neile revisited', in P. Lake and M. Questier (eds.), *Conformity and orthodoxy in the English church, c. 1560–1660* (Woodbridge, 2000), p. 172; TNA: PRO, SP 16/427/46, 428/27, 35, 430/24, 52.

85 John Bridgeman, bishop of Chester 1619–52.

86 Barnabas Potter, bishop of Carlisle 1629–42.

87 Neile's metropolitical visitation of Chester and Carlisle was launched in the summer of 1633, and was completed by May 1634: BI, INST AB 6, pp. 32, 36, 55, 68. Many of the remarks that follow were taken from the report compiled by his visitors – William Easdall, Henry Wickham and John Cosin – which Neile then passed on to Bridgeman of Chester: SRO, D1287/9/8 (A/92).

5. In many places such as heretofore went under the title of Lecturers, and thought all their service they ought to the Church, was only preaching, are brought to yield themselves *in partem Curae*, and become Curates, as well as Lecturers.

6. The dis-respect, that the Ministers have shewed of the publick prayers of the Church hath bred such irreverence in the people, that it is a rare thing in many places to see any upon their knees at the reading of the prayers, or (almost) at the receiving of the Sacrament: and some stick not to say; that, sitting, was the fittest gesture both at the prayers, and at the Sacrament.

7. It was scarce found in any place, that the Communion Table was placed in such sort, as that it might appeare, it was any whitt respected: but so placed, that boyes, and others might sitt about it, and leane upon it; and in many places, by teaching of children in the Church, or Chancell, the Communion Table was the place where the boyes did all their businesse, and oftentimes eate their victualls upon it. For redresse of which abuses in time to come, there is order geven.[88] At Chester the Deane and Chapter have placed their Communion Table, where it ought to stand, and have decently furnished it.[89] But it is not so at Carlile.

8. In some places of these two Dioceses there are some goodly Churches, and reasonably well kept in repayre; but so defaced with galleries, and pewes, as it is not to be endured. For reformation whereof, there is good order geven, if it be performed according to promise made by the Ministers, and Churchwardens.

At Wiggan in Lancashire, (a Benefice of good worth, which the Bishop of Chester[90] holdeth *in commendam*) the Bishop hath built a faire large Chancell.

In most other places the Churches are very miserable, and ruinous in the fabrick, and kept so sordidly within, as would trouble any Christian to see it.

The two Cathedrall Churches are not as they ought to be; and in each of them there is this inconvenience; That they are as well parish Churches, as Cathedrall Churches;[91] whereby there groweth question touching the repayre of the fabrick: And there is by this occasion another inconvenience, That at the same time there is double Service in the same Church. The Service with voices, and Organs in the Quire, and the reading Service in the body of the Church. And when in either place, any part of the Service, that is prescribed, is omitted or mutilated, the answere hath ben; That the one geveth way to the other; and what is omitted in the one, is read in the other part of the Church. The Litanie is scarcely ever heard on Sundayes in the Cathedrall Churches; and Te Deum, Benedictus, the Litanie, Magnificat etc are seldome said, or sung in most of the Churches of the Dioceses, but Psalmes sung in stead thereof. Yet while some men are bold to omitt parts of the prayers prescribed, they have intruded other prayers never appoynted, or authorised to be added to the publick Service.

C.R. It does stand with my pleasur, wherefore see that by the next Yeare ye give me a good If it shall stand with your Maiesties approbation I will, by vertue of the High Commission, take order, that the service of the Cathedrall

---

88 This is Neile's coy reference to his major initiative in 1633–4 requiring churchwardens in York, Chester and Carlisle dioceses to place their communion tables at the top of the chancel, standing altarwise, and to protect them with rails. See Fincham and Tyacke, *Altars restored*, pp. 190–1.

89 They did so just prior to Neile's visitation: SRO, D1287/9/8 (A/92).

90 John Bridgeman.

91 Chester Cathedral contained St Oswald's parish church, Carlisle Cathedral housed St Mary's parish church.

account thereof. Churches, and the service of the parishes be so had, that the one shall not interrupt the other, or be at the same time with the other.

9. In some places it was found, that the Quarter Sessions, the Leet Courts, Court Baron, and other service of that nature with ordinary meetings of Justices, and Jurors be kept in Churches, and Chappells; and there doe their ordinarie businesses of making presentments, and finding Indictments by Juries: And at the Communion Table all these things are done. And in one, or two places, the market being kept neer to the Chappell, if the market day prove rayny, the market folks also keepe market *Richmond*[92] there. And to mend the matter, in one of those places Commissaries Court was sett upp where the Communion Table should stand.[93] For the future avoiding the like prophanation of consecrated places, there is resolute, and peremptorie order geven. Yet I have been lately informed that a steward of one of your Maiesties Courts in Lancashire, at a place called Holcome in the parish of Bury, coming to keepe Courts in the Chappell there, sett a fine of fourtie pounds upon *C.R. I have commanded the* the Churchwardens for keeping the Chappell *Secretarie*[94] *to take order withe* dore lockt, and hindring him of keeping his *this abuse* Courts there. In which case I humbly beseech your Maiestie not only to commaund the taking off of that fine, being imposed by the Steward of your Maiesties courts there; but also to laye your commandement upon me, and the rest of my Bretheren, the Bishops, not to suffer such things to be done in Churches, or Chappells.

10. At Bunburie in Cheshire there is a Grammar Schoole founded by one Thomas Aldersey late Cittizen and Haberdasher of London with exhibition for a preacher and *C.R. I have had the lyke complaint* a Curate;[95] whom the Haberdashers of London *from the Archbishop of* pretend to have power to place and displace at *Canterbury wherefore as I have* their pleasure without any respect of Episcopall *answered him,*[96] *so I tell you that I* Jurisdiction: and their graunts to the preacher *will not endure that anie Lay* and the Curate runne, To have, and to hold, *quam Persone (much lesse a Corporation) diu se bene gesserint*. The place is said to be a *have power to place and displace* good nursery of Novelists, and the Curate, and *Curates or beneficed Preestes at* Lecturer there, were found altogether *ther plasur, therfore you may bee,* unconformable presuming, that the Bishop of *sure of more then my protection* Chester[97] had no power over them, (which I *in this* wonder, that the Bishop of Chester endured.) This Curate and Lecturer being suspended by my Visitors,[98] submitted themselves to subscribe, and have bound themselves to joyne in the due performance of the

---

92   Placed in the margin by Neile.

93   In Trinity Chapel, Richmond: SRO, D1287/9/8 (A/92).

94   Presumably Sir Francis Windebank, to whom Neile submitted his account each year. In his visitors' report on Chester diocese, sent on to Bridgeman, Neile added the comment here that 'It is his Majesties commandment, that consecrated places be not thus abused upon any pretense whatsoever, and also reqireth to be next yeare certified, what is done for reformation thereof': SRO, D1287/9/8 (A/92).

95   In 1594 Thomas Aldersey, citizen and haberdasher of London, was granted letters patent to establish a free school at Bunbury, and the following year granted the rectory and tithes of Bunbury to support a preacher, schoolmaster and usher. *Victoria County History Cheshire*, III (1980), 227.

96   See above, p. 86.

97   John Bridgeman.

98   According to Neile's visitors, Samuel Torshell and John Swan were preachers and 'nonconformalists' and 'the Haberdashers Patentees' at Bunbury: SRO, D1287/9/8 (A/92). For both, see R. C.

whole service, according to the Booke of Common Prayer, and your Maiesties Declaration, and Instructions, and undertaken to certifie their performance thereof; and thereupon obteyned license both for serving the Cure, and for preaching. It may be that the Haberdashers will reprehend them for so doing, as having therein prejudiced their right: which if they shall doe, I shall humbly present the cause to your Maiestie, and crave your Maiesties protection, both on the behalf of the Ecclesiasticall Jurisdiction, and of the poore men, that they may not suffer at the Haberdashers hands by withdrawing their exhibition for doing their duty.

11. Your Maiesties Collegiate Church at Manchester, where the Warden,[99] and fellowes pretend an exemption from all Episcopall, and Archiepiscopall Jurisdiction, and subjection to Canons, was found to be altogether out of order: where there is neither Singing men, nor Quiristers, nor Organ fitt to be used. The Warden and fellowes altogether out of order, scarsely coming to prayers; but never are, when they come, in Collegiate-Quire habit of surplisse, and hoods: but all the service layd upon two poore Chaplens. But upon better consideration, all of them (save one Mr Bourne[100]) reformed themselves, came to the prayers in their habits, and read the Service, which (they say) had not before ben seene. And Mr Bourne himself was contented to read prayers without a surplisse; saying, he refused not, as opposing order, but that he was ashamed now to putt on the surplisse, which in 30 yeares before, of his being Fellow there, he hath not done. The rest have promised reformation for the time to come. And Bourne stands suspended.

C.R. *Let him be so stil except*
he conform

I trust your Maiestie wilbe gratiously pleased to allow of that course, which is taken for reformation, and of remitting of the faults past, so as due reformation, and amendment may ensue. And that, I may hope, it may so come to passe, I will together with the relaxation of my Inhibitions for my Metropoliticall visitation, send to each of my Bretheren, the Bishops of those Dioceses of Chester, and Carlile, all the particulars of the defaults, and of the reformations enjoyned and promised to be performed, and pray them to prosecute the same with effect.[101]

It may be your Maiestie will aske, how it cometh to passe, that things should be suffered to be so generally out of order in those Dioceses, the Bishops being able, and understanding men, professing all conformitie in themselves, and their care of requiring the like in others, subject to their Jurisdiction.

I must ingenuously confesse, I can neither justify, nor excuse them: yet, this I know, they will say, That finding their Dioceses so distracted with Papists, and Puritans, they thought, by a mild way to recover the Puritan part, least that by carrying a severer hand upon the Puritans, then they had power to carry upon the Papists, the Popish party might take heart, and opinion of favour. For the Ordinarie Jurisdiction can proceed no farther against Popish Recusants then to excommunicate, and certifie them, who doe excommunicate themselves.

Richardson, *Puritanism in north-west England* (Manchester, 1972), *passim*; and for Torshell, see also his entry in *ODNB*.

[99] Richard Murray, warden 1609–35. In Feb. 1634 he was prosecuted in the London High Commission, and in June 1635 deprived of his wardenship. F. R. Raines (ed.), *The fellows of the collegiate church of Manchester, part I* (Chetham Society, n.s., 23, 1891), p. 87; CUL, MS Dd. 2.21, fos. 302v, 307v; *CSPD 1635*, pp. 212–14.

[100] William Bourne, fellow of Manchester College and vicar of Whalley. Raines (ed.), *Fellows of the collegiate church of Manchester, part I*, pp. 85–94.

[101] See above, p. 89 n. 87.

It may be they will also say: It is in a manner impossible for the Bishop to know how the publick Service is performed in every Church, and Chappell of his Dioces. The Bishop can but enquire by the othes of Churchwardens, and Sidesmen, who make no conscience of dispensing with their othe, and can hardly be brought to present any thing, be thinges never so farr out of order.[102]

It may also be said in their excuse, that the Bishop executeth his Jurisdiction by his inferior Officers, his Chancellor, his Archdeacons, his Commissaries, and Officialls, and if they be negligent, or corrupt, it is not possible for the Bishop to know, and reforme things, that are amisse. The truth is, if the Bishop be not very vigilant, and resolute to have things kept in order, and exact the same of his Officers, and an accompt of their doings; things wilbe amisse, be the Bishop in his owne person never so well disposed, and affected to governement. And the inferior Officers, that make least advantage of corrections in this kind, may (perhaps) make good advantage of connivence at small faults, as usually they hold such inconformities. And Chancellors, Commissaries, and Officialls, that hold their places by patent for life, stand lesse in awe of the Bishop, then it were fitt they should.

In that it is said before that these Diocesses are full of Recusants, your Maiestie may perhaps aske, how it cometh to passe that in all this discourse of the Visitation, there is nothing said concerning Popish Recusants, as if the whole proceeding hath ben bent against poore unconformable Ministers, and the other not look't after: May it please your Maiestie to be informed; That hundreds of Recusants have ben proceeded against by vertue of your Maiesties High Commission, and fetched out of all parts of the Province, and brought to Yorke, there to compound with your Maiesties Commissioners authorised for that purpose; and your said Commissioners have signified your Maiesties pleasure, that we should forbeare proceeding against such as compounded for their Recusancy and yet, if by any presentments it appeare unto us, that they transgresse the conditions of their said compositions, as by having their children Christened by Popish Priests, or being maried by Popish Priests, or any the like offense of Ecclesiasticall cognizance, we

C.R. The neglect of punishing   doe proceed against them both by the Ordinary
Puritans breedes Papists   Jurisdiction, and by the power of your Maiesties
High Commission.

The Isle of Man.

Having presumed thus much of your Maiesties sacred patience, I desire to informe you of another part of the Province, the Bishoprick of Man.[103]

The Bishoprick consisteth of a Bishop, an Archdeacon, and seventeene parishes.

The Jurisdiction is divided between the Bishop, and Archdeacon, which the Bishop exerciseth the one half of the yeare, and the Archdeacon the other.

The revenue of the Bishoprick, as it now standeth upon the leases lett by the former Bishop is about £150 *per annum*, and *in vero valore*, if it were out of lease, better then £300.

The patronage of the Bishoprick, the Archdeaconry and all the Benefices in the Isle, is in the Earle of Derbie.[104]

---

102 Neile repeated this complaint in later reports: see below, pp. 106, 124.
103 The bishopric of Sodor and Man was currently vacant, following the death of Bishop John Phillips in Aug. 1633, and William Forster was consecrated as the new bishop on 9 Mar. 1634.
104 William Stanley, sixth earl of Derby (1561–1642).

The Archdeaconry is of £60 value *per annum*. The corps whereof is a Benefice with cure in the Isle. The former Bishop[105] had the Archdeaconry *in Commendam*, which confounded the Jurisdiction, and in time would have swallowed up the Archdeaconry into the Bishoprick: but it is now otherwise setled, and the Earle of Derbie hath presented a man of good note for that Archdeaconry.[106]

The Bishop useth also to have a Vicar Generall, one of the Ministers beneficed in the Isle. Which place is of small value, not worth the having.

The most of the Benefices are so in Lay mens hands, that they yield small meanes to them, that serve the Cures. The best of them, which are but two, or three, £40 *per annum*, others £20, and 20 marks, and the greater number of them under £10. By reason whereof, the Clergie there for the most part are unable, and illiterate men, natives of the Island.

Their Divine Service is according to the Booke of Common Prayer of the Church of England, read in some places in English, and in some places in the language of the natives: into which the late Bishop translated our Common Prayer Booke;[107] but how faithfully, I know not; and how much for the good of that people, I leave to your Maiesties better judgement.[108] Under correction, I am of opinion it were well, that all your Maiesties subjects of that Isle, and other places might be brought to the use of the English Tongue.

There is neither Deane, nor Chapter, nor Cathedrall or Collegiate Church; neither doe I understand, that there is any Schoole to breed their children in pietie, or literature, or civilitie: yet I am informed, that there is not a Papist in that Island.

If it shall please your Maiestie to geve me leave, I will in your Maiesties name sollicite the Earle of Derby, and his sonne, the Lord Strange[109] to procure, and settle in this Island some things, that may further the exercise of pietie, the increase of literature, and the education of youth in civility, and the use of the English Tongue.

> I trust your Sacred Maiestie will pardon this boldnes of
> Januarie 1633[110]   Your Maiesties most humble Servant, and
>   Chaplen
>   R. Ebor:[111]

Canterbury province, 1634

January 2 1634.[112]

May it please your most Excellent Majesty. I am at this tyme in obedyence to your

---

105 John Phillips, bishop of Sodor and Man 1605–33.

106 John Broxop, instituted archdeacon of Man on 9 Jan. 1635.

107 Phillips's translation was never published: see his entry in *ODNB*.

108 Neile was a critic of Phillips, believing he had 'filled those parts of the Church with manye unlearnd and unworthye ministers', and wrote to Laud, on Phillips's death in Aug. 1633, urging that the king use his influence with the earl of Derby to ensure a more suitable successor was chosen: BL, Add. MS 64907, fo. 20r.

109 James Stanley, later seventh earl of Derby (1607–51).

110 1634 new style.

111 Richard Neile, archbishop of York 1632–40.

112 LPL, MS 943, pp. 251–7, in the hand of William Dell, Laud's secretary and endorsed 'Lord Archbishop of Canterbury certificate to his Majesty' (p. 258); LPL, Laud's Register I, fos. 215r–216r. The year is 1635 new style.

Sacred Maiesties Commandes to give you an Accompt, how your prudent and pious Instructions for the good and wellfare of the Church of Christ, in your Kingdome, have been obeyed and performed by the severall Bishopps within my Province of Canterbury with all humility and obedyence I here present as followeth.

Canterbury. And first I represent to your Majesty, that I have this yeare, partly by my Vicar Generall,[113] and partly by the Deane of the Arches[114] Visited Seaven Dioceses, beginning (as I am bound by the Ecclesiasticall Lawes) att my owne Metropoliticall Church of Canterbury, and that Diocess; that I might first see what was done at home, before I did curiously looke abroad into other Bishoppes Jurisdictions.[115]

And not to conceale truth from your Majesty, I found in my owne Diocess (especially about Ashford side) diverse professed Separatists with whom I shall take the best and most present Order that I can; Some of them, and some of Maydstone (where much Inconformity hath of late yeares spread) being allready called into the High Commission, where if they be proved as guilty as they are voyced to be, I shall not fayle to doe Justice upon them.[116]

I conceyve under favour that the Dutch Churches in Canterbury and Sandwich, are great Nurseyes of Inconformity in those Partes. Your Majesty may be pleasd to *C.R. Putt mee in mynd of this at* remember, I have complained to your Selfe, and *some convenient tyme when I am* my Lords at the Counsell Board, and humbly *at Councell and I shall redress itt* desyred that they both of the French, Italian, and Dutch Congregations, which are borne Subjects, may not be suffered any longer to lyve in such a Separation as they doe, from both Church and State. And have according to that which I thought might best sorte with your Majestyes Instructions, commanded by my Vicar Generall when he was lately at Canterbury, to beginne fayrely to call them to Conforme with the English Church.[117] Which Busynes I doe hereby humbly bessech Your Majestie to looke upon with a provident Eye, not here onely, but much more in London, for the better Setling of both Church and Common-wealth in that Particular. And your Majestyes Instructions I have for my own part punctually observed them.

The rest of the Diocesses which I Visited this yeare are Rochester, Salisbury: Bristoll: Bath and Wells: Exeter: and Lincolne.[118]

Rochester. For Rochester, I found noe eminent thinge amiss, but the Bishop himself[119] fell into a Palsey, and was thereby forced to goe to the Bath and soe to be longer absent from his Diocess, then otherwise he would have been, and he is now returned, God be thanked much better, though not perfectly well. And for the Diocess, I did not fynde in my Visitation any noted Breach upon any your Majestyes Instructions.

---

113 Sir Nathaniel Brent.
114 Sir John Lambe.
115 LPL, Laud's Register I, fos. 77r–82v.
116 The authoritative study is R. J. Acheson, 'The development of religious separation in the diocese of Canterbury 1590–1660', Ph.D thesis, University of Kent, 1983, pp. 45–97.
117 TNA: PRO, SP 16/278/63–4; see P. Collinson, N. Ramsay and M. Sparks (eds.), *A history of Canterbury Cathedral* (Oxford, 1995), pp. 192–3 and n. 230.
118 LPL, Laud's Register I, fos. 82v–89v, 93r–130v.
119 John Bowle.

Salisbury.   For Salisbury, I found the Bishop[120] had taken a great deale of care about your Majestyes sayd Instructions; and that they might be the better both knowne and obeyed, he hath caused Copyes of them to be sent to most of the Ministers in his Diocess, which hath done a great deal of good.

And though it be not amongst your Instructions, yet I am bold to signify unto your Sacred Majesty, that I fynde the greatest part of Wiltshire overgrowne with the Humours of those men that doe not conforme, and are as backward both Clergy and Layety towards the Repaire of St Paules Church, as any parte of England that I have observed.

The Cathedrall at Salisbury is much pestered with Seates, and I have given *C.R. I doe and will express* Order to remove them, which I hope your *my pleasure (if need be)* Majesty will approve, aswell as you did at *what way you will* Yorke and Durham, and adde your Power if myne be not sufficient.[121]

Bristoll.   For Bristoll, I fynde in my Visitation that the Bishop[122] theire hath taken very good paynes and care since his Comming thither. And that some Clergy men in Dorsettshyre, which gave great Cause of suspicion have quitt themselves in a better manner then was expected, though all be not right in those Partes.[123]

Bath and Wells. Concerning Bath and Wells, I must needs returne to your Majesty, that which I would to God I could doe of all the rest. Namely that all your Instructions are punctually observed, and the Lectures, (as many as are in that Diocess) read not by any particular Factious Persons, but by a Company of learned neighbouring Ministers, which are every way conformable to the Church.[124]

Exeter.   For Exeter, where according to many Complaintes that had been made here above, I might have expected many thinges out of Order, I must doe my Lord the Bishop this Right,[125] that for your Majestyes Instructions, they have been carefully observed. But a great Division there is between the Deane and Chapter. I have twice sett them at Pease yet it breake's out againe. And I doubt there being soe many Brothers and Brothers in Lawe in that Chapter, is not the least Cause of it, the sidinge together for feare of Oppression.

I fynde alsoe there hath been, and is at this present, a great difference between the Deane and Chapter, and the Cittye, about Buryall within the Churchyard of the Cathedrall. I shall doe my best to sett Peace between them, and if I cannot, as I much

---

120 John Davenant.
121 Historical Manuscripts Commission, *Appendix to the Fourth Report* (London, 1874), p. 130. Charles I had visited York Minster and Durham Cathedral on his journey to Scotland in 1633: see Fincham and Tyacke, *Altars restored*, p. 233.
122 George Coke.
123 Laud may have had in mind here John White, rector of Holy Trinity Dorchester. He had instructed Brent on his visitation to examine the conduct of White, especially his covenant of grace. Local forces protected White, although two years later he was to be prosecuted through High Commission. TNA: PRO, SP 16/260/90; D. Underdown, *Fire from heaven* (London, 1993), pp. 173–4.
124 This unqualified (if indirect) praise of the bishop, William Piers, underlines the close relations of the two in 1633–4, for which see Fincham and Tyacke, *Altars restored*, pp. 201–2; and below, pp. 112, 127.
125 For the rather tense relations between Joseph Hall and Laud in the early 1630s which lay behind this comment, see K. Fincham and P. Lake, 'Popularity, prelacy and puritanism in the 1630s: Joseph Hall explains himself', *English Historical Review* (*EHR*), CXI (1996), 856–81.

feare it, I shall be an humble Suitor to your Majesty to take it into your Princely consideration, least it doe more prejudice to both Bodyes, then is yet thought of.

Lincolne.   As for Lincolne, it being the greatest Diocess in the Kingdome I have now reduced that under Metropoliticall Visitation alsoe,[126] and Visited it this present yeare. My Visitours there found Bedfordshire for the bignes most tainted of any part of the Diocess. And in particular Mr Buckley[127] is sent to the High Commission Court for Inconformity. And in Leycester, the Deane of the Arches[128] suspended one Mr Angell who hath continued a Lecturer in that great Towne, for these diverse yeares, without any Lycense at all to Preach, yet tooke liberty enough. I doubt his Violence hath crack't his Braine, and doe therfore use him the more tenderly, because I see the Hand of God hath overtaken him.[129]

For Lincolne it selfe, my Vicar Generall certifye's me,[130] there are many Anabaptistes in it, and that theyr Leader is one Johnson a Baker. And that in diverse partes of that Diocess many both of Clergy and Laity are excessively given to drunkennes. That the Towne of Boston which was a great Nursery of Inconformity, is since the callinge of some of the Magistrates into the High Commission,[131] become very orderly, and settled to obedyence. But the Towne of Loath somwhat to blame.

At Kelsterne dwelle's the wilde younge Gentleman Mr South (concerning whom I have lately spoken, and that often, with your Majesty) he hath committed a horrible Incest, and gotten two Sisters with Childe. I have called him into the High

C.R. The Southewest Wynd is   Commission against the next Terme,[132] and I
commonlie the best, therfore I will hope your Majesty will give me leave to make
not hinder the blowing that way   South blowe West for St Paules.[133]

At Kensworth in Harfordshire, and some other Places, many gad from theyr owne Churches by troupes, after other Ministers. Which is a common fault in the South partes of that Diocess, where the People are said to be very giddy in matters of Religion.

The Cathedrall of this Diocess is not well ordered, eyther for Reparation or ornament, but the Deane and Chapter to whom that care belonges have promised speedy amendment.

For Eaton Colledge within that Diocess, I doe not fynde but that the Provost Sir Henry Wotton hath carryed himself very worthily. The greatest thinges thought to be amiss in that Society are those which are referred to me by your Majesty upon

---

126 Early in 1634 Laud had overcome Bishop John Williams's objections to Lincoln diocese being included in his metropolitical visitation: Laud, *Works*, VI, 345–6, 348–9, 351, 360–1, 365–6, 368; LPL, Laud's Register I, fos. 112v–114v.

127 Peter Bulkeley or Buckley, rector of Odell, Bedfordshire, 1610–35, who then emigrated to New England and became minister at Concord, Massachusetts, 1635–59. See *CSPD 1634–5*, p. 205.

128 John Lambe.

129 John Angel was summoned by High Commission in Sept. 1634 but was given time to conform and retained his lectureship: *CSPD 1634–5*, pp. 205–6; Davies, *Caroline captivity*, p. 166; *ODNB*, 'John Angel'.

130 For Lincoln diocese Laud drew on information supplied by John Farmery, the diocesan chancellor, as well as by Nathaniel Brent, his vicar-general: TNA: PRO, SP 16/271/82, 274/12.

131 CUL, MS Dd 2.21, fos. 102v–264v; *CSPD 1633–4*, pp. 136, 480; P. Thompson, *The history and antiquities of Boston* (Boston, 1856), pp. 428–30.

132 For John South's case, see *CSPD 1634–5*, pp. 354, 496, *CSPD 1635*, pp. 110, 203–4, 234.

133 In other words, a fine earmarked for the restoration of St Paul's.

the Complaint of Kinges Colledge in Cambridge, to which I have noe more to saye till I see whether they of Eaton will declyne the Reference or noe.[134]

Thus farr concerning the Diocesses which I have Visited this yeare. In all which I fynde one great Complaint, and very fitt to be redressed. It is the Generall greivance of the Poore Vicars, that theyr Stipendes are scarse able to feed and cloath them. And which is worse, the Vicars in great Market Townes, where the People are very many, are for the most part worst provided for. But I humbly thanke your Majesty some good hath of late been done for them, and I shall pursue all just and fayre wayes to give them releife; Humbly beseeching you to give your gracious Assistance to me and them.

Winchester.   For Winchester, I fynde my Lord the Bishop[135] there hath been very carefull for all your Majestys Instructions, and that they are well observed through that Diocess, save onely that in two Parishes the Bishop fyndes some defect about Catechizing in the Afternoone, of which he will take great care that it may be remedyed. And I fynde by his Lordships Returne to me, that there are diverse obstinate Recusantes in those partes, which I presume are Certifyed to your Majestys Judges according to Lawe.

London.   The Bishop of London[136] Visited his Diocess this yeare, the Citty and Middlesex in Person, the rest by his Chancellour,[137] by reason of his necessary Attendance upon your Majesty.[138] In this his Visitation he found diverse Complaintes, about Inconformity to the Church Discipline, but the Proofes came home onely against fowre, three Curats, and a Vicar.[139] The Vicar upon Submission hath tyme given him till the next Terme to settle himself, and reduce his Parishioners. And two of the three Curats did presently submitt themselves, and promise Constancy in theyr obedyence to the Church. The third Curat one Philip Saunders of Hutton in Essex, being refractory was suspended, and hath since forsaken the Diocess.[140] It seem's he meane's to settle himself, where he may hope to fynde more favour.

Norwich.   For Norwich, the Bishop[141] Certifye's that he hath put downe some Lectures where factious men performed them, and particularly that he suspended one Bridges, Curat of St Georges Parish in Norwich, for transgressing your Majestys Declaration in his Lectures, but hath of late freed him from that Suspension, upon humble Submission made, and Promise not to offend hereafter.[142] And farther, that he hath lately heard Complaint of Mr Warde of Ipswich for some wordes uttered in Sermons of his, for which he is now called into the High Commission.[143]

He farther Certifye's, that he hath suspended one Enoch Grey[144] for unsound Doctrine preached by him. And that one Simon Jacob, alias Bradshaw, and Ralph

---

[134] Wilkins, *Concilia*, IV, 496.
[135] Walter Curle.
[136] William Juxon.
[137] Arthur Duck.
[138] In his capacity as dean of the Chapel Royal, 1633–6.
[139] The vicar was Thomas Peck of Prittlewell: Webster, *Godly clergy*, p. 206.
[140] *Ibid.*, pp. 206–7, 240.
[141] Richard Corbet.
[142] See M. Reynolds, 'Predestination and parochial dispute in the 1630s: the case of the Norwich lectureships', *JEH*, LIX (2008), 407–25; for William Bridge (1600/1–71), see his entry in *ODNB*.
[143] Samuel Ward, town preacher at Ipswich: see *CSPD 1634–5*, pp. 321, 361.
[144] D. Como, *Blown by the spirit* (Stanford, CA, 2004), pp. 67–8; and see below, p. 142.

Smith, two Wanderers, went up and downe preaching here and there, without Place of Aboad or Authority. And that upon his Summoning them to appeare, they are runne out of that Diocess. Your Majestys Instructions in other thinges have (as he Certifyeth) been carefully observed, both by himself and his Clergy.

Ely.   The Bishop of Ely[145] certifyes, that for any thinge that hath been made appeare to him, all your Majestys royall Injunctions for the good of the Church have been carefully observed throughout his Diocess. And he promises to carry a very watchfull Eye, as he hath ever done, concerning all such Lecturers, as are, or shall at any tyme be in his Diocess.[146]

St Davids. For St Davids, the Bishop[147] is now gone and setled in his Dioces, whence he hath not been absent two monthes these two yeares. He promiseth to be very carefull whom he ordeyne's. The Lecturers in those Partes are not many, yet of late he hath been dryven first to suspend, and afterwardes to dismiss, one Roberts, a Welch Lecturer for Inconformity. And one or two others that have with theyr Giddynes offered to distemper the People, he hath likewise driven out of his Diocess. But his Lordship complaines greivously (and not without Cause) that diverse Impropriators in those Partes have eyther pulled downe the Chancells, or suffered them to fall, to the great debasing of theyr Churches, and leaving them soe open and cold, as that the People in those Mountainous Partes must endure a great deale of hardnes, aswell in the Churches, as in theyr waye to them.

St Asaph.   The Bishop of St Asaph[148] professe's he hath little to returne. And that it is a great part of his Comfort in that remote Place, that the whole Diocess in a manner is peaceable and obedyent, aswell to your Majestys Instructions, as other thinges which concerne the Church. That they are not any where troubled with Inconformity; But hartily wishe's, that they might be aswell acquitted from Superstition and Profaneness.

Landaff.   The Bishop of Landaff[149] certifye's, that this last yeare he Visited in Person, and found that William Erbury Vicar of St Maryes in Cardiff and Walter Cradocke his Curat, have been very disobedyent to your Majestys Instructions, and have preached very Schismatically and dangerously to the People.[150] That for this he hath given the Vicar a judiciall Admonition, and will farther proceed if he doe not submitt. And for his Curat, being a bold ignorant young Fellowe, he hath suspended him and taken awaye his License to serve the Cure. Amonge other things he used this base and Un-Christian passage in the Pulpitt, That God soe loved the <u>World, that for it he sent his Sonne to lyve lyke a Slave, and dye like a Beast</u>.[151]

C.R. This is not much unlike that which was not longe since uttered elsewhere, viz: That the Jewes crucifyed Christ like a Damned Rogue between two Theeves, etc.

He farther Certifye's, that one William Newport Rector of Llangua in Monmouth shire, hath pulled downe the Partition betwixt the Chancell and the Church, and sold

---

145   Francis White.
146   Subsequent reports make no reference to lecturers in Ely diocese.
147   Theophilus Field.
148   John Owen.
149   William Murray.
150   Both Erbury, a future chaplain to the New Model Army, and Cradock, a future Independent, remained thorns in the side of the authorities for the rest of the 1630s: see below, pp. 104, 117, 134; and *ODNB*, 'William Erbery' and 'Walter Cradock'.
151   Underlined by Charles I; the annotation, however, is not in his hand.

parte, and disposed the rest to his owne use, with some other Violences to the great profanation of that Place. For which the Bishop desire's leave to bringe him into the High Commission.

Glocester.   The Bishop of Glocester[152] certifye's, that he is forced to Ordeyne some very meane Ministers in his Diocess, to supply Cures as meane, yet he professeth, that to his knowledge, he never gave Holy Orders to any unworthy Person. And farther he sayth, that he hath put downe some Lecturers, and sett up other some,

C.R. I must bee satisfied that the which he conceyve's he did without offence, *occasions were verie necesary* being done upon different occasions;[153] but *otherwais he shall answer it* sayth that he doth neyther knowe, nor can probably conjecture, that there is any one unconformable man in all his Diocess. Which if it be true, is a great Clearinge of those Partes, which have of late been soe much suspected.

Hereford.   This Bishopricke is voyd.[154]

Oxford.   For the Diocess of Oxford, I fynde the Bishop[155] very carefull and that he hath accordinge to his Promise made to your Majesty built a House at Cuddesden, a Vicarage in his owne Diocess and Guift which he now holdes *in Commendam*. Which House he humbly desyres by your Majestys favour may be annexed to the See of Oxford, which never yett had any House belonging to it.[156] And for the Instructions they have all been observed within his Diocess, save he doubte's some few Lecturers of whom he will make present Inquiry, and hath allready suppressed two, which were not performed as they ought, viz at Dadington,[157] and Woodstocke.

Chichester.   My Lord of Chichester[158] certifye's all very well in his Diocess, save onely in the East parte, which is farr from him, he fyndes that some Puritan Justices of the Peace have awed some of the Clergye into like Opinions with themselves, which yet of late have not broken out into any publike Inconformity.[159]

Peterburgh.   The Bishop of Peterburgh[160] hath Visited his Diocess this last yeare, and begunne soe well to looke to all good Orders, that I hope thinges will goe very well there. But I fynde he is beholding to his Predecessors[161] who tooke very good Care in former years concerning your Majestys Instructions.

This is all the Returne which I have this yeare to make to your Majesty, havinge receyved noe Accompt at all from these Bishopps following. Viz. Worcester;[162] Coventry and Lichfield;[163] and Bangor.[164]

---

[152] Godfrey Goodman.

[153] Underlined by Charles I.

[154] Augustine Lindsell had died on 6 Nov. 1634 and his successor, Matthew Wren, was not consecrated until 8 Mar. 1635.

[155] John Bancroft.

[156] Leters patent authorizing the annexation are dated 26 Mar. 1637: LPL, Laud's Register I, fos. 261r–266r; and see above, p. 81.

[157] Deddington.

[158] Richard Montagu.

[159] For a similar comment by his successor, Brian Duppa, see below, p. 148.

[160] Francis Dee, bishop of Peterborough 1634–8.

[161] Namely William Piers (1630–2) and Augustine Lindsell (1632–4).

[162] John Thornborough.

[163] Robert Wright.

[164] Edmund Griffith, bishop of Bangor 1634–7.

Soe I humbly submitt my Certificat.
W: Cant:[165]

Canterbury province, 1635

May it please your most Gracious Majesty[166]

According to your Royall Commandes I doe here upon the 2d of January 1635[167] *Computi Angliae* present my Accompt both for the Diocess and Province of Canterbury, concerning all those Church affayres which are conteyned in your Majestys most gracious Instructions, published out of your most Princely and Religious care to preserve Unity in Orthodox Doctrine, and Conformity to Goverment within this your Church of England.

Canterbury.   And first for my owne Diocess I humbly represent to your Majesty, that there are yet very many Refractory Persons to the Goverment of the Church of England, about Maidstone and Ashford, and some other Partes, the Infection being spredd by one Brewer, and continued and increased by one Turner.[168] They have been both censured in the High Commission Court some years since, but the hurt which they have done is soe deeply rooted, as that it is not possible to be plucked up on the suddaine, but I must crave tyme to worke it of by little and little.

I have according to your Majestys Commandes requyred obedyence to my Injunctions sent to the French and Dutch Churches at Canterbury, Maidstone, and Sandwich.[169] And allbeit they make some Shewe of Conformity, yet I doe not fynde they have yeelded such obedyence as is required, and was ordered with your Majestys consent and approbation. Soe that I feare I shall be dryven to a quicker proceeding with them.

The Cathedrall Church beginne's to be in very good order. And I have allmost finished theyr Statutes, which being once perfitted will (*mutatis mutandis*) be a sufficyent Direction for the making of the Statutes for the other Cathedralls of the New Erection, which in Kinge Henry the 8[ths] tyme had eyther none left, or none confirmed, and those which are, in many thinges not Canonicall. All which Statutes your Majesty hath given power to me with others, under the Broad Seale of England, to alter or make new, as Wee shall fynde cause.[170] And soe soone as these Statutes

---

165   William Laud.
166   LPL, MS 943, pp. 261–5, in the hand of William Dell, Laud's secretary; endorsed '1635. January. Laud Archbishop of Canterbury certificat to his Majesty' (p. 266).
167   1636 new style.
168   Thomas Brewer of Boxley, a local gentleman, and John Turner, a chandler of Sutton Valence. In 1626 Brewer was labelled 'the general patron of the Kentish Brownists' and Turner as his 'chaplain'. R. J. Acheson, *Radical puritans in England 1550–1660* (London, 1990), p. 90. See also above, p. 95 n. 116.
169   TNA: PRO, SP 16/286/85, 289/5, 7, 298/52.
170   Winchester, another of the 'New Foundations', was given new statutes in 1638, as was Hereford, one of the 'Old Foundations', in 1637. W. H. Hutton, *The statutes governing the cathedral church of Winchester given by Charles I* (Oxford, 1925); J. Jebb and H. W. Phillott (eds.), *The statutes of the cathedral church of Hereford, promulgated AD 1637* (Oxford, 1882); see also Laud, *Works*, III, 253.

for the Church of Canterbury are made ready, I shall humbly submitt them to your Majesty for Confirmation.[171]

There is one Mr Walker[172] of St Johns the Evangelist, a Peculiar of myne in London, who all his tyme hath been but a disorderly and a peevish man, and now of late hath very frowardly preached against the Lord Bishop of Ely his Booke, concerning the Lordes Daye, sett out by authority.[173] But upon a Canonicall Admonition given him to desist, he hath hitherto recollected himself, and I hope will be advised.[174]

London.   For the Diocess of London, I fynde my Lord the Bishop[175] hath been very carefull for all that concernes his owne Person, but 3 of his Archdeacons have made noe returne at all to him, soe he can certifye nothinge but what hath come to his knowledge without theyr helpe.[176]

There have been convented in this Diocess Dr Stoughton of Aldermanbury,[177] Mr Simpson Curat and Lecturer of St Margarets Newfishstreet,[178] Mr Andrew Moline Curat and Lecturer of St Swithyn[179] Mr John Goodwin Vicar of St Stephens Colmanstreet,[180] and Mr Vyner Lecturer of St Laurence in the Olde Jurye,[181] for breach of the Canons of the Church in Sermons, or Practise, or both. But because all of them promised Amendment for the future, and submission to the Church in all thinges, my Lord very moderately forbare farther proceeding against them.

There were likewise convented Mr Sparrowhawke Curat and Lecturer at St Mary Woolchurch,[182] for preaching against the Canon for Bowing at the Name of Jesus, who because he willfully persisted is suspended from Preaching in that Diocess. As alsoe one Mr John Wood a wild turbulent Preacher, and formerly censured in the High Commission Court.[183] But his Lordship forbore Mr White of Knightsbridge, for that his Cause is at this present depending in the Court aforesaid.[184]

Lincolne.   Concerning the Diocess of Lincolne my Lord the Bishop[185] returne's this Information. That he hath Visited the same this yeare all over in Person, which he conceyves noe Predecessor of his hath done these hundred yeares.

[171]   They were confirmed by Charles I in Jan. 1637, and are printed in Laud, *Works*, V, 506–45.
[172]   George Walker (1582?–1651).
[173]   Francis White, *A treatise of the sabbath-day* (1635).
[174]   This proved not to be the case. Walker continued to goad the authorities, rehearsing his trenchant views in *The doctrine of the sabbath*, published in Amsterdam in 1638, and shortly afterwards was arrested for inflammatory preaching: see his entry in *ODNB*.
[175]   William Juxon.
[176]   Juxon had five archdeacons: Henry King, archdeacon of Colchester, Edward Layfield, archdeacon of Essex, Richard Cluet, archdeacon of Middlesex, Thomas Paske, archdeacon of London and Thomas Westfield, archdeacon of St Albans. Juxon repeated this complaint in 1637 and 1639: below, pp. 126, 143.
[177]   John Stoughton, vicar of St Mary Aldermanbury, London 1632–9. For other official moves against him in 1635–6, see his entry in *ODNB*.
[178]   Sidrach Simpson, the future Independent minister; see his entry in *ODNB*.
[179]   At St Swithin 1633–47: see P. Seaver, *The puritan lectureships* (Stanford, CA, 1970), p. 257.
[180]   Goodwin was vicar of St Stephen Coleman Street 1633–45 and 1649–60.
[181]   At St Lawrence Jewry 1633–5: see Seaver, *Puritan lectureships*, pp. 256–7.
[182]   See *ibid.*, p. 258; Webster, *Godly clergy*, pp. 46–7, 242.
[183]   Perhaps the lecturer at St Andrew Holborn and perhaps the same man as John Wood, BD, curate of St James, Duke Place, 1630–9: Seaver, *Puritan lectureships*, pp. 259, 367 n. 56; G. Hennessey, *Novum repertorium ecclesiasticum parochiale Londinense* (London, 1898), p. 118.
[184]   Nathaniel White, curate of Holy Trinity, Knightsbridge. See *CSPD 1635–6*, pp. 87, 94, 518.
[185]   John Williams.

And that he fyndes soe much good done thereby beyond that which Chancellours use to doe when they goe the Visitation, that he is sorry he hath not done it heretofore in soe many yeares as he hath been Bishop.[186]

He farther certifye's that he hath prevayled beyond Expectation for the Augmenting of fower or fyve Small Vicarages. And conceyve's (as your Majesty may be pleased to remember: I have often told you upon myne owne experience) that it is a Worke very necessary and fitt to be done, and most worthy of your Majestys Royall care and consideration.

For Conformity, his Lordship professeth that in that large Diocess he knowes but one unconformable man, and that is one Lindhall, who is in the High Commission Court, and ready for Sentence.[187]

Bath and Wells. My Lord the Bishop of Bath and Wells[188] certifyes, that his Diocess is in very good order and obedyence. That there is not a Single Lecturer in any Towne Corporate, but grave Divines preach by course, and that he hath changed the Afternoone Sermons into Catechizing by question and Answere in all Parishes.

His Lordship further certifye's, that noe man hath been presented unto him since his last Certificat for any breach of the Canons of the Church, or your Majestys Instructions, and that he hath receyved noe notice of any increase of men Popishly affected, beyond the number mentioned in his last Certificat.

Norwich. The Bishop of this Sea dyed[189] allmost halfe an yeare since, and had sent in noe Certificat. But I fynde by my Visitation there this present yeare, that the whole Diocess is much out of order, and more at Ipswich and Yarmouth, then at Norwich it selfe.[190] But I hope my Lord that now is,[191] will take care of it, he shall want noe assistance that I can give him.

Mr Samuel Warde Preacher at Ipswich was censured this last Terme, in the High Commission Court for preaching in disgrace of the Common Prayer Booke, and other like gross misdemeanours.[192]

Oxford.
Sarum.
Elye. ⎫
Chichester. ⎬ These six Bishoppes[193] respectively make theyr Answere that in theyr owne Persons they have observed all your Majestys Instructions, and that they fynde all theyr Clergye very conformable, noe one of them instancing in any Particular to the contrary.
St Asaph. ⎭
Bristol.

---

186 Williams had missed previous episcopal visitations in 1622, 1625, 1628 and 1631.
187 Probably Edmund Lynold, vicar of Healing, Lincolnshire, for whom see J. Martin, 'Edmund Lynold and the court of High Commission', *Lincolnshire Architectural and Archaeological Society Reports and Papers*, V (1953–4), 70–4.
188 William Piers.
189 Richard Corbet died on 28 July 1635.
190 See Brent's report to Laud in TNA: PRO, SP 16/293/128. For Yarmouth, Brent in fact reported 'the town is now quiet', but Laud was alluding to the investigation in 1634–5 in High Commission of the nonconformity of George Burdett, the town lecturer, and the prosecution through Star Chamber in Oct. 1634 of a Yarmouth alderman for slander against Archbishop Neile. See *CSPD 1634–5*, pp. 115, 125, 246, 537–9; R. Cust, 'Anti-puritanism and urban politics: Charles I and Great Yarmouth', *Historical Journal* (*HJ*), XXXV (1992), 1–26; and below, p. 113.
191 Matthew Wren was translated to Norwich on 5 Dec. 1635.
192 *CSPD 1635–6*, pp. 129–30.
193 John Bancroft of Oxford, John Davenant of Salisbury, Francis White of Ely, Richard Montagu of Chichester, John Owen of St Asaph and George Coke of Bristol.

Landaffe.   In this Diocess the Bishop[194] founde in his Trienniall Visitation the former yeare, two noted Schismatickes, Wroth[195] and Erbury,[196] that ledd awaye many simple People after them. And findinge that they willfully persisted in theyr Schismaticall Course, he hath carefully preferred Articles against them in the High Commission Court, where when the Cause is ready for hearinge, they shall receyve according to the merittes of it.[197]

Hereford.   Concerning this Diocess, your Majesty knowe's that the late Bishops Residence upon the Place was necessarily hindred by his Attendance upon your Majestys Person as Clerke of the Closet,[198] but he hath been very carefull for the observance of all your Instructions. And particularly for Catechizing of the Youth. As alsoe for not letting of any thinge into Lives to the prejudice of his Successor. In which he hath done exceeding well, and I have by your Majestys commande layd a strict charge upon his Successor[199] to looke to those particular Leases, which he hath made stay of, that they may be reduced into yeares for the good of that Sea, which abundantly needes it.

Winchester.   My Lord Bishop of Winchester[200] certifye's, that there is all Peace and order in his Diocess. And that himself and his Clergye have dulye obeyed your Majestys Instructions. But he informe's that in the Parish of Avington in Hampshire, one Unguyon an Esquire is presented for a new Recusant, as alsoe three others, whereof two are in Southwark.

Peterburgh. ⎫ These three Bishoppes[201] for theyr severall Diocesses respectyvely
Rochester.   ⎬ make returne, that all Obedyence is yeelded to every of your Majestys
Exeter.   ⎭ Instructions.

St Davids.   The late Bishop of St Davids (now of Hereford)[202] hath in his tyme of Residence taken a great deale of paines in that Sea. And hath caused two to be questioned in the High Commission, and suspended one Roberts a Lecturer for Inconformity.[203] Three or fowre others which were suspended, he hath released, upon hope given of theyr obedyence to the Church, and hath absolutely depryved two for theyr exceeding scandalous lyfe. He complaine's much, and surely with cause enough, that there are few Ministers in those poore and remote Places that are able to preach and instruct the People.

Glocester.   My Lord the Bishop[204] informe's, that that Countye is very full of Impropriations, which make's the Ministers poore, and theyr povertye makes them fall upon Popular and factious Courses. I doubt this is too true, but it is a Mischeife hard to cure in this Kingdome, yet I have taken all the care I can, and shall continue soe to doe.

---

[194] William Murray.
[195] William Wroth, rector of Llanfaches. For his career, see *ODNB*.
[196] William Erbury, vicar of Cardiff; see above, p. 99, and below, pp. 117, 134.
[197] See *CSPD 1635–6*, pp. 89, 95, 110, 474.
[198] Matthew Wren, bishop of Hereford from Mar. to Dec. 1635, was clerk of the closet 1633–6.
[199] Theophilus Field, bishop of Hereford 1635–6.
[200] Walter Curle.
[201] Francis Dee of Peterborough, John Bowle of Rochester and Joseph Hall of Exeter.
[202] Theophilus Field.
[203] See above, p. 99.
[204] Godfrey Goodman.

From the rest of the Bishoppes of my Province I have receyved noe Certificat this yeare, viz.

    Coventry and Lichfield[205]
    Worcester[206]
    Bangor.[207]

Soe I humbly submitt this my Certificat.

W: Cant:[208]

York province, 1635

To the Kings Most Excellent Maiestie[209]

The Certificate of your Sacred Maiesties most humble, and bounden, obedient Servant, and Chaplaine, Richard, Archbishop of Yorke,[210] for himself, and his Brethren, the Bishops of that Province.

It may please your Gracious Maiestie to be informed, that I have carefully sent all your Maiesties letters, and Instructions, directed to me, to be sent respectively, to my Brethren, the Bishops of the Province, and to the Deanes, and Chapters of the Cathedrall, and Collegiate Churches of the Province. Of the receipt whereof by them, I have been certified by their letters, with promise of their due performance of your Majesties commandments.

    I have presumed heretofore to trouble your Maiestie with long discourses touching the state of things in mine owne Dioces, and the rest of the Diocesses of the Province. In which Certificates myself, and my Brethren, (the Bishops) promised all care and diligence for the performance of your Maiesties Most Princely and pious Directions for the better governing of the affaires of your Church, and (I presume) your Maiestie will find by this Certificate the due performance thereof.

For mine owne Dioces:[211]

I assure your Maiestie, (having used the best care I can, by myself, my Chancellor,[212] my Archdeacons,[213] and their Officialls, and other meanes, for the discovery of miscariage in the Ministry,) I scarcely find a Beneficed Minister stiffly unconformable: But, (that finding they must obey,) they doe submit themselves, both in point of doctrine and discipline, and conformitie in their Ministery to the lawes of the Church. A few poore stipendarie Curates, (licensed to serve in Chappells of Ease, and some intruders never licensed, whose dependencie hath been upon benevolences,) have been found unconformable: But most of them, upon being called to

---

205 Robert Wright.

206 John Thornborough.

207 Edmund Griffith.

208 William Laud.

209 TNA: PRO, SP 16/312/84, endorsed 'January 1635. Lord Archbishop of Yorke certificate.'

210 Richard Neile.

211 Of York.

212 William Easdall.

213 Henry Wickham archdeacon of York, Timothy Thurcros archdeacon of Cleveland, John Cosin archdeacon of the East Riding and William Robinson archdeacon of Nottingham.

accompt, have submitted themselves, and made good certificates of their practise of conformitie: And such of them, as refused conformitie, stand suspended.

And, as touching your Maiesties Declaration for setling questions in difference in point of Doctrine,[214] I have not this yeare found disobedience in any of my Dioces. And a watchfull eie is had, if any fly out, to call them presently to accompt for it.

Your Maiesties Directions touching Catechising is carefully observed throughout my Dioces, and, (as I humbly informed your Maiestie the last yeare) hath brought many of the Ministers to performe both catechising and preaching.

Your Maiesties Commandement concerning Lecturers, is carefully put in practise; and hath so prevayled, that many of the Clergie, that were heretofore forward for market-day Sermons in market Townes, finding how negligent the Inhabitants of those places were of coming to the Sermon, and that on the part of the Inhabitants, their preaching was more desired, to draw company to the market, then for the comfort of preaching; they withdraw themselves, and some of them are resolved, rather to imploy themselves hereafter in visiting some of their neighbour Churches, that want preaching Ministers, then to goe to the market Townes, where, oftentimes, some disorders happen, by occasion of eating and drinking, after the sermon. And to all such places, where such weekly sermons are permitted (which are but a very few throughout the Dioces) the Rule is peremptorily geven: Either observe His Maiesties Directions in every particular, or have no Sermon.

For some mens having Ministers in their houses, in the nature of Chaplaines, though they be not thereto qualified, I humbly yielded your Maiestie this reason the last yeare: That some Gentlemen, that have Impropriations, where no vicarage is endowed, but are to find a Curat at the parish Church, or Chappell, doe make the poore Ministers living in their houses, and having their diet with them, a part of the Ministers stipend and relife without which no Minister would be procured to serve such a Cure. But none such are permitted, but conformable men, and Curats allowed by the Ordinarie.

Myself, and all under me, to whom it apperteyneth, doe use our best endeavors to bring the people to the Divine Service in publick prayers, as well, as to the sermons: But through the Churchwardens negligence of doing their duties on that behalf, and daring to dispense with their othes, there is lesse done, then should be.[215] Recusants they doe present, not daring to doe otherwise, because they are publickly knowne. The number whereof I doe with griefe behold.

As touching your Maiesties Declaration to permit lawfull recreations on Sondays, and Holydaies,[216] after all the Divine Service duely frequented, and performed, I have found some reluctancy in a few of the Ministers: but yet, with this petition of some time to consider better of the businesse; and libertie to read my Lord of Elies booke lately written of that subject.[217] Upon reading wherof, they promise, either

---

[214] See above, p. 79 n. 4.

[215] This was a regular complaint by Neile: see above, p. 93, and below, p. 124.

[216] The Book of Sports of 1618, re-issued on 18 Oct. 1633, and ordered to be published 'by order from the bishops through all the parish churches of their severall diocesse respectively' (Fincham (ed.), *Visitation articles*, I, 149–51).

[217] White, *A treatise of the sabbath-day*. Among those required to read the book was the nonconformist Ezekiel Rogers: BI, CP H 2069; and see below, p. 141.

to conforme themselves to your Maiesties command of publishing it, or to submitt themselves to the Ecclesiasticall censure.

All the rest of your Maiesties Directions are carefully observed, as farr forth, as either they concerne me, or my subordinate Ministers: And (I am confident) they are alike observed by others, whom they concerne: vizt, the Deanes and Chapters, and Prebendaries of the Cathedrall and Collegiate Churches.

I crave leave to informe your Maiestie of one, or two other things, vizt,

That, putting in execution your Maiesties Commandment for survey of Churches, and Chancells, and procuring due reparations,[218] I have received Certificates, That, (besides, what I informed the last yeare, that way expended) there hath this yeare, been bestowed in repayring, and adorning of Churches in the Archdeaconrie of Yorke – £4000:[219] In the Archdeaconrie of the Eastriding – £1322 11s 7d. In the Archdeaconrie of Nottingham – £1240 4s. In all £6562 15s 7d besides what hath been expended in the Archdeaconrie of Cleveland, which, (I am informed) hath been a great summe, but have it not by particulars.

I also presume to informe your Maiestie; that, visiting the Collegiate Church of Southwell this yeare, I have taken order for the future maynteyning of the fabrick of the Church, the having a competent number of Vicars Choralls, and Lay-Singing men, and Choristers for the Quire Service there, with some increase of their Stipends.[220]

In the proceedings of the High Commission this yeare, at Yorke, and Southwell, we had sundry persons of base condition censured, some for incests, and others for incestuos mariages, whose punishment was imprisonment, and publick penance, both in Churches, and market places, (to the terror of others,) being otherwaies not hable to pay any fine.

I crave leave to present to your Sacred Maiestie the Certificate, which I have received from my Brethren, the Bishops, in their owne words, without altering, adding, or diminishing any thing.

The Certificate of John Lord Bishop of Chester[221] touching
the observation of His Maiesties pious Instructions,
within the Dioces of Chester for this last yeare, 1635.

1. For residence of the Bishops on their Seas: he hath observed it. For, he hath not been past one moneth out of his Dioces, these three yeares last past.

2. For residence on his Episcopall house. He hath resided there a great part of this yeare; and, some other part thereof resided at his house in Lancashire:[222] partly that he might the better attend his Maiesties service in the sequestration of Whalley

---

218 Namely the royal proclamation of 11 Oct. 1629: Larkin (ed.), *Stuart royal proclamations...1625–1646*, pp. 248–50. For Neile's campaign to restore and beautify churches, see above, p. 71.

219 In his report to Neile of 19 Dec. 1635, Henry Wickham anticipated the 'totall and complete repaire' of all churches and chapels in the archdeaconry of York by the end of the following year. BI, BP C+P XXVII.

220 These orders were incorporated into his injunctions for Southwell issued on 7 Nov. 1636, printed in Fincham (ed.), *Visitation articles*, II, 167–71.

221 John Bridgeman.

222 Namely Chester Palace and Wigan parsonage, an arrangement granted by Charles I and brokered by Bridgeman's patron Thomas Wentworth in 1630: TNA: PRO, SP 16/163/28; SRO, D1287/18/2 (P399/51).

tithes, being neer unto it: and partly because the infection of the small ports hath dangerously raigned in Chester, (and yet doth continue there,) Insomuch, as many have lyen sick thereof even at the gates into his house, so as he could not with safetie goe in. And, in that regard, he craveth libertie to discontinue thence for a while, till he may, without danger, bring his family thither.

3. For setling questions in difference. It is observed.

4. For the solemnity of Ordinations. It is observed accordingly.

5. Concerning Lecturers. They now generally conforme, and such, as have not, are expelled the Dioces, upon presentment brought against them.

6. For countenancing Orthodox Divines. He hath ever done it, unles they prove scandalous in conversation.

7. For Chaplains kept by men not qualified by law. He knoweth none.

8. For frequenting Divine Service. He hath done his best endeavor to see it *C.R. but whether is it performed*   performed.
or not

9. For making leases. It is, for his part, duly observed. And for felling of woods; he hath none to fell.

10. For making leases for 21tie yeares, and not for lives. He hath made no lease for lives, since he first received His Maiesties Letters in that behalf.[223]

11. Touching Benefices *in Commendam*, not to be passed over to others. It is performed accordingly.

12. For geving notice of any notable accident in the Church. It shalbe done, as occasion serves.

13. For certificate to the Metropolitane by the 10th of December. This will shew the performance.

The Certificate of Barnabas Lord Bishop of Carlile.

Most Reverend Father etc. I am now, according to His Maiesties Royall Command, to geve you an accompt of my care to observe those pious, and prudent Instructions, which, this yeare, I received from you. For my particular accompt wherof, I doe withall humilitie, present; as followeth,

1 and 2. To the first, and second. If I were minded to violate them, (which, God forbid) yet (indeed) I cannot. For, (I thanke God) I have neither land, nor lease, nor *Commendam*, not any Episcopall house, but one; where I must alwaies reside:[224] and am more carefull to preserve the woods there, then, if they were myne owne inheritance.

3. The Declaration, for setling all questions in difference, is (I dare say) as duly observed, as in any Dioces.

4. I use the best care, I can; that my Ordinations be solemne, both by examining myself all, that I suspect any waies unworthy, and putting back very many from Order of Priesthood, though the poore stipends of Curats force me, to admitt, but meane Scholars to be Deacons, rather then the people should be utterly without Divine Service.

---

[223] See above, p. 80 n. 8.
[224] Rose Castle near Carlisle.

5. Those foure Directions for Lecturers, I am carefull (as there is occasion) to observe in every point. But, having only three single Lecturers in all my Dioces, a little care will serve the turne.

6. I shall allwaies be willing to countenance and encourage all grave and Orthodox Divines, and may soone learne, how all behave themselves in their sermons; that, if there be cause, I may quickly reforme any disorder.

7. We have not (that I can learne) that keepe any chaplaines in their house, save one, or two; which geve a Minister his table, and some ten pounds a yeare to preach in their parish Church, where they have the tithes.

8. This Royall and religious Instruction is no where more needfull to be observed, then in these parts; wherein I have imployed my paines to the uttermost of my power. But, having no assistance herein from the Churchwardens, (who never present any, *C.R. This I take to his falce, for* for absence):[225] nor from the Justices, (who never *he should cale to the* punish any; I cannot yet effect so much as I *Churchwardens to doe ther* heartily desire, though (I thanke God) I have *deutie. He then hes less to doe.* done much good this way.

9. When His Maiestie shalbe pleased gratiously to looke upon me, and nominate me to another Bishoprick, I shalbe carefull to observe these so Religious and Royall Instructions.

10. I assure your Grace, I have never changed any lease from* lives to yeares; and ** this is miswritten.*[226] since I received His Maiesties Letters to that purpose,[227] I have reduced a lease of lives to yeares. I doe not heare, but that the Deane, and Chapter doe duly observe his Maiesties Commands in that matter: And for the Deane himself,[228] or Archdeacon,[229] or Prebendarie, none of these have any leases at all to lett, either for lives, or yeares.

11. This doth nothing att all concerne me. For, I have neither lease, nor Ecclesiasticall living, nor any other promotions, but my bare Bishoprick; for which I heartily blesse God, and his Gratious Maiestie.

12. We had no alteration, or accident, within this Dioces, which may concerne either Doctrine, or Discipline, but such as your Grace had notice of, sooner then myself.

13. I have been carefull in due time, and, before the day appointed, to geve this accompt. If it come too late, I pray, that the large distance of the place may plead my pardon. If it geve not your Grace content, be pleased to informe me, wherein I have fayled; and I shalbe most ready to reforme myself, and conforme to your godly commands. Thus, wishing etc,

Subscribed
Bar: Carlile.[230]

I have defferred the presenting of this Certificate to your Gratious Maiestie, longer then I should have done, in expectation of my Brethren, the Bishops of Durham,[231]

---

225 Neile often made much the same point: see above, pp. 93, 106, and below, p. 124.
226 Note by Neile.
227 See above, p. 80 n. 8.
228 Thomas Comber (1575–1654), for whom see his entry in *ODNB*.
229 Isaac Singleton, archdeacon of Carlisle 1623–43.
230 Barnabas Potter.
231 Thomas Morton.

C.R. I lyke your diligence, but and the Isle of Man,[232] their certificates; which I
they must bee checked for there have not received: rather adventuring, to take the
slakness. blame upon myself, then that I would seeme to
informe of their negligence.

God of His infinite mercie blesse your Sacred Maiestie withall heavenly, spirituall, and temporall blessings in this life; and reward you with eternall faelicitie for your exceeding great mercie extended to me, my wife, and my sonne in our extreame calamitie; whereby, your Royall goodnes hath delivered us from more then the feare of death: So great was our affliction, till your Sacred Maiesties aboundant mercie, and Royall Pardon releeved us.[233] And therefore, (according to our bounden duty) we pray

O Lord, graunt the King a long life, that his yeares may endure throughout all
generations.

He shall dwell before God for ever: O, prepare the loving mercie, and faithfullnes,
that they may preserve him. Psalm 61: 6.7.

Canterbury province, 1636

May it please your most Sacred Majesty.[234]

According to your Royall Commandes expressed in your late Instructions, for the Good of the Church, I doe here most humbly present my yearly Accompt for my Diocesse, and Province of Canterbury, for this last yeare ending at Christmas 1636.

Canterbury. And first for my owne Diocess, I have every yeare acquainted your Majesty[235] and soe must doe now, that there are still about Ashford and Egerton, divers Brownists and other Separatistes. But they are soe very meane and poore People, that we knowe not what to doe with them. They are said to be the Disciples of one Turner[236] and Fennar[237] who were longe since apprehended, and imprisoned by order of your Majestys High Commission Court. But how this Part came to be soe infected with such a Humour of Separation I know not, unless it were by too much connivance at theyr first beginninge. Neyther doe I see any remedye like
C.R. Informe mee of the particulars to be, unless some of theyr cheife Seducers be
and I shall command the Judges dryven to abjure the Kingdome, which must be
to make them abjure[238] done by the Judges at the Common Lawe, but
is not in our power.[239]

I have receyved Information from my Officers that the Walloon's, and other Strangers in my Diocess, especially at Canterbury, doe come orderly to theyr Parish

---

[232] Richard Parr, bishop of Sodor and Man 1635–44.
[233] On 11 Jan. 1636 Neile's son Paul was pardoned for the manslaughter of Thomas Howton: *CSPD 1635–6*, p. 155.
[234] LPL, MS 943, pp. 267–72, endorsed 'The Accompt of my Province of Canterburye for the yeare 1636 presented to his Majesty January Anno predict' and, in a different hand, 'Apostilled with the King's owne hand etc' (p. 274); LPL, Laud's Register I, fos. 254r–256r.
[235] See above, pp. 95, 101.
[236] See above, p. 101 n. 168.
[237] John Fenner of Egerton. For his views, see Acheson, *Radical puritans*, pp. 91–5.
[238] The matter was raised in the privy council on 21 and 25 Jan. 1637: *CSPD 1636–7*, p. 341.
[239] See below, p. 142.

Churches, and there receyve the Sacraments, and Marrye, etc, according to my Injunctions with that limitation which your Majesty allowed.[240]

There have been heretofore many in Canterbury that were not conformable to Church Discipline, and would not kneele at the Communion, but they are all now very conformable, as I heare expresly by my Officers. And that there is noe falling away of any to Recusancye.

There hath been a Custome that some Ministers thereabouts, have under diverse pretences lyved for the most part at Canterbury, and gone seldome to theyr Benefices, which hath given a double Scandall, both by theyr absence from theyr severall Cures, and by keeping too much Companye, and that not in the best manner. I have seen this remedyed in all save onely one Man, and if he doe not presently conforme, I have taken order for his Suspension.

London.   In the Diocess of London I finde that my Lord the Bishop there (now by your Majestys grace and favour Lord High Treasurer of England)[241] hath very carefully observed those Instructions which belonge to his owne Person. And for the Diocess his Lordship informes me of three great misdemeanours. The one committed by Dr Cornelius Burges, who in a Latyn Sermon before the Clergye of London, uttered diverse insolent Passages against the Bishop's and Goverment of the Church, and refused to give his Lordship a Copye of the Sermon. Soe there was a necessity of calling him into the High Commission Court, which is done.[242]

The 2d misdemeanour is one Mr Wharton a Minister in Essex, who in a Sermon at Chelmesford, uttered many unfitt, and some scurrilous thinges. But for this he hath been convented, and receyved a Canonicall Admonition. And upon his Sorrowe and Submission any farther Censure is forborne.[243]

The 3d misdemeanour which my Lord complaine's of is, the late Spreading and dispersing of some factious and malitious Pamphlets against the Bishoppes and Goverment of the Church of England.[244] And my Lord farther certifyes that he hath reasonable ground to perswade him, that those libellous Pamphlets have been contrived, or abetted, and dispersed by some of the Clergye of his Diocesse, and therfore desire's me to use the authority of the High Commission for the further discovery of this notorious Practise, to prevent the Mischeifs which will otherwise ensue upon the Goverment of the Church. This God willing I shall see performed. But if the High Commission shall not have power enough, because one of those Libells conteyne's seditious matter in it, and that which is very little short of Treason (if any thinge at all) then I humbly crave leave to add this to my Lord Treasurers

C.R. What the High Commission   motion, and humbly to desire that your Majesty
cannot doe, in this I shall supplie,   will call it into a Higher Court, if you finde
as I shall fynde Cause, in a   cause, since I see noe likelyhood but that these

---

240   Namely, that non-natives and strangers could retain their own discipline. See TNA: PRO, SP 16/286/85.I.

241   William Juxon was appointed lord treasurer in Mar. 1636.

242   *CSPD 1635–6*, pp. 472, 479, 487, 497. Burges later recalled that in his sermon, preached at St Alphage London Wall, he had urged the episcopate to be more active preachers: C. Burges, *A case concerning the buying of bishops lands* (1659), p. 28.

243   Samuel Wharton, vicar of Felsted. For his career in the 1630s, see Webster, *Godly clergy*, pp. 33–4, 88, 201, 236, 241, 260.

244   Among them were Henry Burton's *A divine tragedie lately acted* (1636); *A looking-glasse for all lordly prelates* (1636) and *Newes from Ipswich* (1636), both anonymous works by William Prynne; and copies of John Bastwick's *The letany*, then circulating in manuscript.

more powerfooll way[245]   troubles in the Church, it they be permitted, will breake out into some Sedition in the Common wealth.

My Visitation is yet depending for this Diocess, and by reason of the Sicknes I could not with safety hold it, nor thinke it fitt to gather soe much people together but God willing I shall performe that Dutye, soe soone as conveniently I may, and then certify your Majesty at the next returne what shall come under myne owne viewe.[246]

Winchester.   In this Diocesse I finde by my Lords[247] reporte from his Officers that there are diverse Recusants in severall partes of the Country, and that some of them have been seduced away from the Church of England with in these two or three years.

For all thinges else I receyve noe Complaint thence, save onely of three or fowre Ministers that are negligent in Catechizinge, and observe it not at all, or but in the Lent onely. But I shall call upon the Bishop to see this remedyed, and to be as vigilant as he can against any farther increase of Recusants.

Bath and Welles. From Bath and Wells[248] I have receyved a very good and happye Certificat. Both that all your Majestys Instructions have been exactly performed throughout that whole Diocess. And that by Gods blessinge, and the well ordering of Church affayres there have been fewer Popish Recusants presented, then formerly, and that the Number of them is much decreased. And this I cannot but highly approve to your Majesty, if there be not fewer presented, eyther by the overawinge of them which should present, or some cunninge in those which would not be presented.

Norwich.   For this Diocesse my Lord[249] hath given me in a very carefull and punctuall Accompt, very large, and in all Particulars very considerable.[250] And I shall returne it to your Majesty as breifly as I can reduce it. And first he hath for this Summer, but by your Majestys leave lyved (from both his Episcopall Houses) in Ipswich, partly because he was informed, that that side of his Diocess did most need his presence, and he found it soe; And partly because his Chappell at his House in Norwich was possessed by the French Congregation, and soe the Bishop left destitute, but he has given them warninge, to provide themselves elswhere by Easter next.[251]

His Lord founde a generall defect of Catechizinge quite through the Dioces but hath setled it. And in Norwich where there are 34 Churches, there was noe Sermon on the Sunday morning, save onely in 4 but all put of to the afternoone, and soe noe Catechizinge. But now he hath ordered that there shall be a Sermon every morning, and Catechizing in the afternoone in every Church.[252]

---

[245] This request by Laud resulted in the cases against John Bastwick, Henry Burton and William Prynne being transferred to Star Chamber, where they were convicted of seditious libel in June 1637.

[246] LPL, Laud's Register I, fos. 158r–171v. Laud's visitation eventually began in Feb. 1637, but he failed to report on it in his account for 1637. See below, p. 126.

[247] Walter Curle.

[248] William Piers was the bishop.

[249] Matthew Wren, bishop of Norwich 1635–8.

[250] Wren's detailed report to Laud ran to three and half pages: TNA: PRO, SP 16/337/19, partially printed in W. Prynne, *Canterburies doome* (1646), pp. 374–6.

[251] In his report Wren supplied a third reason: 'because, the executrix of the precedent Bishop having not compounded for dilapidations, the Episcopall houses were not then in a readines' (TNA: PRO, SP 16/337/19).

[252] TNA: PRO, SP 16/316/8; Fincham (ed.), *Visitation articles*, II, 159–60.

For Lectures, they abounded in Suffolke, and many sett up by Privat Gentlemen, even without soe much as the knowledge of the Ordinary, and without any due observation to the Canons, or the Discipline of the Church. Diverse of these his Lordship hath carefully regulated according to order, and especially in St Edmondsbury,[253] and with theyr very good content, and suspended noe Lecturer of whom he might obteyne Conformity. And at Ipswich it was not unknowne unto them, that now Mr Warde standes censured in the High Commission,[254] and obeye's not, yet the Bishop was ready to have allowed them another if they would have sought him, but they resolve to have Mr Warde or none, and that (as is conceyved) in despite of the censure of the Court.

At Yarmouth where there was great Division heretofore for many yeares, theyr Lecturer being censured in the High Commission, about two years since, went into New England,[255] since which tyme there hath been noe Lecture, and very much peace in the Towne, and all Ecclesiasticall Orders well observed. But in Norwich one *C.R. Lett him goe wee ar*   Mr Bridge rather then he would conforme, hath *well ridd of him*   left his Lecture, and two Cures, and is gone into Holland.[256] The Lecturers in the Country generally observinge noe Church orders at all. And yet the Bishop hath carried it with that temper, and upon theyr promise and his hopes of Conformity, that he hath inhibited but three in Norfolke, and as many in Suffolke,[257] of which one is noe Graduate, and hath been a Common Stage-Player.[258]

His Lordship humbly crave's direction what he shall doe with such Schollers (some in Holy orders and some not) as Knights and private Gentlemen keepe in theyr Houses, under pretense to teach theyr Children. As alsoe with some Divynes that are Beneficed in Townes, or neare, but lyve in Gentlemens Houses. For my part I thinke *C.R. I approve your judgement in*   it very fitt the Beneficed men were presently *this. I onlie add that care must*   commanded to reside upon theyr Cures. And for *bee taken, that even those*   the rest your Majestys Instructions allowe none *qualified by Law, keepe none,*   to keepe Chaplaines but such as are qualifyed by *but conformeable men.*   Lawe. All which notwithstanding I most humbly submitt (as the Bishop doth) to your Majestys Judgement.

For Recusants, whereas formerly there were wont to be but two or three presented, his Lordship hath caused above fortye to be Endicted in Norwich at the last Sessions. And at the Assizes in Suffolk he delyvered a List of such as were presented upon

---

253 Wren's account is especially full here. See TNA: PRO, SP 16/337/19, printed in Prynne, *Canterburies doome*, pp. 374–5.

254 See above, p. 103.

255 In Feb. 1635 George Burdett was removed from his lectureship by High Commission for 'scandalous, blasphemous, erroneous, heretical and schismatical opinions', and thereafter emigrated to Massachusetts. *CSPD 1634–5*, pp. 537–9; and above, p. 103.

256 Wren's report here adds more detail: 'At Norwich one Lecture is still held by Mr Cock an honest conformable man of whom they make no great regard. Other two have voluntarily relinquished, because they will observe no order, wherof one (Mr Bridge) hath left two Cures and is runne into Holland' (TNA: PRO, SP 16/337/19). For Bridge, see above, p. 98; and M. Reynolds, *Godly reformers and their opponents in early modern England* (Woodbridge, 2005), pp. 191–2.

257 At Diss, New Buckenham and North Walsham in Norfolk, and at Ixworth, Cockfield and 'Wickham' (presumably Wickham Market) in Suffolk (TNA: PRO, SP 16/337/19).

258 At Wickham.

the oath of the Churchwardens, to the Lord Cheife Justice,[259] and his Lordship to the Grand Jury, but they slighted it, pretending the Bishops Certificat to be noe

C.R. Bishops certificates in this Evidence. But the true reason is conceyved to *Case must bee most* be, because he had alsoe inserted such as had *unquaestionable Evidence* been presented to him for Recusant Separatists, as well as Recusant Romanistes.

His Lordships care hath been such, as that though there are about 1500 Clergy men in that Diocesse and many Disorders, yet there are not thirty Excommunicated or suspended, whereof some are for contumacye, and will not yet submitt. Some for obstinate denyall to publish your Majestys Declaration.[260] And some for contemning all the orders and rites of the Church, and intruding themselves without Lycense from the Ordinary for many yeares together.

Last of all he founde that one halfe of the Churches in his Diocesse had not a Clerke able to read and answere the Minister in Divine Service, by which meanes the People were wholly disused from joyning with the Preist, and in many Places from soe much as saying Amen. But concerning this his Lordship hath strictly enjoyned a Reformation.[261]

If this Accompt given by my Lord of Norwich be true, as I beleyve it is (and ought to beleyve it till it can be disproved) he hath deserved very well of the Church of England, and hath been very ill rewarded for it. His humble Suite to your Majesty is that you will be graciously pleased in your owne good tyme to heare the Complaintes

C.R. His sute is granted and that have been made against him <u>that he may</u> *assuredlie his negative* <u>not be overborne by the Outcrye for doing</u> *consequence shall follow* <u>Service.</u>[262]

Oxford.   In the Diocesse of Oxford[263] I finde all your Majestys Instructions carefully obeyed, and there is but one Lecture in the whole Diocesse, and that is read at Henly upon Thames by some Ministers of the Diocesse, Conformable men, and allowed by the Bishop.

His Lordship hath alsoe called upon diverse Recusants, but upon theyr being *C.R. If this bee not, upon* questioned, they plead an Exemption from his *Composition, I understand it not* authority under your Majestys Greate Seale.

Elye.   From my Lord of Elye[264] I have receyved a very fayre Accompt, that his Diocesse is very orderly and obedyent, insomuch that he hath not any thinge of note to acquaint me with.

[259] Sir John Bramston.

[260] The Book of Sports. In his report, Wren stated that he found on visitation that the book had not been read 'in very many places of the diocese' and, having sixty copies to hand, distributed them 'to such persons, as I had most doubt of' and subsequently prosecuted those who refused to comply. TNA: PRO, SP 16/337/19; see also Bodl., Tanner MS 314, fos. 141r–146v.

[261] See Fincham (ed.), *Visitation articles*, II, 157–8.

[262] Underlined by Charles I. Laud toned down Wren's vivid phraseology: 'I may not be for ever overborne with those their false and scandalous clamours, which now do ring all the Land over' (TNA: PRO, SP 16/337/19), probably a reference, in part, to William Prynne's pamphlet, *Newes from Ipswich* (1636), which denounced him as 'little Pope Regulus'; see below, p. 116. Petitions against Wren had been submitted from Norwich and Ipswich: Bodl., Tanner MSS 68, fos. 160r–161r, 70, fo. 103v; Reynolds, *Godly reformers*, pp. 194–8.

[263] The bishop was John Bancroft.

[264] Francis White.

Lincolne.   My Lord[265] in his Certificat[266] mentions two Particulars fitt for your Majestys knowledge. The first is, that one of his Clergye in Bedfordshire, a learned and pious man (as he saith) sett up a Stone upon Pillars of Bricke for his Communion Table, beleyving it to have been the Altar stone. And because this appeared to be but a Grave stone, and for avoyding of further rumours in that Countrye amonge the preciser sorte his Lordship caused it to be quietly removed,

C.R. This may prove a boulde part in the Bishope and the poore Prist in no falte; as, the other day, his information proved concerninge the Ship business at the Council board therefore examine this further

and the ancyent Communion Table placed in the roome of it. But did not farther questione the Partye, because he found him a harmeless man, and otherwise a Deserver.[267] But how deserving soever he be, I must judge it a very bold part in him to attempt this without the Knowledge and approbation of his Ordinary.

The second is that there are risen some Differences in the Southerne partes of his Diocesse, about the Ministers urging the People to receyve at the Railes, which his Lordship saith he hath procured to be placed about the Holy Table,[268] and the People in some Places refusing soe to doe. Now because this is not regulated by any Canon of the Church, his Lordship is an humble Suitor that he may have direction herein. And truly I thinke for this Particular the People will best be wonne by the decency of the thinge it selfe, and that I suppose may be compassed in a short tyme.[269] But if

C.R. Try your way for some tyme

your Majesty shall thinke it fit that a quicker waye be held, I shall humbly submitt.

Salisbury.   From the Lord Bishop[270] of this Diocesse I have receyved noe Particular, but in generall thus. That all your Majestys Instructions are now observed there without repugnance, for ought eyther Chancellour[271] or any other Officer of his hath informed him.

Worcester.   My Lord the Bishop[272] of this Sea certifyes that your Majestys Instructions are carefully observed. And that there are onely two Lecturers in the Citty of Worcester, both very Conformable, and that they shall noe longer continue then they are soe.[273] And that the one of them preache's on Sundayes in the afternoones, after Catechizinge and Service in the Parish Churches, and ending before Evening Prayers in the Cathedrall.

I may not here forbeare to acquaint your Majesty that this Sunday Lecture was ever wont to be in the Cathedrall, and that it is removed because the Citty would suffer noe Prebendary to have it. And Evening Prayers in theyr Parish Churches must needs beginne betymes, and theyr Catechizing be short, and the Prayers at the Cathedrall beginne very late, if this Lecture cann beginne and end in the

---

265 John Williams.
266 See Laud, *Works*, VI, 476–9, for the report and Laud's initial response to it.
267 The clergyman was Jasper Fisher, rector of Wilden. For the incident, see Fincham and Tyacke, *Altars restored*, pp. 254–5.
268 Fincham (ed.), *Visitation articles*, II, 127.
269 For Laud's approach to the issue of reception at the rails, see Fincham and Tyacke, *Altars restored*, pp. 211–13.
270 John Davenant.
271 Marmaduke Lynne.
272 John Thornborough.
273 See Davies, *Caroline captivity*, p. 165.

Space betweene. But if it can be soe fitted I thinke the Deane and Chapter will not complaine of the remove of the Lecture to a Parish Church.[274]

Exeter.   For these three Dioceses my Lords the Bishopps[275] certifye that all
Chichester.   your Majestys Instructions are carefully observed. Neyther doe any of
Peterburgh.   them mention any thinge amisse in the generall eyther for Doctrine or
              Discipline. Onely the Bishop of Exeter hath sent me up two Copyes of the late Libell intituled *News from Ipswich*,[276] which were sent thither to a Stationer with blanke Covers.

Hereford.   These five Diocesses following I have visited this yeare by my Vicar
              generall and other Commissioners.[277] And for Hereford I finde not many thinges amiss, though the often change of the Bishop there which hath of late hapned, hath done noe good amonge them.[278] But some pretensions there are to certaine Customes, which I conceyve were better broke then kept, and I shall doe my best to

C.R. Which ye shall not want   reforme them as I have opportunity, and humbly
if you need   begg your Majestys assistance if I want power.

St Davids.   For St Davids the Bishop[279] is now there, and will take the best care he
              can to see all thinges in order. But there is one Matthews the Vicar of Penmayne, that preaches against the keeping of all Holy dayes, with diverse other as fonde or prophane opinions. The Bishop hath inhibited him, and if that doe not serve, I shall call him into the High Commission Court.

Baronet Rudde is in this Diocesse, the Sonne of a late Bishop there,[280] who is a sober Gentleman. He hath built him a Chappell, and desires the Bishop to Consecrate it. But his Lordship finding one of your Majestys Instructions to be, That none shall keep a Chaplaine in his house, but such as are qualifyed by Lawe, which he

C.R. Since he hath beene at the   conceyve's a Baronet is not, hath hitherto
charge and hath so good   forborne to consecrate this Chappell, as being to
testimonie, lett him have this   be of small use without a Chaplaine, and humbly
desyer with those restrictions   craves direction here in what he shall doe. I
mentioned   humbly propose to your Majesty whether considering the Charge this Gentleman hath been at, and the ill wayes which many of them there have to Church, it may not be fitt to Consecrate this Chappell, and then that he may have a License to use the Minister of the Parish, or any other lawfully in Orders. Always provided, that he use this Chappell but at tymes of some necessity, not making himself or his Family strangers to the mother Church, and that there be a Clause expressed in the License for recalling thereof upon any abuse there committed. And that this License be taken eyther from the Bishop under his Seale, or from the Archbishop of the Province.

---

274   For subsequent developments, see TNA: PRO, SP 16/343/77, 344/107; *CSPD 1636–7*, pp. 496–7.

275   Joseph Hall of Exeter, Richard Montagu of Chichester and Francis Dee of Peterborough.

276   Written by William Prynne and published anonymously as *Newes from Ipswich. Discovering certaine late detestable practises of some domineering lordly prelates* (1636).

277   LPL, Laud's Register I, fos. 171v–175r, 177r–181r.

278   After Bishop Godwin's death in 1633, William Juxon was elected to succeed him but instead was appointed to London, and was followed at Hereford by Augustine Lindsell (1634), Matthew Wren (1635), Theophilus Field (1635–6) and George Coke (1636–46).

279   Roger Mainwaring, bishop of St David's 1636–53.

280   Sir Richard Rudd, first baronet, of Aberglasney, son of Anthony Rudd, bishop of St David's 1594–1615. See G. E. C(ockayne), *Complete baronetage* (6 vols., London, 1983), II, 64.

Landaffe.   For Landaff there is very little found amisse. Onely the Bishop[281] complaine's that wheras Mr Wroth and Mr Erbury[282] are in the High Commission for theyr Schismaticall proceedings, the slowe prosecution there against them, make's both of them persist in theyr by-wayes, and theyr Followers judge them faultles. But for this, I humbly present to your Majesty this Answere, that now the losse of two Termes by reason of the Sicknes hath cast the proceedings of that Court as well as of others behinde hande, and there is noe remedye, where all thinges else staye as well as it.

St Asaph.   In the Diocesse of St Asaph[283] there is noe Complaint but the usuall, that there is great resorte of Recusants to Holywell. And that this Summer Lady Falkland and her Company came as Pilgrims thither, who were the more observed, because they travayled on foote, and dissembled neyther theyr quality nor theyr Errand. And this boldnes of theyrs is of very ill Construction amonge your Majestys People. My humble Suite to your Majesty is, that whereas I complayned of this in open Counsell in your Majestys presence, you would now be graciously pleasd, *C.R. It is don*   that the Order then resolved on for her Confinement may be put in Execution.[284]

Bangor.   For Bangor, I finde that Catechizinge was quite out of use in those remote Partes (the more the Pittye) but the Bishop[285] is now in hope to doe much good, and sees some Reformation in that Particular allready. And I would saye for this, and the other Diocesses in Wales, that much more good might be done there in a Church waye, if they were not overborne by the Proceedings of the Court of the Marches there. And this present yeare in this Diocesse of Bangor my Commissioners for my Metropoliticall Visitation there complaine unto me, that the power which belonges to my Place hath been in them very much wronged and *C.R. I doubt not, but by the*   impeached by that Court. And I doe most *grace of God to agree thease*   humbly beseech your Majesty in your owne *differenses by my hearing*   good tyme to give this my Cause a hearing, if it *of them*   take not a fayre end without that trouble.[286]

Rochester.   For Rochester the Bishop (god comfort him) is very ill of a Palsye,[287]
Glocester.   and that I feare hath made him forgett his Accompt. Neyther hath the
Bristoll.   Bishop of Glocester[288] sent me any, but why I knowe not. And for Bristoll that Sea is voyde.[289]

Coventry and For this Diocesse I have likewise receyved noe Accompt. But I feare
Lichfield.   that whereas the Bishop was lately complained of to your Majesty for making wast of the poore woodes there remaininge, he is not overwilling to give an Accompt of that Particular. Nor of the grosse abuse committed

---

281 William Murray.
282 For Wroth and Erbury, see above pp. 99, 104 and below p. 134.
283 The bishop was John Owen.
284 Elizabeth Cary, Viscountess Falkland (1585–1639); see her entry in *ODNB* and *CSPD 1636–7*, p. 341.
285 Edmund Griffith.
286 See P. Williams, 'The attack on the Council in the Marches, 1603–1642', *Transactions of the Honourable Society of Cymmrodorion*, I (1961), 16–17; Laud, *Works*, IV, 134, VI, 490–1.
287 John Bowle, who died later that year.
288 Godfrey Goodman.
289 George Coke was translated to Hereford on 2 July 1636, and Robert Skinner was not consecrated bishop of Bristol until 15 Jan. 1637.

in the Cathedrall Church by the Lady Davis who I most humbly beseech your Majesty may be soe restrained, as that she may have noe more power to committ such horrible Prophanations.[290]

And soe I most humbly submitt this, my yearly Accompt of my Province of Canterbury to your Majestys Princely wisdome.

W: Cant:[291]

C.R. For the Bishops of Glocester, and Coventry and Lichfield I must know why they have not made ther account. CR
Whythall the 21 of February 1637[292]

York province, 1636

To the Kings Most Excellent Maiestie.[293]
I humbly present to your Sacred Maiestie this Certificate of the due observation of your Maiesties pious directions, and Instructions geven in charge to us, your Bishops of the Province of Yorke. And, though the Certificates of my Brethren, the Bishops of this Province, differ little from their Certificates of former yeares, yet, I crave leave to relate them in their owne words, as they have tendred them to me, to be exhibited to your Most Gratious Maiestie.

The Bishop of Man's Certificate touching His Maiesties Royall
Instructions for the yeare 1636.
1. To the first, touching residence; he saith: That he kept his residence at his poore See, all the summer season; but the extreame coldnes of the country, and the house, (being yet very ruinous) constrayned him to retire into England[294] for the winter season, and no longer.
3. To the third, touching setling of questions in difference; he saith: That the Ministers trouble not their heads with any such matters; the most of them being of no better abilities, then to read distinctly Divine Service.
4. To the fourthe, touching Ordinations; he saith; That necessitie will enforce him to ordeyne, or lay hands on men of meane parts; because the Island is destitute of meanes for good, and learned education; And the Natives, (understanding no other language, then their owne) are not (indeed) capeable of better Service, then such as the Country affordeth.
5. To the fifth, touching Catechising; he saith: That he caused that ancient, and profitable Exercise to be sett up in all the Churches, and warned every Minister upon payne of suspension to be diligent in the same. And, because many of them cannot preach, he caused the Bookes of Homilies to be brought into the Island, and enjoyned every Parish to buy them, for the Parish use, and strictly charged the Ministers to read them every Sunday.

---

[290] Lady Eleanor Davies (1590–1652) was committed to Bethlem hospital. See her entry in *ODNB*.
[291] William Laud.
[292] New style.
[293] TNA: PRO, SP 16/345/85.I, enclosed with a letter from Archbishop Neile to Secretary of State Francis Windebank (1582–1646), dated Jan. 1637 new style (16/345/85). This account has no royal marginalia, and may not have reached the king.
[294] No doubt to his rectory of Eccleston, Lancashire.

6. To the sixth, touching Lectures and Lecturers: he saith: That there are no weekely Lectures in the Island: And for the Ministers conformitie, They are all very obedient to the discipline of the Church, without scruple, or exception against any Ceremonie. 12. To the 12th, touching alteration, or other accident; he saith: That upon St John Baptist day last,[295] he found the people in a Chappell dedicated to that Saint, in the practise of grosse superstitions (too tedious to relate,) which superstitions he caused to be cryed downe, with consent of all the temporall Magistrates, and, in place of them, appoynted Divine Service and Sermons.

For the rest of his Maiesties Royall Injunctions, there is no breach, either in the generall, or in any particular branch of them, to his knowledge.

Ri: Sodor: and Man:[296]

The Certificate of the Bishop of Carlile.[297]

Most Reverend Father in God,[298] I am now, according to his Maiesties Royall Command, and your Graces direction, to geve your Grace an accompt of my care to observe those pious, and prudent Instructions, which I received from your Grace. Where, though in the generall I can justifie my self, that I have not fayled to the utmost of my power to fulfill them all, yet (perhaps) your Grace may expect from me a particular accompt of my carriage in this case. I doe heere with all humilitie present these to your gratious acceptance.

1, 2. To the first and second: If I were minded to violate them, (which God forbid, yet) indeed I cannot. For (I thanke God) I have neither lands, nor lease, nor any *Commendam*, nor any Episcopall house, but one, where I must alwaies reside,[299] and am more carefull to preserve the woods there, then if they were mine owne inheritance.

3. The Declaration, for setling of questions in difference, is (I dare say) as duely observed, as in any dioces.

4. I use the best care I can, that mine Ordinations be solemne, both, by examining myself all that I suspect any wayes unworthy; and putting very many from the Order of Priesthood, though the poore Stipends for Curates, force me to admitt but meane Scholars to be Deacons, rather then the people should be utterly without Divine Service.

5. These four directions for Lecturers, I am carefull, (as there is occasion) to observe in every poynt. But, having only three single Lecturers in all my Dioces, a little care will serve the turne.

6. I shall alwaies be willing to countenance, and, encourage all grave and orthodox Divines, and may soone learne, how all behave themselves in their Sermons; that, if there be cause, I may quickly reforme any disorder.

7. We have none, that I can learne, that keepes any Chaplaine in their house, save one, or two, which geve a Minister his table, and some ten pounds a yeare to preach in their Church, where they have the tithes.

---

[295] 24 June 1636.
[296] Richard Parr.
[297] Barnabas Potter's certificate is virtually identical to that submitted in 1635, but for the final sentence about repair of churches.
[298] Richard Neile.
[299] Rose Castle.

8. This Royall and Religious Instruction is no where more needful to be observed, then in these parts, where I have imployed my paines to the uttermost of my power: but, having no assistance from the churchwardens, (who never present any for absence,) nor from the Justices (who never punish any) I cannot yet effect so much, as I heartily desire, though (I thanke God) I have done much good this way.

9. When His Maiestie shalbe pleased gratiously to looke upon me, and nominate me to another Bishoprick, I shalbe carefull to observe these so religious and Royall Instructions.

10. I assure your Grace, I never changed any lease from yeares to lives. And, since I received His Maiesties letters to that purpose,[300] I have reduced a lease for lives to yeares. I doe not heare, but that, that the Deane and Chapter doe duely observe his Maiesties Command, in that matter; and for the Deane himself,[301] or Archdeacon,[302] or Prebendarie, none of these have any leases to lett, either for lives or yeares.

11. This doth nothing concerne me at all. For I have neither lease, nor ecclesiasticall Living, nor any other promotion, but my bare Bishoprick, for which I heartily blesse God, and his Gratious Maiestie.

12. We have had no alteration, or accident within this Dioces, which may concerne, either Doctrine, or Discipline; but such as your Grace had notice of, sooner then myself.

13. I have been carefull in due time, and before the day appoynted, to geve this accompt. If it come too late, I pray that the large distance of place may plead my pardon. If it geve not your Grace content, be pleased to informe wherein I have fayled; and I shalbe most ready to reforme my self, and conforme myself to your godly commaunds.

By your godly care we have gotten all our Churches (almost) newly seated, and made very fine, and uniforme.[303]

Bar: Carlile[304]

The Bishop of Chesters Certificate.

There is nothing in my Dioces (to my knowledge) which hath happened worth the writing, this yeare: So as, (I conceive your Grace will not expect any farther Certificate to those Instructions, which you lately sent from His Maiestie for Bishops residency, Ordinations, Lectures and leases etc.[305] And though I have nothing more to write, then my last yeares Certificate did impart, if you hold it needfull, I shall obey your will.

And, in a letter of his, it is thus,

In your Metropoliticall Visitation, you began an excellent worke, namely to repayre, and uniforme the Churches of your Province: in pursuance whereof I have ever since laboured to see that perfected, which was then begun, and have brought most of the

---

300 See above, p. 80 n. 8.
301 See above, p. 109 n. 228.
302 See above, p. 109 n. 229.
303 A reference to Neile's metropolitical visitation of Carlisle diocese in 1633 where, as in Chester diocese, his officials ordered the refurbishment of churches. See above, p. 71; Fincham and Tyacke, *Altars restored*, p. 238.
304 Barnabas Potter.
305 A reference to the expanded set of royal instructions, issued on 19 Jan. 1635: see above, pp. 80–1.

Churches in my Dioces to uniformitie, and decencie; wherein the Laitie have most cheerfully bestowed many thousand pounds; and the very shire of Cheshire hath by computation impended some foure or five thousand poundes.[306]

Jo: Cestrien:[307]

The Certificate of the Bishop of Durham.

To the Instructions of his Sacred Maiestie lately geven to the Most Reverend Father in God, Richard, Lord Archbishop of Yorke, his Grace for the Province of Yorke, The accompt of Thomas, Lord Bishop of Durham for this present yeare of our Lord God 1636.

1. For Episcopall residence. I have both duely and dutifully observed it, according to His Maiesties Injunction on my part.

2. This hath been likewise carefully observed, as concerning any waste of woods done in my time; And, as for Land, or Leases, I have none whereon to reside.

3. This hath been putt in practise in my Episcopall Visitation, and in other meetings of the Clergie of this Dioces.

4. This hath been by me reasonably well observed, as I hope.

5. Concerning Lecturers in foure particulars, vizt

    1.   Is duely practised, where the Lecture is read in the Citty of Durham; and so in other places of this Dioces, for any thing that hath come to my knowledge to the contrary.

    2.   Is not ordinarily observed in this Northern Dioces.

    3.   We can hardly procure a sufficient number of competent Ministers to preach a Lecture in our market Townes, by reason of the paucitie of able Ministers. And I know, but one Lecturer in my Dioces, who hath preached in a cloke, which is, because, as yet, his trunke is not come downe from London, as he alleadgeth.

    4.   I know no Lecturer in this Dioces, who would not willingly accept of a Living, with cure of soules, if it shalbe procured for him.

6. There is no Divine, carrying himself discreetly, and moderately, but he receiveth encouragement in his vocation, and so farr as orthodox, by me fully approved.

7. I doe not know, or heare of any persons, by Law not qualified, who is desirous to keepe any Chaplaines in their houses within this Dioces.

8. I have had that care to my power to see Divine Service frequented, as well for prayers, as for catechising: But to bring in Recusants, or their children to catechising (for ought I can learne) is beyond my power.

9. It hath been duely performed on my part.

10. This hath been also strictly observed in my owne particular; nor can I learne, that the Deane, and Chapter of Durham, or any Archdeacon or Prebendary hath transgressed herein.

11. There is no such lease, Benefices, or *Commendam* belonging or used with this Bishoprick.

12. No alteration in doctrine, or discipline hath come to my notice within this Dioces: Only there is one Mr Vincent, who is unconformable in divers degrees,

---

[306] See above, p. 71; Fincham and Tyacke, *Altars restored*, pp. 191, 200, 238.
[307] John Bridgeman.

and is therefore to depart out of this Dioces, so soone as the weather shall become seasonable.[308]

Tho: Duresme.[309]

It now remayneth that I geve your Sacred Maiestie an accompt of mine owne Dioces,[310] which humbly I thus doe,

Ad 1 and 2. I have this yeare (during the time of my being from London) resided at my Episcopall houses of Southwell in Nottinghamshire, and Bishops Thorpe neer Yorke: where I carefully endeavour to doe your Maiestie, and Gods Church, the best service that I can. These two houses at my first coming to them, I found very ruinous; and have been at a great charge in repayring of them, and accommodating of them to more convenient use.[311]

Ad 3. I humbly informe your Gratious Maiestie; That, having this yeare visited the Dioces,[312] I find not in the Clergies preachings any distractions of opinions touching points of Divinitie lately controverted, concerning which your Maiestie published your judicious Directions, and pious Princely Resolution for the peace of this your Church.

Ad 4. I humbly informe your Gratious Maiestie, That I am so carefull nothing may be amisse in my Ordinations, that (in a sort) I abstaine from them. In truth, there hath not these three yeares last past, any man of worth come to me: And upon unworthy men, I will not lay my hands.[313]

Ad 5. Touching the foure points geven by your Gratious Maiestie in charge for Catechising, Lectures and Lecturers, I humbly informe;

1. That, having putt the Churchwardens to it throughout the Dioces, upon their othes, I find nothing to the contrary, but that Catechising is duely performed in all places; and where there is a Preaching Minister, there is usually had on Sundayes, both Catechising, and Preaching.

2. As concerning Lecturers, I scarcely find such a title in all my Dioces, out of the Cathedrall and Collegiate Churches, where the locall Statutes require a Divinitie Lecturer: But otherwise throughout the Dioces I permitt not a license of preaching to any, that is not Parson, or Vicar of some Parish Church: And, if any be admitted for assistance, or Coadjutorship for preaching in any place, his allowance is, but as Curate under the Parson, or Vicar of that Church, and, by his consent if not upon his request. For, by long observation and experience, I have found; that where such a one is sett up, without the good allowance of the Parson, or Vicar of the place,

---

308 John Vincent MA, former fellow of New College, Oxford, was admitted to the curacy of Darlington on 25 July 1634. He evidently left Durham diocese early in 1637, for on 2 Aug. 1637 he was licensed to preach throughout Exeter diocese by Bishop Joseph Hall. Durham Cathedral Library, Sharp MS 49, p. 43; Devon RO, Chanter 43, p. 477.

309 Thomas Morton.

310 Of York.

311 Neile was among a handful of early Stuart bishops who had a reputation for restoring and embellishing his episcopal houses, and was the only one to refer to this activity in these annual accounts. See Fincham, *Prelate as pastor*, p. 53; Foster, 'Church policies of the 1630s', p. 199; and below, p. 140.

312 Neile's second visitation of York diocese took place in 1636.

313 In fact throughout his entire episcopal career (1608–40), Neile was a reluctant ordainer. See Foster, 'Archbishop Richard Neile revisited', p. 172.

there presently followeth distraction of the people, as if there were sett up Pulpit against Pulpit, and Altar against Altar.

3. As for weekely Lectures in Market Townes, preached by a company of neighbouring Ministers; I humbly informe your Maiestie; That I find not any such in my Dioces: whereof I yielded your Maiestie an accompt in my last yeares Certificate;[314] vizt, That, some of the discreeter sort of those Ministers, finding that their paines in that kind upon Market daies, was rather procured to draw companie to the Market, then for the benefit, and comfort of the Word for the Inhabitants there, have withdrawne themselves; and some of them are contented to bestow that their devotion upon some of their neighbour Churches, that have not a preaching Minister. But, if in any place a competent number of learned conformable men, beneficed neer to any Market Towne shall desire, with due and dutifull submission to your Maiesties Orders, to performe such a weekly Sermon, I shall, with your Maiesties good allowance, willingly yield them my consent, and furtherance.

4. And for the 4th point, for a Lecturers yielding to accept of a Benefice with cure, if it might be obteyned for him: I am perswaded, there is not in my Dioces any unbeneficed Minister, that would not gladly accept of a reasonable Benefice, if he could gett it.

Ad 6. I were very unworthie of your Maiesties favour, and the Place, wherein you have placed me, if I should not, (to the uttermost of my power), countenance, and encourage all grave, and orthodox Clergie men: And to them, that are not so; wheresoever I find, or have found any refractary, unconformable Minister, I labour by all good meanes to reclaime and reforme him. And I humbly crave leave to affirme this to your Sacred Maiestie: That howsoever I am, and have been reputed a great adversary of the puritane faction (which I hold myself bound in conscience and duty to God, your Maiestie, and the most happy-established Church of England to be), yet, (having been a Bishop eight and twenty yeares,[315] by my Episcopall power, and Jurisdiction, out of your Maiesties Court of High Commission[316]) I never deprived any man; but have endeavoured their reformation with meeknes and patience. As at this instant, having a poor melancholick, brainsick, unconformable man presented to me, who hath petitioned me to accept of his resignation of his Benefice, rather then that he will conforme himself, I have refused his resignation, and assigned him to conference, with half a yeares respite to be better advised, and not to undoe himself, his wife, and children, and cast himself *in apostastiam Ordinis*.

Ad 7. Of Chaplaines permitted in the houses of other then Noblemen, thereunto by law priviledged, I was bold heretofore humbly to informe your Maiestie, that some Knights, and Gentlemen, that have impropriate Parsonages, where very slender maintenance is allotted for the Curate, as (perhaps) £5, or 20 Nobles, or £10, had Curates, that lived, in their houses, to whom diett, and lodging was a good increase of their Stipend; without which, none of any abilitie to serve the Church, would

---

314 See above, p. 106.

315 Neile had been consecrated bishop of Rochester in 1608, and was subsequently promoted to the sees of Coventry and Lichfield, Lincoln, Durham, Winchester and then York.

316 i.e., excluding sentences in High Commission. For examples of Neile depriving ministers in High Commission, see Fincham, *Prelate as pastor*, pp. 316–17. See also Foster, 'Archbishop Richard Neile revisited', pp. 169–70, 172–4.

be obteyned. And these poore Curates, in these Gentlemens houses doe ordinarily read prayers, and (perhaps) catechise the familie. Which, with submission to your Maiesties better judgement, and resolution, I thinke, would be tolerated; so as the poore men approve themselves to the Ordinarie to be orthodox, and conformable men; and in their domestick prayers, and catechising be held to the forme of the Booke of Common Prayer.

Ad 8. Of your Maiesties godly care, that the publick Divine Service and Catechising be duely frequented, as it ought to be: It becometh me, and all my Brethren, the Bishopps, to be as industrious as we may, for the performance thereof. But the Churchwardens negligence, in dispensing with their othes,[317] when they should present it, and many mens dwelling remote from the Church, and the Justices of Peace not doing their dutie, according to the law in that behalf provided, occasioneth much absence both from Divine Service, and the Catechising. In regard whereof, and consideration of the difficultie of some that dwell 2: 3: or 4 miles from the parish Church, and their coming to the parish Church, there have been in Yorkshire foure Chappells lately built in foure parishes, and this yeare consecrated for the use of Divine Service, and endowed with reasonable meanes, to maynteyne a sufficient Minister in each of those Chappells;[318] yet, with due care, and provision for the indemnity of the parish Church, and of the Parson, or Vicar, incumbents of the Parish Churches. And in pursuance of your Maiesties Proclamation for the repayring of Churches,[319] I have received Certificates of very large summes of money expended in the repayring, and adorning of Churches and Chappells, and making, decent and uniforme Seates.

It may be your Gratious Maiestie will expect of me some information, what the Strangers (Duch and French) in the Levell of Hatfield have done for their frequenting of Divine Service, since your Maiesties late being in these Northern parts;[320] whereof I can only informe your Maiestie: That, upon enquirie made thereof, I find; That, since their Minister, Bonetempes,[321] that came from Leiden, went from them in August last, they have not had any publick assemblies, but have repayred to the parish Churches adjoyning to their dwellings: And, that they now sell away the materialls, that they had provided for a Chappell, which they intended to have built in Lincolne Dioces.[322]

To the rest of your Maiesties Articles, I have nothing to certifie, but as I have formerly done: That, I find not any, whom those your Commandements doe concerne, but that they doe duely, and dutifully observe them.

[317] A point Neile repeatedly had made: see above, pp. 93, 106.
[318] Harwoodale, Wibsey, Hunslet and Attercliffe, consecrated by Bishop Parr of Sodor and Man in Oct. 1636. See BI, INST AB 6, pp. 146–93; G. Lawton, *Collectio rerum ecclesiasticarum de diocesi Eboracensi* (London, 1842), pp. 96, 116, 223, 302.
[319] See above, p. 107 n. 218.
[320] TNA: PRO, SP 16/329/2 lists the king's progress in the summer of 1636, which included Nottinghamshire and Derbyshire.
[321] Peter Bonetemps or Bontemps, ordained in Leiden.
[322] Hatfield Chase was on the borders of York and Lincoln dioceses. In 1636 Neile had written to Laud warning him of the attempt of this 'new plantation' to introduce presbyterian government and worship, apparently with licence from Bishop Williams of Lincoln, and urging that it be required to use the Book of Common Prayer. TNA: PRO, SP 16/310/1 [undated: *c.* 1638], 327/47, 47.I, 331/71; *CSPD 1637*, pp. 195–6; LPL, MS 943, pp. 560–1.

The Eternall Father of mercies, and Fountaine of all goodnes
blesse your Sacred Maiestie with a long life, and prosperous
dayes with the multiplying dayly upon You, and Yours all
spirituall and temporall blessings in this life, and crowne You
with eternall glorie in his heavenly Kingdome: so prayeth,
as in dutie he is bound
Your Maiesties
Most obliged servant and Chaplaine
R: Ebor:[323]

Canterbury province, 1637

In Dei Nomine Amen.[324]
May it please your most Gracious Majesty.
According to your Commandes in your Instructions published for the good of the
Clergye, and my bounden Dutye, I here present my Annuall Accompt for the Prov-
ince of Canterbury for the yeare last past. 1637.

Canterbury.   And first to beginne with myne owne Diocess, I must give your
Majesty to understand that at and about Ashford in Kent,
the Separatists continue to hold theyr Conventicles, notwithstanding the
Excommunication of soe many of them as have been discovered. They are all of the
Poorer sort, and very simple, soe that I am utterly to seeke what to doe with them.
Two or three of theyr principall Ringleaders Brewer, Fenner and Turner[325] have longe
C.R. Keepe these particular   been in Prison, and it was once thought fitt to
parsons fast untill ye thinke   proceed against them by the Statute for
what to doe with the rest   Abjuration,[326] but I doe much doubt they are soe
ignorantly willfull that they will returne into the Kingdom and doe a great deale
more hurt before they will againe be taken. And not longe since Brewer slipt out of
Prison and went to Rochester and other Partes of Kent, and held Conventicles, and
put a great many simple people especially women into great distempers against the
Church. He is taken againe, and was called before the High Commission, where he
stood silent, but in such a geering scornfull manner as I scarce ever saw the like.
Soe in prison he remaine's.

In the Churchyard of the same Towne a Butchers Slaughter house opened to the
great annoyance of that Place, which I have commanded should be remedyed, and
the Dore shutt up.

At Biddenden I have suspended Richard Warren the Schoolmaster for refusing
the Oath of Allegiance, of Canonicall obedyence, and to subscribe to the Articles.
Besides, this precise man willl read nothing but Divinity to his Schollers, noe not
soe much as the Grammer Rules, unless Mars, Bacchus, Apollo, and Pol aedepol
may be blotted out.

---

[323] Richard Neile.
[324] LPL, MS 943, pp. 275–81; endorsed 'My Accompt to his Majesty for the Province of Canterbury
Anno 1637' (p. 282); LPL, Laud's Register I, fos. 289r–291r.
[325] See above, pp. 101, 110.
[326] 35 Eliz. I c. 1, § II, from 'An Acte to retayne the Quenes Subjets in Obedyence'.

The Strangers in Canterbury doe not soe much resort to theyr Parish Churches as formerly they did, at my first giving of my Injunctions.[327] But Visiting this yeare,[328] I have given a publike and strict charge that the Delinquents be presented and punished if they doe not theyr duty in that behalfe.

There is one dwelling in Addisham a marryed man called by the name of Thomas Jordan. He was formerly called Thomas Mounton, because he was found in the Church porch of Mounton in swadling cloathes, left there in all likelyhood by his Mother, who was some Beggar or Strumpet. It is beleyved he was never Christened: I have therfore given order that he shall be Christened with that caution which is prescribed in the Booke of Common Prayer, where the Baptisme is doubtfull.

About Sittingborne there are more Recusants then in any other part of my Diocess. And the Lady Roper Dowager[329] is thought to be a great meanes of the increase of them, but I have given strict charge that they be carefully presented according to Lawe.

There is still a Remainder of Schismatickes in Egerton and the Parishes adjacent. But they are as meane People as those about Ashford, and I am as much to seeke what to doe with them.

London.   My Lord Treasurer[330] complaine's that he hath little assistance of his
          Archdeacons, and I beleive it to be true, and shall therefore if your
C.R. It is most fitt   Majesty thinke fitt, cause Letters to be written
to them to awake them to theyr dutyes.[331]

His Lordship likewise complaine's of some inconformable men which his Chancellour hath mett with in this his last Visitation,[332] but they have receyved such censure as theyr faults deserved, or els submitted themselves. Onely Mr John Knolles a Lecturer at Colchester had forborne to receyve the Holy Communion for two yeares since he came to be Lecturer, and being enjoyned to performe that dutye within a month, he was soe zealous as that he forsooke Lecture and Towne and all, rather then he would receyve the Communion.[333]

I finde likewise in this accompt 25 Ministers convented before the Chancelour for some Inconformityes. And five for Excesse in drinkinge, but there is as good order taken with them as could be.

The Lectures in this Diocess continue many but there is great care taken to keepe them in order.

Winchester.   I finde in the Diocess of Winchester diverse Recusants newly presented,
C.R. I desyre to know the   but whether they be newly perverted[334] doth
certantie of this   not appeare by my Lord the Bishops[335] Accompt
to me.

---

327 See above, pp. 110–11.
328 LPL, Laud's Register I, fos. 181r–185v.
329 Mary Petre, widow of John Roper, Third Lord Teynham of Linsted, Kent, and an active Catholic. See G. E. C(ockayne), *The complete peerage* (14 vols. in 13, London, 1910–59), XII. I, 681.
330 William Juxon.
331 See above, p. 102 and n. 176, and below, p. 143.
332 Juxon's second visitation of London diocese was conducted by his chancellor, Arthur Duck, in the autumn of 1637.
333 John Knowles (*c.* 1606–85) was lecturer at Colchester in 1637 and later emigrated to New England in 1639: see his entry in *ODNB*.
334 Underlined by Charles I.
335 Walter Curle.

There are some five complained of for not Catechizing, which I shall require of the Bishop to see remedyed.

Elye.   Here my Lord the Bishop[336] certifye's, that he is very carefull and sees all things done according to your Majestys Instructions.

Rochester.   My Lord the Bishop of this Diocess dyed before the tyme came that he was to give up his Accompt,[337] soe that I can relate nothing upon certainty, but shall give the succeeding Bishop[338] charge to be very carefull, because his Predecessor laye languishing and was able to looke to little for three whole years before his death.

Salisbury.   The Accompt from hence is very breife, but my Lord[339] is confident that his Diocess is cleane through in good order, and I will hope it is soe.

Peterburgh.   My Lord of Peterburgh[340] hath taken a great deale of paines and brought his Diocess into very good order. Onely he saith there are three Lecturers in the same, one at Northampton but that is read by the Vicar of the Place, one at Rowell which hath maintenance allowed and a third at Daventree mainteyned by the contribution of the Towne. And this last I thinke the Bishop had need take care of.

Bath and Wells.   This Diocess appeare's by my Lords[341] Certificat to be in marveylous good order for all thinges, and a great Reformation hath been wrought there by his care and industrye.

For Popish Recusants the number of them is there much decreased, neyther are any newly presented for Recusancye.

Lincolne.   My Lord the Bishop of Lincolne is not (as your Majesty knowes) in case to make any returne for his Diocess.[342] And since the Jurisdiction thereof came by his Suspension into my handes, I have neyther had tyme nor leysure to make any great Inquiry how conformable in doctrine or discipline men in those partes are. Yet this I finde that both in Buckinghamshire and in Bedfordshire there are many too refractory to all good order. And there are a great number of very poore and miserable Vicarages and Curatshippes in many partes of this large Diocess, and which are allmost past all cure and hope of helpe unless by your Majestys grace and favour some may be had.[343]

Norwich.   My Lord of Norwich[344] hath been very carefull of all your Majestys Instructions, and upon the 24th of September last being then in his

---

[336]   Francis White.

[337]   John Bowle died on 9 Oct. 1637.

[338]   John Warner was consecrated Bishop of Rochester on 14 Jan. 1638.

[339]   John Davenant.

[340]   Francis Dee.

[341]   William Piers.

[342]   In July 1637 John Williams was found guilty in Star Chamber of suborning witnesses, suspended from his offices and imprisoned in the Tower.

[343]   At this time Laud was conducting a survey of the wealth of Lincolnshire vicarages: TNA: PRO, SP 16/378/107–9, 379/6, 21, 31, 53. For Sir John Lambe's advice to Laud on this point, see LPL, MS 943, p. 555.

[344]   Matthew Wren. A copy of Wren's account to Laud, on which Laud's summary is based, is in Bodl., Tanner MS 68, fos. 316r–317r.

Diocess and giving Orders, he refused to admitt five well learned and well mannerd men, because they wanted a sufficient Title according to the Canon of the Church.[345]

I finde that there are in this Diocess six Lectures namely at Wimondham, Northwalsham, East Harling, Norwich, Linne, and Bungay, but they are all performed by conformable and neighbouring Divines, and under such Conditions and rules as my Lord theyr Bishop hath prescribed them.[346] Onely that at Bungay is inhibited for a tyme at the entreaty of some of theyr owne company, and for misdemeanours in it. As for the single Lecturers my Lord hath had a speciall Eye over them.

Your Majestys Letters requiring the Mayor Sheriffes and Aldermen etc, to repayre on Sundayes to Divine Service and Sermons at the Cathedrall in Norwich are very well observed by the most of them.[347] But complaint is brought to the Bishop against one Thomas Kinge, who is held a factious and a dangerous man, and he frequently absentes himselfe from the Cathedrall, and it is doubted that his ill Example will make others neglect theyr dutyes.[348]

Divine Service both for Prayers Catechisme and Sermons is diligently frequented, and that beyond what could suddenly be hoped for in such a Diocess and in the midst of the humourousnes of this Age.

Of those which stood under Episcopall censure, or that fledd to avoyde censure, there are not above three or fowre which have submitted themselves. Yet his Lordship hath had patyence, (notwithstanding a peremptory Citation sent out) hitherto to expect *C.R. Lett him proceed* them: But now must proceed to Deprivation, or *to Deprivation*[349]   suffer scorne and contempt to followe upon all his Injunctions. Nevertheless herein he humbly craves direction, and soe doe I, if it please your Majesty to give it.

His Lordship likewise very carefully and necessarily (as I conceive) crave's direction for these Particulars following.
1.   Diverse Townes are depopulated, noe Houses left standing but the Mannour house and the Church, and that turned to the Lords Barne or worse use, and noe Service done in it though the Parsonages or Vicarages be presentative.
2.   In other Townes the Church is ruined, and the Inhabitants thrust upon neighbouring Parishes, where they fill the church and pay few or noe dutyes.
3.   At Carrowe close by Norwich there are 12 Houses some of them fayre, reputed to be of noe Parish, and soe an ordinary receptacle for Recusant Papists and other Separatists, to the great prejudice of that neighbouring Citty.

---

[345]   However, Wren did ordain twenty-one to the priesthood and seventeen to the diaconate (Bodl., Tanner MS 68, fo. 316r). The reference is to canon 33 of 1604.

[346]   Wren added here 'which I signified in my last years account' (Bodl., Tanner MS 68, fo. 316r), for which see above, p. 113 n. 253.

[347]   Norfolk RO, DN/FCB/1, fos. 10v–11v; see I. Atherton, E. Ferne, C. Harper-Bill and H. Smith (eds.), *Norwich Cathedral: city, church and diocese 1096–1996* (London, 1996), p. 549.

[348]   Thomas King was the town clerk, an opponent of Wren, who emigrated to Holland in 1639 and returned after 1640 to become a founder of the Great Yarmouth congregational church. See Reynolds, *Godly reformers*, pp. 165, 178–9, 196, 230. In his report, Wren described King as 'a very subtile and dangerous man, that not only swaies the City, but is the Oracle of the whole faction in those parts' (Bodl., Tanner MS 68, fo. 316r).

[349]   On 8 Jan. 1638 Wren removed William Bridge from his living of St Peter Hungate Norwich, Thomas Allen from St Edmund Norwich and Henry Porter from Carbrooke, and on 19–20 Mar. William Greenhill from Oakley, Paul Amyrant from Wolterton and Irmingham, Jeremiah Burroughes from Tivetshall and John Philipps from Wrentham. Norfolk RO, Reg/16/23, fos. 179v, 181r.

4. At Lanwood neare Newmarket and in Burwell the mother church standes, but the Roofe suffered to decaye within the memory of man, and the Bells sold, and the Hamlet quite slipt out of all jurisdiction Ecclesiasticall. That church was an Impropriation to the Abbey of Ramsey and is now in Sir William Russells handes.[350]

5. The churchyardes in many places are extremely annoyed and prophaned, especially in Corporate Townes. And at St Edmondes-bury the Assises are yearly kept in a remote side of the Churchyard, and a common Alehouse stande's in the middle of the Churchyarde. The like abuses by Ale-houses, back-dores, and throwing out of filth, with somthinge else not fitt to be related here,[351] are founde at Bungay, at St Marye's ad Turrim in Ipswich, at Wood-bridge, and at Norwich, the Signe posts of two or three Innes stand in the church yard. Of remedy for these abuses the Bishop is utterly in despayre,

C.R. Lett him doe his dewtie unless your Majesty be pleased to take some
and I shall take care that no speciall order for them because they which have
Prohibition shall troble these back-dores into churchyards or common
him in this case passages, will plead prescription, and then a

Prohibition will be graunted against the Ecclesiastical proceedings.

6. Lastly his Lordship certifye's that divers not onely Churches but Townshippes themselves are in danger of utter ruyne by a Breach of the Sea. And there was provision made by Act of Parliament in the seventh yeare of your Majestys royall Father of blessed memory for redress of it,[352] but nothing being since done, it will now cost five tymes as much to remedy as then it would. But the

C.R. Heerin I shall not Bishop is in good hope great good may yet be
faile to doe my part done, if your Majesty will be graciously

pleased to appeare in it, upon such humble Petition as he and I shall make to your Majesty.

Exeter. The Bishop[353] of this Diocess assures me that all thinges are in very good order there. And indeed I thinke the Diocess is well amended within these few years, his Lordship having been very carefull both in his Visitations and otherwise.

This yeare by reason of the returne of diverse that were Captives in Marocco, and having been Inhabitants of those Westerne Partes, there arose in my Lord the Bishop a doubt, how they having renounced theyr Saviour, and become Turkes might be readmitted into the Church of Christ, and under what paenitentiall forme. His Lordship at his late being in London spake with me about it, and wee agreed on a forme, which was afterwardes drawne up, and approved by the Right Reverend Fathers in God my Lords the Bishopps of London, Ely and Norwich,[354] and is now

---

350 Sir William Russell (*c.* 1575–1654), treasurer of the navy. See his entry in *ODNB*.

351 Wren's account is particularly rich here, so Laud might have decided to conceal (i) that 'a very lewd woman' ran an alehouse in a former Abbey outbuilding at Bungay, access to which was through the churchyard; (ii) that a service in St Mary ad Turrim Ipswich had been interrupted by 'a foule swine' which wandered passed the minister's reading desk 'and was not without much disturbance and difficulty kept from going up to the Communion table'; or, most likely, (iii) that Woodbridge churchyard contained a privy house 'in open view' (Bodl., Tanner MS 68, fo. 317r).

352 7 Jac. I c. 20.

353 Joseph Hall.

354 William Juxon, Francis White and Matthew Wren.

setled by your Majestys appointment. And I shall take care to see it registered here,[355] and have given charge to my Lord of Exeter to see it registred belowe,[356] to remaine as a President for future tymes, if there should be any more sadd Examples of Apostacy from the faith.

Oxford.   Whereas your Majesty hath lately been graciously pleased to graunt the ordering of the Woodes of Shottover and Stowe by lease to the Lord Bishop of Oxford,[357] his Lordship assure's me that there is a great deale of care taken, and a great deale of charge layd out by him and his Tenant for the preservation and well ordering of the Woodes there.

He hath likewise been very carefull concerning Recusants within that Diocess, but saith that diverse of them pretend and shewe theyr Exemptions that they should *C.R. Lett mee see those exemptions*   not be troubled for matters concerning theyr *and then I shall declare my further*   Religion in any Ecclesiasticall Courtes, which *pleasure*   hath made his Lordship forbeare till your Majestys pleasure be further knowne.

For Lectures, there are none in that Diocesse, save one at Henley upon Thames, preached by the Incumbent[358] an orderly man and in the Peculiars at Tame and Banbury, but they are out of the Bishops jurisdiction.[359]

Bristol.   My Lord Bishop[360] of this See hath taken great care in his first Visitation, and if he continue that care (as I doubt not but he will) he will quickly settle that Diocess into better order. But he complaine's of the Deane and Chapter (for whose benefit he hath lately made many good Injunctions) that they will not consent that twenty poundes *per annum*, ordered by theyr Statute for the Repayring of High wayes, may be turned to the necessary Supplye of theyr Quire, in regard that £100 *per annum* is lately given by Dr White[361] towards the repayre of the same High wayes. But this and other thinges if your Majesty thinke fitt, I can easily *C.R. Doe so*   alter[362] when I come to revise theyr Statutes or by a Command from your Majesty in the meane tyme.

He farther complaines that his Predecessor Bishop Wright (now Bishop of Lichfield) deteynes in his custodye, all the Writings belonging to Cromhall the lease which your Majesty by your Royall Letters commanded should expire and returne to *C.R. I shall*   the Bishopricke. And sure if this be soe, it is very fitt he be commanded to restore them out of hande.[363]

Lastly he commplaines that they of the Preciser Faction doe every day endeavour to disquiet the People, and that by strange Inventions. And at present they give out that the Liturgye printed for Scotland hath in it sundry notorious pointes of Popery

---

[355]   LPL, Laud Register I, fos. 240r–241v, printed in Laud, *Works*, V, 372–6.
[356]   Devon RO, Chanter 57, fos. 31v–33v.
[357]   John Bancroft.
[358]   Robert Rainsford, vicar there since 1632.
[359]   Both were peculiars in the jurisdiction of the dean and chapter of Lincoln.
[360]   Robert Skinner, bishop of Bristol 1637–41.
[361]   Thomas White (1550–1624). See his entry in *ODNB*.
[362]   Underlined by Charles I.
[363]   Namely Abbots Cromwell, near Tortworth, Gloucestershire: see LPL, Laud's Register I, fo. 241v; Laud, *Works*, VII, 413–15; TNA: PRO, SP 16/387/34, 389/78.

etc, which trouble's the People and doth much harme otherwise.[364] The like is certified me from the Bishop of Exeter[365] concerning Rumors raised in those Partes.

Chichester. My Lord Bishop of Chichester[366] is in a Quartan Ague, besides his old
Diseases of the Stone and the Gout, I pray God comfort him. But I
doe not heare from him that there is much amisse in that Diocess.

Hereford. The Bishop of this Diocess[367] certifye's me that your Majestys
Instructions are in all thinges carefully observed, and he hath used
the utmost diligence he can in reclayming of Recusants, and such as will not
conforme themselves he hath taken a strict course, to have them proceeded withall,
and granted *Significavits* against diverse.

St Asaph. In this Diocess my Lords[368] wordes are, that there is nothinge but
common Peace, and Universall Conformity.

Landaff. My Lord of Landaff[369] hath been very carefull for the setling of the
Rights and Proffits of this Bishopricke, and God hath greatly blessed
his Endeavours therein. And for the Goverment he professe's that in his late Visitation
he hath not founde one Schismaticall Minister or Nonconformist in the Diocess.

Bangor. The Bishop of this See was consecrated but a little before Michaelmas
last,[370] and by your Majestys leave hath not been yet in his Diocess
and soe for this broken part of the yeare is able to give noe Accompt.

Worcester. My Lord the Bishop[371] certifye's that he is less troubled with
Nonconformists since Mr Whateley of Banbury[372] gave over his
Lecture at Stratford within that Diocess. And that during this heavy Visitation[373] at
Worcester he hath caused the Lectures to cease in that Towne.

St Davids. The Bishop of this See[374] hath not had his health of late, and is now
come to Towne to seeke to recover the same, for which he humbly
crave's your Majestys favourable construction. But he certifyes me that all your
Majestys Instructions are duly observed within that Diocess.

From the Bishopps of Lichfield[375] and Glocester[376] I have not receyved any
C.R. Cale for them[377]   Certificats.

And soe with my Prayers for your Majestys longe life and happye Raigne I humbly
submitt this my Accompt for the yeare last past 1637.

W: Cant:[378]

---

364 English knowledge of events unfolding in Scotland in 1637 is analysed in P. Donald, *An uncoun-
selled king* (Cambridge, 1990), pp. 173–90.
365 Joseph Hall.
366 Richard Montagu.
367 George Coke.
368 John Owen.
369 William Murray.
370 William Roberts was consecrated bishop on 3 Sept. 1637, and died in 1665.
371 John Thornborough.
372 See above, p. 84 n. 39. For William Whately (1583–1639), see his entry in *ODNB*.
373 i.e., plague.
374 Roger Mainwaring.
375 Robert Wright.
376 Godfrey Goodman.
377 Wright's certificate reached Laud on 17 Feb. 1638: Laud, *Works*, VII, 413.
378 William Laud.

Canterbury province, 1638

May it please your most Sacred Majesty.[379]

According to my bounden Duty, and your Majestys Commandes expressed in your Instructions for the good of the Clergye, I here present my Accompt for the yeare last past, 1638.

Canterbury.   And first to beginne with my selfe and my owne Diocess, I have been carefull to obey all your Majestys particular Instructions, both for the residing upon my Houses, and preserving of my Woodes etc.

There was one Bedle a Minister of Essex[380] came into this Diocess, and at Harbledowne neare Canterbury (the Curat there being dead) preached very disorderly, three howres together at a tyme, and gott himself many ignorant followers, but soe soone as ever he was enquyred after by my Officers, he fledd the Country, and I purpose God willing to speake with the Chancellour of London[381] concerning him.

I doe not finde that there is eyther any increase or decrease of Papists or Puritans in the Diocess. But the Separatists about Ashford are very busye, miserable poore, and out of that bold against all Church Censure. Soe that without some *C.R. Demande there helpe, and if* temporall assistance from the Judges[382] wee *they refuse I shall make them* knowe not what to doe. And this I have often *assist you*[383] and humbly represented,[384] yet two notorious Separatists being calld in question are fledd the Country, and one of them brake Prison.

At Tenterden some People are somwhat refractory, but the Archdeacon[385] assure's me, he hath great hope to reduce them, which I shall be gladd of.

The Strangers at Canterbury doe reasonably well obey my Injunctions for comming to our Churches, and I shall give them all incouragement, holding it fitting to keepe a moderate hand with them.

London.   In the Diocess and Citty of London there was like to be some distraction both amonge the Ministers and the People occasioned at first by some over-nice curiosityes preached by one Mr Goodwin Vicar of St Stephens in Colmanstreet,[386] concerning the imputation of Christs righteousnes in the justification of a Sinner. But the Differences arising about it were timely prevented by Convention of the Partyes dissenting. And soe God be thanked that busines is at peace.[387]

There is but one noted Refractory Person that standes out in that Diocess, and he is now under Suspension.

[379] LPL, MS 943, pp. 283–7; endorsed 'The Lord Archbishop of Canterbury his accompte to His Majestie for his Province for the yeare ended 1638' (p. 288).

[380] See above, p. 84.

[381] Arthur Duck.

[382] Underlined by Charles I.

[383] Charles I's annotation is incomplete, owing to damage to the manuscript, so the transcription here also draws on *Troubles and tryal of...William Laud*, p. 553.

[384] See above, pp. 95, 101, 110, 125.

[385] William Kingsley, archdeacon of Canterbury 1619–48.

[386] John Goodwin, vicar of St Stephen Coleman Street 1633–45 and 1649–60. See J. Coffey, *John Goodwin and the puritan revolution* (Woodbridge, 2006), pp. 54–6.

[387] But not for long: see below, pp. 142–3.

Winchester.   My Lord the Bishops Certificat,[388] informes me that there are a great many Recusants within that Diocess, and that in some Parishes theyr Children are not brought to be Baptized in the church, which I shall require the Bishop to take speciall care of.

Lincolne.   The Diocess being now in my charge,[389] I doe humbly certify your Majesty that one part of Buckinghamshire, and some Places in Lincolne and Leycestershires are somwhat disorderly, but I doe not finde any man presented unto me for any willfull Refractorynes, save one whom I have caused to be called into the High Commission Court.

There are in Lincolnshire many miserable poore Vicarages and Curatshippes.[390] Might your Majestys Raigne be soe blest, as that they might in tyme finde some releife. But that is quite beyond Episcopall power.

Oxford.   In this Diocess my Lord[391] hath taken care of all your Majestys Instructions and assures me that there is noe Lecture in any Markett Towne within his Diocess except at Henlye, which is performed by theyr owne Minister a discreet man.[392] As for that which was begunne by private Persons in the Chapell of your Majestys Mannour House at Woodstocke, and might have been of very dangerous both Example and consequence, the Bishop hath carefully suppressed it by your Majestys gracious Command upon his Petition.

Worcester.   There is noe Complaint in this Diocess, but onely of one Mr Ephraim Hewett of Wraxhall in Warwickshire, who hath taken upon him to keepe Fastes in his Parish by his owne appoyntment, and hath contemned the decent Ceremonyes commanded by the Church.[393] My Lord the Bishop[394] proceeds against him, and intends eyther to reforme or punish him.

Exeter.   In this Diocess the Bishop[395] assure's me that all things goe very orderly and well, saving that diverse Impropriators suffer willing Ruines (as he conceyves) in the Churches which belonge unto them, wherein he humbly craves both advise and ayde that it may be remedyed.

Hereford.   There was one Mr Workman sometymes a Lecturer at Glocester, and for Inconformity in a very high degree put from that place by Sentence of the High Commission Court. Since that this Man hath been receyved into the house of one Mr Kyrle of Wallford, and lyved there without any Cure, or other knowne imployment.[396] The Bishop[397] hearing of him and resolving to call him in question if he did not conforme himselfe, he hath suddenly left that Diocess, and is gone God knowes whither.

---

[388]   From Walter Curle.
[389]   See above, p. 127.
[390]   See above, p. 127 n. 343.
[391]   John Bancroft.
[392]   See above, p. 130 n. 358.
[393]   Hewett or Huit was minister of Wroxall, Warwickshire, who, for example, described bowing as idolatrous and scandalous. He emigrated to New England in 1639. See E. Huit, *The whole prophecie of Daniel explained* (1644), p. 87; D. Oldridge, *Religion and society in early Stuart England* (Aldershot, 1998), pp. 47, 58, 76–8.
[394]   John Thornborough.
[395]   Joseph Hall.
[396]   For John Workman, see Soden, *Godfrey Goodman*, pp. 170–1, 197–8, 202–8.
[397]   George Coke.

There were some other Complaintes put up, which I certifyed to the Bishop, but his Lordship hath given me a fayre answere, and assures me that by his care and vigilancy they shall all be rectifyed, and that out of hand.[398]

Ely.   My Lord[399] informes me that in his Predecessor Bishop Whites absence he lyving most commonly at London being your Majestys Almoner,[400] there was cutt downe and wasted above 1000 loads of woode.

For all other businesses they are in good condition within that Diocess saving that my Lord the Bishop humbly craves leave hereby to represent a great Greivance to your Majesty which concerne's the Bishoprick, the Dean and Chapter, and all other Clergy men (or indeed rather all your Majestys liege People) inhabiting within the Isle of Elye.

Bristoll.   In this Diocess the Bishop[401] found out one Jeffryes who commonly administred the Blessed Sacrament of the Eucharist being eyther not in Holy Orders at all, or at least not a Preist. Soe soone as he was discovered, he slipt out of the Diocess, and the Bishop thinke's he now serves in a Peculiar under the Deane and Chapter of Wells. I will send thither to knowe the certainty, and see the Abuse punished if I can light upon the Person.

The Bishop further certifyes me that there are very many within that small Diocess who stand Excommunicate, and divers of them onely for not payment of Fees; And againe that many of these are not able to paye them. <u>I thinke it were not amiss that once every yeare in Lent the Chancellor were commanded to take an</u>

C.R. In this ye have very great   <u>Accompt of all the Excommunicats in the</u>
reason, for it is not fitt that the   <u>Diocess, and to cause all to be absolved that</u>
sentence of Excommunication   <u>shall be fitt for Absolution, and particularly to</u>
should stand longer then it   <u>see that noe man be sufferd to continue</u>
needs must   <u>Excommunicated, where nothing but Poverty</u>
<u>hinders the payment of Dutyes or other Fees</u>.[402] The Bishop likewise informes me that Monuments even of obscure and meane Persons are growne very common in those Partes, and prejudiciall both to the walles and Pillars and liberty of Churches, which the Bishop oppose's as much and as fairely as he can, but all is too little.

Landaff.   There were in this Diocess the last yeare but two Refractory Ministers knowne to the Bishop,[403] Mr Wroth, and Mr Erbury. The former hath submitted, but the other would neyther submitt, not satisfye his Parishioners to whom he had given publike offence. Soe he resigned his Vicarage, and hath thereby left the Diocess in peace.[404]

St Davids.   For this Diocess the Bishop[405] humbly crave's your Majestys pardone for his longer staye in London then ordinary, and professes his

---

[398] These complaints related to charges of nepotism, mismanagement of temporalities and irregularities in the cathedral. See Historic Manuscripts Commission, *Cowper II* (London, 1888), pp. 198–201.

[399] Matthew Wren, bishop of Ely 1638–67.

[400] Francis White, who died on 25 Feb. 1638, was almoner 1628–38 (*CSPD 1628–9*, p. 192, followed by *ODNB*, states incorrectly that Barnabas Potter rather than White, then bishop of Carlisle, succeeded George Montaigne as almoner in July 1628).

[401] Robert Skinner.

[402] Underlined by Charles I.

[403] William Murray.

[404] For Wroth and Erbury, see above, pp. 99, 104, 117.

[405] Roger Mainwaring.

Excuse formerly made to your Majesty to be most true viz: That he was forced to it by extremity of sicknes falling upon him in those partes, and forcing his change of Ayre.

That Diocess hath been a little out of quyet this yeare by some Mens medling with those nice questions, which your Majesty hath forbidden should be commonly preached in the Pulpitt. But the relation being somwhat imperfect, I shall informe my selfe farther and then give your Majesty such Accompt as I receyve.

C.R. It is no wunder that this relation is imperfect since since the Bishops sickness gives him an excuse for absence

Bangor.   In this Diocess the Bishop[406] certifyes me two considerable things, and both of them are of difficult cure. The one concerne's his Bishopricke where every thinge is lett for Lives by his Predecessors, to the very Mill that grindes his Corne. The other concerne's the Diocess in generall, where by reason of the Poverty of the Place all Clergymen of hope and worth seeke Preferment elswhere. And he tells me plainly some weake Schollers must be Ordeyned, or else some Cures must be left alltogether unsupplyed.

Glocester.   My Lord of Glocester[407] confesseth he hath been absent from his Diocess a good part of this yeare, being kept from his dwelling houses by the Infection at Glocester, which just cause of absence he humbly submittes to your most gracious Majesty.[409]

C.R. This is well anufe if he have left his desyre of further absenting himselfe[408]

Concerning that Diocess the Bishop speakes not much more. But the Archdeacon[410] at his Visitation finding the Clergy conformable gave them this grave and fitting Admonition, viz That noe man should presume his Conformity should excuse him, if in the meane tyme his life were scandalous. Which was very necessary for that place and these tymes. And the Archdeacon certifyes farther that there are divers which as farr as they dare, oppose Catechizing, and but for the feare of loosing theyr Livings, would allmost goe as farre as Burton and Bastwicke[411] did, which is his owne Expression under his hande.

Norwich.   My Lord the Bishop[412] there complaine's much of the decay of his houses, and the impoverishing of that Bishopricke by some of his Predecessors. And this partly by letting of longe Leases before the Statute restrained it,[413] and partly by a coarse Exchange of some Landes in former tymes.[414] This latter cannot now be helped, but for the decay of his Houses, if he pursue the Facultye which I graunted to his immediate Predecessor, he may helpe a great parte of that

---

406   William Roberts.

407   Godfrey Goodman.

408   An allusion to Goodman's request earlier that year, refused by the king, to travel abroad for his health. See Soden, *Godfrey Goodman*, pp. 279–82.

409   A year later, in Jan. 1640, Goodman was ordered to return to his diocese: TNA: PRO, SP 16/442/38.

410   Hugh Robinson, archdeacon of Gloucester after 1634.

411   Henry Burton and John Bastwick, anti-Laudian writers convicted of seditious libel in Star Chamber in June 1637.

412   Richard Montagu, bishop of Norwich 1638–41. His letter to Laud, on which this summary is based, is in LPL, MS 943, pp. 619–27.

413   1 Eliz. I c. 19 § IV: 'All Grants, etc by Bishops, except to the Crown, for any Term exceeding 21 Years, etc at the usual Rents, declared void.'

414   Principally by Edmund Scambler, bishop of Norwich 1585–94, described by Montagu as 'that *fundi nostri calamitae*' (LPL, MS 943, p. 620).

decaye without much charge. And this God willing I shall putt him in mynde to doe, and give him the best assistance that I can by Lawe.

For the Churches in that Diocess (which are very many) my Lord acknowledges that they are in very decent and good order generally.[415]

The onely thinge which he saith trouble's his Diocess is that the People have been required to come up and Receyve at the Raile, which is sett before the Communion Table, and that heretofore many have been Excommunicated or Suspended for not doing soe. For the thinge it selfe, it is certainly the most decent and orderly waye, and is practised by your Majesty and by the Lords in your owne Chappell, and now allmost every where else. And upon my knowledge hath been longe used in St Giles his church without Creeplegate London, with marveilous decencye and ease, and yet in that Parish there are not soe few as 2000 Communicants more then within any Parish in Norwich Diocess. And when your Majesty had the Hearing of this business in the now Bishop of Elyes tyme,[416] you highly approved it, and therfore I presume you will be pleasd to command that the present Bishop

C.R. I doe so   continue it, and looke carefully to it.[417] And whereas they plead that many stood Suspended for it, the Bishop of Elye in whose tyme it was doth assure me that in above 1300 Parishes there were not 13 eyther Excommunicate or Suspended for refusing of this.[418]

Coventry and   In this Diocess the Bishop[419] gives a fayre Accompt to all your
Lichfield.   Majestys Instructions, soe that I have cause to hope that the Diocess is
                 in reasonable good order. Onely he complaine's that his Predecessors
have leased out part of his House at Lichfield, which puttes him to very great annoyance, but he is entring into a Legall waye for redress of this abuse,[420] in which I
C.R. I shall   presume your Majesty will give him all fayre
and just assistance,[421] if he shall be forced to crave the same.

Chichester.   My Lord the Bishop[422] came but lately to this Sea, and hath not as yet
                 found much amiss.

Peterborough. The Bishop of that Diocess is dead,[423] and noe other yet setled, soe I
                 can have noe Accompt from thence this yeare.

---

[415]   Such comments were common enough in the returns from the northern province, but very unusual from the province of Canterbury. Montagu's report in fact contains interesting detail: 'The Churches in this diocese are many of them extraordinarily fayre, large and bewtifull. All well kept in Norfolke. All with the Altar standing close to the East wall, all rayled about the Altar. I never saw so many bewtifull Fonts as be in many of them. Many also sacrilegiously abused heretofore, and profaned. Many fayre Churches, both in Country and in the City, thatched: but not with strawe but reed, which is dangerous for fire and for lightning, but otherwise bewtifull enough and more lasting then tile or lead, as nowe they are every where deccitfully made' (LPL, MS 943, p. 621). Other contemporaries echoed this praise: see Fincham and Tyacke, *Altars restored*, p. 48.

[416]   Matthew Wren, bishop of Norwich 1635–8, now bishop of Ely. For the hearing, see above, p. 114.

[417]   Underlined by Charles I. For Montagu's subsequent order on reception in Norwich diocese, see Fincham (ed.), *Visitation articles*, II, 218–19.

[418]   See Wren's commentary on Montagu's report: TNA: PRO, SP 16/406/99.

[419]   Robert Wright.

[420]   See TNA: PRO, SP 16/402/43.

[421]   Underlined by Charles I.

[422]   Brian Duppa was consecrated bishop of Chichester on 17 June 1638, and was translated to Salisbury in 1641.

[423]   Francis Dee died on 8 Oct. 1638, and his successor, John Towers, was consecrated on 13 Jan. 1639.

Salisbury.	
Bath and Wells.	These four Bishopps[424] certifye that all thinges are orderly
Rochester.	and well within theyr severall Diocesses.
St Asaph.	

And soe with my Prayers for your Majestys longe lyfe and happy Raigne I humbly submitt this my Accompt for the yeare last past, being 1638.

January 2d 1638–9   W: Cant:[425]

York province, 1638

My most humble and bounden dutie and service to your Sacred Maiestie premised.[426] Fearing, that I have heretofore presumed too much of your gratious patience in presenting to you large narrations, of the certificates received from my bretheren, the Bishops of this province, I now indeavour to make amends for that Errour, by a more compendious way; yet not omitting any thing of substance that they have certified; whereof I may by your gratious favour, make this summary account, that they present, *Omnia bene*; and almost *in eisdem terminis*, with theire certificates of the former yeare.

The Bishop of Man his Certificate

You may be pleased to understand, that concerning this years Certificate by way of answere to his Maiesties Royall Iniunctions; I can say for substance noe more, then an *Omnia bene*; for your servant for his part, is still Resident, And for the Clergie, they are all verie Regular and conformable, both to the Canons of our Church in generall, and likewise to his Maiesties Iniunctions in speciall. I have been very urgent with the Clergie to catechise the younger sorte, in theire severall parishes, and I have this yeare begun to confirme such as were catechised, and in some measure understood the principles of Religion.

R. Sodor: et Man.[427]

The Bishop of Carlile his Certificate

Most Reverend Father in God. I doe here in all humility present unto your Grace[428] a perticuler account of my best care to observe His Maiesties Royall and Religious Instructions, wherein I dare not dissemble and daube up matters, but deale Sincerely to the uttermost of my knowledge.

1. To the First and second I say, I have not been absent from my Episcopall house[429] this yeare, and have been carefull there be noe wast made of the wood:

2. I have not sold one Sticke since I came heere.

3. His Maiesties declaration for setlinge all Questions in difference, is every Synod signifyed, and I am Confident it is very Carefully observed in this dioces:

---

424 John Davenant, William Piers, John Warner and John Owen.
425 William Laud.
426 TNA: PRO, SP 16/412/45; endorsed 'To his Sacred Majestie, the humble Certificate of the Arch Bishop of Yorke. 1638' and 'received 11 February 1638'.
427 Richard Parr.
428 Richard Neile.
429 Rose Castle.

4. My Ordination of Ministers I make as solemne as possibly I can, And seldome ordayne ministers, but put backe some unworthy men.

5. The Fowre perticulers which concerne Lecturers, I am carefull upon all occasions to see them duely observed, And having but two Lectures in this whole dioces, And those performed by two single persons I shall soone see the defects, and Reforme them.

6. I have alwayes been willinge to encourage and Countenance our Grave and Godly divines, And use the best meanes I can, to knowe how every one carries himselfe for lyfe and doctrine.

7. I know not any in this dioces that keepes a Chaplaine, nor any that hath a Minister in his house to teach his Children.

8. I humbly acknowledge this Instruction concernes this Countrey more then any other, And therefore have and shall god willing still strive that it may be strictly observed.

9. I shalbe glad of any Occasion by his Maiesties meere grace and favour to obey this blessed Commaund.

10. I am Resolved God willinge never to change yeares into lives but still watch all good Occasion to doe the Contrary, And soe I am sure the deane and Chapter doe.

11. This doth not at all Concerne mee.

12. I know noe Notable alteration or other accident in doctrine, or discipline of the Church established.

13. And thus according to his Maiesties Royall commaund, which in these Cases I shall rather dye then disobey, I have given your Grace a very Faythfull account, as far as I can learn humbly submittinge them, and my selfe, to your Graces most grave Censure.

Bar: Carlile.[430]

November 28. 1638: The Certificate of the Bishop of Chester
of the Execution of his Maiesties Instructions and Commands
within the dioces of Chester for the yeare 1638.

1. Touching the Bishops Residence within his dioces. It hath bene duly kept, saving onely one Moneth, that hee was at London, in Attendance on his Maiesty, and about other his necessary Occasions this yeare.

2. For Residence on his Lands, Lease, *Commendam* etc. It hath been duly observed this yeare, save that hee hath been sometimes at his house in Lancashire this yeare, according to a Letter of his Maiesties,[431] wherein he is licenced to be there some part of the yeare. And for woods hee never had any in his Time.

3. For setling of Questions in difference etc. It is duely performed as occasion requires.

4. For Solemnity of Ordinations. It is strictly observed.

5. Concerning Lecturers. They are such as is required, or els are Censured according to Law.

6. For countenancing orthodox divines. It is duly done in all Occasions.

---

430 Barnabas Potter.
431 See above, p. 107 n. 222.

7. For keeping Chaplaines by Men not qualified etc. Hee knoweth not any; save Sir William Brereton baronet,[432] and Peter Venables Esquire, Baron of Kinderton;[433] who are specially licenced by his Maiesties Letters, for it.

8. For frequenting divine Service and Catechisme. Hee hath especiall care of it; and (for ought hee can learne) it is duly observed throughout his dioces.

9. For making of Leases belonging to his Bishopricke etc. Hee hath made none this yeare: Save onely hee hath renewed a Lease of Cold-Kirkby in Yorkshire, which was formerly (at the making thereof,) leased out for other Lives.

10. For yearly Certificate to the Metropolitane. It is now, (as formerly it hath been) performed.

11. For giving away of Benefices in *Commendam* etc. Hee hath never done otherwise then the King requires.

12. For notifying of any notable Alterations to the Archbyshop. It hath beene, (and shalbe done) as Occasion is offered.

13. Hee hopeth it is satisfyed: for the tyme of Certifying is not past.[434]

Jo: Cestrien.[435]

The Bishop of Durham his Certificate.

Ad 1 et 2. That his continuall Residence is in his Bishopricke, and on his Episcopall houses, sometimes at one, sometimes at another.[436]

3. That both in his Trienniall Visitations, and in the yearly Synods of the Clergy, his Maiesties directions, for setlinge Questions in divinity, is given in charge, to be strictly observed.

4. That in his Ordinations hee doeth strictly observe his Maiesties Instructions, at the fowre solemne times of ordinations; at which onely tymes hee doeth ordayne ministers.

5. To the fifth concerning Lectures, and catechising; That the same is carefully observed in the fowre branches thereof; vizt that hee is very carefull that catechising be duly had every Sunday afternoone, before the sermon; For the better furtherance whereof, hee sayth, hee hath in a very few yeares dispersed some thousands of Catechismes.[437] Secondly. For the Lecturers reading service before the Sermons: Hee sayeth, that it is usually given in charge in his Visitations; and that hee neither knoweth nor heareth of any that doe otherwise. Thirdly. That there is not any Lecture in all his dioces, by any combination or concurrency of ministers to performe it: But there is one single Lecturer in durham, two in Newcastle, one in Northumberland, and one in Barwick.[438] Fourthly. That there is none of these Lecturers but hath professed hee would gladly take a Benefice, if hee could get it.

432 Sir William Brereton (1604–61), first baronet, of Handforth, Cheshire. See his entry in *ODNB*.

433 See M. F. Keeler, *The Long Parliament 1640–1641. A biographical study of its members* (Philadelphia, 1954), p. 372.

434 The previous year, Bridgeman's certificate had been late, reaching Neile in mid-Jan.: TNA: PRO, SP 16/379/19.

435 John Bridgeman.

436 Durham Castle and Bishop Auckland.

437 See the clause in Morton's visitation articles for 1637 referring to his injunction ordering the distribution of catechisms: Fincham (ed.), *Visitation articles*, I, 116 and n. 21.

438 See the list submitted by Morton for 1633, above, p. 88. Morton here omits the lectureship at St Hilda's, South Shields.

6. That both publikely and privately, hee doeth incourage and countenance ortho-doxe divines, and diligently inquireth into theire behaviour, and when any thing is complayned of, hee is carefull to reforme it.

7. That none in his dioces keepe Chaplaynes in their houses, but such as by Law are qualified.

8. For frequenting divine Service of prayers and catechising as well as Sermons. That it is his greatest care and indeavour. But as touching popish Recusants, as their number dayly increaseth rather then diminisheth, soe by theire late compositions they are freed from the proceedings of the Ecclesiasticall Commissions, whereby to be reduced to order and Conformity.[439]

9. Hee hath ever observed it.

10. Concerning his Maiesties commaund about Church Leases That hee hath strictly given it in charge to the deane and Chapter, and to the Archdeacons;[440] that himself carefully observeth that his Maiesties Commaund; and cannot heare or understand of any act done otherwise.

11. Of Bishops that hold any Ecclesiasticall living in *commendam*, it doeth nothing concerne him.

12. Touching the Bishops giving account to his Metropolitane, if any thing happen which may tend to alteration in doctrine, or discipline. Hee sayeth, there is noe such thing happened: and that if there should (which God forbid) hee would give timely notice thereof.

13. This is the effect of his Certificate, which hee concludeth with his prayer, that God would long preserve his Maiesties Life and gratious Raygne over us.

Tho: Duresme.[441]

It remayneth, that I give your Sacred Maiestie an account of mine owne diocesse,[442] wherein I cannot avoyd the doinge of that, which my bretheren have done before mee, to say of every perticuler of your Maiesties Instructions, as I sayed this time twelve moneth, of the precedent yeare.

1. That my Residence hath beene continually in my dioces and in my Episcopall houses.[443]

2. That by your Maiesties good leave, signifyed by Mr Secretary Windebanke, I have imployed a great quantity of timber in the repayre of the principall house of my Bishopricke, called Cawood castle, and have disbursed in that worke, at the least £1000 since my last Certificate.[444]

3. That my Archdeacons[445] in theire Visitations, doe duly give your Maiesties decla-rations and Instructions in charge, and by diligent inquiry upon oath, cannot finde, but that they are duly observed.

4. I have not had any Ordination this yeare, for that none of worth have desired it of mee.

---

[439] Morton had long complained of these compositions: Laud, *Works*, VI, 334–5.

[440] Gabriel Clark, archdeacon of Durham, and Everard Gower, archdeacon of Northumberland.

[441] Thomas Morton.

[442] York.

[443] From the summer of 1636 Neile had ceased residing for most of the year in London. His 'Episcopall Houses' were at Bishopthorpe, Cawood and Southwell.

[444] See above, p. 122.

[445] Henry Wickham archdeacon of York, John Neile archdeacon of Cleveland, John Cosin archdeacon of the East Riding and William Robinson, archdeacon of Nottingham.

5 & 6. That your Maiesties foure poynts, concerning catechising, lectures, and Lecturers are duly observed. For I indure noe Lecturer, but in the nature of a Curate: Some well disposed beneficed men there are in my dioces, which on some weeke dayes goe and preach in places where there wanteth a preaching minister; whome in theire soe doeing, with other well deserving men in the ministery, I doe with my best indeavour, countenance and incourage.

7. Touching chaplaines, or rather ministers, living in the houses of those that are not legally qualified to have chaplaines, I have heretofore given your Maiestie an humble account how it is done for the releefe of poore men, and obtayning men of reasona[ble] parts to serve the Cures, where the stipends or salaries are so small, that noe men would otherwise serve the Cures.[446]

8. Of your Maiesties royall and Religious care, to have the people hold to the diligent frequenting of the publique divine Service and catechising, my selfe, my Archdeacons, [and] subordinate officers, have that due regard that becommeth us: and use our best indeavours for the performance thereof.

9. I have nothing to informe your Maiestie.

10. Your Maiesties commaundement agaynst turning Leases for yeares into Lives, is duly observed, both by my selfe and all others whome it concerneth, for any thing that I can learne or heare of to the contrary.[447]

11. This doeth not concerne mee.

12. I doe not finde in my dioces any inclination to innovation, in any thing which concerneth either the doctrine or the discipline of the Church of England. Onely I finde, that too many of your Maiesties subiects inhabiting in the east parts of Yorkeshire, are gone into new England, among which there is one Rogers,[448] that had a benefice well worth £240 *per annum*, gone; whome I had laboured by the space of two yeares in sundry conferences to reclayme, and refused to suffer him to Resigne: *C.R. An honnester man must bee*   But at the last, hee going on shipboard for new ☞ *put in place*[449]   England, wrote his letter to mee, acknowledged that I had given him good Counsell, but in vaine; and prayed mee to accept of his Resignation, for gone hee was for New England

I will not presume any further of your Maiesties patience, God of his infinite mercy, blesse, preserve and prosper your Sacred Maiestie; your right virtuous Consort the Queenes Maiestie, the most hopefull Prince Charles, and the rest of your Royall Progenie, with dayly increase of all spirituall and temporall Blessings upon yow, And hee of his infinite goodnes, strengthen your arme, and direct your Counsells, to abate the pride, asswage the malice, and confound the devises of all those, that disturbe your peaceable and pious governement, which is and shall be the dayly prayer of

your Sacred Maiesties most humble and faithfull servant and Chaplaine
R: Ebor:[450]

---

446 See above, pp. 106, 123–4.
447 Neile was less compliant than this comment suggests. See Foster, 'Church policies of the 1630s', p. 199.
448 Ezekiel Rogers (1588–1660), for whom see *ODNB*.
449 A manicule, probably in the king's hand, appears beneath this annotation.
450 Richard Neile.

Canterbury province, 1639

In Dei Nomine Amen.[451]

May it please your most Sacred Majesty.

According to your Royall Commandes expressed in your Instructions for the good of the Church I here most humbly present this my Accompt for the yeare finished now at Christmas 1639.

Canterbury.   And first to beginne with my owne Diocess. The great thinge which is amiss there, and beyond my power to remedye, is the Stiffnes of divers Anabaptists and Separatists from the Church of England, especially in and about the Partes neare Ashford. And I doe not finde eyther by my owne Experience, or by any advise from my Officers, that this is like to be remedyed, <u>unless the Statute</u> *C.R. It wer not amiss to speake*   <u>concerning Abjuration of the Kingdome,</u>[452] <u>or</u> *with the Keeper*[453] *about this*   <u>some other waye by the power of the Temporall</u> <u>Lawe, or State,</u>[454] be thought upon. But how fitt that may be done for the present, especially in these broken tymes, I humbly submitt to your Majestys wisdome, having often complayned of this before.[455]

Many that were brought to good order for receyving of the Holy Communion, where the Rayles stand before the Table, are now of late fallen off and refuse to come up thither to receyve. But this God willing I shall take care of, and order as well as I can, and with as much speed. And the same is now commonly fallen out in diverse other Diocesses.

There was about halfe a yeare since one that pretended himselfe a Minister, who gott many Followers in Sandwich, and some neighbouring Parishes, but at last was found to have gone under three Names, Enoch, Swann, and Grey,[456] and in as severall Habits, of a Minister, an ordinary Layman, and a Royster. And this being discovered he fledd the Country before any of my Officers could lay hold on him. Upon this occasion I have commanded my Commissary and Archdeacon[457] to give charge in my Name to all Parsons and Vicars of my Diocess that they suffer noe man to preach in theyr Cures but such as for whom they will answere, as well otherwise, as for the Poynt of Conformity, which I hope will prevent the like abuse hereafter.

London.   In this Diocess the last yeare[458] there was some Heat struck by opposite Preaching in the Pulpitt, between one Mr Goodwine Vicar of St Stephens in Colmanstreet, and some other Ministers in the Citty, concerning the Act of Beleiving, and the Imputation of Christs' Righteousnes in the Justification of a Sinner. And the Peoples mindes were much perplexed hereabouts. This busines

---

[451] LPL, MS 943, pp. 291–6; endorsed 'Lord Archbishop of Canterbury his accompt of his province for the yeare; 1639:' (p. 298). There is some damage to the right-hand edges of pp. 291, 293 and 295, so the transcription here also draws on *Troubles and tryal of … William Laud*, pp. 558–64.

[452] See above, p. 125.

[453] Thomas Coventry, lord keeper 1625–40.

[454] Underlined by Charles I.

[455] See above, pp. 95, 101, 110, 125, 132.

[456] See Como, *Blown by the spirit*, pp. 67–9; and above, p. 98.

[457] William Kingsley.

[458] See above, p. 132.

was quyeted by my Lord the Bishop[459] and his Chancellor,[460] and a Promise of forbearance made. Yet now lately Mr Goodwine hath preached againe in the same way and the same perplexity is like to be caused againe thereby in the Citty, yet my Lord the Bishop is in hope to settle this alsoe quietly, wherein he shall have the best assistance I can give him.

The Archdeacons in this Diocess and others are too negligent in giving theyr Bishopps due information of such things as are committed to their charge.[461]

Mr Joseph Symonds Rector of St Martyns Iremonger lane, is utterly fallen from the Church of England, and hath abandoned his Benefice and gone beyond the Seas, and soe was deprived in September last past.[462] Mr Daniel Votyer Rector of St Peters in Westcheap, hath been likewise convented for diverse Inconformityes, and promised Reformation, as Mr Symonds alsoe did, but being now called into the High Commission, order is taken for the Officiating of his Cure till it shall appeare whether he will desert it or noe. For he alsoe is gone beyond the Seas.[463]

Mr George Seaton Rector of Bushy in the County of Hertford is charged with continuall Nonresidency, and other misdemeanors, little beseeming a Clergyman. But of this neyther my Lord nor my selfe can say more to your Majesty till wee see what will rise in proofe against him.[464]

Winchester.   My Lord the Bishop[465] of this Diocess give's me a very fayre Accompt of all things regular therein, saving that the Popish Recusants (which he saith are many in that Diocess) doe yearly increase there, and that this may appeare by the Bills of Presentment in his annuall Inquisitions.

Oxford.   My Lord the Bishop[466] informes me that he hath been very carefull in poynt of Ordination as being a Bishop neare the University, and to whom many resort for Holy Orders at tymes appointed by the Church. But he complaines that having refused to give Orders to twenty or thirty at an Ordination, most of them have addressed themselves to other Bishopps, and of them receyved Orders, not onely without Letters Dimissory, but without such qualification as the Canon require's.

In this case I would humbly advise your Majesty that my Lord the Bishop may *C.R. Command him in my name* enquire and certifye by what Bishopps these *to doe so* Partyes soe refused by him were admitted into Holy Orders,[467] that soe they may be admonished to be more carefull for the future, and that this Abuse may not finde incouragement and increase.

For Popish Recusants they have been proceeded against in this Diocess according to lawe, savinge onely such of them as have pleaded and shewed your Majestys Exemption under your Great Seale from being questioned in any Ecclesiasticall Court for matters concerning theyr Religion.

[459] William Juxon.
[460] Arthur Duck.
[461] Juxon had voiced the same complaint in 1635 and 1637: see above, pp. 102, 126.
[462] Rector of St Martin Ironmonger Lane 1632–9, and by 1641 a pastor in Rotterdam. See Hennessey, *Novum repertorium*, p. 284; A. Wood, *Athenae Oxonienses* (4 vols., London, 1813–20), IV, 303.
[463] For Votier's account of his troubles with Laud in the 1630s, see TNA: PRO, SP 16/499/35.
[464] *CSPD 1639–40*, p. 272, *CSPD 1640*, pp. 388, 396, 404; see also *CSPD 1640–1*, pp. 169, 189.
[465] Walter Curle.
[466] John Bancroft.
[467] Underlined by Charles I.

Coventry and I finde by the Bishops Certificat that he[468] hath constantly resided upon
Lichfield.   his Episcopall Houses, but saith that he cannot have his health at
    Eccleshall, and hath therfore since resided in his Pallace at Lichfield,
but with very little comfort, by reason of Inmates left as his Lord saith upon
the Churches possession. His Lordship adde's that he hath an ancyent Pallace at
Coventry in lease, but with reservation of the use thereof, in case the Bishop shall at
C.R. I am content   any tyme come to lyve there.[469] <u>Here he meane's</u>
<u>to reside for a tyme</u>[470] if it shall stand with your Majestys good likinge.

For Popish Recusants his Lordship saith they are presented and prosecuted
according to the Lawe.

Norwich.   This Diocess my Lord the Bishop[471] assures me is as quyet uniforme and
    conformable as any in the Kingdome, if not more. And doth avowe it,
that all which stood out in Suffolke as well as Norfolke at his comming to that Sea,
are come in, and have now legally subscribed and professed all conformity, and for
ought he can learne observe it accordingly. Yet his Lordship confesseth that some of
the vulgar sort in Suffolke are not conformable enough, especially in comming up
to receyve at the Steppes of the Chancell where the Railes are sett.[472] But he hope's
by fayre means he shall be able to worke upon them in tyme.

His Lordship addes that some have endighted a Minister because he would
not come downe from the Communion Table to give them the Sacrament in theyr
Seats.[473] But this your Majesty hath been formerly acquainted with by the Ministers
Petition, which you were graciously pleased to command me to underwrite and send
to the Lord Cheife Justice[474] who ride's that Circuit which I did accordingly and
hope your Majesty will be pleasd to take care that there may be some Settlement
in this Particular.

Elye.   My Lord the Bishop of Elye[475] informes me that Sir John Cutts a
    Gentleman neare Cambridge keeps a Chaplaine, being not thereto (as
he conceyves) qualifyed by Lawe. Sir John pretends that he keeps him as a Curat to
the Parson. The case may it please your Majesty is this. In the Towne of Childerly
there were of old two Parishes Magna and Parva. The one was longe since wasted
and lost. The other yet remaines Presentative. But the whole Towne is depopulated
except the Knights House, and the Church is gone. Upon the decayed walles whereof
stand meane houses of Office, as Brewhouse, Stable etc. Upon this Rectory the
Knight ever provides to have a Titular Incumbent who now is one Mr Rainbowe[476] a
fellow of S. Magdalen College in Cambridge, and houshold Chaplaine to the Earle
of Suffolke.[477] What allowance the Knight makes him is not knowne. Tithes he takes
none. The Knight and his Family goe to noe other church; but he hath a Chappell
which he saith was consecrated by Bishop Heton,[478] and produce's an Instrument

---

[468]   Robert Wright.
[469]   See TNA: PRO, SP 16/310/7.
[470]   Underlined by Charles I.
[471]   Richard Montagu.
[472]   See Fincham (ed.), *Visitation articles*, II, 219.
[473]   This was one of a crop of similar cases: see Fincham and Tyacke, *Altars restored*, pp. 225–6.
[474]   Sir John Bramston; see Fincham and Tyacke, *Altars restored*, pp. 225–6.
[475]   Matthew Wren. His certificate, summarized here by Laud, is in LPL, MS 943, pp. 615–17.
[476]   Edward Rainbowe, bishop of Carlisle 1664–84.
[477]   Theophilus Howard, second earl of Suffolk (1584–1640).
[478]   Martin Heton, bishop of Ely 1600–9.

with Seale purporting That on such a day at Childerly Bishop Heton did consecrate a Chappell by saying Service there himselfe, and having a Sermon. Now upon coulor hereof the Knight enterteynes a Stipendary, who is termed his Chaplaine, and payes him a Stipend, but he is neyther appointed nor payd by the Incumbent.

The Bishop questioning the whole busines, hath required him to attend me, to knowe whether such a Consecration be to be allowed of. And if it be then whether I will allowe of a Chappell in that Place, instead of a Parish church now diverted to other profane uses. Of this I shall take the best care I can by advise of the ablest Civillians, and in the meane tyme certify your Majesty that the Bishop hath reason to be as strict in this as he may, because there is a good Rectory devoured by this meanes, and that allmost in the view of the University of Cambridge.

I likewise finde by my Lord the Bishops Accompt, that there are divers Particulars of moment, and very fitt for redress, presented to him in his late (yet being his first) Visitation, and most of them in the University and Towne of Cambridge. As namely that Emanuel, Sidney, and Corpus Christi Colledges have certaine Roomes, built within the memory of man, which they use for Chappells to all holy uses, yet were never consecrated. That most of the Churchyards within the Towne of Cambridge are annoyed and profaned with Dwelling houses and Shoppes, and part of them turned into Gardens, whereby Digging the Bones of the Dead have been displaced, with divers other Profanations. As namely the Churchyardes of St Michaels, St Maryes, St Bennets, and of St Buttolphes. And farther, that in most of the Chancells of the Churches in Cambridge, there are Common Seates, over high and unfitting that place in diverse respects.[479] In all which businesses, the Bishop hath been very tender both out of his respect to his Mother the University of Cambridge, and because diverse of the Benefices in Cambridge are Impropriations belonging to some Colledges there: yet is pleased to aske my direction herein, and I most humbly doe your Majestys. And herein if your Majesty soe please I thinke it may be fitt to

C.R. It must not bee   consider well of the ill Example, if 3 Colledge Chappells shall be used without any Consecration.[480] And for the Profanations and disorderly Seats, I thinke if an Admonition would amend them, it were well given,

C.R. you ar in the right, if faire   but if that prevaile not, the High Commission
meanes will not, power must   may order it, if your Majesty soe please. And
redress   I hope my Lord the Bishop should not have had all this to doe at his first comming into that Diocess, if I could have held my Metropoliticall Visitation of that Sea before this tyme. From performance of which Duty, I have been bold heretofore to acquaint your Majesty what hath hindred me.[481]

---

[479] In his report, Wren stated that the pews and seats much hindered 'the prospect up to the Communion Table, and the hearing of the Ministers voice' (LPL, MS 943, p. 617).

[480] Underlined by Charles I.

[481] Ely and Oxford were the two dioceses excluded from his metropolitical visitation of the southern province in 1634–7, since Laud was intent on securing the right of visitation over both universities as metropolitan, which he would then visit at the same time as the dioceses which surrounded them. In June 1636 Laud obtained the authority from Charles I to visit both universities, but in the event never exercised it. Later, as a prisoner in the Tower, Laud recalled that about this time 'my troubles began … to be foreseen by me, and I visited them not' (Laud, *Works*, IV, 193). He did, however, conduct a visitation of Ely diocese in 1638, during the *sede vacante*, prior to Wren's arrival as bishop.

There are alsoe diverse poore Cures within six or seven miles round about Cambridge, which are served by some fellowes or other Members of Colledges within the University, who being many of them Stipendaryes, goe or send thither upon Sundayes, and perchance on Holy dayes to read Service, but are absent all the rest of the weeke from all necessarye dutyes of theyr Cure. By this meanes the Parishioners want much necessary helpe and comfort in all tyme of Sickness eyther of them or theyr familyes. Against this I have taken the best care I can in Oxford,[482] but how to effect it in Cambridge I understand not soe well, being not acquainted with the course of that University.

There hapned alsoe in the Towne of Tadlowe a very ill Accident on Christmas day 1638 by reason of not having the Communion Table rayled in, that it might be kept from Profanations. For in Sermon tyme a Dogge came to the Table, and tooke the loafe of Bread prepared for the Holy Sacrament, in his mouth and ranne away with it.[483] Some of the Parishioners tooke the same from the Dogge, and sett it againe upon the Table. After Sermon the Minister[484] could not thinke fitt to consecrate this Bread, and other fitt for the Sacrament was not to be hadd in that Towne, and the day soe farre spent they could not send for it to another Towne. Soe there was no Communion. And this was presented by fower sworne men of the Towne aforesaid.

Lastly it was likewise presented to the Bishop that about forty years agoe one Sir Francis Hynd did pull downe the Church of St Ethelred in Histon to which then apperteyned a Vicarage Presentative, and forced the Parishioners to thrust themselves upon another small Church in the said Towne to the great wronge of the Parishioners thereof. And that the Lead Timber, Stones, Bells, and all other Materialls were sold away by him or imployed to the Building of his House at Madingley. And that now it is called in question, the People (not being able of themselves to reedify the Church) *C.R. Cottington*[485] *would be spoken* can gett noe redresse against the Descendants *withall concerning this* from the said Sir Francis, becaue the Heyre is a Child, and in Wardship to your Majesty.

Hereford.   There is notice come to my Lord the Bishop[486] of some Brownists in that part of his Diocess adjoyning to Wales, which Schismatically preach dangerous Errors, and stirre up the People to followe them. And when they heare of any Inquiry made after them, they slippe out into another Diocess. But the Bishop promiseth to doe his best to order them. But howsoever your Majesty may hereby see, how these Schismes increase in all Partes of your Dominions.

Bristoll.   This Diocess is in good order. And there was lately given tenn poundes *per annum* for 4 solemn Sermons to be preached annually for ever, which the Bishop[487] hath ordered very well.

Peterburgh.   In this Diocess Catechizing in the afternoone by question and answere is generally well observed, though some men doe preach also in the afternoone. In this Particular the Bishop[488] crave's to receyve direction, whether he shall commande them to Catechize onely, and not preach, because your Majestys

---

[482]   See Laud, *Works*, V, 207–9.
[483]   Wren noted that the dog belonged to one William Staple (LPL, MS 943, p. 617).
[484]   Samuel Bradstreet, vicar of Tadlow since 1613.
[485]   Francis Cottington (1579?–1652), master of the Court of Wards.
[486]   George Coke.
[487]   Robert Skinner.
[488]   John Towers, bishop of Peterborough 1638–49.

Instructions seeme to be strict in this poynt. I thinke your Majesty may be pleased to *C.R. So that Catechizing be first* leave the Ministers to preach if they will, soe *dewly performed, let them have* that they doe first Catechize orderly by question *a Sermon after that if they desyre* and answere, and after preach upon the same *it* Heads to the People, for theyr better under- standing of those questions.[489]

Besides some Knights and Esquires keepe Schoolemasters in theyr houses or Schollers to converse with, or dyet the Vicar when his Maintenance is little. And this they saye is not to keepe a Chaplaine, which your Majestys Instructions forbidd. Yet most of these read or saye Service in theyr Houses (which is the Office of a Chaplaine) but they read not the Prayers of the Church according to the Liturgye established. The Bishop crave's direction in this alsoe. And I thinke it be very *C.R. It is most necessarie that* necessary that the Bishop proceed strictly and *the Bishop observe this that* keepe all such that they read or saye noe Prayers *you mention striklie* but those which are allowed and established by the Church in the Booke of Common Prayers.[490]

There are not observed more then seven or eight throughout the whole Diocess which seeme refractory to the Church, and they have made large professions of theyr conformity, which the Bishop will settle soe soone as he can. But this he saith he findes plainly, that there are fewe of the Laity factious but where the Clergy misleades them. And this I doubt is too true in most Partes of the Kingdome. They have in this Diocess come to him very thick to receyve Confirmation, to the number of some thousandes.[491]

Lincolne. There were two Lectures held this last yeare, the one at Wainfleet and the other at Kirton in Lindsey, where some two or three of the Ministers which read the Lecture were disorderly. Amonge the rest one Mr Shove[492] preached very factiously just at that tyme when your Majesty was at Barwicke,[493] and his fellowe Lecturers complained not of him. Hereupon the Chancellor[494] having notice of it, called him in question, and the busines was so foule and soe fully proved, that the Partye fledd the Country, and is thought to be gone for New-England.

Some other smaller Exorbitancyes there are which the Chancellor complaines of, but there is hope that this Example will doe some good among them.

Exeter. In this Diocess one Mr Coxe[495] upon Hosea 4.4 preached a Sermon to prove that the Church of England did not maynteyne the Calling of Bishoppes to be *jure divino*, which Sermon troubled those Partes not a little. My Lord the Bishop[496] after he had had Speech with him sent him to me. When he came it pleased God soe to blesse me that I gave him satisfaction, and he went home very well contented, and made a handsome Retraction voluntarily of himselfe, and satisfyed the People.

---

[489] See Davies, *Caroline captivity*, pp. 139–40.
[490] Underlined by Charles I.
[491] A rare mention of the rite of confirmation in the annual accounts. See above p. 137, and Fincham (ed.), *Visitation articles*, II, 155 n. 12.
[492] Probably Edward Shove, who resigned as vicar of Elsham, Lincs, on 4 Jan. 1638: LPL, Laud's Register II, fo. 7r.
[493] In June 1639, negotiating with the Scottish Covenanters at the end of the First Bishops' War.
[494] John Farmery.
[495] Benjamin Cox (1595–?1663), for whom see his entry in *ODNB*.
[496] Joseph Hall.

St Asaph.   In the skirtes of this Diocess in Shropshire there was a Conventicle of meane Persons layd hold on, and Complaint was made to the Counsell of the Marches. And the Lord President of Wales[497] very honourably gave notice of it both to the Lords and my selfe, and they were remitted to receyve such Censure as the Lawes Ecclesiasticall impose upon them.

Bath and Wells.
Salisbury.
Worcester.
Glocester.   These Bishoppes[498] doe all certifye that every thinge
Rochester.   is well in theyr severall Diocesses, concerning the
St Davids.   Particulars conteyned in your Majestys Instructions,
Landaff.   and otherwise.
Bangor.

Chichester.   The like is certified by the Lord Bishop of Chichester,[499] saving that of late there hath hapned some little Disorder in the East partes of that Diocess about Lewis, which wee are taking care to settle aswell as wee can. And for Nonconformists he saith, that Diocess is not soe much troubled with Puritan Ministers, as with Puritan Justices of the Peace, of which later there are store.[500]

C.R. I hope it is to be understoode that   And soe with my Prayers for your Majestys
what is not certifyed here to be   longe and happy Raigne I humbly submitt
amiss is right, tuching the   this my Accompt January 2 1639.[501]
observation of my Instructions,   W: Cant:[502]
which granted, this is no ill Certificat
10 Feb 1639/40 CR

York province, 1639

It is now the time, that I should present to his Maiesty a Certificate of the due observation, and performance of his Gracious Royall Instructions, throughout this Province.[503] I have heertofore ben bolde to offer his Sacred Maiesty tedious discourses, both of mine owne diocesse, and alsoe such Certificates as I received from my Brethren, the Bishops of the Province, I will now make amends with brevitie; which I pray your Honour[504] to present to his Maiesty; and informe him; That I have received Certificates from each of my Brethren the Bishops of Durham, Chester, Carleil and Man;[505] in which they doe assure mee, that all and every of his Maiesties sayd Instructions are duelie and punctually observed and performed in theire

[497] See above, p. 83 n. 27.
[498] William Piers, John Davenant, John Thornborough, Godfrey Goodman, John Warner, Roger Mainwaring, William Murray and William Roberts.
[499] Brian Duppa.
[500] For a similar comment from Richard Montagu, Duppa's predecessor, see above, p. 100.
[501] 1640 new style.
[502] William Laud.
[503] TNA: PRO, SP 16/441/93; extract from a letter from Archbishop Neile to Secretary of State Windebank. Endorsed '10 January 1639 The Lord Archbishop of Yorke concerning Jenison received 14 answered 17.'
[504] Windebank.
[505] Thomas Morton, John Bridgeman, Barnabas Potter and Richard Parr.

severall diocesses. And for mine owne diocesse, I should be unmannerlie to trouble his Maiesty with thinges not worthy his cognisance, and saying the same againe, which I have sayd in my last yeares Certificate: But I assure your Honour, all his Maiesties Instructions, and directions are, and shall be duely observed by mee and all my Officers; And I trust his Gracious Maiesty will vouchsafe to accept of this for the present …

Bishopthorp January 10 1639[506]   Yours Honours very loving frend and devoted Servant R: Ebor:[507]

---

[506] 1640 new style.
[507] Richard Neile.

4

'POPISH CUT-THROATS AGAINST US': PAPISTS, PROTESTANTS AND THE PROBLEM OF ALLEGIANCE IN EIGHTEENTH-CENTURY IRELAND

Edited by
Robert G. Ingram

urney near Shalene Oct: 12th 232
1764

may it please your Grace —

I can not neglect giving you
an authentic account of a most unparalleld Riot
which happened at Rapho, six miles hence, last Sunday. —
Docter Oswald, the good Bishop, who has much at Heart
the good of Hisstown, the second for size and good Houses in
the county of Donegal, found all His schemes to make the
people happy defeated, by the insolence of a Set of Rioters
who have been ever disturbing the peace of the town, and
had often offerd indignitys even to the great and good Bishop
Goulter in his time. — So remedy this He sent for several
of the Inhabitants, to let them know, that the condition
of geting their Leases renewed was that they should join in his
Discountenance these Rioters, to which purpose He himself
deposited fifty pounds. — and finding that the Ring leader
of this Infamous crew was one Bates who kept a
publick House for vending of whiskey in the town, He
sent His Agent mr. Abraham to him last Saturday to signify to Him, that He must either change His Behaviour
or depart from the town. — Bates, supported by His
clan insulted and Beat the agent, and swore that He
would be revenged on the Bishop. — Accordingly, He
charged a musquet with Ball: and was going out that
night to the castle, in order to shoot the Bishop this the

Introduction*

The Irish problem during the eighteenth century was the problem of allegiance: how could a country filled with Roman Catholics be trusted to obey the protestant monarchs of England? It is now something of a commonplace to argue that the mid-eighteenth century evidenced an increased spirit of tolerance among the English *élite* towards Roman Catholics.[1] Yet, correspondence, which is now housed in Lambeth Palace Library, from William Henry (d. 1768), dean of Killaloe, to Thomas Secker (1693–1768), archbishop of Canterbury, testifies to the tenacity and depth of anti-catholic sentiment among the protestant *élite* on both sides of the Irish Sea.[2] Indeed, that correspondence illuminates the confessional politics of mid-century Ireland and reminds us that many during the era continued to believe that the early modern European wars of religion had not yet been fought to their end.[3]

In an unusually revelatory letter to Frederick Hervey, bishop of Derry, in February 1768, Thomas Secker laid bare his thinking regarding the catholic threat.[4] The proximate provocation for Secker's missive was Hervey's work with the catholic Committee to draft an oath of allegiance whose object, Hervey wrote to one Irish catholic in 1767, was 'to leave your faith entire but to secure your allegiance to the present government and to make you independent of all foreign jurisdiction whatsoever'.[5] Secker, staunchly orthodox but typically no proponent of coercion, would, in this instance, have none of Hervey's eirenical schemes. 'No one can be a heartier Friend to the Civil Toleration of all religious opinions & practices, which are not very prejudicial or dangerous to Civil Society', he protested to Hervey at the outset of his letter.

*   I need particularly to thank James Kelly for his enormous generosity in helping me to identify a number of opaque references, particularly regarding Irish legislation. Nigel Aston kindly provided transcriptions of useful references from the Bowood Archives, which I quote by kind permission of the marquess of Landsdowne and the Bowood Manuscript Trustees. I also thank Bill Bulman, Jonathan Clark, William Gibson, Patrick Griffin, Jill Ingram, Jessica Roney, Gabriel Sewell, Bruce Steiner, Stephen Taylor and Robert Whan for their assistance in the preparation of this piece.

1   Colin Haydon, *Anti-catholicism in eighteenth-century England, c. 1714–80: a political and social study* (Manchester, 1993), pp. 164–203.

2   That correspondence (Lambeth Palace Library (LPL), Secker papers 2, fos. 232–44, 250–77) covers the years Oct. 1764 to Dec. 1767 and runs to just over 15,000 words. Other correspondence between Henry and Secker, save for a few letters now in the Public Record Office of Northern Ireland, is no longer extant.

3   J. C. D. Clark, '"In denial": wars of religion in English discourse, 1639–2008', in *idem, The writing on the wall* (forthcoming). I thank Professor Clark for allowing me to read a copy of his piece in advance of publication.

4   Public Record Office of Northern Ireland (PRONI), D/2798/5/6: Secker to Hervey, 25 Feb. 1768. Unless otherwise noted, the quotations in this paragraph derive from this letter.

5   Quoted in Gerard O'Brien, 'Hervey, Frederick Augustus, fourth earl of Bristol (1730–1803)', *Oxford dictionary of national biography*, ed. H. C. G. Matthew and Brian Harrison (Oxford, 2004) (*ODNB*). For Hervey's work trying to formulate an oath of allegiance for Irish catholics, see Thomas Bartlett, *The fall and rise of the Irish nation: the catholic question, 1690–1830* (Savage, MD, 1992), pp. 78–80, and, more generally, Patrick Fagan, *Divided loyalties: the question of the oath for Irish catholics in the eighteenth century* (Dublin, 1997).

> But I look on the Church of Rome as peculiarly formidable to Protestant States, and especially to these Kingdoms. For it claims absolute Authority over the very minds of men: it is a powerful Body, united under one Head: its Adherents are numerous even in England, much more in Ireland: its Emissaries are disciplined to exact Obedience, zealous to advance its Interest, skillful by Instruction & Experience how to do it: and for that purpose the genuine members of this vast Community are always ready to use Force & Fraud, when it shall be requisite.

For as Secker proceeded to explain in some detail, catholic assurances that 'the spiritual power [of the Church] inflicts only spiritual Censures' or that 'the pope is not infallible' amounted to nothing more than casuistry, and even 'the most learned & moderate' Pope Benedict XIV (1675–1758) 'hath plainly declared in print, that the Divines of that church agree in the Lawfulness of putting Hereticks to Death by the Assistance of the Civil Arm'. Unburdened from penal laws, catholics would quickly prove that their allegiance to the pope trumped their allegiance to their king, so that 'a Protestant State hath no security against papists, but from want of ability in them, & especially in its popish Subjects, to overrun it'. Indeed, Secker warned Hervey, so great was the catholic threat that protestantism still risked annihilation. These nations have peculiar Cause to be on their Guard against Popery', he insisted.

> Their Neighbourhood to France & Spain are an additional Cause. And the Church of Rome will certainly direct its chief Efforts to gain by Degrees a Superiority in the British Islands: because were that once due, Holland & Germany, to say no more, would have little strength to resist.

Thomas Secker normally viewed the contemporary religious, political and geopolitical terrain with gimlet-eyed realism: not so in this instance. Geography and French impotence after the Seven Years War meant that no serious external power stood poised to threaten England's security.[6] Nor could anyone claim creditably during the 1760s that England faced substantive pressure from Roman Catholics. Abroad, the mid-century papacy suffered from the 'humiliating reality of papal weakness',[7] and, indeed, when Clement XIII died in 1769, Horace Walpole, in Italy at the time, wondered whether Clement's successor would be 'the last pope'.[8] At home, Roman Catholics accounted for less than 1 per cent of the English populace and had a demonstrable record of loyalty to Britain's Hanoverian monarchs.[9] England had never been so securely, self-consciously or self-concertedly protestant.[10]

---

6   Paul W. Schroeder, *The transformation of European politics, 1763–1848* (Oxford, 1994), pp. 35–52. But cf. Brendan Simms, *Three victories and a defeat: the rise and fall of the first British empire, 1714–1783* (London, 2007), pp. 555–75.

7   Eamon Duffy, *Saints and sinners: a history of the papacy* (New Haven, 2006), pp. 245. More generally, see Nigel Aston, 'Continental catholic Europe', in *Enlightenment, reawakening and revolution 1660–1815*, ed. Timothy Tackett and Stewart J. Brown (Cambridge, 2006), pp. 15–32.

8   Quoted in Owen Chadwick, *The popes and the European revolution* (Oxford, 1980), p. 368.

9   Haydon, *Anti–catholicism*, pp. 117–66. A 1767 English census of Roman Catholics recorded that there were 69,376 of them in a nation of around 7 million people: John Bossy, *The English catholic community, 1570–1850* (Oxford, 1976), p. 184; E. S. Worrall (ed.) *Returns of papists* (2 vols., London, 1989).

10 J. C. D. Clark, 'Protestantism, nationalism and national identity, 1660–1832', *Historical Journal (HJ)* XLI, 1 (2000), 249–76; Tony Claydon and Ian McBride (eds.), *Protestantism and national identity: Britain and Ireland, c. 1650 to c. 1850* (Cambridge, 1998).

Yet if Secker's hyperventilated analysis of the catholic threat to England related only tenuously to reality, it nevertheless bears closer scrutiny, for he clearly believed that the catholic threat was real. What, other than the clarity of hindsight, accounts for this disconnect between things as they were and things as Secker perceived them to be? At least part of the virulent anti-popery of Secker's letter to Hervey may be chalked up to the public pressure brought to bear upon him and other leaders of the Church of England from a motley crew of anti-dogmatists and heterodox to take a hard line against a supposed fifth column of Roman Catholics within England.[11] Secker himself acknowledged to Hervey that 'any proposals, made by English Bishops, that could bear but the smallest Appearance of being favourable to papists, though proceeding from the sincerest purpose of securing the Establishment in Church & State against them, would raise a Clamour against us, that we should not be able to withstand'.[12]

More importantly, though, Secker's astringent analysis reminds us of another, often overlooked, context: Ireland. Seemingly immune from the strictures upon historians to practise an integrative 'British' history, Ireland nonetheless held an important place in the English official mind throughout the eighteenth century.[13] This was certainly true of Thomas Secker who, buttressed by William Henry's descriptions, looked on Ireland as a confessional dystopia: his response and that of metropolitan officials to this world turned upside down laid bare the limits of enlightenment and revealed clearly the place of Ireland in England's empire. Perhaps even more importantly, the Henry–Secker correspondence testifies eloquently to the burden of history during the eighteenth century, for the previous century's internecine religious wars over 'popery and arbitrary government' cast a long shadow, and nowhere more so than in Ireland, where annual commemorations kept alive memories of the 1641 rebellion and the Jacobite resistance to Williamite rule.[14] Indeed, William Henry's and Thomas Secker's interpretations of the Irish religio-political situation suggest that, within the established Churches of England and

---

11 Robert G. Ingram, *Religion, reform and modernity in the eighteenth century: Thomas Secker and the Church of England* (Woodbridge, 2007). Francis Blackburne, *Considerations on the present state of the controversy between protestants and papists in Great Britain and Northern Ireland* (Dublin, 1770), and *idem, Memoirs of Thomas Hollis* (London, 1780), voice the anti-dogmatic fears about Roman Catholics during the eighteenth century. For context, see Colin Haydon, '"Popery at St. James's": the conspiracy theses of William Payne, Thomas Hollis, and Lord George Gordon', in *Conspiracies and conspiracy theory in early modern Europe*, ed. Barry Coward and Julian Swann (Aldershot, 2004), pp. 173–95, and, more generally, B. W. Young, *Religion and enlightenment in eighteenth-century England* (Oxford, 1998), esp. pp. 19–80.

12 PRONI, D/2798/5/6: Secker to Hervey, 25 Feb. 1768.

13 For works which integrate eighteenth-century English and Irish histories, see D. W. Hayton, *Ruling Ireland, 1685–1742: politics, politicians and parties* (Woodbridge, 2004); J. C. D. Clark, 'Whig tactics and parliamentary precedent: the English management of Irish politics, 1754–1756', *HJ*, XXI, 2 (1978), 275–301; and F. G. James, *Ireland in the empire, 1688–1730* (Cambridge, MA, 1973).

14 For the causes and consequences of seventeenth-century England's wars of religion, see Jonathan Scott, *England's troubles: seventeenth-century English political instability in European context* (Cambridge, 2000). For eighteenth-century evocations of seventeenth-century events, see Toby Barnard, 'The uses of the 23rd of October 1641 and Irish protestant celebrations', *English Historical Review*, CVI (1991), 89–920, and James Kelly, '"The glorious and immortal memory": commemoration and protestant identity in Ireland, 1660–1800', *Proceedings of the Royal Irish Academy: Section C*, XCIV (1994), 25–52.

Ireland, many during the eighteenth century continued to fear that the seventeenth-century 'troubles' might not yet be fully behind them.[15]

I

As it so happened, most Irish also thought that their country was a confessional dystopia. At the lead of the line of complainants stood Roman Catholics, for eighteenth-century Ireland was an English colony with a London-managed protestant confessional state which governed an overwhelmingly catholic people.[16] Ireland's Reformation had failed miserably to convert the nation to protestantism,[17] and by the mid-eighteenth century, Roman Catholics, who accounted for 75–80 per cent of the Irish populace, suffered under penal laws (more often known as 'popery laws') which technically forbade them from owning land, taking leases longer than three decades, practising law, holding government office, serving on grand juries or in the army and navy, studying overseas, or teaching or operating schools in Ireland. Irish catholic priests were likewise harried by legislation aimed at peeling them away from the Jacobite cause: by 1709, most priests had no legal protection under the law.[18] That officials enforced the penal laws relatively laxly did not alter the fundamental fact that Irish Roman Catholics were an oppressed, if mostly quiescent, majority.[19] Nor did it do anything to lessen the grinding poverty among catholics so evident to nearly every observer of Irish life.

Protestants constituted the remaining quarter of eighteenth-century Irish society, with presbyterians comprising the majority of that protestant minority.[20] As John Bowes, Ireland's lord chancellor, explained to Secker in 1763, 'The Northern Counties of Ireland are fullest of Inhabitants, of Scotch Original; Industrious but strongly

---

[15] Caroline Robbins, *The eighteenth-century commonwealthman* (Cambridge, MA, 1959), and Bernard Bailyn, *The ideological origins of the American revolution* (Cambridge, MA, 1967), both argue that many in the eighteenth-century Anglo-American world continued to view their world through seventeenth-century lenses, but both, mistakenly, treat religious concerns as largely epiphenomenal.

[16] Jacqueline Hill, 'Convergence and conflict in eighteenth-century Ireland', *HJ*, XLIV, 4 (2001), 1039–63; Thomas Bartlett, '"This famous island set in a Virginian sea": Ireland in the British empire, 1690–1801', in *The eighteenth century* (Oxford History of the British Empire, vol. II), ed. P. J. Marshall (Oxford, 1998), pp. 253–75, and Toby Barnard, 'Farewell to Old Ireland', *HJ*, XXXVI, 4 (1993), 909–28, anatomize recent historiographical debates concerning the nature of eighteenth-century Irish society. Cf. S. J. Connolly, *Religion, law and power: the making of protestant Ireland, 1660–1760* (Oxford, 1992), and, more implicitly, *idem, Divided kingdom: Ireland, 1630–1800* (Oxford, 2008).

[17] James Murray, *Enforcing the English Reformation in Ireland: clerical resistance and political conflict in the diocese of Dublin, 1534–1590* (Cambridge, 2009); John McCafferty, *The reconstruction of the Church of Ireland: Bishop Bramhall and the Laudian reforms, 1633–1641* (Cambridge, 2007); Alan Ford, *The protestant reformation in Ireland, 1590–1641* (Dublin, 1997).

[18] J. L. McCracken, 'The ecclesiastical structure, 1714–60', in *A new history of Ireland, IV: Eighteenth-century Ireland, 1691–1800*, ed. T. W. Moody and W. E. Vaughan (Oxford, 1986), pp. 91–99; Patrick J. Corish, *The Irish catholic experience: a historical survey* (Dublin, 1985), pp. 95–150. On the penal laws, see Maureen Wall, *The penal laws 1691–1760* (Dundalk, 1967).

[19] Cf. Connolly, *Religion, law and power*, pp. 263–313. For the ways Irish catholics dealt with the penal laws, see Patrick J. Corish, *The catholic community in the seventeenth and eighteenth centuries* (Dublin, 1981), and James Kelly, 'The impact of the penal laws', in *History of the catholic diocese of Dublin*, ed. James Kelly and Dáire Keogh (Dublin, 2000), pp. 144–74.

[20] McCracken, 'The ecclesiastical structure', pp. 99–104; J. C. Beckett, *Protestant dissent in Ireland, 1687–1780* (London, 1948).

attach'd to the Religion of their Ancestors.'[21] Those presbyterians (also known as 'protestant dissenters') likewise bore the burden of penal laws which denied them full citizenship. The relative religious freedom conferred by a toleration act in 1719 and annual indemnity acts failed fully to remove the sting of tithe obligations to the established Church of Ireland, the existence of test acts and other noisome legal disabilities. Throughout the eighteenth century, Ulster presbyterians formed a substantial bloc of immigrants to colonial British North America,[22] while those who remained in Ireland proved less and less willing as the century wore on to accept unquestioningly their second-class status.[23]

Members of the church as established by law – the Church of Ireland – were a minority within the Irish protestant minority, yet they alone enjoyed full civil, political and religious liberties.[24] 'Its bottom is unfortunately very narrow. It is not the religion of the people of Ireland. Its professors, at the very utmost, do not amount to more than one sixth of the Inhabitants…No church, in no Country in the world is so circumstanced', reckoned Edmund Burke of Ireland's state church, whose centres of concentration lay in the north and in towns.[25] Nevertheless, *élite* members of the Church of Ireland – subsequently dubbed the 'protestant ascendancy' – monopolized landed wealth and political power.[26] What about their own disproportionate power could members of the ascendancy possibly have to complain? Perhaps ironically, they refused to acknowledge their colonial status and 'patriots' among them resented the Dublin parliament's emasculation. Try as William Molyneux and others might to argue that Ireland, unlike the North American colonies, was England's sister kingdom, the reality of the ascendancy's political dependency on England was starkly apparent and, by the century's end, increasingly unacceptable. The mid-century Irish patriot aim, though, was not independence, but a closer integration to England, if on terms more favourable to members of the ascendancy.[27]

21 PRONI, T/2872/16: Bowes to Secker, 29 July 1763.

22 Patrick Griffin, *The people with no name: Ireland's Ulster Scots, America's Scots Irish, and the creation of a British Atlantic world, 1689–1764* (Princeton, 2001).

23 Ian McBride, 'Ulster presbyterians and the confessional state, c. 1688–1733', in *Political discourse in seventeenth- and eighteenth-century Ireland*, ed. D. George Boyce, Robert Ecclehall and Vincent Geoghegan (Basingstoke, 2001), pp. 169–92, and *idem*, *Scripture politics: Ulster presbyterians and Irish radicalism in the late eighteenth century* (Oxford, 1998), clearly elucidate presbyterian opposition to Ireland's confessional state.

24 The eighteenth-century Church of Ireland awaits its modern historian. Easily the best introductions to the subject are to be found in Toby Barnard and W. G. Neely (eds.), *The clergy of the Church of Ireland, 1000–2000* (Dublin, 2006), pp. 78–156; Toby Barnard, 'Parishes, pews and parsons: lay people and the Church of Ireland, 1647–1780', in *The laity and the Church of Ireland, 1000–2000*, ed. Raymond Gillespie and W. G. Neely (Dublin, 2002), pp. 70–103; and *idem*, 'Improving clergymen, 1660–1760', in *As by law established: the Church of Ireland since the Reformation*, ed. Alan Ford, James I. McGuire and Kenneth Milne (Dublin, 1995), pp. 136–51. Richard Mant, *The history of the Church of Ireland*, II: *From the Revolution to the union of the churches of England and Ireland, January 1, 1801* (London, 1840)(Mant, *HCI*), remains the most comprehensive treatment of ecclesiastical 'high' politics in eighteenth-century Ireland.

25 R. B. McDowell (ed.), *The correspondence of Edmund Burke*, VIII (Chicago, 1969), 55: Burke to William Fitzwilliam, fourth earl of Fitzwilliam, 21 Oct. 1794.

26 Toby Barnard, *A new anatomy of Ireland: the Irish protestants, 1649–1770* (New Haven, 2003), is the ablest treatment of the social foundations and practical workings of the protestant ascendancy. James Kelly, 'The eighteenth-century ascendancy: a commentary', *Eighteenth-Century Ireland*, V (1990), 173–88, traces the original use of the term 'protestant ascendancy' to the 1780s.

27 Ian McBride, ' "The common name of Irishman": protestantism and patriotism in eighteenth-century Ireland', in *Protestantism and National Identity*, ed. Claydon and McBride, pp. 236–61.

In mid-eighteenth-century Ireland, then, we have a confessional state with an established church whose adherents accounted for but a fraction of the island's populace but who nonetheless monopolized political power. In retrospect, the protestant ascendancy's monopoly proved remarkably sure, not least so because of the permanent presence of an army to defend the 'protestant interest'.[28] But members of the ascendancy did not think their situation so invulnerable at the time. 'Protestant power rested upon conquest, confiscation, and colonization', notes Ian McBride, 'and the continuing awareness of this fact was reflected not just in the popular culture of the native inhabitants but in the sense of insecurity so evident in Protestant consciousness.'[29] Few at the time voiced that protestant insecurity more loudly or clearly than William Henry, and his views should be treated as but the most intense flavor of *élite* Anglo-Irish opinion regarding Irish social, religious and political life and Ireland's proper relationship to England.[30] Henry might not have held the most prestigious offices within the established Church of Ireland, but the Anglo-Irish *élite* regularly gave him public hearings in some of the most visible venues in eighteenth-century Ireland.[31] His message remained constant: Ireland needed improving to stop the rot of popery and protestant dissent from destroying English rule in the kingdom.

II

William Henry dedicated himself to the English cause in Ireland. He did so not from a rung high atop the ladder of ecclesiastical preferment but from more modest posts, which he owed primarily to the patronage of Josiah Hort (*c.* 1674–1751), bishop of Kilmore, and the earls of Shelburne. Brought up in northern Ireland (probably to presbyterian parents) and educated at the University of Dublin, Henry early on gained the favour of Hort, who named Henry one of his domestic chaplains and who presented him to the northern Irish rectories of Killesher (1731) and Urney (1740).[32] Hort's marriage into the extended Fitzmaurice family opened the way for Henry to become one of the family's clients. Certainly by the late 1740s, Henry had established a connexion with the family, and in the autumn of 1750 he could be found writing a condolence letter to Henry Petty, first earl of Shelburne (1675–1751) on

---

28 S. J. Connolly, 'The defence of protestant Ireland, 1660–1760', in *A military history of Ireland*, ed. Thomas Bartlett and Keith Jeffrey (Cambridge, 1996), pp. 231–46.

29 McBride, *Scripture politics*, p. 15.

30 Toby Barnard, 'The languages of politeness and sociability', in *Political discourse in seventeenth- and eighteenth-century Ireland*, ed. Boyce, Ecclehall and Geoghegan, p. 209, argues for Henry as representative of the Anglo-Irish *élite* worldview. There is, of course, a problem of nomenclature regarding the Irish governing class. Its members habitually referred to themselves as 'English' or, as in Henry's case, 'British', but clearly too many at the same time considered themselves Irish 'patriots' and, among the non-imports, identified closely with the land of their birth. For purposes of clarity in this paper, though, I shall refer to the Irish governing class as the 'Anglo-Irish' or 'Anglo-Irish *élite*'.

31 See below, Letters 10, 11, 12. Over half of Henry's published works were sermons given not in his parish church, but to members of the Anglo-Irish *élite* in chapel royal, local assizes, the House of Commons, cathedral pulpits on important political anniversaries and the like.

32 James B. Leslie, *Derry clergy and parishes* (Enniskillen, 1940), pp. 302–3. Cf. Neal Garnham, 'Henry, William [pseudo. Britanno-Hibernus] (d. 1768)', *ODNB*, which suggests that Henry took up Urney in *c.* 1734. It is unclear why Hort took Henry on as a client, though there was a Gloucestershire connexion in both men's families: William Reynell, 'Hort, Josiah (*c.* 1674–1751)', *ODNB*.

the death of Shelburne's only son, James Petty, Viscount Dunkerron.[33] The first earl himself died in 1751, and his estates passed to his nephew, John (Fitzmaurice) Petty, first earl of Shelburne (of the second creation in 1753) (c. 1706–61). Henry and the new earl were rough contemporaries who appear to have got along well with one another, and Henry simply transferred his clientage over to him. In 1756, Shelburne established a linen-producing colony to Ballymote,[34] and through him Henry came quickly to be connected with it: by 1758 Henry was bragging that he intended to provide each of the Ballymote male colonists with 'a bible and backsword to defend it, and to every woman a prayer book and a spinning wheel'.[35] Shelburne also appears to have kept an eye out for more prestigious Irish livings to which Henry might succeed.[36]

Though Henry was a remarkable self-promoter even in an age accustomed to self-recommendation,[37] it took the intervention of the first and second earls of Shelburne, in 1761, to secure him the vacant deanery of Killaloe, a post which Henry held in conjunction with his Urney rectory until his death in 1768. The Shelburnes initially turned for help to Secker who, in turn, sought assistance from Philip Yorke, first earl of Hardwicke, and from Thomas Pelham-Holles, duke of Newcastle, to lobby on Henry's behalf 'for a Bishoprick or good deanery' in Ireland.[38] At the time, Secker respected Henry but did not know him well.[39] However, he thought his case worth promoting 'for the sake of merit and of the publick'. 'I have no other knowledge of him, than from the Letters, which your Lordship hath seen, and from a few little pieces of useful Tendency which he hath published', he explained to Hardwicke at the time, 'and from his general Character, as a worthy man, who hath taken great pains to promote the common welfare, in every way that he could.'[40]

33   Bowood papers, Bowood, S.126, fos. 37–8: Henry to Henry Petty, first earl of Shelburne, 6 Oct. 1750. I thank Nigel Aston for providing me with this reference and for helping me to clarify the nature of the Shelburne–Henry connexion.

34   W. G. Wood-Martin, *History of Sligo* (3 vols., Dublin, 1882–92), III, 243.

35   National Archives of Ireland, Calendar of miscellaneous letters and papers prior to 1760, s.d. 15 Mar. 1758: quoted in Toby Barnard, *Improving Ireland? Projectors, prophets and profiteers, 1641–1786* (Dublin, 2008), p. 38.

36   Bowood papers, S.90, fo. 73: John Fitzmaurice Petty, first earl of Shelburne, to William Petty, lord Fitzmaurice, 16 Mar. 1761. In this letter Shelburne notes that he has 'much obligation to [Henry], but you know that I have more'. I thank Nigel Aston for providing me with this reference.

37   For examples of Henry's self-recommendation for vacant Irish livings, see below Letters 2, 4, 11 and British Library (BL), Add. MS 35597, fo. 268: Henry to Hardwicke, 12 Apr. 1763; BL, Add. MS 32988, fos. 56–7: Henry to Newcastle, 19 Jan. 1768. For background, see William Gibson, ' "Unreasonable and unbecoming": self-recommendation and place-seeking in the Church of England, 1700–1900', *Albion*, XXVII, 1 (1996), 43–63.

38   BL, Add. MS 35596, fo. 278: Secker to Hardwicke, 18 Mar. 1761; LPL, Secker papers 2, fo. 222: Secker to Shelburne, 19 Mar. 1761; *ibid.*, fo. 223: Hardwicke to Secker, 19 Mar. 1761; BL, Add. MS 32926, fo. 370: Secker to Newcastle, 11 Aug. 1761.

39   Henry was thrilled to learn of Secker's translation to Canterbury. 'Are you overjoyed at the promotion of Dr. Secker from Oxford to Canterbury. Since virtue is sought & rewarded, I hope the Golden Age will return', he exclaimed in Apr. 1758: Bowood papers, S.133, fo. 8: Henry to John Fitzmaurice (c. 1706–61), first earl of Shelburne, 6 Apr. 1758. In early 1761, Shelburne wondered how much Secker could do to promote Henry's case: 'The A:Bishop of Canterbury has a high respect for him, but I doubt whether his Grace has weight enough o serve him; pray ponder this matter': Bowood papers, S.90, fo. 73: Shelburne to Lord Fitzmaurice, 16 Mar. 1761. Shelburne died on 14 May 1761, and his son (William Petty, second earl of Shelburne (1737–1805)) took up Henry's cause. I thank Nigel Aston for providing me with these references.

40   BL, Add. MS 35596, fo. 278: Secker to Hardwicke, 18 Mar. 1761.

The 'common welfare' which Henry had 'taken great pains to promote' concerned English control of Ireland. As Secker explained it to Halifax, Henry deserved promotion to an Irish bishopric because he was

> well affected to the general Interest of both nations, & … hath diligently & successfully served the publick there in matters of great Importance to Church & State: particularly by his Superintendency at the Charter Schools, by his Labours to obtain due Restraints agst Spirituous Liquors, & by assisting Ld Shelburne to settle Colonies of industrious Protestants in the South Part of that Country.[41]

In this description, Secker captured something of the scope and intensity of Henry's ambitions. Indeed, since the mid-1730s Henry had been a restless, relentless, unabashed 'improver', a proselyte convinced of English culture's innate superiority and of the inevitable material and moral benefits which would come to the Irish inferiors whom he might improve.[42] To Henry's way of thinking, Ireland's anglicization and anglicanization were its surest routes to improvement, and in this he differed merely in degree, not kind, from others among the Anglo-Irish *élite*. Not surprisingly, he earned the enmity of presbyterians and catholics alike. The former lambasted him as 'that Covetous Man Henry of Urney',[43] while the latter dubbed him 'that little prattling pulpit orator' who had fled his father's presbyterianism into the Church of Ireland and who served as a paid shill for Dublin Castle.[44] Censure of this sort, though, seems only to have emboldened Henry in his improving mission.

Henry's apparently endless list of schemes aimed to improve the material and moral state of Ireland. To begin with, Ireland's very physical geography needed reshaping, by which he meant that it needed to be protestantized. In a work from the 1730s, Henry imagined someone travelling in the predominantly catholic south. There his putative traveller

> at length spies in the midst of a wide waste, a solitary house, the owner of which, without the comfort of doing the least good to mankind, or even enlarging his own fortune, reigns as a petty tyrant over a herd of beasts and a few slaves more wretched than the beasts.[45]

---

[41] LPL, Secker papers 2, fo. 225: Secker to George Montagu Dunk, second earl of Halifax, 22 Mar. 1761.

[42] Barnard, *Improving Ireland?*, p. 13. On the *rôle* of the Church of Ireland clergy at 'the vanguard of the campaign to conquer Ireland for England', see also *idem*, *A new anatomy of Ireland*, pp. 81–104, and *idem*, 'Improving clergymen', pp. 136–51.

[43] PRONI, T/3019/4672: anonymous letter from 'Hearts of Oak', [July 1763]. I thank Robert Whan for providing me with a transcription of this letter.

[44] Robert E. Ward *et al.*, *Letters of Charles O'Conor of Belangare: a catholic voice in eighteenth-century Ireland* (Washington, DC, 1980), p. 117: O'Conor to John Curry, 25 Nov. 1761: 'I like what you sent me as a present from Mr. Henry, that little prattling pulpit orator. His father, a presbyterian parson, lived here, within eight miles of me, under the patronage of Sir Henry King. The son was made a convert to established forms because he lived at the distance of sixty miles from a conventicle. You and I are not men of the *Helvetic turn*; we work honestly, and we work gratis for the public; and we should flatter ourselves that a future historian might mention us as men who did some public service, we will fill a better niche than a Henry or a [Henry] Brooke, who fight in the cause of their country because they are paid.' The charge that Henry was a presbyterian turncoat is repeated by the presbyterian Hearts of Oak in 1763: PRONI, T/3019/4672: an anonymous letter from the 'Hearts of Oak', [July] 1763. I thank Robert Whan for providing me with a transcription of this letter.

[45] National Archives of Ireland, Dublin, M. 2533, p. 450: quoted in Barnard, 'The languages of politeness and sociability', p. 207.

It was far better, Henry insisted, to 'exert our love to our country, [in] the promoting of its improvements by meliorating and enriching the soil, making good roads, navagable canals, erecting comfortable habitations, introducing manufactures, encouraging industry and commerce'. Indeed, before the English imposed their rule on Ireland, the island was but a squalid congeries of 'petty kingdoms'. 'This condition put a stop to arts and sciences, to husbandry and improvements, for to what purpose was it to plough or sow, where there was little prospect of reaping?' he argued. 'This universal neglect of husbandry, and destruction of the inhabitants by intestine broils, covered the face of the country with thickets of woods and briars, and those vast extended bogs, which are not natural, but only the excrescences of the body.'[46] The problem, of course, was that the 'petty kingdoms' had been ruled over and populated by catholics. The protestantization of Ireland, though, promised, among much else, materially to better the country. Hence, Henry reported to the duke of Newcastle in 1765 that the

> wasting consumption, The Emigration of our protestant manufacturers to America, is Stopped. The British Interest in the most popish province is mightily strengthened. It's Extended plains, before almost Desart [sic], Begin to be covered with Men instead of Beasts. And I trust in God, That in Less than fifty years more, *Conaught* will become another Ulster.[47]

If William Henry thought that Ireland's physical landscape needed improvement, even more so did he think that Irish social practices needed ameliorating. The degenerative effects of spirituous liquors on Irish political and social life particularly obsessed him. As he explained to Sir Arthur Gore in 1755 in an open letter requesting legislation to combat the distillation and sale of spirits, it was 'but a Waste of Words' to prove the obvious, that spirituous liquors

> had … nearly extirpated, out of the Minds of our common People, all sense of Religion, Virtue, and Modesty; has often heated them to a Degree of Madness to commit Riots, Thefts, Robberies, and Murders; draws on our Manufacturers into Habits of Idleness and Incapacity for Labour; enervates and dissipates the Courage of our Soldiers; and, to sum up all, destroys the Lives of several Thousands of his Majesty's Subjects in this Kingdom every Year.[48]

It was a subject which continued to worry him throughout the 1760s, as well.[49] Parliament was one venue through which to effect social improvement, and the

---

46 William Henry, *Love of our country. A sermon, preached in the Cathedral Church of St. Patrick, Dublin, March 17th, 1756, being the anniversary festival of St. Patrick* (Dublin, 1756), pp. 17, 19. Henry pursued the same theme in *idem, An account of Lough Lheichs, anglice. lake of the cures in the county of Cavan, in a letter to the Right Reverend Josiah Hort* (Dublin, 1736); *idem, An appeal to the people of Ireland* (Dublin, 1749), pp. 8–9; and *idem, Henry's Upper Lough Erne in 1739*, ed. Charles S. King (Dublin, 1892).

47 BL, Add. MS 32970, fo. 25: Henry to Newcastle, 23 Sept. 1765.

48 William Henry, *A letter to Arthur Gore, Esq; relating to the present abuse of spirituous liquors; and a method to remedy the evil* (Dublin, 1755), p. 5. See also *idem, A dram for drunkards. A funeral sermon, on the terrible death of James Buchanan and Robert Porter, who killed themselves by drinking whiskey* (Dublin, 1759), and *idem, A letter to the Right Honourable John Ponsonby, Esq; Speaker of the Honourable House of Commons; concerning the abuse of spirituous liquors* (Dublin, 1760).

49 In addition to Letters 9, 10, 12, 14, see BL, Add. MS 35592, fo. 231: Henry to Thomas Herring, 21 Dec. 1753.

contents of Henry's correspondence with Secker suggest that he took it upon himself to badger members of parliament about socially ameliorative legislation. But Henry also invested a great deal of effort in Dublin's voluntary social organizations. More densely populated with protestants than anywhere else in Ireland, Dublin served as the centre of England's vice-regal government and the home of the country's law courts, parliament and university.[50] In this eighteenth-century Anglo-Irish hothouse sprang up a number of voluntary societies which aimed to improve the lot of those, especially catholics, who stood outside of the established Church of Ireland. Henry had a hand in most of them, including the Dublin Society, which 'endeavour[ed] the farther Improvement of Husbandry, and other useful Arts'[51] and the Physico-Historical Society, whose stated mission was to survey Ireland's 'antient and present state' in order to enable its future improvement.[52] He took a particular interest in the work of the Incorporated Society for Promoting English Protestant Working Schools in Ireland. In October 1733, George II issued a royal charter for the Incorporated Society, whose mission it was to promote 'Christian Knowledge among the poor natives of the kingdom of Ireland'.[53] Funded by royal grants, voluntary subscriptions and parliamentary subventions, the Incorporated Society went energetically about its business, and by 1748, it ran 30 schools attended by about 900 children.[54] Henry lauded the work of the charter schools and made the explicit point that they were, in point of fact, a 'Scheme of making Ireland a protestant and industrious Kingdom, not by penal Laws, but by the truly Christian and humane Methods of Gentleness and Instruction'.[55] The Incorporated Society was centred in Dublin, but it had a corresponding society in London which held annual sermons by prominent English clerics.[56] Delivering the one for 1757, Secker echoed Henry's thoughts regarding the utility of the charter schools in combating Roman Catholicism. 'The kingdom of Ireland is blessed by Providence with all the means of prosperity; and yet the bulk of the people are in a condition very lamentable', Secker insisted. Yet, though 'the door of Christian freedom is open to them, they continue in thick darkness, voluntary slaves to absurd superstitions. Attached with servile awe to the lowest emissaries of the See of Rome, they imbibe even the dregs of its errors.' As such, so long as they remained in popery's thrall, the Irish threatened England: '[t]ill the generality of the Irish are brought to be protestants, the English are not safe', and

[50] For eighteenth-century Dublin culture, see Toby Barnard, *Making the grand figure: lives and possessions in Ireland, 1641–1770* (New Haven, 2004), pp. 282–309, and *idem*, ' "Grand metropolis" or "The anus of the world"? The cultural life of eighteenth-century Dublin', in *Two capitals: London and Dublin, 1500–1840*, ed. Peter Clark and Raymond Gillespie (Oxford, 2001), pp. 185–210.

[51] *The Dublin Society's Weekly Observations. Volume I* (Dublin, 1739), p. 4. More generally, see James Livesey, 'The Dublin society in eighteenth-century Irish political thought', *HJ*, XLVII (2004), 615–40. For Henry's involvement in the affairs of the Dublin Society, see below Letter 11.

[52] *Dublin Journal* (9 Apr. 1744): quoted in Eoin Magennis, ' "A land of milk and honey": the physico-historical society, improvement and the surveys of mid-eighteenth-century Ireland', *Proceedings of the Royal Irish Academy: Section C*, CII (2002), 199–217, at 199. Henry's 1739 survey of Lough Lerne was done as part of his work on behalf of the Physico-Historical Society.

[53] Quoted in Mant, *HCI*, 510. The Incorporated Society continued the work of a private society for encouraging English schools in Ireland which was founded in 1717.

[54] Kenneth Milne, *The Irish charter schools, 1730–1830* (Dublin, 1997), esp. pp. 177–226.

[55] Henry, *An appeal to the people of Ireland*, p. 13. See also Letter 8 and Milne, *The Irish charter schools*, pp. 135–49.

[56] Of the fifteen published sermons before the London corresponding society during the mid-eighteenth century, eleven were given by bishops.

protestant proselytizing like the charter schools constituted 'carrying the war…into our enemies' headquarters'.[57]

III

The confessional threat which William Henry and Thomas Secker imagined in Ireland proved all too real during the mid-century. The 1745 Jacobite rebellion on the main British isle occasioned no Roman Catholic rebellion in Ireland – where catholic episcopal appointments were still made on the nomination of the Stuart court in exile – but it did rouse William Henry to rhetorical fury in a trio of sermons in which he reminded his listeners of the catholic atrocities committed against protestants in 1641 and of the seventeenth-century Jacobite lord lieutenant Richard Talbot, first earl of Tyrconnell (1630–91), who had 'arm[ed] Popish Cut-Throats against us'.[58] Moreover, he warned his auditors, little had changed since. 'That Church, (or rather Synagogue of Satan) has never yet renounced one of her Errors', he inveighed,

> and tho' she is too Politick to let fly her Fire-brands, Anathemas, Depositions of Princes, Crusadoes, Armys of Holy Cut-Throats, as lavishly as she did, when in the Height of her Power, yet she has this Artillery of Hell still in her Stores; and never fails to make use of it whenever she can do it with Effect.[59]

The lesson, clearly, was not to provide the 'Cut-Throats' a opportunity to do their work.

The Irish Jacobite rising of the mid-1740s might have been non-existent, but the predominantly catholic sectarian-agrarian Whiteboys risings of the mid-1760s, which Henry details in his Lambeth correspondence to Secker, were real enough. And, they only confirmed for Henry what each had argued all along: Roman Catholics were not fully to be trusted.

Henry interpreted the Whiteboys risings in 1765–66 in light of his traumatic experiences during an earlier, predominantly presbyterian, sectarian-agrarian revolt in the summer of 1763, when groups calling themselves the Hearts of Oak briefly seized control of nine Ulster counties from the local landed *élite*. An armed response both to the ballooning county cess (taxes for the upkeep of roads) and to the obligatory tithes owed to the Church of Ireland clergy, the Oakboy risings were, at the

---

57 Thomas Secker, 'Sermon CXXXVII. The pernicious effects to a nation of ignorance and idleness; and the happy consequences of knowledge and industry. Preached before the Society for Promoting English Protestant Working Schools in Ireland, April 27, 1757', in *The works of Thomas Secker*, ed. Beilby Porteus (4 vols., Edinburgh, 1792), IV, 1–2, 6, 14.

58 William Henry, *A Philippic oration against the Pretender's son and his adherents, addressed to the protestants of the north of Ireland* (Dublin, 1745), pp. 7, 15. See also *idem, An appeal to the people of Ireland*, p. 1641. For late seventeenth- and eighteenth-century Irish evocations of 1641, see Barnard, 'The uses of the 23rd of October 1641', 899–920 and Kelly, '"The glorious and immortal memory"', 25–52.

59 Henry, *Philippic oration* 9–10. See also *idem, The remarkable scripture prophecy of deliverance from enemies* (Dublin, 1746), and *idem, The beauty, deliverances, and security of the British constitution, set forth in a sermon, preached in the Cathedral Church of London-Derry, on the first day of August, 1746. Being the anniversary of the deliverance of that city from the siege of 1689; also of the Hanoverian succession in 1714* (Dublin, 1746).

core, confessionally driven.[60] In an open letter to the townsmen of Londonderry, the Oakboys cast their grievances in confessional terms and singled out William Henry for particular abuse.

> It is with astonishment we find your mayor has not obey'd our Orders to him, which were to turn out of the once Loyal City of Londonderry, which Our Fore-fathers so bravely defended against a most Hellish damned set of Papists with their Poltroon James at their head, those high flying Clergy, I mean those of them, who call themselves high Churchmen, Indeed they are only Occasional Protestants, which We call Hipocrites, who would overset the Church of God as by Law Established, & Our most undefiled Church of Scotland. Mind the Solemn League & Covenant those men would turn out our good young King & impose upon us a Papist Stuart, & overset our Constitution that we may become of the Tribe of Antichrist, you know who I mean, the Pope, turn out of your City that Covetous Man Henry of Urney, who turn'd for lucre & now rails against Our Church & People.[61]

At no point in their Londonderry manifesto did the self-described 'sincerely Loyal Hearts of Oak the Reformers of abuse in Church & State' mention the cess or any other secular grievance.[62] Instead, these ultra-protestant presbyterians cast their fight as against papists and crypto-papists within the Church of Ireland, and they lauded the 'Martial brave Actions of Oliver Cromwell, Our first Deliverer, who open'd the way of King William'. This sort of ultra-protestant anti-catholicism as anglican anti-clericalism would have been all too familiar to Thomas Secker, whom many English ultra-protestants had accused of being, at best, a latter-day Laud and, at worst, a crypto-papist.[63]

Henry detailed the Oakboys' progress to Secker and other government officials while on the run from them, and his apocalyptic accounts presented an Ireland on the brink of collapse. To the earl of Northumberland, Ireland's lord lieutenant, he reported on 15 July 1763 that an initial gathering of 1,500 'Disturbers' against an Armagh magistrate who was gathering the cess had swelled to 20,000:

> And it is probable that, unless a Speedy Stop be put to this Disturbance, the whole province of Ulster may be in a flame. For it is carried on by the populace who think it their Interest to Reduce the Landlords, and take away the Rights of the clergy. So they go Hand in Hand, and make it a common Cause.

---

[60] Eoin Magennis, 'A "presbyterian insurrection"? Reconsidering the Hearts of Oak disturbances of July 1763', *Irish Historical Studies*, XXXI, 122 (1998), 165–87, rightly emphasizes the confessional nature of the Oakboys risings. See also *idem*, 'County Armagh Hearts of Oak', *Seanchas Ardmhacha*, XVII (1998), 19–31, and Rev. Theodorus Martin, 'A full and circumstantial account of what happened to me on the eighth day of July 1763', in *Aspects of Irish social history*, ed. W. H. Crawford and B. Trainor (Dublin, 1969), pp. 34–6. But cf. James S. Donnelly, 'Hearts of Oak, hearts of steel', *Studia Hibernica*, XXI (1981), 7–73, which diminishes the confessional dimension of the Hearts of Oak risings.

[61] PRONI, T/3019/4672: an anonymous letter from the 'Hearts of Oak', [July] 1763.

[62] Cf. PRONI, T/2872/16: Bowes to Secker, 29 July 1763, which prioritizes the Oakboys' economic grievances as a cause of the rising.

[63] This is one of the central themes of Ingram, *Religion, reform and modernity*. More generally, see James E. Bradley, 'Anti-catholicism as anglican anticlericalism: nonconformity and the ideological origins of radical disaffection', in *Anticlericalism in Britain, c. 1500–1914*, ed. Nigel Aston and Matthew Cragoe (Stroud, 2000), pp. 67–92.

Worse yet, Henry informed Northumberland, fear had paralysed both the magistrates and Church of Ireland clergy in Ulster into inaction.[64] A few days later found him describing events from within the safety of Londonderry's walls, where many other Church of Ireland clergy from Ulster joined him in refuge. There, on his telling, he tried frantically to embolden the inhabitants and to organize the town's defence against the 30,000 Oakboys bearing down on Londonderry. Indeed, the magistrates even asked him to preach 'to the whole City assembled, and [he] laid before them the great Duty of Obedience to Government, & their Obligations to preserve their happy Constitution'.[65] Having only 30 army regulars to protect it from the marching Oakboys, Londonderry faced being overrun. At this prospect, Henry took matters into his own hands. 'To remedy this Evil, I got a common Hall called this Day, and engaged all the Citizens to stand up for the Constitution, and defend our Walls', he wrote hurriedly to Secker.

> We have got our Cannon well planted, and our Arms ready, and I trust in God our Defender, that We shall stand firm; I have also at my own Expence enlisted all the lately disbanded Soldiers who ply in the City, & pay each Man a Shilling per Day so long as their Service is wanted.

As it turned out, the armed Hearts of Oak never showed up at Londonderry's gates, and so robbed Henry of an 'Occasion to die in Defence of His Majesty's Government, and the Defence of this Important City'.[66] Henry lived to write another day.[67]

By all accounts, the Hearts of Oak risings melted away and the Oakboy leaders went almost wholly unpunished. In part, there was an economic motive for the government's leniency: it feared that an iron-handed response might risk 'driving more of [the Ulster linen manufacturers] into America'.[68] One also has the sense that few among the Anglo-Irish *élite* had the stomach to shed protestant blood in an overwhelmingly catholic country. They showed far less leniency, though, to the catholic Whiteboys.

Whiteboy protests began in Tipperary in 1761 and soon spread throughout other southern counties, including Limerick, Waterford, Cork and Kilkenny. After the initial risings subsided, others popped up in 1764–5, which occasioned much comment from Henry to Secker.[69] Like the Hearts of Oak, the Whiteboys complained of economic inequities, especially enclosure of common land, conacre rents[70] and compulsory tithe obligations, especially on potatoes, to the established Church of Ireland. Also like the Hearts of Oak, they tried to bully local landed *élites*

---

64 PRONI, T/2872/5: Henry to Hugh Percy, first earl of Northumberland, 15 July 1763.
65 PRONI, T/2872/7: Henry to [George Stone], 17 July 1763.
66 PRONI, T/2872/9: Henry to Secker, 19 July 1763.
67 Borthwick Institute for Historical Research, VII/175/3: Secker to Drummond, 28 July 1763, indicates that Secker accepted Henry's account of the Hearts of Oak uprising as authoritative.
68 *Ibid*.
69 Whiteboy activities during the 1760s may be pursued in Thomas P. Power, *Land, politics and society in eighteenth-century Tipperary* (Oxford, 1993), and James S. Donnelly, 'The Whiteboy movement, 1761–5', *Irish Historical Studies*, XXI, 81 (1978), 20–54. In the 1770s, Whiteboy activity revived, for which see Maurice J. Bric, 'The Whiteboy movement, 1760–1780', in *Tipperary: history and society*, ed. William Nolan and Thomas G. McGrath (Dublin, 1985), pp. 148–84, and Maria Luddy, 'Whiteboy support in Co. Tipperary, 1761–1789', *Tipperary Historical Journal*, II (1989), 66–79.
70 *Oxford English dictionary*: conacre is the 'letting by a tenant, for the season, of small portions of land ready ploughed and prepared for a crop'.

and clergymen, often violently. The Whiteboys showed up *en masse* in towns and villages wearing white shirts, levelled hedgerows, burned crops, cut off the ears of gentlemen's horses, buried opponents up to their necks, roughed up clergymen and, occasionally, it was reported, even killed the odd landed gentleman or his agent.[71] Unlike the mainly presbyterian Hearts of Oak, though, the Whiteboys were Roman Catholics of just the 'unimproved' sort that scared Henry and so many others among the Anglo-Irish *élite*. Put another way, if the presbyterian Oakboys unnerved the Anglo-Irish, the Whiteboys positively terrified them, even though they achieved nothing as substantive by way of control as the Oakboys. Improbably, Henry effortlessly connected the two movements, despite their different confessional cores. 'What a sad state are things Brought to by the Oak Boy spirit in the north', he wrote to Secker in late 1764.

> The Clergy Reduced to the Last Distress in other provinces – the priests and shoals of Jesuits making Daily proselytes – and at Least fifty thousand papists in [M]unster, under the name of White Boys, actually engaged by a Sollemn Oath to unite and stand by one another in favour of the French or Spaniards, whenever they shall please to attack us.

This intelligence, he assured Secker, he had got from 'a very wise and Learned privy counselor'.[72]

With rumors like this passing as certifiable fact, it is perhaps not surprising that the horrendous acts imputed to the Whiteboys by the Anglo-Irish *élite* outpaced reality by a long way. Nowhere was this more evident than in the treatment of the Roman Catholic priest, Nicholas Sheehy (*c.* 1728–66), a victim of judicial murder at the hands of the Tipperary Anglo-Irish *élite*.[73] A Tipperary native who had studied in Louvain and was educated in Rome, Sheehy served as parish priest at Clogheen, the epicentre of Whiteboy activity. Though no organizer of the Whiteboys, Sheehy seems nevertheless to have been sympathetic to their cause. Certainly the local landowning *élite* thought him dangerous, for he was indicted repeatedly on everything from being an unlicensed priest to witness intimidation to assault, high treason and rebellion. None of the charges stuck, though, and the government had to issue a proclamation in 1765 which promised a £300 reward for Sheehy's capture. That trial, too, ended in acquittal, but he was finally convicted in February 1766 by a rigged Tipperary jury on charges of having murdered John Bridges a year and a half earlier, despite the fact that there was no evidence that Bridges was even dead. On 15 March 1766, Sheehy died a traitor's death.

Sheehy subsequently came to be seen among Irish catholics as a religious martyr, and with good reason, for the animus expressed against him was expressed almost wholly in religious terms. Shortly after Sheehy's execution, for instance, a letter appeared in a London newspaper from someone who had been present at Sheehy's

---

[71] See, for instance, *Public Advertiser* (14 Oct. 1764); *London Chronicle* (12 Oct. 1765); and James Kelly, 'The Whiteboys in 1762: a contemporary account', *Journal of the Cork Historical and Archaeological Society*, XVIV (1989), 19–26.

[72] See below, Letter 2. For Henry's reporting on the activities and motives of the Whiteboys, see also Letters 4, 7, 8, 9, 10, 11, 13 and 15.

[73] Thomas P. Power, 'Sheehy, Nicholas (1728/9–1766)', *ODNB* synopsizes *idem*, 'Father Nicholas Sheehy (c. 1728–1766)', in *Radical Irish priests, 1660–1970*, ed. Gerald Moran (Dublin, 1998), pp. 62–78, and *idem*, *Land, politics and society*, pp. 260–6.

trial. The letter's author wrote to rebut a recently published defence of Sheehy in the newspaper.

> Shall we … censure so worthy a body of men as the Protestants of the county of Tipperary, and the Judges of the kingdom of Ireland, because a Popish Priest (the tenets of whose religion admit, and in many cases command, a mental reservation) has suffered without confessing the fact?

he asked rhetorically. And the letter's author proceeded immediately and seamlessly to imply that Sheehy's death would send a message to the rebellious Whiteboys.

> The Protestant gentlemen of the counties of Waterford, Tipperary, and Kilkenny, are to a man most firmly convinced that the Roman Catholics in those parts have some mischievous scheme in hand, and, greatly to their honour, have for these months past, most strenuously exerted themselves in suppressing those disturbers of the public quiet

he concluded.[74]

William Henry concurred. He accepted as unquestionable fact that Sheehy had taken up a furze spade himself and personally beat Bridge to death and buried his body. As such, he welcomed Sheehy's death: 'But justice Has now taken place. He and one of His accomplices in that Clonmell murder were convicted on Thursday the 13th[,] and on Saturday morning, were Drawn, Hanged, and Quartered, and their Heads set up on Clonmell goal, murder Being by the Laws of Ireland, High treason', he reported with evident satisfaction to Secker. And, like the anonymous London newspaper correspondent, he reckoned it a matter beyond dispute that Sheehy and his fellow 'popish priests' were the 'principal Directors' of 'a Dangerous conspiracy [that] Has Been carrying on these five years, by the papists in [M]unster, to Keep up a Spirit of Rebellion: That a Sufficient Body of them might be Ready to Support any [F]rench or Spanish attempts to Disturb the Kingdom'.[75] Thankfully, to Henry's way of thinking, there were members of the Anglo-Irish *élite* like the earl of Carrick who dealt more aggressively with Sheehy and the Whiteboys than with the Hearts of Oak.[76] One has the distinct impression that the confessional clarity of the Whiteboy threat was easier for the Anglo-Irish *élite* to understand and to redress than the intra-protestant challenge from the Oakboys. Where the latter froze them into inaction, the latter spurred them to violence. A very few, like Edmund Burke, found Sheehy's

---

74 *Gazetteer and New Daily Advertiser* (14 Apr. 1766). The letter's author signed himself 'A protestant. Middle Temple'. Perhaps it is the same person referred to by Edmund Burke when deploring the brutal treatment of Whiteboys: 'An old acquaintance of mine at the Temple, a man formerly of integrity and good nature, had by living some years in Corke, contracted such horrible habits, that I think whilst he talked on these late Disturbances, none but hang men could have had any pleasure in his company.' Thomas W. Copeland (ed.), *The correspondence of Edmund Burke*, I (Chicago, 1958), 148: Burke to Charles O'Hara, *ante*, 23 Aug. 1762.

75 See below, Letter 13.

76 For Henry's fawning approval of the anti-Whiteboy activities of Somerset Hamilton Butler, first earl of Carrick (1718–74), see below, Letters 4, 8 and 9. For Carrick's own account of the sometimes brutal official response to the Whiteboy threat, see John Fortescue (ed.), *The correspondence of King George the Third, from 1760 to December 1783* (London, 1927), pp. 310–28.

murder and the official response to the Whiteboys morally objectionable: in his response to the Whiteboys, William Henry, suffice it to say, was no Burke.[77]

IV

If William Henry's Lambeth correspondence to Thomas Secker speaks clearly to the depth of Anglo-Irish confessional fears, it also points up the political tensions between the Anglo-Irish political *élite* and their English counterparts. The sort of material and moral improvement advocated by Henry would, he and its other adherents argued, prevent future risings like those of the Hearts of Oak and the Whiteboys. In return, they hoped, the London overseers of Irish affairs would trust the native Anglo-Irish *élite* to undertake the business of English rule. Resentment of the evident English reluctance to place full confidence in the Anglo-Irish *élite* animated mid-century Irish high politics, and Henry himself highlighted two thorny issues which particularly animated 'hiberno-patriots': personnel and parliament.

In Ireland, as in England, bishops in the established church sat by right of office in the House of Lords. A disproportionate percentage of the Irish bench, though, hailed originally from the main British isle, and Secker himself had once been rumored to have been a possible archbishop of Armagh.[78] In 1763, Henry complained to the earl of Hardwicke that only seven of the twenty-two Irish bishops were actually born in Ireland. Might it not be possible, he wondered with evident irritation, that

> the Governours sent to preside over us from our mother country may sometimes think it Good policy to take notice of men of British Descent Born in Ireland, who Have Disinterestedly spent their Lives and fortunes promoting the service of the King, and the common Interest of Great Britain and Ireland?

In addition to opening up avenues for ambitious – Henry preferred to use the adjective 'deserving' – Irish clerics, elevating Irish to the Irish bench would also serve to 'strengthen the affections of the Protestants in Ireland to His Majesty, and to Britain', for it would 'in Ecclesiastical cases, prove the most Effectual means of preserving the Rights of the Church, in this Kingdom'[79] Henry likewise complained of English-born archbishops of Armagh like John Hoadly and George Stone, the latter of whom had devoted himself to politics rather than the Church of Ireland, 'not [to] mention the too great countenance shewn to the Late Rebellious Leaders of the Oak Boys in the north. It was shameful'.[80]

The composition of the Irish episcopate perhaps obviously concerned an episcopal aspirant like William Henry, but non-clerical Irish patriots worried most about English intervention in Irish politics. Though the English relied on Irish 'under-

---

[77] For Burke's extended, though unfinished, assessment of the Whiteboys, see Earl Fitzwilliam and Richard Bourke (eds.), *The correspondence of Edmund Burke* (4 vols., London, 1844), I, 41–5. More generally, see Luke Gibbons, *Edmund Burke and Ireland: aesthetics, politics, and the colonial sublime* (Cambridge, 2003), and Thomas H. D. Mahoney, *Edmund Burke and Ireland* (Cambridge, MA, 1960). It is perhaps worth noting that Burke's mother, Mary (*c.* 1702–70), and his sister, Juliana, were both Roman Catholics; his father, Richard, was a convert to the Church of Ireland from Roman Catholicism.

[78] BL, Add. MS 39311, fos. 52–3: Martin Benson to Secker, 28 Oct. 1746.

[79] BL, Add. MS 35597, fo. 275: Henry to Hardwicke, 28 Apr. 1763.

[80] See below, Letter 2.

takers' to govern the island, Ireland's dependence on England rankled some among the Anglo-Irish *élite*, and the 1750s and 1760s occasioned loudening calls among Irish patriots for more control over their kingdom's political process, especially regarding the Irish parliament's independence. Under Poynings's law, the Dublin parliament could pass no legislation without first receiving the consent of the English king and his privy council.[81] By the eighteenth century, most Irish legislation began as 'heads of bills' in the Irish House of Commons, and while few of these heads of bills were rejected outright, an increasing number during the eighteenth century were amended by authorities on the eastern side of the Irish Sea. Perhaps not surprisingly, these emendations bothered some among the Anglo-Irish *élite*, and both Henry and John Bowes apprised Secker of the Irish problems with the practical operations of Poynings's law.[82]

Yet, Irish patriots raised insufficient objections during the mid-eighteenth century for the process of Irish legislating significantly to be changed. In part, that was because Irish patriotism was a centripetal rather than a centrifugal force: it aimed for Ireland's integration with England not independence from the mother country. More fundamentally, though, the mid-century reluctance to press the matter of Irish legislative independence surely reflected the confessional realities laid bare in the Henry–Secker correspondence. The eighteenth-century Anglo-Irish *élite* monopolized political power because England had long ago forcibly colonized the island, and they enjoyed that monopoly at the expense of Roman Catholics and presbyterians, who accounted for nine out of ten of the island's inhabitants. Everyone recognized this, which helps to explain the fear of confessional rebellion which informed the views of men as different as William Henry and Thomas Secker.

Allegiance in early modern Britain was either signified by oaths or compelled by violence or threats of legal violence.[83] Clearly Thomas Secker thought oaths insufficiently binding upon the consciences of the Irish confessional majority, hence his strident opposition to Frederick Hervey's proposed scheme to liberalize treatment of Irish Roman Catholics. To Secker's way of thinking, the threat of legal violence against Irish catholics remained necessary. 'I wish the severer part of these [penal] Laws were repealed, as no longer necessary, though not as originally unjust: but so as that still they may in some Degree lie at our Mercy, not we at theirs', he wrote to Hervey. 'They should have no Laws in their Favour, which they can abuse to our Disadvantage: and we should have Laws in our Favour, by which we can repress any Attempts of theirs with more Rigour, than I hope we shall ever chuse or need to exercise.'[84] Edmund Burke recoiled with disgust at 'the unfeeling Tyranny of a mungril Irish Landlord, or ... the Horrors of Munster Circuit': Thomas Secker and William Henry thought them the only thing standing between civilization and barbarism in mid-eighteenth-century Ireland.[85]

---

81 James Kelly, *Poynings' Law and the making of law in Ireland, 1660–1800* (Dublin, 2007), is the definitive treatment of its subject.

82 In addition to Letters 8, 9, 10, 12 and 16, see LPL, Secker papers 2, fos. 215–20: Bowes to Secker, 23 Dec. 1760. For the political background, see also Vincent Morley, *Irish opinion and the American revolution, 1760–1783* (Cambridge, 2002), pp. 40–96; James Kelly, *Henry Flood: parties and politics in eighteenth-century Ireland* (Dublin, 1998); and James, *Ireland in the empire*, pp. 251–76.

83 For oaths in eighteenth-century England, see J. C. D. Clark, *Samuel Johnson: literature, religion and English cultural politics from the Restoration to Romanticism* (Cambridge, 1994), esp. pp. 88–124.

84 PRONI, D/2798/5/6: Secker to Hervey, 25 Feb. 1768.

85 Copeland (ed.), *Correspondence of Edmund Burke*, I, 147: Burke to O'Hara, *ante*, 23 Aug. 1762.

Editorial conventions

William Henry's idiosyncratic punctuation and spelling have been preserved in this edition, except where it obscures clarity: clarifications and other editorial interventions have been placed within square brackets. Latin phrases and words and passages underlined in the originals have been italicized. Words which are underlined in the original manuscripts have been printed in italic type. Formulaic conclusions to Henry's letters have been replaced with ellipses, and addresses have been omitted entirely.

Documents

Calendar of correspondence

1. William Henry to Thomas Secker, 12 October 1764

[fo. 232r] [U]rney near Strabane Oct[r]: 12th 1764

May it please your Grace

I can not neglect giving you an authentic account of a most unparallelled Riot which Happened at Rapho[e], six miles hence, Last Sunday.

Doctor Oswald,[1] the good Bishop, who Has much at Heart the good of His town, the second for size and good Houses for the county of Donegal, found all His Schemes to make the people Happy Defeated, by the intolerance of a set of Rioters who Have been ever Disturbing the peace of the town, and Had often offered indignitys even to the great and good Bishop Forster[2] in his time. To Remedy this He sent for several of the Inhabitants, to Let them know, that the condition of getting their Leases Renewed was that they should join in Discontinuance these Rioters. [T]o which purpose He himself Deposited fifty pounds. [A]nd finding the Ringleader of this Infamous Crew was one Bates who kept a public House for vending of whiskey in the town, He [Dr Oswald] sent His Agent M[r]: Abraham to him [Bates] Last Saturday to Signify to Him, that He must either change His Behaviour, or Depart from the town. Bates, supported by His clan insulted and Beat the agent, and swore that He would be Revenged on the Bishop. Accordingly, He charged a musquet with Ball: and was going out that night to the castle, in order to shoot the Bishop thru the [fo. 232v] window of the Room in which His Lordship usually sits. By some incident which providence threw in the way He was Disappointed that evening. But He firmly adhered to His murderous purpose, [and] Determined to Kill the Bishop as He was going into church. The Bishop went that forenoon to the church of Taughboyne six miles from Raphoe, to confirm. He Did not Return untill four o clock, when He took a Bowl of Broth for His dinner and started to go into His Church as the Bell was Ringing. [W]ith some Difficulty He was prevailed on by His Brother[3] and the Rev[d]: Doctor Ledwich[4] to stay at Home, as He was

---

[1] John Oswald (c. 1716–80). An Oxford-educated Scot who came to Ireland as the chaplain to George Montagu Dunk, earl of Halifax (lord lieutenant: 1761–3), Oswald served as the bishop of Clonfert (1762), Dromore (1763) and Raphoe (1763–80). Before coming to Ireland, Oswald served as rector of Marlow, Shropshire, and canon of Westminster (1755–62). Henry Cotton (ed.), *Fasti ecclesiae hibernicae: the succession of the prelates and members of the cathedral bodies in Ireland* (5 vols., Dublin, 1845–60) (*FEH*), III, 357, IV, 171; Joyce M. Horn, *et al.*, *Fasti ecclesiae anglicanae, 1541–1857* (11 vols., London, 1969–) (*FEA*), VII, 91; Mant, *HCI*, p. 635.

[2] Nicholas Forster (c. 1664–1743). An Irishman educated at Trinity College, Dublin, he served as the bishop of Killaloe (1714–16) and Raphoe (1716–43). Contemporaries praised Forster for being a conscientious prelate. *FEH*, III, 355–7; James Todd, *A catalogue of graduates who have proceeded to degrees in the University of Dublin, from the earliest recorded commencements to July, 1866: with supplement to December 16, 1868* (Dublin, 1869), p. 203: Mant, *HCI*, pp. 314–15; *Alumni Dublienses: a register of the students, graduates, professors, and provosts of Trinity College, in the University of Dublin, 1593–1846* (Dublin, 1924) (*Alum Dublin*), p. 300.

[3] Likely James Oswald (1715–69). The bishop of Dromore's younger brother and a friend of Adam Smith's, James Oswald served as an MP in the Westminster parliament (1741–68) and, from 1763, as joint vice-treasurer of Ireland. J. M. Rigg, 'Oswald, James (1715–1769)', rev. J.-M. Alter, *ODNB*; Romney Sedgwick, *The House of Commons, 1714–1754* (11 vols., Oxford, 1970), II, 314–15.

[4] Edward Ledwich (c. 1707–82). A graduate of Trinity College, Dublin (BA, 1729; MA, 1732), Ledwich held a number of livings within the Church of Ireland. At the time of the attack on Bishop Oswald, he served as the treasurer of Kildare (1760–72) and held Derry and Dublin prebends: Leslie, *Derry clergy and parishes*, p. 57; James B. Leslie and W. J. R. Wallace, *Clergy of Derby and Glendalough: biographical succession lists* (Belfast, 2001), p. 816.

much fatigued and warm. They went to church thro' the garden without the Bishop. [O]n their Entrance into the churchyard, they found Bates, and one Thomson His associate, Bates standing with a gun in his Hand, and the other Ready to aid Him. M[r]: Leonard, the Surveyor of Excise coming up at that time to church, and seeing Bates in that posture advised Him to go Home, and attempted to seize the gun. Coll[l]: Oswald, the Bishop's Brother stepped up, and asked Him what He meant. He gave an outrageous answer and instantly cocking his Gunn fired at Coll[l]: Oswald's Breast. But the Coll[l]: Happily Diverted the Ball by catching the muzzell of the gun in His Hand, which Had nearly been fatal to Doctor Ledwich who was coming after, for the shot Grazed by His Leg and Burned his stocking. [O]n this the Col[l]: snatched a stick out of the sextens Hand, and gave Bates a Knock. But Bates immediately Returned it by a Knock on the side of the [fo. 233r] Head which made the [C]oll[l]: Stagger. [A]t the same time, Thomson, Bates's associate, Ran at Him, and gave him such a stroke in the Breast that He fell, and Lay without Life for about 20 minutes. Bates then flew at the [C]oll[l]: to Finish him. But Master Ledwich the Doctors son, a Spirited Boy of 14,[5] seized Bates by the collar, and Held Him, untill the Dean and Congregation Running out of church interposed. Bates Knocked Down young Ledwich and Left Him Sprawling.

Doctor Ledwich, who is a magistrate called the people to assist him. But tho' there were 200 present, none of them Except the Dean and one [T]homson, the Deans manager's son, would assist the Doctor. [W]hereupon the Doctor Himself seized Bates, who in Return took him by the throat. [T]he Bishop Hearing of the Riot came out, and Laid before the people their great wickedness[,][6] while D[r]: Ledwich assisted by the Deans manager, and servants seized Bates[,] and Sent Him under a Strong Guard to Lifferd the county gaol.

I have Read the committal, and seen the Examinations, from which it is very plain, that there was a Deliberate intention to murder this good Bishop, purely for His Desire to Do Good to the country. But Gods providence protected Him. The Coll[l]: is still much indisposed by the Bruises he Received.

I pray God ever to Defend your Grace and all Good men from such wicked men!
…

Will[m]: Henry

I hope to be in Dublin in [N]ovember

2. William Henry to Thomas Secker, 20 November 1764

[fo. 234r] May it please your Grace
I Saw this Day a Letter from an Eminent person in London, saying that our Primate[7]

---

5   Thomas Ledwich (b. 1749). The eldest son of Edward Ledwich, Thomas studied at Trinity College, Dublin (BA, 1768; LLB, 1771). He entered Lincoln's Inn in Nov. 1768 and was called to the Irish bar in 1774. Leslie, *Derry clergy and parishes*, p. 57; *Alum Dublin*, p. 489; *The records of the Honorable Society of Lincoln's Inn. Volume 1: admissions 1420–1799* (London, 1896), p. 462.

6   Cf. Ernest Campbell Mossner and Ian Simpson Ross (eds.), *The correspondence of Adam Smith* (7 vols., Oxford, 1987), VI, 126: David Hume to Smith, 13 June 1767.

7   George Stone (1708–64). Not a pastoral *rôle* model, Stone was one of the leading political figures in mid-eighteenth-century Ireland. An Oxford-educated Englishman who came to Ireland as chaplain to Lionel Sackville Cranfield, duke of Dorset (lord lieutenant: 1730–7, 1750–5), Stone served as bishop

was Given over by all the physicians; and that, in all probability He must be Dead Before that Letter arrived.

To the ministry or people of England this Katastrophe may possibly be of as Little consequence as the fly on the wheel. But to us in Ireland it is an Intelligence which makes an Universal Buzz: and the Appointment of a proper Successor is of the utmost consequence, Both to the civil and Religious Interests of this country.

If any of the Irish Bench is advanced to this High Station, the public voice Has pointed out Doctor Carmichael,[8] the Bishop of Meath, who to His Amiable virtues as a Gentleman Has added the utmost virtue and Dignity in His Ecclesiastical Charracter, which He Has uniformly supported.

But, it is Generally Believed That to fill up this Important post some one [fo. 234v] from the English Bench will be sent, as a Successor to the Irish Apostle S^t. Patrick.

Should this Be the case, may I Hope that your Grace will not think it Impertinence in your servant to Wish, That no one But a person every way fit may be sent to preside over us. This I say from the Love I Bear to my country and the British Interest, and the Zeal I Bear to the protestant Interest, and the very Being of the present Established church in this Kingdom.

Indulge me, my Lord, to say, that I Have Had the Best opportunitys of Knowing Both the Ecclesiastical and political Interests of Ireland Since the year 1724, when I was Adopted by the great Doctor King[9] A:B^p: of Dublin into His particular favour: and By His means into a Successive Acquaintance with most of our Eminent men who Have Lived Here. And upon the whole I am Bold to make this observation 'That the very Existence of the protestant Religion in our present Constitution Depends at this time on the choice which ye shall make of a proper primate.'

When the great and good primate Boulter[10] [fo. 235r] presided over us, every thing went well.

---

8   William Carmichael (1702–65). A Cambridge-educated Scot, Carmichael came to Ireland as the chaplain to William Stanhope, earl of Harrington (lord lieutenant: 1746–50). There he served as the bishop of Clonfert (1753–8), Ferns and Leighlin (1758) and Meath (1758–65) and as the archbishop of Dublin (1765). The second son of the Brigadier-General Sir James Carmichael, the second earl of Hyndford, he was admitted at the Inner Temple in 1719. Before coming to Ireland, he was archdeacon of Buckinghamshire (1742–53) and prebend of Lincoln (1745–53). George E. Cokayne, *The complete peerage of England, Scotland, Ireland, Great Britain, and the United Kingdom, extant, extinct, or dormant* (London, 1910–40) (*CP*), VII, 38; Mant, *HCI*, pp. 606, 609, 641; *FEH*, III, 171; *The clergy of the Church of England database* (www.theclergydatabase.org.uk) (*CCED*); John Venn and J. A. Venn (eds.), *Alumni Cantabrigienses: a biographical list of all known students, graduates and office holders of office at the University of Cambridge, from the earliest times to 1900* (5 vols., Cambridge, 1922–54) (*Alum Cantab*), I, 294.

9   William King (1650–1729). Noted as a pastor, politician and a polemicist, King was one of the leading churchmen in post-revolutionary Ireland. He served as bishop of Derry (1693–1703) and archbishop of Dublin (1703–29) and was educated at Trinity College, Dublin (BA, 1671; MA, 1673; BD and DD, 1688). His early patrons included John Parker, archbishop of Tuam and Dublin; Richard Butler, first earl of Arran (lord deputy: 1682–4); and James Butler, first duke of Ormond (lord lieutenant: 1662–8, 1677–85). S. J. Connolly, 'King, William (1650–1729)', *ODNB*.

10 Hugh Boulter (1672–1742). An Oxford-educated Englishman, Boulter served as archbishop of Armagh (1724–42), being, during that time, a notably strong supporter of the 'English interest' in Ireland. Before coming to Ireland, he served as a fellow of Christ Church, Oxford (1696–1709), chaplain to George I (1719), dean of Christ Church (1719–24), and bishop of Bristol (1719–24). *CCED*; Patrick McNally, 'Boulter, Hugh (1672–1742)', *ODNB*.

His unchangeable Integrity, unfeigned Humility, care in Rewarding merit, zeal for piety, continual attention to good clergymen, close adherence to the Dignity of His Ecclesiastical Charracter, and His unbounded charity flowing merely from this pure Celestial Spring, The Love of God and men made Him the Great Blessing, the Delight of this Kingdom as well as of England: and gave Him uncourted, the Highest Influence in all political affairs, which He Entirely Employed in promoting true Religion: and securing all the British Interests.

I cannot think of His many pubic and private virtues, which His condescension gave me the fullest opportunity of knowing, without a Sigh Breaking out, even at this Distance of time.

His successor, Doctor Hoadly,[11] Did not continue Long to Do either much ~~good~~ good or Harm. He Did not even pretend any great Regard for Religion, for which neglect I Have been witness to good primate Boulter's animadverting on His conduct to His face with some sharpness. He Did not follow the tract of the great Boulter in supporting His Spiritual Character, which He would sacrifice to a trifling Jest[,] and was [fo. 235v] much more solicitous in fattening His Hoggs, than in feeding either the Shepherds or Sheep committed to His charge[,] which occasioned his short Elegy and Charracter, on His Death.

Great Hoadly's Dead, Let Tears wet every Cheek.

Grunt, Grunt, ye Hoggs. Ye pig a-diggin Squeak.

The consequence of such conduct Descended, and made a Kind of Buffoonery in Religion fashionable.

The Spirit of piety Decayed, and people by Degrees grew very Cold and Indifferent about it.

His Successor [Archbishop Stone] Ascended to this Highest pinnacle of Our Temple in the 39th year of His age. He had many virtues and many Advantages. His contempt of Riches, vast munificence and generosity, sweetness of manners, and Inimitable address Disposed the generality to Love and Respect Him: and even Blunted the Darts of Envy which are Let Loose at the favourites of Fortune. All were soon Reconciled to His advancement; and the friends of Religion and the Church Hoped for much good from His Influence.

It soon appeared that all these graces and virtues were pointed at one sole object. Not being much initiated in Ecclesiastical matters, the Church was not His Element. His great Ambition was to Lead and Direct in political affairs. The colledge of the Apostles [fo. 236r] Did not think it consistent with their Duty and Character to *forsake the Word of the Lord to serve tables*. But the Latter was His choice. No attention was paid to spiritual interests. The society of such men was avoided. In Eighteen years [he] never once in person visited His province, tho good Boulter Did it every three years.[12] No man was considered on the account of His merit in the

---

11 John Hoadly (1678–1746). The Cambridge-educated younger brother of the controversial English bishop Benjamin Hoadly (1676–1761), John Hoadly served as bishop of Ferns and Leighlin (1727–9) and archbishop of Dublin (1729–42) and Armagh (1742–6). A protégé of Bishop Gilbert Burnet, Hoadly served, thanks to his patron, as prebend (1706–13), archdeacon (1710–27) and chancellor (1713–27) of Salisbury and as a royal chaplain to George I. Hoadly was not known for his pastoral ardour. Richard Garnett, 'Hoadly, John (1678–1746)', rev. J. Falvey, *ODNB*; John Bergin, 'Hoadly, John (1678–1746)', *Dictionary of Irish biography*, ed. James McGuire and James Quinn (Cambridge, forthcoming). I wish to thank Mr McGuire for allowing me to read this latter article in advance of publication.

12 Stone irregularly visited his Armagh diocese: Magennis, 'Stone, George (1708–1764)'.

church, Let His Services to Religion[,] His King, His country be ever so notorious. On the contrary an appearance of Real merit was His Hindrance. Every Dignity and Emolument was applyed to the Sole point of gaining more clients in the House of Commons. In so much that even in His own great Diocese, the chief Benefices were given, not to His own Clergy. But to young men from other parts whose friends could serve His purposes in the House. Had S^t: Patrick peeped out of His Grave, He would not Have Been able to obtain a Vicars place in His own Cathedral. A neglect, or Rather contempt of merit Became general: The fatal consequence of which on Religion is now too visible.

But this was not All. The church itself Has Been shamefully Abandoned, in order to gain the favour of some Leading members who were Known to be not it's friends. I shall only mention three Instances.

Under His Direction a Bill was Begun in the House of Commons, which passed into a Law pretending to [fo. 236v] provide a Remedy for the clergy to Recover their Ecclesiastical Rights Due by Custom.[13] It prohibited them from all other Remedys: and was so contrived that the Extension of it was found Impossible. This fatal act cut them off from all these Rights for seven years, the term of its duration. And Has Raised Such a Spirit, That I fear it will be Difficult ever again to Recover; to the Ruine of all the poor Vicars.

The parish clerks Being Opposed in their fees; a Law was framed under the Same Influence, which took away all their antient Rights, and in Lieu thereof pretended to give them a tax on the parish, and that But a trifle; for which the churchwardens were made accountable.[14] But this was so artfully contrived, tho twice amended,[15] as to be utterly ineffectual. All our poor parish clerks who Sued thereon by Civil Bill, Have Been Dismissed. And our Churches are Left Destitute, unless where the minister or some good people give them Alms for their service.

A third instance was in the monstrous Bill which, under the pretext of Exonerating some Kinds of Lands from Tythes, was so worded that it would Have taken in at Least two thirds of all the Lands in Ireland.[16] I gave the primate notice of it Early, while it was cooking up in the House of Commons. He promised to take care of it, and made us secure. Yet it passed the councils Here and in England, came over, passed the House of Commons, and was Read a Second time in the House of Lords. in order to be passed [fo. 237r] into a Law. I was uneasy about it and at the Second Reading awakened the attention of some of the Lords. [I] obtained Leave to be Heard by counsell against it. All the Lords were Summoned. [T]he Commons attended, many of them at first offended at my medling, in which some others of the

---

[13] 23 George II c. 12: 'Act for amending, continuing and making more effectual the several acts now in force in this kingdom, for the more easy recovery of tithes and other ecclesiastical dues of small value, and also for the more easy providing a maintenance for parish clerks' (1749): *ILD*.

[14] 33 George II c. 11: 'Act for reviving and amending an act, passed in the 23rd year of his present majesty's reign, entitled, an act for amending, continuing and making more effectual the several laws now in force in this kingdom for the more easy recovery of tithes and other ecclesiastical dues of small value, and also for the more easy providing a maintenance for parish clerks, so far only as the same relates to the more easy providing a maintenance for parish clerks, and to encourage the building of new churches' (1759): *Irish legislation database* (www.qub.ac.uk/ild) (*ILD*).

[15] Two earlier attempts to amend 23 George II c. 12 (in 1755 and again in 1757) failed: *ILD*.

[16] This piece of legislation is difficult precisely to identify. Henry probably refers to the 'Bill to explain and amend an act, entitled, an act to waste and encourage the improvement of barren and waste lands and bogs' (1751): *ILD*.

clergy joined me. But in the End we made it so plainly appear, that the passing of this act would put an End of the present Establishment in Ireland, that the Bill was Rejected. Lord Jocelyne,[17] then Ld Chancellor, many of the Lords and commons, and the judges, came to the Bar, after it was over, and thanked us. [A]nd expressed their joy on our great and narrow Escape.

I need not mention too the great countenance shewn to the Late Rebellious Leaders of the Oak Boys in the north.[18] It was shameful.

Beside all this, when an Ecclesiastic in the Highest Station, neglecting His own province, assumes the Lead in all political affairs, it Raises such an opinion of our Boundless ambition in the Laity: that for such an Error in the Head, they are all Ready to pull Down the whole Body. [T]his Has Done, I fear, Irreparable Hurt to the church in this Kingdom.

What a sad State are things Brought to by the Oak Boy spirit in the north. The Clergy Reduced to the Last Distress in other provinces – the priests and shoals of Jesuits making Daily proselytes – and at Least fifty thousand papists in [M]unster, under the name of White Boys, actually Engaged by a Sollemn Oath to unite and Stand by one another in favour of the French or Spaniards, whenever they shall [fo. 237v] please to attack us.[19] [O]f which fact I am assured by a very wise and Learned privy counsellor.[20]

This Being the State of things: your Grace will forgive my presumption in Entreating you to Interfere in sending some good man, not a meer politician, But an Apostolical man, to Restore true Religion and save the British interest in this poor Kingdom. [P]ardon me, if I Say That the ArchBishops of Canterbury Have always Looked on the state of Religion in Ireland to be within their province.

I can now Have no possible motive in trespassing so far on your condescension, But my warm zeal for the Interest of the protestant Religion, the Honour of His Majesty; and the Security of the British Interest.

This whole nation and many in Great Britain can Bear witness, that for these things, I Have been an Indefatigable preacher and Stickler these 38 years[,] and it Shocks me to think, that unless some care be taken in Due time, I may be so miserable as to [indecipherable] live to see them overthrown ...

Willm: Henry

Kildare Street in Dublin
Novem^r. 20th 1764 –

---

17 Robert Jocelyn, First Viscount Jocelyn (1687/8–1756). An Englishman and protégé of Philip Yorke, first earl of Hardwicke, Jocelyn served as Ireland's lord chancellor (1739–56). G. F. R. Barker, 'Jocelyn, Robert, First Viscount Jocelyn (1678/7–1756)', *ODNB*.

18 For Stone's response to the Oak Boys agitations, see Francis Hardy, *Memoirs of the political and private life of James Caulfeild, earl of Charlemont* (2 vols., London, 1812), I, 89–91. For background, see Magennis, 'County Armagh: Hearts of Oak'; but cf. Donnelly, 'Hearts of Oak, hearts of steel', esp. 8–22.

19 See Donnelly, 'The Whiteboy movement, 1761–5'.

20 Unidentified.

3. William Henry to Thomas Secker, 29 December 1764

[fo. 238r] Kildare Street in Dublin Decem^r: 29th 1764 –

May it please Your Grace,

I should not think the new year fortunate to me, If I Did not first Offer to your Grace my sincerest Wishes, and to Heaven my most ardent prayers, That it may prove a year of Health, Happyness and every comfort to your Grace.

Yesterday, we were surprised with the Sudden Death of The Earl of Shannon,[21] one of our two Lords Justices.

He never was in Better Health or more Lively spirits than on Thursday: Eat His Supper and Drank His usual pint of port after it chearfully, at tea. [W]ent to Bed at Eleven: at one found Himself taken ill: Rung His Bell, and a Little after fell into a fit, from which He soon Recovered, in so much That He Held a conversation with Doctor Barry[22] and the Apothecary. He soon Relapsed into a second, and thence into a third, which carryed Him off at nine in the forenoon. Thus Dyed in His 82^d year, and in the Apparent vigour of Age, the Ablest politician and truly great man, which this Kingdom Has produced. He Had the principal Direction of affairs for 32 years and was ever Distinguished for His warm zeal for the protestant Religion, the British Interest, and a steady adherence to Revolution principles.

[fo. 238v] It is, in the present Situation of Affairs in Ireland, a matter of the utmost consequence to the Existence of the British power in this Kingdom, to appoint such a successor as may be Depended on for His Wisdom, Spirit, and religion.

I Hope that my Lord Chancellor[23] will be thought on, as He is Entirely versed in all the Affairs of Government, Has for more than thirty years [~~indecipherable~~] acted with Dignity and Integrity in public Busyness: and as almost all His predecessors Have Been Honoured with The Authority of Lord Justice.

From the accounts Received of the 15th Date from London since which time we Had no Later pacquet: every one Here concludes that the next pacquet must Bring an account of the primate's Death. Such a vacancy will give an opportunity of filling up the place of another Lord Justice with a nobleman of the greatest weight in parliament, Intrinsick virtue, and Well Directed Zeal for the British Interest, and protestant Religion, that Even Britain it self could ever afford.

The person I mean is Sir Arthur Gore Earl of Arran.[24] As to His personal Character, it Has ever Been most virtuous, Religious, and Amiable. The Happy mixture

---

[21] Henry Boyle, first earl of Shannon (c. 1683–1764). A native Irishman who was educated at Christ Church, Oxford, Boyle was the dominant politician of his time; he served as speaker of the Irish House of Commons (1733–56) and as lord justice fifteen times between 1734 and 1764. Eoin Magennis, 'Boyle, Henry, first earl of Shannon (1681x7–1764)', *ODNB*.

[22] Either Sir Edward Barry (1698–1776) or his son, Nathaniel (later Sir Nathaniel) Barry (d. 1785). Both were prominent Dublin physicians. J. D. H. Widdes, *A history of the Royal College of Physicians of Ireland, 1654–1963* (Edinburgh, 1963), p. 79; Jean Loudon, 'Barry, Sir Edward, first baronet (1696–1776)', *ODNB*.

[23] John Bowes (1691–1767). A boyhood friend of Thomas Secker and protégé of Philip Yorke, first earl of Hardwicke, Bowes served as Ireland's lord chancellor (1757–67). S. J. Connolly, 'Bowes, John, Baron Bowes of Clonlyon (1691–1767)', *ODNB*.

[24] Sir Arthur Gore, first earl of Arran (1703–73). A native Irishman, Gore studied at Trinity College, Dublin (BA, 1722), the Middle Temple and King's Inn. An MP for Donegal (1727–58), Gore, like William Henry, actively supported Irish charter schools. Edith Mary Johnston-Liik (ed.), *History of the Irish parliament, 1692–1800: Commons, constituencies and statutes* (6 vols., Belfast, 2000) (*HIP*), IV, 273–5; *CP*, I, 227.

of the sweetest temper, clear judgment and firmness, Has procured to Him the universal Love of all men in this Kingdom. His country has Long [fo. 239r] Looked on Him, as one of it's first worthys.

In public affairs, He hath ever sought the General good without the Least Byass to His private Interest[,] of which He Gave the Strongest proof, when His country would Have compelled Him to be Speaker, in the Late times of Ferment,[25] He Refused coming into their measures; and tho' He was ungratefully treated, and could Have Ruined all that Had injured Him; His Love to His country Extinguished all His Resentments. His Wisdom and moderation saved this Kingdom from a Civil war.

His Knowledge in political affairs and Intelligence Has Let him into the secret springs and schemes of all those Rioters [the Whiteboys], who are carrying on with Hasty strides yet Great Caution, the interest of popery: and He has often Warned our Governours of the Evil[,] and plainly told them, That unless some effectual Remedys were applyed in time, We should Have the tragedy of 1641 acted over again, upon the first Rupture with France and Spain and officers sent by those powers to Head the papists.[26]

His Knowledge and vigilance with Regard to the Good of His country is universally confessed.

Beside all this, He has more Influence and natural Interest in the House of Commons, by Reason of His numerous family connections, than any other man.[27]

And, as He never made use of this great power, for any other purpose, than to support His Majesty's Government [fo. 239v] and the True British Interests, such a man may be at all times entirely Relyed on. This Kingdom stands in need of such a man. I say these things, not from Interest, But from the pure attraction which, I Hope, my Heart will always feel to virtue[,] and from the perfect Knowledge I Have for near thirty years, that Lord Arran is the most virtuous character this Kingdom affords.

I Went yesterday to pay my Respects to the A:Bᴾ: of Dublin,[28] and sat with Him near an Hour. He is Declining very fast. Has a stuffing in His throat, and much phlegm, Has Quite Lost the use of His Leggs. One of them is greatly Swelled, and Has several little Blisters on it which Require the constant attendance of a Surgeon.

Yet He still sits up in His Armed chair, and Keeps up His Spirit. He has Been a Bishop forty four years, and is now Gradually Dying away, Like a Lamp that Has no more oyl.

As Your Grace may Desire to Know, How I am. Thanks to God I Have Recovered

---

[25] Henry is referring to the money bill dispute of 1753–6, for which, see Eoin Magennis, *The Irish political system, 1740–1765: the golden age of the undertakers* (Dublin, 2000), pp. 62–92.

[26] For the impact of 1641 on the Irish protestant consciousness, see Kelly, '"The glorious and immortal memory"', and Toby Barnard, 'The uses of 23 October 1641 and Irish protestant celebrations', *English Historical Review*, CVI, 421 (1991), 889–920.

[27] The Gore interest was one of the largest family interest in the Irish parliament. Among family members who sat in the Irish House of Commons during the mid-1760s were the Rt Hon. Arthur Saunders Gore (MP for Donegal borough), Henry Gore (MP for Killybeggs), the Rt Hon. John Gore (MP for Co. Longford) and Paul Annesley Gore (MP for Co. Mayo and Co. Sligo).

[28] Charles Cobbe (1687–1765). An Oxford-educated Englishman, Cobbe came to Ireland as chaplain to Charles Paulet, second duke of Bolton (lord lieutenant: 1717–20), and served as bishop of Killala (1720–7), Dromore (1727–31), Kildare (1731–43) and as archbishop of Dublin (1743–65). Thompson Cooper, 'Charles Cobbe (1687–1765)', rev. R. G. Ingram, *ODNB*.

from all my complaints[,] and was able on Christmass Day, to preach and do other dutys to our nobility and gentry, in the Castle Chappell.[29]

That God may long preserve Your Grace as a protector and Blessing to the British and all the protestant Churches, is the fervent prayer of …

Will[m]: Henry

4. William Henry to Thomas Secker, 16 April 1765

[fo. 241r] Kildare Street Apr: 16 1765

May it please Your Grace

I Have for some months Avoided being troublesome: not Having any material occurrencys to communicate.

The Archbishop of Dublin, who Has Been in a Languid State since [J]une last, was taken suddenly ill on Fryday, and Dyed on Sunday, at noon, in his 80th year.[30] He was made Bishop of Killala by the Duke of Bolton[31] in 1720. And A:B[p]: of Dublin in 1742. So that He was the oldest Bishop in Europe. He amassed a Great Estate, which he left to M[r]: Cobbe His only child.[32]

It is Expected Here that He will be succeeded by D[r]: Carmichael,[33] the Worthy Bishop of Meath, who, to the great Regrett of the friends of Ireland, was passed by on the Disposal of the primacy.[34] We suppose that Doctor Dodgson[35] the Lord Lieutenants first Chaplain, will on this occasion be made a Bishop. If after this L[d]: Northumberland[36] continues our Governour, He may Have opportunitys of Extending His favours to some of the Irish Clergy. [T]o this He [fo. 241v] is very well Disposed. If this should be the case The person whom your Grace condescended to Honour with your Recommendation; may Have some Reason to Expect a Benefit; As He Hath, unsolicited, Declared that He intended Him a mark of His favour: and upon the Disposal of the Deanery of Kilmore, went so far as to write to

---

29 Chapel Royal at Dublin Castle: Barnard, *Making the grand figure*, pp. 14–15.

30 For Charles Cobbe's death, see *Dublin Journal*, 3962 (13–16 Apr. 1765).

31 Charles Paulet, second duke of Bolton (*c.* 1661–1722). A staunch whig and MP for Hampshire during the 1680s, Bolton actively supported the exclusion of James, duke of York, from the succession and William of Orange's invasion in 1688. He later served as an Irish lord justice (1697–1700) and lord lieutenant (1717–20). Matthew Kilburn, 'Paulet, Charles, second duke of Bolton (*c.* 1661–1722)', *ODNB*.

32 Thomas Cobbe (1733–1814) served as MP for Newbridge in the Irish House of Commons: *HIP*, III, 438–9.

33 William Carmichael. See above, n. 8.

34 On George Stone's death, the primacy passed to Richard Robinson (*c.* 1708–94): G. Le G. Norgate, 'Robinson, Richard, First Baron Rokeby (bap. 1708, d. 1794)', rev. Eoin Magennis, *ODNB*.

35 Charles Dodgson (*c.* 1723–95). A Cambridge-educated Englishman who came to Ireland as chaplain to Hugh Percy, first duke of Northumberland (lord lieutenant: 1763–5), Dodgson served as bishop of Ossory (1765–75) and Elphin (1775–95). Before coming to Ireland, he kept a school in Cumberland and served as rector of parishes in Yorkshire and Northumberland. *CCED*; *FEH*, II, 287.

36 Hugh Percy, first duke of Northumberland (*c.* 1712–86). Northumberland opposed Walpole during the early 1740s, but transferred his allegiance to the Pelhamite whigs after the Forty-Five. He controlled a small electoral interest in Yorkshire and was thought, for a time, to have a chance to succeed Bute as the first minister in 1763. Instead, George Grenville gained the position, and Northumberland was named lord lieutenant of Ireland. John Cannon, 'Percy [formerly Smithson], Hugh, first duke of Northumberland (bap. 1712, d. 1786)', *ODNB*.

Him a most friendly Letter Declaring His particular Esteem, and Desiring Him to be fully persuaded of His firm Resolution to give Him a proof thereof.[37]

Your Grace must Have Heard various Reports concerning the Disturbances, wherewith the province of Munster, and the county of Kilkenny were threatened by the Insurrections of the papists called White Boys.

The allarm was so great in Cork in January, that the protestants feared a massacre; and on one Sunday Had all the Army under Arms, and the churches Guarded by soldiers all the time of Divine Service.

These Apprehensions were not without some Foundation. For it is notorious that the swarms of Jesuits and some foreign Agents Have for a considerable time past Been Busy in stirring up the papists to mischief. [fo. 242r] No less than thirty two papists, some of them men of property, Had Bills for High treason and Rebellion found against them in the Last Assizes in the County of Typperary.[38]

The Earl of Carrick[39] Having Received informations of treasonable conspiracys, sent them up to the Government, and some of the persons whom He had taken up. Sh[e]ehy,[40] a known Jesuit, who was at the Bottom of their conspiracys, Had a Bill of Inditement for High treason found against Him Last August assizes. The Government offered a Reward of £300 for Apprehending Him.[41] He and His accomplices continued to put out of the way, (some say to Bury alive) the principal witness against Him[,][42] whereupon He Surrendered Himself. The Grand jury of Typperary are so sensible of this, that they Have Subscribed fifty guineas as a Reward to any one who will Discover it. But all their offers will be in vain: for people are intimidated from what was Done in the county of Kilkenny about three weeks ago to M^r: Walsh of Mount Neal.[43]

This man was a papist, But an Honest man, and was said to Have given information of their proceedings [fo. 242v] to The Earl of Carrick. In consequence whereof the sad Catastrophe Happened, which is mentioned in all our Gazettes and public papers. Some malicious persons set fire to His Dwelling House in the Dead of the night, whereby Himself, his wife Big with child, and His six children were Burnt to Ashes.

These are most frightful proceedings. [A]nd the spirit of Rebellion is not yet subdued, as appears by their Rising to the number of 500 at Charlevill in the county of Cork about 12 Days ago, and Destroying M^r: Doulin's Lands. And their Exercising some military Discipline near Thurles.[44] There seems to Have Been an Evil Spirit of Rebellion and contempt of the Laws Let Loose thro' many parts of this Kingdome.

---

37 Henry is referring here to himself.

38 *Dublin Journal*, 3958 (30 Mar. – 2 Apr. 1765); *Gentleman's and London Magazine*, XXXV (1765), 190.

39 Somerset Hamilton Butler, first earl of Carrick (1718–74). An Irishman, he married the daughter of Henry Boyle and lived in County Tipperary: *CP*, III, 60–1.

40 Nicholas Sheehy (1728/9–66). An Irish Roman Catholic priest, Sheehy advocated for the Whiteboys during the early 1760s and was wrongly convicted of murder. Thomas P. Power, 'Sheehy, Nicholas (1728/9–1766)', *ODNB*.

41 For the Feb. 1765 government proclamation concerning Sheehy, see Bric, 'The Whiteboy movement', pp. 157–8.

42 John Bridge, a crucial witness against Sheehy, disappeared in late 1764, and Sheehy was charged with and convicted of his murder.

43 *Dublin Journal*, 3960 (6–9 Apr. 1765); *Gentleman's and London Magazine*, XXXV (1765), 190.

44 *Ibid.* reported that between 400 and 500 Whiteboys 'turn[ed] up the Ground of Mr. Dowling, a Gentleman of repute and Credit'. See also *Gentleman's and London Magazine*, XXXV (1765), 254.

[I]n this city Robberys were so frequent and Barefaced, that for a considerable part of Last Winter, no person could with safety stir out of Doors at night.

But the Spirited Behaviour of the gentlemen, and the vigour of government will I Hope, very soon Reduce all Disturbers to Reason and submission.

The Gentlemen of the county of Kilkenny Have set a good Example. At the Assizes Held there this month, Eight were condemned for High treason, of whom [fo. 243r] Six were Executed on Saturday last. [T]wo Being young Lads, and Led on by their fathers, were thought fit objects of mercy.[45]

Three were condemned for Burning Tythe corn, and are to be Executed. [M]any others were found guilty of Riots &c, and severely punished.

At the Assizes for the county of Tyrone, one M^c:Ghee[46] who Had insulted and impounded Doctor Knight the Rector of Omagh,[47] was found guilty, fined 50 p^ds: Imprisoned for six months, and obliged to find Suretys for His Behaviour for seven years after. This Doctor Knight, as a magistrate, Directed the Kings forces who Reduced the Oak Boys, for which all of that party owed Him malice.

Also, at the Assizes for the county of Donegal, the Grand jury found Every Bill against Bates the wicked villain who intended to Assassinate the good Bishop of Raphoe.[48] [A]nd as Bates Had Escaped out of prison by the negligence, (or Rather Connivance) of Isaack Armstrong the goaler: the goaler was found guilty of an Escape, imprisoned for six months, and fined in fifty pounds. [A]n 100 guineas are now offered for Retaking Bates, who, if taken, will certainly be Hanged, as his crime is now complicated.

[fo. 243v] I see with pleasure a Spirit Rising every where among our Gentlemen to support the Laws, which for a Long time Have Been too much neglected.

It is a peculiar Happyness to this Kingdom, That Lord Chancellor [Bowes] Has Been, at so Critical a time, appointed one of our Lords justices.[49] [F]or His perfect Knowledge of this country, and His Steady zeal for justice, mixed with mercy, support the Dignity of the government and are Daily procuring Reverence to the Laws. He has no jobbs to comply with[,] nothing But the public good to pursue. [S]o can go on in His integrity, impartial, and immoveable.

Upon the whole of what Has Happened among the Disturbers of the public tranquillity: It appears very plain to me; That there Has Been a wicked Rebellious Spirit fomented thro' several parts of Ireland by the Secret Agents of France and Spain: who may imagine, that by throwing this Kingdom into confusion (which will Certainly

---

45 At the Mar. 1765 Kilkenny assizes, men were sentenced to death and executed for murdering Serjeant Johnston and John French, two soldiers when they were conducting some Whiteboys to prison: *Gentleman's and London Magazine*, XXXV (1765), 191. I wish to thank Professor James Kelly for this reference.

46 George Magee: *ibid.*, 190. *Lloyd's Evening Post*, 1210 (10 Apr. 1765), reported that the assizes found Magee ('a most turbulent man') 'guilty for violently assaulting … [Knight]; for making him a prisoner, and detaining him several hours from his lawful occasions, and impounding both him and his horse; and this severe treatment the Doctor received for no other reason than his barely riding over Magee's land to view his corn, his horse not having eaten a blade of his grass'.

47 James Knight (*c.* 1720–67). An Irishman, he studied at Trinity College, Dublin (BA, 1733; MA, 1738; fellow, 1738; BD, 1747; DD, 1736), and served as rector of Drumragh (1758–67). He was noted for his opposition to the Oak Boys in 1763. Leslie, *Derry clergy and parishes*, p. 208.

48 See above, Letter 1.

49 John Bowes served as an Irish lord justice twice (22 Feb. 1765 – 19 Oct. 1765 and 11 June 1766 – 14 Oct. 1767). T. W. Moody, F. X. Martin and F. J. Byrne (eds.), *A new history of Ireland* (Oxford, 1976–2005) (*NHI*), IX, 494.

be the first object of their Attacks, in case of any Future war) they may Embarrass affairs, as to prevent Great Britain from Exerting itself with Spirit and Dignity. The swarms of Jesuits [fo. 244r] who are Daily Flowing into this Kingdom are the principal agents in this Scheme.[50] The commanding officer of my Lord Lorn's Regiment of Dragoons[51] now Quartered at Loughrea in the county of Galway, who came from Loughrea three Days ago, assured me, that two Hundred popish priests are come from abroad into that town, (which is not a Large one) within these three months.

These things Require vigilance.

As your Grace must Have Heard of the most Distinguished Character of Lady Arabella Denny,[52] the patroness of Every good work in this Kingdom; I take pleasure in acquainting you, that she is now perfectly Recovered from the gates of Death in a most violent inflammatory Fever. She was all over seized with nervous convulsions, Her pulse gone, Her Limbs cold, the clammy sweat of Death Had seized her. The physicians gave her up. In this Extremity I ventured to give her D^r: [J]ames's powders, wrenching open Her teeth to get in the tea spoon. It pleased God to give a Blessing. [A]nd now that most valueable Lady Lives and is Doing well: to the Inexpressible joy of this whole Kingdom. Her Recovery Looks Like a Kind of Resurrection. And I know it will be most agreeable to Your Grace's Benevolent Heart.

[fo. 244v] As I am advised to make a tour for the Reestablishment of my Health, as soon as the good weather comes on, It is probable that I may Direct my course to England.[53] In this case, I shall on the first day I see London, pay my grateful Duty at Lambeth …

Willm: Henry

Kildare Street in Dublin
Apr: 16 1765

5. William Henry to Thomas Secker, 16 July 1765

[fo. 250] May it please Your Grace

I should Accuse my Self of unpardonable ingratitude: if after all your Grace's condescension, Kindness, and Friendly solicitude for my Recovery: I Deferred one Hour to acquaint your Grace with my safe arrival at my House in Dublin; in perfect good Health, after a prosperous journey to [P]arkgate[54] in five Days, and a voyage

---

50 For the position of the regular clergy and their numbers, see Hugh Fenning, *The undoing of the friars of Ireland: a study of the novitiate question in the eighteenth century* (Louvain, 1972).

51 General John Campbell, fifth duke of Argyll (1723–1806). A Scot, Campbell was named to lead Lord Lorne's Regiment in 1765. Campbell's father – General John Campbell, fourth duke of Argyll (1693–1770) – served as governor of Limerick (1761–70). *CP*, I, 209–10; Historical Manuscripts Commission, *Report on the Manuscripts of Mrs. Stopford-Sackville* (2 vols., London, 1904), I, 102.

52 Lady Arabella Denny (1707–92). Daughter of the twenty-first lord of Kerry, Denny distinguished herself for her philanthropy, most notably with regard to the Dublin Foundling Hospital and the Magdelan asylum. She was related to the earl of Shelburne, William Henry's patron. Maria Luddy, 'Denny [née Fitzmaurice], Lady Arabella (1707–1792)', *ODNB*; Barnard, *Improving Ireland?*, pp. 179–80, 182–3.

53 Henry did visit London during the early summer of 1765.

54 Parkgate was a Cheshire port town which, during the eighteenth century, was 'the principal port of traffic to and from Ireland': Nikolaus Pevsner and Edward Hubbard, *Cheshire* (London, 1971), pp. 299–300.

of fifty Hours thence to this city where I arrived this forenoon. My Health Encreased every Day on my Journey: and Thanks to God!, seems now to be Quite Re Established. The thanks I owe to Heaven for so speedy and unexpected a Recovery, will, I trust warm my Heart with Redoubled zeal to Do all the good I can. And I never Let slip out of my mind, my Deeply Engraven obligations to your Grace.

Pardon me for troubling your Grace with my Request, that my grateful thanks may be made acceptable to M^{rs}. And Miss Talbot,[55] whose Kind concern for me in my Sickness, and friendly Disposition I must Ever Feel ...

Willm: Henry

Kildare Street
Tuesday July 16 1765

6. William Henry to Thomas Secker, 23 September 1765

[fo. 251r] May it please Your Grace

Since I took the Liberty of troubling your Grace, I Have Been continually Employed in the Dutys of my parish of Urney: or in visiting the Charter Schools.[56] In the course of my visits in the province of Conaught, I came to this place to Attend and Encourage the Spreading colony of protestants whom I Had the comfort of planting in the Dioceses of Killala and Ac[h]onry, which, Blessed be God! Has taken Deep Root, and is Like to prove the Happy means of Spreading the protestant Religion thro the whole country.[57]

Here I met with the account of the Death of the Bishop of Meath.[58] As D^{r}: Hutchinson,[59] Bishop of Killalla is Highly in favour with The Earl of Hertford,[60]

---

[55] Mary Talbot (c. 1694–1784), the widow of Thomas Secker's friend Edward Talbot (1691–1720), and her daughter, Catherine Talbot (1721–70), lived under Secker's roof from 1725 until his death in 1768. Secker and his wife were childless and treated Catherine as their adoptive child. During Secker's archiepiscopacy, Catherine Talbot served at times as his amanuensis and personal secretary. Rhoda Zuk, 'Talbot, Catherine (1721–1770)', *ODNB*.

[56] Milne, *Irish charter schools*, p. 179, records in 1752, the Incorporated Society in Dublin for Promoting Protestant Schools in Ireland charged William Henry and Edward Ledwich (for whom, see above, Letter 1) with being official visitors of Irish charter schools.

[57] Throughout the early and mid-eighteenth century, many Irish landowners sought to promote and to encourage protestants to settle on their estates by offering them preferential leases. In 1756, John [Fitzmaurice] Petty, first earl of Shelburne (c. 1706–61) moved to Ballymote in order to establish a linen manufacturing centre. He brought in seventeen families from northern Ireland to teach those in Ballymote how to work the linen looms: Wood-Martin, *History of Sligo*, III, 243. I wish to thank James Kelly for this reference.

[58] Richard Pococke (1704–65). An Oxford-educated Englishman who came to Ireland as domestic chaplain to Philip Dormer, Stanhope, fourth earl of Chesterfield (lord lieutenant: 1745–6), Pococke served as bishop of Ossory (1756–65), Elphin (1765) and Meath (1765). More noted for his travel narratives than for his pastoral supervision, Pococke died unexpectedly on 25 Sept. 1765 during a visitation of Meath. Elizabeth Baigent, 'Pococke, Richard (1704–1765)', *ODNB*.

[59] Samuel Hutchinson (d. 1780). An Englishman, Hutchinson served as bishop of Killala (1759–80). He matriculated at Queens' College, Cambridge (1718), before migrating to Trinity College, Dublin, in 1721 (BA, 1723; MA, 1727). He held prebends of Down and Connor and the deanery of Dromore before being elevated to the Irish bench. *Alum Cantab*, II, 441.

[60] Francis Seymour Conway, first marquess of Hertford (1718–94). A noted English courtier and politician with Irish estates in county Antrim, Hertford served as Ireland's lord lieutenant (1765–6). William C. Lowe, 'Conway, Francis Seymour, first marquess of Hertford (1718–1794)', *ODNB*.

Our Lord Lieutenant, it is probable that upon this occasion He may be translated to some Better Bishoprick. If this should be the case: and my friends should think me capable of so Important a Trust: I would Hope that my Zealous Labours for the British and protestant Interest, which Have [fo. 251v] Been Laid out in this, the particular county of my nativity, might be carried on with the greater success, should His Majesty think of me, on this occasion.

Your Grace is the Best Judge of the propriety or probability of such a wish succeeding.

I therefore take the Liberty of only Barely mentioning it. Being on the one Hand, fully assured of your Graces great Friendship: and on the other perfectly satisfyed, and Determined to Do my Duty with all Ardour and Disinterestedness, either in my present, or any other station it shall please God to place me ...

Willm: Henry

Ballymote in the county of Sligoe
Septr. 23 1765.

I hope to be in Dublin within a Fortnight

7. William Henry to Thomas Secker, 22 October 1765

[fo. 253r] May it please Your Grace

No words are Sufficient to Express the obligations I feel and must ever feel, for your Letter of the 4th inst:[61] When I Reflect on my own Litleness I am ashamed and Blush at the condescension your Grace Has shewn towards me, and the unwearyed pains you Have taken to place me in a favourable Light with our governours.

Tho' Lord Hertford Declined Entering into any Engagements, I am fully persuaded, that your Graces warm Recommendation will sometime Have the Desired Effect, if He continues to be our Governour for a Longer period than His predecessors.[62] He Landed Here on [F]ryday. I saw Him sworn Lord Lieutenant. [A]nd afterwards, as I was going up to be presented; He prevented His Aid Du Camp, and came up to me very graciously. On Sunday also, He shewed me the Like Respect, at a Crowded Levee; and yesterday sent D^r: Trail[63] the new Bp of Down to Desire me to attend Him as one of His Chaplains. I mention these courtesys, out of gratitude to Your Grace, to whom I owe any Distinction He is pleased to conferr on me.

This Day our parliament met, it was opened by a very Becoming speech from His Excellency, in which He very warmly Recommended our Charter Schools.[64] He professes a great attention to them. We Have, By His [fo. 253v] approbation

---

61 This letter from Secker to Henry appears no longer to be extant.

62 Hertford's predecessors were Thomas Thynne, Third Viscount Weymouth, who was appointed on 5 June 1765 but was never sworn into office, and Hugh Percy, first duke of Northumberland, who served as lord lieutenant from Apr. 1763 until Aug. 1765. Hertford's own lord lieutenancy lasted just over a year (Aug. 1765 – Oct. 1766): *NHI*, IX, 494–5; H. M. Scott, 'Thynne, Thomas, Third Viscount Weymouth and first marquess of Bath (1734–1796)', *ODNB*.

63 James Traill (d. 1783). A Scot, he served as Lord Hertford's tutor chaplain both in Paris and Ireland before being named bishop of Down and Connor in 1765. James B. Leslie and Henry Biddall Swanzy, *Biographical succession lists of the clergy of the diocese of Down* (Enniskillen, 1936), p. 15; *FEH*, III, 211–12; *Lloyd's Evening Post* (2 Oct. 1765).

64 *Lords Journals*, IV, 343.

Drawn up our petition for Aid to the House of Commons. We Have Reason to Hope that His Son Lord Beauchamp[65] will Bring it in[,] and that the Sum Designed to be granted will be £16000. [T]his will make us flourish! and much Less will not Do: for since our own schools are Enlarged, and thro the Late Scarcety of provisions[66] the Expences are much Encreased, The charge of supporting all our schools amounts, on an Average, to one thousand per month. Had it not Been for the £1000 bequeathed by General Wolfe's mother,[67] and other Legacys to the amount of £500 Lately sent us from England, our Fund would Have Been at this time very nearly Exhausted; as appears by our Treasurer's accounts.

The Earl of Hertford is Received among us with universal acceptance: Both on account of His amicable character for Religion and Virtue, and His being a nobleman of Ireland as well as England, whose family Has Long resided here. There Has not been an Irish nobleman Lord Lieutenant Since the Late Duke of Ormond,[68] unless we reckon the Duke of Shresbery,[69] who was Earl of Waterford. But none of His family ever Dwelt among us.

The ArchBishop of Dublin,[70] who Has Been at the point of Death, is now in a good way of Recovery: and is preparing to [fo. 254r] set out Hence for Bath on Saturday. He continues still Exceeding weak; and I fear there is But a Bad prospect for His Ever Returning. [F]or His Fever and Disorder of His Bowells arises from an Obstruction in His Liver. His only Remedy is the Bath waters. I Believe our Physicians send him thither; as they Despair of Relieving him Here.

I Have not seen my Lord Chancellor [Bowes] Look so well these many years as He Does at present.[71] [M]ay God continue the Like Health and good spirits to Him thro the winter!

As his Lordship's time must be taken up in the court, councill, and House of Lords, I shall take the Liberty of writing to Your Grace such accounts of any material transactions During this winter as may be worthy your perusal.

---

65 Francis Ingram-Seymour-Conway, Viscount Beauchamp (1743–1822). Son of Ireland's lord lieutenant, Beauchamp studied at Eton and Christ Church, Oxford. He served as an Irish MP (1761–8), as an Irish privy councillor (1765), and as chief secretary to his father (1765–6). T. J. Hochstrasser, 'Conway, Francis Ingram-Seymour-Conway, second marquess of Hertford (1743–1822)', *ODNB*; *HIP*, VI, 256–7.

66 Ireland experienced one of its periodic subsistence crises in 1765–6. On mid-century Irish harvests, see L. M. Cullen, *An economic history of Ireland since 1660* (London, 1972), pp. 67–74.

67 Henrietta Wolfe (d. 1765) willed £1,000 to the Incorporated Society for Promoting English Working Schools in Ireland: *Annual register, or a view of the history, politicks, and literature for the year 1765* (London, 1766), p. 93.

68 James Butler, second duke of Ormond (1665–1745). An Irishman, Ormond's political sympathies was a tory and anglican who served twice as Ireland's lord lieutenant (1703–7, 1710–13). After the accession of George I, he fled to the continent, where he lived the rest of his life in exile. Stuart Handley, 'Butler, James, second duke of Ormond (1665–1745)', *ODNB*.

69 Charles Talbot, duke of Shrewsbury (1660–1718). A convert from catholicism to the Church of England, Shrewsbury was one of the 'immortal seven' who asked William of Orange to invade England. He served as Ireland's lord lieutenant (1713–14) and was instrumental in securing the Hanoverian succession. Stuart Handley, 'Talbot, Charles, duke of Shrewsbury (1660–1718)', *ODNB*.

70 Charles Cobbe.

71 Bowes suffered from indifferent health during his later years: James Kelly, 'Belvedere House: origins, development, and residents, 1540–1883', in *St. Patrick's College, Drumcondra, 1875–2000: a history*, ed. James Kelly (Dublin, 2006), pp. 28–9.

The good Bishop of Waterford[72] is active in Reviving the committee for Enquiring into charitable Donations. [T]his Enquiry Has already Brought in near £17000. [A]nd this Day, I understand, that Lord Viscount Cuningham[73] Has at Last submitted to pay a charitable Legacy Bequeathed by His uncle Bonnell,[74] which Has Been Kept Back, near 40 years: and will amount to more than £6000.

This good Bishop has shewn to me many Letters concerning the fresh Disturbances of the *White Boys* in Destroying the Rights of the clergy. He is much alarmed at these things. But, I am persuaded that these Riotous proceedings at this time will procure friends to the church, and in the Event Do it service. [fo. 254v] I am well Informed, that Before, Lord Hertford set out for Ireland, M[r]: Ponsonby[75] the Speaker wrote to Him concerning the necessity there was of considering the clergy of Ireland more in the Distribution of Ecclesiastical preferments, than Has Been the custom for some time past. [A]nd that unless this was Done, He could not undertake for Doing His Majesty's Busyness: or that the Ecclesiastical constitution could be long supported.

I inclose the L[d]: L[t]'s Speech which is just come from the press at Eleven o'clock at night.[76] …

Will[m]: Henry

Kildare Street
October 22 1765

P.S. Blessed be God, my Health continues confirmed.

---

[72] Richard Chenevix (1697–1779). A Cambridge-educated Englishman, Chenevix came to Ireland as chaplain to Philip Stanhope, fourth earl of Chesterfield (lord lieutenant: 1745–6). Chenevix's publication of anti-ministerial pamphlets threatened to bar his path to the Irish bench, but through Chesterfield's interventions, he was named to the bishopric of Killaloe (1745). He served subsequently as bishop of Waterford and Lismore (1746–79), and his contemporaries thought him to be a model prelate. H. M. Stephens, 'Chenevix, Richard (1696/7–1779)', *ODNB*.

[73] Henry Conyngham (1705–81). An Irishman, Conyngham was a professional soldier who sat as an MP in both the Irish (1727–53) and Westminster (1747–54, 1756–74) parliaments. Upon the death of his father in 1706, Conyngham and his siblings went to live with their uncle, William Conolly. *HIP*, III, 483; Barnard, *Making the grand figure*, pp. 66–8; *idem*, *A new anatomy of Ireland*, p. 119.

[74] James Bonnell (1653–99). Married to Henry Conyngham's aunt (Jane), Bonnell was an Irish bureaucrat and philanthropist. D. W. Hayton, 'Bonnell, James (1653–1699)', *ODNB*; Toby Barnard, 'Reforming Irish manners: the religious societies in Dublin during the 1690s', *HJ*, XXXV, 4 (1992), 805–38, esp. 818–19. For an account of the Bonnell bequest, and the delay in its payment until the 1780s, see James Kelly (ed.), *Proceedings of the Irish House of Lords, 1771–1800* (3 vols., Dublin, 2008), I, 348–50, 352–6.

[75] John Ponsonby (1713–89). Leader of the major Ponsonby parliamentary connexion, John Ponsonby's manoeuvrings occasionally irked the lords lieutenant. Ponsonby served as speaker of the Irish House of Commons (1756–71). Martyn J. Powell, 'Ponsonby, John (1713–1789)', *ODNB*.

[76] For a copy of Hertford's speech, see *Annual register…1765*, pp. 264–5.

8. William Henry to Thomas Secker, 2 November 1765

[fo. 255r] Dublin Nov[r]: 2 1765

May it please Your Grace

Our Session of parliament Has Hitherto gone on pretty well. In the address to the King and L[d]: Lieu[t]:,[77] an objection was made by Mr. Loftus,[78] against thanking the King for not making use of the *confidential credit*, placed in Him in case the funds Had not Been sufficient. [T]his trust was carped at, as unconstitutional. But, after a Long and trifling Debate, which kept the L[d]: L[t]: and members from their Dinners 'till near nine o clock, the addresses were agreed to. They are grateful, warm, and affectionate.

As the state of the clergy is most miserable in a great part of Munster and Leinster, thro the evil spirit Raised by the White Boy Rebells, and their secret Encouragers, in so much that in many parishes the clergy have nothing at all Left to them: The gentlemen of the House of Commons thought proper to take up this matter. M[r]. Langrishe,[79] a member from Killkenny moved for Leave to Bring in Heads of a Bill, upon this scheme, That all Tythes should be abolished, and that provision should be made for the clergy some other way. He mentioned a Rateable tax on the Lands.[80]

But this appearing to be a Scheme utterly Impracticable (and possibly secretly intended by some to abolish the present subsistence of the clergy, and to substitute nothing Effectual in it's stead, as Has been Done to the parish clerks.) [M]any Lawyers of Eminence in the House spoke largely to it: and it Ended in Leave to Bring in Heads of a Bill, [fo. 255v] 'For the more *Effectual Support* of the Clergy, and The Vindication of their Rights.'[81] We may Hope for some good from this Bill, as the principal Lawyers, who are supposed to be friends to the Ecclesiastical Constitution, are added to M[r]. Langrishe, as a committee for framing this Bill. They are R[t]. Hon[ble]: Ant: Malone,[82] Right Hon[ble]: M[r]: Prime Serjeant,[83] R[t]: Hon: Attorney

---

[77] *The journals of the House of Commons, of the Kingdom of Ireland, from 1613 to 1786* (Dublin, 1753–86) (*CJ*), p. 13 (24 Oct. 1765).

[78] A number of Loftuses sat in parliament in 1765, but the most likely speaker to whom Henry was referring was the Rt Hon. Henry Loftus (MP for Bannow). He succeeded as Fourth Viscount Ely in 1769: *HIP*, V, 105–6.

[79] Sir Hercules Langrishe (*c.* 1729–1811). An Irish MP (1761–1800), Langrishe nevertheless supported the repeal of a number of anti-catholic penal laws. His opposition to the penal laws seems to have rested on financial considerations, not principle, and he opposed either extending the parliamentary franchise to catholics or reforming the tithe system. Thomas G. Fewer, 'Langrishe, Sir Hercules, first baronet (*c.* 1729–1811)', *ODNB*; *HIP*, V, 57–60.

[80] 'Heads of a bill for the more effectual support of the clergy and the vindication of their rights' (29 Oct. 1765): *ILD*.

[81] *CJ*, p. 50 (29 Oct. 1765); *Dublin Journal*, 4019 (2 Nov. 1765); *Public Advertiser*, 9680 (9 Nov. 1765). No bill ensued.

[82] Anthony Malone (1700–76). A lawyer, patriot politician, noted orator and Irish MP (1727–76), Malone was one of the most prominent parliamentarians of the mid-eighteenth century. He vocally opposed the government beginning in the 1750s and lost his place with the exchequer for his participation in the 1761 money bill dispute. Matthew Kilburn, 'Malone, Anthony (1700–1776)', *ODNB*; *HIP*, V, 183–7.

[83] John Hely-Hutchinson (1724–94). A lawyer, Irish MP (1759–94) and prime serjeant (1761–74), Hely-Hutchinson began his parliamentary career as a vocal patriot politician, but, under Bedford's lord lieutenancy, became the government's chief spokesman in the House of Commons. During the Northumberland lord lieutenancy (1763–5), Hely-Hutchinson fell temporarily from governmental favour. Martyn J. Powell, 'Hutchinson, John Hely- (1724–1794)', *ODNB*; *HIP*, IV, 394–403.

General,[84] R[t]. Honble: provost of the colledge,[85] M[r]: Solicitor Gen[l]:,[86] M[r]: Lucius O
Brien,[87] M[r]: Perry,[88] and M[r]: Mason.[89]

There is an absolute necessity, that something very Effectual should be Done;
and that Immediately: to prevent, not only the Ecclesiastical, But Even the *civil*
constitution itself from Being Dissolved. [O]f this necessity there is a plain proof
in the Annexed article, which I Have cut out of the Dublin Journal of this day.[90]
That Authenticity of which may be Entirely Depended on. For it is Drawn up by the
Earl of Carrick who Dwells in County Kilkenny, and Has acted with a true patriotic Spirit in all these Disturbances. He inclosed it in a Letter to M[r]: Faulkner,[91]
Desiring Him to print it, and to mention His Lordship, as the author, to any one
who Enquired.

84 Philip Tisdal (*c.* 1703–77). A client of Archbishop George Stone and an inveterate rival to John Hely-
    Hutchinson, Tisdal served as MP for Trinity College, Dublin (1739–76), solicitor general (1751–60),
    attorney general (1760–77) and secretary of state (1760–77). C. L. Falkiner, 'Tisdal, Philip (bap.
    1703, d. 1777)', rev. Martyn J. Powell, *ODNB*; *HIP*, VI, 405–8.
85 Francis Andrews (*c.* 1718–74). Provost of Trinity College, Dublin (1758–70, 1774), Andrews also
    served as an Irish MP (1759–74). *HIP*, III, 90–1; *Alum Dublin*, p. 13.
86 Marcus Paterson (1712–87). A lawyer and an Irish MP (1756–70), Paterson served as third serjeant
    (1757–64) and solicitor general (1764–9). *HIP*, V, 30–1.
87 Lucius O'Brien (1733–95). A lawyer and Irish MP (1761–90), O'Brien was himself a prominent
    patriot politician. During the late 1760s, he led the opposition to the government's efforts to augment
    the Irish army. A. F. Pollard, 'O'Brien, Sir Lucius Henry, third baronet (1733–1795)', *ODNB*; *HIP*,
    V, 372–5.
88 Edmond Sexton Pery (1719–1806). A lawyer and Irish MP (1751–85), Pery served as speaker of
    the House of Commons (1771–85). He was a prominent patriot politician who, during the 1750s
    and 1760s, attacked the government over money bills, pensions and the kingdom's finances. David
    Huddleston, 'Pery, Edmond Sexton, Viscount Pery (1719–1806)', *ODNB*; *HIP*, VI, 55–9.
89 John Monck Mason (1725–1809). A lawyer, literary scholar and Irish MP (1761–1800), Mason
    supported some easing of penal laws against Roman Catholics during the early 1760s. Arthur Sherbo,
    'Mason, John Monck (1726?–1809)', *ODNB*; *HIP*, V, 201–3.
90 Henry included the following story, which appeared in *Dublin Journal*, 4019 (29 Oct. – 2 Nov. 1765):
    'We hear from Kilkenny, that on Monday the 5th of October, in the Night, a Number of Persons broke
    open a Yard, inclosed with a Stone Wall about eight Feet high, in which some Tythe Corn had been
    placed, at James's green in the Liberties of said City, and that they took the Corn out of the Yard, and
    spread it in the most wet and dirty Parts of said Green, and trod upon it; this Outrage was committed
    in a Place surrounded with Cabbins, and in the Liberties of a City in which a large Body of his
    Majesty's Force, both Cavalry and Foot, are quartered, but it is said the Inhabitants were prevented
    from giving Notice to the Magistrates, by a Guard being set at each of their Doors, who threatened
    them with Death if they opened them – We also hear, that the seven White-Boys who were tried and
    found Guilty last Spring Assizes, and sentenced to be whipped, and confined for one Year, have broke
    out of the County Goal. – We farther hear, that about ten Days since the House of a Man who deals
    in Tythes, near Kilree in the County of Kilkenny, was set on Fire by some malicious Persons, about
    12 o'Clock at Night, and was burnt down to the Ground, together with all the Cloaths, Household
    Furniture, &c, belonging to the Family. Upon this the poor Man was obliged to seek Shelter in a
    neighbouring Cabbin, but on the second Night after his being entertained there, a Number of Persons,
    at least 60, came in the Night to said Cabbin, and by their Threats and Imprecations so far intimidated
    the Owner of it, that he opened the Door, they then declared that they came to search for said Man,
    and as he had concealed himself, they broke open the inner Doors, and thrust an Iron Instrument
    into every one of the Beds, in order to try whether he was hidden in any of them; they at last found
    him, and beat him in a most cruel Manner, took the Tythe Corn he had collected, and spread it in the
    high Road, and there rode over it till it was rendered useless; they then took the Man, with no other
    Covering but his Shirt, above two Miles to Kells, when he was several Times knocked down by them,
    and then forced to take such Oaths as they pleased to direct.'
91 George Faulkner (*c.* 1703–75). A successful printer and bookseller in both London and Dublin,
    Faulkner published the *Dublin Journal*. James E. Tierney, 'Faulkner, George (1703?–1775)', *ODNB*.

A motion was made in the [C]ommons[92] to Enquire into the Legality of the patents granting the office of Master of the Rolls to M[r]: Rigby[93] and of Chancellor of Exchequer to M[r]: Hamilton,[94] Late Secretary to the L[d]. L[t]. For *Life*. Such a grant being Expressly contrary to the words of the Statute of Henry 7th, which Enacts that these officers and all the judges shall Hold, only During the Kings pleasure.[95] All the Eminent Lawyers of the crown spoke to it, and Distinguished away the act of parliament. However [fo. 256r] The House Declined entering into the Subject, as it was not properly their Busyness. They thought it more Respectful to Leave it to the King.

There is another matter of much consequence, which they Have Entered upon, and Have passed an Order.[96] That the proper Officer Do Lay before the House, an Exact List of the Officers on the Revenue Establishment of this Kingdom, for the years ending Lady 1756 to Lady Day 1765, Distinguishing Each year, annexing to each name the Salary, Date of the commission, Security, &c, Distinguishing which are for Excise, and which for Customs, And *which of them Have been Approved of by the Lord Lieutenant, L[d] Deputy, or other chief governours, and privy council, for the time Being*.

This will open a Large field[,] for by the Revenue act of Charles 2[97] it is provided, that all these offices shall be appointed or Approved of by the Governor and privy Council.

This practice Has Been Disused. [A]nd the commissioners of the Revenue Have Disposed of all these places to the great Diminution of the L[d]: L[t]'s Influence. [T]here Being in Ireland about 2000 places of this Kind. The Duke of Bedford[98] attempted to Resume this Right; which was partly the occasion of the outcry Raised against him.[99]

But, as it is now Brought before the House: and the Law is very plain, it seems to be seriously intended. [T]he consequence will be adding much weight to the

---

[92] *CJ*, p. 15 (25 Oct. 1765).

[93] Richard Rigby (1722–88). An Englishman and protégé of John Russell, fourth duke of Bedford, Rigby came to Ireland with Bedford as his secretary when he assumed the lord lieutenancy (1757–61). He took up a seat in the Irish House of Commons (1757–88), serving as Bedford's principal 'man of business' in the Commons. Loathed by the Dublin mob, he was, nevertheless, granted the sinecure of the Master of the Rolls (1759–88). Roland Thorne, 'Rigby, Richard (1722–1788)', *ODNB*; *HIP*, VI, 163–4.

[94] William Gerard Hamilton (1728–96). Nicknamed 'Single-Speech Hamilton', he was an English MP who came to Ireland with George Montagu Dunk, second earl of Halifax (lord lieutenant: 1761–3) to serve as his chief secretary and remained in the position during the Northumberland viceroyalty (1763–5). He was deeply unpopular in Ireland, and returned to England and his seat in the English parliament. Martyn J. Powell, 'Hamilton, William Gerard (1729–1796)', *ODNB*; *HIP*, IV, 354–5; John Brooke, 'Hamilton, William Gerard', in John Brooke and Lewis Namier (eds.), *The history of parliament: the House of Commons, 1754–1790* (3 vols., London, 1964), II, 572–4.

[95] *CJ*, p. 15 (25 Oct. 1765); 10 Henry VII, c. 2: *The statutes at large, passed in the parliaments held in Ireland* (85 vols., Dublin, 1802–30), I, 42–3.

[96] *CJ*, p. 49 (29 Oct. 1765).

[97] 14 & 15 Charles II, s. 4 c. 7: *The statutes at large, passed in the parliaments held in Ireland*, II, 349–65.

[98] John Russell, fourth duke of Bedford (1710–71) was a prominent English politician who began his career as an anti-Walpolean MP and served as first lord of the admiralty and secretary of state for the north before being named Ireland's lord lieutenant (1757–61). Martyn J. Powell, 'Russell, John, fourth duke of Bedford (1710–1771)', *ODNB*.

[99] Magennis, *Irish political system*, pp. 117–19.

Governour; and cutting off the influence of some men who, often under Hand, opposed public measures.

At present, the L^d: L^t. Has Little, in His *Immediate* power, to give, But some church Livings, and Barrackmaster's places.

[fo. 256v] A motion was made to Have a Return made of all members who Had places or pensions[,][100] which was Rejected. In all these Questions, the party who opposed the court, never made a Division of more than 12. So, it is obvious that all things will Run Smoothly.

We of the incorporated Society,[101] with the Speaker [John Ponsonby] our Vice-President, at our Head waited on the L^d: L^t:, and Received the most Earnest assurance of His protection and Countenance.

The good Bishop of Waterford [Richard Chenevix] is going on, indefatigable in His Discovering concealed charitys.[102]

We are in pain for the Archbishop of Dublin [Carmichael], who sailed Hence last Sunday, for [P]ark gate, in a sad state of Health. Lord Chancellor [Bowes] is very well.

These are the particulars worthy of your notice, which at present occur to …

Willm: Henry

9. William Henry to Thomas Secker, 26 November 1765

[fo. 258r] Kildare Street Dublin Nov^r: 26 1765

May it Please Your Grace,

Blessed be God! We Have at Length prevailed against Spirituous Liquors, the Destroyer of this country!

Very early in the Session I applyed to the Speaker, and Leaders of the House of Commons, who approved of my Desire To forward it[.] I printed the Address which goes with this.[103] And Distributed 500 [copies] among the people of the Castle, the Lords, and members of the House of Commons, Lord Mayor, Aldermen and Commons of Dublin, And Had all their Concurrence. Tomorrow the Bill for Restraining the Distilling of any Kind of Grain &c into Spirits, is to be Brought into the House of Commons.[104] [I]t is well Drawn, and I Hope it will not Have one negative.

---

100 *CJ*, p. 60 (31 Oct. 1765).
101 Incorporated Society for Promoting English Working Schools in Ireland.
102 On 11 Nov. 1765, the Lords ordered 'that a Committee be appointed to take into Consideration the several Charities and charitable Donations in this Kingdom and that the Lord Bishop of Waterford, and all the Lords present, be the said Committee': *Journals of the House of Lords of the kingdom of Ireland* (8 vols., Dublin, 1782–1800) (*Lords Journals*), IV, 349.
103 William Henry, *An earnest address to the people of Ireland, against the drinking of spirituous liquors* (Dublin, 1765). This was a reprint of a 1753 pamphlet which Henry published under the same title.
104 On 27 Nov. 1765, Lucius O'Brien introduced the 'heads of a bill to prevent the distilling of spirits from wheat, oats, bere [*sic*], barley, rye, meslin, malt, beans and peas, and from any potatoes, meal or flour of wheat, oats, bere, barley, meslin, malt, beans or peas for a limited time'. The bill was enacted in Dec. 1765 as 5 George III, c. 3: *ILD*.

I send the inclosed Scrap, which contains an Exact account of all the money granted by the [C]ommons. The money Bill will be sent off to England this week.[105] And I Hope to Expedite the Bill against the Distillery[,] that Both may go together. [fo. 258v] Every thing in parliament Has proceeded Smoothly as L^d: Hertford could Wish. He is universally Beloved. The only appearance of an opposition was in some trifling matters, by some friends of Lords Kildare,[106] and Tyrone.[107] Their Highest Division was no more than 39. [I]t Has now Dwindled to 26.

The Earl of Carrick Has Been most active in supporting the constitution against the Rebellious White Boys in the county of Kilkenny. [W]ith the Danger of His Life He took three of them a few Days ago, and Lodged them in Killkenny Goal. Yesterday, He gave notice to the House of peers, that they should all attend tomorrow.[108] For, that He had matter to communicate to them of the Last consequence to this Kingdom. [W]e are all full of Expectation …

Willm: Henry

I saw Ld. Chancellor to Day – He is very well –

10. William Henry to Thomas Secker, 3 December 1765

[fo. 260r] May it please your Grace

Last week the Expectations which the Earl of Carrick Raised terminated in His Laying before the House of Lords (the Bulk of the [C]ommons being present) the unconstitutional practice which Has been followed by the [C]ommons for several years past, and is every Session increasing, of tacking to the Supply granted for the Support of the Establishment, the grant of Several very large Sums for other uses, many of them for private interests no way Relating to His Majesty's Service.[109] The Sums of this Kind granted in the Money Bill Exceed an Hundred thousand pounds for this present Session. When the Bill for the Supply to His majesty comes Back from Great Britain in the form of an act[,] the Lords, who were never consulted in these private grants, are under the Dilemma of either passing the whole tho' contrary to their Sentiments, or Suffering the whole Establishment to Drop. As He had Here a Large field, He painted all this consequences very strongly[,] and concluded That How fatal soever the Remedy Left to the Lords might be, They could not consist-

---

105 The money bill went off to England on 1 Dec.: *Dublin Journal*, 4028 (30 Nov. – 3 Dec. 1765).

106 James Fitzgerald, twentieth earl of Kildare (1722–73). An Irish patriot politician during the mid-century, Kildare gained notoriety in 1753 with his damning memorandum to George II on Irish affairs. Kildare fluctuated between courting and opposing the English viceroys, and in Oct. 1765, he had the new lord lieutenant worried that 'Lord Kildare is preparing for hostilities and will be as active as his power will allow in giving us all kinds of disturbances': *HIP*, IV, 147–9; Eoin Magennis, 'Fitzgerald, James, first duke of Leinster (1722–73)', *ODNB*; idem, *Irish political system*, p. 183.

107 George de la Poer Beresford, eighth earl of Tyrone (1735–1800). Tyrone studied at Trinity College, Dublin (BA, 1754), before serving as an MP in the Irish House of Commons (1757–63). He succeeded his father to the peerage in 1763, at which point he took up a seat in the Irish House of Lords: *CP*, XII, 147, 420–1.

108 *Lords Journal*, IV, 351 (25 Nov. 1765). Lord Carrick is not mentioned in the Lords minutes as the person responsible for making this announcement.

109 The *Lords Journals* does not record Carrick's speech, though the *Lords Journals* did not provide an exhaustive record of all contributions.

ently with their own Dignity: their Established Rules,[110] which were Read: or the trust Reposed in [fo. 260v] Them to 'guard the Subjects against oppression' consent to the passing any Act Hereafter, which Had such Extraneous grants Tacked to it.

Lord Chancellor [Bowes] then made a Speech to the same purpose and observed by what steps this procedure in the commons Had advanced: and to what an Enormous Degree it was increased, to the great prejudice of the Crown, the oppression of the people, and making the House of Lords of no consequence.[111] He said, But with caution and Gentleness, That it was Little Better than *Enslaving them*. That, How shocking soever the consequences of the evil in Rejecting the act of Supply might be[,] yet, unless some Bounds were put to this growing oppression, and that soon, The Evils in Suffering it to go on might prove much greater.

These things were prudently said, by way of a[d]monition to the [C]ommons.[112] However, as the time presses, and it was too Late to Alter the money Bill, it is now gone to England with all the private grants in the old Form. This will occasion some warm altercation when the Bill comes Back, and is Laid before the Lords[,] But will Have no other Effect.

At that time, Lord Carrick Desired that all the Lords might attend on Monday the 2^d ins^t:, That He might Lay Before them the progress of the Rebellious insurgents called the *White Boys* in the South, and His opinion thereon.[113] [fo. 261r] Accordingly, yesterday, the House being very full, and all the [C]ommons being present, His Lordship laid fully before them, the first Beginnings of these Insurrections in 1761, when we were Engaged in war with France and Spain. The oaths taken by their officers and Leaders and the oaths taken by the inferiour sort, to be true to their officers, to join with them whenever called on, and to obey them in all things. He took notice of the weak Efforts which Had at first Been used to suppress them[,] and the most Dangerous then so much favoured by Regimenting them, and sending them to serve in Portugal.[114] The certain consequence of which would Have Been, their Learning the art of war; and Returning at a proper time to cut the throats of the protestants, and shake the British Government, as [P]helimy [O] [N]eal's Irish Soldiers, after Being Disciplined under the Spaniards in Flanders, Did in 1641.[115] He took notice, that since the peace, the same Disturbances Have continued: which He thinks owing to the Influence of their priests, and those officers who Have taken the Lead. [I]t seems, that it appeared from Evidence, That their Leaders were privy

---

110 By a standing order adopted on 30 July 1707, the Irish peers resolved that 'The annexing any Clause or Clauses to a Bill of Aid or Supply, the Matter of which is foreign to and different from the Matter of the said Bill of Supply, is unparliamentary, and tends to the Destruction of the Constitution of this Kingdom': *Rules and orders to be observed in the upper house of parliament of Ireland* (Dublin, 1784), p. 56.

111 *Lords Journals*, IV, 352 (2 Dec. 1765), simply records that 'the House, according to Order, proceeded to the further reading over the Standing Orders of this House, and after some time spent therein, Ordered that the further reading of the Standing Orders be adjourned'.

112 No such motion is recorded in *Lords Journals*, IV, 352.

113 *Lords Journals*, IV, 352 (2 Dec. 1765).

114 Irish protestants strongly resented proposals in 1761–2 to enlist catholic gentlemen in the service of Portugal in order to circumvent the legal prohibition on the admission of catholics to the British army: Maureen Wall, *Catholic Ireland in the eighteenth century*, ed. Gerard O'Brien (Dublin, 1989), p. 119.

115 Sir Phelim Roe O'Neill (1603–53). One of the commanders of the Irish Confederates during the early 1640s, O'Neill was executed in 1653 on charges of treason. Jerrold I. Casway, 'O'Neill, Sir Phelim Roe (1603–1653)', *ODNB*.

to the Designed insurrections of the Oak-Boys in the North before they Began[,] which plainly shows that the whole was a Regular plan, and conducted under the same influence, tho in Different forms, adapting themselves to the Different principles of the people.

From this Regular System, and their still persevering to [fo. 261v] continue and Extend their Ravages in the South, without any plausible pretext, He concluded, 'That there was a Fixed Regular Scheme, underhand carried on, to keep up a Rebellious Disposition among the Lower papists in That they might be Ready, in case of a new war, to take arms, and unite with our Enemys, against the British government and protestant Religion.'

His Lordship Declared, That He had full Examinations to support all He had said[,] and then took notice of some Defects in our present Laws, by which these Rebellious Disburbers Evaded justice.

The Earl of Tyrone,[116] whose Estate is in county Waterford, got up: and in opposition to what L^d: Carrick said, asserted That these insurrections were only Local, and accidental, and not the Effect of Any Scheme[,] and that He Did not give credit to the matters of fact, not Having seen the Evidence. He also said, that we ought not to speak of any Rebellious insurrections in Ireland. That if we did, The *English* would indiscriminately call all the people of Ireland Rebells; as ever since the Rebellion of 1745, all the Scotch were called Rebells thro out England. He said many other Scraps Equally Wise and important. This Roused L^d: Carrick, who insisted on His proposition, and said He had the Examinations and Evidences to produce and appealed to the Bishop of Waterford [Chenevix] for the great number of Letters and Evidences in His Hands. [fo. 262r] Lord Chancellor [Bowes] then interposed and agreed with Lord Carrick in the facts committed by these Disturbers[,] yet hoped, that the prudent steps now taking by Government would soon put an End to them: and in an Healing manner said, that He hoped many of the papists themselves would be Ready to support the constitution and government under which they Enjoyed so much Happyness.

Doctor Cradock, Bishop of Kilmore,[117] made and Delivered very Elegantly a set Speech justifying the conduct of the clergy: and showing How unjustly they were oppressed; and with what Little pretence their property was invaded, and themselves insulted.

L^d: Chancellor [Bowes] agreed with Lord Carrick in the necessity there was of amending some Laws, which were Evaded[,] particularly That it ought to be made Felony to Burn Tythe Corn, out of the Haggards,[118] as well as in them.

That the trifle and malicious Destroying of Corn in any other way as much as Burning, should be Felony.

That the compelling a man by threats to open his Doors for Rioters, should be

---

[116] George de la Poer Beresford, first marquess of Tyrone. See above, n. 107.

[117] John Cradock (1708–78). A Cambridge-educated Englishman, Cradock came to Ireland in 1757 as chaplain to John Russell, fourth duke of Bedford (lord lieutenant: 1757–61), and served as bishop of Kilmore (1757–72) and archbishop of Dublin (1772–8). Before coming to Ireland, he was a fellow of St John's College, Cambridge, and served as rector of a number of parishes, including St Paul's, Covent Garden. B. H. Blacker, 'Cradock, John (1707/8–1778)', *ODNB*.

[118] *Oxford English dictionary*: *haggards* are 'large hurdles with which hay stacks in the field are generally fenced'.

Burglary as much as the Breaking them open by force. And that the compelling men to take unlawful oaths, ought to be made Felony.

So Ended that matter yesterday. Something more will be Done on another Day.

[fo. 262v] I Have the pleasure to say, That the Bill for preventing the Distilling any Kind of Grain or Bread corn into Spirits, Has passed the House of [C]ommons, and is gone to the Castle to be transmitted to England.[119] It is to take place on the 1st Day of January, and to continue untill the 1st of October, with a power to the government and council to continue it Longer, by proclamation, if they shall think it necessary.

Too many Country gentlemen opposed this useful Bill, or threw in Evasions: and I fear might Have Defeated it: Had not the indefatigable pains I took to inform the principal members; and the pamphlet[120] which I put into every members' Hands fully convinced the majority. [T]his they Did your Servant the Honour to own. I Have given this pamphlet also to all the Lords of parliament, to the Lord mayor, and magistracy[,] and to the principal Companys of this city. Blessed be God who Has given us Success!

Having given this wound to this Hydra, I am Determined not to Stop Here. I Have consulted with my virtuous friend Sir Lucius O'Brien; That in order to pave the way for a total abolition of Drinking Spirits, which must be the Effect of Long patience[,] we must convince the Legislature that such a step will Encrease the Revenue of the Crown. [fo. 263r] And, in the mean time, get some public societys who are friends to Religion and virtue, to petition parliament to Redress the sore evills Brought on the Bodys, Religion, [and] Morals of the people: the manufacturers[,] and the Dangers Daily arising against Government, by the Excess of Drinking Spirituous Liquors.

Being invited yesterday to an Entertainment from the corporation of Brewers,[121] where [the] L^d: Mayor[122] and the Sherriffs[123] were present; I proposed to them How much it would tend to the Honour of the city of Dublin to Lead the way in such a virtuous petition.

They all approved. [A]nd my Lord Mayor and Sherriffs promised that, at their next stated meeting in January,

They would prepare and agree to such a petition and Have it ready to send in to parliament.

I Fear, That I Have wearyed Your Grace with the Recital of so many particulars. I shall add no more, But that I am …

Willm: Henry

Dublin Decem^r: 3^d 1765

---

119   *CJ*, p. 145 (2 Dec. 1765); see above Letter 9. The English privy council received the bill on 9 Dec. and sent it to be engrossed on 13 Dec. It became law on 24 Dec. (5 George III, c. 3): *ILD*.

120   Henry, *An earnest address to the people of Ireland*.

121   The Guild of Brewers and Maltsters, which was founded in 1696, was twenty-third in order of precedence in the Dublin city assembly: Mary Clark and Ray Rejaussé, *Directory of historic Dublin guilds* (Dublin, 1993), p. 16.

122   Sir James Taylor served as Dublin's lord mayor (1765–6): Sir John and Lady Gilbert (eds.), *Calendar of ancient records of Dublin* (18 vols., Dublin, 1889–1944), p. xlv.

123   William Rutledge and Richard French were elected Dublin's sheriffs in Apr. 1765.

11. William Henry to Thomas Secker, 12 December 1765

[fo. 264r] May it Please Your Grace,

I send under another cover the Sermon preached by the B^p: of Dromore; as I am of opinion it will please.[124] I was obliged to strip, and curtail it to Bring it within postage.

The noise about pensions in the House of commons Has Dyed away. [T]he Greatest Division was no more than 41.[125]

The Commons are Enquiring into the Rise and progress of the *White Boys*[,][126] and, I Believe will Do Something Effectual to prevent such Disturbances for the future. They have unanimously voted thanks to the Earl of Carrick for His zeal, courage and activity in Striving to Suppress them.

We of the Dublin Society[127] are preparing a Scheme to be Laid Before parliament for maintenance of all the Real poor, and Restraint of Sturdy Beggars and vagrants. [W]e propose to Have in Each of the 32 Countys in Ireland a Large poor-House and work House: in all which may be maintained, at the Rate of 300 in Each county, 3600 Real poor[,] all their poor Children to be taken into our Charter Schools or nursereys. [T]his, if Duely Executed, will be of the Last consequence to this Kingdom, where the poor are Distinguished for their Lazyness. We compute, that the whole Expence will not Exceed forty thousands p^ds: per ann: and will save [fo. 264v] to the public four times that Sum at Least, Beside the good Effect, it will Have on Religion and moralls.[128]

Every pacquet Brings forth accounts, That the A:Bishop of Dublin [Carmicheal], who is at Bath, is hastening to an End. The Candidates for a Succession are the Ar:B^p: of Tuam,[129] The B^p: of Meath,[130] and D^r. Garnet B^p: of Clogher.[131] It is strangely, yet strongly, Reported Here, that D^r: Hughes, (who Had been a Senior Fellow in our

---

124 Henry Maxwell, *A sermon preached in Christ-Church, Dublin, on Wednesday the 23d of October 1765, being the anniversary of the Irish rebellion, before His Excellency Francis Seymour, earl of Hertford, lord lieutenant general,...and the lords spiritual and temporal in parliament assembled* (Dublin, 1765).

125 *CJ*, p. 150 (5 Dec. 1765).

126 'A Committee ... to inquire into the Causes of the Insurrections in the southern parts of this Kingdom, what Means have been used to suppress the same, and what Measures may be the most effectual to put a Stop to, and prevent the same in the future' was appointed by the House of Commons on 3 Dec. 1765. It reported on 20 Dec.: *CJ*, pp. 146, 160–1.

127 Founded in 1731, the Royal Dublin Society was Ireland's premier improving society: H. F. Berry, *The Royal Dublin Society* (London, 1915); Jim Livesy, 'The Dublin Society in eighteenth-century Irish political thought', *HJ*, XLVII, 3 (2004), 614–40.

128 This scheme was devised on the suggestion of Richard Woodward, dean of Dromore: see James Kelly, 'Richard Woodward, bishop of Cloyne', in *Parliament, politics and power: essays in eighteenth-century Irish history* (Dublin, forthcoming).

129 John Ryder (*c.* 1697–1775). A Cambridge-educated Englishman, Ryder served as bishop of Killaloe (1742–43), Down and Connor (1743–52) and Ardagh (1752–75) and as archbishop of Tuam (1752–75). His rapid advancement he owed to his cousin, Dudley Ryder, attorney general during the Pelham ministry. Alexander Gordon, 'Ryder, John (*c.* 1697–1775)', rev. Eoin Magennis, *ODNB*.

130 Arthur Smyth (1706–71). An Irishman who received his education at Trinity College, Dublin, Smyth served as bishop of Down and Connor (1753–65) and Meath (1765–6) and as archbishop of Dublin (1766–71). Leslie and Wallace, *Clergy of Dublin and Glendalough*, p. 1067.

131 John Garnett (1708–82). A Cambridge-educated Englishman, Garnett served as bishop of Ferns and Leighlin (1752–8) and Clogher (1758–82). He came to Ireland as chaplain to Lionel Cranfield Sackville, first duke of Dorset (lord lieutenant: 1730–7, 1750–5). Richard Garnett, 'Garnett, John (1707/8–1782)', rev. Philip Carter, *ODNB*.

University. But was Expelled in the time of the Late provost)[132] is to be advanc'd to the Bishops Bench on this vacancy, thro the Speaker's interest. His character is well known. I hope that the pious and virtuous Lord Hertford will Duely weigh things of So great consequence to Religion.

It will be acceptable to the Great Humanity of M^{rs}: And Miss Talbot, to Know a fresh instance of the wonderful Efficacy of D^r: James's Fever powders.

On Tuesday the 3^d Inst^t: M^{rs}: Henry,[133] by walking too Long in Lady Arbella Dennys fine gardens over the cliffs of the sea caught a sudden cold and shivering. [N]ext Day, was Struck with a most violent Inflammatory fever, which the physician concluded must prove fatal. In this Extremity, I had 12 ounces of Blood Drawn, and Laying aside all Doctors, Administered 7 grains of ye powders. [T]his Quantity I Repeated thrice[,] which, with Gods Blessing, Has Entirely subdued the fever, and carried it off, as by a Regular Crisis.

To the amazement of the apothecary, she is this Day so well, [fo. 265r] as to sit up, without Inconveniency, Seven Hours, Eat some chicken, and Drink three glasses of Claret water.

God be praised for this great mercy and Deliverance.

This Day we Had Handell's Te Deum performed for S^t: Andrews Church, for the Benefit of Mercer's Hospital.[134] We Had the Honour of the L^d: Lieutenants company[,] His Lady, Daughters, and all His family[,][135] and an Audience of more than 400 persons of Fashion. As the Tickets were at 1/2 a guinea each[,] I hope this most useful Charity, wherein I am concerned as a governour, will profit considerably.

I Hope that I may be able to send your Grace more news before Christmass[,] for my attendance at the [Dublin] castle, as chaplain, Begins on Saturday next, and Ends by preaching before the L^d: L^t: on the Sunday Before Christmas ...

Willm: Henry

Kildare Street Dublin
Decem^r: 12 1765

---

[132] Richard Baldwin (*c.* 1666–1758), provost of Trinity College, Dublin (1717–58), expelled Lambert Hughes (1698–1771), chancellor of Christ Church Cathedral, Dublin (1762–71), from his fellowship in Nov. 1739 'for some disrespectful remarks against him in his absence'. Hughes was never elevated to the Irish bench. Leslie and Wallace, *Clergy of Dublin and Glendalough*, p. 750; H. T. Welch, 'Baldwin, Richard (*c.* 1666–1758)', *ODNB*.

[133] It is not known definitively to whom William Henry was married. Leslie, *Derry clergy and parishes*, p. 302, speculates that Henry may have married the daughter of Marcus Dowling in 1738.

[134] *Dublin Journal*, 4031 (14 Dec. 1765). Mercer's Hospital, Dublin, was founded in 1734 by Mary Mercer (d. 1735), the daughter of George Mercer, a prominent Dublin physician. See Horatio Townsend, *The history of Mercer's Charitable Hospital in Dublin, to the end of the year 1742* (Dublin, 1860), esp. pp. 17–27.

[135] In 1741, Lord Hertford married Isabella (1726–82) – the youngest daughter of Charles Fitzroy, second duke of Grafton – by whom he had seven sons and six daughters: Lowe, 'Conway, Francis Seymour, first marquess of Hertford (1718–1794)'.

12. William Henry to Thomas Secker, 26 December 1765

[fo. 266r] May it please your Grace

Last week our parliament was closely Employed in considering and preparing to pass the Bills Returned from England[,] viz. The two money Bills, the Bill to prevent the Distilling of Grain for a Limited time, and that to prevent the Exportation of Corn.[136] An Alteration which was made in this Last in England, gave occasion to those who would seem patriots, to give violent opposition. It came up to the Lords with the other Bills, on [M]onday. And there met with opposition, from the Earls of Westmeath,[137] Tyrone, Charlemont,[138] and L^d: Longford.[139] Tyrone was violent in His opposition, and Entered His protest in which the others concurred. The most violent Declaimer in the House of Commons, on this occasion was D^r: Lucas[,][140] who finding His Oratory Ineffectual there, Had Recourse to His old method of Inflaming the City. [T]o this End He published on [M]onday the address which I inclose.[141] In consequence of such steps, some Incendiary pasted up papers in several places of the *Liberties*, particularly on the [W]eavers' Hall, and a Drum went about calling on the mobb in that Quarter to Assemble, in order to attack the parliament. But they Did not gather to the parliament House untill Eight at night, before which time the House Had Happily Broke up. They threatened to come thither next Day. But, thought Better of it: Especially, as always, on passing our Laws, there is great State Exhibited, all the streets being [fo. 266v] Lined with Soldiers, and the L^d: L^t: Guarded by a Squadron of Horse, and His Battle Axe Guards. As this pamphlet could not answer any purpose, But to Inflame, it is possible that the writer may Hear of it after the Recess, which the commons have fixed for the 23, the Lords for the 27th of Janu^y:

The Earl of Carrick and several other Lords Debated much on the Irregularity of the commons in tacking Occasional Grants, to the amount of more than an Hundred

---

136 *Lords Journals*, IV, 355–6. On the corn export crisis more generally, see Morley, *Irish opinion and the American revolution, 1760–1783*, pp. 54–8.

137 Thomas Nugent, sixth earl of Westmeath (1714–92). The grandson of a prominent Jacobite catholic peer, Westmeath conformed to the Church of Ireland in 1755 and subsequently took his seat in the Irish House of Lords. *CP*, XII, 533; G. Le G. Norgate, 'Nugent, Thomas, fourth earl of Westmeath (1668/9–1752)', rev. Harman Murtagh, *ONDB*.

138 James Caulfeild, first earl of Charlemont (1728–99). After having been the dissolute young man, Charlemont took up his seat in the Irish House of Lords in 1755. Thereafter, he distinguished himself for mediating a money bill dispute. His response to the Hearts of Oak rising in Ulster in 1763 earned him elevation to an earldom in the Irish peerage. He was not, however, an unquestioning supporter of the various vice-regal administrations. James Kelly, 'Caulfeild, James, first earl of Charlemont (1728–1799)', *ODNB*.

139 Thomas Pakenham, third earl of Longford (1713–66). An Oxford-educated Irishman, he served as an Irish MP for the borough of Longford (1745–56). *CP*, VIII, 122–3; *HIP*, VI, 7. For the protest lodged by Lords Tyrone, Westmeath, Charlemont, Longford, and Grandison (John Fitzgerald (otherwise Villiers), earl of Grandison (1684–1766)), see *Lords Journals*, IV, 359–60.

140 Charles Lucas (1713–71). A Dublin physician, Lucas served as an Irish MP (1761–71), but only after having spent a decade in exile after the House of Commons voted that some of the publications he wrote during his 1749 parliamentary campaign were seditious and insurrectionary. Once in the Irish parliament representing Dublin, Lucas proved himself a consistent opponent of the vice-regal administrations. Sean J. Murphy, 'Lucas, Charles (1713–1771)', *ODNB*; *HIP*, IV, 132–5.

141 Charles Lucas, *To the right honorable the lord-mayor, the alderman, sheriffs, commons, citizens, and freeholders of Dublin. The address of Charles Lucas, M.D., one of their representatives in parliament* (Dublin, 1765). The pamphlet is dated 22 Dec. 1765.

thousand pounds, to the money Bills for the support of the civil and military Lists.[142] [A]nd a committee of the Lords is appointed to Enquire into these grants, and the Expenditure of them, since the year 1747, when this practice first Began.

Our L^d: L^t: set out to Day on a tour of 300 miles into several parts, in His private capacity, for His Amusement of shooting woodcocks, and such kind of Exercise. His tour is to L^d: Farnhams near Cavan[143] – thence to L^d: Kingston's at Boyle[144] – to Lord Gore's Enniskillen[145] – and Castle Hume,[146] these three on the famous Lake Erne, all these places Remarkable for wood, water, and all Kind of natural Beautys. I gave His Excellency an Itinerary of every mile, the Kind of Road, and all things worth His Enquiry or observation in this tour. He purposes to be Here again on the 18th of January.

I Had the Honour of Attending His Excellency all the Last week at the castle, and Dining with Him, every Day, either in public or private. I concluded my attendance with preaching before Him, and Dining on Sunday. Finding no Inconvenience to my Lungs from this Service, I complied with the Request of Dean Fletcher, Rector of S^t: Marys,[147] to preach [fo. 268r] yesterday to that great congregation, the most considerable in all Ireland: and afterwards assisted at the communion where we Had 519 communicants, most of them people of Rank and Fashion. I felt a secret joy in this, as I had been appointed curate in that parish by the great and good D^r: King A:B^p: of Dublin, in 1726, where I continued five years.

I mention this, to satisfye Your Grace, How much I am Recovered from the Languid State I was in Last Summer, when I Received all your Kindness at Lambeth.

I pray God to grant your Grace many and Happy new years, and am …

Willm: Henry

Kildare Street in Dublin
Decem^r: 26. 1765.

---

142 *Lords Journals*, IV, 361.

143 Robert Maxwell, first earl of Farnham (1720–79). Before taking up his seat in the Irish House of Lords in late 1761, Farnham served as an MP in both the Irish (1743–59) and Westminster (1754–68) parliaments. *CP*, V, 258–9; *HIP*, V, 227–8; Brooke and Namier (eds.), *History of parliament*, II, 123.

144 Edward King, first earl of Kingston (1726–97). Before taking up his seat in the Irish House of Lords in late 1765, Kingston served as an Irish MP (1749–64). *CP*, VII, 299; *HIP*, V, 20–1.

145 Arthur Saunders Gore (1734–1809) was the son of Sir Arthur Gore, third earl of Arran. He was MP for Donegal borough (1759–60) and, afterwards, county Wexford (1761–8): *HIP*, IV, 277–8.

146 Castle Hume was one residence of Sir Gustavus Hume (1670–1731), MP for Fermanagh. On his death, the estate passed to his daughter, Mary, who married Nicholas Loftus-Hume, later Viscount Loftus: George Hill, *An historical account of the plantation in Ulster* (Belfast, 1877), p. 498; *HIP*, IV, 450–1.

147 William Fletcher (1715–71). Educated at New College, Oxford (BCL, 1739; DCL, 1756), Fletcher served as rector of St Mary's, Dublin (1749–71) and dean of Kildare (1765–71). Leslie and Wallace, *Clergy of Dublin and Glendalough*, p. 633.

urney near Shalane Octr. 12th
1764   232

May it please your Grace —

I cannot neglect giving you
an authentic account of a most unparalleled riot
which happened at Raphoe, six miles hence, last Sunday. —
Doctor Oswald, the good Bishop, who has somewhat at heart
the good of Miltown, the second for size and good houses in
the county of Donegal, found all his schemes to make the
people happy defeated, by the insolence of a set of rioters
who have been ever disturbing the peace of the town, and
had often offered indignities, even to the great and good Bishop
Foulter in his time. — To remedy this he sent for several
of the inhabitants, to let them know, that the condition
of getting their leases renewed was that they should join in
discountenance these Riots, to which purpose he himself
deposited fifty pounds. — and finding that the ringleader
of this infamous crew was one Bates who kept a
public house for vending of whiskey in the town, he
sent his agent Mr Abraham to him Last Saturday to signify to him, that he must either change his behaviour,
or depart from the town. — Bates, supported by his
clan insulted and beat the agent, and swore that he
would be revenged on the Bishop. — Accordingly, he
charged a musquet with Balls; and was going out that
night to the castle, in order to shoot the Bishop ...

5 William Henry to Archbishop Thomas Secker, 18 March 1766 (LPL, Secker 2, fo. 268)

13. William Henry to Thomas Secker, 18 March 1766

[fo. 268r] May it please Your Grace

I Have not been very troublesome of Late; Having caught a violent cold preaching in Christs church on the 30th of January by order from the castle and afterwards seized by a fit of the gout, which as yet Confines me.

Last term Nicholas Sheehy, the popish priest who was in the secret of the Rebellious Disturbances of the papists in the province of Munster, called *White Boys*, who Have Disturbed the Government these five years, was tried by a special jury from the county of Tipperary, for Rebellion.[148] The Evidence was clear and Full, yet, thro' the obstinacy of one or two of the jury, He was acquitted. Hereupon, He was transmitted to Clonmell in Tipperary, to be tryed for the murder of one Bridge, the principal Evidence who Had Sworn to the Examinations for treason against Him.

There, He and one of His accomplices in the murder were Tryed and convicted Last [T]hursday. As I Have it from the officers of the Crown who attended; It fully appeared, That of the two witnesses who Had Sworn to the treason against Him, one was supposed to be poisoned by one of Sheehys followers, who invited Him to a pot of Drink, where of He Dyed the succeeding night.

Bridge the other Evidencer, Remaining at His own House, [fo. 268v] Sheehy the priest came with a Body of White Boys, Drew Him out of His House, carryed Him to a poor Ale House, and there proposed to Him, That He should Retract his Examinations. The poor man was too Honest to perjure Himself. [W]hereupon they Knocked out His Brains with a Furze Spade,[149] Sheehy being present. They Buryed Him with His cloaths on in a Bogghole whence afterwards they Removed the Body to another grave, Disfiguring His face, in such a manner, That he should not be Known, if found.

Having Destroyed these two principal witnesses, Sheehy thought Himself safe, tho a Reward of £300 from the government, and £200 from the Grand jury of Typperary was published in the [Dublin] Gazette for apprehending Him.

He Boldly came in of His own accord and Surrendered. The principal Evidences Being Gone, He was admitted to Bail, whereupon all of His Sort Triumphed and Laughed at Government. His tryal was put off untill the Last term, when other Witnesses appearing proved the treason fully, as I observed, tho by the perjury of some of the jury He was acquitted. But justice Has now taken place. He and one of His accomplices in that Clonmell murder were convicted on Thursday the 13th[,] and on Saturday morning, were Drawn, Hanged, and Quartered, [fo. 269r] and their Heads set up on Clonmell goal, murder Being by the Laws of Ireland, High treason.

[N]ine more of His accomplices for this murder and treason were on their Tryal last Saturday, whose fate I Do not as yet Know.

In the course of the tryal, it appeared that many principal papists of Large fortunes were concerned in Sheehys treasonable proceedings[,] some of whom were apprehended at Clonmell and against the Rest a pursuit is carryed on with vigour.

---

148 *Dublin Journal*, 4058 (18 Mar. 1766). On Sheehy's trial more generally, see Philip O'Connell, 'The plot against Father Nicholas Sheehy: the historical background', *Irish Ecclesiastical Record*, fifth series, CVIII (1967), 372–84; Power, 'Father Nicholas Sheehy (*c*. 1728–1766)'.

149 Furze (whins) is a 'spiny, evergreen shrub with yellow flowers', and a furze spade was a particular type of tool for shovelling it out: *Oxford English dictionary*. See also James Anderson, *Essays relating to agriculture and rural affairs. The fourth edition, with corrections, and large additions* (2 vols., London, 1797), I, 97–101.

Upon the whole, it now plainly appears, notwithstanding the infamous pains that was taken, Even by some protestant lords and gentlemen, to cover the matters, That a Dangerous conspiracy Has Been carrying on these five years, by the papists in [M]unster, to Keep up a Spirit of Rebellion: That a Sufficient Body of them might be Ready to Support any [F]rench or Spanish attempts to Disturb the Kingdom. [A]nd it is not Improbable that the Insolence of the Spanish court who seem to threaten a new war, may Have Been in some measure Buoyed up by a Dependance on these Disturbances, in which the popish priests Have been principal Directors. It is a point perfectly Known, that in case of a new war, Ireland is to be the first object for an attack from the Enemy.

[fo. 269v] I Have many other matters, Relating to our parliamentary proceedings, and the administration Here, to write about. But I Do not think it fit to intermix these things with the Relation I Have given.

It gave me the Sincerest joy to read in the public papers, That Your Grace Had Baptized the young prince of Brunswick,[150] from which Circumstance I comforted my Self, that you were Relieved from the Gout …

Will[m]: Henry

Kildare Street in Dublin
March 18 1766.

The House of Lords Have ordered a Return to be made before the 14th of [A]prill from the clergy of every parish thro the Kingdom, of all the familys in their Respective parishes, Distinguishing, who are protestants, and who are papists[,] as also of all the popish priests and Fryars in their parishes. This Authentic and Distinct Return may be of much Service.[151]

14. William Henry to Thomas Secker, 7 October 1766[152]

[fo. 272r] May it please your Grace

I Have since my coming into my parish in this country, avoided troubling your Grace as I Had nothing material to communicate.

I cannot now Decline the opportunity of presenting to your Grace the Bearer, M[r]: Anthony Sterling,[153] a very Deserving young Clergyman of Ireland, whose Busyness Requires His Stay for some time in London.

He is one of the most Respectable and Staunch Old-Whigg familys in this Kindgom, who Distinguished themselves at the Revolution, and on every occasion in their active zeal for the protestant Religion.

His Worthy father,[154] who is now in London, Hath Been, for many years Clerk of

---

150 *London Evening Post*, 5983 (3 Mar. 1766).
151 *Lords Journals*, IV, 370 (5 Mar. 1766).
152 This letter is filed out of chronological order in LPL, Secker papers 2.
153 Anthony Sterling (1739–99). Educated at Trinity College, Dublin (BA, 1761), Sterling served in a number of Church of Ireland livings. At the time of this letter from Henry to Secker, Sterling was serving as the curate Holy Trinity, Waterford. Henry Cotton, James B. Leslie, William Rennison and Iain Knox, *Clergy of Waterford, Lismore and Ferns: biographical succession lists* (Belfast, 2008), p. 390.
154 Edward Sterling (1711–77): Albert Mack Sterling, *The sterling genealogy* (New York, 1909), p. 153.

the House of commons, and universally Esteemed and Beloved by Every member of the House for His Abilitiys in Busyness, Candour, Benevolence, and Amiable temper. These virtues His son Inherits: and is Regarded greatly for His sobriety, modesty and in all points most conscientious Behaviour as a clergyman. [A]nd I am persuaded [he] will in Due time Become an Ornament to our church. It is merely on this account He Hath got possession of my Heart; and I take the Liberty to present Him to your Grace.

[fo. 272v] This country Hath felt severely that Distress thro want of provisions which Hath Been Diffused over Europe the Last year. Thousands would Have perished Had not the Legislature Early prevented the Distilling of Grain. The act Expired on the 1st instant.[155] The Harvest Hath not answered Expectations, and I fear there is not corn sufficient to supply the people untill May. [A]nd none can be Hoped for from abroad in this general scarcity. If the stills are suffered to go on, the common people will inevitably perish.

In a Letter to M[r]: [P]onsonby the Speaker, and one of our Lords justices, on the 12th of Sept[r]: I Represented these Dangers fully to Him.[156] He Has taken much to Heart the Representation I made; and wrote to me a very full and Long Letter, Lamenting the too apparent prospect of Distress, and the Disability of the commissioners of the Revenue, or even of government to prevent the Destruction of Bread corn, as the Law now Stands. However He has Laid my Letter before the other Lords justices and privy Councill, and Engaged to Do all that is possible to prevent the impending Ruine. I Hope that something will be Done: for the Distillers seem to be afraid of Lighting their fires. [A]nd some who Have attempted it Have been Stopped: or Discouraged.

In England, the King Hath By Law a power to prevent so great a Ruine, and I see by the proclamation of the 26 past, That it is there Done Effectually. Is He not the King and Father of His subjects in Ireland also? And if that maxim be just, '*Salus populi Suprema Lex.*'[157] Why should there not be a Law to Enable His Majesty to Extend His clemency to us?

[fo. 273r] The parliament of Ireland will not meet for a year to come. [I]n the mean time the people may perish. The British parliament meets the 11th of November. [T]hey often Bind Ireland by Laws. Would it not be charitable and Easy to put a clause in the act which will then pass for the Benefit of Great Britain, Enabling His Majesty to take the Like care of His truly affectionate and Loyal Subjects of Ireland?

My Lord, my Heart is melted within me, when I see Daily multitudes of the poor Industrious people flocking to me; and Earnestly Requesting that I may get a Stop put to the Stills which are their Ruine. How can I Help them? I take the Liberty to mention it to your Grace. Your great compassion may perhaps give some Hint of the necessity, to our new Lord Lieutenant, and those in power, who may make the proper provision Before it be too Late.

---

155 5 George III, c. 3: see above, n. 119.
156 If this is, as Henry seems to indicate, a manuscript letter from him to Ponsonby, it appears no longer to be extant. Henry's *A letter to the Right Honourable John Ponsonby, Esq; Speaker of the Honourable House of Commons; concerning the abuse of spirituous liquors* (London, 1760) was published in a third edition in London in 1767.
157 Cicero, *De re publica, de legibus*, trans. Clinton Walker Keyes (Cambridge, MA, 1928), pp. 466–7: 'the safety of the people shall be their highest law' (*ollis salus populi suprema lex esto*).

Having trespassed so far on your condescension, I shall add no more, only my most Ardent wishes for your Graces Health and Long Life, for the public good …

Willm: Henry

Urney near Strabane
October 7th 1766

15. William Henry to Thomas Secker, 27 July 1767

[fo. 270r] May it please Your Grace

I Have carefully Avoided Being troublesome to your Grace since my Retirement into my parish in the country. Yet I cannot Refrain from Deploring the Grievous Loss Sustained by the Death of our Truly Great and Good L^d: Chancellor L^d: Bowes.[158]

This Kingdom hath suffered the greatest Loss it Has Suffered by the Death of any man in it these thirty years. He Determined more Important Causes, and that with the greatest spirit and perspicuity, During the seven years of His Being Lord Chancellor, than Had been Determined in twenty years Before. So truly Did He answer that part of a good Judge's Character, '*Nemini negabimus Justitiam, nemini Deferemus.*'[159]

When the affairs of this Kingdom were in a tottering condition, and the Government Relaxed: thro' the Insurrections of the *White Boys* in the South, and the *Oak-Boys* in the North: and the too great Disposition of great men to shew a timidity or unseasonable Lenity towards one or the Other: His perfect Knowledge of the Constitution, and prudent zeal to support it, put a stop to their Ravages, and Restored the Lustre of Government.

[fo. 271r] [T]he King Has in him Lost the ablest and most upright of all His servants in Ireland.

The Kingdom and the Laws their protector.

Your Grace the most Attached intimate Friend. [A]nd if after such public Loss, it Be not too great presumption to mention it, your poor servant Has Lost a Benefactor who Honoured him with a particular acquaintance, and a Large degree of His Regard for more than twenty years. But the will of God must Be Done.

After sixteen months close Residence in my parish and preaching therein every Sunday, I purpose, God willing to Return to Dublin in September. And, as your Grace is Deprived of the correspondence of so great and Able a friend: I shall, after my Return to Dublin, sometimes take the Liberty to acquaint you with such occurrencys as may be of consequence for your Grace to Know …

Willm: Henry

Parish of Urney
Marstrabane
July 28 1767.

---

[158] Bowes died on 22 July 1767 and was buried in Christ Church, Dublin, where there is a monument to him.

[159] 'We will deny justice to no one; we will condemn no one.' I thank Dr Scott Carson for his help with this translation.

16. William Henry to Thomas Secker, 26 December 1767

[fo. 274r] Kildare Street in Dublin Decemr: 26 1767.

May it please your Grace,

Your most Friendly Letter of the 31st October, which comforted and Refreshed my spirits Beyond Expression, claimed an Immediate grateful acknowledgement.[160] But I Restrained my self, Lest from a principle of Gratitude, I should Stumble into an opposite conduct, by taking up your Grace's too pretious Time, when I Had nothing of Importance to communicate.

The antient Inscription at Lyons came seasonably into my memory. *Dum nimium pia est, Facta est Impia.*[161]

It will be a pleasure to your Grace to Know, That every thing, Relating to His Majesty's Government, good order, and the public good of this Kingdom Has gone on most smoothly, and all Ranks of men, Both in and out of parliament seem to be well pleased.

Some Little Bickerings passed one Day in the House of Commons Relating to the publishing of a proclamation founded on the British act of parliament about Laying an Embargo on Grain.[162] It only gave an occasion to some young members to Display their oratory, and to sensible old patriots to Explain our civil constitution, which was Done with much perspicuity and moderation. After this Instructive and Entertaining Exercise Being continued from two untill ten at night, the Question of Adjournment Being put, it was carried by 123 to 37. [fo. 274v] What contributes much to put all our people in good Humour is their obtaining unaltered the money Bills with the tax of four shillings in the pound, on Absentees, who are in Employment, or pensioners. The pension List amounts to £91000 out of which £70000 Belongs to persons who never Reside. They Have very properly Excepted from this tax all the posterity of our Late Good King[,] and were Strongly inclined to make another Exception in favour of Sir Edward Hawke, whose vigilance and courage saved this Kingdom.[163] But they could not Do it Regularly[,] and they Hope that it will be made up to Him some other way. [T]his tax will produce above £20000 per ann: and is to be applyed to paying off the national Debt, which is now Reduced to five Hundred thousand p^{ds}:

Another good clause in the Money bill is a tax Equall to a prohibition Laid on all French and other foreign Lawns and cambricks. This Has Revived our Sinking Dundalk cambrick manufacture. [I]t is now resumed and carryed on with great vigour, and to the Honour of our Charter Schools, we Have near seventy children out of them apprenticed at Dundalk, and now working on the cambrick Looms.

We got of the public money £12000 towards the support of this great charity.[164] I Hoped that we should Have obtained £16000. For as I was a person appointed to

---

160 This letter from Secker to Henry appears no longer to be extant.
161 'When piousness is overdone, it becomes impiety.' I thank Dr Scott Carson for his help with this translation.
162 A proclamation prohibiting 'the exportation of wheat, oats, bere, barley' and other grains was authorized by the Irish privy council on 24 Dec. 1767 (*Dublin Gazette*, 29 Dec. 1767). I thank Professor James Kelly for bringing this reference to my attention.
163 Sir Edward Hawke (1705–81). Hawke's blockade of the French fleet at Brest in 1759 saved the British Isles from invasion. Ruddock Mackay, 'Hawke, Edward, First Baron Hawke (1705–1781)', *ODNB*.
164 The charter schools were funded by the Irish parliament: see Milne, *Irish charter schools*.

go with the Speaker to attend the L^d: L^t:, I according to my Trust Laid fully before His Excellency every point [fo. 275r] Relating to our Schools, and answered all His Questions to His Entire satisfaction, He appeared very zealous to patronize us. He asked me, what sum I thought Requisite. I said £16000 to make us flourish, tho' £12000 might Keep us up untill next session.

[W]hen it came to be considered in the House; there were so many Demands on government, that tho' we could very Easily have carried the £16000, yet the Speaker thought it more prudent for us to be contented with the £12000[,] as it seems now to be in such a good channell, that we may Rely on the Like supply every session. Had we urged and carryed it for more, it might probably Have Hurt us on a future occasion.

As provisions are this year cheaper in Ireland by near one Half than they Have been in the two preceeding years, I Hope this sum with our other supplys will fully answer all our occasions.

We Had in several schools Losses by unthrifty masters ~~whereupon~~, and sometimes Dishonestt ones; whereupon I proposed a Law, which passed; That no master or mistress shall ever be admitted who shall not give very sufficient security. [W]e feel some good Effects already of this Bye-Law.

[M]uch and very material Busyness is Expected to come on after the Recess which continues untill the 26 of Janu^y:

It is probable, that the Bill for Septennial parliaments, if it Returns from Britain, will then be Debated over again.[165]

It was very Extraordinary, That tho' the Speaker and the [fo. 275v] whole House waited on the L^d: L^t: with this popular Bill and Expressly Desired to transmit it, and at the same time signify to His Majesty, That it was the General Sense of the commons of Ireland[,] yet when the transmittall came to be signed in Council, and six counsellors at Least are necessary, it was signed by seven only. [A]nd among those not one commoner Except the Speaker.

It Has pleased God in His Mercy to Bless this Kingdom Last Harvest with an uncommon Increase of the fruits of the Earth[,]which will Enable us to contribute Largely to the supply of our mother country, which in our Distresses, Has ever been carefull to supply us. [Y]et this plenty was in Danger of being Diverted into another channell. [S]everal ships were Laded from Spain and [P]ortugal, and Large commissions come over, which would Have Drained us of all.

But on Wednesday night Last, the city of Dublin Drew up a petition to parliament.[166] Both Houses joined next Day in an address to the L^d: L^t: to Lay an Embargo on all Exportation of Corn &c for two months, Except to Great Britain. The proclamation was Immediately issued, and all is safe.[167] A Bill is also preparing to Enable the Government at any time Hereafter, in particular circumstances, to Stopp the Distilling of Spirits from any Kind of Grain or potatoes.

This will Save Bread for our manufacturers, and make them Live Soberly. I must

---

[165] The septennial bill was returned and given the royal assent as an octennial act (7 George III, c. 3): *ILD*. For the politics of this measure, see James Kelly, *Henry Flood: patriots and politics in eighteenth-century Ireland* (Dublin, 1998), pp. 125–7.

[166] A petition of several merchants of Dublin on behalf of themselves and the rest of the inhabitants of the city was presented to parliament on 23 Dec. It called for a ban on exports: *CJ*, p. 442 (23 Dec. 1767).

[167] *CJ*, pp. 442, 444 (23, 24 Dec. 1767).

say, that since a Law somewhat similar to this, passed 2 years ago, our common people are Become more Religious, sober, and virtuous than they Had been for some years before.

[fo. 276r] It is no small pleasure and comfort to me, That from the Best observations I am capable of making, The Spirit of Religion and virtue seems Daily to gain ground among us. I take our public Charitys to be the Best Barometre whereby we can judge at the Rising or falling of true Religion. These are continually Encreasing: an Immense contribution was Raised in our Churches Last year to Relieve the Distressed, in time of Scarcity. [A]nd all the charity sermons this season in this City Have produced at Least one third more than upon any preceding occasions.

The spirit of gaming, which Had possessed our people of fashion formerly to such a Degree as to Render them Little Better than Demoniacs, Has Disappeared. And now (*Regis et Reginae ab Exemplum*)[168] pleasing concertos and Rational conversation are introduced into family Entertainments, and even at the Castle.

This Happy course opens the mind, and makes Room for serious and Religious sentiments. The Effect visibly appears in the numbers of people of fashion who frequent of Late Religious services[,] and particularly at the Holy Communion. By the most moderate computation, we Had in the Churches [fo. 276v] of this city, yesterday not Less than Eight thousand communicants. Decency, order, and good Dispositions seem to be every where growing into Fashion, and I hope most people are sincere.

The very papists Have Begun to Drop their Superstition and Biggotry. For these Last two Sundays, King George, His Queen, and the Royal family Have Been publicly prayed for in all the popish chappells of this City.[169] So many men of understanding in the popish Church, Have Lately upon the fullest conviction, Renounced its Errors publickly, That it seems to be tumbling Down apace. M^r: Archibold, one of the most Eminent men of that Church, who Renounced its Errors five years ago, and published His Reasons, Dyed Last summer in Lisburn in the C^{ty}: Down.[170] D^r: Traill, B^p: of Down, attended Him During His whole sickness, and preached His Funeral Sermon, which He will publish.[171] The Bishop told me, that He was greatly Edifyed by His truly Christian Behaviour. A Bull was sent to Archibold from the pope, granting Him plenary absolution for what was past, and inviting Him by the

---

168 'From the example of the king and queen': I thank Dr Scott Carson for his help with this translation.

169 John Brady (ed.), *Catholics and catholicism in the eighteenth-century press* (Maynooth, 1965), p. 129, reports that a prayer for the royal family was said in Cork on 9 Jan. 1768, but it does not record such a prayer being said among chapels in Dublin in Dec. 1767.

170 Richard Archbold (*c.* 1713–67). Archbold was a Jesuit who spent ten years as a missionary in Ireland. In 1755, he publicly renounced his catholicism and converted to the Church of Ireland. This enabled him to inherit a considerable Irish estate. *The Scots Magazine*, XVIII (1755), 153; Thomas A. Hughes, *History of the Society of Jesus in North America* (London, 1917), II, 312.

171 James Traill, *A sermon preached in the parish church of Lisburn, on Sunday, June 28th, 1767. On the occasion of the death of Mr. Richard Archbold, formerly a Jesuit professed, who conformed to the established Church of Ireland, in the year 1755* (Dublin, 1768). Cf. Anonymous, *A letter to the right revd. lord bishop of Down and Connor. Occasioned by a sermon preached by his lordship on the death of Mr. Richard Archbold, formerly a Jesuite* (Dublin, 1768), and Anonymous, *A defence of the character of the late Richard Archbold, Esq; formerly a Jesuit; in confutation of … a popish pamphlet, entitled, A letter to the right revd. the lord bishop of Down and Connor, &c.* (Dublin, 1769). For details of Traill's life, see above, n. 63. For conversion more generally, see Michael Brown, Charles Ivar McGrath and Thomas Power (eds.), *Converts and conversion in Ireland, 1650–1850* (Dublin, 2005).

Highest Rewards to Return into the Bosome of their Church. But He was steady to His principles, and Had more wisdom, and [fo. 277r] virtue, than the unhappy Antonio De Deominis, ~~the unhappy~~ ArchB^P: of Spalano.[172]

[N]otwithstanding this Liberal Spirit which is Daily increasing among the Better sort of people of the Romish church, I am Sorry to find the numbers of papists of the Lowest class Encreasing, even in the protestant [~~indecipherable~~] province of Ulster. This is owing to the vast numbers who flow thither yearly from the province of Conaught to get Bread and Labour, who as soon as they can get any Little pittance to support them, take cottager's tacks or Holdings, and settle in the country: and as the protestants go off to America, settle in their places.

[Y]et the Blind zeal and Biggotry that Distinguished these Lower papists is Daily wearing out.

[V]ery few of the protestant clergy are non Resident, where there is not a manifest Reason. [N]or are any of their Cures neglected on this account. [Y]et an Inquiry was promoted two Days ago in the House of peers into the Residence of the Clergy, and a motion was made by the young Lord Mountmorres, that a Return should be made after the Recess of the names of all the non Resident clergy. [N]o one opposed it, as it must turn out to their Honour.[173] I Desired that the Return upon every clergyman's occasional Absence should be special.

The Act which passed four years ago Enabling the clergy to Recover their Tythes in a summary way, and by a Decree at the assizes for all money and Costs [fo. 277v] certifyed under the Seal of the Ecclesiastical Court, instead of the old way by Excommunication, Has Done some very great Service.[174] As it Expires with this Session, I spoke to the provost of our Colledge,[175] who framed and Brought in this act. [A]nd He has Engaged to Have it continued, and to add any amendments that may make it more useful.

Among the Schemes which are in Embryo, I find there is one for Enabling the Bishops to set the Lands of their Sees in Leases of Lives. This I fear would make sad Havock in the church. [I]t would vastly Enrich the present set of Bishops, But might Beggar their successors[,] and grievously Diminish the Kings patronage. [F]or it is a fact well Know[n] in Ireland, that the present chief tenants under the Bishops, Especially in the northern parts, scarcely pay the tenth part of the Rent which they Receive from the *Terr[e]-tenants* who Hold under them.[176]

As I Do not choose to trouble your Grace unnecessarily, I Have Enlarged my present Letter beyond just Bounds. [W]hen any thing material occurs, I shall Resume

---

[172] Marco Antonio de Dominis (1560–1624) was archbishop of Spalato and a papal critic who emigrated to England, converted to the Church of England during James VI and I's reign and held a number of important clerical livings. In 1622, though, he both returned to Italy and re-entered into communion with the Roman Catholic church. W. B. Patterson, 'Dominis, Marco Antonio de (1560–1624)', *ODNB*.

[173] Hervey Redmond Morres, Viscount Mountmorres (*c.* 1742–97) was an active member of the Irish House of Lords during the late eighteenth century: Robert Dunlop, 'Morres, Hervey Redmond, Second Viscount Mountmorres (1741/2–1797)', rev. Alexander Du Toit, *ODNB*; *Lords Journals*, p. 433 (23 Dec. 1767).

[174] 3 George III, c. 25: 'An act to amend and explain an act made in the 33rd year of the reign of Henry VIII entitled an act for tithes, and for other purposes therein mentioned': *ILD*.

[175] Francis Andrews: see above, n. 85.

[176] John Cowell, *A law dictionary: or, the interpreter of words and terms, used either in the common or statute laws of ... England* (London, 1708): '*Terre a tenens,* Is he who has the actual possession of the Land.'

my pen; But on this condition, that no Return shall be made unless something which I may write Requires an Animadversion.

I Rejoyced to find in the public papers, that your Grace Had Recovered well from your Late indisposition. That God, may for the sake of His Church, continue to your Grace many and Happy years is the fervent prayer of …

Willm: Henry

Dublin Decem^r: 26 1767

5

GEORGE III'S RECOVERY FROM MADNESS CELEBRATED: PRECEDENT AND INNOVATION IN THE OBSERVANCE OF ROYAL CELEBRATIONS AND COMMEMORATIONS

Edited by
Stephen Taylor

6 Beilby Porteus, bishop of London, to Lord Ailesbury, 27 March 1789 (LPL, Porteus Papers 17, fo. 175)

Introduction[*]

At eight o'clock in the morning of St George's Day 1789 the members of the House of Commons began to leave Palace Yard in solemn procession. Slowly they were followed by the judges, the peers and bishops and the royal princes. Eventually, two hours later George III and Queen Charlotte left the Queen's Palace,[1] now better known as Buckingham Palace, to join the end of the procession, which was making its way through Westminster and the City of London to St Paul's Cathedral. Having stopped at Temple Bar to receive the City sword from the lord mayor, the royal party reached the cathedral at midday. At the west door the king and queen were greeted by George Pretyman, bishop of Lincoln, in his capacity as dean of St Paul's, with Beilby Porteus, bishop of London, and the prebendaries of the cathedral. As they entered the cathedral, a rocket fired from the statue of Queen Anne in front of the west end gave the signal for a salute by guns in the Park and at the Tower; a similar salute marked the royal party's departure at the end of the service.[2] As the king and queen made their way to their thrones at the west end of the choir, a moment depicted by Edward Dayes in one of his paintings of the occasion (see Illustration 7), 5,000 charity children, seated under the dome, sang the 100th psalm to begin a specially composed communion service to give thanks for the king's recovery from the illness – the 'malady' or madness – which had afflicted him for four months beginning in October the previous year.[3] The service lasted a full three hours,[4] with the highpoint, and another moment recorded by Dayes, being Bishop Porteus's sermon from the pulpit just in front of the altar rails.[5] Once the king and queen had returned to the Palace, a 'Feu de Joye' was fired by the foot guards. There then followed parties and entertainments across the capital, the 'blaze of illuminations, from one end to the other', continuing the next evening. *The Times* published

[*]   This chapter has its origins in work that I am doing for the project 'British state prayers, fasts and thanksgivings, 1540s–1940s', led by Philip Williamson, Natalie Mears and me, with Alasdair Raffe as the project's research assistant, and funded by the AHRC, grant E007481/1. We shall produce two major publications: an edition of texts, *British national worship: special prayers, fasts and thanksgivings 1530s–2003*, ed. Alasdair Raffe, Philip Williamson, Natalie Mears and Stephen Taylor, for the Church of England Record Society, and a monograph, Philip Williamson, Natalie Mears and Stephen Taylor, *The British nations and divine providence: public worship and the state from the Reformation to the twentieth century*, for Oxford University Press. I am grateful to my collaborators on the project for advice and references, particularly to Natalie Mears for information about sixteenth-century precedents and to Philip Williamson for materials on the nineteenth and twentieth centuries.
[1]   Accounts vary about the times. The *Times*, for example, stated that the king and the queen left at 10.30. *Times*, 136 (24 Apr. 1789), p. 2.
[2]   According to the *World*, 722 (24 Apr. 1789). Accounts of the firing of salutes varied. Compare those from the *Gazette* and the *Times* printed below, pp. 251, 257–8.
[3]   The fullest account of George III's illness is provided by Ida Macalpine and Richard Hunter, *George III and the mad-business* (London, 1969).
[4]   *World*, 722 (24 Apr. 1789).
[5]   An engraving of this painting is reproduced in Derek Keene, Arthur Burns and Andrew Saint (eds.), *St Paul's. The cathedral church of London 604–2004* (New Haven, 2004), p. 368.

7   *The royal procession in St Paul's on St George's Day 1789*, engraving by J. Neagle after E. Dayes (London, 1793)

descriptions of some thirty-nine illuminations on public buildings, businesses and private houses, at the head of which stood the Bank of England:

> On the great front gate was a Crown, with G. R. a bust of the King in a large medallion. In the middle a transparent painting of Britannia, and on her spear the Cap of Liberty, drawn in a car with four horses, and a figure with two children supporting the City Arms. The centre pillars wreathed with varied lamps, and devices of lamps between the side columns round Prince's-street and Bartholomew Lane, with four grand stars at proper distances of the front building. The number of lamps exceeded 12000, and formed, from the great breadth of the building, the most magnificent spectacle ever seen in this country. At the top of each cornice was a lighted flambeau, and all round varied lamps, with *God Save the King*.[6]

The cost of the Bank illuminations alone was estimated to be at least £2,500.[7]

Events such as these will appear familiar to modern readers accustomed to state occasions centred on a royal procession to St Paul's – the Silver Jubilee of 1977, the marriage of Charles, prince of Wales, in 1981 and the Golden Jubilee of 2002.[8] Indeed, many will also be familiar with the 1789 thanksgiving, as the king's arrival at St Paul's forms the final scene of Alan Bennett's play *The madness of George III* and the later screenplay.[9] In 1789, however, very few people alive could remember the last occasion on which a monarch had attended a service in St Paul's. Queen Anne had done so regularly, attending the series of thanksgiving services for military victories during the war of the Spanish succession in 1702, 1704, 1705, June and December 1706, and 1708, and the service celebrating the Union with Scotland in 1707,[10] though plans for a royal procession to the cathedral for the thanksgiving for the peace of Utrecht in 1713 had to be abandoned as a result of the queen's illness. But this tradition, which was itself an innovation – none of Anne's seventeenth-century predecessors ever attended a thanksgiving service at St Paul's, though Elizabeth I had done so in 1588[11] – was abandoned by the Hanoverians after George I went there in January 1715 to celebrate his peaceful accession to the throne.

While the 1789 thanksgiving has only received relatively brief accounts in biographies of George III,[12] it has attracted some attention from scholars in recent years, as interest has grown in the history of loyalism and patriotism in the later eighteenth century and, indeed, as the monarchy itself has re-emerged as a subject of serious

6 *Times*, 137 (25 Apr. 1789), 2c.
7 *Whitehall Evening Post*, 6532 (11 Apr. 1789).
8 John Wolffe, 'National occasions at St Paul's since 1800', in *St Paul's*, ed. Keene, Burns and Saint, pp. 381–91, provides the fullest account of state occasions at St Paul's.
9 Alan Bennett, *The madness of George III* (London, 1992), pp. 93–4; *idem*, *The madness of King George* (London, 1995), pp. 73–4.
10 Nigel Aston, 'St Paul's and the public culture of eighteenth-century Britain', in *St Paul's*, ed. Keene, Burns and Saint, p. 365.
11 For Elizabeth's visit to St Paul's, see John Strype, *A survey of the cities of London and Westminster* (2 vols., London, 1720), I.iii, 169–73. James I and Charles I both attended a sermon at Paul's Cross. For the visit of James I in 1620, see *The letters of John Chamberlain*, ed. Norman Egbert McClure (2 vols., Philadelphia, 1939), II, 297, 299–300, and below, pp. 244–5. It is not clear whether Charles I processed in state to the cathedral on 30 May 1630. See Arthur Hopton, *Hoptons concordancy enlarged* (London, 1635), sig. Q3. I am grateful to Mary Morrissey for these references.
12 John Brooke, *King George III* (London, 1972), pp. 539–40; Jeremy Black, *George III. America's last king* (New Haven, 2006), pp. 281–2.

study.[13] Particularly influential has been Linda Colley's account of the 'apotheosis' of George III, in which the event has a key *rôle* in both changing, and reflecting change in, attitudes towards the king and monarchy on the eve of the French revolution.[14] Matthew Kilburn, in the fullest account of the thanksgiving, emphasizes some of the continuities in the perception and self-presentation of the monarchy through the eighteenth century and provides a useful corrective to the temptation to consider 1789 as marking a sudden shift in attitudes.[15] As will be seen, however, further examination of the thanksgiving, and particularly its relationship to the long-established tradition of fasts and thanksgivings in the Church of England, casts fresh light both on the origins and nature of the event and on its place in the development of modern royal ceremonial.

As Nicholas Rogers has observed, the 'celebrations commemorating the King's recovery were ... an orchestrated show',[16] and nowhere was this more evident than in the procession on 23 April – the choice of St George's Day was itself of enormous symbolic significance. From the moment when the decision had been made that the king would attend a thanksgiving service at St Paul's, considerable efforts were expended to ensure that the visit would be conducted with appropriate ceremony. The records of the lord chamberlain's department have not survived, but the papers of Archbishop Moore and Bishop Porteus, printed below, reveal very clearly the energy devoted to investigating earlier forms and precedents. The bishops – and ministers – were concerned not only with finding guidance about the practicalities of organizing a complicated event but also with ensuring that established forms were observed. In 1789 attention seems to have focused in particular on establishing the precedents for previous royal visits to St Paul's, clarifying the form of the proclamation, and determining the order of the procession. The last issue was of especial importance – precedence carried a great deal of significance for the aristocracy and had the potential to disrupt royal ceremonial, as it had done in 1620.[17] Following William Pitt's formal announcement to the House of Commons of the king's intention, it established a committee to determine the manner of their procession. Meanwhile, the lord mayor of London had issued a series of regulations to ensure that the passage of carriages to and from the cathedral was as smooth as possible.[18] In a

---

13   Among other works, see Hannah Smith, *Georgian monarchy. Politics and culture 1714–60* (Cambridge, 2006); Clarissa Campbell Orr (ed.), *Queenship in Britain 1660–1837. Royal patronage, court, culture, and dynastic politics* (Manchester, 2002); David Cannadine, 'The context, performance and meaning of ritual: the British monarchy and the "invention of tradition", c. 1820–1977', in *The invention of tradition*, ed. Eric Hobsbawm and Terence Ranger (Cambridge, 1983), pp. 101–64; Andrzej Olechnowicz (ed.), *The monarchy and the British nation, 1780 to the present* (Cambridge, 2007).

14   Linda Colley, 'The apotheosis of George III: loyalty, royalty and the British nation 1760–1820', *Past and Present*, CII (1984), 94–129, esp. 113.

15   Matthew Kilburn, 'Royalty and public in Britain 1714–1789', D.Phil. dissertation, University of Oxford, 1997, pp. 227–45, 262.

16   Nicholas Rogers, *Crowds, culture and politics in Georgian Britain* (Oxford, 1998), p. 186.

17   In 1620 the king's 'traine was not so great by reason of many disputes among his followers for place and precedence'. *Letters of John Chamberlain*, ed. McClure, p. 299. There is, however, no evidence that those planning the procession in 1789 were aware of these disputes. For similar problems affecting the marriage of the princess royal to the prince of Orange in 1734, see John, Lord Hervey, *Some materials towards memoirs of the reign of King George II*, ed. Romney Sedgwick (3 vols., London, 1931), I, 264–6.

18   *Journals of the House of Commons*, XLIV, 277; *Report from the committee appointed to consider of*

remarkable survival, which attracted much comment in the newspapers, the raised 'box', in which Queen Anne had sat at St Paul's eighty years earlier, was brought out of storage, restored and enlarged. It was then placed at the west end of the choir, facing the altar, so that the royal family sat in the same position as Anne had done.[19]

Precedent was, therefore, important, and in many respects the 1789 celebrations followed remarkably closely the pattern established by the thanksgivings of Anne's reign. But this is not the whole story. Contemporary accounts of the preparations in 1789 often give the impression that decisions were being made in a hurried, *ad hoc* manner. Perhaps this should not be a surprise – no one involved in the organization of the last thanksgiving procession in 1715 was still alive and the surviving records provided only the barest outline of many of the arrangements. It is clear, for example, that the *rôle* of the children educated in London's charity schools was an innovation. The charity children had played a part in both the thanksgiving for the peace in 1713 and on George I's entry into London in 1714, but on the first occasion they had been seated, singing hymns, in the Strand and on the second occasion they were placed on the south side of St Paul's Cathedral.[20] In 1789, by contrast, they were placed inside the cathedral and given a *rôle* in the service itself. The idea for this appears to have originated with the queen,[21] and it was initially reported that the thanksgiving would be combined with the anniversary meeting of the charity schools, which would be moved from 28 May to St George's Day.[22] If accurate, this report would suggest that the idea for using the charity children in the service came not from earlier thanksgivings, but rather from the highly popular annual services of the London and Westminster charity schools which were also held in St Paul's Cathedral. Any plans to combine the thanksgiving with the anniversary meeting were quickly abandoned and, probably for practical reasons of space, only a 'great portion' of the charity school children were present at St Paul's on 23 April.[23] The arrangements for the music also emphasize a willingness to innovate and borrow from elsewhere. As Porteus noted, from the first discussions of the proposed service the king declared his desire of having an ambitious musical dimension, with 'several Pieces of the best Church Music'.[24] Early discussions about this part of the ceremonial were influenced primarily by the remarkably successful Handel anniversary concerts, pioneered by Joah Bates. George III participated in the planning of the 1784 Handel commemoration, he attended three programmes and he subsequently

the manner of the House of Commons going to Saint Paul's church, on Thursday, the 23d day of April 1789; and of regulations necessary to be observed, for the preservation of order, upon that occasion. Ordered to be printed 21st April 1789* (London, 1789). No similar order was made by the House of Lords, possibly because there were considerably fewer peers. *Journals of the House of Lords*, XXXVIII, 390.

19 *Diary or Woodfall's Register*, 5 (3 Apr. 1789); *General Evening Post*, 8655 (14 Apr. 1789).

20 *Stuart's Star and Evening Advertiser*, 55 (16 Apr. 1789), carried an account of George Vertue's engraving of the 1713 procession. It is far from clear, however, that those at court and St Paul's, who were organizing the procession and service, were aware of the *rôle* of the charity children in earlier processions.

21 *London Chronicle*, 5058 (24 Mar. 1789).

22 *Stuart's Star and Evening Advertiser*, 33 (23 Mar. 1789).

23 *Diary or Woodfall's Register*, 5 (3 Apr. 1789). Some idea of the popularity of these occasions is given by the report of the 1782 meeting in the *General Advertiser and Morning Intelligencer*, 1737 (3 May 1782).

24 See below, p. 228.

became a patron of the Concert of Ancient Music.[25] It is not surprising, then, that the king selected Bates as his director of music for the thanksgiving service and that Bates proposed works drawn exclusively from Handel's oeuvre.[26] In the event, these plans came to nothing. Apparently, despite the king's initial enthusiasm, arrangements for music were simply neglected, though the cost of Bates's scheme may have been at least partly responsible for its abandonment. It took a memorandum from Porteus on 10 April, reminding the king of the urgency of the matter, to elicit the response that he now 'wished to have a good old *Te Deum & Jubilate*'.[27]

What is most striking, however, is how the plans for the procession developed. The idea for the thanksgiving service was very much the king's; there is no reason to doubt what he told Porteus – that he was determined to express his 'Gratitude to God for the mercies he had received … in the most public & solemn manner' or that he made an 'oath' to this effect during his illness.[28] Indeed, there was a concerted effort, in which both the archbishop of Canterbury and, probably, Pitt played a part, to persuade the king to abandon his plans.[29] These reservations may help to explain why the proclamation for the thanksgiving was not issued until 3 April; indeed, *Stuart's Star* reported in mid-March that the idea for the service at St Paul's had been 'entirely laid aside'.[30] But, if the king was determined to give thanks publicly in St Paul's, he was much more ambivalent about the idea of a state procession. The *Whitehall Evening Post* reported as late as 4 April that there would be no such procession, it being the king's intention to avoid anything resembling 'a parade or pageant' and to make his visit to the cathedral 'nothing more, than … a devout thanksgiving to Almighty God made in the most public and solemn manner'.[31] Four days later the king notified the Lords and Commons of his intention to attend St Paul's, but he made it clear not only that he intended to go unrobed, as Queen Anne had done, but also, against earlier precedent, that he expected the peers to be unrobed.[32] He also refused to use the state coach, preferring to travel in 'one of the common coaches', though finally a compromise was reached, the leather panels in the coach being replaced by glass, so that the king could be seen by his subjects.[33]

There is no evidence that the thanksgiving was planned by the court or the ministry for political reasons. Such considerations had often impinged on such events in the past and would again in the future. Queen Anne's visits to St Paul's were highly public statements of her support for the war against France and for her

---

[25] William Weber, *The rise of musical classics in eighteenth-century England. A study in canon, ritual and ideology* (Oxford, 1992), ch. 8, esp. pp. 233–9.

[26] See below, Document 16. The king was well known to be an enthusiast for the music of Handel. *The diaries of Colonel the Hon. Robert Fulke Greville, equerry to his majesty King George III*, ed. F. McKno Bladon (London, 1930), p. 258.

[27] See below, Documents 18 and 19.

[28] See below, p. 227; *Morning Post and Daily Advertiser*, 5004 (11 Apr. 1789).

[29] *Diaries of Robert Fulke Greville*, ed. Bladon, p. 253; *Morning Post and Daily Advertiser*, 5004 (11 Apr. 1789).

[30] *London Gazette*, 13082 (31 Mar. – 4 Apr. 1789), 193; *Stuart's Star and Evening Advertiser*, 27 (16 Mar. 1789).

[31] *Whitehall Evening Post*, 6529 (4 Apr. 1789).

[32] *The later correspondence of George III*, ed. A. Aspinall (5 vols., Cambridge, 1962–70), I, 405: George III to Lord Sydney, 8 Apr. 1789.

[33] *Morning Post and Daily Advertiser*, 5008 (16 Apr. 1789); Kilburn, 'Royalty and public in Britain', p. 234. See the Rowlandson engraving of the procession reproduced in Keene, Burns and Saint (eds.), *St Paul's*, p. 368.

favourite, the duke of Marlborough; her decision not to attend the thanksgivings in 1709 and 1710 revealed Marlborough's fall from grace and the queen's growing sympathy for the tories. Similarly, in 1872 Gladstone believed that a thanksgiving service at St Paul's to give thanks for the recovery of the prince of Wales, attended by Queen Victoria, would be an effective way of countering the republican movement, even of 'getting rid of it altogether'.[34] Pitt himself was very aware of the political uses of thanksgivings. On 28 February 1789 the privy council issued a proclamation announcing the replacement of the prayer for the recovery of the king, which had been included in every church service since 13 November 1788, with one of thanksgiving for his recovery. As the *London Chronicle* observed, this was calculated to be 'the best means of demonstrating the king's right to re-assume the reins of government, without any declaration by the two Houses of his restored capacity for executing the duties of government'.[35] Both the king's recovery to health and the end of the political crisis over the regency, which had convulsed the country for over three months, were communicated to the nation in a manner that both avoided controversy and was consonant with established precedents of issuing special prayers for inclusion in church services.

Despite the popular celebrations which greeted the announcement of the king's recovery[36] and continuing concerns about his health, it seems most likely that the initial opposition from Pitt and at court to the king's plans stemmed from fears about potential protests, directed at either the king or his ministers, as he proceeded along the route from the Queen's Palace to the cathedral. The regency crisis appeared to have deeply divided the country and few at court had any sense of the king's popularity. As Fanny Burney said, before his recovery he 'little … knew the general loyalty and attachment of the nation. The nation knew it not, indeed, itself.'[37] Rather than Pitt and his colleagues devising the thanksgiving as a way of mobilizing support against the whigs, they were the beneficiaries of an unexpected outpouring of sympathy for the king. There is little doubt that the popular mood began to manifest itself clearly, in the capital at least, well before the thanksgiving day – the newspapers were full not only of reports about the preparations, but also of advertisements of properties for let along the exhibition route (two floors of a house in Fleet Street, for example, were going for 60 guineas) and of 'insignia' ('Miniatures of His Majesty, Bandeaus, Sashes, Girdles, Cockades, Sword-knots, &c') for which there was 'an immense demand'.[38] The popularity of 'restoration gloves' carried a clear political message for the whigs.[39] Sections of the press sympathetic to the opposition were reduced to carping criticisms, warning in particular that the procession would bring people out on to the streets and distract them from attending services in their own parish churches, thus undermining the proper religious observance of the day.[40] Growing

34 *The Gladstone diaries. Volume VIII: 1871–4*, ed. H. C. G. Matthew (Oxford, 1982), p. 82; William M. Kuhn, 'Ceremony and politics: the British monarchy, 1871–2', *Journal of British Studies*, XXVI (1987), 133–62.
35 *London Chronicle*, 5047 (26 Feb. 1789).
36 Rogers, *Crowds, culture and politics*, pp. 184–5.
37 John W. Derry, *The regency crisis and the whigs 1788–9* (Cambridge, 1963). Burney is quoted by Kilburn, 'Royalty and public in Britain', p. 262.
38 *The World*, 713 (11 Apr. 1789); *The World*, 720 (22 Apr. 1789).
39 *Times*, 1349 (17 Apr. 1789), 2a.
40 See, e.g., *St James's Chronicle or the British Evening Post*, 4366 (11 Apr. 1789); *Whitehall Evening Post*, 6538 (14 Apr. 1789).

awareness of popular enthusiasm for the thanksgiving may well have contributed to the efforts to create something which resembled more closely a full state procession.

St George's Day itself was a triumph for both the king and the ministry. Along the route of the procession Pitt and Lord Chancellor Thurlow were greeted with cheering. By contrast, the leaders of the opposition – or, at least, those who did not pull down the blinds of their coaches – 'received an universal hiss, which continued with very little intermission until they alighted at St Paul's'.[41] Men who, a few weeks earlier, had been dreaming about their elevation to office under the patronage of the prince regent, were left lamenting sourly that 'the Town is run mad'.[42] All the newspapers, even those sympathetic to the whigs, were agreed that the procession had attracted huge numbers of people. According to the *Public Advertiser*, 'There never were known such a number of people congregated in London on any former occasion. All stages, coaches, and horses have been engaged for a week past a hundred miles around the metropolis.'[43] Letter writers and diarists also testify to the popularity of the event. Mrs Cornwallis observed 'the immense crowds everywhere', described the illuminations the following night as 'the most magnificent that ever were exhibited', and recorded that 'We have nothing here now but rejoicing, feasting and dancing.'[44]

Hitherto this introduction has focused, as have most historians, on the thanksgiving service at St Paul's and on the ceremonial and celebrations which accompanied it. Indeed, most documents in this edition come from the papers of one of the leading actors in those events and are primarily concerned with its organization. It is important, however, to remember that the proclamation ordered a 'General Thanksgiving' to be observed on that Thursday in 'all Churches, Chapels, and other Places of Public Worship' throughout England and Wales. A second proclamation was issued for Scotland, and the marquis of Buckingham, the lord lieutenant of Ireland, was ordered to issue a similar proclamation for that kingdom.[45] The service at St Paul's was, therefore, only one of thousands being held at the same time, though most would have consisted only of morning prayer rather than the full holy communion that was celebrated in the presence of the king. Across the country work stopped as men and women went to church. Even in London, where there was the rival attraction of the procession, churches and chapels 'were better attended than was expected'.[46] The prayers, composed for the occasion by Archbishops Moore and Markham and Bishops Porteus and Hurd,[47] were available not only in the official form of prayer, retailing at the modest price of $3d$,[48] but also in many of the newspapers.[49] All the evidence suggests that most people shared with the king the belief that they had a duty to give thanks to God, 'who hast graciously manifested Thy

[41]   See below, p. 258.
[42]   Brian Connell, *Portrait of a whig peer. Compiled from the papers of the Second Viscount Palmerston 1739–1802* (London, 1957), p. 198.
[43]   *Public Advertiser*, 17809 (24 Apr. 1789).
[44]   Historical Manuscripts Commission, *Report on manuscripts in various collections*, VI (London, 1909), p. 344.
[45]   *London Gazette*, 13082 (31 Mar. – 4 Apr. 1789), 193; *World*, 710 (8 Apr. 1789).
[46]   *World*, 722 (24 Apr. 1789).
[47]   *World*, 709 (7 Apr. 1789).
[48]   *Whitehall Evening Post*, 6531 (9 Apr. 1789).
[49]   E.g., *Whitehall Evening Post*, 6539 (16 Apr. 1789); *Public Advertiser*, 17084 (18 Apr. 1789).

mercy by restoring health to our Sovereign and gladness to Thy people'.[50] Indeed, the desire to give thanks was not confined only to the king's protestant subjects. A thanksgiving mass was published by James Talbot, the vicar apostolic of the London district; reports survive of others in London and Winchester.[51] In Dublin an elaborate mass, drawing on the services of an orchestra and choir numbering 150, was conducted by the catholic archbishop at the Francis Street chapel.[52] The newspapers also reported thanksgiving services held by the Jews and Swedenborgians in London and carried an advertisement for the publication of a Jewish form for use in the Fenchurch Street synagogue on 23 April.[53] Some consideration of the thanksgiving service and, in particular, its relationship to other similar occasions will cast additional light on the themes of tradition and innovation in royal ceremonial.

As has been stated, the last occasion on which a monarch had attended a thanksgiving service at St Paul's had been seventy-four years earlier. However, if royal processions were rare events, the public was familiar with the ordering by the authorities in church and state of special days of thanksgiving and the closely related fast days. Since the accession of George III in 1760 there had been two thanksgiving days (the most recent in 1784 on the occasion of the peace)[54] and eight general fasts[55] – on all these occasions the whole population was required to attend church to participate in specially composed services. In addition, twenty-four special prayers of intercession and thanksgiving were ordered to be incorporated in the daily liturgy prescribed by the Book of Common Prayer, either on a specific day or for a period of time.[56] These 'days' of fast and thanksgiving and these special prayers were an established part of public worship in eighteenth-century England,[57] with a history reaching back to the Reformation.[58] They were firmly rooted in the notions of divine providence which were a key element of English protestantism through the early

---

50 *A form of prayer and thanksgiving to Almighty God; to be used in all churches and chapels ... on Thursday the twenty-third day of April, being the day appointed by proclamation for a general thanksgiving ...* (London, 1789), p. 8.

51 *A thanksgiving appointed to be said for the recovery of our most gracious sovereign King George III* (London, 1789). This pamphlet, the earliest published mass relating to a fast or thanksgiving day of which I am aware, is dated 17 Mar. 1789, but it does not specify a date on which the service is to be used. Given that the royal proclamation for the thanksgiving day was not issued until 3 Apr. 1789, it seems likely that this form was used in one of a number of catholic services to celebrate the king's return to health. A 'solemn high mass', for example, took place in the catholic chapel in York Street, London, on 14 Mar. *London Chronicle*, 5057 (21 Mar. 1789). However, it is clear from other sources that catholic thanksgivings also took place on 23 Apr. See John Milner, *A sermon preached in the Roman Catholic chapel at Winchester, April 23. 1789 &c. Being the general thanksgiving for his majesty's happy recovery* (London [1789]).

52 *Morning Star*, 80 (15 May 1789).

53 *Whitehall Evening Post*, 6518 (10 Mar. 1789); *Stuart's Star and Evening Advertiser*, 35 (25 Mar. 1789); *World*, 720 (22 Apr. 1789). No copy of the Jewish form appears to have survived.

54 In 1763 at the end of the Seven Years War and in 1784 at the end of the American War.

55 All were fasts during wartime: in 1761, 1762, 1776, 1778, 1779, 1780, 1781 and 1782.

56 For military victories in 1761, 1762 (twice) and 1782; for the birth of the king's children in 1762, 1763, 1765, 1766, 1767, 1768, 1770, 1771, 1773, 1774, 1776, 1777, 1779, 1780 and 1783; for daily use during war in 1779 and 1781; for the failure of an assassination attempt on the king in 1786; for use during his illness in 1788; and for his recovery in 1789.

57 The same point can also be made about Scotland, though the form and the history of the events is slightly different. In the eighteenth century separate proclamations were issued for many, but not all, of these events to be observed in the Church of Ireland.

58 There are also continuities with the pre-Reformation period, but the precise nature of these still remains to be elucidated.

modern period and well into the nineteenth and even twentieth centuries.[59] Natural disasters, such as plague and earthquakes, war, rebellion and military defeat were all punishments for individual and national sins, but, more importantly, they were warnings, the expression of God's mercy rather than his anger, calling for repentance and reformation. When combined with notions of the English as God's chosen people, his elect nation,[60] it is easy to see why these events demanded not only individual prayer but also national prayer, with everyone coming together in their parish churches to repent their sins, promise reformation, petition God for forgiveness and give thanks to him for his mercies. Days of thanksgiving were remarkably similar in character. Thanks were due to God not primarily because he had, for example, granted the nation victory over its enemies, but rather because he had stayed his judgments – praise was due to him for his mercies, but, as the services and sermons on thanksgiving days constantly reminded congregations, repentance and reformation were still required to ensure the continuance of God's favour.

Considering the 1789 service in this context reveals it not as a revival of a long dormant tradition but rather as part of an accustomed liturgical response to national moments of crisis and celebration. Indeed, it is worth emphasizing that the general thanksgiving on 23 April was only the last of three similar orders by the privy council relating to the king's illness. First, on 13 November the archbishop was ordered to prepare a prayer for the king's recovery to be added to the daily liturgy in all churches.[61] Outside London and the major cities daily services were rare, but this prayer would have been said every Sunday at both morning and evening prayer until 1 March. On that day congregations in London heard for the first time a new prayer, ordered on 28 February, giving thanks for the king's recovery; in churches elsewhere it was first used on the following Sunday.[62] Finally, the proclamation for the general thanksgiving on 23 April was promulgated on 3 April.[63]

There were many precedents for the special prayers added to Prayer Book services. Such prayers had been ordered during the illnesses of Charles II in 1685, Mary II in 1694 and Queen Caroline in 1737; they had also been said in the royal chapel during Edward VI's illness in 1553.[64] For obvious reasons none of these had been followed by a thanksgiving prayer. But thanksgiving prayers were ordered for the

---

[59] Alexandra Walsham, *Providence in early modern England* (Oxford, 1999), provides the fullest account of protestant notions of providence.

[60] The use of 'English' here is quite deliberate. My focus is on the service prescribed for use in the Church of England (which included Wales), and at least some preachers discussed God's blessings to his chosen people in a way that was specifically anglican rather than generically protestant. However, the fact that proclamations were also issued for Scotland and Ireland complicates the relationship between religion and national identity, and this is a theme which will be explored further in the monograph, *The British nations and divine providence. Public worship and the state from the Reformation to the twentieth century*, which I am writing with Philip Williamson and Natalie Mears.

[61] *London Gazette*, 13042 (11–15 Nov. 1788); *A prayer to be used on litany days before the liturgy, and on other days immediately before the prayer for all conditions of men, in all...churches and chapels ... during his majesty's present indisposition* (London, 1788).

[62] *London Gazette*, 13073 (28 Feb. – 3 Mar. 1789); *A form of prayer and thanksgiving to Almighty God; to be used at morning and evening service, after the general thanksgiving, throughout the cities of London and Westminster ... on Sunday the first day of March 1789; and in all churches and chapels throughout England and Wales, as soon as the ministers thereof receive the same* (London, 1789).

[63] *London Gazette*, 13082 (31 Mar. – 4 Apr. 1789).

[64] *Prayers for the king; to be used in all churches, and chapels immediately before the prayer of S. Chrysostom, both in the morning and evening service* [London, 1685]; *Prayers to be used during the queens sickness, in the cities of London and Westminster* (London, 1694); Lambeth Palace Library,

recovery of Elizabeth in 1562 and Charles I in 1632.[65] Similar in character were the prayers for the preservation from assassination of William III in 1696 and George III in 1786.[66] The most common thanksgiving prayers on royal occasions through the seventeenth and eighteenth centuries, however, were those occasioned by the safe childbearing of the queen.

Remarkably, however, while there were precedents for the prayers of November 1788 and February 1789, there was none for the ordering of a thanksgiving day with special services for the king's return to health. Indeed, the only previous occasion on which a general thanksgiving had been ordered for a royal event was the birth of the prince of Wales to James II and Mary of Modena in June 1688,[67] which would hardly have been an auspicious parallel in the eyes of Englishmen as they celebrated the centenary of the Glorious Revolution. Despite the preoccupation with the search for precedents in 1789, there is no reference to the innovation of the thanksgiving *day* in the surviving sources. But it is inconceivable, especially in a period as resistant to constitutional and liturgical innovation as the eighteenth century, that those advising the king, his ministers and bishops, were not aware of what they were doing. Possibly, this lack of a precedent helps to explain the attempts by Archbishop Moore and Pitt to persuade the king to abandon his plans. Their failure emphasizes the key *rôle* that was still played by the monarch in the ordering of special national forms of worship, especially those concerning the royal family. It was George III's decision to depart from tradition by ordering a general thanksgiving and processing to St Paul's to attend the service in the cathedral of Britain's capital.

The general thanksgiving of 23 April did not create a new tradition. There has never since 1789 been another general thanksgiving to celebrate the recovery of a monarch from illness: in 1820 and 1951 only thanksgiving prayers were ordered, while in 1929 there was no privy council order and a form of prayer was published only for the service in St Paul's Cathedral, though the hope was expressed that 'the same form and order will be used in many churches'.[68] But, in other ways, it has exerted a significant influence over the public religious ceremonial associated with the British monarchy.[69] The success of the 1789 procession undoubtedly encouraged

---

G199.16(15): prayers for the queen, 18 Nov. 1737; *A prayer sayd in the kinges chappell* [London, 1553], STC 7508.

65 *A thanksgiuing for the happy recouery of his maiesties health* (London [1632]), STC 16550.3; Guildhall Library, London, MS 9513/13, part 1, fo. 26r: privy council to Archbishop Grindal, 17 Oct. 1562. It is not clear whether the prayers for Elizabeth were said anywhere other than Paul's Cross.

66 *A form of prayer and thanksgiving, to Almighty God: to be used on Thursday the sixteenth of April next ... for discovering and disappointing a horrid and barbarous conspiracy of papists and other trayterous persons to assassinate and murder his most gracious majesties royal person; and for delivering this kingdom from an invasion intended by the French* (London, 1696); *A form of thanksgiving to Almighty God; for the providential preservation of his majesty's sacred person, in the late attempt upon it, on the 2d day of August, 1786. To be used at morning and evening service, after the general thanksgiving* (London, 1786).

67 *A form of prayer with thanksgiving for the safe delivery of the queen, and happy birth of the young prince. To be used on Sunday next, being the seventeenth day of this instant June, in all churches and chapels, within the cities of London and Westminster...and upon the first day of July next, in all other places throughout this kingdom...* (London, 1688).

68 *Times*, 10 Dec. 1951, p. 4b; *ibid.*, 5 July 1929. It is worth nothing, though, that when George V and Queen Mary attended the service at St Paul's on 25 June 1930 to celebrate the completion of the restoration of the cathedral, the liturgy also included thanks for the king's recovery from illness. Wolffe, 'National occasions at St Paul's since 1800', p. 388.

69 My account of the development of state services for royal occasions in the nineteenth and twentieth

Pitt and the king to revive Queen Anne's practice of attending wartime thanksgiving services in 1797, and the Prince Regent went to St Paul's for the thanksgiving for peace in 1814. Then, after a long gap – Queen Victoria notably did not publicly attend the thanksgiving service for the end of the Crimean War in 1856 – Edward VII went in state to St Paul's for the thanksgiving service at the end of the Boer War,[70] as did George V in 1919 to observe the thanksgiving day ordered to celebrate the signing of the Versailles Peace Treaty. Moreover, while, from the outbreak of the French revolutionary wars, fasts and thanksgivings (and their twentieth-century successors, national days of prayer) in general continued to be ordered for much the same events as they had been in earlier centuries, state prayers on royal occasions proliferated. In 1796 the birth of Princess Charlotte, the daughter of the prince of Wales, was marked by a thanksgiving prayer; this was the first occasion on which a royal birth had been observed for anyone other than a child of the reigning monarch. In 1809 a thanksgiving prayer was issued to celebrate the Golden Jubilee of George III. This was improved upon with the thanksgiving service for Victoria's Golden Jubilee in 1887, the thanksgiving accompanied by a procession to St Paul's in 1897 and then the Silver Jubilee of George V in 1935; in an adaptation of earlier practices to the changed social and religious condition of Britain in the nineteenth century, however, these were marked not by the proclamation of a day of thanksgiving, but by the issuing of special prayers and the proclamation of a public holiday. In 1868 there was a thanksgiving prayer following the failure of an attempt to assassinate the duke of Edinburgh.[71] In 1871 the practice of praying for the health of the monarch was extended to the prince of Wales. It was followed by further innovations: a prayer giving thanks for his recovery and then, in 1872, by a thanksgiving service at St Paul's.[72] In 1901, for the first time, a national service was published for use in all churches to commemorate the death of the monarch; the following year saw a similar innovation for the coronation of Edward VII. By the beginning of the twenty-first century some of these practices had fallen into disuse: prayers have not been issued for the birth of a member of the royal family, other than children of the reigning sovereign, since 1894 and, since the accession of Elizabeth II, they are no longer said on occasion of the monarch's illness.[73] But a 'tradition' of public celebrations, in which church services play a central part, has apparently been established, consisting of coronations, jubilees and deaths of monarchs. And innovation

centuries owes much to discussions with Philip Williamson, who is planning to write an article on these occasions in the period between 1860 and 2002.

[70] In 1902, however, there was no proclamation for a day of thanksgiving nor a privy council order for a form of prayer. Instead, the archbishops issued a selection of psalms, lessons and prayers for incorporation in the services prescribed by the Book of Common Prayer. *Form of prayer and thanksgiving to Almighty God for the restoration of peace in South Africa, issued, under the direction of the king, by the archbishops of Canterbury and York, for use in their respective provinces, on Sunday, June 8th, 1902 ...* (London, 1902).

[71] It was linked with prayers for the Abyssinian expedition.

[72] It is notable that in 1871–2 there was the same pattern of two prayers and then a thanksgiving service as in 1788–9. A full discussion of these events is provided by William M. Kuhn, 'Ceremony and politics', and *idem, Democratic royalism. The transformation of the British monarchy, 1861–1914* (Basingstoke, 1996), pp. 38–47. However, as Williamson notes, Kuhn sometimes conflates the thanksgiving prayer with the service at St Paul's. Philip Williamson, 'State prayers, fasts and thanksgivings: public worship in Britain 1830–97', *Past and Present*, CC (2008), 121–74 n. 174.

[73] *Times*, 22 Feb. 1960, p. 10e; *ibid.*, 12 Mar. 1964, pp. 7f.

still continues: in 2002 special forms of prayer were issued by the archbishops of Canterbury and York to commemorate the death of the Queen Mother.[74] In this story the influence of 1789 has been both direct and indirect. Directly, it became a precedent. Gladstone was well aware of it when trying to persuade Queen Victoria to approve the arrangements for the special thanksgiving service at St Paul's Cathedral for the recovery of the prince of Wales in 1872, though he was also aware that the 'precedents' were not exact.[75] Indirectly, the success of the 1789 thanksgiving helped to alert the British elite to the underlying popularity of the monarchy and its potential to act as a focus for national unity, particularly as its political *rôle* declined. This development was not unproblematic. The failure to follow the precedent of 1789 on George IV's recovery from illness in 1820 almost certainly owed something to his unpopularity at the time of the Queen Caroline affair, and at least part of the impetus for the development of royal ceremonial in the late nineteenth century came from a desire to counter republicanism and make the monarchy more popular, rather than simply to exploit its popularity. But there is no doubt that, over the course of the nineteenth and twentieth centuries, one of the main reasons for the proliferation of royal prayers and services was that they were 'uncontroversial, indeed very popular'.[76] The obvious explanation for the innovation of a service for the queen mother in 2002 is the perception of church leaders (and, presumably, Buckingham Palace) that some focus and structure was needed for the public commemoration of a 'beloved' member of the royal family.[77]

The general thanksgiving for the recovery of George III on 23 April 1789 was a unique event – no general thanksgiving has been held before or since for the recovery of the reigning monarch from illness. Paradoxically, however, it took place in a society which gave enormous weight to precedent in constitutional and liturgical matters, as is revealed very clearly in the documents that follow. This tension between tradition and innovation provides a valuable case study, illustrating the development of state prayers, fasts and thanksgivings in England over the four centuries since the Reformation. One way of understanding the gradual transformation of sixteenth-century fasts and thanksgivings into the national days of prayer and state prayers of the twentieth century is through a series of accounts of how monarchs, churchmen and ministers responded to specific events at a particular time.

Editorial conventions

The spelling, punctuation and capitalization of the originals have been preserved. Abbreviations have also been retained, unless these are obscure, in which case they have been expanded in square brackets. Words which are underlined in the original manuscripts have been printed in italic type.

---

[74] *Special forms of service in commemoration of her late majesty Queen Elizabeth the queen mother* (Cambridge [2002]).

[75] BL, Add. MS 44618, fo. 47.

[76] Williamson, 'State prayers, fasts and thanksgivings', 169; *idem*, 'National days of prayer: the churches, the state and public worship in Britain, 1899–1957', forthcoming.

[77] *Independent*, 1 Apr. 2002.

Documents concerning the 1789 thanksgiving service from the papers of Bishop Beilby Porteus and Archbishop John Moore

The bulk of the documents that follow are taken from the papers of Bishop Beilby Porteus, preserved among the Fulham papers at Lambeth Palace Library. These have been supplemented by the papers of Archbishop John Moore, preserved in the series known as the Archbishops' papers. The Porteus papers comprise a far more substantial deposit than the Moore papers and, within the collection, more survive relating to the 1789 thanksgiving. For this reason the Porteus papers (fos. 137–95 of Lambeth Palace Library, Fulham papers, Porteus 17) form the spine of this edition; Moore's papers (fos. 93–106 of Lambeth Palace Library, Archbishops' papers, Moore 6) have been incorporated into the sequence, omitting two items which duplicate material found in the Porteus papers. It is clear that Porteus's papers relating to the thanksgiving were brought together and re-arranged either by the bishop or one of his secretaries. His papers have been arranged and bound since their arrival at Lambeth Palace Library, but the first folio of this section (fo. 137) is a cover sheet which is endorsed 'Papers respecting / His Majesty's going / St Pauls. – / April. 23. 1789 / T.' and most of the following items are endorsed with a contemporary number in a sequence that runs from one to twenty. Following their re-arrangement at Lambeth, the papers are now bound in strict chronological order. In this edition, however, I have reverted to the contemporary sequence, inserting the small number of items without a number at the appropriate place. As will become apparent, the contemporary sequence does have a logic which helps us to understand some aspects of the organization of the thanksgiving service and the king's procession to St Paul's.

One further item has been included in this edition: extracts relating to the king's illness and the thanksgiving taken from Bishop Porteus's notebooks or diary. These came to Lambeth separately from the Fulham papers and are to be found among the manuscript sequence as MSS 2103–5.

Bishop Porteus's account of the king's illness and the thanksgiving

1.   Extracts from Bishop Porteus's notebooks

Lambeth Palace Library, MSS 2103

Porteus kept a series of notebooks, which he used to record dated entries and other occasional memoranda. The originals survive for the period 1786–1809. Only entries relating to the king's illness or to the thanksgiving service are included here. These notes provide an outline narrative of events from October 1788 to May 1789, as well as revealing some of the bishop's own thoughts and feelings.

[fo. 19r]
Octr. 22. [1788] This Day the first Symptoms of the King's unfortunate Malady.

Oct[r.] 27. Further Symptoms. – Nov[r.] 5. became Violent.

Nov[r.] 16. A Prayer for the King ordered by the Privy Council & composed by the ABp of Canterbury; w[ch] is the constant Usage ...[1]

[fo. 20r]

Febr[y.] 15. This Day administerd the Sacrament at S[t.] James's Chapel to the Prince of Wales as a Qualification for the Regency. But I understood afterwards that according to the usual mode he should not have been qualified till after he was Regent[2] which it so happened that he never was. – The Dukes of York & Cumberland received with Him.

Feb. 17. – From the 5th of November (when the Kings illness became decided) to this time, accounts were regularly published of the Progress of the Disorder & afterwards of its abatement. During this Period the great Question of the Regency was agitated in Parliament the Bill passed the House of Commons & was brought up to the Lords, where it was also warmly debated. On this Day Feb. 17 the King's Physicians, Warren, Pepys & Willis, pronounced the King *Convalescent.*

On the 19th The Lord Chancellor announced this Convalescence to the House of Lords & moved an adjournment & on the 26 D[rs] Bates, Pepys & Willis declared there was an entire Cessation of his Majesty's Disorder –

[fo. 21r]

March 4. This day received a note from Mr Pitt[3] desiring me to be at Kew to morrow at ½ an Hour past 10 or about 2; when the King would probably wish to see me.

– 5. – Went to Kew at half an Hour after ten. In about half an hour the King sent for me.

As I enterd the Kings apartment Dr Warren[4] was taking his Final Leave of his Majesty & going out of the Room.[5]

The King immediately came up to me & addressed me very graciously.

He thanked me for my Sermon at S[t.] James's Chapel on Ash-Wednesday in which I touched briefly on the happy termination of his Disorder. The Queen had sent for the Sermon & read it to him.

He expressed the strongest Sense of Gratitude to God for the mercies he had received; & said it was his desire to manifest that Gratitude in the most public & solemn manner. He had therefore resolved to go to S[t.] Pauls on the Thanksgiving Day. He hoped I would preach on that Occasion being (as he was pleased to call

---

1 *A prayer to be used on litany days before the liturgy, and on other days immediately before the prayer for all conditions of men, in all cathedral, collegiate, and parochial churches and chapels within England, Wales, and the town of Berwick upon Tweed, during his majesty's present indisposition* (London, 1788). The orders for the archbishop to compose the prayer and for its use in all churches were made by the privy council on 13 Nov. 1788. *London Gazette*, 13042 (11–15 Nov. 1788).

2 By the provisions of the 1672 Test Act (25 Charles II, c. 2) the prince of Wales would have been required to receive communion according to the rite of the Church of England within three months of assuming the office of regent.

3 William Pitt (1759–1806); prime minister 1783–1801, 1804–6.

4 Richard Warren (1731–97); educ. Jesus College, Cambridge; succeeded to the medical practice of his father-in-law Peter Shaw; appointed physician to George III in 1762 and to the prince of Wales in 1787. He was 'the most sought-after society doctor of that time'. *Oxford dictionary of national biography* (*ODNB*).

5 'Room' is interlineated over 'Apartment', which has been deleted.

me) his Diocesan, & he proposed having several Pieces of the best Church Music under the [fo. 22r] Direction of Mr Bates.[6]

He said his mind was deeply impressed wth the Truth & importance of the Christian Religion. It had been his great Support through his Illness: He said he had forgot nothing that passed during that Period & he assured me that in the very worst Paroxysms of his Disorder *his Trust in God never forsook him*. This remarkable circumstance I alluded to in my Sermon at S[t.] Paul's; when his Majesty went there to return thanks for his recovery.[7]

He looked in Health but very thin. He wore the undress Windsor Uniform.[8]

I staid till the Bp of Worcester Dr Hurd[9] was announced & then retired.

His Conversation throughout was sensible pious & dignified.

March 15. A Prayer of Thanksgiving Substituted in the Room of the former Prayer.[10]

March 30. Went to Windsor with the addresses of the London Clergy to the King & Queen.[11]

Had much Conversation with the King on the Subject of his going to S[t.] Pauls.

April 23. Thanksgiving Day for his Majesty's recovery. The King Queen & three Princesses [12] went to S[t] Pauls. The Prince of Wales, & the Dukes of York,[13] Gloucester[14] & Cumberland[15] were also there, about 50 Lords, between 2 & 300 of the House of Commons, the Peeresses, foreign Ministers, Lord Mayor & Aldermen &c, &c, &c. The Sermon was preached by me. The Text was Psalm XXVII. 16.[16]

April 25. The House of Commons voted thanks for it.[17]

May 2. The King Ordered it to be printed.

May 16. Went to Windsor to present it to the King & Queen & three Princesses. – His Majesty conversed with me on various Subjects above half an hour in his Library. He then carried me up to the Queen's Apartment where her Majesty was & the three Princesses. I staid there about half an hour more...

[6] Presumably Joah Bates (1741–99); conductor of the Concerts of Ancient Music 1776–93; organizer and conductor of the first Handel commemoration concerts in 1784. *ODNB*.

[7] Beilby Porteus, *A sermon preached at the cathedral church of St Paul, London, before his majesty, and both houses of parliament, on Thursday, April 23d, 1789, being the day appointed for a general thanksgiving* (London, 1789), p. 17.

[8] A dark blue uniform introduced by George III in 1777.

[9] Richard Hurd (1720–1808); educ. Emmanuel College, Cambridge, matric. 1735, BA 1739, MA 1742; preacher at Lincoln's Inn 1765; archdeacon of Gloucester 1767; bishop of Lichfield and Coventry 1774–81; bishop of Worcester 1781–1808; declined George III's offer of the archbishopric of Canterbury in 1783. *ODNB*.

[10] *A form of prayer and thanksgiving to almighty God; to be used at morning and evening service, after the general thanksgiving, throughout the cities of London and Westminster, and elsewhere within the bills of mortality, on Sunday the first day of March 1789; and in all churches and chapels throughout England and Wales, as soon as the ministers thereof receive the same* (London, 1789). The privy council made the order for the discontinuance of the earlier prayer for the king's recovery and the use of this prayer on 28 Feb. 1789. *London Gazette*, 13073 (28 Feb. – 3 Mar. 1789). Porteus's dating is an error.

[11] *London Gazette*, 13082 (31 Mar. – 4 Apr. 1789), 197.

[12] Princesses Charlotte (1766–1828), Augusta (1768–1840) and Elizabeth (1770–1840).

[13] Frederick, duke of York (1763–1827), second son of George III.

[14] Prince William Henry, duke of Gloucester (1743–1805), third son of Frederick, prince of Wales.

[15] Henry Frederick, duke of Cumberland (1745–90), fourth son of Frederick, prince of Wales.

[16] See below, p. 261.

[17] See Document 24 below.

The search for precedents

Many of the documents preserved among the Porteus and Moore papers are copies of proclamations and other documents from the council office, accounts of earlier thanksgivings taken from the London Gazette, *and extracts from the* Journals of the House of Lords, *along with some memoranda based on these documents. The main focus of attention is the precedents for royal processions to St Paul's Cathedral, and the bulk of the documents, therefore, come from the reign of Queen Anne, who attended thanksgiving services in the cathedral on seven occasions. The only other occasion to be noted was the visit of James I to hear a sermon at Paul's Cross in 1620, but it is clear from newspaper reports that contemporaries were aware of other royal visits, including Elizabeth I's in 1588. Some sense of the way in which documents from earlier occasions were later used as models can be gained by comparing the proclamations printed as items 2, 3, 4 and 5.*

2. Proclamation for a general thanksgiving, 3 November 1702[18]

Porteus papers 17, fos. 145–8

At the Court at S[t.] James's the 3[d] of Nov[r.] 1702.

Present

The Queens most Excellent Majesty

Lord Arch Bishop of Canterbury[19]	Duke of Somersett
Lord Keeper[20]	Lord Chamberlain[21]
Lord Treasurer[22]	Earl of Nottingham
Lord President[23]	M[r] Secretary Hedges

Whereas Her Majesty in Council did Yesterday being the 2nd of this Instant November, Order that a General Thanksgiving to Almighty God for the Success of the Arms of Her Majesty and her Allies be Observed throughout the Cities of London and Westminster and elsewhere within the weekly Bills of Mortality[24] upon Sunday next being the 8th instant and in all other places within this Kingdom on Thursday the 3[d] of December next: Her Majesty in Council is this Day pleased to Order that the said General Thanksgiving be Observed throughout the Citys of London and Westminster and elsewhere within the weekly Bills of Mortality upon Thursday next being the 12th of this Instant Nov[r.] instead of Sunday the 8th Instant, and that the following Proclamation signifying Her Majesty's Pleasure herein do bear date this day, and to be past the Great Seal and Printed and Published accordingly.

---

18 Another copy of the preamble to this proclamation is preserved in the Moore papers 6, fos. 95–6. Moore's copy includes the marginal annotation: 'The Queen went to S[t] Pauls on the Day of Thanksgiving.'

19 Thomas Tenison, archbishop of Canterbury 1695–1715.

20 Sir Nathan Wright, lord keeper of the great seal 1700–5.

21 Edward Villiers, first earl of Jersey, lord chamberlain 1700–4.

22 Sidney, First Lord Godolphin, lord treasurer 1702–10.

23 Thomas Herbert, eighth earl of Pembroke, lord president of the council 1702–8.

24 This phrase is used to describe the parishes of London in which mortality statistics were collected between the late sixteenth and the mid-nineteenth centuries. It roughly corresponded to the area which contemporaries would have understood by 'London'.

By the Queen
A Proclamation for a Publick Thanksgiving.

Anne R.

We do most Devoutly and Thankfully acknowledge the great Goodness and Mercy of Almighty God, who hath afforded Us His Protection and Assistance in the Just War, in which, for the Common safety of our Realms and for Disappointing the Boundless Ambition of France, We are now Engaged, and hath given to our Arms in Conjunction with our Allies under the Command of John Earl of Marlborough,[25] Captain General of our Land Forces, a Wonderful and Glorious Current of Success, whereby there hath been gained from Our Enemies many Fortified Townes and large Territories in the Low Countries;[26] and hath blessed the Fleet and Troops of Us and Our Allies, under the Command of James Duke of Ormonde,[27] General of our Forces, on Board our said Fleet, and Sir George Rooke,[28] Admiral of our said Fleet, with the taking and destroying many Ships of War, and great Riches of our Enemies, at the Port of Vigo[29] in the Kingdom of Spain; and has also given us many considerable Successes in the West Indies; and hath rendered our Trade at Sea Secure, beyond what could be expected in the time of War; and thereby made the beginning of Our Reign Happy and Prosperous to ourselfe and Our People; and has likewise given great Success to the Arms of our Allies in Germany and Italy: And therefore duly considering that such Great and Publick Blessings do call for Publick and Solemn Acknowledgements, We have thought fit (by the Advice of Our Privy Council) to Issue this Our Royal Proclamation, hereby appointing and Commanding that a General Thanksgiving to Almighty God, for these His mercies, be Observed throughout Our Cities of London & Westminster, and elsewhere within the Weekly Bills of Mortality upon Thursday the Twelfth day of this Instant November, and in all other Places throughout Our Kingdom of England, Dominion of Wales, and Towne of Berwick upon Tweed, upon Thursday the Third day of December next; and for the better and more Religious and Orderly Solemnizing of the same, We have given Directions to the Arch-Bishops and Bishops of this our Kingdom to compose a Form of Prayer Suitable to this Occasion, to be used in all Churches and Chapels and other Places of Publick Worship, and to take Care for the timely Dispersing thereof through their respective Dioceses.[30] And, We do strictly Charge and Command that the said Publick days of Thanksgiving be religiously observed by all our Loving Subjects, as they tender the favour of Almighty God, and upon pain

---

25 John Churchill, first duke of Marlborough (1650–1722). He had been created captain-general of the army and commander-in-chief of the forces in Holland by Queen Anne immediately after her accession in March 1702. He was created duke of Marlborough in December 1702. *ODNB*.

26 In a series of operations between July and October 1702 Marlborough had removed the French threat to Nijmegen and the river Maas.

27 James Butler, second duke of Ormond (1665–1745). In April 1702 he was appointed to command the land forces in an attack on Cadiz. *ODNB*.

28 Sir George Rooke (*c.* 1650–1709). In the admiralty commission established by Prince George of Denmark in May 1702, Rooke was the senior of four admirals, and was also created vice-admiral of England. He commanded the fleet in the attack on Cadiz. *ODNB*.

29 The attack on Cadiz failed, but the Spanish treasure fleet was subsequently attacked at Vigo, destroying a large part of the French escort and capturing much treasure.

30 *A form of prayer, and thanksgiving to almighty God; to be used throughout the cities of London and Westminster ... on Thursday the twelfth day of this instant November ... For the signal successes vouchsafed to her majesties forces both by sea and land: as also to those of her allies, engaged in the present war against France and Spain ...* (London, 1702).

of suffering such Punishments, as We may justly Inflict on all such as shall contemn or neglect the Performance of so Religious and necessary a duty. Given at our Court at S[t.] James's the 3[d] of November 1702 in the First Year of our Reign.

God save the Queen.

Endorsed: 3rd Nov[r] 1702 / Copy Order in Council / and Proclamation / for a General Thanks/giving on Thursday / the 12 Nov[r.] next. / N[o.] 1.

3.   Account of thanksgiving taken from the *London Gazette*, 12 November 1702[31]

Porteus papers 17, fos. 153–6

Whitehall Nov[r] 12th 1702

This day being appointed by Her Majesty's Proclamation to be observed in London and Westminster and elsewhere within the Bills of Mortality, as a day of public Thanksgiving to Almighty God, for the Glorious Successes of the Arms of Her Majesty and her Allies, particularly of her Majesty's Troops in the Low Countries, under the Conduct of the Earl of Marlborough, and of the Fleet and Troops of Her Majesty and her Allies, under the Command of his Grace the Duke of Ormond and Sir George Rooke at Vigo in Spain: Her Majesty was pleased, for the greater Solemnity of the day, to go to the Cathedral Church of S[t.] Paul's, attended by both houses of Parliament, the great Officers of State, the Judges, and other publick Officers, to return Thanks to God, for these great Mercies and Blessings.

The Proceeding was begun between 8 and 9 in the Morning, by the House of Commons, who went from their own House through S[t.] James's Park, passed before Her Majesty's Palace, down the Pall-mall, and so to St Paul's; the Speaker going first, and the Members following, all in their Coaches. Soon after came the house of Peers; Three of the Knights Marshals Men made way, then came the Clerk of the Crown, the Masters in Chancery, and the Judges, as Assistants to that House; the Peers, being all in their Robes, followed in their Coaches according to their Order of Precedency, as they were Marshalled by the Heralds at Westminster, the youngest Baron going first: Those who are Knights of the Garter wore their Collars of the Order.

Her Majesty came afterwards attended in the following manner; First marched the Knight Marshal on Horseback, with some of his Men; next came one of Her Majesty's Coaches with six horses, wherein were the Gentlemen Ushers; Another of Her Majesty's Coaches, wherein sate the Duke of Somerset Master of the Horse, and the Duke of Ormond, being the Staff-Officer in waiting; Then the Troop of Horse Granadiers; Two more of Her Majesty's Coaches, in which were the Ladies and Maids of Honour; next Her Majesty's Footmen and the Yeomen of the Guard on foot; And then Her Majesty, habited in Purple, wearing her Collar and George, in her Body-Coach drawn by eight Horses, in which were also the Countesses of Marlborough and Sunderland; And last of all Her Majesty's Third Troop of horse Guards.

The Streets were lined from S[t.] James's to Temple-bar by the Militia of Westminster, from thence to Ludgate by the City Trained Bands, and two Companies of

---

[31]   *London Gazette*, 3862 (12–16 Nov. 1702).

Her Majesty's Foot Guards were posted in the Church. The Balconies and Windows of the Houses were hung with Carpets and Tapestry, and the number of Spectators was exceeding great.

At Temple-bar Her Majesty was met by the Lord Mayor in a Gown of Crimson Velvet, and the Aldermen and Sheriffs in their Scarlet Gowns, being all on horseback, and the Lord Mayor surrendered the City Sword to Her Majesty, who having returned the same to him, he carried it before Her Majesty to the Church, the Aldermen and Sheriffs riding before him.

Her Majesty being come to S^t. Paul's, was met at the West Door by the Peers; The Kings and Officers of Arms, with the Gentlemen Pensioners, attending; the Sword of State was carried before Her Majesty from thence into the Choir by his Grace the Duke of Ormond, and Her Majesty walked between the Duke of Somerset and the Lord Chamberlain.

Her Majesty being entered into the Choir, seated herself on her Throne of State, which was placed near the West End of the Choir, opposite to the Altar, the Peers had Seats in the Area, as a House of Lords, the Commons in the Stalls and Upper Galleries on each Side, the Ladies of the Bedchamber, Maids of Honour, and other Ladies of the highest Quality, and the Foreign Ministers, in the two Lower Galleries next the Throne; and the Lord Mayor and Aldermen in the Lower Galleries next to the Altar: The Lord Bishop of London[32] sate in his Throne or Stall; the Dean and Prebendaries within the Rails of the Altar; and the Choir was placed in the Organ-loft. The Prayers and Litany were said and sung by Residentiaries and Minor Canons; the Lord Bishop of London read the Communion Service, and the Lord Bishop of Exeter[33] preached an excellent Sermon;[34] and the Hymn, Te Deum, with several other Anthems, admirably well set to Music, were sung by the Choir.

The Divine Service being ended, Her Majesty returned to S^t. James's in the same State she came. The great Guns of the Tower, and those in S^t. James's Park, were thrice discharged, the first time when Her Majesty parted from S^t. James's, the second at the singing of the Te Deum, and the third when her Majesty came back to her Palace.

The Publick demonstrations given by the Inhabitants of this great and populous City, and places adjacent, of the highest Zeal, Loyalty and Affection, which they were able to express for Her Majesty's Person and Government, and of their extraordinary Joy for the glorious Success of Her Majesty's Arms, were suitable to so great and solemn an Occasion; and the night ended with ringing of Bells, Bonfires, Illuminations, and other Rejoicings.

Endorsed: 1702. / Extract from the / London Gazette. / (N°. 2.)

---

32 Henry Compton, bishop of London 1675–1713.

33 Jonathan Trelawney, bishop of Exeter 1689–1707.

34 Jonathan Trelawney, *A sermon preach'd before the queen, and both houses of parliament: at the cathedral church of St. Pauls Nov. 12. 1702. Being the day of thanksgiving; for the signal successes vouchsafed to her majesties forces by sea and land: under the command of the earl of Marlborough in the Low-Countries; and James duke of Ormond general, and Sir George Rook admiral, at Vigo. As also to those of her allies, engaged in the present war against France and Spain. And likewise, for the recovery of his royal highness the prince of Denmark* (London, 1702).

4.   Proclamation for a general thanksgiving, 17 August 1704

Porteus papers 17, fos. 157–8

By the Queen A Proclamation For a Publick Thanksgiving.
  Anne R.
  We do most Devoutly and Thankfully Acknowledge the great Goodness and Mercy of Almighty God, who has afforded Us His Protection and Assistance in the Just War, in which for the Common Safety of Our Realms, and for Disappointing the Boundless Ambition of France, We are now Engaged, and hath given to Our Arms, in conjunction with our Allies, under the Command of John Duke of Marlborough, Captain General of Our Land Forces, a Signal and Glorious Victory over the French and Bavarian Forces at Blenheim near Hockstet in Germany; And therefore duly considering that such great and publick Blessings do call for Publick and Solemn Acknowledgments, We have thought fit, by the Advice of Our Privy Council, to issue out this Our Royal Proclamation, hereby appointing and Commanding, That a General Thanksgiving to Almighty God, for these His Mercies, be Observed throughout Our Kingdom of England, Dominion of Wales, and Town of Berwick upon Tweed, upon Thursday the Seventh Day of September next, And for the better and more Religious and Orderly Solemnizing the same, We have given directions to the Arch-bishops and Bishops of this Our Kingdom, to compose a Form of Prayer, suitable to this Occasion, to be used in all Churches and Chapels, and other Places of Publick Worship, and to take care for the timely Dispensing thereof through their respective Dioceses.[35] And We strictly Charge and Command, That the said Publick Day of Thanksgiving be Religiously observed by all Our Loving Subjects, as they tender the Favour of Almighty God, and upon pain of suffering such Punishments, as We may justly Inflict on all such as shall contemn or Neglect the Performance of so Religious and Necessary a Duty.
  Given at Our Court at St James's, the Seventeenth Day of August, 1704. In the Third Year of Our Reign.
  God save the Queen.

Endorsed: 17th August 1704 / Copy Proclamation for / a Publick Thanksgiving / upon Thursday the 7th of / September next. / (N°. 3.)

5.   Proclamation for a general thanksgiving, 21 May 1706

Porteus papers 17, fos. 159–60

By the Queen A Proclamation for a Public Thanksgiving.
  Anne R.
  We do most devoutfully and thankfully acknowledge the great Goodness and Mercy of Almighty God who has continued to Us his Protection and Assistance in the Just War in which We are now engaged, for the common safety of Our Realms and for disappointing the boundless Ambition of France and hath given to Our Arms in Conjunction with those of Our Allies under the Command of John Duke

---

[35] *A form of prayer and thanksgiving to almighty God: to be used on Thursday the seventh of September next … for the late glorious victory obtained over the French and Bavarians at Bleinheim near Hochstet, on Wednesday the second of August, by the forces of her majesty and her allies, under the command of the duke of Marlborough …* (London, 1704).

of Marlborough Captain General of Our Land Forces A signal and glorious Victory in Brabant over the French Army and hath restored the greatest part of the Spanish Netherlands to the Possession of the House of Austria in the Person of King Charles the Third[36] by the happy and Wonderful progress of the Confederate Forces, and has also blessed the Arms of Us and those of Our Allies with great Successes in Catalonia and other parts of Spain And therefore duly Considering that such great and Publick Blessings do call for Publick and solemn Acknowledgments, We have thought fit by the Advice of Our Privy Council to issue Out this Our Royal Proclamation hereby appointing and Commanding that a general Thanksgiving to Almighty God for these his Mercys be observed throughout Our Kingdom of England, Dominion of Wales and Town of Berwick upon Tweed upon Thursday the twenty seventh day of June next, and for the better and more religious Orderly solemnizing the same, We have given Directions to the Arch-Bishops and Bishops of this Our Kingdom to Compose a Form of Prayer suitable to this occasion, to be used in all Churches and Chapels and other Places of Public Worship[37] and to take care of the timely dispersing thereof through their respective Dioceses And We do strictly Charge and Command that the said Publick Day of thanksgiving be religiously Observed by all Our Loving Subjects as they tender the favour of Almighty God and upon pain of suffering such Punishments as We may justly inflict on all such as shall condemn [*sic*] or Neglect the performance of so religious and necessary a Duty.

Given at Our Court at Kensington the twenty first Day of May One thousand seven hundred and six, in the Fifth Year of Our Reign.

God save the Queen.

Endorsed: 21st May 1706 / Copy Proclamation for / a Publick Thanksgiving / on Thursday the 27th of / June next. / (N[o.] 4)

6.   Account of thanksgiving taken from the *London Gazette*, 27 June 1706[38]

Porteus papers 17, fos. 161–6

S[t.] James's June 27th 1706.

This day being appointed by Her Majesty's Proclamation to be observed throughout this Kingdom as a Day of Publick Thanksgiving to Almighty God, for his great Goodness in giving to Her Majesty's Arms, in Conjunction with those of Her Allies, under the Command of his Grace the Duke of Marlborough, a Signal and Glorious Victory in Brabant over the French Army, and in restoring the greatest Part of the Spanish Netherlands to the Possession of the House of Austria, in the Person of King Charles the Third; by the happy and wonderfull Progress of the Confederate Forces; and also in blessing the Arms of Her Majesty and Her Allies with great Successes in Catalonia, and other parts of Spain: Her Majesty went to the Cathedral Church of S[t.] Paul's with great Solemnity, to return Thanks to God for these his signal Mercies and Blessings.

---

36 The title given to the Habsburg claimant to the throne of Spain.
37 *A form of prayer and thanksgiving to almighty God: to be used on Thursday the twenty seventh of June next ... for having given to the arms of her majesty, in conjunction with those of her allies, under the command of John duke of Marlborough, a signal and glorious victory in Brabant, over the French army ...* (London, 1706).
38 *London Gazette*, 4240 (27 June – 1 July 1706).

Most of the Lords and Privy Councellors that were in and about the Town met between 9 and 10 in the Morning in the Council Chamber at St James's, the Knights of the most Noble Order of the Garter wearing the Collars of the said Order; and having been marshalled by the Officers of Arms, proceeded about 11 o'clock in their Coaches with Six Horses each towards St Pauls.

Her Majesty came afterwards attended in the following manner: First the Knight Marshal with his Men on Horseback; then the Equeries and Gentleman-Ushers to His Royal Highness in his leading-coach; the Right Honorable the Lord Chamberlain's Coach: One Equery, two Pages of Honour and the Gentleman Usher in Waiting, in her Majesty's Leading Coach: In another of Her Majesty's Coaches, the Women of the Bed-Chamber to Her Majesty: In another the Maids of Honour: His Royal Highness's Body-Coach, with the Lords of His Bed-Chamber: The Ladies of Her Majesty's Bed-Chamber in Two of Her Majesty's Coaches: The Duke of Somerset Master of the Horse, with the Duke of Ormond the Captain of the Guards in Waiting, in Her Majesty's Body Chariot; each drawn by Six Horses: A Detachment of the Horse Gernadiers: Her Majesty's Footmen: After them the Yeomen of the Guard on Foot, some before and some on each side of Her Majesty's Coach: Then Her Majesty, the Dutchess of Marlborough, Grome of the Stole, and the Countess Dowager of Burlington, being the Lady of the Bed-Chamber in Waiting in the Coach of State drawn by Eight Horses, Her Majesty's Third Troop of Horse Guards, closed the Procession.

The Streets through which Her Majesty passed were lined from St James's as far as Temple Bar by the Militia of Westminster; from thence to St Paul's they were railed and Hung with Blue Cloth, the City Trained-Bands lining both sides; and upon Scaffolds erected for that purpose were placed the several Companies in their Gowns, with their respective Flags, Streamers and Musick. A Battalion of Her Majesty's two Regiments of Foot-Guards made a Lane from the West Entrance into the Church to the Door of the Choir. The Balconies and the Windows of the Houses were hung with Carpets and Rich Tapestry, and Crouded with great Numbers of Spectators.

At Temple Bar her Majesty was met by Sir Thomas Rawlinson, Lord Mayor of the City of London,[39] who was Robed with a very Rich Crimson Velvet Gown and wore the City-Collar of S S and Jewel, He was attended by the Aldermen and Sheriffs in Scarlet Gowns, being all on Horseback and by the principal Officers on Foot in Their Formalities who were led up by the City Marshal – When Her Majesty entered the Gate, His Lordship alighted and congratulating Her Majesty's comming into Her most Loyal City of London upon this happy Occasion, he presented to Her Majesty the City Pearl Sword; which She was graciously pleased to return to him; And then his Lordship mounted again, and carried the sword bare Headed before Her Majesty (the Aldermen and Sheriffs riding before him to the Church, where the City sword bearer received it from His Lordship[)].

Her Majesty being come to St Pauls was received at the West Door at Her Alighting out of the Coach, by the Lord Bishop of London in his Robes, and by the Residentiaries and Prebendaries of the Church in their Habits, and was met by the great Officers of State, The Nobility and Privy Councellors, who from thence

[39] Sir Thomas Rawlinson (d. 1709), alderman 1686–7, 1696–1708; lord mayor 1705–6. Alfred B. Beaven, *The aldermen of the City of London* (2 vols., London, 1908–13), II, 111.

proceeded to the Choir in the following Order; First the Officers of Arms then the Privy Councellors who are not Peers two and two; The Peers Temporal and Spiritual two and two; Norroy King of Arms; The Great Officers of State; And Lord Arch-Bishop of Canterbury; The Serjants at Arms with their Maces; Garter King of Arms; and a Gentleman Usher; The Duke of Northumberland with the Sword of State, the Right Honble Perigrine Bertie Esq. Vice Chamberlain of Her Majesty's Household being on His Graces Right Hand; Her Majesty was led by the Right Honble the Earl of Kent, Lord Chamberlain of Her Household, and was followed by the Dutchess of Marlborough, and the Countess Dowager of Burlington; The Duke of Ormond Capt[n] of the Guards and the Duke of S[t.] Albans at the Head of the Band of Gentlemen Pentioners, closed the Procession.

Her Majesty being entered into the Choir, assended a Throne erected at the West End thereof, opposite to the altar, were after her private Devotions, She Seated herself in an armed Chair. Behind Her Majesty were stools for two the Ladies of the Bed-Chamber, and the Great Officers in Waiting attending Her Majesty. The Peers and Privy Councellors were placed on the North Side of the Choir; The Ladies of the Bed Chamber in the Stalls on the South side; and the Maids of Honor and Her Majesty's Bed Chamber Women below them; The Peeresses were placed at the west end of the middle Gallary; and the Foreign Ministers with their Ladies filled the Places prepared for them in the middle Gallary on the same side with the Peers, At the East End of that Gallary were seated the Lady Mayoress and Aldermens Ladies; and at the East End of the South side the Lord Mayor Aldermen and Sheriffs. The rest of the Gallarys were filled by the Ladies and other Persons of Quality that attended at this Solemnity. The Bishop of London sat on his Throne next to the Altar, and the Residentiaries and Prebendaries sat within the Rails of the Altar, except such as Officiated in reading Prayers. The Rev[d.] Doctor Stanhope[40] Dean of Canterbury, Preached.[41] The Hymn, Te Deum with other Anthems were admirably well performed by Her Majesty's Choir & Musick.

Divine Service being ended Her Majesty returned to S[t.] James's in the same Order and State, that she came, The Two Sheriffs riding before her bare Headed to Temple Bar. The Great Guns of the Tower, those upon the River and the Train in S[t.] James's Park, were thrice Discharged, the first time when Her Majesty took Coach at S[t.] James's, the Second at the singing of Te Deum, and the Third when Her Majesty came back to Her Palace.

In the Citys of London and Westminster there were Bonfires Illuminations, Ringing of Bells and all other Demonstrations of Loyalty and Affection to Her Majesty's Person and Government, and of the publick Joy upon so Glorious and happy an Occasion.

Endorsed: 1706. / Extract from the / Gazette – / (No 5)

---

[40] George Stanhope (1660–1728); educ. King's College, Cambridge; chaplain in ordinary to William and Mary, Anne and George I; dean of Canterbury 1704–28.

[41] George Stanhope, *A sermon preach'd before the queen at the cathedral church of S. Paul, London, the xxviith day of June MDCCVI. Being the day appointed for a general thanksgiving to almighty God for success to her majesty's arms in Flanders and Spain, &c.* (London, 1706).

7.   Account of thanksgiving taken from the *London Gazette*, 1 May 1707[42]

Porteus papers 17, fos. 167–8

Whitehall. May 1st 1707

This being the Day appointed for the general Thanksgiving for the happy Union of the Kingdoms of England and Scotland, Her Majesty went in a Coach of State to the Cathedral Church of S[t.] Paul attended by a Magnificent Appearance of the Nobility and Gentry of each Nation, to return Thanks to Almighty God for that great Blessing.

The Streets were lined from S[t.] James's to Temple Bar by the Militia of Westminster; from thence to S[t.] Pauls by the City Trained Bands, the several Companies in their Gowns being placed on Scaffolds erected for that purpose; and a Battalion of Her Majesty's Two Regiments of Foot Guards made a Lane from the entrance into the Church to the Choir. The Balconies and Windows of the Houses were hung with Tapestry, and Crouded with Multitudes of Spectators.

Her Majesty was met at Temple Bar by the Lord Mayor[43] and Aldermen in their Formalities; The Lord Mayor presented to Her Majesty the City Sword, which the Queen being graciously pleased to return to Him, he carried it before her Majesty to the Church.

Her Majesty was received at the entrance into the Church by the Peers; The Sword of State was carried before Her Majesty by the Earl of Seafield. The Lord Bishop of Oxford Preached;[44] and the Te Deum, with proper Anthems, was Sung by Her Majesty's Choir.

Divine Service being ended, Her Majesty returned to S[t.] James's, The Great Guns of the Tower and those of S[t.] James's Park were thrice discharged; the first time when Her Majesty parted from S[t.] James's the second at the Singing the Te Deum, & the third when Her Majesty came back to Her Palace.

The Publick Demonstrations of Joy were suitable to so great an Occasion, and the Day was concluded with Bonfires, Illuminations, and all other Expressions of a General Satisfaction.

Endorsed: 1707. / Extract from the / Gazette / (N[o] 6)

8.   Preamble to the proclamation for a general thanksgiving, 26 September 1710

Moore papers 6, fos. 97–8

26th Sept[r] 1710

At the Court at Kensington

By the Queen, A Proclamation for a Publick Thanksgiving

Whereas it hath pleased Almighty God of His Great Goodness and Mercy to Continue to Us his Protection and Assistance in the just and necessary War, in which

---

[42] *London Gazette*, 4328 (1–5 May 1707).

[43] Sir Robert Bedingfeld (d. 1711), alderman 1697–1711; MP for Hedon 1701. Beaven, *Aldermen of London*, II, 119.

[44] William Talbot, *A sermon preach'd before the queen at the cathedral church of St. Paul, on May the first, 1707. Being the day appointed by her majesty for a general thanksgiving for the happy union of the two kingdoms of England and Scotland* (London, 1707).

We are Engaged for the Safety of Our Realms, and of the Liberty's of Europe, by giving to Our Arms, in Conjunction with those of Our Allies, a wonderfull Course of success this Campaign and more particularly a signal and glorious Victory in Spain:[45] We therefore duly Considering, That such great and publick Blessings do call for a solemn and publick Acknowledgment have thought fitt by the Advice of Our Privy Council to issue forth this Our Royal Proclamation, hereby Appointing and Commanding That a General Thanksgiving to Almighty God, for these his Mercys be Observed throughout England, Wales and Town of Berwick upon Tweed upon Tuesday the 7th Day of Nov[r] next:

Endorsed: 26th September 1710 / Preamble of a Proclamation / for a General Thanksgiving

9. Proclamation for a general thanksgiving, 6 December 1714[46]

Porteus papers 17, fos. 169–70

By the King A Proclamation For a Publick Thanksgiving
    George R.

    Whereas We have received an humble Application from the Arch Bishops and Bishops of England, that a Day may be appointed for a Public Thanksgiving, to Almighty God for his great Goodness in bringing Us to a Peacable and quiet Possession of the Throne of Great Britain, and thereby disappointing the Designs of the Pretender, and the wicked Countrivances of his adherents to defeat Us of Our undoubted Right to the imperial Crown of this Realm and to subvert the establisht Constitution in Church and State; We being well pleased with this Instance of the good Affections of Our People and deeply Sensible of this Signal Providence of God which calls for the most thankfull and solemn Acknowledgements both from Us and Our Subjects, have thought fit by the Advice of Our Privy Council, to issue this Our Royal Proclamation hereby appointing and Commanding that a general Thanksgiving to Almighty God, for these His Mercys be Observed throughout England, Wales and the Town of Berwick upon Tweed on Thursday the Twentieth Day of January next. And for the better and more Orderly Solemnizing the same, We have given Directions to the most Reverend The Arch-Bishops and Right Reverend the Bishops of England, to Compose a Form of Prayer,[47] suitable to this Occasion to be used in all Churches and Chapels, and other places of Public Worship, and to take care for the timely dispersing of the same, throughout their respective Dioceses. And We do strictly Charge and Command, That the said Public Day of Thanksgiving be Religiously Observed by All Our loving Subjects as they tender the favour of

---

45 The 1710 campaign witnessed the fall of Douai and Béthune in Flanders. In Spain Stanhope's defeat of the Spanish at Saragossa was followed by the temporary occupation of Madrid. The former were probably not specifically mentioned because of the hostility of Robert Harley's tory ministry to the duke of Marlborough.

46 Another copy of the preamble to the proclamation is preserved in Moore papers 6, fos. 99–100. On this copy it is noted: 'The King went to S[t] Pauls on the day of Thanksgiving.' Moore endorsed his copy as having been received from Mr Fawkener, for whom see below, n. 165.

47 *A form of prayer and thanksgiving to almighty God; to be used ... on Thursday the twentieth day of January next, for bringing his majesty to a peaceable and quiet possession of the throne, and thereby disappointing the designs of the Pretender, and all his adherents ...* (London, 1714).

Almighty God and upon pain of suffering such Punishment, as We can justly Inflict upon all such who shall contemn or Neglect the same.

Given at Our Court at S[t.] James's the sixth Day of December One thousand seven hundred and fourteen in the first Year of Our Reign.

God save the King.

Endorsed: 6th Dec[r]: 1714 / Copy Proclamation / for a General / Thanksgiving on / Thursday the 20th / Day of Jan[ry] next, / for the Kings happy / accession to the / Throne. / N[o.] 7.

10. Account of the general thanksgiving, 22 January 1715

Porteus papers 17, fos. 171–2

St James's Jan[ry] 22[d] 1714.

Thursday last being the Day appointed for a general Thanksgiving to Almighty God for the King's happy and Peaceable Accession to the Throne His Majesty with their Royal Highnesses the Prince and Princess of Wales attended by the Chief Officers of State, and others of the Nobility, was pleased to go from hence to the Cathedral Church of S[t.] Paul where after the Divine Service appointed for the Occasion a Sermon was preached by the Lord Bishop of Gloucester.[48] The Lord Mayor[49] and Court of Aldermen of London gave their Attendance in the accustomed Manner: The City Companies in their Liveries were in their respective Stands, the Streets being lined by the Militia: The Guns in the Park were fired on a Signal at the singing of Te Deum in the Cathedral as they were all at His Majesty's setting out from and return to His Palace: And at Night there were Illuminations, Bonfires & other public Demonstrations of Joy.

Endorsed: 1714. / Extract from the / Gazette.[50] / No. 8.

11. Memorandum of proclamations for public thanksgivings

Porteus papers 17, fos. 142–4

Memorandum of Proclamations for Publick Thanksgivings.

King Charles the 2nd

14th June 1665.   Proclamation for a general Thanksgiving for a happy Victory over His Majesty's Adversaries at Sea, in London &c[a] 20th of June – the rest of the Realm 4th of July.

N.B. The Gazette not being published until Nov[r] 1665 we have no means of knowing whether the King went in person to S[t] Pauls.[51]

---

48 Richard Willis, *The way to stable and quiet times: a sermon preach'd before the king at the cathedral church of St Paul, London, on the 20th of January 1714. Being the day of thanksgiving to almighty God for bringing his majesty to a peaceable and quiet possession of the throne, and thereby disappointing the designs of the Pretender, and all his adherents* (London, 1715).

49 Sir William Humfreys (d. 1735), alderman 1707–33, 1733–5; director of the Bank of England. Beaven, *Aldermen of London*, II, 121.

50 *London Gazette*, 5296 (18–22 Jan. 1715).

51 There is no evidence that the king went to St Paul's.

6th Augt. 1666.   Proclamation for a General Thanksgiving for the late Victory by His Majesty's Naval Forces against the Dutch.

It appears by the Gazette[52] That His Majesty did not go to St Pauls, but a Sermon was preached before him at Whitehall, which was afterwards published by His Majesty's Order.[53]

King James 2nd – Nil

King William

There are seven Instances of Proclamations for a Day of Thanksgiving during his Reign, but It does not appear by the Gazette, that the King ever went to St Pauls.[54]

Queen Anne

3d Nov 1702.   Proclamation issued for a General Thanksgiving for the Success of the Arms of Her Majesty and Her Allies, on Thursday the 12th of November – and in all other places on Thursday the 3rd of December. Vide Copy No. 1.

On Thursday the 12th of November The Queen went to St Pauls – Vide Account of the Procession &c copied from the Gazette[55] – No. 2.

17th Augt. 1704.   Proclamation issued for a General Thanksgiving on Thursday the 7th day of September next for the Victory at Blenheim in Germany. Vide Copy No 3.

On Thursday the 7th of Septr. Her Majesty went to St Pauls. The Ceremony of the Procession &c is in the Gazette[56] but not copied out being similar to the former.

20th July 1705.   Proclamation issued for a General Thanksgiving on Thursday the 23d of August for the Victory in the Spanish Netherlands.[57]

On Thursday the 23d of Augt. Her Majesty went to St Pauls. The Gazette account of the Procession[58] being much the same as that in 1702 is not coppied.

21st May 1706.   Proclamation issued for a General Thanksgiving for the Victory in Brabant and great Successes in Catalonia on Thursday the 27th of June. Vide Copy No. 4.

---

52 *London Gazette*, 79 (13–16 Aug. 1666).
53 John Dolben, *A sermon preached before the king, Aug. 14. 1666. Being the day of thanksgiving for the late victory at sea* (London, 1666).
54 The days of thanksgiving were 31 Jan. 1689, 19 Oct. 1690, 26 Nov. 1691, 27 Oct. 1692, 12 Nov. 1693, 29 Aug. 1695 and 2 Dec. 1697. The dates given are those on which the thanksgiving was ordered in London; on some occasions it took place later through the rest of the kingdom.
55 *London Gazette*, 3862 (12–16 Nov. 1702).
56 *Ibid.*, 4052 (7–11 Sept. 1704).
57 *Ibid.*, 4143 (23–6 July 1705).
58 *Ibid.*, 4152 (23–7 Aug. 1705).

On Thursday the 27th of June Her Majesty went to St Pauls. The Gazette account of the Procession;[59] vide Copy N°. 5.

19th Novr. 1706. Proclamation issued for a General Thanksgiving for the great and wonderful Successes of Her Majesty's Arms in this Year on Tuesday the 31st of December next.[60]

On which day Her Majesty went to St. Pauls – the Gazette Account[61] not Copied being almost similar.

27th March 1707. Proclamation issued for a Publick Thanksgiving upon the happy Union of the Kingdoms of England and Scotland on the 1st of May next ensuing.[62]

On which day the Queen went to St. Pauls – The Account in the Gazette[63] of the Proceedings upon this Occasion are Copied – Vide N°. 6.

N.B. Subsequent to the Union There has been two Proclamations one for England and one for Scotland – generally both on the same Day, but sometimes not.

A Copy of the Proclamation has also been transmitted to Ireland.

18th May 1713. Two Proclamations issued for a Publick Thanksgiving in England and Scotland upon the Peace with the French King, on Tuesday the 16th of June then next.[64]

8th June Proclamation for enlarging the Time for the Thanksgiving in England to Tuesday the 7th of July.[65]

The Queen being ill did not go to St. Pauls.

King George 1st.

6th Decr. 1714. Two Proclamations issued for a Publick Thanksgiving in England and Scotland upon the Kings accession to the Throne of Great Britain on Thursday the Twentieth day of January then next.[66] Vide Copy of the Proclamation for England N°. 7.

On the 20th of January the King went to St. Pauls – Vide the Account given in the Gazette[67] upon this Occasion – Copy N°. 8.

Endorsed: N°. 9 / Memdum. / of Proclamations issued / for Publick Thanksgivings / also of Entries in the / Gazette.

---

[59] *Ibid.*, 4240 (27 June – 1 July 1706).
[60] *Ibid.*, 4281 (18–21 Nov. 1706).
[61] *Ibid.*, 4293 (30 Dec. 1706 – 2 Jan. 1707).
[62] *Ibid.*, 4319 (31 Mar. – 3 Apr. 1707).
[63] *Ibid.*, 4328 (1–5 May 1707).
[64] *Ibid.*, 5122 (19–23 May 1713).
[65] *Ibid.*, 5128 (9–13 June 1713).
[66] See above pp. 238–9. *London Gazette*, 5283 (4–7 Dec. 1714).
[67] *Ibid.*, 5296 (18–22 Jan. 1715).

12. Extracts from the Journals of the House of Lords, November 1702

Porteus papers 17, fos. 149–152v

Die Mercurii. 4⁰· Novem^ris· 1702.

The Lord Chamberlain (by Her Majesty's Command) acquainted the House that Her Majesty had appointed Thursday the 12th Ins^t. to be observed in London and Westminster as a Day of Publick Thanksgiving to Almighty God on Occasion of the great Successes of Her Majesty's Arms and those of Her Allies and particularly that of Her Troops under the Conduct of the Earl of Marlborough that of the Forces under the Command of the Duke of Ormond at Vigo, and also for the extraordinary Success of the Fleet under the Command of Sr George Rooke And for the greater Solemnity on that Day Her Majesty will be pleased to go to St Paul's Church as has been accustomed in former Times in this Kingdom to return Thanks to Almighty God for the signal and great Success in which not only Her Majesty but all Her Subjects are so highly concerned.

Whereupon it was ordered that this House do attend Her Majesty to St Paul's Church on Thursday the 12 Instant being the Day appointed for a Publick Thanksgiving.

Then Sr Christopher Wren[68] Her Majesty's Surveyor of the Works attending (by Her Majesty's Command) was called in and ordered that convenient Places be provided in St Paul's Church on the Day of Thanksgiving for Eighty Lords not to be mixed with others, and that He attend this House on Friday next to given [*sic*] an Account of what he hath done in Order thereunto.[69]

Die Veneris 6° Novemb^ris 1702.

It is ordered by the Lords Spiritual and Temporal in Parliament assembled That the Earl of Manchester, the Earl of Abingdon, and the Lord Viscount Longueville do go to St Paul's Church and see what Accommodation there is for the Lords of this House to sit there and report to this House at 11 o clock in the Forenoon.[70]

Die Sabbati 7° Novem^ris 1702.

It is Ordered by the Lords Spiritual and Temporal in Parliament assembled That the Herald's and Marshal's Men do attend this House on Thursday the 12th Instant at Ten o clock in the Forenoon.

Ordered by the Lords Spiritual & Temporal in Parliament assembled That no Lord of this House shall go to St Paul's Church with more than Two Horses to his Coach the 12th Instant.[71]

Die Martis 10th Novem^ris 1702.

Ordered by the Lords Spiritual & Temporal in Parliament assembled That Sr Christopher Wren do prepare a Place for the Lords to sit in St Paul's Church agreeable (As near as may be) to the Method of their Lordships sitting in this House.[72]

---

[68] Sir Christopher Wren (1632–1703) held the post of surveyor of the king's works between 1669 and 1715.

[69] *Journals of the House of Lords*, XVII, p. 160.

[70] *Ibid.*, p. 161.

[71] *Ibid.*, pp. 161–2.

[72] *Ibid.*, p. 163.

Die Mercurii 11° Novem^ris 1702.

It is ordered by the Lords Spiritual & Temporal in Parliament assembled That the High Steward of the City of Westminster or his Deputy, together with the Justices of Peace of the said City shall by their Care and Directions to the Constables and other Officers within the said Limits take special Order that no Hackney Coaches be suffered to make any Stay between the Old Palace Yard at Westminster & Temple Bar from Eight o Clock Tomorrow in the Forenoon to Six o clock in the Afternoon of the same Day and that no Carriages Carts or Drays be permitted to pass through any of the Streets between the Old Palace Yard Westminster, and Temple Bar between the Hours aforesaid Tomorrow and herein especial Care is to be taken by the High Steward Deputy Steward and Justices of the Peace as the contrary will be answered to this House.

It is ordered by the Lords Spiritual and Temporal in Parliament assembled That the Lord Keeper of the Great Seal of England do write to the Lord Mayor of the City of London[73] to give Order and take Care to prevent any Stoppages between Temple Bar and the Old Exchange in London Tomorrow from Eight of the Clock in the Forenoon to Six o clock in the Afternoon and that no Carts or Drays be permitted to pass through the Streets between the Hours aforesaid.

It being proposed that the Lords go to S^t. Paul's without their Robes, and Debate thereupon

The Question was put Whether this House shall go in Their Robes Tomorrow to S^t. Pauls's

It was resolved in the Affirmative.

Ordered by the Lords Spiritual and Temporal in Parliament assembled That all the Lords do go in their Robes to S^t. Pauls Church.

Ordered that the Gentleman Usher or his Deputy the Yeoman Usher & Doorkeepers do attend at S^t. Paul's Church Tomorrow.

Ordered That the Orders of this House for the Stalls in S^t. Paul's Church to be kept for this House shall be vacated.

Ordered That the House shall be summoned to attend here Tomorrow at Eight o clock and each Lord acquainted 'That the Lords are to be in their Robes'.

Ordered that the Lords Coaches shall go in the same Places they are called.

Ordered that one Herald and the Marshal's Men attend this House Tomorrow at Eight o clock, and that the Marshal's Men do call the Coaches as directed by the House.[74]

Die Jovis 12 Novem^ris 1702.

Prayers

The House being met in Order to their Proceeding to attend Her Majesty in the Solemnity of the Publick Thanksgiving at S^t. Paul's Church.[75]

Endorsed: N°. 10 / House of Lords / Extract from Journals / Nov 4 1702

---

[73] Sir Samuel Dashwood (d. 1705), alderman 1683–7, 1688–1705; MP for the City of London 1685–7, 1690–5; lord mayor 1702–3. Beaven, *Aldermen of London*, II, 109.
[74] *Ibid.*, p. 164.
[75] *Ibid.*

13. The lords of the council to the bishop of London and dean and chapter of St Paul's, 21 March 1620

Porteus papers 17, fos. 138–9

Whitehall 21st March 1619.

A Lre to the Lo: Bp of London and the Deane and Chapter of the Cathedral Church of St Paule.

Whereas His Majesty out of a religious Zeale to Pietie and Godliness and to stir up others by his Princely example to the Service of God this tyme of Lent, hath a purpose to repaire to that Cathedrall Church of St Paule on Sunday next there to heare a Sermon;[76] And that We are informed that by the West Gate of the Church where the King is to enter there stand two Houses the one a Tippling House and the other a Tobacco House belonging to one Wheatley and one Batchelor; His Majesty hath Commanded us hereby to will and require yr Lop. &ca. presently upon receipt hereof to cause the said two houses to be forthwith prostrated and pulled down to the ground and the Sellers and Vaults filled up, that there be no signe lefte remaining of any such Houses or Vaults there, which his Majesty's expresse pleasure and Command Yor Lp. &ca are to see fully executed and performed. And so &ca.

Endorsed: No. 11 / 21st March 1619 / Copy. / Entry of a Letter / from the Lords of the / Council to the Lord / Bishop of London &a of / The King's intention / of going to St Pauls −

14. Order of the royal procession, 26 March 1620

Porteus papers 17, fo. 140

The Kings Procession to St Pauls 26th March 1620

Messengers of the Chamber	Gentln of the privy Chamr & Bed Chamr in Ordinary
Gentlemen Harbingers, Serjt Porters	Knights of the Bath
Gentn Esqrs The Princes Servts	Knights Embassrs, Ld Presidt & Deputy
Gentn Esqrs The Kings Servts	Vice Admiral & Knt Marshal
Servers the Kings servts	Treasurer of the Excheqr & Masr of the Jewel H[ouse]
Quarter Waiters	Baronets
Gentn Ushers Daily Waiters	Barons Youngr Sons Viscompts Youngr Sons
Clerks of the Signet	Judges of the Coife
Clerks of the Privy Seal	Chief Baron of the Exchr & Ch. Justice of the Comn Pleas
Clerks of the Council	Master of the Rolls & Ch. Justice of the Ks Bench
Clerks of the Parliamt	Chancr of the Dutchy & Chancr & undr Treasr of the Excehqr
Clerks of the Crown	Master of the Wards. Officers of Armes
Chaplains having Dignity (as Deans &c)	Knights privy Councillrs
Aldermen of London	Knights of the Garter
Princes Council at Law	Barons Eldest sons: Earls Youngr Sons
Kings Advocate & Remembrancer	Viscts Eldest Sons. Barons of the Parliamt
Kings Attorney & Solliciter, Genl	Bishops

---

[76] John King, *A sermon at Paules Crosse, on behalfe of Paules church, March 26. 1620 ... Both preached and published by his majesties commandement* (London, 1620).

Serjeants at Law	Marquesses Young^r Sons. Earls Eldest Sons.
King Serjeant	Visc^{ts} – Dukes Young^r Sons –
Masters in Chancery	Marquesses Eldest Sons. Marquesses.
Knights Batchellors	Dukes – Lord Privy Seal
Secret^y of the French & Latin Tongues	Clarenceux Norroy
Esq^{rs} of the Body	Lord Chancel^r, Ld A.B^p of Canterbury
Sewers in Ordinary	
Carvers in Ordinary	Gent^n {Gart^r princ^l { Lord Mayor
Cupbearers in Ordinary	Ushers {King at Arms {

	{Tents	
Masters of	{Revels	
Standing Offices	{Armory	The Prince Serjeants at Arms
	{Wardrobe	
	{Ordinance	The Sword Carried by the Earl of —
Master of Requests		
Chamberlains of the Exchequer		
Trumpets.		The Kings Majestie

Master of the Horse leading a spare Horse. Vice
Chamberlain. Cap^n of the Guards. The Guard.
Footmen & Equeries on Each Side. Gent^n Pentioners
with their Axes on Each Side
Finished

Endorsed: King James & / Queen Anne / At St Pauls. 1620 / 1706[77]

15. Order of the royal procession, 31 December 1706

Porteus papers 17, fo. 141

St Pauls.   Thanksgiving 31st December 1706
     The Queen seated in an arm'd Chair upon the Throne (erected near the West End of the Choir) and another arm'd Chair was set on her left hand for Prince George of Denmark, who being indisposed, was not present, behind those Chairs, were stools for the Dutches of Marlborough and the Lady Fretchville Ladies of the Bedchamber in waiting. The Capt of the Guard Lord Chamberlain, Vice Chamberlain and Clerk of the Closet were all upon the Throne.
     The Ladies of the Bedchamber in the seats before the Stalls on the south Side. And the maids of Honour & bed Chamber women below them.
     Garter Principal K. of Arms and the other Hearlds &^{c} with their Maces. And the Gent^n Pensioners with their Axes, waited on either side the Throne.
     And behind stood the Yeomen of the Guards &^{c}
     The Lord Arch Bishop of Canterbury, the Lord Keeper of the Great Seal, Lord Arch Bishop of York, The Great Officers of State, the Dukes, Earls, Viscounts, Bishops, & Barons, sat in the Body of the Choir in the Manner, as they do in the House of Lords, the Judges & Masters in Chancery placed as usual.
     The Speaker of the House of Commons sat in the Lord Mayors Seat, and the

---

[77] Fos. 140 and 141 are part of the same folded sheet of paper. As originally folded, fo. 141 preceded fo. 140.

members on either hand in the Stalls. And also in opposite Stalls and in upper Galerys on both sides the Choir.

The Peeresses sat in the lower Gallery on the south side West, and the Forreign Ministers with their Ladies, in the opposite Gallery north. At the East End, of that Gallery, were seated The Lady Mayoress & the Aldermens Ladies. And opposite on the south side the Lord Mayor, Aldermen, Recorder & Sherriffs.

The Residentiaries, and Preben^rys sat on Chairs with[in] the Rails of the Altar. Except such as officiated in reading prayers – and without the Rails on Forms, on both sides sat other Eminent Divines.

The Choir and other Musicians filled the Organ Gallery and the Returns of the Gallery on Either side.

The Pulpit stood near the Bishop of Londons Throne.

Planning the music

This group of documents is interesting because it reveals that the king's initial vision of the music to be performed at the thanksgiving service in St Paul's was much more ambitious than what took place. It is also worth noting that Porteus took the lead in the discussions with the king, drawing up the key memorandum that finally elicited a decision about the music. One would have expected that a more prominent rôle would have been played by George Pretyman, bishop of Lincoln, who, as dean of St Paul's, was primarily responsible for liturgical arrangements in the cathedral. It is possible that Porteus was acting in his capacity as dean of the chapel royal, though the fact that early proposals for the musical arrangements would almost certainly not have involved the choir of the chapel royal makes this unlikely. A more plausible explanation of the role of Porteus and Richard Hurd, bishop of Worcester, in this exchange is that the king had personally charged them, probably in conjunction with the two archbishops, with the arrangements for the thanksgiving.

16. Note of the music to be performed at St Paul's, 1789

Porteus papers 17, fos. 173–4

Overture of Esther.[78]
Coronation Anthem.[79]
Dettingen Te Deum.[80]
Handel's Jubilate.[81]
Anthem *My Heart is inditing*.[82]

at the end of the Service
Chorus out of Joseph

---

[78] G. F. Handel, *Esther* (1732), HWV 50b.
[79] Probably a reference to Handel's *Zadok the Priest* (1727), HWV 258, but it could refer to any of the four anthems composed for the coronation of George II (HWV 258–61).
[80] Handel, *Dettingen Te Deum* (1743), HWV 283. It seems unlikely that a performance of the whole work was intended.
[81] Presumably a reference to Handel's 'Utrecht' *Jubilate* (1713), HWV 279.
[82] Presumably a reference to Handel's coronation anthem of 1727 (HWV 259), but it is possible that Purcell's 1685 coronation anthem of the same title is intended.

O Lord who in thy Heavenly Hand.[83]

Endorsed: Nᵒ· 12 / Music for / Sᵗ Pauls. / Brought to me / from the King / by Lord Ailesbury[84] / March 15. 1789.

17. Beilby Porteus, Bishop of London, to Lord Ailesbury, 27 March 1789

Porteus papers 17, fo. 175

St James's Square March 27 1789

My Lord

I take the Liberty of Enclosing to your Lp Mʳ Bates's Letter to me respecting the Music at Sᵗ· Pauls. To this I have only to add one remark. It relates to the last Piece of Music selected for the Thanksgiving Day, *The Chorus out of Joseph*. The Words though extremely solemn and devout are not taken either from our Liturgy or from Scripture. And both the Archbishop of Canterbury and myself have our doubts (which we would humbly submit to his Majesty's Consideration) whether any Words should be introduced into the Service of the Church except such as are to be found in the common Prayer-Book, or in the sacred Writings. This seems to be a clear & distinct Line to draw for Church Music. While this Rule is observed there can be no danger of any improper Compositions of this Sort finding their Way into our Service. But should this be departed from, we are apprehensive it may be alledged as a precedent for introducing Words hereafter from other Oratorios which may be far more exceptionable than those very pious & affecting ones from Joseph.

I understand that on consulting The proper Workmen belonging to Sᵗ Pauls, it is thought very practicable to have the Charity Children arranged under the Dome without obstructing their Majesties' Entrance into the Choir. And Orders for that Purpose are, I believe already given.

I have the honour to be, with great respect, My Lord, your Lordship's / Most obeᵗ· & most humble / Servᵗ· B. London.

Endorsed: To / Lord Ailesbury. / Not sent / March 27 1789

18. Memorandum by Beilby Porteus, bishop of London, about the music for the service

Porteus papers 17, fos. 176–9[85]

A few Weeks ago[86] Lord Ailesbury came to the Bishop of London by his Majesty's Directions with a list of certain pieces of Music which his Majesty chose to have performed at Sᵗ Pauls on the Thanksgiving Day, under the Direction of Mʳ Bates; to whom the Bishop[87] was ordered to Communicate his Majesty's Pleasure on that head. The Bishop of London did so: But was informed by Mr Bates first in Conver-

---

83 'O God, in thy heavenly hand' is the short chorus from Handel's oratorio *Joseph* (1743), HWV 59.
84 Thomas Bruce, earl of Ailesbury (1729–1814); lord of the bedchamber to George III; governor to the prince of Wales and Prince Frederick 1776; created earl of Ailesbury 1776; chamberlain to Queen Charlotte 1780–92.
85 This document is read fos. 176r–v, 177r, 178r–v, 177v. Fo. 179 is blank.
86 'ago' interlineated.
87 'of London' deleted.

sation and afterwards by Letter[88] that in order to perform those pieces of Music in a[89] manner suitable to his Majestys Ideas[90] & the dignity of the Occasion it would be necessary to have a new[91] Orchestra at the East End of the Church, a new[92] Organ & a very considerable Band of Performers; And that[93] these preparations would require a full month from the time of beginning them, & would cost at least 3000£.[94] Mr Bates's Letter containing these Particulars the Bishop of London[95] sent to Lord Ailesbury who gave it to the Queen when her Majesty came to the Drawing Room, & the Bishop understood from his Lordship[96] that her Majesty[97] carried it to the King at Windsor. Nothing more passed till the Bishop of London & the Dean of St Pauls[98] presented the address of the London Clergy[99] to his Majesty at Windsor on Monday the 30th of March.[100] The Bishop then supposed that in Consequence of Mr Bates's Letter He & the Dean of St Pauls would have received his Majesty's express Commands respecting the Music, the Band & the Management of them. – But though some Conversation passed on the Subject His Majesty came to no final Decision on those points, but only expressed his[101] resolution to have no new Orchestra or new Organ; & fixed on[102] the 13th Psalm by Crofts[103] for the Anthem.[104] – These circumstances together with the appointment of so early a Day as the 23d of April for the Thanksgiving Day precluded (according to Mr Bates's Idea expressed in the abovementiond Letter) all Possibility of his Majesty's Original Plan being carried into Execution under Mr Bates's direction. His Majesty however did not point out[105] any other Plan, nor any other Pieces of Music in the Room of those first proposed, nor any Person to conduct them. The B of L. & the D. of St Pauls have been waiting till this time for his Majesty's further commands. But not having receivd any they beg leave now most humbly to represent that if his Majesty chuses to have any thing more than the Common Choir Service, it is now on account of

88   'first...Letter' interlineated.
89   'proper' deleted.
90   'Ideas' interlineated over 'Wishes' deleted.
91   'a new' interlineated over 'another' deleted.
92   'a new' interlineated over 'another' deleted.
93   'to make' deleted.
94   'would ... 3000£.' Interlineated over an illegible deleted word and 'a large Sum of money'. '3000£' is followed by another deleted passage: 'The Bishop desired Mr Bates to put down his opinion [illegible word] of Mr Bates's The Bishop.'
95   'of London' interlineated.
96   'from his Lordship' interlineated.
97   'gave it' deleted.
98   Sir George Pretyman (later Tomline) (1750–1827); educ. Pembroke College, Cambridge, matric. 1768, BA 1772, MA 1775, DD 1784; fellow of Pembroke 1773; effectively private secretary to William Pitt 1783; canon of Westminster 1784; bishop of Lincoln and dean of St Paul's 1787–1820; bishop of Winchester 1820–7. ODNB.
99   London Gazette, 13082 (31 Mar. – 4 Apr. 1789), p. 197.
100 A long passage on fos. 176v and 177r has been deleted, the draft continuing on fo. 178r.
101 'intent' deleted.
102 'on' interlineated.
103 William Croft (1678–1727); organist at the chapel royal 1704; organist at Westminster Abbey and composer to Queen Anne 1708. ODNB.
104 'How long wilt thou forget me O Lord?', from Musica sacra: or, select anthems in score (2 vols., London, 1724–5).
105 'point out' interlineated over 'Substitute' deleted.

the near approach of the Day[106] indispensably necessary to settle immediately what Band[107] there should be, what pieces of Music, & who is to direct & Conduct the whole. But if there is to be nothing more than the usual Choir Service it is only requisite for his Majesty to signify his Pleasure What Te Deum & Jubilate he would have performed.

N.B. The Organ Loft is the only Place now left for a Band & it is to be feared (besides the Shortness of the time for Preparation) that it will not contain a sufficiently [sic] Number to perform the Pieces first proposed in a manner that would meet his Majesty's approbation.

Sent to Lord Ailesbury –
(with Letter) April 10 1789 –

Endorsed [fo. 177v]: Nᵒ· 13 / Memorial to / the King respecting / the Music at / Sᵗ Pauls – / April 10. 1789 / Given by me to Lord / Ailesbury, by him to / Bᵖ Hurd, & by him / shown to the King

19. Richard Hurd, bishop of Worcester, to earl of Ailesbury, 12 April 1789

Porteus papers 17, fos. 180–1

Windsor Sunday Apr. 12ᵗʰ 1789

My Lord

When his Majesty had read the inclosed papers last night, he returned them to me & said, He wished to have a good old *Te Deum & Jubilate*. And I understood his Majesty's pleasure to be that I should communicate this answer to your Lordship. Nothing particular was said about Mʳ Gilbert's proposal.[108]

I thank God, their Majesties & R. family are perfectly well.

I have the honour to be, / My Lord, / Your Lordship's most obedient / humble servant / R. Worcester

Addressed: The Earl of Ailesbury / Semour Place / London

Postmarked: '[A]P13 / 89'[109]

Endorsed: No. 14 / Bᵖ· Hurd to / Lord Ailesbury / April 12 1789

Two accounts of the service at St Paul's Cathedral on 25 April 1789

All the newspapers published accounts of the procession, the service at St Paul's and the later celebrations. Most differed slightly, though there was some copying, as is revealed by the re-printing of the Gazette*'s account in* The diary; or, Woodfall's Register. *Porteus preserved two newspapers, highlighting the errors in the 'official' account printed in the* London Gazette.

---

106 'on account…Day' interlineated.
107 'Band' interlineated.
108 Unidentified.
109 Part of the postmark, presumably 'AP', is missing.

20. *The diary; or, Woodfall's Register*, 25, Monday 27 April 1789[110]

Porteus papers 17, fos. 188–9

London Gazette. Saturday April 25.[111]

Whitehall, April 25.

Thursday last being appointed by his Majesty's Proclamation to be observed as a Day of General Thanksgiving to Almighty God for the signal interposition of his good Providence, in removing from his Majesty the late illness with which he had been afflicted, his Majesty was pleased, for the greater solemnity of the day, to go to the Cathedral Church of St. Paul, accompanied by the Queen, their Royal Highnesses the Prince of Wales, the Duke of York, the Princess Royal, the Princess Augusta, the Princess Elizabeth, the Duke of Gloucester, and the Duke of Cumberland, and his Highness Prince William; and attended by both Houses of Parliament, the Great Officers of State, the Judges, and other publick Officers, to return thanks to God for his great mercies and blessings.

The procession was begun at eight o'clock in the morning by the House of Commons, in their coaches, followed by the Speaker, in his state coach. Next came the Masters in Chancery, the Judges, and after them the Peers, in the order of precedency, as they were marshalled by the Officers of Arms at Westminster, the youngest Baron going first, and the Lord Chancellor, in his state-coach, closing this part of the procession. Such of the Peers as were Knights wore the Collars of their respective Orders.

Afterwards came the Royal Family, in order of precedency, with their attendants, escorted by the parties of the Royal Regiment of Horse Guards.

Their Majesties set out from the Queen's Palace soon after ten o'clock, in a coach drawn by eight cream coloured horses (in which were also two of the Ladies of her Majesty's Bed Chamber,) followed by their Royal Highnesses the Princesses, and proceeded through the gate at Stable Yard, along Pall-mall, and through the Strand, amidst the loyal acclamations of a prodigious concourse of people.

The streets were lined, as far as Temple Bar by the brigade of Foot Guards, the grenadier companies of which were posted in St Paul's Church, and in the Churchyard, and patrolled by parties of Horse Guards. The avenues into the streets through which the Procession passed were guarded by the Queen's Light Dragoons. From Temple Bar to the Church the Streets were lined by the Artillery Company and the Militia of the City; the Peace Officers attending both within and without the City to preserve order.

At Temple Bar his Majesty was met by the Lord Mayor, in a gown of crimson velvet.

The Sheriffs in their scarlet gowns, and a Deputation from the Aldermen and common Council, being all on horseback, when the Lord Mayor surrendered the city sword to his Majesty, who having returned it to him, he carried it bare headed before the King to St Paul's.

His Majesty being come to St Paul's, was met at the West door by the Peers,[112] the

---

110 Only the sections of text relating to the thanksgiving have been extracted.

111 *The diary* reprints the account of the procession given in the *London Gazette*, 13090 (21–5 Apr. 1789), 309.

112 'Peers' is underlined in pen and a 'x' has been added in the margin. This indicates an error in the account – the peers had already taken their seats in the cathedral.

Bishop of London, Dean of St Paul's (Bishop of Lincoln) the Canons Residentiary, and the King's and other Officers of Arms, the Band of Gentlemen Pensioners, and the Yeomen of the Guard attending.

The Sword of State was carried before his Majesty by the Marquis of Stafford[113] into the Choir, where the King and Queen placed themselves under a canopy of state, near the West end, opposite to the altar.

The Peers had their seats in the area, as a House of Lords, and the Commons in the stalls.[114] The upper galleries were allotted to the Ladies of her Majesty's Bedchamber, the Maids of Honour, and such other Ladies of distinction as attended on this occasion. The Foreign Ministers were placed in the two lower galleries, next to the Throne; and the Lord-Mayor and Aldermen in the lower galleries near the altar.

The Prayers and Litany were read and chauted [*sic*] by the Minor Canons. The *Te Deum* and Anthems composed for the occasion were[115] sung by the Choir, who were placed in the organ loft, and were joined in the Chorus, as also in the Psalms, by the Charity Children, in number about Six[116] Thousand who were assembled there previous to their Majesties arrival. The Communion Service was read by the Dean and Residentiaries, and the sermon preached by the Lord Bishop of London.

Divine Service being ended, their Majesties returned with the same state to the Queen's Palace at about half an hour after three o'clock. The guns at the Tower and in the Park were fired three times, first upon the King's setting out, secondly at the singing of the *Te Deum*, and thirdly upon his Majesty's return; after which the Brigade of Foot Guards fired a *Feu de Joye* in St James's Park, being drawn up in the front of the Queen's Palace.

The publick demonstrations of joy and loyalty by the inhabitants of London and Westminster, on the occasion of his Majesty's first appearance in publick since his happy recovery, exceeded all expression; and yesterday evening the illuminations in all parts of this metropolis surpassed in splendor and magnificence all former exhibitions.

(This Gazette contains the following Addresses to their Majesties; from the Bishop and Clergy of the diocese of Carlisle; Protestant Bishops and Clergy of Scotland; the Dean, Sub-Dean, &c. of the Chapels Royal; the Loyalist Clergy, late of North America; Synod of Glasgow and Ayr; the Counties of Montgomery, Chester, Hereford, and Wigtown; Marine Society of London; Medical Society of London; Surgeons of London; Patentees and Comedians of Covent Garden Theatre; Vice Presidents and Governors of St George's Hospital; Borough of Macclesfield; Presbytery of Inverness; Town and Borough of Shaftesbury; Boroughs of Congelton, and Midhurst; Debtors in the Castle Goal [*sic*] of Oxford; Burgh of Inverbervie; Borough of Westbury, Borough of Devizes, Wilts; Counties of Armagh and Wicklow; County of the City of Waterford; and High Sheriff and Grand Jury of the County of Wicklow.) …

---

113 Granville Leveson-Gower, first marquess of Stafford, lord privy seal 1784–94.
114 'and the Commons in the stalls' is underlined in pen.
115 'composed for the occasion were' is underlined in pen and a 'x' has been added in the margin.
116 'Six' is underlined in pen. This probably indicates an error; the account in *The Times* stated 5,000. See below, p. 257.

ON *HIS MAJESTY'S Happy Recovery and Appearance in Public at St* PAUL's, *on the 23d of April,* 1789.

> SEE the best of King's returns,
> Ev'ry heart with rapture burns!
> Heav'n as our only friend,
> Sav'd him from a better end;
> You directed all his ways,
> Let us now our voices raise.
> Subjects happy – blest – and free,
> All unite in praising thee!
> Favour'd nation! People blest!
> Late unhappy and distress'd,
> Banish all your anxious care,
> GEORGE the Third, we now declare,
> Is our lawful King again,
> In his People's hearts to reign!
> Tho' with grief we've been oppress'd,
> Health surrounds the Royal Breast;
> Ev'ry day our joys encrease,
> And our fears are made to cease!
> Subjects shout and huzzas sing
> To the most beloved King!
> See at length Great GEORGE appears,
> Ev'ry face new lustre wears!
> See th' exulting croud surveys
> Britain's pride and Europe's praise;
> Who by Heav'n was design'd,
> Common Patron of Mankind!
> Since Great Britain's best-lov'd Lord
> Is to us again restor'd,
> Guard his life – prolong his reign –
> Give him health devoid of pain:
> All his counsels deign to bless,
> Aid his arms with sure success,
> And assist him to oppose
> All the hopes of home-bred foes!

LORD HEATHFIELD's[117] *ILLUMINATIONS At TURNHAM GREEN*, ON THURSDAY EVENING LAST.

LORD HEATHFIELD exhibited Six large transparencies, the centre one 16 feet by 12, representing Britannia surrounded by Commerce, Plenty, and the Arts, intermixed with groups of dancing children and music, on the right hand of Britannia, is a ship at anchor or safe in port, painted on the stern the George and Charlotte. The whole Illuminated by a blazing sun in its meridian splendor, with the word *Zenith* in the centre, over it the cypher of the King and Queen under an imperial Crown, inscription under the sun, *let your light so shine*. On the right and left, were

---

[117]   George Augustus Eliott, First Baron Heathfield (1717–90); colonel of the First Light Horse 1759–90; governor of Gibraltar 1776–90.

two other transparencies of the same height, but narrower, representing, on one side, Peace, and on the other, Plenty, under the shade dow [*sic*] of a fig tree, with groupes of children regaling on the fruits of the vine, and on one of them a group of children dancing round a garland of flowers wreathed into the cypher of the King and Queen, and at the bottom the motto *under our own fig tree*. His Lordship at the same time gave an ox roasted whole, the fire of which was lighted by a ray from the sun, at the same instant that the whole was set fire to – a match communicated through all the lamps to the fire ball, and to the fire to roast the ox, so that on Lord Heathfield's going out to drink the King's health in some of the porter (of which his Lordship gave a butt away) a Royal salute was fired, and at one touch the whole illuminated. An artillery man by his Lordship's order, fired a Royal salute of 21 rounds which fortunately was so well timed, that his Majesty noticed it. As soon as the rounds were fired, the multitude assembled to eat and drink on the Green, and gave three huzza's.

The illumination had a most striking and brilliant effect, particularly the fire ball, which might be seen at a vast distance in the environs of that neighbourhood, the splendor and brilliancy of it could only be eclipsed by the zeal and loyalty which produced the whole ...

Yesterday morning a vast concourse of people were admitted into St Paul's, at Twopence each, to see the scaffolding erected on account of the King's visit; but they, on seeing a few in the choir viewing the throne on which their Majesties were seated, insisted also on being admitted, which the Verger in waiting could by no means do, not having the Dean's permission to show the choir and throne, these admitted being friends of the head Verger and workmen employed about the Cathedral. Since which, application having been made to the Dean, and he permitting it to be shewn, the same may be viewed this day, at One Shilling each person. – The Verger, whose turn of attendance at the Cathedral being this week, having lost three days, naturally expected the remaining days would be for his own emolument; but this the other Vergers will by no means admit, insisting on its being equally shared, notwithstanding their having had six days clear each.

[118]The soldier-like, intrepid appearance of the *Train Bands*, might have struck terror into the most collected mind. LORD HEATHFIELD seemed astonished: Some were with bayonets, and some without: some with cross-belts, and others with no belts at all: and most of them were so beaten by the populace, that the soldiers were obliged to go to their assistance, and chastise them both.

The *City Militia* yesterday exceeded all bounds of belief. They were overset, and trampled down in all parts from *Temple Bar* to St PAUL's; and had not the regular soldiers taken care of them, not a man of them would have got home safe.

The train'd bands made a most ludicrous appearance, and were rather roughly handled by the mob of Thursday, who pulled the poor fellows by the wig – or the flowing hair – of the little pig-tail – in rather a boisterous manner. This created some confusion; but it did not last long. Many of these city-warriors wore spectacles...

In order to complete our Account of the PROCESSION, *and to give it a Degree of Superiority over what any of our Cotemporaries [sic] can do, we have procured the following exact Disposition of the Inside of the Cathedral, at the Time their*

---

[118]   A cross has been added *here* in ink.

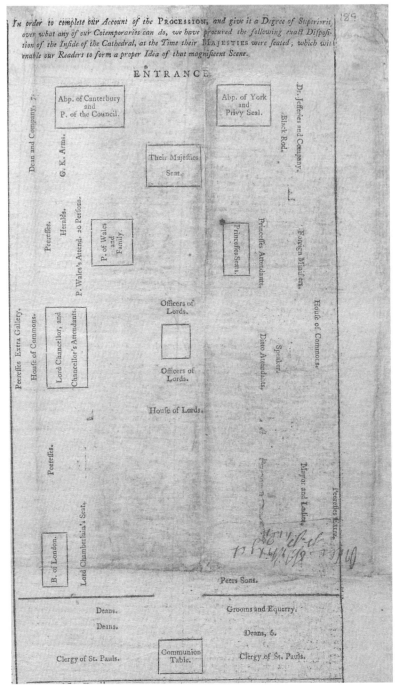

In order to complete our Account of the PROCESSION, and give it a Degree of Superiority over what any of our Cotemporaries can do, we have procured the following exact Disposition of the Inside of the Cathedral, at the Time their MAJESTIES were seated; which will enable our Readers to form a proper Idea of that magnificent Scene.

8 Seating plan of the thanksgiving service for the recovery of George III held at St Paul's Cathedral, 23 April 1789, from *The Diary: or, Woodfall's Register*, 27 April 1789 (LPL, Porteus Papers 17, fo. 189)

MAJESTIES *were seated, which will enable our Readers to form a proper Idea of that magnificent Scene.*

Endorsed: N[o.] 15 / Gazette Account of the / Procession

21. *The Times*, 136, Friday 24 April 1789[119]

Porteus papers 17, fo. 182

… Yesterday his Royal Highness the DUKE of YORK, after his return from St Paul's, gave a grand entertainment to several of the Nobility at York House, Whitehall.

Yesterday at noon the Rev. Dr COURTENAY[120] preached before the Nobility, &c. at the Chapel Royal, St James's.

Yesterday Mr PITT dined with the Bishop of Lincoln[121] at the Deanery, after his return from St Paul's …

ROYAL PUBLIC THANKSGIVING.
TWENTY-THIRD OF APRIL, 1789.

This day will be ever remembered; – it was the day on which the King and his Family went in Procession to St Paul's, to return thanks to the Father of Mercies for that signal blessing which, by restoring him to his people, saved the empire from ruin.

Both Houses of Parliament met at six o'clock in the morning in Palace-Yard, from whence they proceeded in State to receive His Majesty at the Cathedral, in the following

ORDER OF PROCESSION.
MEMBERS of the HOUSE of COMMONS.
The RIGHT HON. MR GRENVILLE, Speaker.
JUDGES.
PEERS.
BISHOPS.
LORD CHANCELLOR,
AND
MARQUIS OF STAFFORD.
DUKE OF CUMBERLAND.

DUKE of GLOUCESTER, with the DUCHESS, PRINCE HENRY, and PRINCESS SOPHIA, preceded by his attendants in a separate carriage.

DUKE of YORK, preceded in like manner.

HIS ROYAL HIGHNESS THE PRINCE OF WALES, in his coach with six gray horses, preceded by another, likewise with six horses.

Royal Family attendants, each coach with six horses, making a Procession of twenty-two carriages, thus:–

---

119   Only the sections of text about the thanksgiving have been extracted.
120   Henry William Courtenay (1741–1803); educ. Christ Church, Oxford, matric. 1759, BA 1763, MA 1766, DCL 1774; prebendary of Exeter 1772–94; prebendary of Rochester 1773–4; rector of St George's, Hanover Square, 1774–1803; chaplain in ordinary to George III; prebendary of Rochester 1783–97; bishop of Bristol 1794–7; bishop of Exeter 1797–1803. *ODNB.*
121   George Pretyman. See above, p. 248 n. 98.

LADIES of the BEDCHAMBER.
MAIDS of HONOUR.
EQUERRIES.
CHAMBERLAIN to the QUEEN.
MASTER of the QUEEN'S HORSE.
The KING'S ATTENDANTS.
LORD CHAMBERLAIN of the HOUSEHOLD.
MASTER of the HORSE to the KING.
A PARTY of the HORSE GUARDS.
HIS MAJESTY and the QUEEN, attended by the LADIES HOLDERNESS and
EGREMONT, in his carriage, drawn by eight cream coloured horses, decorated
with blue ribbons.
PARTY of the HORSE GUARDS.
LADIES attendants on the PRINCESSES.
PARTY of the HORSE GUARDS.
The PRINCESSES ROYAL, AUGUSTA, and ELIZABETH, in a coach and six, attended by
one of the Ladies of Honour.
Another PARTY of HORSE GUARDS closed the Procession into the City,
TEMPLE BAR.

At 10 o'clock, the Lord Mayor,[122] attended by the Sheriffs and four Common
Council, arrived near Temple Bar, where they waited for the Royal Family, in the
House of Messrs Hoare and Co. The Lord Mayor came in his private coach, – the
Sheriffs in their state chariots: attendants were in waiting with their horses, which
were most beautifully caparisoned, and decorated with blue and white ribbons.

On the approach of the Royal Family being announced, the Lord Mayor and
Sheriffs mounted their horses at Temple Bar, and on the arrival of the Royal Family,
the Lord Mayor complimented each as they passed, congratulating them on their
entrance into the City.

On the King's entrance under Temple Bar, the Lord Mayor dismounted, and in
a bending posture presented his Majesty with the City Sword of State, through the
window of his coach, which the King very graciously received, and returned.

The procession was here interrupted for a considerable time, and their Majesties
waited under the gateway upwards of a quarter of an hour.

From thence the procession was increased by the artillery company, the company
of Troxophilites,[123] and the city officers on foot, who preceeded [sic] the Royal
Family. The four Gentlemen of the Common Council; the two Sheriffs, and the Lord
Mayor rode immediately before their Majesty's carriage.

In this order they proceeded to
THE ENTRANCE OF ST PAULS.
where the arrival of their MAJESTIES being announced by a discharge of the Tower
guns, they were preceded first by the Committee appointed to meet them at Temple
Bar,
The City Officers,
Archbishops of Canterbury and York,
The Lord Chancellor,

---

122 William Gill (d. 1798); alderman 1781–98. Beaven, *Aldermen of London*, II, 136.
123 The toxophilites, or archers, were 'clad in green and gold, with their bows and quivers'. *Public Advertiser*, 17809 (24 Apr. 1789).

The Prince of Wales and Dukes of York, Gloucester and Cumberland,

The SOVEREIGN,

The QUEEN,

The PRINCESSES ROYAL, AUGUSTA, and ELIZABETH,

The Ladies of the Bedchamber, Maids of Honour, and the Lords of the Bedchamber.

On their Majesties entering the cathedral, the drums and fifes played a slow march, which was succeeded by the 100th psalm, sung to the old tune, and accompanied by the organ.– The words 'All people that on earth do dwell', being excellently adapted to an occasion where universal thanksgiving and general joy pervaded what may be truly called the people.

In this psalm the charity children, to the number of 5000, with ribbons across their shoulders, on which were painted the words 'God save the King' joined; and though they might not be in perfect musical concord of voice, their little hearts panted with harmony of sentiment, and they felt more than they could express.

Their Majesties were not inattentive witnesses, and passing through this scene of infant loyalty, the impression it made on the Queen was too much for female sensibility. The tears fell – and they fell from more than Royal eyes – the audience was much affected.

After the psalm, divine service commenced, and was chanted and said in the cathedral manner, by the Gentlemen and Boys of the Choir and Chapel Royal.

The *Bishop of Lincoln* as Dean of St Paul's, assisted by the Bishop of Bristol,[124] performed the communion service.

The Sermon was preached by the Bishop of London, who took his text from the 16th verse of the 27th psalm.

'O tarry thou the Lord's leisure: be strong and he shall comfort thine heart: and put thou thy trust in the Lord.'[125]

When divine service ended their Majesties returned to the Queen's house,[126] only with this difference in the order of procession: they were followed instead of preceded by the two Houses of Parliament.

The children, on the Royal Family retiring, sung the 104th psalm.

The Bishops of London and Lincoln attended nearest to his Majesty's person on his entrance and departure, and he conversed with them in a familiar manner on the subject of the day, with all that condescension and affability for which he is so highly extolled in every court of Europe.

Lord Heathfield also attended his Majesty, but he was so very feeble and so much impaired in his health as to require support.

The arrangements at the Cathedral were most excellently judicious, and not marked by the least confusion, notwithstanding the numerous assemblage of all the Lords and Commons now in town, without distinction of Party – The Prince of Wales, Duke of York, Duke of Glocester, Duke of Cumberland and all their suits of

---

124 Christopher Wilson (*c.* 1714–92); educ. St Catharine's College, Cambridge, matric. 1733, BA 1736–7, MA 1740, DD 1753; prebendary of St Paul's 1745; rector of Barnes, Surrey, 1768–92; bishop of Bristol 1783–92. J. and J. A. Venn, *Alumni Cantabrigienses, a biographical list of all known students, graduates and holders of office at the University of Cambridge, from the earliest times to 1751* (4 vols., Cambridge, 1922–7).

125 As printed in the Psalter.

126 Now known as Buckingham Palace, it had been acquired by George III in 1761.

attendants, with a selection of the principal Ladies of Fashion, Ambassadors, City Magistrates, &c.

The King set off from the Queen's house about half past ten, which was announced by a rocket from St James's, that was followed by a rocket from Blackfriars, to give signal to the Artillery at the Tower, who gave a discharge of forty guns.

The discharge of the same number was repeated when his Majesty arrived at St Paul's, and when the service was over.

DRESSES.

His MAJESTY wore the full-dress Windsor uniform.

Her MAJESTY AND THE PRINCESSES in garter blue, richly trimmed with gold fringe, and bandeaus in their head dresses, with the motto of 'God save the King'.

The Prince of WALES, the Duke of York, Gloucester, and Cumberland, in full-dress Windsor uniforms, with insigina's of their several orders.

The ladies were all in full dress, complimentarily similar to that of the QUEEN: Mr Pitt and many other of the King's particular friends were in the Windsor uniform.

The Lord MAYOR in purple velvet, richly trimmed with gold. A rich crimson velvet robe embroidered with gold, hung across his shoulders.

The Lord CHANCELLOR was in his State Robes, and so was the Speaker of the House of Commons.

All the Royal Liveries were made up new for the occasion.

––––––––

During the time the coaches of their Majesties, and the Prince and Princesses, passed through the Strand and Fleet-street, the bells were every where rung; and on each side of Temple-Bar there was a band of music, which performed as the Royal Family passed.

The LORD CHANCELLOR was received in every avenue to the Cathedral with the most unbounded shouts of applause, particularly at the bottom of Fleet-street, where the Procession stopped near half an hour. The multitude here shewed particular respect to his Lordship, by standing uncovered the whole time he was in sight. Mr PITT, in the early part of the morning, and Earl Bayham[127] afterwards, were likewise received with the most repeated huzzas.

Mr Fox[128] and Lord Loughborough,[129] at St Martin's Church, and in passing through Temple-Bar, were recognised, and received an universal hiss, which continued with very little intermission until they alighted at St Paul's.

Lord STORMONT,[130] though very finely dressed in brown and gold, had not much opportunity to shew it, for on approaching Temple-Bar, and finding some disapprobation, he very prudently pulled down the green blinds of his chariot, and sat *perdu*.

Some of the Members of the Opposition experienced similar marks of public hatred.

---

[127] Presumably John Jeffreys Pratt (1759–1840), Viscount Bayham, the son of Earl Camden, MP for Bath and a lord of the admiralty.

[128] Charles James Fox (1749–1806), the leader of the whig opposition in the House of Commons.

[129] Alexander Wedderburn (1733–1805), Baron Loughborough; lord chief justice of the common pleas 1780–93; first commissioner of the great seal 1783; lord chancellor 1793–1801; created earl of Rosslyn 1801. A member of the Fox–North coalition, he supported the whigs through the 1780s. *ODNB*.

[130] David Murray (1727–96), Viscount Stormont; secretary of state 1779–82; lord president of the council 1783, 1794–6; succeeded as earl of Mansfield 1793. A supporter of the Fox–North coalition, he continued to vote with the whigs until 1793. *ODNB*.

All the avenues to town, as well as the streets appeared to be alive, the croud moving to the line of Procession, and hurrying some with draggled tails, others with dripping heads, through thick and thin as fast as their legs could carry them to see once more the face of their recovered monarch, and miserable did *they* think themselves who were prevented from enjoying that happiness.

About ten o'clock the Houses in those streets through which the Procession passed, made one of the finest appearances that can be conceived. They looked like a continued gallery of female charms, where the pencil of nature had finished in the highest perfection a selection of the most beautiful faces in the universe, among which appeared numbers that were quite new in the metropolis, some celestial rosy cheeks as yet unpolluted by late hours, or ruined with the *meretricious* fashion of *paints* and *cosmeticks*.

In proportion as the Royal carriage approached so did the countenance of the public brighten up with joy. There was a kind of anxious impatience, mingled with delight, perceptible in every eye, which gave to the contour of the face, an emanation that cannot be truly described.

What their Majesties felt on this glorious day was visible in their looks. – Religion, – Joy, – Gratitude, – Affection and Benevolence, beamed in each feature, whilst the time beating pulse to the heart kept the countenance in perfect unison with the sentiments of the mind.

The ideas of the PARTY at this sight, where loyalty shone with conspicuous lustre among the people, were such as Milton describes *Satan* to have felt when he beheld the SUN in fully glory; and if they spoke from their hearts, if they were for a moment as undisguised in expression, as the Poet's Fallen Angel was on that occasion, the address must be alike–

–'To tell thee how I hate the beams!'[131]

We have not heard of any accident that happened during the whole day, except where the Westminster mob attempted to close the procession; which the Oxford Blues[132] soon settled without Injury to a single individual.

———

Amongst the shops most conspicuous for the beauty and elegance of their visitors, and which made no mercenary traffic of them, were those of those eminent haberdashers, WLELS [*sic*] and FISHER,[133] and that fashionable jeweller – TOWNSHEND;[134] – both in Fleet Street: – there were upwards of 250 Ladies of distinction at the house of the former, and the latter was filled with company of equal rank.

A trick was played off by one of the Common Council, who asked a Member of the House of Commons for his ticket, on entering the church; by which means the Palace Yard Member was refused for sometime, and the City Member admitted in his stead.

---

131 'O Sun, to tell thee how I hate thy beams, / That bring to my remembrance from what state I fell.' John Milton, *Paradise Lost*, IV, 37–8.

132 The Royal Horse Guards Blue, also known as the Oxford Blues from their re-formation in 1661 as the Royal Regiment of Horse, or Horse Guards.

133 'Wells, Fisher, Wells and Headeach' are listed as haberdashers of 52 Fleet Street in *The London directory for the year 1789; containing an alphabetical arrangement of the names and residences of the merchants, manufacturers and principal traders of the cities of London and Westminster...* (London, 1789), p. 158.

134 The *London directory*, p. 151, only lists one Townsend in Fleet Street: Elizabeth Townsend, whose hardware shops were at 73–4 Fleet Street.

The Duchess of Cumberland's carriage by some means fell into the Procession a short space West of the City, and so got into St Paul's. – The idea of the Lady being *Royal* in the cavalcade could not be admitted in the etiquette from the Palace.

The Duke of York's regiment were drawn up after the King returned, and first a *Feu de Joye*, by order of his Royal Highness.

Mrs Fitzherbert[135] was at Newberrys[136] in St Paul's Church Yard. What were her sensations on this joyful occasion?

In the Royal Suite were twenty-two coaches.

His Majesty looked remarkably well, and as usual was particularly devout during Divine Service.

The Choir was too limited for the company. There was a general complaint from those invited for want of room.

The pickpockets were numerous, and those who did not take our advice[137] of leaving their valuables at home, repented not observing the precaution. A Gentleman handing a Lady into her carriage from Mr Parker's glass shop[138] in Fleet-street lost a very valuable gold watch.

The price of seats lowered from three guineas to three shillings. – This was the fate of extortion.

At Temple Bar the Lord Mayor's horse was conspicuous – it was conspicuous from its supporters – two of the city militia walked on each side, holding the bridle with one hand, and, with a saving caution, holding the other over his Lordship's legs, in order to correct any accident that might disturb the equipoise of the body. It is but on very particular occasions the Lord Mayor is obliged to ride, and therefore horsemanship is not considered as any part of his duty.

Sir *Benjamin Hammett*[139] was fortunately astride one of *Hughes's* horses;[140] – it was a tractable animal, and would have done any thing. The Knight was therefore safe: – even if he did not understand riding, the horse taught him what he should do.

Surgeon Wadd,[141] Mr Dixon,[142] Deputy Leekey,[143] and Deputy Birch,[144] were also mounted on horses belonging to the Circus. The decorations were pretty; and the 'God Save the King' on the front of the bridles had a good effect.

The coach in which their Majesties went was not the State carriage – it was prepared for the occasion, and had glasses in the panels so as to give a full view of the Royal Pair. The carriages in which the princesses rode was open in the same manner.

---

135   Maria Fitzherbert (1756–1837), who had unlawfully married the prince of Wales on 15 Dec. 1785. Their relationship had been a source of public controversy throughout the king's illness and the regency crisis in 1788–9.

136   Francis Newbery was a merchant at 55 St Paul's Church Yard. *London directory*, p. 112.

137   See *Times*, 135 (23 Apr. 1789), p. 2c.

138   William Parker and son, 'glass-manufacturers, were located at 69 Fleet Street. *London directory*, p. 116.

139   Sir Benjamin Hammet (d. 1800); MP for Taunton 1782–1800; alderman of London 1785–98. Beaven, *Aldermen of London*, II, 138.

140   Charles Hughes (1746/7–97) was a circus proprietor, who had opened the Royal Circus and Equestrian Philharmonic Academy at Blackfriars Road, St George's Fields, in 1782. *ODNB*.

141   Solomon Wadd (d. 1821), a surgeon who practised in Basinghall Street, London.

142   Unidentified.

143   Gabriel Leekey was a watch-maker at 15 Basinghall Street. *London directory*, p. 98.

144   Possibly Thomas Birch, a linen draper, of 122 Cheapside. *London directory*, p. 26.

The English Factory at Lisbon have determined on a *fete*, to be given in honour of his MAJESTY'S recovery.

As a contrast to the Royal Thanksgiving at the Cathedral, a correspondent desires us to present our readers with the following, which was received last week by a Clergyman in Kent, about 70 miles from town:– ' Steven Soundy desires to retoren Gode thankes for a long and dangras illnesse. – To be menchend if you plees, Sur.'

'*To the Worthie Vicker of* ——.'

A Correspondent observes, that among the many curious devices intended as marks of loyalty and affection, by a generous and Patriotic People, for the approaching general illumination, on the happy recovery of our most gracious Sovereign, the East as well as the West end of the town, has to boast its particular beauties, not only the Bank, India House, and the different Fire Offices, but at a tin plate manufactory, in White Chapel; where there is a brilliant and beautiful display of elegant varigated lamps. At the upper part of the house is the following judicious and well chosen motto, 'Glory to God'; below and underneath a Superb Crown, is added 'Our King's Restored', the one expressive of the goodness of providence, the other the use a of [*sic*] our exultation, which together form a pious and grateful ejaculation to that Great Being by whom 'Kings Reign'; this with a magnificent, G. R. is intended for this evening, and will no doubt attract the admiration of the public, on so joyful an occasion.

Endorsed: N⁰· 16 / Ceremony at Sᵗ Pauls

Printing the sermon

Porteus's sermon was very popular, rapidly going through six editions. While the exchange of letters printed here makes clear the king's approval of the sermon, it is largely concerned with clarifying who was responsible for ordering the sermon to be printed and how that order should be issued. Again, we can see the importance attached to precedents. The confusion on this issue can be attributed to the fact that, after the middle of George I's reign, the fashion for printing court sermons, which had been a staple of the religious press in the seventeenth century, rapidly died out.[145]

22. Earl of Ailesbury, to Beilby Porteus, bishop of London, [24 April 1789]

Porteus papers 17, fo. 183

Friday

Lord Ailesbury presents his Compliments to the Bishop of London & hopes He will gratify the Queen with a Sight of the excellent Sermon He preached at Sᵗ Paul's Yesterday which Her Majesty is particularly desirous of reading: the Queen Lᵈ A– is likely to see this Evening.

Endorsed: Lᵈ Ailesbury / April 24. 1789

---

[145] Stephen Taylor, 'The clergy at the courts of George I and George II', in *Monarchy and religion. The transformation of royal culture in eighteenth-century Europe*, ed. Michael Schaich, Studies of the German Historical Institute (Oxford, 2007), pp. 129–51.

23. Robert Smith[146] to Beilby Porteus, bishop of London, 26 April 1789

Porteus papers 17, fos. 184–5

M[r] Robert Smith presents his Compt[s] to the Bishop of London, & being desired by the House of Commons to present to his Lordship the Thanks of that House for his Sermon preached on Thursday last, Mr Smith proposes to wait upon the Bishop tomorrow at twelve o Clock.

Should that time happen to be inconvenient, M[r] Smith will wait upon the Bishop at any Hour on Tuesday Morning, that his Lordship may please to appoint by a Line sent to M[r] Smiths House in S[t] James's Place.

Hampstead Sunday Ap[l] 26. –[147]

Endorsed: H. of Commons

24. Order of the House of Commons, 25 April 1789[148]

Porteus papers 17, fos. 186–7

Sabbati 25 die Aprilis 1789.
    Ordered,
    That the Thanks of this House be given to the Lord Bishop of London for the excellent Sermon by him preached before His Majesty and both Houses of Parliament at Saint Paul's Church on Thursday last the Day of Public Thanksgiving appointed by His Majesty; and that Mr Robert Smith and Mr Wilberforce[149] do attend his Lordship with the Thanks of this House.

J Hatsell[150]
Cl. Dom

Endorsed: N[o.] 17 / Thanks of the / House of Commons / April 25. 1789

25. John Warren, bishop of Bangor,[151] to Bishop Porteus, Great George Street, London, 28 April 1789

Porteus papers 17, fo. 190

The Bishop of Bangor presents his Compliments to the Bishop of London, & believes the following account contains an accurate List of the several Preachers at St Paul's, on the seven days of Thanksgiving, at which Queen Anne was present.

---

146 Robert Smith (1752–1838), MP for Nottingham 1779–97.
147 '1789' has been added in a different hand.
148 *Journals of the House of Commons*, XLIV, p. 289.
149 William Wilberforce (1759–1833), leading evangelical layman; MP for Kingston-upon-Hull 1780–4, Yorkshire 1784–1812, Bramber 1812–25.
150 Clerk to the House of Commons.
151 John Warren (1730–1800), having been educated at Caius College, Cambridge, was ordained deacon in 1753 and priest in 1754. He served as chaplain to two bishops of Ely, Matthias Mawson and Edmund Keene, before being nominated to the bishopric of St David's in 1779. He was translated to Bangor in 1783. A strong supporter of Pitt's ministry, he enjoyed the particular confidence of Lord Chancellor Thurlow and his younger brother was physician to George III. *ODNB*.

X   On the 12th Nov[r.] 1702, D[r] Trelawney, Bishop of Exeter, preached – Joshua 23. 8.[152]

X   On the 7th Sep. 1704, D[r] Sherlock, Dean of St Paul's, preached.[153]

On the 23[d] of Aug[t] 1705, D[r] Willis, Dean of Lincoln, preached. Isaiah 11th 13, 14.[154]

X   On the 27th of June 1706, D[r] Stanhope, Dean of Canterbury, preached. Deuterom. 33. 29.[155]

X   On the 31st Dec[r.] 1706, D[r] Burnet, Bishop of Salisbury, preached. Psalm 72. 4.[156]

X   On the 1st May, 1707, D[r] Talbot, Bishop of Oxford, preached. Psalm 133. 1.[157]

X   On the 19th August 1708, D[r] Fleetwood, Bishop of S[t] Asaph, preached. Ezekiel 36. 32. See his Works pag. 435.[158]

Great George Street
28th Ap. 1789.

Endorsed: Preachers at S[t.] / Pauls.

26. Archbishop Moore to Lord Sydney, 1 May 1789 [draft]

Porteus papers 17, fos. 191–192r

My Lord,

I find upon inquiry in the Houses of Parliament that it is not consonant to the usage of either of them that a motion should be there made for the Printing & Publishing the Bishop of London's excellent Sermon preached at St Pauls before his Majesty on the late happy day of Thanksgiving; & I conceive their reason to be, that it would not be respectful to his Majesty for them to take any measure of that kind in relation[159] to a Sermon preached by his Majestys Command. I find too in looking back to the Thanksgivings at St Pauls, when Queen Anne attended in Person, that the Sermons there preached were printed & published *by her Majestys special Command*. Three of them I am in possession of, which were preached by Dr Stanhope Dean of Canterbury, by Bishop Burnett, and Dr Talbott Bishop of Oxford.

---

152 Trelawney, *Sermon preach'd before the queen*. The text was Joshua 23. 8–9.

153 William Sherlock, *A sermon preach'd before the queen, at the cathedral church of St. Paul, London, on the seventh of September, 1704. Being the thanksgiving-day for the late glorious victory ... at Bleinheim ..., on Wednesday the second of August, by the forces of her majesty and her allies, under the command of the duke of Marlborough* (London, 1704). His text was Psalms 58. 11.

154 Richard Willis, *A sermon preach'd before the queen, at the cathedral church of St. Paul, London, on the 23d day of August 1705. Being the thanksgiving-day for the late glorious success in forcing the enemies lines in the Spanish Netherlands, by the arms of her majesty and her allies, under the command of the duke of Marlborough* (London, 1705).

155 See above, p. 236 n. 41.

156 Gilbert Burnet, *A sermon preach'd before the queen, and the two houses of parliament, at St. Paul's on the 31st of December, 1706. The day of thanksgiving for the wonderful successes of this year* (London, 1707).

157 Talbot, *Sermon preach'd before the queen*. The text was Psalms 133. 1–3.

158 William Fleetwood, *A compleat collection of the sermons, tracts, and pieces of all kinds, that were written by the right reverend Dr William Fleetwood, late lord bishop of Ely* (London, 1737), pp. 435–43. The sermon was also published separately in 1708.

159 'of that kind in relation' has been interlineated above 'with respect', which has been deleted.

Now[160] the Publication of the Bishop of Londons Sermon being eagerly wished for & expected, I[161] request your Lordship to inform me whether you have received his Majestys Commands on that Subject, presuming at the same time to submit it to your Lordships better Judgment, whether[162] under the circumstances above stated it may not be proper to take[?] his Majestys Commands if you have not rec^d them.

I have &c

27. Archbishop Moore to Bishop Porteus, 1 May 1789

Porteus papers 17, fo. 192v

Friday.

My dear Lord, Having learnt from the best Authority that the regular & best Channel of suggestion to the King, on the subject of your Publication, w^d be thro' the Secretary of State; I sent a letter for that purpose to Ld Sydney, by whom it will be sent in the Green Bag of this Evening, as I understand.

The other side of this Paper exhibits to you the rough draught of the letter; what I sent was more correct but in Substance just the same.

Yrs faithfully / J. Cantuar.

Endorsed: N° 18 / Abp Moore / to Lord Sydney / May 1. 1789.

28. George III to [Lord Sydney], Windsor, 2 May 1789

Porteus papers 17, fo. 193

Windsor May 2^d 1789.
m/10 p^t 5. P.M.

The proper mode of directing the Bishop of London to print the Sermon He preached at St Pauls on the Thanksgiving seems to be for Lord Sydney to intimate to the Archbishop of Canterbury that it is my desire he should express to the Bishop of London my Wish that this Sermon may be published.

G.R.

Endorsed: N° 19 / King's di/rections / about / printing the / Sermon

29. Archbishop Moore to Bishop Porteus, 30 May 1789

Porteus papers 17, fos. 194–5

30 May 1789

My dear Lord,

I have not a word of information to give you from any Authority in respect to his Majestys intentions of being at St James's or not on the Birthday. I have some reason to imagine that point is not yet decided upon. The Duke of Glocester asked me yesterday[163] Whether you did not intend to send copies of your Sermon to the

---

[160] 'Now' has been interlineated over 'I find', which has been deleted.
[161] 'I' has been interlineated over, '& beg' which has been deleted.
[162] 'it' deleted.
[163] 'yesterday' is interlineated.

Royal Family, and before I could make any reply added that he wished me to say to you that he sh^d. be glad to have one. He seemed to think that it was customary to send copies to the Family when the King ordered a Sermon to be printed. How far that opinion is founded I know not. I was about ordering my horse with an intention of riding over to you when your Servant called; but I find it w^d. not have been practicable to [s]pare the time. I am faithfully / your Servant / J. [Ca]ntuar.

Addressed: The Lord Bishop / of London

Endorsed: N°. 20[164] /Abp. Moore / May 30. 1789.

Postscript

The final group of papers reveals how the 1789 thanksgiving was itself later cited as a precedent.

30. William Fawkener[165] to Archbishop Moore,[166] council office, 24 September 1795

Moore papers, 6, fos. 93–4

My Lord

I have the honour of inclosing a copy of a Letter written by your Grace to the Lord President of the Council,[167] communicating His Majesty's commands on the subject of the Thanksgiving for his Recovery; and a copy of the Minute made with respect to the form of Prayer to be used on that occasion; the Order for preparing which, was not, for a very obvious reason, made by his Majesty himself, as is usually the practice: and I, likewise, inclose an Order so made, by His Majesty in Council, in the case of a single Prayer. I do not find among the Council Papers any letter from an Archbishop of Canterbury, to a President of the Council, communicating the King's commands, except when a Proclamation was to issue for a General Thanksgiving or a Fast, but the form for a single prayer, will be the same.

If your Grace should have any further commands for me, I need not say with how much pleasure I shall obey them.

I have the honour to be, with the greatest respect / My Lord / Your Graces most obedient / & most humble Servant / W. Fawkener

Council Office Septr 24th 1795

Endorsed: A Letter from M^r / Fawkener with / 3 Papers relative / to Orders of Council / for Thanksgiving / Prayers – / 1763 1788 1789 Preambles to Proclamations for General Thanksg[ivi]ngs. / N° 57

---

164   '19' has been crossed out.
165   William Augustus Fawkener (*c.* 1750–1811) was appointed a clerk of the privy council in 1779.
166   John Moore (1730–1805), educ. Pembroke College, Oxford, matric. 1745, BA 1748, MA 1751, BD and DD 1763; prebendary of Durham 1761; canon of Oxford 1763; rector of Ryton, Durham, 1769; dean of Canterbury 1771–5; bishop of Bangor 1775–83; archbishop of Canterbury 1783–1805. *ODNB.*
167   Charles Pratt, First Earl Camden, lord president of the council 1784–94.

31. Order to prepare a form of prayer, 12 August 1762[168]

Moore papers 6, fos. 101–2

At the Court of S[t] James's the 12th Day of Aug[st] 1763.
Present The King's Most Excellent Majesty in Council.
His Grace the Lord Archbishop of Canterbury[169] was this Day Ordered to prepare a Form of Thanksgiving for the safe Delivery of the Queen, and Birth of a Prince.[170]

Endorsed: Extract from the Council / Register. 1763

32.   Minutes of the privy council, 13 November 1788

Moore papers 6, fos. 103–4

At the Council Chamber Whitehall the 13th of Nov[r.] 1788.
By the Lords of His Majesty's Most Hon[ble] Privy Council.

Present

Arch[bp] of Canterbury	Earl of Effingham[171]
Lord Chancellor[172]	Earl of Denbigh[173]
Arch[bp] of York[174]	Bishop of London
Lord President	Lord Sydney[175]
Lord Privy Seal[176]	Lord Amherst[177]
Duke of Chandos[178]	Mr Pitt
Duke of Richmond[179]	Mr Grenville[180]
Marq[s] of Carmarthen[181]	Master of the Rolls[182]

---

[168]   '1763' in this document is presumably an error for '1762'. The future George IV was born on 12 Aug. 1762; Frederick, duke of York, was born on 16 Aug. 1763.

[169]   Thomas Secker, archbishop of Canterbury 1758–68.

[170]   See *A form of prayer and thanksgiving to almighty God; to be used at morning and evening service, after the general thanksgiving, throughout the cities of London and Westminster, and elswhere within the bills of mortality, on Sunday the fifteenth of August, 1762; and in all churches and chapels throughout England and Wales, on the Sunday after the ministers thereof receive the same; on the safe delivery of the queen, and happy birth of the young prince...* (London, 1763).

[171]   Thomas Howard, earl of Effingham (1747–91); privy councillor 1782; treasurer of the household 1782–3; master of the mint 1784–9; governor of Jamaica 1789–91.

[172]   Edward, First Lord Thurlow, lord chancellor 1783–92.

[173]   Basil Feilding, earl of Denbigh (1719–1800); privy councillor 1760; lord of the bedchamber 1763–1800.

[174]   William Markham, archbishop of York 1777–1807.

[175]   Thomas Townshend, Viscount Sydney (1733–1800); home secretary 1782–3, 1783–9.

[176]   See above, p. 251 n. 113.

[177]   Jeffrey, Baron Amherst (1717–97); privy councillor 1772; commander-in-chief 1778–82, 1793–5.

[178]   James Brydges, duke of Chandos (1731–89); privy councillor 1775; lord steward of the household 1783–9.

[179]   Charles Lennox, duke of Richmond (1735–1806); privy councillor 1765; secretary of state 1766; master-general of the ordnance 1782–3, 1783–95.

[180]   William Wyndham Grenville (1759–1834); MP for Buckingham 1782–4, for Buckinghamshire 1784–90; privy councillor 1783; joint paymaster general 1784–9; speaker of the House of Commons Jan.–June 1789; created Baron Grenville 1790.

[181]   Francis Godolphin, marquess of Carmarthen (1751–1837); privy councillor 1777; lord chamberlain to the queen 1777–80; foreign secretary 1783–91; succeeded as duke of Leeds 1789.

[182]   Sir Richard Pepper Arden, master of the rolls 1788–1801.

The Lord President acquaints the Bond [*sic* ?Board] with the Object of the Meeting of Their Lordships, namely to consider of the Steps proper to be taken, for causing Prayers to be put up to Almighty God, for the restoration of His Majesty's Health – and thereupon the following Orders were made by Their Lordships.

It is this Day Ordered by Their Lordships that His Grace the Lord Archbishop of Canterbury do prepare the form of a prayer to Almighty God for the recovery of His Majesty from the Severe Illness with which it hath pleased the divine Providence to afflict Him.[183]

And it is hereby further Ordered, That His Majesty's Printer do forthwith print a competent number of Copies of the said Form of Prayer, that the same may be forthwith sent round and read in the several Churches of England and Wales, and the Town of Berwick upon Tweed.

It is this Day Ordered by Their Lordships That every Minister, or Preacher, as well of the Established Church in that part of Great Britain called Scotland, as those of the Episcopal Communion, protected and allowed by an Act passed in the 10th year of Her late Majesty Queen Ann, c. 7 – Intituled 'An Act to prevent the disturbing Those of the Episcopal Communion in that part of Great Britain called Scotland, in the exercise of their religious Worship, and in Use of the Liturgy of the Church of England; and for repealing the Act passed in the Parliament of Scotland, intituled An Act against irregular Baptisms and Marriages' do at some time during the Exercise of the Divine Service in such respective Church, Congregation or Assembly, put up their Prayers to Almighty God for the Recovery of His Majesty from the Severe Illness with which it hath pleased the Divine Providence to afflict him.

Endorsed: Extract from the Council / Register – 1788 / Prayers for king's health[184]

33. Archbishop Moore to Earl Camden, 31 Mar. 1789

Moore papers 6, fos. 105–6

My Lord.

I have it in command from His Majesty to communicate to your Lordship his Determination to have a Day of general Thanksgiving on Thursday the 23[d] of next Month, for the signal Interposition of the Divine Providence, in his recoving [*sic*] from his late Illness – For which it is his Pleasure that a Proclamation should be forthwith prepared.

His Majesty signified at the same time also his Intention of attending Divine Service in the Cathedral of S[t] Pauls on that Day.

I have the honor to be, / with the utmost respect, / My Lord, / Your Lordship's / most obed[t.] / humble servant / J. Cantuar

Lambeth House March 31st 1789

Endorsed: Copy / Letter from His Grace the Arch / Bishop of Canterbury to the / Lord President of the Council / on the Subject of the Proclamation / for a General Thanksgiving on / His Majesty's Recovery. / 1789.

---

183 *A prayer to be used on…during his majesty's present indisposition.*
184 'Prayers for the king's health' is added in pencil, possibly in a modern hand.

6

'MY UNFORTUNATE PARISH': ANGLICAN URBAN MINISTRY IN BETHNAL GREEN, 1809–*c.* 1850

Edited by
Arthur Burns

9 Bishop Blomfield, bust by William Behnes, 1833

Introduction*

Lambeth Palace Library holds rich material for both local and social historians. For example, the Fulham papers (previously housed at Fulham Palace) incorporate correspondence of several bishops of London concerning diocesan administration. Some bishops have left disappointingly thin archives; at the other extreme, the papers of Charles James Blomfield (bishop of London 1828–56) are an extraordinary resource for both the national and local history of the church, not least because, alongside in-correspondence, the collection contains sixty of Blomfield's 'letterbooks', preserving carbon copies of out-correspondence. Fifty-seven of these relate primarily to the administration of the diocese. The originals are exceptionally fragile, and are not available to researchers; fortunately a microfilm edition has been published by World Microfilms Publications. The value of this deposit and of the Fulham papers more generally for parochial history can be exemplified by examining them in relation to a single (but remarkable) parish during the first half of the nineteenth century: Bethnal Green. Such was the significance of this parish, and so remarkable the events that transpired there, moreover, that the correspondence illuminates several themes of central importance to nineteenth-century ecclesiastical and religious history: among them the dynamics of reform, the development of ministry in a period of rapid urbanization and the development of the clerical profession.

I

On 18 November 1809, the Rev. Joshua King, MA and fellow of Brasenose College, Oxford, was instituted rector of St Matthew's Bethnal Green on the college's presentation. Aged thirty on his appointment,[1] he would remain rector until his death aged eighty-one on 15 February 1861. King was the second son of a Cheshire clergyman, Bryan King,[2] when Joshua was born perpetual curate of Birkenhead on the Wirral, although by the time Joshua matriculated at Brasenose in 1796, Bryan had moved up in the world and a mile or two west to become rector of Woodchurch, of

---

*   I would like to thank Richard Palmer and the staff of Lambeth Palace Library, the staff of the Tower Hamlets Local History and Archives Library, Bancroft Road, the staff of the London Metropolitan Archives and Elizabeth Boardman, archivist of Brasenose College, Oxford, for help in preparing this edition. I also owe a debt to Elizabeth Kerr of Wall-to-Wall Productions, for it was while researching for an edition of *Who do you think you are?* that I first got to grips with this topic. The Rev. Kevin Scully of St Matthew's Bethnal Green has been unfailingly helpful, and I owe a particular debt to Julian Woodford for sharing with me so generously the fruits of his remarkable research regarding Joseph Merceron for his as yet unpublished biography, *The boss of Bethnal Green*.

1   He was born on 20 Nov. 1778 (http://www.familysearch.org, accessed 23 Feb. 2009).

2   Ord. d., p. Chester, 1774–5; licensed cur. Bidston, Cheshire 1775; perp. cur. Birkenhead 1776 nominated by Bishop Markham; rect. Woodchurch 1792–1820 [CCE-id 113065]. The eldest son was William (1777–1816). There were also daughters: Margaret (b. 1783), Mary (b. 1784), Ellen (b. 1788) and further sons George (b. 1780) and Bryan (1793–1822).

which Bryan's wife Ellen (d. 1833) was co-patron. Joshua's own parochial career would also begin in the diocese of Chester, when he served as perpetual curate of the proprietary chapel of St Stephen's, Byrom Street, Liverpool, from 1807 to 1808 following ordination on the title of his fellowship by Bishop Randolph of Oxford.

At Bethnal Green, King succeeded the recently deceased William Loxham, another north-western Brasenose man, appointed in 1766. Loxham died at his family home in Longton, Lancashire, and would later be remembered in Bethnal Green as never having set foot in the parish; certainly he was rarely if ever present after his first six months.[3] King, however, would be different: in 1809 Bethnal Green experienced the novelty of a resident incumbent.

Bethnal Green was precisely the sort of parish which critics of the effects of non-residence and pluralism on the Church of England would shortly seek to highlight. A couple of miles north-east of St Paul's Cathedral, by the early nineteenth century it was becoming one of the most remarkable parishes in the diocese of London, and indeed in the Church of England. It was of comparatively recent origin, legislation creating it from the ancient parish of Stepney in 1743: the act authorized the rate to finance the building of St Matthew's, which after some travails was finally consecrated on 15 July 1746.[4] The act explained that the hamlet of Bethnal Green was 'computed to have more than fifteen thousand inhabitants' crammed into 1,800 homes, and that the absence of a church 'hath been a great cause of the increase of dissoluteness of morals, and a disregard of religion, too apparent in the younger and poorer sort', this encouraging 'the better sort' to up sticks. The size of the population reflected an influx initially into the western reaches of Bethnal Green of what were described in the Commons in 1743 as 'journeymen weavers and other inferior artificers belonging to the weaving trade who by hard labour and industry can scarcely in the most frugal way of life maintain themselves', some of whom were Huguenots, and most of whom were connected with the silk industry. Growth continued throughout the century and beyond: by 1811 King's parish contained some 5,715 inhabited houses; twenty years later there were 10,877, and the population was estimated at 62,018, making it second only to St Pancras (population 103,548 in 1831) in London.

One of King's first tasks as rector was to respond to a diocesan circular inquiring into the spiritual provision in London's most populous parishes (Document 1). As his replies indicate, the parish was poorly served: St Matthew's itself might accommodate over a thousand at a sitting, but to list alongside it 'the French church' – St Jean's, Spitalfields, established in the 1680s in St John Street at the north end of Brick Lane, which conducted services using the liturgy of the French Reformed Church – was surely to overstate the 'anglican' presence. Dissent was not especially better served, however. King could only talk vaguely of the chief places of worship: the independent (congregationalist) chapel under the ministry of John Kello, which by 1818 was described as 'decayed'; the Middlesex chapel in the Hackney Road which he also classed as Independent (but which a year later was described as Wesleyan methodist); the 'methodist' 'Gibraltar' chapel (in fact another congrega-

3   K. Leech, P. J. E. Eyre and J. Oldland, *The history booklet of St Matthew's Bethnal Green*, rev. J. Oldland (London, 1989), p. 6; Brasenose College, Oxford (hereafter BNC), Hurst, Bethnal Green 3, J. King to R. Heber, encl. with King to A. T. Gilbert 12 Mar. 1823; Loxham [CCE-id 113066].
4   16 Geo. II, c. 28. What follows draws extensively on T. F. T. Baker (ed.), *A history of the county of Middlesex*, XI, *Victoria county history* (*VCH*) (London, 1998), pp. 87–263.

tional meeting house); the 'methodist' Bethel chapel, which *VCH* tentatively identifies with a later baptist chapel in Austin Street; and a 'Brick Lane Meeting House' which *VCH* (again tentatively) identifies as congregationalist. King calculated the combined accommodation these afforded at 1,150.

As the fact of the enquiry indicates, such disproportion between ecclesiastical provision and population was becoming a source of concern, only amplified by the absence of additional clerical provision (another near contemporaneous return indicates that King was not employing a full-time curate, although there was an unendowed lecturer at St Matthew's inherited from his predecessor).[5]

Full-time assistant curates were not as yet as ubiquitous as they would be in the 1830s and 1840s: nonetheless, this may also have reflected a second obstacle to effective ministry in the parish, the rector's poor remuneration. The finances of the new parish were troublesome from the start and, as finally settled, the rector was denied both great tithes (which remained with the patron of both Stepney and now Bethnal Green, Brasenose College), and small tithes which, with 'garden pennies', Easter offerings and burial fees, went to the churchwardens. The latter paid the rector a stipend of £130 per annum, to which he added the surplice fees.[6] Even if the incumbent had had the inclination there were thus limited resources to support either charitable expense or clerical assistance beyond his private means. In 1812 King moaned to the vestry that he was

> so fully occupied in parochial duties, in filling up and signing testimonials and certificates for the relatives of sailors and soldiers, in writing letters of recommendation for the poor to different charitable institutions, in searching the registers, in baptizing infants, in visiting the sick, and in burying the parish poor (all which duties are performed gratuitously), that my whole time is completely devoted. Permit me, then, to ask, whether I am adequately repaid?[7]

He sought an increase; and in 1813 a new act raised his stipend to a much more respectable £400 per annum. By the time of the Ecclesiastical Duties and Revenue report of 1835, drawing on figures for 1829–31, moreover, King returned his average net income as £614, reflecting the not inconsiderable contribution to be expected from surplice fees in so populous a parish.[8]

At the time King took office, the climate engendered by on the one hand the evangelical revival and on the other the political and social tensions associated with the French Revolution and wars had raised issues of pastoral and missionary strategy and encouraged a more sympathetic and supportive atmosphere for launching new initiatives (although their form remained highly contentious). One such initiative was the British and Foreign Bible Society, founded in 1804 for the printing and

---

5   Lambeth Palace Library, Fulham papers, Randolph 14, fo. 65: return on duty in London churches to Bishop John Randolph, 27 Nov. 1812. The lecturer was William Lowfield Fancourt, lic. 25 June 1807 [CCE-id 57979].

6   16 Geo. II, c. 28.

7   Tower Hamlets History Library and Archives, Bancroft Road, London (hereafter THL), BG274, fo. 386 (27 Feb. 1812). See also BNC, D148, *From the rector to the inhabitants of the parish of St Matthew, Bethnal Green*, 14 Feb. 1812.

8   53 Geo III, c. 113, § 2; Parliamentary papers (hereafter PP) 1835, XXII, *Report of the commissioners appointed … to inquire into the ecclesiastical revenues of England and Wales*, p. 637. In 1812, however, King calculated his income from surplice fees as only £100, from which he deducted £40 to pay 'an occasional assistant'.

distribution of bibles at home and abroad on an explicitly interdenominational basis, and which disturbed orthodox high churchmen (notably those later referred to as the 'Hackney Phalanx') with its implied challenge to the Society for Promoting Christian Knowledge (SPCK) and plan of circulating the Bible without an accompanying Book of Common Prayer. King's own response to a meeting of a Bethnal Green auxiliary in 1814 (Documents 3–6) clearly establishes his own churchmanship, but the extent of the furore also indicates that both parish and incumbent generated unusually intense conflicts. As will emerge, in King's case this was partly a matter of temperament, and partly a result of the close connexions he perceived between church affairs and wider matters of public order; in the case of the parish, however, it reflected the exceptionally troubled nature of both its constitution and its culture.

Perhaps the most distinctive and immediate challenge which the incumbent of Bethnal Green faced – and indeed that which King argued accounted for the absenteeism of his predecessor – was the conduct of parochial affairs, and in particular of the vestry. The condition of the parish administration in 1810 was succinctly and only partly anachronistically summarized in 1906 by Sidney and Beatrice Webb when they entitled a section dealing with Bethnal Green in their seminal volumes on *English local government* 'The rule of the boss'.[9]

The 'boss' in question was Joseph Merceron (1764–1839). As an historical figure Merceron is only now emerging from the shadows thanks to the assiduous researches of Julian Woodford; hitherto details of his life were as obscure as he was clearly shady in real life.[10] The Spitalfields son of pawnbroker James Merceron and christened at the French *la Patente* church in Brick Lane,[11] Merceron had gradually worked his way to achieve a stranglehold on the operation of parish administration, beginning as a collector of the poor rate. From 1787 he became a dominant influence on the 'Directors of the Poor' and their funds. He took his place on the Watch Board and the Board of Street Commissioners, while outside the vestry he sat on the Commission of the Peace for Middlesex and Tower Hamlets. By 1800 the concentration of power in his own hands and the presence of dependants and followers throughout the parish bodies made him appear to the Webbs as 'an almost irresistible dictator'.[12] The constitution of the vestry (all rated at more than £15 per annum were members) meant that its meetings could potentially be attended by thousands; therefore one essential element in maintaining Merceron's position was the ability when necessary to rally supporters in large numbers to control its proceedings, whether by voting or an intimidatory presence.

Merceron was nonetheless an able parish administrator. The Webbs acknowledged that he made proceedings more businesslike; but his control and influence over parish finance underpinned his growing stake in local property (by 1816 he owned 11 public houses and collected rents from 16 more) if not through large-scale embezzlement then through misappropriating balances for his own ends, while as

---

[9] Sidney and Beatrice Webb, *English local government*, I: *The parish and the county* (London, 1963; first pub. 1906), pp. 79–90.

[10] I thank Julian Woodford for showing me the manuscript of his as yet unpublished book, *The boss of Bethnal Green*, which will be the definitive study. References to this refer to the chapter numbers. In the meantime, see Ian Doolittle, 'Merceron, Joseph (c.1764–1839)', rev., in *ODNB*.

[11] See Woodford, *Boss of Bethnal Green*, ch. 1; and *passim* for further detail on his career as charted below.

[12] Webb and Webb, *Parish and the county*, p. 82.

magistrate he actively protected some disreputable establishments controlled by tenants and supporters. Rating assessments appeared to favour Merceron's associates and were punitive for his enemies, while the operation of parochial charities also seemed open to question. In 1816, King would testify that Merceron 'has amassed a large fortune without any ostensible means; takes care to elect the most ignorant and the lowest characters on whom he can depend to fill all parochial offices, and to audit his accounts'.[13] Whatever the precise nature of their interaction, in combination Merceron's legitimate and illegitimate activities ensured that at his death his estate was valued at some £300,000 (some £20,000,000 in modern terms), and there were plenty in the parish who could count the cost of crossing him – whether financial or damage to property or person.[14]

In 1804 the vestry appointed a committee to audit the parish accounts, prompting Merceron's resignation as treasurer, only to be reappointed when no rival candidate emerged. This was the first challenge to his regime; the next came when King arrived. The Webbs describe King as a 'new and public spirited rector'; whatever his actual motivation, he was central to a determined effort to challenge Merceron, and the most remarkable early documents printed here relate to this struggle (Documents 2, 7–8, 11, 14).

The modern researcher struggling to disentangle the intricacies of the conflict is consoled by the knowledge that the Webbs themselves confessed defeat. The vestry minutes which survive make gripping reading, not least because by the early twenties the competing parties were electing rival parish clerks who would simultaneously attempt to read minutes to the assembled vestry.[15] An early incident followed King's effort to secure an increased salary as part of the revision of the legislation governing the parish: having secured a unanimous resolution in support in February 1812, by the end of the year the proposed new act was a source of division, Merceron persuading the vestry to oppose the bill particularly over changes proposed to the rating system until a compromise was eventually effected. The change in tone reflected the fact that King had instituted legal proceedings indicting Merceron both for fraudulent alterations to the rates pointed out to him by the vestry clerk and for perjury in court. This prosecution was abandoned in mysterious circumstances which suggest that King's legal team had been 'got at'. Merceron's triumph was complete when a vote to defray his legal expenses was surreptitiously engineered at a vestry in August 1813.

It was war. In 1814 King issued a written appeal for support from his parishioners; on 11 April the vestry condemned it as a gross libel, and an attempt to rescind this resolution only resulted in another stating that King 'has forfeited all claim to their respect and confidence' being passed 324 to 25; then in 1816 King and others attempted to pass a motion condemning electoral malpractice and Merceron for withholding funds, only to see it defeated and a congratulatory address to the treasurer passed by a majority of 200 to 1. King later complained that in order to prevent a proper audit Merceron would 'instigate his creatures to riot and clamour, even within the walls of the church; … lately he has adjourned all public vestry meetings to the churchyard, where a mob has collected to support him'. The Webbs

---

13 PP 1816 (510), 'Report from the committee on the state of the police of the metropolis: with the minutes of evidence taken before the committee', p. 153.

14 For his will, see The National Archives, Kew, PROB/11/1916.

15 For the minutes, THL, BG274 (1782–1813), BG275 (1813–20), BG276 (1820–3), BG277 (1823–8).

wrote of Bethnal Green becoming a 'saturnalia of turbulent disorder', with King bemoaning the bull-baiting, dog-fights and duck hunts encouraged in the proximity of the church and even into the churchyard during divine service. That King was able to give such testimony to a Commons select committee in 1816 which lengthily quizzed Merceron and the vestry clerk over alterations to assessments, indicated, however, that the tide was beginning to turn.[16]

With James May, the vestry clerk of thirty years cast into the wilderness by Merceron following his testimony to the committee, King now built an alliance against Merceron culminating in a second prosecution led by the resident magistrate Lawrence Gwynne focusing on Merceron's legal expenses in the earlier case (silently charged to the parish) and his licensing of public houses which permitted debauchery. This time Merceron could not escape, and he was sentenced to a total of eighteen months imprisonment and a £200 fine.[17] The shift in power was instantly apparent at the vestry of 23 March 1818: a proposal that Merceron be re-elected treasurer found only 29 supporters in a vestry of over 1,000; the vestry clerk was reinstated; the next day Gwynne headed the polls for vestrymen and commissioners of the poor.[18]

King now enjoyed a brief period in the sun. A celebratory dinner was convened; a project for a national school, long frustrated, now proceeded (Document 9); a hundred householders were sworn as special constables to tackle disorder.[19] But it did not last. Gwynne switched allegiance, and in 1821 King alleged under oath that immediately after Merceron's conviction Gwynne had offered him and the other prosecutors £10,000 to drop the case (Gwynne maintained that all he had sought was proper restitution to the parish while attempting to spare the Merceron family), an extraordinary offer even so dwarfed by a subsequent proposal that he should receive twice that sum.[20] Merceron was released; a prosecution of those associated with Merceron (including William Francis Platt, minister of Holywell Mount congregational chapel in Shoreditch – something no doubt no surprise to the tory rector and suggesting that this issue and his opposition to the Bible Society may have seemed to him not unconnected)[21] was dismissed as vindictive. By 1820 Merceron's camp were strong enough to elect a rival parish clerk, Merceron's son-in-law Robert Brutton, with Merceron himself reappearing in the vestry and with his allies beginning to reassert their place in parochial government. The vestry was once more no place for the faint-hearted, and a new complex of alliances was formed leading to new legislation which would produce a select vestry less liable to disorder, and more amenable to Merceron, who was a chief promotor of this measure. The act received

16 THL, BG275, fos. 40, 45, 73 (minutes 11 Apr., 4 May 1814, 24 Apr. 1816); Webb and Webb, *Parish and the county*, p. 85; PP 1816 (510), pp. 151–6.
17 See W. B. Gurney, *The trials of Joseph Merceron Esq for fraud, as treasurer of the poor rate funds of St Matthew Bethnal Green* (London, 1819).
18 THL, BG275, 23 Mar. 1818.
19 Webb and Webb, *Parish and the county*, p. 87.
20 See *Morning Chronicle*, 13 Dec. 1821, 'Law intelligence'; *Times*, 25 May 1818, p. 3F, 29 May 1818, p. 3B; BNC, Hurst, Bethnal Green 3, King to A. T. Gilbert, 12 Mar. 1823.
21 In a letter to the principal of Brasenose (BNC, Hurst, Bethnal Green 3, 12 Mar. 1823), King alleged that in 1812–13 Merceron had thrown 'himself into the arms of the methodist preachers for protection, and from that time they have not only been his strenuous supporters and eulogisers, but have incessantly persecuted, harassed and defamed the rector and anyone who possessed principle enough to discountenance Mr Merceron's crimes'.

the royal assent on 12 May 1823.[22] Less than ten days later came the tumultuous vestry meeting recorded in King's letter to Bishop Howley of 26 May 1823 (Document 14), at which a key component of the new vestry was to be elected.

It is difficult to reconcile the act with the various competing interpretations on offer, both contemporary and modern. The large and participatory vestry would now be replaced by a new body: all male inhabitant rated householders would have a vote in the election of 'vestrymen, governors and directors' from among those rated at £15; the act named sixty such vestrymen, who would retire annually in cohorts of ten until sixty elected vestrymen took their place. The dispute at the vestry seems to have turned on the interpretation of clauses 6 and 7 of the act. The first specified that all persons possessed of property worth £80 per annum should be 'electors of vestrymen, estate governors and directors of the poor'; the second that 'the electors of vestrymen, estate governors and directors of the poor, duly qualified as aforesaid' should meet to elect thirty residents of the Tower Hamlets to be 'electors of vestrymen, estate governors and directors of the poor' alongside the sixty already named. To the casual reader, King's proposed interpretation – that these thirty were to be elected by the wide constituency that would in future also select the sixty others – seems the most natural reading of the text: the marginal labelling of clause 6, however – stating that it gives 'Qualifications of electors of estates governors and directors of the poor' – might imply that it establishes a separate franchise for these posts in contrast to that for the 'governors and directors' mentioned earlier, although there is no clear indication that the posts are in fact distinct. By 1830, however, when Brutton and others were examined on the workings of the vestry, they were clear that the vestry consisted of sixty elected men rated at £15 per annum or above and thirty rated at £80 rental who 'represent the property of the parish', elected by those 150–200 persons possessing property worth more than £80. Whatever else, the account of the 1823 vestries here belies Brutton's assertion to the 1830 select committee that the 'bill passed in 1823, and the parish has been in a state of perfect tranquillity ever since'.[23] King had thus been defeated; and indeed humiliated, as the former promoter of parochial order was presented as the fomenter of a disturbance which had necessitated the reading of the Riot Act.

And so for the time being ended the experiment of a fully resident rector in Bethnal Green. King's father had died in 1820, and his family possessed the presentation to his living of Woodchurch in Cheshire, to which Joshua was duly instituted on 3 March 1821. With a population of 748 in 1831, and an average net annual income at the same date of £827, Woodchurch must have offered a pleasing contrast to his troublesome London living from the outset; and the travails of 1823 settled the matter. From 1823 King would take services for only part of the year; from 1828 he ceased to take any share in the duty of the parish.

---

[22] 4 Geo. IV, c. 21.
[23] PP 1830 (215), 'Report from select committee to inquire into laws and usages under which select and other vestries are conducted', pp. 106–10.

II

Thus *Exit King, stage right*(eous)! Merceron remained. This helps explain how after his death in 1839 despite his convictions, Merceron was remembered locally as 'an active and public spirited local administrator, who had suffered harsh treatment from the malignant prosecution of unscrupulous enemies'.[24] Today his name is celebrated in 'Merceron House' in Globe Road. Does this reflect a classic east end exercise in romancing the criminal, a Melmottian figure being recalled in ways that prefigure the later selective amnesia regarding the Kray brothers who operated in the same streets, and whose funerals, like Merceron's, would be grand affairs conducted at St Matthew's? A less Ackroydian reading might associate it more with his ability in his last decade to stand unapologetically among the Great and the Good of the parish as philanthropist, bequeathing money to the parochial schools, and in the year of his death his name appearing on the committee for the Bethnal Green churches fund alongside those of Gladstone and King's nephew.

No doubt the continuing local presence of the Merceron family, whom the Webbs hinted bought up incriminating publications, also ensured a constituency keen to pour scorn on the absent rector. But if Merceron was a complex figure, so was King. As Julian Woodford's researches make clear, his outspoken public assaults on Merceron may have in part reflected his consciousness that he had already supped with the devil; the increase in his salary in 1813 had been purchased with a compromise on the then current prosecution which for some reason Merceron later felt no need of.[25] In so far as King was a reformer, he was a reformer of the Sydney Smith generation, whose concern lay primarily with the rights and responsibilities of property (and the propertied); however, while the whig canon could by the mid-1830s appreciate the irony of his situation, telling Gladstone that 'When you meet a clergyman of my age, you may be sure that he is a bad clergyman', the tory King emerged a much more bullish reactionary. Not only would his ongoing rectorship ensure that he remained a consideration in all future reform initiatives in the parish, but his activities in Cheshire attracted national attention.

This had already proved the case with the legal proceedings consequent on King's attempt to poison game belonging to Sir Thomas Stanley; in the 1830s it would be his outspoken platform oratory that caught the eye. In 1835, the reformist *Morning Chronicle* prominently reported King's address to a South Cheshire election dinner as 'worthy of the days of Sacheverell', with its talk of the 'diabolical purposes' of 'Dissenters of the Independent denomination that are *independent of every obligation, civil, moral and religious*', encouraged by an '*unprincipled, time-serving and mob-governed* [whig] *administration* who pandered to a vulgar and unprincipled appetite for change, which they took infinite pains to create', as well as 'intriguing with that vagabond O'Connell'.[26] The *Chronicle* mocked tory support for this pugilistic champion, who offered similarly combative addresses to electors in 1837:

> 'Clear the way!' – a ring! A ring!
> Hail our hero, Joshua King!

---

[24] Webb and Webb, *Parish and the county*, p. 90.
[25] Woodford, *Boss of Bethnal Green*, ch. 9.
[26] *Morning Chronicle*, 23 Jan. 1835, editorial.

Champion of our Church he stands,
Ready with his Reverend hands,
Dealing vengeance on her foes,
Right and left, with bloody blows!

Cheer him now, this chief of thumpers,
Back'd by Squires and primed with bumpers –
All who love the milling trade
Cheer, O! cheer this dauntless blade.[27]

Hostile commentators immediately linked King's anti-reform stance to his clerical career, the *Chronicle* speculating that he had been chosen to deliver the address as 'the greatest pluralist present'. This proved a red rag to King, who toasting 'The Lord Bishop and the Clergy of the Diocese' at another tory dinner in October boasted that it was 'True, *he held two church livings* – the one his patrimonial property, the advowson having been for centuries in the family – the other being the reward of merit or good fortune, having been presented to him by his College.' After adverting both to the sanctity of property and the familiar defence of clerical inequalities as 'great prizes' necessary to attract talent, he went on to 'fearlessly ask, what was it that either the one or the other of his parishes lost by his being a pluralist?' The *Chronicle* had an answer:

> That … King should prefer Woodchurch to Bethnal-green, though in the latter there is more room for the zealous exertions of a Christian Minister, may appear strange to those who deem the care of souls the object to which the labours of such a person ought to be directed. But we live in the nineteenth century and not in the age of the Apostles. There are no foxes or hares in the vicinity of Bethnal-green … and it is one of the advantages held out by our Establishment to distinguished men like the Rev. JOSHUA KING to enter it, that they can derive a good income from a large city population to spend in a parish where there is good coursing and fox-hunting. … The Rev. JOSHUA KING is not an ordinary pluralist; for let it be borne in mind that he has been singled out by a distinguished College as the fittest man to take charge of 50,000 souls.[28]

Such copy helps explain another feature of King's post-1823 career: his worsening relations with the diocesan. It is clear that, even for William Howley, at times King went too far – as when he denied his services to charity children as part of his war with Merceron (Documents 7–8). But when Charles James Blomfield succeeded Howley at London in 1828, it would have been hard to imagine a superior less likely to look kindly on King. Not only was Blomfield an advocate of the poor law and church reform that featured in King's indictments of the whigs, who by the end of the decade had pluralities explicitly in his sights. Even worse, he was translated to the see from the bishopric of Chester, where no doubt he had seen and heard much of King (earlier a near neighbour of Blomfield when the latter was rector of St Botolph's Bishopgate 1808–24), not least since while there he 'strongly deprecated in his clergy the pursuit of field sports'.[29] Even without the additional tensions

---

[27] *Morning Chronicle*, 31 Jan. 1835. For 1837, see e.g. *Manchester Times and Gazette*, 14 Oct. 1837.
[28] *Morning Chronicle*, 15 Oct. 1835.
[29] A. Blomfield, *A memoir of Charles James Blomfield*, 2nd edn (London, 1864), p. 77.

generated by the Bethnal Green scheme itself, therefore, it is hardly surprising that the letters from the bishop to one whom a newspaper headline proclaimed to be 'A Pluralist Fox-Killing Parson'[30] were at best stiff, while in correspondence with others Blomfield openly stated his belief that King should not have been granted permission to hold Woodchurch and Bethnal Green in plurality.

III

With King's departure, we enter a period in which the focus of the church authorities increasingly lay in efforts to extend the pastoral provision for the inhabitants of the parish, the first efforts towards which were a further source of controversy in his last years in residence. With the events of the previous quarter century reinforcing a conviction that it behoved the state actively to reinforce the established church, the end of the Napoleonic Wars saw a concerted effort to bolster anglican provision in centres of growing population. In 1818 the government announced a million pound grant in aid of church extension to be administered over a decade by a church building commission (including Howley, leading members of the high church Hackney Phalanx and several London clergy). This aimed to elicit voluntary subscriptions in support to erect up to 200 new churches with an emphasis on free accommodation being available to the poor.[31] As early as November 1818 Howley suggested to the commission that Bethnal Green should be an early beneficiary, though also noting that the absence of a large propertied class of sympathetic churchgoers in the parish would make the chances of securing additional church rates in support of a new building remote. This proved prescient, for even when in 1819 the commissioners undertook to finance two new churches in the district entirely from their own funds provided the vestry provided the sites, they received a hostile response stressing the priority of poor relief during a recession (Merceron himself leading opposition to King's efforts to secure sites).[32] In 1822 a compromise saw the original plan for a site on Bethnal Green itself substituted by a location just to the south (where King feared services would be disrupted by noise from the neighbouring lunatic asylum), and only in 1826 did John Soane receive £15,999 to finance a utilitarian variation on his standard commission design (Merceron exhibited his local patriotism in unsuccessfully petitioning the commission for an extra £500 to extend the stubby bell tower by a few metres as the proposed scheme elicited 'only complaints coupled with ill-natured observations'). St John's was consecrated as a chapel of ease to St Matthew's on 18 October 1828, the cost having risen to £17,346, covered by a grant of £18,266: the new church provided 2,000 sittings, of which 800 were in rentable pews and 1,200 free.[33]

As a (perpetual) curacy created from St Matthew's, the patronage of St John's fell to Brasenose College, Oxford, which nominated a series of alumni to enjoy what in 1831 was an annual net income from the pew rents of £198 (but no parsonage or surplice fees). In 1837 the church after long discussions was assigned a district to

30 *Bell's Life in London and Sporting Chronicle*, 31 Jan. 1836.
31 For what follows, the best source is M. H. Port, *600 new churches: the church-building commission 1818–1856* (Reading, 2006), esp. pp. 78, 213.
32 THL, BG275, 13 Jan. 1819.
33 Port, *600 new churches*, p. 327.

the east of the Cambridge road (as King noted, encompassing the most prosperous part of the parish), and with it half of the surplice fees derived from ceremonies conducted there until the next voidance of St Matthew's, when they would all come to the minister; negotiations no doubt being smoothed by the fact that the first cleric to benefit was Joshua King's nephew Bryan, who remained in post until appointed to another Brasenose living, St George's in the East, in 1842.[34] However, the family resemblance was limited: Bryan had developed tractarian views while at Oxford, and at St George's in 1859–60 would be the focus for some of the most violent anti-ritualist demonstrations in London. Even while at St John's, however, he would be a much more active presence than his uncle in the next phase of church reform in Bethnal Green.

The provision of a new church took some pressure off St Matthew's, but in Joshua King's absence the burden of work fell heavily on his own curates. The first record we have of a full-time stipendiary assistant to King comes from July 1823, when an unlicensed curate was appointed by the newly absentee rector. This was James Mayne, who was to remain curate of St Matthew's until 1842, and whose work in the parish was explored for an episode in the BBC series *Who do you think you are?* It is unnecessary here to explore in depth Mayne's interesting career, discussed elsewhere by Richard Palmer in an article arising from the research done for the programme.[35] But Palmer's research makes all too apparent the remarkable scale of activity required of the curate, who in the three years from 1828 to 1831 performed each year some 800 christenings, 180 marriages and 670 funerals. The letters relating to Mayne reproduced here (Documents 15–19, 30) illustrate the close monitoring of such substitute clergy which formed the second prong of episcopal efforts to improve pastoral provision in urban areas, involving in February 1832 the first recorded example of Blomfield's willingness to confront King with the prospect of being dispossessed of the rectory. This provoked the embattled incumbent to complain to his college of 'our lordly despot, who seems an exact counterpart of the notorious Bonner'.[36] The documents can be read in contrasting ways. On the one hand, it is possible to view the non-graduate Mayne, a late entrant to the profession from obscure circumstances, as an overburdened and zealous pastor, a prisoner of circumstance forced into an economy of makeshifts of multiple insecure employments (the lectureship at St Matthew's, the chaplaincy at the lunatic asylum, schoolmastering) and threatened with a loss of salary to satisfy the bishop's desire for more clerical manpower without unduly inconveniencing the rector. According to a surprised and condescending Bryan King, Mayne would welcome his daughter's marriage to a journeyman walking-stick finisher as a good match: 'none of your professions for me, in which a man must often starve his belly in order to clothe his back'. But perhaps he should instead be understood as a clerical entrepreneur, with an eye for money-making opportunities to add to a not inconsiderable income (at £150, his stipend far exceeded both the London and national averages for assistant curates – £99 and £81 in 1831 – even without taking account of the use of the parsonage as a residence). In fact he suffered no loss in income when

---

[34] *London Gazette*, 31 Mar. 1837, p. 877; order in council of 28 Jan. 1837. See also BNC, Hurst, 3, King to A. T. Gilbert, 22 Sept., 4 Oct., 9 Dec. 1832.

[35] Richard Palmer, 'James Mayne [CCE-id 70753], curate of Bethnal Green', *CCEd Online Journal N&Q*, II (2008) http://journal.ccedb.org.uk/archive/cce_n2.html.

[36] BNC, Hurst, Bethnal Green, 3, King to A. T. Gilbert, 17 Feb. 1832.

Thomas Davies was finally licensed as a second curate in 1832, the rector taking the hit of £75 (and Bryan King also hinted at some sharp practice regarding fees). It is important nevertheless to recognize a second dimension to Mayne's ministry, invisible in the documents here: his activity in relief work and political agitation in the parish, taking a leading *rôle* in the creation of a committee to relieve the distressed poor in Spitalfields and Bethnal Green in 1829, as a campaigner for the Reform Bill in 1831–2, serving as treasurer of the Royal Adelaide Provident Institution and in 1841 becoming president of an Association for the Relief of the Destitute Poor of Bethnal Green. In 1831 King had told Blomfield that Mayne delivered 'universal satisfaction'; and it is unlikely that he would have received a Lambeth MA as he did in 1832 had not the bishop taken a kinder view of his labours than apparent in the letters here. And unlike King, he established a good relationship with the vestry, which issued him a handsome tribute when he left to become vicar of Hanslope with Castlethorpe in 1842. In both his charitable and parochial activity he thus often found himself working alongside the ageing Merceron. In fact, anyone who has examined his career closely, noting the fact that Mayne was allowed to chair the vestry unmolested only a few years after 1823, may find it hard to avoid the conclusion that he had entered into some sort of 'accommodation' with Merceron of the kind King had (intermittently at least) resisted.[37]

During the 1830s the effectiveness of the established church in Bethnal Green was thus dependent on the dedication and initiative of a small number of individuals. Concerned though Blomfield was to see the parish better served, he was unwilling to depend on those agencies beyond the parochial system which had also identified the parish as a high priority. Thus he was unwilling to provide full backing to the ministry of the interdenominational London Society for the Promotion of Christianity among the Jews whose chapel in Palestine Place was licensed by Howley in 1814, accompanied by schools and a training institution for converts (Documents 21, 23). Later he was reluctant to endorse another interdenominational evangelical missionary enterprise of a different character, the London City Mission, which in 1843 proposed to direct its efforts to Bethnal Green and appointed 20 missionaries to that end. In this latter instance one of the promoters was the evangelical brewer Robert Hanbury, dismayed at what he perceived as the tractarian influence pervading the parochial system in Bethnal Green. After rejecting Hanbury's grounds forcefully, Blomfield nonetheless joined with Bishop Sumner of Winchester to inaugurate a strictly Church of England Scripture Readers Association the following year to deploy lay agency within the parochial system (Documents 42, 44–5).

That system, in Blomfield's eyes, however, needed significant reinforcement in the context of his rapidly developing see city, and thus it was in April 1836 that he launched an initiative in urban church extension, unprecedented in its ambition in a single locality, that came to focus especially on the parish of Bethnal Green and which provides the context for much of the correspondence reproduced here.

---

37 Palmer, 'Mayne', paras 21–7; William Crouch, *Bryan King and the riots at St George's in the East* (London, 1904), pp. 22–3. I fully endorse Woodford's suspicions regarding Mayne's relation with Merceron.

IV

By 1836 the ecclesiastical commission of which Blomfield was one of the driving forces had powerfully articulated the case for church extension in England's booming conurbations, and also provided a suggested model for the redistribution of existing church revenues in order more effectively to match resource and pastoral need (although Blomfield and his fellow commissioners still held out hopes of further direct state aid of the kind received in the wake of the Napoleonic Wars – could not parliament impose a 2d. levy on each ton of coal imported into London to fuel its expansion?). Blomfield now sought to mobilize in addition private giving, principally from London commercial and property-owning interests to build or purchase – and also partly endow – a total of fifty new churches or chapels in the metropolis.[38] A committee was duly formed and a public appeal launched: the Metropolis Churches Fund. Blomfield himself donated £2,000; two women each anonymously gave £5,000; and by the end of the year £106,000 had been raised. Inevitably, after this initial rush of enthusiastic support, donations tailed off, in the third year amounting only to £5,600. Supporters considered how to reinvigorate the project. Thomas Chalmers, who had headed a major established church extension movement in Scotland which built more than 220 new churches between 1834 and 1841, had from the start advocated a different approach:

> The bishop's scheme is on too grand a scale: advise him to be more moderate in his views: let him show the effect of the parochial system in one great parish, and he may then proceed by degrees to other parishes; but if he insists on expatiating over the whole metropolis by building fifty churches at once, his whole scheme will be nothing more than a devout imagination, impossible to be realised.[39]

It was now decided to try an approach reflecting Chalmers's instincts. In March 1839 a new appeal was issued in the context of, but distinct from the wider scheme, and led by one of the founders of the church building commission in 1818, William Cotton (1786–1866), a wealthy London merchant and director of the Bank of England, who habitually set aside a tithe of his income for charitable purposes and whom Blomfield described as his 'lay archdeacon'. With Cotton as treasurer, and Bryan King and Henry Mackenzie as secretaries, a committee was assembled to promote contributions for the creation of ten additional districts in the parish of Bethnal Green, each to be provided with 'the means of public worship, instruction, and pastoral superintendance'.[40] The committee brought together representatives of a wide range of London interests, including the Hackney Phalanx (H. H. Norris and George Cambridge), lay evangelicals (Robert Hanbury and Thomas Baring), a leading high church politician (W. E. Gladstone) and 'local notables' (most notably, Captain Sotheby, RN, and both Joshua King and one Joseph Merceron, replaced on his death shortly after by his son Henry).

---

[38] For the Metropolis Churches Fund, see Blomfield, *Blomfield*, ch. 9; *Final report of the Metropolis Churches Fund from July 1836, to May 1854* (London, 1854); A. Saint, 'Anglican church-building in London, 1790–1890: from state subsidy to free market', in C. Brooks and A. Saint (eds.), *The Victorian church: architecture and society* (Manchester, 1995), pp. 34–9.
[39] Quoted Blomfield, *Blomfield*, p. 178.
[40] *Spiritual destitution of the parish of Bethnal Green, London* (London, 1839).

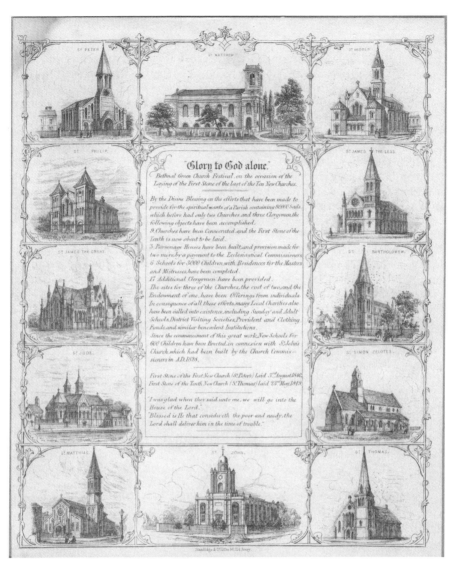

10 Commemorative record of the twelve churches of Bethnal Green issued on the occasion of the Bethnal Green Church Festival celebrating the laying of the foundation stone of the tenth new church in 1850 (reproduced by permission of Tower Hamlets Local History Library and Archives)

Like the broader scheme, the Bethnal Green fund had an extremely promising start. Shortly after its commencement, it could already report that Blomfield had himself pledged another £500, as had Brasenose, the Bank of England, the East India Company, the Grocers' Company, Henry Hoare and an individual identified only as 'P'; an anonymous cleric and his sister promised no less than £6,000, while 'Commercial Prosperity' pledged £2,000. Several livery companies gave munificently alongside the queen dowager and the archbishop of Canterbury, who matched Joshua King's £100. Sermons delivered by the evangelicals Thomas Dale and Henry Melville generated collections worth some £320; smaller donations from the parish itself raised more than £160; Captain Sotheby gave the site for one of the churches. The committee was also able to factor in a promise of £10,000 from the Metropolis Churches Fund, £5,000 from the church building commissioners and £1,000 from the City Corporation to be divided equally among the ten church-building projects.[41] By the time the foundation stone of the first of the projected churches, St Peter's, was set in place on 3 August 1840, more than £52,000 had been raised for the scheme.[42]

St Peter's was consecrated in July 1841; then St Andrew's (South Conduit Street) in December. St Philip's (Freard's Mount) and St James the Less (St James's Road) followed in 1842. Annual reports from the committee plotted steady but relentless progress – St Bartholomew's and St James the Great in 1844, St Jude's in 1846, St Simon Zelotes' in 1847 and St Matthias's, Hare Street in 1848 – until the consecration of the last of the ten new churches, St Thomas's, built at the sole expense of William Cotton as a memorial to his son, on 19 June 1850. By the time a retrospective final report on the scheme was issued in 1854, there was understandable pride in having raised a grand total of almost £115,000 and in the revolution effected in the ecclesiastical statistics of the parish of Bethnal Green, and not only in the number of anglican churches (each with an accompanying parsonage). In 1839 the parishioners had enjoyed the services of 5 clergymen and a single national school; by 1853 there were 22 clergy, 10 schools, 10 scripture readers, 19 pupil teachers and 244 Sunday school teachers and 129 district visitors.[43] Over the 1840s the annual total of baptisms had risen from 768 to 2,030.

Bethnal Green served as a model for other concentrated church-building initiatives, notably that focused on St Pancras, which formed the cornerstone of the remarkable programme of church extension that defined Blomfield's tenure as bishop of London (some 200 churches being consecrated in the diocese as a whole). Posterity, however, has not been kind to the Bethnal Green scheme, its progenitors or personnel. It has not helped that Blomfield was caricatured as a bureaucratic and partisan bully (how King would have cheered) by critics from both evangelical and tractarian wings of the church eager to find fault (not without assistance from satirists such as Sydney Smith, Disraeli and Trollope), his reputation not really recovering until the mid-twentieth century. Nor is the modern observer predisposed to a favourable judgment by a perambulation of the parish in search of the ten new churches: St Peter's and St James the Less remain open for worship, but St James the Great and St Bartholomew's are now redeveloped as housing, while St Andrew's, St Jude's, St

---

41 *Ibid.*, pp. 3–7.
42 For this and much of the information in the following paragraph, *Final report of the Metropolis Churches Fund*, appendix IV, which reproduces the annual reports of the Bethnal Green Fund.
43 Blomfield, *Blomfield*, p. 182.

Matthias's, St Philip's, St Simon Zelotes' and St Thomas's have disappeared without trace. But less superficial reactions have been equally unfavourable: Andrew Saint, writing in the context of one of the most perceptive accounts of Victorian London church extension, views the Bethnal Green scheme as coming 'close to disaster', and correctly notes that his opinion had contemporary precedents. Not only does he cite Timothy Gibson's eminently quotable private verdict on his clerical colleagues (as curate of St Matthew's from the early 1840s), (Document 181) but that of the social reformer Charles Booth, who at the end of the century judged that there had been 'wasted effort to such an extent that even now "remember Bethnal Green" is apt to be thrown in the teeth of those who try to inaugurate any great movement in the city on behalf of the Church'.[44] Even as the last of the churches was consecrated, supporters of the scheme had to acknowledge that 'it has been significantly said that the churches of Bethnal Green have not answered'. The documents reproduced here can perhaps suggest a more nuanced verdict.

V

Criticisms of the Bethnal Green scheme have pointed to shortcomings in planning, execution and personnel. It can, for instance, be presented as a representative example of an anglican insistence on working through the parochial system and a costly programme of church building in a rapidly changing urban environment that called instead for a more light-footed, flexible and swift response – the kind often identified with the early methodist mission to industrializing areas. Writing of the ten churches, Saint thus suggests that such buildings should have been 'the icing on the cake, only to be built once an infrastructure of parish life was in place'.[45]

Such a critique possibly undervalues the *rôle* church buildings played in Victorian urban religion as explored in recent scholarship by Sarah Williams and others, which also suggests that the effectiveness of the anglican approach to urban mission should not be so readily dismissed.[46] But more importantly, the Bethnal Green scheme was in fact striking for the fact that, following Chalmers's example, as it was implemented it attempted to integrate the church-building project with a variety of complementary approaches to the parish. The 1839 appeal attached equal importance to the means of instruction (schools) and pastoral superintendence, which were envisaged as part and parcel of an integrated vision of ministry. Thus parsonage houses would ensure that the churches would have resident ministers: Blomfield claimed that 'no other mode of endowment yields so large an interest for the money laid out' (Document 115). Schools proved a key issue, £18,812 having been spent by 1854; three years before the annual report noted that 6,000 children were now under instruction in the seven schools by then complete[47] (and our documents also reveal Blomfield's backing for further school initiatives outside the parochial structure so long as they did not distract clergy from their parochial duties (Documents 80, 125)). It is also

---

[44] Saint, 'Anglican church-building', pp. 36–8.

[45] *Ibid.*, p. 38.

[46] Sarah Williams, *Religious belief and popular culture in Southwark c. 1880–1939* (Oxford, 1999); see also J. Cox, *Religion in a secular society: Lambeth 1870–1932* (Oxford, 1982); R. Gill, *The myth of the empty church* (London, 1993).

[47] *Final report of the Metropolis Churches Fund*, appendix IV, p. 87.

important to recognize that Bethnal Green was an early experiment with the creation of pastoral districts in advance of the construction of churches. This approach
was greatly facilitated by the passage of Peel's New Parishes Act of 1843 (6 & 7
Vict., c. 37) under the auspices of which it became possible to constitute districts
without any existing church building as the basis for a future parish, and it was
under this legislation that districts were constituted for St Bartholomew's, St James
the Great, St Jude's, St Matthias's, St Simon Zelotes' and St Thomas's in 1843–4,
in the last case six years before the related church building was complete. From
the outset clergy were assigned and pastoral strategies developed – for example,
Joseph Brown, the first minister of St Matthias's, consecrated in 1848, was from
October 1844 licensed to conduct services in the former French church on St John
Street, and worked alongside his own assistant curates. During the ceremony to
lay the foundation stone of the new church in 1846 Brown was presented with a
silver salver in recognition of services already rendered. Other elements of parish
organization also predated the appearance of this church: indeed, at its consecration
in 1848, 200 adults and 700 children were served a celebratory libation of Alexis
Soyer's 'famine soup', originally developed for the Irish potato famine, from his
adjacent 'Parochial Model Kitchen'.[48] In the case of St Bartholomew's and St James
the Great, moreover, Blomfield appointed *de facto* curates before either districts or
churches formally existed, and in these instances moved on candidates who did not
live up to his expectations for the first incumbents once more permanent arrangements were established (Documents 37, 46).

Such an attempt at an integrated approach required a degree of co-ordination that
could only come from an engaged bishop. In itself, the sheer volume of correspondence relating to Bethnal Green in the papers of a bishop with a major national *rôle*
and a diocese of more than 650 parishes testifies to the unusual degree of episcopal
oversight it received; and several documents (Documents 25–8, 41) chart the process
by which Blomfield sought even greater control through acquiring the patronage of
both St Matthew's and the new churches, the transfer taking place in 1843. Blomfield's opponents seized on the growth in episcopal patronage consequent on the
Metropolis Churches Fund as evidence of his self-aggrandizing tendencies, but it is
clear that in exchanging Weeley in Essex for St Matthew's Blomfield surrendered
a potentially useful reward for a protégé for a challenging and merely moderately
remunerated post which only a dedicated pastor would contemplate accepting on
the condition of residence on which the bishop would have insisted (had King not
outlived him). As his letters to those considering or holding one of the district
ministries indicate (Documents 51, 61), moreover, he was under no illusion that his
newly acquired livings represented choice preferment; there can be no question that
while the shortcomings of the clergy appointed may have been exaggerated, the
quality of the candidates available to take up such demanding posts was a factor in
the difficulties the scheme experienced. The exchange was also necessary to make
possible some of the financing of the new livings to be extracted from the ecclesiastical commission, and no reader of these letters more generally will be left in
any doubt as to the virtuosity of Blomfield and Cotton in tapping all available and
compatible agencies to support the pastoral effort in Bethnal Green, including the
commission, the church building commission (which supported eight of the ten

---

48 *Lloyd's Weekly London Newspaper*, 20 Sept. 1846; *The Era*, 27 Feb. 1848.

new churches), and the Additional Curates Society (Documents 85, 106, 132) and the National Society (Document 86). If necessary, new agencies with the capacity to raise funds were created, as was the case with the Scripture Readers and District Visiting Associations (Documents 53, 75). Blomfield also made full use of his epis-copal powers to vire income across his diocese: in 1847 an order in council author-ized a raid on the revenues of St Katherine Coleman (some £1,100 per annum for a cure consisting of 700 souls) for £400 to be distributed between five of the new churches and St John's, some compensation for the failure seven years earlier of the bill by which he had hoped to appropriate the revenues of the Finsbury prebend in St Paul's to the scheme, which had left something of a hole in the original budget.[49] More locally, new local legislation in 1845 to regulate the parochial finances in St Matthew's provided the bishop with the opportunity to create a 'special fund' from burial fees in the parish to supplement clerical incomes (Document 162).

If the bishop's acquisition of patronage was controversial, this was in part a consequence of the heated climate of clerical partisanship which characterized the late 1830s and early 1840s. Across England, church parties scrutinized appoint-ments in order to detect indications of episcopal bias and the balance of advan-tage between competing groups (in 1844 the editor of *The Times* went so far as to compile a record of the leanings of as many of the London clergy as he could, the results of which for Bethnal Green are recorded in the list of clergy on pp. 298–305).[50] Tensions in London were especially acute in the 1840s after Blomfield's 1842 charge condemned tractarianism and he then bungled an attempt to impose the surplice as a badge of unity. It is clear from the letters that one source of disquiet with the Bethnal Green scheme was a belief among some evangelicals that Blom-field was using it to advance extreme high churchmen (Documents 42, 63). Taken overall, however, they confirm that while clearly aligned with the moderate high church party and cautious regarding the interdenominational activism of some evan-gelicals, Blomfield was supportive and appreciative of the pastoral endeavours of the evangelical clergy and leading laymen in the parish, and while personally impressed with the tractarian Nathaniel Woodard, would not allow his scruples regarding the latter's sacramental teaching to be overcome in order to secure his undoubted ener-gies for the parish (Documents 46, 48, 50). The *via media* was a difficult one in the 1840s, but Blomfield tried to pursue it.

Blomfield could certainly be a bully and brusque – hence in parts the accusations of imperiousness. It is nonetheless hard not sympathize with the note of exasperation that often enters his letters, and which, together with the tone of the in-correspond-ence, raises the *rôle* of personalities in the failings of the Bethnal Green experiment. In his discussion Saint claims that the Bethnal Green clergy 'found themselves operating in impecunious isolation, outside the middle-class cultural milieu natural to them. ... As a result, they took to gimmickry or became lonely, eccentric and perverse.'[51] Here his account is certainly coloured by the clerical freakshow staged by Timothy Gibson for the edification of Henry Mackenzie (the former secretary of the fund) in 1859 (Document 181). One incumbent is memorably termed 'a slug in the lord's vineyard', and a roster of ministerial crimes and misdemeanours

---

[49] See *London Gazette*, 22 June 1847, pp. 2263–6.
[50] Bodleian Library, Oxford, MS Add. C. 290, 'The principal clergy of London classified according to their opinions on the great Church questions of the day.'
[51] Saint, 'Anglican church building', p. 38.

from adultery and seduction to peculation is painstakingly recounted. But though Gibson concluded 'I heartily wish I could have given a more satisfactory [account] – but indeed I have "nothing extenuated nor set down in malice"', he was hardly a disinterested observer. His own St Matthew's was one of three churches presented as a success, and as curate of the mother church of the parish, he had particular reasons to resent the competition for funds with the clergy of the district churches. It also apparent, from his complaints at self-indulgent ritual and high Calvinism, that his own moderate evangelicalism had little time for churchmanship of different persuasions.

Regarded with a cooler eye, the 'personnel issues' clearly apparent in Bethnal Green have a more complex character. Saint's model of alienation might fit the case of many nineteenth-century clerics (though in the country as much as the town, as the case of the suicide James Skinner memorably illustrates).[52] But it is not clear that it is especially relevant to Bethnal Green. First, 'isolation' seems to have been a less of a problem than the clergy tripping over each other, sometimes in the courts (Documents 98, 140–1), as they competed for revenue or authority; in the end, there were perhaps too many districts, even though barely enough clergy. Second, the clergy did not share a 'common milieu', but a striking variety of backgrounds. The strong Brasenose contingent, mainly born in the north-west (but of a variety of theological affiliations), worked alongside Cambridge men from London, the midlands and East Anglia, and non-graduates whose birthplaces are obscure. Moreover, their careers as clerics were equally diverse: some, like Edward Relton, followed a classic path from college via ordination to a spell as curate and then an incumbency and perhaps higher preferment; others, like Mayne and Gibson, endured long years of insecurity as curates before finally acquiring a living for themselves. The Trinity College Dublin educated Irishman John Espy Keane had spent many years in Australia, establishing a pioneer church in territory where gangs were even more a feature of everyday life than in Bethnal Green (James Coghlan's early career had similarly been in the empire, in his case Canada). And although George Alston had spent time at Cambridge, he had migrated to Trinity College Dublin for the degree he completed after an abortive ambition for a career in the law and naval service; in 1848 he would write to *The Times* that the horrors of the cholera at St Philip's surpassed even his experience of 'the cock-pit of a line-of-battle ship (the *Boyne*) filled with wounded seamen after a general engagement'.[53]

'Gimmickry' too deserves a second look. Clearly a variety of pastoral styles and initiatives were found in the Bethnal Green districts. In part this reflected the financial situation of the clergy: they had to make-do, forging a pastoral economy of makeshifts which could frequently incur the ire of their bishop or rector. But it also reflected the fact that in the 1840s a widely accepted model of what constituted a successful urban ministry was yet to emerge, in contrast to a wealth of guidance available to incumbents of rural parishes. By the end of the century specialist urban ministers had developed along with the idea of the 'slum priest' and the muscular

---

52 H. and P Coombs (eds.), *Journal of a Somerset rector, 1803–34* (Oxford, 1984).

53 *Times*, 23 Aug, 1848, p. 3. The *Boyne* was a 98-gun second rate; could the engagement have been the action in which the *Boyne* and *Caledonia* clashed with the French *Romulus* off Toulon in 1814, which resulted in two deaths and forty wounded in the ship's complement? If so, Alston was only fourteen at the time: William James, *The naval history of Great Britain from ... 1793 to the accession of George IV*, 6 vols., ed. Rev. Frederick Chamier (London, 1837), VI, 256.

Christian brand of urban evangelism associated later in Bethnal Green with the Settlement movement. The early Victorian generation were still grasping after ideas. We know from other sources that James Mayne, for example, was active in a variety of initiatives to relieve the distress in Bethnal Green as well as speaking out in favour of the 1832 Reform Act in a manner that prefigures the politicized urban ministry of later Christian socialists in the parish; ten years later it seems to have been easier for the local clergy to collaborate in initiatives concerned with parochial relief of the poor than in more ecclesiastical causes, all ten district clergy writing to *The Times* in defence of the Metropolitan Visiting and Relief Association's work in Bethnal Green.[54] It is noticeable how in the later letters here an interest in sanitary reform, a key issue in Bethnal Green particularly once cholera struck, begins to appear a central clerical concern, while Blomfield, himself increasingly interested in issues of hygiene and a supporter of Edwin Chadwick's reforms, cautioned his clergy against taking the lead (Documents 118, 119, 131, 150). For a later generation, active alignment with the social and political campaigns of the marginalized would in contrast appear a precondition of effective ministry in the slum.

If only half of Gibson's claims about the personal lives of his colleagues were true, then it would be hard to avoid the conclusion that the Bethnal Green clergy had significant and sometimes literally criminal shortcomings. Defending his father's reputation, this was the line taken by Alfred Blomfield in his account of the scheme in 1863: 'it was not always easy for the Bishop to find clergymen who by means, ability and character were well fitted to take charge of the new churches'.[55] Clearly a Bethnal Green ministry could appear the incumbency of last resort; especially to a generation that had grown up with a decidedly different set of expectations of what it was to be a successful anglican incumbent, even within the diocese of London, which at this date took in large tracts of rural Essex and Hertfordshire. Gibson had no hesitation in trying to sort the saints from the sinners; but there are grounds for being more circumspect. The letters reveal the feet of clay of some of those spared by Gibson, notably the 'worthy' John Graham Packer, whose financial travails (Documents 39, 61, 94, 120, 128, 146, 167, 170) led to a spell in the Queen's Bench prison; on the other hand, Joseph Brown and George Alston, who both got short shrift, emerge with greater credit. Brown's mass excursions could be seen in a much more favourable light as an early example of parochial social work,[56] and it is clear that the bishop was most anxious to retain and appreciative of his services at St Matthias's, situated in one of the poorest parts of the parish (Documents 86–7, 144). Alston in particular exemplifies the difficulty of identifying a 'good' cleric: his financial embarrassments and aggressive challenge to King clearly alienated Gibson and Blomfield, yet the latter clearly appreciated his pastoral work (Document 32), as did parishioners who in 1846 presented him with a silver communion service; Alston's letters to *The Times* also testify to a heartfelt response to the impact of cholera and poverty on his 14,000 parishioners, squashed into a square quarter of a mile bereft of drainage, which he described in 1849 as a 'charnel house'.[57] Keane of St Jude's appears in Blomfield's correspondence as a perpetual irritant concerned largely to alter his church, find a way round the ban on pew rents and exploiting

54 *Times*, 5 Nov. 1844, p. 6.
55 Blomfield, *Blomfield*, p. 183.
56 See the account in *Daily News*, 9 July 1849, 'A poor man's picnic'.
57 *John Bull*, 16 May 1846; *Times*, 12 Mar. 1847, 21 Nov. 1848, 23 Aug. 1849.

a clerical assistant (Documents 89, 92, 95, 109, 121, 157, 172–3); yet his earlier incarnation in the demanding *rôle* of a government chaplain in Australia suggests that for at least some of his career he was not without a strong sense of vocation. While the clergy may not have been driven to eccentricity or perversion by the experience of Bethnal Green, it may not be implausible to suggest that they may have been affected by their close engagement in a community where bribery and corruption and illicit subsidies had long fuelled the dynamics of a parish where life could be a struggle. It is unlikely that they entered into any accommodation of the kind earlier hinted at for Mayne, but it may be that for some – maybe, for example, Thomas Davies, Alston, and John Graham Packer – their 'moral compass' became less true as they struggled to make ends meet themselves, in much the same way that a few years later Trollope would feel contaminated by his contact with urban electoral politics. Certainly, a sorely tried Blomfield would nonetheless remark of Packer that 'Nothing can be alleged against him beyond excessive imprudence and those departures from the line of straightforwardness and plaindealing which are apt to be gradually produced by pecuniary difficulties' (Document 170).

Any assessment of the impact of personalities on the Bethnal Green scheme is, however, incomplete if like Gibson's, and indeed Blomfield's memoir, it omits that of the rector himself. The popular association of non-residence with neglect too often obscures the close interest which an absentee had of necessity to take in protecting his interests in a parish, and this was very much the case with King. Long after his departure he remained a focus for much contention in the parish. Although admitting that in some respects his ministry had its shortcomings (he declined to write his own sermons, preaching those penned by previous generations) his family in Woodchurch later recalled him as 'a fine portly man, fond of sport and a very good shot,…a strong tory…kind-hearted like his father and very liberal; there were few poor clergy in the neighbourhood who had not received benefits and kindness from him'.[58] This last observation would surely have provoked a wry smile from the district clergy of Bethnal Green in the 1840s. They would have been less amused by King's verdict on them writing to Blomfield in 1843:

> I regret to find that the clergy of the different districts seem disposed to act with an entire disregard either to my wishes, or authority and interests…We have an imperium in imperio. Each clergyman opposes me, and pursues a perfectly inde-pendent course of action in his particular district – and that the result of their labours, instead of being an exhibition of conspicuous and consistent unity and uniformity, is little better than utter confusion [or, as he put it in a letter to William Cotton at the same date, 'confusion, disorder, and every evil work'].

King threatened to withdraw his co-operation with the scheme in protest.[59] For all King's protestations of support for improved pastoral provision, the replies Blom-field dispatched to the non-resident cleric make plain the nature of the missives to which he was forced to respond, and make it hard to view the rector, and his vitu-perative letter-writing, as other than one of the chief obstacles to success. Two points might be entered in mitigation. First, as already indicated, he belonged to an earlier

---

[58] W. F. Irvine and F. C. Beazley, *Notes on the parish of Woodchurch* (Liverpool, 1902), pp. 18–19.

[59] Letters copied to the principal of Brasenose: BNC, B12, King to Blomfield, 31 May 1843, King to William Cotton, 8 June 1843.

generation which had seen in the protection of the inviolability of property from arbitrary interference by the state or other self-appointed authority a key underpinning of liberty. Secondly, that King should view his interests in St Matthew's in this light as well as simply being concerned to maximize his personal income was in part the result of his understanding of his *rôle* in safeguarding the interests of his college and patron, Brasenose, and later of future incumbents presented by the bishop, a theme that animates his correspondence with successive principals in Oxford.

He was also, in fact, right to identify the devil as being in the detail of the arrangements, particularly those relating to finance, under which the new districts were constituted, and which few if any previous appraisals have bothered to explore. For all the money directed at Bethnal Green, as Blomfield conceded in his letters, it was not enough to support effective ministry readily either in terms of ministerial salaries or the costs of services and maintenance of the churches. We frequently see Blomfield carping at what he regarded as unnecessary or unauthorized expenditure (e.g. Documents 78, 110); but in places short-term scrimping had long-term consequences. By 1869, for example, St Jude's church was already in disrepair; parsonages had no drains, and, when it was inspected at the end of the century, the kitchen floor at St Simon's parsonage was of bare earth, covered in white mould.[60]

The documents also demonstrate just how difficult it was for the clergy of the new districts to fight the temptation to establish a system of pew rents and lettings (Documents 97, 172), traditionally of great significance to the economy of urban ministries (and still vital to the viability of St John's on the Green (Document 24)), despite the emphasis on the provision of free accommodation in securing funds for the Bethnal Green scheme (Documents 95, 97). In their absence, a new model for financing the urban clergyman in a new church was required, and despite the assistance received towards endowments, these could not easily support either the family life or work expenses expected of some of the clergy – this latter point seems to have been H. P. Haughton's (perhaps specious) justification for not opening schools or employing curates at St James the Less. If the clergy were not to institute pew rents, or humiliate themselves or the church as Packer seems to have done by effectively begging for financial support on an individual basis (Document 128), alternative sources were needed.

The documents usefully highlight the consequences that followed for an often overlooked dimension of ministerial income, fees for services. The creation of new churches where rites of passage could be conducted inevitably had consequences for the income of the rector of the mother church. Similarly, the question of who was to pay for repairs and fittings in the new churches in the parish was a matter of concern to its churchwardens and (thanks to the fact that legislation designed to facilitate church building and parochial division raised hitherto unexplored issues and was subject to frequent amendment as new acts superseded each other in rapid succession), a source of confusion and dispute (Documents 40, 52, 57, 73, 126). All concerned had to be clear under which act any one district or church had been inaugurated. By the time the group of districts created under Peel's 1843 act were established, a scheme for compensating the rector for loss of fees was in place; in the earlier instances, it had been agreed that he should retain a proportion of the

---

fees for marriages, churchings, registration of baptism and burials: half at St John's, and two-thirds at St Philip's, St Peter's, St Andrew's and St James the Less. This became the greatest source of complaint from King and his curate Gibson against the ministers of the district churches. George Alston at St Philip's was the chief thorn in King's flesh. Blomfield was at first inclined to applaud the pastoral benefits of Alston's decision not to seek fees for registering baptisms from poor members of his flock and scold King for forgetting the true relation of the fee and the rite (Documents 32–4, 49). King, on the other hand, told Cotton that while he too had agreed to remission in cases of real distress, Alston, 'a man of sanguine temperament and shallow judgement', had refused to investigate individual circumstances, and had instead proclaimed that no fees would henceforth be taken for either baptisms or churchings, thus upsetting the carefully calculated balance of pastoral profit for pecuniary loss on which King had agreed to parochial division, not least as other district clergy copied Alston's example.[61] Tensions escalated, and by 1846 King was complaining to the ecclesiastical commission (Document 98) that Alston was claiming that were it not for the rector marriage fees too would be cancelled and was withholding all fees due to the rector. King reported that he was on the verge of seeking legal redress, which he duly did in 1847, being awarded £30, though not before a hearing in which Alston challenged King's legal right to be rector in view of his pluralism, a theme which remained the ostensible justification for his subsequent continued defiance and Alston's own legal action against King in the Court of Arches in 1849.[62] King had law on his side in this matter, but had lost the moral high ground, and though Blomfield had by now lost patience with Alston (whose own residential arrangements also left something to be desired as did his questionable financial dealings (Documents 158, 171)), he offered no more than a perfunctory defence of the rector. The struggle over fees had wider repercussions. As Gibson complained in 1851, Alston had effectively undercut the fees charged at the parish church for marriages by 6s from shortly after his appointment, leading to a dutch auction (at times advertised in handbills posted around the parish) between the clergy as they competed for a share in revenues until Alston was charging only 2s 6d as opposed to the 13s charged at St Matthew's at the start of the process (which King had eventually been forced to cut to six).[63] Alston's scheme no doubt had pastoral benefits (though in years to come cheap or penny weddings led to scandal at St James the Great), but it threatened the already fragile financial framework that sustained his fellow district clergy, who in 1851 sought an agreed fee which Blomfield felt too high (Document 180). It was in such technical matters, and the small print of orders in council, that at least some of the fortunes of the Bethnal Green scheme were determined.

[61] BNC, B12, King to Cotton, 12 June 1843, enclosed in letter of same date to R. Harington; King to R. Harington, 10 June 1843.
[62] *Daily News*, 30 Nov. 1847.
[63] *Guardian*, 17, 24, 31 Dec. 1851, 7, 14 Jan. 1852; *Daily News*, 29 Dec. 1851.

VI

There has been a tendency in the past to regard favourable contemporary verdicts on the Bethnal Green scheme as self-deluding exercises in self-justification. Clearly it cannot be judged as a runaway success. But such an outcome was never likely in this particular urban environment with its rapidly and ever-changing population. This is nowhere more eloquently illustrated than in the case of another of the French protestant churches situated on the fringes of the district, established in 1743 on the corner of Fournier Street and Brick Lane, and which testifies to the truth of the motto inscribed by its builders on the sundial which crowns its frontage: *umbra sumus*, 'we are shadows'. Its original use was superseded when it was taken over by the London Society for Promoting Christianity amongst the Jews in 1809; then followed a spell as a methodist chapel; in 1898 it became the *Machzike Hadath*, the Spitalfields Great Synagogue; then in 1976 it underwent a final transformation as the *Jamme Masjid* or Great London Mosque, serving the Bengali immigrants now settled in the area.

In the circumstances, the fact that in 1851 the religious census recorded more than 23,000 attendances from the population of 90,193 then attributed to the parish of Bethnal Green was perhaps more of an achievement than has sometimes been acknowledged, and we have already noted the roster of statistics relating to provision that were compiled as the scheme drew to a close.[64] More pessimistic readings have perhaps been encouraged by the fact that at the end of the nineteenth century the district once more witnessed a remarkable outburst of pastoral energy, but this time more dependent on personal commitment and sacrifice among clergy and lay Christians, institutes and settlements than the ecclesiastical organization and planting of the 1840s. But it is important not to read the efforts of the earlier era only in the light of the later enterprise. The Bethnal Green scheme was formulated by men in their middle age in the 1830s, a generation who thought vice and sin needed to be tackled, but not poverty *per se*, which only moral improvement could address, in contrast to a later generation whose incarnationalist theology encouraged much more direct concern with social issues and their place in pastoral strategy. Moreover, the earlier cohort's memories stretched back to the first years of the nineteenth century. By juxtaposing the scheme with King's earlier encounter with Merceron as we have done here, it is perhaps easier to appreciate some of the verdicts offered in the 1850s. The documents reproduced certainly demonstrate just how much the understanding of what it was to be an urban clergyman and the task confronting the church as an institution changed in the first half of the nineteenth century, leaving a figure like King appearing increasingly an embarrassing anachronism; but they also suggest that it was more than poverty and disease that made Bethnal Green appear such a high priority for action, and coloured understandings of its impact.

Despite the emphasis on church building in the scheme, church attendance was not as strongly to the fore in assessments of its results as one might anticipate. There was more interest in issues of the impact on a wider community through the take up of rites of passage on the one hand, and the tone and atmosphere of the district on the other. Much was made of the contrast between the scene at the consecration

---

[64] See above, p. 285.

of St Peter's when 'fearful' language had been shouted and an 'infuriated ox' (of the Merceron tradition) driven among the children assembled, with the good order prevailing among a crowd including 7,000 pupils at the consecration of St Thomas's. A select committee on divine worship in populous parishes in the late 1850s found William Cotton confident that Bethnal Green was in a better condition than neighbouring parishes, while John Colbourne of St Matthias's reported that long-term residents felt that it was now much safer to walk the streets of what nevertheless remained a rough district. It was in the same spirit that the churchwardens of 1850 had claimed that the churches did 'answer': 'We see it in the good order, the improved moral and religious habits of the people.'[65] If there had been an improvement in the feel of the parish, this owed much to developments outside the scope of this discussion. But it would be wrong immediately to dismiss the contribution of the scheme, and indeed of its church buildings. We might beg to differ from the correspondent for *John Bull* who found significance in the fact that the well-ordered festival accompanying the laying of the foundation stone of St Thomas's occurred on a church site which the year before had witnessed a Chartist 'riot', but would have more sympathy with the accompanying reflection that the same scene had earlier witnessed the murder by the London burkers John Bishop and Thomas Williams of a friendless Italian boy for the purposes of selling his corpse for dissection in a medical school.[66] The institutionalized vice of Merceron's early nineteenth-century Bethnal Green perhaps may also have given additional importance to an institutional presence of church buildings as rival centres of influence, even though as we have seen that vice had permeated St Matthew's itself. Perceptions of change may reflect the creation of new solidarities and contexts for significant numbers of parishioners which should not be lightly dismissed. The church still struggled, but it was a more autonomous and active presence in the aftermath of the scheme than it had managed to be in the early nineteenth century. In a sense the changes of emphasis which led later generations of East End clergy to disparage their predecessors' efforts, although on occasion hampered by the burden of the infrastructure bequeathed by them, may also have only been possible on the back of the immense amount of resource and energy mobilized by Blomfield and his allies.

It is perhaps fitting to end this introduction with a brief reflection on the author of the majority of the documents included in this selection, Charles James Blomfield. It is not the intention of this edition to 'vindicate' the Bethnal Green Scheme, or to judge either Joshua King or the district clergy for their contributions to its progress and failings. One might, however, pause and reflect for a moment on the fact that a favourite jibe aimed at the former classical scholar Blomfield by his contemporaries was that he was a 'Greek play bishop', who had only received his preferment through his tutoring of aristocrats; Sydney Smith in 1838 was withering in condemning what he regarded as the ego-inflating impact of advancement on a power-crazed 'man who has had no opportunities of seeing the world, whose parents were in very humble life, and who has given up all his thoughts to the Frogs of Aristophanes and the Targum of Onkelo'.[67] If nothing else, it might be suggested that

---

[65] PP 1857–8, IX (387), 'Report from select committee on divine worship in populous districts', pp. 42–3, 72; Blomfield, *Blomfield*, p. 183.

[66] *John Bull*, 26 May 1849, p. 323.

[67] See Arthur Burns and Christopher Stray, 'Greek play bishops (*act.* 1810–1840)', *ODNB*, online edn, May 2009 (http://www.oxforddnb.com/view/theme/96575, accessed 9 July 2009).

a perusal of Blomfield's correspondence concerning a single parish will leave the reader firmly of the opinion that Smith's witticism was grotesquely inadequate as an appraisal; and that a bishop who not only knew the world, but made such ceaseless and indefatigable efforts to improve it, deserved better.

Editorial conventions

The edition that follows reproduces almost all the documents in the Fulham papers clearly identifiable as relating to the parish of Bethnal Green and its clergy between the institution of Joshua King as rector in 1809 and the completion of the tenth new church constructed under the auspices of the Bethnal Green churches scheme in 1850. The only documents omitted are those relating purely to pastoral matters concerned with individual parishioners, those where the contents effectively reproduce those of a letter already included or where the letterbook microfiche is of such poor quality as to render the document illegible. The majority of the letters which survive are out-correspondence from the bishops, but there are also some important letters sent to the bishop, and documents sent as enclosures by his correspondents. In addition, the edition includes a number of letters from the first years after the completion of the scheme which allow themes prominent in earlier correspondence to be followed through to the early 1850s. Two important documents from the Church of England Record Centre collections (currently accessed through Lambeth Palace Library) sent to the ecclesiastical commissioners at the height of the scheme have also been included, and finally the edition reproduces the remarkable letter of 1859 written by Timothy Gibson to Henry Mackenzie to offer a retrospective of the scheme. The original is in private hands, but a photocopy is included in the copy of the final report of the Bethnal Green churches scheme held at the Tower Hamlets Local History Library and Archives, Bancroft Road, London, and it is from this that the current edition was prepared.

Each document has been assigned a number and this is employed in cross-referencing in the edition. Unless otherwise stated, all documents are from the Fulham papers, the document references indicating the volume of the bishop's papers in which they are held and the folio or item number. The place of writing is often indicated by an abbreviation, and where the writer was a cleric associated with a particular district of the parish, that is indicated by a letter code which can be identified from the list of districts and their clergy which follows (as the mother parish, St Matthew's is not assigned such a code).

Capitalization and minor punctuation has been brought in line with modern practice in all but one case, document 10, where it was essential to convey a sense of the original. Words which are underlined in the original manuscripts have been printed in italic type. Abbreviations have been silently filled out, and the lining of the final salutation/signature compressed. In the references both in the introduction and to the documents, those to newspapers and parliamentary papers are given to the originals, but were researched using a series of online resources: *The Times digital archive, 19th-century British Library newspapers, 19th-century UK periodicals, House of Commons parliamentary papers, UK statutes (Justis)* and the *London Gazette*. Some lay individuals resident in Bethnal Green have been identified with the help of a variety of London street and postal directories, *The Old Bailey online*, and the help of Julian Woodford.

Abbreviations

BG	Bethnal Green
CCE-id	Clergy of the Church of England Database personification number
CJB	Charles James Blomfield
cur.	curate
d.	deacon
F(P)	Fulham (Palace)
L(H)	London (House)
min.	minister
ODNB	*Oxford dictionary of national biography*
ord.	ordained
p.	priest
perp. cur.	perpetual curate
rect.	rector
vic.	vicar
WH	William Howley

The churches and clergy of Bethnal Green, 1809–1850

What follows draws on the Clergy of the Church of England Database 1540–1835, alumni lists for Oxford, Cambridge, Trinity College Dublin and individual colleges, the *Clergy list*, *Crockford's clerical directory* and manuscripts held at the Guildhall Library, London: in particular curates' licensing books (London Diocesan papers, MS 10,300/7–10), revocations of licences (MS 10,300B) and the bishop's act books (MS 9532A/3–4). In 1844 an account of all the clerics active in London churches at the time was prepared for the editor of *The Times* (Bodleian Library, Oxford, MS Add. C. 290 'The principal clergy of London classified according to their opinions on the great church questions of the day'), and where clergy here merited a mention, it is reproduced. For each district, all the incumbents identified for the period 1809 to 1850 are listed, together with any assistant clergy mentioned in the documents. The terms used to describe offices are those found in the diocesan archive. The initial date run indicates when the cleric appears to have been active as seen in the *Clergy list* and/or documents, while after the name come the licences and appointments found in the diocesan papers. Each district church is assigned an identifying code used in the documents to associate clergy with their specific locality. Details of districts assigned are drawn from the *London Gazette*, where the orders in council were gazetted.

ST MATTHEW'S

Rectory, parish church since 1746; patron Brasenose College, Oxford, until 1843, then the bishop of London.

Rectors

1809–61 King, Joshua (1778–1861)
Son of Rev. Bryan King; born Ches.; Brasenose Oxford BA 1800, MA 1802, fellow 1803; ord. d., p. Oxford 1803–4; perp. cur. St Stephen's Byrom Street, Liverpool 1807–8; rect. Woodchurch, Ches. 1821–61 [CCE-id 34812].

Assistant clergy

1823–41 Mayne, James (*c.* 1775–1851), licensed *curate* 5 Dec. 1828, stipend £150 and use of parsonage (but serving from 1823), *afternoon lecturer* 7 Aug. 1829.
Ord. d., p. Chester 1814–15; cur. Stoke, Ches., 1814; cur. Little and Great Witchingham, Norf. 1821; Lambeth MA 1832; vic. Hanslope with Castlethorpe, Bucks., 1842–51. See Richard Palmer, 'James Mayne [CCE-id 70753], curate of Bethnal Green', *CCEd Online Journal N&Q*, II (2008) *http://journal.ccedb.org.uk/archive/cce_n2.html*.
1832–5 Davies, Thomas, licensed *assistant stipendiary curate* 27 July 1832, stipend £75; revoked 27 Nov. 1835 [CCE-id 94941].
1841–5 Hunter, Evan Haynes, licensed *stipendiary curate* 19 Dec. 1841, stipend £75.

Shrewsbury School, Trinity Cambridge, BA 1839, MA 1849; ord. d., p. London 1841–2; cur. St Anne's Limehouse 1845–8; cur. St George's Southwark 1846–8; cur. St John the Evangelist's Charlotte Street, London 1850–1; cur. Ickham, Kent 1851–3; cur. St Thomas's Stamford Hill 1854–8; cur. Lymm, Ches. 1858–61; cur. Little Drayton, Salop 1861–2. Last *Crockford* entry 1865.

1842–61 Gibson, Timothy (*c.* 1793–1864), licensed *senior stipendiary curate* 9 Dec. 1842, stipend £120 and use of rectory house; also *afternoon lecturer* 1842–61. Ord. d., p. 1836–7 (Salisbury); perp. cur. Ash, Salop, 1838; lecturer St George's Southwark, and All Hallows Lombard Street 1850–8; rector St Matthew's Bethnal Green 1861–4. [*Times*: 'Is a very popular preacher and an active working clergyman. Decidedly evangelical.']

1842 Fawcett, John Turner Coleman (1805–67), licensed *stipendiary curate episcopal chapel St John Street*, stipend £100 9 Dec. 1842.
Son of John, Westminster, armiger; Christ Church Oxford BA 1827, MA 1829; ord. d., p. Oxford, 1827–9; cur. Owersby, Lincs. 1829; vic. Kildwick, Yorks., 1843–67 [CCE-id 27516].

1846 Neville, William Latimer (1802–61), assistant cur. in 1846–7, but not licensed. B. Birmingham; Queen's Oxford, BA 1826, MA 1828; ord. d., p. Winchester 1826, 1828, cur. Holy Trinity Brompton, superintendant West Indian mission to Western Africa, where he died. Author of many tracts [CCE-id 82424].

ST ANDREW'S [A]

Church consecrated 21 Dec. 1841; district assigned 17 June 1843; patron bishop of London.

Curates

1841–3 Lawson, William de Lancy (1809–85), active as curate 1841–3.
B. Westmorland; schools Sedbergh, Beverley; St John's, then Magdalene Cambridge BA 1834, MA 1837, fellow; ord. d., p. Ely 1835; cur. Oakham, Rut., 1836–40; cur. Kentish Town, London, 1840–1; min. St John's Chapel, Uxbridge, Mdx, 1845–51; cur. St John's, Bradford, Yorks., 1854. Of Fishponds, Bristol, 1855–70. Published *Arithmetic explained: questions and examples* [CCE-id 7179].

1843–64 Parker, George Hargreave (1813–64). licensed *curate* to district chapel and curacy 7 July 1843.
Son of Rev. William Parker (secretary to SPCK and prebendary of St Paul's); Charterhouse and Oakham schools; ord. d., p. Ripon 1838–9; admitted St John's Cambridge as ten-year man 1839; cur. Anstey, Leics. to 1841; cur. Groby, 1842–3. Author, religious. Married 1843, Henrietta, d. of William Rowe of Leics. [*Times*: 'Son of Parker the bookseller on the Strand. Strong evangelical. Not I fear very active…Very low church, abhor[s] the Tractarian heresy'.] Died of bronchitis in Hackney.

ST BARTHOLOMEW'S [B]

District church; district constituted 23 May 1844, church consecrated 8 June 1844; patron bishop of London.

Ministers/perpetual curates

1841–3 Woodard, Nathaniel (1811–91), given sole charge of St Bartholomew's district as curate.
Son of John Woodard, farmer of Basildon Hall, Essex; Magdalen Hall, Oxford matr. 1834, BA 1840, MA 1866; ord. d. London 1841; given sole charge as cur. of St Bartholomew's. Raised money to complete the church and furnish a school. Cur. New Shoreham, Suss. 1846–50; began school leading to opening of several institutions which became known as the 'Woodard schools', concentrating on middle-class education, including what became Hurstpierpoint and Lancing Colleges. By the end of the twentieth century the Woodard schools were the largest educational body in England with the exception of the state. Canon residentiary Manchester Cathedral 1870. A strong high churchman, involved in several controversies over the years, beginning with that which led to his departure from St Bartholomew's.
1844–53 Relton, Edward William (1816–1893), licensed as *minister* of district 4 June 1844.
Son Rev. John Rudge Relton; b. Warlingham, Surr.; Christ's Hospital, Pembroke Cambridge, BA 1839, MA 1842; assistant master Bruton School, Som.; ord. d., p. York 1840–1; cur. Sheffield; vice-principal Sheffield Collegiate School 1840–2; cur. St Peter's Stepney 1843; vic. Ealing 1853–86, rural dean 1859–63. Publ. *Hints for Sunday school teachers*. Latterly of Carshalton, Surr. [*Times*: 'A most industrious young clergyman – the best the Bishop has appointed to this district. Is high church from education and example…A leaning towards the Tractarian party'.]

Assistant clergy

1847–9 Peckston, Thomas Snowden, licensed *assistant stipendiary curate* with stipend of £100 2 July 1847.
Trinity Cambridge BA 1841, MA 1845; Ord. d., p. Lincoln 1845–6; headmaster Beverley Grammar School, Yorks., 1842–5; Maths. master Collegiate Grammar School, Southwell, Notts., 1845–6; assistant min. St John's, St Peter's and St Matthias's, Bethnal Green, 1849–60; of St Andrew's, Bethnal Green, 1853–6; of St Jude's, Bethnal Green, 1860–5. Subsequently resided at Cambridge Heath. Disappears from *Crockford*, 1875.

ST JAMES THE GREAT [C]

District constituted 23 May 1844, church consecrated 4 June 1844; patron bishop of London.

Ministers/perpetual curates

1842–3 Lewis, Edward Thomas, active as minister to 1843.
Son of Rev. Thomas of Llanstephan, Carmarthen; St John's, Queens' Cambridge, BA 1831; ord d. and p. St David's 1832–3; 1843 licensed as assistant cur. St Philip's Dalston; vic. Glascomb, Radnorshire, 1847–51.

1843–52 James, William, licensed as *minister* of district of St James the Great 4 June 1844. Resigned *perpetual curacy* 16 July 1852.

Apparently a literate, but described as BA in 1852 in *Morning Chronicle* announcement of preferment. 1852–5 inc. Plymstock w. Turnchapel, Devon. [*Times*: 'An inactive clergyman. High church, but utterly without influence…Tractarian'].

ST JAMES THE LESS [D]

Church consecrated 19 July 1842; district assigned 17 June 1843; patron bishop of London.

Ministers/perpetual curates

1842–5 Coghlan, James (1798–1858), licensed *minister* of episcopal chapel in St John Street[1] 1 July 1840; licensed *curate* of district chapel and chapelry St James the Less 23 June 1843.

B. Hampshire; Sidney Sussex, then Queens' Cambridge BA 1829, MA 1840; ord. d. Canterbury 1828; p. Quebec 1829; licensed to officiate in province of Canterbury; rect. of Markfield, Leics., 1845–58. Author, *A popular companion of the Holy Scriptures* [*Times*: 'A very hardworking pastor – High church, but no influence… Tractarian'] [CCE-id 113733].

1845–59 Haughton, Henry Philip (1813–59), licensed *perpetual curate* of district church or chapel and chapelry 19 Dec. 1845.

Son of cleric; Brasenose Oxford BA 1834, MA 1837; ord. d. Carlisle on letters dimissory from Norwich 1835; cur. Carleton Rock 1835; rec. Markfield, Leics., 1844–5. Translator of *The classical student's translation of Horace* (1844) [CCE-id 5980].

ST JOHN'S [E]

Parochial chapel to St Matthew's consecrated 18 Oct. 1828, district assigned 28 Jan. 1837; patron Brasenose College, Oxford, to 1843, then bishop of London.

Curates/perpetual curates

1828–9 Stone, William (1801–82), licensed *curate* 7 Nov. 1828.

B. Ches.; Brasenose Oxford BA 1822, fellow 1822–30, MA 1825; ord. d. Oxford 1826, p. London 1829; rect. Christ Church Spitalfields 1829–56; canon of Canterbury 1855, rect. St George's the Martyr and St Mary Magdalene's, Canterbury 1858–66 [CCE-id 21749].

1829–31 Maddock, Henry William (1805–70), licensed *perpetual curate* 29 Apr. 1829.

B. Chester; St John's Oxford BA 1827, fellow Brasenose 1827–36, MA 1830; ord. d., p., Oxford 1827–8; vic. Kington, Herefs. 1835–50; perp. cur. All Saints St John's Wood, London, 1850–70 [CCE-id 35330].

1831–4 Parry, John (*c.* 1805–52), licensed *curate* 21 Jan. 1831.

---

1   The former French Church of St Jean's Spitalfields.

B. Lancashire; Brasenose Oxford BA 1825, MA 1828, fellow; ord. d. Oxford 1828, p. Peterborough 1829, rect. St John's Wapping 1834–52 [CCE-id 21103].

1834–7 Casson, George (b. *c.* 1810), licensed *curate* 16 May 1834.
B. Chester; Brasenose Oxford, BA 1831, fellow 1831–43, MA 1834; ord. d. Oxford 1833, p. London 1834; rect.. Wold, Northants. 1842–70 [CCE-id. 24498].

1837–41 King, Bryan (1811–95), licensed *curate* 23 June 1837.
B. Liverpool; school Shrewsbury; Brasenose Oxford BA 1834, MA 1837, fellow 1835–43; ord. d., p. Oxford, 1836–7; rect. St George's in the East, 1842–62; vic. Avebury, Wilts., 1863–94. Publ. *Sacrilege and its encouragement* (an account of the St George's riots); *The recovery of the lost sheep of the Church of England by home missions in her large and destitute parishes*. [*Times*: 'In private life he is as remarkable for his extreme pride and hauteur...he is notorious for want of propriety and discretion in the administration of his duties appertaining to his public function... Strong tractarian'.]

1842–5 Jones, Edward Rhys (*c.* 1818–), licensed *curate* 2 Dec. 1842.
B. Liverpool; Brasenose, Oxford BA 1839, fellow Queen's Oxford 1841–3, MA 1842, fellow Brasenose 1843–51. [*Times*: 'Talented, industrious and popular. Decidedly evangelical. Relies greatly on the judgement of Mr Champenys of Whitechapel.']

1845–66 Tagg, John (1819–99), licensed *perpetual curate* St John's 27 Mar. 1846.
B. London; Pembroke Cambridge BA 1841, MA 1845; ord. d., p. London 1842–3; cur. St Mary's Whitechapel 1842–5; rect. Mellis, Suff. 1867–89.

ST JUDE'S [F]

District constituted 23 May 1844, church consecrated 13 July 1846; patron bishop of London.

Minister

1844–68 Keane, John Espy; licensed *minister* of district 7 June 1844.
Graduate of Trinity Dublin, BA 1823, MA 1824. Had emigrated to Australia in 1825 on a free passage on the *Henry Porcher*, where as a government-sponsored chaplain he became the first minister appointed west of the great dividing ridge near Sydney in 1825. He was appointed to the parish of Bathurst at Kelso, helping establish the church of Holy Trinity, Kelso, although he returned to Sydney for a time in his first year on account of his wife's health. He was, however, taking services there in 1836.[2] He also served as chaplain at Kissing Point (1826) and as the (reforming) master of the Female Orphan School in the colony in the same year. From December 1837 to October 1840 he was performing duties at St John's church, Wilberforce, in the Hawkesbury region of New South Wales, as he did at St James's Pitt Town from 1838 to January 1841. Later chaplain to Bethnal Green Union. [*Times*: 'An active clergyman. Wants judgement. Evangelical.']

---

[2] See colonial secretary's papers, New South Wales State Archives: http://colsec.records.nsw.gov.au/ indexes/colsec/k/F30c_ka-ke-02.htm; Hawkesbury on the net, church registers: http://hawkesbury. net.au/church/index.html.

Assistant clergy

1846–7 Valentine, James, licensed *assistant stipendiary curate* district church of St Matthias's, 18 Apr. 1846; licensed *assistant stipendiary curate* in church of St Jude's 24 July 1846.

Listed with no degree as assistant curate, in *1847 clergy list*, but BA in licence.

c. **1850 Gore, John**, not identified.

ST MATTHIAS'S [G]

District constituted 23 May 1844, church consecrated 24 Feb. 1848; St John Street chapel (former French church) licensed as fit place for services by Joseph Brown, minister of district 25 Oct. 1844; patron bishop of London.

Ministers/perpetual curates

1844–9 Brown, Joseph (1800–67), licensed *minister* of district 7 June 1844.

From Suffolk; Queens' Cambridge, matric. 1826, BA 1830, MA 1833; ord. d. 1829; p. (Lincoln) 1830; cur. Barkeston and Plungar, Leics., 1829; vic. St Paul's, Mill Hill, Mdx, 1833–44; rect. Christ Church, Southwark, 1849–67; chaplain of Government Schools at Norwood; organized home for servants out of employment, and Albert Institution, Blackfriars. Chief promoter Cholera Orphan Home at Ham, Surr. Publ. *Hymns and psalms for divine worship*; *Sermon on the death of William Wilberforce, preached at St Paul's, Mill Hill* [*Times*: 'Extremely low church. Prepared to take any step against Tractarianism. A working clergyman. Is supported in this incumbency by Mr Kingscote and other leaders of the party who give him large sums for his schools, &c. pay *two curates*. Of course he has some influence with this class.'] [CCE-id 45629].

1849–54 Edwards, Allen Thomas (1818–1904), licensed *perpetual curate* new parish and church 5 Oct. 1849.

Son Thomas Edwards, London; b. Birmingham; Rugby school; St Catherine's Cambridge BA 1848, MA 1851; ord. d., p. Ely 1847–8; cur. St Andrew-the-Less Cambridge 1847–9; chaplain of Trinity Alms House Mile End; Metropolitan District secretary British and Foreign Bible Society 1854–8; vic. St Paul's Chatham 1858–63; vic. St Philip's Lambeth 1863–86.

Assistant clergy

1846–8 Hall, William, licensed *assistant stipendiary curate* district church 18 Dec. 1846, stipend £100.

Possibly from Wales, Corpus Christi then Clare, Camb BA 1835, MA 1838 (the licence states MA), fellow 1836–48; ord. d. Ely 1836; poss rect. Lower Saxham, Suff. 1952–85.

ST PETER'S [H]

Chapel consecrated 28 July 1841; district assigned 17 June 1843; patron bishop of London.

Curate/minister

1841–73 Packer, John Graham (1812–83), *assistant curate* St Matthew's 1837–41, licensed *curate* in district chapel St Peter's 23 June 1843.
Born London; Eton; Trinity Cambridge matr. 1833, BA 1837, MA 1840; ord. d. York 1836; p. London 1838; cur. Kirk-Smeaton, Yorks., 1836; rect. Wootton, Kent, 1873–9; vic. Arreton, Isle of Wight, 1879–82. Published *Companion to Euclid*; *Theopolis*. [*Times*: 'Very high church but wholly devoid of any influence, personal or moral. Would scarcely be worth mention here except as one of the Bethnal Green clergy who are now influential, because a numerically strong body.'] His wife, Ann, died in 1847.

Assistant clergy

1844–50 Fenn, David (1802–50), licensed *assistant stipendiary curate* 2 Aug. 1844, stipend £70.
Son of Nathaniel Fenn of London; Queens' Cambridge BA 1832, MA 1836; ord. d. Ely 1833, cur. Olney, Bucks., 1833; cur Astwood, Bucks., 1841–4; died at St Peter's parsonage [CCE-id 58240].

ST PHILIP'S [I]

Chapel consecrated 27 April 1842; district assigned 17 June 1843; patron bishop of London.

(Perpetual) curate

1842–51 Alston, George (1800–79), licensed *curate* of district chapel and chapelry 23 June 1843; conditionally resigned *perpetual curacy* and district chapelry 27 Nov. 1851 dependent on institution to vic. Horndon on the Hill.
Son G. Alston, attorney of Nayland, Suff.; studied law and afterwards went to sea before Queens' Cambridge 1832, migrated to Trinity Dublin 1834, where BA 1836; ord. d. Dublin 1836; p. Ripon 1838; cur. Kirkheaton, Yorks., 1841; vic. Horndon-on-the-Hill, Essex, 1852–3; rect. Studland, Dors., 1854–78; lived latterly at Clifton, Bristol, married 1828 Anne Charlotte, d. of Sir Henry Oxenden, Bart., of Broome Park, Kent; later Isabel, d. of Sir Eaton Travers, widow of Rev. Charles Smythies of Colchester.

Assistant clergy

1847–8 Dodsworth, George, licensed *assistant stipendiary curate* stipend £80 and to reside in Hackney 26 Nov. 1847.
Ord. d. and p. Chester 1823–4; cur. Danby Wiske, 1823; missionary and chaplain to HM Forces, Newfoundland; St Catherine's Cambridge as ten-year man from Danby Hill, Northallerton 1832, BD 1834, DD 1839; cur. Harewood, Yorks., 1849–54, chap. to Viscount Ranelagh; assistant minister HM chapel, Cumberland lodge [CCE-id 113292].

ST SIMON ZELOTES' [J]

District constituted 23 May 1844, church consecrated 26 July 1847, patron bishop of London.

Ministers/perpetual curates

1844–7 Guyon, Gardiner Guion (1816–88), licensed *minister* to district 14 June 1844; resigned *perpetual curacy* 17 Aug. 1847.
Fifth son of John Guyon, Commander, RN, of Richmond, Surr.; St John's, Cambridge, 1835, migrated to Peterhouse, BA 1840, MA 1844; ord. d. Gloucester and Bristol 1841; p. Llandaff 1842; cur. Newchurch, Monmouth, 1841–2; cur. Charlton-next-Dover, Kent, 1843; cur. Little Hadham, Herts., 1847–52; married 1843, Harriott, dau. of Thomas Price, lived latterly Richmond, Surr. [*Times*: 'A young man recently appointed. Very High Church, seemingly with the impresson that the clergy require to be *reverenced* in order to be more influential…Strong Tractarian'.]
1847–57 Ansted, Joseph Board (1821–1914); licensed *perpetual curate* 20 Aug. 1847.
Son of William Ansted, London; Christ's Cambridge BA 1843, MA 1846; ord. d. and p. London 1843–4; cur. Whitechapel 1843–7; vic. Stony Stratford, Bucks., 1857–9; vic. Longdon, Staffs., 1859–61; rect. Morborne, Hunts., 1861–90.

ST THOMAS'S [K]

District constituted 23 May 1844, church consecrated 8 July 1850; school room licensed for divine service by Kerry 27 Oct. 1847.

Minister

1845–64 Kerry, William (d. 1887), licensed *minister* of district of St Thomas's 3 Jan. 1845.
Son of William Kerry of Brook Street Grosvenor Square, London; King's College London school, St John's Cambridge, BA 1842, MA 1845; ord. d., p. London 1842–3; cur. St Andrew's Holborn 1843–4; vic. St Jude's Bristol 1864–84.

The documents

1. Return of places of worship, 1810

Randolph 13, fos. 125–6[3]

House of Lords, Tuesday, 19th June 1810
Ordered, – That an humble address be presented to His Majesty, that He will be graciously pleased to direct the archbishops and bishops of each diocese to report to His Majesty what place or places of divine worship, according to the Church of England, there is or are within every parish which appears to contain a population of 1,000 persons or upwards; what number of persons they are capable of containing; and also, what other place or places of divine worship there is or are in every such parish.

Reverend sir
Having received instructions from the archbishop of Canterbury to make a report to His Majesty in pursuance of the above address, and finding that your parish contains a population of 1,000 persons or upwards, I send you the following queries, to which you will be pleased to return full and distinct answers, and to forward the same to me in the inclosed cover before the 20th of November next.
I am, rev. sir, your obedient humble servant, J. London,[4] Fulham Palace, Oct 20th, 1810.

Query 1st. – What place or places of divine worship according to the Church of England is or are there within your parish, and how many persons are they each capable of containing? Answer: Two. The mother church – and a French church.[5] The mother church is capable of containing about 1,100 persons – The French church about 550.

Query 2d. – What other place or places of divine worship is or are there within your parish? Answer: There are two Independent meeting houses – one on the Green capable of containing about 300 persons[6] – and one in Hackney Road, called Middlesex Chapel, capable of containing about 350 – Besides these there are three Methodist meeting houses – called Gibraltar Chapel, Bethel Chapel and Brick Lane Meeting House.[7] The first will contain about 200 persons – the other two – about

---

3   A printed document with handwritten answers supplied by Joshua King.
4   John Randolph, bishop of London 1809–13.
5   St Jean's Spitalfields, on St John Street, founded *c.* 1682. It employed the liturgy of the French Reformed church.
6   The congregationalist chapel under the ministry of John Kello on Cambridge Road. By 1818 this was described as 'decayed'.
7   Gibraltar chapel (in fact congregationalist), in Gibraltar Place off Bethnal Green Road; Brick Lane possibly also a congregationalist meeting house; possibly originated in 1760. Closed 1877.

150 each. There is also a newly created chapel on the Green built on speculation – which when finished and occupied will contain about 500.[8]

St Matthew Bethnal Green, Joshua King, population – 30,000 at least

2. Rev. Joshua King, to WH, BG 14 March 1814

Howley 25, fos. 270–2

My lord

The king's annual letter[9] with your lordship's exhortation and the lord mayor's annexed was sent me on Saturday last by the churchwardens of this parish, and immediately remitted to them for the following reasons.

Before it is read in the parish church, I consider it my duty to inform your lordship that possessed with a thorough conviction that the King's Bounty had never been properly applied (if applied at all to the purposes for which it was sent) in order to secure a distribution of the money I caused notice to be given last year that it would be distributed on a certain day in the vestry. The churchwardens and the three trustees thro' whose hands the money had for years passed objecting to such publicity overruled the measure – but at length agreed that each person who received a portion for private distribution should send in a list of the names and residence of the persons whom he had relieved within a fortnight after the distribution. Finding this agreement but partially complied with, and not at all satisfied with the appearance of shrinking from investigation, I requested at the chamberlain's office that the names of the following gentlemen viz. Josiah Boydell, Robert Wrightson, Thomas Pedley, and James Racine[10] might be added to the list of trustees, and received an assurance that my request should be complied with. This was done with a view to counteract the overwhelming influence of the present trustees, and to secure a proper distribution of the money in future. Here, however, I was again foiled. For Mr Key the chamberlain's clerk paid the £5 last week to the churchwardens not only without having annexed those respectable names aforementioned to the list but even without my signature, although the draft expressly specified that the money shall not be paid without the signature of the minister as well as churchwardens.

If the town clerk considers an application from me under these circumstances not of sufficient weight to be attended to – yet I have been assured that if your lordship or the lord mayor were but to express a wish as to the augmentation proposed, that that would be immediately complied with.

---

8   Ebenezer or Park chapel, built as an Independent or Independent Calvinist chapel under the Rev. Robert Langford in 1811. It had accommodation for 650 by 1838. It closed in 1876.

9   Each year the bishop of London issued a letter exhorting a public subscription in favour of the King's Bounty, a royal donation of £1,000 paid annually to the chamberlain of London. The chamberlain apportioned the fund to the various parishes according to their size and at his discretion.

10   Josiah Boydell: either (1752–1817), artist and publisher, studied under Benjamin West and produced portraits and historical paintings, alderman of Cheap ward (1804–9) with a print publishing business at Cheapside, or the coal merchant of 221 Upper Thames Street; Robert Wrightson, 'gun-carriage maker to the government' (1805), resident of Bethnal Green and long-term opponent of Merceron; Thomas Pedley, wholesale salesman of 3 Union Row, Bethnal Green; James Racine, Huguenot dyer based in Hare Street.

Before therefore I proceed to read the king's letter, or assist for the time to come in collecting money from house to house without being enabled to secure its proper appropriation, I respectfully wait your lordship's further commands and remain, with all due respect, your lordship's most obliged humble servant,
Joshua King

3. Rev. Joshua King to WH, BG 11 November 1815

Howley 25, fo. 273

My lord
Hand-Bills have been stuck up about this parish in every direction purporting that a meeting of the auxiliary Bible Association[11] in this district will be held at the parish church of St Matthew Bethnal Green on Tuesday Nov. 14th 1815 at 6 o'clock in the evening – at which all the labouring classes of the community are requested to attend. In pursuance of this notice, my church will doubtless be forcibly entered by a host of Dissenters, and converted into a meeting-house. Therefore I am desirous of obtaining your lordship's opinion as to the most advisable measures to be adopted – convinced that both prudence and firmness are requisite to prevent further encroachments. The frequenters of the Conventicle are now coming forwards under the immediate sanction of the churchwardens and other parish officers to take possession of the church in open defiance of its legitimate rector. I deemed it necessary to advise with your lordship's secretary upon the subject who seems to be of opinion that I should order the church doors to be locked, and keep the keys in my own possession – that I should desire some police officers to attend to prevent riot – and should write to the chairman and churchwardens to prohibit the meeting. If these measures meet your lordship's approbation they shall be adopted – Or if anything more desirable should suggest itself I shall be most happy to follow your lordship's directions.
I am with great respect, your lordship's most obedient humble servant,
Joshua King

4. Rev. Joshua King to WH, BG 15 November 1815

Howley 25, fo. 276

My lord
I feel particularly obliged for your lordship's kind and paternal advice. It fortunately happened that the presence of the police officers, and the notice of prohibition had the desired effect of preventing the meeting in the church. I did not however venture to act until I had advised with Dr Swabie[12] as to the right of taking possession of the keys of the church. His decided opinion, and the promise of cordial cooperation from Mr Gifford the police magistrate[13] who warmly entered into my

---

[11] I.e., of the British and Foreign Bible Society, founded 1804 to print and distribute bibles at home and abroad on an interdenominational basis.

[12] Maurice Swabey (1753–1826), advocate of Doctors Commons and chancellor of Rochester diocese.

[13] John Gifford (1758–1818), historian and Pittite political writer, founder and editor of the *Anti-Jacobin Review* (1798–1806); appointed police magistrate in Shoreditch and then Great Marlborough Street as a reward for his six-volume *Political life* of Pitt published in 1809. Described in the *Annual*

views, and your lordship's silence which I construed into assent determined me as to the line of conduct to be pursued. Orders had been given by the churchwardens for the erection of a stage in the place of the pulpit, and for the church to be filled as full of candles as it could hold. These appendages were conveyed to Gibraltar Chapel, a Methodist meeting-house in the neighbourhood,[14] to which place the disconcerted dissenters and unwary churchmen adjourned their meeting. Of the conduct of Mr Crosbie the curate of Shoreditch,[15] who has long been ingratiating himself among the Methodists, I have great cause to complain. He lavished abuse upon me most unmercifully for not allowing them to meet in my church – declared his determination to give up the church at Shoreditch on all occasions – And expressed a wish to be always with them whether they met at chapel or at church – and that whether at the meeting-house or at church he would always advocate their cause.

Having done, I hope, with the Bible Society – I take the liberty of reminding your lordship of a promise made by the churchwardens of this parish that new stoves should be erected in the church against this winter. So far from intending to do this – and because it was known that my health was materially affected by the exhalation arising from the coals and the drying putty with which the stoves were pro tempore cemented together – and because the sulphur was particularly annoying to many of the congregation – it has therefore been determined that the old stoves shall again be used this winter. If your lordship would be pleased to prevent the fulfilment of this unfeeling determination another would be added to the many favours already conferred upon your lordship's most obedient humble servant,

Joshua King

5. Rev. Joshua King to WH, BG 21 November 1815

Howley 25, fo. 278

My lord

I have enclosed a note received from Mr Willson[16] a respectable inhabitant of this parish who attended the meeting on the 14th inst. at my particular request. He, knowing the cause of the present enquiry, has, I am persuaded, extenuated rather than aggravated Mr C's[17] offence. I have nothing to add to a former detail respecting Mr C except that I have seen his name once or twice exhibited on printed bills at the corner of streets as being about to take the chair at a meeting-house within Shoreditch. And as he farms the fees from Mr Plimley[18] he finds it tends not a little to his emolument to identify himself with the strong dissenting interest in this parish thereby obtaining from me some baptisms, many churchings, and still more marriages. So accommodating are Mr C's religious sentiments that, in a conversa-

---

biography and obituary (1819) as 'a strenuous member of the Church of England, and deemed its prosperity and security essentially necessary to the state'. See *ODNB* and E. L. de Montluzin, 'The *Anti-Jacobin* revisited: newly identified contributions to the *Anti-Jacobin Review* during the editorial regime of John Gifford, 1798–1806', *The Library*, IV (2003), 278–302.

14 See n. 7.
15 Robert Crosby MA (1771–), licensed lect., St Lawrence Jewry and St Mary Magdalen Milk Street 1812; licensed cur. St Mary Haggerston, Shoreditch, 1827 [CCE-id 91964].
16 Below, no. 6.
17 E.g., Robert Crosby. See n. 15.
18 Henry Plimley MA (1764–1841), vicar of St Leonard's Shoreditch [CCE-id 64885].

tion I held with him about four months' ago respecting the Bible Society and the diffusion of Calvinism from our pulpits, he said he thought it advisable to fall in with the popular opinions of the day.

The printed paper contains a copy, tho' not a very accurate one, of my letter to the churchwarden, and the very liberal comment put upon it by the members of the Bible Society. That they have subjected themselves to an action for a gross and malicious libel is unquestionable – and it appears that they are subject to a double penalty for having exhibited the placards in many of their windows without any printer's name affixed to them. I am strongly urged by some friends to prefer an indictment against the parties. But the uncertainty, the expense, and anxiety attending a legal process militate strongly in my mind against seeking redress in this way. Probably the best and least objectionable method would be to call upon the most prominent offenders publically to apologize for their conduct, and to give up the author of the libel. In default of a compliance with these conditions to summons them before Mr Gifford[19] who would punish them by inflicting the penalty of £20 upon each offender – which money might with very good effect be expended in bibles for the use of the poor belonging to the church. It is a duty I owe to myself and to the Establishment not to allow an offence of such magnitude to be passed over unnoticed and I am persuaded your lordship will not advise that I should permit an aspersion of so black a die to be cast upon with me with impunity. Silence under such circumstance will be construed into guilt – and would only encourage the ill-disposed to proceed to still more outrageous acts.

I am, with great respect, your lordship's most obedient humble servant,
    Joshua King

6. John Willson to Rev. Joshua King, 2 Copthall Court, Throgmorton Street,[20] 21 November 1815

Howley 25, fos. 280–1

Reverend sir

In answer to your favour of yesterday I have to state that I was present at the meeting of the Bible Society held in your parish and heard the Rev Mr Crosby speak upon the occasion – Altho' I do not feel competent to particularize words or sentences yet I will positively state as to meaning and general inference – Mr Crosby commenced his address by lamenting the prohibition of the use of the parish church upon that occasion and that any unfortunate difference between yourself and your parishioners should have been the means of throwing an impediment in the way of so truly good and laudable an institution, intimating that had he been in your situation he would gladly and cheerfully have contributed to the advancement thereof by permitting the use of the church and was sorry that upon that occasion you had so far forgot yourself as to refuse it, hoping and trusting that at the next meeting of the Society those differences would have subsided and the Society allowed the free use of the church.

---

[19] See n. 13.
[20] Just to the north of the Bank of England site. This appears to identify the sender as John Willson, attorney, in 1815 giving his address as 13 Angel Court, Throgmorton Street in *Kent's Directory*. The letter was enclosed with no. 5.

In fact the whole of his address was an indirect praise of himself at your expense and an attempt to lessen you in the estimation of the auditors on the foundation of your refusing the use of your church, making strong professions on his part of support to the Society either in churches, chapels or elsewhere and stating that notwithstanding your refusal he had no doubt but that the society would be bene-fitted thereby – this is from the best of my recollection the purport of his address but not having an idea of being asked for particular words or sentences I cannot state it otherwise than in this general way.

I am, reverend sir, respectfully your very obedient servant,
    John Willson

7. Rev. Joshua King to WH, BG 27 January 1817

Howley 25, fo. 282

My lord

I have reason to believe that it is the intention of the churchwardens of this parish, acting under the influence of Mr Merceron,[21] to lay an information against me probably in the shape of a presentation to your lordship at the next visitation for not reading the Prayers on Wednesdays and Fridays. I will briefly state what is, and invariably has been the practice. I have ever been in the habit of reading the Prayers when there have been two persons in the church besides the charity children[22] with their masters – and make a point of inviting the women who come into the vestry-room preparatory to being churched to go into the body of the church in order to constitute a congregation. But I have always considered the children in the same light as the clerk, sexton and pew-openers who attend from necessity and not from choice, and who do not assemble for purposes of devotion. Under this impression – and because I have not felt inclined to become chaplain to the charity children from compulsion, especially as my interference has been objected to and my name struck out of the list of those who are to receive subscriptions for the charity – and as the most obnoxious persons are continually obtruded upon me to preach their sermons – I have felt additionally justified in not reading the Prayers unless there has been a congregation exclusive of the children. This statement will enable your lordship to appreciate the merits of the case and to advise me what you would consider fittest to be done. For altho' the least deviation from the constituted practice would at the moment afford the enemy cause for triumph – yet I should consider it my duty to pursue that course which might be deemed the most prudent and the best.

I remain your lordship's most obedient humble servant,
    J. King

---

[21] Joseph Merceron. See introduction, pp. 274–7 and n. 11.
[22] The children attending the Green Coat School, Bethnal Green, a parochial charity founded in 1763 to school and clothe girls, joined by boys two years later; by 1816 there were thirty-five of each sex being taught on the junction of Church Street (later Bethnal Green Road) and Gibraltar Walk. The school was supported by a mixture of sermons, donations, school pence and legacies. It closed in 1930.

8. WH to Joshua King, F 29 May 1817

Howley 5, no. 86

Dear sir

I have seen with pain & much disapprobation the malicious attacks which have been levelled against your character; and should very reluctantly be made instrumental in furthering this system of persecution. But, on thinking over the present case, I am apprehensive of being placed in a very awkward situation if it comes before me. I do not see how any distinction can be made between different descriptions of person who come to church as part of the congregation. The clerk, the sexton, &c, attend as officers of the church, & have therefore an ostensible business there, besides participating in the prayers, though this also should form part of their business. But the charity children do not come for the purpose of assisting in the performance of the duty. They are brought by compulsion, perhaps, to say their prayers: but the act of their coming proves that is considered by their superiors as right that they should pray at those times. The service of the church is designed for them as well as others; and if it is proper they should come at all, they must, I think, be considered as an effective part of the congregation. On these grounds, I am of the opinion the custom which has hitherto been followed cannot be sustained; and I apprehend that in refusing to read the service to them when a requisition is formally made you would give a greater advantage to your enemies than by compliance. They certainly would not fail to represent the matter in a very invidious light; and in my view of the case, you will consult your dignity, as well as peace, in not insisting on a custom, which you adopted merely because you found it established by others. It is my decided wish to give you all the support in my power. Your health, I hope has been improved by your late absence.

    I remain, &c,

      WL

9. William Frederick, duke of Gloucester, to WH, Gloucester House[23] 16 April 1819

Howley 7, fo. 197

My dear lord

I lose no time in acknowledging the receipt of your letter and in expressing my regret at not having been at home when you were so good as to call here this day.

It is quite impossible for either the duchess[24] or myself to hesitate respecting our answer to the application you tell me is to be made to us by the Committee for erecting a National School in the parish of Bethnal Green after your lordship's statement & recommendation; We shall therefore have great satisfaction in complying with the request.

---

23 Prince William Frederick, duke of Gloucester and Edinburgh (1776–1834), nephew of George III, chancellor of the University of Cambridge 1811–34 (though nicknamed 'Silly Billy' on account of his limited intelligence), field marshal 1816; advocate of the abolition of slavery and Catholic emancipation, supporter of Queen Caroline according to *ODNB* 'priggish and extremely pompous', though 'religious and charitable'. Gloucester House was his London residence, demolished in 1904 – it stood at 137 Piccadilly.

24 Princess Mary, duchess of Gloucester (1776–1857), daughter of George III.

I am with the highest esteem, my dear lord, very sincerely yours,
William Frederick

10. Ed. H– to WH, 16 June 1820

Howley 7, fos. 198–198a[25]

Most Revd Lord

Your Lordship having most Graciously Condescended to Give a Sermon on Sunday next the 18 Inst. for that Most Excellent Charity the National School belonging to the Parish of St Matthew Bethnal Green, Your Lordship will then have an Opportunity of seeing the aforesaid Church, will scarcely Contain 3 Thousand of its Inhabitants, Was it not for the Episcopal Chapell Erected for the Conversion of the Jews,[26] the Aforesaid Inhabitants would not have a place to attend Divine Worship, as the Said Parish Contains Upwards of Thirty Thousand people, and more than Six Thousand Houses and many of them far from the Aforesaid Church, and many of them not Being Able to Attend divine Service in the Morning, your Lordship I hope will have the Goodness to let the Church be opened for an Eveng Lecturer for the Use of the Poor as might Be willing to Attend, as it Might be the Means of Many of them that Frequently Attending public Houses on Sunday Evenings would have A place to have the Most Blessed Gospel of Almighty God our Heavenly Father, as it may be of Service to the Poor here and thereafter, As having been Informed by some of the Inhabitants as it might be of Service and making them Acquainted of some Knowledge concerning their religious duty towards God – and Man, which might be accomplished at A triflying Expence to the Inhabittants as Follows

Supposing that 5000 Houses at an annual Contribution of 2–6 Each House would amount to the sum of £625–0		£	s
	Afternoon Lecture	75	– 0
	Evening Do.	75	– 0
	Candles for Do,	180	– 0
	Firing	20	– 0
	Organist Sixton		
	Attendance on pews &c	90	– 0
To pay the Whole Expense 440 – 0	Total	£440	– 0
Balance due £185 – 0			

The Balance to be Appropriated towards repairing of Aforesaid Church, and it would be of great Service to some Member of the Established Church who has But a small Sufficiency to Maintain him, If the Following Plan is not Approved of it might be Accomplished by the Small Tythes which at this Present is 3 pence in the Pound by Raising them to 5 Pence, their will be much Opposition to the Plan as it may Effect some that has many Houses, as small Expences be most Convenient to them as they think, May the Blessing of Almighty God, Assist your Pious Endeavour

---

[25] In this instance spelling and punctuation have been preserved to give a better sense of the original letter. 'Ed. H' has not been identified.

[26] In 1814. See introduction, p. 282.

to the Honour of his Most holy name and the Salvation of your and all the flock of your Diocese Immortal souls, is my most sincere wish

I remain your Lordships Humble Servant,
        Ed H–

11. Rev. Joshua King to WH, BG 7 August 1820

Howley 25, fo. 286; enclosure fo. 288

My lord

I am about to leave town this morning for a few weeks to try the effects of the Cheltenham waters – and as your lordship is likely to be applied to during my absence concerning the Green Coat charity school[27] in my parish, it may not be improper to anticipate the application by putting your lordship in full possession of a few prominent facts.

Mr Merceron, of public notoriety, was by a complete trick appointed on the 1st of June last treasurer of the school in question, and a resolution was adopted that I and the other trustee should transfer the stock belonging to the charity, now vested in our names in the Bank of England, into Mr Merceron's hands. The accompanying resolutions demonstrate the sense of a numerous and most respectable body of the subscribers upon the subject – And I have positively refused to allow any sermons to be preached in my church for the institution unless the subscribers will supersede their monstrous appointment.

The object of Mr Merceron's electors will be to solicit your lordship's interference.

A different line of conduct on my part would, I apprehend, have had the effect of sanctioning crime and might have caused the rising generation to suppose that the high-road to preferment and to distinctions in Bethnal Green was unblushingly to perpetuate offences of a most demoralizing tendency, and with callous effrontery to brave them out in defiance of common decency and public opinion. And I am not without hopes of succeeding, by withdrawing for a time my support from the charity, in extricating the school out of Mr Merceron's hands, and getting it eventually incorporated within our national school.

I am, my lord, with great respect, your most obedient humble servant,
        Joshua King

Saint Matthew Bethnal Green

At a numerous meeting of the subscribers to the Green Coat Charity School held at the White Hart Tavern Bethnal Green road on Friday the 9th day of June 1820 to take into consideration the extraordinary proceedings of Thursday the 1st of June instant at the Committee Room in the Workhouse[28] relative to this charity, and to adopt such measures as shall be deemed advisable

The Revd Joshua King in the chair

Resolved unanimously

1st: That it is the opinion of this meeting that the treasurer of any charitable insti-

---

27 See n. 22.
28 A parish workhouse erected on the corner of Hare Street and Winchester Street just to the south of St Matthew's in or around 1766.

tution ought to be a man of known honour and integrity, and capable of affording in his own person the benefit of moral example to those objects of whose support and protection he is made pecuniary guardian.

2ndly: That from certain information disclosed, it appears to this meeting that the proceedings adopted in the election of treasurer to the Green Coat Charity School on Thursday the 1st June instant were irregular and illegal, and contrary to the rules and regulations passed for the government of the charity

3dly: That it is also the opinion of this meeting that the trustees of the Green Coat Charity would not be justified in transferring the stock vested in their names in the funds to those persons nominated at the aforesaid meeting on the first instant.

4thly: That the subscribers to these resolutions protest against the election of treasurer at the meeting aforesaid, and hereby

Resolve: That in consequence of such proceedings their respective subscriptions to the charity be *not paid*, until such measures be adopted as may correct the evils, and remove the objections set forth in the foregoing resolutions.

Signed by the chairman and seventy subscribers

12. Rev. Joshua King to WH, Woodchurch 26 September 1820

Howley 25, fo. 290

My lord

Since my arrival here the melancholy task has devolved on me of depositing the remains of a revered father[29] in the grave, who, after having laboured in the vineyard for nearly 50 years with utility and honour, departed this life esteemed and lamented by all who knew him, more especially by those delegated to his pastoral care. The family, especially my widowed mother and sister are overwhelmed with grief, and I cannot but be fully alive to the fearful responsibility to the numerous and singularly delicate as well as difficult duties which this calamitous event has imposed upon me. I believe your lordship is aware that the perpetual advowson of the rectory of Woodchurch[30] is vested in the family, and consequently descends to me. It is at present my intention (and I hope it will meet with your lordship's acquiescence) as far as practicable to divide my residence between Bethnal Green and Woodchurch. The object of the present application is to entreat a licence to remain here from the 7th October to the latter end of November or December should it be needful to remain so long for the purpose of adjusting my father's affairs and administering to the comfort and consolation of the family.

I remain, my lord, with the highest sentiments of esteem, your lordship's most obedient humble servant,

      Joshua King

---

[29] Bryan King: for King's family, see introduction, pp. 271–2 and n. 2.
[30] On the Wirral, Cheshire.

13. Rev. Joshua King to WH, Woodchurch 4 March 1822

Howley 25, fo. 292

My lord

Your note of the 26 ultimo has been forwarded to me into Cheshire where I am now in residence and where I hope to continue till the beginning or middle of next month in expectation of recovering from the farmers, who are greatly distressed, but a small portion of what they are indebted to me for the last year's tithes.

As the object of your lordship's communication seemed only to be to ascertain my opinion as to the eligibility of sites for churches in the parish of Bethnal Green I may possibly be enabled to communicate my sentiments as satisfactorily by letter as I could have done personally.

If two churches are to be built, I beg to give it decidedly as my opinion that I should consider the Garden-ground[31] beyond the green between Globe Lane and the Mile End Road near Twig-Folly[32] as the most eligible situation for the one – and a plot of ground near the Hackney Road, formerly occupied by a school for the Jews, now in the occupancy of a Mr Wilson and called, I think, Cambridge Academy, as the best situation for the other. In pointing out these sites, I have in view the present and future wants of the whole parish more especially of two populous districts, where the population is daily increasing, both equally remote from the parish church and from each other.

Should your lordship wish for more satisfactory and distinct information, Mr May a Solicitor who resides in Bethnal Green Road,[33] or Mr Masterman of Bacon St[34] who formerly appeared before your lordship and the Commissioners on the subject would cheerfully wait upon you with a map of the parish. I have the honour to remain your lordship's most obedient humble servant,

Joshua King

14. Rev. Joshua King to WH, BG rectory 26 May 1823

Howley 25, fos. 294–5

My lord

Although I feel great reluctance in trespassing upon your valuable time with any matters relative to myself or my unfortunate parish – yet as the best interests of society, & my own personal safety, are deeply involved in the proceedings about to be detailed (and in which Mr Thomas Gable[35] bore a most prominent part) I trust the magnitude of the objects at stake will plead my apology for soliciting the favour of your lordship's friendly advice. Before I proceed further, it will be necessary to inform your lordship that an Act has recently been obtained for this parish[36]

---

31   Farmland.

32   Off Green Street, part of a new development *c.* 1810.

33   James May, solicitor, resident at no. 2 Bethnal Green Road, the vestry clerk who worked with King against Merceron in 1816, having formerly been a client of Merceron's (–1841).

34   Charles Stanley Masterman, builder, of 41 Bacon Street.

35   A Mr Gable was named in 1822 as one of the governors of the Bethnal Green workhouse involved in maltreatment of inmates alongside Robert Brutton. Otherwise, he seems not to have played a conspicuous part in parish affairs. I am grateful to Julian Woodford for this information.

36   4 Geo. IV, c. 21, *An act for appointing select vestrymen, governors and directors of the poor of the*

by Merceron and his partisans whose attempt to invade my ecclesiastical rights I successfully resisted before the Committee, & succeeded, to the great mortification of the promoters of the Bill, in getting some clauses introduced which were likely to be of general utility to my parish. Under this new act a vestry meeting was called on Wednesday last for the election of 30 'Estate Governors'. As a doubt had arisen, who were the persons qualified to vote upon the occasion, I refused to preside at the meeting, altho' urgently solicited, unless counsel's opinion was obtained respecting the admissibility of the votes of the electors of vestrymen mentioned in the 2nd clause.[37] Mr Adolphus'[38] opinion was consequently obtained, which is positive that they are admissible. Upon this opinion I acted – But before it was produced to the meeting, from which all the electors of vestrymen were excluded vi et armis[39] altho' I repeatedly ordered their admission, I exhorted the Estates Governors to act upon the principle so strongly recommended by the Committee of the House of Commons that 'the Bill should be considered by all Parties as an act of conciliation and no cause of triumph should be given to either' – and therefore recommended that 15 persons should be proposed by each party, & elected. This proposition was received by Merceron, Gwynne, Gable etc with the greatest disdain, & violent exclamations 'that they wanted none of my speeches, that I had no right as chairman to dictate to them – that I ought to be ashamed of myself – that they were not going to give up the advantages they had gained by the Act &c &c'. I then produced the before-mentioned opinion, upon which I was assailed on every side with the vilest calumny & abuse, with hissing, hollowing, shouting & most violent exclamations – Gwynne[40] (who is a magistrate, & against whom it has been proved in evidence upon his conviction before the Court of King's Bench of a libel that he offered me £10,000 to pervert the ends of justice if I would assist him in protecting his friend Merceron from being called up for judgment) said I was at my old tricks again – that I did it to involve the parish in endless litigation – insinuated that I had been guilty of perjury in the evidence given against him in the King's Bench – & reproached me with laying poison to poison Sir Thomas Stanley's cattle.[41] All was

---

parish of St Matthew Bethnal Green in the county of Middlesex, and for altering and amending two acts passed in the thirteenth and fifty-third years of his Late Majesty King George III, relating to the same (12 May 1823). Under its second clause, all male householders assessed for poor rates resident for at least six months would constitute the electorate for vestrymen, governors and directors of the poor; under clause 6 those persons holding property worth more than £80 per annum would also qualify to vote whether or not they were resident. The vestry itself would in future consist of ninety vestrymen, governors and directors of the poor, with ten retiring each year in rotation. To qualify for election, candidates would have to be inhabitant householders rated at more than £15 per annum. Sixty individuals were named in the act; clause 7 required the election of thirty more within a month of the act's passing, leading to the events described here. In addition the rector, the churchwardens, the treasurers of the poor rate funds and overseers of the poor (in the case of the lay officers both while in office and for one year after standing down) would be members of the vestry. Clause 11 specified that the rector, if resident and present, was to chair meetings of the vestry.

37 I.e., all resident male householders assessed to the poor rate.

38 John Adolphus (1768–1845), lawyer and author of *Biographical memoirs of the French Revolution* (1799).

39 'with force of arms' (Latin).

40 Lawrence Gwynne (1772–1854), mathematician, astronomer and former lieutenant and commander RN; magistrate and deputy lieutenant for county of Middlesex, and sheriff of London and Middlesex 1818–19.

41 In April 1820 King and his brother Bryan were tried at the Chester assizes for conspiracy 'to poison his majesty's subjects, distributing poison for the destruction of cattle, conspiracy to poison swine',

confusion, although I luckily kept my temper & did not utter a single irritating expression amidst all the abuse heaped upon me for about three hours. Merceron & his party were pertinacious in refusing admission to the electors of vestrymen – I in urging their admission. I proposed an adjournment of the meeting to next week that another opinion might be obtained, upon which I pledged myself to act. This was refused – At length, to avoid being kept at the workhouse all night, where the meeting was held, I agreed to take the votes of the Estate Governors present by ballot, & to declare the numbers for each list viz. for Gwynne & Wrightson[42] – but that I should not consider their votes *decisive* of the election – & would only receive them *conditionally* without prejudice to the question – & that after I had received their votes by themselves, I would immediately proceed to perceive the votes of the electors of vestrymen. The number for Gwynne's list, as all the persons whose names were included in that list voted for themselves, was 81 – For Mr Wrightson's list 5, none of the Governors whose names were included in this list having voted for their own election. Merceron & co. then became clamorous for an adjournment, which I refused, till the electors of vestrymen had tendered their votes. They took the law into their own hands, superseded the authority of the chairman – & upon the question of adjournment being put by Gwynne, which was carried, many of them left the room. Benches upon which Merceron's creatures seated themselves, in addition to locks, bars & bolts, were placed against the door to prevent any of the electors of vestrymen from entering, & I was again assailed with the vilest abuse and insult. Several of the creatures approached in menacing attitude, & said 'they were better fellows than me, they would not be bullied & dictated to by me' – added 'Mr Rector I am going to piss – Mr Rector I am going to s**t'. After my ears had been thus offended for nearly an hour – & receiving a positive declaration from the constable and overseers that no person should be admitted, I adjourned the meeting to the vestry-room, & there received 179 votes for Wrightson, & 5 for Gwynne. From eleven o'clock in the morning till ten at night I was occupied in this painful business.

and having laid poison to this end. The case was widely followed in the press from its origins in the Knutsford quarter sessions in Oct. 1819. King, who wrote to the *Morning Chronicle* to call on the public to reserve judgment despite the finding of a true bill on the 'absurd and malicious' charges (26 Oct. 1819), had obtained a writ removing the case from the Cheshire courts to King's Bench, his counsel insisting that the nature of the case and the involvement of the Stanleys made a fair trial unlikely in Cheshire (*Ipswich Journal*, 20 Nov. 1819). Prosecuting, the attorney general argued that on visits to his father's parish of Woodchurch, King had enjoyed field sports, leading Sir Thomas Stanley to bring an action under the game laws. King in revenge had plotted to destroy foxes (which as vermin he assumed were not protected) and partridges on the estate, the plot coming to light through the discovery by a 'poor cottager' rummaging through rubbish of a partly destroyed letter to one of King's brothers. The prosecution further alleged that Stanley's gamekeeper claimed to have seen Bryan King and an accomplice distributing poisoned cake and bait in one of Sir Thomas's fox coverts to which pigs and cattle had access. The defence in reply claimed only to be protecting the right of the Kings to shoot foxes on their own freehold against the intimidation of Sir Thomas and the 'fox-hunting party'; before the case could be elaborated further the bench intervened to throw out the indictments and instruct the jury to return a verdict of not guilty. The only charge that might have stuck, relating to the poisoning of game, had not featured in the indictments. In summer 1820 Bryan King brought an action for malicious prosecution against Stanley in the Chester assizes, and was awarded 40*s* in damages. Stanley's counsel argued in King's Bench that a miscarriage of justice had occurred, but despite accepting that Stanley had a case, the court declined to order a retrial in view of the small amount of damages involved (*Morning Chronicle*, 17 Apr. 1820, 22 May 1821).

42   Robert Wrightson: see n. 10 above.

On the Thursday, I again went to take the chair – my access to it was interrupted by Gwynne, who disputed my right to preside & wanted to put it to the vote. While he was abusing me, I sprang over the table, & got possession of the chair, which I told him I claimed by virtue of my office as well as in conformity with the act, & that I would not be dispossessed. I then reported, after having read the notice for convening the meeting, the result of the ballot the day before, & pronounced the persons contained in Wrightson's list to be duly elected. They were however refused admission into the room, while those in the other list were already there. A rush was made to get in – several blows & bruises followed – the Riot Act[43] was called for – the result was, the Governors elected by the vestry were forced out of the room – & the whole disturbance was, of course, attributed to me, because I ordered them to be admitted. Imagination can scarcely picture the gross personal insults I then received. As soon as a little order could be restored, I protested against the exclusion of those who had been duly elected – pronounced the object of the meeting, which was to supersede the appointment of the vestry clerk, churchwardens and other officers who had been legally elected in the church on Easter Monday & Tuesday last by an ex post facto appointment, *to be illegal* – and therefore on both these accounts adjourned the meeting sine die. On quitting the room, the most discordant yells were set up, & I was literally hunted like a wild beast, amidst the vilest exclamations. Merceron & co then elected their own chairman, & proceeded, after having lavished the most copious abuse upon me, to the election of officers, who, with closed doors, have taken upon themselves the administration of the affairs of the parish, & who by locks, bolts, & open violence exclude those who were legally appointed from attending their meetings. Such conduct becomes no longer a matter of consideration solely with reference to myself as rector, although my life may fall a sacrifice to vindictive rage, but affects materially the interests of the Established Church & the public peace. I may venture to say, that the misrepresentations which have gone forth, as to my own conduct, & the foul though groundless imputations which have been cast upon me, have had a direct tendency to make me a most obnoxious individual to all the unprincipled & undiscerning part of my parish – therefore unless some remedy can speedily be applied to evils of such an alarming magnitude, I shall be driven to the unpleasant necessity of retiring for ever from the parish, & leaving it entirely at the mercy of that lawless faction by which I have been constantly assailed. Whether this would be a case to lay before the secretary of state for the Home Department, or for the attorney-general, your lordship may probably be enabled to determine. For after the enormous sums I have already expended in vindicating the rights of the Church, & in bringing offenders within my parish to merited conviction & punishment & after witnessing as little good arising therefrom, I should not feel again disposed to seek a remedy upon my own responsibility.

I have the honour to remain, your lordship's most obliged and obedient servant,
    Joshua King

---

[43] *An act for preventing tumults and riotous assemblies, and for the more speedy and effectual punishing the rioters*, 1 Geo. I, st. 2 c. 5 (1714) allowed local authorities to declare a gathering of more than twelve people unlawful and demand they disperse.

15. CJB to Rev. Joshua King, L 9 December 1831

Blomfield 2, fo. 44

Revd sir

I wish to draw your attention to the very inadequate provision made for the duties of your parish of St Matthew Bethnal Green, the whole of which, including those of lecturer, are left to be discharged by Mr Mayne,[44] with the occasional aid of a clergyman named Davis,[45] who is quite disabled by bodily infirmity from taking any active part in the office of parochial visiting etc. This state of things of course excites great dissatisfaction, as it is quite impossible for any one clergyman, however active & zealous, to look after the spiritual wants of such a population. I have therefore to express my earnest hope that you will make some arrangement for a second curate. Mr Mayne will not object to a deduction from his present income of £40 or £50, and I trust that you will be ready to add as much more, with a view to restoring to your parishioners a more effectual superintendence and a more satisfactory performance of the duties of this church.

I remain, revd sir, your faithful servant,
C. J. London

16. CJB to Rev. James Mayne, LH 17 December 1831

Blomfield 2, fo. 51

Revd sir

Mr King informs me that you have lately accepted a chaplaincy at a lunatic asylum[46] & opened a school. It being impossible that the parochial duty of Bethnal Green, including that of lecturer, should be properly discharged in conjunction with other avocations, I must press for a new arrangement of the curacy, and as Mr King objects to pay any additional stipend, it will be necessary that a part of your emoluments should go to a second curate. With respect to the lunatic asylum, I must beg to see you again on Friday

I remain, revd sir, your faithful servant
C. J. London

17. CJB to Rev. Joshua King, L 13 February 1832

Blomfield 2, fo. 74

Revd sir

Your answer to the letter which I addressed to you on the subject of the curacy of St Matthew Bethnal Green is of such a nature as to preclude all further argument

---

[44] See above, pp. 281–2; Richard Palmer, 'James Mayne [CCE-id 70753], curate of Bethnal Green', *CCEd Online Journal, N&Q*, II (2008) http://journal.ccedb.org.uk/archive/cce_n2.html.

[45] See above, p. 298.

[46] Bethnal House lunatic asylum originated in the eighteenth century and in 1800 was acquired by Thomas Warburton, who already owned another asylum in Hackney. The asylum took in paupers paid for by their parish, who made up 654 of the 933 inmates in 1829–30. By 1831 Warburton had built a 'Red House' for men to accompany an existing 'White House' now confined to women only. The presence of two medical officers from 1828 seems to have curtailed the abuses previously reported.

on my part. I shall therefore content myself with informing you that unless a more adequate provision be made for the spiritual duties of your important parish, I shall probably feel myself called upon to take measures for declaring the living void. You are doubtless aware that it was rendered *voidable* by your institution to Woodchurch, and that it may be declared actually void either by the patron or the bishop.

I am, revd sir, your faithful servant

C. J. London[47]

18. CJB to Rev. Joshua King, L 20 February 1832

Blomfield 2, fos. 82–3

Revd sir

I have to acknowledge the receipt of your letter consenting to the appointment of a second curate. You remark that I might have spared the threat of declaring your living void. You will be pleased to remember that I did not intimate any such intention, till I had received a peremptory *refusal* to my request, which has been acceded to only in consequence of such intimation.

Whatever any other bishop might have done under such circumstances you may be assured that I should have put into execution, if necessary, a measure which was not resolved upon without proper advice.[48] If upon the avoidance so declared, the patron of St Matthew Bethnal Green had represented you, the living of Woodchurch would have become *ipso facto* void, & upon your being again presented to it St Matthew's would have been rendered voidable. But I am certainly very glad that all this has been prevented.

I am, revd sir, your faithful servant

C. J. London

19. CJB to Rev. James Mayne, LH 26 April 1832

Blomfield 3, fos. 17–18

Revd sir

When I last saw you here you informed me that Mr Davies[49] was disabled by bodily infirmities from all active exertion, and I then told you that I should press upon Mr King the necessity of appointing an efficient coadjutor to you in the curacy, especially as you had undertaken duties which I considered to be incompatible with the proper care of the parish. I am therefore rather surprised that without further communication with me, you should have recommended Mr Davies to be the assistant curate and am now at the necessity of desiring that he will not continue to

---

47 King wrote to the principal of Brasenose in the wake of this letter that Blomfield was a 'lordly despot, who seems an exact counterpart of the notorious Bonner': BNC archives, D148, King to A. T. Gilbert, 17 Feb. 1832.

48 In his letter of 17 Feb. to Gilbert, King quoted from his reply to Blomfield: 'The patrons are much too honourable to take any such unfair advantage of an incumbent – and I trust that there is not upon the bench a bishop who under the peculiar circumstances of this case could act as our lordship insinuates.'

49 Thomas Davies: see Document 15.

officiate in the church at Bethnal Green without my licence. I shall be out of town till the 5th of May; after which date I will trouble you to call on me

I remain, revd sir, your faithful servant

C. J. London

20. CJB to Rev. Joshua King, L 10 January 1833

Blomfield 5, fo. 52

Revd sir,

Mr Parry[50] will probably be ready to acquiesce in any arrangement which I may suggest to him; but I wish to learn from you what proportion of the surplice fees taken at St John's you think should be paid to you.[51] If the *whole* were to be handed over to you, and it were known that no part went to Mr Parry, most probably there would be very few surplice fees given at St John's, as they are generally considered as a compliment to the officiating clergyman. I have been prevented from various causes from answering your letter before

I am, revd sir, your faithful servant,

C. J. London

21. CJB to Rev. James Boardman Cartwright,[52] Southend, 16 September 1834

Blomfield 9, fo. 36

Revd sir

I have to acknowledge the favour of your letter, conveying to me a request from the Committee of the London Society for Promoting Christianity amongst the Jews,[53] that I would admit Mr Farman, one of their missionaries, into holy orders; and I am sorry that I do not feel myself at liberty to comply with that request. I do not admit any person, not being a graduate, as a candidate for ordination, except under the provisions of the 59 Geo. 3 c. 60[54] which relates to the ordination of persons for the service of the Church in '*His Majesty's foreign possessions and colonies*'; nor can I ordain any person who is not appointed to exercise his ministry in some particular place, a practice, which if it were to prevail to any extent, would be productive of much inconvenience.

I remain, revd sir, your faithful servant,

C. J. London

---

50 See above, pp. 301–2.

51 Fees payable to the incumbent for marriages and burial in the parish (not necessarily conducted by him). King had been in discussion with the church building commissioners, and had proposed the retention of half the surplice and half the regular fees by the rector, noting that the location of St John's amidst 'the more opulent of the parishioners' would entail a loss to the rector. See BNC, D148, King to A. T. Gilbert 4 Oct., 9 Nov. 1832.

52 James Boardman Cartwright MA (1798–1861), minister Jewish Episcopal Chapel, Bethnal Green, 1831–61 [CCE-id. 47156].

53 The LSPCJ was founded in 1809 on an interdenominational evangelical basis similar to that of the Bible Society to take the Christian message to the Jewish community.

54 *An act to permit the archbishops of Canterbury and York and the bishop of London for the time being to admit persons to holy orders specially for the colonies.* Samuel Farman was in fact ordained deacon by Blomfield on 12 Dec. 1834 as a colonial clergyman [CCE-id 112761].

22. CJB to Rev. Thomas Davies, F 23 November 1835

Blomfield 11, fo. 41

Revd sir

The fact of your having appropriated to your own use money which you had received as subscriptions to the Bethnal Green national schools having been admitted, I deem it upon further consideration unnecessary to institute an enquiry respecting the other charge which has brought against you.[55] Upon the former ground, independently of other considerations, it becomes my painful duty to revoke your licence, and to forbid your officiating in my diocese.[56]

I remain, revd sir, your faithful servant,

C. J. London

23. CJB to Rev. James Boardman Cartwright, F 5 July 1836

Blomfield 12, fos. 59–60

Dear sir

It is not necessary for me to explain the reason of my having so long delayed in answering your letter of the 4th May. I am now through God's mercy convalescent, though not yet equal to any exertion.

I am very sensible of the kind opinion which has led the Committee of the London Society for Promoting Christianity amongst the Jews to express a wish that I should become a patron of that institution: but the view which I have long taken of the great question of converting the Jews, and of the best method of promoting that object, is such that I am obliged to decline complying with their wish. At the same time I am disposed to afford them every facility, which I consider to be not incompatible with the interests of the church, in the prosecution of their benevolent design.

You allude to the religious destitution of the district in which your ministry is exercised. It has always been a subject of painful solicitude with me, and I hope that, with the blessing of God upon the project which I have now in hand, for building additional churches in the metropolis, something may be done in the way of remedy.

I remain, dear sir, your faithful servant

C. J. London.

24. CJB to Rev. Bryan King [E],[57] Ravensworth Castle[58] 26 September 1838

Blomfield 17, fo. 47

Revd sir

I see no objection to the alterations which you propose to make in the pew rents at St John's Church Bethnal Green, except the chance of persons not taking seats at £1 who are ready to pay 15s – But of this you will be able to judge pretty well from previous inquiry. It will be necessary that a new scale of pew rents should be

---

55 *Sic.*
56 The formal revocation came on 27 Nov. 1835. See Guildhall Library, LDP, MS 10300B.
57 See above, p. 302.
58 County Durham; the home of Sir Thomas Henry Liddell, First Baron Ravensworth (1775–1855).

prepared, and signed by you with the churchwardens, & then by me. This can be done after my return home.

I remain revd sir, your faithful servant

C. J. London

25. CJB to Rev. Ashurst Turner Gilbert,[59] LH 18 November 1840

Blomfield 26, fos. 87–8

My dear sir,

I am desirous of appropriating, with the consent of the Ecclesiastical Commissioners, some part of the income of certain largely endowed benefices in my gift, to the endowment of some of the new churches built by means of the Metropolis Churches Fund, in the parishes of Stepney & Bethnal Green. You are aware that it is our intention, in every case where it is practicable, to provide residence houses for the ministers of these churches. Each house will cost us about £1,200. I propose, in addition to this endowment, to assign to each church, as far as the resources at my disposal will go, a permanent endowment of from £50 to £100 per annum, payable out of the income of the benefices alluded to. But this can only be done, under the 74th sect of the 3 & 4 Vict. c. 113[60] where the benefices to be endowed belong to the same patron.

I wish therefore to learn whether Brasenose College will consider this proposal as bringing the churches to be endowed within the limits of the offer which they have already made, of giving to the bishop of London the patronage of each of the new churches in Stepney and Bethnal Green, as he may find the means of endowing.

Believe me my dear sir, with much esteem, yours very faithfully

C. J. London

26. CJB to Rev. Ashurst Turner Gilbert, LH 5 May 1841

Blomfield 28, fos. 64–5

My dear sir

The Ecclesiastical Commissioners will raise the income of district churches with a population of 2,000 and upwards to £150 a year, where they are in public patronage, which description does not include benefices in the gift of colleges. The church of All Saints Mile End[61] new town and most, if not all of the Bethnal Green churches, will have nothing to depend upon in the shape of pew rents, beyond what may be required to defray the expenses of divine service. I wish therefore to inquire, whether the college will consent to place those of the new churches, which may be so situated as to render it necessary to look for an endowment to the Ecclesias-

---

59 Ashurst Turner Gilbert (1786–1870), principal of Brasenose Oxford from 1822. An orthodox high churchman, initially supportive of the tractarians who later turned against them; in 1842 he was appointed bishop of Chichester [CCE-id 29358].

60 The Ecclesiastical Duties and Revenues Act/Ecclesiastical Commissioners Act, 1840. § 74 allowed a bishop to apportion income between benefices with a common patron subject to the latter's approval.

61 In 1841 Mile End new town was constituted a district chapelry of St Dunstan's Stepney. All Saints had been built in 1838–9 under the auspices of the church building commission with support from the Metropolis Churches Fund. It was demolished in the 1950s.

tical Commissioners, in the patronage of the bishop as a preliminary step towards obtaining such endowment.

You are aware that my expectation of being able to provide endowments for all these new churches, by means of the Finsbury Prebend, were disappointed by the rejection of my Bill by the House of Commons, after it had passed the Lords.[62]

I have not laid aside my purpose of making some provision for these churches from the proceeds of one or two of the larger benefices in the City of London but that cannot be done immediately.

Believe me, my dear sir, with much regard, yours very truly,

    C. J. London

27. CJB to Rev. Ashurst Turner Gilbert, F 29 July 1841

Blomfield 29, fos. 55–7

My dear sir

I certainly understood from a former communication, that the college had consented to vest the patronage of the new churches in the bishop in cases in which he should provide an endowment as well as the expense of building the church. Nothing was said as to the source from which the endowment was to be derived; although I had held out, in my printed proposals, the prospect of endowments from the prebends of St Paul's. The plan of endowing out of the proceeds of particular stalls has been suspended by the more comprehensive scheme of the Eccl Commissioners, but the endowments now offered to these new churches may fairly be regarded as coming from that source, the Commissioners having already in their possession the estates of several of the prebends of St Paul's. It is to be borne in mind that I have also provided for each of these churches an endowment of not less than £1,200, in the shape of an excellent parsonage house.

At all events I hope that the college will come to some decision on the question as soon as possible, for until the endowments take effect, we shall have to provide stipends for the ministers of the churches in the poorer districts, out of the fund intended for the building of the churches; and in some instances out of my own pocket. I have already paid a large sum in this way.

I think you will easily perceive that as pieces of patronage these churches are far from being desirable; but I can see no method of obtaining for them a competent endowment if they are not to be in the gift of the bishop and certainly we should not have spent as much money on parsonage houses to improve the patronage of the college who, I insist,[63] should defray that expense in all cases where they retain the patronage for themselves

Believe me my dear sir, yours very truly

---

[62] The bill, 'An act to enable the prebendary of the prebend of Halliwell and Finsbury, within the Cathedral Church of St Paul's London, to sell to the mayor and commonality and citizens of London the prebendal estate, the purchase monies to be paid to the governors of the Bounty of Queen Anne and to be applied to the endowment of churches in and near the metropolis' (in fact within five miles of the west doors of St Paul's and Westminster Abbey) had been introduced in June 1840 on Blomfield's behalf by the prebendary of Finsbury since 1816 Hugh Percy, by now bishop of Carlisle and holding the prebend *in commendam*. Parliamentary Archives, Houses of Parliament, London, HL/PO/JO/10/8/1334, 674.

[63] Barely legible: 'insist' is the most likely reading.

C. J. London

PS I consecrated the first of the Bethnal Green churches yesterday.[64]

28. CJB to Rev. Ashurst Turner Gilbert, F 7 September 1841

Blomfield 29, fos. 83–4[65]

My dear sir

I intended to thank you long before this for your letter of 31 July; but have been prevented by various causes from doing so. With respect to that part of it which alludes to a proposal made in your letter of the 16 Dec 1840 that the selection of the churches to be endowed should be left with the College, I beg to observe, that from the nature of the case this cannot be done. It is only with a certain class, those of which the income is under £150, that the Commissioners can deal; they are prepared to augment all such churches, being in public patronage and if any selection were to be made it must be made with reference to the circumstances of the church & district; of which the bishop must necessarily be the best judge. The endowment, to be given by the Commissioners will be a fixed sum calculated upon a past average of receipts from pew rents and other sources of income; necessary outgoings being deducted. For instance, if the pew rents, fees etc amount to £150, and the expenses of the church be £80 the Commissioners will give £90 per annum to bring the net income up to £150. In the case of All Saints Stepney,[66] if I remember rightly, not more than £20 remains, after payment of expenses. The augmentation having been once fixed, will not be suspended or withdrawn, if the income arising from other sources should afterwards exceed £150.

Believe me, my dear sir, yours very truly

C. J. London

29. CJB to Rev. Nathaniel Woodard [B],[67] F 9 October 1841

Blomfield 30, fo. 36

Dear sir

I am glad to learn that your prospects of usefulness in your new charge[68] are so encouraging. With respect to persons who do not know whether they have been baptised, and who are desirous of being so, and are qualified, you may administer baptism in the hypothetical form presented by the rubric.

With regard to the objects which you are endeavouring to accomplish, the most important is the erection of sufficient schoolrooms: and until this is done, I should be sorry to see any part of the money collected by you (except such parts thereof as may be given for that specific object) laid out on the erection of a spire, although I agree with you in thinking such addition desirable if it be made according to a design of the architect who builds the church: not otherwise

I am, dear sir, your faithful servant

C. J. London

---

64 St Peter's.
65 A letter making the same points in shorter form was also sent on 3 Aug. (Blomfield 29, fo. 62).
66 I.e., All Saints Mile End.
67 See above, p. 300.
68 St Bartholomew's district.

30. CJB to Rev. Joshua King, F 6 December 1841

Blomfield 31, fo. 77b

Dear sir

I am not prepared to agree with Mayne's suggestion that one curate will suffice for the parish church of Bethnal Green to which, when all the new churches are built, there will still, I imagine, be attached at least 10,000 souls – If however you wish the whole question to stand over till Mr Mayne is about to leave, Mr Hunter[69] had better not be ordained as his assistant curate. He would certainly not do for the office of principal curate.

I remain, dear sir, your faithful servant,
    C. J. London

31. CJB to Rev. John Graham Packer [H],[70] LH 30 March 1842

Blomfield 33, fo. 30

Dear sir

I have no power to do what you suggest, and if I had, I doubt whether it would be proper to exercise it in this instance. Your district is already larger than I could wish it to be.

There is no reason why those pews, *which are not hired by persons* residing within the district, should not be let to persons living in another parish, if the incumbent does not object; which he would hardly do, where the parties are out of reach of their parish church. But they must not occupy pews to the exclusion of persons within the district who may wish to hire them.

I remain dear sir, your faithful servant
    C. J. London

32. CJB to Rev. Joshua King, F 19 November 1842

Blomfield 34, fos. 71–3

Dear sir

The enclosed letter from Mr Alston[71] has given me very great concern. It is an answer to one of mine, in which I expressed the pleasure I had derived from his successful ministrations in a most neglected and destitute district,[72] and especially at his having prevailed upon very great numbers of poor creatures, living in an almost heathen state, to bring their children to be baptised, who, if they had been required to pay the fees would never have presented their little ones to be admitted into the Church of Christ. It is clear that nearly all these cases are of that description; so that you do not really *lose* any part of your actual income, by the remission of the fee for registration, and you ought not in reason to look for any *gain*. But the truth is, that you appear to mistake the law of the case which is this. No clergyman can

---

69 Evan Haynes Hunter was in fact ordained by Blomfield in Dec. 1841, and licensed to St Matthew's. See above, pp. 298–9.
70 See above, p. 304.
71 See above, p. 304.
72 The district of St Philip's.

legally demand a fee for baptism nor refuse the sacrament if it is not paid. A fee is due by custom, for *registration*, but the clergyman is bound by law to register every baptism, & *having so done* he may demand the customary fee and sue for it, if it be withheld. Were I to hear of any clergyman demanding it *beforehand*, and delaying baptism till it was [paid], I should proceed against him if he persisted in the practice in the spiritual court. It would be an intolerable thing, if an infant were to die unbaptised because its parent could not pay the clergyman a fee. I wish once more to remind you that the fee is for *registration*, and cannot legally be demanded till the registration has taken place. I trust, therefore, that you will see the necessity of renewing, *at least*, the permission given to Mr Alston, especially as you are not likely to be an actual loser by it; for it has been ascertained that while so many poor children have been christened in the district churches the numbers of baptisms in the parish church has not been diminished. The question is not whether the children shall be baptised in the district churches or the parish church, but whether they shall be baptised in the district churches, or *not at all*.

With regard to Mr Fawcett,[73] whom I directed to write to you, and who has undertaken to explore and enlighten the very worst part of your parish, all that is required is a written request from you that I will license him to officiate in the parish.

As I have not hitherto met with any opposition on your part in the measures which have been taken to lessen the fearful amount of spiritual destitution which prevails within the limits of your charge, I hope that this representation will have weight with you, and that you will give us a cordial measure of concurrence & assistance – all the more cordial, seeing that you are not able to discharge in person the duties of your enormous parish.

I remain, dear sir, your faithful servant,
       C. J. London

33. CJB to Rev. Joshua King, F 28 November 1842

Blomfield 35, fo. 1

Dear sir

I send you Mr Alston's remarks upon your letter which I forwarded for his perusal. In those remarks I entirely concur. All the inquiries I have made satisfy me as to their correctness. I wish to recall your attention to the fact stated in my last letter, that no clergyman is at liberty to refuse baptism; and that no fee is due till *after* registration. Were any clergyman to refuse baptising a child till the parents had agreed to pay him for registering the baptism he would subject himself to punishment.

We desire that you should not suffer any *loss* by the necessary labour to relieve you from a part of those pastoral duties which you cannot perform either by yourself or your curates; but you cannot reasonably expect to have your burthen lightened & your emoluments *increased* at the same time – especially as you are not resident on your benefice. The plan which you propose with respect to baptism is at variance with the Rubric and is moreover impracticable.

I remain, dear sir, your faithful servant,
       C. J. London

---

73   John Turner Coleman Fawcett, see p. 299.

34. CJB to Rev. Joshua King, F 5 December 1842

Blomfield 35, fos. 7–8

My dear sir

Your proposal of delaying the baptism of poor children for 3 months is contrary to the Rubric which directs that 'the curates of every parish shall often admonish the people that they defer not the baptism of their children longer than the first or second Sunday next after their birth – unless upon great & reasonable cause, to be approved by the Curate'. The 68th canon directs that 'no minister shall refuse or delay to christen any child that is brought to him to the Church upon Sundays or Holy days'.

A fee for registration is due by custom, & may be demanded *after* registration. No stipulation is to be made before baptism: nor can a clergyman insist upon payment of the fee before registration. If I was driven to make this publicly known the effect may probably be the almost total loss to incumbents of registration fees: but I shall not do so, if I can avoid it; but I cannot acquiesce in any regulation which shall have the effect of deterring parents from bringing their children to be baptised.

I remain, dear sir, your faithful servant,

C. J. London

PS With respect to the Registration Act,[74] I have on more than one occasion spoken very strongly in the House of Lords upon its mischievous operation.

35. CJB to Rev. Edward Rhys Jones [E],[75] Sevenoaks 20 April 1843

Blomfield 35, fos. 93–4

Dear sir

I feel some difficulty respecting your proposal of substituting a weekly evening service for the daily morning prayers. The expense of lighting the church and paying the attendants would still further diminish the too scanty income of the minister. There is an evening service at the Episcopal Jews Chapel in the immediate neighbourhood, which would probably suffice for all who might be disposed to avail themselves of it; and I fear that when you have been a longer time in the district you will hardly be equal to the continued exertion of one additional sermon in the week.

There is an obvious objection to the discontinuance of the morning prayers, once commenced. People will not come to them all at once, but must be accustomed by degrees. I feel that I cannot directly sanction the discontinuance, but must leave you to the exercise of your own discretion as to a change; but with the understanding that in any case there must be morning prayers on Wednesdays & Fridays.

I remain, dear sir, your faithful servant,

C. J. London

---

[74] The Civil Registration Act of 1836, 6 & 7 Will. IV, c. 85.
[75] See p. 302 above.

36. CJB to Rev. Joshua King, LH 5 June 1843

Blomfield 36, fo. 14

Dear sir

I took the opportunity of my confirming at Bethnal Green to inspect your rectory house which I am sorry to say I found disgracefully out of repair. The circumstance of your non-residence on that important benefice makes it the more necessary for me to interfere, and to require you to leave no time in having the house thoroughly repaired, under the provisions of the 1&2 Vict. c. 106 sect. 41.[76] It is my intention to send a surveyor (Mr Marsh) to inspect the house & report to me; but I will wait for your answer before I do so.

I remain, dear sir, your faithful servant,

C. J. London

37. CJB to [?Rev. Edward Thomas Lewis],[77] Cheshunt 14 June 1843

Blomfield 36, fo. 26

Dear sir

After the most anxious & painful consideration of the case I am compelled to inform you that I cannot alter the decisions which I have already made known to you. It would endanger the success of all the means which have been employed to provide for the spiritual destitution of the metropolis, by means of churches built and endowed upon voluntary contributions placed at my disposal were I appoint you to any of the new churches so built, after what has happened & is now generally known. The determination which I have been bound to form has given me the greatest pain, & I trust that some method may be found of lessening the inconvenience which it will occasion to you, as much as possible.

I remain, dear sir, your faithful servant

C. J. London

38. CJB to Rev. Joshua King, F 27 June 1843

Blomfield 36, fo. 27

Dear sir

I have good reason for believing that your registration fees have increased rather than diminished since the erection of the new churches in Bethnal Green, so that you have no grounds for complaint on that score. For my view of the general questions of fees for baptism & registration I refer you to my letter of the 19th of November last,[78] by which I mean to abide.

---

[76] The Pluralities Act 1838. Clause 41 required non-resident incumbents to keep parsonages they did not occupy in good repair, authorizing the bishop to commission a survey which if it revealed disrepair would lead to a monition requiring action by the incumbent. If this did not ensue, the incumbent would be liable to penalties for non-residence.

[77] No name is given, but the catalogue suggests the surname of the recipient was Lewis, and the details fit the case. For Lewis, see p. 300.

[78] Document 32.

With respect to your house, the tone of your answer to my letter has determined me to proceed under the act of parliament referred to in my last letter. I know from my own observation that it is disgracefully out of repair.

I am, dear sir, your faithful servant,

C. J. London

39. CJB to Rev. John Graham Packer [H], F 8 July 1843

Blomfield 36, fo. 49

Dear sir

It was distinctly stated that you were to receive a payment from the Bethnal Green Fund on account; to be repaid, upon your obtaining an augmentation. I am surprised and concerned at your attempting to evade the fulfilment of that agreement, and entirely agree with Mr Cotton[79] in his view of the question.

I am, dear sir, your faithful servant

C. J. London

40. CJB to the churchwardens of St Matthew's Bethnal Green, LH 13 July 1843

Blomfield 36, fos. 58–9

Gentlemen

It is my duty to direct your attention to the present state of St John's Church, Bethnal Green, which is in urgent need of repairs. I am informed that the vestry have recently declined entertaining the question, but upon what grounds I do not know. There can be no doubt as to the liability of the parish to repair the church, under the express provision of the 58 Geo. III c. 45 s. 70,[80] which enacts that the churches of district parishes shall be repaired by the districts to which they belong, and that those *built by the Commissioners*, which are not made district churches, shall be repaired by the parishes in which they are built. Now St John's was built by the Commissioners, and constituted, not the church of a district parish, but the chapel of a district chapelry. The vestry need not entertain any apprehension lest their repairing St John's should involve any question as to the repairs of the new churches, built by means of the Bethnal Green Churches Fund, which are on a different footing.

---

[79] William Cotton: see introduction, p. 283.

[80] *An act for building and promoting the building of additional churches in populous parishes* (30 May 1818) set out the workings of the £1 million church-building grant of 1818 and established the church building commission. The act empowered the commissioners to erect chapels of ease within existing parishes, or fully to divide parishes in which churches were erected by order in council on the next vacancy if the patron consented. A third and complex option was to create 'district parishes', which would become perpetual curacies (the nomination belonging to the patron of the mother church) for ecclesiastical purposes only within existing parishes, with the incumbent to be paid from pew rents. In this instance the mother parish remained the civil unit and continued to receive all glebe, tithe and moduses. Up to the next vacancy all marriages, burials and christenings would be conducted at the mother church, whose incumbents would also be compensated for any demonstrable loss of income. Moreover, for twenty years after the creation of a district parish it would remain liable for repairs to the mother church. § 70 made the parish churchwardens responsible for repairs to all such chapels not designated district churches.

I trust that the vestry will reconsider the matter, and fulfil their legal obligations without driving me to the necessity of having recourse to legal proceedings.

I remain, gentlemen, your obedient humble servant,

C. J. London.

41. CJB to Rev. Richard Harington,[81] F 24 July 1843

Blomfield 36, fos. 77–8

My dear sir

At length I am prepared to make a proposition of the exchange of the advowson of Bethnal Green for that of a country living.

As near as I can learn, the *net* income of Bethnal Green is £535 per annum; which will most probably be reduced, in the course of a few years, in consequence of the fees which will belong after Mr King's incumbency, to the ministers of the new churches.

The living which I have to offer in exchange is that of Weeley, about ten miles from Colchester in the Tendring hundred, where a good house has been erected within the last few years by the present incumbent, Mr Mercer.[82] I send you his account of the annual value. Amongst the outgoings the payment to the governors of Queen Anne's Bounty will be less every year till it ceases altogether.[83]

With respect to the new churches, I can hardly consider the patronage of them to be of any value to the college. The duties are onerous, and the income so scanty that it will always be difficult to find suitable persons to take charge of them. I must take the patronage of Bethnal Green, if an exchange is made, subject to the present rector's life, seeing that he is not a person to whom I could think of offering preferment, if I had any which was tenable with his living in Cheshire.

I remain, my dear sir, your faithful servant

C. J. London

42. CJB to Robert Hanbury,[84] Tunbridge Wells 5 September 1843

Blomfield 37, fos. 72–5

My dear sir

A letter of yours has been placed in my hands which has given me great pain, and which I think affords me some grounds of remonstrance if not of complaint.

---

81 Richard Harington, DD, principal of Brasenose Oxford 1842–53.

82 The rectory of Weeley, Essex, in the bishop of London's patronage. Average net income in 1831–2 £375. Thomas Warren Mercer (*c.* 1798–1876), Trinity Oxford MA, incumbent of Weeley since 1833. The exchange being discussed was effected by an order in council on 13 Dec. 1843, giving the bishop of London the patronage of St Matthew's Bethnal Green and that of all chapels then or in the future erected in the parish.

83 Founded in 1704 to receive first fruits and tenths earlier confiscated by Henry VIII for the purpose of augmenting poorly endowed livings. By the 1840s it could make loans and disbursements for building parsonage houses.

84 Robert Hanbury (1796–1884), evangelical brewer and philanthropist. Cousin of Thomas Fowell Buxton. Partner in Truman, Buxton and Co. Actively involved in the London City Mission. Built and endowed anglican churches at Thundridge and Ware, Hertfordshire.

You mention your determination to assist in bringing the City Mission[85] into Bethnal Green and state, as a reason that 'the clergymen are altogether unfit for the important offices they have undertaken, most of them being decidedly in favour of the Oxford doctrines, and none of them, you fear, truly evangelical and devoted men.'

Now this is a very serious charge, and one which it concerns me, as well as the clergy themselves, to refute, if possible. I must really beg of you to state which of the Bethnal Green clergy you consider to be 'decidedly in favour of the Oxford doctrines', by which I conclude you mean those opinions made public in the Tracts for the Times, which at variance[86] with the Articles of our Reformed Church. I know only of *one*[87] who can be fairly charged with holding those opinions; and I am sure you will believe me when I say that I would not knowingly have appointed *any* persons of that description. That one is about to leave Bethnal Green, and of those who will remain I am not aware that any one is open to the same imputation. Some of them, I know, are labouring very hard amongst the poor, and they have at least laid the foundation of much future ground by the establishment of new schools.

It was not to be expected that the churches would be numerously attended for a long time to come. People maintained in ignorance, & long accustomed to darkness, will not all at once come to the light. The effect of the schools and of the pastoral visitation of the clergy will by degrees be perceived in increasing congregations, unless indeed their efforts are frustrated by those of the agents of the City Mission, persuading the people to attend other places of worship. I have no right to complain of your having recourse to Dissenters, to do that which the Church has not yet had time to do, if you think it a point of conscience to employ their agency, but what I do complain of is your charging the clergy of the new churches by wholesale, with holding opinions which I am persuaded they would disclaim, and against which indeed some of them have earnestly protested: and I think I am entitled to request that you will specify the persons to whom you allude. The small number of persons attending of late St Andrew's Church may be ascribed to the unfortunate state of Mr Lawson's[88] health which obliged him for some months to be non-resident, and finally to resign. I think I can venture to promise that in the course of a very short time the state of things there will be much altered.

It is rather hard that no credit is given to these clergymen for their zealous and effective labours amongst the poor children of that neglected parish.

Believe me my dear sir, yours faithfully,

    C. J. London

---

[85] The London City Mission. An important interdenominational mission to the London poor established in 1835 by David Nasmith, employing lay agents to visit them. The absence of clerical control made many high church anglicans suspicious.

[86] *Sic.*

[87] Presumably Nathaniel Woodard; see p. 300. As the biographical notes indicate, however, *The Times* saw it differently.

[88] William de Lancy Lawson, see p. 299.

43. CJB to Rev. Timothy Gibson,[89] F 21 October 1843

Blomfield 38, fo. 47

Dear sir

The addition which you suggest to the churchyard of the parish church would undoubtedly be desirable, but it cannot be effected unless the parishioners are willing to purchase. I know of no other source from which funds for that purpose could be looked for. I am not yet patron of Bethnal Green; but the college has agreed to transfer the patronage to the see of London in exchange for that of a living in Essex.[90]

With respect to the lectureship in Southwark,[91] I cannot but think that *all* your energies are required for your duties in Bethnal Green. I have objected to the ministers of the new churches taking any additional duty. And it appears to me that there is still stronger ground of objection in your case.

I remain, dear sir, your faithful servant
C. J. London

44. CJB to Rev. Frederick Charles Cook,[92] F 25 November 1843

Blomfield 39, fos. 55–6

My dear sir

I will thank you to see Mr Owen[93] and tell him that having had a conference with the clergy of Bethnal Green I have found, to my surprise, that the lay agents of which he spoke,[94] have been for some time already employed in that parish; and that their operations have been for the most part not only conducted in a manner at variance with Church principles, but in some cases expressly directed against the Church in favour of Dissent; and that there is no possibility of their acting under the superintendence of the clergy & in subordination to them. Under these circumstances, I feel myself to be under the necessity of declining to give my sanction to the measure which Mr Owen – with the most benevolent intentions – has undertaken to carry into effect.

I remain, my dear Sir, your faithful servant,
C. J. London

45. CJB to Rev. Timothy Gibson, F 2 December 1843

Blomfield 39, fos. 87–8

Dear sir

The City Mission I consider to be in its constitution at variance with Church principles and it is certainly so in its operations. In leaving the clergy of Bethnal

---

[89] See above, p. 299.
[90] See Document 41.
[91] At St George's.
[92] (1804–89), secretary to London Diocesan Board (1841) and inspector of schools in London and Middlesex (1844). Later a conservative biblical scholar (having studied with Niebuhr in his youth).
[93] Not identified.
[94] Presumably those of the London City Mission.

Green at liberty to avail themselves of the services of any visitors to be approved of by themselves and paid by Mr Owen, out of the monies which certain benevolent individuals have placed in his hands I did not intend to give any sanction to the principles of the City Mission. If Mr Hanbury & other gentlemen interested in the spiritual state of Bethnal Green are willing to pay the salaries of a certain number of persons members of the Church of England, and approved by the clergy to act as their assistants & under their direction, I see no objection to the clergy availing themselves of such assistance; but I must candidly say that I have no expectation of any cordial cooperation with the clergy on the part of the City Mission Society. If upon full consideration of the question you should think it desirable to try the experiment of such assistants as I have described, I would advise you to accept them at the hands of Mr Hanbury or Mr Owen: as churchmen; and not from the Society: and in any case you ought to have the selection of your own assistant agents.

I enclose the nomination with my signature & remain, dear sir, your faithful servant

    C. J. London

46. CJB to Rev. Nathaniel Woodard [B], F 15 December 1843

Blomfield 74, fos. 53–4

Dear sir

You appear to have understood my words in a sense different from that in which I used them. I remarked that no doubt the doctrine which you had preached on the subject of absolution[95] would increase your influence among the people; for that no doctrine would obtain greater influence than that of the Romish priest himself, which makes it so easy for a sinner to obtain complete absolution. With respect to your future plans, I recommend that you should endeavour to obtain an assistant curacy under an able and discreet incumbent and pass two or three years of probation in that capacity. It will then be seen how far you are qualified for the sole charge of a parish or district. In order to put an end to the present inconvenient state of things, I must request you to resign the cure of your present district at the expiration of the present month.

I remain, dear sir, your faithful servant,

    C. J. London

---

95 In May 1843 Woodard preached a sermon commending the use of confession and absolution as provided for in the Book of Common Prayer, provoking churchgoers to complain to Blomfield, and the correspondence seen here, as well as comment in the national press. He resigned his post at the end of 1843, and was appointed curate at St James's Clapton.

47. CJB to Rev. Timothy Gibson, F 23 December 1843

Blomfield 74, fo. 89

Dear sir

Before I give you a final answer as to Mr Hunter's[96] case, I should wish to have some conversation with you, and I will thank you to call at London House on Friday next, when you can also speak to me on the subject of Mr Alston's baptisms.[97]

I remain, dear Sir, your faithful servant,

C. J. London

48. CJB to Rev. Nathaniel Woodard [B], F 26 December 1843

Blomfield 74, fo. 97

Dear sir

Your last letter makes it necessary for me to adopt some decisive measure. It is quite true that when you took charge of a district in Bethnal Green it was with an understanding that you were to become, in due time, the incumbent of that district. You have since that time preached & maintained doctrines at variance with those of the Church of England; and I am therefore compelled by a sense of duty to do that which is extremely painful to me, & to decline the responsibility of placing you as incumbent in the new Church which is about to be consecrated.

I remain, dear sir, your faithful servant,

C. J. London

49. CJB to Rev. Timothy Gibson, LH 10 January 1844

Blomfield 74, fos. 164–5

Dear sir

Mr Alston assures me that the parties whom he sent to have their baptisms (performed by him) registered at the parish church, were refused, unless they paid 1/6, and that therefore he sent no more.

I have more than once informed Mr King that this kind of proceeding is illegal; and that the clergy are bound to register all baptisms; & not to demand the fee till *after* registration. Mr Alston erred in this, that he did not send *certificates* to you to be entered instead of sending the parties themselves, unless they brought with them such certificates, in which case all was right. I trust that the baptisms in question will be registered *somewhere*.

I remain, dear sir, your faithful servant,

C. J. London

---

[96] E. H. Hunter was licensed by Blomfield as assistant curate.

[97] A reference to a dispute which in June 1843 saw King write to Cotton and Blomfield to complain that Alston was refusing to take fees for baptismal registration ostensibly on the grounds of the poverty of the applicants, thus effectively evading an agreement to pay a proportion of his fees for these and churchings to the rector. Fearing a significant loss of income, King had asked Alston to refer all such cases to Gibson. See BNC archives, B12, King to A. T. Gilbert, 12 June 1843. The dispute over fees was to be a long-running one: see Documents 49, 70, 98, 100, 102, 129, 137–41, 165–6, 174, 180.

50. CJB to Rev. Nathaniel Woodard, LH 27 January 1844

Blomfield 74, fos. 236–8

Dear sir

Nothing can be more contrary to my wishes or intentions than a design 'to crush you' – On the contrary I would gladly promote any arrangement which might lessen the inconvenience which, I am well aware, must result to you from my not making you the incumbent of St Bartholomew's: but I cannot conscientiously entrust you with the permanent charge of a district church, in the exercise of the patronage vested in me, knowing you to hold opinions which I believe to be, I will not say heretical, but not in strict accordance with the doctrines of our Church – It is as *patron* of St Bartholomew's that I feel this insurmountable difficulty. Although you are not regularly licensed, I am quite ready, if it can be done, to give you the privilege which you would possess, if you were licensed, of appealing against my decision to the archbishop: but I doubt whether his Grace would entertain the appeal, as not being strictly under the provisions of the Curates Act;[98] and it would be for you to consider, whether if the appeal were made and my decision confirmed, your position would not be the worse for it.

I do assure you that I am deeply grieved at the necessity by which I feel myself bound to follow this course of proceeding: but I cannot help observing, that the difficulties of your position have been greatly increased by your not having more readily acquiesced in my determination.

It appears that I was *not* misinformed, as to your having taken the keys of the church into your own keeping, although you have since parted with them.

If you wish to see me, I shall be at liberty to receive you on Monday at eleven o'clock.

I remain, dear sir, your faithful servant,
C. J. London

51. CJB to Rev. Joseph Brown [G],[99] LH 6 February 1844

Blomfield 74, fo. 264

My dear sir

I am afraid that I misled you as to the income of the Bethnal Green new churches. I believe I said £200 per annum. I ought to have said £150 per annum & a house. In case it may be in my power to offer you one of these districts, I fear it will not be possible for me to sanction an arrangement by which you should continue to hold your office at Norwood,[100] even though that arrangement should be temporary.

I am, my dear sir, yours faithfully
C. J. London

---

[98] 53 Geo. III, c. 149, the Stipendiary Curate's Act of 1813.
[99] See above, p. 303.
[100] Chaplain of government schools.

52. CJB to Robert Brutton,[101] LH 19 February 1844

Blomfield 74, fos. 306–7

Sir

When I had the pleasure of receiving you with a deputation from the vestry of Bethnal Green, I told you I did not consider that the parish was liable, by law, to the charge of repairing any of the new churches which have been built there, except St John's.

I think it right to inform you, that some doubt has been cast on the correctness of that opinion, and would therefore desire to be considered as not having given it. But one thing is certain, that by repairing St John's Church, their legal obligation to do which is plain & undoubted, the parishioners will in no way affect the question of their liability to repair the other churches, which is at least doubtful.

I remain sir, your obedient humble servant

     C. J. London

53. CJB to Rev. George Alston [I], n.d. (13 March 1844?)

Blomfield 74, fos. 389–91

Dear sir

I am desirous that the clergy of Bethnal Green should accept an invitation which will probably be made to them to meet some gentlemen at the rectory house, for the purpose of considering whether some plan cannot be decided for rendering available to the spiritual good of the parish the bounty of several laymen who are willing to furnish the clergy with scripture readers, to be approved of by them, and to act under their directions: this to be done quite apart from the City Mission, and under my sanction. The spiritual wants of the parish are so far beyond the reach of the clergy themselves, without some such auxiliary means as these, that I cannot but think it very desirable to try the experiment, provided that it be done in a manner consistent with Church order, which I think may be effected.

If *all* the clergy of Bethnal Green are not inclined to avail themselves of this opportunity, I shall be ready to sanction such a proceeding on the part of those who are. I shall be obliged to you if you will communicate this letter to the other clergy of the new districts. In case any such plan as I have hinted at should be adopted, the visitors, or scripture readers should meet the clergyman weekly & give him an account of what they have done, and receive his instructions.

I remain, dear sir, your faithful servant

     C. J. London

---

101   The vestry clerk of St Matthew's Bethnal Green from the conflict in 1820 until 1857, son-in-law of Joseph Merceron.

54. CJB to Rev. Timothy Gibson, LH 13 March 1844

Blomfield 74, fo. 392

Dear sir

I have suggested to Mr Kingscote,[102] that the clergy of Bethnal Green might, with your permission, be invited to meet at the rectory house for the purpose of consulting with him and some of the gentlemen who undertake to provide the means, whether scripture readers might not be employed, approved of by the clergy, and acting under their direction, quite apart from & independent of the City Mission, and under my sanction.

I have written to Mr Alston on the subject.

I am, dear sir, your faithful servant,

C. J. London

55. CJB to Rev. George Alston [I], LH 4 April 1844

Blomfield 74, fo. 449

My dear sir

I see nothing to object to in the questions which you have sent me.[103] Some of them are the same as those which the Committee[104] intend to propose. With respect to the 6th question, about not engaging in any secular business, it is a point which I did not mention to the Committee: you had better ascertain their intentions respecting it.

I propose that every scripture reader should have my express sanction in writing. The rules drawn up by the Committee appear to me to be satisfactory.

I am, my dear sir, yours faithfully,

C. J. London

56. CJB to Mr Graves,[105] LH 9 May 1844

Blomfield 40, fo. 79

Sir

I wish to call your attention to the present state of St John's church Bethnal Green, which is discreditable to the parishioners, who are bound by law to repair it. About their obligation there can be no doubt; and whatever apprehension they may entertain concerning their liability to repair any of the other new churches, which

---

102 Henry Robert Kingscote (1802–82), converted after nearly drowning in the late 1820s, he was an evangelical friend of Blomfield, with whom he founded the Church of England Scripture Readers' Association and the Metropolitan Visiting and Relief Association. He was a generous benefactor of St Matthias's. Later he was a founder of the British and Colonial Emigration Society and of the National Orphan Asylum at Ham Common, Surrey, in 1849.

103 To be asked of prospective lay scripture readers.

104 On 18 March the Association for Providing Scripture Readers in Connexion with the Church of England was formed under the sponsorship of Blomfield and the evangelical bishop of Winchester, Charles Sumner. Its committee included Kingscote (the honorary secretary) and Robert Hanbury. It decided that the committee would set questions to be asked by clergymen. Readers would be immediately assigned to the Bethnal Green districts. *Times*, 6 May 1844, p. 3.

105 Not identified.

feeling I am told operates on their minds, that liability can in no way be affected by their repairing of St John's Church which is on a different footing, and which they are unquestionably bound to repair.

I am very unwilling to have recourse to legal proceedings against the church-wardens, but I cannot allow the church to remain any longer in its present state. The delay will only increase the ultimate cost to the parish

I remain, sir, your obedient humble servant,
      C. J. London

57. CJB to Mr Graves, F 16 July 1844

Blomfield 41, fo. 85

Sir

I am not a little surprised at the contents of your letter. I explained to you so distinctly, that I thought it impossible for you to mistake, that the order in council, of which you speak, constituted St John's Bethnal Green an *ecclesiastical district*, under the provisions of the 59 Geo. III c. 134 s. 16,[106] and *not a District Parish*, under the 58 Geo III c. 45 s. 21,[107] and that therefore the parishioners at large are bound to repair St John's Church, by the 3 Geo IV c. 72 s. 20.[108] I should be glad to know whether this statement, which I made to you by word of mouth, having before made it to Mr Brutton by letter, was laid before the vestry.

It is my intention to institute legal proceedings against the churchwardens, for their neglect of duty & to compel them to repair St John's Church.

I remain, sir, your obedient servant,
      C. J. London

58. CJB to Robert Brutton, F 16 July 1844

Blomfield 41, fo. 85

Dear sir

I will thank you to request Mr Graves to let you see the letter which I have

---

[106] *An act to amend and render more effectual an act passed in the last session of parliament, for building and promoting the building of additional churches in populous parishes* (13 July 1819). § 16 allowed the church building commissioners to assign an ecclesiastical district to an existing or new chapel to be under the care of a curate subject to the incumbent of the parish church. The commissioners and bishop would determine how fees would be allocated and whether marriages etc. could be celebrated; it could not become a benefice through augmentation of the salary.

[107] See n. 80 above. § 21 set out the means by which a formal district could be assigned to a new chapel by an order in council.

[108] *An act to amend and render more effectual two acts passed in the fifty-eighth and fifty-ninth years of his late majesty for building and promoting the building of additional churches in populous parishes* (22 July 1822; 'The Church Building Act, 1822'). Under § 12, this allowed the commissioners and bishop to apportion part or all of fees for services at the new church to the mother parish subject to five-yearly review. § 15 allowed patrons to surrender patronage to commissioners and bishop to facilitate changes to status; and to convert district chapelries to district parishes on the next vacancy or with the consent of incumbent where compensation for lost income was agreed and accommodation for the new incumbent provided. § 20 established that if no other provision was made in the foundation of the chapel, responsibility for repairs remained with the parish vestry. § 22 allowed the commissioners with the bishop and patron's consent to assign up to a moiety of glebe, tithe, moduses etc. to chapels of ease within parishes even where no division had taken place.

written to him in answer to one which I have received from him, and which has greatly surprised & disappointed me. I can hardly believe that the vestry were not informed by him, or by you, of the real law of the case, as it had been repeatedly explained to you by me. I shall lose no time in putting the churchwardens into the spiritual court, as I am resolved to be no longer trifled with.

I remain, dear sir, your faithful servant,

C. J. London

59. CJB to Rev. Edward William Relton [B],[109] F 23 July 1844

Blomfield 41, fo. 107

Dear sir

The formation of the new districts in the parish of Bethnal Green has not in any way altered or affected the liability of the inhabitants of those districts to the payment of church rates made by the parish vestry

I am dear sir, your faithful servant,

C. J. London

60. CJB to Rev. George Alston [I], F 27 July 1844

Blomfield 41, fo. 117a

My dear sir

We find it impossible to get possession of the school adjoining your church[110] at present, and we are precluded by our original agreement, it appears, from erecting schools on the other side of the church. Indeed, I doubt whether we should be justified in doing so, seeing that the existing schools will ultimately fall into our hands. Besides these circumstances all that can be done is to erect schools in the neighbourhood as soon as a site can be found.

I am sorry that you think of resigning your charge. You will not do so of course till after the expiration of three months.

I am, my dear sir, yours faithfully,

C. J. London

61. CJB to Rev. John Graham Packer [H], F 2 August 1844

Blomfield 41, fo. 120

Dear sir

I should be very glad, were it in my power to hold out to you, and to your fellow labourers in Bethnal Green, a prospect of more competent provision in the way of permanent endowment: but I do not at present entertain any hope of our being able to do so.

I am quite aware of the inadequacy of your remuneration, but it must be borne in mind that it was never represented to you as likely to be greater than it actually is. If, after a trial, you find it insufficient, I cannot advise your continuance in your present

---

109 See above, p. 300.
110 St Philip's.

post. Above all things, I trust you will avoid incurring any fresh *debts*, without any prospect of being able to pay them.

I remain, dear sir, yours faithfully,

C. J. London

62. CJB to Rev. Joseph Brown [G], Chester 23 Sept. 1844

Blomfield 41, fos. 190–1

My dear sir

I have objected to the appointment of the clergy of the new churches in Bethnal Green to the chaplaincies of union workhouses on the grounds that the charge of their own districts is more than sufficient for them and that the money subscribed for the erection of those churches was given in the confidence that their ministers would be required to give their undivided energies to the improvement of that most neglected parish. Upon this ground I refused permission to Mr Fenn,[111] Mr Packer's curate, to become a candidate for the chaplaincy to which you have been elected. I now feel some doubt whether I might not with propriety have permitted him to seek for that appointment, as being an *additional* clergyman in the district to which he belongs. If you will call upon me at London House on Friday Oct 4 I will speak to you on the subject.

I am, my dear sir, your faithfully

C. J. London

63. CJB to Rev. Baptist Wriothesley Noel,[112] F 29 October 1844

Blomfield 41, fos. 260–2

My dear sir

The pressure of business has hitherto prevented me from answering your letter; and indeed I should perhaps not have answered it at all, however little I might be satisfied with it, did I not think it right to notice some misapprehensions, under the influence of which you appear to have written it.

There is no doubt a difference between a Queens Letter and my circular.[113] The former is a command, issued in virtue of the royal prerogative, and it is the duty of the bishops to require & enforce obedience to it on the part of the clergy. This duty I must fulfil. In my circular letter to the clergy on the subject of collections for church objects, I have been careful not to assume an authority which may be thought not to belong to me, & I have limited myself to a *request* that they would carry out my wishes.

The doing so, or not, is left to their own discretion: but I think it not unreasonable to expect, that those clergymen who do not think it fit to comply, should write to me

111 David Fenn. See above, p. 304.

112 (1799–1873), from an aristocratic background, ordained in 1823, attracted large evangelical audience at proprietary chapel of St John's Bedford Row; prolific author on evangelizing the urban poor, strong supporter of London City Mission and Evangelical Alliance. In 1848 he seceded to join the baptist church.

113 Queen's Letters were an important fund-raising device for national charities, abolished in 1855.

& state their reasons. It is hardly consistent with common courtesy (to say nothing of the respect due to an ecclesiastical superior) to take no notice of my letters.

With respect to the Metropolis Churches Fund, it would surely have been well that you should have made yourself acquainted with the facts of the case before you grounded your objection to preaching for it, upon that circumstance of the bishop of London's possessing the patronage of the churches built by the Fund. I have not a list at hand, to refer to, of the churches built by means of this fund, but I can at once mention *22* which are not in the patronage of the bishop: e.g. 3 at Islington, which are in the gift of the vicars, 2 in Upper Chelsea, in that of the rector, 3 in Stepney in the patronage of Brasenose College. Of the ten new churches in Bethnal Green, five were to have been left to the College, but they have now passed into the bishop's patronage, in consequence of my having exchanged the advowson of a living in Essex for the less valuable but more important rectory of Bethnal Green. It is not true that several of the new churches are almost empty, and I know of only *one*, the minister of which urges the doctrines to which you allude.[114] The churches are well attended in the evening, and if they were not, I should not be surprised. Poor ignorant people who have been utterly neglected for many years past cannot all at once be brought to Christ; but the congregations are steadily improving, and the schools will, we hope, train up a generation of worshippers. I am glad that you have now stated plainly your objections, because to a certain extent they may be easily answered, but I must say that I think I deserved an earlier & more candid explanation from you.

I am, my dear sir, your faithful servant,

C. J. London

64. CJB to Robert Brutton, F 6 November 1844

Blomfield 41, fos. 277–8

Dear sir

In your letter to me of the 19 July last, you informed me that the churchwardens had laid my letter of July 16[115] before the vestry, and that it was ordered to be taken into consideration the following week. You stated that you would immediately communicate the result. I have heard nothing further on the subject, and I have now to request you to direct the churchwardens to inform me without delay whether they intend to repair St John's Church forthwith, or not. In case of their refusal I shall have the less scruple in instituting legal proceedings against them, as I understand that they have funds in hand out of which the necessary repairs might be paid for. But whether they have or not, it is my duty to compel them to do their duty.

I am, dear sir, your faithful servant,

C. J. London

---

[114] Possibly John Graham Packer, although both William James and James Coghlan were also described as tractarian by *The Times*. Gardiner Guion Guyon of St Simon Zelotes's is the other possible candidate, but his church was not yet complete.

[115] Document 58.

65. CJB to Rev. William James [C], F 21 December 1844

Blomfield 41, fo. 369

Dear sir

I cannot with propriety sanction your baptizing Mr Wicking without the consent of the clergyman in whose district he resides. I do not understand why a feeling of shame should influence him with respect to one clergyman more than another.

With regard to your stoves, inquiry was directed to be made whether all the apertures made for the purpose of ventilation were closed. The stoves now in the church ought to be sufficient to moderate the extreme cold. At all events the church must be much warmer than St Paul's Cathedral, or Westminster Abbey, which are well attended in the coldest weather and where there are *no* stoves.

I really can hardly recommend the committee to incur any further expense here for a warming apparatus.

I am, my dear sir, your faithful servant
    C. J. London

66. CJB to Rev. Timothy Gibson, F 7 January 1845

Blomfield 42, fo. 16

My dear sir

It is not possible for me to hold out any inducement to you to remain at Bethnal Green which should weigh against the offer of preferment elsewhere, and therefore although I shall regret the loss of your services in that important parish, I cannot dissuade you from taking a living, if offered to you.

I shall be ready to bear testimony to your qualifications, if inquiry be made of me by any of the Chapter of St Pauls,[116] but it would be contrary to my established practice to interfere, in the way of direct recommendation, with the patronage of that body.

I remain, my dear sir, yours faithfully,
    C. J. London

67. CJB to Rev. Timothy Gibson, F 9 January 1845

Blomfield 42, fo. 24

My dear sir

I have informed Mr Northall that I do not think he has any just cause of complaint. The clergy should of course make a reasonable allowance for unforeseen cause of delay; but this can hardly be expected to extend much beyond a quarter of an hour, & in no case except where infection is apprehended, ought they to bury after dark. I have told Mr Northall that in this parish the clergy have so many duties to perform, that if people will not keep their appointments it is impossible for them to get through them all.

I am, my dear sir, yours faithfully,
    C. J. London

---

[116] St Paul's Cathedral.

PS. I think it right to add, that in this case I should have been inclined to put myself to a little inconvenience rather than give the parties the trouble of a second attendance.

68. CJB to Captain Charles Sotheby RN,[117] LH 13 March 1845

Blomfield 42, fos. 160–1

My dear sir

It has been owing to unforeseen contingencies that the burial ground of St James the Less Bethnal Green has not been consecrated before this time. It is my intention to consecrate it as soon as the fencing can be completed. It will be destined primarily to the use of the inhabitants of the district parish, but I have no power by law to prevent the internment of non-parishioners. I am, however, desirous of providing a much larger cemetery in that neighbourhood, which will probably have that effect.

The churchyard in question will hardly be surrounded by buildings, as towards the canal it will be almost open to the Victoria Park.[118] It is not possible to provide cemeteries for the poor which shall be remote from all houses, on account of the distance to which they would have to go. Burial grounds which were in the country twenty years ago are now in crowded neighbourhoods. If proper regulations for interment be made & observed, no serious inconvenience can be occasioned, where the ground is not very confined.

Believe me, my dear sir, yours very faithfully,

    C. J. London

69. Richard Jones to CJB, tithe commission, 4 April 1845

Blomfield 61, fos. 203r–6v

My lord

I have the honour to send you the opinion of the law officers of the Crown on a case submitted to them as to the Bethnal Green tithes – It was drawn by Mr White and embodies I take it for granted all his views and points. The opinion accords with that which I had been led to form from a perusal of the papers.

I regret that no great prospect seems to exist of obtaining from the parish a reasonable endowment for the new churches, but I have some doubts as to the fund for spiritual purposes being much if at all less than it would have been had no compromise or legislation ever taken place.

The idea of acquiring for the purposes of the church £1,200 a year, an amount to be made up by what is called the supplemental rate, has been throughout illusory. Every advance from the rates is distinctly illegal except so far as it may be necessary to make up the sum by which the tithes, Easter offerings &c may prove insufficient when properly collected to pay the £400 a year.

A rate constituting a surplusage beyond that deficiency is most clearly an illegal

---

[117] (1782–1854). Midshipman at the battle of the Nile, succeeded to family estate at Sewardstone, Essex, dying as a rear-admiral. The family owned an important estate in Bethnal Green, and Sotheby donated one of the sites for the new churches.

[118] Opened in 1845.

rate and non-existent in the eye of the law and has been judicially decided to be so: see page 12 of case.

If therefore the churchwardens had been declared mere trustees for spiritual purposes all they could have been treated as holding for such purposes would have been the surplus of such dues, tithes and offerings after the £400 a year was paid.

The difficulty and expense of collecting Easter offerings closely from a population of 70,000 people, many of them poor, would have been enormous. The liability of small courts and curtilages to the payment of 3/6 as garden pennies would have been a constant source of squabble and litigation.

Much of the income would have been liable to parochial assessment and if the parish guarantee a minimum £500 a year clear of *rates* and expenses as they propose to do I am inclined to think it will constitute nearly if not quite as large a net sum as could have been secured by pushing to the utmost such rights as the church would have had if no act had been passed. Clearly the income will come in a more desirable and peaceful form. If this be so it is the less to be regretted that the churchwardens cannot be considered as trustees for any surplus applicable to spiritual purposes. The wording of the Act which I have directed to be subjoined to the opinion have it appear made this appear certain to the Law Officers as I confess it does to me

With these views I think your Lordship will secure not such a sum as is desirable, but as great a one as it is practicable to get by acceding to the proposition made by the parish and letting the bill now in parliament proceed.[119]

As your lordship did me the honour to ask for my opinion I have thought it right to give it plainly. I have the honour to be, my lord, your lordship's faithful servant,

Richard Jones

NB as the case is a long one I have directed a separate copy of the opinion also to be sent.

70. Petition to the ecclesiastical commissioners received 1 May 1845

Ecclesiastical Records Centre, EC 526, 751/45

To the Right Honourable and Right Revd the Ecclesiastical Commissioners of England

The memorial of the undersigned clergy of Bethnal Green respectfully showeth that your memorialists are the incumbents of the first four churches of Bethnal Green, and in consequence of their churches having been consecrated previously to the passing of Sir Robert Peel's Act for the formation of Districts for Ecclesiastical Purposes[120] they are placed in a very unequal and disadvantageous position

---

119   The bill became law on 31 July 1845 as 8 & 9 Vict., c. 180, *An act for extinguishing garden pennies, small tithes, and Easter offerings within the parish of St Matthew's Bethnal Green in the county of Middlesex, and for providing a fund for the payment of the stipend of the rector of the said parish*: Parliamentary Archives, HL/PO/PB/1/1845/8&9V1n267 c. clxxx. Its chief provisions were: (i) the abolition of garden pennies, small tithes and easter offerings to be replaced by a parochial composition rate; (ii) from this the churchwardens to pay the rector's stipend of £400 per annum; (iii) additional rates and dues from graveyards in the parish to be applied 'for ecclesiastical purposes' in the parish by the bishop, and to raise at least £100 and up to £150 for church repairs and services and salaries at St Matthew's and St John's, with any shortfall being added to the composition rate; (iv) detailed rules on how to deal with evasion.

120   6 & 7 Vict., c. 48, 'New Parishes Act', 1843.

as compared with the clergy who have recently been appointed to churches under the provisions of that Act. Your memorialists refer to their being compelled to pay two-thirds of all their fees to the non resident rector of the parish, and that having to bear every expense connected with the performance of divine service in their respective churches, and also being responsible for the maintenance of their national schools, to neither of which purposes does the rector contribute anything whatever, their incomes are so reduced as to make their position one of extreme difficulty. Your memorialists therefore very respectfully solicit that your Right Honourable Board will be pleased to give the rector such compensation as you have already given in the cases of the more recently formed districts in the parish[121] and thereby liberate your memorialists from any obligation to account to him for their fees.

J. G. Packer, MA, incumbent of St Peter's
Js Coghlan, MA, incumbent of St James the Less[122]
Geo. Alston, BA St Philip's
George Hargreave Parker, incumbent of St Andrew's.[123]

71. CJB to Rev. George Alston [I], F 3 July 1845

Blomfield 43, fo. 3

My dear sir

I know & lament the inadequacy of the incomes provided for the clergy of Bethnal Green; but I know of no means from which they can be augmented *at present*, and they are not less, but rather higher, than they were at first represented to be – the *gross* income of your church was I believe stated at less than £200 per annum, whereas it is in fact £224. I do not consider that the salary of an organist, sexton, or pewopener ought to be paid by the clergyman, nor indeed that of the beadle. I expect to have some means under the new local act[124] of adding to the income of the new churches & you are probably aware of my intention to augment them at a period which cannot be very remote.

I remain my dear sir, yours faithfully,
    C. J. London
PS No part of the General Fund can be spared for the expenses of divine service etc.

72. CJB to Rev. John Espy Keane [F],[125] Boreham vicarage, 29 July 1845

Blomfield 43, fo. 10

My dear sir

You must not fancy that I am displeased because I cannot always enter at length into subjects brought before me. You did very right in stating to me Mr Kellday's project;[126] but I told you that I feared there were insuperable difficulties of a legal

---

121 I have not been able to establish the sum involved.
122 James Coghlan, see above, p. 301.
123 See above, p. 299.
124 8 & 9 Vict. I, c. 180 (1845), see n. 119 above. This refers to the income from graveyards.
125 See p. 302 above.
126 Possibly John Kelday, pawnbroker, of 10 Durham Place East, Hackney Road? His project is unidentified.

nature in the way, and I expressed a wish to have a more precise statement of the proposals made to me. I have been expecting to receive it. In the meantime I am unable to give any definite opinion on the subject. I am quite convinced of your zealous desire to do that in your line for the good of the poor people committed to your charge, but you are not to be disheartened if I cannot always sanction the particular mode of doing so which you may suggest.

I remain, my dear sir, your faithful servant

C. J. London

73. CJB to Robert Brutton, F 18 November 1845

Blomfield 43, fo. 145

Dear sir

By the new Bethnal Green Act[127] the parishioners are bound to provide whatever is necessary for the performance of divine service in St John's. A *font* is indispensably necessary for the administration of baptism and the 81st canon requires that it shall be provided.

There is no doubt but that the Court of Queens Bench would grant a mandamus[128] enforcing this requisition, upon the strength of the act above referred to, but I should be very sorry to be driven to have recourse to legal proceedings, so soon after a settlement which I had hoped was a *bona fide* one on the part of the vestry. I will thank you to read this letter to the churchwardens, & to let me know their final decision, that no time may be lost by me in enforcing, if necessary, a compliance with my decision.

74. CJB to Rev. John Tagg, [E][129] F 18 December 1845

Blomfield 43, fo. 212

My dear sir

I do not entertain any doubt as to the liability of the churchwardens to provide for lighting the church for divine service, but I think it expedient to take legal advice on the subject; and if I am right in my opinion, I shall apply to the Court of Queens Bench for a mandamus. I wish you therefore not to acknowledge *your own* liability, or that of any other parties than the churchwardens, but to provide in the best you can further lighting of the church till the question is determined, & to make a formal demand to the churchwardens to light it.

If, as might be the case, you have district churchwardens for St Johns, *they* are the persons who ought to make this demand. I will thank you to let me know at what times the gas is required in your church.

I am, my dear sir, your faithful servant,

C. J. London

---

127 8 & 9 Vict. I, c. 180 (1845), see n. 119 above.
128 A writ to compel an officer to perform an official duty.
129 See p. 302 above.

75. CJB to Rev. George Alston [I], F 24 December 1845

Blomfield 43, fo. 23

My dear sir

Not having been able to attend the Committee meetings of the District Visiting Society in Saint Martin's Place[130] of late, I am not aware of the reasons which have influenced them in determining the amount of their grants: but I cannot help thinking that what they have done for you on former occasions ought to have protected them against the charge of unfairness which you have brought against them.

I have forwarded your letter to the Committee, & have no doubt but that it will receive due consideration.

I am, my dear sir, your faithful servant,

    C. J. London

76. CJB to Robert Brutton, F 31 December 1845

Blomfield 43, fos. 244–5

Sir

Having been informed by the Revd Mr Tagg, that the churchwardens of the parish of Bethnal Green had refused to provide for the lighting of St Johns Church at the time of evening service, I have thought it right, though not entertaining any doubt on the subject, to take legal advice as to their liability, under the provisions of the act of parliament passed in the last session, to take order for having the church lighted during the performance of divine service when the daylight is not sufficient, Having been advised that there is no question as to such liability, I have to request you to inform the churchwardens that it is my intention to apply to the Court of Queens Bench for a mandamus to compel them to do their duty in that respect.

I am told that they have agreed to place a font of stone in St John's Church, in conformity with the canon, but I have not received any official answer to my requisition on that subject.

I have to desire that before the font is placed in the church, a plan may be submitted to me, that I may fix upon the proper position.

I am sir, your obedient servant

    C. J. London

77. CJB to Rev. Henry Philip Haughton [D],[131] F 5 January 1846

Blomfield 43, fo. 256

My dear sir

I am prepared to sanction your appointment as chaplain to the Workhouses of the Whitechapel Union, provided that you employ an assistant curate & that the services in your church are not interfered with by those in the workhouses.

---

130 The Association for Promoting the Relief of Destitution in the Metropolis, and for Improving the Condition of the Poor, by Means of Parochial and District Visiting under the Superintendence and Direction of the Bishop and Clergy (founded 1844). Blomfield was president and the trustees included Henry Kingscote, R. H. Inglis and William Gladstone.

131 See above, p. 301.

I am, my dear sir, your faithful servant,
    C. J. London

78. CJB to Rev. Henry Philip Haughton [D], F 15 January 1846

Blomfield 43, fo. 271

My dear sir

I approve of your proposed arrangement of the services in your church. I have no objection to the alteration which you suggest as to the stove, and the branches – but who is to pay for it? You must not look to the Metropolis Churches Fund for any further aid.

I am, my dear sir, yours faithfully,
    C. J. London

79. CJB to Henry Merceron,[132] 5 March 1846

Blomfield 43, fos. 342–3

Sir

You are no doubt aware that we are about to build one of the Bethnal Green churches[133] in Hare Street, on a site lately covered by some ruinous houses. I went yesterday to look at the place, and find that there are some very miserable houses in Edward Street, belonging to you, but leased to Mr Lisiness [?], which will stand between the end of the church & the street and will greatly disfigure the building and destroy its architectural effect.

We should not be indisposed to treat for the leasehold interest of these houses, with a view to taking them down, if we could hope that you would give us the reversion of the freehold, and considering the immense improvement of your property, in common with that of other proprietors in the parish, by the erection of our new churches, and the increased value which it will derive from them, I hope that we may, without presumption, calculate on your liberality in this particular. It appears that 49 years of the lease are unexpired.

I was glad to see the new school rooms in the rebuilding of which you took so active a part, presenting so handsome a front.

I have the honour to be, sir, your most obedient servant,
    C. J. London

80. CJB to Rev. John Espy Keane [F], LH 4 March 1846

Blomfield 43, fo. 347

My dear sir

I cannot say more on the subject of the theological department of King's College[134] than this, that I should be prepared to receive young men with the proper certificates

---

[132] Blomfield clearly names the addressee as 'Jos.'. This may be a Freudian slip: it was probably Henry Merceron, Joseph's son, who was addressed; there was no Joseph Merceron in the next generation of the family.

[133] St Matthias's.

[134] Opened in 1846, for the training of anglican ordinands.

of having passed through the regular course of study and examination *without* a University degree.

With respect to a commercial school[135] which would probably be beneficial to your neighbourhood, I would advise you to consult with Mr Russell, who has such a school, and with the secretary of the London Diocesan Board of Education the Revd Rd Burgess (79 Pall Mall).[136] I should be ready to give my sanction to any such school established upon the right principles.

I remain, my dear sir, yours faithfully

C. J. London

81. CJB to Rev. John Espy Keane [F], LH 9 March 1846

Blomfield 43, fo. 352

My dear sir

I am not prepared at present to state, as a general regulation, that I can admit any non-graduates as candidates for ordination who have not gone through the regular course of study in the theological Department of King's College London.

I am, my dear sir, yours faithfully,

C. J. London

82. CJB to Rev. John Tagg [E], LH 7 April 1846

Blomfield 43, fo. 392

My dear sir

In order to my providing for a mandamus, it will be necessary that you should address to me a representation, stating that you have applied to the churchwardens to light St John's Church for the evening service, and that they have refused to do so. This representation must be verified by affidavit or declaration before a magistrate.

I shall then make an order upon the churchwardens to light the church; & if it be not done within a reasonable time, I shall then move the Court of Queens Bench for a mandamus.

I am, my dear sir, your faithful servant

C. J. London

83. CJB to Rev. John Espy Keane [F], LH 9 April 1846

Blomfield 43, fo. 394

My dear sir

I cannot approve of any plan for the raising of certain pews in your church above the level of others.

Your faithful servant,

C. J. London

---

135 Aimed at boys preparing for a trade.
136 Richard Burgess BD (1796–1881), a convert from Roman Catholicism who became a strong evangelical; rect. Holy Trinity, Chelsea.

84. CJB to Rev. Timothy Gibson, LH 21 April 1846

Blomfield 44, fo. 16

My dear sir

I have no objection to Mr Neville's[137] assisting you, but I think it advisable that he should do so for a month or two *before* he is licensed, that you may have an opportunity of judging how far he is likely to be a suitable coadjutor to you.

I am, my dear sir, your faithful servant,
        C. J. London

85. CJB to Rev. George Alston [I], LH 29 May 1846

Blomfield 44, fo. 69

My dear sir

I am very much concerned that you should have committed an imprudence which has entailed upon you the alleged necessity of absenting yourself from your duties, for the sake of evading a legal demand. This step cannot but be seriously detrimental to your own character & usefulness as a clergyman, and to the interests of the Church in Bethnal Green. It is truly lamentable that *three* of the clergy there should be implicated in such proceedings. You say nothing of the provision which you have made for your duty. If you have left it to the care of a curate who is paid from the Additional Curates Fund,[138] his stipend will of course not be continued.

I must beg of you to inform me what arrangement you have made.

I am my dear sir, yours faithfully,
        C. J. London

86. CJB to Rev. Joseph Brown [G], F 9 June 1846

Blomfield 44, fos. 108–9

My dear sir

Before I take any further step towards supplying your place, I am anxious to learn whether it be not possible for us to retain the benefit of your services at Bethnal Green where they are duly appreciated and will be greatly missed.

It is very much to be lamented that you should leave the harvestfield after having as it were only sown the seed, just as the blade is springing up, & requiring the care and watchfulness of the husbandman.

I am informed that the expense of the schools has fallen very heavily upon your private resources, & interfered with your means of domestic comfort. Now this, I think, might be provided for, by friends who are very desirous of securing, if possible, a continuance of your labour amongst the poor people, of that neglected neighbourhood; and that some of the expense and probably all that of house rent, might be spared you. I have reason to believe that a sum of £100 per annum might be provided in this way. It is possible also that some grant might be obtained for a

---

[137] William Latimer Neville. See above, p. 299.
[138] The Society for Promoting the Employment of Additional Curates, founded in 1837 through the efforts of Blomfield to provide additional clergy for parishes rather than substitutes and partly a riposte to the more evangelical Church Pastoral Aid Society.

year or two from the National Society's Special Fund towards the maintenance of your schools. When the church is built and consecrated your labours will be of a more agreeable and encouraging kind.

I wish to learn from you with what addition to your present income you would be inclined to remain at your present post of usefulness, at all events for a year or two longer.

Be so good as to keep this communication *quite private*; & believe me, my dear sir, yours very truly,

C. J. London.

87. CJB to Rev. Joseph Brown [G], F 18 June 1846

Blomfield 44, fos. 122–3

My dear sir

I thank you very much for your kind answer to my letter.

I saw yesterday a deputation from your parishioners, who brought me a memorial most numerously signed, praying me to secure, if possible, your continuance among them, & stating the blessings which you have already been the means of securing to them. It would have cheered and encouraged you to hear the way in which the poor people spoke of you, & would, I think, have confirmed you in your determination to continue among them. I told them that I had some hope of your being induced to remain, & that I would do what I could, but that I could not then promise more.

Of course you cannot be expected to stay many years at your present post; but even two or three more would be of very great benefit, & I think not only to your own particular district.

Believe me, my dear sir, yours very truly

C. J. London

88. CJB to Rev. Henry Philip Haughton [D], F 20 July 1846

Blomfield 44, fo. 181

My dear sir

I shall be better able to judge of your proposed scale of fees when I see the sums stated in detail. There must be no difference between rich and poor funerals, as to the mode of performing the service; *all* must be taken into church. I am not clear that the rector will be entitled to any portion of the fees. It will in some measure depend upon the terms of the order in council[139] which assigned a district to St James the Less.

I am my dear sir, yours faithfully,

C. J. London

---

[139] Order in council of 3 Apr. 1843, published in *London Gazette*, no. 20235, 20 June 1843, pp. 2068–71. This specified that two-thirds of the fees for marriages, baptisms, burials and churchings should during the incumbency of the rector be paid to him.

89. CJB to Rev. John Espy Keane [F], F 8 August 1846

Blomfield 44, fo. 211

My dear sir

I have requested the archdeacon to visit your church and to give me his opinion as to the reading desk. Your complaint against Mr Clutton[140] is not just. When an architect has completed a church, with suitable internal fittings & ornaments, any arbitrary alteration which is made without consulting him is a reflexion upon his skills. He knew that everything had been approved by the Metropolis Churches Committee and by me, and he did quite right in making known to us any alterations which had been made without my sanction.

In saying that you 'protest against the vestry' you use a very improper phrase. You may think it too small as I do; but that is the fault of the Committee in permitting it to be so built and as no part of the cost was defrayed by you, you have no right to protest against any part of it.

I am, my dear sir, your faithful servant,
C. J. London

90. CJB to Rev. Henry Philip Haughton [D], F 10 August 1846

Blomfield 44, fo. 215

My dear sir

As I intend before long to call upon the clergy of my diocese to make collections for the Metropolis Churches Fund, I cannot sanction the plan of a general appeal from the pulpit on behalf of the Bethnal Green schools.

I am happy to say that I have just secured a donation of £2,000, one half of which is to go towards the endowment of the schools of St James the Great, and the other half to the general fund for the schools in Bethnal Green.

I am my dear sir, your faithful servant,
C. J. London

91. CJB to Rev. John Espy Keane [F], F 14 August 1846

Blomfield 44, fo. 224

My dear sir

The archdeacon does not think that the reading desk is improved by the addition which has been made to it. It may therefore remain as it is; but I must request that no further alteration be made to your church without my sanction first obtained.

I am, my dear sir, your faithful servant
C. J. London

---

140 Henry Clutton (1819–93), architect of St Jude's, who studied with Edward Blore, designed many anglican churches before converted to Roman Catholicism in 1857; given the original commission for Westminster Cathedral.

92. CJB to Rev. John Espy Keane [F], F 14 August 1846

Blomfield 44, fo. 230

My dear sir

I cannot venture to sanction the outlay of any more money upon your church without the authority of the committee which cannot be obtained at the earliest before October. It will be easy to provide for lighting the pulpit *temporarily* with candles.

I am, my dear sir, yours faithfully,

C. J. London

93. CJB to Rev. George Alston [I], Trinity College, Cambridge, 14 October 1846

Blomfield 44, fos. 331–2

My dear sir

I am sorry to be under the necessity of saying that I strongly disapprove of your determination not [to] pay Mr King his legal dues at the usual time, as well as of the general tone of your letter. In such a matter you are bound to consider not your own convenience, but his legal rights; and the circumstances of his having called upon you as you state, to pay him that which did *not* belong to him, clearly does not justify you in holding back from him that which *does*. The case is so plain, that I cannot help wondering at your seeing it in any other light than that in which I have here put it.

You are altogether mistaken as to the right by which Mr King holds his rectory. He has no need of dispensation. He held the living as a voidable living, before the passing of the Benefice Plurality Act,[141] which made no difference in his tenure, although no *new* incumbent could so hold the living. A voidable living may be declared void by the bishop, or the patron may at any time present a clerk for institution, as though it were void, but no *other* party can interfere.

I am ready to protect the clergy of the new churches from unjust demands, but I cannot encourage them to withhold that which is the lawful property of another person. I must therefore beg that you will pay Mr King his dues in the same manner as your brother incumbents pay them.

I am my dear sir, your faithful servant,

C. J. London

94. CJB to Rev. John Graham Packer [H], F 22 October 1846

Blomfield 44, fos. 349–50

Dear sir

I feel myself called upon to remonstrate with you very strongly against the course which you are pursuing, of begging money in all directions. I hear it spoken of with disapprobation in various quarters, and it is obvious that it is calculated to bring the clergy & the church and our charitable efforts for Bethnal Green into discredit.

---

[141] The Pluralities Act, 1 & 2 Vict., c. 106 (1838).

Having urged this consideration upon you on a former occasion, I had hoped that you would have desisted from this system of mendicancy, and if it be not laid aside I shall feel it necessary to take some decided step for the purpose of putting a stop to it. Much as I feel for the difficulties in which so many of the clergy are placed, such proceedings as yours are calculated to destroy all sympathy for you while they are injurious to the success of any general measures which may be resorted to for improving the condition of the poorer clergy.

I remain, dear sir, your faithful servant,
    C. J. London

95. CJB to Rev. John Espy Keane [F], F 21 November 1846

Blomfield 44, fos. 388–9

My dear sir

I stand pledged to the public, and to the Ecclesiastical Commissioners, that no pew rents nor any payment equivalent to pew rents shall be taken in any of the new churches in the parishes of Bethnal Green; and I owe it to them as well as to the poor inhabitants of the parish to take care that this undertaking is *bona fide* adhered to.

The plan which it appears has been adopted by your churchwardens was no doubt well meant, and I do not wish to cast any blame upon them beyond that of not having consulted me in the first instance. But the plan is quite inconsistent with the understanding to which I have alluded, and I must beg that it may be laid aside; and that no collections for the expenses of the Church be made except in the church itself.

I sincerely hope that no further change will be attempted in the system which has been established in the new churches of Bethnal Green and which if it be departed from in *one* church must be given up in all.

As to whether the collections shall be made at the offertory, or from pew to pew when the offertory sentence are not read, or at the doors, these are questions which I leave to the direction of the clergy to determine for themselves, although I myself greatly prefer the first mode.

I remain, my dear sir, your faithful servant
    C. J. London

96. CJB to Rev. Henry Philip Haughton [D], F 21 November 1846

Blomfield 44, fo. 390

My dear sir

The contributors to the Bethnal Green Church & School Fund gave their money on the faith of an assurance that no money was to be taken for sittings in any of the new churches, and I am bound to take care that this condition is faithfully observed.

I consider that the mode which has been resorted to in the case of your church is not consistent with the principle of perfectly free sittings, and I must beg that it be discontinued, and that all collections made for the purpose of defraying the expense of divine service be made in the church itself; either at the offertory, which is the more regular mode, or from pew to pew when the offertory sentences are not read, or at the doors, as you may think best.

I am my dear sir, yours faithfully,
    C. J. London

97. CJB to Rev. Henry Philip Haughton [D], F 14 December 1846

Blomfield 45, fos. 30–2

Dear sir

I am obliged in candour to state, that I consider your proceeding in the matter of pew rents, by no means a fair one. You were distinctly told by me, when you were licensed to St James the Less, that there would be no pew rents; but an endowment from the Ecclesiastical Commissioners of £150 per annum, and probably an addition of £50 per annum from another source in the course of a few years. Undoubtedly I should never have consented to the exchange with Mr Coghlan[142] had I thought it possible that you should turn round upon me & upset all my plans for the spiritual good of the poor of Bethnal Green. But this is a question which I cannot allow to be so easily disposed of.

The first appeal to the public for aid towards supplying that destitution evidently supposed the absence of pew rents, for it said 'the poverty of the inhabitants renders it essential that some provision should be made for the support of the clergyman',[143] and from that time it was an understood thing, & known to all the clergy who were appointed to the new churches, that no pew rents were to be taken. It was on the faith that none would be taken that the Ecclesiastical Commissioners endowed the church to the amount of £150 per annum. In Mr Coghlan's application for endowment it is distinctly stated that '*all* the sittings were *free*'. Had it been otherwise, had the pews for instance been let for £50 per annum, the Commissioners' grant would have been less by that amount. To let the pews, therefore, is in some sense a fraud upon the Commissioners; unless the amount, up to £150, be returned to them, to be applied to the augmentation of poor livings.

The fact of the *Church Commissioners* having declared a certain number of sittings to be *appropriated* without fixing any pew rents is a proof that no such rents were contemplated, for no pews can be lawfully let in any consecrated church, except under the authority of the Church Commissioners, at a scale fixed by them. No such scale having been fixed in this case, no pew rents can be legally taken, and if the churchwardens permit it, they may be proceeded against in the spiritual court.

Dr Lushington[144] says that 'in churches not built by the Church Building Commission pew rents cannot be legally taken' – sittings may be appropriated without being let, as they are in all parish churches.

To this view of the question I adhere, and intend to act accordingly.

I remain, dear sir, your faithful servant,

C. J. London

---

142 Haughton had exchanged his Leicestershire rectory of Markfield for St James's the Less with his predecessor James Coghlan.

143 *Spiritual destitution of the parish of Bethnal Green* (1839), p. 1.

144 Stephen Lushington (1782–1873), a distinguished civilian lawyer, judge of the London consistory court from 1828, and from 1858 dean of the Court of Arches. MP for Tower Hamlets 1832–41, a whig-liberal, but a conscientious churchman. See S. M. Waddams, *Law, politics and the Church of England: the career of Stephen Lushington, 1782–1873* (Cambridge, 1992).

98. Rev. Joshua King to ecclesiastical commissioners, Woodchurch, 18 December 1846

Church of England Record Centre, EC526, 4427/46

My Lords & gentlemen

Previous to my consenting to the parish of St Matthew's Bethnal Green being apportioned out into districts an assurance was held out to me that my rights & privileges would be respected, & my emoluments be unimpaired. Good faith seems to have been observed as regards the first four churches built in my parish to which districts were assigned, the clergymen appointed to those churches being made accountable to me for two thirds of the fees they received. One of them, however, a Mr Alston, soon manifested a disposition to violate the engagement into which he had entered by refusing to receive any fees for the churching of women, & the registration of baptisms. Being desirous of imposing some check upon this wholesale mode of proceeding, the ire of Mr. A. was raised to such a pitch that he placarded me through the parish setting forth that he would not receive a fee for a marriage were he not compelled by me. This conduct thro-out has been most reprehensible, attempting to render me obnoxious to my parishioners & to evade the fulfilment of an agreement into which he voluntarily entered. He is one of the district clergy who has recently been implicated in the disgraceful practice of negotiating fictitious bills – and now sets me at defiance – declares he will no longer be accountable for any fees – dares me to bring an action against him for their recovery, & is instigating others of the district clergy to conspire and cooperate with him in this dishonest act.

It occurs to me that the unpleasantness and exposure consequent upon bringing this matter into court might be avoided by allowing those ministers of the district churches who are accountable to me for a portion of the fees to retain the whole themselves, provided you, out of the funds at your disposal, would be pleased to allow me a compensation for the loss sustained. I venture respectfully to offer this suggestion in hopes of averting from the Church the great scandal that must inevitably ensue should such disreputable conduct obtain notoriety (as it otherwise will do) in a court of law.[145]

I have the honour to be, my lords & gentlemen, your very obedient humble servant,

Joshua King.

99. CJB to Rev. John Tagg [E], F 28 December 1846

Blomfield 45, fo. 40

My dear sir

I am prepared to sanction your table of fees: with the alterations proposed in your letter of the 26th instant. It appears to me that of the fees accruing from the erection of tablets & the sale of vaults in St John's Church, a part at least might properly go towards forming a fund, either for the purchase of a house, or for the augmentation

---

[145] King did resort to the courts, the case of *King* v. *Alston* being heard on 29 Nov. 1847 at Queen's Bench. King was awarded £30 by the court. See *Liverpool Mercury*, 3 Dec. 1847, p. 7; *Daily News*, 30 Nov. 1847, p. 4. For the troubled history of marriage fees at St Philip's, see n. 203 below.

of the incumbent's income, the *interest* being appropriated to the *latter* purpose, the *capital* to the former.

I am, my dear sir, yours faithfully,

C. J. London

100. CJB to Rev. George Alston [I], F 31 December 1846

Blomfield 45, fos. 43–5

My dear sir

I have read Mr Kenyon's[146] opinion, and have no doubt as to the correctness of his conclusion, viz: that the word *commendam* was used in the Bethnal Green Act[147] with reference to the rectory being held by a bishop: had it been intended to prohibit its being held in plurality with another benefice, the word *dispensation* would have been added.

I think that you are hardly justified in using such very strong language as you have employed in speaking of Mr King as holding two livings. It may be questioned whether he ought ever to have been permitted to hold Bethnal Green with Wood-church; but he was permitted to do so by the patrons, who might have presented another clerk, upon his institution to another living. It has been at all times since that event, competent to either the patron, or the bishop, to declare the living of Bethnal Green void; but until that is done, Mr King is the legal incumbent.

Finding him to be in possession, and having been in possession for several years, when I became bishop of London, I did not feel myself at liberty to dispossess him and now, of course, I feel still greater delicacy, being myself the patron.[148] Still, however, I should probably not scruple to take that step if Mr King were to do anything which might seem to require it: but I cannot consider that his claiming his undoubted legal dues, secured to him by the order-in-council, constitutes an offence for which he deserves even my censure.

Of course it is very annoying to me, that in my endeavours to provide for the spiritual good of the people of Bethnal Green, which I am bound to say Mr King in no way withstood or discouraged, the arrangements which I was in justice bound to make for the purpose of securing him, as far as could reasonably be expected, the continued enjoyment of his lawful rights should be disturbed and set at nought by any of the clergy whom I had been the means of introducing into his parish, and it was on this account that I said, in my last letter, that *I* as well as *he* had some ground of complaint.

Mr King has sent in a very strong memorial to the Ecclesiastical Commissioners,[149] which I am desirous of having withdrawn if possible: but this I cannot do, if you persist in your refusal to pay him his dues.

I remain, my dear sir, your faithful servant,

C. J. London

---

[146] Probably John Kenyon (1807–80), DCL, judge of the Oxford consistory court and Viverian professor of common law.

[147] The act of 1743, § 33.

[148] Presumably lest it appear he be seeking to put his 'own' man in.

[149] Document 98.

101. CJB to H. J. Hodgson,[150] F 31 December 1846

Blomfield 45, fo. 40

Sir

I shall be very glad if it be found possible to raise an endowment fund for St John Bethnal Green, if any thing like the amount which is specified in the Resolutions you have sent me a copy, and I shall most readily become a contributor to such Fund; especially if it should be the means of enabling Mr Tagg to retain his pastoral charge.

When you have ascertained which of the gentlemen named in your second resolution will consent to sit on the committee, you will perhaps let me hear from you again.

I remain, sir, your obedient servant,

    C. J. London

102. CJB to Rev. Timothy Gibson, F 2 January 1847

Blomfield 45, fo. 53

Dear sir

I am sorry to say that I have failed in my endeavour to induce Mr Alston to pay Mr King his legal dues; and I have no means of compelling him to do so. Mr Alston is possessed with a notion that Mr King is not legally the rector of Bethnal Green, because the local act provides that the living shall not be held *in commendam*. I do not think he is right in this opinion. I have first both as patron & ordinary, to declare the living void; but until that is done I consider Mr King to be the legal incumbent.

I remain, dear sir, your faithful servant,

    C. J. London

103. CJB to Rev. John Tagg [E], LH 15 February 1847

Blomfield 45, fo. 108

My dear sir

I should be inclined to endow St John's Bethnal Green with £150 per annum out of the tithes of St Catherine Colman Fenchurch Street, on condition that the sum of £5,000 or a rent charge to the amount of another £150 were *secured* so as to make the income of the clergyman £300 a year; and on condition also that all the sittings in the church should be declared free.[151]

I wish you to submit this proposition to your endowment committee as soon as possible

I am, my dear sir, yours faithfully,

    C. J. London

---

[150] Probably Henry John Hodgson (1817–92), barrister.
[151] The scheme had to be scaled down: see Document 115.

104. CJB to churchwardens of St Jude's Bethnal Green, F 18 January 1847

Blomfield 45, fo. 72

Gentlemen,

In answer to your letter of the 23d ulto. I beg to state that it has in no degree altered the opinion which I expressed to Mr Keane in the letter which I addressed to him on the 21st of November,[152] and in which I hoped he had acquiesced. I can by no means approve of a plan which if persisted in would break up the system which I have been so desirous of establishing in the Bethnal Green churches.

I am, gentlemen, your obedient servant,

    C. J. London

105. CJB to Rev. John Tagg [E], LH 25 May 1847

Blomfield 45, fo. 246

Private
My dear sir

I am advised by counsel that an application to the Court of Queens Bench for a mandamus to compel the churchwardens of Bethnal Green to provide for the lighting of your church would fail. I wish this not to be known, in the hope that by some other means they may be inclined to perform their duty. I know of no funds out of which this expense can be defrayed, except that which may be raised by subscription amongst your congregation. I am sorry that I cannot give you a more satisfactory answer to your inquiry.

I am, my dear sir, yours faithfully,

    C. J. London

106. CJB to Rev. Henry Philip Haughton [D], F 23 June 1847

Blomfield 45, fo. 271

My dear sir

After full consideration of the subject I feel myself compelled to object to your taking any duty which will involve the leaving of the whole of one of the services in your church to your curate. Nor do I see how you would be a gainer by such an arrangement, for the Committee of the Additional Curates Fund[153] would of course withdraw their grant, which is made for the purpose of providing the services of an additional clergyman, not of relieving you from any part of your duty which you could perform.

It gives me great concern to be under the necessity of interfering with any arrangements which might improve your income

I am, my dear sir, your faithful servant,

    C. J. London

---

[152] Document 95.
[153] See above, n. 138.

107. CJB to Rev. Timothy Gibson, F 25 November 1847

Blomfield 46, fo. 197

My dear sir

I am concerned to hear of Mr King's [154] serious illness – of which I knew nothing till I received your letter; nor have I had any application respecting his absence from his living.

I have no other objection to the plan which you propose for supplying his place than this, that the whole time of the second curate of St Matthew's ought to be devoted to the parish – and the whole time of Mr King's substitute to the parish of St George – Be so good as to let me know whether Mr King has an assistant curate and if you can, meet me at London House on Saturday at half past two,

I am my dear sir, your faithful servant,

C. J. London

108. CJB to Rev. John Graham Packer [H], F 26 November 1847

Blomfield 46, fos. 205–6

My dear sir

The archdeacon has sent me a full and detailed report of the conferences which he had with you *and* your churchwardens.

After the most careful consideration of the subject I am disposed to concur in the recommendation made by the archdeacon, and cordially assented to by the churchwardens, that there should be a communion on the 1st & 3rd Sundays of every month, as well as on the great festivals, & that the offertory should be made by the whole congregation; the prayer for the Church Militant not being read on the other Sundays.

The collection at the offertory from the whole congregation & the reading of the Church Militant prayer before the departure of the communicants on two Sundays in every month, without apparent objection, will be a great point gained; so great, that it will, I think, be well purchased at the price of some concession on other points. I entertain considerable doubt as to the expediency of a weekly communion in parish churches in the present state of religious principle & failing in the mass of our people, although in some places, peculiarly circumstanced, it may be desirable.

Upon the whole it appears to me that the churchwardens, as representing a certain portion of your congregation, have made larger concessions than I had expected they would make, and that this is one of the cases in which it is right for us to act upon the principle of St Paul, to 'bear the infirmities of the weak' & to 'please our neighbour for his good to edification';[155] nor do I see that in acceding to the proposed arrangement you will be guilty of any dereliction of the duty which you owe to the Church.

I am, my dear sir, yours faithfully,

C. J. London

---

[154] Bryan King at St George's in the East.
[155] Romans 15:1, 15:2.

109. CJB to Rev. John Espy Keane [G], 29 November 1846

Blomfield 46, fo. 212

My dear sir

It has been stated to me that you have moved the stoves in your church to the west end, & have put up two unsightly chimneys which disfigure the building. You are perhaps not aware that no such erection can be lawfully made without the sanction of the bishop or archdeacon, and I must beg of you not to allow any change whatever to be made, for the future, either in the fabric itself of the church, or in the internal decorations & arrangements, until the archdeacon has inspected the church, and given permission for the proposed alterations

I am, my dear sir, your faithful servant

C. J. London

110. CJB to Rev. Henry Philip Haughton [D], F 29 November 1847

Blomfield 46, fos. 209–11

My dear sir

I fear that I shall not be able by reason of indisposition to meet you at London House on Wednesday. I wished for an opportunity of speaking to you more fully than I can well do by letter, on the subject of your church etc.

I wish that you had not expended any sum of money beyond that of which I sanctioned the outlay, on your churchyard; or rather I should say that I wish that you had applied to me before you expended it, which you could easily have done by letter. The expenditure itself was, I dare say, necessary, but I am sure you must see that what one of the Bethnal Green incumbents does in this way, *all* may do, and that then the small fund entrusted to me by the Act of Parliament would not be at my disposal, but at theirs.

I am willing however to direct the payment of £10, £1.13.9, £6 and £2.2.0. making altogether £19.15.9. Upon receipt of the different bills I will direct Mr Silk to hand you a check for that amount. But I must request you to bear in mind that in future I shall not consider myself at liberty to repay any sums, however small, of which I have not first sanctioned in writing the outlay. I am sure that you will readily perceive the necessity of this restriction.

I much regret that no alteration may be made in the position of the stoves, affecting the walls or architectural appearance of the church without the previous sanction of the archdeacon, given after his personal inspection.

I remain, my dear sir, your faithful servant

C. J. London

111. CJB to Rev. John Graham Packer [H], F 29 November 1847

Blomfield 46, fo. 215

My dear sir

I am sorry to find, upon referring again to the archdeacon's letter, that I made a mistake as to the nature of his proposal, which I now see, recommended two monthly sacraments, but only one general collection at the offertory from the whole congregation.

But even with this modified proposal I am disposed to recommend your compliance: and I could see such an arrangement as it contemplates established in other churches in my diocese.

I am, my dear sir, yours faithfully,
      C. J. London

112. CJB to Rev. William Hall [G],[156] F 9 December 1847

Blomfield 46, fo. 239

Dear sir

I can have no difficulty in answering the question which you have professed to raise. Mr Brown would not wish to interfere with the exercise of your private judgement as to signing the Lord's Day petition,[157] but he has a right to expect that you do not move any questions of a religious nature amongst his parishioners without his consent.

I remain, dear sir, your faithful servant
      C. J. London

113. CJB to the churchwardens of St Peter's Bethnal Green, F 10 December 1847

Blomfield 46, fo. 241

Gentlemen

It gives me the liveliest satisfaction to learn, from your letter, as from one which I have received from Mr Packer, that you have come to an amicable understanding with him respecting the mode of conducting divine services, and I earnestly hope that nothing may occur to disturb the good feeling which now exists.

I remain, gentlemen, your faithful servant,
      C. J. London

114. CJB to Rev. John Graham Packer [H], F 10 December 1847

Blomfield 46, fo. 242

My dear sir

I am heartily glad to hear of a pacification. I wish it may not *prove* to be a truce instead of a *treaty*; but from an expression in the letter which I have received from the churchwardens I am led to fear that upon their quitting office there may be some danger of renewed dissatisfaction. I earnestly hope that such may not prove to be the case.

I am, my dear sir, yours faithfully,
      C. J. London

---

[156] See above, p. 303.
[157] I.e., a sabbatarian petition.

115. CJB to Rev. John Medows Rodwell,[158] F 11 December 1847

Blomfield 46, fo. 243

My dear sir

My object, and that of the Ecclesiastical Commissioners with respect to St Johns Bethnal Green, is to get as large an endowment as we can to meet the £150 per annum which I have reserved for it out of the Rectory of St Catherine Colman. In the first instance I named a large sum: but I fear there is no prospect of obtaining more than £1,000, and if that can be got, I shall acquiesce.[159]

I think that whatever sum may be obtained cannot be better expended than in erecting a parsonage house. No other mode of endowment yields so large an interest for the money laid out.

I am, my dear sir, yours faithfully,
    C. J. London

116. CJB to Rev. John Tagg [E], F December 1847

Blomfield 46, fo. 246

My dear sir

I have received a letter from Mr Brookes, your churchwarden, on the subject of lighting your church. I do not like to tell him plainly that my legal advisors are of opinion that I should not succeed in an endeavour to compel the parish church-wardens to pay the expenses, but I wish you to say to him as from me that the legal difficulties are so great that I cannot venture to specify any fixed time at which it is probable that the matter will be settled. In the meantime I think, considering what has been done for the church in the way of endowment, the congregation might exert themselves to provide the necessary funds.

I am, my dear sir, yours faithfully,
    C. J. London.

117. CJB to Rev. John Espy Keane [F], F 22 December 1847

Blomfield 46, fo. 267

My dear sir

I do not remember if Mr Valentine[160] was licensed to your curacy. If not, it is necessary that he should be so. The question of folding doors to your schoolrooms is one on which I feel myself hardly competent to give an opinion without inspecting the rooms & hearing what is to be said for & against the proposals. I hope you have shaken off the influenza.

---

158 (1808–1900); b. Suffolk; lect. St Andrew's Holborn 1836–43; rect. St Ethelburga's Bishopgate 1843–1900; prebend of St Paul's; secretary Additional Curates Fund 1843–58. Distinguished oriental scholar. See *ODNB*.

159 In Oct. 1849 it was reported that £1,000 had been raised by the parishioners towards permanent endowment, and the bishop duly appropriated £150 per annum from St Katherine Colman on condition that 337 sittings be declared free in addition to the 800 existing ones. *John Bull*, 6 Oct. 1849, p. 626; see also order in council of 20 May 1847, *London Gazette*, no. 20746, 22 June 1847, pp. 2263–6.

160 See p. 303.

I am, my dear sir, yours faithfully,
C. J. London.

118. CJB to Rev. Henry Philip Haughton [D], F 15 January 1848

Blomfield 46, fo. 271

My dear sir

I am glad to hear that you have made a movement in the cause of sanitary improvement. I hope it may awaken your people to the importance of the subject.

With respect to the sanitary commissioners, it must be borne in mind that their authority at present extends only to inquiry. The power of *interfering* will probably be given by Lord Morpeth's Bill.[161] The Guardians of the Union have power at present to apply to magistrates for the removal of nuisances, & for enforcing the cleansing and whitewashing of tenements.

I am, my dear sir, your faithful servant,
C. J. London

119. CJB to Rev. Timothy Gibson, LH 9 February 1848

Blomfield 46, fos. 369–71

My dear sir

As the parochial clergy are from the nature of their duties, more conversant with the actual state of the poor than any other class of persons, they may be naturally expected to be the first to press a consideration of that state upon the attention of those who possess the means of improving it. But what those means are, and the wisest & best mode of applying them, is a proper subject of consideration for others as well as the clergy.

The destitute condition of the poor is a subject which ought to interest *all* the members of the community as well as the ministers of religion; and it appears to me to be the duty of the clergy in the first instance to bring that subject under the notice of their parishioners, the lay authorities of their districts, and other benevolent persons, and to invite their cooperation and advice. This, I think, is what they ought to do, not, in the first instance, to take upon themselves the responsibility of convening a public meeting, for the purpose of considering a plan which they have themselves devised, without having any communication with others. Such a step would be likely to excite jealousy & to awaken suspicion.

The distress, of which you speak, is not confined to the parish of Bethnal Green, but exists also in Spitalfields, and, though perhaps in a less degree, in Whitechapel & St George's East. In any movement which may be made for the relief of that distress, the clergy of all the parishes should, if possible, act together, & at all

---

[161] The Public Health Bill introduced by George Howard, Viscount Morpeth (1802–64), shortly after (Oct. 1848) the seventh earl of Carlisle, as a minister in Russell's whig-liberal cabinet. The resulting act (11 & 12 Vict., c. 63) drew on Edwin Chadwick's investigations, and established central and local boards of health (which could be imposed on any locality with mortality rates in excess of 23:1,000). The local boards might take responsibility for sewerage, street cleaning and paving, the water supply, and regulate slaughterhouses, burial grounds and employ an inspector of nuisances, an officer of health and surveyor.

events, be in communication with one another. But they ought also, in my judgment, before any public step is taken, to communicate with the local authorities, the churchwardens & overseers, the magistrates, and those benevolent individuals who are always ready to support any plan for the benefit of their poor neighbours, such as Mr Hanbury, Sir E. Buxton[162] etc. Any measure which may be determined upon after such communication, and generally approved by all parties, I shall be ready to take into consideration, but I cannot encourage the precise form of proceeding which is suggested in your letter.

I am, my dear sir, your faithful servant,

C. J. London

120. CJB to Rev. William Scott,[163] LH 19 February 1848

Blomfield 46, fo. 384

My dear sir

I thank you for your letter. I saw Mr Packer & Mr Alston sometime since and made a suggestion regarding the demands of Mr Packer's creditors, the result of which I expected to have learned from Mr Packer. I can do nothing more for him; he has not acted in such a manner as to encourage any one to come forward to his assistance. If the scandal which is likely to be occasioned to the Church by his proceeding could be prevented now, it would only be for a time.

I am, my dear sir, yours faithfully

C. J. London

121. CJB to Rev. John Espy Keane [F], LH 18 April 1848

Blomfield 47, fo. 77

My dear sir

I did not answer your first letter, being persuaded that a very little consideration would be sufficient to make you perceive the great indelicacy & impropriety of making any application to me on the subject to which it related; a subject, to which for obvious reasons I must decline making any further reference.

I have been told within the last few days that doors have been recently fixed to nine of the sittings in your church. The archdeacon, who tells me that he has not sanctioned any such alterations, has been directed by me to inquire into the case and, if he finds it to be as stated, to order the removal of the doors.

I am, my dear sir, your faithful servant,

C. J. London

---

162   Edward North Buxton (1812–58), second baronet, son of Thomas Fowell Buxton, liberal MP for Essex South. For (Robert) Hanbury, see n. 79.

163   (1813–72), Queen's Oxford MA 1839; perp. cur. Christ Church Hoxton 1839–63; vic. St Olave's Jewry 1860–72. Editor *Christian Remembrancer* and one of founders and contributor to *Saturday Review*. Known as 'Scott of Hoxton'; tractarian. See *ODNB*.

122. CJB to Rev. John Espy Keane [F], LH 24 April 1848

Blomfield 47, fo. 81

My dear sir

I know nothing of the letter to which you allude. Mr Humphrey has been for some time absent from London, & I have not heard from him on the subject of any communication from you – I cannot imagine why you should hesitate to disobey the Queens commands respecting the special form of prayers.[164] You did not state to me any scruple about the form of prayer for General Fast nor could you have any reason for supposing that I did not approve of the prayer in the present instance. I really wish, my dear sir, that you would exercise your common sense & not give me so much trouble. – more than all the Bethnal Green clergy together.

I am, my dear sir, your faithful servant

C. J. London

123. CJB to churchwardens of St Jude's Bethnal Green, F 12 June 1848

Blomfield 47, fo. 158

Gentlemen.

I have to acknowledge the receipt of a memorial transmitted to me by you respecting the pulpit in St Jude's church, and beg to inform you that I have referred it to William Cotton esq & Mr Clutton,[165] the architect of the church, to report to me thereon.

I cannot but remark that when I preached at the consecration of the church I made particular enquiry as to whether I was audible or not, and was informed that I had been distinctly heard in the remotest parts of the church.

I remain, gentlemen, your obedient servant,

C. J. London.

124. CJB to Rev. Timothy Gibson, F 12 July 1848

Blomfield 47, fos. 207–8

My dear sir

As I do not approve of the system of lectureships paid by voluntary contributions & still less of the making collections in church for that purpose, I cannot give any direction in the matter to which your letter refers. But at the same time, as I do not think it necessary to interpose my authority to prevent the continuance of an established custom except under special circumstances, I must leave the point in question to the discretion of the churchwardens & yourself. I doubt whether a collection can be legally made in church without the consent of the churchwardens; but I do not advise the churchwarden to interfere with a customary collection of the kind to which you refer.

I thought I had informed you in a former letter that I never give my name as a

---

[164] Probably the request for prayers for peace and tranquillity issued on 15 Apr. 1848, though possibly those of thanksgiving for the safe delivery of a daughter to the queen on 18 Mar. The prayer for a general fast had been issued on 9 Mar. 1847 in response to a food shortage.

[165] See p. 283 and n. 140.

subscriber to any theological work, for very obvious reasons, but I shall be ready to take two copies of your History of Joseph.[166]

I am, my dear sir, your faithful servant,

    C. J. London

125. CJB to Rev. Joseph Brown [G], F 24 July 1848

Blomfield 47, fos. 218–19

My dear sir

After careful enquiry & consideration I have decided upon giving my sanction & support to the proposed ragged schools[167] for Bethnal Green and at my recommendation a grant in aid has been made by the London Diocesan Board.

I believe that the circumstance of their being entirely *free* schools will have the effect not of diminishing, but of increasing the number of scholars in the national schools,[168] where a payment is made. All parents who care about their children's education & can possibly afford it will rather pay a small sum for that object in a national school, than send them to a ragged school were nothing is paid, looking upon the former as the more respectable. Many little tradesmen & mechanics would send their children to a national school if the most destitute and ragged children went elsewhere – the respectability of the school would in their estimation be increased.

I hope therefore that before long you may see reason to alter your present opinion with respect to these intended schools, it being most desirable that there should be no important difference of sentiment between the clergy of Bethnal Green, as to the best mode of providing for the education of poor children in that great parish.

I am, my dear sir, yours faithfully,

    C. J. London

126. CJB to Robert Brutton, F 14 September 1848

Blomfield 47, fo. 294

Dear sir

I should have returned an earlier answer to your letter, but that I wished to take a legal opinion upon the question to which it relates.

It seems hard upon Mr Eagles[169] that he should not be able to take away the organ for which he has received only a part of the price; but I am advised that it cannot legally be done, and that the churchwardens are not at liberty to permit it. I do not see what can be done in the matter except to have from time to time collections for the purpose of raising the sum required for the purchase of the organ.

I remain, dear sir, your faithful servant

    C. J. London

---

166 T. Gibson, *Lectures on the history of Joseph* (London, 1848). The volume was dedicated to Lady Mary Hoare, and subscribers included many residents of Bethnal Green, including two Mrs Mercerons and Henry Merceron (two copies apiece), as well as Ansted and John Tagg of its clergy. Joshua King was not a subscriber.

167 Ragged schools were independently established schools providing free education for those too poor to pay. The Ragged School Union (founded 1844) was chaired by Lord Shaftesbury, and the term itself introduced by the London City Mission.

168 I.e., a school in association with the National Society.

169 James Eagles, organ builder of Shoreditch. See Document 127.

127. CJB to James Eagles, Cambridge 30 September 1848

Blomfield 47, fo. 301

Sir

It is certainly very hard that you should not be paid the remainder of the price which was agreed upon for the organ in the church of St James the Less: but I know of no source to which you can look for such payment, except the voluntary contributions of the parishioners. I have always cautioned clergymen and committees against putting up organs unless they were sure of being able to pay for them. All that I feel myself at liberty to consent to is this: that if before Christmas 1849 money cannot be raised for the payment of what is due to you, you shall be at liberty with consent of the incumbent & churchwardens to exchange the present organ for a smaller one, according to the proposal contained in your letter of the 26th inst.

I am sir, your obedient servant
    C. J. London

128. CJB to Rev. John Graham Packer [H], F 9 December 1848

Blomfield 47, fo. 368

My dear sir

I have learned with great regret that you are again going about and asking *in forma pauperi* for eleemosynary contributions. This is realty a most undesirable course of action and brings disgrace upon the church as well as yourself, while it discourages those friends who have done so much for Bethnal Green and damps their ardour in the cause.

If you persist in this course in spite of my repeated remonstrances I shall feel it to be my duty to make *publicly* known my strong disapprobation, and to state some of the *facts* of the case of which I am cognisant.

I am, my dear sir, your faithful servant
    C. J. London

129. CJB to Rev. Joshua King, F 26 December 1848

Blomfield 47, fos. 389–91

My dear sir

I saw Mr Alston on Friday last, and re-stated to him my opinion respecting the non-fulfilment of the conditions, or rather the understanding upon which he took the district of St Philip's. He said nothing about any intention of bringing into question further than he has already done, your tenure of the rectory, nor do I believe that he has any such proceeding in view.

No dispensation can now be granted, under the provisions of the Plurality Act;[170] and it is but fair to say that if such dispensation were legal, I should object to it. Although I refrain, under present circumstances from *disturbing* the arrangements which I found existing when I came to the see of London yet, as I consider it to be

---

[170]   The Pluralities Act, 1 & 2 Vict., c. 106 (1838).

in itself objectionable, I could not do any thing to *confirm* it. If Mr Alston takes any steps to have the living declared void it will not be with my consent or approval.

You seem not to be aware that even before the passing of the Pluralities Act, no dispensation could be granted for holding two benefices more than 45 miles apart. Such benefices could be held together only by permission of the patron & ordinary, either of whom might at any time declare the first taken benefice void.

I remain, my dear sir, your faithful servant,

    C. J. London

130. CJB to Rev. George Dodsworth [I],[171] F 27 December 1848

Blomfield 47, fo. 392

Revd sir

I have told Mr Alston that as he cannot reside within his district himself, I must call upon him to appoint a curate who will take up his abode in it or close upon it; and I have further intimated to him my wish that his assistant should be a young man, strong & active and able to take a greater share in the *pastoral* duties of this district than you have been able to do. Mr Alston agrees with me as to the propriety of such changes.

I remain, reverend sir, your faithful servant

    C. J. London

131. CJB to Rev. William Kerry [K],[172] LH 8 January 1849

Blomfield 48, fos. 21–2

My dear sir

Since I saw you at London House I have considered Dr Rayner's[173] objection to having laymen on any committee which may [be] formed for instituting a dispensary, or for other charitable purposes in the parish of Bethnal Green, I am strongly of opinion that such objection ought not to be insisted on; but that the cooperation of some of the more respectable of the lay parishioners should be invited, and their advice asked, for instance Mr Brutton, Mr Racine, Mr Williams, churchwarden of St Peter's. No good will be done by any attempt to place a monopoly of the management of local charities in the hands of the clergy, and I must object to the constitution of any committee which does not comprise a certain proportion of laymen.

I shall be glad to see you on Friday next at London House.

I am, my dear sir, yours faithfully,

    C. J. London

---

171 See p. 304. Dodsworth had resided at Hackney while stipendiary curate.
172 See p. 305.
173 Dr Thomas Ottery Rayner, MD, of St Matthew's Place, Hackney Road, and associate of King's College, secretary to the Royal Maternity Charity. A doctor of the same name died in 1874 aged sixty-three at Temuka, Timaru, in New Zealand, having been on the electoral register there in 1862. See New Zealand Historical Data, http://homepages.paradise.net.nz/~dchamber/home.htm accessed 21 June 2009.

132. CJB to Rev. John Espy Keane, F 18 January 1849

Blomfield 48, fo. 26

My dear sir

I must beg that you will as quickly as possible supply Mr Valentine's place; as I cannot advise the Committee of the Additional Curates Fund to pay the stipend if a curate does not give his *whole* time to duties of the curacy.

I am, my dear sir, your faithful servant

      C. J. London.

133. CJB to Rev. Joshua King, LH 19 February 1849

Blomfield 48, fos. 80–1

My dear sir

I am sorry to be under the necessity of sending for your information a paper which I have received within these few days from Doctors Commons.[174] You will see that Mr Alston persists in his intention of trying the validity of your tenure of the rectory of Bethnal Green, which I thought he had laid aside, in consequence of my expressed disapproval of it.

I have submitted the case to Dr Lushington[175] informing him of my unwillingness to be made accessory to declaring the living void. He advises me that under the Church Discipline Act[176] I have no discretion, but that I am bound to allow Mr Alston to prosecute his suit. I will, however, delay answering the letter which I have received from the proctor, till I hear from you. I must trouble you to return me the case & opinion.

I remain, my dear sir, your faithful servant

      C. J. London

134. CJB to Rev. John Tagg [E], LH 26 February 1849

Blomfield 48, fo. 91

My dear sir

I find upon further inquiry that the governors of Q.A.B.[177] are not likely to make any objection to the application of the £1,000 towards building a house. With respect to free pews, I do not approve of their being all thrust back to the western end of the church, and I think it will be much better to make one whole row, from 1 to 22, free. You had better inquire at No 13 Great George St[178] whether the authority of the church commissioners is requisite to give effect to the new arrangement of sittings. When this is done, and the money paid into Q.A.B., the payment of the augmentation will commence.

I am, my dear sir, yours truly,

      C. J. London

[174] The college of advocates practising in the ecclesiastical and admiralty courts, dissolved in 1857.
[175] See n. 144.
[176] 3 & 4 Vict., c. 86 (1840).
[177] Queen Anne's Bounty.
[178] At this time the office for the commissioners for building new churches.

135. CJB to Rev. Joshua King, LH 1 March 1849

Blomfield 48, fo. 100

My dear sir

Dr Lushington after carefully reconsidering the question is still of opinion that the Act of Parliament is imperative, and that if Mr Alston persists in his application I am bound to permit him to institute a suit. I have, however, had some further conversation with Mr Alston, and he says that in deference to my wish he will forebear from proceeding provided that he can make some amicable arrangement with you to prevent dispute or annoyance respecting the fees.

It appears very doubtful whether, notwithstanding the exchange of advowsons, the nomination to the rectory would not be in the College supposing you to vacate it.

I am, my dear sir, your faithful servant

C. J. London

136. CJB to Rev. Joshua King, LH 10 March 1849

Blomfield 48, fos. 117–18

Dear sir

It having been solely & entirely owing to my intervention & remonstrance that Mr Alston abandoned his intention of prosecuting his intended suit, which must have issued in your being ousted from the rectory of Bethnal Green, I must say it was not very gracious on your part, to insinuate in your letter of the 6th instant that I was not serious in my wish to prevent matters coming to that extremity, because I had told you that I should be obliged to act upon Dr Lushington's advice if Mr Alston should persist in his intention.

A little reflexion will satisfy you, that whatever may be the weight due to the opinion of Dr Addams,[179] or of any other lawyer, I could not do otherwise than follow the advice of Dr Lushington not only on account of his eminence as an ecclesiastical lawyer, but because he is my chancellor and as such my advisor in all legal questions, except those which are likely to come before him as judge of the Consistory Court.

Although I would not willingly have allowed Mr Alston to proceed, I should have felt less difficulty in doing so, had the necessity arisen, in consequence of my having ascertained that if the living had been declared void, the presentation would have been for this turn with the *College,* and not with *me*: and I am bound to add that I consider Bethnal Green to be a living which ought not to have been allowed, in the first instance, to be held with any other, unless the rector had been bound to residence for at least half the year

I am, dear sir, your faithful servant

C. J. London

---

[179] Jesse Addams (1786–1871), a proctor at Drs Commons and advocate in the consistory court, who was later Henry Phillpotts's advocate in the Gorham case.

137. CJB to Rev. George Alston [I], LH 21 March 1849

Blomfield 48, fo. 138

My dear sir

I sent your letter, with its enclosure, to Mr King. It appears from his answer, that he is not disposed to accede to your proposal. It seems to me that the proper course to pursue would be that you should both agree to refer the matter to the arbitration of some impartial person. I must decline all further interference

I am, my dear sir, your faithful servant,

C. J. London

138. CJB to Rev. George Alston [I], LH 23 March 1849

Blomfield 48, fo. 147

My dear sir

It appears to me that Mr King can hardly be expected to acquiesce in your demand to its full extent. I do not see why you should retain money which has been proved to be legally due to Mr King.

It seems to me that the questions at issue between you had better be referred to the arbitration of some impartial person or persons; and that both you should agree to abide by his or their decision.

I am, my dear sir, your faithful servant

C. J. London

PS Mr King is willing to exonerate those of the district clergy who pay a portion of their fees to him from all such payments in future.

139. CJB to Rev. George Alston [I], LH 2 April 1849

Blomfield 48, fo. 165

My dear sir

I do not admit the justness of Mr Philipp's argument, either in law or in equity. But I must request you to state by letter to Mr King what you have stated to me, as I can no longer act as mediator between you. I must again repeat that I strongly disapprove of your original proceedings with regard to the fees due to Mr King.

I am, my dear sir, your faithful servant

C. J. London

140. CJB to Rev. Joshua King, L 11 April 1849

Blomfield 48, fo. 175

My dear sir

I have received a letter from Mr Alston's proctor renewing his demand of Letters of Request to the Court of Arches.[180] I very much wish that you could obviate the

---

180 The provincial ecclesiastical court of Canterbury. Letters of request enabled cases to be sent direct to the court bypassing the diocesan courts.

necessity of such a proceeding; but if he persists I shall not be at liberty to refuse compliance with his demand.

I am, my dear sir, your faithful servant

C. J. London

141. CJB to Rev. Joshua King, L 18 April 1849

Blomfield 48, fo. 194

My dear sir

It must be admitted that you take a very strange method of acknowledging the efforts I have made to dissuade Mr Alston from prosecuting his intended suit when you insinuate that 'I feel little sympathy with you & am not disposed to prevent Mr A's indulgence of his fiendlike & vindictive intentions.'

It is solely from feelings of personal sympathy or compassion that I have made these efforts; not from any opinion that such a case of plurality as yours could be defended, but being reluctant to disturb an arrangement which had been so long suffered to continue.

I have again consulted Dr Lushington; and he advises me in the strongest manner not to wait for a mandamus to compel me to do what he holds to be my clear duty, and accordingly, have once more signified to Mr Alston my disapproval of this proceeding. I have signed Letters of Request to the judges of the Court of Arches.[181]

I could not possibly consent to the arrangements which you propose.

I remain, my dear sir, your faithful servant,

C. J. London

142. CJB to Rev. Henry Philip Haughton [D], LH 25 April 1849

Blomfield 48, fo. 195

Dear sir

As you have declined acting in concert with the other clergy of Bethnal Green in carrying out the plans which I have suggested and sanctioned for the good of the parish[182] I cannot give any contribution to the object of your present appeal.

I am my dear sir, your faithful servant,

C. J. London

143. CJB to Rev. John Graham Packer [H], LH 25 May 1849

Blomfield 48, fos. 231–2

My dear sir

The committee of the B. G. Churches Fund is not responsible for the payment of any expenses incurred without its previous sanction. After consulting with Mr

---

[181] See Lambeth Palace Library, Court of Arches, H749/1 for the letters of request, dated 28 Apr. 1849. There is no indication in the file that the case went further.

[182] See Document 181.

Cotton I am willing to allow £10 from the fund at my disposal towards the liquidation of Mr Tolley's bill,[183] to be paid by me to him

I am dear sir, your faithful servant

C. J. London

144. CJB to churchwardens of St Matthias, F 30 July 1849

Blomfield 48, fo. 304

Gentlemen

I am sorry to be under the necessity of declining to comply with any request made to me by persons who have shown themselves to be so much attached to the Church, but I am obliged to state at once and distinctly that I cannot appoint Mr Proctor[184] to succeed your late excellent incumbent Mr Brown.

I remain, gentlemen, your very faithful servant,

C. J. London

145. CJB to Rev. Edward William Relton [B], Bowness 24 August 1849

Blomfield 48, fo. 341

My dear sir

If the Queen Dowager's donation[185] be *recoverable* I dare say that Her Majesty would permit some portion of it to be applied to the purchase of the school room; but there seemed to be some doubt, when I last inquired, as to what had become of the money.

I am, my dear sir, yours very truly,

C. J. London

146. CJB to Rev. John Graham Packer [H], Bowness 6 September 1849

Blomfield 48, fo. 347

Dear sir

I am sincerely sorry for the trials with which it has pleased God to visit you; but I think it my duty to say very frankly that after all that has taken place I cannot

---

183 Perhaps Temple George Tolley, bricklayer, of 37 Lamb Street, Spital Square.
184 Several candidates were in orders, none obvious!
185 Queen Adelaide (1792–1849 – she died on 2 Dec.), widow of William IV. In Jan. 1849 it was reported that Adelaide had given 100 guineas and Blomfield 50 towards a new dispensary to be called the 'Royal Adelaide Dispensary' in Bethnal Green: *John Bull*, 20 Jan. 1849, p. 44. As the events in letters 131, 147, 150–1 also chart, it appears that disputes arose over the composition of the governing body, and that Dr Rayner (see n. 173) was dismissed from his position as secretary to the original project but continued, with the funds, on a rival version using the same title (perhaps easier after Adelaide's death?). Certainly a Queen Adelaide Dispensary was duly opened in Bethnal Green in 1850 in Warner Place, with a resident medical officer, ceasing work as a dispensary only in 1961. It has not proved possible to establish as yet which of the two projects this reflected, but it would appear that the foundation was not straightforward. On 9 Nov. 1851 the *Era* reported that Dr Rayner had successfully defended an action in Southwark County Court to recover some £22 for drugs supplied to the Dispensary which 'had ceased to exist in February last' leaving £100 in a bank in the name of Rayner and Thomas Peckston (here 'Paxton') over which Rayner claimed to have no control, having never been more than an honorary secretary to the project.

consider that you have any claim upon me, and that there is no prospect of my removing you to another incumbency.

I enclose a check for £10 and must request you to consider it the last time that I can assist you in that way

I am, dear sir, your faithful servant

C. J. London

147. CJB to Dr Thomas Ottery Rayner[186] and Rev. Thomas Snowden Peckston [B],[187] F 1 October 1849

Blomfield 48, fo. 374

The bishop of London presents his compliments to Dr Rainer and the Rev. Thomas Peckstone, and begs to state that he is authorised by the Queen Dowager to request that the sum of £100 paid to them as a donation from Her Majesty may be paid to the bishop's account at his bankers Messrs Jones Loyd & Co., 43 Lothbury, for the purpose of its being applied to certain charitable objects in the parish of Bethnal Green.[188]

148. CJB to Rev. William Kerry [K], Earls Colne 22 October 1849

Blomfield 49, fo. 7

My dear sir

I have received a letter from Dr Rayner, who refuses to transfer any part of the Queen Dowager's donation although the object for which it was given cannot be attained. His letter is written in such a tone that it is impossible for me to take any notice of it, or to have any communication with him. It now rests with the committee, under whom Dr Rayner and Mr Peckston acted, to take such steps as they may think proper.

I am, my dear sir, yours faithfully

C. J. London

149. CJB to Rev. Thomas Snowden Peckston [B], LH 24 October 1849

Blomfield 49, fo. 10

Dear sir

The £100 contributed by the Queen Dowager was given towards the establishment of a dispensary, *in* and *for* Bethnal Green only, to be under the management of a committee, consisting of the parochial clergy and some respectable laymen. This project having failed, I applied for permission from the Queen Dowager to appropriate her Majesty's subscription to other charitable objects connected with this parish. This permission was readily granted, but Dr Rayner refuses to give up any part of this money. It appears however that it stands at the bankers in the joint

---

186 See n. 173.
187 See p. 300.
188 See n. 185.

names of Dr Rayner and yourself, and I feel it my duty to caution you not to consent to the transfer of any portion of it without having first obtained my sanction.

I remain, dear sir, your faithful servant,

    C. J. London

PS I wish you to lay this letter before the committee originally formed

150. CJB to Rev. John Fortunatus Stansbury,[189] F 10 December 1849

Blomfield 49, fo. 74

Revd sir

I quite approve of a movement for the purpose of establishing baths and wash-houses for the parish of Bethnal Green, and shall be ready to cooperate with its promoters to the best of my power, in any way but that of personal attention to the plan which it will not be in my power to give. I think it should be made an indispensable condition that the parish should take advantage of Sir Henry Dukin-field's Act,[190] although it may be deemed advisable to assist them with a voluntary subscription.

I remain, reverend sir, your faithful servant,

    C. J. London

151. CJB to Rev. Edward William Relton [B], F 18 January 1850

Blomfield 49, fo. 118

My dear sir

I am very much concerned to think that you should find it necessary to relinquish your charge at Bethnal Green, and especially from so painful a cause –

I do not think you should advertise for a curacy; but I advise you first to have leave of absence, say for 6 months, and see what air is best suited to Mrs Relton's health, before you bind yourself to a particular spot. If you can call at London House on Monday at ¼ before 12, I will speak to you on the subject.

I am, yours very truly,

    C. J. London

152. CJB to Rev. Joseph Brown [G], LH 13 February 1850

Blomfield 49, fos. 164–5

My dear Mr Brown

Your former curate Mr Hall[191] has thought fit to associate himself with Dr Rayner despite the dismissal of the latter from the office of joint secretary to Queen

---

[189] (1805–94), headmaster of Oundle School 1848–76.

[190] The 1846 Baths and Wash-Houses Act (9 & 10 Vict., c. 74) enabled parishes to finance bath-houses out of loans from the poor rates. Dukinfield was vicar of St Martin's in the Fields. See E. H. Gibson III, 'Baths and washhouses in the English public health agitation, 1839–48', *Journal of the History of Medicine and Allied Sciences*, IX (1954), pp. 391–406, which also notes the *rôle* of both William Cotton and Blomfield in the agitation.

[191] See above, p. 303.

Adelaide's Dispensary,[192] & has been soliciting contributions to another charity, to which they have given the same name, representing it as being under my patronage, although he admits that he was aware of my having refused to have anything to do with it, and of my having protested against Dr Rayner's proceedings. This conduct, which I do not scruple to call dishonest, he tells me has your approval. He says that you consider him to have done quite right. I cannot believe that you have said any such thing, but I wish to have your own denial of it.

Believe me, yours very truly
C. J. London

153. CJB to Rev. William Hall [G],[193] LH 15 February 1850

Blomfield 49, fos. 175–6

Revd sir

After what passed at our interview on Monday last you can be at no loss to know the reason which led me to state that I should demur to licensing you in my diocese. By your own admission you have been soliciting contributions to a charity,[194] as being one which I patronise, although you knew at the time that I had withdrawn my name from it, & had openly expressed my disapproval of the methods which had been resorted to by some of its supporters.

I designated this as a proceeding not to be reconciled with the plainest rules of truth and honesty; and I expected from you a proper acknowledgement of your error. Instead of this, you defended your conduct, and told me that Mr Brown quite approved of what you had done. Thinking this to be very improbable I wrote to inquire of Mr Brown[195] whether your statement was true. He assures me, as I expected, that he has said nothing of the kind, but that on the contrary he told you plainly that you were altogether wrong in the matter, and advised you at once to withdraw from the charity alluded to. I am willing to attribute your misrepresentation of what Mr Brown said to nervousness & agitation rather than to a wilful intention of stating what was not true, but it certainly does not diminish the necessity of a proper apology on your part for having made an improper use of my name and until this has been offered, I must desire you not to officiate in my diocese.

I am, reverend sir, your faithful servant
C. J. London

154. CJB to Rev. William Hall [G], LH 18 February 1850

Blomfield 49, fo. 178

Reverend sir

His Royal Highness the duke of Cambridge[196] has been pleased to forward to me a letter received from you and dated the 15th inst., some days after you had seen me. This letter contains statements so evidently intended to mislead & deceive his

---

192 See nn. 173, 185.
193 See p. 303.
194 The Queen Adelaide's Dispensary: see n. 185.
195 I.e., the Rev. Joseph Brown of St Matthias's.
196 Prince Adolphus Frederick, duke of Cambridge (1774–1850), tenth child of George III.

Royal Highness that I feel it to be my duty to persist in my prohibition, & to forbid your officiating in the diocese of London.

I am, revd sir, your faithful servant
    C. J. London

155. CJB to Rev. William Hall [G], LH 26 February 1850

Blomfield 49, fo. 193

Revd sir

I must leave it to you to determine for yourself how far it is right for you to continue in connexion with an institution which has assumed a name to which it is not entitled,[197] & which has been set on foot in opposition to one which *is* entitled to the name, and which has the sanction of the bishop of the diocese, and of the clergy of the parish for the benefit of which it has been established.

I am, revd sir, your faithful servant
    C. J. London

156. CJB to Rev. Edward William Relton [B], F 25 July 1850

Blomfield 49, fo. 388

My dear sir

I have delayed answering your letter much longer than I had intended owing partly to a very great pressure of business, and partly to indisposition. Immediately upon receiving it I paid Mr Cotton[198] £15 as my quota of the sum promised to you and shall be ready to repeat the payment at the proper time. You need have no scruple about receiving it as both Mr Cotton and I gladly avail ourselves of this method of testifying our sense of the manner in which you have fulfilled your duties.

With respect to the future I wish I would see more clearly what advice to give you. The most obvious course to pursue is that you should seek to offer an exchange of preferment with some clergyman who would be likely to take up and carry on your plan at St Bartholomew's. But I fear it will be difficult to find any one who would be willing to remove from the country to Bethnal Green.

I should be glad if I had an opportunity to remove you to some quieter sphere of duty, but the claims upon me are so many, and some of them urgent, that it is very uncertain when such an opportunity may occur, and it would not be right to hold out a prospect which I may not be able to realise.

With the assurance of my sincere wishes for your health and comfort, I remain, my dear sir, yours very truly
    C. J. London.

---

[197] The Queen Adelaide Dispensary.
[198] I.e., William Cotton.

157. CJB to Rev. John Gore [F],[199] F 30 November 1850

Blomfield 50, fo. 181

Revd sir

In such a parish as Bethnal Green it is not possible to lay down an exact scale of duty for an assistant curate defining what he shall do and what he shall not do, but generally speaking he must do whatever his principal requires him to do. As it appears that you are not likely to come to an understanding with Mr Keane as to your share of the parochial duties, I am inclined to advise your leaving him after due notice.

I am, revd sir, your faithful servant,

C. J. London

158. CJB to Rev. George Alston [I], F 16 December 1850

Blomfield 50, fo. 228

My dear sir

I am much concerned to hear of your giving up your evening service, so useful in a district like yours. I don't quite understand why you should find it more difficult to keep it up than the other clergy of Bethnal Green unless it be that you reside so far from your people, which I cannot help regretting.

I am, my dear sir, your faithful servant

C. J. London

159. CJB to Rev. George Alston [I], LH 3 February 1851

Blomfield 50, fo. 365

Dear sir

I believe the third service at your church to have been a part of the additional duty, in consideration of which the Committee of the Additional Curates Society made you a grant. I have thought it my duty, in forwarding your petition for a renewal, to state to the committee the fact of your having discontinued that service, but I have not grounded thereon any recommendation.

I remain, dear sir, your faithful servant,

C. J. London.

160. CJB to Rev. Henry Philip Haughton [D], F 5 February 1851

Blomfield 50, fo. 375

Dear sir

The fund at my disposal will not suffice for the repair of all the parsonage houses in Bethnal Green. The incumbents must do in this respect as the incumbents of other small livings are obliged to do, who have no special fund to resort to. I am ready to allow something towards the expense of laying on water. If you will send me the bill (£7.5.0) receipted, I will send you a check for £6.

---

[199] Not definitively identified.

I am, dear sir, your faithful servant,
    C. J. London

161. CJB to Rev. George Alston [I], LH 24 February 1851

Blomfield 51, fo. 51

My dear sir
    I return your solicitor's letter which has in no respect changed my opinion as to the course which you are bound in honour to pursue. The only question which the case admits of, is one of *amount*
    I remain, dear sir, your faithful servant,
    C. J. London

162. CJB to Mr Lawless, 5 March 1851

Blomfield 51, fo. 72

Sir
    I have no such fund as you suppose. The Bethnal Green Special Fund, accruing from the burial fees paid over to me yearly[200] have not been considered applicable to the purpose of making provision to clergymen for doing duty.
    I am sir, your obedient servant,
    C. J. London

163. CJB to Rev. Henry Philip Haughton [D], LH 12 April 1851

Blomfield 51, fo. 139

Dear sir
    I know of no other means of providing for the expense of divine service in the church of St James the Less than those which are common to all the incumbents of the new Bethnal Green churches. After what has happened you can hardly expect me to make any special effort on your behalf.
    The exchange between you & Mr Coghlan[201] was entirely your own measure. I had nothing to do but to give my consent to it.
    I am, dear sir, your faithful servant
    C. J. London

164. CJB to Rev. George Alston [I], F 25 July 1851

Blomfield 51, fo. 276

My dear sir
    As my objection to the exchange which you propose is insuperable, and as I do not feel it necessary to explain it, no good would be done by my seeing Mr Verity.[202]

---

200 See n. 119.
201 See n. 143.
202 E. A. Verity, perp. cur. of All Saints, Habergham, Whalley, Lancashire, since 1845.

I am, my dear sir, your faithful servant
    C. J. London
PS It does not follow, because I object to this exchange, that I am unwilling to admit
Mr Verity into the diocese.

165. CJB to Rev. George Alston [I], F 26 July 1851

Blomfield 51, fo. 282

My dear sir
    I am sorry to learn that the arrangement which I recommend with respect to fees
has not been made, in consequence, as it seems, of Mr Haughton's holding out. His
district is so entirely on the edge of the parish, separate from the rest, that I think
you need not have regarded his opposition.
    I should be sorry to be under the necessity of interfering publicly to put a stop
to the present very objectionable system.
    I am, my dear sir, your faithful servant
    C. J. London

166. CJB to Rev. George Alston [I], F 30 July 1851

Blomfield 51, fo. 292

My dear sir
    I do not consider that the reasons you have assigned at all justify your proceed-
ings with regard to the marriage fees;[203] and I hope that some method may be found
of putting a stop to such a discreditable system as that which some of the clergy
have adopted.
    I am, dear sir, your faithful servant
    C. J. London

167. CJB to Rev. John Graham Packer [H], F 1 August 1851

Blomfield 51, fos. 293–4, 296

Dear sir
    I am extremely sorry, both on your account and that of the Church, for the trouble

---

203 In 1851 Gibson complained publicly in a letter to the *Guardian* that from the consecration of St
    Philip's Alston had charged 7*s* for marriages as opposed to the 13*s* at St Matthew's and 10*s* 6*d* at
    other district churches, siphoning the marriage business into his church so that more than 500 were
    solemnized there in the year before, forcing other clergy including A. T. Edwards at St Matthias's
    to reduce their fees, and King himself to cut the fees at St Matthew's to 6*s*, with Alston in response
    cutting his first to 5*s*, then half a crown (2*s* 6*d*). Gibson claimed to have attempted to secure an
    agreed rate at a meeting, to which Alston would not agree. An exchange of letters followed, in which
    Alston denied opposing an agreed sum provided that it was unaminously adopted, prompting Gibson
    to claim that Alston was hiding behind H. P. Haughton's unwillingness to collaborate on the issue.
    The parties also disputed Blomfield's opinion on the most desirable level at which to set a rate. The
    correspondence was prompted by a report in the *Guardian* that handbills had appeared on the streets
    advertising rival church's rates. See *Guardian*, 17, 24, 31 Dec. 1851, 7, 14 Jan. 1852; *Daily News*,
    29 Dec. 1851, and Documents 174, 180.

in which you are involved,[204] and I should be quite prepared to advance the money which you want, if I could believe that it would really put an end to your difficulties and prevent their recurrence. But the experience of the past convinces me that each would not be the case, and after consulting Mr Cotton, who is aware of the extent of your liabilities, I am satisfied that until they are done away by some summary proceeding any moderate sum of money advanced to you would be thrown away.

I am very sensible of the evils which flow from the inadequate endowments of the Bethnal Green churches; but it was such as we could provide, and an addition of £50 per annum has been made which you had no reason to expect when you were appointed to St Peter's. You were then cautioned as to the difficulty of maintaining a family on so small an income, and questioned as to your being free from debt. On this point you deceived Mr Cotton and me. Had I been aware of the amount of your debts I should have refused, out of kindness to yourself, to appoint you to St Peter's.

I do not wish to dwell upon the sad acts of imprudence which you have since committed, your drawing bills etc. and I earnestly hope that I may not be forced to state them publicly: but as to any disgrace which may come upon the church, and the parish of Bethnal Green, *that* has been already inflicted.

When you are once more secured from future demands on the score of liabilities heretofore incurred, I shall be very ready to come forward and assist you; but at present I am persuaded that any money which might be advanced would be thrown away to no good purpose as former advances have been.

I remain, dear sir, your faithful servant
    C. J. London

168. CJB to Rev. John Gore [F], F 4 August 1851

Blomfield 51, fo. 300

Dear sir

As there appears to be no hope of your getting on comfortably with Mr Keane, I again advise you to give him notice of quitting his curacy at the end of three months. This will be better than your quitting upon notice from *him*, which I must permit him to give you, if necessary.

I am, my dear sir, your faithful servant
    C. J. London

169. CJB to Rev. John Gore [F], F 11 August 1851

Blomfield 51, 315

Dear sir

It being evident that you and Mr Keane can never cordially cooperate in the pastoral duties of his district, I have consented to his giving you 6 months notice

---

[204] It was serious: on 19 Aug. 1851 the *London Gazette*, no. 21237, p. 2145, reported that an order had been made vesting the estates of John Graham Packer ('in the Queen's Prison') in a provisional assignee. He had been arrested for debt: the Queen's prison was the successor to the former King's Bench prison in Southwark. The *Daily News* of the same date reported from the Insolvent Debtors Court that Packer had been released from prison pending his hearing.

to quit the curacy; but I strongly recommend you to take, if possible, an earlier opportunity of leaving.

I am, dear sir, your faithful servant
    C. J. London

170. CJB to Rev. Brathwaite Armitage,[205] F 18 August 1851

Blomfield 51, fos. 316–17

Revd sir

I wish I could give you a perfectly satisfactory account of poor Mr Packer.[206]

Nothing can be alleged against him beyond excessive imprudence and those departures from the line of straightforwardness and plaindealing which are apt to be gradually produced by pecuniary difficulties. We have paid what we believed to be the whole amount of his debts on a former occasion, & have advanced him money at other times. But we were not made aware of the real state of the case; and on the present occasion, well knowing that no moderate sum of money would clear him from his liabilities, nor afford more than a partial & temporary relief, I have declined after consulting others who know the state of his affairs, to advance him any more money, but I have sent a certain sum for the benefit of his children to the Revd William Scott of Christ Church Hoxton,[207] who has kindly promised to see what can be done for them. Mr Packer is active and useful in his district, & liked by his parishioners.

I remain, revd sir, your faithful servant,
    C. J. London

171. CJB to Rev. George Alston [I], F 12 August 1851

Blomfield 51, fo. 319

Dear sir

I think it would have been more seemly, and more suitable to your relation to me as your diocesan, if instead of announcing to me that you were about to publish my letters, you had asked my permission to do so. However, you must follow your own course, but it may very probably be necessary for me, in case you should do what you propose, to make public some other letters which have passed between us, and certain other circumstances which have interfered with the complete attainment of the object which Mr Cotton & I had in view when we undertook to provide for the spiritual wants of Bethnal Green.

I am, dear sir, your faithful servant,
    C. J. London

---

205 (1804–78); vic. Peterchurch, Herefordshire, 1832–75.
206 I.e., John Graham Packer of St Peter's. See n. 204.
207 See n. 163.

172. CJB to Rev. John Espy Keane [F], Bolton Bridge, Skipton 15 August 1851

Blomfield 51, fo. 324

Dear sir

I send you a letter from Mr Gore which I will thank you to return to me as soon as you can. Is his statement true with respect to the letting of your seats to persons not in your district, or to what extent is it true?

If such is indeed the case it will be my duty to interfere and put a stop to a system in itself wholly illegal, and utterly at variance with the object for which your church was built.

I am, my dear sir, your faithful servant,

C. J. London

173. CJB to Rev. John Espy Keane, Bolton Bridge, Skipton 22 August 1851

Blomfield 51, fo. 343

My dear sir

I object in the strongest manner to your bringing the questions at issue between yourself and Mr Gore before your parishioners. These questions are to be decided not by them, but by me, & an appeal to a public meeting would be quite derogatory to my authority. When I require the testimony of your parishioners I will ask for it, but not through the medium of a public meeting. It was easy for you to collect from my last letter that I attached little or no weight to Mr Gore's accusations, but the one point, which related to a simple matter of fact, & which I did speak of as important, you have passed over in silence: I mean the letting of the seats in your church to strangers, and the non-reservation of sittings for the poor of your own district. This is the one point to which I desire to call your attention & if which I beg a full and particular explanation.

I remain, my dear sir, yours faithfully,

C. J. London.

174. CJB to Rev. Timothy Gibson, Bolton Bridge 28 August 1851

Blomfield 51, fo. 355

My dear sir

I wrote to Mr Alston on the 26th ulto.[208] expressing my regret that my recommendation had not been attended to, and my opinion as to the unimportant nature of Mr Haughton's opposition. In answer to this, Mr Alston stated his reasons for not having complied with my suggestions. I wrote again on the 30th ulto. and said that I did not consider these reasons sufficient; & that I hoped some method might be found of putting a stop to the discreditable system now pursued. If Mr King thinks fit to lower the scale of marriage fees at the parish church, I have no objection to his doing so, but I regret that he should have been forced to it by what I consider a very improper proceeding.

I am, my dear sir, your faithful servant

C. J. London

---

[208] Document 165.

175. CJB to Rev. George Alston [I], Bakewell 5 September 1851

Blomfield 51, fo. 365

Dear sir

I am sorry to be under the necessity of declining to sanction your proposed exchange with the incumbent of Kelham.[209]

I am, dear sir, your faithful servant

C. J. London

176. CJB to Rev. George Alston [I], F 6 October 1851

Blomfield 52, fos. 33–4

Dear sir

I do not admit the justice of any such claim as that which you have advanced in your letter of the 3rd inst. Considering how many times you have had occasion to confer with Mr Cotton and me on money matters, it seems strange that this claim should now be put forward for the first time.

We paid £1,100 to the Ecclesiastical Commissioners which they met with a like sum for a *house*; and as a house could not be built so soon as we had hoped, the interest of these two sums has been regularly paid to you as a matter of favour, not of right; and to this amount both St Phillip's and St Andrew's have been better off than any of the other churches for which parsonages have been built except St James endowed by Mr Harrold. Be so good as to send me Mr Cotton's letter from which you have quoted a passage.

I am, dear sir, your faithful servant,

C. J. London.

177. CJB to Rev. Timothy Gibson, F 6 November 1851

Blomfield 52, fo. 84

My dear sir

Considering that I might at any time have declared the living of Bethnal Green void, and have foreborne from doing so, I think Mr King's assertions & reflexions are really too bad.

So far is his supposition about Brasenose College from being true, that when I inquired whether if Mr King were ejected the college would do anything to replace him I received an assurance that they would not. His conduct is such that I am strongly inclined to declare the living void at once & to put an end to a great scandal.

I have told him that I will not in any way pledge myself regarding his residence at Bethnal Green.

I am, my dear sir, yours faithfully,

C. J. London.

---

[209] Nottinghamshire. Robert N. Sutton rect. since 1844.

178. CJB to churchwardens of St Jude Bethnal Green, F 20 November 1851

Blomfield 52, fo. 120

Gentlemen

I am sorry to receive your report of the state of your church. I cannot help reminding you that a good deal of money has been laid out in altering the church without my sanction which would have sufficed to put it into thorough repair. With respect to the roof, tiles were used in preference to slate after mature consideration as being warmer in winter & cooler in summer. Under any circumstances it would not be possible to make any alteration in the church at this time of year and in the present state of the fund at my disposal I cannot think of applying any part of it to cleaning or colouring of the church.

I remain, gentlemen, your faithful servant,

C. J. London

179. CJB to Rev. George Alston [I], L 10 March 1852

Blomfield 53, fo. 212

Dear sir

I am greatly surprised at your having taken the liberty (to use no sharper phrase) of referring your poor tradesmen to me for the payment of debts contracted by *yourself* without any authority from the District Visiting Association. But I have a proposal to make. If you will pay me the money which you owe me (£50) I will hand it over to Mr Trevitt[210] for the purpose of discharging the bills, or so much of it as may be required for that purpose.

I remain your faithful servant

C. J. London

180. CJB to Rev. Timothy Gibson, LH 31 March [1852]

Blomfield 53, fo. 268

My dear sir

I understand that the clergy of Bethnal Green have agreed a marriage fee of 10/6. This seems to me much too high for such a neighbourhood. What I understood from the clergy, when I saw them at London House, was that 7 or 7/6 was to be the fee. 10/6 will have the effect of driving the people to the Registrar – I suppose I shall receive a communication on the subject

I am my dear sir, yours faithfully,

C. J. London

---

[210] George Alston's successor. See n. 218.

181. Rev. Timothy Gibson to Rev. Henry Mackenzie,[211] 25 April 1859

Tower Hamlets Local History Library and Archives

Anent the B.G. churches I send the following statement.

St Matthew's, the mother church, notwithstanding the erection of ten additional ones, is much better attended now than it was 17 years ago, when I became the curate.

St Peter's still retains Mr Packer[212] as incumbent – who is a worthy man, without *much* energy, – the church about half filled on Sundays – whilst the schools are flourishing.

St Andrew's has been most unfortunate with respect to the clergy who have been successively appointed there – Mr Lawson,[213] the first incumbent – though an excellent & a learned man – and I may add a truly good & pious man – yet he was too much of an ascetic in his habits – and his sermons too erudite and recondite – for B.G. so *he* was not the right sort of man. Mr Woodard – or Woodward[214] – who succeeded him was too Romanising in his views and practices – and after a sermon of his – on the power of the *priesthood* to *forgive* sins, had been condemned by our late good & ever lamented bishop – he soon withdrew for Shoreham near Brighton, where his doings have been too notorious for years to be ignorant of them. The present incumbent, Mr Parker,[215] who came from Plymouth, had been one of the late Dr Hawker's school[216] – and his sentiments were so highly Calvinistic as to be bordering on Antinomianism – since then he has become a great politician and tells the *very few* people who attend him – that they should read nothing but the Bible and the *newspaper* – the destinies of the French Empire form the perpetual theme of his sermons – and the substance of Sunday pamphlets with which he has attempted to enlighten the part of the public residing in his locality. His schools are shut up. – his church almost empty – he himself is now very ill – at Brighton for three months – and it is thought he can never recover – atrophy seems to be his disease.

St Philip, where your young kinsman and namesake is, – was for years – the scene of Mr Alston's[217] vagaries – who annoyed the bishop – & tormented and defrauded the clergy by marrying for 2/6 (including all charges) thus he brought people from all parts of London to be married at his church – and used frequently to join together 50 couples per diem.

Mr Trevitt his successor – is a most amiable man – but a disciple of Kingsley – and Maurice[218] – very lax and *liberal* in his notions – stating that being obliged to sign & swear conformity to an agreement with the articles & liturgy is one of the

[211] Henry Mackenzie (1808–78), master of Bancroft Hospital Mile End 1837–40 and secretary to the Bethnal Green scheme, by this date incumbent of Tydd St Mary's, Lincolnshire, and prebendary of Lincoln Cathedral. From 1870 suffragan bishop of Nottingham.

[212] John Graham Packer.

[213] William de Lancy Lawson. See p. 299.

[214] Nathaniel Woodard. See p. 300. Gibson assigns him to the wrong church.

[215] George Hargrave Parker. See p. 299.

[216] John Hawker (1773–1846), curate of Stoke Damerel and later minister of Eldad chapel, built for him by adherents when he seceded from the Church of England in protest at catholic emancipation.

[217] George Alston.

[218] I.e., of Charles Kingsley and Frederick Denison Maurice, Christian socialists and broad churchmen. James Trevitt, b. 1813, St Alban Hall Oxford MA 1864; ord. d. and p. London 1843–4; cur. Thorndon on the Hill, Essex, 1843–52; licensed perp. cur. St Philip's, Bethnal Green, 28 Nov. 1851.

greatest curses of our church. He also marries at a lower price (not so low as 2/6) than any of the rest of us – and hence carries on a successful trade in that way – but his church is very poorly attended – and but very little salutary impression made on the surrounding neighbourhood. – he is also away out of health – and I hear many speak highly of the zeal assiduity and success of your namesake – who has recently come there.

St James the Less, Victoria Park, has proved a uniform failure until recently – Mr Coghlan[219] was a most extravagant and worldly man – & after being there some years to the injury and disgrace of the church – left over head and ears in debt for some chaplaincy at Berbice[220] – which he afterwards left – and came to England where about two years ago he died in the very depths of poverty and misery. He was succeeded by a Mr Haughton,[221] whose wife was sister to some lady of title – he had an aversion to coming into contact with poor people – had boxes affixed to the inner doors of the church as watering places for the morning and evening contributions of the congregation in lieu of pew rents – you may imagine the disgust this movement excited – he would have no schools built – for he would neither do anything towards keeping them up, if built – nor would he take any trouble concerning them – he was a sort of perpetual blister to good Mr Cotton & to our late good bishop. He however contrived to realise a clear £2,000 out of his burial ground after the surrounding churchyards were closed by Order of Council in 1854.

When he was no longer allowed to bury – he effected an exchange with the present incumbent, Mr Grundy[222] – he is of the Hugh Allen or Spurgeon sort[223] – has filled the church to overflowing – has had the schools built – and they were recently opened by a sermon in the morning from the bishop – and a tea meeting in the evening at which there were sundry specimens of oratory. W. Cotton, esq, in the chair – Thos Jackson, our old friend, Mr Ayrton, MP for the Tower Hamlets[224] – and your humble servant being the chief speakers. Mr Grundy…has gone away for three months to recruit his health. I hear from several who know him well that he is far from being a hardworking man – his wife goes to bed last and gets up first – she superintends provident club – schools – meets the district visitors – and thus takes the greater part of the work out of his hands – he thinks of little else but preaching – and it is said he has preached *all* his best sermons – and is too idle to make more, – if so I fear he will prove only a flash in the pan.

St James the Great, BG Road – Mr Lewis[225] – who was to have been the first incumbent – & who, for some time before the consecration of the church lived with his family in the parsonage, – was dismissed by the bishop for being one of the never to be forgotten 'Coal Hole Party'. He after became curate of Mr Wright

[219]   James Coghlan.

[220]   The name for the former Dutch colony united with Demerara-Essequibo to form British Guiana in 1831.

[221]   Henry Philip Haughton.

[222]   William James Grundy, literate, ord. 1851–2, rect. Kilverton, Nottinghamshire; perp. cur. St James's the Less 1859.

[223]   Charles Spurgeon (1834–92), baptist Calvinist preacher whose success led to the building of the Metropolitan Tabernacle; Hugh Allen (1806–77), anglican evangelical preacher, who played a prominent *rôle* in the ritualist disturbances at St George's in the East in 1859.

[224]   The Rt Hon. Acton Smee Ayrton (1816–86), liberal MP for Tower Hamlets 1857–74.

[225]   See p. 300.

of Dalston[226] – from there he went to Wales – to take possession of a small living there – but died of consumption a few years ago, His successor, Mr James,[227] proved a very inefficient and immoral man, his wife and children being in the country, – & he remaining at home – he went to bed with his servant maid; – this was in some sort hushed up – but the matter was so well known in the parish that his usefulness was at an end here – therefore he exchanged livings with the present incumbent, Mr Coke[228] – who came from Plymstock, Devon, – James there seduced a servant girl whose mother lived in the parish and was a communicant, He asked the bishop of Exeter for leave of absence for two years – his lordship said he intended to institute a commission for inquiry – and James rather than risk an examination threw up his living – and has since without character or employment resided in Exmouth – having no means of obtaining a livelihood except such as are furnished by his good and excellent wife's little property.

Mr Coke out-Herods Herod – when at Plymstock he walked about the village and the surrounding neighbourhood in a curiously made cassock with a long girdle or sash hanging down his right side, He played various odd pranks and vagaries and so disgusted the people there that they caused the bells to be rung when they knew he was to leave them – here he has shut up his schools – although they have an endowment of £1,000, having bought a house for his wife and family at Tottenham, he is seldom in residence. Every winter – and all through the year he collects for the poor large sums by advertisements – and no one knows what becomes of the money; about 4 weeks ago he knocked down a pauper in his hall who asked him for a receipt for some shillings he had been sent with from the chairman of our board of guardians as payment for his copies of marriages for the quarter – and sprained the poor man's leg as well as nearly broke his arm – a warrant was issued for his appearance at Worship St Police Office – but he prevailed on the Registrar General to send for our vestry clerk and obtained a promise from him that the pauper man should not bring him into court – but that the matter should be compromised – he had to pay £5 to the poor man whom he had injured – and £5 more for expenses. He told me a year ago that he is a Roman Catholic at heart – he seldom has 20 people in his church and I am sorry to be compelled to say that at St James the Great it is indeed *'death in the pot'*.[229]

St Bartholomew has a most worthy active & hardworking clergyman in Mr Vivian,[230] his church is well attended – his schools, reading rooms and District Visiting Society in full and successful operation and he is universally respected and beloved.

St Matthias in Hare St was for some years under the care of the Rev. Joseph Brown – now rector of Christ Church Blackfriars – he was the most scheming and contriving man I ever knew – famous for obtaining great notoriety for his excur-

---

226 Thomas Preston Wright, perpetual curate of St Philip's, Dalston 1844–60.
227 William James.
228 Edward Francis Coke (1817–97), b. Jamaica, Brasenose Oxford BA 1840, MA 1845; ord. d. and p. (Hereford) 1840–1; cur. All Saints Hereford 1840–3; perp. cur. Plymstock 1842–52; perp. cur. then vic. St James the Great Bethnal Green 23 July 1852–97.
229 2 Kings 4:40.
230 Francis Henry Vivian (1828–1909), b. Helston, Cornwall, Trinity Cambridge BA 1851, MA 1854; ord. d. and p. London 1851–2; assistant cur. St Thomas's Bethnal Green 1851–3; perp. cur. St Bartholomew's 1 Apr. 1853–61; perp. cur. St Peter's Stepney 1861–3; vic. Stoughton, Sussex, 1863–97.

sions with thousands of poor men, women & children[231] – and for hitting on some expedient for bringing grist to his own mill – he was much patronised by Lord Shaftesbury[232] – and some others of that clique – but certainly was and is the most precious & successful clerical humbug I ever met with and Mr Allen T. Edwards,[233] his immediate successor and nominee (for the late bp who had long before taken his mental dimensions allowed him to choose & recommend a successor) as also the present incumbent Mr Colbourne[234] recommended to the bishop by Mr Allen – each of these gentlemen is an exact facsimile of the illustrious Joseph Brown.

Mr Colbourne has a full church – and his schools are well attended – he also seems indefatigable in circulating bills of sermons which he preaches – of tea meetings – scientific lectures – but every move of the sort is but a pretext for getting money – none but high Calvinists beside himself are admitted into his pulpit – of course the Bp forms an exception – St Jude has for its incumbent a Mr Keane[235] an eccentric Irishman – and red-hot evangelical – he disgusted the Bp (I mean the late Bp) by letting his pews and other disorderly proceedings– insomuch that our good friend Charles James told him more than once he was sorry he had ever known him.

St Simon Zelotes had for its first incumbent Mr Ansted[236] – a truly excellent man – but he was so much out of health that for the most part he was compelled to be from home – and when in residence his illness destroyed all his energies – and his wife was a forward meddling and quarrelsome person who by her frequent indiscretions did real injury to the district.

The present incumbent, Mr Christie,[237] is only a slug in the Lord's vineyard – consequently he has scarcely any congregation and the schools are in a languishing state.

St Thomas, the last of the 10 new churches – has for incumbent Mr Kerry[238] – who is a perfect gentleman and a kind-hearted man. However, he fraternizes so much with the Romanizing party in our Church – and has introduced such novelties into his mode of conducting divine service in the church that his usefulness by these things is much retarded.

Such proceedings may do for Belgravia but as to *Bethnal Green* it is one of the most absurd things in the world to think of introducing them here. Mr Tagg,[239] of St Johns on the Green – has become a married man – has a rising family, goes on very well and is as much respected as ever.

Thus I have scribbled for you – as briefly as I could – an account of the two old and the ten new churches in B.G. I heartily wish I could have given a more satisfactory one – but indeed I have 'Nothing extenuated nor aught set down in malice'.[240]

---

[231] See the account of one such 'poor man's picnic' for over 1,200 parishioners at Havering-atte-Bower in 1849 in *Daily News*, 9 July 1849.

[232] Anthony Ashley Cooper (1801–85), evangelical activist and philanthropist.

[233] Allen Thomas Edwards. See p. 303.

[234] John Colbourne (1827–91); Peterhouse Cambridge BA 1852; ord. d. 1852, p. 1855; cur. St George's Birmingham 1852–4; perp. cur. St Matthias's 1854–65; vic. Hinckley, Leicestershire, 1865–74.

[235] John Espy Keane.

[236] Joseph Board Ansted. See p. 305.

[237] Campbell Manning Christie, St Bees, ord. d. and p. Chester 1841–2; perp. cur. Stony Stratford, Buckinghamshire, 1851–7; perp. cur. St Simon Zelotes', 1857.

[238] William Kerry.

[239] John Tagg.

[240] *Othello*, act 5, scene 2: 'nothing extenuate, nor set down aught in malice'.

I have endeavoured to set before you a true and faithful discussion of the real state of things here – of course I should not *thus* write to any *indifferent* person – but knowing as I well do the interest and anxiety you felt – and the incessant & long continued labours you underwent whilst actively and most efficiently employed in carrying out the favourite project of our late good bishop and of the excellent Mr Cotton – I felt it but due to you that I should comply with your request – and I am only sorry that I could not owing to the Lent services, send you this account before.

I remain, my dear sir, with good esteem and respect, yours most truly

T Gibson.

PS Mr Haughton the late incumbent of St James the Less, has recently died.

7

CHARLES JAMES BLOMFIELD, BISHOP OF LONDON, AND CHURCH ARCHITECTURE AND ORDERING

Edited by
M. H. Port

11 Interior of St Stephen's, Hammersmith, from *The Builder*, 27 April 1850

Introduction*

Charles James Blomfield was eminent among nineteenth-century anglican prelates for his strenuous church-building efforts. It might be said that he had more opportunity than most of his fellows, as bishop of London from 1828 to 1856, when the pressure for new churches for the increased and increasing population was at its height, and London's population growth was at its most vigorous. Nevertheless, his achievement in this work was outstanding: he was a leading figure on the church building commission, and dominated the Incorporated Church Building Society, the two principal national engines for church extension at this period. Although in 1836 he still hoped for a further instalment of state aid for that purpose,[1] he accepted that direct and immediate action was needed,[2] and therefore promoted voluntary subscriptions, first diocesan, and then local.

As bishop of London Blomfield had to be a key ecclesiastical statesman, and his 'ungovernable passion for business' ensured that he was a protagonist in the church reform dramas of the 1830s. In his First Charge to the diocese of London, in July 1830, Blomfield stressed the value of the parochial system, and acknowledged the deficiency of church room in London.[3] His practical disposition however suggested a third service on Sundays as an immediate help in that respect. He pointed out that recent legislation (the repeal of laws limiting the *rôle* of dissenters and Roman Catholics in the state) had placed the Church of England in a new position, an implicit admission that further grants of state aid for church-building were unlikely. Four years later, he remarked on the growth of hostility to the established church, and spoke more specifically about the need for new churches: allowing a church and two clergy for every 3,000 inhabitants, he calculated that there was a diocesan deficiency of 99 churches and 210 ministers.[4] In his Third Charge he discussed the most recent parliamentary measures, defending the church and ecclesiastical commissions (in which he played a significant *rôle*) as seeking the greatest possible efficiency in the exercise of the church's spiritual functions, citing the commission's second report as identifying two indispensable objects to that end: to 'improve the condition of... benefices' of large population but small endowment; and 'to add to the number of clergymen and churches' to enable 'adequate provision for the religious instruction of a rapidly increased and increasing population'.[5] He recognized that this was an on-going situation, not one that could be resolved once and for all, as an earlier generation had seemed to think. Although, with the revival of conservative feeling in the electorate, Blomfield envisaged the possibility of a renewal of state aid, he

---

[*] Unfortunately, Blomfield's use of the wet paper form of copying does not always leave a legible image. I am most grateful to the staff at Lambeth Palace Library for help in elucidating these texts.

[1] *Proposals for the creation of a fund to be applied to the building and endowment of additional churches in the metropolis by Charles James Lord Bishop of London* (London, 1836), p. 13.

[2] *Ibid.*, p. 4.

[3] *A Charge delivered to the clergy of the diocese of London at his first visitation in July MDCCCXXX by Charles James lord bishop of London* (London, 1830).

[4] *A Charge delivered ... MDCCCXXXIV ...* (London, 1834).

[5] *A Charge delivered ... in October, MDCCCVIII ...* (London, 1838), pp. 36–7.

was certain that it would not come before the church had 'first done all in its power
to supply the religious wants of the country, by an improved application of its actual
resources'.[6]

In this process, Blomfield included the generosity of churchmen, though admitting it was too slow and uncertain to resolve the 'enormous immediate evil'.[7] In
1836 he had, as mentioned above, launched a diocesan subscription, the Metropolis
Churches Fund for building at least fifty new churches in London. A district with
cure of souls would be assigned to each, and a stipend independent of pew rents
(partly deriving from the suppression of prebends at St Paul's Cathedral). Thirty-four
parishes in London with a population of 1,137,000 had only sixty-nine churches,
with accommodation for 101,682. Supposing church room should be provided for
one third of the population, and allowing a church for every 3,000, another 210
churches were needed.[8] He therefore called for large donations, though he did not
renounce the church's claim on the state, and recurred to the eighteenth-century
device of a tax on coals, proposing 2d a ton as an amount that would not be felt
by consumers.[9] A meeting of nobility and gentry at London House, the episcopal
residence in St James's Square, launched the fund, Blomfield himself contributing
£2,000, and £106,000 was raised within the year. But thereafter contributions came
in more slowly, in 1838–9 only £5,600.[10] This attrition led to a suggestion for establishing local funds. William Cotton,[11] a banker with interests in East London, started
a subscription for building ten churches in Bethnal Green, one of the most densely
populated parishes in East London, that raised £60,000. In his Fourth Charge Blomfield called his clergy's attention to the effectiveness of these appeals to the laity:
already forty-one new churches had been provided for.[12] This was perhaps somewhat misleading, as the funds had only made contributions towards providing these
churches, and grants were dependent on the efforts made locally: when the Metropolis Churches Fund was wound up in May 1854 it had paid entirely for only thirteen
churches, contributing towards a further sixty-five.[13]

But Blomfield constantly struck a note of encouragement. In his Charge of 1846
he recurred to the usefulness of his fund, which had raised nearly £180,000, and
commended the Bethnal Green Fund, which had raised £60,000, between them
providing for sixty-three new churches, of which forty-four had been completed.
But underlying this gain was the reality of contending with a population steadily
increasing at 30,000 a year. 'Is this not a case', he asked, 'in which the resources of
the State might be equitably and profitably employed, if not to do all that is wanted,
yet at least to aid the provisions and charitable endeavours of private Christians?'
But the need could not wait; a fresh subscription had been opened, and he told his
clergy to urge the fund's claim 'on your wealthier parishioners', not a few of whom

---

6   *Ibid.*, pp. 44–5.
7   *Ibid.*, p. 43.
8   *Proposals for ... a fund*, pp. 4–5.
9   *Ibid.*, p. 13. The current cost of coals in London was from 25s to 35s a ton. A coal tax was levied for
    metropolitan improvements until 1889.
10 G. E. Biber, *Bishop Blomfield and his times* (London, 1857), pp. 183–7.
11 1786–1866; governor of the Bank of England, 1843–5; called by Blomfield his 'lay archdeacon'. See
    Oxford dictionary of national biography (*ODNB*), *sub nomine*.
12 *A Charge delivered...in October MDCCCXLII...* (London, 1842), p. 63.
13 Biber, *Bishop Blomfield*, p. 188. The fund raised £266,000, received £23,000 in interest, and its
    expenses totalled £5,100; the total cost of the seventy-eight churches was £536,000 (*ibid.*).

'might annually build and endow a church, without abridging themselves of a single comfort, or even luxury'.[14]

There can be no doubt, then, that the building of large numbers of new churches, each the seat of at least one clergyman, was a primary aim of Blomfield's episcopate. But what sort of a bishop was he? In his First Charge he promised 'that if you find me a plain-spoken and candid monitor, and an uncompromising assertor of what I esteem the sacred principles of clerical duty, you will also find me accessible to reason, and thankful for advice'.[15] In roundly attacking private baptisms, in the same Charge, he avoided imposing a prohibition, remarking 'I am disposed rather to try, in the first instance, what can be effected by this public declaration of my opinion.'[16] Recurring to this issue in 1838, Blomfield expressed himself strongly, but still with paternal consideration: 'I do not want to interfere unnecessarily with the discretion of the Clergy.' He insisted, however, that departure from the Prayer Book rubric would be very difficult to justify.[17]

Similarly, in the controversy over ritual promoted by the Oxford Movement, Blomfield asserted that he 'was not unwilling to pause and be silent for a time, in the hope that those, who have engaged in the controversy, would see the evils which must ensue to the church from its continuance, and be led to modify, or at least to keep within their own bosoms, what I considered to be extreme opinions'.[18] This is evident in his attitude towards Upton Richards's conduct in the Margaret Street Chapel (Letters 7, 17). Avoidance as far as possible of controversy, a commonsensical approach to problems, and an adherence to the rules were the characteristics of his episcopal attitude, exemplified in the correspondence that follows (notably Letters 9, 13, 15); the clergy had a duty to comply with the Rubric and the Canons. 'Conformity to the Liturgy implies, of course, an exact observance of the Rubric. We are at no more liberty to vary the mode of performing any part of public worship, than we are, to present doctrines at variance with the Articles of Religion', he had told the clergy of his Chester diocese in 1825, and reiterated this in his fourth London Charge in 1842.[19]

A further relevant question is what sort of a man he was. Professor Owen Chadwick remarks somewhat unsympathetically that 'Endowed with high practical talents he was all his life remote from practical men, never invited familiarity or possessed the common touch...Blomfield commanded neither the art of charm nor the virtue of tact...He mastered detail and liked quick decisions.'[20] The letters that follow show, in my view, a hard worker in the vineyard indeed, but a reasonable one, seeking to harvest all the vines. His colleague Copleston of Llandaff, Dean of St Paul's 1827–49, hardly knew Blomfield's equal as a man of business, who was moreover 'a most accomplished man, not only learned and acute, but possessed of wit, pleasantry, and good taste; a proficient in music; conversant with the fine arts and general literature, modern as well as ancient'.[21] We might expect him then

14 *A Charge delivered...in October MDCCCXLVI...* (London, 1846), pp. 36–8.
15 First Charge, 1830, p. 12.
16 *Ibid.*, p. 24.
17 Second Charge, 1834, p. 48.
18 Third Charge, 1838, p. 6.
19 *Ibid.*, p. 31.
20 Owen Chadwick, *The Victorian church*, Pt 1 (London, 1966), pp. 133–4.
21 A. Blomfield, *A memoir of Charles James Blomfield, with selections from his correspondence* (1863), II, 92.

to show a lively interest in architecture, an art about which controversy currently raged.

So what was his attitude towards the building and design of the new churches he was promoting? The answer is that he saw these questions purely in terms of practicalities.

For essentially Blomfield was organization man. A populous district lacked a conveniently situated church: one must be provided. How large a church did the needs of the district require?[22] What was the best site for it? The bishop would help to secure a site (Letters 3, 6).[23] What local resources were there?[24] He would encourage the raising of funds – perhaps give a donation himself, but certainly promise to see what might be obtained from the various grant-giving bodies in which he played so powerful a *rôle*:[25] the Incorporated Church Building Society, the church building commissioners, the ecclesiastical commissioners, the Metropolis Churches Fund; check whether the proposed plans afforded the appropriate accommodation and were cost-effective.[26]

To style he was indifferent: 'A Church', he might almost have said, 'is a machine for worshipping in.' It was, however, a particular form of worship, for which long chancels were unsuitable (Letter 2). Design was something to be left to the architects, provided that it complied with the rubric: 'I am aware that the situation of the font in some churches is such, that a recurrence to ancient practice would not answer the [baptismal] object of publicity and solemnity: in such cases the proper course is, not to depart from the rubric, but to move the font.'[27] In a new church, such matters must be resolved at the outset, and then the architect be left free to exercise his peculiar skill. He wrote to that effect to the Rev. J. E. Keane, incumbent of St Jude's, Bethnal Green (8 August 1846):[28]

> I have requested the Archdeacon to visit your Church and to give me his opinion as to the Reading Desk.
>
> Your complaint against Mr Clutton[29] is not just. When an Architect has completed a Church, with suitable internal fittings & ornaments any arbitrary alteration which is made without consulting him is a reflexion upon his skills.
>
> He knew that everything had been approved of by the Metropolis Churches Committee & by me: and he did quite right in making known to us any alteration which had been made without our sanction.

[22]	See, e.g., Lambeth Palace Library (LPL), Blomfield papers, vol. 6, fo. 80 (Abridge), vol. 19, fos. 145–6 (Hammersmith).

[23]	See, e.g., Blomfield to Rev. F. T. Atwood, 22 Nov.1851, stating that he had seen a local clergymen about the need for a new church in Hammersmith: 'A site may probably now may [*sic*] be obtained without much difficulty, which, if the matter be delayed, would be unattainable … I shall gladly promote [the undertaking] by all means in my power' (LPL, Blomfield papers, vol. 52, fo. 123; see also fo. 127, vol. 53, fos. 99, 112, 119, and vol. 54, fo. 78).

[24]	E.g., LPL, Blomfield papers, vol. 6, fos. 40–1, 16 May 1833, respecting new chapel at Abridge, Essex.

[25]	As at Abridge and Chrishall, Essex, LPL, Blomfield papers, vol. 6, fo. 40, vol. 2, fo. 42.

[26]	As those of 1832 at Hampstead were not, LPL, Blomfield papers, vol. 3, fo. 19.

[27]	Second Charge, 1834, p. 48.

[28]	LPL, Blomfield papers, vol. 44, fo. 211. I am grateful to Professor Arthur Burns for drawing this letter to my attention.

[29]	Henry Clutton (1819–93), partner of William Burges in the Lille Cathedral competition, which they won.

Ornamental features, such as stained glass windows, or mural paintings, must accord with anglican doctrine (Letter 14). But the bishop's *rôle* was to concentrate on essentials;[30] to secure a church, a building for a specific purpose, not to determine whether it should be First or Second Pointed.

In 1848 Blomfield proposed to the ecclesiastical commissioners (of whom he was a key member) the creation of a Peel parish[31] in Hammersmith, so close to his seat at Fulham; he would then 'undertake to provide a Church ... sufficient for the accommodation of the inhabitants upon a plan to be approved of by the Commissioners.'[32] This project was duly executed, St Stephen's, Shepherds Bush, rising in 1849–50 to the designs of Anthony Salvin.[33] Here, surely, Blomfield would express his taste. As the *Ecclesiologist*, the organ of the pro-Gothic movement, commented, this church 'has a peculiar value, as indicating how far our diocesan is willing to take the peculiar responsibility of those various features of the arrangement and decoration, which from desuetude had become to a great extent novelties in England when we first advocated their revival'.[34]

We have little evidence, however, that Blomfield sat down with Salvin to provide him with a stylistic or ornamental brief. Early in 1849 Blomfield did write to Salvin:[35]

> I did not get your letter in time to see you before you left town. There are two or three details in the plan respecting which I should wish to speak to you before they are finally settled.
>
> If you will let me know a few days beforehand when you will be in London I will attend your office.
>
> I quite agree with you as to the course to be pursued with respect to the contract & will thank you so to answer it.

These 'two or three details' are most likely to have concerned liturgical arrangements, such as the position of the font in relation to the entrance, rather than any matter of architectural design. 'One thing is evident', remarked the *Companion to the almanac* in its review of new churches in 1849, 'that medieval character is now universally affected for churches as the only legitimate ecclesiastical style.'[36] St Stephen's was a pretty standard work by one of the leading Gothic Revival architects: that is to say, it was in the ecclesiologists' approved style, the 'flowing Middle Pointed' or Decorated. Built like so many Victorian churches of Kentish ragstone, with Bath stone dressings, St Stephen's enjoyed a 'very well developed chancel' (perhaps surprisingly, but then, again, does this indicate Blomfield's distancing himself from matters architectural?), and a lofty, open-roofed five-bay nave, aisled

---

30 'The great object is to get a new Church. I am of opinion that the most desirable thing would be to make it the Parish Church but if that be objected to by any considerable body of the Parishioners, I would not make it a *sine qua non*: that would be, to endanger a greater good for the sake of a less.' LPL, Blomfield papers, vol. 53, fo. 99: Blomfield to Rev. F. Taunton, 30 Dec. 1851.

31 Under Sir Robert Peel's act of 1843 the ecclesiastical commissioners could create a district parish before a church was built.

32 LPL, Blomfield papers, vol. 59, fos. 145–6, 7 Aug.1848.

33 Anthony Salvin (1799–1881) was a pioneer Gothic Revival architect of a Northumberland gentry family.

34 *Ecclesiologist*, XI (new series VIII) (1850), 62–3.

35 LPL, Blomfield papers, vol. 59, fo. 184, 10 Feb. 1849.

36 *Companion to the almanac 1849* (London, 1849), p. 227.

and clerestoried, with an asymmetrical tower and spire. The main entrance was by a north porch, adjacent to the road, and the font appropriately and symbolically stood near to the entrance. The sanctuary was 'separated from the chorus by a rail' and was 'fitted with an altar correctly vested'; a double sedilia was recessed on the south side; and the lower parts of the chancel walls were diapered – an uncontroversial form of decoration, like the scroll-work painted in the spaces between the rafters of the chancel roof (cf. Letter 8). Sanctuary and chancel were paved with Minton's encaustic tiles, and the chancel was 'fitted with seats stallwise'. The reading- or prayer-desk , however, stood unecclesiologically under the pulpit, outside the chancel to the south, with a 'westerly desk for the Lessons'. All the seats were open benches. Most of the windows had stained glass by Wailes, but not, according to the *Ecclesiologist*, of his best designs. But the windows, like the organ, were gifted by relations, friends and clergy.[37]

All the evidence suggests that Blomfield had no critically formed taste in archi- tecture; he went along with the taste of the circles in which he moved: 'Middle Pointed' (Decorated Gothic); non-Romanizing; stained glass windows of uncontro- versial subjects. I have found but one instance (Letter 1) in which he expressed an aesthetic view about a church building – his objection to long chancels (Letter 8) was liturgical, not aesthetic. Early in his episcopate Blomfield became involved in repairs of the abbey church of St Albans, then a parish church (the Lady Chapel housing the grammar school) in the London diocese. The architect Lewis Wyatt had been called on to survey the semi-ruinous fabric in 1818, and again in 1827 when his estimate for restoration came to no less than £30,000.[38] Although other architects were consulted, nothing was done until in February 1832 a section of wall collapsed. As diocesan, Blomfield served on a committee to organize the repair work. The involvement at this point of architect Thomas Leverton Donaldson (1795–1885), an alumnus of the St Albans School, caused Blomfield to record this unique comment on design (Letter 1). But his deprecation of Holy Trinity, Brompton, was almost universal among the reading classes.[39]

Nearly all the following letters from Blomfield are focused on the plans of All Saints, Margaret Street, St Marylebone, as they represent his most explicit inter- vention in the design of a church. But it is an intervention concerned with internal fittings that had an explicit relationship with the character of divine worship to be offered therein. And these letters also present his characteristic pastoral qualities, his reasonableness, his eirenic qualities, the overriding desire to further a good work and to move to solve a problem, but only within the limits that the rules imposed. The irony is that Blomfield here misinterpreted the purpose of the rule on which he relied; he failed to take into account the rubric before 'Morning Prayer' in the 1559 Prayer Book, as in 1552, ordering that the chancels remain as they had done in time past, i.e., separated in some distinct manner from the rest of the church; or the Royal Injunctions of 1559; or the injunctions of his seventeenth- and eighteenth- century predecessors. The chancel was to be separated from the nave by a partition with gates, to provide 'a special part in the church where the faithful might assemble

[37] *Ecclesiologist*, X (new series VII) (1850), 62–3; XI (new series VIII) (1850), 62–3; *Builder*, 27 Apr. 1850, 199.
[38] J. Myles, *L. N. Cottingham 1787–1847: architect of the Gothic Revival* (London, 1996), p. 89.
[39] See, e.g., 'J.I.C.' (Carlos) in *Gentleman's Magazine*, 1830, pt 1, p. 579.

for the Holy Mysteries without interruption or disturbance from intruders'.[40] Here it was rather Alexander Beresford Hope who was the architectural upholder of the anglican tradition, though his intentions might be contrary to that tradition; Blomfield, had he realized it, was advocating, in terms of structure, the policy of church restorers and progressive churchmen to clear away obstacles between the nave and the altar.[41]

Editorial conventions

In editing these letters I have included all those that I could discern from the Index to the catalogue of Blomfield's correspondence that related to All Saints, Margaret Street, as well as those few letters to architects that gave an indication of his architectural tastes. I have preserved Blomfield's spelling (including capitalization) and punctuation, so far as the 'wet copy' method he employed permits it to be deciphered. Words which are underlined in the original manuscripts have been printed in italic type.

[40] G. W. O. Addleshaw and F. Etchells, *The architectural setting of anglican worship* (London, 1948), p. 49, citing specifically here Hooker, *Works* (1888 edn), II, 53.
[41] Addleshaw and Etchells investigate in detail the character and function of the post-Reformation chancel in their first two chapters.

A selection of letters from C. J. Blomfield relating to architectural questions and church order, taken from the Blomfield papers in Lambeth Palace Library

To T. L. Donaldson, Esq., Fulham, 9 August 1832

Vol. 3, fos. 64–6

Absence from home prevented me from returning an immediate answer to your Letter.

Having received several communications informing me that many persons who were desirous of contributing to the restoration of St Albans Abbey Church were prevented from doing so by a want of confidence in the Reports[1] on which the Committee were acting, I thought it my duty to make known the same to Mr Small,[2] and to Lord Verulam,[3] being prevented from attending a Meeting of the Committee held at that Nobleman's house. In one or both of these Letters (I think only in one) I stated that one of the gentlemen who had communicated with me, a person very conversant with our ancient church architecture, had said that his doubts respecting your competency were in part grounded upon your want of success in the Church at Brompton,[4] and that there were others who had the same feeling. This, as far as I recollect, was the extent of what I said on this subject: and this it was my duty to say, as a Member of the Committee and as being to a certain extent responsible for the proper application of the money which might be subscribed.

I am not aware of having mentioned the matter to any other persons; but having myself viewed the Abbey Church a few weeks ago, I expressed my decided opinion that all necessary repairs might be done for less than half the amount of your Estimate, agreeing as it did, very nearly, with that of Mr Wyatt.[5] With regard to your *Architectural Skill* in design, it would be presumptuous in me to give an opinion – I have certainly said, on other occasions, that I thought the exterior of the Church at Brompton most unsightly; but that it was not altogether the architects fault, the funding for its decoration having fallen short.

I am sorry that any communication which I have made officially to the Committee sh^d have given you pain, but I do not feel that I could have abstained from making such communications after the representations which I have received on the subject.

---

1   See E. Roberts, *The hill of the martyr: an architectural history of St Albans Abbey* (Dunstable, 1993), pp. 191, 195–7; J. Myles, *L. N. Cottingham 1787–1847* (London, 1996), pp. 89–90.
2   Rev. Henry Small, rector and dean of St Albans, 1817–35.
3   1775–1845. Lord lieutenant of Hertfordshire 1823–d. High Steward of St Albans 1809–d.
4   Holy Trinity, Brompton, London, designed by Donaldson and erected 1826–9 at a cost of £10,407, of which the church building commissioners (of whom Blomfield was one of the most active) paid £7,407; the remainder by public subscription. It was denounced by the architectural critic E. J. Carlos (1798–1851) as an outstandingly complete specimen of 'Carpenter's Gothic' (*Gentleman's Magazine*, 1830, pt I, 579). Illustrated in M. H. Port, *Six hundred new churches*, 2nd edn (Reading, 2006), p. 186.
5   Lewis William Wyatt (1777–1853); his 1827 report costed repairs at £30,000.

2. To George Gilbert Scott, Esq., Fulham, 3 December 1851

Vol. 53, fos. 19–20

As I am quite unconscious of having spoken disparagingly of you, and having in fact the highest opinion of your architectural skills and taste, I should very much like to know the particular observations to which you allude, & to whom they were made.

The only remark which I remember to have made, which could be construed in that way was, that I thought you were rather too fond of long Chancels, which, however architecturally correct, are not well suited to our forms of worship.

With reference to the proposed new Church at Westminster,[6] what I said to Mr Anstrum [?] was, that if your plan which I thought was a very good one, was found to be more costly than was consistent with the funds provided for it's execution, a less expensive building must be erected, it being of the greatest importance that no further delay should take place; but that I doubted whether you would be willing to make your plan less perfect, in order to save expence.

The Church which you are building at Ealing is very beautiful,[7] and, as far as I could judge from one inspection, contained no features which I could wish to be altered.

If you should wish to see me I shall be glad to receive you at London House on Friday at Twelve o'clock.

All Saints, Margaret Street

3. To the duke of Portland, Fulham, 19 November 1846

Vol. 58, fos. 275–276v

I beg leave once more to trouble Your Grace on the subject referred to in my last letter.

The Solicitor of the parties who are desirous of building a church on the site now occupied by Margaret Street Chapel,[8] and the adjacent houses, has ascertained that

---

6 St Matthew, Great Peter Street, 1849–51, was built in the midst of slums; burned 1977 and rebuilt on a smaller scale.

7 Christ the Saviour, 1852, 'in correct Second Pointed style … plenty of naturalistic carving of capitals and corbels inside. An impressively tall, rather busy W. tower … Lofty interior with tall arcades and clerestory'. B. Cherry and N. Pevsner, *The buildings of England. London 3, north west* (London, 1991), p. 165.

8 Margaret Street Chapel, a proprietary chapel built in the mid-eighteenth century, had been acquired by a Tractarian congregation that by 1845 had raised £2,000 to rebuild it 'as a church more fitting to their ritualistic tastes' (Paul Thompson, 'All Saints' Church, Margaret Street, reconsidered', *Architectural History*, VIII (1965), 74). The incumbent since 1839, Rev. F. Oakeley (1802–80), chaplain and fellow of Balliol College, Oxford, then converted to Rome and gave up all his preferments. After lengthy negotiations involving the crown, the duke of Portland as freeholder, and the ecclesiastical commissioners, it was in 1847 agreed to rebuild it as a parish church; the Rev. Upton Richards (see n. 18 below) was appointed incumbent. The congregation agreed that the Ecclesiological Society should conduct the rebuilding as their 'model church', to suit their ritual requirements and English medieval architectural forms. The Society appointed A. J. Beresford Hope (1820–87), an enthusiastic amateur of church architecture, and Sir Stephen Glynne to supervise. Hope was a major financial contributor, and dominated proceedings.

the leasehold interests of the Houses which will be required, can be purchased for £3700. They have desired me to make known this fact to Your Grace, and to enquire how far Your Grace would be inclined to authorize your Agent to state the terms on which you would convey to them the freehold for the premises in question as they are desirous of ascertaining whether it will be in their power to proceed with the undertaking or not.[9]

They will have to purchase Margaret Street Chapel of the Crown.

4. To Rev. Charles Baring,[10] Fulham, 23 December 1848

Vol. 59, fos. 247–249v

I am placed in circumstances of considerable embarrassment by your determination with respect to the proposed new Church in your parish.[11] The late Rector, the Dean of Chichester[12] gave to that proposal his full sanction, and encouraged the promotion of the scheme to proceed. I had therefore little or no hesitation in consenting to it, it being understood that all the arrangements with respect to the constitution of the new Church, and the mode of celebrating Divine Service therein, were to be subject to my approval & direction.

Upon the declarat[io]n[?] of this double consent, on the part of the Rector & the Bishop, the promoters of the plan proceeded to expend a very large sum of money, not less, I believe, than £9000 in the purchase of the freehold of the present Chapel in Margaret Street and of the houses immediately adjoining.

It does not seem to me likely that this site can be abandoned, and another purchased, except at a considerable pecuniary loss; and indeed as a large part of the money already expended was furnished by persons residing in the neighbourhood of the Chapel, and accustomed to attend Divine Service there, it is not probable that they would consent to forgoing the advantages which they anticipated from a Church in that precise spot.

Under these circumstances I feel that I should be hardly justified in revoking the consent which I gave in the first instance, to a plan which I had no reason to suppose would be objected to.

It appears that I expressed an opinion at an early stage of the business that the new Church should not have a District assigned to it. Of this I have myself no recollection; and it is certainly quite contrary to my general view of such cases, which is that every Church should, if possible, have its own District under the exclusive care of its own Minister; I see no reason, why the Church in Margaret Street, if one is to be built, should be an exception to that rule.

9   Hope had raised about £9,000, mainly from his mother and one Henry Tritton, a banker, who anonymously paid much of the building costs. H. W. Law and I. Law, *The book of the Beresford Hopes* (London, 1925), p. 162.

10 Rev. Charles Thomas Baring, MA (1807–79), son of Sir Francis Baring, 2nd bart.; rector of All Souls, Langham Place, St Marylebone, 1847–56; bishop of Gloucester and Bristol, 1856–61; bishop of Durham, 1861–79.

11 Margaret Street was within the parish of All Souls, Langham Place, one of the four new parishes created out of St Marylebone in 1825.

12 Very Rev. George Chandler, DCL (1778–1859), rector of All Souls, 1825–47, and dean of Chichester, 1830–59.

5. To A. J. Beresford Hope, Fulham, 10 January 1849

Vol. 59, fo. 267v

I have been in correspondence with Mr Baring respecting the proposed new Church in Margaret Street, and I send for your perusal [?] his last letter to me.

His determined opposition places me in a very painful and embarrassing situation; and I cannot but earnestly wish that, if it be possible, the site may be changed. I am aware that that cannot be done except at considerable pecuniary sacrifice; but it will be well worth while to avoid a contest which would be very injurious to the Church, at some cost [?].

I am sure that you will perceive the difficult position in which I am placed and will be desirous of relieving me from it.

6. To Rev. Charles Baring, Fulham, 16 January 1849

Vol. 59, fos. 283v–286v

I thought it right to shew your letter to Mr Hope, as the chief contributor to the intended new Church in your parish. In his answer to me he says, with his usual kindness and consideration, that he, with the other promoters of the plan will endeavour to find a site elsewhere, although it must necessarily be at a large pecuniary sacrifice.

I will therefore suspend my final decision till I learn the result of their inquiry.

Mr Hope remarks, with some justice, that the first part of your letter to me would have come more gracefully from you on your first induction, before you had, by your apparent goodwill, encouraged him & his friends to go on, & incur such trouble & expence. Your argument drawn from the existence of St Andrews,[13] he observes, shews a misapprehension of the case; for at the time when their plan was arranged St Andrews' was in course of erection, and entered into all their calculations.

St Andrews is built on the extreme western verge of the new parish, containing 5000 souls. St Margarets would be nearly on the extreme Eastern verge of a District containing 2000. The new church would hold between 600 & 700. A population of 7000 is entitled to two Churches, if they can be had; and no other site could be procured. The plan of bringing thither 'Sisterhood of Charity'[14] has long been abandoned.[15] I feel rather hurt, that in the present state of the question you should have thought it necessary to threaten me with the St Marylebone Vestry.[16]

---

[13] St Andrew's, Wells Street, St Marylebone, by S. W. Daukes (1811–80), was built in 1847. The *Ecclesiologist* remarked: 'considered in a ritual point of view, it is the most satisfactory church which has yet been built in London' (new series VIII (1850), 80).

[14] Referred to in Blomfield's letter to Hope of 28 Feb.1846: statements made to him caused him to hesitate about approving connecting the institution with the new church until he had made further inquiry, LPL, Blomfield papers, vol. 59, fo. 61v.

[15] According to the Laws, 'with the Bishop of London's consent a Sisterhood was established in an adjoining house [to the old chapel]' on its re-opening in November 1847. Law and Law, *Book of the Beresford Hopes*, p. 162.

[16] The old parish of St Marylebone was governed between 1832 and 1855 by a ratepayer-elected body termed the 'vestry'; it had no ecclesiastical connotations.

7. To A. J. Beresford Hope, Fulham, 11 January 1851

Vol. 50, fos. 311–12

The understanding to which I came with Mr Richards, on the occasion to which you refer, was to this effect, that although I could not approve of some of the forms observed in Margaret Street Chapel, I would not interfere to prohibit them, so long as divine Service should continue to be performed in that Chapel, but that no additional forms could be allowed. Mr Richards promised that none such should be introduced.

But it has all along been understood and I have two or three times reminded both you and Mr Richards, that in the new Church, when consecrated, no forms were to be introduced, which were not sanctioned by the Rubric, or by established custom. Mr Richards's own proposal respecting the new Church made to me Jan. 30 1846 was that

'The Rubric should be fully carried out *but nothing* more.[']

By this principle I am ready to abide, but I am not, & never have been, ready to admit, that all the practices adopted in the Margaret Street Chapel are rubrical. Whether they are so, or not, is a question to be determined at the proper time. I am sure you would not desire me to go beyond this.[17]

I should be glad to see the plans of the New Church, if you will let them be brought to London House on Wednesday next at half past two.

8. To Rev. W. U. Richards,[18] London House, 9 May 1851

Vol. 51, fos. 174–5

I am sorry to find, by the letter, which Mr Hope has addressed to you, that he has decided upon making his completion of the Church which he has so munificently undertaken to build,[19] contingent upon my consenting to have the Chancel entirely divided from the body of the Church, by a Screen with Gates. To a low Screen, not intercepting the view of the officiating Clergy from the congregation, nor entirely separating the chancel from the body of the Church I do not so much object, although I would prefer it's being omitted: but I decidedly object to its being closed by means of gates. I approve of the custom of adorning the Chancel more highly than the other part of the Church;[20] but I disapprove of such a mode of dividing it from the body of the sacred edifice, as shall have the appearance of

17 In a further letter to Hope, 19 Feb. 1851, Blomfield referred to his attitude regarding the ritualistic practices of the Rev. J. Murray at St Andrew's, Wells Street, St Marylebone, in which he felt himself 'hampered by the concessions which I unfortunately made with great reluctance, in the case of Mr Richards, although those concessions were distinctly stated to be only temporary'. That had 'taught me a lesson as to the course to be pursued by me in future'. LPL, Blomfield papers, vol. 51, fos. 25–7.

18 Rev. William Upton Richards, MA (1811–73), was an assistant in the Manuscripts Department of the British Museum when he was appointed incumbent of the Margaret Street Chapel in 1847, half his stipend then being paid by Hope. In 1849 he was appointed vicar of the new parish, which he retained until his death.

19 The plans were submitted to the Metropolitan Buildings Office (for approval of structural adequacy) on 1 Mar. 1850, as a result of which the width of the north aisle had to be reduced. Thompson, 'All Saints' church', 75.

20 As in his church of St Stephen's, Shepherds Bush, where the chancel ceiling was enriched with scrollwork painting.

excluding the Laity, and of reserving the Chancel altogether for the Clergy & for those who assist them in the Choral parts of the Service.

I am therefore under the painful necessity of declining to accede to Mr Hope's wish with respect to the *Gates* of the Screen.

9. To same, London House, 20 May 1851

Vol. 51, fos. 196–7

I have no doubt as to the correctness of Mr Hope's statement that there were gates to the Screen in the drawings which were shown to me in the first instance, although I have no recollection of that feature of the plan, my attention not having been directed to it. When Mr Hope brought the plans to me in Town in Dec[r] last,[21] I noticed the Gates, and stated my strong objections to them.

I cannot help thinking that this is a point which Mr Hope should concede to my scruples. In two churches now building in the diocese of Oxford, in which screens, with gates formed part of the plans, the gates were given up at the request of the Bishop.

In the plans for your intended New Church I have allowed some things of which I did not altogether approve, but which I thought might be permitted, out of deference to Mr Hope's wishes.

I think I may fairly expect him, on the other hand, to give way on a point to which I feel a strong objection in principle.

10. To same, Fulham, 7 July 1851

Vol. 51, fo. 259

I have already admitted that in the drawings which Mr Hope exhibited to me of his intended Church, there was a screen with gates. But my attention had not then been drawn to the purpose which these gates might be intended to answer; viz: the entire exclusion from the Chancel of all persons but the Clergy and their Assistants (excepting of course those who partake of the Holy Communion at the time of their receiving it).

I wish to know whether it be your intention, or Mr Hopes, that the Chancel should be so set apart exclusively for the Clergy and their Assistants.

11. To same, Fulham, 6 August 1851

Vol. 51, fo. 307

I now send you my final decision of the question relating to the Screen. I should have sent it some time since, but that I did not think it right to intrude upon the first moments of your grief, under a heavy calamity.[22]

In the assurance of my sympathy & my prayers.

---

[21] This timing is interesting: Butterfield's working drawings were amended in the summer of 1850 to provide for granite pillars and an encrustation of tiles and coloured marbles, instead of paintwork, and were quantified in about July; the contract with the builder was signed on 1 Sept. 1850. Thompson, 'All Saints' church', pp. 5–6.

[22] Richards's wife had died.

12. To same, Fulham, 6 August 1851

Vol. 51, fos. 303–6

I have to thank you and Mr Hope for your candid admission that it is your intention to have the Chancel set apart exclusively for the Clergy and their Assistants, and that this is to be effected by means of a screen with gates.

Supposing it to be right that the Clergy should have a separate place in the Church, apart from the Laity, I consider that the principle is sufficiently maintained by the practice which has obtained since the time of Archbishop Laud, by whom it was introduced, of railing off a space in front of the Communion Table, within which the officiating Clergy may remain when not in the Reading Desk or Pulpit. If the entire Chancel is to be set apart for the carrying out of this principle, an undue importance is given to the principle itself, and a large space is left unoccupied, which in the present state of our population can ill be afforded. It has been decided by the ecclesiastical Courts, that where the body of the Church does not afford sufficient accommodation for the parishioners, the Bishop may order them to be seated in the Chancel.

If it be said that the place where the Holy Communion is celebrated ought to be set apart, I answer that this principle, supposing it to be incontrovertible, is sufficiently indicated by the usual railing before the Communion Table.

It is certain that at the first, and least protestant period of our Reformation, it was not thought necessary to exclude the laity from the choir, or chancel. This appears from the rubric in the Prayer Book of 1549, following after the Offertory Sentences

'Then so many as shall be partakers of the holy Communion shall tarry still in the quire, or in some convenient place nigh the quire, the men on one side, and the women on the other side. All other (that mind not to receive the said Holy Communion) shall depart out of the quire, except the Ministers and Clerks.' From which it appears that even non-communicants remained in the *quire* till after the reading of the Offertory Sentences.

It seems probable, looking to this rubric, & to the practice in Roman Catholic churches at the present day, that before the Reformation the whole congregation assembled in the choir at the celebration of the Mass. This practice has been continued to the present day, and now universally prevails in our Cathedrals.

It appears to me therefore that the reservation of the whole Chancel to the Clergy and their Assistants is unnecessary, and at variance with true Christian feeling, ancient practice, and the custom of our own Church; and that a screen, or barrier, with gates, visibly & practically asserting such reservation, is a thing which ought not to be allowed.

I have therefore to request that you will make known to Mr Hope my determination not to consecrate any Church, in which the Chancel is separated from the body of the Church by a Screen with Gates.

13. To same, Fulham, 28 November 1851

Vol. 52, fos. 135–6

I have carefully considered the reasons which you have urged, in your letter of the 14th instant, for my retracting the decision which I had announced to you respecting a Screen with Gates.

My objection to the Gates is not removed; and if the question were now *res integra*, I should persist in it. But I must admit, that as I have inadvertently approved of the plan, in which the Gates were shewn, the case is somewhat different, and I am therefore prepared to withdraw my objection in the present instance; it being understood that the gates will be always open in the time of Divine Service, and that lay members of the Congregation who may be competent to take part in the musical parts of the service will be admitted to sit in the Chancel.

14. To same, Fulham, 30 December 1851

Vol. 53, fo. 95

A printed Circular signed by you has just been shewn me, respecting the intended decoration of your Church.[23]

I must beg that none of the 'Fittings for the Altar', nor 'Mural Paintings in Fresco', nor 'mural decorations in Coloured Tiles' nor 'Painted Glass', be determined on, till they have received my approval or consent.

15. To same, Fulham, 19 January 1852

Vol. 53, fo. 142

I cannot but feel some surprise as well as regret, at Mr Hope's not having at once acceded to my proposal, which I consider to be in itself reasonable; and which the experience of the last twelve months has proved to be necessary.

It is surely much better that I should have an opportunity of *considering* beforehand, whether there is any ground of objection to the proposed decorations of your Church, than to take objection when they have been executed; and a brief conversation would not allow sufficient time for such consideration.

16. To same, Fulham, 26 January 1852

Vol. 53, fo. 151

The proposal which I have made with respect to the intended decoration of your new Church, is so reasonable that I feel myself to be fully justified in adhering to it.

The language in which Mr Hope has thought fit to signify his objections to it, is unbecoming *him*, and disrespectful to *me*.[24]

---

[23] The carcass of All Saints' was approved by the Metropolitan Buildings Office surveyor in December 1851, and the clerestory glass was fixed by the end of the year. Hope had commissioned frescoes from William Dyce in the chancel and J. C. Horsley in the nave already in 1849, although 'Dyce did not start work until November 1853 and Horsley's commission was never taken up'. Thompson, 'All Saints' church', 79.

[24] 'Hope thereupon refused to see the Bishop and told [the ecclesiologist the Rev. Benjamin] Webb "he cannot interfere with the Church, inasmuch as it is my freehold".' Hope eventually called on Blomfield with the designs, 7 Feb. 1853, 'and the pair made up their differences in criticism of Richards' romanizing tendencies'. Law and Law, *Book of the Beresford Hopes*, p. 166.

17. To Rev. J. E. Hall, London House, 13 March 1852

Vol. 53, fo. 220

I have been prevented by the pressure of business from returning an earlier answer to your letter.

Mr Richards introduced the custom of lighting candles on the Communion Table,[25] not only without my sanction, but in violation of a direct agreement with me.[26]

After some time I heard of what he had done, & remonstrated with him on the subject: but I was induced to consent to his making no change till his new Church should be consecrated which I then expected would take place before this time,[27] telling him distinctly that I would not permit it to be done in that Church. This conversation took place on the 3ᵈ April 1852 [*sic*].

I have no objection to your stating this to any other persons.

---

[25] Part of his 'romanizing tendencies' that Hope and Blomfield alike objected to.
[26] See 7 above, Blomfield to Hope, 11 Jan. 1851.
[27] Lack of money delayed completion of All Saints' until April 1859, after Blomfield's resignation and death. Law and Law, *Book of the Beresford Hopes*, pp. 166–7.

8

WILLIAM DODSWORTH:
AN AUTOBIOGRAPHICAL MEMOIR

Edited by
Richard Palmer

On the . of March 1829. I first performed the duty at Margaret Chapel — an eventful era for me, and fraught with consequences then little foreseen by me. I came indeed with great fear & trembling, & with most sincere misgivings as to my own powers for fulfilling the duty now devolving upon me. However I set to with the utmost vigour that I could command — I had two full duties every Sunday (at that time daily service was never thought of) I had intended also to visit all my flock — But my first attempt was unfortunate. The family of a Tailor had a pew in my chapel. I called upon them — but only found the tailor, who first thought that I came to be measured, & on explaining to him the real object of my visit he said that he supposed "I wanted the pew rent". It turned out that he was an infidel & that his wife & daughters only attended Church; and that my visit had only brought them into difficulties. This was a considerable relief to my zeal & I found it needful to be more circumspect. However I made it known

12 William Dodsworth's account of his spiritual progress for 1829, when he became minister of Margaret Street Chapel, London (LPL, MS 4727, fo. 104)

Introduction

Year by year Lambeth Palace Library acquires archives, manuscripts and printed books to encourage new research and to facilitate the writing of the history of the church. One such resource, a small cache of papers of William Dodsworth (1798–1861), was purchased by the Friends of Lambeth Palace Library in 2007.[1] It includes a previously unknown autobiographical memoir, written by Dodsworth for his children in 1857.[2]

The life of William Dodsworth represents a spiritual progress which throws light on the shifting religious currents of his day and on those painful transitions from evangelical to tractarian and, finally, Roman Catholic, which were the subject of David Newsome's classic study.[3] Brought up in a context of conventional anglican piety, Dodsworth became a fervent evangelical at the age of nineteen in the summer of 1817. It was the first major turning point in his life, redirecting him towards a career in the church. From 1821 to 1828 he held four curacies in Lincolnshire, Essex and Surrey, where he exercised a passionate evangelical ministry often in the face of opposition.

Between 1826 and 1829 Dodsworth was drawn steadily into the study of prophecy within the orbit of the British millenarian revival. He came to be on intimate terms with Henry Drummond and Edward Irving, and he took part in the influential series of conferences on prophecy which were held at Albury between 1826 and 1830. These involvements led him away from evangelicalism and from what he perceived to be the narrowness of its opposition to the prophetic movement. These were the Adventist years in Dodsworth's theological development, culminating in 1829 when Henry Drummond appointed him minister of the Margaret Chapel, London. Dodsworth may well have been expected to pursue an Irvingite agenda in London. However, he was unable to accept the charismatic occurrences in Scotland in 1830 and broke away at this time, taking no part in the catholic apostolic church which Irving and Drummond brought into being in the years from 1832.

Instead, the Margaret Chapel developed in a different direction during Dodsworth's ministry from 1829 to 1837. Prior to the publication of the first of the *Tracts for the times* in 1833, Dodsworth had introduced a weekly communion service and the observance of saints' days. From 1834 he was drawn progressively into the tractarian fold, coming into friendship with Newman, Pusey and Manning, and he became a leading figure in the introduction of tractarian principles in London. In 1837 he was appointed perpetual curate of a new church, Christ Church, Albany Street, London, where he put the ideals of the Oxford movement more fully into effect, creating a model parish for the next generation of anglo-catholic endeavour.

---

[1]   The papers had descended through the family of Dodsworth's daughter, Anna Harriet Drummond (1841–1915), and were purchased from Mrs Jo Drummond. The papers are now bound as MS 4727. The memoir is in Dodsworth's hand throughout, an original draft which, with a few exceptions, he left uncorrected.

[2]   MS 4727, fos. 62–140.

[3]   David Newsome, *The parting of friends* (London, 1966).

His pastoral vision extended to the care of the whole community, including schools and a string of charities for the poor. In partnership with Pusey he also established the first anglican sisterhood at Park Village West.

As the 1840s advanced Dodsworth found increasing difficulty in maintaining Catholic principles within the protestant establishment. Impelled in print to uphold the *via media* and to reprimand converts to Rome, in private he struggled to find compatibility between Catholic principles and the thirty-nine articles. Visits abroad, sometimes accompanied by Manning, exposed him to Roman Catholic worship and generated a reverence for it. He was shocked by the Hampden case and the Gorham judgment which seemed to reveal an Erastian control of the Church of England by the state. On the last day of 1850 he was received into the Roman Catholic church.

He began this new phase of his life with an apologia addressed to his former flock at Christ Church, Albany Street,[4] and with a pamphlet war with Pusey, his former friend and colleague. Until this time he had been a prolific author, but he published nothing more from 1852 to 1856, living quietly in Italy as a layman, being debarred by his marriage from entering the Roman Catholic priesthood. These were years of acute personal unhappiness caused primarily by the rift in his family which arose from his change of religious allegiance. His obituary by Frederick Oakeley speaks of 'his gait of depression, and countenance of agony at that period…a countenance which was but a speaking tablet of days and nights of anxiety'.[5] The unexpected conversion of his wife Elizabeth, some weeks before her death in October 1856, changed everything.[6] It led, six months later, to the autobiographical memoir in which he reviewed the course of his life. This marked a release, a resumption of work as a Catholic writer and polemicist in the years 1857–8 before his literary career was ended by a stroke in 1859.

With the exception of the obituary by Oakeley in *The Tablet*, William Dodsworth received scant biographical attention in his own century and, as an apostate, was largely omitted from the historiography of the Oxford movement. His *rôle* as the apostle of tractarianism in London was not fully appreciated until the appearance in 2003 of a perceptive full-length study by Stephen Young.[7] The subsequent emergence of Dodsworth's autobiographical memoir enhances knowledge of his religious development and allows his own voice to speak.

Frequently the narrative confirms what could previously be only guessed in the absence of documentation. It speaks, for instance, of Dodsworth's association with Charles Simeon at Cambridge and identifies James Brownbill as the priest who eventually received him into the Roman Catholic church. In addition the memoir provides much new information and sometimes springs a surprise. We learn, for example, of his unhappy experience of Richmond Grammar School under its

---

4   William Dodsworth, *Anglicanism considered in its results* (London, 1851).
5   *The Tablet*, 21 Dec. 1861, p. 810.
6   Newman recorded Elizabeth Dodsworth's conversion in a letter in November 1856: 'she was in her last illness – and, to Dodsworth's surprise,…she suddenly asked him whether he thought she could be saved out of the Roman Church. *He said he would not pronounce upon it*, in the case of individuals… Presently, she got him to send for a Priest.' See John Henry Newman, *The letters and diaries*, ed. Charles Stephen Dessain (32 vols., London, 1961–2008), XVII, 467–8.
7   Stephen Edward Young, 'William Dodsworth 1798–1861: the origins of tractarian thought and practice in London', PhD thesis, Open University, 2003. Young also wrote the article on Dodsworth in the *Oxford dictionary of national biography* (*ODNB*) (Oxford, 2004), XVI, 441–2.

admired headmaster, James Tate, of whom Dodsworth paints an unexpectedly hostile portrait. More significantly, we discover that Dodsworth was not brought up as an evangelical, but underwent a conversion, along with his mother and sisters, in 1817. His zeal as an evangelical clergyman – described somewhat ruefully from his standpoint in 1857 – forms one of the principal themes of the narrative. The memoir also provides new information on the opposition which his ministry provoked at this time, leading to his withdrawal from a previously unknown curacy at Gainsborough and from another at Stisted. The memoir is also important in documenting friendships and associations which influenced Dodsworth at significant moments of his life. We learn, for example, of the closeness of his friendship with Hugh McNeile and of their companionship in prophetic studies at Albury, and also of an early Catholic influence on Dodsworth at this time in the person of Edward Vaughan, vicar of St Martin's, Leicester.

Written as it was for his children, Dodsworth's memoir gives an inside view of his family and of the personal life which lay behind his public persona as a preacher, pastor and man of letters. His father, John Dodsworth, emerges as free-thinker who scoffed at the evangelicalism of his wife and children, and whose losses in business and reckless expenditure cast a shadow over his family. William Dodsworth's life-long pursuit of earnestness in religion can perhaps be seen as a reaction. Ironically, his spiritual journey produced a division in his own household as acute as that in the home of his parents. His marriage in 1830 to Elizabeth Buller-Yarde-Buller, a member of his congregation at the Margaret Street Chapel, represented a leap in social status and a return to the wealth of his early childhood. His wife was the daughter of a baronet and counted, amongst her siblings, a baronet, a baron and a countess.[8] The marriage enabled him to set up home amongst the elegant terraces of Regent's Park. From 1834 the couple shared the home at York Terrace of Elizabeth's mother, Lady Buller, on the understanding that Dodsworth would be the head of the household. It proved an uncomfortable arrangement since Dodsworth's increasingly Catholic sympathies alienated both his wife and, even more, his evangelical mother-in-law.

Entry into the Roman Catholic church deepened the rift between Dodsworth and his wife and brought total estrangement from Lady Buller. The convert protagonists of David Newsome's study were largely men whose wives had already died or couples who accepted the Roman allegiance together.[9] Dodsworth's memoir documents a more difficult and painful situation, and one which also raised questions about the upbringing of his children. At the time of his reception in 1850 the children comprised five daughters aged between nine and seventeen, and two sons aged

---

[8] Elizabeth Dodsworth was the daughter of Sir Francis Buller (afterwards Buller-Yarde-Buller), second baronet, and his wife Eliza Lydia (known as Lady Buller), daughter and heiress of John Halliday of Dilhorne Hall, Staffordshire. She was the sister of John Buller-Yarde-Buller (afterwards Yarde-Buller), third baronet, first baron Churston, Sir Edward Buller-Yarde-Buller (afterwards Manningham-Buller), first baronet, and of Susan Elizabeth, whose first marriage was to the sixteenth earl of Morton. Under the will of her mother, Lady Buller, proved in 1851, Elizabeth Dodsworth received the use of an investment of £28,000 and the residue of the estate (The National Archives (TNA), PROB 11/2141).

[9] Newsome, *The parting of friends*. Of those who converted between 1846 and 1854, Henry Manning and Robert Wilberforce were widowers, George and Sophia Ryder and Henry and Mary Wilberforce converted (more or less) together.

13 William Dodsworth, engraving by W. Walker, after E. Walker (London, 1834) (reproduced by permission of the Master and Fellows of Trinity College, Cambridge)

six and eight.[10] Dodsworth tells us that the sons, being so young, 'of course' became Roman Catholics with him.[11] The daughters, however (with the exception of the youngest, Anna Harriet), were beyond an age to be dragooned without their consent. After much heart-searching, Dodsworth decided to keep all of the girls together in the family home with their mother. All five daughters were still at home and outside the Catholic fold when their mother died six years later. It was to them (although ostensibly to all his children) that Dodsworth addressed his memoir, and perhaps especially to Anna Harriet whose descendants preserved it.

For the memoir is not merely the memorializing of an influential life. The writing of autobiographies and reminiscences was a common element in both the evangelical tradition and the Oxford movement; there was a desire to memorialize and to affirm faith for the benefit of others.[12] For those who took the ultimate step of entry into the Roman Catholic church there was also a need to justify and to explain. There might also be a polemical and public context, as in the case of Newman's *Apologia*.[13] By contrast Dodsworth's memoir is private and informal, written at speed and not polished for a public audience, uneven in its coverage of the various phases of his life, and sometimes with spaces left for dates which were never added. Its purpose emerges only in its final querulous paragraph. His daughters, he wrote, had been impressed by the conversion of their mother and had undertaken to consider their own position, but in the months that followed they had not fulfilled their promise. He could only hope that the grace of God would prevail in them. On this awkward note the narrative comes abruptly to its end, and Dodsworth's discomfort in writing it is palpable.

How then were the autobiography and its concluding plea received? Of the religious development of the two oldest daughters, Elizabeth Jane and Olivia, almost nothing is known, except that in later life Olivia maintained a friendship with Manning and was sufficiently devoted to her father's memory to propose the publication of a memoir.[14] However his third and fourth daughters, Emma and Georgiana Augusta, seem to have taken his plea to heart. Both became Roman Catholics in the year after it was written, and by 1860 both had entered Roman Catholic religious

---

10   The children were Elizabeth Jane (b. 1833), Olivia (1834–1901), Emma (b. 1836), Georgiana Augusta (1839–1906), Anna Harriet (1841–1915), William Edward (1842–59) and Cyril (1844–1907). Dodsworth's family and household at Gloucester Lodge and York Terrace, Regent's Park, are recorded in the censuses of 1841, 1851 and 1861 (TNA, HO107/684, HO 107/1493, RG 9/83).

11   The elder son William predeceased his father in 1859. The younger, Cyril, with Cardinal Wiseman as his godfather and mentor, was sent to school at Oscott and Downside. He became a Redemptorist priest: his preaching, evangelizing and pursuit of poverty in his ministry in the West Indies, Canada and USA displayed all the earnestness of his father. See Paul Lavendure, 'Biography of Cyril Dodsworth, C.Ss.R', *Redemptorist North American Bulletin*, 13th issue (June 2000), 20–3.

12   Christopher Tolley, *Domestic biography. The legacy of evangelicalism in four nineteenth-century families* (Oxford, 1957). From the standpoint of the Oxford movement there are points of comparison in the autobiography of Isaac Williams, written for his children in 1851 with additions in 1859 (Lambeth Palace Library (LPL), MS 4477), published as Isaac Williams, *The autobiography*, ed. Sir George Prevost (London, 1892).

13   John Henry Newman, *Apologia pro vita sua*, ed. Martin J. Svaglic (Oxford, 1967).

14   Olivia married in 1867 John William Philips (1827–91), manufacturer and deputy lieutenant for Staffordshire, the widowed husband of her cousin Adelaide Manningham-Buller (Sir Bernard Burke, *A genealogical and heraldic history of the landed gentry*, 9th edn (2 vols., London, 1898), II, 1182, Philips of Heybridge). Elizabeth Jane and Anna Harriet were living with them at their Knightsbridge home at the time of the census of 1871. Olivia's letter to H. P. Liddon in 1887 suggesting a memoir, never published, is recorded in Young, 'William Dodsworth', p. 16 n. 2.

orders.[15] Anna Harriet followed a more circuitous path, entering an anglican sisterhood, the All Saints Sisters of the Poor, a society influenced by the Park Village
Sisterhood which Dodsworth had helped to establish. She left subsequently and
married an anglican clergyman, Arthur Hislop Drummond (1843–1925), assisted by
a ruling from Archbishop Tait that she was no longer bound by her vow of celibacy
after leaving the sisterhood.[16] Later, it seems, she too became a Roman Catholic, for
in 1889 Cardinal Manning wrote to Drummond in reply to a question from him as
to the date of 'Mrs. Drummond's reception'. Manning believed that it had occurred
in May of that year.[17] Anna Harriet died in 1915 in a Roman Catholic nursing home
attached to St Michael's Convent, Clacton, kept by the Sisters of Mercy. She was
buried not with her husband, but with her father William Dodsworth, at St Mary's
Catholic cemetery, Kensal Green.[18]

As to Dodsworth's memoir itself, there is little to suggest that it was ever widely
known, although there exists amongst the Dodsworth/Drummond papers a single
page of an edited transcript, evidence that it may have received some limited circulation beyond the family.[19] This appears to be in the hand of Henry Wilberforce
(1807–73) and the editorial excision of personal matter implies that it may have
been intended for publication, but no edition has been traced. Later, if a tanta-
lizing reference to Dodsworth's 'journal' can be taken to refer to the memoir, it was
perused by Cardinal Manning. In 1889, following a visit from Dodsworth's daughter
Olivia, Manning wrote:

> I shall read your dear Father's journal with a lively interest. He and I were in such
> perfect agreement of mind and sympathy in the trials of those years that it cannot
> fail to bring back to me a most vivid memory of times and men, anxieties and
> doubts, ending at last in a great calm.[20]

---

[15] Young, 'William Dodsworth', p. 264, citing Dodsworth's will dated 28 Jan. 1860. In the census of
     1861 Emma is recorded as a member of the Sisters of Mercy at the Community of the Good Shep-
     herd, Hammersmith; Georgiana as a member of the Society of the Sacred Heart at the Roehampton
     Convent (TNA, RG9/24, fo. 139, RG9/1680, fo. 48). Georgiana entered the order on 3 Feb. 1860
     and died at its house at Roscrea, Ireland, in 1906 according to the index of nuns maintained by the
     Catholic Family History Society.
[16] Papers of Arthur Drummond, acquired by LPL with those of Dodsworth, are now MS 4727. They
     include the ruling signed by Tait (fo. 145); further documentation is contained in the Tait papers
     (vol. 237, fos. 20–5). From these sources it appears that Anna joined the sisterhood in or after 1873
     (since her vow was received by Richard Meux Benson, who became chaplain to the sisterhood in
     that year). She left in or by 1878, the date of Tait's ruling and of her marriage. Arthur Drummond, a
     widower with children at the time of the marriage, was vicar of All Saints, Boyne Hill, Maidenhead,
     an honorary canon of Christ Church, Oxford, and a prominent member of the English Church Union.
     He was a distant cousin of Henry Drummond of Albury.
[17] LPL, MS 4727, fo. 150r.
[18] The burial took place on 20 Dec. 1915. I am grateful to the registrar for information on the Dods-
     worth/Drummond grave, no. 7295.
[19] LPL, MS 4727, fo. 141r.
[20] LPL, MS 4727, fo. 147r.

Editorial conventions

The memoir was written by Dodsworth on a single leaf followed by 39 bifolia. He numbered the bifolia 1–39, probably indicating that they were separate one from another when the text was written and afterwards crudely sewn to form a booklet. When acquired by Lambeth Palace Library the booklet was without covers (and may never have possessed any), and the initial and final leaves were worn and frayed, with loss of text at the ends of lines. Letters or words missing from the text, either from physical damage or because Dodsworth left blank spaces in the text for dates or other details which were not readily to hand, are represented in this edition by square brackets [ ]. The booklet has been conserved and re-foliated as fos. 62–140 of Lambeth Palace Library MS 4727.

Dodsworth wrote his memoir at speed for the private use of his family. The text is written on the rectos of the leaves. A few corrections were made subsequently with equal haste – sometimes confusing the original text – and a few additions were made on the versos of fos. 63, 64, 67 and 130. For the most part, however, the text remained uncorrected and unpolished. As a result, and perhaps also because of the informal nature of the memoir, Dodsworth's approach to punctuation and spelling was casual. In this edition the original spelling and wording have been preserved, even where a word has been repeated or some other obvious mistake has been made. Punctuation and capitalization however have been modernized in the interest of producing a more readable and intelligible text.

William Dodsworth: an autobiographical memoir

[fo. 62r] I have drawn up the following little sketch of my life for the use of my children. It so happens that my lot in life has been cast far away from the place of my birth, and that I have had but little intercourse with my kinfolk in that part of the world. I am naturally uncommunicative on such subjects – so that I feel my early life and associations would be scarcely known to my children unless I leave some such record. It may be well also that they should know my innermost thoughts on some more recent passages of my life.

[fo. 63r] I was born at Kirk-ella, a beautiful little village it then was, about four miles from Kingston-upon-Hull. My father, of a good Yorkshire family, was a merchant and owner of ships in Hull, and possessed a sort of villa residence at Kirk-ella.[1] I was born in a house next opposite the church, afterwards the residence of Mr Jo[] Sykes. But before I was old enough to notice anything my father removed into a better house on the road to West-ella, which had beautiful grounds attached to it and which was afterwards occupied by Mr Jo[] Sykes who I think died in it.[2] It was long the residence of his widow and I believe is in possession of the family to this day.

My family originally came from the neighbourhood of Helmsley, on the Hambleton Hills, a very beautiful part of Yorkshire. But in the time of my grandfather or greatgrandfather (I am not certain which) they removed to York – a place of great resort for Yorkshire families of that day. My grandfather or his father filled the office of Lord Mayor of York [fo. 64r] which was often brought to our minds as children by our having, as a play thing, a large gilt staff or pole which had belonged to the lord mayor.[3] At that period this office used to be held by gentlemen, so late as my own time I remember its being held by Mr Dundas, the eldest son of

---

[1] William Dodsworth was born at Kirk Ella, the son of John Dodsworth (1765–1818) and his wife Harriet, on 19 Mar. 1798. See Young, 'William Dodsworth', ch. 1.

[2] The mercantile and property interests of John Dodsworth were closely associated with those of his friends, the Sykes family, especially Joseph Sykes of West Ella Hall (1723–1805), mayor of Hull 1761 and 1777, and his sons John Sykes of Kirk Ella (1763–1813), mayor of Hull 1792, and Daniel Sykes (1766–1832), MP, who was executor of John Dodsworth's will and guardian of his children. See Joseph Foster, *Pedigrees of the county families of Yorkshire* (5 vols., London, 1874–5), V: *North and East Riding*, and Young, 'William Dodsworth', ch. 1. Damage to fo. 63 renders the christian names of the two members of the Sykes family unreadable with certainty, but the first is more probably Joseph and the second John.

[3] Ralph Dodsworth (*c.* 1732–94), grandfather of William Dodsworth, was lord mayor of York in 1792. He was the eldest son of John Dodsworth of Nawton, in the parish of Kirkdale, near Helmsley. See Robert H. Skaife, 'Civic officials of York' (manuscript in York Central Library). Ralph Dodsworth was a raff, or timber, merchant who, in partnership with William Osbourne of Kingston-upon-Hull, purchased the forest of Glenmore from the duke of Gordon and founded a ship-building yard at Kingston at the mouth of the river Spey. His eldest son John, father of William Dodsworth, was born and christened on 9 Dec. 1765 in the parish of St Mary Bishopshill Senior, York (the entry in the parish register in the Borthwick Institute for Archives: 'John, son of Mr Ralph Dodsworth, wood merchant...' corrects the *International genealogical index* and Young, 'William Dodsworth', p. 19, where John's father is named as John). John Dodsworth (1765–1818) followed his father Ralph as a timber merchant and shipbuilder.

the then Lord Dundas, and afterwards Lord Zetland.[4] The clan of Dodsworth in Yorkshire is very numerous and of various grades. My father was the head of the family. [Added note on fo. 63v] I mention this because it might *possibly*, tho' not probably, be of use to my eldest son, for since my brother Ralph has no children, my eldest son will be the head of the family and heir-at-law, if no nearer can be found. [fo. 64r continued] My mother was, before her marriage with my father, Miss Harriet Haydon, the daughter of a banker of Guildford, Surrey. The offspring of this marriage was four sons and three daughters in the following order, 1. John, 2. Jane, 3. Harriet, 4. Ralph, 5. William, 6. Sarah Elizabeth, and 7. Benjamin. John was to have succeeded to my father's mercantile business in Hull, which was kept open to him. But after my father's death, and when he had reached the age of about 30, he chose to go to College to prepare himself for anglican orders. He entered himself as fellow-commoner at Queens' College Cambridge, and after going through the university course was ordained to the curacy of Papworth St Agnes, Cambridgeshire, and afterwards was presented to a small living near Leeds.[5] Afterwards he took the curacy of Shadwell near to a small estate which he had in [fo. 65r] the neighbourhood of York. In the year 1838 he was killed in a fall from a gig.[6] Jane, my eldest sister, married her cousin Thomas Haydon. Harriet some years after followed her example and married his brother Joseph Haydon. In the year 1842 she had a coup-de-soleil at Brighton. She was never afterwards herself and died at Guildford in 1844. Ralph went to Australia as a settler, mined himself, returned home with nothing, and has ever since been in poor circumstances. [Added note on fo. 64v] Ralph married a person of low station in life but a respectable woman, whom I have never seen. [fo. 65r continued] Sarah Elizabeth died at Stisted in Essex where she lived with me, unmarried, when I held that curacy. Benjamin died young about the year 1818 while I was at College. My father died, at the age of 52, a few months before him at Carleton Hall, where we then lived, and was buried at Kirk-Ella.[7] My mother died at my house in York Terrace in the year 1837 at the age of 73.

My childhood so far as I can recollect was very happy while we lived at Kirkella. From stories since told of me I suppose I was a lively and somewhat impertinent boy. I can remember being rebuked for slapping my aunt's face on some occasion for having offended me. Also I used to be laughed at for the following adventure. One day after dinner my [fo. 66r] brother and I stole into the dining room and emptied the wine bottles by which I became somewhat elevated. On being called to give an account, I said we had so much red wine and so much white 'and finished off by matrimony' meaning a mixture of the two wines. A rich old gentleman, Mr Sykes of West-ella, was a sort of hypochondriac, and would have a doctor from Hull to visit him every day to whom he gave a fee of two guineas. I had heard this mentioned and the next time of the Doctor passed, the road skirting our garden wall, I had perched myself on the wall and cried out There goes two guineas. I suppose I could not be more that five or six years old. I got punished for my impertinence, but the Doctor

4   Lawrence Dundas (1766–1839), lord mayor of York 1811–12, afterwards second baron Dundas and first earl of Zetland

5   A later pencil note on fo. 63v identifies this living as Roundhay, Yorks. See also J. A. Venn, *Alumni Cantabrigiensis, Part II, II* (Cambridge, 1944), p. 315.

6   *The clergy of the Church of England database* gives his date of death as 28 Sept. 1839.

7   John Dodsworth died Apr. 1818; Benjamin Dodsworth died Dec. 1818, Young, 'William Dodsworth', p. 34.

always after this went another way. These are trifling things but they are traits of character not very favourable to me I fear. Another curious thing I remember at this age, that I had an extraordinary dislike to ladies. I would always run away when they wanted to kiss me and to this day I have a lively recollection of being bribed to allow a Mrs Maister, a friend of my mother's, to kiss me by a beautiful red purse, with a wax figure of Napoleon upon it. I can even recollect the struggle I had between love of the beautiful purse and dislike of being kissed. But I was vanquished and got the purse. This is the more curious because [fo. 67r] afterwards I was at least as susceptible to the tender passion as my neighbours, which this memoir will shew. I remember very little else of this early period. I rather think that I was not apt to learn, as I found myself behindhand when I went to school. This I think was at the age of seven. I was sent to Beverley Grammar School, which had possessed a very high character under Dr Jackson, but was then on decline under a new master who came about six months after I got there, Mr Neale.[8] This man proved to be a great scamp. I can well remember his coming first into the school and making a flowery speech about making every boy his friend etc.

About this time my father gave up his mercantile affairs in Hull, and bought an estate in Holderness, Carleton Hall, at which we went to live. It was a very retired place, at a distance, most from [sic] friends.[9] My father took to farming his estate and we boys in our holidays indulged in all kind of field sports. We had horses and dogs almost at our will, and we made great use of them. I remember the pride which I had in riding my father's hunters, and, being a lightweight, [fo. 68r] sometimes leading the field. Farming I fancy did not answer to my father who lost much money in it and yet, in expectation of another estate which was to come to him at the death of his uncle, he never restricted his expenses within his income. [Added note on fo. 67v] I believe I may trace to these circumstances the too great tendency to economy which has characterised my life. My father though very reckless in expenditure used from time to time to break out into sore expressions about our hastening into poverty. I well remember being so disturbed with such expressions that I drew some comfort from looking at our furniture and thinking that we could not be so very near absolute poverty. [fo. 68r continued] Here our difficulties began. He always used to say that all would come right when he succeeded to this inheritance. But my great uncle lived to an advanced age, while we were each year accumulating debts, so that in fact perhaps the value of the estate was expended before it came to us, which was but a short time before my father's death.

In the mean time it had been discovered that I was not making progress at Beverley School, from which therefore it was determined to remove me. My father fixed upon

8   John Jackson (1754–1813), Fellow of Trinity College, Cambridge, 1778, master of Beverley Grammar School 1780–1808, curate of Beverley Minster 1807–13. He does not appear to have held a doctorate and is described as 'John Jackson, A.M.' on a memorial inscription in Beverley Minster. William Henry Neale (1785–1855) was appointed master of Beverley Grammar School in Feb. 1808 and dismissed in 1814 as 'an unfit person to be entrusted with the education of youth'. See John R. Witty, *A history of Beverley Grammar School*, revised 1986 edn by R. Michael Scrowston, typescript in the possession of the school. Witty also recorded a commendation of Dodsworth 'in the Boadicea of Cowper' at the school speech day in 1809, *The Bevertonian*, Apr. 1927, p. 26.

9   Carleton Hall, Holderness, lay in the parish of Aldbrough, about twelve miles north-east of Hull. Young explains the move to Carleton Hall, also known as East Carleton Farm, 'in the remote and unfashionable area of Holderness' as resulting from a downturn in the family's mercantile affairs, Young, 'William Dodsworth', pp. 24–5.

two other schools, and gave me the choice between them, Richmond and Ripon. My choice was determined I believe by hearing that at Richmond School there was no flogging – and so to [fo. 69r] Richmond I was sent. In one respect the selection was good. James Tate, the master, was a first rate scholar, and certainly turned out very good men for the universities.[10] I here found myself very much behindhand, and never can I forget the misery which I had to endure from being bullied by an usher of the name of Willis. He used to delight in exposing my ignorance. I was a little deceived also about the flogging. True, there was none in the strict sense of that term – there was no birch rod used. But Tate used to go into the most violent unrestrained passions and then his wrath was really terrible. He seemed to have a special spite against the foundation boys, although he himself had been one at this very school. I have seen him take his heavy walking stick and strike a thick headed boy of this class over the head – there must really have been danger of splitting his head open. He was more gentle with us but still I was terribly afraid of him although he never once lifted his hand against me while I was there. Still I [fo. 70r] was not a favourite and my excessive dread of him proved a great disadvantage. When I came under his personal instruction I think I made tolerable but not distinguished progress. In the latter part of my time there I suffered from a foolish love affair. The second master of the school in whose house I lodged had a very pretty sister-in-law about 19 or 20, when I was 18. He threw us much together, not, I think, without a design and I, silly boy that I was, fancied myself deeply in love – and like love stricken swains neglected my books.

The upper boys too had a great deal too much liberty. We did almost what we pleased and there were some very dissipated youths. I remember on one occasion, at the proclamation of peace, assisting to take home Tate himself in a state of intoxication. It was not likely therefore that we should put any great restraint upon ourselves. We got into habits of occasionally taking too much wine, and from this I date some [of] my misfortunes in life.

I went to College – Trinity at Cambridge – a fair classical scholar and more advanced than my equals in mathematics to which I had [fo. 71r] a particular liking.[11] But I went with this set from Richmond. Some of my chief friends were steady reading men, but others, especially two very clever men who had great influence over me, were very free livers though clever men, one of whom afterwards greatly distinguished himself. The result was that during my first year at Cambridge I tried to unite hard reading with free living. However I read enough to have done pretty well. My nearest friends expected me to come out in the first class of our College examinations. And I believe I should have done so but from one of those untoward circumstances which sometimes exercise so great an influence on the future. In our viva voce examination we had to translate a book of Thucidides. I had the book well up, with the exception of one passage which had puzzled me and which I had passed by under the notion that out of the whole book surely this one passage would not fall to me – for there were about fifty of us, taking our parts in rotation. It so happened that this one passage [fo. 72r] did fall to me, and I believe my blundering in it lost

---

10 James Tate (1771–1843) transformed Richmond into one of the leading classical schools of his day. Dodsworth's portrait of Tate contrasts with that in Young, 'William Dodsworth', pp. 25–8, and in the *ODNB*, where Tate is presented as an inspirational teacher 'rejecting corporal punishment and refusing to rule by fear'.

11 Dodsworth matriculated at Trinity College, Cambridge, in the michaelmas term, 1816.

me a place in the first class – I came out high in the second class. This however was a great disappointment to me, and I believe had great influence on my future life.

I went home for the long vacation. My mode of life and reading together had told upon my constitution. I was far from well. My disappointment in the classes did me no good. In this vacation however a great change came upon me.

I think I may say that, as long as I can remember, I had always some religious feelings about me. My mother who was herself punctual in her duties, without any particular seriousness in religion, used to make us say our prayers, and taught us after her own method. I cannot remember the time when I had not a very strong fear of hell and other religious feelings. My father, I fear, was a free thinker and used to reflect upon my mothers *presbyterianism* – I believe because earnest religion was almost confined, amongst protestants, to the dissenters at that day. It may be supposed then that our religion, as children, was of a very loose kind. We used to go to church regularly and laugh at methodism, and so it continued till I came home from College at the long vacation in 1817. One partial exception however I must [fo. 73r] mention, the remembrance of which has much struck me in recent years. When I was at Richmond School one of our frolics was to go into the dissenting meeting houses either for fun or at least out of mere curiosity. I remember once going into the catholic chapel, the first I believe that I had ever entered. I can remember at this moment the cross on the back of the priest's chasuble. There was no fun or joking there, I remember being impressed with something as really supernatural. It might be a mere superstitious feeling; but it is curious that I never remember to have entered a catholic chapel again without having some some such feeling of reverence for what I did not comprehend.

When I returned from College after my first year in 1817, a great change had taken place in my home. My sisters had been on a visit to their cousins Haydons of Guildford,[12] and had come back thoroughly imbued with the religion called evangelical. My dear mother, now under very great trial from the conduct of my father, had always been ready for anything which indicated more earnestness in religion, and now was more than ever open to its influence. She too had earnestly embraced the same opinions. At the same time some members of a family (the Sykes) who had always been amongst our chiefest friends, became imbued with the same kind of religion, and my eldest brother who much wished to marry [fo. 74r] one of the girls was inclining the same way. So when I came home I was brought into the very thick of it and on all sides beset with arguments and persuasions. For a long time I resisted, but I could not resist the reasoning that after St Paul the 39 Articles taught 'justification by faith alone'. This so far as I can remember was a turning point with me. Then I do think I was inclined to be more earnest in religion than I had been and this system seemed to offer it. Added to which my eldest brother's influence over me at that time was very great, and from whatever motives he was inclined to profess himself an evangelical. These various influences prevailed, and in October I returned to Cambridge a confirmed 'evangelical', and this was also attended with a change in my future destiny.

My father had always stood strongly on the point of allowing us to choose our own future in life. I had long chosen the law, chiefly I think in the first instance

---

[12] Dodsworth's mother was born Harriet Haydon, from a family of leading bankers centred in Guildford, Young, 'William Dodsworth', pp. 19, 35–6.

because amongst all the visitors at our house when I was a boy I liked Mr Daniel Sykes, a barrister, the best. So when I was mere child I was bent upon being of the same profession. Curiously enough, when I came to be older, I had a real liking for the study of law and have often been told by my friends, (perhaps it is a doubtful compliment) that I should have [fo. 75r] succeeded in that profession. Now however, having imbibed these 'evangelical' opinions, I conceived an ardent desire to take orders in the church, and my sisters and other religious friends seemed to take it for granted that I should take this course. My father was angry when he found out my new religious opinions but said that as I had got such notions I was only fit to be 'a methodist parson': so he consented to my change of profession, perhaps the more readily as he had now become very embarrassed in his circumstances and my outfit for the law would have been much more expensive.

I went back to Cambridge, then, with my new religion and with very impaired health. I immediately attached myself to the 'evangelical' party. I frequented Mr Simeon's church and his sermon parties, as they used to be called.[13] They were parties of young men whom he received to tea once a week and instructed in the composition of a sermon. His method was too formal but still no doubt not without use. My new opinions were a great injury to my progress in universities [sic] studies. At that time great contempt was generally thrown by the 'evangelical' party on all worldly distinction. It was represented rather as a temptation, than a desirable acquisition, and to me under the novelty of my 'conversion' my new born zeal for religion threw everything else into the shade. I must do Mr Simeon the justice to say that he often urged us to pursue our secular studies and held up Henry Martyn, who had been senior wrangler, as an example to us.[14] But this advice made little impression on minds newly awakened to the importance of heavenly [fo. 76r] and eternal things. A 'sphere of usefulness' in which to preach the Gospel was regarded as a far higher object of pursuit than any university distinction, and, generally speaking, of course not without exceptions, the Simeonites, as we used to be called, though studious men in their own way, did not aim at high honours. This I think partly influenced my future career. A country living where I should have opportunities of teaching what seemed to me of more value than ten thousand worlds, became the object of my desires.

But there were other circumstances also which hindered my reading for university distinction. As I have said, I returned to Cambridge with impaired health, but read steadily one term. I then went to Guildford for the Christmas vacation at Guildford and there had all my religious feelings deepened, and was flattered with extraordinary attention from some of my cousins. Again I returned to College, and in January or February 1818, I broke a blood vessel. One evening as I was walking with a friend on the Trumpington Road, I can remember the place quite well, my mouth filled with blood. It was thought right that I should go home, and Dr Alderson, our family physician, took a very serious view of my case.[15] I think the result has gone far to shew that his view was an exaggerated one. However he thought that without any delay I ought to go out to Madeira. Contrary winds [fo. 77r] detained me till

---

13 Charles Simeon (1759–1836), the influential evangelical leader and one of the founders of the Church Missionary Society.

14 Henry Martyn (1781–1812), missionary and translator. Martyn graduated in 1801 as senior wrangler and winner of several prizes. See *ODNB*, XXXVII, 36–7.

15 John Alderson, MD (1758–1829), the leading physician in Hull.

78

mishap, unless being becalmed for two days under
a burning sun might be accounted one. We reached
Gibraltar on June 2nd or 3rd. I remember being on shore
on the 4th which was then the king's birth Day
and kept by the garrison with great display. One
way in which my religious zeal had them thoroughly
was in taking out numerous tracts from the
Religious Tract Society. Many of these I remember
leaving on the benches on the grand Parade
they were in various languages. & so I flattered
myself that I was sowing good seed which
in time would bear fruit.
a few days later
The homeward bound Mediterranean
Packet called at Gibraltar. & in her the Louisa
I took my passage home. A high church Clergyman
such as were in those days - "high & dry" - was
on board. considering what my opinions were
it is strange that I should have got on so well
with him. I mention this as in a case afterwards, it seems to vindicate that I must at
that time have had some high-church
principles, notwithstanding my evangelicalism
we struck up a friendship & parted with mutual
regret.
After a good, but rough passage, we landed
at Falmouth on a Saturday. I would by no means
travel on Sunday. So there I spent the day scarcely
do I remember walking on Sunday afternoon

14 William Dodsworth recounts his voyage home from Madiera in 1818 (LPL, MS 4727, fo. 78)

the beginning of April. We had a terribly stormy voyage out. One night a tremendous sea broke in our bulwarks. I thought we were going to the bottom, and well I remember jumping out of my berth, clasping my hands together, and offering, as I thought, my last prayer, the cabin being ankle deep in water. However we weathered the storm and arrived safely in Madeira.

In the meanwhile I had recovered my health, the Spring was far advanced, and I had only about six weeks to stay at Madeira until the heat made it desirable to go homewards. The time had passed very pleasantly amongst the hospitable English merchants at Funchal and in its neighbourhood. There was then no English chapel and I used to assemble a few English people to hear me read the church service and a sermon.[16] I used to visit the catholic churches and convents as a matter of curiosity, but do not remember any particular impression produced by them, except some disgust at the dirt and spitting.

I returned home by way of Gibraltar, accomplishing the voyage from Madeira to that place in a Spanish felucca – the only Englishman on board, and not without fear that we might be boarded by pirates, who were not infrequently met in those seas. We had a beautiful voyage without any [fo. 78r] mishap, unless being becalmed for two days under a burning sun might be accounted one. We reached Gibraltar on June 2nd or 3rd. I remember being on shore on the 4th which was the then king's birthday, and kept by the garrison with great display.[17] One way in which my religious zeal had shewn itself was in taking out numerous tracts from the Religious Tract Society. Many of these I remember leaving on the benches on the Grand Parade. They were in various languages, and so I flattered myself that I was sowing good seed which in time would bear fruit.

A few days later the homeward bound Mediterranean packet called at Gibraltar and in her, the Louisa, I took my passage home. A high church clergyman, such as were in those days 'high and dry' was on board. Considering what my opinions were it is strange that I should have got on so well with him. I mention this as, in a case afterwards, it seems to indicate that I must at that time have had some high church principles, notwithstanding my evangelicalism. We struck up a friendship and parted with mutual regret.

After a good, but rough passage, we landed at Falmouth on a Saturday. I would by no means travel on Sunday. So there I spent the day and well do I remember walking on Sunday afternoon [fo. 79r] to a small church beautifully situated in the neighbourhood where 'the Gospel was preached' according to the common slang of the day. By some mischance my letters had not reached me: and I determined to take Guildford in my way home. On arriving there Joseph Haydon very abruptly told me of the death of my father, which had occurred a few weeks before. It was the first death in our family, and the grief and strangeness of it almost drove me distracted. I remember that, on receiving the intelligence, I walked off on the Stoke road to indulge my feelings alone, until my cousin Tom came and found me out and brought me back.

---

16   There was no English church in Madeira until the opening of the consular chapel in 1822. The consular chaplain from 1818 to 1819 was W. G. Cautley; possibly Dodsworth's visit preceded his taking up the post. See H. A. Newell, *The English church in Madeira* (Oxford, 1931), pp. 11, 46.

17   George III was born on 24 May 1738. His birthday was perceived to fall on 4 June after the introduction of the new style calendar in 1752.

The long vacation had now commenced, so there was no returning to College until October. I spent this summer at home at Carleton, and was thrown much into the society of a very beautiful girl, F.S. She was of the same religious opinions and I fancied myself violently in love with her. Perhaps I really was so, as she perhaps was with me, and we set up a sort of indirect correspondence through my sisters. This was another hindrance to me when I got back to College. The time however for distinguishing myself in any way was now past, and although I was still what might be called a [fo. 80r] reading man, it was in a very desultory way and not such as would get me a name. I took up Hebrew and also mineralogy, though I never made much progress in the latter study. I kept on partly with mathematics from liking the subject. But my whole heart was fixed upon going into orders and my reading was chiefly with that view. In my third year's College examination I passed tolerably well, the authorities enquired why I would not go up for honours. This was now out of the question; but I passed creditably for my degree being 11th amongst the 'oi πολλοι.[18]

I took my degree of BA in January 1820. More than a year had to elapse before I should be 23, that is of age to take orders. By the death of my father our home had been broken and the estate was to be sold. My elder sister had recently married Tom Haydon, and I gladly accepted their invitation to spend this year with them at Guildford. I proposed to my guardian Mr Sykes to take pupils which he very much approved.[19] The plan however came to nothing; because I would not engage myself for a day beyond the time at [fo. 81r] which I should be ready to take orders. I now first became acquainted with Henry Drummond whom I visited at Albury Park, with the view to taking as a pupil the son of Lord Kinnoul [sic].[20] However it came to nothing. There I also met for the first time Spencer Percival [sic].[21] I remember thinking that their religion was of a very odd kind. I was myself at this [time] full of religious zeal with very little knowledge. Often I used to walk out to call at the cottages in the neighbourhood to talk to the people about religion, and I remember reproaching myself, if I saw people working in the fields, for not having the courage to go to them and speak of their souls. I used to ask myself how I could answer it at the day of Judgment that, knowing the Gospel which could save them, I left them in ignorance of it. This feeling grew upon me until it made me quite unhappy. I thought myself called upon to convert everybody. I was excessively puritanical both in opinion and practice, and had a tendency to extremes. I thought all balls and plays absolutely sinful, games of chance I thought an unjustifiable appeal [fo. 82r] to providence, and I even objected to social parties, unless they involved prayer and the exposition of scripture. I thought myself fully acquainted with the gospel, and held in very light esteem all who were not of my own way of thinking.

At length the time drew near when I was to take orders, and here I determined to throw myself entirely on Divine Providence as I thought. Indeed I think this was

---

[18] The *hoi polloi*, the rank and file.
[19] Daniel Sykes (1766–1832), MP.
[20] Henry Drummond (1786–1860), politician and banker, of Albury Park, Surrey. He was the sponsor of the Albury conferences and co-founder of the catholic apostolic or Irvingite church in the years 1832–5. Drummond was married to his cousin, a daughter of the tenth earl of Kinnoull. However the identity of the prospective pupil is obscure. The children of the tenth earl were in adulthood by 1820; the eldest son of the eleventh earl was not born until 1827.
[21] Spencer Perceval (1795–1859), eldest son of the prime minister. He became an Irvingite Apostle in 1833.

so real a feeling that I believe I was guided by Him, in the midst of all my self sufficiency and perverseness. I resolved therefore not to have a choice in my first curacy. It would have naturally gratified me to be near my sister Jane. We had always been very much attached to each other and I should have enjoyed exercising 'my office' amongst my relations. However I would admit no bias of this kind. I made it known amongst my friends and acquaintances that I wanted a curacy with a title and I resolved with myself to accept the first that offered wherever it might be. This [fo. 83r] happened to be the joint parishes of Glentworth and Saxby in the Diocese of Lincoln, situated about eleven miles north of the city of Lincoln. I unhesitatingly accepted this curacy. The duties of it were to perform two full services every Sunday, one at Glentworth and one at Saxby. My rector, Mr Bassett,[22] resided at the former parish, containing about 300 inhabitants, and made himself responsible for visiting the sick and for all the week-day duties; while I had the sole charge of Saxby, a little village of about 130 inhabitants about two miles at [sic] Glentworth. The parsonage house which was a mere cottage was occupied by a farmer and his wife, the best rooms being given to me as a lodger. To this cure I was ordained on April 1, 1821 by Dr Pelham, bishop of Lincoln, in Quebec chapel, St Marylebone.[23] It happened to be out of the usual time of administering orders. My examination was by the bishop himself. It was exceedingly slight, chiefly I think consisting in a translation of the Greek Testament. The bishop had been a life's guardsman promoted by [fo. 84r] George IV. He was a man of no learning and enquired nothing about my doctrine, a circumstance I shall have hereafter to allude to.

Everything, during my residence at Guildford had tended to exalt my views of the office of a clergyman, so that he was, as it was termed, a Preacher of the Gospel. The Haydons made much of every such person and honoured him above all others. My own feelings in reference to eternal things were at this time very vivid. I was beyond measure elated at becoming a clergyman, partly, and I fear in great measure from motives of vanity, and partly I must hope and think from some little appreciation of the difference between temporal and eternal things. Certain I am that I would not have changed my office for a throne could it have been offered me. As 'an ambassador for Christ' I justly esteemed myself as possessing a higher than any earthly office, and amidst all my ignorance and vanity and other sins, I do believe that *then* I was entirely free from motives of worldly interest. At least so far as this, I feel that it would have made no difference in my choice of profession, if I had been certain [fo. 85r] to remain a poor curate all my life long. If I desired a living it was that I might be my own master, and manage my parish in my own way, and beyond a doubt I had an overweening confidence and self conceit of my own 'faithfulness' and efficiency.

I went down to my curacy full of this spirit and full of zeal and earnestness, expecting to achieve great things in my assault on Satan and his kingdom. When I came near to the village, the coach put me down at the Lodge of Fillingham Park,

---

22 Henry Bassett (*c.* 1778–1852), rector and patron of North Thoresby and vicar of Glentworth and Saxby.
23 George Pelham (1766–1827), bishop of Lincoln. He had held a commission in the guards before changing his vocation. The Quebec chapel was a non-parochial chapel in the parish of St Marylebone, London. The date is cited by Young, 'William Dodsworth', p. 38, as Sunday 31 Mar. 1821. However 31 Mar. fell on a Saturday in that year.

where I was to be met by someone from my rector at Glentworth.[24] While waiting in the Lodge, I engaged the woman who kept it in a religious conversation, and ended by reading the scriptures and praying with her. I mention this because it was brought against me afterwards in a quarter which I little expected. My first sermon was from the text 'I determined to know nothing amongst you but Jesus Christ and him crucified.' I still have the sermon and I believe there is little in it which I might not now say, but much omitted which I should now insert. It gave great satisfaction to my rector and his wife, and greatly did I feel flattered by their warm approval of it. This was at Glentworth church. In the afternoon I preached [fo. 86r] [at] Saxby from the words 'Behold the Lamb of God which taketh away the sin of the world'. How well I remember the feeling of elation as I rode up to the church yard and remarked the people *waiting for me to preach to* [sic] *the Gospel to them*. Filled I fear I was with spiritual vanity.

I lived at Saxby for eighteen months alone. My cottage was not large enough to receive my mother or one of my sisters who would have come to me. I look back upon that time with mixed feelings. That I was really religious, and really feared God, I cannot doubt. I read much; chiefly my Bible, and books of 'evangelical' piety. I spent much time in the composition of my sermons. As the parishes were two or three miles apart, my rector kindly urged upon me that one sermon would do for both. But I was flattered by observing that some people came to both churches and this even from other parishes at considerable distance. One man of little education I remember walk [sic] *six miles* every Sunday rain or fine *to hear me*. Consequently I would make two sermons per week, that they might not be discouraged from coming to both churches. [fo. 87r] This occupied much of my time. There I read for priest's orders, and I may name it as certainly an advantage which I feel to this day, that in course of my preparation for priest and deacon's orders, I made a complete analysis of Butler's Analogy and Pearson on the Creed, and the fifth Book of Hooker's Ecclesiastical Polity.

My churches were crowded with hearers which brought me no goodwill from the neighbouring clergy and as several of the people came from the neighbouring villages, in defiance of ecclesiastical order, of which I then thought very lightly, I did not scruple to visit them, and I can well remember how my foolish heart rejoiced in the incense of flattery which ever these poor uneducated people offered me, and I fear that I was often vain enough to seek it. My religious state was then a very mixed one. Nothing perhaps apparently was wanting in me. I was diligent in my duties, though never satisfying my own conscience, especially in the matter of visiting those of my flock who might be unwilling to receive. I was naturally very shy, and my conscience was always reproaching me for backwardness in *aggressive* efforts to convert [fo. 88r] the sinful. Much of this I think now rose from ignorance because these people are not to be won by too much interference; but I was too much influenced by what I thought 'faithfulness', testifying to them 'whether they would hear or whether they would forbear'. I used to be a good deal upon my knees, but my prayers were very desultory and unsatisfactory. On the whole I cannot but think that I was earnest and sincere but withal vain and self sufficient, and so I lived in my little cottage during the year of my diaconate.

---

[24] Fillingham, nine miles north-west of Lincoln. Dodsworth probably refers to the gateway with attached lodges of Fillingham Castle.

In the beginning of April 1822 I went up to London to receive priest's orders, and here a strange sort of reception awaited me. The bishop of Lincoln, Dr Pelham, had an abhorrence of 'evangelicalism'. He had admitted me to deacon's orders without any suspicion of what I was, and nothing in my slight examination had then elicited my opinions. But it appears that my own abundant zeal had now been reported to him, and especially my having read and prayed with the woman at Fillingham Lodge when I went to my curacy. He rebuked me for this extraordinary zeal. The examination too was such as to draw out my opinions on doctrine, with which he expressed himself not a little displeased. However, having satisfied him or his chaplain, [fo. 89r] in the matter of scholarship, which was not difficult, he could not well refuse me orders. So I was ordained priest in St Marylebone church (the same in which I was afterwards married) on 12th April 1822.[25] I paid a short visit to Guildford and was much elated by the kind of attention paid me by my sisters, and the great approbation expressed at my sermons and expositions. They were empty enough, but had no doubt a strong savour of evangelicalism in them.

I returned to my parishes in Lincolnshire, and accepted the appointment of honorary secretary to the Bible Society at Gainsborough, about 12 miles from Saxby. This brought me into connection with that town: and I soon after had the offer of the curacy at the parish church, from Mr Beckett the newly appointed vicar.[26] The emolument was somewhat less. At Saxby I had received £120 per annum; and I may mention that from the extreme economy of my mode of life, I have never had more money *to spare*, than I had then, besides keeping my horse. However I can truly say, that at this time emolument was very little considered by me. I was far more attracted by a large church to preach in, and 'an extensive sphere of usefulness'. [fo. 90r] The matter of my own fitness did not much trouble me. Of course, I acknowledged myself unfit for any post; but I had a strong faith or feeling, perhaps it was no more, that God would supply my defects and be my sufficiency. It was quite in keeping with the evangelical opinions which I had imbibed to hold myself in readiness for everything. I do think that my genuine feeling was 'Behold here I am send me', and under this I was ready to take any office, however difficult, or if the way had been opened to me 'to go to the ends of the earth'.

The offer of the curacy at Gainsborough therefore seemed to me 'as an opening of Providence', and I at once accepted it, at the reduced stipend of £100 per annum. In my zeal I fear I did not much consult the wishes of my rector at Glentworth, who, I afterwards found out, did not think I had used him well in leaving him so soon, and who I believe was quite satisfied with my services. Indeed I received nothing but kindness from him and his wife. But I was abundantly selfish and thought that everything ought to give way to my desire for 'greater usefulness' and so [fo. 91r] I removed to Gainsborough in the autumn of the same year 1822.

Here I had the supreme delight of preaching to a crowded church of more than 1000 persons, and my vanity was salved over with the plausible pretext that my pleasure arose from being so very useful. Here I might have gone on for I know not how long, if it had not been for the reputation of over-zeal which I had gained with the bishop. For when my licence was applied for, without actually refusing it, he expostulated with the vicar for appointing a gentleman of my sentiments. A good

---

25 Young, 'William Dodsworth', cites the date as Sunday 14 Apr. 1822.
26 George Beckett (1793–1843), vicar of Gainsborough 1822–43.

deal of correspondence ensued, but nothing was decided for six months, during which I continued to exercise my 'acceptable' ministry. The people had not been used to so 'earnest' a ministry, and I believe I was really much liked by them. At length, my licence being still in suspense, my vicar suggested that I should relieve him from a difficulty by resigning the cure. On my own principles, this was 'a leading of Providence' and without hesitation I followed it and resigned the cure.

During my residence at Gainsborough I had cultivated the acquaintance of an evangelical clergyman, Rev. Thomas Dykes of [fo. 92r] of [sic] St John's, Hull, whom I had known before we left Carleton.[27] I had preached in his church, and it so happened that when I was on the point of resigning my curacy at Gainsborough, a friend of his, Mr Escreet, curate of Stisted in Essex, was just dead.[28] The rector, Dr Seale,[29] had no sympathy with Mr Escreet's evangelical sentiments; but on the whole had been pleased with him, and with his sister, who lived with him, and on this account was disposed to listen to a recommendation from his friends. If they did not immediately recommend some one the probability was that Dr Seale would appoint some one who would not 'preach the Gospel' to the poor people who had learned to appreciate Mr Escreet's ministry. Here then seemed to be a providential call. 'The preaching of the Gospel' to this people seemed to depend upon my immediate acceptance of the offer, so without hesitation I acceded, and forthwith removed to Stisted.

This was a very different sphere of action. All the duties of the parish of about 800 souls fell upon me. Dr Seale was advanced in years, and although once or twice a year on great [fo. 93r] [festivals] he would preach and often read prayers in the morning, with these exceptions I had the whole work to do, with two sermons in Summer and one in Winter, an arrangement with which the Doctor would allow no interference. Here my evangelicalism received a spur which did me no good. My predecessor Mr Escreet had held the curacy about three years. He had been entirely one of this school, very zealous and earnest, so the people expected a good deal, and it was my great ambition, I fear not of the purest character, to equal if not surpass my predecessor. I gave myself completely up to the work. Besides my two services on Sunday, I used to have a familiar exposition of Scripture in the chancel of the church in the evening, and on a week day evening at the work-house. We had also very efficient schools, so that my time was fully occupied in active duties. Here I obtained a lodging, humble enough indeed, but enabling me to receive my two sisters Harriet and Elizabeth who came to live with me. My zeal carried me on. I rebuked the Squire of the parish for taking [fo. 94r] God's name in vain, and I had no indisposition to preach truths which were not very palatable to my old rector. Still we went on together with much comfort, and I believe I was much liked by the poor people, not so much by the farmers.

Here I began to feel the painfulness of our reduced circumstances. While I had been alone, it was a matter of little consequence; but my pride was hurt at seeing my sisters in my poor abode, and of course much shut out from society. I believe it was this feeling which inclined me to seek an East India Chaplainship which was thrown

27 Thomas Dikes or Dykes (1761–1847), priest-in-charge of St John's, Hull, 1791–1846, a leading evangelical preacher. He had performed the marriage of Dodsworth's sister Jane to her cousin Thomas Haydon in 1819, Young, 'William Dodsworth', pp. 22–3.

28 John Escreet, born at Hull c. 1797. Died 8 Mar. 1823.

29 John Barlow Seale (1753–1838), vicar of Stisted 1792–1838.

in my way about this time. The stipend was an increasing one, beginning with £800 per annum. I thought I should be able to make my mother and sisters a handsome allowance out of this; and the sort of enterprise itself was perhaps not distasteful to me. But the notion of my going to India distressed my mother beyond measure. When first she heard of it she was residing at Guildford and well do I remember her coming at once to Stisted without notice (at which I was more annoyed than I ought to have been) to stop me. She positively declared that she would not receive one shilling of my stipend, and that my going to India would make her miserable. So there [fo. 95r] was nothing to be done but to give up the plan, which I did with a very ill-grace.

So I remained at Stisted for nearly three years when my youngest sister Elizabeth died in my house at the age of 23. I was exceedingly attached to her, the only sister younger than myself. She died after [*sic*] typhus fever after a few days illness.[30] This unexpectedly led to my removal from Stisted.

During my residence at this place I paid occasional visits to my sister Jane at Guildford, and there I first met Mr McNeile whom Henry Drummond had recently presented to the Living of Albury.[31] We at once struck up a very intimate friendship. I admired his open hearted bearing as a friend as well as eloquence as a preacher, and we became exceedingly intimate. My sister's death had excited a very strong feeling in my parish at Stisted, where she was much beloved for kindness to the poor, and as I was anxious to make the most of this feeling, I engaged my friend McNeile to come and preach the funeral sermon. In order to this I was compelled to exchange duties with him, and so I did not hear his sermon, but it was very offensive to my old rector. [fo. 96r] He did not like the doctrine, nor the action, nor the sermon being extemporaneous; besides which he had himself preached a sort of funeral sermon which he thought might have sufficed. On my return home he expostulated very freely with me on having introduced such a fire brand into the parish. In the mean while I had ordered a tablet, with a long inscription upon it for my deceased sister. It was of a very 'evangelical' character, and doubtless it was very imprudent in me to propose it being placed up in the church. Although perhaps there was nothing positively objectionable in it, yet it had that kind of party aspect about it, which in later times would have made it objectionable in my own eyes. Dr Seale positively refused his permission to its being placed in the church without the alteration of one or two expressions to which I most reluctantly consented. I expostulated on my side, and offered to give up the curacy, I believe under the impression that he would not like to part with me. However this might be, he replied, that unless I would engage not to bring into the parish such preachers as the 'Wild Irishman' as he called McNeile [fo. 97r] he thought it was better that we should part. I was far too self-willed to enter into any such engagement, and so I agreed to go. On such little matters do the greatest consequences of our life seem to hang. For had I staid [*sic*] at Stisted, how greatly altered had been the course of my future life. I cannot even conjecture what my future would have been, only something certainly very

---

30 Sarah Elizabeth Dodsworth, christened at Kirk Ella, Nov. 1799. Young, 'William Dodsworth', p. 47, gives her age at death as twenty-six, citing an announcement in the *Hull Advertiser*, 30 Oct. 1825.

31 Hugh Boyd McNeile (1795–1879), or Hugh M'Neile, initially a fervent evangelical preacher, was rector of Albury 1822–34, and moderator at the Albury conferences. He and Drummond became leading supporters of Edward Irving and shared his views on the premillenial second advent of Christ. He was afterwards dean of Ripon.

15 William Dodsworth, lithograph by C. Baugniet (London, 1845) (reproduced by permission of the National Portrait Gallery, London)

different from what it has been. I had made several friendships while at Stisted, Mr Strutt, afterwards Lord Rayleigh, Mr Marsh, Mr White, Mr Ware, the Savile Onleys of course and many others.[32] I believe I was very much liked here; and I am ashamed to confess the sort of gratification which I felt that I should be much missed. I fear that this was a stronger feeling than that of distress that my poor people were to be left to the tender mercies of my old rector, who was sure to avoid appointing another 'evangelical firebrand' like myself, as it turned out. I remember being presumptuous enough to warn them of the loss they might sustain by my leaving them though I must in candour say that this was done a good deal in imitation of what I had heard that Mr Escreet had done before me.

I had great excitement in leaving Stisted, [fo. 98r] many of the people coming to take most loving leave of me, which I think so much flattered my vanity as to soften the pain of separation. However I had some real regrets in bidding adieu to a people who I believe really loved me and valued my services such as they were.

In [] of [] 1826 I removed to Chiddingfold, a parish to which the dean of Salisbury had just presented himself as rector.[33] He engaged me as assistant curate, expressing his intention of residing part of the year himself. This intention however he never fulfilled, so that in fact for the first time I undertook the sole care of a parish. The preceding rector had been a kind charitable man, but of the 'dry' school, so very little had been done for the people in the way of bringing the people to earnest religion. I applied myself to this work with great vigor [*sic*]. I established a second sermon, and cottage lectures, but it was very uphill work. Still I believe some good was done. In other respects my curacy was very comfortable. I had an excellent rectory house and gardens, and my mother [fo. 99r] and sister Harriet lived with me until the latter married her cousin Joseph Haydon which she did during my residence at Chiddingfold.[34] I was but 11 miles from Guildford. My sister Jane and her family used to come and spend the summer months with me. The country was beautiful and altogether I was extremely well satisfied. Here a friendship for McNeile and Henry Drummond was much ripened, and I had very frequent intercourse with them. This led to important results.

I had hitherto belonged to what is called the evangelical party, and yet I had never felt entire sympathy with it. I can call to mind some little things which indicated this. At first going to Saxby I remember being disturbed, although I scarcely knew why, at the people in the crowded little church sitting upon the communion table. This may be [*sic*] now be regarded as a monstrous sort of liberty; but such things were entirely disregarded amongst low-church people of those days and I doubt not that my sort of instinctive objection would have been thought very preposterous then. In all such matters the feeling of the evangelicals was generally identical with

---

32 John James Strutt, second baron Rayleigh (1796–1873) underwent a religious conversion in 1822 and became a keen supporter of evangelical causes. He took part in the Albury conferences and was for a time associated with Irving and his circle. William 'Millenial' Marsh (1775–1864) made his parish in nearby Colchester a focus for evangelicals throughout Essex, and for the development of prophetic studies. On the Savill-Onley family of Stisted Hall, see Burke, *A genealogical and heraldic history of the landed gentry*, II, 1123.

33 Dodsworth omits the exact date of his move to Chiddingfold. Young, 'William Dodsworth', p. 49, indicates that he was officiating there from at least December on the basis of the parish registers, and cites his nomination as a stipendiary curate dated 28 Dec. 1826. The dean of Salisbury was Nicholas Pearson, a prominent evangelical.

34 Harriet Dodsworth married Joseph Haydon at Chiddingfold on 7 Apr. 1828.

that of dissenters, and indeed we none of us had any difficulty or compunction in attending dissenting worship. I can remember [fo. 100r] also being much disgusted with the apparent inconsistency of crying out against 'the world' while the evangelicals had 'a world' of their own. Still almost all real earnestness in religion seemed to be confined to that body, and of course I was classed as one of it. My intercourse at Albury Park however soon began to open my mind to many things of which I had hitherto been ignorant. Here I first met Lewis Way in 1826 and soon after Edward Irving.[35] In McNeile I found a man of very congenial disposition. Owing to the society we met at Albury Park we took up together the study of unfulfilled prophecy. Irving's book on the Revelations, and the translation of Lacunza, a Spanish catholic, and conversation with Lewis Way, opened our minds to this subject very much.[36] I now first began to feel the very great *narrowness* of the evangelical system and the greater part of that party resisted the study of prophecy in a very absurd way. As an instance I remember a most foolish and unargumentative book of Dr Hamilton of Scotland being in great repute amongst them.[37] The evangelical organ the '*Record*' newspaper took up the matter warmly against the study of prophecy. Then came Irving's remarkable book on 'The signs of the times' which in a most masterly way exposed the emptiness of the evangelical system.[38]

[fo. 101r] The result of all this was very much to shake me out of the evangelical system, though still belonging to that party, as in fact it was the only earnest one. But we saw great faults in it. McNeile went hand in hand with me, and about this time published a sermon called 'evangelical idolatry', the purport of which was to shew that the evangelicals put 'doctrines' in the place of Christ himself.[39] Now too 'the Albury Meetings' took place, which were the assembly of many clergymen and dissenting ministers to consider the subject of prophecy.[40] Still there was amongst us great enmity to the catholic church. Indeed the prevailing sentiment was that the pope was 'Antichrist', an opinion very much built upon the 1260 day-year system, which, as will be ultimately seen, had a very important influence on my own future.[41]

At the second of these 'Albury Meetings', Advent 1828, Mr Edward Vaughan of Leicester was present.[42] He broached some views on the authority of the church, which were comparatively new to us all. They very much commended themselves

35 Lewis Way (1772–1840), evangelical clergyman and promoter of the conversion of the Jews. Edward Irving (1792–1834), preacher and a leading voice in the premillenialist movement in evangelicalism; afterwards a founder of the catholic apostolic, or Irvingite, church.

36 Irving was the translator of Manuel Lacunza y Diaz, *The coming of the Messiah...by Juan Josafat Ben-Ezra* (London, 1827). His studies on the Book of Revelation at this time included *Babylon and infidelity foredoomed of God; a discourse on the prophecies of Daniel and the Apocalypse* (Glasgow, 1826) and *Lectures on the Book of Revelation* (London, 1829).

37 William Hamilton (1780–1835) DD, evangelical Church of Scotland minister at Strathblane, author of *A defence of the scriptural doctrine touching the second advent of Christ from the erroneous representations of modern millenarians* (Glasgow, 1828).

38 Edward Irving, *The signs of the times* (London, 1829).

39 *Evangelical idolatry. A sermon...by a clergyman of the established church* (London, 1829). The authorship of this sermon does not appear to be recorded in the British Library or other catalogues

40 From 1826 to 1830 Henry Drummond hosted week-long annual conferences on prophecy at his estate at Albury Park, Surrey. Dodsworth was a participant and preached at the 1829 conference, Young, 'William Dodsworth', pp. 52–3.

41 The day–year principle interprets a day in biblical prophecy to represent a year of actual time. References to 1,260 days in the Books of Daniel and Revelation were taken in some protestant circles to prophesy the reign of the pope as antichrist for a period of 1,260 years.

42 Edward Thomas Vaughan (1772–1829), vicar of St Martin, Leicester, 1802–29.

to my mind, which had already imbibed opinions tending that way. Still however these were rather views and opinions than principles. McNeile went the full length with us in them, and preached a sermon in [fo. 102r] St Clements Dane's [*sic*] about this time upon the text, 'Obey them that have the rule over you' which astonished his evangelical admirers.

Things went on in this way until the autumn of 1828, when my rector, the dean of Salisbury, gave me notice that he intended to come and reside in the rectory of Chiddingfold, which of course turned me out, and as there was no other adequate accommodation in the parish for my mother, involved the necessity of my leaving the curacy. Mr Drummond had recently purchased Margaret chapel, Cavendish Square, and offered the appointment of minister to it to me.[43] I had really very great difficulty in accepting it. First I disliked the thought of living in London. Second I disliked the system of pew-rents by which the chapel was supported. Third I had a sincere diffidence in my own powers for such a sphere. But when I was ordained I set out on a principle to which I was resolved to adhere. I would not choose for myself. I would take what Providence seemed to offer me. Had any country cure come in my way, suitable for me, how gladly should I then have taken it in preference to this London opening. Nothing however did come in my way, and so reluctantly I accepted Mr Drummond's [fo. 103r] with the express stipulation that I was to have nothing to do with the temporal affairs of the chapel. I was to receive the fixed salary of £300 per annum, whether the chapel filled or not. This in a great measure took off one of my objections.

In the meanwhile I had to leave Chiddingfold immediately, while Margaret chapel would not be ready for me till Lady Day 1829. How was I to fill up the intermediate time? Here an offer came to me from Mr Zachary Biddulph who had just been appointed to the Living of Shoreham.[44] He could not enter upon it for six months and wanted some one to fill up the intermediate time. This exactly suited me, and in [] 1828 I removed from Chiddingfold to Shoreham, where I took a lodging close to the church. Here I went on for six months. My ministry was abundantly successful in one way. The churches were well filled and I found a most willing and teachable people. I had far greater satisfaction in this charge than any that I had yet had, and I remember well, ardently wishing that I might have been allowed to give up Margaret chapel and remain at Shoreham. But this was not to be.

[fo. 104r] On the [] of March 1829, I first performed the duty at Margaret chapel; an eventful era for me, and fraught with consequences then little foreseen by me. I came indeed with great fear and trembling, and with most sincere misgivings as to my own powers for fulfilling the duty now devolving upon me. However I set to with the utmost vigour that I could command. I had two full duties every Sunday (at that time daily service was never thought of). I had intended also to visit all my flock. But my first attempt was unfortunate. The family of a tailor had a pew in my chapel. I called upon them, but only found the tailor, who first thought that I came to be measured, and, on explaining to him the real object of my visit, he said that

---

43 The Margaret chapel was a proprietary chapel within the parish of St Marylebone, London. Proprietary chapels were largely free of episcopal control. Drummond may have intended that the Margaret chapel should be a centre for spreading Irvingite thought. On this period in Dodsworth's life, see Young, 'William Dodsworth', pp. 44–122.

44 Zacchariah (or Zachary) Henry Biddulph (born *c.* 1792) was instituted to the vicarage of Shoreham, West Sussex, 4 Sept. 1828 (*Clergy of the Church of England database*).

he supposed 'I wanted the *pew rent*'. It turned out that he was an infidel and that his wife and daughters only attended church; and that my visit had only brought them into difficulties. This was a considerable rebuff to my zeal, and I found it needful to be more circumspect. However I made it known [fo. 105r] as widely as I could that it was my desire to visit those members of my congregation who wished to see me.

In the meantime my theological associations were undergoing a new phase. I fell in with Mr S. R. Maitland at Henry Drummond's.[45] In intercourse with him I became convinced that the 1260 day-year system had no ground to stand upon; which confirmed suspicions which I had before entertained that 'the papacy' was not marked out for condemnation in the prophecies. At this time also Mr Irving began to teach that church ought to possess the Gifts of the Holy Ghost, and certain supposed manifestations of these Gifts occurred in Scotland.[46] McNeile took up the subject warmly in favour of the church possessing such gifts, without however pretending to decide on these particular manifestations. I took essentially the same view of the matter, but I think somewhat less warmly than McNeile, the difference being that while he contended that the church ought to exercise them and preached a sermon in S. Clements [*sic*] Danes (I think) to that effect, I rather maintained what even now I believe to be the truth, that the indwelling of the Holy Ghost invests the church with the power of gifts and miracles; while the act of exercising them may for various causes be in abeyance. The ignorance of the evangelical body in general on such subjects was only equalled by its prejudice and the whole matter was met by these people [fo. 106r] with such senseless virulence as to predispose candid minds in the opposite direction. I was now on intimate terms with Edward Irving. His church was much frequented by us all; both on account of his eminent talents and of his teaching on prophecy. In those days no objection was felt to church people frequenting a presbyterian place of worship.

Altogether the subject of gifts and miracles was one of great perplexity, and the strange manifestations which occurred in various parts of the kingdom seemed not to be accounted for on motives of intentional deception. Mr Baxter of Doncaster, who was supposed to be endowed with these gifts, and was recognised as an 'apostle' by Mr Irving and his followers, was at length convinced that he was under a delusion. His withdrawal from them was an indication of his *honesty*, and he published an account declaring himself to have been under a supernatural power, which he could not continue, the power of evil as he now thought it.[47]

My reason for mentioning these matters is to account for that special prayer which now rose from many hearts 'to be guided into all truth.' We were in great

---

45 Samuel Roffey Maitland (1752–1866). Maitland attacked the folly of equating the 1,260 days in prophecy with calendar years in *An enquiry into the grounds on which the prophetic period of Daniel and St. John has been supposed to consist of 1260 years* (London, 1826). He became Lambeth Librarian in 1838.

46 In 1830 the final Albury conference was called to consider reports of occurrences in Scotland of ecstatic utterances (speaking in tongues), miraculous healing and inspired interpretations of scripture. These were associated with the visionary Margaret Macdonald (d. 1840) of Port Glasgow and Isabella and Mary Campbell of Rosneath. See Columba Graham Flegg, *Gathered under Apostles: a study of the catholic apostolic church* (Oxford, 1992), pp. 41–6. A report on a visit to the Macdonald family by the Plymouth Brother John Nelson Darby is among Dodsworth's papers (LPL, MS 4727, fos. 1–8).

47 Robert Baxter, a lawyer from Doncaster, attended Irving's church in London from 1831 and became endowed with prophetic utterances. He became disillusioned and wrote a *Narrative of facts characterizing the supernatural manifestations in members of Mr Irving's congregation ... and formerly in the writer himself* (Doncaster, 1833).

perplexity without any guide on earth, and it made us most earnestly pray for guidance from heaven. It seemed really as if religion had perished from the land. The old 'high and dry' looked on with contempt, [fo. 107r] the evangelicals positively scoffed, and the sort of religionism without religion which now began to prevail amongst them was most painful. The more earnest seemed groping their way in the dark. Prayer seemed our only resource and certainly we did most earnestly pray not to be allowed to reject anything that was from God, and that we might be kept from all delusions.

I am far from disinclined to trace my subsequent course to the most sincere and earnest prayers which I then offered up for divine guidance. Fully conscious indeed I am of much sin and imperfection in them, and in my general conduct at that time: nevertheless I may truly say that I was sincere and earnest in seeking light and I think no world sacrifice would have stood in the way of my embracing anything which I believed to be truth.

In the meantime my chapel was well attended. Amongst many others Lady Buller and her daughter became regular attendants as early as Easter 1829.[48] It is a curious circumstance that although, as I find from my wife's papers, that they were anxious to make my acquaintance, as I also certainly wished to know all my flock, my [fo. 108r] first visit to them at 7 York Terrace was not until July [] 1829. Nor was I at first struck with any admiration of her who was destined to be my future wife. Our acquaintance went on somewhat slowly at first: but by degrees we were drawn together by some attraction. In December 1829 I made my offer, which I considered as virtually although not formally accepted, and on October 28, 1830 we were man and wife.

The few years that followed were certainly those of the highest earthly enjoyment. I believe that nothing in this world could exceed out mutual love and mutual enjoyment in each other. Indeed we loved each other too well, shall I say *idolized* each other. It may be that it was this which brought upon us a just retribution from Him, who has called Himself a jealous God. Our sentiments were congenial. My dearest wife looked up to me as her guide, as well as her chief joy. On the other hand I thought nothing good enough for her, and while I may still say that in the ordinary sense I was attentive to my clerical duties, my delight [fo. 109r] was to be with her alone.

About the year 1834 two changes were in operation which began to mar this too sweet enjoyment of life. The one was that by the death of Mrs Willot, an old friend of Lady Buller, she was left alone.[49] I think it had always been a plan of my wife that whenever this event should take place her mother should live with us. To this proposal I could raise no possible objection, nor was I in the least inclined to raise any. I was very fond of Lady Buller and I believe that she had a mother's affection

---

48 Dodsworth married Elizabeth Buller-Yarde-Buller (1799–1856) at St Marylebone parish church on 28 Oct. 1830. She was the daughter of Sir Francis Buller-Yarde-Buller, second baronet (1767–1833) and his wife Elizabeth Lydia, *née* Halliday (*c.* 1774–1851), daughter and heiress of John Halliday of Lincoln's Inn and Dilhorne Hall, Staffs. *See* George Edward Cokayne, *Complete baronetage* (6 vols., Exeter, 1900–9), V, 261–2, and *Burke's peerage* under Baron Churston. In her will Lady Buller is named as 'Dame Eliza Lydia Buller'.

49 Elizabeth Willott, otherwise Willot, spinster of York Terrace, Regent's Park. Her will was proved in the Prerogative Court of Canterbury in March 1834 (TNA, PROB 11/1829). A substantial bequest to Lady Buller was transmitted in the latter's will to her daughter Elizabeth Dodsworth (PROB 11/2141).

for me. The arrangement for our ménage was very liberal on her part. The family was to be entirely ours, and she became our permanent guest. Certainly if such an arrangement is desirable under any circumstances there was a fair prospect of success in our case. [fo. 110r] and yet in the end it turned out very unhappily.

The other event to which I refer as occurring about this time is the opening of my own mind to catholic truth. This indeed took place very gradually, and it is difficult to say exactly when it began. Indeed I had long had feelings and tendencies in that direction. Certainly before I came to reside in London in 1829 I had a keen perception of the absurdities and inconsistencies of evangelicalism which was increased by my intercourse with Edward Irving; while my high church tendencies were strengthened by conversation with Edward Vaughan of St Martin's, Leicester. But as yet there was no 'high church party'. I had no sympathy with the 'high and dry', and so I still had chief intercourse with evangelicals, although I was regarded as somewhat of a black sheep amongst them. About this time however the [fo. 111r] publication of 'the Tracts for the Times' commenced and with that arose a 'high church party' which united zeal for the salvation of souls with the maintenance of church principles.[50] As a Cambridge man however I had little acquaintance with the Oxford School, and so was still very much left to my own resources. I had sometime before this established weekly communion, and the observance of saints' days at Margaret chapel; and I had diligently taught attendance on the ordinances of God as such, against the 'evangelical' tone which elevated preaching at the expense of other things. Before I came to London also I had begun to practise fasting on Ash Wednesday and Good Friday, which I carried to an undue length. So altogether I was well-prepared to sympathise with the party which now began to rise into notice at Oxford.

The first thing which caused any serious difference between my wife and myself was my beginning the practice of fasting every Friday. Even the Ash Wednesday and Good Friday's fasts, which I had observed from the first [fo. 112r] had been a trial to her: but when this came to be repeated every week, it became really intolerable to her. Had I been in the catholic [church] I might on this ground have obtained a dispensation. Had I not been a clergyman I perhaps might have dispensed myself; but I was placed in this dilemma. I felt myself bound to teach self-denial and in this the slight approximation to it in the weekly fast. And how could I teach what I did not myself practise? So in this our sorrows began. My wife could not bear to see me fast. When I persevered she tried to do it herself, with the worst effect for it increased her irritability. Her mother too was wholly opposed to this teaching, and was unhappy if she did not eat. I also was strongly opposed to her attempting to fast, first from her not being equal to it, and secondly from her avowedly not doing it from a right motive, i.e. only because I did it. So our Friday miseries were certainly very great. [fo. 113r] Another bad consequence was that the irritability made her look unfavourably and suspiciously at my teaching. Often she misinterpreted me and I can remember often and often coming home after sermon not knowing whether I would be met with black looks and repulsive manner. This I began to feel had an unwholesome effect on my ministry. It seemed to me that my wife interfered with me far too much and I in my turn became vexed and irritated.

---

50 The *Tracts for the Times* were published from 1833 to 1841. On the Oxford movement and its voluminous literature, see Peter Nockles, *The Oxford movement in context* (Cambridge, 1994).

All this however came on more gradually, so that although I mention the year 1834 as *about* the time my mind began to open to catholic truth, it is impossible to fix *any time* for the commencement of our domestic trials. They came on by degrees, and here certainly arose a great disadvantage in her mother living with us. No doubt her discomfort greatly aggravated my wife's [fo. 114r] feelings against my teaching, and Lady Buller's state of mind, combining what appeared to me a strong innate worldliness with all the strong features of 'evangelicalism', was a constant discomfort to me and probably acted as a spur to me in an opposite bearing. Then again, as our children grew, it became a constant source of uneasiness to see them more or less under their grandmother's influence although I must do her the justice to say that I never knew of her teaching them anything directly opposed to me. But it could not be otherwise than that her influence should have an opposite tendency to mine.

Then again, had we been alone, my wife would have leant more entirely on me. As it was an opposing interest was present, and she divided a dependence which ought to have been wholly mine. Not that I have the least reason to suspect that [fo. 115r] her mother directly influenced her against me or that she knowingly allowed other feelings to interfere with her allegiance to her husband. But it is not in the nature of things that such influences should be inoperative – in this instance I know that from some circumstances in my wife's early life, before she knew me, they were very powerful.

I would here repeat then, for the guidance of my children, my strong disapprobation of an arrangement which leaves a mother with a daughter in early married wife [*sic*]. It may be less injurious in later years when the habits of married life are fixed. If it had not been for my change of religious faith, no doubt we should have gone on better. Whatever might be her other faults, my mother-in-law was excessively amicable except in her hatred of the catholic church and of everything tending towards it. But even apart from this change of faith, I have experienced enough in married life to convince me, that it is at least [fo. 116r] exceedingly undesirable that a mother should live with a married daughter.

In 1836 I preached and published a short course of sermons on 'romanism and dissent'.[51] They shew the state of my mind at this period. I was in the *Via Media*. I thought that 'the Church of England' had found the happy line between two opposing systems of error, and to shew how very gradually our dissentions whether in church or family came on, I may say that these sermons were quite approved of at home, and even amongst many of my evangelical friends – in fact there was nothing like disruption at this time. Of course my teaching was looked upon with suspicion by the more extreme evangelicals, but on the whole I was liked well enough. I had overflowing congregations at Margaret chapel, and about this [time] I received the offer of the new church, which was to [be] built in Albany Street. A large portion of my flock came from Regents Park in that neighbourhood, so I had the less reluctance in accepting this [fo. 117r] proposal. In July 1837 the new church, Christ Church, Albany Street, was consecrated, and I was collated to it by the bishop of London in whom the presentation was vested.[52]

---

51 William Dodsworth, *The Church of England a protester against romanism and dissent* (London, 1836). The sermons were published in separate parts under this title.
52 Christ Church, Albany Street, London, the first church to be built under Bishop Blomfield's church extension scheme, was consecrated on 13 July 1837. Dodsworth was perpetual curate from 1837 to

16   William Dodsworth, engraving by an unknown engraver (reproduced by permission of the National Portrait Gallery, London)

This was a new sphere. I had a large parochial charge of about 14,000 souls, and I set about it with all the vigor [*sic*] I could command. I began with two curates, to whom I soon added a third from a fund raised at the offertory. I think that my increased responsibility helped me forward towards the catholic church, for I felt more and more how little hold protestantism could give over the people. I certainly did my utmost to put all forces to work. I established daily service, frequent lectures, a regular system of district visiting, communion on every Sunday and saint's day etc. etc.

I think we did make some little impression upon the poor – or rather on a small number out of my 14,000 people. My church was very largely attended and matters seemed to go on prospering enough. But in the mean while I was drawn closer and closer in my sympathies with the Oxford School. My teaching became more and more [fo. 118r] high-church. I began a close friendship with Dr Pusey and offended many of my friends by placing him in my pulpit, for he was everywhere spoken against and, although I well knew what odium I should incur, I thought it ungenerous not to shew the sympathy which I really felt with him.[53] Soon after we established the protestant nunnery and Dr Pusey's imprudence, and the excessive absurdity of these good ladies, who delighted to display their character of nuns, brought great odium upon me.[54] Many of my friends began to cool towards [me]. My church got a bad name as tractarian or romanising. Many forsook it.

The first indication of this was from the strong evangelicals. They took offence at my teaching sacramental grace and their defection took place before there was anything else to object to. I remember being much impressed with the hollowness of what is called 'influence'. I was supposed to have a good deal, certainly many had shewn considerable attachment to my ministry and had removed from Margaret chapel to Christ Church to follow it, [fo. 119r] and here I was working my heart out among the people. And yet no sooner did I attempt to lead these persons on to something beyond what they had been used to, and *to practice* [*sic*] *it*, than they forsook me for proprietory chapels where 'the minister' just attended for Sunday duty and spent the remainder of the week in some suburban villa. It was a result which did me good. However though I soon lost these strong evangelicals, others remained, and others were drawn to me, so that for long my church suffered no sensible diminution in numbers. But by degrees this consequence also followed, my congregation began to drop off, more especially when the Gorham case arose in the years 1848, 1849, but here I am rather anticipating.

In the year 1841 I first went abroad. I had been down in Scotland to the consecration of a protestant church, recently [fo. 120r] built by Lady Lothian at Jedburg,

---

1850, *Survey of London*, XXI (1949), 150–2. On Dodsworth at Christ Church 1837–50, see Young, 'William Dodsworth', pp. 156–254.

53 Edward Bouverie Pusey (1800–82). Young, 'William Dodsworth', pp. 170, 196, shows that he was a regular, if not frequent, preacher at Christ Church, Albany Street from Easter 1840 onwards; between 1845 and 1849 he preached on a dozen occasions.

54 The Sisterhood of the Holy Cross, known as the Park Village Sisterhood, was the first anglican religious community, founded in 1845. Dodsworth and Pusey were largely responsible for its foundation and development, although Dodsworth committed himself to working under Pusey's direction. See Thomas Jay Williams and Allan Walter Campbell, *The Park Village Sisterhood* (London, 1965). Dodsworth was against any revival of medieval religion and regretted that the sisters thought of themselves as nuns. See Young, 'William Dodsworth', p. 203. He and Pusey became increasingly estranged after 1848.

and here I ought to record a most providential escape from death which I had at this time.[55] Before going to Lady Lothian's I had a desire to see Loch Catherine and Loch Lomond, and with this view arrived at Callendar, where to book a gig to carry me to the Trossachs.[56] In going down the hill, the traces of the horse became loose. The horse ran violently away and began to kick. The driver jumped out and left me to the mercies of Providence. At the bottom of the hill, the horse ran up a bank and upset the gig. I was dashed to the ground and taken up completely stunned, my face much injured, the effects of which I sometimes feel to this day. It was a very narrow escape.

I went to Lady Lothian's, [and] wonderful to say was able to preach within a week. Here I received an invitation from Lord Campden [*sic*] to visit him at Brussels.[57] I felt it an opportunity for seeing foreign lands not to be lost, and accordingly I went.

[fo. 121r] Even at this time I was wonderfully prejudiced against the catholic church. But I sincerely desired to try everything by what I believe to be God's truth, and God blessed my sincere desires. Although I thought that there was much superstition, and was specially offended with the large dolls of B.V.M., I was very much impressed with the devotion of the people, and as I remember offending my friend Hook[58] by writing to Lady Lothian that 'the Belgians seemed to have attained what we were only looking for'. I think that from this moment I began to look upon the catholic religion in a very different light from that in which I had hitherto regarded it. I had thought of it as formal and external, chiefly consisting in forms and ceremonies. Here I saw these very forms and ceremonies accompanied with life and power. Still I was far from the church and indeed then thought it [fo. 122r] impossible that I should ever become a catholic. I had a strong conviction that the Church of England was the catholic church in this country, and my appreciation of foreign catholicism led to more than remove some prejudices. My feeling long after this was that if the Roman communion was more blessed than ours that was no reason why I should leave the Church of England. Nor indeed would it have been if this had really been a portion of the church.

In 1837 my mother had died. It comforts me to remember how much she had within her of the catholic ethos. How self denying she had been for many years! How patient under one of the greatest calamities that could befall a wife, and how humbly she had submitted herself to worldly losses and deprivations. Surely the root of the matter was in her. She could not be said to have rejected the catholic religion, for it never was presented to her acceptance, she had no more than that dim hazy

---

55 Cecil Chetwynd Kerr, marchioness of Lothian (1808–77), one of the earliest sponsors of tractarianism in Scotland. The consecration of St John's episcopal church, Jedburgh, built at her expense, was on 15 Aug. 1843, attended by Hook, Keble and other high churchmen, *ODNB*, XXXI, 410–11. See also T. Clarke, 'A display of tractarian energy: St John's episcopal church, Jedburgh', *Records of the Scottish Church History Society*, XXVII (1997), 187–219. Dodsworth appears to be incorrect in recording 1841 as the first year he went abroad if this followed his visit to Jedburgh.

56 Callander, Perthshire, a centre for visitors to Loch Lomond, Loch Katrine and the Trossachs.

57 George Charles Pratt, second marquess Camden (1799–1866). On his co-operation with Dodsworth in 1844–5 in founding the Park Village Sisterhood, see Henry Parry Liddon, *Life of Edward Bouverie Pusey* (4 vols., London, 1893–97), III, 13, 21.

58 'B.V.M.' indicates the Blessed Virgin Mary. Walter Farquhar Hook (1798–1875), vicar of Leeds 1837–59 and subsequently dean of Chichester. He preached frequently from Dodsworth's pulpit at Christ Church (Young, 'William Dodsworth', p. 170), representing an older style of high churchmanship rather than tractarianism.

knowledge of it which then belonged to the mass of [fo. 123r] protestants. She died while with me in York Terrace. May God forgive me for all my undutifulness to this excellent mother, whose chief fault perhaps was to love me too well. How often is such love abused by ill requitals!

In 1844 I lost my dear sister Harriet, who had long been a sufferer from a coup de soleil which she received at Brighton two years previous. She was greatly attached to me and from her great candour of mind I think she might have become a catholic if the subject had ever been fairly brought before her.

About this time I think the feelings of my wife began to undergo a change towards me; not, I would fain hope, that there was any real diminution of love, but chiefly from want of sympathy with my growing convictions. There was an estrangement. She became suspicious of me, and as I thought very unreasonable, especially in grudging me the least absence from her, suspecting me [of] things far from my mind, misinterpreting my teaching, and putting ill construction on all that I did. All this I really think amounted [fo. 124r] to disease in her. She often said she could no longer trust me, and I may mention it as really indicative of disease, that upon one occasion urging her to give reasons for this painful distrust, she could allege nothing more than that I had taken a house at St Leonards which she disliked, and which was dirtily furnished; the fact being that it was the only house at liberty and certainly not unsuitable for us. It had been a year or two before occupied by Baron Alderson and his family.[59] This is a slight matter to mention but it is a consolation to me to think that there was never anything really serious between us, except on the matter of religion. I am conscious indeed of innumerable failings, and although I cannot honestly reproach myself with any feelings towards her at any time except those of love and affection, I was certainly not unoften irritated by what I thought an undue interference in my ministry and by other things which seemed unreasonable.

I believe I may say that these ten years, commencing about 1840, were the great trial of my life. It was not indeed until towards the end of them that I had any thought of becoming a catholic. Many of my protest [] [fo. 125r] were still in full force, and I contemplated nothing beyond the carrying out of catholic principles within the protestant establishment. But this caused constant irritation to my wife and positive dislike in my mother-in-law, not, I sincerely believe, to me personally, for she always professed to love me, but to my ways of proceeding. To add to my trial it was the time when my wife was bearing children, and the sorrow which I was compelled to occasion her I believe really risked her life. Such was my position. I loved her dearly and tenderly. Often and often my convictions of truth and duty had to struggle with that love and overcome it. I was but groping my way to light and doubtless was guilty of errors and inconsistencies in conducting the affairs of my church, which were quickly laid hold of by my wife. I had to contend against great opposition in my parish. I offended many of my old evangelical friends. My children now growing up were exposed to opposite influences. I had no peace either at home or abroad. My place [fo. 126r] of shelter was my church, where, amidst many desertions and oppositions, I was training up a goodly number in a stricter life, many of whom came to me for auricular confession.

---

[59] Sir Edward Hall Alderson (1787–1857), judge, a baron of the exchequer. He was one of the wardens of Christ Church, Albany Street. *See* Williams and Campbell, *The Park Village Sisterhood*, p. 87.

During these ten years I paid two or three visits to the Continent, which were always accompanied with increasing veneration for the catholic church:[60] but still there were points to which I had, as I thought, insuperable objection, and I was still strong in the conviction that is would be sinful to leave 'my own communion'. In the year 184[] I preached a sermon on 'allegiance to the church' to that effect.[61] But I think I was more and more approaching to the feeling that it would have been a mercy to have been born within the catholic church, but that being an 'English catholic', as I thought, I had no choice in the matter. To one point I stood most pertinaciously which was that as long as I continued a minister of the established church [fo. 127r] I was bound by every principle of honor and honesty to minister its doctrines and its practices faithfully. If it was catholic, still it was obviously antagonistic to Rome, a point which could not be evaded or overlooked. Hence I felt not a little scandalised by some high tractarians, who, with less tendency towards the Roman Catholic church than myself, adopted and recommended their books, not such early ones as might on our principles be claimed as belonging to both communions, but even the recent Roman works. I had much difficulty in keeping them out of the Sisterhood established in my parish, and indeed they were introduced secretly, to my great distress.[62] Indeed I must say that I had the greatest difficulty in keeping the institution to the character in which it had been represented to the bishop of London.

I now began to suspect that the most favourable interpretation of the Thirty Nine Articles would scarcely be found compatible with the tenets which I [fo. 128r] considered to be taught by the catholic church. Although I could not quite accept 'Tract Ninety' I had found considerable alleviation by the line taken in that able treatise.[63] Again, I avoided as much as possible all controverted points on which the Articles had spoken, and as I had honestly subscribed them when called upon to do so, I persuaded myself that I might now put them aside for a while, being certain that I never contradicted them, but rather keeping in abeyance the question whether if *now* called upon, I could *ex animo* subscribe them. For instance, I taught strongly the Real Presence; but I left the question of transubstantiation untouched, never teaching it, and yet never contradicting it. I was conscious that this position could only be temporary and provisional.

About 1848/9 I was invited to allow myself to be proposed for a Scotch bishopric (Glasgow) and I had reason to believe that had I consented I should have been elected.[64] I hesitated for some time. As one of my difficulties was the Erastianism of the Church of England, this seemed [fo. 129r] so far to open a way of deliverance. But on more mature reflection I saw this was more in appearance than in reality: for beyond a doubt the Scottish episcopal church (a name sufficiently offensive) owes its existence and preservation to the English church, and seeks on every occasion to identify itself with it. At the same time, I should have been giving up a more arduous and responsible duty, and should have been leaving my people under a perplexity

---

[60] Dodsworth travelled on the continent with Manning in 1844 and 1847 and was in Paris in May and June 1850. *See* Young, 'William Dodsworth', pp. 215, 228.

[61] William Dodsworth, *Allegiance to the church: a sermon* (London, 1841).

[62] Young, 'William Dodsworth', p. 203, on the discovery of Roman Catholic books in the Sisterhood in 1848 causing Dodsworth to fear 'romanizing'.

[63] John Henry Newman's famous tract 90, *Remarks on certain passages in the thirty-nine articles* appeared in Jan. 1841.

[64] The Scottish episcopal see of Glasgow and Galloway became vacant in 1848 when Walter John Trower was appointed.

in which I had contributed to bring them. On laying the question before my friend H.E.M. he also strongly dissuaded me from the change.[65] So after no little trial I wrote to decline the proposal.

In the meanwhile matters were drawing to a crisis at Christ Church. Two of my curates, Mr Gordon and Mr New, became catholics.[66] The third, Mr Garside, felt it necessary to relinquish his post from tendency towards the same result.[67] This state of things compelled me to speak out. Also in some instances I was called upon, as I fairly might be, to use my influence to restrain others from submitting themselves to the catholic church. Of course I undertook the duty, but I was [fo. 130r] too lukewarm in the cause of protestantism to give much satisfaction. In fact though still shrinking from many things in the catholic church which I misunderstood, and misinterpreted, I could no longer adopt the common protestant language towards her. This could not be otherwise than a great trial to a clergyman who honestly desired to act up to the spirit of the Church of England. I admitted indeed, and still admit, the distinction between the positive belief of that body as professed in the Creed, and its protests in the Articles which might fairly be regarded as temporary and accidental. And this I think might fairly exempt any one from the charge of dishonest subscription, *so long as he could see no absolute contrariety between the Articles and his own faith and so long as he was no party to anything which he believed contrary to the law of Christ.*

But events were now occurring in the Church of England which seemed to force upon every enquiring mind an examination into the very foundations upon which it stood as separated from the rest of the catholic world. In 1848 Dr Hampden was nominated by the crown to the see of Hereford.[68] This gentleman had been censured by the University of Oxford for holding heretical [fo. 131r] opinions, and a very strong opposition was made by several of the bishops, as well as by others, to his admission into the episcopate. The case indeed in itself was lame enough, for although the university had censured him, it had allowed him to officiate within its walls a Professor of Divinity. The question however of his title to be admitted to the anglican episcopate did not turn upon the fact of his being heretical or otherwise. The law officers of the crown openly and avowedly maintained that assuming him to be a heretic there was nothing in the law of Church of England which could resist the power of the crown to appoint him. The Attorney General in memorable words asserted, without any contradiction from the Judges on the Bench (Denman, Patteson, Coleridge and Erle) that 'if the queen chose to make a bishop of a convicted felon, the church was bound to accept her nomination'.[69]

---

65 Henry Edward Manning (1808–92), afterwards Cardinal Manning.

66 John Gordon, curate at Christ Church 1842–6 was received into the Roman Catholic church in 1847, becoming an oratorian and one of Newman's closest friends. See Young, 'William Dodsworth', p. 176. Francis Thomas New, curate at Christ Church from 1840, *ibid.*, p. 176, converted with his wife in 1847 and became a solicitor (W. Gordon Gorman, *Converts to Rome* (new edn, London, 1910), p. 200.

67 Charles Brierley Garside, curate at Christ Church 1844–7, transferred to the Margaret chapel and was received into the Roman Catholic church in 1850 (Young, 'William Dodsworth', p. 176). He became a Roman Catholic priest (Gorman, *Converts*, p. 115).

68 Renn Dickson Hampden (1793–1868), nominated to the see in Nov. 1847 and consecrated in March 1848. High church opposition made the appointment a *cause célèbre*.

69 The Hampden case came before the Queen's Bench in Jan. 1848, when the attorney general, Sir John Jervis (1802–56) appeared as counsel for the archbishop of Canterbury before Thomas Denman, first

[Added note on fo. 130v] Note/ about the same time Dr Lee, nominated to the see of Manchester, was accused of drunkenness, on which ground his confirmation to the bishopric was resisted.[70] The question however was not allowed to be discussed. Whether a drunkard or not, it was contended successfully that the queen's will could not be resisted. [fo. 131r continued] The event seemed to justify the assertion, for the confirmation of the bishop was sustained, and all enquiry into his fitness disallowed. This was a strong indication of the Erastianism of the established church, and certainly was a severe blow to my allegiance to it. Still it seemed to me to have too much the character of an accident about it to affect me seriously. It was a difficulty, but then every difficulty was not fatal, and it rather affected persons than doctrine. Of course it was a grave consideration that an heretical bishop might [be] [fo. 132r] forced on the church, but then the question of his being heretical was never mooted. The University of Oxford was not an ecclesiastical body and had Dr Hampden been put upon his defence he might have cleared himself of the obnoxious imputation. We do not condemn even the notorious murderer without a trial.

But soon a case arose to which no such extenuating pleas could be applied. This was the Gorham case.[71] Mr Gorham had been presented to the living of Bampford [sic] Speke.[72] Dr Philpot [sic] the bishop of Exeter[73] refused to institute him on the ground that he held heretical opinions on the subject of baptism. The case was brought before the Court of Arches. The ecclesiastical judge, Sir Herbert Jenner Fust, decided in favour of the bishop of Exeter, on the ground that Mr Gorham denied the efficacy of Holy Baptism. Mr Gorham adhered to his doctrine and appealed to the judicial committee of privy council. The committee, composed entirely of lay-men, one or two of them being dissenters, took up the question and ultimately reversed the sentence of the church court below and imposed upon the archbishop of Canterbury the duty of instituting Mr Gorham.[74] By this proceeding many important questions were opened and forced upon the attention

1.   The entire subjection of the Church of England both in theory and practice to the civil power.
2.   The question of jurisdiction.
[fo. 133r] 3. The decision in favour of false doctrine.

The special relationship between church and state in England had long lain dormant. My own impression, and I believe it was the general impression of the clergy, was that at the time of the so called 'Reformation' the temporalities which it was supposed that the pope had usurped were handed over to the crown, and the spiritualities to the episcopate, or the dormant body 'Convocation'. Unquestionably great ignorance prevailed on the whole subject. The mention of the crown as 'supreme in all causes ecclesiastical as well civil' might have opened men's eyes.

baron Denman, Sir John Patteson, Sir John Taylor Coleridge and Sir William Erle (Richard Jebb, *An account of the case of the Right Rev. R.D. Hampden...* (London, 1849).

[70] James Prince Lee (1804–69), the first bishop of Manchester, was nominated to the see in 1847. An allegation of drunkenness led to a successful prosecution of his accuser for criminal libel in 1848.

[71] On this *cause célèbre* concerning George Cornelius Gorham (1787–1857) see J. C. S. Nias, *Gorham and the bishop of Exeter* (London, 1951).

[72] Brampford Speke, some four miles from Exeter.

[73] Henry Phillpotts (1778–1869), bishop of Exeter.

[74] The judgment of the judicial committee was given on 8 Mar 1850. Dodsworth's involvement in anglo-catholic meetings called at the time of the judgment is recorded in Newsome, *The parting of friends*, p. 351.

But in the first place, for many years they were mere words never put in force, and in the second place they might be loosely interpreted as recognising the right of the crown to see justice done to all its subjects in ecclesiastical as well as civil matters. Ignorance on this subject however was no longer possible. In the case of Mr Gorham a lay court had to decide upon a pure matter of doctrine of the most sacred character, and the helplessness of the church was perhaps made even more manifest by there being present three bishops who did not form part of the court, and had no voice in the matter. It would be impossible indeed that the complete subjection of the established church [fo. 134r] to the state could have been more fully shewn. The lay court reversed the decision of the ecclesiastical court, remitted the case back to it, and required the ecclesiastical court to force the institution of a clergyman whom it had already pronounced to be heretical: that is, it decided a purely spiritual matter without the intervention of any spiritual authority; and it did not even execute its own decision, but required the ecclesiastical authorities to do so. It was no mere act of power, like imprisoning a refractory bishop, or taking his authority into its own hands, but it exacted obedience from the bishops and they obeyed. No case could more plainly shew the entire subjection of the church to the state. If the Church of England professed to have the authority of Christ, it makes His authority subject to that of the crown; it is a state of treason against Him.

2. This case brought into clearer revelation the question of jurisdiction. First, as respected the ecclesiastical courts, second, as distinguished from orders. Hitherto attention had been so little drawn to a matter left entirely in abeyance, that I believe the fact was realised by few, that the jurisdiction of the English bishops and of course of their courts also is derived simply from the crown [fo. 135r] so that any decision even of the ecclesiastical courts has no higher than a temporal authority, and again the church, and not the state, has the power to send forth missions, to establish bishoprics. It belongs to the church not merely to ordain, but also to send forth. And again there was a general confusion prevailing between orders and jurisdiction: for instance the power of absolution was attached generally to orders, whereas an ordained priest has no real authority to remit sin unless he has received jurisdiction thereto.

These questions seemed to involve the necessity of examining into the very foundations of anglicanism, and into the grounds of the so called Reformation in England. We could no longer in honesty ignore such questions. The result of my own examination was the proof that the Church of England owes all its jurisdiction to the temporal power. In ordination, and even in the consecration of bishops, the Church of England is in a manner independent. The crown cannot ordain or consecrate, but in all matters of jurisdiction the crown is absolute and can confer episcopal jurisdiction even [fo. 136r] upon a layman, as Henry VIII did upon Cromwell.

3. These conclusions seemed almost to override the question of false doctrine. Still the decision of the privy council in favour of Mr Gorham had its own insuperable difficulties. By enforcing his institution and by the submission of the church through its bishop to that act, it constituted the efficacy of baptism an open question. The bishop of Exeter indeed at first talked of excommunicating the archbishop of Canterbury, who had to execute the order of the privy council, but he afterwards virtually retracted by recognizing Mr Gorham as vicar of Bampford [sic] Speke and exhorting the parishioners to obedience to him and in fact by continuing to communicate with the established church. Henceforth Mr Gorham taught the inefficacy of baptism, with just as much authority as the bishop taught its efficacy. In fact it

was ruled by the court of last record that the Church of England had not decided the question. Henceforth then it became the duty of every clergyman to examine whether he could honestly continue to set forth a sacrament in this point of view. For my own part nothing had been clearer to my mind than [fo. 137r] that, so long as I continued a clergyman of the Church of England, I was bound to teach as the church taught. If then the church left this question open, I might still indeed teach the true doctrine *as my opinion*, but I could no longer teach it *as her doctrine*. The result was quite obvious, which experience has since fully verified, that from this time this fundamental article of the Creed would become a mere matter of opinion.

Of course all these matters more than shook my confidence in the Church of England and forced upon me the question of 'unity' and of the grounds the English Reformers took against the authorities of the Roman Catholic church. Still I was slow to learn. The Gorham judgment was given early in March 1850 and it was not until the very last day of that year – a memorable day for me – 31 December 1850, that I yielded subjection to the one holy catholic church. I placed myself in the hands of Cardinal Wiseman, who after much kind converse remitted me to Father Brownbill, S.J.[75] who received me into the church, giving me conditional baptism.

The sacrifice which this act cost me can only [fo. 138r] be known to myself. It must be buried in my own bosom. Whatever in it meets the outward eye, loss of friends, of influence, of money etc is as nothing compared with what can only be known to me. Even my dearest wife never knew one half. The struggle which I had to endure was terrible, but God gave me the victory at last.

It was of course a great blow to my wife, and it was absolute estrangement from her mother. It created a great difficulty about our children. Happily my two boys were too young to create any difficulty with them. They, of course, became catholics with me. Four of our daughters were too old to be influenced otherwise than by reason, and of course I could not separate them from their mother. The fifth was my difficulty. She might have been sent to a catholic school and of course at her tender age would have conformed. But there would have been the seeming cruelty of separating her from her mother, and the breach of an understood and often expressed resolution that we would never allow our girls to go from under our own roof. I took some advice upon the matter, which fell in with my own bias to leave her with the others, first from the apparent hardship of separating her from them [fo. 139r] and secondly, from the hope that such a concession would be most likely to soften my wife and lead to her conversion also, by which we hoped all would be gained over. I confess that I have been sometimes tempted since to regard this as too worldly reasoning, and that I ought to have made sure of a soul while it was within my reach. Still *perhaps* such a course might have raised an opposition so powerful as to have deprived me of that blessing which is now the great solace of my life – the conversion of my dearest wife.

Lady Buller was now becoming very infirm so that we could not break up our establishment at Gloucester Gate. This was to me an additional trial, as it left me in the midst of my former parishioners and friends. Let me testify however that God gave me inestimable peace and joy in my own soul. It was as the beginning of new

---

[75] Nicholas Patrick Stephen Wiseman (1802–65), cardinal-archbishop of Westminster. Dodsworth conversed with Wiseman on 30 Dec. 1850 (Young, 'William Dodsworth', p. 239), and was received into the Roman Catholic church the following day by James Brownbill (1798–1860), a Jesuit who received many converts.

life to me, and yet great was my misery if for one moment I looked back, or took off my eyes from the one spring and source of my joy. The 1st of November 1851 my mother-in-law died. Olivia's[76] health required that we should go to Torquay, where we staid until July, and then partly for her sake, and partly for change of scene, we went abroad and spent three years in [fo. 140r] Italy. During that period I occasionally [] a tolerably full diary, which I need not here []. In December 1855 we returned home. Here my dearest wife began to sicken. After spending some months in London, 24 Chester Square, in August we removed to Lyne Grove, where I had my greatest joy and greatest sorrow.[77] My dearest wife became a catholic, and then was snatched from [me] yet never to be really separated ----.[78]

My daughters seemed at the time a good [] impressed, and here perhaps I erred again. [I] thought it ungenerous to press them under their sorrow. I refrained from saying anything on the subject of religion, under an eng[agement] from them, that they would in due [course] give the matter their full consideration. Engagement alas! they have not ful[filled] and I see I can do no good in pressing it up[on them]. I can only hope and pray and the same grace [which] brought their mother to the foot of the cross, may bring them also.

19 May 1857.

---

[76] Olivia, Dodsworth's daughter, born 1834. She married John William Philips in 1867.

[77] Chester Square, London SW1, an elegant square laid out between 1828 and 1840. Lyne Grove, a mansion at Chertsey, Surrey.

[78] Elizabeth Dodsworth died 20 Oct. 1856 at Chertsey. On her conversion, a few weeks before her death, see Young, 'William Dodsworth', pp. 248–50.

9

ARCHBISHOP DAVIDSON'S VISIT TO THE WESTERN FRONT, MAY 1916

Edited by
Michael Snape

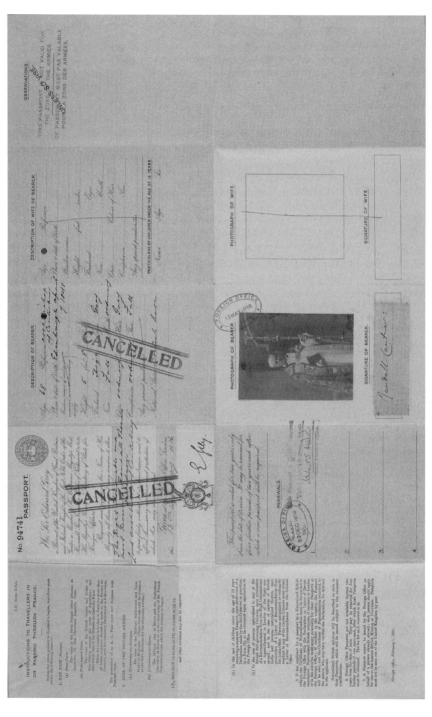

17 Archbishop Davidson's passport for his visit to the Western Front, May 1916 (LPL, Davidson 799/1)

Introduction*

It was the fate of Randall Thomas Davidson (1848–1930) to be archbishop of Canterbury throughout the supreme national crisis that was the First World War. While it introduced novel dilemmas involving clerical conscription and the rules of war (particularly as they concerned the use of poison gas and the aerial bombing of German civilians in reprisal for air raids on Great Britain), it also lent a new urgency to a host of pre-war issues and concerns within the Church of England, among them temperance, social purity, prayer book reform (especially as it touched on holy communion and prayers for the dead), ecumenical relations, the church's apparent estrangement from the working class and the manifold problems and constraints of establishment. Despite his Scottish presbyterian background and his chronic ill health (the result of a shooting accident as a child, an issue which had dogged his earlier years at Rochester and Winchester and had twice precluded his appointment as bishop of London), in other respects Davidson was ideally qualified to lead the Church of England through these turbulent years. Cautious, conciliatory and normally astute in his approach to political and ecclesiastical affairs, he did not shrink from confronting powerful government figures or from courting public odium, as when he opposed the bombing of German civilians in 1917. Nevertheless, he always retained the ability to mix comfortably in the House of Lords and in governmental circles. Widely popular on his retirement, and not least because of his mediation during the general strike of 1926, in Stuart Mews's judgment Davidson's great achievement as archbishop of Canterbury from 1903 to 1928 (the longest tenure of the see of Canterbury since the Reformation) lay in the fact that he preserved the 'comprehensiveness of the Church of England', he upheld 'liberty of thought' and he sustained a Christian influence on British public life 'at a time when international and class conflict could have obliterated institutional religion'. It was, undoubtedly, a remarkable performance and one that was suitably honoured in the bestowal of a baronetcy by King George V in 1928 and in the publication of George Bell's monumental biography in 1935.[1]

Despite being a rather fragile sixty-eight-year-old, as archbishop of Canterbury Davidson visited the Western Front from 16 May to 24 May 1916. At this stage of the war, the battle of Verdun was in progress, Allied preparations were in full swing for the battle of the Somme and the great, albeit indecisive, naval battle of Jutland lay but a few days ahead. Indeed, during the course of his own visit to the Western Front, on 21 May Davidson was to witness the intense bombardment that preceded a successful German attack on the Vimy Ridge sector, an attack that resulted in a significant loss of ground and in nearly 2,500 British casualties.[2] Although this was, as Davidson rightly noted, a unique visit for an archbishop of

* The editor is grateful to Dr John Bourne and Mr David Blake for their assistance with some biographical details.

[1] G. K. A. Bell, *Randall Davidson* (2 vols., London, 1935); *Oxford dictionary of biography* (*ODNB*); *Who's who in World War One,* ed. J. M. Bourne (London, 2001), p. 69.

[2] N. Cave, *Arras: Vimy Ridge* (Barnsley, 1996), pp. 52–63.

Canterbury to undertake, the advent of the steamship and the worldwide growth of the anglican episcopate in the nineteenth century had ensured that anglican bishops had already established themselves as potential visitors to war zones across the world. In 1854, for example, Bishop Tomlinson of Gibraltar had visited British troops in Constantinople, a crucial base for operations in the Black Sea and the Crimea, confirming several thousand soldiers and sailors and returning to recount his edifying experiences at public meetings in Great Britain.[3] During the Boer War, British troops were conspicuously well served by the anglican bishops of the South African province. W. M. Carter, bishop of Zululand, endeavoured to volunteer as a chaplain while A. G. S. Gibson, the coadjutor bishop of Capetown, visited a military hospital at Deelfontein in July 1900 in order 'to dedicate the graveyard [and] to hold a Confirmation service in the Church'. Some months previously, in December 1899, their colleague, Bishop A. H. Baynes of Natal, had helped to bury the dead after the battle of Colenso.[4] These precedents set, the outbreak of an increasingly global war in the late summer of 1914 ensured that anglican bishops would become frequent visitors to Britain's far-flung expeditionary forces. Before Davidson arrived in France in May 1916, the British Expeditionary Force (or BEF) in France and Belgium, by far the closest and largest of these, had already been visited by the archbishop of Armagh (J. B. Crozier) and also by the bishops of Birmingham (Henry Russell Wakefield), London (A. F. Winnington-Ingram), Pretoria (Michael Furse) and northern and central Europe (Herbert Bury).[5] These sometimes lengthy visits had often been accompanied with a good deal of publicity. The visit of the inimitable bishop of London at Easter 1915 was covered by *The Times* and the *Daily Mirror* and was described at considerable length in *The bishop of London's visit to the Front* (1915), an account that was written by his domestic chaplain, Guy Vernon Smith. Similarly, *The Times* published the bishop of Birmingham's account of his visit to the Western Front in September 1915, an account that later appeared as *A fortnight at the Front* (1915) and which was also featured in *The war illustrated* of September 1917.[6] If the visit of the bishop of Pretoria, Michael Furse, took place with less fanfare, it was no less significant for it marked an unprecedented intervention in purely military affairs. After spending an entire month 'in Northern France and Flanders', Furse complained of the BEF's acute shortage of shells in a letter to *The Times* in May 1915, thus adding fuel to the 'Shell Scandal' that had broken earlier in the month following the battle of Aubers Ridge and which led to the appointment of Lloyd George as minister of munitions.[7] Hence, when Davidson arrived in France in May 1916 the commanders of the BEF were already used to, and had cause to be more than a little wary of, the visits of influential churchmen.

Yet still they came. The mobilization of the Territorial Force, the raising of Kitchener's vast 'New Army' of wartime volunteers and, from early 1916, the unprecedented conscription of males of military age meant that never had the British

---

3   *Times*, 2 Nov. 1854, p. 9.

4   M. Blunden, 'The anglican church during the war', in *The South African War: the Anglo-Boer War 1899–1902*, ed. P. Warwick and S. B. Spies (London, 1980), pp. 279–91 at p. 286; *Church Times*, 3 Aug. 1900, p. 119, 2 Feb. 1899, p. 135.

5   Anon., 'The churches and the armies', *The Times History of the War* (22 vols., London, 1916), VIII, 313–52, at 328.

6   *Times*, 10 Jan. 1933, p. 7.

7   S. P. Mews, 'Religion and English society in the First World War', D. Phil. dissertation, University of Cambridge, 1973, p. 83; *Times*, 25 May 1915, p. 7.

army been so representative of the nation at large. For compelling political reasons, therefore, and also in the interests of military and civilian morale, the commanders of the BEF in particular had to play host to a long succession of ecclesiastical and other dignitaries, figures who ranged from King George V to Ben Tillett, the radical dockers' leader, whom Haig noted was a declared 'Socialist Revolutionary'.[8] Davidson's visit, which was timed to coincide with preparations for the battle of the Somme, Britain's largest offensive to date on the Western Front, was followed in July 1917 by that of Cosmo Lang, the archbishop of York.[9] Here again, Lang's twelve-day visit coincided with preparations for a major British offensive on the Western Front, namely the third battle of Ypres; indeed, Lang delivered addresses 'to six brigades of the [Fifth] Army, just before they made an attack' and he returned to England on the very day that the offensive commenced with the battle of Pilckem Ridge.[10] Episcopal visits continued into 1918, when the visiting bishop of Kensington, J. P. Maud, was pointedly not invited to lead 'a special service of thanksgiving and intercession' at GHQ to mark the fourth anniversary of the outbreak of war, Haig preferring that this be led by 'our own Military Chaplains'.[11] Even after the Armistice in November 1918, the Western Front remained an important destination for eminent churchmen. Davidson himself returned for a longer trip in January 1919, a trip that also included the British zone of occupation in the Rhineland and in which meetings with officers and chaplains concentrated on themes such as 'Church Unity, Reform, Demobilization, Church and Labour, [the] Y.M.C.A., Permanent Diaconate, etc.'. Furthermore, on his visit to the temporary school of instruction for prospective ordinands at Le Touquet, Davidson reiterated his earlier pledge that finance would no longer be permitted to serve as an insurmountable obstacle to those of modest means.[12]

Nor were other battle fronts or, indeed, the Royal Navy neglected. In two theatres of war, Egypt and East Africa, this was mainly due to the presence of displaced bishops. Unable to proceed to Palestine after his consecration as bishop of Jerusalem in Westminster Abbey on 28 October 1914, the day before Turkey commenced hostilities against the Allies, Rennie MacInnes went to Cairo instead, where he 'spent much time with the troops of the [Egyptian Expeditionary Force], helping the chaplains and confirming men from every part of the Empire'.[13] Similarly, British troops in east Africa were served bodily and spiritually by Bishop Frank Weston of Zanzibar, who raised and commanded the Zanzibar Carrier Corps from 1916.[14] In terms of visitors proper, Bishop Price of the Chinese diocese of Fuhkien visited the Gallipoli peninsula in October 1915 (he later joined the Army Chaplains' Department);[15] Lang visited the ships of the Grand Fleet at Scapa Flow,

8   G. Sheffield and J. Bourne (eds.), *Douglas Haig: war diaries and letters 1914–1918* (London, 2005), p. 247.

9   J. G. Lockhart, *Cosmo Gordon Lang* (London, 1949), pp. 257–8.

10   University of Birmingham, Church Missionary Society (CMS) Archives, XCMS ACC 18/F1/50–4, diaries of L. H. Gwynne, 31 July 1917; Lockhart, *Cosmo Gordon Lang*, p. 258.

11   G. J. De Groot 'The Reverend George S. Duncan at G.H.Q., 1916–1918', in 'Military miscellany I', ed. A. J. Guy, R. N. W. Thomas and G. J. De Groot, *Publications of the Army Records Society*, XII (1996), 265–434, at 403–4; G. S. Duncan, *Douglas Haig as I knew him* (London, 1966), p. 129.

12   Bell, *Randall Davidson*, II, 942–4; A. Wilkinson, *The Church of England and the First World War* (London, 1978), pp. 277–8; see below, p. 477 n. 34.

13   *Times*, 28 Dec. 1931, p. 12.

14   *Times*, 4 Nov. 1924, p. 19.

15   Imperial War Museum Department of Documents, 90/7/1 C.I.S. Hood, 31 Oct. 1915; W. Ewing, *From Gallipoli to Baghdad* (London, 1917), p. 59; Price was commissioned on 9 Feb. 1916 and seems to

Invergordon and Rosyth in July 1915;[16] Winnington-Ingram made a similar tour in 1916 and visited British forces in Salonika in 1918,[17] while the bishop of Nagpur, Eyre Chatterton, toured the expeditionary force in Mesopotamia in 1916 and 1917.[18] Nor were other denominations to be outdone in such public demonstrations of pluck and pastoral concern. The bishop of London's visit to France and Belgium in 1915 was quickly succeeded by the descent of Andrew Wallace Williamson, minister of St Giles's Cathedral, Edinburgh, and a former moderator of the Church of Scotland (indeed, these two visits led the young John Reith to wonder why his father, who was then moderator of the United Free Church, 'had not been invited to visit the troops in France').[19] Similarly, Cardinal Francis Bourne visited the Western Front in February 1915 and again in October 1917; he was the guest of Admiral Jellicoe and the ships of the Grand Fleet in the summer of 1916 and, in January 1917, he visited a British squadron at Taranto, shortly after he had presented a party of a hundred British sailors to Pope Benedict XV.[20] Another early visitor to the Western Front was the Chief Rabbi, J. H. Hertz, who came in June 1915 and who was entertained by the then commander-in-chief of the BEF, Field-Marshal Sir John French, and by its adjutant-general, Sir Nevil Macready.[21] By dint of its wide-ranging educational and religious work, the non-denominational YMCA added more names to this list of eminent church visitors to British troops in France and Belgium; John Kelman of Edinburgh, a United Free Church minister and a skilled propagandist for the Allied cause in the United States, made an unusually favourable impression on Sir Douglas Haig in 1917 while 'Gipsy' Smith, the most celebrated evangelist of his day, preached the good news on two extended visits to France in 1916 and 1917.[22]

Naturally, these excursions were presented to the British public as purposeful, salutary and even courageous exercises. Given the public debate over combatant clergy (and, as the war dragged on, over the clergy's exemption from conscription) of particular value was the element of danger they posed to senior ecclesiastics. If Sir John French had forbidden the bishop of London from visiting the front line in 1915, *The Times* stressed that Winnington-Ingram had nevertheless been 'well within the range of the German guns' and Vernon Smith was also careful to explain that 'Although he did not actually enter the trenches, the Bishop was often very close to the firing line, and once at least shells fell at no great distance to us.'[23] In a similar vein, the bishop of Birmingham was keen to emphasize that he had actually visited the trenches in September 1915, hearing the 'occasional ping' of a rifle bullet 'against a sandbag' and being warned off a road that was 'a favourite

---

have served the standard twelve-month term of a temporary chaplain; he rejoined the Department in 1918 and was appointed assistant bishop and archdeacon of Ely in 1919. *Monthly army list*, July 1916, 1793a; *Crockford's clerical directory*, LI (1920), p. 1218.

[16] Lockhart, *Cosmo Gordon Lang*, p. 257.

[17] S. C. Carpenter, *Winnington-Ingram* (London, 1949), pp. 289–90.

[18] Royal Army Chaplains' Department (RAChD) Archive, Amport House, 'Report on A.C[h].D. Mesopotamia'; E. J. Thompson, *The Leicestershires beyond Baghdad* (London, 1919), pp. 51, 108.

[19] *Times*, 12 July 1926, p. 19; J. Reith, *Wearing spurs* (London, 1966), p. 182.

[20] *Tablet*, 13 Feb. 1915, p. 208; Anon., *A British cardinal's visit to the Western Front* (London, 1918), p. 10; F. Bourne, *The cardinal archbishop's visits to the fleet* (London, 1917); E. Oldmeadow, *Francis Cardinal Bourne* (2 vols., London, 1944), II, 108 and 115.

[21] *British Jewry book of honour*, ed. M. Adler (London, 1922), p. 36.

[22] *The back parts of war: the YMCA memoirs and letters of Barclay Baron, 1915 to 1919*, ed. M. Snape, Church of England Record Society, XVI (Woodbridge, 2009), pp. 61–2, 78–80.

[23] G. Vernon Smith, *The bishop of London's visit to the Front* (London, 1915), p. 46.

target' for German machine-gunners.[24] Later in the war, shells fell within '25 yards' of the archbishop of Armagh and within 'fifty yards' of the archbishop of York.[25] However, and notwithstanding such quasi-heroics, reactions among the recipients of these visits could be mixed to say the least. George Duncan, who was effectively Haig's personal chaplain from early 1916 to the end of the war, was keenly aware that the commander-in-chief found the whole business rather irksome. As Duncan later remarked, Haig felt 'an instinctive dislike…to visitors from civilian life, and not least to churchmen, unless they came on a highly responsible mission'.[26] Indeed, faced with what he was prone to regard as clerical junketing, Haig was inclined to be quite severe in judging his guests. Of Cardinal Bourne, whom he met in 1917, Haig wrote: 'The Cardinal is neither eminent in appearance or in conversation but I expect means well'; however, an even harsher verdict was returned on Bishop Maud the following year, a prelate whom Haig judged to be 'an ordinary type of man, and scarcely up to the standard of Intelligence which ought to be expected in a Bishop'.[27] Furthermore, if Haig seemed to be 'rather taken' by Archbishop Lang when they met in 1917, he soon fell to lecturing the archbishop on the future of the Church of England. As Haig told Duncan: 'I told [Lang] that the church would have to alter its ways after the war: and one would like to see one great Church for the British Empire: and he was quite open &sympathetic'; in response, a sceptical Duncan 'told the Chief this was not the Cosmo Lang that we unfortunately knew in Scotland'.[28] Evidently, Davidson escaped quite lightly in comparison with similar visitors to GHQ.

However, visiting churchmen could not expect an unequivocal welcome even from their chaplains. If Roger Bulstrode, who attended Second Army's chaplains' conference at Talbot House on 17 May, described Davidson as 'a great and simple-hearted Christian who commended himself to all',[29] another infantry chaplain, Julian Bickersteth, was deeply disappointed by his encounter with the archbishop at the conference of Third Army chaplains two days later. Here, and prior to a rather chaotic and fruitless debate on the National Mission, 'the Archbishop spoke somewhat haltingly, his theme being the importance of our work and the amazing opportunity we had of influencing not only the coming generation, but the course of the world's history for the next hundred years'; at the end of the conference, so Bickersteth wrote, 'I think most of the chaplains agreed that the day was rather wasted, and the Archbishop's address quite lacking in fire or inspiration.'[30] However, such was the intense animosity felt by certain Irish Catholic chaplains towards the archbishop of Westminster that one of their number wrote in February 1915:

Cardinal Bour[n]e came for a bit of advertis[e]ment to this country. The King came to see his troops; yes, Card[i]nal must come to[o] to 'the front', but he always kept a day's journey from the range of the German guns. … This is not a safe place for a coward … Boulogne, Le Havre, Rouen, would supply a swell crowd of admire[r]s, and that was just what he wanted. The Archbishop of Rouen

---

24 *Times*, 14 Sept. 1915, p. 7.
25 Anon., 'The churches and the armies', p. 328. Lockhart, *Cosmo Gordon Lang*, p. 258.
26 Duncan, *Douglas Haig*, p. 130.
27 *Haig's autograph Great War diary* (microfilm, Brighton, 1987), 21 Oct. 1917, 4 Aug. 1918.
28 De Groot, 'George S. Duncan', p. 368; Duncan, *Douglas Haig*, p. 130.
29 Imperial War Museum Documents, 87/10/1 R. Bulstrode.
30 *The Bickersteth diaries, 1914–1918*, ed. J. Bickersteth (London, 1996), pp. 81–2.

invited him to the celebration of St. Jeanne D'Arck's [*sic*] feast or Beatification. Bourne could not come 'on principle', because the English burned her.[31]

These visits also met with a mixed response from officers and other ranks. While Davidson's tour was relatively low key (his health may have precluded the preaching marathons which marked the visits of Lang and Winnington-Ingram) that of other bishops was quite the reverse, involving a supporting cast of thousands of troops who were paraded to hear their words of wisdom and encouragement. Still, Winnington-Ingram, a popular figure in the metropolis and a long-standing chaplain to the London Rifle Brigade, seems to have been welcome enough. Frank Meryon Chance, a young subaltern in the 1/24th London Regiment (The Queen's), was disappointed not to have heard the bishop speak: 'On the Tuesday of Easter Week dear good Ingram came and preached to the Brigade. But I, who have always longed to hear him was not allowed to go, as I had some special trench work to do. I was very grieved at this, but I could fortunately easily see him.'[32] Other churchmen had, however, a lesser claim on their audiences; on Sunday 29 July 1917, for example, the anglicans of the 62nd (2nd West Riding) Division were paraded for a massive service led by the archbishop of York simply because they belonged to 'a Yorkshire Division'.[33] Five days earlier, Lang had addressed different brigades at five separate locations.[34] One of his numerous auditors in 1917 was Bernard Martin, a lieutenant in the 1st North Staffordshire Regiment, who tellingly confused Lang with the archbishop of Canterbury and recalled:

> I don't remember even his subject and I doubt if anyone in the battalion paid much attention – just another boost of morale ... as I watched his dignified performance with several attendant chaplains, my thoughts wandered amongst my war experiences ... all leading me to believe the war would inevitably bring changes in the established Church. Now I had doubts sufficient to stir again the disillusion I thought I'd overcome. What did Establishment leaders living in safety and comfort, know about war or any need for reconsidering beliefs [?] In bitterness I fancied the Archbishop back in Blighty, telling the House of Lords 'I've just returned from a visit to the Front ... our boys in high spirits ... won't be long before we have good news ... very soon now.'[35]

If widely assumed to be good for morale, the official purpose of these visits could vary considerably. However unenthusiastically he may have been received, Cardinal Bourne could at least claim that he had been vested 'by the Holy See with the spiritual care of all the Catholics in His Majesty's Army and Navy' and also that he was 'the ecclesiastical superior of the Catholic Chaplains in both services'.[36] Nevertheless, the situation was different for Bourne's anglican counterparts. With the chaplain-general, Bishop John Taylor Smith, officially in charge of their chaplaincy matters the visits of anglican bishops were emphatically not for the inspection

---

31 I. Fennessy, 'Fr. Peter B. Bradley and Irish Franciscan chaplains in World Wars I and II', *Irish Sword*, XXIII (2003), 449–61, at 451–2. I am grateful to Mr John Brennan for this reference.

32 University of Leeds, Liddle Collection, F. M. Chance.

33 CMS Archives, diaries of L. H. Gwynne, 29 July 1917.

34 Lockhart, *Cosmo Gordon Lang*, p. 258.

35 B. Martin, *Poor bloody infantry: a subaltern on the Western Front 1916–17* (London, 1987), pp. 146–8.

36 *Tablet*, 13 Feb. 1915, p. 208.

and direction of army chaplains. Furthermore, if in more distant theatres of war, such as the Dardanelles and Mesopotamia, these visits continued to be essential for confirmations and for the consecration of military cemeteries,[37] on the Western Front the need for such services declined over the course of the war. In April 1915, the bishop of London embarked on what was billed, significantly, as an Eastertide 'Mission' to the troops in France,[38] one that was intended 'to bring a word of love and greeting from friends in England' and which included a few confirmations and the consecration of military cemeteries.[39] However, with the appointment of Bishop Gwynne as deputy chaplain-general on the Western Front in July 1915, and the tightening of episcopal control that came with it, the need for a civilian bishop to conduct confirmations in France and Belgium diminished; furthermore, and as Davidson was to discover, the consecration of British military cemeteries ground to a halt in the face of understandable objections from the French authorities.

In essence, therefore, Davidson's visit was intended as a fact-finding and morale-boosting tour of the BEF. In terms of gathering information, Davidson's agenda involved surveying the British sector of the Western Front, meeting the commanders of the BEF and gauging the condition of France and the mood of the French church. The latter was of particular interest in the light of Winnington-Ingram's and Russell Wakefield's separate meetings in 1915 with the archbishop of Rouen and with Abbé Lemire of Hazebrouck, whose conciliatory views and gestures had led the bishop of Birmingham to conclude that 'there are great instances of breadth to be found within the ranks of Rome' and to declare that 'out of this war should come a possibility of a better understanding between the various religious bodies whose men are fighting for the Allies'.[40] In terms of morale, Davidson was largely concerned with meeting the anglican chaplains of the BEF and with discussing plans for the forthcoming National Mission of Repentance and Hope. However, and as Julian Bickersteth remarked, discussion of the National Mission could give rise to strong and confused debate, a phenomenon that was simply a reflection of the fundamental incoherence of the wider enterprise, of which the mission on the Western Front was intended to be but an 'echo'.[41] Envisaged by its early advocates as a collective act of self-examination and fundamental reorientation by England's national church,[42] in practice the National Mission was variously understood, poorly executed and widely criticized. Even its title proved puzzling to many and William Temple, perhaps its foremost champion, had to concede that there had been much dispute over the meaning of 'Repentance' in this context.[43] Furthermore, while wiser heads had counselled that this was an undertaking best left until after the war,[44] the

---

37 W. Wand, *Changeful page* (London, 1965), p. 82; The National Archives, WO 95/4989 principal chaplain [Mesopotamia] war diary.
38 *Times*, 12 Apr. 1915, p. 4; Vernon Smith, *Bishop of London's visit*, pp. 19, 44–5.
39 *Times*, 12 Apr., p. 4; Vernon Smith, *Bishop of London's visit*, pp. 10, 30–1, 56–7.
40 Vernon Smith, *Bishop of London's visit*, p. 81; *Times*, 14 Sept. 1915, p. 7.
41 L. Gwynne, *Religion and morale: the story of the National Mission on the Western Front* (London, 1917), p. 7.
42 Bell, *Randall Davidson*, II, 768.
43 D. M. Thompson, 'War, the nation, and the kingdom of God: the origins of the National Mission of Repentance and Hope, 1915–16', in *The church and war*, ed. W. J. Sheils, Studies in Church History, XX (Oxford, 1983), pp. 337–50, at p. 346; F. A. Iremonger, *William Temple* (Oxford, 1948), pp. 210–11; Wilkinson, *Church of England*, pp. 76–7.
44 Thompson, 'War, the nation, and the kingdom of God', pp. 346–7.

mission, which had been in gestation for more than a year, went ahead in October and November 1916, thus coinciding with the closing stages of the biggest, length-iest and bloodiest battle in British history. This unfortunate timing was not helped by the fact that individual dioceses were left to plan and carry out the mission as they saw fit,[45] although posters, literature and speakers were provided at a national level in order to supplement its services and public meetings.[46] If the National Mission's supporters could draw comfort from the fact that it took place at all, that it generated new committees and reports and that it strengthened the call for reform in the post-war Church of England, the non-churchgoing population remained largely unmoved by it.[47] While this seemed to reveal the depths of popular indifference towards the established church, the National Mission was also subjected to some trenchant criti-cism. To Horatio Bottomley, the super-patriot of the popular press, in view of the manifest nobility of the nation and of its soldiers at the present time the mission appeared to be 'an insult and [an] impertinence';[48] to Conrad Noel, the radically left-wing vicar of Thaxted, it was simply a 'Mission of Funk and Despair', while to the sardonic and cerebral Hensley Henson, then dean of Durham, it was all too clearly 'a grave, practical blunder',[49] one that Adrian Gregory has recently compared to the battle of the Somme – 'that other great national effort of the year' – in terms of disappointed hopes and wasted effort.[50]

If the National Mission misfired at home in the autumn of 1916, it took place somewhat later in the BEF, in 'December 1916, and the early months of 1917'.[51] Planning commenced within a fortnight of Davidson's departure, with the minutes of the newly established conference of senior anglican chaplains noting:

> National Mission of Repentance and Hope. The D.C.G. [Bishop Gwynne] called attention to the forthcoming attempt of the Home Church to face the problems raised, and to deepen the religious sense awakened, by the war. The S.P.C.K. had produced literature preparatory to it, and the recent visit of the Archbishop of Canterbury to the Front had, as one of its objects, the enlistment of the Expedi-tionary Force in the Mission.[52]

In August, B. K. Cunningham, the renowned clergy trainer, was invited to France in order to address gatherings of chaplains from each army; the same meeting also noted with evident approval the fact that Roger Bulstrode had begun to publicize the impending mission 'by means of circulars'.[53] At the November conference, and with the battle of the Somme now over, much of the discussion was given over to planning the details of the mission.[54] Cunningham made his anticipated tour the following month, his guidance helping 'towards the attainment of a common

---

[45] Bell, *Randall Davidson*, II, 768; Wilkinson, *Church of England*, pp. 73–4.

[46] Iremonger, *William Temple*, pp. 211, 213; A. Gregory, *The last great war: British society and the First World War* (Cambridge, 2008), p. 327 n. 49.

[47] Iremonger, *William Temple*, pp. 214–16; Wilkinson, *Church of England*, pp. 79–80; Gregory, *The last great war*, p. 171.

[48] Gwynne, *Religion and morale*, p. 56.

[49] Thompson, 'War, the nation, and the kingdom of God', p. 337; Iremonger, *William Temple*, pp. 209–10.

[50] Gregory, *The last great war*, p. 171.

[51] Gwynne, *Religion and morale*, p. 13.

[52] RAChD Archive, 'Proceedings of A.C.G.'s conferences', 6–7 June 1916.

[53] *Ibid.*, 17–18 Aug. 1916.

[54] *Ibid.*, 28–9 Nov. 1916.

message',[55] and the messengers ('all chaplains of the B.E.F.') began their work in their allotted districts at the end of December. Here, their missions took the form of 'an eight-day course of sermons, beginning and ending with a Sunday', this being supplemented by 'visits to outlying units, officers' meetings, and the like'.[56] If it could be claimed that their message was at least fairly consistent, the impact of the mission was inevitably uneven; despite its extended time frame, not 'every member of the Force heard the Message of the Missioners, for some of the divisions were actually fighting, and many units were on the move'.[57] Furthermore, its impression on those who were involved was uncertain. As Gwynne rather cagily put it:

> Perhaps little fruit has been gathered in, the barns have not yet been stocked, but soil has been prepared, and much seed has been sown; and at any rate the strong insistence upon the ideal side of the war has, we hope, contributed something to the morale of the British Army in the Field.[58]

Furthermore, it was clear that much useful discussion had been provoked and, so Gwynne rather pointedly remarked, 'whatever divergent opinions are held as to the value of the National Mission at home there can be no hesitation as to its usefulness out here'.[59]

While Davidson was keen to nurture the fruits of his visit, sending a letter of support to Gwynne in December 1916 in which he spoke of his hopes for the National Mission in France and of his 'imperishable recollection of the scenes and circumstances' of the chaplains' work,[60] he was also determined to ensure that a proper record was kept of his remarkable expedition. Only four days after his return, he dictated a full account to his secretary, Mary Mills, based on jottings he had made throughout his visit (in fact, he was working on this account as his train pulled into Victoria Station from Folkestone on the evening of 24 May). Subsequently, a typed version was produced which was illustrated with maps, postcards and his passport for the visit. This archiepiscopal scrapbook, as it were, was subject to further alterations and additions, in Davidson's own hand. What seems clear is that the account as it stands was never meant for publication at the time. In addition to the particulars of individuals and personal meetings which it contains, to say nothing of its military details, the publicity surrounding similar visits had clearly raised the ire of the military authorities and Davidson was, in any case, hardly a showman or a self-publicist. In short, what we have is a very personal account of the archbishop's experiences and reflections during a visit that marked a critical juncture in the course of the First World War and the history of the Church of England.

Editorial conventions

The spelling, punctuation, capitalization and underlining of the originals have been preserved. Davidson's later insertions and additions are shown in italic.

---

[55] Gwynne, *Religion and morale*, pp. 13–14.
[56] *Ibid.*, pp. 8, 14.
[57] *Ibid.*, p. 8.
[58] *Ibid.*, p. 46.
[59] *Ibid.*, p. 11.
[60] *Ibid.*, pp. 60–1.

Archbishop Davidson's war diary during May 1916

I begin to dictate this on Sunday afternoon, May 28th, 1916, Mary Mills being my amanuensis. It is to tell in brief outline the story of a visit (very memorable in my own life) to the Army in the Field and in the fighting line. It is dictated from rough notes made by me in pencil *day by day*, and expanded considerably in what I am now setting down.

I had wished last year, 1915, to accept the cordial invitation given to me to come to the Front on a full visit, but I was ill and absolutely forbidden to attempt it. A few months ago Bishop Gwynne, as Deputy Chaplain-General,[1] asked earnestly whether it would not now be possible. He had the warm concurrence of Sir Douglas Haig,[2] as Commander-in-Chief, and of the other Generals, with whom he had talked it over, and it was arranged that I should go in May when locomotion would be easier and mud would be less, so as to cover as much ground as possible. A good deal of preliminary business was necessary about papers and passports, and my own passport caused some amusement at the different places of examination and check, as my portrait, which had to be stuck in it, was a postcard portraying me with cope and crozier – not quite usual in a passport office. It was arranged that Bishop Gwynne should meet me at Boulogne, and that Canon Pearce, as Assistant Chaplain General,[3] should go with me thither from London. Accordingly we left

[1] Llewellyn Henry Gwynne (1863–1957), a product of St. John's College, Highbury, went to the Sudan as a CMS missionary in 1899, in the wake of its reconquest by Lord Kitchener, and was consecrated suffragan bishop of Khartoum nine years later. On leave at home when war broke out, he promptly offered his services as an army chaplain and arrived in France at the end of Aug. 1914. After several months serving as a chaplain in base areas and with an infantry brigade, he was appointed deputy chaplain-general (DCG) in July 1915 with responsibility for all anglican chaplains in the BEF. The creation of this new post, the promotion that accompanied it and the local schism that it represented in the organization of the Army Chaplains' Department (AChD), proved highly controversial among Gwynne's contemporaries. *Times*, 4 Dec. 1957, p. 13; M. Snape, *The Royal Army Chaplains' Department 1796–1953: clergy under fire* (Woodbridge, 2008), pp. 187–9, 256–7; H. C. Jackson, *Pastor on the Nile* (London, 1960).

[2] Douglas Haig (1861–1928) succeeded Field Marshal Sir John French as commander-in-chief of the BEF on 19 Dec. 1915 and remained in command until the end of the war. A devout, paternalistic and relatively innovative commander who attained the status of a national hero in the aftermath of the war, the scale of the losses incurred by the BEF under his command (largely unavoidable according to Haig's defenders, wholly unforgivable according to his detractors) and the mendacious and self-serving volumes of Lloyd George's *War memoirs* (1933–6) helped to undermine his reputation in the interwar period, to the extent that he is now widely seen, in anglophone countries at least, as the First World War's ultimate 'butcher'. Despite vigorous scholarly attempts to rehabilitate his reputation, Haig's performance as commander of the BEF remains a source of fierce controversy among historians. *ODNB*; *Who's who in World War One*, ed. Bourne, pp. 117–19; Sheffield and Bourne (eds.), *Douglas Haig*, pp. 1–43; M. Snape, *God and the British soldier: religion and the British army in the First and Second World Wars* (London, 2005), pp. 61–7.

[3] Canon Ernest Harold Pearce (1865–1930), formerly of St Peter's College, Cambridge (BA 1887, MA 1891), was treasurer of Westminster Abbey and was appointed honorary assistant chaplain-general (ACG) in Jan. 1916 in order to assist the chaplain-general, Bishop John Taylor Smith, with the running of anglican matters in the AChD. Formerly professor of bible history at Queen's College, London, and previously a chaplain in the Territorial Force, Pearce shared the chaplain-general's evan-

Charing Cross at 8.20 a.m. on Tuesday May 16th. At the station, besides our own circle (E.M.D., M.C.S.M., and Bell and Quick)[4] the Chaplain General[5] *with characteristic kindness* presented himself, and we went off in the officers' train to Folkestone. The steamer was crammed with soldiers, and one felt what a prize these loaded boats would be to the enemy. Ours was one of two boats crossing together, and the whole decks were a mass of khaki, the men being packed like sheep. The sea was smooth, and one felt how horrid it would have been if it were rough. *Lifebelts were available for everybody, but a great many did not wear them.* At Boulogne there were further passport identifications. Bishop Gwynne met me at the gangway with John Macmillan,[6] who is Military Chaplain at Tréport and was to be with me through my stay. We lunched at the Officers' Club in Boulogne, together with Gooch, senior Chaplain at Boulogne,[7] and Woodward, *of Southwark*,[8] who was

gelical background and outlook and was known as having 'great capacity as a man of affairs'. Like the post of deputy chaplain-general, that of ACG was a wartime creation. At the same time that Pearce was appointed to lend a hand in the chaplain-general's office, anglican ACGs were also appointed to each home command and to each army and major base on the Western Front. Pearce became archdeacon of Westminster in June 1916 and bishop of Worcester in Jan. 1919. *Times*, 29 Oct. 1930, p. 16; Anon., 'The churches and the armies', p. 320.

4   Edith Murdoch Davidson (1858–1936), the second daughter of Archbishop Archibald Campbell Tait and Davidson's wife of forty years, *Times*, 27 June 1936, p. 16; Mary Mills, Davidson's secretary, *Times*, 30 May 1930, p. 16; George Kennedy Allen Bell (1883–1958), Davidson's biographer and later bishop of Chichester, formerly of Christ Church College, Oxford (BA 1905, MA 1910), trained at Wells and ordained deacon in 1907 and priest in 1908, appointed as one of Davidson's two domestic chaplains in 1914, *ODNB;* Bell, *Randall Davidson*, I, 715; Oliver Chase Quick (1885–1944), another of Davidson's domestic chaplains, formerly of Corpus Christi College, Oxford (BA 1909), trained at Farnham, ordained deacon in 1911 and priest in 1912, *Crockford's clerical directory*, XLV (1913), p. 1233.

5   Namely Bishop John Taylor Smith (1860–1938). A product of St John's College, Highbury, and formerly a CMS missionary and bishop of Sierra Leone, Taylor Smith was appointed chaplain-general in 1901, his principal qualifications being his episcopal rank and his personal links with the royal family. An earnest evangelical who had been raised a Wesleyan, he divided opinion in the Church of England during the early months of the war, being denounced by some critics as a bigot who discriminated against Anglo-Catholic candidates for chaplains' commissions. Whatever else, the appointment of Bishop Gwynne as DCG on the Western Front in July 1915, and of Canon Pearce as an honorary ACG in Jan. 1916, were symptoms of the extent to which he had lost the confidence of the wider church by the time of Davidson's departure for France. However, Taylor Smith remained in office, retiring as chaplain-general in 1925. *Times*, 29 Mar. 1938, p. 18; Snape, *Royal Army Chaplains' Department*, pp. 174–9, 185–9; M. Whitlow, *J. Taylor Smith: everybody's bishop* (London, 1938).

6   John Victor Macmillan (1877–1956), formerly of Magdalene College, Oxford (BA 1899, MA 1902), was trained at Farnham before being ordained deacon in 1903 and priest in 1904. He had been one of Davidson's domestic chaplains for more than a decade (1904–15) before he was commissioned into the AChD on 26 Oct. 1915. Macmillan ended his career as bishop of Guildford. *Crockford's*, 1913, p. 973; *Monthly army list*, July 1916, 1792b; Bell, *Randall Davidson*, I, 46 and II, 1415; *Times*, 16 Aug. 1956, p. 11.

7   Actually, Thomas Sidney Goudge (1870–1954). Formerly of Merton College, Oxford (BA 1893, MA 1912), Goudge was ordained deacon in 1893 and priest in 1894. After serving as a curate in England, he was commissioned into the AChD in South Africa on 1 July 1901, having served as an acting, or probationary, chaplain since 1898. Goudge was a chaplain Third Class on the outbreak of war, with the relative rank of major, and he was promoted to temporary chaplain First Class, with the relative rank of colonel, on 24 Apr. 1916. He was still serving as the senior anglican chaplain in Boulogne at the end of 1917. http://www.thePeerage.com, p. 24478, consulted 30 July 2009; *Crockford's*, 1913, p. 595; *Quarterly army list*, June 1914, p. 1741; *Monthly army list*, July 1916, 1789; RAChD Archive, 'Proceedings of A.C.G.'s conferences', 7 Nov. 1917.

8   Clifford Salisbury Woodward (1878–1959), formerly of Jesus College, Oxford (BA 1901, MA 1904), was ordained deacon in 1902 and priest in 1903 after training at Wycliffe Hall. A chaplain of Wadham

going out as Chaplain, and a few others. After luncheon I paid my respects to the Military Commandant in his office,[9] and then Mac and I drove off in Gwynne's car, with him, to the great base station at Etaples.[10] It was rather a new country to me, among the sand dunes and fir trees, and then undulating fields with women working everywhere. The same sight became familiar in the days which followed, and one grew accustomed to seeing respectable tradesman-like women, or farmers' wives, in black, driving all the carts, and girls and older women working in all the fields. *Naturally, in May-time* I did not see any ~~actual~~ *of them actually* ploughing, but many were driving harrows and other machines, and in the villages there were literally no Frenchmen to be seen, only women and our own khaki-clad soldiers. In one case a few days later I saw a woman shoeing a great Flemish horse, with its foot upon her knee, like an ordinary blacksmith. I was struck throughout by the quietness and simplicity of their working, and, as always in France, every yard of soil is cultivated.

We got to Etaples, some fifteen miles off, about 4 p.m. This great base was a wonderful sight – camps for sick men and sick horses; training schools of different sorts; rows of hospital huts and tent hospitals. Blackbourne, the Senior Chaplain, whom I had known years ago,[11] is in general charge of the clerical department and seems to do it well. There was a gathering of chaplains and officers for tea, and I had *plenty of talk with most of them and* an initiation into the rules and systems of the great place, extending literally for miles. A healthier looking spot one could hardly imagine – hills and fir trees and dry sand and bushy copses. We walked through parts of the camp and I visited some of the wards in the hospital and made friends with the American ladies who are there in force as nurses, being part of the hospital gift from the United States.[12] A long hut ward is converted into a Chapel,

College and a lecturer at Wycliffe Hall from 1910, in 1913 Woodward became rector of St Saviour with St Thomas, Southwark. During his incumbency he became known for his practice of holding open-air prayer services during Zeppelin raids. Commissioned into the AChD on 15 May 1916, he won the MC while serving with the 47th (London) Division on the Somme. Woodward was wounded in Oct. 1916 and returned to England. He went on to become bishop of Bristol in 1933 and bishop of Gloucester in 1946. *Crockford's*, 1913, pp. 1677–8, and 1920, p. 1677; *Monthly army list*, July 1916, 1794b; *Times*, 15 Apr. 1959, p. 15; B. Baron, *The doctor: the story of John Stansfeld of Oxford and Bermondsey* (London, 1952), pp. 30 and 161.

9   Colonel Herbert William Wilberforce, great-grandson of William Wilberforce, grandson of Bishop Samuel Wilberforce and son of the Ven. Albert Basil Orme Wilberforce (1841–1916), archdeacon of Westminster and chaplain to the House of Commons. Archdeacon Wilberforce had died only three days previously. A. F. Becke, *History of the Great War based on official documents. Order of battle part 4. The Army Council, G.H.Q.s, armies, and corps 1914–1918* (Uckfield, 2007), p. 16; *Times*, 15 May 1916, p. 4.

10   A base later made famous by the Etaples mutiny of Sept. 1917, the most serious outbreak of collective indiscipline in the British army during the course of the First World War. Nevertheless, its scale was relatively minor and its nature restrained in comparison with outbreaks of unrest in other armies during the last two years of war. In its aftermath, only four charges of mutiny were pressed and only one of the defendants executed. R. Holmes, *Tommy: the British soldier on the Western Front 1914–1918* (London, 2004), pp. 347–8.

11   Jacob Blackbourne (1862–1936), formerly of University College, Durham (BA 1896), was ordained deacon in 1885 and priest in 1886. He was commissioned into the AChD on 14 Apr. 1898 after having served for two years as an acting chaplain at Aldershot and, before that, as a curate and vicar in Lincolnshire. He saw active service in the Boer War and in Somaliland and had served in a number of home and overseas garrisons before Aug. 1914, by which time he was a chaplain First Class. From the particulars of Blackbourne's career, it is unclear in what capacity he had become known to Davidson. *Crockford's*, 1913, p. 139; *Quarterly army list*, June 1914, p. 1741; *Times*, 28 Mar. 1936, p. 14.

12   Although neutral until Apr. 1917, as 'an English-speaking, liberal, non-militaristic nation', American

and there I met all the chaplains. Gwynne conducted some intercessory prayer and I addressed them, together with Church Army *Captains* and other *male* lay-workers.[13] I tried to arrange to visit the Church Army huts afterwards, but it was too late, as we had a very long drive before us. We got off soon after six, and drove first up the river Canche to Montreuil, now our Army Headquarters.[14] The country was beautiful – Montreuil a most striking place, the old village standing on a steep hill and glowing in the evening sun. We did not go up to the hill, but walked by the river, and found the charm of scenery which has attracted artists for many generations. Mac had known it well, having been there several times in childhood and boyhood. Then we drove on to the north-east, some parts of the country being beautiful and all glowing in spring greens. It is curious to think of this as the country of Creçy and Agincourt.[15] We passed through the striking village of Fauquembergues [*sic*], which we were afterwards to know well, about eleven or twelve miles from St. Omer. We got to St. Omer before 8.30. I was lodged with Mac in one of the houses which Bishop Gwynne occupies, an ordinary French house in a very French street. He himself sleeps in another, but takes his meals *in the one we occupied, using it* there, using the one we occupied as a kind of guest-house. His two staff officers, Drury[16] and Thorold,[17] both regular chaplains, and nephews respectively of Bishop

public opinion (with the significant exceptions of its Irish-American and German-American constituencies) tended to sympathize with the Allies. In addition to selling the Allies vast amounts of war materiel, a significant amount of humanitarian help was also forthcoming from the United States. In June 1915, the Chicago Medical Unit arrived in France to work with the BEF, taking over No. 23 General Hospital at Camiers, then part of the base at Etaples. T. Wilson, *The myriad faces of war: Britain and the Great War, 1914–1918* (Cambridge, 1988), pp. 90–1; C. Messenger, *Call-to-arms: the British army 1914–18* (London, 2005), p. 408 footnote.

13 An array of civilian religious organizations worked with the British army in France and Belgium. These included the Church Army, the YMCA, the Salvation Army, the Catholic Women's League, the Friends Ambulance Unit, Catholic Huts for Soldiers Abroad, the Scottish Churches Huts, the Army Scripture Readers' and Soldiers' Friend Society and the Navvy Mission Society. Hundreds of male and female volunteers worked with the Church Army on the Western Front during the course of the war including, by the beginning of 1918, nearly 300 anglican clergymen. The organisation was answerable to Bishop Gwynne after his appointment as DCG in July 1915. Lambeth Palace Library, Davidson papers, vol. 254.

14 The General Headquarters (or G.H.Q.) of the BEF was relocated from St. Omer to Montreuil in Mar. 1916. Duncan, *Douglas Haig*, p. 20.

15 Fought, respectively, on 26 Aug. 1346 and 25 Oct. 1415. Both were bloody and spectacular English victories over the French, a historical irony that was not lost on educated Britons. R. Holmes (ed.), *Oxford companion to military history* (Oxford, 2001), pp. 9, 234–5.

16 William Drury (1876–1943), the nephew of Thomas Wortley Drury, Bishop of Ripon, was formerly of Corpus Christi College, Cambridge (BA 1898, MA 1906), and was ordained deacon in 1899 and priest in 1900 after training at Ridley Hall. After a brief curacy in Birmingham, he became an acting chaplain in Dec. 1901 and was commissioned into the AChD on 22 Feb. 1903. Drury served in South Africa during the later stages of the Boer War and had risen to chaplain Third Class by Aug. 1914, after having served as a garrison chaplain in Woolwich and in Singapore. He was promoted to temporary chaplain Second Class, with the relative rank of lieutenant-colonel, on 16 Nov. 1914 and was appointed assistant to Bishop Gwynne on 6 Aug. 1915. J.C. Welch, 'The Klip river manouevres of 1903', *Journal of the Society for Army Historical Research*, LXXVI (1998), 111–125; *Crockford's*, 1913, p. 438; *Quarterly army list*, June 1914, p. 1741; *Monthly army list*, July 1916, 1789.

17 Ernest Hayford Thorold (1879–1940), the nephew of Anthony Wilson Thorold, Davidson's predecessor as bishop of Rochester (1877–91), was formerly of Queen's College, Oxford (BA 1901, MA 1908), and was ordained deacon in 1904 and priest in 1905. Following a curacy in Battersea, Thorold was commissioned into the AChD on Christmas Eve 1906, having been an acting chaplain since the previous Aug. Thorold served as a garrison chaplain in England and South Africa and was a chaplain Fourth Class, with the relative rank of captain, in Aug. 1914. He was promoted to temporary chaplain

Drury and Bishop Thorold, dined with us, also the Provost-Marshall [*sic*], a lively and interesting man.[18] I found a good deal to ponder over in my first day's experiences. At night in *the* silence one could hear the guns *continuously booming* in the distance eastwards.

Wednesday May 17th. At 8 a.m. we had a Celebration in the improvised Chapel, made out of an office and forming the ground story [*sic*] of a large recreation room for the soldiers above.[19] The neighbouring chaplains, some fifteen in all, and the Church Army officers etc. were present. I celebrated and gave a short address. After breakfast, Mac and I left Gwynne in the office, and went off in Gwynne's car to Poperinghe. The drive was flat at first and then we had to cross the hill of Cassel, which is the Headquarters of our Second Army, under General Sir H. Plumer.[20] It is a most striking and picturesque place, the only hill in the flat plain, having glorious views. It is said that in very clear weather the coast of Kent is visible, and it is always possible on a clear day to see the sea near Dunkirk. We saw it on the occasion of the visit described below, p. [513]. We got down and walked about the town. Plumer was in London and had had tea with us *at Lambeth* on Monday. From Cassel we passed by Steenworde, across the Belgian frontier (passports again) to Poperinghe,[21] some 24 miles from St. Omer. There, at Talbot House,[22] the building

---

Third Class on 8 Mar. 1916. A talented staff officer and administrator, Thorold became chaplain-general in 1931. *Crockford's*, 1913, p. 1500; *Quarterly army list*, June 1914, p. 1743; *Monthly army list*, July 1916, 1791; Snape, *Royal Army Chaplains' Department*, p. 279; J. Smyth, *In this sign conquer* (London, 1968), p. 309.

18 Brigadier-General William Thomas Francis Horwood (1868–1943). Commissioned into the 5th Lancers in 1888, Horwood had left the army to serve as chief of police on the London and North Eastern Railway in 1910. He rejoined the army in 1914 and served as provost-marshal of the BEF from Dec. 1915 until the end of the war. He was appointed commissioner of the Metropolitan Police in Apr. 1920. *Times*, 20 Apr. 1920, p. 15; *ODNB*.

19 This model is very much that of a late Victorian anglican soldiers' institute, a model that was also followed in the configuration of Talbot House at Poperinghe. Snape, *Royal Army Chaplains' Department*, pp. 142–3; see below, n. 82.

20 Herbert Charles Onslow Plumer (1857–1932) commanded Second Army from May 1915 to Nov. 1917 and from Mar. 1918 to the end of the war. Although Plumer's walrus moustache and rotund stature inspired the cartoon character of Colonel Blimp after his death, he emerged as the most popular British general of the First World War, partly due to Second Army's prolonged defence of Ypres and its successful offensive at Messines in June 1917, but also due to his genuine paternalism and to his singular talent for public relations. In the interwar period, 'Daddy' Plumer's reputation as the British soldier's favourite general was cemented by his high-profile support for the fledgling Toc H movement. A devout high churchman, Plumer frequented the chapel at Talbot House in Poperinghe and, according to Charles Harington, his principal biographer and former chief of staff, he marked the commencement of the battle of Messines by kneeling in prayer for his attacking troops. *Times*, 18 July 1932, p. 17; *Who's who in World War One*, ed. Bourne, pp. 234–5; P. Simkins, 'Herbert Plumer', in *Haig's generals*, ed. I. F. W. Beckett and S. J. Corvi (Barnsley, 2006), pp. 141–63; Snape, *God and the British soldier*, pp. 67–8.

21 Poperinghe, a sizeable market town, was an important railhead for the BEF and served as the gateway to the Ypres Salient. Although not ravaged to the same extent as Ypres, it often came under fire from German heavy artillery. *Letters from Flanders: some war-time letters of the Rev. P.B. Clayton (Tubby) to his mother*, ed. B. Baron (London, 1932), pp. 42–3; L. MacDonald, *They called it Passchendaele* (London, 1993), pp. 15 and 78.

22 Inspired by Neville Talbot and originally leased from a local brewer, 'Talbot House' (or 'Toc H' in the signaller's phonetic alphabet of the time) was opened in Dec. 1915. It is still unclear whether it was named after Neville Talbot or after his younger brother, Gilbert, who had been killed outside Ypres in July 1915. Home to a soldiers' club known as 'Everyman's Club', Talbot House also comprised an impressive attic chapel known as 'The Upper Room'. Despite its striking egalitarianism (proclaimed by a famous placard that read 'ALL RANK ABANDON YE WHO ENTER HERE'), the model for

which Neville Talbot had formed into an Officers' Club [*sic*] *(*the officers giving it the name, in spite of his protests*)* we met Neville Talbot,[23] Clayton,[24] McCormick,[25] and some others who were expecting us. The car left us, going back all the way to St. Omer, to fetch Gwynne for the afternoon. We walked about Poperinghe and

Talbot House was that of the pre-war Church of England soldiers' institute. These institutes had originated in Aldershot in 1880 and spread to the larger garrisons of the British empire in subsequent decades. Often linked to individual dioceses, these facilities sought to provide wholesome recreation for ordinary soldiers and were intended to bring them into contact with their chaplains in surroundings where the formalities of rank could be set aside. University of Birmingham, YMCA Archives, K24 YMCA War Work No. 4 religious, letter of E. S. Talbot, Easter 1919; F. H. Brabant, *Neville Stuart Talbot* (London, 1949), p. 61; Snape, *God and the British soldier*, pp. 216–18; Snape, *Royal Army Chaplains' Department*, pp. 142–3.

23 Neville Stuart Talbot (1879–1943) was the second son of E. S. Talbot, the distinguished theologian and bishop of Southwark (1905–11) and Winchester (1911–23). Commissioned into the Rifle Brigade in 1899, Neville had seen active service in the Boer War. However, in 1903, and by now a staff officer in South Africa, he chose to resign his commission in order to study at Christ Church College, Oxford. He was ordained deacon in 1908 and priest in 1909, when he was also elected chaplain of Balliol College. Neville was commissioned into the AChD on 30 Aug. 1914, along with his brother, Edward Keble Talbot of the Community of the Resurrection, and he enjoyed rapid promotion while serving on the Western Front. He became senior chaplain of the 6th Division in 1915 (in which capacity he was the driving force behind the creation of Talbot House), senior anglican chaplain of XIV Corps in Apr. 1916 and ACG of 5th (or Reserve) Army in Sept. 1916. He was also awarded the MC in Jan. 1916. During the course of the war, Talbot also became an outspoken champion of reform in the Church of England and, from 1917, he was a strong supporter of the Life and Liberty movement. *ODNB*; Brabant, *Neville Stuart Talbot*; *Monthly army list*, July 1915, 1793a; University of Birmingham, CMS Archives, XCMS ACC/18/Z/1, army book of L. H. Gwynne, p. 227; N. S. Talbot, 'The training of the clergy', in *The church in the furnace: essays by seventeen temporary chaplains on active service in France and Flanders*, ed. F. B. MacNutt (London, 1917), pp. 267–87; N. S. Talbot, *Thoughts on religion at the Front* (London, 1917); Snape, *Royal Army Chaplains' Department*, pp. 188, 237–9; *The National Mission of Repentance and Hope: reports of the archbishops' committees of inquiry. The worship of the church, being the report of the archbishops' second committee of inquiry* (London, 1919), p. 39; *Crockford's clerical directory*, LXVI (1937), p. 1297.

24 Philip Thomas Byard Clayton (1885–1972), formerly of Exeter College, Oxford (BA 1909, MA 1912), was ordained deacon in 1910 and priest in 1911 and was serving as a curate of St Mary's, Portsea, on the outbreak of war. He was commissioned into the AChD on 26 May 1915 and his first posting in France was to Le Tréport as a hospital chaplain. From there Clayton was posted to the 16th Infantry Brigade in Nov. 1915, a brigade which was then part of 6th Division, whose senior anglican chaplain was Neville Talbot. Although briefly posted to Boulogne in June 1916 and to the 29th Division that Aug., Clayton spent the greater part of his war in and around the town of Poperinghe. He was its garrison chaplain from Sept. 1916 and, while he also distinguished himself ministering to artillery units in the Ypres Salient, he is principally remembered for his incumbency and ministry at Talbot House and for his work in connexion with the later Toc H movement. *Monthly army list*, July 1915, 1791; *ODNB*; *Letters from Flanders*, ed. Baron, pp. 10–13; P. B. Clayton, *Tales of Talbot House* (London, 1920), pp. 147–9; Snape, *God and the British soldier*, p. 60; CMS Archives, Army book of L. H. Gwynne, p. 44.

25 William Patrick Glyn McCormick (1877–1940), formerly of St John's College, Cambridge (BA 1899, MA 1907), was ordained deacon in 1900 and priest in 1901. Following a short curacy in London, he served as an acting chaplain during the closing stages of the Boer War and remained in South Africa as a missionary, where his sporting prowess worked to his advantage in the mining areas of the Rand. McCormick was commissioned into the AChD on 28 Aug. 1914, was senior chaplain of the Guards Division from 1915 to 1917 and deputy assistant chaplain-general of XIV Corps from 1917 to 1918. In 1919 he was ACG at Boulogne. McCormick had a colourful, high-profile career in the post-war church, making numerous radio broadcasts and being the first clergyman to appear on British television. He became vicar of Croydon in 1919 and vicar of St Martin-in-the-Fields in 1927. *Crockford's*, 1913, p. 959; *Monthly army list*, July 1916, 1792b; *ODNB*.

18   Postcard of Fauquembergue church, see pp. 469 and 479–80.
(LPL, Davidson 583, fo. 9)

19 Fauquembergue, postcard of Impasse Guerlet, post office and church (LPL, Davidson 583, fo. 9)

20 Postcard of Cassel, 'vue générale', see pp. 473 and 513 (LPL, Davidson 583, fo. 13)

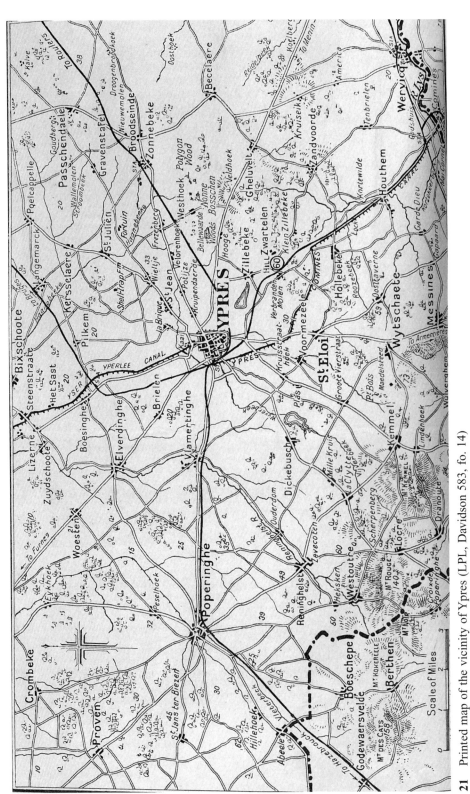

21 Printed map of the vicinity of Ypres (LPL, Davidson 583, fo. 14)

found Norman Davidson[26] at headquarters office, and his car then took us, i.e. Norman, Mac, Neville Talbot and myself, to Ypres. It is an absolutely straight road of about nine miles, and we were now within *the near* sound of the constant guns, and as we *approached* neared Ypres the road grew more and more war-strewn, the trees all broken, every house smashed and uninhabited – the road itself ploughed up by shell marks everywhere and being constantly repaired. It is the only road into Ypres this way and consequently has at night to be used for all the *road* transport, and the Germans therefore shell it continuously. Before getting near Ypres we had to put on steel helmets,[27] furnished to us at Poperinghe, and each to carry the gas mask in a bag ready for use at a moment's notice.[28] The shelling at Ypres was still going on, but was quiet at the time we were there, or at least not severe enough to make General Fielding [*sic*][29] prohibit our going there *about the shattered streets*. I afterwards learned from General Plumer, in command of the Second Army, that if he had been in France he would have forbidden my going to Ypres. Fortunately he was not.

The scene in Ypres itself is indescribable.[30] The Cathedral and the Cloth Hall are simply piles of ruins, lying in heaps, both inside and outside the rectangular remains of the shattered walls.[31] The broken Cloth-Hall tower is upstanding in a tottering and mutilated condition. Also part of the Cathedral. I brought away with me a piece of the Cathedral glass. There are practically no houses in the town undestroyed, and our soldiers are occupying dug-outs or cellars. We walked through the ruins every-where, and I visited some of the men in their cellars and dug-outs and examined their quarters. Those I saw had grown used to the life and its conditions and perils, and were very quietly going about their avocations, or taking their rest, or (several) shaving, and all were most ready to talk. Our own guns concealed among ruins were

---

[26] A son of Davidson's younger brother, Henry. Lieutenant-Colonel Norman Randall Davidson DSO of the Royal Horse Artillery died near Ypres on 5 Oct. 1917. Bell, *Randall Davidson*, II, 780; http://www.cwgc.org. consulted 30 July 2009.

[27] These were something of a novelty at the time of Davidson's visit, having only been issued to soldiers of the BEF from the autumn of 1915. A. Rawson, *British army handbook 1914–1918* (Stroud, 2006), pp. 245–6.

[28] The Germans had first used poison gas on the Western Front in Apr. 1915. At this point of the war, the commonest British gas mask, or gas helmet, consisted of a flannel bag with glass eyepieces, treated with a compound of glycerine, sodium carbonate and thio-sulphate. Rawson, *British army handbook*, p. 246.

[29] Major-General Percy Thynne Feilding (1866–1932) was commissioned into the Coldstream Guards in 1888 and served with distinction during the Boer War. In Aug. 1914 he was commanding the 3rd Coldstream Guards but was given command of the 149th Infantry Brigade, 50th Division, in Apr. 1915. On 3 Jan. 1916 Feilding was appointed to the command of the Guards Division, a post that he held until Sept. 1918. *Times*, 24 Oct. 1932, p. 9; A. F. Becke, *History of the Great War based on official documents. Order of battle part 1. The regular British divisions* (Uckfield 2007), p. 25.

[30] By the end of 1914, Ypres was the only Belgian city still in Allied hands. During the course of the war, it was subjected to constant bombardment and the Germans made determined attempts to take the city in 1914, 1915 and 1918. Together with those of St Martin's Cathedral, the ruins of the city's thirteenth-century cloth hall soon became the 'twin architectural icons' of Ypres' 'epic ruination'. P. Gough, '"An epic of mud": artistic interpretations of Third Ypres', in *Passchendaele in Perspective*, ed. P. Liddle (London, 1997), pp. 409–21, at pp. 412–13.

[31] Although his earth and masonry ramparts had long been outgrown, Ypres had been fortified by the great French military engineer Sébastian le Prestre de Vauban in the late seventeenth century. Holmes, *Tommy*, pp. 21–2.

22 Postcard of the interior of the chapel of Talbot House, Poperinghe, Easter 1916. See pp. 477–8 (LPL, Davidson 583, fo. 21)

23 Potcard of the market place at Fauquembergue, see pp. 479–80 (LPL, Davidson 583, fo. 25)

firing fairly continuously. We went to the gate of the Eastward, the Menin Gate,[32] and walked about the ramparts, formerly a wooded promenade, now a tangle of broken trees, barbed wire, dug-outs, and shell-holes. Nothing more devastated can be imagined. Then we rambled back through the town. Shelling was going on, but no shells were falling in Ypres itself while we were there, though our own guns were noisy, and Norman being with us we were allowed to examine some of them in their hidden places among the ruins. After leisurely examination of it all we drove back to Poperinghe, which had been bombed by an aeroplane during our absence. The aeroplane passed over Ypres while we were there, on its return eastward, and our guns fired at it continuously and, so far as we could judge, harmlessly. We watched the shells bursting round it.

At Poperinghe we lunched with General Fielding and his staff, among whom Norman is an obvious favourite. Neville Talbot and Fielding had a vehement disputation about Haldane etc.[33] of which I got rather tired – wanting to see more and being very familiar with the sort of conversation. Then we went to Talbot House, where in the garden, there was a large gathering of Church of England chaplains, some sixty (?) in number. We had a fairly lively discussion on the question of the relation of Army work at present to the National Mission; on a possible supply of new ordinands after the war,[34] and on other kindred topics. Then a stand up and walking about tea at which the Presbyterian and other non-Anglican chaplains joined us, including 'Ralph Connor' the Canadian (Mr. Gordon).[35] I think I had a talk with every man, and some of them were full of interest. I was very much struck with the quiet simplicity, and even the unconscious dignity of the chaplains, some of whom I had known quite well; and all of them seemed to me to have 'grown' in the best sense. Then we went to an exceedingly 'upper room', a long garret which has

---

[32] Subsequently the site of Sir Reginald Blomfield's memorial to the missing of the Ypres Salient, which was unveiled by Lord Plumer in June 1927, http://www.cwgc.org/search/cemetery_details. Consulted 24 Dec. 2008.

[33] Richard Burdon Haldane (1856–1928), Liberal secretary of state for war from Dec. 1905 to June 1912 and subsequently lord chancellor. In the face of much opposition and criticism, as secretary of state for war Haldane had carried out far-reaching reforms of the British army, including the creation of the Territorial Force, the establishment of the Officers Training Corps and the preparation of the BEF as a deployable entity. Despite the fact that he made an unrivalled contribution to preparing the British army to fight another European war, with the outbreak of war with Germany he was hounded by the right-wing press for his alleged pro-German sympathies and was dropped from the new coalition government in May 1915. *Who's who in World War One*, ed. Bourne, pp. 119–120; *ODNB*.

[34] The future recruitment of working-class ordinands, especially former soldiers, became a key demand of reform-minded chaplains during the course of the war; indeed, 'Tubby' Clayton even kept his own register of prospective ordinands at Talbot House. Swayed by this pressure, in Feb. 1918 Davidson informed Convocation that he had formally assured the chaplain-general that 'all really suitable and qualified men who desire to be candidates for Orders, and who are chosen as suitable for it' would not be precluded from training due to their 'financial difficulties'. Bell, *Randall Davidson*, II, 884; Snape, *God and the British soldier*, p. 29; Snape, *Royal Army Chaplains' Department*, pp. 250–1; S. Mews, 'Clergymen, gentlemen and men: World War I and the requirements, recruitment, and training of the anglican ministry', *Nederlandsch Archief Voor Kerkgescheiden*, LXXXIII (2004), 435–47.

[35] Charles William Gordon (1860–1937) was a presbyterian chaplain who served on the Western Front with the Canadian Expeditionary Force. A popular novelist before the war, he preferred to write under the name of Ralph Connor. D. Crerar, *Padres in no-man's land: Canadian chaplains and the Great War* (Montreal, 1995), pp. 46–7.

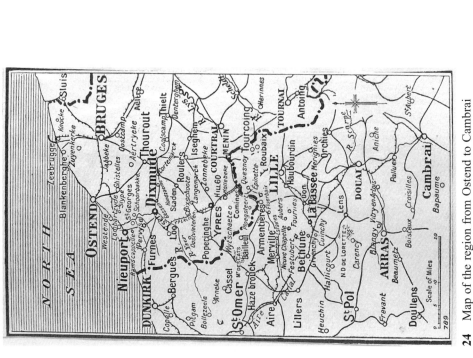

25 Map of the region from Bethune to Amiens (LPL, Davidson 583, fo. 28)

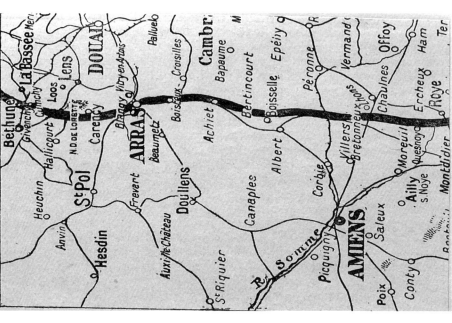

24 Map of the region from Ostend to Cambrai (LPL, Davidson 583, fo. 28)

been cleverly transformed into a Chapel at the top of Talbot House.[36] There in an overflowing meeting we had prayers and a full address from me upon the uniqueness of our present responsibilities and the splendour of our opportunity. Gwynne had by this time joined us. After the address the chaplains left, except those who were concerned in the ensuing confirmation. Clayton presented about 36 or 40 men, a few of them officers, and all of them keen.[37] The chapel was crowded with others and the scene was to me indescribably pathetic. Guns firing outside, though a little way off, and the men presenting themselves for confirmation with obvious and unabashed earnestness, corresponding with the courage they show in thus coming forward among their fellows. I spoke to them shortly and simply. All had been admirably arranged by Clayton.

Then we drove back to St. Omer, the road seeming to me in my tiredness rather interminable, and found Dr. Simms, the head Presbyterian chaplain,[38] awaiting us for dinner. I was glad to get the opportunity for [a] full talk with him, and of showing our appreciation and sympathy with his difficulties. He strikes me as being more of an officer than an ecclesiastic. But he is keen and quiet and digni-fied, and quite obviously in earnest on behalf of the men and the organisation. It did not altogether surprise me that he should have proved himself so thin-skinned on questions of comparative rank and dignities. I tried to 'rub in' the fact that our chaplains have no wish for military rank, and only accept it because of War Office rules and orders.[39]

Thursday May 18th. Dr. Simms came to breakfast at 8 and we had more talk. At 9 Gwynne, Mac and I drove via Fauquembergues, where a great market was going on in the square which we had seen so quiet on Tuesday. We walked about the market, where our Tommies were being, so far as I could judge, rather shamelessly charged

---

36 The ornate chapel of Talbot House was captured in picture postcards of the time (see illustration 22). Its hangings (which had formerly adorned the bishop's chapel at Southwark) were donated by Bishop Edward Talbot, its altar was a renovated carpenter's bench (unrailed, in keeping with the ethos of Talbot House) and various units and individuals supplied its fixtures, fittings and memorials. The existence of this 'Upper Room' reflected necessity as well as invention and devotion for anglican chaplains were normally debarred from using catholic churches in France and Belgium. Snape, *God and the British soldier*, pp. 216–18; Snape, *Royal Army Chaplains' Department*, p. 233.

37 This confirmation is but one illustration of a religious revival that was widely experienced by the BEF prior to the battle of the Somme. Much commented upon in numerous quarters at the time, it has been too readily dismissed as illusory by subsequent historians. Snape, *God and the British soldier*, pp. 164–8; *The back parts of war*, ed. Snape, pp. 75–8; N. E. Allison, 'Baptist chaplains' revivalism at the Front (1914–1918)', *Baptist Quarterly* , XLII (2007), 303–13.

38 Dr John Morrow Simms (1854–1934) was an Irish presbyterian minister who was commissioned into the AChD on 29 Mar. 1887. He subsequently saw active service in the Sudan, South Africa and in Somaliland. As the most senior of the department's First Class chaplains, Simms was principal chaplain of the BEF from Aug. 1914 to Nov. 1918. However, his jurisdiction was much depleted with the appointment of Bishop Gwynne as DCG in July 1915. As a regular chaplain with twenty-eight years service, Simms was understandably aggrieved that Gwynne's appointment was accompanied by a temporary promotion to the relative rank of major-general, a slight that was also decried by presbyterians at home. In the event, Simms's resignation was averted and some backstairs political lobbying ensured that he received the same promotion in 1916. By 1919, Simms's stature was such that he was elected moderator of the Presbyterian Church of Ireland and, in 1922, he entered the Westminster parliament as Unionist MP for North Down. *Times*, 30 Apr. 1934, p. 16; *Quarterly army list*, 30 June 1914, p. 1741; Snape, *Royal Army Chaplains' Department*, p. 193.

39 This was disingenuous to say the least. Anglican chaplains were very much divided on the merits of chaplains holding relative rank, with even reformist chaplains such as Harry Blackburne and Neville Talbot differing on the subject. Snape, *Royal Army Chaplains' Department*, pp. 237–9.

by the market-women for the beads and brooches and other trifles they were buying. I helped some of them with their bargains! The drive was long. It was via St. Pol, Doullens etc., skirting Amiens, passing through its suburbs, but not entering the city. Then on to Querrieux which is the Headquarters of the Fourth Army under Sir H. Rawlinson.[40] I think the drive from St. Omer was about 60 miles in all. Rawlinson occupies a fine chateau. We lunched in company with him and a large staff, including General Sutton, Lord Halifax's son-in-law, [41] Sir Richard Sutton (a young aide-de-camp with a fortune of £130,000 a year), and a great many more.

After lunch I went with Rawlinson to his room, where he explained everything, showing me the large scale photographs of trenches and their place on the map etc. and making all clear.

Then I drove with Archdeacon Southwell, who is Senior Chaplain of the Fourth Army,[42] and is doing admirably, and Bishop Gwynne, to Corbie, some [blank] kilometres off. There we found a wonderful muster of some 70 chaplains, which had been arranged by Archdeacon Southwell and Chadwick,[43] the admirable chaplain there. We met in the Kinema Theatre erected for our troops. We first had, as on the previous day, a simple intercession service, conducted by Gwynne, and then before going to conference, I gave a full address much like that on the previous day. Then we Bishops unrobed and had a conference of chaplains, whereat Southwell and Ted Talbot[44] and some others spoke exceedingly well, and the talk was, I thought,

[40] Henry Seymour Rawlinson (1864–1925) became commander of Fourth Army in Feb. 1916, which he commanded until Feb. 1918 when he was appointed British military representative on the Allies' supreme war council at Versailles. Reappointed to Fourth Army in Apr. 1918, Rawlinson remained in command until the end of the war. Having performed poorly on the Somme in 1916 (he was largely responsible for the debacle of 1 July, the bloodiest day in the history of the British army), Rawlinson partly redeemed himself as an army commander in the summer and autumn of 1918 – the so-called 'advance to victory'. Widely regarded as an ambitious and shifty character, Haig had no illusions as to the conditional nature of Rawlinson's loyalty and Rawlinson was known among his peers as 'The Fox' and even as 'The Cad'. *Times*, 28 Mar. 1925, p. 17; *Who's who in World War One*, ed. Bourne, pp. 244–5; I. F. W. Beckett, 'Henry Rawlinson' in *Haig's generals*, ed. Beckett and Corvi, pp. 164–82.

[41] Major-General H. C. Sutton (1867–1928) was deputy-adjutant and quartermaster-general of Fourth Army in May 1916. Charles Lindley Wood (1839–1934), Second Viscount Halifax, was the leading Anglo-Catholic layman of his day and served continuously as president of the English Church Union from 1868 to 1919. Becke, *Order of battle part 4*, p. 99; *Times*, 18 Apr. 1928, p. 18; *ODNB*.

[42] Henry Kemble Southwell (1860–1937), formerly of Magdalene College, Oxford (BA 1884, MA 1886), had served as an acting army chaplain in the Boer War. He became a canon of Chichester in 1911 and was appointed archdeacon of Lewes in 1912. A strong if progressive high churchman, he was deeply involved with the schools of the Woodward Foundation and was provost of Lancing at the outbreak of war. He proved a popular ACG of Fourth Army, where he was known for his tact and sympathy, being 'held in the highest regard by the chaplains who worked under him'. Southwell became bishop of Lewes in 1920. *Times*, 11 Mar. 1937, p. 18.

[43] Frederic William Evans Chadwick (?-?), a graduate of the University of London (BA 1892), was trained at Lichfield and ordained deacon in 1893 and priest in 1894. He was commissioned into the AChD on 15 May 1915, having been chaplain of Winwick Asylum and a curate in a succession of Lancashire parishes. *Crockford's*, 1913, p. 259; *Monthly army list*, July 1916, 1791c.

[44] Edward Keble Talbot (1877–1949) was the eldest of E. S. Talbot's three sons. Formerly of Christ Church College, Oxford (BA 1900, MA 1910), he trained at Cuddesdon and was ordained deacon in 1904 and priest in 1905. Talbot joined the Community of the Resurrection in 1910, having served as a curate in London, and was commissioned into the AChD on 23 Aug. 1914. A talented and forceful preacher, he was soon identified as a potential messenger for the National Mission in France. Wilkinson, *Church of England*, pp. 342–3; *Crockford's*, 1913, p. 1466; *Monthly army list*, July 1916, 1793b; RAChD Archive, 'Proceedings of A.C.G.'s conferences', 6 June 1916.

much more useful than on the previous day. The National Mission, ordinands, new plans for services after the war, the nature of the impression made on the men, the sort of worship that suits best, and so on.[45] We then went to the beautiful garden of the chateau occupied by General Congreve,[46] in command at Corbie, and a regular 'garden party tea' took place. General Congreve was much to the fore and is an admirable man. He is a nephew of Father Congreve,[47] and apparently sympathetic with that school. He knew all about Corbie and its history as a monastery. The garden in which we met had been the monastery garden up to the French Revolution, when the monastery was destroyed, the Church, however, remaining – rather striking. It is now the garden of an ugly suburban chateau, occupied by our General under the 'paid hospitality' of a French lady, on whom I called to thank her for her kind arrangements for tea etc. In the garden I met General Jacob, the Bishop's cousin,[48] lately wounded very badly, but recovered, and many other officers, and I got [a] quiet talk with at least a score of the chaplains *including Ted Talbot*. Many of *them* ~~whom~~ had pointed things to say, and *nearly* all of *them* ~~whom~~ made on my mind a very favourable impression as to the work they are doing, the wisdom they are showing therein, and the vigour and sometimes originality of their plans.

Then in the General's car I drove with Southwell to a high bit of ground several miles off, overlooking the town of Albert, where I met by appointment General Rawlinson. We had a fine view of the whole valley, with the English and German trenches, and Rawlinson took me to the brow of the hill and explained the whole lie of the country, pointing out the villages on the opposite slopes about which he said we should hear more before very long. We could see Fricourt, Thiepval,

---

45   These topics were being addressed in a survey undertaken by the bishop of Kensington, J. P. Maud, in his capacity as the chairman of the committee for the Preparation of the Church for the National Mission of Repentance and Hope. A questionnaire had been sent to 1,300 army chaplains and 300 naval chaplains at the beginning of May and, three months later, its results were summarized in a report compiled and written by George Bell. G. K. A. Bell, *The National Mission of Repentance and Hope. A report on the chaplain's replies to the Lord Bishop of Kensington* (London, 1916).

46   Lieutenant-General Sir Walter Norris Congreve (1862–1927), commander of XIII Corps in May 1916. Despite the comfortable surroundings described by Davidson, Congreve, who had won the Victoria Cross during the Boer War, was notable for his visits to front-line trenches and for conducting aerial reconnaissance missions in person. In fact, he was the only corps commander to be wounded during the First World War, losing his left hand to a German shell near Vimy Ridge in June 1917. He also lost his only son, Major William La Touche Congreve VC, on the Somme in July 1916. That Apr., Congreve had confided to him, 'I don't feel I can ever make a general for I cannot face having men killed in the ruthless way generals must do.' Becke, *Order of battle part 4*, p. 209; J. M. Bourne, 'Lions led by donkeys', http://www.firstworldwar.bham.ac.uk/donkey/congreve.htm, consulted 22 July 2009.

47   George Congreve of the Society of St John the Evangelist, an anglican religious order better known as the Cowley Fathers. In defiance of the formal appointments process, and as commander of 18th Infantry Brigade, Walter Congreve had taken Fr P. N. Waggett SSJE to France as an unofficial chaplain in Sept. 1914; Waggett was not to be commissioned into the AChD until the following Dec. *Crockford's*, 1913, p. 313; B. Taylor, 'The Cowley Fathers and the First World War', in *The church and war*, ed. Sheils, pp. 383–90, at p. 384.

48   Claud William Jacob (1863–1948) became commander of II Corps on 28 May 1916, having previously distinguished himself as commander of the Meerut Division and, subsequently, of the 21st Division. The only officer of the Indian army to achieve high rank in the BEF, he acquired a reputation for moral courage, efficient staff work and for his interest in the welfare of his troops. His cousin was Edgar Jacob, bishop of St Albans from 1903 to 1919. *Who's who in World War One*, ed. Bourne, p. 143; *Times*, 3 June 1948, p. 6; *Crockford's*, 1913, p. 1318.

26 The 'Golden Virgin' of the basilica of Notre Dame de Brebières, Albert, see p. 483. Cutting from a magazine (LPL, Davidson 583, fo. 32)

Contalmaison, and many more on the slopes and hills with encircling hills.[49] The shelling was going on vigorously on either side, and we watched the shells tearing the ground and sending up clouds of earth and dust. There were also German and French aeroplanes overhead being fired at by their respective enemies, but not, so far as I could see, firing at one another, though the shells were bursting round both.[50] Just below us was the town of Albert, its Cathedral spire broken, and on its top the great figure of the Virgin and Child hanging down at an angle and looking as though they must fall.[51] The General was an admirable and keen exponent, and I learned to appreciate the situation in quite a new way. Then we went with him into some of our back line trenches, and he explained the detail of construction etc. Unfortunately John Mac and Bishop Gwynne had, in the Bishop's car, missed the road and did not reach us till we had observed all this for some time. Then I drove back to Querrieux with Southwell, and had a great deal of useful talk about the chaplains, their needs, their work, their usages, including such questions as non-communicating attendance and evening Communion etc. etc. This was most interesting and Southwell described to me his own position as greatly modified by his experience in the war.[52]

At Querrieux we left Southwell (he joined us later at Amiens for dinner) and drove to Amiens with Bishop Gwynne and Mac. We had rooms reserved in the Hotel du Rhin. The hotel was full of English officers and their guests, and we could not at first get a *dinner* table. Southwell joined us and after dinner we sat long in the garden talking. Suddenly, about 10 p.m., came a brisk fusillade all over the

49 In essence, Rawlinson was showing Davidson the prospective battleground of the 1916 Somme offensive, then being planned at Fourth Army headquarters. Fricourt, Thiepval and Contalmaison were all in German hands in May 1916 and had been identified as first-day objectives only two days previously. In the event, and although they should have been taken on 1 July, Fricourt was taken the following day, Contalmaison on 10 July and Thiepval on 26 Sept. P. Hart, *The Somme* (London, 2005), pp. 64–6; C. McCarthy, *The Somme: the day-by-day account* (London, 1995), pp. 33–4, 44, 121.

50 The primary function of aircraft at this stage of the war was aerial reconnaissance and artillery spotting; purpose-built fighters (or 'scouts'), designed to play an offensive *rôle* against other aircraft, did not begin to appear until 1915 and only in the following year, with the battles of Verdun and the Somme, did a fully-fledged struggle for air superiority commence on the Western Front. J. H. Morrow, 'The war in the air', in *The Oxford illustrated history of the First World War*, ed. H. Strachan (Oxford, 1998), pp. 265–77, at pp. 267–71.

51 Known as the 'Golden', 'Leaning' or 'Hanging' Virgin of Albert, this gilded statue of the Virgin and child was dislodged from its original position atop the tower of the basilica of Notre Dame de Brebières by German shellfire in Jan. 1915. Temporarily secured by French engineers, the statue was visible to British, French and German soldiers alike throughout the 1916 battle of the Somme. Given its sacred nature and precarious situation, various stories circulated as to its significance, the most common being that the war would end when the statue fell to the ground, a prophecy that remained unfulfilled after it was toppled by British shellfire in Apr. 1918. G. Gliddon, *When the barrage Lifts* (London, 1987), p. 2; Snape, *God and the British soldier*, pp. 44–5.

52 Many high churchmen and Anglo-Catholics insisted on fasting communion and thus the early morning was regarded as the ideal, if not the only, time for partaking. Furthermore, and although it had found a few advocates with the growth of the Oxford movement, the presence of non-communicants at communion services had been discouraged by the anglican tradition. If the Report of the Royal Commission on Ecclesiastical Discipline of 1906 had already reinforced and legitimized a widespread desire for liturgical change, the bishop of Kensington's survey met with 'a constant request' for 'greater elasticity' and, as Bell remarked, one of the 'altogether surprising' demands it elicited was that 'Holy Communion should be explicitly treated as the principal Service of the Sunday'. D. Gray, 'Earth and altar', *Alcuin Club Collections*, LXVIII (1986), 16–17; H. Davies, *Worship and theology in England. The ecumenical century, 1900–1965* (London, 1965), pp. 290–1; Bell, *Report on the chaplain's replies*, pp. 40–1.

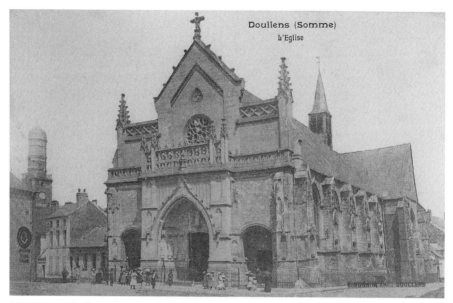

27 Postcard of Doullens, church, see p. 485 (LPL, Davidson 583, fo. 36)

28 Postcard of German troops leaving Doullens, 9 September 1914 (LPL, Davidson 583, fo. 36)

town, firing at hostile aeroplanes – *(Taubes)*.[53] We could not see the hostile aircraft owing to the garden trees, but could see the shells. It lasted about fifteen minutes. At midnight, after I had just written the above note, came a terrific cannonade, much more noisy than before, which lasted for about a quarter of an hour *and was repeated, less strenuously, later*. I had no notion that there could be so hot a firing into the air in the middle of a great town from guns of all sorts without apparently any *great* damage to the town itself. Yet next morning when we came down we heard that, except for the breaking of a good deal of glass, no harm had been done by the French guns. There had been three German aeroplanes dropping bombs, especially near the barracks, and three motor wagons had been injured or destroyed. But, unless we were misinformed, that was all the damage.

I had rather a wakeful night, meditating upon all the new things I had seen that day, and listening to the artillery at intervals! One felt more and more the fearsomeness of all this going on between Christian peoples and the helplessness of religious leadership to intervene and per contra the gain and opportunity which is coming to the manhood of England and France, and an obligation to use it.

After breakfast on <u>Friday May 19th</u> I had the first quiet time since I left England – going to the Cathedral alone and remaining there a full hour. Stacks of sandbags hide the sculpture of the West front *half way up the walls* and most of the groups of the internal figures.[54] The general effect is to make the Cathedral into a rather unquiet and undevotional place, as there are workmen everywhere – not women this time. However I greatly appreciated the hour's quiet.

Then Gwynne and Mac arrived with the car, picked me up in the Cathedral, and *we* drove off to St. Pol, a long way. <u>En route</u> we stopped for nearly an hour at Doullens and took a walk through its streets and the interesting and well-kept old Church, and then through the riverside woods, full of our ammunition and commissariat wagons, with a great many men hard at work, loading, cleaning etc. We got some talks with a few of them and I found one man from Folkestone and another from Southwark. Some miles on we again took a walk round the town of Fremont, some [blank] miles short of St. Pol. In the Church a Catechism class for girls was being conducted by a lady, no priest being present. We had also seen both at Doullens and at Amiens, little gatherings of women in the Church one of them leading a group of others in intercessions of a litany sort.

Arrived at St. Pol, Headquarters of the Third Army, we went straight to General Allenby's[55] Headquarters – a chateau even finer than Rawlinson's – situated in the

---

53 The Taube ('Dove') was a monoplane designed by the Austrian engineer Igo Etrich in 1910. Manufactured under licence by several German companies, it was practically obsolescent by 1916. Slow and stable, it saw varied use by the German Army Air Service as a reconnaissance aircraft, a bomber and eventually as a trainer. J. H. Morrow, *The Great War in the air* (Washington, 1993), pp. 19, 37–8, 73, 103; S. Pope and E. A. Wheal, *The Macmillan dictionary of the First World War* (London, 1995), p. 465.

54 Although theoretically protected by the Hague Convention of 1899, the need to protect the churches of France against German shelling was illustrated not only in the fate of the basilica at Albert (see above, p. 483 n. 51), but also in the destruction of Rheims cathedral in Sept. 1914. A. Clayton, *Paths of glory: the French army 1914–18* (London, 2005), p. 51; A. Becker, *War and faith: the religious imagination in France, 1914–1930* (Oxford, 1998), p. 15.

55 Edmund Henry Hynman Allenby (1861–1936) became commander of Third Army in Oct. 1915 and was relieved in June 1917 after his poor performance at the battle of Arras (Apr.–May 1917). The following month he lost his only son on the Western Front. Transferred to the command of the Egyptian Expeditionary Force, Allenby redeemed his reputation by breaking the Turkish lines in Palestine

29 Postcard of Doullens, citadel
(LPL, Davidson 583, fo. 38)

30 Postcard of Doullens, bell-tower
(LPL, Davidson 583, fo. 40)

middle of the town with large gardens stretching countrywards. All looked fresh and beautiful, but it *is* said to be a dank place in winter. We had lunch with him and his staff, Lord Dalmeny,[56] of whom Allenby spoke in high praise, a young aide-de-camp, Agnew, from New College, and a very clever and capable General Chief of the Staff, who had been a lecturer on military history, and had a few years ago brought his students to study the battle-fields of this very region, including St. Pol.[57] I had much interesting talk with him about old warfare and new, and the effect of motors, telephones etc. He is not sanguine of any early close of the war. Allenby was kindness and courtesy itself, and I had a further repetition of what Rawlinson had done for me on the previous day at Querrieux – Allenby taking me into his room and there going over the large scale maps, including a curious contour map all raised to scale which he has fashioned. He taught me the geographical facts about the Vimy ridge and our battling there – the guns being audible in the distance while we talked.[58] He explained it most carefully and interestingly. After all this he went on to talk with great freedom and with an unexpected largeness of view and breadth of sympathy about the German atrocities, and, as he thinks, the exaggerated accounts of them which find currency, and about Morgan's book on the German War Spirit, and what he regards as unfairness to Germany. Morgan had been to see him and he had talked it all over with him.[59] Allenby dislikes the Germans immensely

and by capturing Jerusalem in Dec. 1917. He then pursued the Turkish army through Palestine and into Syria until Turkey's capitulation in Oct. 1918. Despite his imposing physical stature and his infamous temper (attributes that were to earn him the nickname of 'The Bull') Allenby was a quietly committed anglican who, in stark contrast to the Kaiser on an earlier visit to Jerusalem, chose to enter the Holy City on foot, as a pilgrim. *Who's who in World War One*, ed. Bourne, pp. 5–6; M. Hughes, 'Edmund Allenby', in *Haig's generals*, ed. Beckett and Corvi, pp. 12–32; Snape, *God and the British soldier*, pp.70–1.

56 Albert Edward Harry Mayer Archibald Primrose (1882–1974) later became sixth earl of Roseberry and second earl of Midlothian. The son of the fifth earl of Roseberry, Liberal prime minister from Mar. 1894 to June 1895 and a personal friend of Davidson's, Dalmeny was a celebrated cricketer and the youngest MP to be elected in the general election of 1906. Although the launch of his political career required that he resign his commission in the Grenadier Guards, he returned to the army on the outbreak of war and eventually became military secretary to the irascible Allenby, with whom he enjoyed a good relationship. One of Allenby's corps commanders, James Aylmer Haldane, wrote that '[Allenby] is a prime bully. I pity his poor staff as they have a hard time with him and fortunately for Dalmeny the Bull is a snob and grovels to anyone senior to him or still better has a title.' *ODNB*; Hughes, 'Edmund Allenby', p. 16.

57 Major-General Louis Jean Bols (1867–1930), major-general general staff of Third Army from Oct. 1915 to May 1917. Educated at Lancing and the son of a Belgian diplomat, Bols had lectured at the Staff College for some years prior to the war. By all accounts, his cheerful and emollient character stood in stark contrast to Allenby's dour and acerbic demeanour. *Who's who in World War One*, ed. Bourne, pp. 30–1; Becke, *Order of battle part 4*, p. 89; *Times*, 15 Sept. 1930, p. 14.

58 Vimy Ridge, in Artois, was a key position in the sector between Loos and Arras. In Allied hands, it was anticipated that it would serve as an artillery platform from which to disrupt German movements in the Douai plain to the east. Clayton, *Paths of glory*, pp. 66–7.

59 A reference to John Hartman Morgan (1876–1955), professor of constitutional law and legal history at University College, London, and Rhodes lecturer to the University of London in the law of the empire. The son of a Welsh congregationalist minister and his Swiss wife, Morgan was a staunch Liberal who, though he volunteered for combatant service on the outbreak of war, was soon appointed to the adjutant-general's staff of the BEF as a home office commissioner. As his staff *rôle* was to 'inquire into the conduct of the Germans in the field', Morgan conducted extensive investigations in France and Belgium and his findings were conveyed to the British public in several publications, most notably *The German war book* (1915), 'a literal translation of the handbook on the usages of war issued by the German army', *War, Its conduct and legal results* (1916), *German atrocities: an*

and 'would like to kill every German' he sees, but he thinks that in judging their behaviour we are apt to apply a standard of conduct which would be too severe for any Army that every existed, and certainly for our own.[60] The talk interested me particularly because he is a man from whom I should have expected a *somewhat more* ~~very~~ conventional view.

After lunch Agnew, the aide-de-camp, took me to see the office of the Army Headquarters, with its amazing signalling arrangements, the telephone and tele-graph etc. These are under the Command of General Newbigging,[61] who gave me an amazing explanation of the ramified and elaborate plans necessary. From the house where all these centre there are 145 sets of wires going to every part of the region and far beyond it, e.g. to Rouen, *to* Paris, and to England, though this last is via GHQ, which has a separate wire to the War Office. A great number of telephone and telegraph clerks from the G.P.O. in London are ceaselessly at work, and they have wonderful systems of tape repetition and amplifications of messages etc. It is bewildering in its extent and elaboration, and set one wondering what would be the result if a shell or a bomb dropped into the building, which is, as a matter of fact, the Law Court of the Department, and shattered everything.[62] They assured me that a very few hours would set things straight again, though perhaps they would for a time have to confine themselves to the leading lines which they could pick up quickly outside the damaged place.

After this explanation we went to a hall where I found 65 chaplains, under the charge of Day, the Senior Chaplain of the Third Army,[63] and we had a close repetition of yesterday's procedure – intercessions and address and conference – the speaking being good and interesting and several points well debated. Among the chaplains who took part well were Kidd *(*of All Hallows, Barking*)*,[64] Macleod Campbell,[65]

---

official investigation (1916) and *Leaves from a field note book* (1916). *Times*, 21 Apr. 1955, p. 11, and 28 Apr. 1955, p. 15; *ODNB.*

60   As a career officer and veteran of the Boer War, Allenby was no doubt conscious of the moral limita-tions of the British regular soldier and of the sometimes brutal conduct of the British army towards Boer civilians in South Africa. *ODNB.*

61   Actually, Colonel W. P. E. Newbigging, deputy director of signals. Each army had its equivalent of Newbigging and also its own signals company of Royal Engineers. At this stage in the war, these companies were largely composed of former employees of the General Post Office. Becke, *Order of battle part 4*, p. 89; Rawson, *British army handbook*, p. 110.

62   A striking observation in which the archbishop anticipated one of the primary objectives of later, *blitzkrieg*-style warfare. M. Cooper, *The German Army 1933–1945* (London, 1990), p. 114.

63   Edward Rouviere Day (1867–1948), a graduate of Trinity College, Dublin (BA and Divinity Testi-monium 1891), was ordained deacon in 1891 and priest in 1892. He was commissioned into the AChD on 18 Jan. 1900, having served as an acting chaplain at the Curragh and at Woolwich since 1893. Thereafter, he served in the Boer War and in various British and overseas garrisons and was a chaplain First Class on the outbreak of war. He served as ACG of Third Army from 1916 to 1918. *Quarterly army list*, June 1914, p. 1741; *Monthly army list*, July 1916, 1790, and July 1918, 1790.

64   Joseph Henry Kidd (?-?), a graduate of the Royal University of Ireland (BA 1900), was ordained deacon in 1902 and priest in 1903. Following a succession of Irish curacies, he became curate of All Hallows, Barking, in 1911 and was commissioned into the AChD on 22 Feb. 1916 at the age of thirty-eight. Crockford's, 1913, p. 859; *Monthly army list*, July 1916, 1792a; RAChD Archive, Amport House, card index.

65   John McLeod Campbell (1885–1961), formerly of Balliol College, Oxford (BA 1906, MA 1910), was trained at Farnham and was ordained deacon in 1909 and priest in 1910. From 1909 he was chaplain of Hertford College, Oxford; he also served as examining chaplain to the bishop of Oxford, Francis Paget, and to the archbishop of York, Cosmo Gordon Lang. Like many of his more distinguished contemporaries at Oxford (including Neville Talbot, William Temple and 'Tubby' Clayton) Campbell

Geoffrey Gordon,[66] and Day himself. We then adjourned to tea in a neighbouring inn, all very well arranged, and I got the opportunity of talking to a great many of the chaplains, usefully I think. The whole gathering impressed me with a sense of the excellence of the work which is being done by these men and the splendid effect on them of their experience. Among others I met there *McCalman* my own ordinand,[67] Lord Harris' friend, also young Romanes, Mrs. Romanes' son,[68] who had found me out.

We drove home in the evening to St. Omer, but were delayed by two troublesome punctures which proved hard to remedy – one of them taking nearly an hour – and we did not get to St. Omer till towards 10 p.m. and found there two men waiting for us for dinner – a General Franks R.A., commanding the Royal Artillery in the Second Army, who had been a friend of Gwynne's in the Sudan,[69] and Harry Blackburne, the very efficient Senior Chaplain of the First Army,[70] which we were to visit the next day.

was heavily involved in the Oxford and Bermondsey Mission. He was commissioned into the AChD on 14 Aug. 1914, possibly helped by the fact that the chaplain-general was a strong supporter of the OBM, and he rose to become senior chaplain of the 4th Division. Described by one admirer as 'an outstanding Army chaplain', in 1924 Campbell was appointed principal of Trinity College in Ceylon; however, he ended his life as master of Charterhouse and as chaplain to the Speaker of the House of Commons. *Crockford's*, 1913, p. 237; *Monthly army list*, July 1916, 1791b; *Times*, 28 Feb. 1961, p. 16, 4 Mar. 1916, 1961, p. 8, 7 Mar. 1961, p. 15; *The back parts of war*, ed. Snape, pp. 4–7.

66 James Geoffrey Gordon (1881–1938), formerly of Trinity College, Cambridge (BA 1903, MA 1907), had been president of the Cambridge Union and was called to the bar in 1906. He later trained at Cuddesdon and was ordained deacon in 1909 and priest in 1910. After serving two curacies in London, he was commissioned into the AChD on 18 Jan. 1916. His wartime writings – notably *Papers from Picardy*, which he co-wrote with Tom Pym, and 'Membership and loyalty', on the subject of the church and the soldier, which he wrote for *The church in the furnace* – championed the cause of reform in the Church of England. Gordon ended his career as bishop of Jarrow. *Crockford's*, 1913, p. 592; *Monthly army list*, July 1916, 1791e; T. W. Pym and G. Gordon, *Papers from Picardy* (London, 1917); J. G. Gordon, 'Membership and loyalty', in *The church in the furnace*, ed. MacNutt, pp. 147–71.

67 Hugh McCalman, apparently a non-graduate, was ordained deacon in 1912 and priest in 1913. He was commissioned into the AChD on 15 Jan. 1915, at the age of twenty-five. *Crockford's*, 1913, p. 956; *Monthly army list*, July 1916, 1792b; ; RAChD Archive, Amport House, card index.

68 Mrs Ethel Romanes (1856–1927) was the widow of the scientist George John Romanes (1848–94), a close friend of Charles Darwin and the founder of the Romanes lectureship at Oxford. Widowed in 1894, she became a well-known writer on religious subjects and a lecturer of international stature. An Anglo-Catholic who was active in the Pan-Anglican Congress and in the Christian Social Union, she converted to Roman Catholicism in 1919. The son alluded to is probably Lieutenant-Colonel J. G. P. Romanes of the Royal Scots. *Times*, 1 Apr. 1927, p. 16; *ODNB*.

69 Major-General George Mckenzie Franks (1868–1958) was major-general of the Royal Artillery in Second Army from Dec. 1915 to July 1917. As a younger officer, he had distinguished himself during Kitchener's reconquest of the Sudan. *Who's who in World War One*, ed. Bourne, p. 97; Becke, *Order of battle part 4*, p. 79; *Times*, 15 Oct. 1958, p. 15.

70 Harry William Blackburne (1878–1951), formerly of Clare College, Cambridge (BA 1901, MA 1904), was ordained deacon in 1901 and priest in 1902. Blackburne volunteered for the West Kent Yeomanry while an undergraduate and saw active service in the ranks during the Boer War. After ordination, and following a curacy in Warwickshire, he became an acting chaplain on 15 Oct. 1903 and was commissioned into the AChD on 14 Feb. 1904. He then served in various garrisons at home and in South Africa and was chaplain to the Royal Military College at Sandhurst, holding the rank of chaplain Third Class, on the outbreak of war. Once in France, Blackburne rapidly became senior chaplain of the 1st Division and was appointed ACG of First Army in Jan. 1916. In this capacity he distinguished himself as one of the most competent, innovative and vocal chaplains of the war, becoming a passionate supporter of the Life and Liberty movement. To the surprise of many, Black-

31 Map of the region from Dunkirk to Arras (LPL, Davidson 583, fo. 41)

I had had a good deal of quiet thinking-time, as I stayed behind with the car while its intestines were under treatment – Gwynne and Mac walking on – and thus got my thoughts into shape and said my prayers – made keener by what we had been seeing and doing all day. I also got a good deal of talk with the Tommies who were billeted in the village where we broke down. One of them a very interesting quite young soldier from Tooting, who had got some keen and rather original thoughts about the war and its lessons for him and others. I felt when I got to bed that the day had been a fruitful one.

Saturday May 20th. The quietest morning I have had this week. I went with Mac to the Cathedral, or Church of Notre Dame, at St. Omer, and we were lucky enough to find there an archaeologist – a very interesting Abbé Augustin Dusantoir – who took us round and poured forth wonderful stories and comments on everything, intermingling his volvuble and sometimes humorous remarks with bits of bad English which made him quite unintelligible. The Church is a wonderful place, full of beautiful carving which by a miracle escaped destruction at the time of the Revolution.

At 12.30 we drove off with Bishop Gwynne to the Headquarters of the First Army near Aire. It is a large chateau, the very house in which our King was laid up after his accident last year.[71] The house is occupied by ~~Monro~~ Sir Charles Monro,[72] commanding the First Army, but Monro was at the moment in England, and his place as host was taken by Sir H. Wilson.[73] He was kindness itself and poured forth information ceaselessly. I think him one of the most remarkable expounders and

---

burne was not appointed chaplain-general on Bishop Taylor Smith's retirement in 1925 but, as an obituarist remarked, his natural independence, outspokenness and impatience was 'not the way to a bishopric!' Bishop Gwynne once described him as 'a hell-for-leather, don't care a d— Assistant Chaplain-General' but also fretted in Nov. 1916 that '[Blackburne] is an excellent chaplain with wonderful powers which qualify him for his present job, but he lacks humility and does not know his limitations.' Blackburne ended his career as dean of Bristol. *Crockford's*, 1913, p. 140; *Quarterly army list*, June 1914, 1742; *Times*, 3 June 1963, p. 10; CMS Archives, diaries of L. H. Gwynne, 9 Nov. 1916; H. W. Blackburne, *This also happened on the Western Front* (London, 1932); H. Blackburne, *Trooper to dean* (Bristol, 1955).

71 King George V (1865–1936) made no fewer than five visits to the Western Front during the course of the war. On 28 Oct. 1915 he was thrown from his horse during a visit to First Army. The accident caused the king 'stiffness and bruises' and Haig, who was then the commander of First Army, much consternation. *Who's who in World War One*, ed. Bourne, pp. 104–5; Sheffield and Bourne (eds.), *Douglas Haig*, p. 167.

72 A sound administrator rather than a gifted field commander, Charles Carmichael Monro (1860–1929) became commander of Third Army in July 1915 and was appointed commander-in-chief of the Mediterranean Expeditionary Force three months later. In this capacity, Monro took the courageous if controversial decision to evacuate the Gallipoli peninsula, a phased evacuation that was conducted with remarkable success from Dec. 1915 to Jan. 1916. That Feb., Monro was sent back to the Western Front to take command of First Army. However, his subsequent operational record proved to be an unhappy one; First Army lost part of Vimy Ridge to a German attack in May and it mounted a bloody, fruitless and unnecessary attack at Fromelles the following month. That Oct., Monro was appointed commander-in-chief in India, where he spent the remainder of the war successfully reorganizing the Indian army. *Times*, 9 Dec. 1929, p. 17; *Who's who in World War One*, ed. Bourne, p. 210; J. Bourne, 'Charles Monro', in *Haig's generals*, ed. Beckett and Corvi, pp. 122–40.

73 Better known for his Unionist sympathies and for his involvement in the notorious 'Curragh Incident' of Mar. 1914, despite his penchant for intrigue Henry Hughes Wilson (1864–1922) was a capable staff officer who had planned and executed the mobilization and deployment of the original BEF in Aug. 1914. At the time of Davidson's visit, Wilson was commanding IV Corps, then part of First Army. However, having gained the ear of Lloyd George whilst commander of Eastern Command in Great Britain, Wilson rose to represent Britain on the Allies' supreme war council and to become chief of the imperial general staff in Feb. 1918. His career was terminated by Irish republican assas-

32   Postcard of the cathedral of Nôtre Dame and the Palais de Justice, St Omer
(LPL, Davidson 583, fo. 49)

lecturers I have ever met – strong, capable, cheery, thoughtful, with plenty to say
and saying it exceedingly well. I had much talk with him at luncheon, and, feeling
the value of a lecture *from* ~~with~~ him, I fortunately concluded an arrangement with
him that he should, after the function *at Bethune* in the afternoon, take me to the
hill of Notre Dame de Lorette (near Vimy) which he is himself defending with great
keenness.[74] It is an observation point of the first importance and a strategic centre
for the whole of the First Army. I shall return to this.

  After luncheon I drove to Bethune with Gwynne and Mac – a good many miles
away. There in a large private house with a beautiful garden we had a gathering
of chaplains. They met in a dismantled drawing-room and filled it. I think about
70 were there, under the very efficient marshalling of Harry Blackburne, whom
everyone recognises as a man of quite remarkable powers of organisation and of
attraction to soldiers. The intercessions and address were like those of the last three
days, but perhaps a little more crisp and pointed, the speeches of the chaplains
with regard to the Mission etc. being lively and suggestive. We discussed the same
subjects as on other days, and all went well.

  At 4.45 the Generals of the Army, whom Blackburne had invited from all the
region round, began to arrive and soon we had in the garden about 40 Generals.
I managed to get a short conversation –sometimes quite short – with nearly every
one of them, and in the majority of cases I got to the point about which I greatly

sins in June 1922. *Who's who in World War One*, ed. Bourne, p. 306; Sheffield and Bourne (eds.,),
Douglas Haig, p. 510.
[74] Notre Dame de Lorette was wrested from the Germans by the French 10th Army during the second
   battle of Artois of 9 May–18 June 1915, the only significant gain in an offensive that cost the French
   army some 300,000 casualties. Clayton, *Paths of glory*, pp. 64–6; Cave, *Arras: Vimy Ridge*, pp. 16–17.

cared, the work of our chaplains, their fitness for it, any suggestions which could make matters better, and the help the Generals are giving and can give. As before, I was immensely struck with the keen appreciation shown by every one of these leading officers as to the first-rate character, capacity, courage and perseverance of the chaplains and how very much has now come to turn on their work. Nearly every General spoke of them as being just the men who ought to be there and of having got a real grip upon their troops and cheering them in every way. The gathering in the garden was a striking instance of the pulling together of padres and officers and their mutual appreciation of one another. I found links of connexion or acquaintance with a great many of these officers. Nearly all were delightful to talk to, the only exceptions being perhaps the medical men of whom there were one or two in high office. I purposely went on trying to draw out the criticisms of one of these, but could not find any substance in them. I found Bernard Montgomery among the officers,[75] one of the few who was not a General. He was looking well and keen, and several people spoke very warmly of him and his work.

Tea was over at 5.40, and Sir Henry Wilson had arranged to have a strong rapid car waiting in which he whirled off Mac and me, together with his own aide-de-camp, Locker-Lampson,[76] who had been at Eton with Mac. We drove to the ridge of Notre Dame de Lorette, some miles off. It is a long ridge which Wilson compared to the Hog's Back, but it is not so steep or high. As we went up the side road near Bovigny, through villages greatly broken by shell fire and among the dug-outs of the wayside, a shell of the smaller sort, which Lampson called a 'pipsqueak', burst not far behind us to the surprise and, I think, a little to the disquiet of our military hosts. Locker Lampson tried hard to find out where it fell, but it was not clear, only it was not far away. I was glad to have the experience. It was an isolated spot with no special reason for being shelled. We got to some open ground on the top of the hill, with a French cemetery of rows and rows of little graves, many hundreds with little crosses, about half the crosses having names. They are some of those who fell in the gaining of the ridge by the French. It is said to have cost them 150,000 casualties. We walked along the ridge near the edge of the Bois de Bovigny, and there Sir H. Wilson pointed out the whole lie of the land – with Loos[77] in the

---

75 Bernard Law Montgomery (1887–1976). Son of Henry Montgomery, bishop of Tasmania (1889–1902), and a grandson of Dean Frederic William Farrar, Montgomery had been commissioned into the Royal Warwickshire Regiment in 1908. Severely wounded at Ypres in Oct. 1914, his injury meant that he served as a staff officer for the rest of the war. At the time of Davidson's visit, Montgomery was brigade major of 104th Infantry Brigade, then part of the 34th Division. He went on to become the most celebrated – and controversial – British general of the Second World War. M. Carver, 'Montgomery', in *Churchill's Generals*, ed. J. Keegan (London, 1992), pp. 148–65; N. Hamilton, *The Full Monty* (London, 2002), pp. 66–80.

76 Oliver Stillingfleet Locker-Lampson (1880–1954) had been Conservative MP for North Huntingdonshire since Jan. 1910. He was commissioned into the Royal Naval Air Service in Dec. 1914 and was promoted commander the following year. Significantly, the use of armoured cars by the British on the Western Front had been pioneered by the Royal Naval Air Service and Locker-Lampson served with naval armoured car units throughout the war, first in Belgium and, subsequently, with the Russian army on the Eastern Front. In 1916, the vehicles of the Royal Naval Armoured Car Division on the Western Front were in the process of being handed over to the army. *Times*, 9 Oct. 1954, p. 8; Messenger, *Call-to-arms*, pp. 175–8.

77 The mining town of Loos gave its name to the failed British offensive of 25 Sept. – 4 Nov. 1915, a battle that cost 60,000 British casualties and which contributed to the replacement of Sir John French by Sir Douglas Haig as commander-in-chief of the BEF in Dec. Holmes (ed.), *Oxford companion to military history*, p. 518.

33 Map of the region from Ostend to Arras (LPL, Davidson 583, fo. 53)

distance on the North-East, down towards Arras South-East on the right, and the Vimy ridge in the left foreground, a little south of east, and the shattered village of Souchez,[78] between the Lorette and Vimy ridges, corresponding, as Wilson pointed out, to the position of Guildford on the Hog's Back.[79] We were standing just above a farm called Marqueffles, in which, as Sir H. Wilson explained, he had *three* 9.2 inch guns concealed, which the Germans were always trying to find out. 'Now and then they have shelled the neighbouring fields, but they have never found the exact place of the guns which are there in those buildings, just below us' – say 250 yards. He had hardly said this when Locker Lampson called out 'I hear a German shell whistling,' and the great shell came with a scream and whistling sound and landed plump among the buildings which we were looking at, with an earth-shaking explosion. The General was much excited – 'The brutes! They have got us. What splendid shooting! They have the very spot!' Then came another shell almost on the same spot. We went a little nearer after this so as to observe better, and two more shells came. It was all as if it had been got up as an exhibition for us, and nothing could have been clearer or more absorbingly interesting. There was nothing to show us the exact effect of the shooting upon the hidden guns. We could only see the considerable smashing of earth and buildings, and the General said he would not know till later on at night when a report would come in to him. Then we went on examining the English and German trenches through our glasses and could watch the rifle fire going on between them, and occasional guns, ours and theirs, further off, but well within sight. Meanwhile a very plucky airman of ours was circling just overhead and the Germans kept firing shells at him, all of which we could watch quite close. It was a wonderful object lesson of a varied sort, and as Locker Lampson said afterwards – 'You had simply an extraordinary exhibition because of your higher standpoint and the visibleness of everything.'

We were to have gone on through the woods eastwards to look at the panorama, but it had become late and a little hazy, so we did not don the helmets which we had brought with us, but drove down across the broken ground to the south of the ridge near Ablain, the General showing us his trenches and discussing the superiority of the Germans as trench diggers and barbed wire entrenchment makers – 'Our men won't work on this sort of job as theirs do. Their disciplined energy is incredible.'[80] When we got lower down he pointed out the rivulet source of the Souchez stream among concealed guns, chiefly machine guns, ready, as he said, 'in case of falling back. But we must not fall back. We do not mean to, and to give up Notre Dame de Lorette would be intolerable.' He then told us the story of how the French who had won Lorette at a cost of 150,000 casualties had lamented being sent off to Verdun

---

78   The scene of fierce fighting during the second battle of Artois (see above, p. 492 n. 74), Souchez was finally captured by the French on 26 Sept. during the third battle of Artois (25 Sept. – 11 Oct. 1915). Clayton, *Paths of glory*, pp. 67–70; Cave, *Arras: Vimy Ridge*, p. 33.

79   Part of the North Downs in Surrey, the Hog's Back is situated between Guildford in the east and Farnham in the west.

80   Standing largely on the strategic defensive on the Western Front since the autumn of 1914, the Germans had been generally free to choose their own ground. Hence, after nearly two years of occupation, the German positions on the Somme in the summer of 1916 were, in Winston Churchill's words, 'undoubtedly the strongest and most perfectly defended positions in the world'. R. Prior and T. Wilson, *The Somme* (New Haven, 2005), p. 38.

and handing over the ridge to the English.[81] The Germans knowing this, circulated at Verdun a report that the English had at once lost the ridge. So distressed were the French soldiers, though Joffre reassured them,[82] that they insisted on sending back two staff officers to Lorette to find out that it was a lie. All this he described to us with great keenness, showing us his arrangements, e.g. what looked like a stack of straw carefully and neatly made, but which was really a concrete house covered with straw and containing a gun.[83]

We drove back, through the trenches, to the rest village of Gouy-Servans where our men were in rest billets,[84] and then much further back to the General's house at Rouchicourt, close to Rebreuve, a really beautiful chateau. There he had, with extraordinary kindness, arranged to have ready for us a great Rolls Royce car which he had borrowed for the purpose, and, after examining his garden, we drove back in it at incredible speed, about, I suppose, 40 miles, to St. Omer, where Gwynne (who had returned straight from *Bethune* Aire after the conference) was awaiting us for dinner with a few officers, including young Kingsmill of *from* Hampshire.

Sunday May 21st. Starting from St. Omer soon after 9 a.m., Gwynne, Mac and I drove via Fauquembergues and Fruges to Hesdin. It was a long drive on a beautiful morning of bright sunshine, the roads being dusty, but everything else was beautiful. I never saw so many partridges – we were putting up pairs of them everywhere along the road. They were *basking* in the dust, and the outcome of so many pairs must be prodigious. We passed practically across the field of Agincourt. Arrived at Hesdin, we met Canon MacNutt,[85] who had arranged a parade service in the 'champ de manoeuvres' close to the town.[86] This was a large field, with thick soft grass, one

---

[81] The German offensive at Verdun commenced on 21 Feb. 1916 and the battle had run only three months of its ten-month course by the time of Davidson's visit. Such were the demands made on the French army during this, the longest battle of the First World War, that three-quarters of the French army's divisions were committed to it at one point or another. Clayton, *Paths of glory*, p. 127.

[82] Joseph Jacques Césaire Joffre (1852–1931) was appointed chief of the general staff of the French army in 1911 and was its commander-in-chief from Aug. 1914 to Dec. 1916. Although he remained an Allied hero due to his performance during the battle of the Marne in Aug.–Sept. 1914, Joffre's costly offensives in 1915, his failure to foresee Germany's offensive at Verdun in Feb. 1916 and the ultimate failure of the Somme offensive in its summer and autumn months led to his dismissal at the end of the year. *Who's who in World War One*, ed. Bourne, pp. 146–7.

[83] A rather clumsy description of a pillbox.

[84] By 1916 a British infantryman could expect to spend only a small proportion of his time in the front line. Unlike the French army, the BEF rotated its units between front-line positions and billets in the rear, which meant that in practice, and when it was actually at the front, 'a battalion could expect, on average, to spend just ten days a month in the trenches'. G. Corrigan, *Mud, blood and poppycock: Britain and the First World War* (London, 2003), pp. 89–94.

[85] Frederic Brodie MacNutt (1873–1949), formerly of Jesus College, Cambridge (BA 1900, MA 1904), trained at Ridley Hall and was ordained deacon in 1901 and priest in 1902. Vicar of St Matthew's, Surbiton, a canon of Southwark Cathedral and author of *Preparation for confirmation* (1909) and *The inevitable Christ* (1912), he was commissioned into the AChD on 1 July 1915. A 'persuasive and forceful preacher' and another outspoken advocate of church reform, MacNutt was the editor of *The church in the furnace* (1917), 'commonly known as "The fat in the fire"', to which he also contributed an essay entitled 'The moral equivalent of war', a trenchant critique of conventional piety, belief and church life. Although a firebrand in his younger days, he ended his career as a canon of Canterbury. *Crockford's*, 1913, p. 976; *Times*, 19 July 1949, p. 9; *Monthly army list*, July 1916, 1792b; F. R. Barry, *Period of my life* (London, 1970), p. 58; *The church in the furnace*, ed. Macnutt.

[86] Despite its many critics, regular church attendance, which for anglicans normally took the form of a formal parade service on the Sabbath, was a mandatory part of life in the British army until 1946. Snape, *God and the British soldier*, pp. 139–42.

side was a natural parapet or bank, with umbrageous trees under which they had arranged a desk etc., and we read and spoke from there, the men being in a hollow square below. The service was not a special one to which men from a distance had been summoned (this was what I had been anxious to avoid owing to the stories which reached me about that kind of service in the Bishop of London's visit), but the ordinary parade service of Sunday morning. Some 1500 men in all were present, including the H.A.C., the Artists' Rifles, King Edward's Horse, and some other units.[87] Canon MacNutt *of Surbiton*, with a splendid voice, read a shortened service; Bishop Gwynne read, at my request, a lesson from Revelations 3 – the epistle to Sardis – and I spoke for about 10 or 12 minutes. I think we were all well heard. Our chauffer, who was at the very back, professed to have heard every word. After service, and after seeing the men march past and off the ground, many officers were introduced – no one so far as I know of special distinction. We unrobed in a splendid new hut which has just been erected in connexion, I think, with the Church Army, and then we drove *miles* to Montreuil, the present General Headquarters. In the striking town on the top of the hill we visited the Adjutant General, Fowke,[88] with whom I had a long private talk of a very useful kind on the chaplaincy question, with special reference to certain difficulties about cars and so on. Then, with General Butler, a most interesting talker,[89] I drove to the General's house, a fine chateau, a mile *or more* from Montreuil. Oddly enough no one whom I asked seemed to know its exact name. I did not ask Haig himself. There the Commander-in-Chief, Sir Douglas Haig, received us most cordially. With him were Lord Cavan,[90] General Dobell,[91] General Fowke, and a great many more.

---

[87] This seems to have been a congregation largely composed of troops drawn from the more prestigious Special Reserve and Territorial regiments. The 1/1st Honourable Artillery Company and 2nd King Edward's Horse were serving as GHQ troops while the 1/28th London Regiment (Artists Rifles) was serving as an officer training unit. Holmes, *Tommy*, pp. 125 and 131; E. A. James, *British regiments 1914–18* (Uckfield, 1998), pp. 15–16.

[88] Lieutenant-General George Henry Fowke (1864–1936) was an exceptionally able staff officer who had previously served as the BEF's engineer-in-chief. As its adjutant-general from Feb. 1916 to the end of the war, he was responsible for its personnel and financial affairs. *Who's who in World War One*, ed. Bourne, pp. 95–6; Becke, *Order of battle part 4*, p. 12; Rawson, *British army handbook*, p. 51.

[89] Major-General Richard Harte Keating Butler (1870–1935) was deputy chief of the general staff at GHQ from Dec. 1915 to Feb. 1918. Although very loyal to Haig, on whose staff he served for three years, Butler chafed at being confined to this *rôle*. Despite his chatty response to Davidson, his relations with certain army commanders, who were obliged to seek access to Haig through him, were often much more strained. Sheffield and Bourne (eds.), *Douglas Haig*, pp. 496–7; *Who's who in World War One*, ed. Bourne, pp. 46–7.

[90] Frederick Rudolf Lambart (1865–1946), tenth earl of Cavan, had left the army in 1913 but was recalled from retirement on the outbreak of war. A highly competent brigade and divisional commander, he graduated to the command of XIV Corps in Jan. 1916, a command which he held with distinction until Mar. 1918. Although Davidson does not mention this, Cavan was a cousin of 'Tubby' Clayton's. A staunch churchman, Cavan frequented the famous chapel at Talbot House and became a strong supporter of the Toc H movement after the war. Becke, *Order of battle part 4*, p. 215; *Who's who in World War One*, ed. Bourne, p. 163; Snape, *God and the British soldier*, pp. 71, 218.

[91] Major-General Charles Macpherson Dobell (1869–1954) had recently completed the protracted Allied conquest of the German colonies of Togoland and Cameroon. Like Davidson, Dobell was merely a visitor to GHQ and went on to take command of the Western Frontier force in Egypt the following month. *Who's who in World War One*, ed. Bourne, p. 74; Becke, *Order of battle part 4*, p. 28; *ODNB*.

I found Haig rather shy and difficult to talk to at first, but when he thawed he was delightful in his quiet, earnest frankness of conversation. I pressed him for criticism about the work of the chaplains, but I could not elicit anything except laudation. He was strong on the great value of the changed administrative order which now encourages the chaplains to go forward into the trenches, if they will do so, instead of being, as formerly, kept behind at the casualty clearing stations, or even further back.[92] Haig was enthusiastic about the fine type of young Padre now at work in all parts of the line. There was hardly one whom he knew he would wish changed. He has himself a great affection for the Presbyterian Chaplain, Duncan, who is attached to Headquarters,[93] and whose ministry Haig himself, who I suppose is a semi-Presbyterian, often attends.[94] Both Haig and Fowke spoke in terms of real affection about Bishop Gwynne, and the tact and vigour of his administrative work. It is remarkable how Gwynne's simple goodness has evidently been his passport to the affection of these people, while his efficiency wins their respect.

I spoke to Haig fully about the need of a car for the use of the senior chaplain of each Army, now called in each case Assistant Chaplain General, four in all, besides the four at the Bases.[95] Haig and Fowke had each of them spoken of the gain arising from the administrative gradation of the chaplains throughout our Force, instead of

---

[92] From Aug. 1914 until Jan. 1916, a War Office directive had forbidden chaplains (who were non-combatants and who were classed as ambulance personnel under the Geneva Convention of 1864) from being in the front line other than for the purpose of burying the dead. At Haig's instigation this policy was abandoned by the BEF in Jan. 1916, his purpose being to maximize the contribution of chaplains to the morale of its citizen soldiers. Strongly criticized and widely flouted at the time, the ban later served to give a spurious credibility to Robert Graves's tales of malingering anglican chaplains in *Goodbye to all that* (1929). Snape, *Royal Army Chaplains' Department*, pp. 216–19, 268–9.

[93] George Simpson Duncan (1884–1965) was ordained as a minister in the Church of Scotland in 1915 after being offered an army chaplaincy. A rising academic, he was commissioned on 9 Sept. 1915 and, on arrival in France, was posted to GHQ at St Omer, where he first met Haig on Sunday 2 Jan. 1916. The day had been appointed by King George V as a National Day of Prayer and, although the setting was 'a small dingy concert-hall' in the town, his impressive oratory made a permanent and profound impression on the new commander-in-chief. Duncan spent the rest of the war as Haig's *de facto* personal chaplain; he moved with Haig to his new G.H.Q. at Montreuil in Mar. 1916 and Haig often entered summaries of Duncan's sermons in his personal diary; Simms even likened their relationship to that of Moses and Aaron. After the war, Duncan succeeded to a chair in biblical criticism at St Andrews and became a distinguished New Testament scholar; he was elected moderator of the general assembly of the Church of Scotland in 1949. *Times*, 9 Apr. 1965, p. 17; *ODNB*; *Monthly army list*, July 1916, 1794; Duncan, *Douglas Haig*, pp. 17–20; Snape, *God and the British soldier*, pp. 62–7; De Groot, 'George S. Duncan', *passim*.

[94] As a student at Clifton College, an undergraduate at Brasenose College, Oxford, and a career officer, Haig seems to have worshipped as an anglican. However, his early upbringing under a pious mother had been presbyterian. Riled by party rivalries within the Church of England and burdened by the enormous pressure of command, under the influence of Duncan's preaching Haig returned to his presbyterian roots while commander-in-chief. According to Duncan's diary, in July 1917 Haig even told Archbishop Lang that he had not found anglican preaching helpful in his new *rôle*: 'I told him ... that before I was made Com. in Chief I used always to go round [i.e., to the Church of England]: and that for 3 Sundays or so afterwards I did so out here: but one fellow told me what to do with our spare money, but it was only Duncan who told us straight what we ought to do and to be regarding the big things of the present.' Snape, *God and the British soldier*, pp. 61–3; De Groot, 'George S. Duncan', p. 368.

[95] The position of ACG had been created in Jan. 1916, partly at the instigation of a small advisory committee on anglican chaplaincy which had been formed the previous summer by the War Office. Snape, *Royal Army Chaplains' Department*, pp. 187–9.

the old-fashioned level uniformity of chaplains in the different classes.[96] I cordially agreed as to the gain of this decentralization and of throwing responsibility on the Assistant Chaplain General, but I pressed strongly that the gain might quite easily be neutralised, or lost, if the men thus appointed were not enabled to move about throughout the region wherein their subordinate officers are at work. It was like choosing with much pride four first-rate horses and then insisting that they should remain in the stable. Haig went into the matter carefully, pointing out his difficulty, namely that the War Office in London were insisting on a considerable diminution in the number of cars and consequent expense, and that the moment was not propitious for the new departure of giving cars to the four Chaplains. However, he recognised quite frankly the truth of what I had said and repeated more than once – 'I think you have made out a case. We must see what can be done. I shall do my best to arrange it.' He did not commit himself as to the manner in which this was to be effected, i.e. whether from home or from himself, and spoke with his usual quietness and reserve. But I do not think his words were merely formal. He went on to urge me to write to him, either about that or anything else, and I promised to do so.

Upon the general question of chaplains of different denominations, I did not find any trace of what I heard him quoted as saying, namely that the Anglican chaplains were inferior to the Presbyterians and Roman Catholics. Indeed, his words to me were all I think incompatible with such an opinion.[97]

We discussed the question of visits of Bishops. He was very emphatic and spoke with a quiet gravity about it. 'We don't want books written about visits to the Front. We don't want our men and their ways exploited, and we certainly don't want men of a different type to come out for joy rides about the country.' This referred, not obscurely, to Bishop Russell-Wakefield of Birmingham. But he went on – 'Visits like yours for quiet consultation with us and for giving stimulus to officers and chaplains, and speaking to the gatherings of men which you come across naturally, are of very real good.' I then spoke of the gain which might ensue from a visit of the Archbishop of York a little later. On that point he was cautious and reserved

---

96 Since 1859, and besides the chaplain-general, there had been four classes of chaplain in the AChD and promotion had largely been by seniority. However, by 1914 this had resulted in a top-heavy department where there were too few chaplains young and fit enough to take the field. The introduction of the post of ACG (and, eventually, that of deputy assistant chaplain-general) created a new hierarchy among a large body of chaplains who, whether regular, Territorial or temporary, were overwhelmingly in the lowest (the Fourth) class. Snape, *Royal Army Chaplains' Department*, pp. 102, 191.

97 Since being admitted to the Chaplains' Department in the late 1850s, in the tightly knit regimental world of the regular army presbyterian and Roman Catholic chaplains had enjoyed a key advantage over their anglican counterparts. Whereas anglican chaplains were appointed to garrisons, whose composition was subject to frequent changes, Presbyterian and Roman Catholic chaplains were treated as chaplains to Scottish and Irish regiments respectively. However, while their *de facto* regimental status tended to enhance their reputation, Haig had already expressed some exasperation at anglican in-fighting, noting in his diary on 30 Mar. 1916 how 'the clergy of the Church of England are squabbling terribly amongst themselves over High Church and Low Church methods'. In a subsequent meeting with Gwynne on 2 Sept. 1916, Haig also voiced his suspicion that the anglican bishops were seeking to 'promulgate ritualism' in the army and spoke 'disparagingly of the men who took orders when he was at Oxford'. Haig's insistence on the unity of his chaplains and his wariness of 'sacramental religion' were probably factors in Davidson's subsequent decision to request the bishop of Kensington *not* to publicize the findings of his earlier survey (see above, p. 481 n. 45). Snape, *Royal Army Chaplains' Department*, p. 141; *Haig's autograph Great War diary*, 30 Mar. 1916; CMS Archives, diaries of L. H. Gwynne, 2 Sept. 1916; Mews, 'Religion and English society', pp. 202–3.

and seemed to show that there is a something in the background. He did not say what it was, but I imagine that it is the continued flicker of the absurd legend of pro-Kaiserism which was manufactured from the Archbishop's speech a year ago.[98] He did not say this, but I feel pretty sure that that was what he referred to, and, indeed, a friend of Haig's, whom I will not name, told me definitely, and without prejudice, that such an idea is still afloat. I pointed out the gain of a visit from such a man as Ebor, *which* would certainly be helpful to everybody, and he agreed in his quiet way that after a good interval, (he emphasised and repeated those words,) it might be a desirable thing, and he invited me to write to him about it again 'towards autumn.' I did not feel it wise to say or do more, and I undertook to write later.* [* But circumstances led to all visits of that sort being discouraged, and Gwynne thought I should do harm instead of good if I raised the matter again at the time I had intended to do so.][99]

My talk with Haig was long. We sat together in his room discussing the situation as a whole. He was restrained in his expression, but seemed hopeful as well as determined, while obviously feeling intensely the gravity of the situation, the immensity of the task ahead, the certainty that the French have no more reserves to fall back upon, that they have reached the zenith of what they can do, and must now begin to decline in strength, and consequently must rely more upon us and so on.[100] What I liked about him was the quiet earnest emphasis with which he gave his opinions, and the total absence of mere optimistic talk of a conventional sort. We parted I think the best of friends.[101]

---

[98] Like his friend Richard Burdon Haldane, Archbishop Cosmo Gordon Lang (1865–1945) fell victim to anti-German hysteria early in the war. In Nov. 1914, and while speaking at the Empire Music Hall at York (without notes, as was his wont), Lang decried popular caricatures of the Kaiser and spoke of his 'sacred memory' of 'the Kaiser kneeling beside King Edward VII at the bier of Queen Victoria'. These words haunted him for the rest of the war, Lang becoming the subject of a deluge of obloquy and the recipient of 'Hundreds of letters and scurrilous postcards'; his postbag also included no fewer than twenty-four Iron Crosses. Unsurprisingly, Lang's 'sacred memory' of the Kaiser impaired his ability to speak with real authority on the war and, as late as 1918, a meeting in Middlesbrough at which he was due to speak was the subject of a public boycott. *ODNB*; Lockhart, *Cosmo Gordon Lang*, pp. 248–51.

[99] Negotiations in the late summer of 1916 over a future visit by Archbishop Lang were no doubt precluded by the 1916 battle of the Somme (1 July – 18 Nov.).

[100] This was reflected in Allied planning for the Somme offensive. Originally designed to be an Anglo-French offensive, the critical situation at Verdun meant that the contribution of the French army was reduced from forty to sixteen divisions. Clayton, *Paths of glory*, p. 116.

[101] In his personal diary, Haig summarized Davidson's visit and their discussion thus:

> We had quite a large party of clerics at lunch. The archbishop of Canterbury and his chaplain, Bishop Gwynne (Deputy Chaplain General), the Principal Chaplain (Rev. Dr. Simms), Lord Cavan, and General Dobell (from the Cameroons) also lunched. The archbishop was very pleased with all he had seen and the work the various chaplains are doing. The latter told him how much they have been helped in their work of late by all Commanders, 'so different to the old days' whatever that may mean.
>
> In reply to a question, I told the Archbishop that I had only two wishes to express and I had already explained them to Bishop Gwynne, and these are:
>
> First that the chaplains should preach to us about the objects of Great Britain in carrying on this war. We have no selfish motive, but are fighting for the good of humanity.
>
> Secondly. The chaplains of the Church of England must cease quarrelling amongst themselves. In the field we cannot tolerate any narrow sectarian ideas. We must all be united.
>
> The Archbishop thought his people were very united now, but possibly six months ago some were troublesome!
>
> *Haig's autograph Great War diary*, 21 May 1916.

Then Gwynne and Mac and I drove back to Montreuil and called upon General Maxwell, who is now Quarter-Master-General, and a delightful man, brother of Father Maxwell.[102] He occupies a beautiful house in a garden near the ramparts. We sat with him there and then walked on the ramparts which overlook the whole plain down to the sea. The view was simply glorious – sunshine flooding the whole plain, and the varied greenery of everything being such as I have hardly ever seen. His beautiful garden reaching to the ramparts, with abundant birds, beautiful trees and shrubs, make it an ideal place, and most unlike 'roughing it' in any way. We reluctantly left it for the long drive across the country to Arras. We carried this out at good speed vîa St. Pol, though with some minor car troubles. It had been arranged that we should go for tea to General ~~Cooper~~ Cowper [sic][103] at the chateau he occupies near Warlus, a few miles west of Arras. When we arrived we found that the General and his aides-de-camp had gone to a little hill above the grounds where he has an observation post, in order to watch the bombarding which had just been opened in great force on the Vimy ridge and in the valley which separates it from Notre Dame de Lorette. We joined him there and he pointed out all that was happening – the terrific cannonade upon the trenches and slopes above Souchez. It was several miles off, but everything was perfectly clear to the naked eye, and with glasses, of which we had several, the bursting of each shell could be watched. I had never realised what a terrific thing a violent bombardment of this sort is – the ceaseless roar and flash and explosions – I felt it one of the most solemnly dreadful sights one could conceive. One can hardly picture the endurance of those who are in the actual fall of these shells. The General bid us watch it as quite exceptional in its violence, and our position enabled us to see it with perfect clearness. The interest for us was greatly enhanced by the fact that the region being shelled included the very slopes on which we had, just 24 hours before, been examining everything with General Wilson.

At General Cowper's request, an aide-de-camp telephoned to General Dudgeon at Arras[104] to know whether he would regard it as safe for me to go down and attend the voluntary service being held in the town at 6.30. General Dudgeon replied naturally enough that it depended upon what we meant by 'safe'. Arras is under shell fire, and the Germans hold the eastern *or southern* suburb,[105] and some form of firing is going on ceaselessly, but he did not think the danger was such as to be prohibitive if I would like to come, and anyhow the service would take place. Of course this was just what I wanted, and we accordingly drove into Arras with the General's aide-de-camp, the General lending us his car in order that ours, which needed some

102 Ronald Charles Maxwell (1852–1924) became quartermaster-general of the BEF on 27 Jan. 1915. In this capacity, he was responsible for its supplies and communications and also for the transportation of its wounded. Despite his efficiency, Maxwell was replaced in Dec. 1917 on the grounds of his age. He was the brother of Fr Gerald Speirs Maxwell, who became superior general of the Society of St John the Evangelist in 1907. *Who's who in World War One*, ed. Bourne, p. 203; Rawson, *British army handbook*, p. 50; *Times*, 22 July 1924, p. 16; *Crockford's*, 1913, pp. 1013–14.

103 Actually, Major-General Victor Arthur Couper (1859–1938), then commanding the 14th (Light) Division. *Times*, 17 May 1938, p. 18.

104 Brigadier-General Frederick Annesley Dudgeon, then commanding 42nd Infantry Brigade, one of the three component brigades of the 14th (Light) Division. A. F. Becke, *History of the Great War based on official documents. Order of battle part 3a. New Army divisions 9–26* (Uckfield, 2007), p. 46.

105 This problem was largely eliminated as a result of British gains in the opening days of the battle of Arras (9 Apr. – 15 May 1917). Wilson, *Myriad faces of war*, pp. 450–4.

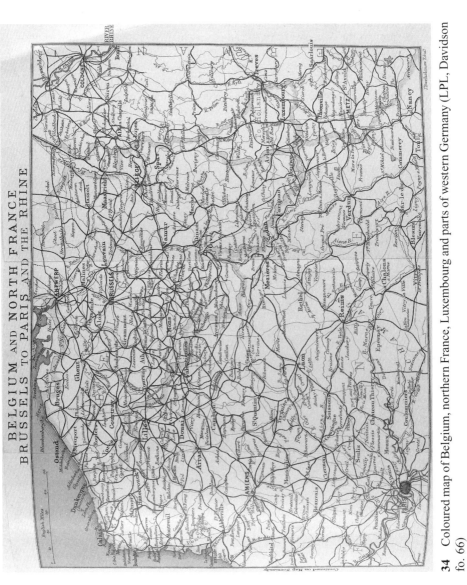

34 Coloured map of Belgium, northern France, Luxembourg and parts of western Germany (LPL, Davidson fo. 66)

attention, might receive it while we were absent, in view of the long drive before us later. We picked up General Dudgeon at his office, and went on with him to a large building, a convent and girls' school, which had been horribly shelled, the chapel and some other parts were in ruin, but some rooms were used by our men. A service was being held in a large hall, or schoolroom, close to the ruined chapel. Meantime the German guns, both machine guns and others, were ceaselessly firing a few hundred yards to the S. East at our aeroplanes, which were overhead, and in addition to this there were shells passing over Arras fired by the Germans from Neuville Vitasse, south of Arras, towards, or at, Mont St. Eloi and Neuville St. Vaast, north of Arras near the Vimy ridge. So the scene was not exactly a quiet one. The room was crowded to extremity by the men, who had come naturally, without any intimation of my visit, but evidently welcoming me with real interest. I spoke straightly and simply to them, but I think helpfully. Among the officers we met in Arras (though I rather think he could not come to the service) was Bernard Paget,[106] who expressed himself specially glad to see me, and with whom I got some minutes quiet talk. He is on the staff as Brigade Major[107] and looked very well and keen. The streets of Arras were a sad spectacle – houses every here and there being quite shattered, and the whole place suffering from almost ceaseless bombardment of some kind. It has been quite definitely explained to us that of course a German shell might drop among us at any moment.[108] But it did not, and in the oddly methodical way the Germans follow in these respects, this was not, they said, exactly the hour for it.

(About a fortnight after getting home I received a letter from Mrs. Annesley, General Dudgeon's sister, who wrote –

'I thought it might interest you to hear what my brother, Brig.-General Dudgeon, said about your visit to France. I will quote his words:- "The Archbishop of Canterbury paid us a visit last Sunday and came to my Headquarters. I took him round to one of my regiments and he arrived while Evening Service was going on in a ruined building. He made such a nice address and the men were <u>delighted</u> at his visit. German shells were bursting quite close to where he was. He is a charming old gentleman and I enjoyed my talk with him."')

The ruined Chapel in the Convent was a sad spectacle. It has been a very fine building. I brought away a scrap of one of the windows lying among the wreckage which piled the floor.[109] The whole scene was striking – the service so perilously surrounded, so noisily accompanied, the soldiers growing quite used to it, and

---

[106] Bernard Paget (1887–1961) was the third son of Francis Paget, bishop of Oxford from 1901 to 1911, and was commissioned into the Oxfordshire and Buckinghamshire Light Infantry in 1907. Considered to be 'one of the stars of his generation', he rose to high rank in the British army. He taught at the Staff College in the interwar years, served with distinction in Norway in 1940 and became commander-in-chief home forces in 1941. However, he was supplanted by General Bernard Law Montgomery, another bishop's son, as commander of the 21st Army Group in Jan. 1944, five months before D-Day. At the time of Davidson's visit, Paget was on the staff of the 42nd Infantry Brigade. *Times*, 18 Feb. 1961, p. 10; R. Mead, *Churchill's lions: a biographical guide to the key British generals of World War II* (Stroud, 2007), pp. 336–41.

[107] Deemed by B. L. Montgomery to be 'the most interesting of all Staff jobs', the task of the brigade major, a relatively lowly staff appointment, was to deal with administration relating to his brigade's operations, intelligence, organization and training. Messenger, *Call-to-arms*, pp. 342–6.

[108] The obvious danger posed by German shelling meant that church services in the trenches were usually forbidden. Snape, *Royal Army Chaplains' Department*, pp. 236–7.

[109] As we have seen, Davidson had also taken a scrap of broken glass from the ruins of St Martin's Cathedral in Ypres. According to Robert Graves, the filching of glass from ruined churches on the

Bailey, the Chaplain, one of our Edmonton men,[110] under Boyd,[111] arranging all quite simply and happily. *When they sang 'There is a green hill far away' I found it difficult to restrain myself.*

On our return drive towards Warlus, in the General's car, we narrowly escaped a grave accident. We were going along a fortunately *straight* safe road at a reasonably fast pace when a tremendous bump came and the whole *hinder* wheel on the near side bounded over the bank into a cornfield. Somehow we did not upset, but we were a mile or two from anywhere, and the only people near us were the gunners working the concealed guns at each side of the road. Fortunately before long one of our cyclists came up, the aide-de-camp commandeered him in the General's name and sent him off to Warlus to fetch our own car. Meanwhile we walked on and had opportunity of seeing the concealed guns beside the road which are in constant use for bombarding the German end of Arras.

The *different* manners of concealment *are* is interesting. The most effective apparently is the spreading over them *on stakes eight or ten feet high* a large piece of wire net on which great turfs are laid at intervals, and it is said that from an aeroplane it is almost impossible to distinguish a gun thus concealed from the rest of the ground. After a time our own car arrived and we started on the long drive back to St. Omer. We were not very clever, I think, about the roads, and lost our way among some small side roads before reaching St. Pol. We wandered as far off the road as Avesnes. However, we got to St. Omer before 11 p.m. and were getting some supper when guns began firing in the streets and the Cathedral bell rang to proclaim danger from bombs. The female folk in our house were greatly alarmed- a ridiculous girl *little daughter of our landlord* going into artificial hysterics and standing on the stairs screaming. Mac was very sympathetic, and I was very cross with her and told her not to be foolish. They wanted us to go into the cellars, but we would not be disturbed and finished our supper. In the morning it turned out that no bomb had fallen in the actual town, but that the gunners had fired freely at aeroplanes, which they heard, though I am by no means sure that they actually saw them. Such at least was the opinion of the orderly who was waiting on me, and he is a personal friend of some of the gunners.

Altogether it had been a very long and very memorable day, brimful of interest and of grave suggestion as to the magnitude, complexity, and difficulty of our extraordinary task, and the nature of the dangers which are every day going on. <u>Monday May 22nd</u>. I had to attend to some business about chaplains etc. early, and

Western Front could be seen as sacrilegious, and therefore unlucky, by front-line soldiers. R. Graves, *Goodbye to all that* (London, 1960), p. 100.

[110] Charles Henry Bailey, formerly of University College, Oxford (BA 1905), trained at Wells and was ordained deacon in 1907 and priest in 1908. Following a curacy in Birmingham, Bailey went to Canada, joining the Edmonton Mission, in the diocese of Calgary, in 1910. He was commissioned into the AChD on 7 Dec. 1914 at the age of thirty-two. *Crockford's*, 1913, p. 61; *Monthly army list*, July 1916, 1791; RAChD Archive, Amport House, card index..

[111] Arthur Hamilton Boyd (1869–1955), a non-graduate, was trained at Edinburgh Theological College and ordained deacon in 1896 and priest in 1897. He became rector of Slaugham in 1901 after serving two curacies in Sussex. A pre-war chaplain to the 4th Royal Sussex, a battalion of the Territorial Force, Boyd was commissioned into the AChD on 24 Sept. 1914 and he won the Military Cross on the Western Front five months later. He was senior chaplain of the 3rd Cavalry Division at the time of Davidson's visit. *Crockford's*, 1913, p. 168; *Monthly army list*, July 1916, 1791a; http://www.chailey1914–1918.net/arthur_hamilton_boyd.html, consulted 30 July 2009.

at 10 o'clock arrived Captain Nosworthy,[112] aide-de-camp to General Sir Charles Fergusson, commanding a corps of the Second Army,[113] whose headquarters are at Bailleul. He had been sent to take us to a vantage point for seeing the sector of the line south of Ypres before going on to lunch with Sir Charles Fergusson. In the General's car we drove by Cassel, Abeele and Boeschepe to Westoutre, across the Belgian frontier. I managed to stop there in order to see what I had been anxious to see, one of the great laundries and mending places for the Army. In some long huts adapted from existing sheds, 150 stalwart Flemish girls were working in what seemed to me a quiet and orderly way at the washing and mending of the clothes of the men from the Front. Each is paid three francs a day.[114] *An English* A non-commissioned officer was in charge of them when we were there and he took us round, his superior being absent. He assured us they behaved extremely well, but I felt the arrangement to be open to some difficulty.[115] The girls were less alert or giggly than English girls would I think have been in like circumstances as we ploughed our way through wash tubs and the mending rooms. An immense deal of work was going on. The piles of clothing seemed quite appalling. No men work with them, but there are forewomen, one or two of whom, we were told, had been in 'Homes' in England, which did not perhaps suggest all that might be desired, but it enables communications to pass between the girls who speak Flemish, not French, and the men in command.

Thence we drove on to a certain well-known height with a windmill which has been used as an observation post for showing Royal and other people this part of the line. The visitors included, we were told, our own King, King Albert,[116] Mr. Asquith,[117] and some others. It is called Scherpenberg. We walked up through some

112 Francis Poitiers Nosworthy (1888–1971), who was commissioned into the Royal Engineers in 1907. During his years on the Western Front Nosworthy 'was wounded twice, mentioned in dispatches six times, and awarded the French War Cross, D.S.O. and Bar [and] M.C. and Bar'. He was appointed a general staff officer third grade on 17 Jan. 1916. *Times*, 12 July 1971, p. 14; *The London Gazette*, 18 Feb. 1916, p. 1809.

113 Lieutenant-General Sir Charles Fergusson (1865–1951), seventh baronet of Kilkerran, had commanded II Corps on the Ypres sector since Jan. 1915. However, he was transferred to the command of XVII Corps, in Third Army, three days after meeting Davidson. *Times*, 21 Feb. 1951, Becke, *Order of battle part 4*, pp. 137, 233.

114 Salvage, repair and recycling were great preoccupations of the BEF and, by Sept. 1918, its efforts were saving the British taxpayer £4 million per month. By 1917, and in Le Havre alone, around 1,500 French women were employed in cleaning items of equipment retrieved from the front. Messenger, *Call-to-arms*, pp. 234–5.

115 The question of sexual morality in the army concerned Davidson throughout the war. In Mar. 1918 he clashed with the adjutant-general, Sir Nevil Macready, over the right of army chaplains to report directly to him on the issue of army-regulated brothels in France, a scandal that had raised a public outcry the previous month. At the same time, Davidson forced a debate in the House of Lords over the 'morals and health' of the soldiers of the BEF. As a result of this debate in Apr. 1918, the War Office felt obliged to convene a conference of doctors and churchmen on the subject, a conference that resulted in a War Office circular which emphasized that 'continence and self-control' were 'the only real safeguard' against venereal disease. Bell, *Randall Davidson*, II, 891–7.

116 Albert I (1875–1934), king of the Belgians. Despite the virtual conquest of Belgium in the summer and autumn of 1914, under King Albert's command the Belgian army remained in being throughout the war, holding its own sector on a narrow strip of Belgian territory between Ypres and the North Sea. *Who's who in World War One*, ed. Bourne, p. 2.

117 Herbert Henry Asquith (1852–1928), Britain's Liberal prime minister from Apr. 1908 to Dec. 1916. His eldest son, Raymond Asquith, was killed on the Somme in Sept. 1916. *Who's who in World War One*, ed. Bourne, p. 11.

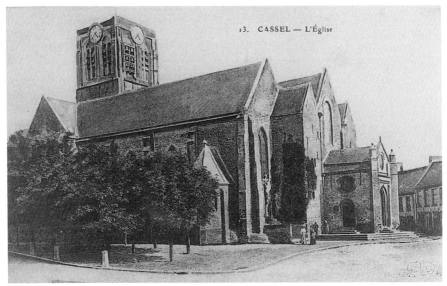

35   Postcard of Cassel church (LPL, Davidson 583, fo. 110)

36   Postcard of Cassel town hall
(LPL, Davidson 583, fo. 111)

copse wood to the windmill which is well placed for seeing the whole country round. The hill was swarming with troops in rest billets *and I got some talk with some of them*. It is within range of shells, but it is, as a matter of fact, very little shelled. From the top one can see the whole Ypres salient, and the range of country round, and Nosworthy pointed out to us all the English and German lines and the notable points in the country beyond them. It was a little hazy for the distant places, but we could easily watch the intermittent shelling which was going on along the ridge of Messines,[118] and also see south-east towards Armentieres, in the nearer distance Bailleul, and other places. We had very clear explanations from Nosworthy, a nice boy who had been badly wounded at Ypres, where he had evidently shown great courage and received the Military Cross. He told me that when he was taken into the hospital, the surgeon who examined him said to the nurse 'We had better go on to the next case. This poor fellow will be dead in half an hour.' Nosworthy added that he felt he would have liked to jump up and kick him – 'whether what he said was true or not, and I did not believe him, he certainly had no business to say so in my hearing, and I wanted to tell him so. But I could not move.'

He is an enthusiastic friend of Archdeacon Southwell's, to whom he says he owes everything, and he struck me as being an admirable specimen of the young officer product of first-rate chaplaincy work.[119] I had lots of time for quiet talk with him during our drive. Mac was sitting in front.

After a leisurely inspection of the whole front from this excellent observation point, and much endeavour to make out different places through the increasing haze, we drove on to Bailleul and there had lunch with Sir Charles Fergusson and his staff in their big *house* huts in the centre of the town. Bailleul is a place in which gas has been used against the town.[120] Whether this was accidental or intentional, it was somewhat appalling in its effects, civilians as well as the soldiers being made exceedingly ill by it. E.g. the matron of the Casualty Clearing Station[121] which I visited, and with whom I had much talk, described to me its effect on her. It rather interested me to find how fairly and reasonably the officers discussed this. 'The Germans are within their rights in doing it. If people stay here they must take the consequences however unpleasant.' Fergusson had a few hours before we arrived been appointed to the command of a Corps in the Fourth Army[122] near Souchez, the

---

118   Messines Ridge was taken in spectacular fashion by Plumer's Second Army on 7 June 1917. Holmes (ed.), *Oxford companion to military history*, p. 580.

119   Although hardly their preserve, the officer corps was the natural home for the alumni of Britain's public schools and universities. Given that younger officers were the future leaders of society, and as it was commonly accepted that its officers set the tone of army life, ecclesiastical observers were greatly concerned about the state of religion among them, especially in the light of their earlier religious education. Snape, *God and the British soldier*, pp. 147–51.

120   Banned under the terms of the Hague Declaration on Asphyxiating Gases of 1899, to which Germany had subscribed, the German army nevertheless pioneered the use of poison gas in the First World War. After experimenting on the Russians in Jan., the first mass gas attack on the Western Front was unleashed against the French near Ypres on 22 Apr. 1915. A. Roberts, 'Land warfare: from Hague to Nuremberg', in *The laws of war*, ed. M. Howard, G. J. Andreopoulos and M. R. Shulman (New Haven, 1994), pp. 123–4; Holmes (ed.), *Oxford companion to military history*, p. 200.

121   Casualty Clearing Stations, which effectively served as field hospitals some distance behind the front line, were vital links in the British army's chain of treatment and evacuation of its sick and wounded, and had become 'the hub of the medical system in the field' by 1916. Messenger, *Call-to-arms*, pp. 415–17.

122   Actually the Third Army, see above, pp. 505 n. 113.

very region of the hard, and as we now heard successful German attack which we had watched yesterday from above Warlus. He was kindness and friendliness itself, and of course we had many links in common. He is nephew of Mrs. Kennion and of Sir Charles Dalrymple. He is one of Gwynne's strongest upholders in religious matters, and is evidently extremely popular. We had abundant talk and he gave me a very curious account of the friendly relations subsisting between the combatant airmen of the opposing countries when an aerial battle is over, each honouring and caring for the other. They fight with the utmost violence in the air, but as soon as one of our airmen comes down in German lines they send up an aeroplane which drops a message with streamers to say (or words to the effect) 'Your gallant officer, Captain – is we regret to say injured. We are doing everything for him that is possible,' or again 'Captain – is we grieve to say dead. We are burying him with full military honours.' This is reciprocated on our side, and seems not to correspond closely with what happens in other branches of the services.[123]

I also met at Fergusson's table General Radcliffe, a son of old Sir Polloxfen [sic] Radcliffe,[124] whom I had known so well in Drummuir days. This man I had, as he remembers, seen more than once when he was a little boy, and he startled the officers at mess by saying – 'The Archbishop taught me to shoot.' Apparently he had walked with me in shooting days at Drummuir, and learned something from me.

After lunch and talk we went off on a round of local visitations, seeing Church huts, Y.M.C.A. huts,[125] the kinema huts, hospital clearing station etc. The huts at Bailleul are much like those near Canterbury, and indeed some of the workers had been working at Canterbury. It struck me, however, that the soldiers were, as is natural, much more keen and absorbed. Outside one hut a little class was being conducted by a Sergeant about pigeon posts.[126] We remained to listen, and he went into it all for us and we learned much about the success of the pigeon-flying system from the trenches. The pigeons return to the dovecots, which are their permanent

[123] Despite its prosaic and often brutal nature, the conflict in the air was greatly romanticized in the war years. As late as 1917, Lloyd George described contemporary pilots as 'the knighthood of this war, without fear and without reproach' and even Manfred von Richtofen, the most ruthless and lethal of all German fighter aces, received a funeral with full military honours when he was shot down over British lines in Apr. 1918. Nevertheless, 'Mick' Mannock, the top-scoring British ace of the war, revealed more of the realities of the air war when he famously said of Richtofen's demise: 'I hope the bastard burned the whole way down.' D. Jordan, 'War in the air: the fighter pilot', in *The Great World War 1914–45. Volume 1. Lightning strikes twice*, ed. P. Liddle, J. Bourne and I. Whitehead (London, 2000), pp. 80–98, at p. 81; *Who's who in World War One*, ed. Bourne, pp. 194–5, 248–9.

[124] Brigadier-General Percy Pollexfen de Blacquiere Radcliffe (1874–1934) was the only son of General Sir William Pollexfen Radcliffe, a veteran of the Crimean War and of the Indian Mutiny, and was commissioned into the Royal Artillery in 1893. He graduated from the Staff College in 1905 and served throughout the war as a staff officer. At the time of Davidson's visit he was brigadier-general general staff in II Corps, and in that capacity was involved in the evaluation of military intelligence and in the planning of operations. Becke, *Order of battle part 4*, p. 137; Rawson, *British army handbook*, p. 62; *Times*, 10 Feb. 1934, p. 14.

[125] The Young Men's Christian Association was the largest civilian religious organization working with the BEF. Relations between the interdenominational YMCA and individual denominations could be rather strained, as Davidson goes on to illustrate. However, as archbishop of Canterbury Davidson was a vice-president of the Association and, at the opening of a YMCA hut at Folkestone earlier in the year, he had acknowledged that the YMCA was 'first and foremost among societies working for the well-being of soldiers'. *The back parts of war*, ed. Snape, pp. 18, 29.

[126] A pigeon service had been established in 1915 and, by this stage of the war, carrier pigeons were normally issued to infantry battalions at the rate of two per day. Rawson, *British army handbook*, p. 312.

Flemish homes, or more interestingly, to our own lorry transport dovecots, which the pigeons will find directly, even if the lorry has moved several miles away from where the pigeon had last seen them. Of course there is no possibility of sending messages by this means to the trenches, only from them.

One of the Y.M.C.A. men was a Canadian Congregationalist Minister with a post at Toronto. I felt a little in the atmosphere of a rather determined and independent Y.M.C.A. religion which owes no allegiance to any Church; but perhaps I was wrong.[127]

I inspected a clearing hospital pretty thoroughly. It was a pathetic sight – a great row of stretchers of wounded men had just been brought in. They were being seen to. Then I spoke to a row of amputation cases recently operated upon – some of them rather proud of their stumps. Then the wards of sick, not wounded, men, and some wards of officers, including an Australian Brigadier-General. These were in cubicles, the place being ordinarily a great boarding-school. Among them was a Belgian officer, who *on learning* had learned my identity (he was very ill) reverently craved my blessing, and tried to kneel to receive it. I gave it in Latin.[128] The matron seemed a capable lady, the daughter of old [blank] Chaplain to Queen Victoria and the Duke of Edinburgh. The medical men, two young Scotsmen, impressed me rather less than she did. These inspections took some time, and then we drove off, having our first taste of rain, via Estaires to Lestrem, where we found General Pinkey [*sic*][129] who commands the Bantams.[130] He too was in a chateau surrounded by a moat where he entertained us at tea, and then, in slight rain, he drove us off in his car, the others following in Gwynne's car, to see first a captive balloon and its manner of working. We had all its mechanism and that of its parachutes explained to us.[131] From this we drove on to some open fields to inspect two Battalions of Bantams. They were in separate places near Paradis, a couple of miles apart. I found

---

127 For precisely these reasons, relations between Canadian chaplains and the Canadian YMCA were notably poor. Crerar, *Padres in no-man's land*, pp. 75–80.

128 A significant and poignant incident given that Pope Leo XIII (1878–1903) had pronounced anglican orders to be 'absolutely null and utterly void' in his bull *Apostolicae Curae* of 18 Sept. 1896. The bull followed Lord Halifax's ingenuous efforts to promote a reconciliation between Rome and Canterbury, efforts that Davidson had watched closely and critically as bishop of Rochester. Bell, *Randall Davidson*, I, 228–37.

129 Actually, Major-General Reginald John Pinney (1863–1943). Pinney was the eldest son of an anglican clergyman, namely John Charles Pinney, vicar of Coleshill in Warwickshire, and was commissioned into the Royal Fusiliers in 1884. He graduated from Staff College in 1890 and, after the outbreak of war, was given command of the 23rd Infantry Brigade. In July 1915 he was moved from this regular formation to become commander of the 35th Division, a formation composed of Kitchener volunteers, and was moved to the 33rd Division (a mixture of regulars, Territorials and Kitchener volunteers) in Sept. 1916. Here he famously stopped the issue of the traditional rum ration; for this, or so Frank Richards later claimed, Pinney (who was known to be 'a devout, non-smoking teetotaller') was widely decried as 'a bun-punching crank and more fitted to be in command of a Church Mission hut at the Base than a division of troops'. *ODNB*; *Who's who in World War One*, ed. Bourne, p. 234; F. Richards, *Old soldiers never die* (London, 1983), p. 217.

130 'Bantams' was a term coined to denote Kitchener volunteers who were under the army's initial height requirement of five feet three inches. The first 'Bantam' battalion was raised in Cheshire in Nov. 1914 and eventually two divisions of Bantams were raised, namely the 35th and the 40th. Messenger, *Call-to-arms*, pp. 106–8.

131 Fixed balloons were first deployed by the BEF in 1915 and were operated by the Royal Flying Corps for the purpose of artillery observation. Usually deployed in pairs in order to enhance the accuracy of their spotting, their vulnerability to air attack meant that balloon crews were the only British airmen to be permitted the use of parachutes. R. Barker, *The Royal Flying Corps in France: from*

myself called upon to make a speech to each, after inspecting them in detail – first to the Royal Scots in a field at Lacoture, and then to the West Yorkshires, nearer Paradis.[132] The men had just come in from the trenches near Neuve Chapelle,[133] and I was rather distressed to find they had been stopped before reaching their billets in order that I might see them and speak to them. However, they seemed to enjoy it and they looked *a* very tough and vigorous group of little men. They were grimy and muddy, but quite brisk and very ready to talk, so far as inspection etiquette permitted. I had not been prepared for these addresses, but both Mac and Gwynne thought that what I said was ~~specially~~ right and stimulating. Many of the Scotsmen came from Edinburgh which gave me opportunity.[134]

Then we drove back to St. Omer, via Merville and Hazebrouck. We were a little late for dinner, and found Colonel J. Campbell, Cawdor's nephew,[135] and Major *Crawford*, both of the Coldstreams, to dinner. They are dear friends of Bishop Gwynne's, and had just arrived at St. Omer with their men. With them Gwynne was more amusing and anecdotal than I have ever known him. Major Crawford knew Ernest[136] and had stayed at Grey Walls.[137] They both seemed quite admirable specimens of the British officer.

I had been greatly impressed on the roads with the huge array of motor lorries loaded with ammunition, or with food stores, or other equipment.[138] The sight of these great rows of them, hundreds together, ranged on side roads, waiting for night-fall to make their way forward, gave one, when one thought of it, almost a keener notion of the organisation needed, than anything else did. I was amused to find that one of the biggest and most formidable looking of these ranges of cars, turned out

---

Mons to the Somme (London, 1995), pp. 89–93; Pope and Wheal, *Macmillan dictionary of the First World War*, p. 57.

132 These details indicate that Davidson addressed the 17th Royal Scots and the 17th West Yorkshires of 106th Infantry Brigade. A. F. Becke, *History of the Great War based on official documents. Order of battle part 3b. New Army divisions 30–41 and 63rd (R.N.) Division* (Uckfield, 2007), p. 54.

133 Neuve Chapelle was the scene of an attack by First Army, which was then commanded by Haig, on 10 Mar. 1915. Though initially successful, it failed to break through the German lines owing to a lack of support and the offensive was called off three days later. Pope and Whelan, *Macmillan dictionary of the First World War*, p. 338.

134 The 17th Royal Scots had been raised in Edinburgh in Feb. 1915. James, *British regiments*, p. 43.

135 John Vaughan Campbell (1876–1944) was commissioned into the Coldstream Guards on 5 Sept. 1896. His father had been killed in the Anglo-Zulu War of 1879 and he was a nephew of the third earl of Cawdor, a Conservative politician who had served as first lord of the admiralty. Campbell had seen active service in the Boer War, where he earned a DSO, and he won the Victoria Cross while commanding the 3rd Coldstream Guards on the Somme in 1916, gamely rallying the survivors of his battalion with his hunting horn during its attack on Ginchy on 15 Sept. Promoted to brigadier-general in Nov. 1917, he commanded the 137th Infantry Brigade of the 46th (North Midland) Division until Nov. 1918, when he was given command of the 3rd Guards Brigade in recognition of his leadership at Bellenglise in Sept., where his brigade had led an attack that pierced the defences of the vaunted Hindenburg Line. *Times*, 9 Jan. 1914, p. 9; 'Lions led by donkeys', consulted 30 July 2009.

136 Ernest Davidson, the archbishop's youngest brother (1856–?). Bell, *Randall Davidson*, I, 7.

137 Grey Walls, near Muirfield and its golf links, had been built as a holiday home by Alfred Lyttelton (1857–1913), a barrister, Liberal Unionist politician and well-known sportsman. Designed by Edwin Lutyens, it had later played host to Edward VII. *ODNB*; http://www.greywalls.co.uk, consulted 3 Sept. 2009.

138 By the end of 1916, there were more than 18,500 lorries in the BEF in addition to nearly 8,000 cars, vans and ambulances. *Statistics of the military effort of the British empire during the Great War, 1914–1920* (London, 1992), p. 593.

on closer inspection to be not great heavy lorries after all, but London omnibuses painted slate colour and looking most imposing and as unlike <u>buses</u> as possible.

<u>Tuesday May 23rd.</u> At 11 a.m. after a stroll in St. Omer, we three drove off to Hazebrouck to see Abbé Lamire [*sic*],[139] who is the only Deputy now sitting in the Chamber who is also a priest. Besides this he is Mayor of the town, and is altogether a person of great importance and much personal charm. We had a long talk with him and he struck me as a man of real capacity, earnestness and certainly eloquence. He is suspended by Papal Order from the exercise of his functions as a priest because he refused to ask the sanction of his Bishop to his standing for the Chamber of Deputies. He said he did not ask it because he thought it very probably would be refused in which case *if he had asked for leave* he could not stand; therefore he preferred to do it without getting leave. I did not gather that they place him at any disadvantage beyond forbidding his officiating.* [*I learned subsequently that a few months later this ban had been removed and he is again in good favour.]

I asked him about the outcome of the war in its effect on religion in France. He was not very sure of his hopes. Religion, he thinks, has obtained a fresh footing, but he wonders whether it is religion of a robust kind. He thought that Sacré Coeur would be in lieu of the Cross, and that the religion was rather unmanly and of a narrow type.[140] All this would be very foreign to his nature or wish. The problem of the schools is the most difficult of all, and he feels no certainty that these things will be right after the war as regards the re-admission of religion to the schools from which it is banished.[141] He described how a great many women are now teaching in the schools in order to get the opportunity of influencing the children religiously, most of these ladies having been Sisters, but as religious orders cannot now teach in Government-aided schools, they have dropped their garb, with full ecclesiastical consent and sanction, and teach simply as Mdlle.——. He thought they were doing much good. He went on to say that the men of France are not really irreligious.

139 Jules Auguste Lemire (1853–1928), first elected to the chamber of deputies in 1893, was the most influential figure in a new generation of French 'democratic priests'. These emerged during the pontificate of Leo XIII and were committed to the principles of democracy and social justice (Lemire, for example, was a keen advocate of workers' allotments). However, priests like Lemire fell under a cloud during the pontificate of Pius X (1903–14), when liberals and modernists were equally unpopular at the Vatican, but this cloud largely dispersed under Benedict XV (1914–22). Nevertheless, in 1914 Lemire got into trouble over a question of obedience, namely by defying his bishop in standing for the chamber of deputies for the sixth time while also acting as the mayor of Hazebrouck. The dispute was of brief duration, however, and the ban on Lemire saying mass was quickly lifted. Lemire has been described as 'a Fleming with a rough face and a down-to-earth mode of expression [who] was as wily as a peasant and as simple as a Church student'. Nevertheless, his populist instincts also meant that he tended to get 'carried away … by the applause of the radicals and socialists and was sometimes too ready to point out the political errors of the Church in France'. A. Dansette, *Religious history of modern France. Volume II. Under the Third Republic* (Freiburg and Edinburgh, 1961), pp. 127–8.

140 A more traditional, right-wing catholicism was on the march in wartime France. The cult of the Sacred Heart, long associated with royalism and with conservative nationalism, enjoyed a dramatic resurgence and the cults of female saints (and putative saints) also intensified, the three 'most popular intercessors' during the war years being the Virgin Mary, Joan of Arc and Thérèse of Lisieux. Becker, *War and faith*, pp. 79, 85–96.

141 As a result of two waves of anticlerical legislation under the Third Republic, religious instruction had been removed from the curriculum of state schools in 1882 and catholic teaching orders and their schools had been suppressed in 1904, the year before the formal separation of church and state in France. R. Price, *A concise history of France* (Cambridge, 1997), pp. 197–8, 203.

38   Postcard of the tomb of Monseignor de Croy, Cathedral of Nôtre Dame, St Omer (LPL, Davidson 583, fo. 119)

They had been forced into opposition to the Catholic Church though they ought not to have yielded to the force. But they wished their children to be religiously taught and to go to Mass, even if they did not go themselves, but a great many were going now. All the parents here in Hazebrouck sent their children to Catechism and to First Communion.

We then passed to the condition of France in other respects, and he was not inclined to be very buoyant. He is himself quite clear and determined about the war, but he says that in many parts of France the people are losing patience – 'You English have more patience than we have. You know our temperament, especially in the south. It is not satisfactory to me to see how many people are beginning to be impatient for peace, however it may be obtained.' (I ought to say that this was vehemently contradicted to me afterwards by men who profess to know.)

The Abbé edits a newspaper which has now a peculiar character. It is called 'Le Cri des Flandres', and instead of carrying on its old character it now consists entirely of news as to the whereabouts and well-being of people in different parts of France who want their friends in the part occupied by [the] Germans to know about them. They pay something for a few lines of insertion and the paper consists of nothing else. He gave me a copy of it. It was dated last January, but he says it is of the same kind still. When our aeroplanes are going over part of the Germanly-occupied France they drop quantities of these which are circulated among the population who find out about their relations or concerns in this way. The Germans take no great exception, and even in some cases allow the newspapers to be exhibited in shop windows. But they would not allow a more open or avowed circulation lest it should be made use of by giving, in cipher, or otherwise, military information. Such was the Abbé's story, and I have kept the copy of the paper. I left him after this long talk with the sense that he is a fine specimen of a liberal-minded religious

Frenchman. Before I left he knelt down and asked for my blessing. What his Bishop would have said I do not know. I gave him the full benediction from our Communion Office in Latin as we use it in Convocation. He was pleased with this and asked afterwards to have the words said again that he might know them.[142]

Then we drove on to Cassel, walking the last part of the way so as to enjoy the sun and views from the hill of Cassel. Sir H. Plumer had arrived the previous evening from London. He welcomed us very cordially in his interesting house on the very top of the hill of Cassel. It is an awkward enough building of staircases, but it has marvellous views from the coast line southwards and eastwards, and is eminently the place for a headquarters staff. Plumer and some of his officers told me that they believed Cassel to be the scene of the rhyme about the Duke of York commanding 100,000 [sic] men, who marched his army up the hill and marched them down again! But they were not sure of the identity of the place. I undertook to find out for them in return for the hospitality they had shown me. I may therefore add here that on getting back to London I set to work on what proved an impossible task – the identification of the hill in question. I consulted John Fortescue of Windsor, Sir F. Kenyon and Mr. Pollard of the British Museum, Mr. Tedder of the Athenaeum, who again consulted Mr. Hilaire Belloc, and I think Mr. Buchan.[143] But it was all in vain. The Duke of York, George III's son, was no doubt in Flanders, and not far from the Hill of Cassel, but he did nothing which corresponds to the rhyme.[144] What is more important, Tedder unearthed the fact that the rhyme is older than his date, and that if the Duke of York is the right person it must refer to James II, and not to Flanders at all. Again the rhyme appears to have another form which substitutes the King of France for the Duke of York. The correspondence about the matter I sent to Plumer. All this is by the way.

We had abundant talk with Plumer. He began by saying that had he been on the spot when we wished to go to Ypres, he would have forbidden it. I told him that I was profoundly thankful that he had been in England as I had greatly appreci-

---

142 It is hard to avoid the conclusion that Davidson's meeting with Lemire, and other positive contact with French and Belgian catholics in May 1916, helped to prepare the way for Davidson's *rôle* in the Malines Conversations with Cardinal Mercier of 1921–6. Bell, *Randall Davidson*, II, 1254–302.

143 In 1916 Sir John Fortescue (1859–1933), a younger son of the Third Earl Fortescue, was librarian at Windsor Castle and was in the midst of writing what would become a thirteen-volume history of the British army, a history that he published between 1899 and 1930. Sir Frederic Kenyon (1863–1952) was a classicist and biblical scholar who was director of the British Museum from 1909 to 1930. Albert Frederick Pollard (1869–1948) was professor of constitutional history at University College, London, a former president of the Historical Association and editor of its journal *History*. Henry Richard Tedder (1850–1924) was a member of the royal commission on public records and had been librarian of the Athenaeum since 1876. Besides his literary distinction and his standing as a former Liberal MP, Hilaire Belloc (1870–1953) was a popular historian and a vocal commentator on military affairs. Already famous as the author of *The thirty-nine steps* (1915), John Buchan (1875–1940) was the principal author of *Nelson's history of the war*, which appeared in twenty-four volumes from 1915 to July 1919; in June 1916 he joined GHQ in France with the task of writing its official communiqués. *Times*, 23 Oct. 1933, p. 19, 25 Aug. 1952, p. 8, 5 Aug. 1948, p. 7, 2 Aug. 1924, p. 15, 17 July 1953, p. 8; *ODNB; Who's who in World War One*, ed. Bourne, pp. 43–4.

144 Frederick Augustus, duke of York and Albany (1763–1827), took command of an Allied army in Flanders in 1793. The following year, and after several major battles, the French drove his army into Holland and the hapless duke of York returned to England. Decades later, the Duke of Wellington said of this unfortunate campaign: 'I learned what one ought not to do, and that is always something.' *The encyclopedia of military biography*, ed. T. N. Dupuy, C. Johnson and D. Bongard (London, 1992), pp. 825–6; M. Glover, *Wellington as military commander* (London, 2001), p. 33.

ated the Ypres opportunity. He showed me carefully his maps, as the other Army Commanders had done, and we had a good deal of talk about the relative difficulty of each sector of the four. We also discussed the chaplains and their work, and the gain of the permission given them to be in the trenches. His view of the good they are doing corresponded with what I had heard from all the rest. Plumer was rather grave about the bombarding of the Souchez to Vimy region on Sunday which we had witnessed. He thinks it *gives* additional evidence of the unimpaired strength of Germany and their absence of any anxiety about ammunition. He sees the gravity of the work before us, the real need of men, even inadequately trained men, for training might be completed after they are in France. Kitchener, he said, had asked him whether he would consent to having 200 untrained men in each battalion. He had said he would gladly take them rather than have the battalions remain short of their full strength. He thinks it quite a mistake to describe such men as useless. However we have come to this that it must be a war of attrition now and nothing else. He does not expect fireworks, but there is danger to us, though he hopes to Germany also, of too long a prolongation of the preparation months. We are already late in the field. When the men have *been enlisted in England* come in in June under the new Act,[145] they will not be ready to take the field before September at the very earliest. Then winter will be coming on. It was all thoughtful, useful, reasonable, and grave. Not depressed, but definitely grave. He shares the nervousness some feel about French perseverance, and he was interested in all I told him about the Haze-brouck conversations with Lemire. Plumer is surprised, as I am, at the scrappiness of the information obtainable in France about those parts of France which are under German rule. No accounts of really atrocious behaviour on the part of the German officers occupying Eastern France seem to have reached any of the Generals to whom I had talked about it, but Plumer thought there were isolated instances of wrong-doing, due probably to the vagaries of particular German officers, who were either undisciplined or vicious.* [* Of course all this was before the beginning of the deportations from Lille and elsewhere of which we have heard so much since.][146]

I found my whole talk with Plumer wholesome and sobering.

We got back to St. Omer in the afternoon and I spent its later hours in visiting various places with Gwynne. First the hospital which is now also a casualty clearing

---

[145] A reference to the Military Service Act (No. 2) of May 1916, which was about to receive the royal assent and that extended conscription to married men. The original Military Service Act of Jan. 1916 had introduced conscription for single men aged between eighteen and forty-one who were resident in mainland Britain and who had no dependants. Rawson, *British army handbook*, p. 34; I. Beckett, 'The nation in arms, 1914–18', in *A nation in arms: a social study of the British army in the First World War* , ed. I. F. W. Beckett and K. Simpson (Manchester, 1985), pp. 1–35, at pp. 12–13.

[146] For the civilian population, conditions in occupied France were very severe, as were those in occupied Belgium. Its population of more than two million were subjected to the systematic requisitioning of food, goods and raw materials. While the Germans took hostages (including the bishop of Lille) as early as the autumn of 1914, forced labour and deportations started in 1916. Resisters of all kinds were subject to summary trials and executions and it was indicative of the depth of German paranoia about partisan activity that at least sixteen pigeon fanciers were executed for not surrendering their birds. A. Becker, 'Life in an occupied zone: Lille, Roubaix, Tourcoing', in *Facing Armageddon: the First World War experienced*, ed. H. Cecil and P. H. Liddle (London, 1996), pp. 630–41; M. Atack, 'The experience of occupation: northern France', in *The Great World War 1914–45. Volume 1*, ed. Bourne, Liddle and Whitehead, pp. 533–50; S. Audoin-Rouzeau and A. Becker, *1914–1918: understanding the Great War* (London, 2002), pp. 54–64.

station. It is normally a great school. I went all over it and spoke to the doctors, matron, nurses, and most of the patients who were well enough to converse. It was a sad sight in many ways, but seemed to me well managed and the Chaplain and Matron are on good terms. I did not feel quite so sure about the surgeons. Their largest ward was formerly the chapel of the school and is a huge place, not I thought so satisfactory as many, as the lighting is indifferent for patients who want to read etc.

From the hospital I went with Mac to visit the Monro Institute – an excellent Church club and recreation room erected close to the Barracks.[147] I talked there both with workers and men. Then I met Colonel Campbell of the Coldstreams, and with him went over the Barracks. I was greatly struck by his close touch with the men and their evident affection for him. He brought his staff *and* non-commissioned officers, including one rather heroic sergeant-major, to talk to me. The Barracks, which are ordinarily occupied by French troops, are less unlike our home barracks than I had expected. About the men there was an obvious seriousness which betokened what they had gone through, *near Ypres*, and might yet have to go through, and it was in a sort of awestruck way that some of them spoke about the fearful fighting in the trenches. No one, they said, could wish to go back to it, though they were quite ready to go when they were wanted, not light-heartedly, but determinedly.

After these rounds, Mac and I had a walk as tourists round the town, inspecting again the Cathedral, the Tour St. Bertin, and other things including the vast building which was once the Jesuit College where our Irish clergy were trained. It belonged to England till, I think, 1840, and it was then sold at a great price to France as a military hospital.[148]

At night the remaining Army General, Sir Charles Monro, who had been in England when I visited the First Army (which he commands) came to dinner. It had been to me a great advantage to go over the ground with Sir Henry Wilson, and then to be able, thirty-six hours later, to discuss it with Sir Charles Monro. We had abundant talk. A delightful man, forthcoming in all ways. I do not think I elicited much that was new, but he was able to summarise and correlate what I had already been trying to learn.

Wednesday May 24th. I took the Early Service in the Chapel, or Oratory, which Gwynne has in his other house, i.e. the house in which he sleeps, not that in which he eats and sleeps his guests. The other chaplains, some half a dozen, who were in and near St. Omer, and were available, attended. At 10 a.m. we started on my homeward journey. Half-way along the road to Boulogne, say 20 miles from St. Omer, we

147 In contrast to Britain, conscription was a fact of life in pre-war France. In Aug. 1914, the French army had more than 820,000 men under arms and nearly 3,000,000 reservists. Consequently, and due to the regional organization of the French army, substantial barracks were a ubiquitous feature of larger provincial towns. Clayton, *Paths of glory*, p. 32; P. Haythornthwaite, *The World War One source book* (London, 1992), p. 173.

148 Established by Robert Parsons in the early 1590s for the purpose of educating English catholics, the Jesuit College at St Omer was, in its origins and history, an emphatically English institution. Accordingly, when the Society of Jesus was suppressed in France in 1762, the buildings passed into the possession of the English College at Douai, which was run by secular priests, and a new school was created. Although its staff and students were in turn evicted in 1793, its buildings were returned to the executors of a former president after the restoration of the Bourbon monarchy and were eventually sold to the French government. 'Catholic Encyclopaedia: College of St. Omer', http://www.newadvent.org, consulted 3 Sept. 2009.

stopped to visit General Tommy Pitman,[149] who occupies a huge chateau with his staff. He is in command of the cavalry,[150] and is evidently showing his accustomed vigour, training them and stimulating them in all ways. He was full of cheerful manly talk, and I found it interesting to go over with him some of the questions I had been puzzled about. He had not seen so much as I had seen of the whole line, but of course he knew his own part exceedingly well. In his great garden, which like those of the other chateaux, is full of rank grass, tall poplars, stagnant ponds, and a general look of what would be called in England 'unsatisfactoriness' in a garden, he had been fashioning under the trees a wonderful map or model on a huge scale, made in [?] sand, which grows hard. It gave a great tract of country eastwards over which the cavalry may one day have to pass, and he had marked all the levels of hills and valleys and every village, and almost every tree. He thought it very useful for his officers that they might thoroughly understand the country which he hopes they are to traverse 'when the push does come.' One of his men, Keith Falconer, was at work on it when we saw it. I was very glad to see him in harness, and he is characteristically bright and hopeful about the Army and its doings, and begged me to cheer up Ernest, who insists on getting into the dumps about it.

Then we drove on and about 12 o'clock reached Boulogne where I at once met all the chaplains, about 21 or more, in the office of Gooch, the Senior Chaplain. There we had short prayers and an address from me, and then I managed to get a separate few words with each of them. They included Canon Hannay ('George Birmingham')[151] and young Balleine, son of the Dean of Jersey,[152] who is doing

[149] Brigadier-General Thomas Tait Pitman (1868–1941) began the war as a colonel, commanding the 11th Hussars. He commanded the 4th Cavalry Brigade from May 1915 to Mar. 1918, when he took command of the 2nd Cavalry Division. He was promoted to major-general the following month. The Pitman family were relatives of the archbishop. Marquess of Anglesey, *A history of the British cavalry 1816 to 1919. Volume 7: the Curragh incident and the Western Front, 1914* (London, 1996), pp. 159, 258; Becke, *Order of battle part 1*, pp. 9–10; Bell, *Randall Davidson*, I, 195; II, 1418.

[150] Although commonly viewed as redundant, even with the advent of the tank (which was to see its debut on the Somme in Sept. 1916) for the generals of the First World War mounted troops remained the best available means of exploiting a breakthrough. This goal, however, remained elusive for the BEF until 1918. Pope and Wheal, *Macmillan dictionary of the First World War*, pp. 107–8.

[151] James Owen Hannay (1865–1950), a graduate of Trinity College, Dublin (BA 1887, Divinity Testimonium 1889, MA 1896), was ordained deacon in 1888 and priest in 1889. A popular novelist and writer, he served a curacy in Wicklow from 1888 to 1892 and was rector of Westport, Mayo, from 1892 to 1913. He was also a canon of St Patrick's Cathedral, Dublin, from 1912 to 1922. He adopted the pseudonym 'George A. Birmingham' after his writing antagonized some local opinion in Westport. Expelled from the Gaelic League in 1914 for his supposedly objectionable portrayals of Irish rural life, Hannay left Westport in 1913 and embarked upon a lecture tour of the United States from which he returned in 1915. He was commissioned into the AChD on 11 Jan. 1916 and served in France for a year, the standard length of a temporary chaplain's contract at that time. He contributed to *The church in the furnace* with an essay entitled 'Man to man', in which he appealed for a greater concentration on the essentials of faith and morals; the following year he published *A padre in France* in which he described his work as an army chaplain. Hannay's post-war career was unsettled. He left Ireland in 1922 and served the British legation at Budapest before finding a living at Mells in Somerset; however, in 1929 the rectory was destroyed by fire. He ended his professional life as vicar of Holy Trinity, Kensington. *Crockford's*, 1913, p. 654; *Monthly army list*, July 1916, p. 1792; CMS Archives, Army book of L. H. Gwynne, p. 151; Snape, *Royal Army Chaplains' Department*, p. 184; *The church in the furnace*, ed. MacNutt (London, 1917), pp. 335–46: J. O. Hannay, *A padre in France* (London, 1918).

[152] The Balleines were an important clerical family on the island of Jersey; two Balleines were the incumbents of livings on Jersey in 1913 and two were serving as anglican chaplains in 1916. Austen Humphrey Balleine, formerly of Exeter College, Oxford (BA 1907, MA 1910), trained at Leeds,

excellent work, and some other attractive men, and I was glad to be able to give them a word of cheer about the special difficulty and importance of their work at the Base, without the glow and glamour of the fighting line.[153]

Then Gooch, Balleine, and I drove up to the British soldiers' cemetery where an enormous number of our men who have died in Boulogne from wounds or otherwise are buried. The graves are arranged in long rows along the top of a hill, and although quite simple, seemed admirably ordered. It is in charge of an English corporal, who is a gardener, and he looks after the whole with great care. Funerals go on daily from the great hospitals. The ground has not been formally consecrated, as there were difficulties raised by the French Government about certain consecrations which had taken place at the hands of the Bishop of London and Bishop Furse of Pretoria. So it was decided that all should remain as it is till after the war, when proper arrangements will be made for consecration etc.[154] Meantime there is virtually a consecration of each grave before the interment takes place in it. The number has been so great that it is impossible to have quite separate graves for each, but it is managed in a most orderly and reverent way. I went into the arrangements carefully.

Then we lunched at the Officers' Club, as I had done on my arrival at Boulogne from England. Colonel Wilberforce, son of Basil, who is Base Commandant, and Colonel Lister, who is a Chief Medical Officer, and especially an oculist, lunched with us. Then Mac left me for his own work at Le Treport. No companion could have been more helpful than he during these nine days. After a futile attempt, by request, to catch Princess Victoria of Schleswig-Holstein at her hotel (she is here on Y.M.C.A. work)[155] I went with Gooch and Balleine to two large hospitals – one for officers in an ex-German hotel, where I found among the patients some delightful men, and a much larger one for men in the great Casino which has huge light halls,

---

was ordained deacon in 1908 and priest in 1910. After serving a curacy in Lancashire, from 1912 he was a domestic chaplain to the bishop of Wakefield. He was commissioned into the AChD on 22 Sept. 1914 at the age of thirty. Robert Wilfred Balleine (?–?), formerly of Pembroke College, Oxford (BA 1903, MA 1906), was ordained deacon in 1904 and priest in 1905. He had served a number of curacies in Lancashire and had acted as chaplain to the bishop of Manchester and as the diocesan inspector of schools. He was appointed archdeacon of Manchester in 1910 and was commissioned into the AChD on 12 Sept. 1914. *Crockford's*, 1913, p. 70; *Monthly army list*, July 1916, 1791; RAChD Archive, Amport House, card index.

153 Morals and morale at the army's great bases were notoriously poor. Besides the moral dangers that were posed by their proximity to major towns, without the stimulus of immediate danger 'Permanent Base' men were deemed to be hopelessly unresponsive to religion. As one ACG later put it:

Combatants are infinitely more responsive, of course, than non-combatants. Even at the Base, in the reinforcement camps where the men are congregated before being drafted up to the Front, a good chaplain can get any number of candidates for Confirmation or men wishing to make their Communion, Confession, etc. Units permanently on the Line of Communication or at Base would break the heart of almost any priest.

D. S. Cairns, *The army and religion: an enquiry and its bearing on the religious life of the nation* (London, 1919), p. 175.

154 Despite initial difficulties, it became a matter of policy for the French and Belgian governments to surrender the sites of British military cemeteries in perpetuity. M. and M. Middlebrook, *The Somme battlefields* (London, 1991), p. 8.

155 Princess Helena Victoria, King George V's first cousin, was president of the YMCA's Ladies' Auxiliary Committee, a committee formed early in the war to collect comforts for the troops and to recruit female volunteers for YMCA work. *The back parts of war*, ed. Snape, p. 32; *Times*, 15 Mar. 1948, p. 7.

and makes an admirable hospital with views everywhere to the sea.[156] I went all round and talked to scores of men. It is easier to do so now that one has been over the ground and can say so much more about particular places.

Again I was less impressed by the medical men who accompanied us. The matron seemed capable, but I gather that she does not interest herself much in the work of the chaplains, who, however, were on very friendly terms with the men. Many of the men were lying in the garden and were lively and mirthful. ~~Many~~ *Some* of those in the garden had had limbs amputated and were waiting for the day to return to England. These hospitals certainly call for great administrative ability in their organisation, and, so far as I am able to judge, the head medical and surgical men who are guiding the whole are doing *it* quite admirably. They correspond to the Staff Officers whom I had everywhere ~~soon~~ *seen* and who impressed me so much. The question always arises whether the junior officers, either in the ordinary Army, or in the Medical Service, are qualified to follow adequately the high lead given to them. About this I had no means of judging.

On leaving the hospital I was accompanied to the boat by kindly officials, embarkation officers and others, who smoothed my path through the passport office etc, where again documents had to be signed, photographs examined, identity established, and so on, to a degree which struck me as rather ludicrous in my own case with the Commandant and Bishop Gwynne accompanying me. Gwynne and Gooch and Balleine also came to see me off, and Canon Pearce, who had come over on purpose to fetch me, as he had crossed with me to Boulogne at the start, was kind and attentive in every way. We got off at 4.35 – two boats both crowded with troops returning home on leave. Apparently we were less protected by destroyers than on our outward voyage, but they may have been protecting us more than I knew. The crowds of soldiers were got into the train at Folkestone by 6.15, which had now become 7.15 ~~by~~ *owing to* the English time changing its hour under the Daylight Saving Act while I was absent.[157] The train was delayed en route, and we did not reach Victoria till about 10 p.m.

So ends, as I rough-hew it in the train which is crawling into London, the record of a journey unique in my own experience as a man, and I think unique historically in the experience of an Archbishop. I have seen more or less the whole front line held by the English from north of Ypres to the Somme, and much of the hinterland twenty or thirty miles back. I have not seen the great Bases at Rouen and Havre, and this is a distinct loss, but it was impossible to do everything. We have been blessed throughout by splendid weather, by the extreme kindness of everybody without exception, and by the smooth working of the carefully made arrangements. To Bishop Gwynne I owe more than I can easily express. Unfailing in kindness,

---

[156] Base hospitals, to which the wounded and sick from the front were evacuated from Casualty Clearing Stations (see above, p. 507 n. 121), were classed as 'Stationary' or 'General', the distinction being increasingly one of size rather than function. The latter, the larger of the two, were frequently established in requisitioned premises of suitable size, such as hotels or municipal buildings. There were three base hospitals in Boulogne at the time of Davidson's visit, namely No. 7 Stationary, No. 13 Stationary and No. 13 General. Messenger, *Call-to-arms*, pp. 418–21; Rawson, *British army handbook*, pp. 142–3; http://www.1914–1918.net/hospitals.htm, consulted 4 Sept. 2009.

[157] As a response to wartime needs, the first Summer Time Act advanced the clock to one hour ahead of Greenwich mean time, with effect from 2.00 a.m. on 21 May 1916. The act had received the royal assent only four days earlier. 'History of legal time in Britain', http://www.srcf.ucam.org, consulted 3 Sept. 2009.

inspiring in work and good spirits, and, above all, continuing instant in prayer, he has impressed me more and more each day. I thank God for all the lessons of these nine days, and I trust I may find it possible to do my work a little less inadequately in consequence. Quod faxit Deus.[158] If I were doing it all over again there are a few things which I should endeavour to manage more thoroughly than I have succeeded in doing. I should like to have had more talks with the men themselves – the average Tommy in rest billets and elsewhere. I did have such talk fairly frequently, perhaps more frequently than the above records show. But I should like to have done it more – I think it would have been fruitful both to them and to me. I talked abundantly to wounded men, but less abundantly to those who were in good health. This was of course because of the ceaseless rush and movement of my every hour, but I might perhaps have done better than I did. One saw daily evidence of their good spirit and endurance and their readiness for all that they may have to do. Their humour shows itself among other ways in the endeavour everywhere to give names to the trenches corresponding to English streets, villages, etc, Oxford Street, Piccadilly Circus, Leicester Square, the Strand etc. are frequent, and some of the names have been so long in use that they are regularly used, even officially.[159] It is all part of the cheery way of dealing with the daily work. Again, I have not seen as much as I should have liked of the head doctors, perhaps had I been at the Bases I should have seen them more. I have seen the fighting Generals, but not the medical Generals, or very little. One may however have opportunity hereafter of seeing most of them at home. One other point which I do not think I have mentioned above. I was constantly impressed when looking across the Front at fighting times by the absence of physical men – guns are firing, shells exploding, and aeroplanes are overhead, and you know that within the few miles which you are looking at there are thousands and thousands of men, but they are all in trenches, and the country sometimes looks as though it were uninhabited. I had not been prepared for this.[160]

Perhaps I ought to try to sum up the results, or the impressions, made on my mind by what I have seen and done. I do not think I can do so very usefully. I have been in touch throughout with men of the first order, and my appreciation of them and their words and ways is apparent in what is above written. I do not feel that any one of them stands out as a man of supreme genius, but the level, both of capacity and of personal tone, is very high. I have had no experience justifying me in expressing an

---

158   What God does.
159   This tendency is still reflected in the names of some of the cemeteries now maintained by the Commonwealth War Graves Commission (CWGC). While there is a Strand military cemetery south of Ypres and a Euston Road and Knightsbridge cemetery on the Somme, the most notable example is Tyne Cot cemetery outside Ypres, the largest CWGC cemetery in the world, so called because a barn on the original site was dubbed 'Tyne Cot' by men of the Northumberland Fusiliers. http://www.cwgc.org, consulted 3 Sept. 1916.
160   The new and somewhat disquieting phenomenon of the 'empty battlefield' was very much a function of the weight and lethality of modern firepower. Some of Davidson's unsettlement is echoed in the words of Captain Stanhope in *Journey's end* (1928) by R. C. Sherriff, who served as an infantry officer on the Western Front:

I was looking across at the Boche trenches and right beyond – not a sound or a soul; just an enormous plain, all churned up like a sea that's got muddier and muddier till it's so stiff it can't move. You could have heard a pin drop in the quiet; yet you knew thousands of guns were hidden there, all ready cleaned and oiled – millions of bullets lying in pouches – thousands of Germans, waiting and thinking.

R. C. Sherriff, *Journey's end* (Harmondsworth, 1983), pp. 45–6.

opinion about the officers of lower rank. All of whom I have met have been agreeable and interesting, but of course my intercourse with them has been very slight.

About the Chaplains I can speak with unreserved thankfulness. They have had the most splendid opportunity that has perhaps ever fallen to the clergy of our own or any other Church. I honestly believe they are rising to it and using it effectively and well. All of them are, I think, impressed, as are also the Staff Officers of whom I have seen so much, with a sense of the horribleness of this great war, and the inadequacy of any reason for its occurrence. But I have heard no single voice suggesting that we can do other than carry it through with the utmost vigour to the victorious end for which we pray.

10

LAMBETH 1920:
THE APPEAL TO ALL CHRISTIAN PEOPLE
An account by G. K. A. Bell and
the redactions of the Appeal

Edited by
Charlotte Methuen

LAMBETH CONFERENCE 1920

July 5 - August 7

Rough Notes.

It is difficult to sum up in any brief statement the impressions formed by the Lambeth Conference of 1920. The great feeling which underlies anything is one of profound thankfulness for the whole sense and spirit of the Conference itself.

In a way the beginning of the Conference was came a a prophecy of the end. At the luncheon at S. Augustine's (July 3) the demonstration of affection felt by all the Bishops present for the Archbp of Canterbury as they stood upon their feet as one man when he rose to make his speech showed in a conspicuous way the remarkable influence wh. the Abp' works exert on all his brother Bishops — an influence of affection and unbroken patience and not of authority or command. And again at the opening of the sessions on July 5 (it was the A of C's words), taken from the gospel for the previous day (Trinity V) "Launch out into the deep" that, echoed by many Bps in the course of the conference, gave a stimulus as it were, and supplied an interpretation to

39 G. K. A. Bell's account and impressions of the 1920 Lambeth Conference from his diary for the period 1919–21 (LPL, Bell 251, fo. 75)

Introduction

Looking back on the Lambeth Conference of 1920, most participants and observers agreed that the Appeal to All Christian People was its most significant result. Thus, presenting the Appeal to the Church of England's National Assembly in November that year, Cosmo Gordon Lang, the archbishop of York,[1] commented that, although the conference had produced many important resolutions needing the sanction of the anglican communion, 'I think that by universal agreement it is felt that the resolutions which were issued by the conference on the great subject of the union of the Church of Christ possess a character and an importance of their own.'[2] Church reunion – or ecumenism, as we would now call it – was a critical question in 1920. In the wake of the First World War, there was a strong sense that the 'war to end war' must usher in a new era of peace. As the Paris Peace Conference failed to bring about the hoped-for settlement for Europe, the new government in Russia descended into tyranny, and the League of Nations became pawn in the domestic politics of the USA,[3] 'it was becoming more and more apparent that any true internationalism must have a spiritual, that is a Christian, foundation'.[4] Many people in the European Churches felt a new imperative towards unity: that the church should witness to the unity that society seemed unable to achieve.

The impulse towards unity came from elsewhere as well. Missionaries and mission churches were aware that denominational division rooted in the processes of European history could be damaging for the message of the gospel when it was preached in Africa, or India or the East; competition between churches did not make much sense in the frontier settlements of North America or the colonies of Australia and New Zealand. Calls for reunion of separated churches were coming from around the world:[5] from North America, in the form of the Philadelphia Plan, a proposal for organic union of all protestant denominations, which despite its failure on a larger scale had prompted the drafting of a concordat between the protestant episcopal church of the USA (PECUSA) and the congregationalist churches in the USA; from India, with proposals for church union between the anglican church, the South India united church and the Syrian Mar Thomas church; and from East Africa, with the Alliance of Missionary Societies in British East Africa, drawn up

1   Biographical notes to all bishops mentioned in Bell's account of the Lambeth Conference can be found in the footnotes to that account below.
2   *The appeal of the Lambeth Conference: two speeches by the archbishop of Canterbury and the archbishop of York at the meeting of the National Assembly of the Church of England Thursday November 18 1920* (London, 1920), p. 4.
3   These are the factors identified by Frank Theodore Woods, Frank Weston and Martin Linton Smith in their *Lambeth and reunion: an interpretation of the mind of the Lambeth Conference of 1920* (London, 1921), pp. 10–11.
4   *Ibid.*, 12.
5   Texts relating to all these proposals are detailed in *Documents bearing on the problem of Christian unity and fellowship, 1916–1920*, ed. G. K. A. Bell (London, 1920). For further literature, see Charlotte Methuen, 'The making of "An Appeal to All Christian People" at the 1920 Lambeth Conference', forthcoming.

at Kikuyu in 1918, and rebutted by Frank Weston, the bishop of Zanzibar, who had accused the anglican bishops of Mombasa and Uganda of heresy for presiding at a 'united communion service'.[6] Mission churches in China and in Australia were exploring ways of working more closely together. In England discussions had taken place amongst anglicans about the status of nonconformist ministers, with proposals for recognition of their orders put forward by a conference at Mansfield College, Oxford and counter proposals from a gathering at Pusey House.

As early as 1915, the archbishop of Canterbury, Randall Davidson, felt it necessary to issue a statement ruling that 'full intercommunion' was for the present impossible:

> Members of non-episcopal Churches might and would be welcomed at the Holy Communion in Anglican Churches, when temporarily isolated from their own. Bishops could not, however, bid their own Church members, similarly isolated, seek the Holy Communion at the hands of Ministers not episcopally ordained. Such ministers might be invited to preach on occasion in Anglican Churches.[7]

Davidson's response attracted criticism from those, such as Herbert Hensley Henson, then bishop of Hereford, who hoped for the recognition of the orders of other protestant churches by anglicans. Tensions over questions of unity were running high, and it was clear that this would be a major theme at the Lambeth Conference. Reflecting on the period before the conference, Davidson remembered:

> I was by no means easy in my mind for we had to deal for the first time, as I frequently pointed out in conversation, with the probability that we should find a minority in the Conference who would not be content to be an acquiescent minority, but might march out denouncing us, or raise cohorts outside.[8]

A clear steer of the direction that Davidson hoped would be taken was given through an article published in *The Times* on the eve of the conference. Noting that 'there can be little doubt that of all the subjects before the bishops, that on the subject of reunion will excite the most general attention', the article traced the history of discussions of reunion at previous Lambeth Conferences and in other contexts, including the interim reports of the committee preparing for the first world Faith and Order Conference, which would take place in Lausanne in 1927, focusing particularly on the question of the episcopate and noting: 'It is now agreed by all who signed the second interim report on Faith and Order, whether belonging to the Episcopal or Non-Episcopal Churches, that the continuity with the historic episcopate is to be effectively preserved.' It conceded, however, that this was 'a subject which obviously bristles with difficulties, and if not handled wisely, may easily provoke increased antipathies, instead of promoting fellowship'.[9] Lang, who was to chair the committee on reunion, was well aware of the difficult task he faced. He wrote to his friend and former chaplain, Wilfred Parker: 'I only hope that the Spirit of

6   *New York Times*, 4 Jan. 1914. (All citations from the *New York Times* refer to articles accessed via ProQuest Historical Newspapers: http://www.proquest.com/en-US/catalogs/databases/detail/pq-hist-news.shtml.)

7   *Documents 1916–1920*, ed. Bell, p. 45.

8   Memoir of the Lambeth Conference 1920 (unpublished), in Davidson papers, 14, fo. 40. Unless otherwise stated, all references to unpublished materials are to collections held at Lambeth Palace Library (LPL).

9   *Times*, 2 July 1920, 7, col. D.

God may get hold of us, enabling us to do something more than arrive at a series of platitudinous compromises on every subject.'[10]

On 2 July 1920, 252 anglican bishops gathered in London for a 'day of devotion' at Fulham Palace, with addresses by Charles Gore, the former bishop of Oxford. They were 'from all parts of the world and of the most diverse traditions and experiences', as an editorial in *The Times* commented towards the end of the conference:

> We need but little imagination to see them in their different dioceses. This Bishop is accustomed to travel over long stretches of land in the back blocs of Australia, another lives most of his time in the snows of North-West Canada, another must march through the jungle from one station to the next in Central Africa, another's work compels him to spend a large part of his time in boats which take him in turn to the widely scattered islands of Melanesia or the West Indies.[11]

The 1920 Lambeth Conference welcomed one native Indian and two African bishops.[12] However, at this date the vast majority of colonial or missionary bishops came either from England or the USA (fifty-two bishops were present from the PECUSA), a system which, for all its faults, did mean that a significant proportion of the bishops present had worked in more than one province of the communion.

On Saturday, 3 July, the bishops travelled to Canterbury for a reception in the Cathedral, and on Sunday, 4 July Holy Communion was celebrated at Westminster Abbey with a sermon given by Bishop Ryle, the dean of Westminster, previously bishop successively of Exeter and of Winchester. The conference met at Lambeth Palace from 5 July until 7 August. The first week was dedicated to plenary presentations of the themes to be discussed, which included, besides reunion, Christianity and international relations; the League of Nations, spiritualism, Christian science and theosophy; the position of women in the councils and ministrations of the church; industrial and social life; marriage and social morality; and the development of the provinces of the anglican communion. The bishops then divided into committees to discuss each of these themes over the following fortnight, with a final two weeks of plenary sessions to approve the reports of individual committees from 26 July until 7 August. The conference concluded with a service of Holy Communion at St Paul's Cathedral on Sunday 8 August, at which Thomas Gailor,

---

[10] Lang to Wilfred Parker, 27 June 1920, LPL MS 2883, fo. 243v. Parker (1883–1966) had been Lang's chaplain from 1909 until 1913, when he moved to Johannesburg. Returning in 1915, he was assistant priest at St Martins-in-the-Fields and chaplain to the forces. In 1919 he became rector of St George's Parktown, Johannesburg, where he remained until 1923. He then worked in St Cyprian's Native Mission, Johannesburg until 1931, when he was appointed archdeacon and director of native missions in the diocese of Pretoria. In 1933 he was consecrated bishop of Pretoria. He retired in 1950. *Who was who*, VI (1961–70; 2nd edn, London, 1979), 871. Online edition of *Who's who*, incorporating all volumes of *Who was who* (Oxford University Press, Dec. 2007), at www.ukwhoswho.com.

[11] *Times*, 7 Aug. 1920, 11, col. C.

[12] These were Vedanayakam Samuel Azariah (1874–1945), bishop of Dornakal; Isaac Oluwole (1852–1932), bishop of West Equatorial Africa; and Adolphus Williamson Howells (1866–1938), who had been consecrated bishop of the Delta Pastorate church in the Niger diocese in June 1920. For Howells, see *Who was who*, III (1929–40; London, 1941), 671. For biographical notes on Azariah and Oluwole, see nn. 21 and 63 to Bell's account of the Lambeth Conference, below. The first Chinese bishop had also been consecrated but he spoke no English and did not attend the conference (Woods, Weston and Linton Smith, *Lambeth and reunion*, pp. 23–4).

bishop of Tennessee and acting presiding bishop of the protestant episcopal church of the USA, preached.[13]

Lang introduced the theme of reunion and took the chair of the committee. On 9 July, he wrote to Wilfred Parker from Lambeth Palace:

> We are now concluding the first week of the Conference. I had to make a very difficult speech introducing the vast theme of Christian unity, but I am very grateful for all the kind things that were said about the lead which I tried to give. I could not go into the details, but only tried to indicate the spirit in which we must approach our task. I have a Committee of more than 60 Bishops to deal with, containing every variety of opinion, from Zanzibar and Nassau to Durham, and my heart fails when I think of the difficulties.[14]

He resolved that it was necessary first to come to an agreement about the definition of the unity which must be striven for; only then could more practical steps be considered. The result was the Appeal to All Christian People, which is resolution 9 of the 1920 Lambeth Conference resolutions, accompanied by a series of resolutions on questions relating to table and pulpit fellowship.

As was customary, the report of the Lambeth Conference gave no indication of the discussions leading to the Appeal, or of its drafting. Commentators at the time were conscious of the need to write 'without violating that privacy which has, with undoubted propriety, marked its deliberations'.[15] However, minutes of the discussions of the committee on reunion were taken by George Nickson, bishop of Bristol,[16] and Edwin James Palmer, bishop of Bombay, who were secretaries to the sub-committee for relations with episcopal churches and sub-committee for reunion with non-episcopal churches respectively.[17] As chairman, Lang took detailed notes of the proceedings.[18] Additionally, the archbishop of Canterbury's chaplain, George Bell, who had a keen interest in questions relating to reunion and ecumenism,[19] attended most of the sessions on reunion, taking his own notes,[20] commenting on

---

[13] A notice regarding this service in *The Times* suggests that this service was open to the public, but added: 'We are asked to announce that only the Bishops were expected to communicate.' *Times*, 7 July 1920, 4, col. C.

[14] Lang to Wilfred Parker, 9 July 1920, LPL MS 2883, fo. 245r–v. Names and biographical information for all the bishops mentioned in Bell's account are given in footnotes to that account.

[15] Woods, Weston and Linton Smith, *Lambeth and reunion*, p. 46.

[16] George Nickson (1864–1949) was educated at Southport School, Trinity College, Dublin, and Corpus Christ College, Cambridge. Ordained in 1888, he served concurrently until 1897 as tutor and bursar of Ridley Hall and lecturer in divinity at Selwyn College, and as curate of Holy Trinity, Cambridge until 1890 and was vicar of St Benedict from 1891 until 1894. In 1897, he moved to Fairfield, Liverpool, and in 1905 to St Andrew's, Southport. He was consecrated bishop-suffragan of Jarrow in 1906, and in 1914 became bishop of Bristol, where he remained until his retirement in 1933. *Who was who*, IV (1941–50; 5th edn, London, 1980), 850.

[17] These minutes are to be found in Lambeth Conference (LC) 115, 'Committee A, relations to reunion with other churches' (minutes taken first by Nickson, then by Palmer), and LC 117, 'Committee A (b): reunion with non-episcopal churches' (minutes taken by Palmer).

[18] Lang papers 208; Lang also wrote an account of the conference: Lang papers 209.

[19] For Bell's ecumenical engagement at this stage of his career, see Charlotte Methuen, '"Fulfilling Christ's own wish that we should be one": the early ecumenical work of George Bell as chaplain to the archbishop of Canterbury and dean of Canterbury (1914–1929)', in *Kirchliche Zeitgeschichte*, XXI (2008), 222–45.

[20] Bell papers 253–4: volumes 253 and 254 contain Bell's notes from the plenary sessions; volume 255 contains his notes from the reunion committee.

the proceedings in his diary[21] and subsequently writing a vivid and moving account of the conference with pen-sketches of some of the participating bishops.[22] This account is the first of the texts reproduced below.

The minutes books make it possible to trace the discussions of the committee, and this is aided by a series of redactions of the texts which eventually became the Appeal to All Christian People and its associated resolutions. These make up the second, and most substantial set of texts given below.[23] The redactions as discussed in the sessions are pasted into the minutes book of the sub-committee on reunion with non-episcopal churches, from which the Appeal originally arose. A series of amended texts, indicating intervening stages of the drafting process, together with a full set of proofs of report of the committee on reunion, can be found in the papers of John A. Douglas.[24] This series of redactions indicates that the drafting of the Appeal involved three main stages, indicated by the Texts A, B and C below. Two early texts of the resolutions exist (Texts F and G below), also found in the Minutes book and the Douglas papers. These are supplemented by a series of amendments found in the Douglas papers (Text H).

The redactions indicate that Lang's attempts to begin by establishing a vision of the unity to be sought was reasonable successful. The vision of 'a living fellowship in which the various gifts and graces bestowed by God upon each shall be no longer kept in separateness, but used and enjoyed for the enrichment of the whole body', found in the first draft, clearly informs the final Appeal:

> The vision which rises before us is that of a Church, genuinely Catholic, loyal to all truth, and gathering into its fellowship all 'who profess and call themselves Christians', within whose visible unity all the treasures of faith and order, bequeathed as a heritage by the past to the present, shall be possessed in common, and made serviceable to the whole Body of Christ. Within this unity Christian Communions now separated from one another would retain much that has long been distinctive in their methods of worship and service. It is through a rich diversity of life and devotion that the unity of the whole fellowship will be fulfilled.

The basis of the profession of faith was the Lambeth quadrilateral, agreed by the 1888 Lambeth Conference, with the first three articles appearing virtually unchanged.[25] It was noted that this was not a stumbling block to any church. The final article, however, does not appear in its original form, and it is clear from the

---

21 Bell papers 251, fos. 61–75r.

22 Bell papers 251, fos. 75v–86r.

23 Precise indications of where these texts can be found are given below.

24 Douglas papers 1, drafts of the appeal: 356–7, 366–70; drafts of resolutions: 356, 361–3; proofs: fos. 409–12. The presence of these drafts and proofs in his papers suggests that Douglas may have offered administrative support to the 1920 Lambeth Conference, perhaps to the sub-committee for relations with episcopal churches, although Bell's diary does not indicate his presence. Douglas (1869–1956) was vicar of St Luke, Camberwell, from 1909 until 1933; he was a leading figure in anglican–orthodox and anglican–old catholic dialogue. See *Who was who*, V (1951–60; 4th edn, London, 1984), 314–15.

25 Lambeth Conference 1888, resolution 11: 'That, in the opinion of this Conference, the following articles supply a basis on which approach may be by God's blessing made towards home reunion:
    a. The Holy Scriptures of the Old and New Testaments, as "containing all things necessary to salvation", and as being the rule and ultimate standard of faith.
    b. The Apostles' Creed, as the baptismal symbol; and the Nicene Creed, as the sufficient statement of the Christian faith.

notes on the discussions and from the different redactions of the appeal that the committee's discussions centred on episcopacy, and in particular on the orders of those not episcopally ordained. Henson and a few others wished to recognize all non-conformist orders and be done with it; at the least they wanted to move away from the requirement of episcopal ordination and the acceptance of the historical episcopate as a prerequisite for union,[26] although, as observed above, the tone set by the *Times* article at the beginning of the conference had made it clear that this route was unlikely to be followed. Nonetheless, successive drafts of the Appeal suggest that the sub-committee for relations with non-episcopal churches was prepared to go as step further in affirming the orders of those churches than was the full committee. Texts B2 and C include a paragraph which has been removed from the final Appeal:

> We want this, and all other ministries of grace, to be available for the whole Fellowship Church. For there are diversities of gifts, but the same Spirit. There are differences of ministries, but the same Lord. We desire to share the gifts and inheritances of Grace held in trust by the other groups. It is GOD's will that they should operate freely within the one body.

The Appeal committed anglicans in the name of reunion to receive 'a form of commission or recognition which would commend our ministry to their congregations', expressing the hope that ministers of other churches would be prepared to 'accept a commission through episcopal ordination' in their turn. In the case of such a step, Text B affirms that 'in our judgement such a step would imply no question as to the spiritual reality of the ministries at present exercised by them'; Text C2, and with it the final text of the appeal, states more cautiously, 'In so acting no one of us could possibly be taken to repudiate his past ministry', describing that ministry as 'a past experience rich in spiritual blessings for himself and others'. There is a subtle distinction here between successive drafts, moving from an affirmation of the spiritual reality of the ministry of those not episcopally ordained to a recognition of the spiritual blessings that ministry has conferred. At the same time, as some nonconformists were quick to point out, room is left for interpretation of the episcopate as being of the *bene esse*, rather than the *esse* of the church.[27]

Discussions of the resolutions focused on the question of intercommunion, which was not to be generally allowed, pulpit exchange, which was permitted if the preacher to be invited took the same view of unity as that defined by the appeal, and the *rôle* of confirmation. However, and very importantly, the resolutions allowed for exceptional cases when churches were entering into schemes to reunion. This flexibility was crucial in the Indian context. It was made possible, as Bell recounts, not least by the inspirational contribution of Frank Weston, bishop of Zanzibar,

---

c. The two sacraments ordained by Christ himself – Baptism and the Supper of the Lord – ministered with unfailing use of Christ's words of institution, and of the elements ordained by him.

d. The historic episcopate, locally adapted in the methods of its administration to the varying needs of the nations and peoples called of God into the unity of his Church.'

www.lambethconference.org/resolutions/1888/1888–11.cfm, accessed 10 July 2009.

[26] A detailed account of the discussions which shaped the appeal is beyond the scope of this introduction. See Methuen, 'The making of "An Appeal to All Christian People"' for a more extended consideration.

[27] This distinction had been the subject of discussion at an early stage in the proceedings, particularly by Henson and Palmer. See Bell papers 255, fo. 15v (Palmer), 17r (Henson). For this as an interpretation of the appeal, see the letter of MacFadyen discussed below.

'whose ... conciliatory Spirit, large heartedness, clear mindedness and passionate desire for reunion together with a quite remarkable power of draftsmanship were predominant forces in the working out of the Appeal and its attached Resolutions'.[28] Bell emphasizes also the importance of Lang's chairmanship, which not only gave rise to the Appeal but took it through the difficult stage of its presentation to the whole conference. Davison remembered: 'The Reunion subject loomed largest, and the Archbishop of York's speech in introducing the Report of his Committee was a masterpiece.'[29] Lang, however, was nervous to the last, as he wrote to Wilfred Parker:

> Having got things through Committee, I was afraid that the remaining 200 Bishops, who had not worked together as we had for a fortnight of ceaseless toil, would cut the thing to bits. Instead of that, when I presented the Report it seemed to be taken out of my hands and what Neville called 'a rushing mighty wind' seemed to sweep away difficulties and criticism, and instead of days of anxious discussion the appeal and its accompanying resolutions were adopted in less than one day with only a handful of Bishops objecting. I think most of us who were present will not forget that day, for it was difficult – to me impossible – to think that this wind was other than the wind of the Spirit: anyhow, I must believe that somehow God has a purpose in a thing which came with to much unanimity from 200 Bishops who really prayed and asked for guidance at a critical time.[30]

'Carried 3.15 p.m. Friday 30 July 1920 with 4 dissentions', reads a note on Douglas's copy of the proof. 'The Conference sang the doxology on the suggestion of the Bishop of Worcester.'[31]

The sense that something important had taken place was strong. Davidson commented on the atmosphere that had developed in the committee as it grappled with its vision of unity:

> [In his final speech, Lang] was able to speak in a very different tone of hope and thankfulness from what had been possible for him in the opening debate some three weeks earlier. A great deal has been said and printed about the amazing spirit of harmony and even of unanimity which marked the Reunion discussions and Resolutions, as well as the full and most difficult Report of the Committee.[32]

In his closing sermon, Gailor too affirmed the 'wonderful unanimity with which 250 bishops from many lands reached agreement on the essential principles of Catholic reunion', which, he said 'must live in their memories as a blessed experience'. What ever the response to the Appeal, the bishops could 'take comfort that they had prayed and studied and taken counsel, in order to search out and forsake whatever in their presentation of the Gospel might seem to stand in the way of visible reunion of he Universal Church'.[33] Lang had a similar sense of the deepening of fellowship amongst the bishops, and saw this as being of great importance to the anglican

---

28 Bell papers 251, fo. 77v; see p. 537 below.
29 Davidson papers 14, fo. 48.
30 Lang to Wilfred Parker, 10 Aug. 1920, LPL MS 2883, fos. 248–9.
31 Douglas papers 1, fo. 410v.
32 Davidson papers 14, fos. 48–9.
33 Report of Gailor's sermon in *Times*, 9 Aug. 1920, 7, col. A.

communion; he was affirmative too of the *rôle* of the archbishop of Canterbury, as president of the conference:

> There was a really admirable spirit of fellowship; this is important, as it is only this sense of brotherhood among the bishops which keeps all these independent churches which now form the Anglican Communion together. The President proved to be not only an excellent Chairman but also a very real head of this brotherhood.[34]

The Appeal was released ahead of the conference Report on 12 August with a press conference the previous afternoon. Bell noted in his diary:

> A special conference of pressmen summoned in Library on Aug 11 at 5 p.m. … RTC [i.e., the archbishop of Canterbury] and Peterboro' addressed them on Report. RTC spoke perhaps a little more freely than he might have done if he had realised that his remarks themselves w[oul]d be published, e.g. about Rome: but confession led to genuine object of Appeal being quoted for a guide. An explanation of the Appeal by Peterboro' was handed round (with Appeal) to reporters … Zanzibar & Nassau had interpreted Appeal to Church Times. Rhinelander had written article for Br. Weekly. … The result of this (but mainly due to the Appeal) was extraordinarily encouraging.[35]

Immediate reactions to the Appeal were positive. In a letter to *The Times*, the president of the Wesleyan methodist conference, John Wardle Stafford[36] wrote that the Appeal had been received with great satisfaction by Wesleyan methodists, affirming, with element of hyperbole, that it had 'already stirred Christendom to the uttermost parts of the earth'. He went on:

> Whatever comes of these proposals, it would seem impossible that Christian Churches should ever again resume the attitude of mutual hostility, or even 'armed neutrality', which unfortunately obtained in days not long past. The practical issue will not be unimportant, but the influence of the appeal will be more powerful than any results that may be tabulated.[37]

Other voices of approval were raised to welcome the Appeal, and by the end of August, Lang could report to Wilfred Parker:

> Here is dear old Halifax[38] writing that few things in his life have given him more pleasure [than the appeal]: That he thinks that it will do untold good. And on the other hand here is Scott Lidgett[39] saying that [it] is the most remarkable thing since

---

34 Lang to Wilfred Parker, 10 Aug. 1920, LPL MS 2883, fo. 247.

35 Bell papers 251, fo. 69r–v.

36 John T. Wardle Stafford (1861–1944) was a Methodist minister, in 1920 serving in Scarborough. In 1923, he moved to Toronto to take charge of the Methodist church there, and was a delegate to inaugural meetings of the United Church of Canada. *Who was who*, IV, 1090.

37 *Times*, 21 Aug. 1920, 4, col. B.

38 Charles Wood, Second Viscount Halifax (1839–1934) was a strong supporter of ecumenical relations, especially with the Roman Catholic church. For further details of his life and career, see *Oxford dictionary of national biography* (*ODNB*), I–LX (Oxford, 2004), LX, 74–5. The *ODNB* is also available online at www.oxforddnb.com.

39 John Scott Lidgett (1854–1953), a methodist minister, co-founder of the Bermondsey Settlement in 1891, had been president of the Wesleyan Methodist Conference and also of the National Council of the Evangelical Free Churches of England and Wales. He was later president of the Uniting Confer-

the Reformation. Shakespeare,[40] saying that it is the Finger of God. Horton[41] that it creates a new epoch. And Zanzibar pleading with all his fellow Catholics that they will make it their guiding vision for years to come. How can one doubt with all this in mind, that there is some purpose of God in this thing?[42]

He felt awed and privileged by having been a part of its drafting.

Determining the theological and practical implications of the Appeal was more difficult. Lang continued to emphasize the importance of having established the aim of unity, affirming in a sermon on 15 August reported in *The Times* the next day: 'The unity of the church was not to be made or remade. It existed, and had only to be made real and visible.' Philip Rhinelander, bishop of Pennsylvania, concurred:

> In the Bishops' view unity is something already given to and present in the Church, which is to be manifested and maintained. It is not a humanly devised expedient, incidentally and almost accidentally forced to the front by the pressure of untoward circumstances. It is an enabling gift or endowment of the Holy Spirit present in the Fellowship from the beginning, waiting, like all other gifts, for human realization and acceptance, but definitely and irrevocably the plan of Divine wisdom and the goal of Divine will. Hence unity takes its place as a primary, moral obligation resting on the whole company of Christ's disciples.[43]

For Rhinelander, the important aspect was the 'self-denying ordinance' explicitly expressed in the Appeal, which he saw applying to anglicans as much as to members of non-episcopal churches:

> Unity is to be sought, and sacrifices made for its attainment, in order that the whole Body of Christ in all its rich and divinely given diversity of thought, character and temperament may be enriched and edified; that all the nations and groups, with all their 'peculiar differences' and special gifts, may flow into the Kingdom and find their home and sanctification there, and be made 'one man in Christ Jesus'.[44]

---

ence of the Methodist Churches, and became the first president of the united church in 1932. *Who was who*, V, 660–1.

40 John Howard Shakespeare (1857–1928) was a baptist minster who worked for unity within the baptism movement as well as in the wider church context. He was secretary of the Baptist Union of Great Britain and Ireland, 1898–1924; European secretary of the Baptist World Alliance; moderator of the Federal Council of the Evangelical Free Churches of England, 1919–21; joint secretary of the Federal Council of the Evangelical Free Churches of England (1921–8). *Who was who*, II (1916–28; 5th edn, London, 1992), 736; *ODNB*, XL, 938–9

41 Robert Forman Horton (1855–1934) was a congregationalist minister, and one of the first generation of nonconformists to study at Oxford, where he took a first class degree in Greats at New College in 1878. After graduation, Horton remained in Oxford as lecturer in history and fellow of New College. In 1883, the University's Congregation refused approval of his nomination as examiner for the paper 'The rudiments of faith and religion'. Horton left Oxford and was ordained in 1884 to serve the Hampstead congregational church, where he remained for forty-six years. Horton served terms of office as chairman of the London Congregational Union, of the Congregational Union of England and Wales and president of National Free Church Council. In 1927, he founded the Oxford Conference for bringing modern knowledge and Christian belief together. *ODNB*, XXVIII, 214–16; *Who was who*, III, 665–6.

42 Lang to Wilfred Parker, 21 Aug. 1920, LPL MS 2883, fo. 250r–v.

43 Philip M. Rhinelander, 'The Lambeth ideal of unity', *Constructive Quarterly* (Mar. 1921), 9–18, here 16.

44 *Ibid.*, 18.

Woods, Weston and Linton Smith agreed, although they thought that anglicans would find themselves submitting to the requirements of episcopal, rather than non-episcopal, churches.[45] Lang, however, saw the importance of the appeal primarily as giving anglicans the impetus they needed to engage in the process of union:

> The Appeal marked a new epoch, for it brought a new spirit and a new outlook to members of the Anglican church. Some of them, accustomed to the traditions and conventions perhaps of a rigid churchmanship, might find it disquieting, but remember the urgency of the great need. The new age demanded that we should have courage to think anew, to act anew. Some of them that desired immediate steps to be taken towards union, especially with the Nonconformists, might be disappointed, but short cuts often led astray, and we could not rightly take any steps until we knew the goal of our journey.[46]

Bishop Welldon, dean of Durham,[47] preaching at a joint service of the Established and United Free Churches affirmed that the appeal had changed attitudes of denominations to one another, bringing about a 'policy of Christian sympathy':

> It means that the Churches will think well and not ill each of the others, that they look, not so much for points of difference as for points of agreement each with the others. It means that they will go back for the conditions of Fellowship to the original principles of the Gospel. ... Christians never will think alike, but they may be friends and not enemies. They may show the world the spectacle of a Christendom no longer torn and rent by dissension, but reunited in Christ.[48]

In an era in which members of the Free Churches still found it hard to gain acceptance by the establishment, these were significant gains. Dugald MacFadyen, secretary of the British Council for the Interchange of Preachers and Speakers between Britain and America,[49] saw in the Appeal a more specific – and very promising – theological step, for in his view, the Appeal had shifted the emphasis of the fourth article of the Lambeth Quadrilateral 'from the episcopate to ministry':

> It asks for a ministry acknowledged by every part of the Church as possessing not only the inward call of the Spirit, but also the commission of Christ and the authority of the whole body. ... If episcopacy is necessary for the well-being of the Church, but not for its being, for its convenience rather than its essence, it may be discussed rationally and on the basis of experience, and the verdict given accordingly to the balance of the evidence.[50]

In *Lambeth and Reunion*, however, Woods, Weston and Linton Smith, although they emphasized 'the any graces and blessings showered by God upon the non-episcopal

---

45 This is clear from the discussion of 'The realisation of the ideal', in Woods, Weston and Linton Smith, *Lambeth and reunion*, chs. 4 and 5.

46 Sermon by the archbishop of York on Sunday 15 Aug., reported in *Times*, 16 Aug. 1920, 7, col. A.

47 James Cowell Welldon (1854–1937) was headmaster of Harrow School (1895–98), bishop of Calcutta (1898–1902), canon of Westminster (1903–6), dean of Manchester (1906–18) and dean of Durham (1918–33). *ODNB*, LVII, 1001–2

48 As reported in *Times*, 6 Sept. 1920, 7, col. E.

49 Dugald MacFadyen (1867–1936), was a congregational minister who had served in Hanley, Staffs., and in Highgate before becoming secretary of the British and American Interchange Council. *Who was who*, III, 855.

50 *Times*, 17 Aug. 1920, 6, col. C.

communions', maintained the need for churches entering into a union based on common faith to 'accept the episcopate' in terms which indicated that the emphasis had shifted less than MacFadyen had hoped.[51] The nearly two decades of discussions between the Church of England and the Free Churches which followed, and their eventual failure, bore witness to this tension.

'It cannot be said that all the high hopes raised by [the Appeal] and other ecumenical ventures were fulfilled', asserted Neill in his account of the ecumenism of the interwar period. Nonetheless, 'all the time, in all the continents, in all the great confessions, with a persistence and passion perhaps unknown in any previous epoch, the search for closer outward fellowship and corporate unity was going on.'[52] If it was nothing more, the Appeal to All Christian People issued by the Lambeth Conference of 1920 was an important impetus to that movement and a strong encouragement for anglicans to join it. But the Appeal was more: it offered a formulation which made it possible for anglicans to recognize and affirm the faith taught and held by other churches, and which has borne fruit in later ecumenical agreements; it articulated a vision of unity which encouraged flexible and creative thinking about what relations to other churches might look like; and it laid the foundations for an approach to union which made it possible for churches to 'regain' the historic episcopate. Most importantly, the story of the making of the Appeal to All Christian People is the story of a finding of agreement where there was none: and in that it is itself a model for all who still seek the unity of the church.

Editorial conventions

The spelling, punctuation and capitalization of the originals have been preserved, unless clearly erroneous, in which case they have been silently corrected. Words which are underlined in the original manuscripts have been reproduced with single or double underlining as used by the author. Abbreviations have been expanded in square brackets.

---

[51] Woods, Weston and Linton Smith, *Lambeth and reunion*, pp. 63–9.
[52] Stephen Charles Neill, 'Plans of union and reunion 1910–1948', in *A History of the Ecumenical Movement 1517–1948*, ed. Ruth Rouse and Stephen Charles Neill (2nd edn, London, 1967), pp. 445–508, here p. 448.

Texts

I   Lambeth Conference 5 July – 7 August 1920, by George K. A. Bell, Bell papers, vol. 251 (diary 1919–26), fos. 75v–86r

Lambeth Conference 1920
July 5 – August 7
Rough Notes

It is difficult to sum up in any brief statement the impressions formed by the Lambeth Conference of 1920. The great feeling which underlies everything is one of profound thankfulness for the whole sense and spirit of the Conference itself.

In a way the beginning of the Conference came as a prophecy of the end. At the luncheon at S. Augustine's (July 3) the demonstration of affection felt by all the Bishops present for the Archb[isho]p of Canterbury[1] as they stood upon their feet as one man when he rose to make his speech shewed in a conspicuous way the remarkable influence wh[ich] the A[rch]b[isho]p was to exert on his brother Bishops – an influence of affection and unbroken patience and not of authority or command. And again it was the A[rchbishop] of C[anterbury]'s words at the opening of the sessions on July 5, taken from the gospel for the previous day (Trinity V) 'Launch out into the deep' that, echoed by many B[isho]ps in the course of the Conference, gave a stimulus as it were, and supplied an interpretation to [fo. 76r] all that was done. A curious contrast on the one hand to B[isho]p Ryle's[2] impassioned plea in the Abbey (July 4) that the great fruit of the Conference might be to add 'Holy' before 'Catholic' in the Nicene Creed, and on the other to the dazed bewilderment with which the A[rch]b[isho]p of Algoma[3] (like a kindly Rural Dean of the old school)

---

[1]   Randall Thomas Davidson (1848–1930) was archbishop of Canterbury from 1903 until his resignation in 1928. Davidson had been chaplain to two successive archbishops of Canterbury, Archibald Campbell Tait, who was also his father-in-law (1877–82), and Edward White Benson (1882–3), before being appointed dean of Westminster and domestic chaplain to Queen Victoria (1883–91), during which time he advised on senior appointments in the Church of England, acted as assistant secretary to the Anglican Conference of 1881 and helped to shape public opinion during the ritualist controversy. In 1891, he published his *Life of Archbishop Tait*. In 1891, Davidson was consecrated bishop of Rochester, and in 1895 was translated to the see of Winchester, where he remained until he became archbishop of Canterbury in 1903. He continued to be involved with questions of ritualism and to seek a way forward which would keep the Anglo-Catholic party within the Church of England. Davidson was also influential in matters of education and social policy. *ODNB*, XV, 318–25; see also G. K. A. Bell, *Randall Davidson, archbishop of Canterbury*, 3rd edn (Oxford, 1952).

[2]   Herbert Edward Ryle (1856–1925), was at this time dean of Westminster, a post he held from 1911 until his death. A biblical scholar, and advocate of the historical study of the Old Testament, Ryle was Hulsean professor of divinity at the University of Cambridge (1887–1901), bishop of Exeter (1901–3) and of Winchester (1903–11). Ryle had headed the delegation sent to Sweden in 1909 to explore the possibility of closer relationships between the Church of Sweden and the Church of England. *ODNB*, XLVIII, 483–5.

[3]   George Thorneloe (1848–1935), was bishop of Algoma (Canada) from 1897 to 1926. Thorneloe was a broad churchman and an excellent administrator who provided strong leadership to a rapidly expanding diocese, travelling extensively on the new railways, and encouraging the growth of strong

announced that he listened to the expression of liberal sentiments in an assembly which he had every reason to expect would be staunchly conservative. 'The A[rch]-b[isho]p of C[anterbury] is a wonderfully wise man' said the A[rch]b[isho]p of Armagh[4] to me well on in the sessions, and dwelt on his fairness, his open mindedness and his patience in a way which practically all the Bishops wd have endorsed. The A[rch]b[isho]p of Armagh told me also how the A[rchbishop] of C[anterbury] had explained to him that it was his consistent policy in such an assembly of Bishops not to act as the ordinary chairman, but to treat every Bishop with the utmost deference, so that none might say hereafter that the view of any Bishop of the Church had not had a fair hearing. The Assembly, only held every ten years, was far too solemn and important to admit of any method savouring of suppression [fo. 76v] or rush. And the incident which may perhaps illustrate the A[rch]b[isho]p's feeling of his relationship to this brother Bishops was his very definite request to the Chapter at Canterbury that it should not place the High Altar on the lower platform in the sanctuary, as they had decided to do, till after the Lambeth Conference was over: so that his place In S. Augustine's Chair might be in front of the altar still and not behind and as it were over it in the guise of a Pope or Patriarch!

(It is only fair to add, when talking of the A[rchbishop] of C[anterbury]'s patience, that there were moments at the end of the day when several Bishops thought the tolerance of verbal amendments was carried too far! But in the end the policy was abundantly justified.)

One small personal note may be inserted. In the first of the session[s] the A[rch]-b[isho]p was suddenly smitten with lumbago, a very painful bout: and for some days was terribly crippled, and sat in his chair with rugs over him and (to his disgust) a hot water apparatus under him.[5] But it gradually went off during the Committee weeks.

[fo. 77r] As to the work before the Conference, as marked out on the Agenda Paper, naturally by far the most important part was the work on reunion. And it was most moving. Not only was the progress of that work of extraordinary interest, but the moment when the Appeal was finally accepted with but four hands raised against

---

parish organizations. Under his care, Algoma ceased in 1906 to be a missionary diocese run by the Provincial Synod and became an autonomous diocese able to elect its own bishop and manage its affairs through its Synod. See www.dioceseofalgoma.com/handbook/history.htm, accessed 24 June 2004.

4   Charles Frederick D'Arcy (1859–1938) was archbishop of Armagh from 1920 until his death. D'Arcy published *A short study of ethics* (London, 1895) and *Idealism and theology* (London, 1899) which secured his reputation as a theologian. In 1903 he became bishop of Clogher, being translated in 1907 to the see of Ossery, Ferns and Leighlin, and in 1911 to Down, Connor and Dromore. In 1912, D'Arcy signed the Ulster Covenant indicating his strong support for the Unionists. He became archbishop of Dublin in 1919, and archbishop of Armagh in 1920. D'Arcy was a strong supporter of church reunion, especially with the presbyterian church, although he was more cautious in his relations to the Roman Catholic church, and was closely involved in the Lausanne Faith and Order Conference in 1927. *ODNB*, XV, 123–4.

5   Davidson was susceptible to lumbago due to a back injury resulting from a shooting accident when he was fourteen. *ODNB*, XV, 318.

it (Vermont,[6] Long Island,[7] Milwaukee,[8] and Accra[9])[10] was the greatest moment of this or any previous Lambeth Conferences, a moment full of the sense that the Spirit itself had led the Bishops and ending with a burst of heartfelt praise in the singing of the Old Hundredth by all present standing on their feet.

A very large part of the successful issue of the Appeal, its wording, the acceptance of conciliatory language on either side, the redrafting and revision and its quality of inclusiveness and generosity, was due to the chairmanship of the Reunion Committee, the A[rch]b[isho]p of York.[11] And yet while this is abundantly true, and while probably no other Chairman could have so carried first the Committee and then the Conference to precisely that goal, nothing on [fo. 77v] anything like the

---

6   Arthur C. A. Hall (1847–1929) was bishop of Vermont from 1894 until his death. Hall was born near Reading and took his degree at Oxford. On graduation in 1869, he joined the Society of St John the Evangelist and was ordained the following year. In 1873, he was sent to Boston Massachusetts, where he soon gained a reputation as an excellent preacher and retreat conductor. In 1891, Hall was recalled to England after a dispute over his involvement with the election of Phillips Brooks as bishop of Massachusetts. He remained there until 1893, when he was elected bishop of Vermont and released from the SSJE. Charles Hill, 'In memoriam Arthur C. A. Hall: fourth bishop of Vermont. A Sermon (revised) preached in Christ Church, Ballston Spa, New York, on Quinquagesima Sunday, March 2, 1930', http://anglicanhistory.org/usa/acahall/hill1930.html, accessed 2 July 2009.

7   Frederick Burgess (1853–1925) was bishop of Long Island from 1901 to 1925. Burgess was born in Providence, Rhode Island, the nephew of Bishop George Burgess of Maine. He studied at Brown and at General Theological Seminary, also spending one year in Oxford. He served in parishes in Connecticut, Pennsylvania, Detroit and Brooklyn before being elected bishop of Long Island in 1901. His obituary recorded that he 'was known to be a conservative in theology, rather inclined to high churchmanship'. *New York Times*, 16 Oct. 1925, 4.

8   William Walter Webb (1857–1933) was bishop of Milwaukee from 1906 until his death. Webb was educated at Trinity College and Berkeley Divinity School, Middletown, Connecticut. He served in parishes in Middletown, Connecticut and Philadelphia before becoming professor of dogmatic theology at Nashotah House in 1892. In 1897 he became President of Nashotah house, a post he held until he was consecrated Bishop Coadjutor of Milwaukee in 1906. He became Diocesan Bishop later that year. Webb was known for being 'a high churchman, and an ardent Anglo-Catholic.' *Dictionary of Wisconsin History*, www.wisconsinhistory.org, accessed 2.07.09.

9   Mowbray Stephen O'Rorke (1869–1953) was bishop of Accra from 1913 to 1924. O'Rorke was educated at Wesley College, Sheffield, and the University School, Nottingham. Originally a businessman and lawyer, he studied theology at Trinity College Dublin and served in parishes in Jarrow and Durham before moving to be dean of St Paul's Cathedral, Central Queensland, in 1910, from where he moved to Accra in 1911. In 1924 he returned to England, becoming rector of Blakeney with Langham Parva and guardian of the Shrine of Our Lady of Walsingham, and subsequently chaplain to St Audries School and King's College, Taunton, until his retirement in 1939. *Who was who*, V, 836.

10   Bell may, however, be mistaken in including O'Rorke in this list. The proofs of the debate include the note: 'Dissentions: Bishops Osborne [i.e., the Bishop Coadjutor of Springfield], Vermont, Milwaukee, Long Island. Some (4 or 5) including Barking did not vote at all' (Douglas papers 1, fo. 410v). In his diary, Bell wrote of the final vote: 'Only two spoke against. Vermont, sadly but temperately & earnestly: Osborne in somewhat rasping & critical tones. Then the Appeal was put: & four hands only were held up against it. The Conference had done some g[rea]t thing, whatever else it did or left undone' (Bell papers 251, fo. 81v; see p. 524 below).

11   Cosmo Gordon Lang (1864–1945), archbishop of York (1908–28); archbishop of Canterbury (1928–42). Lang served his curacy in Leeds under Edward Stuart Talbot (see n. 23 below) before becoming dean of Magdalen College, Oxford, and vicar of the University Church. In 1896 he moved to Portsea, and in 1901 became bishop of Stepney, succeeding Arthur Winnington-Ingram. From Stepney, he was translated the archbishopric of York in 1908. *ODNB*, XXXII, 456–61.

same scale could have been done had it not been for the Bishop of Zanzibar,[12] whose speech at in the first week struck the note of the Appeal – catholicity inclusive of groups within the Catholic church – and whose further study in Committee, conciliatory Spirit, large heartedness, clear mindedness and passionate desire for Reunion together with a quite remarkable power of draftsmanship were predominant forces in the working out of the Appeal and its attached Resolutions. So large-minded and so ready to go to almost all lengths was the B[isho]p of Z[anzibar] that there were moments when some feared that the next day w[oul]d bring repentance, and a frank confession that he had made a mistake and must withdraw from all further share in the Committee or even the Conference proceedings. One of the most interesting features, by the way, in the Committee stage was the cooperation in the draftsmanship and in the finding room for different p[oin]ts of view, of the Bishops of Zanzibar and Durham,[13] at the speaker's lectern or the platform in the Library, or in the chaplain's room between the sittings.[14] Up to the end the B[isho]p of Z[anzibar] c[oul]d not abide the B[isho]p of D[urham]. [fo. 78v] (so he told me) but he never shewed it, hiding this and much else perhaps with his strange smile. He told me too that it was Henson who as vicar of Barking had taught him so much of the Catholic faith, at a time when he did not hesitate to proclaim the Nonconformists to be emissaries of Satan.

In the C[ommit]tee the two main days were <u>July 19</u> when the first draft of the Appeal (then quite short and called merely a Statement[15]) was presented after a most disappointing and depressing first week, and <u>July 20</u> when the sensational Resolution

---

[12] Frank Weston (1871–1924), was bishop of Zanzibar from 1908 to 1924. After ordination he served as curate at St John's Stratford East and at St Matthew's Westminster before being sent to Zanzibar by the Universities' Mission to Central Africa in 1892, where he became chaplain and principal of the school at St Andrew's Training College, helped to run St Mark's Theological College, and also served as chancellor of the diocese of Zanzibar. He became bishop of Zanzibar in 1908. His strong opposition to what he saw as the blurring of denominational boundaries proposed by the Kikuyu conference in 1913 brought him notoriety in England and elsewhere. He was president of the Anglo-Catholic Congress in 1923, and was regarded by many in Britain as 'unreliable and unpredictable'. *ODNB*, LVIII, 287–9, quote 289.

[13] Herbert Hensley Henson (1863–1947) was bishop of Hereford 1918–20, and bishop of Durham from 1920 until his death. After a complex nonconformist childhood, Henson studied modern history at Oxford, without college affiliation until he was elected a fellow of All Souls in 1884. He was much influenced by Charles Gore, and was ordained priest in 1888. His views were initially Anglo-Catholic, but he later became much more critical of Anglo-Catholics and advocated reunion with nonconformists. In 1909, Gore forbade Henson to preach at Carr's Lane congregationalist Church in Birmingham; Henson ignored the prohibition. In 1912, Henson became dean of Durham, and in 1912 he was appointed bishop of Hereford by Lloyd George, against Davidson's wishes. A group of prominent Anglo-Catholics, led by Gore, protested that Henson's views made him unfit to be bishop; however, Davidson was satisfied as to Henson's orthodoxy. In 1920, Henson was translated to Durham. Although referred to in Bell's account as 'Durham', at the time of the Lambeth Conference he was in fact bishop of Durham elect, having been appointed after the death of his predecessor in May, but not yet installed. To his annoyance, he appeared on the list of bishops attending as bishop of Hereford. *ODNB*, XXVI, 612–15.

[14] Bell's wife, Hettie, wrote later: 'I remember coming upon the group *very* late one evening in Lollard's Tower – Jimmy Bombay sitting cross-legged on the floor like an Indian Buddha, Neville Talbot draped along the mantelpiece, cups of tea everywhere, and George, pen and notebook in hand, correlating all the words of wisdom' (R. C. D. Jasper, *George Bell, bishop of* Chichester (London, 1967), 57.

[15] This is Text B below.

drafted by the B[isho]p of Zanzibar was first discussed by the C[ommit]tee.[16] It was after the latter that the A[rchbishop] of York expressed his wonder whether after all Z[anzibar] w[oul]d wake up to find he had gone too far! (The Z[anzibar] Resolution appears in final form as Res. 12). The first work had indeed been disappointing; the witnesses seemed rigid dogmatists or 'boneless' enthusiasts for the most part. 'It is devilish' said Neville Pretoria[17] at the end of the worst day when Gore, Ryle, J. A. Robinson & Turner had held forth.[18] The main work, it is true, was done in C[ommit]tee – but a vast amount was done outside, in conversation on the lawn at Lambeth after luncheon, with [fo. 78v] Tinnevelly,[19] Warrington,[20] & Zanzibar arm in arm, or in confabulations at night between e.g. Zanzibar and Dornakal[21] when D[ornakal] finds Z[anzibar] ready in the end to give everything D[ornakal] c[oul]d want provided that (what is irregular is not formally resolved by the Lambeth Conference and that) the future is secured and satisfactory guarantees of Episcopal

[16] Draft resolutions by the bishop of Zanzibar, text G below.
[17] Neville Stuart Talbot (1879–1943) was educated at Haileybury College, Christ Church, Oxford, and Cuddesdon College, before serving in the Rifle Brigade during the Boer War. He served his curacy at Armley, before being appointed tutor and chaplain of Balliol College, Oxford, in 1909. From 1914 to 1919, he served as chaplain in France, and was consecrated bishop of Pretoria in 1920. In 1933, he returned to England to become vicar of St Mary, Nottingham, and assistant bishop in the diocese of Southwell. He was the son of Edward Stuart Talbot, bishop of Winchester (see note 23 below), and younger brother of Edward Keble Talbot, who was later superior of the Community of the Resurrection, Mirfield. *Who was who*, IV, 1131–2.
[18] This was a day on which 'expert witnesses' were invited to contribute. According to the committee minutes, Lang first presented his text (Text A below) and then invited the "learned doctors', Charles Gore, former bishop of Oxford; Bishop Ryle, dean of Westminster (see p. 534 n. 2); Dr Armitage Robinson (dean of Wells), and Mr C. H. Turner (fellow of Magdalen College, Oxford) to speak (Lambeth Conference papers (LC) 115, minutes book for 'Committee A, relations to reunion with other churches', fo. 16). On 16 July, the sub-committee for relations with non-episcopal churches was also addressed by Rev. Dr John Howard Shakespeare, moderator of the Federal Council of Evangelical Churches, and other free church 'witnesses' (LC 117, minutes book of 'Committee A (b): reunion with non-episcopal churches', fos. 2–4). Bell noted in his diary of these presentations: 'Gore, Robinson & Turner all frankly reactionary – though Gore was more rigorous than the other two. Much antiquarianism. Ryle meagre, and inconsiderately "broad"' (Bell papers 251, fo. 65v).
[19] Edward Mansfield Waller (1871–1942) was bishop of Tinnevelly and Madura (India) from 1915 to 1922. After taking his MA in classics at Cambridge, Waller was tutor at St John's Hall before being appointed vice-principal of St Paul's Divinity School, Allahabad, in 1897. In 1903 he was made principal, and in 1907 became principal of Jay Narayn's School in Benares, and then secretary of the Church Missionary Society (CMS) in India. In 1915 he was appointed bishop of Tinnevelly, and in 1923 was translated to Madras, where he remained until 1941. *Who was who*, IV, 1195.
[20] Martin Linton Smith (1869–1950) served curacies in Whitechapel, Aston, Limpsfield and South-wold; was rector of St Nicholas, Colchester; vicar of St Saviour, Liverpool; St Nicholas, Blundell-sands; chaplain to the forces; and rector of Winwick, Warrington, before being appointed bishop of Warrington (suffragan to Liverpool) in 1918. In 1920 he became principal of Hereford as Hensley Henson's successor, and in 1930 was translated to Rochester, where he remained until his retirement in 1939. *Who was who*, IV, 1072
[21] Vedanayakam Samuel Azariah (1874–1945), was bishop of Dornakal from 1912 until his death 1945. Azariah was a founder of the indigenous Indian Missionary Society. At the Edinburgh Missionary Conference in 1910, he appealed for friendship across the barriers of race and empire. In 1911, Whitehead, bishop of Madras, nominated Azariah to be first bishop of the newly created diocese of Dornakal, and in 1912 he was consecrated the first Indian bishop of the anglican church. Azariah led the joint committee on church union in South India which after his death brought about the merger of the anglican church in South India with other protestant churches. *ODNB*, LVIII, 663; *Encyclopaedia Britannica* online, accessed 24.June 2009.

supervision are provided in the interim. (If you are one of the B[isho]ps of the S[outh] I[ndia] United Church I shall be entirely satisfied.)

– The chief work of all – the Appeal – was itself due to a little self-appointed C[ommit]tee meeting in Lollard's Tower on Friday m[ornin]g July 16 when the full C[ommit]tee did not meet, as Ebor[22] and others went off to Cambridge for Hon[orary] degrees, a c[ommit]tee or caucus (Zanzibar, Winton,[23] Bombay,[24] Pretoria, Chichester,[25] Peterboro',[26] Pennsylvania,[27] Brent,[28] Warrington (?)[29]) who talked on the lines of Zanzibar's proposals, chiming in with similar speeches of

---

22 I.e., the archbishop of York.

23 Edward Stuart Talbot (1844–1934) was bishop of Winchester from 1911 to 1923. A historian and senior student of Christ Church, Oxford, in 1869, Talbot was appointed first warden of Keble College and was ordained deacon, and priest the following year. He contributed to *Lux mundi*, supported the founding of Lady Margaret Hall, one of the first colleges for women in Oxford, was a strong supporter of the Oxford Mission to Calcutta and an important influence in the founding of Oxford House in Bethnal Green. In 1889, he moved to become vicar of Leeds, where he remained until 1895, when he became bishop of Rochester, and worked to establish the diocese of Southwark, of which he became the first bishop in 1905. He was translated to Winchester (=Winton) in 1911. *ODNB*, LIII, 684–5.

24 Edwin James Palmer (1869–1954), bishop of Bombay 1908–28. Palmer was fellow and latterly chaplain of Balliol College, Oxford, from 1891 until his appointment as bishop of Bombay in 1908. Once in Bombay he worked to give the proposed church union a constitutional structure which would, in his understanding, preserve apostolicity whilst defining a practice acceptable to other churches. On retirement, Palmer returned to England and was assistant bishop to Arthur Cayley Headlam, bishop of Gloucester. *ODNB*, XLII, 486–8.

25 Winfrid Oldfield Burrows (1858–1929), was bishop of Chichester from 1919 until his death in 1929. After taking degrees in classics and mathematics and serving as tutor at Christ Church, Oxford, Burrows became principal of Leeds Clergy School in 1891. He served in parishes in Leeds and Edgbaston and as archdeacon of Birmingham before becoming bishop of Truro in 1912. *Who was who*, III, 196.

26 Frank Woods (1874–1932), bishop of Peterborough 1916–23. Woods was took his degree at Trinity College, Cambridge, before serving in parishes in Huddersfield, Brixton, Kersal, Auckland and Bradford. In 1919 he became bishop of Peterborough, and in 1924 was translated to Winchester. After Lambeth 1920, Woods, together with Henson and Weston, published *Lambeth and reunion*. *Who was who*, III, 1485.

27 Philip M. Rhinelander (1869–1939) was bishop of Pennsylvania from 1911 until 1923, when he retired due to ill-health. Born in Newport, Rhode Island, Rhinelander studied at Harvard and then Oxford. From 1896 he was rector of St Mark's Washington, before becoming professor of ecclesiastical history and homiletics at Berkeley Divinity School, Middletown, Connecticut in 1903. In 1907, he moved to Cambridge, Massachusetts, to take up the professorship for the history of religion at the Episcopal Theological School. After his retirement he became trustee of Washington Cathedral and warden of the College of Preachers. Rhinelander was known as a high churchman who was a strong advocate for church unity. *New York Times*, 22 Sept. 1939, 30; see also Henry Bradford Washburn, *Philip Mercer Rhinelander: seventh bishop of Pennsylvania, first warden of the College of Preachers* (New York, 1950).

28 Charles Henry Brent (1862–1929), was bishop of Western New York from 1918 until his death in Lausanne in 1929. Brent studied at Trinity College, Toronto, and served at St Paul's Cathedral, Buffalo, before moving to parishes in Boston. In 1902 Brent was chosen to be the first missionary bishop of the Philippine Islands, where he was active in opposing the opium trade. He was appointed chaplain general of the American Expeditionary Forces in 1917, and received wide recognition for his work, including the Companion of the Order of the Bath. Elected bishop of Western New York in 1918, Brent was a strong advocate for the USA's membership of the League of Nations. In 1927, he presided at the World Conference of Faith and Order at Lausanne. He was responsible for the episcopal parishes in Europe from 1918 until 1927. In 1928, he took leave of absence in order to recover from a period of ill-health, but died whilst in Europe. *New York Times*, 28 Mar. 1929, 27.

29 *Sic*: writing up his notes, Bell was clearly unsure as to whether or not the bishop of Warrington had been involved in this group. Bell's diary is of no help on this point.

Brent, Pennsylvania and Pretoria, and bade Peterboro' and Zanzibar & Pennsylvania draft a statement for submission to Ebor and then if possible to the big C[ommit]tee.

– Again the very presence of Dornakal, with the knowledge of the definite plan for union in South India, [fo. 79r] of which he was brimful, constituted an immense stimulus in itself. There was a genuine sense that here was a κρισις, and that every step should be taken to help which could be. The immediate fruit may be seen in Res. 12 A (iii). He did not say a great deal: what he did say was sound and keenly felt: but it was he and his which meant much. Then there were Madras,[30] with his hair puffed out all round his head a little like an old lady with kind humorous eyes, & Tinnevelly, sallow & lean, both almost too insistent on the S[outh] India p[oin]t of view & anxious to test everything by how it w[oul]d look to their friends there: the Bishop of Uganda, earnest & God-fearing & still (and knowing all he stood for) yet supporting the B[isho]p of Zanzibar with his whole heart: Warrington sensibly and persuasively interpreting one school to the other: Peterborough, with his six feet odd, rising to appeal for accord: Brent's calm seriousness, vision, and authority: Hankow[31] with his cry for union from China – and how many more!
Yet there were a few that must be named!

Notably perhaps the B[isho]p of Durham (perched from the start in his place as Dunelm in the front [fo. 79v] bench between London[32] and Winchester and resenting any reference to him as B[isho]p of Hereford. 'I am Bishop-elect of Durham.') He had a definite policy – one definite step to be taken by this Conference, the formal recognition of presbyterian orders, and at first all his arguments and appeals were turned this way. He had an ally, to begin with, in Armagh: a strange partnership, thought Brent; but Armagh parted from D[urham] as the argument wore on, and became wholehearted for the Appeal. Durham was extraordinarily able – the ablest man of them all, so far as 'ability' went – he always had an admirable argument (whatever the subject) and an equally admirable from of expression: but a 'solitary'. He voiced the feelings of a few inarticulate B[isho]ps maybe and of very many laymen outside, but not perhaps in a way they would have thought very persuasive. Yet he was a remarkable speaker to hear! Not only on Reunion but on practically any

---

30 Henry Whitehead (1853–1947), bishop of Madras 1899–1922. Whitehead was the elder brother of the mathematician and philosopher Alfred North Whitehead. After studying classics at Oxford and serving as preacher in Abingdon, he was appointed principal of Bishop's College, Calcutta, and moved there in 1883; in 1890, he became additionally head of the Oxford Mission to Calcutta. Whitehead sought ways of encouraging the Anglo-Catholic Oxford Mission to work more closely with other Christian bodies in India and supported Indian Christians in their aspirations to self-government. After his consecration as bishop of Madras, Whitehead welcomed Dalit people ('untouchables') into the church. He was a close friend of V. S. Azariah (see p. 538 n.21). *ODNB*, LVIII, 663–4.

31 Logan H. Roots (1870–1945) was missionary bishop of Hankow in China from 1904 to 1938. He was born in Illinois, studied at Harvard and the Episcopal Theological School and went to China in 1896. On his retirement to the USA, he became a leading figure in the Moral Rearmament movement. Gerald H. Anderson (ed.), *Biographical dictionary of Christian missions* (Grand Rapids, 1999), pp. 576–7; *New York Times* 25 Sept. 1945, 22.

32 Arthur Foley Winnington-Ingram (1858–1946), bishop of London 1901–39. He took his BA in classics at Keble College, Oxford, and served as a curate in Shrewsbury and then as chaplain to W. A. Maclagan, bishop of Lichfield, before being appointed head of Oxford House, Bethnal Green, in 1888. He transformed the work of Oxford House, and in 1897, was consecrated bishop of Stepney. In 1901 he became bishop of London, and would remain for thirty-eight years. Although he worked hard to improve the conditions of the poor in his diocese, he was largely unsuccessful in holding together the different tendencies within his diocese. He was particularly known for his outspoken support for Britain's efforts in the First World War. *ODNB*, XXIX, 280–2.

other subject he had a masterly independent contribution of his own. He called me the honeybee of the conference because it was my fate to absorb all the eloquence, and give forth none. On Reunion [fo. 80r] he fought every stage in C[ommit]tee – the chief fight was on Res. 9 § viii – and though accepting amendments agreed between himself and Zanzibar he felt that after all the Appeal & Resol[utio]ns were not straight and w[oul]d meet the fate of not being straight – at the very end of the C[ommit]tee after threatening a minority report he secured the insertion of a closing paragraph suggesting an element of discord. 'I could kill that man', said Bombay to me in a fury when this last move was made, in the Crypt at the very conclusion of the C[ommit]tee! But hostile and critical as Dunelm had been in C[ommit]tee he maintained absolute silence in the Conference itself while the Appeal was being discussed – to his immense credit in the eyes of all – and did not vote against it.

Then there was the Bishop of Bombay, one of the Secretaries to the Reunion C[ommit]tee, a very explosive force – full of passion for Reunion, & breaking into vehement speech on how 'The Great Church Awakes'. A busy figure pressing his way through, with his smoked glasses, & his two patent leather satchels with its steel handles, sometimes stamping his feet with indignation, sometimes bursting into tumultuous [fo. 80v] speech, half-don and half-prophet. Very restive under opposition, and difficult as secretary to Ebor, not caring for interference nor to be told <u>how</u> to do what he had been told to do. Not perhaps an easy collaborator with anybody. But a wonderfully powerful pen and mind. He gave much, especially in the first week of the Conference, to the formation of ideas, and the digest on non-episcopal churches was his work. But he gave a good deal all through. And his main work was the drafting of the Encyclical, in which he characteristically scrapped the contributions which other draftsmen had laboriously compiled for certain of its sections! Very impatient of one yoke fellow Boutflower[33] 'old stick in the mud', as he called him, who does not understand the difference between being right and being bright. (He very emphatically prayed that he might never again be secretary to Ebor!) A curious picture he made in the 'Encyclical circle' sitting on the mat in the A[rch]b[isho]p's study with his legs crossed like a gnome, thinking or interjecting remarks: while around Brent, Peterborough, Ely, Boutflower & RTC[34] sat in a [fo. 81r] group drinking the midnight tea and eating the late (Huntley & Palmer) biscuit. One pleasing moment in the Reunion discussion was the tribute paid by Manchester[35] to Neville Pretoria whose speech about the younger generation had convinced him – a tribute greatly appreciated by his Father Winchester. Winchester, too ill, just after his golden wedding, for the first week of the Conference and only gradually recov-

---

33   Cecil Henry Boutflower (1863–1942) was educated at Uppingham and Christ Church, Oxford, before being ordained in 1887. He was curate at St Mary, South Shields, and was then chaplain to the bishop of Durham, and vicar, and later archdeacon, of Barrow-in-Furness. Boutflower was consecrated bishop of Dorking in 1905; in 1909 he was appointed bishop of South Tokyo. In 1921 he was translated to Southampton where he served until 1933. *Who was who*, IV, 124–5.

34   I.e., the archbishop of Canterbury (RTC = Randall Thomas Cantuar).

35   Edward Arbuthnott Knox (1847–1937) was bishop of Manchester from 1903 to 1920. Knox was a scholar at Corpus Christi, Oxford, before becoming fellow, dean, tutor and chaplain of Merton College. In 1891 he moved to become vicar of Aston, Birmingham, where he became suffragan bishop of Coventry, archdeacon of Birmingham and rector of St Philip's Church which later became the cathedral. He helped to lay the foundation for the new see of Birmingham. As bishop of Manchester from 1903, Knox was recognized as one of the leaders of the evangelical party within the Church of England. *ODNB*, XXXII, 8–9.

ering as the C[ommit]tee wore on was very warmly cheered on his first appearance in the full Conference, to which he made many useful contributions.

I have already said how much the B[isho]p of Zanzibar did to make the Appeal in its full form possible. More than this he made the crowning plea for its unanimous acceptance, [a] plea addressed especially to his brother bishops of the catholic school. Truly he swept the Conference into magnificent unanimity, as he addressed it immediately after the luncheon interval. But the tide was flowing fast the whole of that momentous Friday morning (July 3): from the A[rchbishop] of York's most informative opening speech, with its solemn reading of the Appeal, onwards – much helped no doubt by Oxford's[36] petition that the Appeal [fo. 81v] sh[oul]d be taken en bloc. There was a real sense of the Spirit of God. The incredible had happened in C[ommit]tee, was being continued in a very marked way in Conference. It was a time of deep religious experience. Some of the best speeches, as RTC reminded the Conference, before the luncheon adjournment, [as] had happened to Cicero, were never delivered. Only two spoke against. Vermont, sadly but temperately & earnestly: Osborne[37] in somewhat rasping & critical tones. Then the Appeal was put: & four hands only were held up against it. The Conference had done some g[rea]t thing, whatever else it did or left undone.

No doubt the main work of the Conference was done in the final week of the reserved sessions: that is the Resolutions on Reunion (all but the last few episcopal Resol[utio]ns) and on Ministry of Women. The Women Resol[utio]ns were admirably piloted by the Bishop of Ely. One the motion that the Report be received the B[isho]p of Z[anzibar] made a rigorous speech of protest, opposing such large liberties being conceived to women p[ar]tly as against Catholic tradition, p[ar]tly as furnishing and extra big 'scandal' in the eyes of [fo. 82r] Moslems. Z[anzibar]'s catholic 'history' was however severely dealt with by Ely. Z[anzibar] opposed altogether the idea of Holy Orders from women, only allowing them apparel of the same sort of place as exorcists or similar 'ministries'. Finally it was he who demanded a record of the voting on Resol[utio]n 52.

In the last week there were periods of reaction from the achievements of the previous six days. The most contentious and troublesome of all the subjects was proved to be the Resolutions on Marriage – Sex problems: very largely due to the somewhat sketchy character of the Report & the Resol[utio]ns prepared by a C[ommit] tee headed by distinguished bachelors. The B[isho]p of Durham delivered himself in burning words of Divorce, & when the final Resol[utio]n on that subject was passed asked to have his dissent recorded in the Minutes and promised to proclaim it publicly at an early date. But the chief bone of contention was Birth Control. On this there was

---

36   Hubert Murray Burge (1862–1925) was bishop of Oxford from 1919 until his death. After taking his BA in classics at University College Oxford, he taught at Wellington before returning to University College as fellow and tutor, and later dean. In 1900 he was appointed headmaster of Repton School, but in 1901 moved to become Headmaster of Winchester. In 1911, he accepted the bishopric of Southwark; during his time there he built up good relationships with the people of his diocese. He supported Hensley Henson in his conflict with Gore, bishop of Oxford, and was appointed to Oxford on Gore's retirement. He was an early supporter of ecumenism, and especially of the World Alliance Movement for Promoting Friendship through the Churches. *ODNB*, VIII, 749–50.

37   Bishop E. W. Osborne had been bishop coadjutor of the diocese of Springfield from 1906 to 1916. He had previously been rector of the church of St John the Evangelist of Boston, and was superior of the American branch of the Society of Mission Priests of St John the Evangelist. *New York Times*, 4 Aug. 1904, 7; www.episcopalspringfield.org/Bishop/FormerBishops.htm, accessed 24 June 2009.

prolonged debate and all sorts of printed amendments were submitted dealing with the possibility of exceptional cases being allowed. Strong things were said on either side, particularly by one side as to the wrecking character of a Resol[utio]n wh[ich] contained [fo. 82v] exceptions. The B[isho]ps of Winton, Fredericton,[38] Durham were foremost spokesmen on the side of leaving it to individual consciences while solemnly asserting the general rule: Zanzibar, Southwell,[39] Vermont, London were foremost the other way. Bishop of Norwich[40] *median patrem tenit*, and his form of amendment was about to be put and carried at the end of prolonged debate in a somewhat diminished house when Zanzibar strode to the rostrum and said rather ominously that the did not like to determine his relation to the Lambeth Conference by a vote on such a Resolution in a House of such a size. It looked like a threat. Anyhow the debate was adjourned, and finally a new Resolution, framed by Nassau was put two or three days later, & generally agreed (save for Durham).

Missionary Problems and the rest went pretty well: and the chairman of each c[ommit]tee did his part with skill both weeks. Oxon presented his report on psychical matters – a good and liberal report – with ability, but with the air of detachment as though he really was not interested in the subject and willingly let things go. Perhaps the authorization of 'healers' was let go a little too easily, & timidly, by the Conference [fo. 83r] to the initial disappointment of Assam and (in lesser degree) of Brent (who thought it an opportunity missed).

– There is much more to describe, but where can one begin and how make choice? I shall not easily forget the Metropolitan of Demotica, who came – a typical Oriental of the older School – straight from Constantinople with Komninos, a lay professor, as his expert in attendance: was received by the Lambeth Conference in full session where he exchanged grave speeches, interviewed by the Episcopal Committee, by the Eastern Churches C[ommit]tee, photographed with the A[rch] b[isho]p of Canterbury, by himself, and with his delegation, and sat in place of honour in the Abbey & St Paul's. I seem to see him now visiting Lambeth with Komninos & taken from room to room by Jenkins & myself on July 31; and afterwards sitting on the seat under the trees in the garden at the end of the long walk below the windows of the Palace, waiting for his taxi. He was a gentle old man, with a quaint humour. 'Ah c'est terrible, notre histoire', said he to me as he told of the fearful indignities which the Patriarch used to endure in the old days when visiting the Grand Vizier at Constantinople, kneeling & grovelling on he floor like a dog. He spoke of the Patriarch's lodgings in a monastery at Const[antinople] – contrasting their narrow range with the splendour of Lambeth. Then, when he finally [fo. 83v] came to bid the A[rch]b[isho]p goodbye after friendly talk and expressions of hope on either side for closer relationship between the two churches, leading to Union, the A[rch]b[isho]p of Canterbury said 'Mais pas trop vite' and the words were echoed

---

38 John A. Richardson (1868–1938) was bishop of Fredericton, Canada, from 1906 until his death, becoming also metropolitan of Canada from 1934 to 1938. *Anglican bishops of Canada*, http://bishop.blogsome.com/category/fredericton/ accessed 24 June 2009.

39 Edwyn Hoskins (1851–1925) was bishop of Southwell from 1904 until his death. Hoskyns had served in several parishes, including Stepney and Bolton, before being appointed bishop of Burnley in 1901. *Who was who*, II, 520.

40 Bertram Pollock (1863–1943), bishop of Norwich from 1910 until his resignation in 1942. He had previously been headmaster of Wellington. A good administrator, Pollock was less interested in matters of liturgy and church government and would later lead the campaign against the Prayer Book revision. *ODNB*, XLIV, 769–70.

with gusto by the Metropolitan 'pas trop vite'. (Note Germanos, Metropolitan of Seleucia, originally named as delegate, seems to have been much more progressive: he went to Faith and Order Conference at Geneva).

– As to the personelle of the Conference as a whole it was said by those who might know that the general level of ability was higher but that there were fewer peaks. A natural leadership belonged to the better known English diocesan B[isho]ps – and the reason was clear. The overseas Metropolitans did not on the whole provide the most remarkable B[isho]ps. Brisbane[41] was the most rigorous & adventurous. Sydney[42] was in minorities with Manchester, neither strong nor conciliatory. Capetown[43] a kind old gentleman. Rupertsland[44] a fine looking old Moses with patriarchal beard & manly sense & a twinkle in his venerable eyes (a Scot). Calcutta[45] modest, capable, straight but perhaps did not do himself justice.

– Among the Americans, Brent & Rhinelander stood out in character & ability. Vermont an old [fo. 84r] warrior, full of kindness & humour, foremost on the moral question. Tennessee[46] admirable teller of stories, admirable also in putting aggres-

---

41 St Clair George Alfred Donaldson (1863–1935) was educated at Eton and Trinity College, Cambridge, where he took a double first in classics and theology before going to Wells Theological College. After a period as chaplain to the archbishop of Canterbury and curate in Bethnal Green, he moved to Hackney Wick and then to Hornsey. He was appointed bishop of Brisbane in 1904 and became archbishop in 1905, remaining there until 1921. He considerably increased the number of Australian-born clergy in the diocese, and worked to break the legal ties between the Australian Church and the Church of England. In 1921, Donaldson was translated to Salisbury where he remained until his death in 1935. *ODNB*, XVI, 514–15.

42 John Charles Wright (1861–1933) was archbishop of Sydney from 1909 until his death, and also primate of Australia from 1910. Born in Lancashire, he was educated at Manchester Grammar School and Merton College, Oxford, where his tutor was a leading evangelical, Edmund Knox, later bishop of Manchester. After serving in Bradford and Ulverston, and Leeds, Wright moved to Manchester to become Knox's chaplain and rector of St George's, Hulme. Wright was influenced by Knox's theological conservatism and emphasis on order and discipline, but he shared with other younger evangelicals a wish to embrace modern scholarship and an awareness of social questions. In 1910 he was elected archbishop of Sydney, where he appointed clergy of moderate views, and rigorously enforced canon law in matters of vestments, requiring all clergy licensed in Sydney to agree not to wear the chasuble. As primate of Australia, Wright worked towards a new constitution to enable autonomy from England, but although agreement seemed close in 1926 and 1932, it was not eventually reached until 1961, nearly thirty years after Wright's death. *Australian Dictionary of Biography*, http://adbonline.anu.edu.au/biogs/A120655b.htm, accessed 24 June 2009.

43 William Marlborough Carter (1850–1941) was archbishop of Cape Town 1909–31. Educated at Eton, where his father was fellow, and then at Pembroke College, Oxford, he served in West Bromwich, Bakewell and then in the Eton Mission, Hackney, before being appointed bishop of Zululand in 1891. In 1902 he was translated to Pretoria, before becoming archbishop of Cape Town in 1909. *Who was who*, IV, 195.

44 Samuel Pritchard Matheson (1852–1942) was born at Kildonan, Manitoba, and educated at St John's College, Winnipeg. He was Professor of Exegetical Theology at St John's College and Canon of St, John's Cathedral before becoming dean of Rupert's Land (1892). Matheson was elected archbishop of Rupert's Land in 1905, and primate of Canada from 1910; he held both positions until his death. www.mhs.mb.ca/docs/people/matheson_sp.shtml, accessed 2 July 2009.

45 Foss Westcott (1863–1949) was bishop of Calcutta from 1919 until his retirement in 1945. As metropolitan of India, he oversaw the development of the anglican church in India as an autonomous province and was closely involved in the formation of the church of South India.

46 Thomas F. Gailor (1856–1935) was bishop of Tennessee from 1898 until his death. Gailor was born in Jackson, Mississippi, and educated at Racine College, Wisconsin, and the General Theological Seminary City. After a curacy served in Pulaski, Tennessee, he was appointed professor of ecclesiastical history and polity at the University of the South, a position he held until 1893, when he was consecrated bishop of Tennessee. In 1916 Gailor was elected chairman of the House of Bishops and

sive American Bishops in their place e.g. S[outh] Carolina,[47] and in summing up with fairness and humour the American position. Harrisburg,[48] the B[isho]p of whom most of his brother bishops warned the rest of the Conference as a terror, told wonderful stories of how he had practically established Reunion with the East on a formula of his own C[ommit]tee's, produced an Old Catholic Polish B[isho]p suddenly, black looking, gruff, but not unkind: with deaf wife, dazzling daughter and a chaplain son immaculately dressed. Massachusetts,[49] obviously influential but too liberal for his American brethren, a good speaker and careful for the rights of the General Convention! Connecticut,[50] descendant of Elder Brewster of the Mayflower. S[outh] Florida,[51] delivering a wonderful speech about women: a speech to which Durham listened, he said, with an enjoyment greater than his agreement.[52] S[outh] Carolina with a strong pro-American vein: W[est] Missouri[53] with his amazing flow

elected president of the National Council of the Episcopal Church, and thus presiding bishop of the PECUSA, in 1919, a position he held until 1925. *Tennessee encyclopedia of history and culture*, http://tennesseeencyclopedia.net/imagegallery.php?EntryID=G001, accessed 2 July 2009.

47 William A. Guerry (1861–1928) was bishop of South Carolina from 1908 until his death, which was the result of being shot by a former priest of the diocese. Born in South Carolina, he studied at the University of the South before returning to his home state where he served in a number of parishes. In 1893, Guerry was appointed chaplain and professor of homiletics and pastoral theology at the University of the South, which positions he held until his return to South Carolina in 1907 as bishop coadjutor. *New York Times*, 10 June 1928, 18.

48 James Henry Darlington (1856–1930) was bishop of Harrisburg from 1905 until his death. Born in New York, Darlington studied at New York and Princeton Universities and Princeton Theological Seminary. After ordination he served in only one parish, Christ Church Brooklyn. Darlington was known as a leader in international philanthropy and the ecumenical movement. *New York Times*, 15 Aug. 1930, 13; 19 Nov. 1930, 19.

49 William Lawrence (1850–1941) was bishop of Massachusetts from 1893 until he retired in 1927. Lawrence studied at Harvard and the Episcopal Theological School. After serving in a parish for six years, he returned to the Episcopal Theological School in 1883 as professor of homiletics and later dean, where he remained until he was elected bishop of Massachusetts in 1893. During his episcopate, Lawrence founded the church pension system of the episcopal church. *New York Times*, 5 May 1893, 9; 7 Nov. 1941, 23.

50 Chauncy Bunce Brewster (1848–1941) was bishop of Connecticut from 1899 to 1928. He was born in Connecticut and attended school in New Haven before studying at Yale and at Berkeley Divinity School, Middletown, Connecticut. He served in parishes in Middletown, Rye, NY, Detroit and Baltimore before being elected bishop coadjutor of Connecticut in 1897. His obituary noted: 'he was known as a scholarly, liberal leader who sought to adapt the traditions of an ancient faith to the social needs of a changing modern world'. *New York Times*, 10 Apr. 1941, 24.

51 Cameran Mann (1851–1932) was bishop of South Florida from 1913 until his death in 1932, during a period of growth and development which in 1922 saw the diocese created out of the Missionary Jurisdiction of Southern Florida, largely on Mann's initiative. Born in upstate New York, he trained at General Theological Seminary and served in several parishes in New York State, including Watkins, where his father had been the previous incumbent. In 1901, Mann was sent to be missionary bishop of North Dakota, and in 1913 appointed in South Florida. *New York Times*, 9 Feb. 1932, 25.

52 Bell writes in his diary for 8 July of this speech (fo. 64r): 'Henson spoke in afternoon of S Florida's eloquent speech[,] all of which he enjoyed, and with much he agreed, "but my enjoyment was greater than my agreement".'

53 Sidney Catlin Partridge (1857–1930) was bishop of West Missouri 1911 until his death. Partridge was born in New York City, educated at Yale and Berkeley Divinity School, Middletown, Connecticut, and ordained deacon in 1884, going to Shanghai as a missionary to teach at St John's College. From 1887, he was a missionary in Wu-Chang, China, and rector of Boone School. He was consecrated missionary bishop of Kyoto, Japan in 1900, returning to the USA to become missionary bishop of Western Missouri in 1911. *New York Times*, 23 June 1930, 16; David Shavit (ed.), *The United States in Asia* (New York, 1990), p. 384.

of missionary speech (Diarrhoea in expression, said B[isho]p Trower,[54] constipation in thought.) And two score more, as to each of whom almost one might have something else to pick out!

It is impossible to describe all the Bishops, even in a [fo. 84v] line in such rough and cursory notes as these. I can only jot down a few impressions very briefly of some individual B[isho]ps not mentioned hitherto. Antigua[55] with brown beard, skull cap & glasses, & Inverness cape to ward off the anti-tropical cold, making his way to the platform from time to time in defence of catholic principles on different issues. Kampala[56] with his smooth hair & youthful face bubbling with enthusiasm over internationalism & everything else: Glou[ce]ster[57] with his long grey locks, shaking a forefinger in emphasis & warning: Chichester with his gouty leg stretched half the time on a campstool before him – and the other half leaping up like a schoolmaster to correct: Aberdeen[58] dark haired & chiefly chaffing the English B[isho]ps on their provincial English attitudes – the establishment and so forth –: Molony[59] in gentle & persuasive tones speaking of Provincial organisation & the relation of it to the C.H.S.K.H.[60] a name greeted at first by a surprised Conference with a ripple of mild

---

[54] Name difficult to read: probably Gerard Trower (1860–1928), who was bishop of North-West Australia 1909–27. Trower was born in Hook, Yorkshire, and educated at Merchant Taylors' School, Keble College, Oxford, and Ely Theological College. He was ordained deacon in 1888 and priest in 1889, serving curacies at St Mary's, Redcliffe, and St Alban's, Birmingham. In 1895 he moved to Sydney as rector of Christ Church St Laurence, where his high church leanings and introduction of altar lights and vestments provoked some controversy. In 1901 he was consecrated bishop of Likoma, Nyasaland (now Malawi), where he established schools, a hospital, a cathedral and a theological college. In 1910 he was enthroned as first bishop of North-West Australia, and worked, not always successfully, to establish a mission to the Aborigine people. He ordained the first Aboriginal deacon, James Noble, in 1925. In 1927 he resigned and returned to the UK to serve on the Isle of Wight where he died in 1928. *Australian dictionary of national biography*, http://adbonline.anu.edu.au/biogs/A120298b.htm?hilite=Trower, accessed 3 July 2009.

[55] Edward Hutson (1873–1936) was bishop of Antigua from 1911 until his death, becoming also archbishop of the West Indies from 1922. Hutson was born in Antigua and educated at Codrington College, Barbados, and Durham University (by affiliation), being ordained in 1896. He served as curate to his father at All Saints, Antigua, and was rector of St Paul, St Croix, before being consecrated bishop of Antigua in 1911. *Times*, 23 Oct. 1936, 19B; *Who was who*, III, 686.

[56] John Jamieson Willis (1872–1954) was educated at Haileybury College, Pembroke College Cambridge, and Ridley Hall. Ordained in 1895, he served a curacy in Great Yarmouth before going with CMS to be a missionary in Ankole, Entebbe and Kavirondo, where he was archdeacon. In 1911, Willis was consecrated bishop of Uganda. He returned to the UK in 1934, and was assistant bishop in the diocese of Leicester from 1935 to 1949. *Who was who*, V, 1176.

[57] Edward Charles Sumnor Gibson (1848–1924) was bishop of Gloucester 1905 until 1922. Gibson was educated at Charterhouse and Trinity College, Oxford. He was ordained deacon in 1871, and served as chaplain and then vice-principal of Wells Theological College, returning after a period as principal of Leeds Clergy School to become principal in 1880. In 1895, he was appointed vicar of Leeds, before being consecrated bishop of Gloucester in 1905. *Who was who*, 310.

[58] Frederick Llewellyn Deane (1868–1952) was educated at Keble College, Oxford, and ordained in 1891. After serving in Kettering and Leicester, he moved to Glasgow where he was rector of St Mary the Virgin from 1904 and provost of St Mary's Cathedral from 1908. Deane was consecrated bishop of Aberdeen and Orkney in 1917. He retired in 1943, becoming assistant bishop in Glasgow and Galloway in 1947. *Who was who*, V, 291.

[59] Herbert James Molony (1865–1939) was born in Dublin and educated at Pembroke College, Cambridge, and Ridley Hall. Ordained in 1888, he served a curacy at St Stephen's, Newcastle, before being sent by CMS to India, working in Mandla from 1890 and in Jubbulpore in 1905. In 1908 he was consecrated bishop to the British Missionary Area in Chekiang, China, where he remained until 1928. From 1929 to 1937, he was rector of Teston, Kent. *Who was who*, III, 953.

[60] Chung Hua Sheng Kung Hui, the anglican church in China, was founded in 1912 from the churches

laughter: Banister[61] & Cassels[,][62] veteran Chinese missionaries, both of them, the former uttering a vehement appeal for the suppression of the opium traffic in China. Gilbert White,[63] the B[isho]p who has walked across Australia, tall, spare, with shaggy beard & the [fo. 85r] clear blue eye of a Christian counsellor, not a mystic, noting much (like his ancestor the naturalist) but saying little. Oluwole[64] with his vigorous air, stately words of simple manly self-sufficiency. Barking[65] striding up bulldog-like to the platform to deliver his message whoever may be already there & whatever ruling the President may be about to give. Mike Furse[66] with strident voice,

---

pioneered by anglican missions to China in the nineteenth and twentieth centuries, but was not recognized by the anglican communion until the Lambeth Conference of 1930. For more details of its history, see www.ttc.edu.sg/csca/skh/ accessed 3 July 2009. *Who was who*, II, 38.

61 William Banister (1855–1928) was first anglican bishop of Kwangsi and Hunan, China, serving from 1909 until 1923. Banister was born in Lancashire, and trained at the CMS College in Islington. Ordained deacon in 1879 and priest in 1880 by the bishop of London, Banister served a brief curacy in Blackburn, Lancashire before being sent by CMS as a missionary to Foochow and Ku Cheng in 1880. He became principal of the CMS Theological College in Foochow in 1893, CMS secretary to Hong Kong in 1897 and archdeacon of Hong Kong in 1902.

62 William Wharton Cassels (1858–1925) was bishop of Western China from 1895 until his death. Born in Portugal, Cassels was educated at Repton School and St John's College, Cambridge. He was ordained in 1882 and served a curacy at All Saints, South Lambeth, until 1885, when he sailed for China as one of the 'Cambridge Seven' to join the China Inland Mission. Cassels worked initially in Shansi and Taning, North China, before moving to West China and setting up a mission in Paoning, where the first church was dedicated in 1893. The work in Western China was interdenominational, which caused George Evans Moule, bishop of Mid-China, some concern. In 1895, Cassels was consecrated bishop of the newly established diocese of Western China, being taken on to the payroll of CMS for the purpose. In 1907, he was offered, but refused, the bishopric of Mid-China after Moule's resignation. *Who was who*, II, 140; Marshall Broomhall, *W. W. Cassels: first bishop in Western China* (London, 1926).

63 Gilbert White (1859–1933) was first bishop of Willochra, Australia, from 1915 until his retirement in 1925. White was born in Rondebosch, in the South African Cape Colony, but the family returned to the UK in 1861. White was educated at Fettes College, Edinburgh, and Oriel College, Oxford, where he read classics and theology. He was ordained in 1883, and after serving a curacy in Helston, Truro, emigrated to Queensland in 1885 where he became rector of Charters Towers, moving to Herberton in 1886, and becoming archdeacon of North Queensland in 1890. He was consecrated first bishop of Carpentaria in 1900 and was translated to Willochra in 1915. In 1925, White was Australian delegate to the World Conference on Life and Work, Stockholm. He retired to England in 1926. *Who was who*, III, 1444; *Australian dictionary of biography*, http://adbonline.anu.edu.au/biogs/A120521b.htm, accessed 3 July 2009.

64 Isaac Oluwole (1852–1932) was bishop of West Equatorial Africa (assistant to the bishop of Lagos) from 1893. Oluwole was born in Sierra Leone. He attended the premier West African College, Fourah Bay, where he earned a Durham affiliated BA. From 1879 he was principal of the CMS grammar school in Lagos, in 1879. He was ordained deacon in 1881 and priest in 1884. In 1893 he was consecrated bishop of West Equatorial Africa in St Paul's Cathedral, London, and received a DD from the University of Durham. *Dictionary of African Christian biography*, www.dacb.org/stories/nigeria/oluwole_isaac.html, accessed 3 July 2009. For a somewhat unsympathetic portrait of Oluwole's appointment and ministry, see Emmanuel Ayandele, *'Holy' Johnson: pioneer of African nationalism, 1836–1917* (London, 1970), especially pp. 249–51, 318–23.

65 James Theodore Inskip (1868–1949) was bishop of Barking (suffragan to Chelmsford) from 1919 until his retirement in 1948. Inskip was educated at Clifton College, Bristol, and Corpus Christi College, Cambridge, where he read classics, and Ridley Hall. Ordained in 1891, he served his curacy at St James', Hatcham, before becoming vicar of St Paul's, Penzance, in 1894. In 1900, he moved to Leyton, in 1907 to Jesmond, Newcastle-upon-Tyne, and 1916 to Christ Church, Southport. From there he was consecrated bishop suffragan of Barking in 1919. He served concurrently as archdeacon of Essex (renamed West Ham in 1922) from 1920. *Who was who*, IV, 589–90

66 Michael Bolton Furse (1870–1955) was bishop of St Albans from 1920 until 1944. Furse was educated at Eton and Trinity College, Oxford. From 1895 he was fellow and dean of Trinity College,

sometimes lowering & stormy like a giant prize fighter. Exeter[67] dashing in with a fine aimless frenzy of his own yet with intermittent inspiration. Jerusalem[68] a dapper figure, well-groomed, well informed, delivering himself in eloquent and effective but somewhat narrow minded speech on the sinister forces at work in the Zionist movement. Deaf Athabasca[69] with his ear trumpet perched on a table in a front row; and last of all the nearly 90 year old (?) Willis of Tonga[70] who though he sits in the place vacated for him by Premier Bishop Plunket of Meath[71] immediately below the Presidential Chair yet heard never a word or barely a word the whole five weeks.

The Conference ended on Sat Aug 7 with a memorable scene. A motion that the A[rch]b[isho]p leave the Chair and the A[rchbishop] of Y[ork] take it was put & carried: a further motion that Mrs Davidson suitably attended enter the library was also agreed. All [fo. 85v] the B[isho]ps present, including for the first time the Americans, had united to present the A[rch]b[isho]p with a primatial cross of ebony & silvergilt as a mark of their gratitude. Speeches were made by York, Tennessee (who made the presentation), Armagh, Calcutta showing the depth of affection & admiration felt for the President who has so wisely & patiently brought all so safe to port. It wd be difficult to say too much of the unanimity with which the expressions of gratitude were greeted, or the enthusiasm with which the whole Conference received the A[rch]b[isho]p as he rose to give thanks for the words spoken about him, and the gift of the cross. It shewed once more the warmth of the almost love for

Oxford, being ordained deacon by the bishop of St Albans in 1896 and priest by the bishop of Oxford in 1897. In 1903 he was appointed archdeacon of Johannesburg, and in 1909 was consecrated bishop of Pretoria. He returned to England in early 1920 to become bishop of St Albans. *Who was who*, V, 402.

67   Lord William Gascoyne Cecil (1863–1936) was educated at Eton and University College, Oxford. Ordained in 1887, he served his curacy in Great Yarmouth, becoming rector of Bishops Hatfield in 1888 and being consecrated bishop of Exeter in 1916, where he remained until his death. *Who was who*, III, 233.0

68   Rennie MacInnes (1870–1931) was bishop of Jerusalem from 1914 until his death. MacInnes was educated at Harrow and Trinity College, Cambridge. He was ordained in 1896 and served a curacy at St Matthew's, Bayswater, before going to Cairo, Egypt, with CMS as a missionary in 1899. From 1902 to 1914 he was CMS secretary in Egypt and North Sudan, and from 1909 canon of St George's Jerusalem in 1909. *Times*, 28 Dec. 1931, 12D; *Who was who*, III, 860.

69   Edwin Frederick Robins (1870–1951) was bishop of Athabasca, in the province of Rupert's Land, Canada, from 1912 to 1930. Robins was born in London and trained at the CMS College in Islington. Ordained deacon in 1894, he went as a CMS missionary to the Punjab, returning to London in 1897 when he was ordained priest. He served curacies at St James, Paddington, and in Widcombe, and was vicar of Thorpe-Le-Soken, near Colchester, before being appointed archdeacon of Athabasca in 1909. After resigning as bishop of Athabasca in 1930, he returned to England to be vicar of Wicklewood and assistant bishop in the diocese of Norwich. *Who was who*, V, 937.

70   Alfred Willis (1836–1920) was assistant bishop of Tonga, diocese of Polynesia from 1902 until his death. Willis was born in Greatford, Lincs., and educated at Uppingham, St John's College, Oxford, and Wells Theological College. Ordained in 1856, he was curate of Strood and then St Mark's, New Brompton, Kent, until his appointment as missionary bishop to Honolulu in 1872, supported by the Society for the Propagation of the Gospel. After a stormy ministry in Honolulu (there were petitions for his resignation from 1890 onwards), he moved to Tonga in 1902, and the see of Honolulu passed to the PECUSA. *Blain biographical directory of anglican clergy in the diocese of Honolulu 1862–1902*, http://anglicanhistory.org/hawaii/blain_directory.pdf, accessed 3 July 2009.

71   Benjamin Plunket (1870–1947) was bishop of Meath from 1919 to 1925. Plunket was the son of the Fourth Baron Plunket, archbishop of Dublin. He was educated at Harrow and Corpus Christi College, Cambridge, and ordained in 1896 to a curacy at St Peter, Dublin. In 1902 he was appointed rector of Aghade with Ardoyne, and in 1907 vicar of St Ann's, Dublin. He was consecrated bishop of Tuam, Killala and Achonry in 1913, whence he was translated to Meath in 1919. *Who was who*, IV, 921.

their President felt by the B[isho]ps who had come to attend the Lambeth Conference from all parts of the world. After Mrs Davidson in a few words, charged with feeling, expressed her thanks, with the new Cross in his hand the A[rch]b[isho]p gave the final blessing to all present. The Conference, save for an afternoon sitting to complete the Encyclical, was over. On the next day all the B[isho]ps went to S Paul's to offer thanks, & receive Communion together (as all did receive it). The A[rch]b[isho]p spoke his last words of farewell: gave his blessing: & so g[rea]t hopes [fo. 86r] were crowned: and g[rea]t events in the history of the Church were set afoot.

II The making of the Appeal to All Christian People: redactions and draft resolutions

1. Redactions of the Appeal to All Christian People

Text A, drafted on 13 July, presented to the sub-committee on 14 July: 'Statement of the committee on re-union'. In: LC 115, fos. 18–21; a slightly amended version (A2), probably representing the discussion on 14 July, in: the Douglas papers 1, fos. 356–7.

Text B, drafted on 16/17 July, presented to the sub-committee on 19 July: pasted into LC 117, minutes book of the committee for reunion with non-episcopal churches, fos. 14–18, with a revised version (B2) dated 19 July 1920 – Douglas papers 1, fos. 354–5a.

Text C, presented for discussion on 22 and 23 July: carbon copy in: Douglas papers 1, fos. 366–70, with a revised version (C2) in: LC 115), fos. 24v–28 (§§ 1–6) and fos. 31–3 (§§ 7–9).

Final text: from the anglican communion's Lambeth Resolution Archive: www.lambethconference.org/resolutions/1920/1920–9.cfm (accessed 8 July 2009).

Text A: presented on 14 July	Text B: presented on 19 July	Text C: presented on 22 and 23 July	**Final text** **Resolution 9**:
COMMITTEE ON RE-UNION	A STATEMENT OF OUR POSITION	*An Appeal from the Bishops assembled in the Lambeth Conference of 1920 To all Christian People*	The Conference adopts and sends forth the following Appeal to all Christian people:
			An Appeal To All Christian People from the Bishops Assembled in the Lambeth Conference of 1920
		We, the Bishops of the Anglican Communion [C2: *We, Archbishops, Bishops Metropolitan, and other Bishops of the Holy Catholic Church in full communion with the Church of England, two hundred and in number and*] in Conference assembled, realising the responsibility which rests upon us at this time, and sensible of the sympathy and the prayers of many, both within and without our own Communion, make this appeal to all Christian people. We acknowledge all those who believe in our Lord Jesus Christ, and have been baptized his name [C2: *into the name of the Holy Trinity*], as sharing with us membership in the universal Church of Christ which is his Body. [C2: *We*	We, Archbishops, Bishops Metropolitan, and other Bishops of the Holy Catholic Church in full communion with the Church of England, in Conference assembled, realising the responsibility which rests upon us at this time, and sensible of the sympathy and the prayers of many, both within and without our own Communion, make this appeal to all Christian people. We acknowledge all those who believe

believe that the Holy Spirit has called us in a very solemn and special manner to associate ourselves in penitence and prayer with all those who deplore the divisions of Christian people and are inspired by the vision and hope of a visible unity of the whole Church.]

I. We believe that God wills fellowship. By God's own act this fellowship was created through and in [C2: *made in and through*] Jesus Christ, and its life is in his Spirit and its objective is the accomplishment of His will and the promotion of His glory.
We believe that God intends this fellowship so far as this world is concerned, to be an outward, visible, and united society, with [C2: *having*] its own recognized officers, using the GOD-given means of grace, and inspiring all its members for a [C2: *to the*] world-wide service for [C2: *of*] the Kingdom of God. This is what we mean by the Catholic Church.

II. This united fellowship is not visible in the world today. On the one hand there are the other ancient episcopal Communions in East and West, to whom we are [*ours is*] bound by many ties of common faith and tradition. We cherish the earnest hope that it may be possible for us again to be united with them in completeness of fellowship.
On the other hand there are the great non-episcopal Communions, standing for rich

in our Lord Jesus Christ, and have been baptized into the name of the Holy Trinity, as sharing with us membership in the universal Church of Christ which is his Body. We believe that the Holy Spirit has called us in a very solemn and special manner to associate ourselves in penitence and prayer with all those who deplore the divisions of Christian people, and are inspired by the vision and hope of a visible unity of the whole Church.

I. We believe that God wills fellowship. By God's own act this fellowship was made in and through Jesus Christ, and its life is in his Spirit.

We believe that it is God's purpose to manifest this fellowship, so far as this world is concerned, in an outward, visible, and united society; holding one faith, having its own recognized officers, using God-given means of grace, and inspiring all its members to the world-wide service of the Kingdom of God. This is what we mean by the Catholic Church.

II. This united fellowship is not visible in the world today. On the one hand there are the other ancient episcopal Communions in East and West, to whom ours is bound by many ties of common faith and tradition.

On the other hand there are the great non-episcopal Communions, standing

1. The unity of the Church which is the Body of Christ exists by His act, and embraces all those whom he has drawn, [A2: *or is drawing,*] into fellowship with Himself, both those who have departed this life, and those who are yet in it. It is the duty of the Church on earth at any time to devote itself to the purpose of God, by striving to let this Unity be visible in common life, witness and service.
[*Accepted*]

2. This unity is now obscured through the sins and failures of Christians, which have led to, and still maintain, the divisions of Christendom. Our desire is that we and all our fellow Christians should join [A2: *Our desire is to invite our fellow Christians to join with us*] in a sincere confession of these sins and in an earnest and

I. We believe that GOD wills fellowship. By GOD's own act this fellowship was created through and in Jesus Christ. Its life is in His Spirit, and its objective is the accomplishment of His will and the promotion of His Glory. We believe that GOD intends this fellowship as far as this world is concerned, to be an outward, visible, and united society, with its own recognized officers, using GOD-given means of grace, and inspiring all its members for a world-wide service [B2: *for the Kingdom of God*]. This is what we mean by the Catholic Church.

II. This united fellowship is not visible in the world today. Christians are organized in different groups, each one keeping to itself gifts that rightly belong to the whole fellowship, and tending to live its own life apart from the rest.

deliberate endeavour to heal these divisions.

[Accepted]

III. This condition of broken fellowship we acknowledge to be sinful [handwritten correction substitutes: _contrary to God's will_], and we desire frankly to confess our share in the guilt of thus crippling the Society of Christ and hindering the activity of His Spirit.

III. [C2: _The causes of division lie deep in the past, and are by no means simple or wholly blameworthy. Yet none can doubt that self-will, ambition, and lack of charity among Christians have been principal factors in the mingled process, and that these, together with blindness to the sin of disunion, are still mainly responsible for the breaches of Christendom._] This condition of broken fellowship we acknowledge [C2: _We acknowledge this condition of broken fellowship_] to be contrary to GOD'S will, and we desire frankly to confess our share in the guilt of thus crippling the Society [C2: _Body_] of Christ and hindering the activity of His Spirit.

III. The causes of division lie deep in the past, and are by no means simple or wholly blameworthy. Yet none can doubt that self-will, ambition, and lack of charity among Christians have been principal factors in the mingled process, and that these, together with blindness to the sin of disunion, are still mainly responsible for the breaches of Christendom. We acknowledge this condition of broken fellowship to be contrary to God's will, and we desire frankly to confess our share in the guilt of thus crippling the Body of Christ and hindering the activity of his Spirit.

---

elements of truth, _liberty_ and life which might otherwise have been obscured or neglected. With them we are closely linked by many affinities, racial, historical and spiritual. [C2: _We cherish the earnest hope that all these Communions, and our own, may be led by the Spirit into the unity of the faith and of the knowledge of the Son of God._] But [C2: _in fact_] we are all organized in different groups, each one keeping to itself gifts that rightly belong to the whole fellowship, and tending to live its own life apart from the rest.

---

for rich elements of truth, liberty and life which might otherwise have been obscured or neglected. With them we are closely linked by many affinities, racial, historical and spiritual. We cherish the earnest hope that all these Communions, and our own, may be led by the Spirit into the unity of the faith and of the knowledge of the Son of God. But in fact we are all organized in different groups, each one keeping to itself gifts that rightly belong to the whole fellowship, and tending to live its own life apart from the rest.

IV. The times call us to new outlook and new measures. The faith cannot be adequately apprehended and the battle of the Kingdom cannot be worthily fought while the body is divided, and is thus unable to grow up into the fullness of the life of Christ. The time has come, we believe, for all the separated groups of Christians to agree in forgetting the things which are behind and reaching out towards the goal of a reunited Catholic Church. The removal of the barriers which have arisen between them will only be brought about by a new comradeship of those whose faces are definitely set this way.

The vision which rises before us is that of a Church, genuinely Catholic, loyal to all truth, and gathering into its fellowship all 'who profess and call themselves Christians', within whose visible unity all the treasures of faith and order, bequeathed as a heritage by the past to the present, shall be possessed in common, and made serviceable to the whole Body of Christ. Within this unity Christian Communions now separated from one another would retain much that has long been distinctive in their methods of worship and service. It is through a rich diversity of life and devotion that the unity of the whole fellowship will be fulfilled.

IV. The times call us to a new outlook and new measures. The faith cannot be adequately apprehended and the battle of the Kingdom cannot be worthily fought while the Body is divided, and is thus unable to grow up into the fullness of the life of Christ. The time has come, we believe, for all the separated groups of Christians to join together [C2: agree] in forgetting the things which are behind and reaching out towards the goal of a reunited Catholic Church. The removal of the barriers which have arisen between them will only be brought about by a new comradeship of those whose faces are definitely set this way.

The vision which rises before us is that of a truly Catholic Church within which many groups would retain their characteristic systems of life and worship in one organic, visible friendship, and all the treasures of faith and order, possessed at present separately, would find full scope, and be available for the whole body.

[C2: *The vision which rises before us is that of a Church, genuinely Catholick because loyal to all truth, and gathering into its fellowship all 'who believe and call themselves Christians', within whose visible unity all the treasures of faith and order, bequeathed as a heritage by the Past to the Present, shall be possessed in common, and made serviceable*]

3. Our aim, therefore, is not merely or mainly [A2: *primarily*] that some of the Churches, into which the one Church has been split up, should be united with ours, but that all should co-operate in manifesting in one visible body the fullness of the diverse gifts of the Spirit.

Thus our ideal is neither the absorption of these churches into one uniform system, not their alliance in a loose federation, but a living fellowship in which the various gifts and graces bestowed by God upon each shall be no longer kept in separateness, but used and enjoyed for the enrichment of the whole body.

[Accepted]

IV. The time has come, we believe, for the separated groups of Christians to join together in forgetting the things which are behind, and reaching out towards the goal of a reunited Catholic Church. We have a vision of many groups retaining their own systems while combined in one organic fellowship, in which all the treasures of faith and order, possessed at present separately, may find full scope and be available for the whole body.

4. We acknowledge all those who believe in our Lord Jesus Christ, and have been baptized into the name of the Holy Trinity [A2: *into His name*], as sharing with us membership in the universal Church of Christ, which is His body.

We confess that in and through the existing divisions of Christendom we have all alike become involved in a state of schism, of which we have all need to repent, and from which we must all seek to be set free.
[Accepted]

V: This means an adventure of goodwill, and still more of faith, for nothing less is required than a new discovery of the creative resources of GOD. To this adventure we humbly believe that God is now calling all the members of his Church.

VI: We urge that this visible unity of the Church will be found to involve a wholehearted acceptance of:–
(a) The Holy Scriptures, as the record of GOD's revelation of Himself to man, and the Creed commonly called Nicene.
(b) The corporate life of the whole fellowship as expressed for all in the divinely instituted

[C2: The Holy Scriptures, as the record of God's revelation of Himself to man, and as being the rule and ultimate standard of faith:

V. This means an adventure of goodwill and still more of faith, for nothing less is required than a new discovery of the creative resources of God. To this adventure we are convinced that God is now calling all the members of his Church.

VI. We believe that the visible unity of the Church will be found to involve the wholehearted acceptance of:
The Holy Scriptures, as the record of God's revelation of himself to man, and as being the rule and ultimate standard of faith; and the Creed commonly called Nicene, as the sufficient statement of the Christian faith, and either it or the Apostles' Creed as the baptismal confession of belief; the divinely instituted sacraments of Baptism and the Holy Communion, as expressing for all the corporate life of the whole fellowship

---

to the whole Body of Christ. Within this unity some of the Christian Communions separated from one another might still retain much that has long been distinctive in their methods of worship and service. It is through a rich diversity of life and devotion that the unity of the whole fellowship will be fulfilled.]

V. This means an adventure of goodwill, and to this adventure we are now called.

VI. We believe that this visible unity of the Church will be found to involve the wholehearted acceptance of
(a) The Holy Scriptures, as the record of God's revelation of Himself to man, and the Creed commonly called Nicene.
(b) The corporate life of the whole fellowship as expressed for all in the divinely instituted sacraments of Baptism (normally completed in the laying on of hands) and the Holy Communion, with wide liberty for each group to authorise such additional rites and customs of worship and devotion as

---

5. We believe that the visible unity of the Church will be found to involve at least (a) the acceptance of the canonical scriptures of the old and new Testaments as containing all things necessary to salvation, and the Nicene Creed as the sufficient statement of the Christian faith, (b) the acceptance of the two Sacraments of Baptism and the Supper of the Lord, as ordained by Christ Himself, and (c) a common Ministry which

possesses [A2: *a Ministry which will be accepted by every part of the Church, as possessing*] the commission of Christ and the authority of the whole Body. This Common Ministry, we believe, can only be secured through episcopal ordination. [This sentence is replaced in A2 by: *In view of the position of episcopacy in the past history and present life of the Church, we believe that this common ministry is to be secured through episcopal ordinations.*]

[Accepted subject to reconsideration of (b) with regard to confirmation in view of certain statements about confirmation made by the doctors]

are found by experience to minister to its spiritual needs.
(c) A Ministry acknowledged by every part of the Church as possessing the commission of Christ and the authority of the whole body. Considerations alike of history and of present experience point to the Episcopate as the one means of providing such a ministry.

sacraments of Baptism (and the Holy Communion, with wide liberty for each group to authorise such additional rites and customs of worship and devotion as are found by experience to minister to its spiritual needs.
(c) A ministry acknowledged by every part of the Church as possessing the commission of Christ and the authority of the whole body.

and of the Creed commonly called Nicene, as the sufficient statement of the Christian faith, and either it or the Apostles' Creed as the Baptismal confession of belief: The divinely instituted sacraments of Baptism and the Holy Communion, as expressing for all the corporate life of the whole fellowship in and with Christ:
A ministry acknowledged by every part of the Church as possessing not only the inward call of the Spirit, but also the commission of Christ and the authority of the whole body.]

in and with Christ; a ministry acknowledged by every part of the Church as possessing not only the inward call of the Spirit, but also the commission of Christ and the authority of the whole body.

6. While expressing this belief with regard to the authority necessary for the Ministry of the whole Church, we yet gladly acknowledge, that God has been pleased to confer gifts of His Holy Spirit upon the Ministry of Churches which have not accepted Episcopal ordination, and to use the Sacraments administered in

[VII.] We confidently claim a place by the side of the ancient episcopal communions of East and West, awaiting hopefully such mutual re-union as will again unite us in completeness of fellowship.
We believe that in the future as in the past, the Episcopate will prove to be the most effective means of maintaining the unity and continuity of the Church. But

May we not reasonably claim that considerations alike of history and of present experience point to the Episcopate as the as the one means of providing such a ministry?

VII: Moreover, to our brethren who do not possess the episcopate, we would urge that it is now and will prove to be in the future the most effective means of maintaining the unity and continuity of the Church. But we greatly desire

VII. May we not reasonably claim that the episcopate is the one means of providing such a ministry? It is not that we call in question for a moment the spiritual reality of the ministries of those Communions which do not possess the episcopate. On the contrary we thankfully acknowledge that these ministries have been manifestly blessed and owned by the Holy Spirit as effective means of grace. But we submit them as effectual means of grace. [Accepted]

7. We believe that the acceptance of the Historic Episcopate would not only secure for the whole Church a common Ministry, but also prove in the future, as in the past, to be a powerful means of maintaining the Unity and continuity of the Church. [Accepted with 4 dissentients]

we greatly desire that the office of the Bishop should be increasingly exercised in a representative and constitutional manner in accordance with the ideals of the early and undivided Church.

VII. We want this Ministry to be available for the whole Fellowship.

B2: VIII. We want this Ministry and other ministries to be available for the whole Fellowship. For there are diversities of gifts, but the same Spirit. There are differences of ministries, but the same Lord. We desire to share the gifts and the inheritances of Grace held in trust by the other groups.

that the office of a Bishop should be increasingly [C2: everywhere] exercised in a representative and constitutional manner in accordance with the ideals of the early and undivided Church [C2: and more truly express all that ought to be involved for the life of the Christian family in the title of Father-in-God]. Nay more, we eagerly look forward to the day when through its acceptance in the whole Church we may unitedly [C2: all] share in the gifts of the Spirit [C2: the members of] the whole body in the apostolic rite of the laying-on of hands, and in the joy and fellowship of a Eucharist in which as one Fellowship we may together, without any doubtfulness of mind, offer to the one Lord our worship and service.

 [C2: share that grace of the Holy Spirit which is] pledged to [C2: the members of]

VIII: We want this, and all other ministries of grace, to be available for the whole Fellowship [C2: Church]. For there are diversities of gifts, but the same Spirit. There are differences of ministries, but the same Lord. We desire to share the gifts and inheritances of Grace held in trust by the other groups. It is GOD's will that they should operate freely within the one body.

that considerations alike of history and of present experience justify the claim which we make on behalf of the episcopate. Moreover, we would urge that it is now and will prove to be in the future the best instrument for maintaining the unity and continuity of the Church. But we greatly desire that the office of a bishop should be everywhere exercised in a representative and constitutional manner, and more truly express all that ought to be involved for the life of the Christian family in the title of Father-in-God. Nay more, we eagerly look forward to the day when through its acceptance in a united Church we may all share in that grace which is pledged to the members of the whole body in the apostolic rite of the laying-on of hands, and in the joy and fellowship of a eucharist in which as one family we may together, without any doubtfulness of mind, offer to the one Lord our worship and service.

VIII. We believe that for all, the truly equitable approach to union is by way of mutual deference to one another's consciences. To this end, we who send forth this appeal would say that if the authorities of other Communions should so desire, we are persuaded that, terms of union having been otherwise satisfactorily adjusted, bishops and clergy of our Communion would willingly accept from these authorities a form of commission or recognition which would commend our ministry to their congregations, as having its place in the one family life. It is not in our power to know how far this suggestion may be acceptable to those to whom we offer it. We can only say that we offer it in all sincerity as a token of our longing that all ministries of grace, theirs and ours, shall be available for the service of our Lord in a united church.

[C2: IX: We believe that for all, the truly equitable approach to Union is by way of mutual submission to one another's consciences. To this end, we who send forth this appeal would say in all sincerity that if the Authorities of other Communions should so desire, we are persuaded that terms of union having been otherwise satisfactorily adjusted, Bishops and Clergy of our Communion would willingly accept from these Authorities whatever a form of commission or recognition which would commend our ministry to their congregations, as having its place in the one family life.

To this end we would say in all sincerity that if the authorities of other Churches should so desire, we are persuaded that Bishops and Clergy of our Communion would be willing to accept from them such fitting ordination or commission as would commend our ministry as having its place in the one family life.

On the other hand, we desire to share in the inheritances of Grace held in trust by the other groups; and should the authorities of these groups so desire we are persuaded that Bishops and Clergy of our Communion would be willing to accept from them some suitable recognition or commission which would commend our ministry as having its place in one family life.

It is God's will that these gifts should operate freely within the one body, and to this end, should the authorities of these Churches so desire we are persuaded that Bishops and Clergy of our Communion would be willing to accept from them such suitable ordination or commission as would commend our ministry as having its place in one family life.

VIII. [IX.] We hope that the same motive will lead their ministers to accept such ordination as will secure for them a full recognition throughout the whole Fellowship. And we solemnly affirm that, in our judgement, such a step would imply no question as to the spiritual reality of the ministries at present exercised by them which we thankfully acknowledge to be manifestly blessed and owned by the Holy Spirit as effective means of Grace. God forbid that any man should repudiate a past ministry rich in spiritual experience, both for himself and others.

IX: We hope that the same motive would lead their ministers to accept such ordination as will secure for them a full recognition throughout the whole fellowship. And we solemnly affirm that in our judgement such a step would imply no question as to the spiritual reality of the ministries at present exercised by them. We thankfully acknowledge these ministries to be manifestly blessed and owned by the Holy Spirit as effective means of Grace. God forbid that any man should repudiate a past ministry rich in spiritual experience, both for himself and others.

It is our hope that the same motive would lead ministers who have not received it to accept a commission through episcopal ordination, as obtaining for them a ministry throughout the whole fellowship. In so acting no one of us could possibly be taken to repudiate his past ministry. God forbid that any man should repudiate a past experience rich in spiritual blessings for himself and others. Nor would any of us be dishonouring the Holy Spirit of God, whose call led us all to our several ministries, and whose power enabled us to perform them. We shall be publicly and formally seeking additional recognition of a new call to wider service in a reunited Church, and imploring for ourselves God's grace and strength to fulfil the same.

It is our hope that the same motive would lead ministers who have not received it to accept a commission through Episcopal Ordination at our hands, as obtaining for them, so far as we are able to secure it, a ministry throughout the whole fellowship.

In so acting no one of us can possibly be taken to repudiate his past ministry. God forbid that any man should repudiate a past experience rich in spiritual blessings for himself and others: nor would any of us be dishonouring the Holy Spirit of GOD, Whose call led us all to our several ministries, and Whose power enabled us to perform them. We shall be publicly and formally seeking additional recognition of a new call to wider service in a re-united Church, and imploring for ourselves GOD's grace and strength to fulfil the same.]

IX. [X.] The moral leadership to be exercised by the Catholic Church in days to come depends upon the readiness with which each separated group is prepared to make sacrifices for the sake of a common fellowship, a common ministry, and a common service to the world.

This appeal we make to all who love our Lord Jesus Christ in sincerity.

19th July 1920

X: The spiritual leadership of the Catholic Church in days to come, for which the world is manifestly waiting, depends upon the readiness with which each group is prepared to make sacrifices for the sake of a common fellowship, a common ministry, and a common service to the world.

We place this ideal first and foremost before *ourselves and our own people*. For many of them doubtless it must mean a conversion from longstanding prejudices to a new outlook. We call upon them *and all other Christian people whom our words may reach* to make this effort for the cause of Christ [C2: *the effort to meet the demands of the new age with a new outlook.*] To others also we make the same appeal. It is not primarily that we ask them to unite with the Anglican Church [C2: *Our appeal is not that they should consent to be absorbed in the Anglican Church*], but rather that we and they together should unite in one new and great endeavour to build up the Body of Christ, and to manifest to the world that visible unity for which He prayed [C2: *to recover and to manifest to the world the unity of the Body of Christ for which he prayed*].

IX. The spiritual leadership of the Catholic Church in days to come, for which the world is manifestly waiting, depends upon the readiness with which each group is prepared to make sacrifices for the sake of a common fellowship, a common ministry, and a common service to the world.

We place this ideal first and foremost before ourselves and our own people. We call upon them to make the effort to meet the demands of a new age with a new outlook. To all other Christian people whom our words may reach we make the same appeal. We do not ask that any one Communion should consent to be absorbed into another. We do ask that all should unite in a new and great endeavour to recover and to manifest to the world the unity of the Body of Christ for which he prayed.

2. Redactions of the practical recommendations arising from the appeal

Text F, drafted on 19 July, presented on 20 July: resolutions drafted by the archbishop of York, in: LC 117, fos. 21–2 (with a further copy in: Douglas papers 1, fo. 358).
Text G, presented on 20 July: resolutions drafted by the bishop of Zanzibar, handwritten versions in Bell papers 255, fos. 50v–51r, and in Douglas papers 1, fos. 359–60: typed version with *amendments* (G1) in: Douglas papers 1, fos. 361–2.
Text H, discussed on 21 July: typed list of amendments, with *further; handwritten amendments*; in: Douglas papers 1, fo. 363.
Final text: resolution 12: www.lambethconference.org/resolutions/1920/1920–12.cfm.

Text F: Draft resolutions archbishop of York	Text G: Draft resolutions bishop of Zanzibar	Text H: Amendments	Resolution 12
Resolutions	**Draft Resolutions** *(Bishop of Zanzibar)*		**Resolution 12**

Text F: Draft resolutions archbishop of York

Resolutions

1. We acknowledge the Ministry of Non-Episcopal Churches as a Ministry possessing the gifts of the Spirit, and the Sacraments administered by them as effectual means of grace.
2. Future Ordinations in any united Church of which we can be a part must be Episcopal.
3. The ground for this assertion is that Episcopal Ordination is in fact the means by which a common Ministry possessing the Commission of Christ and the authority of the whole body secured.
4. It will not be regarded as breaking our fellowship if a Province makes regulations to allow Ministers, who have not been Episcopally ordained but are taking a definite part in the work of re-uniting the Church, to preach in the congregations of the Churches which are attempting to re-unite.

Text G: Draft resolutions bishop of Zanzibar

Draft Resolutions
(Bishop of Zanzibar)

THAT this conference, affirming its conviction that the Holy Eucharist, wherever celebrated by a Priest episcopally ordained, is the one official offering of the whole Catholic Church, and that all celebrations of the Lord's supper apart from such a priest lack the note of universality and are contrary to Church order, declares: -

THAT *[marginal note: in ac[cordance] with the principles of the order laid down according to the Pref[ace] of the ordinal attached to the BCP [it cannot approve] in Anglican Ch[urche]s of the celebration of the H[oly] C[ommunion] by non-episcopally ordained minister[s for members of the Anglican Ch[urch]]* it cannot countenance approve *within the Churches of the Anglican [Communion], celebration of the Holy Communion by Non-Episcopal*

Text H: Amendments

Forms of second clause for consideration at 11 a.m. [on 21 July]

By the Bishop of Zanzibar

Nor does it with a united voice approve the reception by Anglican Communicants of the Lord's Supper administered by such ministers in their own Churches

The Bishop of Winchester's amendment to substitute for all of the above written words: -

Resolution 12

The Conference approves the following statements as representing the counsel which it is prepared to give to the bishops, clergy and other members of our own Communion on various subjects which bear upon the problems of reunion, provided that such counsel is not to be regarded as calling in question any canons or official declarations of any synod or House of Bishops of a national, regional, or provincial Church which has already dealt with these matters.

A. In view of prospects and projects of reunion:
i. A bishop is justified in giving occasional authorisation to ministers, not episcopally ordained, who in his judgement are working towards an ideal of union such as is described in our Appeal, to preach in churches within his diocese, and to clergy of the diocese to preach in the churches of such ministers.
ii. The bishops of the Anglican Communion

will not question the action of any bishop who, in the few years between the initiation and the completion of a definite scheme of union, shall countenance the irregularity of admitting to Communion the baptized but unconfirmed communicants of the non-episcopal congregations concerned in the scheme.

iii. The Conference gives its general approval to the suggestions contained in the Report of the Sub-Committee on Reunion with Non-Episcopal Churches in reference to the status and work of ministers who may remain after union without episcopal ordination.

5. After an Act of Union has been concluded by a Province the Province may further make regulations under which the Ministers, who at the time of the Act of Union were not episcopally ordained, may minister the Sacraments in the united Church in such congregations as may be ready to receive their ministrations.

6. We are bound by the example of the Apostles to regard Confirmation as a part of the practice of the Universal Church, and, therefore, to commend it to those Churches that do not now practice it as a means by which God wills to endow every member of the Church with gifts of the Holy Spirit for life and service within it.

7. During negotiations looking towards corporate Re-union Communicant members of Churches involved, although unconfirmed may be admitted by Priests of our Church of Communion when they have no opportunity of receiving Holy Communion from their own Ministers.

8. After a Province has completed an Act of Union those who were at the time of the Act of Union Communicant Members Churches which have united, my be admitted to Holy Communion by Ministers episcopally ordained if otherwise admissible even though they be not confirmed.

Or, save in quite exceptional circumstances, the reception by Anglican Communicants of the Lord's Supper administered by such ministers in their own Churches.

The Bishop of St Albans' amendment

Or the reception by Anglican Communicants of the Lord's Supper administered by such ministers in their own Churches, save in quite exceptional circumstances, by special permission of the Bishop.

Ministers the ministrations of Non-Episcopal ministers at Anglican altars, nor can it with a united voice approve *save in quite exceptional circumstances* the reception by Anglican Communicants of the Lord's Supper administered by such ministers in their own Churches, or the invitation of separated Christians to communion at Anglican altars, or the interchange of pulpits.

Nevertheless, the Bishops are unanimously agreed: -

(a) THAT no Priest has canonical authority to refuse Communion to *anyone kneeling before the Holy Table, person kneeling before the Holy Table,* unless he be excommunicate by name, or, in the canonical sense of the term, a cause of scandal to the faithful,

(b) THAT a Bishop is justified in admitting to his pulpits occasionally for good reason; *authorizing an occasional interchange of pulpits between his own clergy and* ministers of separated bodies who have publicly and formally assented *openly assented* to and are whole-heartedly working for the proposals put forth above, (i.e. the Appeal).

[marginal note (amendment put by the Bishop of Durham): *ministers non-episcopally ordained who have publicly certified their acceptance of the three first articles of the Lambeth Quadrilateral [and] in his judgment are working for the ideal of this [Re-union?] such as is described above.*]

[fo. 363r] *and in the spirit of this same principle it requires as the general observance of the Church that Anglican non-communicants shall not receive Holy Communion at the hands of such ministers and this same principle requires) that as the general rule {for our?} church* Anglican communicants should receive the Holy Communion only at the hands of ministers of their own church or of churches in communion with it.

[fo. 363v] *It cannot with a united voice give an affirmative answer to those who have asked for its approval of schemes for invitations to communion {made to such ?} churches or members of non-episcopal congregations and the interchange of pulpits and that this Conference ???* [regretting? noting?] *its inability to speak unanimously in these points seeing that in ???? to be God's ??? [will in?] issuing an appeal for union that may make all such schemes unnecessary.*

B. Believing, however, that certain lines of action might imperil both the attainment of its ideal and the unity of its own Communion, the Conference declares that:

i. It cannot approve of general schemes of intercommunion or exchange of pulpits.

ii. In accordance with the principle of Church order set forth in the Preface to the Ordinal attached to the Book of Common Prayer, it cannot approve the celebration in Anglican churches of the Holy Communion for members of the Anglican Church by ministers who have not been episcopally ordained; and that it should be regarded as the general rule of the Church that Anglican communicants should receive Holy Communion only at the hands of ministers of their own Church, or of Churches in communion therewith.

C. In view of doubts and varieties of practice which have caused difficulties in the past, the Conference declares that:

i. Nothing in these Resolutions is intended

9. Apart from negotiations for Re-union we do not think that Communion should be refused by Priests of our Church to devout Communicant members of non-Episcopal bodies who are temporarily deprived of the opportunity of receiving the Holy Communion from their own Ministers.

20th July, 1930

[fo. 362] (c) THEY will not hold to blame *They will not question the action of any Bishop* who in the few years, during which the proposals *an definite scheme of union* (for re-union) are *is* maturing, shall countenance the irregularity of permitting members of separated bodies to receive communion at Anglican altars, provided that those who are so received have publicly and formally assented to the above proposals and are whole-heartedly working towards their fulfilment, *admitting to communion baptized {and confirmed ?} communicants of the non-episcopal congregations concerned* and

(d) THAT they confidently commit to the *local ecclesiastical authorities* (various Provinces & national churches) of the Anglican Communion the task of effecting re-union with (their separated brethren) *other Christian communities* on lines that are in general harmony with these proposals and resolutions.

20th July, 1920

Furthermore this Conference affirms its conviction that except in such cases as shall be {below?} mentioned invitations to communion in Anglican Churches ought not to be extended to members of non-episcopal nor interchange of pulpits permitted and declares that the general rule {of our ?} church is ?????

(While) this conference cannot approve of a general scheme of / invitation to intercomm[union] or exchange of pulpits, but not right to see resolutions as intended to indicate that the rule of confirmation as conditioning admission to Holy Communion must necessarily apply to the case of baptized persons who seek communion under conditions which in the bishop's judgement justify their admission thereto.

to indicate that the rule of confirmation as conditioning admission to Holy Communion must necessarily apply to the case of baptized persons who seek Communion under conditions which in the bishop's judgement justify their admission thereto.
ii. In cases in which it is impossible for the bishop's judgement to be obtained beforehand the priest should remember that he has no canonical authority to refuse Communion to any baptized person kneeling before the Lord's Table (unless he be excommunicate by name, or, in the canonical sense of the term, a cause of scandal to the faithful); and that, if a question may properly be raised as to the future admission of any such person to Holy Communion, either because he has not been confirmed or for other reasons, the priest should refer the matter to the bishop for counsel or direction.

III   Chronology of the making of the Appeal to All Christian People at the 1920 Lambeth Conference

Date		Reference	Redaction
3 July	reception in Canterbury Cathedral	Bell papers 251, fos. 61r–62r	
4 July	service at Westminster Abbey	Bell papers 251, fos. 62v–63r	
5 July	Opening sessions	Bell papers 251, fo. 63v	
6 July	First plenary session – Reunion: speech Ebor	Bell papers 251, fo. 63v	
7 July	First meeting of Reunion Committee Discusses procedure	LC 115, fo. 3	
12 July	Committees begin – Bell attends Reunion p.m. 2 p.m. York gives opening speech; presents four points for preliminary discussion [LC 115, fo. 7] Ely presents views in letter; Committee addressed by Armagh, Bombay, Zanzibar, Durham, Norwich	Bell papers 251, fo. 65r–v LC 115, fos. 9–11	
13 July	Reunion Committee meets: 'Admirable speech by Bp of Pennsylvania'; Durham suggests episcopacy not of the *esse* of the Church; general discussion Afternoon: H Knight, Ebor, Bombay, Bristol 'concoct … "Prologomena" on unity'	Bell papers 251, fo. 65v	Text A
14 July	Experts (Gore, Ryle, JA Robinson, CH Turner); presentation of prolegomena 'got one very little further than the old Lambeth Quadrilateral' – Neville – 'it's devilish' discussion 'On returning to Lambeth [from debate at House of Lords] I suggested to the Abp a possibility of Zanzibar, Talbot & Brent (and one or two others!) getting together to [fo. 65r] articulate Zanzibar's proposals of a Great Church in which the denominations of Noncon. origin shd be groups. He agreed that there may be something in it and told me to set NST[albot] at Zanzibar.'	Bell papers 251, fo. 65v	Changes leading to Text A2
15 July	'I got at NST, who at once fell in with suggestion of group conference and made plans accordingly.' a.m. Shakespeare gave evidence p.m. S India proposals discussed – 'Bishop of Dornakal leading off in a most moving way. Many frank questions and answers. A little fire between Bombay and Madras. Crucial issue is interim position of non-Episcopally ordained ministers.'	Bell papers 251, fo. 66r	
16 July	'Ebor, Ely & others in Cambridge. … No meeting of Reunion or women's ctees. But Neville, Brent, Pennsylvania, Bombay, Winton, Peterboro', Chichester, Zanzibar all meet as group in Lollards to thrash out Zanzibar scheme. It seems like [it has been] been satisfactory.'	Bell papers 251, fo. 66v	First draft of Text B
17 July	'Neville told me that Peterboro', Zanzibar & Rhinelander were set to draft the "statement on Reunion". I saw it & made one or two slight suggestions. The draft was revised in evening and given to Ebor. In Reunion Ctee Quick, Tatlow, Lacey, Temple all gave evidence. Uganda expounded Kikuyu, & Rhinelander the American Concordat.'	Bell papers 251, fo. 66v	

18 July	Bell: 'Brent, Rhinelander, Peterboro' & co to Abbey. Spent afternoon revising the "Statement" until all agreed.'	Bell papers 251, fo. 67r	Text B
	Davidson: 'On the middle Sunday of the Conference, during the Committee fortnight, a little group sat all afternoon, under the tree on the lawn. It consisted of the two Archbishops, Bishop Rhinelander of Pennsylvania, Bishop Brent, the Bishop of Peterborough – Edith was also with us. We went through the various drafts, resolutions etc. which had been suggested, but on the whole decided to turn it into an Appeal of a consecutive sort. The Bishop of Peterborough wrote a draft beginning with the words "God wills fellowship etc." This draft was manipulated considerably afterwards by the Archbishop of York and much improved. It was, however, the outcome of that afternoon's conversation.'	Davidson papers 14, fo. 49	
19 July	19 July: At Reunion Ctee all day. … In afternoon York presented draft Appeal composed by Zanzibar, Perteboro', Brent & Co. York suggests Appeal; promises Resolutions	Bell papers 251, fo. 67r	Discussions leading to Text B2
	York makes 'statement'; followed by reading of 'A Statement of our Position'	LC 117, fo. 19 Bell papers 255,	
	H Knight, Bombay, Bristol & York draft Resolutions on specific pts.	fo. 44r–v	Text F
20 July	At Reunion Ctee all day. Zanzibar proposes a long Resolution of his own in place of the 'Official' Resolutions drawn up by York & Co. Zanzibar's accepted as basis – he proves most conciliatory. Interesting to see Durham & Zanzibar hobnob. Today the crucial day – an extraordinary spirit of fraternity & conciliation displayed. Zanzibar the chief.	Bell papers 251, fo. 67v	Text G
	Minutes of discussion with Resolutions as proposed & passed		
		LC 117, fos. 20ff	
21 July	A little Reaction at Reunion Ctee, … Zanzibar wonders whether he has committed himself to opposing a joint communion.	Bell papers 251, fo. 67v	
	Minutes of further discussion and amendment of resolutions		
		LC 117, fos. 25–8	Text H
22 July	Reunion Ctee. [no further comments]		
	Discussion of clauses 1–6	LC 115, fos. 23–4	Text C with
23 July	Reunion Ctee: Zanzibar tells me he is glad he came to L[ambeth] C[onference] approves of work of Ctee, cannot abide Henson, though at Barking H[enson] had taught him Non-coms were emissaries of Satan. Henson like me has reservation whether things have been quite straight. Zanzibar on his own principles ought not to have assented to the Resolutions.	Bell papers 251, fos. 67v–68r	discussion leading to Text C2
	Discussion of clauses VIII–X	LC 115, fos. 29–30	
24 July	Bp Durham suggests minority report draft Report of the Committee for Reunion discussed	LC 117, fos. 29–30	
27 July	Discussions of Committees reports begins (until 5 Aug)		
28 July	Lang introduces Appeal		
4 Aug	Amendments to Appeal and Reports of the Committee for Reunion agreed; Encyclical distributed	Bell papers 251, fo. 68v	
5–6 Aug	Amendments to Encyclical		
7 Aug	Encyclical presented; Message to Men & Women of Goodwill; presentations		
8 Aug	Closing service at St Paul's		

11

ARCHBISHOP TEMPLE'S OFFER OF A LAMBETH DEGREE TO DOROTHY L. SAYERS

Edited by
Peter Webster

24, NEWLAND STREET,
WITHAM,
ESSEX.

7·9·43

Your Grace,

Thank you very much indeed for the great honour you do me. I find it very difficult to reply as I ought, because I am extremely conscious that I don't deserve it. A Doctorate of Letters – yes; I have served Letters as faithfully as I knew how. But I have only served Divinity, as it were, accidentally, coming to it as a writer rather than as a Christian person. A Degree in Divinity is not, I suppose, intended as a certificate of sanctity, exactly; but I should feel better about it if I were a more convincing kind of Christian. I am never quite sure whether I really am one, or whether I have only fallen in love with an intellectual pattern. And when one is able to handle language it is sometimes hard to know how far one is under the spell of one's own words.

Also, you know, I am just a common novelist & playwright. I may not – in fact I almost certainly shan't – remain on the austere level of <u>the Man Born to be King</u> & <u>the Mind of the Maker</u>. I can't promise not to break out into something thoroughly secular, frivolous or unbecoming – adorned, if the story requires it, with the language of the rude soldiery, or purple passages descriptive of the less restrained & respectable passions. I shouldn't like your

39 Dorothy L. Sayers to Archbishop William Temple, 7 September 1943, reacting to Temple's offer of a Lambeth degree (reproduced by permission of David Higham Associates and the Estate of Dorothy L. Sayers) (LPL, W. Temple, fo. 273)

Introduction*

Among the papers of William Temple at Lambeth is a short correspondence from the summer of 1943 between the Archbishop and the novelist and writer Dorothy L. Sayers, in which Temple intimates his wish to award Sayers the Lambeth Doctorate of Divinity. The ensuing exchange, at the end of which Sayers was to turn down the offer, is illustrative of the views of both Temple and Sayers on the relationship between the Church of England and the arts, and stands as an epitome of many of the unresolved tensions in that relationship.[1]

In order to place the offer in its fullest context, a brief account of the previous six years' development in Sayers's work is necessary. For the editor of Sayers's letters, 1937 was a turning-point in her career, at which the transition from detective novelist to playwright began.[2] The year saw the production of her first attempt at religious drama, *The zeal of Thy house*, for the Friends of Canterbury Cathedral, which was staged in June. The play was successful enough to transfer to the Westminster Theatre in London, and marked a new phase; as one of her biographers has noted, views that might previously have been attributed to characters in her novels were now voiced by angels and archangels in a story of the building of a cathedral, and as such were bound to be attributed to her personally.[3] It was from this point on that Sayers's correspondence gradually became swollen with invitations from clergy and lay Christians to write or speak on religious matters; despite her later protestation that she had never intended to become embroiled in apologetics, or to 'bear witness for Christ', this was to be the effect.[4] Prominent articles began to appear, such as 'The greatest drama ever staged is the official creed of Christendom' in the *Sunday Times* in April 1938.[5] Sayers's profile as Christian apologist grew, and by 1939 she was receiving letters 'by every post imploring one to open bazaars at Penzance or South Shields'.[6]

At some point in the immediate pre-war period Sayers caught the attention of William Temple, at that point still archbishop of York.[7] Late in 1939 Temple, according to his biographer a devotee of detective fiction, wrote to J.H. Oldham

---

* I am indebted to Melanie Barber, Mark Greengrass, Margaret Hunt and to the staff of Lambeth Palace Library for their assistance at several stages of the preparation of this edition.

[1] Lambeth Palace Library (hereafter LPL), William Temple papers, vol. 39, fos. 267–80. The Sayers letters were included in the second volume of the edition of her correspondence edited by Barbara Reynolds (5 vols., Cambridge, 1995–2002), at pp. 429–32. It is briefly summarized in Reynolds, *Dorothy L. Sayers: her life and soul* (London, 1993), pp. 372–4, and by James Brabazon, *Dorothy L. Sayers* (London, 1981), at pp. 214–15. It is not mentioned in Ralph E. Hone, *Dorothy L. Sayers. A Literary Biography* (Kent, OH, 1979).

[2] *Letters*, II, xiv.

[3] Brabazon, *Sayers*, pp.161–2.

[4] Sayers to John Wren-Lewis, Good Friday 1954; *Letters*, IV, 139.

[5] *Sunday Times*, 3 Apr. 1938.

[6] Sayers to her son, 22 Mar. 1939; *Letters*, II, 123.

[7] Sayers was guest of honour at a luncheon of the Old Queens Society, chaired by Temple in Feb. 1938. *Times*, 7 Feb. 1938.

exclaiming 'how magnificent Dorothy Sayers is!'[8] Sayers turned down a request from the archbishop in the summer of 1940 to write a play for use in the diocese of York, and in November 1941 declined an invitation to be involved in a prospective religious 'Brains trust' broadcast by the BBC.[9] Temple was, however, successful in persuading Sayers to contribute to his Malvern Conference of January 1941.[10]

Temple's offer of the Lambeth DD was in recognition of the impact of two works in particular: the series of radio plays *The man born to be king*, and the earlier book *The mind of the maker*. Published in 1941, *The mind of the maker* may fairly be regarded as Sayers's most enduring work of theology proper.[11] Temple clearly thought highly of it, describing it as 'a really original approach to the doctrine of the Trinity, of great theological and apologetic value' (Letter 4). V. A. Demant thought the work to be of 'inestimable value', having 'as to method, in my opinion, revived theology as it should be written in any constructive and seminal sense'.[12] Developing ideas already present in *The zeal of Thy house*, it contains an extended analogy between the creative work of the Trinity and human creativity.[13] In so doing, it lays out a doctrine of the status of work of the highest possible dignity, and makes some very trenchant claims for the independence of the artist and the importance of works of art in and of themselves; views which, it will be argued, were in part behind her decision to refuse the Lambeth degree.

If *The mind of the maker* was quietly successful, *The man born to be king* was a sensation. Before the plays were even broadcast, agitation had begun in the press against Sayers's use of modern speech, and against the direct portrayal of Christ by an actor, since any such portrayal was still disallowed on the stage under the censorship powers of the lord chamberlain. The greater impact, however, unfolded as the plays were broadcast at monthly intervals between December 1941 and the following October.[14] In his foreword to the printed edition of the plays, James Welch, director of religious broadcasting of the BBC, reproduced a sample of the hundreds of letters of thanks he had received, showing, in his view, that the plays had been massively successful in reaching the majority of the listening public who were not regular churchgoers, and who had not been reached hitherto by the more standard BBC provision of broadcast services and religious talks.[15] As Welch put it whilst

---

[8] F. A. Iremonger, *William Temple, archbishop of Canterbury. His life and letters* (London, 1948), p. 477; quoted in a letter from Oldham to Sayers, dated 28 Dec. 1939, in Brabazon, *Sayers* p. 188.

[9] Sayers to Temple, 30 Aug. 1940, *Letters*, II, 177; Sayers to Temple 24 Nov. 1941, *Letters*, II, 321. On her view of the existing BBC programme of that name, see Sayers to James Welch, 2 Jan. 1941; *Letters*, II, 217–21.

[10] Sayers's paper on 'The church's responsibility' was included in *Malvern 1941. The life of the church and the order of society* (London, 1941), pp. 57–78. The conference itself is described in Iremonger, *Temple*, pp. 428–33.

[11] On the work's originality, see John Thurmer, 'The theology of Dorothy L. Sayers', *Church Quarterly Review*, 168 (Oct.–Dec. 1967), 452–62. See also several of the pieces in Thurmer, *Reluctant evangelist. Papers on the Christian thought of Dorothy L. Sayers* (Hurstpierpoint, 1996).

[12] Demant, 'Analogy of creation' (a review), in *Christendom. A Journal of Christian Sociology*, XII, 45 (Mar. 1942), 49–53, at 49.

[13] *The zeal of thy house* (London, 1937), pp. 110–11.

[14] The making, broadcasting and reception of the play are described in depth in Kenneth M. Wolfe, *The churches and the British Broadcasting Corporation 1922–1956. The politics of broadcast religion* (London, 1984), pp. 218–38.

[15] Foreword to Dorothy L. Sayers, *The man born to be king* (London, 1943), pp. 12–15. The printed version had itself gone through some twenty-four impressions by 1969.

suggesting the idea of the Lambeth degree to Temple in June 1943, 'these plays have done more for the preaching of the Gospel to the unconverted than any other single effort of the churches or religious broadcasting since the last war' (Letter 1). Cyril Forster Garbett, archbishop of York and chairman of the BBC's Central Religious Advisory Council at the time, later described the plays as 'one of the greatest evangelistic appeals made in this century'.[16]

Welch's confidence that Sayers would be delighted with such an offer was not borne out by her first response (Letter 6). Whilst professing herself honoured, and recognizing that the degree was not intended as a 'certificate of sanctity', she nonetheless expressed doubt as to whether she was enough of a 'convincing Christian', and not simply 'in love with an intellectual pattern'. Her letters contain ample evidence of this diffidence, which clearly ran much deeper than a conventionally humble declaration of *nolo episcopari*. The opening words of her address to the Malvern Conference gave some warning of her view: her feelings on treating any question relating to the church were of embarrassment, since 'I am never quite sure how to identify it or whether, in anything but a technical sense, I feel myself to belong to it.'[17] Sayers later professed herself personally unsusceptible to religious experience or emotion, but instead sustained by a purely intellectual conviction; a theme that recurred elsewhere in her correspondence.[18] As she put it to Temple, part of her was perhaps trying to preserve a 'bolt-hole'; an insurance against an irrevocable public step of personal commitment.

There is in addition some evidence of a degree of personal lassitude in her own attendance at public worship. Brabazon has noted an infrequency at public worship when visiting Sayers's parental home in Cambridgeshire.[19] There also survives amongst the Lang papers evidence that this had come to the attention of the archbishop himself. In 1941 George Bell, bishop of Chichester, had been warned by a clergyman in his diocese, on the basis of confidential information from clergy in Essex where Sayers lived, that she was apparently not a communicant member of her own parish church. It would be kindest therefore, suggested Bell, not to press Sayers too far forward as a spokesperson for the church, but to allow her the space to make up her own mind. Lang professed his surprise, but had noted rumours of an apparent movement towards Rome in any case, and continued '[b]ut apart from this I have lately been thinking that the Church of England tended to make too much of her and put her too much on its front-window'.[20] It is not clear whether or not Temple was aware of this correspondence when making the offer of the degree.

Sayers's first response also made the point that as a mere 'common novelist and playwright', she could not guarantee in the future to abstain from writing 'secular, frivolous or unbecoming' work, full of the language of the 'rude soldiery' or descriptive of the less respectable passions; 'I shouldn't like your first woman D.D. to create

16 Charles Smyth, *Cyril Forster Garbett. Archbishop of York* (London, 1959), p. 211.
17 *Malvern*, p. 57.
18 Sayers to John Wren-Lewis, Good Friday 1954: *Letters*, IV, 136–7; Sayers to L. T. Duff, 10 May 1943, *Letters*, II, 401. See Marjorie Lamp Mead, 'Rejoicing in truth: Dorothy L. Sayers and the "good of the intellect"', in *Further studies on Sayers. Essays presented to Dr Barbara Reynolds on her 90th birthday*, ed. Christopher Dean (Hurstpierpoint, 2004), pp. 23–30.
19 Brabazon, *Sayers*, p. 118.
20 Correspondence between J. A. Bouquet, Bell and Lang, at LPL, Bell papers, vol. 208, fos..245–8: Lang to Bell 16 May 1941, fo. 248. Such a move to Rome was apparently mooted from time to time in the Roman Catholic press; Sayers to V. A. Demant, 2 Oct. 1941, *Letters*, II, 306.

scandal, or give reviewers cause to blaspheme' (Letter 6). Temple evidently took the lightness of tone at face value, responding with a quip about the detective novels of Cyril Alington, dean of Durham (Letter 7). It seems probable, however, that behind the apparent levity was a fear, of which Temple could have had no notion, of the possible disclosure of details of Sayers's private life. Brabazon has suggested that the one doctrine of the church with which Sayers was in emotional engagement was that of sin, and in her case, the consciousness of the church's certain view, were it to know of it, of her marriage to a divorced man.[21] Even more pressing was the matter, known only to her and a handful of others, of her illegitimate son, John Anthony, born in 1924 and being raised by Sayers's cousin, Ivy Shrimpton.[22] Barbara Reynolds has suggested that these private considerations played no part in her decision to refuse, and that the reasoning expressed in the letter was sufficient.[23] The point clearly cannot firmly be established one way or the other. However, being the first female recipient of the Lambeth DD whilst continuing to work in the still morally ambiguous environments of secular literature and the theatre would have brought pressures of which she was surely likely to have been sensible, and which cannot but have been a factor to have been considered.

There may well have been therefore very pertinent personal issues behind Sayers's initial reluctance. Temple was however not deterred, and took further advice from Oliver Quick, regius professor of divinity at Oxford, as to whether his intention could be as well fulfilled by the award of a D.Litt., which Sayers had suggested instead (Letters 6 and 7). Quick's advice, in a letter that has not survived, appears to have been that a D.Litt. would not quite have the same import, and so Temple returned to the subject once again, hoping that Sayers might accept (Letter 8). In fact, the D.Litt. had been awarded only once before in the twentieth century, and not on that occasion for the sort of 'Letters' that Sayers had in mind.[24] After a request for more time, Sayers responded on 24 September with her longest statement, which Temple accepted, professing that he should do the same in her position (Letters 9 and 10). Her letter made two main points, which shed much light on the position of both the Christian apologist and the Christian artist in relation to the institutional church in this period.

The first concerns the effect, deleterious in Sayers's view, of too close an association between the apologist and the church. Almost from the beginnings of Sayers's growing involvement as an apologist, her letters show a persistent sense that both the amount and the profile of such involvement ought carefully to be controlled, lest its effectiveness be blunted. As early as January 1939, she wrote to the Roman Catholic bishop of Nottingham that she was already trying to avert the risk of her 'perpetual appearance in the pulpit' detracting from the force of what she might

---

[21] Brabazon, *Sayers*, pp. 214–15. See also Sayers to John Wren-Lewis, Good Friday 1954; *Letters*, IV, 137.

[22] *Letters*, II, 437–41.

[23] Reynolds, *Sayers*, footnote to p. 374. The judgment is offered without any (to this author) compelling evidence to discount the suggestion, which has been made by Brabazon, *Sayers*, pp. 214–15.

[24] Francis Carolus Eeles, secretary of the Central Council for the Care of Churches, was thus honoured in Mar. 1938. The D.Litt. was not awarded again until May 1962, to the first female recipient of any Lambeth degree, the ecclesiastical historian Margaret Deanesly. The register books of degrees are to be found at LPL, Faculty Office, FVI/1/3 and F VI/1/4 (1931–53 and 1953–74 respectively.) Separate summary lists exist at Faculty Office, F VI/2/7A (1947–70), and MS 1715, pp. 89–113 (1848–1948).

have to say.[25] Archbishop Lang's caution in this regard has been noted above, and at least one observer of the national scene agreed, arguing in 1941 that the church had mishandled its reception of T. S. Eliot, having 'worked his name to death in our propaganda as we are now doing also with Miss Dorothy Sayers'.[26] By December 1942 it had become clear to her that, despite her best efforts, she had already come to be viewed as 'one of the old gang, whose voice can be heard from every missionary platform'; it was therefore time to withdraw somewhat.[27] So it was that she explained to Temple that the status of outsider was necessary in the 'present peculiar state of public opinion', in order to avoid becoming, in the phrase of the *Daily Herald*, '"the pet of the bishops"'.

Sayers's second point in this final letter would appear to be simply a restatement of her earlier fear about future writing on secular subjects proving an embarrassment to Temple in the future. However, an examination of her other writings reveals that her fear of 'a sort of interior inhibition in the handling of secular work', here phrased very gently, was part of a much more robust view of the independence of the artist, and of the record of the church's patronage of the arts up to that point.

The mind of the maker, to which Temple was concerned to give recognition, contained in the chapter on 'The love of the creature' a gentle insistence on the artist's duty to protect, as it were, the interests of their creature.[28] This conviction was more strongly expressed when challenged, as in the case of a protracted and bitter disagreement with the BBC over editorial intervention in the scripts for *The man born to be king*.[29] One particular letter to Welch justifies an extensive quotation:

> I am bound to tell you this: that the writer's duty to God is his duty to the work, and that he may not submit to any dictate of authority which he does not sincerely believe to be for the good of the work. He may not do it for money, or for reputation, or for edification...or for any consideration whatever. ... The writer is about his Father's business, and it does not matter who is inconvenienced or how much he has to hate his father and mother. To be false to his work is to be false to the truth: 'All the truth of the craftsman is in his craft.'[30]

Such a high view of the duty of the artist to God and to his work had added force when considered alongside Sayers's jaundiced view of the relationship between the church and the arts; a view shared by many other artists, as the present author has shown elsewhere.[31] As early as 1938, Sayers had been sufficiently aggrieved by the lack of financial support from the church for the provincial tour of *The zeal of Thy house*, 'a play written and performed for her honour', that she was prompted

---

25 Sayers to Neville S. Talbot, 25 Jan. 1939; *Letters* II, 116–17.
26 'Clericus', *The crisis in the church. An open letter to the archbishop of York* (London, 1941), p. 23. 'Clericus' was apparently an anglican clergyman based in London.
27 Sayers to Eric Fenn (BBC), 14 Dec. 1942; *Letters* II, 382.
28 *The mind of the maker* (London, 1941), pp. 102–7.
29 The dispute is described in Wolfe, *Churches and the BBC*, pp. 220–3. Sayers's side of the correspondence is at *Letters*, II, 196–236.
30 Sayers to Welch, 2 Jan 1941; *Letters*, II, 217–21. The final quotation is from *The zeal of Thy house*, voiced by the Prior in scene III, 59.
31 Peter Webster, 'The "revival" in the visual arts in the Church of England, c.1935–c.1956', in *Revival and resurgence in Christian history*, ed. Kate Cooper and Jeremy Gregory, Studies in Church History, 44 (Woodbridge, 2008), pp. 297–306.

to write to the *Times* about the matter.[32] However, the problem ran much deeper than mere parsimony, and was a constant theme in Sayers's correspondence. The church was widely associated, in her view, with 'artistic frivolity and intellectual dishonesty'.[33] It had seemed unable to grasp that 'the divine Beauty is sovereign within His own dominion; and that if a statue is ill-carved or a play ill-written, the artist's corruption is deeper than if the statue were obscene and the play blasphemous'.[34] What was necessary was 'a decent humility before the artist', and an absolute insistence that a work of art must be good in itself, before it could possibly be good religious art.[35] Sayers, in common with several of her contemporaries in the arts, suspected the church of holding to an inadequate understanding of the absolute necessity of beauty.

This point is more precisely focused if one considers for what exactly it was that Sayers was to be honoured. Amongst the muniments at Lambeth survives some guidance, from the time of Archbishop Davidson, on the award of Lambeth degrees. It stipulated, in line with the practice of Davidson's predecessors, that degrees be awarded only to 'persons eminent' in the various fields, and in practice, in the case of the DD, to those 'in the Foreign and Missionary Work of the Church by some special service, generally of a literary character; e.g. translating the Scriptures into a new language'.[36] Despite the fact that, in practice, the DD had been awarded almost exclusively to clergy, *The man born to be king* would seem to be just such a 'special service' of a literary character for the mission of the church. Welch's initial suggestion was clearly that it was as the author of *The man born to be king*, a 'work of Christian evangelism', that Sayers might be offered the degree (Letter 1). Temple agreed that the plays were 'one of the most powerful instruments in evangelism which the Church has had put into its hands for a long time past'; the 'most effective piece of evangelistic work, in my judgment, done in our generation' (Letters 2 and 4). Oliver Quick agreed, and suggested that C. S. Lewis might also be offered a degree: 'They are the two people who seem really able to put across to ordinary people a reasonably orthodox form of Xty' (Letter 3).

Despite Welch's description of the work as Sayers's 'magnum opus', conspicuously absent from this exchange was any broader sense of the plays being honoured *as plays*; any sense that there was some worth in a play that was well crafted, regardless of its 'effectiveness' as an evangelistic tool. It was, however, precisely this (apparently) instrumental view of the arts that so exercised Sayers. The commissioning practice of 'asking writers to produce stories and plays to illustrate certain doctrine or church activities' showed how little such 'pious officials' understood of the mind of the artist. In these productions doctrine was not allowed to emerge spontaneously from the inherent dynamic of a narrative imagined by the artist; instead, action and characters were inevitably distorted for the sake of the doctrine that had been preordained for exposition, with disastrous consequences.[37] As Sayers told the Malvern Conference, the church was thus guilty of fostering corruption 'by condoning and approving a thing artistically vicious provided that it conforms

---

32 *Times*, 24 Nov. 1938.
33 Sayers to the Rev. G. E. Wigram, 14 Jan. 1943; *Letters*, II, 383.
34 *Malvern*, p. 75.
35 Sayers to Brother George Every, 21 May 1941; *Letters*, II, 261.
36 Printed leaflet on 'Lambeth degrees', LPL, MS 1715, pp. vii–ix, at p. vii.
37 Sayers to Brother George Every, 21 May 1941; *Letters*, II, 261.

to moral sentiment'.[38] However, no sooner than Sayers had sat down after having 'harangued' the conference thus, George Bell (as she later recalled) 'toddled amiably onto the platform and said: "And I do agree with Miss Sayers that the Church must manage to get hold of the Arts again". – Oh, dear! The C. of E. does suffer a great deal from her bishops.'[39] The notion of the church 'getting hold of' the arts clearly rankled, as it appeared in later letters, and Sayers was to restate her point, in gentler terms, at the conference on 'The Church and the Artist' that Bell himself convened in Chichester in 1944.[40] In accepting Bell's invitation to that conference, she named as the 'text' for her oration a phrase of Charles Williams: 'Religion itself cannot order poetry about; the grand act is wholly autonomous.'[41]

It may well be argued that Sayers's view of the church was too negative, and did not take into account the work of a number of key figures. Bell himself was capable of defending the freedom of the artist against opposition, as in the case of John Masefield's play *The coming of Christ*, for Canterbury Cathedral in 1928. His agency in the setting-up of the subsequent Canterbury Festival plays was by this point well known, and Sayers could hardly have been unaware of it.[42] It was also the case that both Temple and Quick held much more developed views on the relationship between theology, the church and the arts than the tone of their letters here reproduced would suggest.[43] However, even if Sayers were aware of this work, the accumulated record of the wider church in its actual patronage (as opposed to theological writing) meant that the balance was overwhelmingly negative. Sayers was in fact to return to the theme some ten years later, in an article entitled 'Playwrights are not evangelists', and a sense that little progress had been made can be detected amongst other commentators in the 1950s and beyond.[44]

In passing Sayers suggested an alternative way in which the Church of England might usefully honour artistic work (Letter 11). Rather than attaching the accolade to the individual, she suggested a scheme more analogous to the *nihil obstat* commonly attached to Roman Catholic publications, but more honorific in intention. Attaching the approbation to the individual work would both free the artist later to range across genres and subjects which may be 'descriptive of the less restrained and respectable passions', and at the same time protect the church from association with such work. The present author has described elsewhere a tension between different approaches in anglican patronage of the arts in this period, between the individualistic approach of a patron such as Walter Hussey, later dean of Chichester,

---

38 *Malvern*, p. 75
39 Sayers to Count Michael de la Bedoyere (editor of the *Catholic Herald*), 7 Oct 1941; *Letters*, II, 309.
40 See Sayers to an unidentified correspondent, 28 Nov. 1941; *Letters*, II, 334. Bell's notes on the proceedings of the conference are at LPL, Bell papers, vol. 151, fos. 190–6.
41 Sayers to Bell, 4 Sept. 1944; LPL, Bell papers, vol. 151, fo. 169. The text is from Charles Williams, *The figure of Beatrice. A study in Dante* (London, 1943).
42 See Peter Webster, 'George Bell, John Masefield and "The coming of Christ": context and significance', *Humanitas. The Journal of the George Bell Institute*, X, 2 (2009), 111–25; on a later instance of Bell's defence of the artist, see Paul Foster, 'The Goring judgement: is it still valid?', *Theology*, CII (1999), 253–61. On the probability of Sayers's awareness of Bell, see Hone, *Sayers*, p. 84. On Bell's work in general, see Webster, 'The "revival" in the visual arts'.
43 See, by Temple: *Mens creatrix* (London, 1923), ch. 10 ('The nature and significance of art', pp. 93–128), and *Nature, man and God* (London, 1934), pp. 135–65. See also Quick, *The Christian sacraments* (London, 1927), ch. 2 ('Aesthetic sacramentalism'), pp. 19–42.
44 'Playwrights are not evangelists', *World Theatre*, V (1955–6), 61–6. Webster, 'The "revival" in the visual arts', pp. 297–8, 306.

and the more institutional approach characteristic of George Bell.[45] It may have been that Temple's approach was the only way in which, under the pressures of war-time, he could conceive to use the limited institutional tools at his disposal. It would seem that he had not the time to pursue Sayers's idea, or to explore it any further privately, and the suggestion does not appear to have gained any traction with his successors or indeed anywhere else in the Church of England. Temple's offer, had it been accepted, would however have been greatly innovative amongst Lambeth degrees. It would have been the first award to a woman, the innovative nature of which becomes apparent in light of the fact that the first subsequent award to a female candidate (of the lesser degree of MA) was not made until 1958, and the first doctorate (a D.Litt.) not until 1962.[46] The lack of a ready means by which to honour 'freelance' writers and apologists was further demonstrated by the hesitation by Archbishop Fisher over awarding a doctorate to the writer Leslie Paul; he was, after much internal consultation, awarded the MA in 1959.[47]

It also remained the case that no easy means was found to honour artists. The Lambeth degree of Mus.Doc. had long been awarded to senior cathedral organists and also to composers such as Martin Shaw (1932), and had achieved a status as a professional qualification, being awarded on the testimony of others in the field.[48] It is a measure of the difference between the church's relationship with church musicians and that with practitioners in the visual and dramatic arts that the first award for work in the arts (other than music) was not made until 1971, to the theatre director Martin Browne, whose first dramatic collaborations with George Bell in the diocese of Chichester had begun in the early 1930s.[49] The whole exchange remains a highly revealing episode in the relationship between the church and the arts.

Editorial conventions

Manuscript amendments to typescript or manuscript letters that are clearly authorial have been adopted without comment. Obvious spacing errors in type have been corrected without comment. Misspellings have been retained, as have errors of grammar and syntax. Words which are underlined in the original manuscripts have been printed in italic type.

---

[45] Webster, 'The "revival" in the visual arts', p. 302.

[46] LPL, Faculty Office FVI/1/4. Register Book 1953–74. The MA was awarded to Diana Mary Snow (Mother Clare of the Deaconess Community of St Andrew) and Mrs Mildred Betty Ridley, in both cases 'in recognition of conspicuous services in the Church of England'.

[47] LPL, Fisher papers, vol. 223, fos. 154–64.

[48] On the existence of a church-musical 'establishment', see Ian Jones and Peter Webster, 'Anglican "establishment" reactions to "pop" church music in England, 1956–c.1900', in *Elite and popular religion*, ed. Kate Cooper and Jeremy Gregory, Studies in Church History, 42 (Woodbridge, 2006), pp. 429–41, at p. 430.

[49] LPL, Ramsey papers, vol. 207, fos. 12–14. R. C. D. Jasper, *George Bell, bishop of Chichester* (London, 1967), pp. 121–2.

The letters

The correspondents

William Temple, archbishop of Canterbury

Dorothy L. Sayers, writer and dramatist

Oliver Chase Quick, regius professor of divinity in the University of Oxford, and canon of Christ Church

Dr James W. Welch, director of religious broadcasting for the BBC

Sir Henry T. A. Dashwood, legal secretary to the archbishop

1. Welch to Temple 18 June 1943

TS, LPL, William Temple papers, 39, fo. 267

My dear Archbishop,

I hope you have now received a specially bound copy of THE MAN BORN TO BE KING. We had three copies specially bound for you, the Archbishop of York[1] and the King.

Two letters happen to have come in the post this morning about these plays and I really think it worth while asking you to read copies of them, because they bear on the main subject of this letter.[2] They are typical of the letters that continually keep on coming in.

If you are able to read my introduction, you will know something of how the plays got on the air and what we think of their religious value. But much the most important part of the book is the brilliant introduction by Dorothy Sayers herself. These plays seem to me to be her *magnum opus*; she spent more than two years studying her sources and books and writing these plays, and I know something of the terrific labour that went into their making. I have done a good deal of travelling up and down the country recently, talking mostly to parsons and lay-people, and I have been astonished at the religious effect of these plays on regular churchgoers; but very much more striking than that is the way in which the Gospel has been made to mean something to people totally divorced from the churches to whom the Christian Gospel has little relevance or meaning. My serious judgment is that these plays have done more for the preaching of the Gospel to the unconverted than any other single effort of the churches or religious broadcasting since the last war – that is a big statement, but my experience forces me to make it.

And so I wonder, not knowing the rules of this particular game, whether it would

---

[1] Cyril Forster Garbett, archbishop from 1942 to 1955, who was also chairman of the BBC's Central Religious Advisory Council from 1923 until 1945; *ODNB*. Biographical information has been derived from the *Oxford dictionary of national biography* (*ODNB*) unless stated otherwise.

[2] These letters have not been retained.

be possible and right to offer Dorothy Sayers a Lambeth D.D. for this fine piece of Christian evangelism. This may be quite impossible, but I thought I would suggest it. I have not asked Dorothy Sayers, but I think I know her well enough to say that nothing would give her such deep pleasure as the conferring of that degree. And I think such an honour would have the support of church people throughout the country.

Your devoted servant,

2. Temple to Welch 21 June 1943

TS copy, fo. 268

My dear Welch,

Your letter raises a most interesting suggestion; I will take a few soundings about it at once and should be very happy if it seemed possible to do what you have proposed.

I did received [*sic*] the specially bound copy and wrote to thank the Director-General for it; I am delighted to have it.[3] I have also got the ordinary edition.

I have read nearly the whole of the plays now. I think they are extraordinarily effective, and while they are full of interest to somebody who knows the story, I am sure you are right in thinking that they are one of the most powerful instruments in evangelism which the Church has had put into its hands for a long time past. Also I entirely agree with you about the introduction, which is a brilliant piece of work.

Yours very sincerely,

3. Quick to Temple 24 July 1943

MS, fos. 269–70

My dear William,

I'm sorry for the delay in answering your letter. It only reached me last night. I'm on a holiday & staying for the moment at Hugh's prep. school which has been evacuated here. It is Hugh's last term, after which he follows Anthony to Shrewsbury.

I'm all for Dorothy Sayers being given a D.D., & shd like C.S. Lewis to have one too. They are the two people who seem really able to put across to ordinary people a reasonably orthodox form of Xty. But I don't think it wd be the least use *my* trying to suggest D.S. or C.S.L. either for an Oxford D.D. Hon. D.D.s are entirely in the hands of the Hebdomadal Council[4] – I am not a member of it & I am never consulted by it. I did on one occasion try to suggest a name to the Council; but I only got 'rapped over the knuckles' for my [fo. 269v] pains. It was F.R. Barry, just after he had been made a Bishop.[5] He clearly ought to have been given a D.D by Oxford, & at the Vice Chancellor's suggestion I wrote a long letter to Council, stating his case & dwelling on his services to the University & to theological teaching. All the answer I got was a curt note to the effect that as the Council had not granted a D.D to one

---

3   This presentation copy would appear not to have been deposited in the archbishop's library at Lambeth Palace.

4   The chief administrative body of the University of Oxford.

5   Frank Russell Barry, bishop of Southwell, 1941–63; obituary in *Times*, 25 October 1976. He in fact received a Lambeth DD in 1947: LPL, MS 1715, p. 113.

or two other recent bishops, they could not without unfairness grant one to Barry. Their attitude seemed to me to be quite typically unimaginative & unintelligent. I was obliged to tell F.R.B. that, if he were to send in his published work for D.D. & B.D. 'by accumulation' in the ordinary (& expensive) way, the result would be doubtful. (N.P. Williams[6] whom I consulted privately thought Barry's work clearly not good enough & even Hodgson[7] considered it 'a border-line case'. Of course in this case, which wd be decided by the Board of the Faculty, *nothing* but the quality of the actual work submitted could be considered). The result [fo. 270] was that Barry, naturally enough, decided not to apply for a D.D., & there is no means of giving him one. I was fed up by the whole business, over which I took much trouble to no purpose. And I am sure that to start again over Dorothy Sayers would only lead to the same result, in spite of the fact that N.P.W. is no longer there to oppose, as he certainly would.

But, as I say, I'm all for D.L.S. having her D.D. & shd be delighted if she were to receive one from Lambeth.

Yours affectionately,

4. Temple to Dashwood 31 July 1943

TS, fo. 271

My dear Dashwood,

After consulting several people, including the Archbishop of York and the Bishop of London, who cordially approve, I should like to offer the Lambeth D.D. to Miss Dorothy Sayers, whose book 'The Man Born to be King' represents a great amount of study and is the most effective piece of evangelistic work, in my judgment, done in our generation, and her former book, 'The Mind of the Maker', was a really original approach to the doctrine of the Trinity, of great theological and apologetic value.

But I suppose it has never been given to a woman before. I consulted the Regius Professor of Divinity at Oxford, who entirely approves my going forward. All Degrees there are now open to women as to men and the Doctorate has been given to several women, though not, I think, in Divinity.

[fo. 271v] Before I write to Miss Sayers, I just want to be sure that you can see no objection from the point of view of regulations.

Yours sincerely,

5. Temple to Sayers 4 September 1943

TS, fo. 272

Dear Miss Sayers,

I am writing to ask if you would allow me to confer upon you the Degree of D.D. in recognition of what I regard as the great value of your work especially The Man Born to be King and The Mind of the Maker. I have consulted the Regius Professor

6   The late Norman Powell Williams, Lady Margaret professor of divinity and canon of Christ Church, who had died in May of that year. *ODNB*.
7   Leonard Hodgson, regius professor of moral and pastoral theology from 1938. He succeeded Quick as regius professor of divinity after Quick's death in 1944. *ODNB*.

of Divinity at Oxford who cordially approves my going forward. There are I am afraid certain fees to be met amounting to about £70. This sounds exorbitant but any proposal to reduce the fees for the Lambeth Degrees would, at least a little while ago, have met serious resistance from the Universities. There is a little ceremony of admission to the Degree which we can fix at any time convenient to both of ourselves. You would be the first woman actually to receive the Degree though there has in the past been a [fo. 272v] proposal to confer it upon one other but that never actually took place.

Yours sincerely,

6. Sayers to Temple 7 September 1943

MS, fo. 273

Your Grace,

Thank you very much indeed for the great honour you do me. I find it very difficult to reply as I ought, because I am extremely conscious that I don't deserve it. A Doctorate of Letters – yes; I have served Letters as faithfully as I knew how. But I have only served Divinity, as it were, accidentally, coming to it as a writer rather than as a Christian person. A Degree in Divinity is not, I suppose, intended as a certificate of sanctity, exactly; but I should feel better about it if I were a more convincing kind of Christian. I am never quite sure whether I really am one, or whether I have only fallen in love with an intellectual pattern. And when one is able to handle language it is sometimes hard to know how far one is under the spell of one's own words.

Also, you know, I am just a common novelist & playwright. I may not – in fact I almost certainly shan't – remain on the austere level of *The Man Born to be King* & *The Mind of the Maker*. I can't promise not to break out into something thoroughly secular, frivolous or unbecoming – adorned, if the story requires it, with the language of the rude soldiery, or purple passages descriptive of the less restrained & respectable passions. I shouldn't like your [fo. 273v] first woman D.D. to create scandal, or give reviewers cause to blaspheme.

My husband says, helpfully, that after all I could scarcely be more scandalous than Dean Swift![8] He also says (being military-minded) that I should probably do as the Archbishop says & not argue. Perhaps he is right. Probably I am only trying to keep a bolt-hole open into which I can retreat, crying: 'I never really committed myself to anything – I only wrote books!' I don't know. I find it very difficult to tell where conscience ends & pride, or cowardice, begins.

I expect I had better leave it to your judgement. If you tell me that I ought to accept, I will. It is a very great honour, and I am deeply sensible of it. I feel as though I had not expressed myself very graciously or gratefully, but I do appreciate it very deeply & I thank you...

I shall be in town from to-morrow till Saturday morning if you would like me to come & see you or anything. My address is 24, Great James St., W.C.1. Or I could come up at any time.

Yours very sincerely, and indeed gratefully,

---

8   Jonathan Swift (1667–1745), satirist and dean of St Patrick's Cathedral Dublin. *ODNB*.

7. Temple to Sayers 10 September 1943

TS, fo. 274

Dear Miss Sayers,

I am rather moved by your letter and the anxiety you shew. Let me say at once that if you would feel easier in letting the Degree be a Doctorate of Letters, I would readily agree to that; but I should like first to consult Canon Quick. I do not think there is the least harm in a Doctor of Divinity writing detective stories or any similar literature: Cyril Alington is not only a Doctor of Divinity but also a Dean and has several such stories to his credit – or discredit; frankly I am not quite sure which, because though they amused me, knowing him as I do, I don't think they are very good![9]

I am very sorry I can[']t arrange for you to come and see me just now, but I am in Canterbury all this month. I am going to send your letter on to Canon Quick and ask for his reactions, making no comment of my own to give him any lead, and I will write again when I have heard from him.

Yours sincerely,

8. Temple to Sayers 15 September 1943

TS, fo. 275

Dear Miss Sayers,

I have now had a letter from Oliver Quick[10] which I cannot send because it contains some other matter, but entirely agreeing with me that it would be a great mistake to suppose that a D.D. is to be regarded as anything like a certificate of sanctity or incompatible with the production of thoroughly secular work in literature. I think that the object I have in view would not be quite fully met by a D. Litt., and I am therefore hoping more than ever that you will be ready to accept the D.D. If so, we will lay plans for the moment of conferring it.

Yours sincerely,

9. Sayers to Temple 18 September 1943

MS, fo. 276

Your Grace,

Thank you very much for your letters. I quite see that a D.Litt. wouldn't be the same thing from your point of view. I only mentioned it as the kind of thing I should have no qualms about accepting.

I do still feel a little uneasy about it. Will your Grace forgive me & not think I am making a silly and ostentatious fuss if I ask for two or three days more in which to consider? I seem to be behaving very ungraciously, but I can't help feeling horribly like the jay in peacock's feathers,[11] with a touch of Judas Iscariot.

Yours very sincerely,

---

[9]   Cyril A. Alington, dean of Durham since 1933. The *ODNB* describes his detective fiction as 'clever, witty, but quickly perishable'.

[10] This letter has not survived.

[11] A reference to one of the fables of Aesop.

10. Temple to Sayers 22 September 1943

TS, fo. 277

Dear Miss Sayers,

I am so sorry to have put you all in a flutter! I am most anxious that you should not feel pressed in this matter. It would be to me a satisfaction if you allow me to confer the degree; it is a considerable satisfaction to have offered it; but if on reflection you are disposed to think it better that it should not be conferred, do not a moment hesitate to say so. Perhaps however, in that case, I might have your permission to mention privately to friends that I had made the proposition but that you preferred not to become *doctrix*?

Yours very sincerely,

11. Sayers to Temple 24 September 1943

MS, fos. 278–9

Your Grace,

Thank-you very much for your letter. I have been thinking the matter over very carefully, & have consulted, confidentially, one or two people whose advice I thought would be valuable, & have come to the conclusion that it would be better for me not to accept the D.D. My consultants all felt on the whole the same way about it, though not all for the same reasons. (If you cared to have their names, I am sure they would readily explain to you why their judgement supported my instinctive feeling about it).

Quite apart from my reluctance to sail under anything that might appear to be false colours, there are certain practical considerations. The first, & perhaps the most cogent from the Church's point of view is this: that any good I can do in the way of presenting the Christian Faith to the common people is bound to be hampered & impeded the moment I carry any sort of ecclesiastical label. In the present peculiar state of public opinion, it is the 'outsider' with neither dog-collar nor professional standing in the Church who can sometimes carry the exterior defensive positions by the mere shock of a surprise assault; but the power to do this depends largely on remaining a free-lance. The moment one becomes one of the regular 'religious gang', or (in the elegant phrase used by the *Daily Herald*) 'the pet of the bishops', everything one says is heavily discounted. That is why I have lately been refusing to appear on the platform at religious meetings, or to sign protests & manifestoes – the oftener one's name appears in such contexts, the less weight it carries.

Also, knowing the world of journalism as I have only too much reason to do, I think we might find ourselves up against some very disagreeable [fo. 278v] publicity. It is, I think, your generous intention that the recognition given to my work should be publicly known. But women are 'news' in a way that men are not, & peculiarly subject to the attentions of the sensational press – some of which does not love me very much. There might well be some rather disagreeable comments, impossible to refute or argue about, whose barb would stick, ranging from, 'Thriller-writer Dorothy Sayers, having made Christ a best-seller to the tune of 30,000 copies, has been rewarded with a D.D.' to 'This not very seemly farce, dealing cynically & light-heartedly with divorce (or what not) is by Miss Dorothy Sayers, D.D., & will probably make the Archbishop rather sorry that he ever ...' and so forth. And to the extent that this might happen, & that one would not wish it to happen, there would always be a sort of interior inhibition in the handling of secular work. I know, of course, that there is nothing to prevent the writing of detective stories – mostly a very innocuous form of entertainment; but there would always be the strain of an obligation to *be* innocuous & refrain from giving offence, & that is a strain under which no writer can work properly.

By all means say to those people who have been demanding that 'something should be done about' the author of the books that you have offered her a Degree, & that she has, with a deep sense of appreciation, thought it nevertheless better to decline the honour. I understand very well, I think, the purpose you had in mind – & indeed I have often felt, and said, that it would be a good thing & helpful to the work of what it is fashionable to call the Lay Apostolate, if their books could receive some form of official recognition – not in order to reward the writer so [fo. 279r] much as to establish the orthodoxy of his doctrine. As it is, the reader is only too apt to suppose that Christianity interestingly presented is not historical Christianity at all, but a new 'interpretation' deriving from the author's individual taste & fancy. (As, only too often, it is.) But I would suggest, with submission, that the best way would be to accord recognition, not so much to the workman as to the work. If, for example, the Church had something analogous to the power of the French Academy to 'couronner' the actual book, when it appeared to be both orthodox & valuable to God's work.[12] I am not thinking of anything quite like a medal or a 'prize', but something which would act both as a 'nihil obstat' & as a mark of honour – which would say, in effect, 'This book, though readable & even exciting, stands within the Catholic tradition, & the Church commends it.' This should satisfy any writer who was not making Divinity his life-work, & would also be of some guidance to the reader (who at present is in some uncertainty about what is & is not 'in the tradition'); while the Church would not have committed herself to approving any subsequent errors and extravagancies [sic] into which the amateur theologian might (through sin or ignorance) so easily fall. (I often wonder what the Popes think of the FID. DEF. on English coins, & if they ponder on the rashness which conferred that title on Henry VIII!)[13]

But all this is by the way. I hope very much that Your Grace will [fo. 279v] understand why, after very careful deliberation, I have come to the conclusion that I must refuse the very great honour offered to me, & will believe that I have done so in no ungrateful spirit.

Yours very sincerely,

12. Temple to Sayers 30 September 1943

TS, fo. 280

Dear Miss Sayers,

I am extremely grateful for your most kind letter. I think I do fully understand the situation: indeed you have persuaded me that if I were in your position I should have

---

12 Probably a reference to the *Grand prix du roman*, awarded by the Académie Française. I am indebted to Mark Greengrass for his advice on this matter.

13 *Fidei defensor*, the title conferred on Henry VIII in 1521 by Pope Leo X, in recognition of his *Assertio septem sacramentorum*, of the same year.

reached your conclusion. Meanwhile I am still glad that I made the proposal and that you are willing for me to mention it to some of those who have been eager that the Church should show some real recognition of the great value of your Plays and also the book 'The Mind of the Maker'.

Yours very sincerely,

12

'IMPROPER AND EVEN UNCONSTITUTIONAL': THE INVOLVEMENT OF THE CHURCH OF ENGLAND IN THE POLITICS OF THE END OF EMPIRE IN CYPRUS

Edited by
Sarah Stockwell

Τῷ Σεβασμιωτάτῳ 'Αρχιεπισκόπῳ Καντουαρίας καί Πρωτιεράρχῃ
πάσης 'Αγγλίας,ἐν Χριστῷ τῷ Θεῷ λίαν ἡμῖν ἀγαπητῷ καί περισπουδά-
στῳ ἀδελφῷ , Κυρίῳ Τζιόφφρεΰ , χαίρειν ἐν Χριστῷ 'Ιησοῦ τῷ Θεῷ .

Πρόθυμοι ἀποστέλλομεν τῇ 'Υμετέρᾳ ἀγαπητῇ Χάριτι τά
ἀδελφικά ἡμῶν ταῦτα Γράμματα, ἵνα ἐξαγγείλωμεν Αὐτῇ τήν,ἀπείρῳ
Θεοῦ συγκαταβάσει, ἐκλογήν ἡμῶν καί ἀνάρρησιν εἰς τόν 'Αγιώτατον
'Αρχιεπισκοπικόν Θρόνον Κύπρου, χηρεύσαντα διά τῆς πρός Κύριον
ἐκδημίας τοῦ ἀειμνήστου 'Αρχιεπισκόπου Μακαρίου τοῦ Β', καί
τηλεγραφικῶς ἤδη Αὐτῇ ἀνακοινωθεῖσαν .

'Απευθύνοντες τῇ 'Υμετέρᾳ Σεβασμιότητι ἐγκάρδιον ἐν
Χριστῷ ἀσπασμόν, διαβεβαιοῦμεν 'Υμᾶς, ὅτι περί πλείστου ποιούμενοι
τάς μεταξύ τῆς 'Ορθοδόξου 'Εκκλησίας καί τῆς 'Αγγλικανικῆς ὑφιστα-
μένας ἀγαθάς σχέσεις, πᾶσαν, τό ἐφ'ἡμῖν, καταβαλοῦμεν προσπάθειαν
πρός ἔτι στενοτέραν τούτων σύσφιγξιν καί ἀνάπτυξιν .

Θερμήν δ'ἀναπέμποντες εὐχήν πρός τόν "Ύψιστον ὑπέρ τῆς
'Υμετέρας Χάριτος καί ὑπέρ τῆς σεβασμίας 'Εκκλησίας τῆς 'Αγγλίας ,

διατελοῦμεν
Τῆς 'Υμετέρας περισπουδάστου Σεβασμιότητος
πρόθυμος ἐν Χριστῷ ἀδελφός

'Εν τῇ 'Ι.'Αρχιεπισκοπῇ Κύπρου
τῇ 26η 'Οκτωβρίου 1950

ὁ Κύπρου Μακάριος

40   His Beatitude Archbishop Makarios III sending warm brotherly greetings to Archbishop Fisher, 26 October 1950 (reproduced by permission of his Beatitude Archbishop
Chrysostomos of Cyprus) (LPL, CFR OC, fo. 114)

Introduction*

The Church of England had a singular, if ambiguous, relationship to British imperialism. It had long provided chaplains to British military and naval personnel;
its clergy accompanied British settlers overseas, establishing new churches in the
Americas and elsewhere; and like churches of other denominations, it dispatched a
great many missionaries overseas. By the twentieth century, this extensive overseas
missionary activity and the creation of an overseas anglican episcopate had brought
into being the worldwide anglican communion, broadly but by no means wholly
coterminous with existing and former regions of the British empire. Through the
anglican communion's significant overseas episcopal, clerical and missionary presence the central church authorities generated a substantial archive relating to empire
and, more widely, to foreign and overseas issues, including the correspondence of
the bishops of London (in the Fulham papers) with churches in the West Indies
and the American colonies over which in an earlier period they had jurisdictional
oversight; regular correspondence between Lambeth Palace and anglican overseas
bishops and metropolitans; papers relating to the meetings of the worldwide anglican
communion held every ten years at the 'Lambeth Conferences' and correspondence
with the principal officers of the anglican missionary societies.

This contribution to the anniversary volume is hence intended to highlight the
potential of the archives at Lambeth Palace Library for the scholar of modern colonial and imperial history, as well as of modern anglican history – and not just in
relation to what might seem the most obvious conjunction of church and empire,
overseas missionary activity. The documents that follow relate to the British Mediterranean colony of Cyprus in the 1950s, where there was no missionary interest
and only a limited anglican clerical presence. More specifically, the documents
concern one significant year in British efforts to deal with the political and guerrilla campaign for *enosis* (union with Greece) among the island's majority Greek
population: 9 March 1956, the day on which the spiritual head of the Greek-Cypriot
community, Archbishop Makarios III, was arrested by the British authorities and
flown to exile in the Seychelles, until 6 April 1957 when Makarios and his fellow
detainees were allowed to leave. Makarios failed to secure the island's union with
Greece, but after a political settlement was reached between Britain, Turkey and
Greece, which set the terms for the British retreat, Makarios finally returned to a
hero's welcome in Cyprus in March 1959. He was elected as the island's president
in December and the following year led the island to independence.

These developments in 1950s Cyprus constitute one part of the story of the British
retreat from empire after 1945. Sandwiched between the south Asian transfers of
power and the British withdrawal from Palestine in the 1940s, and the second great
phase of British decolonization from the late 1950s and early 1960s, what have been
dubbed the 'ambiguous fifties' appear as something of an interlude in the history of

* I am very grateful to staff at Lambeth Palace Library for their assistance and especially to Clare
 Brown and Gabriel Sewell, as well as to Melanie Barber and Arthur Burns, for advice and encouragement, and to Diana Markides for help with identifying Greek Cypriots from the period.

British decolonization.[1] After Labour was ousted from power in 1951, the Conservative governments of Churchill (1951–5) and Eden (1955 – January 1957) sought to 'contain' colonial political change, flying in the face of mounting anti-colonial nationalism, continued British economic weakness and American anti-colonialism. As some historians have seen it, they even aimed at imperial reassertion, continuing counter-insurgency in Malaya, launching the notorious Anglo-French invasion of Egypt in 1956 ('Suez') and embarking upon new military campaigns in Kenya as well as in Cyprus.[2]

British (and, indeed, European) decolonization concerned the Church of England in a variety of ways, not least because of the church's continued missionary work in many colonies, but also because it encouraged the church to push forward its own 'decolonization' project, with accelerated localization of the overseas episcopate and the creation of independent provinces in those areas still under Lambeth's jurisdiction. The anglican hierarchy, and in particular Geoffrey Fisher (archbishop of Canterbury, 1945–61), became involved perhaps to a surprising degree in the events that culminated in the transfers of political power in a number of British colonies, especially in eastern and central Africa, where the process of colonial political change gave rise to thorny issues around race and violence.[3]

The anglican church's involvement in Cyprus in the 1950s is in part explicable within the same broad explanatory framework as its engagement with the process of ending empire elsewhere: the exercise of Christian leadership in the face of what it sometimes perceived as the increasing moral bankruptcy of British policy. But, as already remarked, the absence of the 'missionary' factor differentiates the involvement of the church in Cyprus from its part in the politics of other British colonies in the 1950s. Instead the degree to which the church became involved is accounted for by the developing international ecumenical movement, and in this way the Cyprus documents also tie in with a significant theme in the twentieth-century history of the church: ecumenicism. Cyprus, as one clergyman at the Church of England Council on Foreign Relations (CFR) wrote in summer 1952,

> appears to be a problem not only of the Colonial Empire, but of church relations. Other problems in the Colonial Empire on which the churches have recently spoken are sure to be taken care of by the concern of the missionary societies in those areas. In the case of Cyprus, however, it seems that only the Church of England is likely to take note of the concern of the Orthodox church there for Enosis.[4]

---

[1]   W. D. MacIntyre, *British decolonization, 1946–1997. When, how, and why did the British empire fall?* (London, 1998), ch. 3.

[2]   D. Goldsworthy, 'Keeping change within bounds: aspects of colonial policy during the Churchill and Eden governments, 1951–1957', *Journal of Imperial and Commonwealth History*, XVII (1990), pp. 81–108; Martin Lynn (ed.), *The British empire in the 1950s. Retreat or revival* (London, 2005), intro., p. 11.

[3]   See Sarah Stockwell, 'Splendidly leading the way? Archbishop Fisher and decolonisation in British Africa', *Journal of Imperial and Commonwealth History*, XXXVI, (2008), 545–64; also published as Robert Holland and Sarah Stockwell (eds.), *Ambiguities of empire. Essays in honour of Andrew Porter* (London, 2009).

[4]   Lambeth Palace Library (LPL), CFR, File OC 105: W. H. McCartney (asst. general secretary, CFR) to Sir Kenneth Grubb (BCC), 30 June 1952, and reply by K. P. Drake, secretary to Grubb. McCartney suggested that the Cyprus issue be given a 'thorough airing' by the B[ritish] C[ouncil of] C[hurches], but the BCC international department did not think that it was appropriate at this time to take action.

By generating new lines of communication with the leaders of other Christian churches, not only at home through anglican participation in the British Council of Churches (BCC), but also internationally in the World Council of Churches (WCC), inaugurated in 1948 at a meeting attended by representatives of all the Christian churches except Roman Catholic and Soviet orthodox, ecumenicism had opened a new flank to the church's overseas engagement. From 1950 a newly formed Council for Ecumenical Co-operation reported on both the BCC and the WCC to the Church of England's legislative body the Church Assembly (comprising the Convocations of Canterbury and York and the House of Laity). Archbishop Fisher served as president of the BCC as well as from 1948 to 1954 as one of six joint presidents of the WCC. George Bell, bishop of Chichester, a pioneer of the ecumenical movement, was also, until his death in 1958, closely involved in its affairs, in recognition of which he was made an honorary president.[5]

The selected documents illustrate how 1950s Cyprus had the potential to complicate relations between the anglican church and other churches in the ecumenical movement. It also became an issue between the church and the Conservative governments of the 1950s, making the documents of significance to those concerned with the history of church and state. Another aspect of the interest of these documents lies additionally in the snapshot they provide of policy-making within the post-war anglican church, and especially of the influence of advisory bodies, in this case the Church of England CFR, located in Lambeth Palace and established to advise archbishops and to act with their consent in all relations with foreign churches. Much of the correspondence arriving at Lambeth and concerning foreign affairs and relations with other Christian churches was 'processed' by the officers of the council, who, where necessary, provided translations for the archbishop and produced draft responses for his consideration. Many of the documents reproduced below come from the as yet un-catalogued CFR papers.

If Lambeth Palace Library is an obvious starting point for researching themes of ecumenicism and church and state, what might be less apparent is their value to historians not primarily interested in, or even concerned at all with, the history of anglicanism. For example, the documents at Lambeth are a potentially useful source for historians of both Cyprus and orthodoxy. Until 1964, when he was persuaded of the value of record-keeping, Makarios burnt his own papers.[6] Historians researching his key role in the politics of the island are forced back on a variety of other archives and memoirs: those at Lambeth constitute one such resource.

Lambeth Palace Library is home to an enormous volume of correspondence and other papers on Cyprus and even once the decision had been taken to focus the scope of this contribution to the anniversary volume to the year of Makarios's deportation hard choices had still to be made about the selection of material. Some brief comment on the principles of editorial selection is therefore in order beyond that of their potential to illuminate the themes already sketched above. First and foremost, the intention has been to try as far as possible to construct a coherent 'story' and, while illustrating the different dimensions of the episode as they affected the anglican church, this has entailed ignoring other possible 'stories' that could be told around the history of the church and Cyprus at this time: I return to some of these other areas at the end of this introduction. The documents reproduced here and the rest of the introduction focus therefore on the church's response to Makarios's deportation. They concentrate in particular on Fisher's involvement in policy and constitutional questions: although the archbishop was by no means the only senior anglican to become drawn into Cypriot affairs, with George Bell's sustained interest particularly noteworthy, Fisher is arguably the more intriguing figure, engaging as he did with the details of British policy. The selected documents reflect all Fisher's major political interventions over Cyprus during the year and there is consequently a bias in the documentation towards examples of correspondence or other communications with British government ministers. Secondly, in order to illuminate the church's own 'policy'-making processes, documents have been selected with a view to showing the variety of sources influencing Fisher's response to the deportation and Cypriot political issues; others illustrate Fisher's own input.

Because far more is omitted from the contribution that follows than could possibly be included, linking passages (in italics) have been used before some documents in order to help provide essential context where it is not already evident from the introduction or the documents themselves. Where possible the link passages trace the 'paper trail' behind each document and, in some cases, the response to, or consequences of, correspondence or particular initiatives detailed in the documents. Material from government papers in The National Archives is used to shed light on ministerial and Whitehall attitudes to Fisher and his proposals.

We now turn to a brief narrative of the historical background to events in Cyprus in the 1950s and of how these related to the anglican church. A more detailed account of the period of Makarios's deportation is then given, before the introduction ends with an analysis of the significance and nature of the church's involvement with Cyprus in this period.

I

The eastern Mediterranean island of Cyprus had passed only comparatively recently under British control.[7] While nominally remaining under the suzerainty of the Ottoman Empire, the island was declared a British protectorate in 1878. It was annexed to the British Empire with the outbreak of war in 1914. Despite many years of Ottoman rule and the island's geographical proximity to the Turkish coast, only about one fifth of the population was Turkish whereas about 80 per cent was culturally and linguistically Greek, and had long favoured union (*enosis*) with Greece. Under Ottoman rule, the ancient church of Cyprus, independent within the Greek orthodox communion, had been allowed a powerful position within the Greek-Cypriot community, providing secular as well as ecclesiastical leadership, with the archbishop of Cyprus designated *ethnarch* of his people. When the transfer of sovereignty from the Ottomans to Britain was confirmed in the 1923 Treaty of Lausanne, and two years later Cyprus became a crown colony, Greek-Cypriot agita-

---

[7] This account of historical background and of the politics of 1950s Cyprus draws on R. F. Holland, *Britain and the revolt in Cyprus 1954–1959* (Oxford, 1998). For an excellent short introduction, see R. F. Holland and D. Markides, *The British and the Hellenes. Struggles for mastery in the eastern Mediterranean 1850–1960* (Oxford, 2006), ch. 9.

tion for *enosis* became stronger. The church was at the forefront of this campaign. Its formal powers and privileges were whittled away under British administration; sponsoring *enosis* became one way in which the church could underpin its support base in the Greek community.[8] In 1931 the unrest sparked riots in the capital, Nicosia. The British administration responded by suspending the island's Legislative Assembly and exiling two of three of the island's bishops. Regulation passed in 1937 forbad the election of a non-Cypriot as archbishop of Cyprus and in the absence of the bishops of Kitium and Kyrenia, the church was unable to hold elections for a successor after the death of the incumbent archbishop; instead the bishop of Pathos acted as *locum tenens* for some years.

By the late 1940s although the Labour government withdrew the legislation preventing a new archiepiscopal appointment[9] and embarked upon constitutional reform with a view to the restoration of representative government on the island, the factors which were to lead to the 1950s conflict were falling into place. After Britain withdrew from its mandate in Palestine in May 1948 Cyprus assumed enhanced strategic importance in the eyes of British policy-makers as the only territory in the region remaining under direct British control. Indeed British chiefs of staff now argued not just for the retention of bases on the island but for Cyprus itself as a base; an assessment that only gained more weight with the growing uncertainty over the future of the Suez base (eventually settled with the agreement reached in 1954 with Egypt for a staggered withdrawal of British forces).[10] Anxious to preserve British sovereignty over the island, the British government was reluctant to permit discussion of *enosis* or to concede the legitimacy of Greek interest in the politics of the island. Even if it had not been for the island's strategic value, its 'mixed' population complicated any transition to self-government, with the island's minority Turkish population and the Turkish government in favour of the continuation of British rule.[11] In Cyprus, however, the Greek-Cypriot archbishop confronted by the growing strength of the communist party AKEL, founded in 1941 and campaigning for Cypriot self-government, rallied support around *enosis*. British constitutional proposals unveiled in 1948 allowing for limited representative government fell short of this aim and were rejected by the Greek Cypriots. The Orthodox church organized a plebiscite on the issue in January 1950 among Greek-Cypriots; unsurprisingly the result found overwhelming support for union. Later, after it had effectively lost the battle for Greek-Cypriot popular support, AKEL was to fall in behind the *enosis* banner, although the party continued to have an uneasy relationship with the church. When on 28 June 1950 the incumbent archbishop Makarios II died he was succeeded by the former bishop of Kitium, Makarios III.

Archbishop Makarios III had only recently returned from the United States where he had been studying theology at Boston, financed by a World Council of Churches scholarship. Better travelled than some Cypriot clerics, Makarios set about 'internationalizing' the Cyprus question, travelling to Greece (where he was to become

8   Rolandos Katsiaounēs, *Labour, society and politics in Cyprus during the second half of the nineteenth century* (Nicosia, 1996), pp. 75–8.
9   LPL, CFR, File OC 112: Arthur Creech Jones to Fisher, 22 Oct. 1946.
10 Holland and Markides, *British and the Hellenes*, p. 223.
11 Diana Markides, 'Britain's "new look" policy for Cyprus and the Makarios–Harding talks, January 1955–March 1956', *Journal of Imperial and Commonwealth History*, XXIII (1995), 479–502, see esp. 479–80.

an influential figure in Greek popular political and religious life) to try and get the Greek government to sponsor a debate on the island at the United Nations, and to America to attend the UN in autumn/winter 1952.[12] As a wealth of material in Lambeth Palace demonstrates, both Makarios and other orthodox churchmen also used ecclesiastical statesmanship in their attempt to mobilize support for *enosis*.

Until the mid-1950s, however, the Greek government remained unwilling to champion *enosis* at the expense of traditional Anglo-Hellenic friendship or to risk its developing friendship with Turkey.[13] But relations between Britain and Greece became more strained with the British refusal to discuss sovereignty and a change of government in Greece in November 1952. Foreign Secretary Anthony Eden's careless dismissal of the *enosis* case when raised by new Greek Prime Minister Field Marshal Alexandros Papagos in September 1953 at the very time that Eden was enjoying the Greek government's hospitality while convalescing from surgery altered the Greek perspective, and in 1954 Papagos acceded to Makarios's request to take the issue to the UN.[14] An ill-judged statement in the House of Commons in 1954 by Henry Hopkinson, minister of state at the colonial office, to the effect that there were 'certain territories...that can never expect to be fully independent' (remarks widely interpreted as referring to Cyprus), and the introduction by the British administration in Cyprus of anti-sedition legislation, further inflamed Greek-Cypriot opinion. After the UN decided against adopting a resolution on Cyprus in December 1954, Makarios decided the time was ripe to open a new flank in the campaign for union with Greece. In April the following year EOKA (the National Organization of Greek Cypriot Fighters), led by Colonel George Grivas (a right-wing Greek-Cypriot who had acquired some notoriety in his military resistance to Greek communism after the war) embarked upon a terrorist campaign in Cyprus initially aimed at the British and Greek-Cypriot 'traitors' rather than at members of the Turkish minority.

Until this time British ministers had sought to portray Cyprus as a purely British colonial question, but from summer 1955 British policy shaped by new Foreign Secretary Harold Macmillan ensured that this would change. By then, considerations to do with Turkey had increased in significance following Britain's entry to the Turco-Iraqi ('Baghdad') Pact in spring 1955. At the same time, Macmillan, still unwilling to relinquish sovereignty over Cyprus, but conscious that Britain needed to be seen to be advancing the island politically – not least in American eyes and in the context of Greek sponsorship of the Greek-Cypriot campaign at the United Nations – favoured bringing Turkey more closely into the frame to allow Britain to use Turkish concerns to circumvent *enosis*. With this end in view he invited both Greece and Turkey to London (the 'Tripartite Conference') from 29 August to 7 September 1955, at which he proposed that both Greece and Turkey be given a *rôle* in the governance of the island and set out proposals for limited Cypriot self-government; predictably the conference failed in the face of Greek and Turkish differences.

That month, with continued violence in the island, Eden, now prime minister, appointed as new governor a military man, Sir John Harding, then chief of the Imperial General Staff. Makarios and Harding engaged in extended talks over

---

[12] See Demetris Assos, 'Makarios: a study of anticolonial nationalist leadership, 1950–1959', Ph.D. dissertation, Institute of Commonwealth Studies, University of London, PhD, 2009, esp. ch. 3.

[13] Assos, 'Makarios', pp. 71–5.

[14] Holland, *Britain and the revolt in Cyprus*, pp. 31–2.

the winter of 1955–6, but got nowhere. Although some commentators questioned British sincerity in participating in these discussions, others concluded that Harding entered upon them in the very real hope of achieving a political breakthrough.[15] As Harding's account of the talks in a letter written later to Fisher (Document 10) illustrates, when, in November 1955, Harding secured cabinet's agreement to a statement acknowledging the Cypriot right to self-determination but, crucially, hedged around with qualifications to the effect that it could only be achieved when strategic considerations permitted, he appeared genuinely shocked by Makarios's immediate rejection of it.[16] But the Cypriot archbishop's ability to compromise was hamstrung by a need to satisfy Greek-Cypriot expectations and maintain his authority in the face of potential opposition from more hard-line supporters of *enosis*. For its part, Eden's government, conscious of the wider imperatives of British Middle Eastern policy and fearful of being charged with 'retreat' by right-wing Conservative MPs, was unwilling to concede more.

Diplomacy having failed, Harding switched tactics, arresting Makarios and three others, including the more extreme Bishop Kyprianos of Kyrenia, on 9 March 1956. They were taken to exile in the British colony of the Seychelles. In Cyprus, Harding oversaw a counter-terrorism campaign in many respects characteristic of the British response to colonial insurgency elsewhere in the 1950s: curfews; the execution of summary justice through special courts, which, although on nothing like the scale that occurred in British colonial Kenya in the 1950s, saw death sentences handed down to several alleged members of EOKA resulting in nine executions; the creation of detention camps and a British military and intelligence campaign that prompted allegations of brutality and torture.

Anglican archbishops and advisers had long viewed events in Cyprus with mixed reactions. They were impatient with what appeared to be the British administration's needless trampling of orthodox sensitivities. British interference in the 1930s with the archiepiscopal succession had proved a particular red rag to anglican leaders and they had made repeated attempts to try and persuade successive British governments to repeal the legislation concerned. But anglicans were alert to the degree to which the Cypriot church was immersed in politics, and were only too conscious that by the 1950s Cypriot and Greek orthodox churchmen were keen to pull them into the *enosis* campaign.[17] 'How inconvenient', Fisher complained on receipt of one letter on the subject in August 1950, 'of the Archbishop of Athens to write to me about Cyprus.'[18] Like the orthodox churchmen, the British government also on occasion sought the help of the anglican church in dealing with Cyprus, although that they did so was because the church was already involved and so offered a potentially useful channel through which to approach Greek Cypriot leaders. Becoming too closely associated with the British state carried its own risks for the anglican church, however, as Herbert Waddams, secretary at the CFR, was aware. When, in 1948 Labour secretary of state for the colonies Creech Jones asked Fisher to see if he could use his influence to dissuade the Orthodox church in Cyprus from

---

15 Markides, 'Britain's "new look" policy', pp. 489–90.

16 *Ibid.*

17 See e.g., LPL, CFR, File OC 105: Rev. G. L. Prestige (actg. sec. CFR) to R. C. Barnes, foreign office, 17 Aug. 1950, on efforts to prevent the bishop of Kyrenia from securing an interview with Fisher.

18 LPL, CFR, File OC 105: Fisher to Prestige, 28 Aug. 1950.

'provocative acts' in 'defiance of the law' in support of *Enosis*,[19] Waddams warned Fisher that any public action by the church could adversely impact upon his 'prestige with the orthodox by making it appear that you are an instrument of British government policy'.[20]

Ironically in view of what was to come to pass, Reverend Donald Goldie, the anglican archdeacon of Cyprus and chaplain at Nicosia (within the diocese of Jerusalem), greeted the appointment in 1950 of Makarios III with qualified enthusiasm: he looked forward to what he hoped would be an easier relationship with the new, younger prelate and a 'more confident understanding with the church here on spiritual grounds'. He recognized that 'Makarios is a politician, and if he were not then he certainly would not be occupying his present position', but concluded that 'I am sure he is not *merely* a politician'.[21] Fisher had had the opportunity to judge the new archbishop for himself when Makarios visited London in 1953, and again in October 1954. On the second of these occasions, when the two met at Makarios's request, it was Fisher who steered the conversation towards political issues, recently made more heated by Hopkinson's 'never' statement in the Commons. Fisher ventured the opinion that he himself believed a period of self-government followed by further discussion of the island's future to be the best course for the island, remarking that he feared the British government had not 'handled the matter [of the political development of the island] very well'.[22] Nonetheless as the terrorist campaign on the island got under way, anglican leaders were increasingly frustrated at their failure to persuade the Cypriot archbishop to condemn the violence.[23] Of Makarios's claims that he dare not openly do so, Archdeacon Goldie believed the 'truth was otherwise' and that 'he [Makarios] was personally implicated in and wholly sympathetic towards EOKA'.[24]

By March 1956, then, the anglican church had already been drawn into the conflict, occupying a sometimes uneasy position between the British state and its fellow Christian clergy in Cyprus and Greece; a position which, as Waddams correctly surmised, would only be rendered more complicated by the deportation (Documents 1 and 2).

The news that Makarios had been exiled provoked strong reactions around the world. Lambeth was bombarded by telegrams from other Orthodox church leaders expressing their concern at the turn of events. Documents 12–14 provide some illustration of the degree to which the deportation drew Fisher into discussion with various interested constituencies. These included the oecumenical patriarch in Constantinople, Archbishop Athenagoras,[25] with whom the anglican church was

---

[19] LPL, Fisher papers 41, fos. 264–5: memorandum of meeting between Arthur Creech Jones, Lord Winster and Fisher. 15 Dec. 1948.

[20] *Ibid.*, fo. 266, Waddams to Fisher, 17 Dec. 1948. At Waddams's suggestion, Fisher chose to contact Athenagoras, newly elected oecumenical patriarch asking if he could intercede with the Cypriot church.

[21] The emphasis is Goldie's. LPL, CFR, File OC 114: Goldie to McCartney, 2 Nov. 1950.

[22] LPL, CFR, File OC 114: 'Note for the file', by Waddams, 29 Oct. 1954, of meeting between Fisher and Makarios, 28 Oct. 1954.

[23] LPL, Fisher papers 155, fo. 71: Archdeacon Goldie to Fisher, 6 Apr. 1955; and LPL, CFR, File OC 105: record of conversation between Goldie and Makarios, 27 June 1955 (written just before Goldie left the island and his successor, A. W. Adeney, arrived).

[24] LPL, CFR, File OC 106: confidential memorandum, 'The deportation of Archbishop Makarios' by Goldie (written following Goldie's return to the UK), 10 Mar. 1965, sent to Waddams at CFR.

[25] The patriarch of Constantinople and the spiritual leader of eastern orthodoxy had been styled 'oecu-

in increased communication as a result of earlier Anglo-Orthodox conversations, as well as more recently shared interest in resisting attempts by the Russian Orthodox church (encouraged by Stalin) to supplant the *rôle* of the oecumencial patriarch in providing orthodox leadership. Athenagoras had no formal jurisdiction over the Church of Cyprus, but was most immediately concerned with the repercussions of developments on the island for the Greek minority in Constantinople. This community had already been the victims of anti-Greek rioting on 6 – 7 September 1955 on the occasion of the tripartite conference between the British, Greek and Turkish governments over Cyprus. Indeed the international complications of *enosis* were a major blow to the improved relations between the Greek minority and the Turkish government and people that had developed in the post-war period and that had achieved a particular high-point with the succession of the Turkish candidate, Athenagoras, as patriarch.[26]

The deportation also drew anglican leaders into a series of exchanges with the officers of the World Council of Churches. They too were under pressure from orthodox churchmen to respond to events: one, Englishman Francis House, an associate general secretary of the WCC,[27] felt after a call from Athens as if he was a 'Western ecclesiastic who had been in personal contact with a Byzantine Bishop immediately after the sack of Constantinople by the Crusades!' When the WCC's general secretary, Wim Visser't Hooft, upped the stakes for the anglican church by unilaterally issuing a 'personal' statement on the deportation, Fisher issued a stinging rebuke, reprimanding Visser't Hooft for acting without first securing the agreement of the other officers of the WCC or of the British churches (Document 3). Waddams believed that Hooft had fallen 'right into' the trap the 'Orthodox were providing for him'.[28]

The storm of correspondence that followed the deportation was probably inevitable. Moreover, a certain minimum response by the anglican church to events was necessitated simply by the church's communion with the Church of Cyprus and the interruption which the exile of its head posed to normal formalities between the two. Some of the correspondence in Lambeth concerns gestures of friendship between the churches, for example when it was agreed to send Makarios a little reading matter to leaven his days in exile (the lives of three previous anglican archbishops were duly despatched to the Seychelles, although it is difficult to know what the archbishop, who spent some of his time in exile learning English, made of the three volumes).[29]

But if Fisher faced significant calls from all sides to intervene (from the 'Cyprus

---

menical patriarch' since the sixth century (although the Turkish government recognized him only as Greek orthodox patriarch of the Greek minority in Turkey). As senior orthodox leader his primary responsibility was for relations between the autocephalous (including Cyprus) and autonomous Orthodox churches.

26 Alexis Alexandris, *The Greek minority of Istanbul and Greek–Turkish relations 1918–1974* (Athens, 1983), pp. 234–59, at p. 270.

27 Edward Carpenter, *Archbishop Fisher: his life and times* (Norwich, 1991), p. 422.

28 LPL, CFR, File 106: note for Fisher, 13 Mar. 1956, by Waddams recording telephone call with Dr Payne (of the WCC executive committee); further note by Waddams also 13 Mar., dated 'Later'; House to Waddams, 16/17 Mar. 1956; Waddams to House, 20 Mar. 1956.

29 LPL, CFR, File OC 114, see correspondence from bishop of Jerusalem (from whom suggestion first arose), 5 Oct. 1956.

ANYTHING CAN HAPPEN NEXT...

41 'Anything can happen next': cartoon of Archbishop Fisher and Archbishop Makarios III by Vicky [Victor Weisz] published in the New Statesman on 5th May 1956 (reproduced by permission of The British Cartoon Archive, University of Kent, www.cartoons. ac.uk)

is Turkish' party as well as from the Greek-Cypriots),[30] the degree to which he chose to engage with the whole question of Cyprus is striking (as reflected in Illustration 41) – and provides another example of Fisher's very active involvement with the process of colonial political change to add to his interventions in the politics of other areas of the colonial empire. Furthermore the very wholehearted way in which Fisher intervened gave rise to greater expectations among Greeks as to what he could do to ameliorate the situation. The Greek response in turn appears subsequently to have persuaded the archbishop of Canterbury that he had acted to good effect (see e.g., Document 12). Speaking in the House of Lords on 15 March 1956, Fisher, apparently influenced by Waddams's recent experience in Cyprus,[31] set out a series of proposals that in their insistence on the importance of constitutional progress and of negotiation – including, however unpalatable, with Makarios – were in broad terms to remain the basis of all his subsequent public and private interventions over Cyprus.[32] In what his biographer, Edward Carpenter, calls one of the 'most effective' speeches Fisher ever delivered in the Lords,[33] the archbishop appealed to all sides to condemn terrorism, but also suggested that the British government appoint a constitutional adviser and resume negotiation. Fisher's strongly pragmatic approach was reiterated in letters written to Governor Harding and to Conservative secretary of state for the colonies, Alan Lennox-Boyd (Documents 5–6).

Fisher's ideas elicited a mixed response. One of those in contact with Fisher, the Greek Cypriot, Nicos Rossos, wrote that from his discussions with 'persons close to' Makarios it seemed that 'people here are convinced that the constructive proposals put forward by the Archbishop of Canterbury offer the only visible key to conciliation'.[34] Sir Charles Peake, British ambassador in Athens, wrote to express his admiration for Fisher's intervention; he concurred with Fisher's emphasis on continuing negotiation with Makarios, finding it difficult to believe that Britain would find anyone else 'with whom to do business in the future'.[35] For his part Lennox-Boyd conceded that the Lords speech was 'nicely balanced between constructive suggestions and round condemnation of Makarios for his inactivity over violence'.[36] Harding also saw some merit in the suggestions, but only as part of a wider attempt to deal with the problem and he concluded that for the time being he could not advise the government to resume negotiation with Makarios.[37] If nothing else Fisher's intervention required the colonial office and administration in Cyprus to respond, and at this critical time in the Cyprus question Harding drafted a twelve-page reply to Fisher, sent after thorough consultation with London (Document 10).

As the weeks wore on Fisher became more impatient with what he perceived to be the British government's intransigence and his exchanges with ministers increasingly heated, as evident in further letters written to Lennox-Boyd in April (Documents 7 and 8). On 19 April 1956 the government announced the appointment of

---

30 See LPL, CFR, File OC 106: telegrams received in Mar. 1956; and Fazil Küçuck to Fisher, 14 June 1956.
31 See The National Archives (TNA), Kew Gardens, colonial office (CO) 926/194, no. 6: minute by W.A.M. [orris] on meeting with Fisher's chaplain J. R. Satterthwaite, Mar. 1956.
32 *House of Lords debates*, 1955–6, vol. 196, 15 Mar. 1956, cols. 468–73.
33 Carpenter, *Archbishop Fisher*, p. 621.
34 LPL, CFR, File OC 106: N. Rossos to Satterthwaite, 29 Mar. 1956.
35 LPL, Fisher papers 170, fo. 124: Peake to Fisher, 1 May 1956.
36 TNA, CO 926/194, no. 4: Lennox-Boyd to Sir John Harding, 28 Mar. 1956.
37 TNA, CO 926/194, no. 16: Harding to Lennox-Boyd, 15 Apr. 1956.

Lord Radcliffe as constitutional commissioner. The move corresponded to Fisher's own proposal, but Radcliffe's terms of reference were vague and Radcliffe himself did not see his *rôle* as being to produce a 'recommended' constitution.[38] Moreover, on 17 April Prime Minister Eden had declared that there could be no talks over Cyprus until the cessation of violence.[39] Fisher's impatience with the government was aired publicly when he spoke out at a meeting of the British Council of Churches on 24 – 5 April – with consequences for Fisher's relations with Conservative ministers and Eden (see Document 11). The experience led Fisher to advise the BCC that since he himself was in bad odour it would be better if a delegation they proposed sending in early June to the colonial office was not led by him.[40]

Fisher's intervention was also causing irritation among members of the British administration in Cyprus. The monthly intelligence appreciation for Famagusta for June 1956 referred to the 'wholly artificial importance attached to Dr Fisher's incursions into the field of Cypriot politics'. It went on:

> It may be incredible to us that the Archbishop of Canterbury while feeling that communion between the Anglican and Orthodox Church is too close for a small matter like the Cyprus problem to come between then, should feel unable to suggest (or should not have thought of suggesting) that both churches should make a joint denunciation of violence. But it is not at all incredible to the Cypriots. Dr Fisher's efforts undoubtedly provided propaganda material for Britain's enemies and gave indirect encouragement to the terrorists, for it appeared that he regarded the Orthodox Church's holding a gun to our head (or our back) as a matter of very little consequence.[41]

Wearily one British official in Cyprus requested that the secretary of state see Fisher as he had heard that the 'Arch. of Canterbury has another "plan"' to launch and it was necessary to try and 'limit [the] damage' of further possible intervention from Lambeth.[42] In London, however much Cyprus was causing ructions between Fisher and the government, officials at the colonial office were rather more circumspect, noting that the commissioner in Famagusta did not 'know all the facts', including the details of Fisher's most recent speech in the Lords when he had revealed his efforts in correspondence with Makarios to get the Cypriot to denounce violence.[43] To Harding's suggestion that the secretary of state and Lord Radcliffe might on the latter's return 'usefully discuss the question of how to handle the Archbishop', it was noted in Whitehall that 'This seems to be a case of judging too hastily.'[44]

After the initial flurry of activity, the rate of correspondence and discussions about Cyprus within the church slowed over the summer of 1956. Fisher continued to express exasperation with the government (it had, he wrote to Kenneth Slack at the BCC in July, handled Cyprus 'about as stupidly as anyone conceivably could'

---

38 TNA, foreign office (FO) 371/123888, at RG 1081/907, Moreton (CO) to Hancock (FO), 5 May 1956, enclosing correspondence from Radcliffe to Sir John Martin, 29 Apr. 1956.

39 *House of Commons debates*, 1955–6, vol. 551, 17 Apr. 1956, cols. 846–7.

40 LPL, Fisher papers 170, fo. 170: Fisher to Kenneth Slack, BCC, 4 June 1956.

41 TNA, CO 926/194, 'Extract from monthly political appreciation of Commissioner, Famagusta' , 4 June 1956, enclosed with no. 41, G. Sinclair (government of Cyprus) to Sir John Martin, CO, 29 June 1956.

42 *Ibid.*, Sinclair to Martin, 29 June 1956.

43 *Ibid.*, minute on no. 41 by W. A. Morris, 4 July 1956.

44 *Ibid.*, no. 45, Harding to Melville, 26 July 1956; minute on no. 45, possibly by Melville.

and it would be 'an advantage if one or two people could go and really bark at him [Lennox-Boyd]'),[45] but Fisher's attentions switched to doing what he could to facilitate negotiation, especially as no Greek Cypriot had agreed to meet with Lord Radcliffe. He urged reconciliation in a speech in the Lords in late July (as well as regretting the British government's insistence that violence must end before negotiations resume),[46] and he tried to use his influence with some of the Greek Cypriot leaders to persuade them to meet with the constitutional commissioner (see Documents 16 and 17). Although they still declined to do so, Fisher's intercession was perceived in Whitehall as potentially useful. By the end of July Harding informed London that there seemed to be a significant body of opinion within the Greek Cypriot community, perhaps influenced by Fisher, that was opposed to the attitude adopted by the ethnarchy council (an assembly comprising mostly lay Greek Cypriots) in its refusal to enter talks with Radcliffe, with pressure having apparently been brought to bear by the 'Rossos-Pavlides' (both of whom were among Fisher's contacts – see Document 12) clique on Nicos Kranidiotis, chief aide to Makarios, to support their line against that of the ethnarchy.[47] From Downing Street the prime minister approached the colonial office enquiring about Fisher's offer to help.[48]

Nevertheless by September the church increasingly found itself caught between a rock and a hard-place. The balance of domestic British opinion against Makarios shifted more decisively with the discovery in late August of the 'Grivas' diaries, bringing firmer evidence of Makarios's complicity in the terrorist campaign. From Cyprus, Goldie's successor as archdeacon, Reverend Arthur Adeney, wrote asking whether the time was right for 'an agonizing reappraisal of Makarios's character'. In his response Fisher showed characteristic pragmatism: 'all that has happened is that he is proved blacker than was before certain. The important thing is that he is still alive and is still a factor in the Cyprus situation, and something has to be done about him.'[49] Whatever the new evidence, at the WCC Visser't Hooft was anxious about orthodox concern at the 'silence' of the Council over Cyprus. He worried lest the fall-out from the whole issue might 'create an earthquake in Orthodoxy' if a rumoured move of the orthodox patriarchate from Istanbul to Mount Athos were to occur. Since 'the whole Greek world sees the problem of relations between Turkey and Greece in terms of the Cyprus issue it would be felt that the Western World and particularly Britain was really responsible for what in their eyes was a great disaster for Orthodoxy'.[50] Fisher himself was more sceptical as to whether the issue would bring about a relocation of the patriarchate[51] but was anyway mindful of quite different criticism from closer to home since his Lords speech and perceived failure to condemn Makarios for condoning violence had angered members of the British armed forces in Cyprus.[52]

45 LPL, Fisher papers 170, fo. 187: Fisher to Kenneth Slack, BCC, 10 July 1956; fo. 199, Fisher to Slack, 23 July 1956.
46 *House of Lords debates*, vol. 199, 25 July 1956, cols. 221–5.
47 TNA, CO 926/194, no. 47, Harding to Lennox-Boyd, 29 July 1956.
48 *Ibid.*, no. 49, J. J. A. Howard to Drake, CO, to P. F. de Zuleta, private secretary to prime minister, 7 Aug. 1956.
49 LPL, Fisher papers 170, fos. 216–17, Adeney to Fisher, 1 Sept. 1956; fo. 220, Fisher to Adeney, 17 Sept. 1956.
50 *Ibid.*, fos. 221–2, Hooft to Fisher, 21 Sept. 1956.
51 *Ibid.*, fos. 238–41, Fisher to Hooft, 11 Oct. 1956.
52 *Ibid.*, fos. 223–9, Adeney to Fisher, 25 Sept. 1956.

Under pressure from these different quarters, Fisher continued to focus on the practical help he could offer to bring about a breakthrough in the impasse. A truce organized by Grivas in August had come to nothing after Harding responded only by setting out the terms on which he would accept the surrender of EOKA men.[53] Now, spurred on by indications that he might be able to exert influence on some Cypriots (see Document 18), Fisher wrote to Lennox-Boyd on 11 October 1956 (Document 19) suggesting – somewhat extraordinarily – that he might be able to secure a second truce. Against the advice of his officials – who queried whether it was right for the secretary of state to write such a candid letter to Fisher especially without clearing it first with the foreign office – Lennox-Boyd wrote back to Fisher on 31 October, declining the offer at least for the time being and suggesting that the first truce had played into Grivas's hands.[54]

By December tensions on Cyprus were rising. There was an escalation in EOKA violence, and a stepping up in the British counter-insurgency campaign. In these circumstances (and rather contrary to the interpretation being advanced at the Council on Foreign Relations – see Document 18), Harding sought to impress the cabinet with the need for constitutional action, perhaps along the lines envisaged by Lord Radcliffe who had submitted his report in October. Although he was prevented by the terms of his appointment from considering the question of British sovereignty over the island, the report proposed the restoration of the legislature in which the Turkish minority would be given a privileged position.[55] But with British policy towards Cyprus dictated by the imperatives of Britain's wider Middle Eastern policy which had culminated in the joint Anglo-French military action over Suez in Egypt from 31 October, Lennox-Boyd delayed publication of the report. With no success in securing the cabinet's agreement to progress on the constitutional front, Harding continued a policy of repression on the island. A series of uncompromising statements by the governor on TV and in radio broadcasts provoked criticism in Britain and led to a debate on the Cyprus regulations in the Lords on 6 December 1956. Facing American pressure as well as domestic (including from Fisher, with whom he and Harding had recently met – see Document 21), Lennox-Boyd travelled to Athens and Ankara for discussions with the Greek and Turkish governments. He was unable to reach a satisfactory agreement with the former while the latter pressed him to proceed with the island's partition, an option now being discussed by Britain if only as a bargaining counter in negotiations with the Greeks. On his return, Lennox-Boyd published the Radcliffe constitutional proposals, promised to introduce a new constitution once violence had ceased and reaffirmed the British government's willingness to revisit the question of self-determination when the 'international and strategic situation permits', but, told the Commons, partition could not be ruled out.[56]

The continued complications of Fisher's position throughout these months are illustrated by the story of a telegram sent to Makarios at the end of the year with customary Christmas greetings, accompanied by a request to denounce violence and

[53] Holland, *Britain and the revolt in Cyprus*, p. 150.

[54] LPL, Fisher papers 170, fos. 251–5, Lennox-Boyd to Fisher, 31 Oct. 1956; see also TNA, CO 926/194, no. 51, minute by Lennox-Boyd, 30 Oct. 1956, on letter.

[55] *Constitutional proposals for Cyprus: report submitted to the secretary of state for colonies*, CMD, 42, HMSO, 1956; *House of Commons debates*, 1955–6, vol. 562, 19 Dec. 1956, cols. 1267–9.

[56] Holland, *Britain and the revolt in Cyprus*, pp. 152–67.

initiate negotiation: approved by the colonial office, it was sent via official channels to Makarios in the Seychelles as a matter of 'urgency', but with the request from Waddams that the Seychelles governor make it clear – if not too 'unduly embarrassing' – that the archbishop 'has taken an independent attitude during the whole of the Cyprus affair and that some of his comments have been critical of the Government'.[57]

The new year and the accession of Harold Macmillan as new Conservative leader to power following the resignation of Anthony Eden seems to have encouraged Fisher – led by advice from Waddams (Document 23) – to hope that the time might be ripe for a new approach to the Cyprus question. He wrote to Macmillan in early February 1957 (Documents 24–5); the letter was described by one senior official in the CO as 'pathetically naïf [sic]', although he conceded that 'the intention is honourable and some of his conclusions not so far short of their mark'. He further commented: 'I had always been taught that this degree of interference by the church in a political issue was improper and even unconstitutional.'[58] The prime minister met with the lord president of the council and the foreign and colonial secretaries to discuss the letter, and the two departments prepared drafts as a basis for a reply, which when eventually sent rebuffed the arguments given in Fisher's letter and in length returning, as one official commented in Macmillan's office, 'tit for the Archbishop's tat'.[59] This correspondence seem to have reached a dead end: Fisher responded to Macmillan's reply, noting how 'Every available answer to support British policy has been long utworn, and I am left in the miserable state of having no constructive answer to give people'; to which Macmillan replied curtly 'surely there is no constructive answer against sin except redemption'.[60] Simultaneously, Fisher kept up the pressure on Lennox-Boyd, urging the latter to release Makarios even if he should not be allowed to return to Cyprus (Document 28).

Despite the sharp tenor of these exchanges, a breakthrough over Makarios's position came shortly after. In late March 1957, following a new EOKA ceasefire, Lennox-Boyd announced that the British government had accepted an offer from NATO's secretary general to assist with conciliation over Cyprus and was willing to release Makarios as soon as he denounced violence. A week later came the news that Makarios, having satisfied the British government on this front, would indeed be allowed to leave.[61] Fisher's relief was palpable. He now focused on trying to get Makarios to respond constructively to British actions. The last document reproduced here is Fisher's letter to Makarios on the occasion of his release. It marks the conclusion of one phase in the church's involvement over Cyprus in the 1950s.

The story did not of course end there. Refused permission to return to Cyprus, Makarios stayed in Athens from where his grip over Grivas and developments on the island was weaker. Greek Cypriots continued to seek Fisher out, treating him almost as if he were a spokesman for Her Majesty's government. For example, in

---

57 TNA, CO 926/194, no. 62, Waddams to CO, 22 Dec. 1956; no. 69, minute by Sir John Martin, 1 Jan. 1957.
58 TNA, CO 926/632, minute by Melville, 7 Feb. 1957.
59 TNA, prime minster's office (PREM) 11/2268, minute by C. R., 14 Feb. 1957. For Macmillan's reply see: LPL, Fisher papers 186, fos. 144–50, 17 Feb. 1956.
60 LPL, Fisher papers 186, fo. 151, Fisher to Macmillan, 26 Feb. 1957; fo. 152, Macmillan to Fisher, 27 Feb. 1957; TNA, PREM 11/2268.
61 *House of Commons debates*, 1956–7, vol. 567, statement by Lennox-Boyd, 20 Mar. 1957, col. 392; further statement, 28 Mar. 1957, cols. 1355–6.

mid-April Phidias Doukaris, described as one of the ethnarchy's British delegates, met Fisher, asking his advice as to how best negotiations between the Government and Makarios might re-commence.[62] Perhaps because Fisher had become accustomed to being consulted in this way, he reacted angrily when at one point Makarios wrote directly to Macmillan without first consulting him. To the Cypriot prelate he wrote expressing his disappointment that he should only have heard of Makarios's letter through the press: 'Your Beatitude will readily understand that it is not easy for your friends here who have the well-being of Cyprus at heart to take useful steps to advance a settlement if they are kept in ignorance of your Beatitude's intentions and not asked for their advice on matters of importance.'[63] To Spyros Kyprianou, another ethnarchy delegate in Britain, Fisher complained that Makarios had been foolish to write directly to the British government when it would have been better to use a 'wise person of an impartial character privately going' between Makarios and British ministers.[64]

Fisher also remained in contact with the British ambassador to Greece, Sir Charles Peake, meeting him on 27 June 1957, when Peake told him that he had accepted an invitation from Lennox-Boyd to act as the latter's adviser on Cypriot affairs with a view to bringing about a change in attitude in the press. Peake told Fisher in confidence that his first step was to secure bi-partisan agreement to the proposition that the only way forward in Cyprus was to 'uphold the Consitution as the only ground on which free discussion can hopefully take place' and secondly to achieve a change of policy in Cyprus, for which it was necessary that Harding be removed as governor. Peake explained to Fisher: 'When such a change is made all the barriers and barbed wire fences should come down and every risk be squarely met. If a civilian Governor was thus assassinated, that is a fair price to pay, if it is the only way by which the situation can be redeemed.'[65]

By the end of the year Sir John Harding had as Fisher proposed been replaced. His successor, Sir Hugh Foot, made an immediately good impression at Lambeth, with Fisher noting that the new governor 'inspired immense confidence by the clarity and decisiveness of his plans and their essential rightness'; the archbishop believed too that the 'C. Office [sic] will not find him an easy man to push off his self-chosen path unless he agrees that he must abandon it'.[66]

The church's involvement in the political process declined at this point, probably because the pattern and degree of anglican interest reflected the centrality to developments of the Orthodox church and with Macmillan refusing to negotiate with Makarios preferring instead to liaise with the Greek and Turkish governments, the Cypriot churchman was increasingly sidelined, forced back upon the co-operation of the Greek government to speak for Greek Cypriots. At this stage it was Turkish-Cypriot terrorism which posed the greater challenge to British security, with many Turks now demanding the island's partition – a prospect in no small part evoked by Macmillan as a means of keeping Greek demands in check. In these circumstances in summer 1958 Macmillan unveiled a new plan, entailing the appointment of permanent Greek and Turkish representatives to Cyprus who would provide

---

[62] LPL, Fisher papers 186, fos. 177–81, Fisher's note of a meeting, 16 Apr. 1957.

[63] Ibid., fos. 188–9, Fisher to Makarios, 18 June 1957.

[64] Ibid., fo. 187, Fisher to Kyprianos, 17 June 1957.

[65] Ibid., fos. 190–1, 'Secret' record of conversation between Fisher and Peake, 27 June 1957.

[66] Ibid., fo. 192, record of Fisher's meeting with Foot, annotated by Fisher, 19 Nov. 1957.

the means for Greek and Turkish 'association' with Britain in its administration of the island. The Turkish government, facing problems elsewhere in the Middle East especially following the 1958 revolution in Iraq, entered into direct negotiations with the Greek government (since December 1956 led by Constantine Karamanlis), proposing independence for the island, as favoured by the Americans and also the NATO secretary general. With Makarios (for whom the Macmillan plan was an anathema providing as it did for a permanent Turkish presence on the island) on board, agreement was reached between Turkey and Greece at Zurich in February 1959 favouring an independent Greek–Turkish Cyprus under international guarantee; these proposals were then put to and ratified by Britain and the other parties at Lancaster House from 17 to 19 February 1959. After further protracted negotiations to resolve the question of the geographical size of bases Britain would be permitted to keep on the island (a question over which Fisher once more intervened to try and persuade Makarios to reach an arrangement),[67] the colony's transition to independence was achieved on 16 August 1960.

If the church was less involved in the negotiations from 1958 to 1960, the controversy surrounding the church's invitation to Makarios to attend the 1958 Lambeth Conference ensured that Cyprus remained a live issue between Fisher and Macmillan's government. The invitation infuriated some in the government and also prompted widespread public criticism. This response left Fisher justifiably cross: the invitation had first been mooted in discussions between Herbert Waddams and members of the foreign office a year previously and, as the result of an enquiry by Macmillan was to show, Whitehall officials had assured the church then and subsequently that the invitation was a purely 'ecclesiastical affair'. Feeling himself to be the victim of an injustice, Fisher wrote to the prime minister seeking to set the record straight. He was nevertheless sufficiently perturbed by the breach to church–state relations at home that he broke ranks with his advisers to declare that he would not have invited Makarios if he had known of the reaction it would cause among government ministers. Further evidence of Makarios's combustible approach to politics provided the reason (whether genuine or simply a convenient excuse is unclear) for Fisher to reconsider the invitation, and using intermediaries the church advised Makarios that it would be preferable to send a representative in his stead; a course of action with which Makarios concurred.[68]

II

As indicated earlier in this introduction, the documents selected for inclusion here represent only a tiny proportion of the hundreds of pages of material in Lambeth Palace Library, even for the comparatively short period of Makarios's deportation, and as previously stated the edited documents by no means capture all elements of the church's interest in Cyprus. One area of concern for the church both during and after this period which is not documented here relates to allegations of brutality levelled against the British police and security forces as well as Fisher's attempts

[67] LPL, CFR , File OC 114: Satterthwaite to W. K. Blackburn (new archdeacon in Cyprus), 21 Apr. 1960.
[68] See among other papers on this those in LPL, CFR, File OC 114.

to intercede on behalf of some of those handed down capital sentences for their activities with EOKA. Questions of morality and violence were also among those exercising George Bell. The bishop of Chichester's own involvement in Cyprus culminated a few months before his death in a visit to Greece in March 1958 at the suggestion of Queen Frederica, wife of King Paul I who had succeeded to the Greek throne in 1947.[69] During this visit Bell met secretly with Makarios at the instigation of the Greek king and queen.[70]

Notwithstanding the inevitable limitations, the documents included here, selected from the papers of Fisher, Bell and the CFR, enable a nuanced view of the church and Cyprus, illuminating the importance of personality, as well as relations between Fisher and his advisers. Taken together the documents expose the degree to which the church engaged with the political as well as the ecclesiastical affairs of Cyprus and acted as both critic and advocate of British government policy. It is important to remember that Cyprus constituted just one strand of many in Fisher's on-going discussions with the colonial office and others about different areas of the colonial empire.[71] The time Fisher devoted to the affairs of Cyprus needs therefore to be multiplied to arrive at a full picture of his engagement with the process of British decolonization: it follows also that the strains imposed by Cyprus on relations between church and state need to be viewed *in situ* alongside all the other areas of interaction over colonial affairs. That Fisher became so intensely engaged with constitutional and political questions might be said to be a consequence of the leader of the established church offering moral leadership to the British people as indeed he did in relations to questions of race and British policy in colonial Africa. Such an explanation holds some water. But the issues concerning Cyprus were more complicated than an interpretation of this kind fully permits. Popular outrage at terrorism on the island, especially among those associated with the British forces, was such that Fisher's continued communication with Makarios, his criticism of British policy and, above all, his 1958 invitation to Makarios, adversely affected Fisher's own reputation.

The 'Cyprus question' presented Fisher with a genuine dilemma. The church had, as it did in relation to other regions of the colonial empire, its own agenda, quite distinct from that of the British state: in this case it was that of ecumenicism and retaining good relations with the Orthodox churches, and although some, notably Bell, were more concerned with these than Fisher himself, Fisher was nonetheless committed to the ecumenical project both at home and internationally. Fisher was also genuinely exasperated by what he perceived as the mistakes of the British administration, while remaining deferential to the British government and concerned with British public opinion.

While Fisher displayed an unswerving, even arrogant, belief in his own proposals, it is hard to avoid the conclusion that his appreciation of developments in Cyprus was narrow – even naïve. Although Fisher was always careful to seek out corroborating evidence, he was fed information from Greek and orthodox churchmen, information which was then presented to him by Waddams, general secretary at the

---

[69] See LPL, Bell papers 92, fo. 308, Prince George to Bell, 21 June 1957. The suggestion was communicated via Frederica's brother, Prince George of Hanover (a descendant of Queen Victoria's eldest daughter and the German emperor, Frederick III).

[70] See LPL, Bell papers 297 (diaries), fos. 55–98 (notes of visit to Greece).

[71] See Stockwell, 'Splendidly leading the way'.

CFR since 1945, whose judgment appears sometimes questionable. Fisher, and more particularly Waddams, showed in some of the correspondence marked pro-Greek sympathies and in many ways distinct anti-Turkish bias. The Lambeth Cyprus documents show how others used the church to pursue their own interests: one might argue that this was because Greeks, accustomed to a very different relationship between church and state, attributed more influence to Fisher than was in fact the case; but the anglican church also offered a useful channel through which some of those otherwise marginalized by the political process could seek to advance their views.

Indeed the Church of England appears in these documents as an organization perhaps surprisingly permeable to external lobbying. For example, although cautious about their orthodox colleagues, various anglican churchmen offered an open door to orthodox churchmen and to their Greek advocates, some of whom obtained significant leverage with the church. Waddams relied heavily and one might say uncritically on his 'close friend' Alexander Pallis, described by Waddams as a 'former Balliol man' who was 'in charge of information for the Greek Government at Athens' and 'in touch with everyone of importance both here and in Athens';[72] his faith in Pallis was at times to provoke consternation at the foreign office, as Bell records in his diary (Document 26). It is hard to avoid the conclusion that in this period at least the CFR strayed beyond its brief that it should limit itself where possible to religious and theological questions.[73] Bell's own most regular correspondent on Cypriot affairs seems to have been Jerome Cotsonis (Ieronimus Kotsonis), chaplain to King Paul and secretary of the Greek organization for Cypriot union with Greece, with whom he had been very favourably impressed when the two first met at the WCC meeting at Evanston in America in 1954. Bell subsequently tried to engineer meetings between Cotsonis and Lennox-Boyd. If some British commentators were prone to complain that the Greeks and Cypriots assumed greater political influence over the anglican church than was the case, anglican churchmen were arguably guilty in turn of not taking sufficient account of the highly political nature of their orthodox colleagues.

The 'open door' did not stop with fellow churchmen. Instead, the Cyprus issue, like other colonial political questions, saw Fisher and some of his colleagues collaborate with a variety of interested Britons of different political persuasions (see, for example, Document 23). As will be apparent from the documents, the Greek-speaking Labour MP, Francis Noel-Baker, who had in early 1956 served as mediator between Governor Harding and Makarios, secured particular influence with Fisher. For Noel-Baker, Fisher not only appeared like-minded, but, as the MP's own initial influence waned, the anglican primate appears almost to have become a form of proxy through whom he could seek to put his own views to government (Documents 9, 14, 20, 27).

That Fisher apparently became so reliant for information on a variety of interested Greek and British individuals was also because he lacked access to the intelligence available to the British government (a problem acknowledged in Whitehall as reflected in the discussion as to what information should be disclosed to Fisher) as well as the government's strategic perspective. Perhaps in part because of this

---

[72] LPL, CFR, File OC 107: Waddams to Fisher, 25 Sept. 1956.
[73] See *Proceedings of the church assembly*, vol. 25, no. 1 (1945–6), p. 43, 6 Feb. 1945, answer given by bishop of Gloucester to question about the CFR.

Fisher continued to press the British government to bring Makarios back into nego-tiations from summer 1955, at a point at which British policy, increasingly under the direction of Macmillan, first as foreign secretary and from January 1957, as prime minister, was developing along quite different lines. While Fisher and his advisers blamed Governor Harding for what they saw as the British reliance on coercion rather than negotiation, we now know that Harding was more anxious to see political progress than was fully apparent to contemporaries.[74]

Moreover, the church found it difficult to know how to read Makarios. They were not alone in this. He had, as the anglican Archdeacon Adeney commented, 'very charming ways',[75] and an irritating tendency to belie his sometimes accommo-dating demeanour in private by speaking with greater inflexibility in public.[76] That Makarios was complicit in the terrorist campaign was revealed with the discovery of Grivas's diaries, but nonetheless it is only subsequently that the full extent – and limits – of Makarios's involvement has become clearer. A recent assessment concluded that Makarios, although not 'the man of blood' the British portrayed him as, was the 'political leader of EOKA'.[77]

As the foregoing discussion indicates, the documents that follow provide, then, a particular, sometimes oblique perspective on the Cyprus question in the mid-1950s, and therein lies much of their interest. Turkey looms less large than considerations to do with Greece and the Orthodox church; and although the colonial office is prominent in church dealings over Cyprus, the foreign office features very little.

There remains the question of the wider significance of these documents and of the history of the church's involvement with Cyprus in the 1950s. For historians of modern British imperialism they provide ample illustration of the complex domestic impacts of decolonization.

Perhaps more pertinent to readers of this volume is the issue of how the study presented here intersects with the wider history of British church and state. The Cyprus episode illustrates the approach of the 'schoolmaster' Archbishop Fisher to affairs of state; for their part the Cyprus case led some in Whitehall to question whether it was appropriate – 'improper and even unconstitutional'– for the church to intervene politically to the degree to which it was doing. If irritated Whitehall offi-cials understandably occasionally drew upon a language implicitly if not explicitly evocative of ideas of disestablishment, the question nonetheless remains of whether Fisher's involvement did indeed push the accepted boundaries of the role of the primate of the established church.

Throughout most of the nineteenth and twentieth centuries bishops in the Lords had exercised a self-denying order, confining their interventions within the House to issues either of direct relevance to the church or to moral and religious ques-tions and avoiding overtly political and especially party-political issues – although the question of what constituted 'political' was open to considerable ambiguity

---

[74] For an assessment of Harding's governorship, see Holland, *Britain and the revolt in Cyprus*, esp. pp. 211–12.

[75] LPL, Fisher papers 170, fos. 7–8: Adeney to Waddams, 6 Mar. 1956.

[76] Assos, 'Makarios', p. 236.

[77] *Ibid.*, pp. 95–6, 111. Makarios at the suggestion of a former Greek minister of military affairs, Georgios Stratos, recruited Grivas in May 1951 to fulfil the role of a military leader, although Assos argues that Makarios, hoping to achieve his goal by sabotage, always opposed full-scale guerrilla tactics. See also Stanley Mayes, *Makarios. A biography* (London and Basingstoke, 1981).

and latitude of definition. This approach had been maintained even in the face of the rapid growth in the early decades of the twentieth century of Christian social ideals among anglican churchmen notwithstanding intervention in the 1926 general strike.[78]

Fisher himself is generally regarded as less 'political' than his predecessor as archbishop, William Temple, although he did sometimes speak critically of government domestic as well as overseas policy (as his interventions over the introduction of premium bonds show).[79] Indeed Fisher had been appointed by Churchill to succeed Temple in preference to Bell precisely because he appeared the safer 'pair of hands', in part because of Bell's outspoken criticism of British wartime aerial bombing campaigns.[80] But it seems likely that Fisher, whose period as archbishop was distinguished by his reform of canon law and his administrative capability, was more inclined to engage with complex colonial political issues than others might have been. We might further speculate as to whether the problems caused by the post-war British retreat from empire had particular potential to pit church versus government – and not only when, as in the case of Cyprus, they had implications for the church's own standing overseas. As Conservative governments in the 1950s resorted to greater force to deal with anti-colonial nationalist movements for change, they flew in the face of international opinion while moving further and further from the rhetoric and ideal of a British imperial 'civilizing Christian mission'. British colonial and imperial policy hence raised precisely the questions of morality on which the church felt beholden to get involved, perhaps all the more so in view of the church's increasingly confident leadership from the 1930s over what Matthew Grimley identifies as a 'moral community' extending well beyond the ranks of anglican church-goers.[81]

Fifteen years on from the conflict discussed above, Cyprus again hit the news following the brutal Turkish invasion of the island on 20 July 1974. In Cyprus, Makarios had continued as both ecclesiastical and secular leader, although he was deposed in a coup five days before the invasion, but in Britain, Fisher had long retired. When orthodox ecclesiastics once again appealed for anglican intervention, Fisher's successor Michael Ramsay, on the eve of his own retirement, was said to be reluctant to 'make any personal intervention which could only be thought political'. Instead the church had 'at every stage' been in consultation with the Foreign and Commonwealth Office 'so that anything we did would not be out of step with the secular authority';[82] this may have been because Ramsay preferred to avoid becoming mired in the controversies that had bedevilled his predecessor, but more likely that Cyprus, now an independent country, no longer had the same potential for conflict between the anglican church and the British government and was also consequently no longer perceived as a region for which the anglican church needed

---

[78] See Edward Norman, *Church and society in England 1770–1970* (Oxford, 1976), esp. pp. 73–5, 188, 222, 400.

[79] David Hein, *Geoffrey Fisher. Archbishop of Canterbury 1945–1961* (Eugene, Ore., 2007), pp. 87–8. See also Carpenter, *Archbishop Fisher*; William Purcell, *Fisher of Lambeth: a portrait from life* (London, 1969).

[80] Carpenter, *Archbishop Fisher*, p. 130; Hein, *Geoffrey Fisher*, pp. 40–1.

[81] Matthew Grimley, *Citizenship. Community, and the Church of England. Liberal anglican theories of the state between the wars* (Oxford, 2004), see esp. chs. 5, 6 and conclusion.

[82] LPL, CFR, File OC 110: Michael Moore (canon for foreign relations) to the bishop of London, 12 Sept. 1974.

to offer particular moral leadership. But as these tentative reflections indicate, enormous scope remains to explore the as-yet under-researched recent history of the church and state.[83] As historians begin to see beyond secularizing narratives and write religion more fully into later twentieth-century British history, the potential of the extensive archival resources in Lambeth Palace Library to illuminate diverse aspects of recent modern history is considerable.

Editorial conventions

The spelling, punctuation and capitalization of the originals have been preserved. Abbreviations have also been retained, unless these are obscure, in which case they have been expanded in square brackets. Words which are underlined in the original manuscripts have been printed in italic type.

---

[83] For important recent contributions, see, as well as Grimley, *Citizenship*; S. J. D. Green, 'Survival and autonomy: on the strange fortunes and peculiar legacy of ecclesiastical establishment in the modern British state c. 1820 to the present day', in *The boundaries of the state in modern Britain*, ed. D. Green and R. Whiting (Cambridge, 1996), pp. 299–324; Keith Robbins, *England, Ireland, Scotland, Wales. The Christian church 1900–2006* (Oxford, 2008).

Documents[1]

1. CFR, File OC 106: 'Note. For the archbishop', 8 March 1956, by Rev. Herbert M. Waddams (general secretary, CFR)

The document which follows was written one day before the arrest and deportation of Makarios III, when rumours were rife in London and Cyprus that the British government intended to act against the Cypriot archbishop. There is no evidence that Fisher acted on the suggestion made below that he write to the prime minister. As well as working with Fisher in his capacity as general secretary at the CFR, Waddams had also spent eighteen months working in Lambeth Palace on second-ment from the Council.[2]

I think that you ought to consider in advance what attitude you will adopt in case of a worsening situation in Cyprus. It seems to me quite likely that, if the situation does get worse, as it well may, the British Government may arrest and/or deport Archbishop Makarios. Any such action is quite likely to throw a very great strain on Anglican/Orthodox relations generally. If Makarios were arrested I should expect a very strong and probably intemperate protest from the Archbishop of Athens[3] appealing to you to join him in protesting to the British Government. If you were to decline to do this, or attempt to justify the British Government's action, he might well announce the end of Anglican/Orthodox relations and refuse to permit the Church of Greece to take part in any talks with the Church of England and other Churches of the Anglican communion. The Oecumenical Patriarch would then find himself in a difficult position. Although he is likely to take a much more balanced view he might find it necessary to decline to have any further talks on the grounds that they were inopportune in the present conditions. Such a development would effectively torpedo any attempts for general Anglican/Orthodox conversations in 1957.

From a purely political point of view I think the arrest or deportation of Makarios would be very ill-advised. If he alone were taken it would leave a free field to the Bishop of Kyrenia who is far more extreme and uncontrolled in his anti-British statements.[4] If Makarios and Kyrenia were both arrested it could be made to look like an attack on the Church as such. The deportation of the majority of bishops after the 1931 riots is not a good precedent for following the same practice now. It

---

1 Biographical and some other details given in footnotes to the documents from: *The Oxford dictionary of the Christian church*, ed. F. L. Cross, 2nd edn, rev. F. L. Cross and E. A. Livingstone (London, 1974); *Oxford dictionary of national biography* (Oxford, 2004); *Crockford's clerical directory* (Oxford, pub. annually since 1858); and *Wikipedia*.

2 On Waddams see, Carpenter, *Archbishop Fisher*, p. 191.

3 Spyridon, archbishop of Athens and All Greece, 1949–56.

4 Kyprianos, bishop of Kyrenia, had initially sought to succeed Makarios II as archbishop but had been forced to withdraw his candidacy in view of the popularity of Makarios, then bishop of Kitium. Kyprianos, the leading figure within the 'Kyrenia Circle', remained a rival focus within the Cypriot Church, exploiting any sign that Makarios was willing to retreat from *enosis*. He was exiled with Makarios in 1956.

took a great many years representations from the Archbishop of Canterbury to H. M. Government before the Labour Government permitted the bishops to return.[5] Such action against the bishops would also be a ready-made propaganda weapon in the hands of the Russians who could contrast the excellent conditions of the Orthodox in Russia with the opporession [sic] suffered by the Orthodox at the hands of the British in Cyprus.

[In this connexion the general crisis in the Middle East may also affect anglican relations with the Christian minorities there. Ecclesiastical contacts will appear very much less acceptable in countries where British influence has ceased to have any noticeable affect on muslim governments.]

If the Cyprus situation develops badly I think you ought to be prepared if quite necessary to publish your letter to Makarios of June last year in which you appealed to him to oppose violence and hatred, together with his reply declining to do so.[6] This, of course would not help relations with Makarios but it might be necessary to do this in order to safeguard your reputation at home and to show that you have tried to help towards a better atmosphere.

I think you ought to approach the Government now, possibly by writing to the Prime Minister, to say that you hope he will not be provoked into arresting ecclesiastics and that the deportation or arrest of Makarios is likely to do nothing to better the situation and will simply add to the difficulties of the Government. If he is arrested and deported in spite of this and protests are received from Athens, as they surely will be, I suggest that delaying tactics be adopted as long as possible so as to avoid a direct clash with the Archbishop of Athens, if that can be done. I do not know how seriously Greek feelings were aroused over the 1931 affair, but I have the impression that they are more acute now.

H.M.W.

2. CFR, File OC 106: confidential memorandum for the archbishop, 13 March 1956, by Rev. Herbert M. Waddams

As Waddams advocates in this memorandum, Fisher did speak in the Lords debate on Cyprus on 15 March. He also wrote to Governor Sir John Harding and to Alan Lennox-Boyd later in the month: see Documents 5 and 6. For his part, Waddams telephoned William Clark at the foreign office and asked him whether the Government could say that the deportation was only 'temporary'. Waddams explained that this would make the situation easier for the church ('Confidential note for file' by Waddams, 14 March).

---

5   It is arguable how far Creech Jones's decision to allow the return of the bishops in 1946 was a result of anglican lobbying, and how far it was alternatively part and parcel of the new Labour government's bid to restore constitutional government in Cyprus.

6   Sent 3 June 1955. Fisher wrote: 'I am…worried that the absence of any clear statement from the Church authorities and particularly from you as their undisputed leader may cause persons to suppose that the Church is in fact supporting such outrages as have occurred. Would it not therefore make a signal contribution to better feeling and to the exorcism of the spirit of hatred and evil if your Beatitude were to give a lead to the people to look to you for spiritual leadership and guidance?' Makarios replied on 24 June 1955: 'I am sincerely afraid that an official condemnation of events by myself, would not find at the present stage the necessary response, but would involve the risk of exposing me rather unprofitably.' No copy of this correspondence survives in the Fisher papers, but it can be found in TNA, PREM 11/2268.

I had a long talk with James Virvos[7] last night who is, as a matter of fact, as pro-British as he is Greek and who, I believe, intends to take British nationality as soon as he retires and plans to spend the rest of his life here. He cannot do that while he is in charge of the Greek Cathedral. I say this because it is relevant to his views.

We discussed the Greek and Cyprus situation fairly thoroughly. He feels that it is of the greatest importance that something should be said by Your Grace to soften Greek and Orthodox opinion which is at present as bad as it can be.

There is some evidence, which of its nature cannot be conclusive, that a compromise was being planned in Athens for Makarios's visit, which he was prevented from paying by his deportation.[8] The fact is that the British Government removed him from the scene when the bargaining was still in progress from the Greek point of view, whatever may have been the impatience of Sir John Harding or Mr. Lennox-Boyd. Mostras, the Greek Ambassador, was practically in tears when he heard, tearing his hair and saying 'How can any reasonable man understand such action?'[9]

The situation in Greece is also difficult. Karamanlis has only a narrow majority and the Greeks are very fearful that if the united front of the Left do get in Communism would be back with a vengeance.[10] The Left is trying to organise demonstrations about Makarios so as to provoke such a riot as will bring the Government down. This also is something which ought to be borne in mind.

In spite of the irritations and failures of Makarios, my view is, and there is some evidence to support it, that he was a moderating influence and that the heat came from the Ethnarchic Council.[11] You will perhaps have observed that Bishop Kyprianos of Kyrenia made a speech condemning violence the day before, or two days before his deportation. This may have been the result of a letter from Virvos who knows him well, urging him to do this.

No evidence has yet been produced by the Government that Makarios or Kyprianos had any direct hand in the campaign of violence and terrorism even though their attitude may have been thought to encourage this. I am therefore exceedingly uneasy on general grounds to see the arbitary [sic] arrest of a British citizen and his deportation without trial; this is the negation of our principles and practice of justice. When this arbitary [sic] action has the effect of depriving a Church of its leaders on the grounds that the Government does not like their political opinions – which is what it appears to boil down to – it strikes me as very serious.

I therefore think that you ought to speak in the House of Lords debate on Thursday and suggest that you might take this sort of line:

Deportation, whether justified or not, is evidently a sign that the British Government has given up hope of reaching agreement with the leaders of the people of Cyprus. The Government's view that other people will come forward who can be regarded as representative is optimistic in the extreme, not to say unrealistic. But it is at least quite evident that the British Government has closed the door on this

---

7   Bishop James Virvos of the Greek orthodox cathedral of Saint Sophia of the Archdiocese of Thyateira and Great Britain, Bayswater, London.
8   Makarios was arrested at the airport from where he had planned to travel to Athens to continue discussions with the Greek government.
9   Vassilios Mostras, Greek ambassador to Britain.
10 Constantine Karamanlis, right wing prime minister of Greece from Oct. 1955 until June 1963. Greece had only recently emerged from civil war between the communists and the royalists.
11 As archbishop of Cyprus, Makarios was also ethnarch and head of the ethnarchy, a body to which he selected representatives and which served in an advisory rather than executive capacity.

particular series of negotiations. It would be fatal if this were regarded as the end of everything and the Church may properly speak to urge all those concerned to new efforts at reconciliation and at the solution of this particular problem.

The Government should be appealed to to take new steps which would result in the return of these Church leaders at the earliest possible moment. It is impossible to regard them, as is suggested in one of the official statements, simply as political leaders. The Church of Cyprus cannot function properly without their presence and the attempt to keep them in exile for a long time cannot be regarded as anything but a counsel of despair. Nobody in these days would wish to create a new benefit of clergy by which bishops were exempt from the ordinary laws, but deportation without trial of British citizens is not in the tradition of British justice and cannot be regarded as more than a crisis measure. Although Heads of Churches are not exempt from the law they cannot be removed without serious effects on Church life, and the Government must take such matters into consideration. 25 years ago a similar measure was taken by the British Government in exiling three of the bishops of the Island. If we look at the situation in 1956 this measure does not seem to have produced any change in the attitude of the Greek-speaking people of the Island, on the contrary they are more openly committed to *Enosis* than they were before. The previous banishment of the bishops meant that for fourteen years the British Government was made to appear as one which interfered with the proper freedom of religion by preventing access of bishops to their people.[12]

I think an appeal to the Government to re-open negotiations should be made and that Your Grace should offer to mediate in any way that appeared hopeful of results so as to break the present deplorable impasse.

      H.M.W.

3. Fisher papers 170, fos. 13–14: Archbishop Geoffrey Fisher to Dr Wim A. Visser't Hooft, general secretary of the World Council of Churches, Geneva, 16 March 1956 (copy)

This letter was written by Fisher in response to Visser't Hooft's 'Personal State-ment' about Makarios's deportation made on 13 March 1956. Visser't Hooft had begun this statement by noting that he was not yet in a position to 'give more than a personal expression of opinion, since it will take some time to consult with the officers of the World Council of Churches and the Executive Committee, and we have not yet heard from the churches in Britain or had the opportunity to study the full statement of the British Government's policy'. He went on to refer to the concern and shock expressed by orthodox and Christian opinion around the world. He also stated that the WCC had always emphasized the importance of self-determination, a commitment that had been expressed specifically in relation to Cyprus by the Churches' Commission on International Affairs in 1954.[13] Nonetheless Fisher had been angered by the statement as the letter reproduced below demonstrates. The BCC also wrote to Visser't Hooft expressing its dismay at his statement.[14] Fisher's letter seems to have crossed one sent to him by Visser't Hooft also on 16 March.

---

12 See above p. 589 and also document 1.

13 There is a copy of the statement at LPL, Fisher papers 170, fo. 10.

14 LPL, Fisher papers 170, fo. 16: Kenneth Slack, general secretary to the BCC, to Fisher, 16 Mar. 1956.

Here Visser't Hooft wrote in conciliatory tone in response to critical remarks Fisher had already made about his statement in his speech in the Lords, explaining that there were precedents for making a 'personal statement' and asserting that he had expressed feelings which as 'far as I can ascertain, are practically universal outside the British isles'. Visser't Hooft wrote a (further) friendly letter on 23 March 1956 in which he thanked Fisher for a message he had recently sent (possibly to smooth relations after the letter reproduced below), and in which Visser't Hooft commented that 'The raspberry is swallowed. The bath is taken.'[15]

Personal

My dear Visser't Hooft,

I write this letter in my personal capacity and with no connection with my office as Archbishop of Canterbury:

You might like to have a copy of the speech which I delivered in the House of Lords yesterday, and accordingly I enclose it. I should also report that when Lord Salisbury[16] was speaking and mentioned the Bishop of Chichester's reference to the World Council of Churches I got up and interjected the following statement: 'I am sorry that the Bishop quoted the secretary of the World Council of Churches, who (to my mind) exceeded all his rights in issuing that statement at all'.

As you will see I take very strong exception to the personal statement put out by you on 13th March. It is no good calling it a personal statement: it is bound to be a statement by the General Secretary of the World Council of Churches: as such I must regard it as a most improper statement to be made by the General Secretary. Like you I have received telegrams from Patriarchs and Archbishops, and I shall be writing to them to-day to explain my position (I enclose a copy of my letter to them). But it is really intolerable that I should be compelled also to justify my position to you as Secretary of the World Council of Churches.

I should make the following detailed comments on your statement:

Paragraph 1

If you said 'I am not yet in a position to express any opinion since …' that would have been entirely in order. There is no kind of reason why the world should expect an immediate pronouncement by the World Council of Churches any more than it can expect an immediate pronouncement by the United Nations Organisation. A single paragraph thus amended would have been entirely in order.

Paragraph 2

This paragraph falls into a statement of entire partiality. Having said that it is impossible to separate in the minds of the people the activities of the Archbishop as ecclesiastical and political leader, you go on to approve the resentment caused by the treatment of this *ecclesiastic* without any reference at all to the resentment caused by the activities of this *politician* which has had such serious consequences already.

Paragraph 3

You state that Christians of other member Churches of the World Council will have various desires, one of them being that justice should be done. The implication clearly is that at present injustice is being done which must be remedied. As you will

---

15 *Ibid.*, correspondence at fos. 17–18, 28.
16 Robert Gascoyne-Cecil, fifth marquess of Salisbury (1893–1972) leader of the House of Lords and lord president of the council from 1952, a strong imperialist who resigned from the cabinet over the release of Makarios in 1957.

see from my speech in the House of Lords it is perfectly clear that grave mistakes were made on both sides in a political sense, but so far as bare justice is concerned there is no doubt that Makarios' political activities had led to violence, terrorism and murder. It is certainly not for you to publish in connection with the World Council of Churches your decision that justice lies on one side and not on the other.

Paragraph 4

9 [*sic*]   You correctly judge that Christian opinion demands that the dispute in Cyprus should be settled by negotiation. I think you imply that the *sole* responsibility for breaking off negotiations rests with the British Government: if so, I disagree. You then refer to force and acts of violence 'on one side or the other' as though the force behind Makarios, which included murder and public disorder, was comparable in moral terms with the steps taken by the British Government to support law and order.

Paragraph 5

You refer to responsible public opinion in many countries. It is perfectly obvious that much responsible public opinion deplores the deportation. I do not know what steps you took to find out whether there was also responsible public opinion which approved of it. In any case it is very improper of the Secretary of the World Council of Churches to declare, with all the prestige of his office, upon the merits or demerits of British statesmanship without the full approval of the officers of the World Council of Churches or of the British member Churches.

You then put forward a condition which you call essential to the continuation of negotiations, saying that a great many Christians in many countries and churches would support you in this. In how many countries and in how many Churches have you tried to ascertain whether or no the general opinion regards the recall of the Archbishop (without apparently any regard to the demands of law and order in Cyprus) as an essential preliminary? I am always extremely chary of claiming to speak on behalf of the Church of England: while there are some in the Church of England who would agree with you on this point, there are a great many others who would disagree with you in such an unqualified statement. But if I find it difficult to assess the general opinion in the Church of England, how can you, with such confidence, assess the opinion of all the Churches in the World Council of Churches at such short notice and, I suspect, without any enquiry? Certainly you made no enquiry at all of what the general opinion was in England, since if you had wished to do that you would hardly have failed to consult me.

Yours sincerely

4. Fisher papers 170, fo. 15: Rev. A. W. Adeney (anglican archdeacon in Cyprus) to archbishop Geoffrey Fisher, 16 March 1956

16/3/56 (subsequent to letter to Waddams)[17]

Your Grace,

I have today heard for the first time the summary of your statement in the House of Lords on Cyprus. (We have been without papers for 4 days, English or local).

---

[17] Probably that of 6 Mar. 1956, copy at LPL, Fisher papers 170, fos. 7–8.

As you know the negotiations took place in this house.[18]

I believe the Archbishop was trying to get out of a situation wh. [*sic*] he had himself created by inviting terrorists to this island. The link between his ecclesiastical status, Enosis and terrorism is very difficult to disentangle. e.g. several political discourses in church which ended (in the middle of the Mass) with Eoka leaflets showered from the galleries. These leaflets were very likely printed on his own Press. And as you know bombs were actually found being manufactured in his garden.

I have not access to intelligence reports, but I believe the link to be closer than I knew at the time of the talks.

Our feeling here is that the Greek Govt. is the nigger in the woodpile. We have no certainty that terrorism wd [*sic*] not continue after the constitution began to be worked [?]. Enosis must bring a violent Turkish reaction.

For these reasons I cannot feel that your statement just now presents a possible solution. But I have been reflecting [?] to the deputy governor that we cannot for long keep the Abp confined & the question of how we are to release him must be envisaged & when.

When other Bishops returned (in 1945)[19] after promise to refrain from activities (political etc [?]) the promise was not kept: nor can I see how Apb Makarios would agree on his return to condemn violence. He is too heavily compromised & has refused to do so on many occasions. We can now see why. Unfortunately the man with the gun can command silence, or cause cessation of [word illegible]; the way to his suppression will not be short or easy.

We are in good heart here & the efficiency of the terrorists is exaggerated. But the local people fear them. They all fear a sudden amnesty.

With respect, your grace,

Yours faithfully

    A.W. Adeney

5. Fisher papers 170, fos. 22–3: Archbishop Geoffrey Fisher to Field Marshal Sir John Harding, governor of Cyprus, 19 March 1956 (copy)

I see from the papers that at a press conference you were asked about my speech in the House of Lords. I judge from your comment that you had not seen the whole speech and did not know the context in which I referred to resuming negotiations with Makarios. Accordingly I venture to send you a copy of the speech.

You will understand that I was trying to speak not only to British people but to the Orthodox Churches and many Christians in other parts of the world who have been put into a state of vehement indignation by Makarios' deportation. As I said,

---

18 Adeney had at the governor's request loaned his house as a venue for the governor's talks with Makarios on two occasions in January 1956. Adeney wrote elsewhere that 'My part was limited to welcoming both parties and keeping my family clear!. The Archbishop seemed quite glad to come here and the Governor expressed his gratitude. The meetings consisted of long discussions over a document. The Greek press seemed to welcome the meeting being held at the archeaconry, but I of course have also to think of relations with the Turkish community and am myself unwilling to commit myself on the merits of Enosis': LPL, CFR, File OC 106, note (by Adeney) 'Meetings of Archbishop Makarios and Governor in Archdeacon's House', Jan. 1956.

19 See above p. 589.

my only purpose is to seek reconciliation – that is my duty, just as the restoration of law and order in Cyprus is your duty.

A peer said to me after my speech that I had taken my stand firmly on both sides – that of course was my intention. You cannot begin to reconcile people unless you stand in with both of them enough to gain their confidence. I did not spare Makarios nor did I acquit the British Government.

As always when people are quarrelling the only hopeful thing is to get them to lay all their quarrels aside and concentrate on the practical thing to be done. My suggestions were directed to help everybody to forget their passions and look to the future.

My suggestion about restoring Makarios and negotiating with him was point no: 3. The first and most important point was point no: 1.[20] I still think there is something in it and it has gained a remarkable range of support from some newspapers and some very responsible people.

If the Government appointed an independent person now to draft a constitution along the lines contained in your correspondence with Makarios seeking such advice and help as he wanted,[21] it would I believe assist everyone to lay their passions and resentments aside. It would take him some months but the general principles are sufficiently clear and since he would not be representing either party he could use his best judgment for submission later on to the interested parties.

Any question of letting Makarios return or of negotiating with him would arise only if this draft constitution was in being. And then provided that Makarios renounced all forms of terrorism, negotiations would begin again from the basis of the draft. As I said in the Lords, I am perfectly certain Makarios would find it far more difficult to make trouble when discussing a draft – in the recent negotiations he was free to make bogies and raise demands at his own will.

I do not doubt your statement that Makarios' ambition is to be the sole arbiter in Cyprus. For my own part I do not wish to question too much the rightness or wrongness of his deportation. I have had plenty of evidence of my own of his complicity with terrorism: the fact remains that to the Greek Orthodox and to many Christians in many parts of the world he will appear as a martyr to British Colonialism just as Stepinac in Jugo Slavia (who was a very bad man in many ways) was proclaimed by the Roman Catholic Church as a martyr to Tito.[22] We gain nothing by saying that Makarios shall not return ever or within the foreseeable future: to bring him back to discuss a constitution already in draft which would make it perfectly clear that he could not be the only arbiter of Cyprus would be a great gain.

May I say finally how deeply I sympathize with you in your hateful task and how much I admire the way in which you have tackled it all through. You will understand that my task is a different one; the particular suggestions I have made may be right or wrong, but they have helped a great number of people who found from the Government no evidence that they had anything in mind except to wait

---

[20] The appointment of a constitutional adviser: see *House of Lords debates*, 1955–6, vol. 196, 15 Mar. 1956, cols. 472–3.

[21] Published as Cmnd 9708, *Correspondence exchanged between the governor and Archbishop Makarios* (1956).

[22] Catholic archbishop of Zagreb since 1937 who in 1946 was arrested by the Yugoslav government on charges of Nazi collaboration, forced conversion to catholicism of Serbs, and treason against the Yugoslav government. He subsequently served five years in gaol.

for some new leaders to turn up in Cyprus with enough courage to start negotiating with us again.

Yours sincerely

G.C.

6. Fisher papers 170, fos. 39–40: Archbishop Geoffrey Fisher to Sir Alan Lennox-Boyd, secretary of state for the colonies, 29 March 1956 (copy)

*The letter below was sent in response to a letter dated 28 March from Lennox-Boyd
in which the latter thanked Fisher for sending him a copy of his letter to Harding
and referring to Fisher's speech in the Lords. Lennox-Boyd sent a brief reply to the
letter below explaining that he was about to leave for a week's holiday but would
arrange a meeting with Fisher on his return.[23]*

29th March 1956

My dear Lennox-Boyd,

Thank you for your letter of the 28th March referring to Cyprus, and my speech
in the House of Lords. Perhaps I might say a word further even though what I
suggest may be regarded as impossible.

At the moment the parties to the dispute are the British Government and Archbishop Makarios speaking for the Church and people in Cyprus. The world in
general and the Orthodox Church in particular are inclined to think that of the two
the British Government is more to blame for the breakdown of negotiations. They
may be wrong but that is widely held.

You say that real progress in drafting a constitution would not be possible until
discussion on the spot has shown what would be acceptable to the Greek Cypriots
and Turk Cypriots in terms of concrete details. I wonder if you are there on the right
lines? The Greek Cypriots from their side of the quarrel would be inclined to say
we will not discuss until Makarios is back to speak for us. We are thus still in the
same dilemma. Which side has got to climb down first?

What I suggested was that the British Government should appoint a man of independent position and mind to draft a constitution in the light of the correspondence
between the Governor and Makarios: in doing so he could make what enquiries
he liked but the draft would be his own responsibility and nobody else's. Neither
side would be climbing down while this independent person drew up a draft which
seemed to him to best meet the circumstances, and I added that a time table should
be attached – that is to say that the draft would include some kind of directions as to
when control of internal security should pass to the Cypriot Government and so on.

The immense advantages of this step are (a) that is tells everybody that something is being done (b) what is being done does not require either side to the dispute
to climb down (c) it provides a new starting point of discussion to which both sides
– the British Government and the Cypriots – can come uncommitted to look at the
thing on its merits.

When the independent person has thus got a draft various pre-conditions become
possible as a step to starting negotiations upon it. The British Government can quite
rightly require from Makarios an undertaking to condemn and oppose any violence
and terrorism. If Makarios refuses he puts himself out of court. Makarios can quite

---

23 LPL, Fisher papers, fos. 37–8: Lennox-Boyd to Fisher, 4 Apr. 1956; fo. 53 Lennox-Boyd to Fisher.

rightly ask that he should be allowed to return to Cyrpus for the negotiations – if the British Government refuses it puts itself out of court. In fact both sides ought to be ready to do what was required in order to enable negotiations to proceed on the draft.

And the draft being there, it is far easier for them to deal with concrete points of detail with the general presupposition that everybody will try to agree and not to disagree. Any disagreement which cannot be got over would then be known to the world for what it is: not a disagreement about suspicions but a disagreement about a particular proposal put forward by an independent adviser.

As I say this may not be possible; it may be unusual though after all if [*sic*] has some kinship with what Sir Keith Hancock did in Uganda.[24] But you are not afraid of the unusual as Malta shows.[25] If the whole of my proposal fails then everything else has got to wait till the British Government itself enters into negotiations with Cypriots (presumably Cypriots less Makarios) to discover in what terms acceptable to everybody the British Government should be willing to draft a constitution. That does nothing to resolve the dilemma. My suggestion, I still believe, does do a great deal to resolve it.

I am down in Canterbury until April 10ᵗʰ or thereabouts. If after that a talk would be useful I would welcome it but I have really tried to put on paper for what it is worth what was in my mind.

Yours sincerely

G.C.

7. Fisher papers 170, fos. 50–1: Archbishop Geoffrey Fisher to Sir Alan Lennox-Boyd, 4 April 1956 (copy)

4th April 1956

My dear Lennox-Boyd,

Forgive my writing about Cyprus. But every day that passes only worsens the position and the possibilities. As I am sure you realise the important thing now is not really what may happen in Cyprus but what is happening in the hearts of Greek Orthodox and Greeks all over the world and in the hearts of friendly and hostile critics of the exile of Makarios. In their eyes we have done a bad thing. We cannot convince them that we have done a good thing, by merely saying so. Nothing will enable a reasonable judgement and a friendly attitude to return except a clear indication that the British Government is trying at the earliest possible moment to heal by some constructive act.

One of my correspondents is Archbishop Michael, Head of the Greek Orthodox Church in the U.S.A.,[26] a person of very great power and of very strong and even violent opinions as we have learned to know in the World Council of Churches. He sent me a violent telegram when Makarios was deported. I replied and now

---

[24] Historian Sir Keith Hancock led an independent constitutional commission to Uganda in 1954.

[25] A referendum had been held on the British island of Malta in February 1956 in which a large majority voted for the island's political integration with Britain (with the islanders retaining their own assembly but with Maltese MPs attending the British parliament). Although the British government agreed to experiment with constitutional arrangements of this kind, the Maltese subsequently rejected the proposals.

[26] Of the Greek archdiocese of North and South America; and a president of the WCC.

have had a letter back from him. I venture to enclose a copy of it.[27] It strikes me as a triumph of the Spirit of Christ that such a man as he is should in this reply be obviously trying to restrain himself and not to worsen the situation. But you see the strain upon him. Nothing but *some* speedy sign of a desire to heal by the Government will touch him.

So I come back to my last letter. I still believe that my suggestion is the best. The Government cannot yet announce that it will reopen negotiations because there is no one to negotiate with; at present it can do almost *nothing* which will not be misunderstood.

What can it do *now* – and speed is really essential – which can begin to restore confidence? I suggest it appoints a really competent man with no other terms of reference than the correspondence between the Governor and Makarios with a roving commission to draft what seems to him the best constitution he can contrive so that the draft when finished can become a basis of fresh negotiation.

Have you any better suggestion? The only alternative that would help would be that suggested by Archbishop Michael, to bring Makarios to Switzerland and negotiate with him there. Would you like that suggestion any better than mine? The one fatal thing is to leave this wound to fester and go gangrenous. You cannot yourself provide the dressing and the bandage, for in the eyes of the Orthodox and others you inflicted the wound: and it is not an answer to them to say that you had to. But you could openly before the world commission someone else, as I suggest, to prepare the dressing and the bandage. Is not that sense? I write out of a great desire to help you and the whole Christian world out of this perplexity.

Yours sincerely
    G.C.
Dictated, but not signed personally owing to absence.

8. Fisher papers 170, fos. 62–3: Archbishop Geoffrey Fisher to Sir Alan Lennox-Boyd, 19 April 1956 (copy)

In response to the letter below, Lennox-Boyd rang Fisher on 23 April, explaining that since his return from holiday he had not yet had the time to reply properly to Fisher's letter, and reiterating the government's position that until the restoration of law and order there could be no negotiation.[28]

My dear Lennox-Boyd,
    The British Council of Churches meets on Tuesday of next week, and the subject of Cyprus is bound to come up. As you realise the Prime Minister's statement in the House of Commons helps not at all.[29] By my speech in the House of Lords I was able to build a bridge of continuing sympathy not only with the Greek Orthodox Church in Greece and in the United States, but with Christian opinion in all parts

---

27 Dated 27 Mar. 1956. Original at Fisher papers 170, fos. 33–4.
28 LPL, Fisher papers 170, fos. 72–3, see note of conversation and also the interim reply Lennox-Boyd sent shortly after receipt of Fisher's letter.
29 That there could be no negotiation until the restoration of law and order in Cyprus: *House of Commons debates*, 1955–6, vol. 551, 17 Apr. 1956, cols. 846–8.

of the world. By the skin of my teeth I even managed to keep Bishop Dibelius[30] in a state of suspending judgement although he is engaged in bitter conflict with the East German Government and his natural sympathies would be all against you.

I wonder whether you realise what has been done by Christian people to save the Government from unrestrained indignation and denunciation by a vast number of non-political [*sic*] minded people. The only reason why I was able to help them was because I turned their thoughts from judgement on the past to the hope of some constructive step soon to be taken: and I made a suggestion which even the secular press in England very largely welcomed.

My speech was made five weeks ago to-day. All through this time we have been saying to your critics: 'Keep quiet, the Government must be mediating some constructive step'. Then came the question on Tuesday in the House of Commons:[31] all the Prime Minister can say is that the there is no question of negotiation in Cyprus until Law and Order is restored. The Prime Minister says this is a definite and clear position on which to rest. In fact, of course, it merely puts the whole initiative into the hands of the terrorists. Everything is immobilised until Law and Order is restored.

This question has been a long battle for the retention by the British Government of the moral initiative. They lost it long ago when they said to Cyprus 'never'. Slowly in the course of negotiations they recovered the moral initiative. The deportation brought everything to an end and left a blank. I gave an invitation to the Government to resume the moral initiative, and for five weeks they have made no move, and the Prime Minister says that they do not intend to do make any move in this moral field.

As I say, this is bound to come up at the British Council of Churches. I so admire your devotion and eagerness and right thinking in all this field of colonial relations that it will distress me terribly to have to say that the Government had thrown away its chance of resuming the moral initiative: but is there anything else I can say?[32]

My suggestion may have been unworkable, though nobody has told me why. It seems to me better than Listowel's[33] suggestion of a Parliamentary Committee.[34]

---

[30] Otto Dibelius, bishop of the Lutheran church in Berlin, and from 1954 a president of the WCC.

[31] The prime minister spoke in response to a question by Aneurin Bevan.

[32] In the event Fisher did criticize the government in his BCC speech, expressing a 'little indignation' 'quite simply against our own Government for apparently and as far as we are allowed to know, doing nothing constructive at all': see press reports: *Times*, 25 Apr. 1955.

[33] The Labour peer was a former secretary of state for India and also minister of state at the colonial office.

[34] Lord Listowel had written to Fisher on 2 Apr. enclosing a statement prepared by members of the all-party committee formed to promote conciliation in Cyprus and expressing his hope that Fisher would support their policy. Members included the MPs Aneurin Bevan, Jo Grimond and Tony Benn. The statement proposed the formation of a parliamentary commission to be sent to Cyprus to assist in the re-opening of negotiations and to make recommendations for the progressive repeal of the emergency legislation. Fisher replied to the effect that he believed the Statement's insistence on immediate self-determination (as opposed to the acceptance of its desirability in practice) unwise and unrealistic in view of the British government's position (Fisher added here that 'In my view "self-determination" is not an absolute right, but is always limited by the duty regarding the rights and the needs of others') and added that he believed negotiations with Makarios as well as Makarios's release should only occur once the archbishop had disowned violence. Listowel responded that they felt unable to agree with Fisher on these points. LPL Fisher papers 170, fo. 46, Listowel to Fisher, 2 Apr. 1956 (enclosed draft statement at fos. 48–9); fos. 56–7, Fisher to Listowel, 5 Apr. 1956; fo. 60, Listowel to Fisher, 18 Apr. 1956.

Anyhow surely the Government cannot be content to be barren of ideas for five weeks, apart from the attempt to prevent terrorism which is a purely negative and unconstructive operation.

Yours sincerely,

9. Fisher papers 170, fos. 96–8: memorandum on meeting between Archbishop Geoffrey Fisher and Francis Noel-Baker MP, 26 April 1956

I saw Noel-Baker yesterday: he talked very fully for half an hour without stopping. I note such things as I can recall:

1. My first speech made a good impression amongst the Greek Orthodox.
2. The feeling in Cyprus is still astonishingly good both among ordinary Cypriots and among our soldiers. A government initiative, therefore, would still have fruitful soil.
3. They all respect Harding deeply as a man.
4. Harding thinks it will take at least six months to end terrorism. On the Prime Minister's statement that would mean no negotiation for six months.
5. All the moderates are completely pro-Makarios. There will be nobody else to negotiate with. No Cypriot will come forward or dream of trying to take the place of Makarios. Noel-Baker himself got to know Makarios extremely intimately and is convinced that whatever knowledge he had of the terrorist he was himself seeking agreement and was really anxious to reach it. Noel-Baker agreed that perhaps he had been a bit cowardly in resisting the terrorists, and there is, of course, the possibility that they sometimes make him stand when he wanted to give in on a point.
6. A political move from our side must be taken.
7. Part of the tragedy was that Harding was given no competent political adviser and had no liaison officer with the Archbishop. Thus he was pitch forked into this situation completely unequipped. There is a liaison man now, Reddaway,[35] who is no more than a former officer of humble origins who is being consulted: he has no real qualifications: he is married to a poor kind of Cypriot woman which Cypriots do not like, and he has really not got his heart in reconciliation.
9. Makarios by being exiled is in a very strong position and if in the end he forbade terrorism would have great moral power behind him provided that it cannot be said that he is doing this to buy his freedom from us.
10. The Greek Prime Minister and others are sick of Cyprus and want to get it settled, and Noel-Baker told me that in fact it was paralyzing any restoration of stability in Greece itself.
11. Noel-Baker tells me that the decision to deport Makarious was not made by Lennox-Boyd, but imposed by a cablegram from Anthony Eden who has all along retained control of this matter. He thinks that Lennox-Boyd might have been wiser if not controlled by Eden.
12. Noel-Baker's plan is that the Government should produce a draft constitution: discuss it privately with the Greek Prime Minister and with the Turks, and then

---

[35] John Reddaway was an official in the British administration who had married a local woman and achieved influence as a Greek-speaker: see Holland, *Britain and the revolt in Cyprus*, pp. 99, 111, 221–3. Noel-Baker was not disinterested himself on this front, having previously acted as mediator, including in February at Makarios's request: *ibid.*, p. 111. For Noel-Baker, see p. 603.

publish it with the simultaneous appeal from the British and Greek Governments and from Makarios for the cessation of terrorism. But this would mean at some stage negotiation with Makarios who ought to be brought nearer than the Seychelles and even to this country. There should also be discussion with some Cypriots. All parties are really now agreed that the issue of self-determination must be postponed. The question now is the establishment of self-government on a proper basis.

13.   I stated my reason for thinking that it would be wiser for the Government to appoint a commissioner to draft a constitution. He would have a certain degree of independence: he could consult with anybody he liked including indeed Makarios; if he wanted he to he might never have to move out of England. What he produced would then be for discussion, but since it would be produced by him and not by the Government friendly discussion might thereby be helped. I agreed that Makarios must be brought nearer, and perhaps here. We agreed that Noel-Baker would go on trying to see the Prime Minister and urging the matter from his point of view: I would do my best with Lennox-Boyd, and might even try to involve R.A. Butler.[36]
      sG.C.

10. Fisher papers 170, fos. 84–95, Governor Sir John Harding to Archbishop Geoffrey Fisher, 26 April 1956

Harding's reply to Fisher's letter of 19 March 1956 was only sent after the Governor had consulted the colonial office and the colonial office in turn conferred with the foreign office over the propriety of informing Fisher about diplomatic correspondence between Britain, the US and Greece.[37] As a result of the consultation with the colonial office, Harding's original draft to Fisher was changed (to remove a comment that went further than current UK policy in 'rejecting for all time an possibility' of renewed negotiations with Makarios).[38] In the letter below the governor also gave the archbishop confidential evidence of Makarios's complicity in terrorist activity and this information does seem to have influenced Fisher.[39] The archbishop replied to Harding, but, although the governor then drafted a full response to this further letter, the colonial office, worried lest in his response the governor was revealing too much confidential information (that HMG was considering 'conciliation' by means of an approach to both the Turkish and Greek governments that it was not appropriate to reveal 'even to the Archbishop of Canterbury'), eventually advised against sending it, preferring instead to see the correspondence brought to an end.[40] In the letter below Harding narrates circumstances leading to the collapse of his five-month talks with Makarios.

My dear Archbishop,

I have now heard from Alan Lennox-Boyd and, with his agreement, am sending you the considered and comprehensive reply to your letter of the 19th March, which

---

[36] Conservative politician who was at this point lord privy seal and leader of the House of Commons.

[37] TNA, CO 926/194, no. 1, Harding to Lennox-Boyd, 19 Mar. 1956; no. 15, J. A. Thomson (FO) to D. M. Smith (CO), 12 Apr. 1956.

[38] *Ibid.*, no. 20: Lennox-Boyd to Harding, 24 Apr. 1956

[39] With CO permission: *ibid.*, no. 1: Harding to Lennox-Boyd, 19 Mar. 1956. Lennox-Boyd replied that although Fisher's representatives had not been shown security reports from Cyprus he believed nonetheless that the archbishop was aware of Makarios's character.

[40] TNA, CO 926/194, minute on draft Harding to Fisher at no. 38 by D. Smith, 18 May 1956.

I promised in my note of the 27th March. I am sorry not to have been able to write before.

It was good of you to take the trouble to write to me about your suggestion that negotiations should be resumed with Archbishop Makarios once order had been restored and a constitution drafted. I am sorry if anything I am reported as having said at my press conference gave the impression that I had taken this suggestion out of its context. It was clear to me from the summary of your speech that the third suggestion was dependent on the fulfilment of the two preceding suggestions. But here in Cyprus it is naturally the return of Makarios and the reopening of negotiations with him which have been seized upon.

My attitude to the political problems of Cyprus is based on the firm conviction that in the present international context the full use of the whole of the Island for military purposes is indispensable to the fulfilment of British policy and the maintenance of British influence in the Middle East as a whole. I believe, moreover, that in the present world situation the maintenance of British influence in the Middle East is indispensable to the security and stability of the whole Free World. Therefore, I could never have accepted an agreement which made Enosis at an early date inevitable.

As regards my dealings with Archbishop Makarios the problem of forming a judgment on another man's motives lies at the heart of the matter. Mine has been formed gradually over a period of five months and I will try to give you some idea of the process by which I reached my final conclusion.

I have now read and re-read your speech, and would like to say at once that I fully appreciate and greatly admire the high and responsible motives that impelled you to speak as you did. Also, if I may be permitted to say so, I find your speech wise and constructive, and there is much in it with which I wholeheartedly agree. If I am unable to go the whole way with you in your conclusions, it is not because I question your main thesis regarding the need for reconciliation. It is because I do not believe reconciliation is to be found in the resumption of negotiations with Makarios.

When I came here last October there were many who assured me that he was essentially a moderate man and at heart well disposed towards some reasonable accommodation between Greek-Cypriot aspirations and British interests in Cyprus. According to their advice all we had to do was to accept the principle of self-determination as applicable to Cyprus and we would then find him willing to co-operate in the restoration of peace and order and in the development of constitutional government.

There were others who said that I would be wasting my time in negotiating with him because he was the arch-Enosist. There was already a certain amount of information about his connections with the terrorists which seemed to support such views.

There were still others who held the view that whatever his private sentiments might be, he was indistinguishable from the extremists in practice because he was unable or unwilling to stand up to them in matters of importance.

However, I decided to see what could be done by negotiation. Having committed myself to that course I treated him as one who was sincerely anxious to reach a reasonable settlement. Throughout our discussions I persisted in so regarding him in spite of the accumulating evidence of his identification with the violence and intransigence of the extremists. I was determined to pursue the path of negotiation to the absolute limit of conciliation and concession.

In deciding to pursue this course I assumed a heavy responsibility. Had I then foreseen that the negotiations were going to drag on for five critical months, I might have decided differently. During this time the urgent task of restoring law and order had to take second place to political considerations. The security forces have had at times to be told to hold their hand in order not to prejudice political developments, such as the consultations with the Greek Government, the results of the Greek elections and, above all, the course of the negotiations with Makarios himself. During that time forty-two lives have been lost and one hundred and fifty-seven persons have been wounded. During that time, too, the terrorists, by the most brutal intimidation and the most cynical exploitation of nationalist emotions have strengthened their hold on the Greek Cypriot public, and have had considerable success in deadening the public conscience to the brutality and wickedness of their methods, and in passing themselves off as a national liberation movement.

It is possible that, if on my arrival I had decided to give over-riding priority to all the rigorous and unpleasant measures heeded to restore law and order, the terrorists would never have established to the same degree their hold on the Greek Cypriot public. It is certain that, had I done so, we should by now be definitely nearer to the end to terrorism and lawlessness. There are some who say I was wrong to attempt negotiation. For myself, I am convinced it was the right thing to do. And if a genuine settlement could have been reached, peace and order would have been restored more quickly and with less hardship and bitterness.

During my first series of meetings with Makarios,[41] he produced his own three-point plan. This was to the effect that H.M.G. should first recognise the principle of self-determination as applicable to Cyprus, that he would then co-operate in framing and bringing into operation a constitution, and that when it was working H.M.G. should undertake to discuss the political future of the Island with the elected representatives of the people. This seemed to me a more constructive approach than might have been expected, and I took up with Ministers the possibility of producing proposals which would meet Makarios' views while safeguarding our own position. The whole purpose was to establish a basis on which he could agree to co-operate in the development of constitutional government and to advise his fellow-countrymen to do the same. A formula was devised and shown to both the Greek and Turkish Governments. This formula was the first version of that which later appeared in the White Paper;[42] it was subsequently amended four times in the effort to satisfy Makarios. The first reaction of the Greek Foreign Minister was that it would be an act of bad faith not to accept it. The Greek Prime Minister described it as 'very constructive'. King Paul found it 'constructive and helpful' and asked his government to convey that opinion to Makarios. The U.S. Government said that they regarded our move as 'very constructive'. The Turks were apprehensive, but did not press their objections. I should be grateful if you would treat this information about the foreign reactions to our formula as personal and confidential to yourself since it has not so far been made public.

I again took the initiative in inviting Makarios to resume our discussions and I presented the formula to him on the 21st November.[43] He rejected it out of hand,

---

[41] In Oct. 1955.

[42] See above p. 591.

[43] Harding persuaded Eden's government to concede the principle of self-determination, although it stated that present circumstances did not allow for its immediate application.

and we began examining what more we could do to meet him. On the 7th December Makarios made a public statement to the Ethnarchy Council in which he said that he was not interested in anything but 'the easy and quick exercise of self-determination'. Nevertheless, we continued our endeavours to put forward proposals acceptable to him. Again consultations with the Greek and Turkish Governments were necessary.

Early in January I once more took the initiative in resuming the discussions, in which I put revised proposals to him. He raised further objections which I reported back to London. Towards the end of January I went home to discuss these points with Ministers, and I was authorised to present our proposals to him in the manner indicated in the first of my letters in the White Paper. The final stages of the negotiations are recorded in the subsequent correspondence.

As I read the record of the debates in Hansard, it seems to me that there has been some doubt and confusion about why the talks broke down. To me the answer is simple. They failed because Makarios was determined to secure Enosis quickly and without compromise – and that we could not accept. The demands he produced in the last stages of the negotiations settled for me the perplexing problem with which I had been confronted on my arrival here, the problem of what his real motives were.

There are, of course, several different roads by which a Cypriot leader determined to achieve Enosis might pursue his aim. Since his election as Archbishop, Makarios seems to me to have explored four. He has tried local defiance, non-co-operation and intransigence under the slogan 'Enosis and only Enosis' which he inherited from his predecessor. That produced a mere deadlock. He has tried the international approach, seeking through the Greek Government and the United Nations Organisation to bring such external pressure to bear upon H.M.G. as to force them to yield Enosis. When that failed to produce results, he countenanced a resort to violence. While violence still continued and had, let us admit, had some effect in causing the British authorities to take Enosis claims more seriously than before, he entered into the discussions with me and apparently decided that the constitutional road to Enosis was worth exploring.

At the end of our long-drawn-out negotiations he left me in no doubt that his purpose was to secure conditions which would have made him master of the Island, a position he could then exploit to make Enosis a virtual certainty in a short space of time. The demand for an amnesty was designed to leave the terrorist organisation intact, its cadres in being and its weapons in readiness for the next round. The control of public security was to be transferred to a Cypriot Minister 'as soon as law and order had been restored' – a state of affairs which, as I had emphatically pointed out to him, might be entirely superficial. The whole control of internal public affairs, including the means of influencing public opinion, was to be handed over to a legislature in which the elected Greek majority could in present circumstances only be nominees of the Archbishop or EOKA or of both .jointly. All this was to occur quickly while the terrorist stranglehold on public expression was still absolute and before the decent, law-abiding, moderate elements had recovered the power to think and speak for themselves.

Please do not think I am criticising him for being devoted to the cause of Enosis. That is his right, though I deplore the methods he has seen fit to use. But the point I wish to make is the futility of my negotiating further with him once it has been established – to my mind beyond all doubt – that his aims are irreconcilable with those of H.M.G.

It has been represented here and in London that our offer of self-government was a sham unless it included Cypriot control of the police and other aspects of public security. What a travesty that is. We had offered to elected Cypriot Ministers control of finance and the revenue-earning departments, of all legal and judicial affairs other than those relating to public security, of agriculture, forestry and water resources, of medical and welfare services, of education (surely an overwhelming proof of our sincerity after the shameful way in which the schools have been used against us), of public works, roads, harbours and communications. But without Cypriot control of public security this, we are told, was a sham and not worthy of the name of self-government.

My considered view is that, in the particular circumstances which exist here, our military requirements, which are our over-riding interest, cannot, even if peace and order were restored, be properly safeguarded without control of public security. After all that has happened here in the past twelve months, it seems to me utterly unrealistic that anyone should suggest that we should hand over these grave responsibilities to Greek Cypriot control unless our purpose were to make Enosis inevitable. I took considerable pains to explain to Makarios the nature of the responsibilities which public security entailed and the reasons why, in present circumstances and for a long time to come, the Governor could not reasonably be expected to hand over such responsibilities to Cypriot Ministers. I assured him, however, that I believed the time would come when, as confidence and co-operation developed, it would be increasingly possible for the Governor to associate Cypriot Ministers with his discharge of these responsibilities and even, in time, for him to hand them over. My explanations had no effect, and I was left with the firm impression that Makarios was unwilling to consider the matter on its merits, but was guided simply by his determination to use constitutional government as an instrument to bring about his personal political aims and ambitions.

It has been said in some quarters – that I went further than I should have done in trying to meet him on this crucial point. We had originally lumped public security with defence and external affairs as subjects which would have to be reserved indefinitely to the Governor. I had hoped that, if Makarios' protestations of the personal confidence he felt in me meant anything at all, it might have been possible to dispel any genuine doubts he might have on this point by separating public security from defence and external affairs and by making its retention as a reserved subject dependent on the Governor's personal judgment. This failed to satisfy him and at our last meeting on the 29th February he said that he could not accept what I had suggested because 'it provided neither a time limit nor any conditions dependent on facts or circumstances to determine how long public security should be reserved to the Governor; the criterion was entirely subjective and the decision depended merely on the Governor's judgment.' I do not see how it could be otherwise.

Since the breakdown of the negotiations there has been a deliberate attempt to put it about that the real cause of the breakdown was our refusal to concede the principle of a Greek elected majority. I have indicated above the real reason for the breakdown. Procedurally speaking, the breakdown occurred over all three points – amnesty, public security and the elected majority – and of the three points the least crucial was the last. It has, however, clearly been chosen by our critics as the one on which it is easiest to attack us. I thought Alan Lennox-Boyd made a good point in the House when he drew attention to the amount of time which had been spent in discussing this point at our last meeting with Makarios in comparison with the time spent on the other two points.[44] When, after nearly two hours on the amnesty and public security, we finally reached the question of the elected majority, Makarios had already made plain his rejection of what we had offered on the previous two points.[45] The negotiations had, in fact already broken down on those points. As for the elected majority, Makarios conceded that we had substantially met his point. He said that 'by a syllogism' one could deduce that we had, in fact, conceded that the Greek Cypriots should have a clear elected majority in the Assembly. I suppose he meant that, since we had promised to define the elected majority in accordance with 'normal liberal constitutional doctrine' and since such doctrine required that representation in a mixed community should reflect the composition of the population, therefore we had conceded that the elected Greek Cypriot representatives should have a clear majority. He said, however, that the form in which this was stated was not satisfactory to him and he remained obdurate on this in spite of our explaining why it would not be in the interests of anyone – and not least of his own community – to provoke the Turkish minority into boycotting the constitutional consultations (which would certainly have been the result of our attempting to tie the hands of the Constitutional Commissioner further than we already had done at that stage).

If I required further confirmation of my conclusion that Makarios was not open to compromise, such confirmation was provided in a document which was taken from him at the airport when he was taken into custody. It was the text of a speech he was proposing to deliver to the Greek Press on his arrival in Athens. In a significant passage he referred to the proposal we had made for the appointment of a Constitutional Commissioner. This, he said, he would have been prepared to accept provided that the Commissioner were elected 'by the free vote of the people of Cyprus' and provided that any constituent assembly over which he might preside 'would have full authority' to determine the form of the constitution.[46] Thus, we were not only to commit ourselves to certain principles which would have made Makarios the sole arbiter of the Island's future, but even the details of the constitution, including the safeguards for the Turkish minority, were to be settled by a person elected by the Greek Cypriot majority in the Island and by an assembly in which their voice would be overwhelming. I think this bears out in a striking manner not only my own conclusion about Makarios' motives, but also the point made by the Prime Minister in the House when he said that, even if we had yielded on the three points over which the talks broke down, 'other demands would immediately have been flung up in their place'. Again I must ask you to treat this information in this paragraph as personal and confidential since it has not so far been made public.

Once I had reached the firm conclusion that Makarios was uncompromisingly intent on nothing but the early realisation of Enosis, it followed that I had then to reconsider my whole attitude towards him and to examine afresh the distasteful possibility of having to remove him from the Island. In the result I decided – after much anxious thought – that, once his motives had been indisputably established as being fundamentally and. immediately opposed to our over-riding strategic interests in Cyprus, and since while he remained no one else would be prepared to

---

44 Lennox-Boyd flew to Cyprus to participate in the final discussion between Harding and Makarios.
45 Lennox-Boyd would not accept a general amnesty or the transfer of responsibility for security to a Greek-Cypriot minister, but was willing to concede a Greek-Cypriot majority (although the British cabinet subsequently refused the last, for fear of the Turkish reaction): Assos, 'Makarios', pp. 136–7.
46 The letter is annotated with large, pencil exclamation marks at this point, presumably by Fisher.

come forward, I had no choice but to regard him as 'a major obstacle to a return to peaceful conditions'. His stubborn refusal to denounce murder in itself amounted to a condonation [*sic*] of terrorist methods. Once the possibility of bringing violence to an end by a political agreement with the Archbishop had been exhausted, I was forced to consider his refusal to denounce violence in the light of his long record of association with the organisers of terrorism, and I came to the conclusion that he was using his great influence and his high office to support murder and violence against the State. I decided that his 'influence must therefore be removed from the Island in the interest of promoting peace, order and good government'.

I am afraid I have written at great length. But I was anxious, if I could, to convince you that there are substantial grounds why I could not advise H.M.G. to contemplate any resumption of negotiations with Makarios. I am convinced that there would be no point in doing so unless we were prepared to admit an early abdication to Enosis, and that, as I said at the beginning of this letter, is something which I believe would be utterly contrary not only to our own interests in this Island and in the surrounding region, but also to those of the whole Free World.

For the rest, there may well be advantage in drafting and publishing a constitution so that the suspicions of our intentions which Makarios has raised can be put to rest. A joint appeal by the Greek and Turkish Governments to the Greek Cypriot people to end terrorism does not seem to me a prospect which can be usefully pursued at present. On more than one occasion Her Majesty's Government have asked the Greek Government to use their influence with Makarios to this end but there is no evidence that they have done so. Indeed, as you know, there is ample proof that the Greek Government have used Athens Radio to encourage violence and there is some evidence that they may, directly or indirectly, have encouraged it in more material ways. The Greek Government have recently made it plain on repeated occasions that they support Makarios in every way. I can therefore see no prospect of their agreeing to denounce Eoka at present. The Turkish Government have made it plain that they consider that the restoration of law and order is a prerequisite to any constitutional advance. However, these are matters on which I must reserve my position until I have discussed them thoroughly with H.M.G.

I myself believe that the answer to this perplexing problem must be looked for along the lines which Alan Lennox-Boyd indicated towards the end of his speech on the 14th March. We must first of all create conditions in which people in Cyprus can speak and think for themselves. We must ensure that British military requirements are fully met, and we must press on with measures on the social and economic front. At the same time we must continue to study and work for ways and means of reconciling the conflicting interests which are at the root of the political problems.

Briefly they are :-

(a) British military requirements,

(b) Greek and Greek Cypriot emotions and aspirations, and

(c) Turkish and Turkish Cypriot anxieties and fears.

I fully agree with the statement you made in your speech that 'Reconciliation generally begins not by asking any party to change his tune at once but by devising some temporary next steps on which they can all agree'. What better 'next steps' than co-operation in putting an end to violence and in framing a constitution could there possibly have been? The Archbishop's refusal to take them unless and until he had made certain that the final outcome was entirely to his liking has convinced me that the means of reconciliation cannot be found in resuming negotiations with him.

Yours sincerely
    John Harding

11. Fisher papers 170, fos. 131–2: Prime Minister Sir Anthony Eden to Archbishop Geoffrey Fisher, 4 May 1956

This letter follows Fisher's speech at the British Council of Churches in April 1956. Fisher's remarks ('The complete inaction of the Government as it appears in the Prime Minister's statement does indeed justify indignation: but the Colonial Secretary is an able, an eirenic and a liberal minded person')[47] *angered members of the government. 'So bitter is the Cabinet over Dr. Fisher's accusation of inaction', declared an article in the* Sunday Express *on 29 April, 'that all precedents are to be broken by a Government rebuke to the Primate of All England in the Commons.' Fisher, accused of suggesting a difference between the approaches of the prime minister and his colonial secretary towards Cyprus, wrote to several ministers, including Lennox-Boyd, as well as to Prime Minister Eden, to refute the charge. This is Eden's reply.*

May 4, 1956
My dear Archbishop,
    Thank you for your letter of April 28 and for correcting what has seemed to be a misunderstanding. Actually I can assure you that I had not been worried about remarks on personalities. What has distressed me is that you should have so misunderstood our policies. It has never been in our minds to impose a constitution on Cyprus without consulting the people of the island. Our difficulty has been that we could not consult them until law and order have been restored. We were very willing to secure the Archbishop's co-operation in establishing a constitution if he had been willing to work with us. But unfortunately, as you know, he was not.
    As I thought we had made quite clear, since he was deported, our offer of a liberal constitution has remained open. It remains our policy to enlist the co-operation of the whole Cypriot population, both Greeks and Turks, in framing this constitution. I most earnestly hope that neither you not anyone else will make this prospect more remote by anything that may tend to discourage the moderates from standing out against terrorist pressure, and that all in positions of authority in this country will use their influence to encourage them to come forward and talk to the Governor. I am a little afraid that your recent remarks, however high their intention, may have had the former effect.
    The Governor is coming over within the next two weeks to give us an up-to-date report on the situation.
    I would like to assure you that I am always at your disposal if you would like to have a talk before making a speech on this terribly thorny subject. If you had been able to do this on the present occasion I feel pretty sure that we could have avoided these misunderstandings, which I regret as much as you.[48]
    Yours sincerely
        Anthony Eden

---

[47] LPL, Fisher papers 170, fos. 78–9, draft speech.
[48] To which Fisher replied that he had sought consultation with Lennox-Boyd for some weeks but by the time the colonial secretary eventually rang the text of the BCC speech had already passed out of his, Fisher's, hands. TNA, PREM 11/2268, Fisher to Eden, 10 May 1956.

12. CFR 96, File OC 106: note of an 'Interview with Archbishop Athenagoras [the oecumenical patriarch] and the bishop of Melita [the oecumenical patriarch's representative in Geneva], 14 May 1956', by Archbishop Geoffrey Fisher

Despite Fisher's heading above his notes of this meeting, it appears from what follows that Athenagoras was not in fact present, especially as in paragraph 4 Fisher reports that the bishop of Melita 'had been in touch with Athenagoras', although in Documents 13 and 15 Fisher refers to talks he has had with Athenagoras about Cyprus – perhaps on the telephone. Fisher visited Athenagoras in 1960, becoming only the second archbishop of Canterbury to visit an oecumenical patriarch.[49]

The Bishop of Melita made four points:
1. The Ecumenical Patriarch asks me to give every help that I can.
Marshal [corrected to 'martial'] law is still in operation: as long as that is so the Greek population feel insecure, and don't know what may happen. Not a penny of compensation has yet been paid, and no money is forthcoming. Some people have had some miserable compensation, but quite inadequate and, in fact, it is true to say that nobody has really got any adequate compensation at all as yet.[50]
2. So long as the Cyprus question is inflamed, the Greeks in Istanbul are open at any moment to Turkish attacks. At any moment the Turks may say 'Well, our fellow Turks in Cyprus are getting a raw deal or somebody has been murdered or something is irritating us' and they can turn and attack the Greek population forthwith. Thus a hundred thousand people, Greeks in Constantinople, are in a state of intense and continuous fear.
3. He has been talking to Visser't Hooft. The World Council of Churches is in general behind my line of advance, and they ask whether there is anything which can be done from Geneva to help. I told them again that we must see what is said in the House of Commons to-day, and thereafter we must consider what the next step can be. Francis Noel Baker is working along his line: Kenneth Grubb[51] whom I saw this afternoon is ready to take action after the Commons debate, if any action seems possible, and he is at least quite certain that there must be some further clear and definite statement from the Christian side before he goes to Hungary for the meeting of the Central Council.[52] Unless the British Churches have something positive to say, and if possible some advance to show, they will be shot to pieces there.

On my side I must wait too until I have seen the Commons debate: it looks to me as though the way is open for me to ask to see either the Prime Minister or Lennox-Boyd from their last letters: if there is any advantage that I can see of urging them along a line of constructive action, then I must go and see them.
4. The Bishop of Melita had been in touch with the Ecumenical Patriarch: he is entirely in favour of Anglican Orthodox conversations in 1957. He wants them to be held at Halki[53] which in itself would give immense encouragement to the Greeks

---

49 Hein, *Geoffrey Fisher*, 77 n. 23.
50 For damage sustained during the anti-Greek riots of Sept. 1955.
51 Sir Kenneth Grubb, president of the Church Missionary Society and chair of the Commission of Churches on International Affairs, which was jointly sponsored by the WCC and the International Missionary Council.
52 The central committee of the WCC had accepted an invitation to meet in Hungary in 1956 in the belief that the churches in Hungary wished to participate in the ecumenical movement: Carpenter, *Archbishop Fisher*, p. 186.
53 The Theological School at Halki, Constantinople, where Athenagoras himself had studied.

in Constantinople. The theologians in Athens are ready to be brought in and it can all therefore be looked forward to with confidence. He suggests a date after Easter, possibly at the end of April because they get involved in other Conferences later in the Summer.

I looked at Waddams' note after he had seen the Archbishop of Athens: the Archbishop had obviously been slow to commit himself to anything, but he had said that if the Ecumenical Patriarch was for it he was for it too: and it is clear that the Ecumenical Patriarch is entirely for it.

The Bishop of Melita did mention the attempts of Moscow and I said that we were well aware of that, and I explained why we had to have conversations with Moscow to bring things up to date since 1917, our last theological contact, and I explained the quite different purpose of our discussions at Halki which have a long period of proved agreement behind them.[54]

13. CFR 96, File OC 106: confidential note of an interview with Sir Paul Pavlides,[55] Mr Rossos,[56] and Bishop Virvos, 14 May 1956, by Archbishop Geoffrey Fisher

They began by giving me the attached personal message from the Bishop of Kitium.[57] Rossos then made the following points:

Delay is making the situation far worse: far worse for the Oecumenical Patriarch: far worse for the Greek-Turk relationships: far worse for Eastern N.A.T.O. Makarios had accepted the postponement of self-determination:[58] he had accepted that the interests of international sscurity [*sic*] and strategic security must take precedence, and there the thing stuck. Meanwhile the economic life of the Island and the school life of the Island is disorganized: unemployment is beginning: 71,000 children are on the streets instead of being in schools, many of them elementary schools – that means that about 80% of the children of school age are not going to school.[59]

The whole community is deteriorating. No-one will come forward to negotiate: they would have no foIlowing if they did: they would not know what to say or propose because they would have no mandate from anyone. Prominent people have from time to time denounced the terrorism, but they get no hearing of any sort and there is no kind of hope in going on as the Government now does. John Clerides Q.C., an ex-mayor of Nicosia and an ex-member of the Executive-Council denounced terorism [*sic*] but nobody listened, and he now has resigned from the Executive Council.[60]

---

54 On the oecumenical patriarch and the Russian Orthodox church, see above p. 593.
55 Resigned from the Cyprus executive council in Sept. 1955.
56 Described as a 'Cypriot layman'. See also pp. 595, 597.
57 No longer with the document. The bishop of Kitium had not been deported with Makarios and the bishop of Kyrenia.
58 In the negotiations with Harding Nov. 1955 – Feb. 1956. The chief obstacle to securing an agreement was believed by the British government to be its refusal to agree to an elected Greek majority on the legislature. See pp. 624–5.
59 Young people were to the fore in unrest in Cyprus in the autumn/winter 1955. By March most secondary schools on the island had shut (4 or 5 by government order, others for safety) and about 275 (around half) of all elementary schools were closed: see LPL, CFR, File OC 106; A. W. Adeney to Waddams, 6 Mar. 1956.
60 John Clerides, the only remaining Greek on the executive council, resigned following the deportation; Holland, *Britain and the revolt in Cyprus*, p. 120.

Here Sir Paul took over – more vociferous: delay only fosters an intense and growing hatred of the English. The Archbishop gave up two important things:

(a) He gave up self-determination now, and

(b) He gave up opposition to the ballot box and elections: it had always been held that to give way on this would be a grave error and would be the grave of self-determination, since once they had a Government of their own and powers to vote they would get too fond of self-government and would abandon any desire for self-determination.

That point too Makarios surrendered. He retreated as far as he could, and could not go any further. All who advised him, like Sir Paul, said that no further retreat was possible. He repeated that no-one can now negotiate at all forward. He then looked backwards and made the following points:

(a) The original requirement of H.M.G. was that strategic and political needs should govern the situation. Then H.M.G. agreed to strike out political, but treaty obligations and strategic requirements remained. Then Makarios asked 'who is to decide when the needs on strategic grounds have come to an end'. Makarios proposed an international body to decide that. H.M.G. (I agreed very naturally) turned that down. Makarios totally accepted this situation: that is to say he just dropped it and discussions went on on the basis that H.M.G. would decide when the needs had ceased to require priority.

Sir Paul went on to say that he and others were perfectly ready to drop further conflicts about the police, about internal security and about the amnesty: it all came down to the elected majority.

He then referred to various passages from Command Paper 9594, Miscellaneous Number 18, 1955, and especially page 42. This gives various statements by Macmillan and Nutting,[61] I suppose at N.A.T.O.[62]

We then came on to discussing further steps: everybody agreed that the first thing to do is to get a draft Constitution going. It is no good sending a commissioner to Cyprus: less good to send a parliamentary commission there. All the facts are known: the Commissioner need not go away from London: he could read the papers: then draft his Constitution. What then? Sir Paul said he could consult the Greek Government. He had suggested that to the Colonial Office when he saw Lennox-Boyd and Hare.[63] The answer was that they could not consult with the Greek Government who spent their time abusing the British. Then said Sir Paul 'much better consult Archbishop Makarios – go there, or send someone there with a representative of the Ethnarchy'. The World Council of Churches also said 'go and see Makarios and talk about it and then get an agreement'. They pointed out that Makarios does not

---

[61] Sir Anthony Nutting, minister of state in the foreign office.

[62] In fact the command paper comprised the published proceedings of the tripartite conference organized by Foreign Secretary Harold Macmillan between Britain, Greece and Turkey: Cmnd 9594, *The Tripartite Conference on the eastern Mediterranean and Cyprus, August 29 – September 7 1955* (London: HMSO, 1955). P. 42 detailed proposals made by Macmillan at the conference, including, (i) the introduction of a new constitution to allow for fullest possible measure of self-government in present circumstances; and (ii) the establishment of a 'tripartite committee' in London to draw up a constitution. Appendix III, pp. 44–6, reproduced the text of a speech made by Nutting at the UN, 23 Sept. 1955.

[63] John Hare, minister of state at the colonial office, 1955–6.

have any information at all about Cyprus – neither radio or papers nor anything else. There must be an Ethnarchy representative to inform him of the present situation. And Sir Paul said 'when the Government has got so far as that with their draft, and have discussed it with the Greek Government and Cypriots, then let them put it to Makarios and say take it or leave it'.

He added that it all turned on the elected majority: that was the one point. If out of the 21 members, 11 were elected; 9 should be Greek and 2 Turk in due proportion. Out of the other ten, 3 would rightly be ex-officio officials, 7 nominated: of the 7 nominated Sir Paul said 5 must be Greek. That would mean that the Greek members would be 9 plus 5 which equals 14, and the Turkish two plus two which equals four. I said that that was all very well, but even so the Turks could always be outvoted: it did not really matter how big or small the Greek majority was: there must be a security for the minority. To this Sir Paul agreed and said that he had discussed with the Colonial Office, drawing up a whole list of subjects to be protected so that the Turks might not be open to abuse. I replied to that, that a great list is no good at all. You can always find a way round a list. What must be there is an absolute veto, vested in the Governor, of any measure which seemed to be in any way unfair to the Turkish minority. And really they agreed to this.

We agreed also that the only way forward was to get down to drafting. I pointed out that there were some advantages in my idea of the Government appointing an independent commissioner and having him on his own responsibility to take what consultations he liked in Greece, Cyprus, the Seychelles, or anywhere else; being, so to speak, on his own, he could have informal conversations with all sorts of people without bringing in the Government and all the anti-Government feeling which is prevalent in Greece and Cyprus. When he had got a draft, then it could be privately discussed by the British Government, the Greek Government, by the Cypriots and even by Makarios, without harm. And if there was then a drawing together and an obvious agreement in sight, then a meeting could be called here in London, or somewhere, for final negotiations to which necessarily Makarios would have to be invited, as no final settlement could be made without him.

This same point arose when I was speaking to the Bishop of Melita and Archbishop Athenagoras. They said 'should not Makarios come back to London'. I said that to begin at that point was fatal. The Government would certainly say no. The thing should begin with the drafting of a Constitution in one way or another: then would come discussions with the Greek and Turkish Goverments, with the Cypriots and others: then would come by the sheer force of events the necessity to call in Makarios once more. That was the right way to go to work.

There this long conversation of an hour and a half with Sir Paul and Rossos came to an end. They concluded finally that my suggestion or something like it, to begin with drafting, had the terrific backing of everybody in Cyprus: something along that line must be done. That was why they really looked to me as the salvation of the situation. The same, as I hear, is true in Greece. By one means or another we must as tactfully as we can persuade and lead the British Government to the point of doing something positive to start the drafting of a constitution once more. That must carry on simultaneously with the restoration of law and order. To leave it out would expose us to all the attacks and abuse which is inevitable from those who regard G.B. as violating the principles of freedom in this matter.

G.C.

14. CFR 96, File OC 106: Archbishop Geoffrey Fisher's note of an interview with Mr Francis Noel Baker MP, 14 May 1956

I saw Noel Baker for a brief time immediately after my interview with the Cypriots. There were really two points arising out of an interview which he had a day or two ago with the Prime Minister.

1. Noel Baker conveyed to Eden the private message from the Greek Prime Minister that he, the Greek Prime Minister, was ready and willing at any time to enter into informal conversations with a representative of the British Government towards finding a constitutional settlement. After a long talk Eden said that he would give Noel Baker a message in reply in writing the next morning. The next morning Noel Baker was told that there was no such message ready, but that there would be a message ready later: in the evening Noel Baker received a message from one of the Prime Minister's Secretaries giving him the following – that the Prime Minister was interested in what Noel Baker had told him, and that any future discussions would be carried on through Sir Charles Peake in Athens,[64] which is another way of saying 'mind your own business'. That is all profoundly disappointing. Really Eden ought to have been able to send some message back: his excuse was that he did not know what use would be made of it in Athens.

2. Eden also revealed why he was so angry with my speech to the B.C.C. He told Noel Baker that, in fact, he, Anthony Eden was just engaged in meditating some step along the lines I had suggested: then when I spoke he could do no more about it. Why he couldn't I don't know. But that throws a lurid light on my earlier letter to Lennox-Boyd. On the Thursday before I sent Lennox-Boyd a letter saying what was in my mind and asking if there was anything else I could say. If the Prime Minister had really had in mind then some step of starting constitutional discussions, a message could certainly have been sent to me before late on Monday evening: and on the Monday evening when Lennox-Boyd rang me up he never gave any hint that they had any intention, but merely repeated that nothing could be done so long as law and order was not restored, which is precisely what Anthony Eden had said in the House of Commons and which impelled me to speak as I did at the B.C.C.

We agreed that we must wait and see what happened in the Commons to-day: we agreed that two lines of action must be pursued simultaneously – restoration of law and order and reopening of the drafting of a Constitution. The Government's fatal mistake is to do the first and do nothing about the second. They must both go hand in hand, and this agrees entirely with what was said early this morning with the Cypriots.

    G. C.

15. CFR, File OC 106: letter from Archbishop Geoffrey Fisher to Rev. Herbert Waddams, 14 May 1956 (copy)

My dear Waddams,

I am grateful for the various messages which reach me from time to time through Satterthwaite,[65] and for your letter of 5th May. While you are doing this field work, we are having great times here at home. You have avoided a lot of trouble by being

---

64 British ambassador in Athens.
65 Rev. John Satterthwaite was assistant general secretary at the CFR.

away and Satterthwaite has carried the burden with most commendable quietness and competence. Whether I have been quiet and competent is another matter. The one thing which is quite clear is that by my original speech in the House of Lords I have won the sympathy and the confidence of the Greek Cypriots to a remarkable degree, and also of Greeks in Athens. For five weeks our Government did nothing at all. I felt that at the British Council of Churches I must say something further. On the Thursday before the meetings [of the BCC] I wrote to Lennox-Boyd, told him what was in my mind, and asked him if there was anything else I could say. I got no reaction at all until late on Monday evening when Lennox-Boyd rang up on the telephone and was very angry that I should say what I had told him I was going to say: and simply went on that law and order must be restored before anything else could happen. I was all the more justified in saying what I did say on the Tuesday at the British Council of Churches. I got rapped over the knuckles by the Government for it, but I am quite impenitent: and a large body of opinion is behind me in this matter.

To-day I spent an hour and a half talking to Sir Paul Pavlides and Mr. Rossos from Cyprus. I have had a talk with Noel Baker. I have had a long talk with Archbishop Athenagoras plus the admirable Bishop of Melita whose seat is in Geneva where he represents the Ecumenical Patriarch. Well I will not go on with all that. There is a debate in the House of Commons to-day. When I have seen what they say I will decide what further action if any I can take. It can only, I think, be by insisting upon a talk with Lennox-Boyd or with the Prime Minister, or with both, to make clear to them that they must take some open action about the making and drafting of a Constitution.

The other thing I might mention is that the Bishop of Melita told me with certainty that the Ecumenical Patriarch was all in favour of Anglican Orthodox discussions in 1957 at Halki. He said that being at Halki would bring great encouragement to the Greeks in Istanbul. I read again your note on the conversation you had with Archbishop Dorotheos in Athens.[66] He was obviously being more cautious and cagey, but he said in the end that if the Ecumenical Patriarch was for it, he would be for it too. And the Bishop of Melita assured me that the Greek theologians were all set to come to Halki. I hope you will find all this confirmed when you get to Istanbul, and that such conversations will be arranged. He suggested that immediately after Easter, at the end of April, might be the best time.

So we go on, cheerful in spite of all things. All good wishes to you on your journeys.

Yours sincerely,

Geoffrey Cantuar.

16. Fisher papers 170, fol. 188: Archbishop Geoffrey Fisher to the bishop of Kitium, 16 July 1956 (copy)

This letter (as well as Document 17) was written to persuade the bishop of Kitium, who remained in Cyprus, to co-operate with British constitutional expert, Lord Radcliffe.

---

[66] Dorotheus had succeeded Archbishop Spyridon as archbishop of Athens and All Greece on 29 Mar. 1956.

My dear Bishop,

I sent a hurridly written letter yesterday.[67] I venture now to send a copy of another letter which I have sent to some Cypriots whom I have seen in London recently.[68] It may add a little to what I said in my earlier letter to you.

I cannot tell you how important I think it to be that you and other leaders should see Lord Radcliffe and should talk out such things as I mention in a quiet and friendly manner.

May God guide you all with the comfort and wisdom of his Holy Spirit.

Yours sincerely,

17. Fisher papers 170, fos. 189–90: draft letter from Archbishop Geoffrey Fisher, 16 July 1956

Fisher explains in Document 16 that he is sending the letter reproduced below to some 'Cypriots I have seen in London'. It seems likely that these were Sir Paul Pavlides and Nicos Rossos (see Document 12). If so, this letter seems to have had some impact at least with Pavlides and Rossos (see p. 597). As Fisher admits towards the end of this letter, he appears to have written it without prior consultation with either Lord Radcliffe or the colonial office but his comments on government policy, including over the issue of an elected majority, may have been influenced by the content of Sir John Harding's April letter (see Document 10 and n. 44). Fisher raises the question of how best Cypriot representatives might consult Makarios over possible constitutional proposals arising from the Radcliffe mission and promises to use what influence he can to facilitate such consultation. Fisher subsequently took this issue up with Lennox-Boyd and Harding (see Document 21).

I rejoiced when I heard that the Government was sending Lord Radcliffe to Cyprus and had charged him with the duty of making preliminary enquiries with a view to the drafting of a Constitution. This was, if you remember, the first of the three steps which I proposed when I spoke in the House of Lords. But now I see from the papers that there is some reluctance among Cypriots to cooperate with him. I have sent a letter to the Bishop of Kitium imporing [*sic*] him to speak freely and generously with Lord Radcliffe. May I ask you to use all your influence with the Bishop and to do everything you can yourself to help Lord Radcliffe.

In my conversation with you, it really seems as though all obstacles could be overcome. To my mind there are only three important points:

1.   Self-determination: Archbishop Makarios before he was deported had agreed with the Governor to leave this question in abeyance for the time being. I am sure that is necessary. The recent difficulties our Government has had make that yet clearer. As we can all see the question of self-determination raises big political issues and affects N.A.T.O. and none of us really wish to press that particular point to a devision [*sic*] at the moment, since any decision would be fatal to the true interests of Cyprus and of peace. I hope that all of you in Cyprus, therefore, will continue to say to Lord Radcliffe that the issue of self-determination can be post-

---

[67]   There is no copy in LPL, Fisher papers 170.

[68]   See next document.

poned altogether until there is some general agreement between the Government, the Greeks and the Turks in Cyprus.

2.   An elected majority. I am perfectly sure you have only to ask for that to get it, and of course you will rightly ask for it.

3.   Safeguards for the Turkish minority. On every democratic principle there must be safeguards. Lord Radcliffe will know how to provide them in a Constitution. I hope that you will all show yourselves as generous as possible in this matter.

I need not go further. I believe that on the above lines a constitution could be devised without great difficulty which would sufficiently satisfy all parties. From the papers I realize that some people will wish to make the point that they cannot negotiate with Lord Radcliffe unless Archbishop Makarios is brought back to Cyprus. I earnestly hope that this point will not be pressed. In any dispute it is always fatal for either party to make a demand which they know must be refused by the other. Here, as so often, the longest way round is the shortest way there. As I have said to the Bishop of Kitium I see the matter in three stages:

a)   All of you in Cyprus should now speak to Lord Radcliffe without prejudice saying what is in your minds and showing, as I trust, a helpful and generous spirit. This commits you to nothing and there is no reason at this point for any direct reference to Archbishop Makarios.

b)   After these conversations Lord Radcliffe will prepare, no doubt, a first draft of a Constitution. It is at that point that negotiations begin, and there you would very rightly feel it necessary to be in touch with Archbishop Makarios. For my part I should hope that our Government would at that stage allow representatives of the Cypriots to go to the Seychelles for direct conversation with Archbishop Makarios, and I should certainly do everything in my power to urge the Government so to act. Thus Lord Radcliffe's first draft would be fully discussed and Archbishop Makarios would have a full say in these discussions. I should hope and pray that as a result agreement would be reached as to what should be put into the second and final draft.

c)   For the final draft there should be an official meeting in England or in the Mediterranean at which all the parties would be represented. Archbishop Makarios himself would be there, and would join with the British Government in signing the agreement about a new Constitution. At that stage, if not before, Archbishop Makarios would join with us and with all of you in a forceful call to end all violence and terrorism in Cyprus. That having been done and the agreement signed Archbishop Makarios would return to Cyprus.

I have no idea of what is in Lord Radcliffe's mind or in the mind of the Colonial Secretary. I only set out here what is in my own mind. If good people like yourself in Cyprus would work wholeheartedly along these lines I believe a solution would be reached in Cyprus and in the world outside, and would at last bring peace. I pray earnestly it may do so.

Yours sincerely,

18. CFR, File OC 107: confidential note to the archbishop on 'Cyprus' by Rev. Herbert Waddams, 3 October 1956

I went to talk confidentially with C. M. Woodhouse, Director-General of Chatham House about Cyprus. He was political advisor to the guerrillas in Greece during the war and knows Greece backwards. I discovered that it was his initiative which led to the truce which was recently called by the terrorists.[69] He wrote to Pallis[70] and Mostras (London Ambassador at present in Athens). The whole thing was completely spoilt by Harding who apparently took his line without consulting anybody at home.[71] As a consequence the Greeks, of course, regarded the surrender call as a challenge. Woodhouse thinks that there may still he a chance of getting the guerrillas to call off their violence again and that you could help in this by privately appealing to some suitable people in Greece. He suggested George Soferiadis[72] who is at present in the Ministry of Foreign Affairs and whom I know quite well. It would, of course, be necessary for you beforehand to get some assurances from the Government that if it was successful the same mistake would not be made again. He also tells me that the Colonial Office are absolutely determined that in no circumstances will Makarios ever be negotiated with and that the permanent officials are deliberately acting in such a way as to make it as impossible as possible (excuse the expression) for any Government to bring Makarios back.

He thinks that if you are to make an appeal of this kind it will have to be strictly private, with no publicity whatever, and because Pallis and Mostras succeeded on the last occasion when nothing came of it, it would be wise to choose someone else this time since their previous efforts might be accounted a failure.

All this is rather important and I think that it would be very well worth your while to ask Woodhouse to come and talk things over with you. In private correspondence with Eden he received a clear assurance that the conceding of the principle of self-determination was absolutely sincere and genuine though its application could not of course be considered just now.

You will realise that all this is strictly confidential but I thought you would like to know it before seeing Pallis tomorrow. I hope to be here with him if you want me present at your talk.

H. W.

19. CFR, File OC 107: Archbishop Geoffrey Fisher to Sir Alan Lennox-Boyd, 11 October 1956 (copy)

Fisher's letter mentions the 'Radcliffe Constitution', a reference to Lord Radcliffe's report submitted to Lennox-Boyd in October 1956. Lennox-Boyd replied to Fisher on 31 October. In response Fisher wrote the Colonial Secretary another letter agreeing that Makarios had to show a 'change of heart about terrorism' before negotiations with the archbishop could be resumed, but nevertheless restating his conviction that Makarios needed to be brought back into negotiations and commenting that 'at

---

[69] The truce was announced by Grivas on 16 Aug. 1956 probably as a result of pressure from the Greek government. In Cyprus Harding relaxed security, but, in view of the assessment of his military advisers that Grivas had declared the cease fire in order to gain a 'breathing space' in which EOKA could re-group, Harding's official response agreed only to a limited amnesty for some EOKA fighters but did not offer an end to the Emergency or to open talks with Makarios: Holland, *Britain and the revolt in Cyprus*, pp. 148–50.

[70] Sir Alexander Pallis; see above p. 603.

[71] In fact Harding was handicapped by the British government's refusal at this stage to enter into conciliatory discussions with the Greek government over Cyprus: Holland, *Britain and the revolt in Cyprus*, pp. 149–50.

[72] Probably George Seferiades, also known as George Seferis, Greek poet and ambassador to London 1957–62.

that stage you might find some way of letting Makarios consult outside Cyprus'. He reiterated his offer to help by making contact with Cypriot leaders or Makarios.[73]

My dear Lennox-Boyd,

As you can imagine Cyprus is again very much in my mind. The approaching completion of the new Constitution will present us all with what may be a last hope. I know how anxious you will be to secure that it has as good a chance as possible of fair consideration, and I am anxious to do anything I can to help.

The Times leader today says almost everything that in my judgement ought to be said at this moment about Cyprus. I have no doubt that the proposals of the Radcliffe Constitution will satisfy the Times' requirements that they should be promising: and my contacts with Cypriots encourage me to think that they will be ready to accept the kind of contribution under contemplation.

The remaining difficulty is to secure an interlude during which the constitutional proposals can be considered without prejudice and without distracting emotions.

The first desideratum, as the Times says, is for a new truce offer by the terrorists. As no doubt you know the suggestion of the first truce offer and part of its wording came from your friendly Greeks in Athens who were really desiring to get an interlude for some discussion. I am bound to say that in my opinion the meeting of this offer by a call to surrender was a terribly serious mistake of psychological understanding. It obviously makes it more difficult to secure a repetition of the offer. But it is not impossible. I have contacts with those who had a hand in engineering the first truce offer. They think a second could be secured.

Would you welcome a second truce? Have you your own plans for inviting it? Or would you encourage me to do what I can through those known to me who can make direct contact with the terrorists?

There remains one other desideratum. I doubt whether the terrorists would think of offering another truce. I doubt whether the Cypriot leaders will give any impartial thought to the new proposals – unless they know what is to be done about Makarios. You may not be able to commit the Government: but terrorists and Cypriot leaders must have some reasonable expectation in this matter as soon as possible.

The irreducible minimum for them, I think, would be a request (which seems to me entirely reasonable in itself) that as soon as the proposals are known to them they must be enabled to have direct, free and unfettered discussion about them with Makarios. It does not seem to me to matter much *where* such discussions take place. The Government may not like London for them and I rather agree. The Cypriots would certainly refuse the Seychelles as Makarios would still be under duress. The essential point is that there should be this opportunity for free discussion between Makarios and his followers.

Is that contemplated? Would you object to my telling those known to me that such a course would be strongly put before the Government here in England with some good hope?

All this assumes that if a final settlement is reached, Makarios will sign it as the accepted leader of the Cypriots and will return to Cyprus. Is it reasonable of me to make that assumption? I cannot believe that that result can be avoided, though it requires one proviso. The proviso is that Makarios ex animo abjures terrorism.

---

[73] LPL, CFR, File OC 107: Fisher to Lennox-Boyd, 6 Nov. 1956 (draft).

If a new atmosphere can be generated, I do not doubt that he would. Surprisingly enough the famous Diaries,[74] though they show Makarios as fully implicated and the final authority, show also that Grivas found him rather dilatory and half hearted!

The question here is as to when Makarios can be called on to abjure terrorism? Before he is allowed to return to Cyprus? Most certainly, yes. Before he is asked to negotiate directly with the British Government the final settlement? Yes, certainly. Before he is allowed to have direct discussions with his Cypriot followers? I should say, no. All he should be asked at first to do would be to accept fully with his followers in Cyprus the Truce to enable discussions to take place in which he would have a part. It is desirable, however, that these should take place somewhere civilised where moderating pressure cold be brought to bear upon him from the Greek Government and elsewhere. Again I ask is there anything you would like me to do (or would allow me to do) in the matter of Archbishop Makarios.

I have put on paper the points most in my mind. If I can help in any way, I am of course at your disposal, and would gladly talk the matter over.

Yours sincerely,

G.C.

20. CFR, File OC 107: confidential 'Note to the archbishop' by Rev. Herbert Waddams, 7 December 1956

I went to the house of Francis Noel-Baker this evening to discuss with him the Cyprus situation. He entrusted to me for your eyes only the accompanying notes of important interviews which he had two months or so ago with Mr Karamanlis, the Greek Prime Minister and with Mr Menderes the Turkish Prime Minister. There are also interesting accounts of his conversations in Cyprus and his impressions there.

He thinks that the points which could and should be put to the Colonial Secretary and the Governor can be phrased in the form of questions, which I have put down on the attached piece of paper. I have myself changed their phraseology and order somewhat and added to them a little. In addition to these points it is desirable that you should be ready with answers to points which may be made against your point of view, and especially against the proposal to bring the Archbishop of Cyprus into the picture again.

It is important to note that Francis Noel-Baker thinks it essential that the new proposed constitution should be shown to the Greek and Turkish Governments and to Archbishop Makarios *before* publication: otherwise there will be grave risk of its being unacceptable.

Sir John Harding is always saying in public that he is not intending to negotiate. He said it again this evening on TV. By this it appears that he means that he is not prepared to call in question the basic points of a Constitution which has been prepared as a whole. It is desirable that his words should not be taken to mean that no discussion of marginal points is to be considered.

Noel-Baker himself would like to know whether the government are in earnest about finding a solution and whether they think that he can be of any use. He has carefully remained polite and detached for a long time and is prepared to continue if it will help, but he finds the situation rather frustrating. He asked the Colonial

---

[74] See above p. 597.

Secretary (through Sir John Martin)[75] a day or two ago to send a telegram to Makarios from himself conveying his personal greetings and asking if there was anything Makarios would like to tell him for his own guidance at the present moment. He does not know whether it was sent.

He is prepared to go out and see Makarios or to do anything else that might be useful, if asked. He thinks (probably rightly) that he still has Makarios's confidence and that he is the only person in politics to enjoy it.

7.12.56

Points to be prepared to answer.
Obj.
Makarios is so stained with violence that he cannot be dealt with.
Resp.
He showed himself ready to take advantage of the threat of violence as a political weapon. But he promised to denounce it when agreement was reached. The Grivas diaries added nothing to the general indictment, and he appears in them rather as a moderating influence.
Obj.
Other leaders will appear.
Resp.
None has done so so far. Things have got worse and not better in spite of the huge number of troops and extremely severe penalties. Greeks do not react like the British. Policy hitherto has made it almost impossible for responsible leaders to co-operate without Makarios. Other alternatives are worse than he.
Obj.
The Turks won't agree.
Resp.
The Turks in the island will probably do what they are told to do by Ankara. There is good reason to believe that the Turkish government is ready for an accommodation on the basis of (a) a standstill on enosis (b) the cessation of violence and (c) adequate protection for their minority. The Greeks cannot be expected to give up their support for eventual enosis and the Turks cannot be expected to give up their opposition to it. They can however agree that the propaganda activities on the subject should be dropped, and this is what is meant by a standstill on enosis. It should be agreed that the question of enosis should be left to a later date. This had already been agreed in principle before the deportation of Makarios.
Obj.
Terrorism must be put down before anything else can be done.
Resp.
The cessation of violence of course must be the first aim. But there is more than one way to reach this goal and repression is the worst of all ways. The most probable way of achieving it quickly is by a political settlement in which Makarios is brought back.
Questions
Do the authorities agree that the atmosphere in Cyprus has deteriorated very much in the last few months?
Do they agree that it is continuing to deteriorate so fast that there is a serious danger

---

[75] Assistant under-secretary, colonial office.

that soon it will be impossible to get any political co-operation between the communities – British, Greek and Turkish?

Do they agree that the promulgation of the Radcliffe Constitution gives a new opportunity for getting an acceptable political settlement? And that, so far as one can foresee, this is likely to be the last chance for a long time?

Do they agree that the present terrorism and repression together with the savage punishments which can be inflicted, is a condition to which every possible remedy must be sought? As a matter of urgency?

Do they see the Radcliffe proposals as a serious attempt to reach a settlement or as a propaganda move to prove by their rejection that the Cypriots cannot be satisfied? In other words – is the attempt to reach a settlement to be a serious one with all that this implies? Are they ready for a really determined effort to reach agreement all-round and to try everything to persuade the Cypriots to accept it?

This means the greatest care and time will have to be spent on the matter including the Greek and Turkish governments to back the Constitution – and Archbishop Makarios.

Do they agree that there are no signs of anyone else who will replace Makarios as representative of the Cypriots?

Are not the alternatives to Makarios worse than he – the Communists, Grivas or the Bishop of Kyrenia (also in Seychelles)?

Whether Makarios is thought to be a wicked man or not by the Governor, is that not an evasion of the point, which is to bring the bloodshed to an end as soon as possible? If it can be done by bringing Makarios into the picture again is there not a moral duty to do it to save further loss of life in the island?

Makarios might be brought to London where discussions could be held. Whatever the outcome it could be agreed that he should not return to the island until after he had condemned violence and until after violence had ceased for a month or some other period. But it would be necessary to permit him to continue to play his part in the island's political life after his return. If constitutional politics begin to work he will not long remain a politician.

21. Fisher papers 170, fos. 278–81: note on a meeting between Archbishop Geoffrey Fisher, Sir Alan Lennox-Boyd and Sir John Harding, 10 December 1956

This meeting was held at Fisher's request.[76]

Cyprus

I saw Lennox-Boyd and Harding on 10th December, 1956. It was friendly throughout and we ended on very happy terms, though after a great deal of straight argument. In reply to Lennox-Boyd's question I said that there were two things I wanted to raise:

1.   Is the situation in Cyprus deteriorating?
2.   If so, how did they propose to launch their new Constitution?

On deterioration Harding demanded to know my evidence. I said it came from England, from Greece and from Cyprus. He said I could ignore anything which came from Athens. I did not name Pallis,[77] but I described his career and said that he

---

[76]   LPL, Fisher papers 170, fo. 263: Fisher to Lennox-Boyd, 30 Nov. 1956.
[77]   See above, p. 603.

was very pro-British and entirely reliable. Harding then really admitted that the situation was deteriorating, and that every delay in taking up the Constitutional question increased the deterioration, but it had not yet gone beyond recovery. (I forebore to say that this was a strong proof that if they had taken my advice last April, and started constitutional discussions then it need not have deteriorated at all.)

We then went on to the Radcliffe Constitution, and at this point got into a bit of a wrangle which was useful. I said frankly I had tried to help them, that I had to defend them against very severe criticism at home and abroad, that I had done not a little to soften criticism, but that they had given me no weapons at all with which to defend them: they had slogged away at suppressing terrorism and nothing else.

Lennox-Boyd protested that to Makarios he had insisted on the need for a Constitutional settlement and had even mentioned Radcliffe's name. I asked if he had ever said that in public, and he said 'no', and I once more tried to make them realise that they had to have a plain answer to their critics that they had done everything that justice required, and a bit more: but at any moment Lennox-Boyd was liable to go off emotionally about the murder of British soldiers and the rest, and there is no doubt that Harding and he have, for a long time, regarded the suppression of terrorism as the only thing that mattered.

Radcliffe's Constitution is to be drawn up in the form of an Order in Council, but before the Order is finally passed there would be time for tiny alterations: but in essence when it is public it will be in its final form. They are proposing to discuss it privately with the Greek and Turkish Governments in case any small adjustments were called for to get acquiescence.[78] They appeared to think that the Turks were now the most prominent and difficult partners to the negotiations, but they hoped to get a settlement with these two Governments before publication.

I argued that they should ask the Greek Government to sound Makarios before publication. This they resisted fiercely saying that the Turks would go through the roof if Makarios was made a partner to the negotiations. I argued that there was no question of his being a partner to the negotiations, but it would help the Government if they knew beforehand what his reaction was likely to be. If the Greeks said it was going to be acceptable the whole position is won: if unacceptable, at least, we could say that through the Greek's best friend, Makarios, we had tried to get good will.

Clearly they were not prepared to make any approach beforehand to Makarios. When Lennox-Boyd made a statement in the House he would say that a copy of the Constitution was that afternoon being given to Makarios in the Seychelles, and to the Cypriot Leaders. I asked whether he would say also that facilities would be given for the Cypriot leaders to discuss the Constitution with Makarios. He at once became cagey and looked at Harding, and Harding looked at him, and Lennox-Boyd said that it might be said in answer to an inspired supplementary question.[79] I said that it was the critical question whether the Cypriots should be allowed to have direct discussions with Makarios before declaring their opinion. Lennox-Boyd said that he

---

78 Lennox-Boyd sent Fisher a brief note two days later to give him confidentially advance notice that he was leaving on 13 Dec. for talks in Greece and Turkey about the Radcliffe Report: LPL, Fisher papers 170, fo. 282, 12 Dec.
79 In the event Lennox-Boyd responded to a question from Labour MP James Callaghan to the effect that the British government would provide the 'necessary facilities' to enable Makarios to engage in consultation about the proposals.

would have to let the Turks see the House of Commons statement beforehand, and if this was in the statement it might send the Turks off the deep end as they regard Makarios as a bad man who must be given no place in the negotiations at all. But if it was done in a supplementary he need not tell the Turks beforehand. I do not think he had really thought much about the importance of the point. The one thing I achieved was to make him realise that other people might go off the deep end if he did not say clearly that the Cypriot Leaders would have this facility. It had obviously been in his mind and rather put in the background, and not seen to be the important point that it is.

My general impression was that they are now terrified of the Turks more than anybody else, though whether this is a genuine judgement or is, at least, encouraged by the fact that it gives them added reason for being tough with the Cypriots and Makarios I do not know.

     G.C.

P.S.

I do not think they have got so far as to consider where they would be if after the Constitution was published Makarios and the Cypriots said no. Nor had they considered the need for themselves to shew [*sic*] to the world that they had taken every possible step to encourage them to say yes, and to help them to do it before the no was said. In their own thinking they have really dismissed Makarios as no longer relevant, seeing no half-way house between that and letting him become again the arbiter and the negotiator. I pointed out that whether they liked it or not he is still the arbiter: and there is no evidence that even the Cypriots that do not want to see him back will try to dispense with him.

They pressed me to give the names of the Cypriots with whom I was in touch. This I refused to do: Lennox-Boyd tried to represent it as a duty, and I said that I could not possibly do it without their leave.

22. CFR, File OC 108: confidential 'memorandum' dated 3 January 1957 prepared by Rev. Herbert Waddams on his talk with the Turkish ambassador in London on 2 January 1957

Waddams ensured that this memomorandum was widely circulated. He sent a copy to Francis Noel-Baker, who passed it on to the foreign secretary. Waddams also sent a copy to W. H. Young at the foreign office, to Alexander Pallis, to Kenneth Younger (Labour MP and former minister of state at the Foreign Office), and to Jo Grimond (Liberal MP). Younger, although sceptical about the veracity of Waddams's report, passed the letter on to James Callaghan, who had recently taken over as Labour spokesman for colonial affairs. Grimond noted in reply that: 'of course they (Turkey) are more and more encouraged in their attitude when our Government makes them an excuse for their present policy in Cyprus'. By then Waddams had already met with a British diplomat in Turkey who suggested that there was no likelihood of the Turkish government allowing a massacre of the Greek community in Turkey.[80] The Turkish Ambassador himself disputed the record of the interview, and Waddams's alarmist memorandum of the interview led officials in Whitehall to doubt his judg-

---

[80] LPL, CFR, File OC 108: Younger to Waddams, 8 Jan. 1957; Grimond to Waddams, 12 Jan, 1957; and 'Note for the file', Waddams, 5 Jan. 1957.

ment: it was one of two specific examples of Waddams's 'unwisdom' cited by Lord Winster in conversation with Bell: see Document 26.

Yesterday I had an interview lasting fifty minutes with the Turkish Ambassador in London. I had written to him to say that I had some anxieties about the position of the Oecumenical Patriarchate. This is a short notice summarizing my main impressions.

The Ambassador began by emphasising the extremely low standard, both morally and educationally, of the Greek Orthodox clergy and stressed that their influence (he excepted the Patriarch) was anti-Turkish.

I had previously mentioned three points: The September 1955 riots; the introduction of a private members bill in Parliament to expel the Patriarch, and the arrest of some leading members of the Greek community, including a bishop.

In regard to the riots he said that they were notable for the fact that there was no loss of life, and the Turkish Government could easily put right the material damage, but he went on to say that if provocation by the Greeks continued in Cyprus and elsewhere, it was more than likely that there would be another riot, only this time it would be a massacre and the police and the troops would probably be on the side of the rioters. He added that life was cheap in the Mediterranean, that fighting was the Turkish national sport, and the Turks outnumbered Greeks by three or four to one.

He then went on to say that the Radcliffe proposals for Cyprus, though by no means perfect, would be accepted by the Turks as the basis for further development. If, however, the Greeks refused this the Turks would ask for Partition of the Island, and, if this were refused the Turks would insist on the revision of the Treaty of Lausanne, which would end the matter once for all by exchanging the whole of the Greek population of Turkey-in-Europe for the Turks in Trace and elsewhere.[81]

I said twice very emphatically that any such solution would be a calamity. The only positive thing he said was that if the Cyprus matter was settled there would not be any further trouble.

My own comment on this is that I very much fear that it may be true. As regards the last point, the Ambassador definitely assured me that this was the official policy of the Turkish Government. I recognize, of course, that the Ambassador may have regarded me as an impressionable and simple clergyman who could be used conveniently for bringing pressure to bear upon the Archbishop of Canterbury and upon Orthodox personalities. But even allowing for this it seems to me remarkable that such threats could be uttered in cold blood in London, for surely it must show that he is quite convinced that the British government would permit the Turks to carry out these threats without any serious results to the Turks.

It was quite plain from the Ambassador's remarks that he was bent on expelling the Greeks and Armenians if possible. This means in fact all the Christians and from a historical point of view any such step would be an immense catastrophe. Quite apart from the fact that exchange of populations causes intense misery to the individuals concerned, it is also a confession of utter bankruptcy from the human and political point of view. But besides this the expulsion of Greek Christians from the

---

[81]   According to the terms of the Treaty of Lausanne Turkey had been forced to accept the rights of some 100,000 Constantinople Greeks to remain in the city (and in return a Muslim minority of similar size was allowed to remain in Western Thrace) who were thus exempted from the compulsory Greek–Turkish population exchange: Alexandris, *Greek minority of Istanbul*, pp. 317–19.

city which they founded and built 1650 years ago as one of the great historic centres of Christianity would be a crime of the greatest magnitude. The massacre of the Armenians in the last seventy years and the capital levy of the last war, however, will show that the Turks will have no moral scruples about such matters. Self interest is the only thing which will weigh with them, and this means that the future safety of the minorities in this ancient and historic corner of Europe can only be assured if the British and American Governments, particularly the latter, are prepared to make it clear to the Turkish Government that they will in no circumstances countenance any such development as that suggested by the Ambassador, and that they require guarantees of some sort that the Turkish Government is civilized enough to ensure the safety and well-being of the minorities within the boundaries of its State.

H.W.

23. CFR, File OC 108: 'Note for the file', by Rev. Herbert Waddams, 25 January 1957

This document, reporting on a meeting that Waddams attended with journalists, MPs and others interested in Cyprus, provides some context to the decision taken to send a personal letter from Fisher to new Prime Minister Harold Macmillan (see Document 25). The meeting took place at the instigation of a Mrs J. C. Carras, who is described as a Greek resident in London. Mrs Carras had earlier written to Waddams at the CFR expressing anxiety about the political repercussions for the Karamanlis government and possible boost to communism in Greece should the next attempt to elicit the support of the UN (spring 1957) over Cyprus fail. She proposed that a group of MPs and journalists be brought together to discuss the island, and suggested that 'only the Church could succeed in getting such a group as these together'. Although Fisher declined her request to do this himself, he agreed to let Waddams act instead.[82]

On Monday evening last, 21st January, I attended a gathering at the house of Mrs. Carras to discuss Cyprus and what could be done to get out of the present situation. Mr. Grimond[83] was in the chair, and there were about 50 or 40 present, including the Greek Charge d'Affaires and a young man Mr. Ducharis from the London Office of the Cyprus Ethnarchy.[84] The presence of these two people was very unfortunate since they could do very little more than put forward (at great length) the Government or Ethnarchy line. This had the result of damping down the discussion. I made some remarks about the urgency of the situation and Honor Balfour[85] added to then. Apart from this there were some useful and helpful remarks by Desmond Donnelly,

---

[82] LPL, CFR, File OC 107: 'Note to the archbishop', by H. M. W.[addams], 23 Nov. 1956; Waddams to Mrs J. C. Carras, 21 Avenue Road, London, 29 Nov. 1956.

[83] Jo (later Lord) Grimond, leader of the Liberal party, 1956 – 67.

[84] Phy[i]dias C. Doukaris, a UK delegate of the ethnarchy. Doukaris (also spelled Ducharis) visited Fisher in Apr. 1957 to discuss Cyprus: see p. 600.

[85] Honor Balfour, journalist and broadcaster, was a Liberal although closely associated with Donnelly (see next note).

M.P.,[86] Mr. Callaghan, M.P.,[87] and Cyril Falls.[88] Sir Robert Boothby[89] intervened with a statement that there had been a great change of opinion among the rank and file of the Conservative Party, including the Suez Group,[90] and that it was more than likely that, after a certain time, they would get out of Cyprus in rather the same way as they got out of Palestine. The Turks would then take over and conquer the Island in 24 hours. I do not quite know what his object was by saying that. It may have been to frighten the Greeks, but I very much fear it will have the opposite effect, and will encourage both the Cypriots and Greeks to be more intransigent and not less. I left half an hour before the party broke up at 11.50 p.m. and I gathered that not very much more was said except that Bessborough[91] made a rampageous speech about rooting out violence.

There did, however, seem to be a general feeling that the advent of the new administration might be an opportunity for a new start and I think that this opinion adds point to the proposal that the Archbishop should write a letter to Macmillan at an early date.

24. CFR, File OC 108: draft letter from Archbishop Geoffrey Fisher to Prime Minister Harold Macmillan, January 1957

This draft letter seems to have been prepared at the CFR and may have been influenced by points that Francis Noel-Baker suggested to Waddams needed to be put to Harold Macmillan – see Document 20. The draft also reflected Waddams's recent interview with the Turkish ambassador in London (Document 22). A draft of the letter was circulated to Kenneth Slack (general secretary, BCC), Rev. J. Pitt-Watson (professor of practical theology, Glasgow, and member of the Church of Scotland) and to Rev. Ernest Payne (general secretary of the Baptist Union of GB and Ireland) for comments. Both Slack and Payne sought clarification as to whether the letter was intended to be sent in a personal capacity by Fisher or on behalf of all British churches.[92] On the second page of the draft letter Fisher handwrote his own suggestions (see end of document for these). On the CFR file from which this document is taken there is also an extract from a further draft as well as more notes by Fisher (not reproduced here). Fisher's suggestions seem to have been incorporated in the version of the letter which was finally sent on 4 February 1957 and which is also printed here (Document 25).

As you know I have been personally very anxious about the Cyprus situation for a very long time. I have felt bound to do all I could to find some way out of the appalling impasse which seems to have been reached. To this end I have several times approached Lennox-Boyd offering to help in any way he thought suitable, but

---

86 Desmond Louis Donnelly, Labour MP 1950–70 (but expelled from Labour party in 1968, subsequently founding the Democratic party, and later joining the Conservative party).
87 James Callaghan, future leader of the Labour party and prime minister, and shadow spokesman for colonial affairs.
88 Cyril Falls, military officer, historian and writer.
89 Robert (later Lord) Boothby, Conservative politician and MP.
90 A group of Conservative MPs opposed to the withdrawal of British forces from the Suez Canal zone and to retreat in the Middle East (including Cyprus).
91 Frederick Ponsonby, tenth earl of Bessborough and Conservative politician.
92 LPL, CFR, File OC 108: Slack to Waddams, 18 Jan. 1957; Payne to Waddams, 21 Jan. 1957.

he has not found it advisable to do anything specific. I did, on my own initiative, appeal to Archbishop Makarios, the Archbishop of Athens, and leading personalities in Cyprus to try to use the opportunity provided by the Radcliffe proposals for a new start which would give promise of suitable development in the future. I recognize too that Sir Anthony Eden had himself been personally concerned with the whole Cyprus problem, and it is for this reason that I have thought it well to ask you to consider one or two points in regard to it, for changes of Government can often be used as an occasion for making a fresh start so as to escape from difficult conditions.

I have been in rather close touch with a number of persons directly concerned with the problems of Cyprus outside the circles of the British Government, especially in Cyprus and Greece. Their united testimony fills me with alarm at the continued and very grave deterioration of conditions in Cyprus. It seems likely that these are so embittering relations between Greek Cypriots and the British as to render future friendly co-operation increasingly difficult. There is even a danger that if they persist such co-operation may become altogether impossible. There is a risk that a stalemate will, while keeping political conditions as they are, simply provide the framework for a progressively [sic] worsening of the atmosphere. This seems to me to give the whole problem an urgency which can only be disregarded at our peril.

Apart from the position in Cyprus itself I think the present situation is doing serious damage to our reputation in many parts of the world, especially among African and Asian leaders. Of course I fully recognize the provocation and scandalous behaviour of many of our adversaries, and I am sure I could, if I tried, make just as good a case for our policy as any member of the Government. But that is not the point with which I am concerned. It seems to me that all men of good will ought to concentrate on finding a way out and doing everything that is humanly possible to put an end to the insane slaughter of people in Cyprus, and to do something to repair the damage to our international friendships.

It is a great disappointment to me that the Radcliffe proposals have so far been so negatively received. Here again I do not think that anyone will be served by trying to lay the blame on one side or the other. Actions were not all well judged and the new point of departure seems to be in danger of being missed. I do, however, have some slight indications that the Greek Government might reconsider its attitude if its appeal to the United Nations fails, but there is no doubt that the appeal itself will do further damage to friendly relations.[93]

I do not like to raise such subjects as this without making any attempt to provide positive proposals, and I should like to make some tentative suggestions in regard to two points.

The first is the cessation of violence. It seems to me that there has been some lack of imagination in trying to stop the violence. When EOKA called off the campaign a very valuable opportunity of using that break was missed by the unimaginative action of our authorities, and I believe that there is still some chance of getting a repetition of such cessation if the Government is ready to use it in a positive way. This brings me to the second point, namely the position of Archbishop Makarios. It would, of course, be very easy to call for a cessation of violence if Makarios was to be brought back into the picture rather more fully. The actions of the Government

---

93 The Greek government persuaded the UN to adopt a resolution (1013 (XI)) calling for the resumption of negotiations over Cyprus in spring 1957.

in relation to the Radcliffe proposals seem to me to amount to a recognition that Makarios is an indispensable factor in the situation and that no settlement is likely without his support. But when he is incommunicado in the Seychelles and is allowed only extremely limited communications with the outside world it makes it almost impossible to approach him so as to enable him to co-operate effectively with the British government. Moreover even if Makarios was willing to give some assurance in the Seychelles there is a serious risk that it might not be accepted on its face value by Greek and Cypriots because he would be regarded as giving it under duress. Would it not be possible, after careful preparation, to appeal to EOKA to cease violence while Makarios was brought to Malta and there given all the opportunities of discussing with anybody he likes the whole problem of the Island?

It would be very important that any such suggestion should be carefully prepared both by Greeks and Turks and other interested parties. Constitutional proposals could be put forward again in a rather more friendly spirit and it could be made clear both to the Turks and Greeks that they could be subject to amendment by agreement on one condition, namely, that both Turks and Greeks would recognize one another's interests and be prepared to reach a reasonable compromise. There is evidence that this might be achieved if properly approached. One feature of the situation which causes me some disquiet is the attitude of the Turkish government, apparently as a result of British readiness to give way to their susceptibilities. The Turkish Ambassador, in an interview the other day, indicated that the Greek population of Istanbul might well be massacred if the Greeks provoke the Turks in Cyprus, and added that it was the official policy of the Turkish Government to insist on a revision of the Treaty of Lausanne together with the expulsion by way of exchange of all the Greek population of Istanbul if neither the Radcliffe proposals nor Partition were acceptable to the Greeks. I am astonished that the Ambassador of Turkey in London could express such views, and I can only conclude that he believes that the British authorities will not object to him doing so.

As I said at the beginning my only excuse for writing to you at such length is that Cyprus weighs heavily upon my heart and conscience, and I hope that your formation of a new Government may give another chance of making a fresh start which will lead to the end of violence and towards a friendly settlement. I need hardly say again that if there is anything I can do I shall be very glad to help towards a constructive solution.

Yours sincerely,

Fisher's handwritten annotations on above:

* Turkish ambassador

* A new Governor the only hope? Eg Walter Monckton[94]

25. CFR, File OC 108 (also Fisher papers 186, fos. 140–2): Archbishop Geoffrey Fisher to Prime Minister Harold Macmillan, 4 February 1957 (copy)

This is a revised vision of Fisher's letter to Macmillan. It reads quite differently to the draft (Document 24) circulated by Waddams, and, with its emphasis on the

---

94 Walter Monckton, First Viscount Monckton of Brenchley, politician and lawyer, adviser to Edward VIII during the abdication crisis. He was Conservative minister of defence 1955–6 and in 1957 was paymaster general.

appointment of a new governor, would seem to reflect Fisher's own input as indicated by Fisher's annotations on the draft. It also gives much more emphasis to the position of the oecumenical patriarch. It is in addition interesting for Fisher's apparent credulity: he seems to have accepted surprisingly unquestioningly the suggestion by Waddams that there might be a Turkish massacre of the Greek community in Turkey.

My dear Prime Minister

I had a few words with you recently about Cyprus. May I return to that unhappy topic at some length?

I am increasingly alarmed by the information which reaches me from many quarters, and I get the impression that political opinion here is beginning to despair of finding any healing or constructive solution. To my mind to lose patience or hope would be a final disaster. The situation as it is is one of stalemate. Some new point of departure is needed. In the hope that it may help you to find one, I venture to put forward the result of my own anxious search. It does at least lead to a concrete proposal.

I.   The situation is now dominated by the Turks. They are not in a mood to make any concession towards Greeks or Cypriots. On the contrary, even at the highest diplomatic levels they are talking in terms of ruthlessness against the Greeks in Istanbul. Killing is to Turks and Greeks alike a familiar occupation, and with or without further provocation the Turks might repeat the riots of September, 1955, in a worse form and massacre the Greeks in Istanbul. The position of the Oecumenical Patriarch is daily increasing in difficulty and danger, despite the fact that he is an enlightened person (he came to his office from the U.S.A.)[95] and has established good personal relations with the Turkish Government. If there were a massacre, it would probably mean the end of the Patriarchate in Istanbul: and the extrusion of the Oecumenical Patriarch would be a disaster for the whole Orthodox Church. The Soviet would no doubt pose as the champions of the Greeks: the Russian Church would claim to succeed to the leadership of the Orthodox Church: of Constantinople with its historic place in the story of Christendom if it became exclusively a Moslem city the final 'Ichabod'[96] would be spoken.

II.   We must recognise that it is unsafe to give the Turks any excuse for a massacre of the Greeks. Yet we must not let the Turks suppose that they have nothing to fear from us whatever they do. We cannot just abandon the Cyprus problem to them. Indeed the danger of some Turkish outburst is so great that at the diplomatic level strong warning ought to be given to the Turks now that any anti-Greek movements in Istanbul would antagonise us, ruin their own case, and frustrate their own ends. Apart from that our most urgent task now is to save the Greeks from the worst consequences of their own violence, and that in a double sense:

    (a) I am told that the civil administration in Cyprus is finding a real difficulty in controlling the general population there. The unrest and distress might easily lead to a general strike and with it widespread lawlessness. Such a thing

---

[95] Athenagoras had previously been orthodox archbishop of North and South America, 1930–48.

[96] According to the Books of Samuel, Ichabod was the son of Phinehas and born on the day that the Ark was taken into Philistine captivity and his father and grandfather (the priest Eli) killed. The name is said (1 Sam. 4, 21) to be a reference to the fact that 'the glory has departed' (from Israel), either in reference to the death of his father or Eli or a reference to the loss of the Ark.

with clashes between Cypriot and Turks might have terrible repercussions in Istanbul.

(b) But the only way of saving the Greeks from themselves is in some striking way to turn their thoughts away from their grievances to a positive hope of a reasonable and satisfying solution to their troubles.

Thus the need is for a new constructive plan of action which will not antagonize the Turks afresh but will give Cypriots and Greeks another and a substantial reason for coming to an agreement. The new plan must, to be effective, really give us all a feeling of 'a fresh start'. The launching of the Radcliffe constitutional proposals was meant to do just this, but so far it has failed. Even so I believe we can recreate the conditions for a fresh start.

III. Our desire to establish a peaceful constitutional settlement in Cyprus has been bedevilled by the terrorists and by the poisonous encouragement of it from Athens.[97] Terrorism (and Archbishop Makarios's association with it) has been blocking our way all the time, Unless we can somehow circumvent it as a political issue there can be no 'fresh start'.

It is often the way of wisdom and of reconciliation to treat a thing as finished before it really is. Terrorism has not been exterminated: perhaps it never can be altogether by present method: But as an organized force E.O.K.A. has I understand from the Press been seriously damaged. Anyhow an opportunity is offered of saying and saying truthfully that the chief part of the suppression of E.O.K.A. is accomplished.

Here then is the moment for the Government to give striking evidence that its chief concern is now no longer with terrorism but with constitutional settlement. Since Makarios was deported, the former has ranked first in statements of Government policy. Now it could be said boldly that it is to be subordinate to the constitutional settlement.

How is the change of policy to be made evident and given a fresh start. I dare to suggest by a change of Governor. General Harding has carried through his hateful task in such a way as to enhance his great reputation. He has borne the brunt. He can truthfully say that he had done what he was especially charged to do and has smashed E.O.K.A. But now the need is for constitutional settlement, for one known to the world as a civil administrator and not as a soldier. Is it not a very proper moment at which he could hand on his task with a real sense of achievement and with universal gratitude and honour to another kind of Governor to meet a now changed situation?

The new Governor would of course have to have (as General Harding now has) the help of a competent soldier to carry on the suppression of terrorism. But the Governor would bring no record of association with the suppression with him. By his mere arrival he might turn all the better sort of Cypriots and general public opinion with them away from violence to hope of peace. He should be known as a skilful and sympathetic healer of divisions. If I name two names, it is simply to indicate fields of action from which such a new Governor would come. So I say e.g. Sir Walter Monckton, a pastmaster at reconciliation or e.g. Cohen[98] who was Governor of Uganda and saw the Kabaka out and back again and still kept the confidence of

---

[97] Presumably a reference to the Greek government.
[98] Sir Andrew Cohen, former assistant undersecretary for African affairs at the colonial office and governor of Uganda, 1952–7.

the Buganda.[99] The new Governor could not be Lord Radcliffe since what is desired is a fresh start. Radcliffe like Harding could not but carry something over from the past which excellent in itself could be regarded as psychologically a stumbling block to the Greeks whom we are now trying to save from themselves.

My argument takes me a stage further. A new Governor would have the task of negotiating the Radcliffe Constitution. As such he could at once legitimately say that he must talk with Archbishop Makarios in person. Here again an obstacle could be circumvented. The Government has said that it will not negotiate with Makarios until he disavows violence: Makarios like any other martyr for a cause refuses to let his side down. There seems no way out. Some have suggested to me that Makarios might be invited to agree that 'there is no further place for violence at this time'. I should prefer the more honest way which I suggest. The Government appoints a new Governor. The new Governor on his own responsibility asks the Government to allow Makarios to come to see him. No one's face is lost. A sensible, indeed an inevitable, thing is done. Where should. [*sic*] Where should they meet? Perhaps best in London. What if no agreement is reached? Shall Makarios go back to the Seychelles? That is hardly possible. Why should not he (like the Kabaka) be kept in England until a settlement *is* reached and violence ended, and then be allowed aback to Cyprus or permanently exiled.

I submit that along such lines a hopeful 'fresh start' can be made: and if I may say so, the fact that you come in as Prime Minister for the first time is a very important factor. Anthony Eden, Harding and Radcliffe have all played their part: out of their endeavours has come this present moment of opportunity of averting otherwise certain failure and possible disaster. But like Moses, it is not for them to hope for the Promised Land. A new Prime Minister putting forward this fresh start with a new Governor (and a new chance for Makarios involved in it too) and Radcliffe's constitutional proposals would, I believe, convince the world as well as Cyprus that there was hope. And in such a situation Lennox-Boyd's tremendous enthusiasm and eirenic purpose would remain to be the bridge over the Jordan.

IV. One thing remains – self-determination. If I were free to follow my opinion, I should say that self-determination should not be referred to at all by any of the parties concerned for fifty years, if then. But that would not be well received. Anyhow the Government has already publicly committed itself to the principle of self-determination. All that can be done now is to find a sufficiently delaying formula. The Turks now say they will not have self-determination at any price. For the Greek Cypriots it is an essential demand. The best perhaps that can be done is to include as part of the 'fresh start' a declaration that by general consent it will be forbidden to raise the issue of self-determination in the proposed Cypriot Parliament for a period of 10 years.

There is much talk of handing Cyprus over in some way to N.A.T.O. jurisdiction. I believe it is essential to keep Cyprus as a domestic issue. But within the frame work outlined above, there is of course room for military arrangements with N.A.T.O.

---

[99] The Kabaka, the traditional ruler of the Christian kingdom of Buganda, had been deported by Britain from Uganda in 1953 over tensions arising over the Bugandan kingdom's future place within an independent state of Uganda. He was returned to Uganda in 1955. Fisher knew the Kabaka and his involvement in British–Bugandan negotiations parallels that of his *rôle* over Cyprus: see Stockwell, 'Splendidly leading the way', 207–8.

So I conclude. It is only the gravity of the situation which makes me impose such a document upon you. My justification is that whatever may be the demerits of the plan I have outlined, it seems to me better than any other suggestions I have heard.

Yours sincerely

G.C.

26. Bell papers 297 (Bell's diary 12 November 1956 – 6 July 1958), p. 12 reverse – p. 13, entry: 'Foreign office and C.F.R., 24 February 1957'

Some parts of this extract from the diary of the bishop of Chichester, George Bell, proved difficult to transcribe accurately. The extract nevertheless illuminates foreign office reactions to the church's involvement in the Cyprus issue.

Ch[rist] Ch[urch Rec[tory], St Leonard's[-on-Sea]

Sir Charles Peake, British Ambassador at Athens, had asked Percy Maryon-Wilson[100] to see me confidentially, to tell me of certain anxieties he and the Ambassador at Ancora (and it seems some of the FO too) feel about the Church & politics, the Abp. of C. and the CCFR and especially Waddams. It boiled down to a criticism of 'independent initiatives' being taken by Waddams: and a failure on Abp's part and CFR's to recognize that the Greek politician *cannot* dissociate the action of church leaders from that of the govt. There was a feeling of complaint perhaps that action was sometimes taken by or on behalf of the Abp. without consultation with FO: yet Abp. cd. at any time get F.O. opinion – coming to Lambeth e.g. There is disappointment in govt. quarters naturally that govt policy in Cyprus is not more widely supported – and not backed by Church. I pointed out the poor way in which the Cyprus question has been handled – the rudeness [?] of Eden – the deadlock etc – the inability of Govt to climb down, perhaps this Govt wld not do so. /[*sic*] Percy had many opportunities in Athens of meeting politicians – esp. opposition politicians, at Mser [?] Venizelos.[101] F.O. has wanted him to put British policy across to them: but I don't know how far he did/ [*sic*].Two instances in particular Percy gave me of Waddams' unwisdom (1) letter to A. Pallis strongly criticizing Ld Radcliffe's Cyprus proposals. This letter (on CFR paper) had gone to Avaros (G[ree]k rep[resentative] at UN) and Tsatsos (acting Foreign Minister) and was taken by them to show some move by *govt* a way for abolition of Radcliffe's proposals. Peake had been satisfactory [?] by Waddams – had replied to W. but had *not* told him he thought it a pity to write such letters to Pallis (a not very safe man, moving between Athens & London. This letter also critical of Lennox-Boyd. (2) The other instance was Waddam's account of his interview with late Turkish Ambassador in London. Much too highly coloured and not seriously taken to be a fair representation of what Ambassador said, about massacre etc. British Consul General saw the Patriarch later (?early January) found him unalarmed, & [?] friendly to Turkish [Bell subsequently deleted 'Turkish'] government of Istanbul, spoke gratefully [?] of compensation so far paid for damage in Sept 1955 riots. //Abps. letter to Makarios did not make favourable impression – 'very ill considered letter on political grounds'

---

100 Sir (George) Percy Maryon-Wilson, rector of Christ Church St Leonard's-on-Sea and canon of Chichester Cathedral.
101 Sophocles Venizelos, liberal politician and former Greek prime minister.

(Peake) – critical and delicate situation not improved by his intervention. Percy was asked whether Chichester had any influence on the Abp. of C? They been sorry Abp favours enosis, could not Chichester dissuade him? (seriously ignorant of either his or my attitude!) Percy said when he asked general about church parade how many soldiers wd go if not compelled, General replied all would go – *not* to go was to advertise oneself a communist! No hotel allowed to be built, without chapel in it!

27. CFR, File OC 108: 'Note for the archbishop', Rev. Herbert Waddams, 19 March 1957

This note records a telephone conversation between Waddams and Noel-Baker that took place a few days after EOKA had announced a second truce. The government proposed to respond to the truce on 19 March, but in the event Macmillan, facing differences within his cabinet, stalled. He departed the next day for talks with President Eisenhower in Bermuda.

Francis Noel-Baker rang me up this morning to say that he was very much afraid that the opportunity provided by the cease fire in Cyprus was again going to be bungled. Apparently Callaghan had returned very depressed from an interview with Lennox-Boyd yesterday. He thought that the Government might make some one or two inadequate gestures, but refer it again to NATO where they thought that the Turks would effectively stymie anything acceptable to the Greeks. He also had the impression that Archbishop Makarios might be let out and allowed to go anywhere except Cyprus, but not permitted to talk. Meanwhile repressive measures were to continue.

A statement was due to be made at 3.30 to-day by Lennox-Boyd, but he thought that it would probably be an interim statement.[102] He would like you to bring any influence you have to bear on the matter if you possibly can, and would very much appreciate a short talk with you either at Lambeth or the House of Lords at an early moment.

He takes a certain amount of credit for the cease fire for which he has been working for some time. It is always impossible to say what caused such a move, but I think that Francis Noel-Baker's efforts probably did have something to do with it. He will be in London until the end of the week.

H.M.W.

28. CFR, File OC 108: Archbishop Geoffrey Fisher to Sir Alan Lennox-Boyd, 22 March 1957 (copy)

My dear Lennox-Boyd,

As you know ever since the Cyprus trouble came to a head a year ago I have been urging Archbishop Makarios and all who can influence him that he must renounce violence. After the last Government statement[103] I am in doubt as to what to think or what to urge upon Makarios, and I should be grateful if you could clear the matter up a little for me.

---

[102] Lennox-Boyd merely said he would make a statement the next day: *House of Commons debates,* 1956–7, vol. 567, 19 Mar. 1957, col. 218.

[103] See above, p. 599.

The proposal is that if Makarios now renounces violence he should be allowed to leave the Seychelles and go anywhere except Cyprus. Makarios, however misguided, is according to his lights a Patriot fighting for a particular end, and regarded by his people as a martyr. Looking at the offer from his point of view, what advantage is Makarios supposed to get out of it? Merely to be free is for him not an inducement but a temptation to be resisted as a piece of self-indulgence. To ask him now on pure grounds of absolute morality to confess that he has been wrong all these years, and that he will never resort to violence again is surely as psychologically short-sighted as when a parent locks his boy up and says: 'I shall not let you out until you say you are sorry'.

So I come to my own judgement on the matter. That depends on what the Government really means by its offer. If it is to ask Makarios to say he is wrong and to offer him nothing in return except freedom of movement outside Cyprus, it seems to me an offer psychologically wrong to make and one which is very difficult to urge him to accept. The real question is whether if he renounces violence and is released the Government then mean to take him into consultation in the interests of peace in Cyprus. I see that in the House of Lords Lord Perth[104] was pressed on this point. He was asked: 'shall we then be prepared to negotiate with Archbishop on the Radcliffe report' and the answer was: 'we want to do first things first' the first thing being the appeal to N.A.T.O., an appeal which may be open to all kinds of delays and hazards and barren results. It gives Makarios no comfort to know that whether or not he will be negotiated with still remains completely obscure. Personally I think the Government must declare now what it means so that Makarios may be able to understand what the offer means. Again if what the Government means is that in certain circumstances, after N.A.T.O. has digested this matter, it. may possibly turn out that we shall find ourselves willing to talk with Makarios but equally we may find ourselves still unwilling to (even if ex-hypothesi he has renounced violence) then Makarios would be a complete fool to accept the offer from his point of view.

To make the offer mean anything Government must now say more, and my own feeling is that every consideration of psychological wisdom and generous spirit compels the conclusion that the Government should now say that if Makarios renounces violence not only will he be released but at the earliest, possible moment we will bring him into consultation as to the future Constitutional position in Cyprus taking as our basis the Radcliffe Constitution. That would be an offer which Makarios could properly be urged to accept: but, as I say, I cannot see any reason why he should wish to accept anything short of that, or how I could urge him to accept anything short of that.

I would myself go a step further. The Government statement has, as you realise, merely started a fresh round of barren argument with the Opposition here and the Greek Government and all the other partners to this sinful condition. There is only one policy which is always beyond cavil whatever its result and that is the policy of generosity. I cannot myself see what point is gained by anybody at all by trying to extort from Makarios the renunciation of violence when whatever the lips say (to quote Euripides) there is no kind of guarantee that the heart has consented thereto and anyhow we have got far beyond the stage where policy has got to be settled by going over old ground and trying to sweep up spilt milk. The moment has come

---

[104] John Drummond, seventeenth earl of Perth, minister of state at the colonial office 1957–62.

when only an act of generosity can possibly solve the problem. I believe myself that the only thing to do (since Makarios must come back into this picture somehow if there is ever to be peace) is to say openly to the world 'we are now going to release Makarios; our intentions have been made clear in the Radcliffe Constitution: we are prepared to enter into discussions on that Constitution with Makarios if he, on his side, promises to bring to the discussions a sincere desire to reach agreement. If, in the end, that fails, we shall never allow him to go back to Cyprus, but we shall never put him back to the Seychelles.' For all practical purposes by saying this you are no worse off than you are now, and on all grounds of moral authority and generous spirit you have got on to firm and unassailable ground.

You will see what I must know before I can make a judgment, or speak about it. I should hope that now the Government would decide on the generous policy I have indicated. If the answer to that is no, then may I ask this question: is the Government willing to say that if Makarios renounces violence and is released it is the Government's intention at the earliest possible suitable moment to enter into discussions with him on the Constitutional future of the Island.

Yours sincerely,

29. CFR, File OC 108: Archbishop Geoffrey Fisher to Francis Noel-Baker MP (copy), 4 April 1957, enclosing letter to Archbishop Makarios (see Document 30)

This letter was sent following the announcement on 28 March that Makarios would be released from the Seychelles. He left the island on 6 April, but not before he had made what Fisher judged an ill-advised statement to the press. The anglican bishop of Madagascar, Thomas Parfitt, also called on Makarios during the latter's stop-over on Madagascar, and reported to Fisher that the Cypriot still seemed too much the 'politician'.

My dear Noel Baker,

I am delighted to know that you are going out to meet Archbishop Makarios in Mombassa. I enclose a letter unsealed: if, after reading it, you think that it could do no harm, I should be very grateful if you would deliver it to him. If you think it better not to, then please deliver in your own words a message of good will on my behalf.

If in conversation you wish to refer to me about future plans, I can summarise my views in the following brief form:

1. The Government's action was meant to be and is a generous action. It is essential that it be met by a similar generous spirit on Makarios' side. No quarrel can ever be ended except by mutual accommodation. In a grave quarrel like this each side has an unanswerable case, and yet Christian charity only begins to operate when each side discusses what they can do to meet the other side in trust and in self-sacrifice.

2. I regret that Archbishop Makarios had at once to answer newspaper correspondents: thereby he was compelled to define things much better left undefined. The next step must be quiet conversation, not yet negotiation, still less public utterances which in effect limit one's freedom to follow where God may at any moment guide us. I trust, therefore, earnestly that Archbishop Makarios will refuse to make any further public statements until he has had an opportunity of discussion with all responsible parties.

3.   I would finally add a most serious warning. I regard partition as a counsel of despair. I am sure Archbishop Makarios would deplore such a solution: but as a student of history and of modern political affairs I must warn him that if he stands out too much for all that he desires, without any give and take, the almost certain result of it will be partition. I should regret that terribly. I hope that the Archbishop will see that if he is to avoid that final result he must do it by winning the good will of the Christian Churches in general, and of his friends in this country, by showing a spirit of reason, of generosity, and of just simple common sense by which a reconciliation and settlement can be achieved.

   Yours sincerely,
       Geoffrey Cantuar.

30. CFR, File OC 108: Archbishop Sir Geoffrey Fisher to Archbishop Makarios (copy), 4 April 1957, enclosed with Document 29

My dear Archbishop,
   May I be allowed to say how greatly relieved I was when the Government announced that you were to be set free to go where you would, with the exception of Cyprus. It has been my hard task all through these tragic months to move now one side, and now the other, to action which, in my judgment, was required by what we know of Our Lord's mind. You will recall that all I have said in public and in my letter to you was dictated by the desire to promote peace. It was a joy to me that in this positive way our Government has now taken a step which I regard as right in itself and generous in its intention: but peace demands that both sides simultaneously should move in a spirit of reconciliation.

   I send this greeting through Mr. Francis Noel Baker, a very good friend of yours and mine. He will be able to say what is in my heart and what I now hope for. In this note I merely greet you in Christian fellowship, thanking God for your release and praying that at every step you and your fellow countrymen, and we in this country, may be obedient to the heavenly vision and to the guidance of the Holy Spirit.

   I remain, your loving brother in Christ,
       G.C.

13

HOMOSEXUAL LAW REFORM, 1953–1967

Edited by
Hugh McLeod

30th June, 1965.

Dear Mrs. Goodhew,

Thank you for your letter. I have just this to say
in reply. You appeal to me to bear in mind that Christ
condemned sin. That is certainly true. We find in the
7th Chapter of St.Mark's Gospel a series of sins which
Christ says defile a man: clearly his condemnation of
all of them is severe, and so should ours be. When we
look at the list of sins there given one or two of them
have to do with sex: but the rest have nothing to do
with sex at all. Some of the sins in that list are crimes
in English Law: others are not. It seems to me that an
enlightened Christian morality does require that we avoid
suggesting that sexual sins are necessarily more terrible
than others because Christ does not suggest that. Equally
we need a well thought out principle as to which sins should
be crimes and which should not.

These are serious questions for us to face, and I do not
think the matter is dealt with fairly by suggesting that those
who try to face these questions in a new way are "condoning sin".

Yours sincerely,

Mrs. Goodhew,
Fifteen Cowley Street,
S.W.1.

42 Archbishop Ramsey to Mrs Suzanne Goodhew, in response to her criticism of his
support for Lord Arran's Sexual Offences Bill, 30 June 1965 (LPL, Ramsey, fo. 78)

Introduction*

In May 1938 the archbishop of Canterbury, Cosmo Gordon Lang,[1] received a letter from Dr R. D. Reid, who had been headmaster of King's School, Taunton, until his conviction the previous year of a homosexual offence. Reid condemned the 'brutal attitude of law and society' to 'the unfortunate class of people' to which he belonged. As a 'loyal member of the Church of England' (and presumably an anglo-catholic, as he referred to his confessor) he deplored his church's 'ostrich' attitude, and appealed to Lang to give his support to a change in the laws. In a reply marked 'Private', Lang expressed sympathy, stating that he had 'constantly to deal with clergy, some of otherwise high character, who have given way to the instincts about which you write'. But he was opposed to any change of the laws.[2]

During the next fifteen years there is no sign in the archives of Lambeth Palace that archbishops of Canterbury were interested in the laws relating to homosexuality or that anyone was trying to make them take an interest. Then in October 1953 Geoffrey Fisher,[3] archbishop since 1945, received a letter from the same Dr Reid, complaining that homosexuals were victims of a home office pogrom, and asking Fisher's support for an official inquiry.

I

1953 was the year when homosexuality and the laws punishing sexual acts between males became a central area of public concern and debate in Britain, and they remained so until the passage of the Sexual Offences Act in 1967. During this period the laws relating to homosexuality were perhaps uniquely divisive. For one section of the public they were a symbol of British morality, and any relaxation of the laws would bring about not only a rapid moral decline, but very possibly a decline in British power and standing in the world; for another section of the public these laws were coming to be seen as a relic of 'Victorianism' and a symbol of all that was wrong with Britain. The long-drawn-out, but ultimately successful campaign to reform the laws was pursued by a diverse coalition. Its members often differed in religion, politics, approaches to sexual morality – and indeed sexual orientation. But they worked together in parliament, the press and campaigning organizations. The Homosexual Law Reform Association, founded in 1958, reflected this diversity: its most prominent leader, Anthony Grey, was gay and a humanist, while the first

---

* The most important discussion of this topic is now Matthew Grimley, 'Law, morality and secularisation: the Church of England and the Wolfenden Report, 1954–1967', *Journal of Ecclesiastical History*, LX (2009), 725–41, which appeared after this Introduction was written.

1 Lang (1864–1945) was primate from 1928 to 1942. The standard biography is J. G. Lockhart, *Cosmo Gordon Lang* (London, 1949).

2 Lambeth Palace Library (LPL), Lang papers 164, fos. 266–72. See also G. I. T. Machin, *Churches and social issues in twentieth-century Britain* (Oxford, 1998), pp. 98–9.

3 Fisher (1887–1972) was archbishop between 1945 and 1961. See Edward Carpenter, *Geoffrey Fisher – his life and times* (London, 1991).

secretary, the Rev. Andrew Hallidie Smith, was a married clergyman. The other key organizer, A. E. Dyson, was gay and was described by Grey as a 'God-botherer'.[4]

Many of the campaigners for reform were themselves homosexual, including some who had been in prison. But many were not. What needs to be emphasized is that those campaigning for a change in the law included many who regarded homosexuality as a regrettable condition and homosexual acts as 'abnormal' or even 'sinful'. In arguing that the laws were nonetheless harmful and must be repealed, they were influenced by one or more of the following overlapping considerations: arguments by psychiatrists that homosexuality was an 'abnormality' resulting from damaging experiences in childhood and adolescence, for which the 'sufferer' should not be blamed; the pastoral concerns of Christian clergy who wanted to 'help' homosexuals, and believed that the intervention of the law was counter-productive as well as cruel; recognition of the evils associated with or resulting from the present laws, including the repulsive methods of entrapment used by the police and the blackmailing of public figures who were homosexual; and the claim (strengthened by the experience of war against Nazi Germany and the Cold War against the Soviet Union) that the individual should have the right to a 'private life', free from interference by the state. A number of books or films also played a part in persuading many people that the laws ought to be changed, including Alfred C. Kinsey's work on human sexual response (1948–53), which suggested that the number of people of both sexes who had had homosexual experience was much higher than hitherto realised; *Against the law* (1955) a personal testimony by Peter Wildeblood, one of those imprisoned as a result of the notorious Montagu trial; and *Victim* (1961), a film starring Dirk Bogarde playing a gay lawyer who, following the suicide of his former lover, confronts a gang of blackmailers.

II

Fisher's response to Reid's letter was brisk, unequivocal and less sympathetic in tone than Lang's had been: he could see no reason for a change in the laws.[5] As headmaster of Repton during the First World War he had expelled two boys accused of homosexual activities,[6] and his attitude to sex between men continued to be entirely negative, though he seems to have avoided the expressions of contempt and disgust employed by many churchmen, as well as politicians, journalists, judges and policemen, when discussing the subject.[7]

But this was now an issue that would not go away. During the next four years Fisher gradually modified his views, and by September 1957 when the Wolfenden committee published its historic recommendation that the sexual activities of 'consenting adults in private' should no longer be subject to the law, Fisher gave his support – attracting a number of hostile letters.[8] Fisher might be termed a reluctant convert, and he was probably not unduly upset when Macmillan's Conservative

---

4   Obituary of Dyson by Anthony Grey, *Gay and Lesbian Humanist*, Autumn 2002.
5   LPL, Fisher papers 126, fos. 293–4, 298 (see below, Documents 1 and 2).
6   Carpenter, *Fisher*, p. 19.
7   There are numerous examples of these in Patrick Higgins, *Heterosexual dictatorship* (London, 1996), e.g. pp. 271–7
8   For instance LPL, Fisher papers 194, fos. 187–8 (see below Document 7).

government failed to implement this recommendation, on the grounds that the public was not yet 'ready' for it.[9] On the other hand, Michael Ramsey,[10] who succeeded Fisher in 1961, believed passionately in the need to change the laws and he took an active part in the debates both in the church and in parliament which culminated in 1967 with the Sexual Offences Act, legalizing sex in private between men aged twenty-one and over.[11] The act contained various exclusions that continued to be debated over the following decades. It prescribed a higher age of consent for homosexuals than that applying to heterosexuals; sex between men serving in the armed forces and the merchant navy continued to be prohibited; and, unlike many of the other legal reforms of the 1960s, the act applied only to England and Wales – Scotland and Northern Ireland followed suit in 1980 and 1982 respectively.[12]

Until 1967 there was a range of laws, not to mention bye-laws, which could result in the arrest and possible imprisonment of male homosexuals. (The law took no notice of lesbians.) Sodomy had indeed been a capital offence until 1861, after which those convicted were liable to life imprisonment. The 'Labouchere Amendment' of 1885 defined all forms of male homosexual activity as 'acts of gross of indecency', liable to two years' imprisonment. There were also many arrests arising from acts of 1898 and 1912 which prohibited 'persistently importuning for an immoral purpose'.[13] The number of 'offences known to the police' rose sharply in the years after the Second World War, reaching a high point in 1955.[14] Most commentators have followed Reid in seeing this as a result of a 'home office pogrom' directed by Sir David Maxwell-Fyfe, home secretary from 1951 to 1954, aided and abetted by Sir Theobald Mathew as director of public prosecutions.[15] Houlbrook, however, dismisses this view, pointing out that the increase in arrests began during the Second World War and continued during the years of the post-war Labour government, and arguing that it was due to changes in police methods rather than any direction from the top.[16]

Our concern here is not with the causes of the upsurge in prosecutions in the 1940s and early 1950s, but with its impact on public opinion and, in particular, on the Church of England. In April 1954 Maxwell-Fyfe persuaded his cabinet colleagues to agree to the setting up of a home office departmental committee on homosexual offences and prostitution, which became known as the Wolfenden committee, as it was chaired by John Wolfenden, vice-chancellor of Reading

---

9 Mark Jarvis, *Conservative governments, morality and social change in affluent Britain, 1957–64* (Manchester, 2005), pp. 98–9.

10 Ramsey (1904–88) was primate from 1961 to 1974. See Owen Chadwick, *Michael Ramsey, a life* (Oxford 1990).

11 *Ibid.*, pp. 145–9.

12 See, for instance, Stephen Jeffery-Poulter, *Peers, queers and commons: the struggle for gay law reform from 1950 to the present* (London, 1991).

13 Higgins, *Heterosexual dictatorship*, pp. 155–7.

14 Jeffery-Poulter, *Peers, queers*, p. 22.

15 Jeffrey Weeks, *Coming out: homosexual politics in Britain from the nineteenth century to the present*, 2nd edn (London, 1990), pp. 158–64. Maxwell-Fyfe (1900–67), who was lord chancellor, 1954–62, with the title of Lord Kilmuir, was to be a leading opponent of the bills to legalize homosexuality in the 1960s.

16 Matthew Houlbrook, *Queer London: perils and pleasures in the sexual metropolis, 1918–1957* (Chicago, 2005), pp. 33–6.

University.[17] Wolfenden was himself an anglican and several other members of the committee were either clergymen or committed church members. In establishing the committee the government was influenced by a series of events that had thrust the 'problem' of homosexuality to the forefront of public attention. Most obviously the increasing numbers of arrests and the regular newspaper reports of homosexual men being imprisoned raised the spectre for one section of the public of a nation in moral decline, re-enacting the last days of Rome, while it galvanized others to challenge the laws. Furthermore the defection to Moscow in 1951 of the diplomat Guy Burgess, who was homosexual, and of his bisexual colleague, Donald Maclean, together with the Montagu trials in 1953 and 1954, inspired sensational reports in the popular press focusing on the dangers posed by homosexuals to state security as well as innocent youth and public morals. On the other hand, the growing respect accorded to psychiatrists was opening the way for a different approach, according to which homosexuality, or 'inversion', as it was commonly termed, was an unfortunate 'condition', often the result of inadequate parenting, which should attract pity and maybe 'treatment', but not blame. While the sensationalist *Sunday Pictorial* had in 1952 run a series headed 'Evil men', which unequivocally opposed any relaxation of the law,[18] *The Sunday Times* attempted a more balanced treatment of what it called 'A social problem' in November 1953, attracting thereby a large volume of letters.

One of the most substantial contributions to this debate, unpublished but widely circulated, was *The problem of homosexuality*, a report by a study group of the Church of England's Moral Welfare Council (MWC). Completed in December 1953, several hundred copies of the report were printed and sent to a select list including members of parliament, churchmen, social workers and doctors – but certainly not to the press (an exception being made for *The Times*).[19] It was claimed in December 1953 that Maxwell Fyfe was waiting to read the report before deciding what to do next, and in February 1954 a copy was sent to him.[20] Though the report was never published, requests for copies and comments on its contents were soon coming in, some from abroad. One of these was from Alfred C. Kinsey, who was generally approving, in spite of some points of disagreement.[21] The Labour MP Desmond Donnelly referred to it when calling for a royal commission on homosexuality in April.[22] It featured again in the House of Lords debate the following month, leading the Rev. E. N. Millard, archdeacon of Oakham to boast:

> One thing sticks out a mile; and that is that our pamphlet is of mighty importance and has achieved much already. It has been a real score for the C of E. ... I do feel personally that a change in the law is an essential part of what is necessary, the

---

[17] Andrew Holden, *Makers and manners: politics and morality in post-war Britain* (London, 2004), pp. 66–7; John Wolfenden, *Turning points: the memoirs of Lord Wolfenden* (London, 1976), pp. 129–46. Wolfenden (1906–85), after a brief career as an academic philosopher, was a public school headmaster, then vice-chancellor, and later director of the British Museum.

[18] Higgins, *Heterosexual dictatorship*, pp. 288–97.

[19] Church of England Record Office (CERO), MWC/HOM/1: Hugh C. Warner to bishop of St Albans, 26 Feb. 1954. Warner, was education secretary of the Church of England's MWC, and the bishop was its chairman.

[20] Unsigned letter to dean of Windsor, 17 Dec. 1953; note in files of MWC, 9 Feb. 1954, *ibid.*

[21] CERO, MWC/HOM/3: Kinsey to Warner, 3 Aug. 1954.

[22] *House of Commons debates*, 28 Apr. 1954, col. 1748.

problem is a practical one to some of us; and no-one who gets involved in the task of trying to help and advise these folk can escape the immense sense of grievance and injustice which colours all their thinking and makes advice sometimes quite unacceptable to them.[23]

The 'Inversion Group' which produced the report seems to have been the brain-child of the council's 'Central Lecturer', the Rev. Dr Derrick Sherwin Bailey, who was conducting research on the biblical and historical background to the laws on homosexuality. His article of February 1952 in *Theology* appears to have started the anglican debate,[24] and he later published the ground-breaking *Homosexuality and the western Christian tradition* (1955). In April 1952 he urged the MWC to set up a study group, and he gained the support of the Rev. Hugh Warner, the council's education secretary, although it took several months for his plan to come to fruition. In November 1952 Warner wrote to *The Times*, calling for a departmental committee on the question and asserting that people should not be punished for a condition for which they were not responsible.[25] The study group first met on 9 March 1953.[26] It included doctors, a lawyer, clergymen and theologians, but the key member seems to have been Bailey, who ultimately wrote their report.[27] Though few minutes of their meetings have survived, some of their concerns and working methods are apparent from correspondence between members of the group or between the group and other members of the MWC, as well, of course, as from the report they eventually produced. As the title of their report indicates, they regarded homosexuality as 'a problem' – not least for many homosexuals. The group was driven partly by the need for more understanding of the nature and causes of 'inversion', partly by concern for the suffering of many 'inverts' and the need to provide better pastoral support, and partly by a sense of the unfairness of the law which punished what was regarded as immoral behaviour by male homosexuals, but not by heterosexuals or lesbians. Warner, as chairman of the group, made it clear that he regarded sex outside of marriage as sinful, but, in a distinction that would be adopted by Wolfenden and would become a commonplace, he did not think it was the function of the law to regulate private morality – and indeed he regarded the present laws as positively harmful.[28]

Although in early 1954, the MWC insisted that the report was the responsibility of the study group, and not an official statement by the council,[29] it seems to have provided the basis for the evidence which the council submitted to the Wolfenden committee in 1955.[30] Drawing especially on Kinsey, they stressed human 'sexual diversity' and 'adaptability'. They saw the causes of 'inversion' as lying mainly in family background or in sexual segregation, whether at school in adolescence or later in such institutions as prisons or the armed forces. They saw 'war and its

---

23 CERO, MWC/HOM/5: archdeacon of Oakham to Warner, 20 May 1954.

24 Peter Coleman, *Christian attitudes to homosexuality* (London, 1980), pp. 172–3.

25 CERO, MWC/HOM/1: copy of letter dated 27 Nov. 1952.

26 See notes for the first meeting in CERO, MWC/HOM/1.

27 Coleman, *Christian attitudes*, p. 175.

28 See his letter to the editor of *The Times*, dated 2 Nov. 1953, in LPL, Fisher papers 126, fo. 297.

29 Undated and unsigned document in CERO, MWC/HOM/4.

30 There is a copy of their submission in CERO, MWC/HOM/7. Peter G. Richards, *Parliament and conscience* (London, 1970), pp. 63–84, claims that it was the most influential of the submissions to Wolfenden, while Higgins, *Heterosexual dictatorship*, p. 35, plays down its significance.

consequences' as a major factor – including the long absences or premature deaths of the fathers who were supposed to be providing appropriate male *rôle*-models for growing boys. (Precisely the same point would be made by the Labour MP Leo Abse some ten years later when introducing the Sexual Offences Bill in the House of Commons.[31]) In answer to the main objection to reform, they denied that homosexuals posed any greater threat to children and adolescents than heterosexuals. They stressed the 'loneliness' of many homosexuals, and condemned the existing laws as unjust, based on a false conception of the proper scope of the law, and preventing effective research on the causes of 'inversion'. They concluded by recommending that the laws prohibiting homosexual activity in private should be repealed and that there should be a common age of consent of seventeen applying both to homosexuals and heterosexuals.

Geoffrey Fisher, like many other leaders of the Church of England, was moving in the same direction, but very much more cautiously. Indeed as early as 30 November 1953 he was claiming 'there is full agreement that the law needs revision'[32] (in contradiction to what he had told Dr Reid earlier in the same month), but for long he remained entirely vague as to what kind of revision was needed. He also made occasional attempts to dampen the reforming enthusiasm of his MWC. As archbishop and leader of the anglican communion he had a host of other pressing concerns, and homosexual law reform was never high on his agenda. The apparent inconsistencies between his statements and actions relating to this issue may have arisen from the fact that he was generally responding to a specific situation, and needed to reconcile a number of often conflicting considerations, relating to an issue to which he had given little concentrated attention. Some years later, in responding to a letter asking him to condemn the anti-reform views of Gerald Ellison, bishop of Chester, Fisher replied that bishops did not have to think alike, and that while York and Exeter stood on one side and Chester on the other, he was somewhere in the middle.[33] Rather than a clearly worked out position this may have reflected a considerable degree of ambivalence, mixed with a sense that other issues were of higher priority. The recognition that some revision of the law might be needed had been contained in a letter to Frances Temple, widow of Fisher's revered predecessor William Temple. The correspondence concerned a letter which Temple had sent to Dr Reid, presumably in reply to a letter on similar lines to the one, quoted above, which Reid had sent to Lang. Temple it seems had been more encouraging than Lang, not only with regard to possible changes in the law, but with regard to the much more controversial topic of the moral status of homosexuality. Fisher was insistent that the letter ought not to be published.

Even if Fisher was already accepting the need for some changes in the law, an episode in February 1954 was revealing of his attitude to those who fell foul of these laws. Four months earlier, one of Britain's most famous actors, Sir John Gielgud, had been arrested for importuning, though he escaped with a fine.[34] When it was

---

[31] *House of Commons debates*, 19 Dec. 1966, col. 1078.

[32] LPL, Fisher papers 126, fo. 317: Fisher to Frances Temple, 30 Nov. 1953.

[33] LPL, Fisher papers 194, fo. 169: Fisher to Harry Williams, 23 Oct. 1957, Fisher papers 194, fo. 169. Harry Williams, dean of Trinity College, Cambridge, was one of the more active anglican supporters of homosexual law reform in the 1950s, and a leading member of the Cambridge group of radical theologians in the 1960s, at which time he also 'came out' as gay.

[34] See Higgins, *Heterosexual dictatorship*, pp. 268–72.

announced that he would be appearing in a radio play, the bishop of Birmingham received complaints, which he directed to Fisher. The archbishop immediately wrote a letter marked 'Private and Confidential' to General Sir Ian Jacob, director-general of the BBC, suggesting that Gielgud should be blacklisted for a period as a mark of disapproval for his offence: a privately run theatre was one thing, but the BBC as a national institution had an obligation to uphold the moral values of the nation. The tone of the letter was that of a friendly, though far from intimate, fellow member of the Establishment, who preferred to deal with such matters discreetly and expected to be heard. In the event, Jacob found a way of side-stepping Fisher's demand.[35]

In May 1954 Maxwell Fyfe wrote to Fisher asking him to suggest an anglican representative on the projected committee. Cyril Garbett, archbishop of York, favoured Warner, but Fisher describing him as 'too much of a professional on the subject', chose the Oxford theologian, V. A. Demant.[36] Fisher's reservations about the more enthusiastic advocates of reform were made more explicit after the MWC gave evidence to Wolfenden. Fisher told one of the council's members that '"we were rather falling backwards in gentleness". So long as a man was an invert probably many people knew nothing about him, but when he committed a homosexual act, then society had to take notice.' He was not persuaded by the sharp distinction between 'public' and 'private' posited by the MWC, which was to be a central assumption of the Wolfenden Report. He agreed that 'the law should be the same for homosexuals and heterosexuals', but he wondered if the way forward might be not a more lenient treatment of the former, but a stricter, treatment of immoral behaviour by the latter.[37] While Fisher continued to toy with the idea that there might be legal penalties for adultery, he came to accept the 'public'/'private' distinction, partly because of the realization that effective regulation of the private would require the kinds of state powers associated with totalitarian states.[38]

If in early 1955 Fisher was keeping a distance between himself and the MWC, by September 1957 when the Wolfenden Report was published, Fisher was a supporter and Wolfenden wrote to express his gratitude.[39] He was even more pleased when in November the Church Assembly voted by 155–138 to approve the committee's recommendations on homosexuality, and he noted that five years before such a vote would have seemed impossible.[40] Even then some members of the MWC were less happy, feeling that a more emphatic endorsement from Fisher would have produced a larger majority.[41]

In the years following, the Conservative government refused to take any action and the Labour party remained officially neutral, in spite of the demands from some Labour MPs for the implementation of Wolfenden's recommendations. The

---

35 LPL, Fisher papers, 142, fos. 350, 352–3, 354, Fisher to Jacob, 13 Feb. 1954; Jacob to Fisher, 16 Feb. 1954; Fisher to Jacob, 22 Feb. 1954 (see Documents 3–4). Jacob (1899–1993) left a military career for the BBC, acting as director-general 1952–60.

36 For discussion of Demant's role on the committee, see Higgins, *Heterosexual dictatorship*, pp. 109–11.

37 CERO, MWC/HOM/8, unsigned memo in MWC files, dated 22 Jan. 1955, and beginning 'I managed to have a word with the Archbishop this week…'.

38 LPL, Fisher papers 194, fos. 192–3 (see below, Document 8).

39 LPL, Fisher papers 194, fo. 159: Wolfenden to Fisher, 24 Sept. 1957.

40 *Ibid.*, fo. 181: Wolfenden to Fisher, 19 Nov. 1957 (see below, Document 6).

41 CERO, MWC/HOM/8: archdeacon of Oakham to Ena Steel, 15 Nov. 1957. Steel was general secretary of the MWC.

first attempt, in 1960, to press the case in the House of Commons failed by a considerable margin.[42] Meanwhile 1958 had seen the formation of the Homosexual Law Reform Society, apparently prompted by a letter to the *Spectator* from the indefatigable Dr Reid. Described by Higgins as 'effectively a front organisation for the liberal establishment', it was supported by a mix of Christian, humanist, literary and academic luminaries, ranging from Bertrand Russell and A. J. Ayer to Trevor Huddleston and Donald Soper.[43]

III

If Fisher remained ambivalent to the last, there could be no doubt where Michael Ramsey stood. He too regarded homosexual acts as sinful, though he warned against any exaggerated stress on sexual sins, or any claim that everything that is sinful must be punished by the law.[44] He was also concerned at the damaging pastoral effects of the interference by the police and the courts. As archbishop of York he had declared his support for Wolfenden, and as primate from 1961 he placed all of his considerable weight behind the reform cause.

The leaders of the reform movement were eager to obtain Ramsey's declared support. When in May 1965 Lord Arran introduced the first of several reform bills in the House of Lords, he asked Ramsey to speak in support.[45] Ramsey did so, prompting a large number of hostile letters, many containing threats to leave the church in protest.[46] By June 1966 he had received so many letters of this kind that he produced a standard letter of response stating that although homosexual acts were sinful homosexuals could best be helped by a change in the law.[47] Ramsey, through his lay chief of staff Robert Beloe, also pressed other bishops to join the debate. Beloe, who was evidently on friendly terms with Arran, acted in effect as a whip on his behalf, sending out numerous reminders to bishops and trying to ensure that at least one of them would speak in support of the bill.[48] He received many apologies, usually on the grounds of longstanding engagements in their dioceses, though the bishop of Leicester did say that he was not very keen on the Wolfenden recommendations anyway.[49] The result was that at each stage of the long-running debate there was usually at least one bishop speaking in support of Lord Arran and those bishops who were present all voted for reform. Dependent as they were on private members without government support the various bills introduced by Arran in the Lords and by Humphrey Berkeley and Leo Abse in the Commons repeatedly failed to go through all the required stages, in spite of majority votes in both Houses. By June 1966, a desperate Arran was asking Beloe to appeal to Ramsey to put pressure on the government to give its support for the bill.[50] In fact it would be another private

---

[42] Richards, *Parliament and conscience*, pp. 75–6.
[43] Higgins, *Heterosexual dictatorship*, pp. 124–7.
[44] LPL, Ramsey papers 78, fo. 175: Ramsey to Suzanne Goodhew, 24 June 1965 (see Document 12).
[45] Ibid., fo. 24: Robert Beloe to Ramsey, 22 Mar. 1965.
[46] E.g. Ibid., fos. 115–17: Lady Angela Brocket to Ramsey, 1 June 1965.
[47] For examples of letters to Ramsey and his replies, see LPL, Ramsey papers 98, fos. 269–81.
[48] E.g. LPL, Ramsey papers 78, fo. 25.
[49] Ibid., fo. 30.
[50] LPL, Ramsey papers 98, fo. 243: Arran to Beloe, 3 June 1966.

member's bill, introduced in the Commons later that year, that would become law in July 1967. In the final vote in the Lords in 1967 seven bishops, including Ramsey, voted in favour and none against. The leading opponent of reform, Lord Dilhorne, blamed the bishops for the failure of his crusade.[51]

None of the speakers in the parliamentary debates was prepared to state unequivocally that homosexuality was a legitimate option, in no sense inferior to heterosexuality. Wearied by the long battle for reform, Abse, Arran and their allies were prepared to make many compromises, and their arguments were shaped to attract the widest possible range of support. Abse, who was a keen believer in the joys and virtues of family life and who also had a strong interest in psychoanalysis, pleaded for compassion for homosexuals who were denied these joys, mainly, he suggested, because of inadequate parenting or other things that had gone wrong in their upbringing.[52] So far as Christian opinion was concerned, *Towards a Quaker view of sex* (1963), with its much more positive view of homosexuality and its insistence that sexual morality must not discriminate between those of differing sexual orientation, marked the beginning of a new era, but as yet had no impact on the political debate. Medical opinion generally promoted sympathy for homosexuals, but a sympathy starting from the premise that heterosexuality was 'normal' and that any other orientation was a result of an abnormal development which required special explanation.

IV

The Church of England played a part in several of the liberalizing reforms passed in the 1960s,[53] also including the decriminalization of attempted suicide (1961), suspension of the death penalty (1965), the extension of the grounds for legal abortion (1967) and divorce law reform (1969). These measures are often seen as a package, but this is wrong: there were indeed those who supported all of them or opposed all of them, but there were many people who strongly supported some of the changes, while opposing or at least being ambivalent about some of the others. So far as the Church of England leadership was concerned there was overwhelming support for the first two of these measures and very widespread, though more cautious, support for homosexual law reform, whereas opinions on abortion and divorce law reform was more divided, with the desire to reduce the numbers of abortions and divorces being balanced against an awareness of the faults of the existing laws.

Interpretations of the *rôle* of the Church of England and other churches in the enactment of these reforms have varied widely. At one extreme is Callum Brown, who minimizes this *rôle*, seeing the Sexual Offences Act, as well as the legislation relating to suicide, abortion and divorce, as an aspect of the 'dechristianization' of British society.[54] It should be sufficiently clear from what has been said above

---

51 Chadwick, *Ramsey*, p. 149. Dilhorne (1905–80) had as Sir Reginald Manningham-Buller been the Conservative attorney-general 1954–62 and was lord chancellor 1962–4.

52 See his highly idiosyncratic memoirs, Leo Abse, *Private member* (London, 1973).

53 For an extended discussion, see Hugh McLeod, *The religious crisis of the 1960s* (Oxford, 2007), pp. 215–39.

54 Callum G. Brown, *Religion and society in twentieth-century Britain* (London, 2006), pp. 267–70.

that this interpretation underestimates the part played by the Church of England. Moreover, it is wrong to take the criminalization of homosexuality as an index of the Christianity of a society or decriminalization as an index of dechristianization. Communist governments, as well as the Nazis, have often been harsh in their treatment of homosexuals, whereas most west European countries, many of them quite as Christian as the United Kingdom, decriminalized homosexuality in the nineteenth century or the first half of the twentieth.[55] On the other hand, Cate Haste claims, speaking generally of the legislation relating to sexual behaviour, that 'The conversion of the Church of England to liberalism was crucial.'[56] While agreeing that the church occupied a strategic position in a number of the key debates, I would question two points in her argument. First, anglican support for such reforms did not necessarily imply a conversion to 'liberalism': as I have argued elsewhere,[57] it is necessary to distinguish between 'liberal' and 'pragmatic' Christians, who both supported liberalizing measures, but often for different reasons. Second, she is wrong, at least in respect of homosexual law reform, to suggest that the anglicans were jumping on a secular bandwagon: as has been shown above the MWC played a significant part in setting the wagon in motion, and its subsequent rate of progress was too slow to attract those jumping on from opportunistic motives.

Three other points seem to me stand out. First, there is the *rôle* of the MWC, which is a striking example of the way in which a small group of energetic and well-informed people can play an important part in public debate on a taboo topic, and in winning over the leaders of their own institution. The Wolfenden committee was particularly open to the arguments of the MWC, partly because Wolfenden was looking for a general principle that would provide a consistent basis for their recommendations, and the MWC provided this in their distinction between 'public' and 'private', 'crime' and 'sin'.[58] Second there is the continuing value attached to support from the Church of England generally and archbishops of Canterbury in particular by the proponents of reforming legislation in the 1950s and 1960s. How much difference such support actually made is difficult to assess, and there certainly were occasions when governments chose to ignore strongly stated episcopal objections to their policies. However, there was a widely shared perception both among proponents and opponents of reform that bishops made a difference. Sydney Silverman, for instance, understandably nervous about the House of Lords which had rejected his anti-hanging bills in 1948 and 1956, made great efforts to persuade Ramsey to pilot his abolitionist bill through the Upper House in 1965, though eventually Ramsey refused, contenting himself with a strong abolitionist speech.[59] Third, the *rôle* of Ramsey and his colleagues in some of the major legal changes of the 1960s is a reminder that these reforms were carried through with the support of middle-aged and elderly legislators who were in no sense part of the 'Swinging Sixties', but who were convinced on humanitarian or pragmatic grounds, sometimes reinforced by questions of legal principle that the laws needed changing.

---

[55] Jeffery-Poulter, *Peers, queers*, p. 135.
[56] Cate Haste, *Rules of desire* (London, 1992), p. 213.
[57] McLeod, *Religious crisis*, pp. 228–33.
[58] Wolfenden, *Turning points*, pp. 134–5, explains the importance he attached to basing the report on general principles..
[59] Chadwick, *Ramsey*, pp. 160–1.

Editorial conventions

The Fisher and Ramsey papers contain a considerable number of letters and memoranda relating to homosexuality and, more especially, to homosexual law reform. These come mainly from the years 1953–7 (promoted by the appointment and deliberations of the Wolfenden committee and its subsequent report) and 1965–7 (relating to the various reform bills debated in parliament during this period). The largest category comprises correspondence between the archbishops and those anglican laypeople or clergy who wrote to support or (more often) to question the stance taken by the primates or other representatives of the church. A second category consists of memoranda by Robert Beloe concerning the House of Lords debates or correspondence relating to these debates between Ramsey or Beloe and anglican bishops – mainly urging them to speak and/or vote in favour of Lord Arran's reform bill. Third, there is correspondence between Fisher, Ramsey or Beloe and other public figures, including home office ministers, Lords Arran and Dilhorne, and Sir John Wolfenden. I have presented here examples of documents of all three kinds, including correspondence between Fisher and the director-general of the BBC. The latter is particularly revealing of Fisher's own thinking, especially his assumption that some issues could best be dealt with by a discreet word to a fellow member of the establishment, who was almost inevitably an acquaintance, if not a friend. I have not included any examples of a fourth important category, also revealing of Fisher's personality and ideas, namely the correspondence between the archbishop and members of the MWC, relating especially to their evidence to Wolfenden. A fifth category relates to a conference of the Modern Churchmen's Union in July 1967, where Canon Hugh Montefiore (vicar of Cambridge's university church, and later bishop of Birmingham) gave a paper in which he suggested that Jesus may have been homosexual. Ramsey was deluged with letters demanding disciplinary action, but I have not included either these, or the letters subsequently exchanged between Ramsey and Montefiore, and between Ramsey and the bishop of Ely.

In all cases I have retained the punctuation and spelling of the originals. Words which are underlined in the original manuscripts have been printed in italic type.

Documents from Lambeth Palace Library

1. Dr R. D. Reid to Archbishop Geoffrey Fisher,[1] 27 October 1953

Fisher papers 126, fos. 293–4

My Lord Archbishop,

A short time ago you sent a very kindly reply to a suggestion of mine that the time had come for an enquiry into the treatment of homosexual people in this country. Now there has arisen as is obvious to anyone, a veritable program [*sic*] against us. Before this, the law has been described by such a Christian authority as Dr Sherwin Bailey as a SHAMEFUL INJUSTICE and its repeal urged by such responsible authorities as the Magistrates' Association and the B.M.A.[2]

I must repeat that I do not condone offences against children or public decency. Both are caused by the present law and are not peculiar to homosexual people.

It is clear from directives issued by the Home Office that the present campaign has official backing, probably not unconnected with a 'coronation clean up'.[3] It is tragic that our dear and sovereign lady's name should thus be associated with such beastly cruelty. It is a beastly part of a primitive urge to persecute the peculiar, and only those with inside knowledge can know of the wave of misery, frequently causing suicide,[4] which is passing through the country.

I have purposely been brief when so much might be said.

I make a heartfelt and final appeal to your grace to come to our aid with some declaration of Christian sympathy with our cause. All we ask is investigation. It is a small thing.

I have the honour to be,
Your Grace's obedient servant,
R. D. Reid

2. Fisher to Reid, 3 November 1953

Fisher papers 126, fo. 298

Dear Dr Reid,

I do not at the moment recall my previous correspondence with you but perhaps there is no need to refer to it. As to the present situation I think you must be perfectly clear about the matter. Homosexuality is against the Christian law of morals and is rightly regarded as a social menace if it becomes in any sense widespread. There is

---

[1] Fisher was for many years a headmaster before becoming a bishop, and critics detected the influence of his former profession in the hectoring tone that he often adopted in his correspondence.

[2] British Medical Association.

[3] The coronation of Queen Elizabeth II had taken place on 2 June 1953, and it was claimed that overseas visitors were shocked by the visibility of prostitution on the London streets. Higgins, *Heterosexual dictatorship*, pp. 255–6.

[4] See *ibid.*, pp. 104–8.

an accumulation of evidence that homosexuality is becoming a real social evil, and I know cases where homosexuals are enticing men and persuading men who are not by nature homosexual at all into this practice.

You will have seen what the magistrates have said. Quite obviously society must protect itself against this as against any other anti-social moral perversion. This is hardly the moment at which to put in a plea for a better law or for public sympathy. I hope that all homosexuals will stop at once to realise that whatever their physical infirmities or their natural tendencies any indulgence of them is against Christian morals and the public welfare. They should seek priest and psychiatrist for help.

Yours sincerely,

Geoffrey Cantuar

3. Fisher to Lt Gen Sir Ian Jacob, 13 February 1954

Fisher papers 142, fo. 350

PRIVATE AND CONFIDENTIAL

My dear Jacob,

Here is a rather urgent matter. I have had a letter from a Bishop in the Midlands referring to the fact that Sir John Gielgud is announced to be broadcasting on the Third Programme[5] on Sunday February 21st at 3 o'clock. Some people in Birmingham are asking him to take public action by way of protest. I have told him that I should like first to approach you confidentially.

You will remember that quite recently Sir John Gielgud was convicted for importuning for immoral purposes. I agree with the Bishop that it would be a grave scandal if the B.B.C. allowed him to broadcast while this incident is still in the public mind. If I remember rightly, after Professor Joad[6] was convicted of travelling on the railway without a ticket, with intention to defraud, he disappeared from B.B.C. programmes for some time. Gielgud's offence is far worse than Joad's, and must, as it seems to me, be marked by total exclusion from the B.B.C. for some time. If it be said that the B.B.C. cannot discover the private morals of people who broadcast, the answer is that there is here no question of private morals, but of conviction in open court of a crime. …

Yours sincerely,

Geoffrey Cantuar

4. Jacob to Fisher, 16 February 1954

Fisher papers 142, fos 353–4

My dear Archbishop,

Your letter of the 13th February raises a question which has much exercised our minds, and I would like to tell you what our thoughts have been. I should say first

---

5   The BBC's Third Programme, specializing in music and talks, catered for a highly educated radio audience and had somewhat more latitude than the Home Service or Light Programme to introduce taboo topics.

6   C. E. M. Joad (1891–1953), professor of philosophy at Birkbeck College, London, was a popular radio pundit, though tending to be distrusted by other professional philosophers – and according to the *Oxford dictionary of national biography* (*ODNB*) was 'a habitual fare-dodger'.

of all that we have arrangements for noting down those people who are convicted of offences or who otherwise become notorious, so that consideration can be given to their employment in broadcast programmes. Each case has, of course, to be considered separately.

This machinery came into action in the case of Sir John Gielgud. We had to take into account what exactly he had been convicted of doing. He was charged with persistently importuning for an immoral purpose. He pleaded guilty, but said that he was tired and had had a few drinks and was not responsible for his actions. The magistrate warned him of the seriousness of taking more drink than he was able to control and told him to see a doctor. The magistrate finally said 'I suppose on this occasion I can treat you as a bad case of drunk and disorderly'.

On this basis it was felt that after an interval of four months it would be permissible to allow him to appear as an actor in a broadcast.

The case is not quite parallel with that of Professor Joad in this way. Joad was taking part in 'The Brains Trust', a programme in which all kinds of questions were discussed, including those involving moral issues. Joad was in fact inclined to take up attitudes in the discussions on moral grounds. This being so, it was felt that it was impossible to keep him in the programme after his conviction for fraud. Gielgud is appearing as a professional actor, which is a rather different kind of occupation.

These questions are, as you say, most difficult. We recognise that greater care has to be taken in a service that goes into people's homes than, for instance, on the London stage where Gielgud is at present appearing in a play, but in view of the circumstances I have outlined above we came to the conclusion that the engagement could be made. Our conclusion might have been different if there had been no doubt about the case.

Yours sincerely,
Ian Jacob

5. Sir John Wolfenden to Fisher, 24 September 1957

Fisher papers 194, fo. 159

My dear Archbishop,

I am most grateful to you for your generous letter. If you genuinely feel that I shall not be an albatrosss round the neck of the new Social Responsibility Board, I will gladly try to do what you ask.[7] ...

We are all deeply in your debt for your timely and friendly words about 'the Report'. It is, of course, inevitable that with such a wide canvas, composed entirely of tricky and distasteful problems, we should provide plenty of scope for people to disagree with us. But, as you have so pointedly observed, what I believe we have done is to make clear the difference – incredibly unnoticed by so many of our fellow-countrymen – between crime and sin. Our modest concern was with crime; and it is now for the Churches to take the opportunity of teaching the appropriate lessons about sin. I (as I need hardly say to you) am not a theologian; but I have been trying to 'plug' this distinction as hard as I can, and I am profoundly grateful that you and others have found it possible to press it. Of course to make the distinction

---

[7] Wolfenden had been invited to be chairman of the church's new Board of Social Responsibility, of which the MWC would be a part.

is only one step. The next is the much more controversial one of deciding which sins ought to be also crimes; and clearly there is room for genuine differences of opinion among honest men about that. … To say that I am heartily sick of the whole topic would be an under-statement; and I am afraid that that you may well find the proportion of obscene abuse in your post-bag increased as the result of what you have said and written; I am therefore the more deeply grateful to you. …

Yours very sincerely,

J. F. Wolfenden

6. Wolfenden to Fisher, 19 November 1957

Fisher papers 194, fo. 181

My dear Archbishop,

Thank-you very much for your letter of yesterday. I read the accounts of the Church Assembly with growing admiration. I wish I could have been there to listen; this unfortunately was impossible, but I had reports from the Bishops of St Albans and Sheffield at lunch time on that day. So I was given the half-time score then. Mortimer[8] was splendid and obviously there were others who supported bravely. I do not think one need worry very much about Powell;[9] he represents a point of view, but my guess is that he represents it so violently as not to be quite convincing. The incredible thing about the Assembly's vote was not that it was, as the Times said, 'by a majority of only 17'. The staggering thing is that the Church Assembly should vote by any majority at all in that direction. If you or I had said five years ago that in November 1957 the Church Assembly would decide by a majority that adult consenting homosexual acts should be taken out of the criminal law, we should have been removed to a lunatic asylum. I find it difficult to express my gratitude to the Assembly and, especially, to you for your magnificent summing-up statement at the end. …

With renewed and humble gratitude,

Yours very seriously,

J. F. Wolfenden

7. Colonel Hugh S. Browne to Fisher, 27 November 1957

Fisher papers 194, fos. 187–8

PERSONAL

My dear Archbishop,

You will remember me as Organising secretary for S.P.G.[10] for the Dioceses of Canterbury, Rochester and Chichester from 1945 to 1949.

---

8 Robert Mortimer (1902–76), bishop of Exeter and an anglo-catholic, was for many years regarded as the Church of England's leading moral theologian and came to special prominence in the 1960s as chairman of the church committee which produced the influential report on divorce, *Putting asunder* (1966).

9 Powell, a stipendiary magistrate at Clerkenwell and one of the lay representatives from the diocese of Southwark, who was one of the strongest critics of Wolfenden in the Church Assembly.

10 Society for the Propagation of the Gospel, the Church of England's principal high church mission society.

Further to my letter of September 25th last, which dealt with the Wolfenden report, & which your Chaplain acknowledged on October 1st, I write again on that subject, because I think that in your position you are not able to gauge correctly the true effect on the people of this country of the Church assembly's agreement (by a majority of 17, so the papers said) with the section of the Wolfenden report that deals with homosexuality. You are bound to be dependent on what people tell you at second hand.

There was a question on the 'Any Questions'[11] programme on Friday November 15th which asked whether the Church has thrown away its moral leadership by agreeing with that section of the Wolfenden report; and in the 'Any Answers' programme on the following Thursday the Chairman said that 90% of the letters received on that subject were against the Wolfenden Report. If I understood him aright one man went so far as to say that he would not take Communion any longer in the Church of England ...

The law should punish all sin if it could, but some it cannot punish. Those sins which it can punish, we put under the heading of 'crime'. And homosexuality, whether between adults or juveniles, can be punished by law, & must, in the interests of the nation as a whole, & also of the men concerned, remain a crime.

It is utter nonsense to try & make out that some men can no more help themselves committing the crime of homosexuality than they can help the colour of their hair. There is no man who cannot be cured of the habit if he *wants* to be cured. You might as well say that a man should not be punished for murder or for stealing material things because he cannot help doing it.

And to say that, because we are not strict enough over fornication &/or adultery, therefore we must be more lenient towards homosexuality, is, of course, an argument which does not hold water for a moment.

The texts which I have come across so far in the Bible which support my view (& I have found none which do not) are:-
Genesis XIX, 1–30
Leviticus XVIII, 22
Judges, XIX, 21–25
Romans, I, 27
Jude, verse 7.[12]

I do beg of you to consider carefully & fully what I have said. The only way that I can see of counteracting the enormous harm which the decision of the Church Assembly has done, not only to the Church of England but to Christianity as a whole, is by you yourself coming out openly & strongly in favour of retaining homosexuality between all men as a crime punishable by law.

---

[11] A radio programme in which four pundits, usually including representatives of the main political parties, answer questions from an audience, and which is followed a few days later by 'Any answers' where listeners send in their own views.

[12] Leviticus states unequivocally (according to the Authorized Version) 'Thou shalt not lie with mankind as with womankind: it is an abomination.' The Genesis passage describes the destruction of Sodom and Gomorrah (allegedly for the sin of 'sodomy' – though Sherwin Bailey, in particular, disputed this interpretation). Jude is a reference to Sodom and Gomorrah, and Judges tells a similar story, though with different consequences. Paul in Romans includes in a list of sinful practices 'men, leaving the natural use of the woman, burned in their lust one toward another'. For discussion of these and related passages, see Coleman, *Christian attitudes*, pp. 38–88.

Nothing would undermine the manhood if the nation more quickly than making it legal.

I would be grateful if you would let me know that you yourself have read this letter.

Ever yours sincerely,

Hugh S. Browne (Colonel)

8. Fisher to Browne, 3 December 1957

Fisher papers 194, fos. 192–3

Dear Colonel Browne,

I must send a brief answer to your letter, making just these two points:

It really astonishes me how unwilling people are in these days to allow other people to differ from them without taking it as a source of moral insult. It must be obvious to anybody that two views can be taken as to the expediency of applying the Wolfenden Committee's recommendations about homosexual offences. I don't get angry and threaten to leave the Church of England because a very large minority in the Church Assembly take a different view from the majority, and I cannot see how any sane person should count it against the Church of England that on such a matter, by a small majority, the Church assembly take a view from which they happen to differ. Really there is common sense and charity in discussing these matters which all Christian folk ought to maintain.

The Church Assembly by a larger majority approved the principles of the Wolfenden report; in particular they took clear notice of the distinction between a crime and a sin. You can if you like of course maintain the principle that the law should punish all sin if it could, but you would find practically no considering person to agree with you, for if it be true then the only right system of Government is that of the totalitarian system which seeks to invade not only a man's private house, but his private thoughts, and punish people for wrong thinking. I cannot believe that you really uphold that astonishing thesis. The law could only conceivably be justified in punishing all sin if it had a divine and unerring knowledge of what sin was, and even then if it punished every sin as a crime by force, it would be strangely unlike the general behaviour of Almighty God towards His creation, who leaves men free to sin if they wish so to abuse their freedom, although it has the power to stop them doing it at any moment. ...

Towards the end of your letter you say that it is nonsense to make out that some men are unable to save themselves from homosexuality; I entirely agree –and I have never said a word to the contrary. You say that nothing could undermine the manhood of the nation more quickly than making homosexuality between consenting adults in private free from the criminal law. I would reply that nothing could more quickly restore the manhood of the nation on a far wider scale, and rescue homes and families, than making adultery a crime. I wonder what you would think of that?

Yours sincerely,

Geoffrey Cantuar

9. Memo, dated 22 March 1965, from Robert Beloe,[13] intended recipient not stated

Ramsey papers 78, fo. 25

Debate in the House of Lords on the Wolfenden Proposals for Homosexuality

Lord Arran[14] telephoned on the 19th March to consult the Archbishop about the debate that he said he had mentioned to him when they met and in which the archbishop had agreed to take part on the 12th May.

I said that we had not got this in the diary but Arran said that the Archbishop had put it in his diary. I said that the Archbishop would not be back in London until lunch-time and was due to go to Chichester in the evening. Arran said that he hoped he would speak second in the debate after him.[15]

I said that of course the Archbishop could not sit right through the debate if he was to keep his engagement in Chichester. Arran then told me the names of the Peers Spiritual who belonged to the Homosexual Law Reform Society:-

York[16]

London[17]

St Albans[18]

Manchester[19]

Southwark[20]

Birmingham[21]

Exeter[22]

Winchester[23]

He said that he would like the Archbishop's advice as to which one of these should be invited to speak. I said that I thought the Archbishop would probably advise St Albans and advised Arran to approach him. Arran said that he would also write to the other Bishops on his list to invite them to be present and support him.

---

13 Robert Beloe (1905–84), formerly chief education officer for Surrey, was lay chief of staff at Lambeth Palace from 1959 to 1969, having been appointed by Fisher who gave him the job of ensuring the presence of bishops in important debates in the House of Lords. See Carpenter, *Fisher*, pp. 398–9.

14 Lord Arran (1910–83), a Conservative peer, sponsored a series of bills for homosexual law reform between 1965 and 1967 including the one that was ultimately successful. Leo Abse, his counterpart in the Commons, suggested that Arran's campaign was 'an act of reparation' for the unhappiness and premature death of his elder brother, who was homosexual. See Jeffery-Poulter, *Peers, queers*, p. 84.

15 Ramsey did in fact speak second in the debate, and in support of Arran on 12 May, and supporting speeches were also made by the archbishop of York and the bishops of Worcester and Southwark.

16 Donald Coggan (1909–2000), archbishop of York 1961–74, and then archbishop of Canterbury, the first evangelical to hold that office for more than a century.

17 Robert Stopford (1901–76), bishop of London 1961–73.

18 Michael Gresford Jones (1901–82), bishop of St Albans 1950–70, and chairman of the MWC at the time of its evidence to Wolfenden.

19 William Greer (1902–72), a former secretary of the Student Christian Movement and bishop of Manchester 1947–70, also well known as a critic of nuclear armaments and capital punishment.

20 Mervyn Stockwood (1913–95), bishop of Southwark 1959–80 and anglo-catholic, socialist, and one of the highest-profile bishops, described in the *ODNB* as a homosexual, but one whose romantic relationships were platonic.

21 Leonard Wilson (1897–1970), bishop of Birmingham 1953–69. As bishop of Singapore he was interned by the Japanese during the Second World War; later president of the Modern Churchmen's Union.

22 Robert Mortimer.

23 Falkner Allison (1907–93), bishop of Winchester 1961–75 and an evangelical.

… He did not propose to tell the Bishops of Carlisle[24] and Chester[25] who he believed were opposed to his proposals.

R.B.

10. Michael Ramsey, archbishop of Canterbury, to Lord Arran, 25 May 1965

Ramsey papers 78, fo. 70

My dear Arran,

On my return from Scotland this morning I am delighted to see the great success which you had in the House of Lords last night.[26] I am glad that you showed yourself ready for improvements and I shall be glad to try and helping that direction. I wonder what would be the best way for us to keep in touch over amendments? Would it be a good idea if Beloe could make some plans with you about this?

With my best wishes,

Yours very sincerely,

Michael Cantuar

11. Arran to Ramsey, 26 May 1965

Ramsey papers 78, fo. 71

My dear Archbishop,

Thank-you for your letter of 25th May which rejoiced me. I am very proud to belong to such a responsible and progressive body as the House of Lords.

About amendments – I will certainly keeping touch with Mr Beloe, and no doubt we can find the necessary formulas. I like to think there is no great difference of view between your Grace and myself as to what these should be.

But, as I said in the Debate, best of all would be if the amendments were tabled by yourself. The House could not fail to be impressed, and I think the Bill would have a better chance of getting through, if it were felt that the Lords spiritual were behind it.

The Bishops spoke splendidly.[27]

Yours most sincerely,

Buffy Arran

---

[24] Thomas Bloomer, bishop of Carlisle 1946–66.

[25] Gerald Ellison (1910–93). Bishop of Chester 1955–73, and later bishop of London. Generally regarded, according to the *ODNB*, as an 'arch conservative' (though his biographer wished to qualify this description).

[26] The House of Lords voted 94–49 to give a second reading to Arran's Sexual Offences Bill – the first time that either House had shown a majority in favour of legalizing homosexual acts between consenting adults in private.

[27] The bishops of Chichester and Southwark spoke in support of Arran, and the bishops of Lincoln and Ripon also voted for his motion.

12. Ramsey to Suzanne Goodhew,[28] 30 June 1965

Ramsey papers 78, fo. 175

Dear Mrs Goodhew,

Thank-you for your letter. I have just this to say in reply. You appeal to me to bear in mind that Christ condemned sin. That is certainly true. We find in the 7th Chapter of St Mark's Gospel a series of sins which Christ says defile a man.[29] Clearly his condemnation of all of them is severe, and so should ours be. When we look at this list of sins there given one or two of them have to do with sex: but the rest have nothing to do with sex at all. Some of the sins in that list are crimes in English Law: others are not. It seems to me that an enlightened Christian morality does require that we avoid suggesting that sexual sins are necessarily more terrible than others because Christ does not suggest this. Equally we need a well thought out principle as to which sins should be crimes and which should not.

These are serious questions for us to face, and I do not think the matter is dealt with fairly by suggesting that those who try to face the questions in a new way are 'condoning sin'.

Yours sincerely,
        Michael Cantuar

---

[28] Suzanne Goodhew was married to (though later divorced from) the right-wing Conservative MP for St Albans, Victor Goodhew. She had written to Ramsey criticizing his support for Arran's Bill.

[29] According to the *New English Bible*, these are evil thoughts, fornication, theft, murder, adultery, ruthless greed, malice, fraud, indecency, envy, slander, arrogance and folly.

Index

PUBLICATIONS

1. VISITATION ARTICLES AND INJUNCTIONS OF THE EARLY STUART CHURCH. VOLUME I. Ed. Kenneth Fincham (1994)
2. THE SPECULUM OF ARCHBISHOP THOMAS SECKER: THE DIOCESE OF CANTERBURY 1758–1768. Ed. Jeremy Gregory (1995)
3. THE EARLY LETTERS OF BISHOP RICHARD HURD 1739–1762. Ed. Sarah Brewer (1995)
4. BRETHREN IN ADVERSITY: BISHOP GEORGE BELL, THE CHURCH OF ENGLAND AND THE CRISIS OF GERMAN PROTESTANTISM 1933–1939. Ed. Andrew Chandler (1997)
5. VISITATION ARTICLES AND INJUNCTIONS OF THE EARLY STUART CHURCH. VOLUME II. Ed. Kenneth Fincham (1998)
6. THE ANGLICAN CANONS 1529–1947. Ed. Gerald Bray (1998)
7. FROM CRANMER TO DAVIDSON. A CHURCH OF ENGLAND MISCELLANY. Ed. Stephen Taylor (1999)
8. TUDOR CHURCH REFORM. THE HENRICIAN CANONS OF 1534 AND THE *REFORMATIO LEGUM ECCLESIASTICARUM*. Ed. Gerald Bray (2000)
9. ALL SAINTS SISTERS OF THE POOR. AN ANGLICAN SISTERHOOD IN THE NINETEENTH CENTURY. Ed. Susan Mumm (2001)
10. CONFERENCES AND COMBINATION LECTURES IN THE ELIZABETHAN CHURCH: DEDHAM AND BURY ST EDMUNDS, 1582–1590. Ed. Patrick Collinson, John Craig and Brett Usher (2003)
11. THE DIARY OF SAMUEL ROGERS, 1634–1638. Ed. Tom Webster and Kenneth Shipps (2004)
12. EVANGELICALISM IN THE CHURCH OF ENGLAND c.1790–c.1890. Ed. Mark Smith and Stephen Taylor (2004)
13. THE BRITISH DELEGATION AND THE SYNOD OF DORT 1618–1619. Ed. Anthony Milton (2005)
14. THE BEGINNINGS OF WOMEN'S MINISTRY. THE REVIVAL OF THE DEACONESS IN THE NINETEENTH-CENTURY CHURCH OF ENGLAND. Ed. Henrietta Blackmore (2007)
15. THE LETTERS OF THEOPHILUS LINDSEY. VOLUME I. Ed. G. M. Ditchfield (2007)
16. THE BACK PARTS OF WAR: THE YMCA MEMOIRS AND LETTERS OF BARCLAY BARON, 1915–1919. Ed. Michael Snape (2009)
17. THE PAPERS OF THE ELLAND SOCIETY 1769–1818. Ed. John Walsh and Stephen Taylor (forthcoming)
18. FROM THE REFORMATION TO THE PERMISSIVE SOCIETY. A MISCELLANY IN CELEBRATION OF THE 400TH ANNIVERSARY OF LAMBETH PALACE LIBRARY. Ed. Melanie Barber and Stephen Taylor with Gabriel Sewell (2010)

Forthcoming Publications

BRITISH STATE PRAYERS, FASTS, THANKSGIVINGS AND DAYS OF PRAYER 1540s–2002. Ed. Alasdair Raffe, Philip Williamson, Natalie Mears and Stephen Taylor

LETTERS OF THE MARIAN MARTYRS. Ed. Tom Freeman

THE PARKER CERTIFICATES. Ed. Ralph Houlbrooke, Helen Parish and Felicity Heal

THE CORRESPONDENCE OF ARCHBISHOP LAUD. Ed. Kenneth Fincham and Nicholas Cranfield

THE DIARY OF JOHN BARGRAVE, 1644–1645. Ed. Michael Brennan, Jas' Elsner and Judith Maltby